ECC Essentials

TEACHING THE EXPANDED CORE CURRICULUM TO STUDENTS WITH VISUAL IMPAIRMENTS

Carol B. Allman and Sandra Lewis, Editors

Susan J. Spungin, Consulting Editor

Printed in the United States of America

Library of Congress Cataloging-in-Publication Data

ECC essentials : teaching the expanded core curriculum to students with visual impairments / Carol B. Allman and Sandra Lewis, Editors ; Susan J. Spungin, Consulting Editor.

pages cm

Includes bibliographical references and index.

ISBN 978-0-89128-498-7 (pbk. : alk. paper) — ISBN 978-0-89128-680-6 (online subscription) — ISBN 978-0-89128-681-3 (ascii download) — ISBN 978-0-89128-682-0 (mobi) — ISBN 978-0-89128-683-7 (epub) 1. Children with visual disabilities—Education—Curricula—United States. 2. Teachers of the blind—United States—Handbooks, manuals, etc. I. Allman, Carol B.

HV1638.E44 2014

371.91'10973—dc23

2014016868

The American Foundation for the Blind removes barriers, creates solutions, and expands possibilities so people with vision loss can achieve their full potential.

It is the policy of the American Foundation for the Blind to use in the first printing of its books acid-free paper that meets the ANSI Z39.48 Standard. The infinity symbol that appears above indicates that the paper in this printing meets that standard.

To all past, present, and future teachers of children with visual impairments, with heartfelt thanks for your passion for our special field of visual impairments and your dedication to the unique children we serve.

—C.B.A. and S. L.

Contents

Foreword

The expanded core curriculum (ECC) is not a new idea. Professionals who work with students who are blind or visually impaired have always needed to identify and define the unique needs of these students and the skills that would enable them to attend school, work, and pursue independent lives in the world. Starting in the early 1940s, educators in the visual impairment field began to study their students as well as the literature of the times to articulate more specifically their students' unique needs. Mackie and Dunn (1955), Mackie and Cahoe (1956), and Spungin (1977), for example, attempted to define the skills that were necessary for these students as a result of their visual impairments—which were then described as disability-specific competencies—and began to define a curriculum for the teachers who worked with them.

Some form of a disability-specific curriculum has, in fact, been recognized as necessary for children who were blind or visually impaired for many decades, as far back as the 1900s. To some extent the original purpose of such a curriculum was to promote social skills. However, this curriculum, its definition, and the role it was to play, as well as the way in which it was to be taught, all took on greater importance when the traditional residential school placement that was common in the 1940s and 1950s and earlier in the century began to give way to the mainstreaming of more and more children with visual impairments into their local public schools. When the Education for All Handicapped Children Act (now the Individuals with Disabilities Education Act [IDEA]) was passed in 1975, this trend accelerated: Students with disabilities were to be placed in the least restrictive educational setting that was appropriate for them, and the majority of students with disabilities, including students who were blind or visually impaired and those with multiple disabilities, were increasingly placed in their neighborhood schools. By 1986, 72 percent of all blind and visually impaired children attended public school (Curry & Hatlen, 1988), and by the beginning of the 21st century this number had grown to more than 90 percent (APH Annual Report 2012). Although students received the benefits of attending school in their home communities alongside other students who were not disabled, they did not receive the kind of ongoing specialized instruction that residential schools in general provided.

The Need for a Special Curriculum

It soon became evident that many of the unique needs of children with visual impairments were not being met in public schools, for a number of reasons. First, the focus of education of students who were blind or visually impaired in local school programs was almost exclusively on a core curriculum of academic subjects that paralleled what their sighted peers received, which visually impaired students had difficulty accessing. Little attention was paid to the nonacademic skills students also needed to learn as a result of their disability. Thus a significant aspect of students' needs for specialized instruction was not addressed in general education classrooms. Second, a lack of trained teachers who might help these students acquire needed skills was apparent and persists to this day. And third, students who had other disabilities besides a visual impairment often were not recognized as needing the intervention of a trained teacher of students with visual impairments, since visual impairment was usually not considered to be their primary disability.

Another factor that made it difficult to meet students' needs in public schools is the itinerant teaching model of service delivery used by the vast majority of school districts in this country; most teachers of students with visual impairments were and are itinerant. This model allowed teachers to cross district and state lines, requiring them to travel over large geographic areas and handle large caseloads of children who are visually impaired. As a result, visually impaired students who attended public schools sometimes had little or no access at all to a teacher of students with visual impairments. Teachers were allowed too little time to address each student's individual needs, and most often had to pull students out of the classroom to address the development of disability-specific skills. Consequently, many students often missed time focusing on their core academic work or socializing with their classmates.

Formalizing the Expanded Core Curriculum

In the early years of mainstreaming, children who were blind or visually impaired attended local school programs, and many teachers were convinced that all these students would need from the school was the same or similar instruction that sighted students received. Educators in the visual impairment field at that time believed that the specialized instruction students needed would in the main be provided in the home and community. Once it became apparent that this assumption was not true, other approaches needed to be considered. From this effort was born the expanded core curriculum.

The movement toward what became known as the expanded core curriculum covered most, if not all, the instruction children who were blind or visually impaired needed that was unique to their disability. The areas of the ECC included instruction not needed by sighted students, who typically gained many of the skills encompassed in the ECC through incidental learning. The lack of instruction ordinarily received by visually impaired students in these areas became more and more apparent as students who had never entered the door of a school for the blind began to graduate from local school programs without the skills needed to participate in adult life after leaving the school system. While the concept of the ECC evolved over time, in response to the growing awareness of students' needs, there nevertheless was no organized or formalized approach defined for the education students needed.

A more formal presentation of the ECC began in 1988 when Sandra Curry and Philip Hatlen published their landmark article, "Meeting the Unique Educational Needs of Visually Impaired Pupils through Appropriate Placement," in which professionals and parents were alerted to the impact of students' failure to learn the elements of the ECC. The need for a dual curriculum—an *expanded* core curriculum in addition to the core curriculum—was explained: This disability-specific curriculum would allow teachers to instruct all students with visual impairments in ways in which to access the same academic curriculum as their classmates, but often using different techniques. In addition to covering the unique skills required to access the core curriculum, this curriculum would also prepare students with the skills to be successful in life's everyday activities.

The importance of the ECC for students with visual impairments has grown steadily, emerging strongly over the past three decades. Instruction has taken place in different ways. Some residential schools and some teachers of students with visual impairments took it as their responsibility to teach all nine areas identified as part of the ECC, while other teachers have worked on one area of the ECC at a time.

ECC Essentials

The value of a disability-specific curriculum has become so firmly established among educators of students with visual impairments over the years that today the discussion has shifted to defining what in essence this curriculum comprises. In the chapters of the book that follows, the components of the expanded core curriculum are considered to be the following: compensatory access, sensory efficiency, assistive technology, orientation and mobility, independent living, social interaction, recreation and leisure, career education, and self-determination. The visual impairment field in general has accepted the concept of an expanded core curriculum as defining the skills necessary for students who are blind or visually impaired to face their education and their lives on an equal basis with their sighted classmates. However, teachers of students with visually impairments, especially itinerant teachers, often feel that they cannot find the time in the day to address all the components of this curriculum in their already overloaded schedule of teaching.

In fact, this issue of time, given the mostly itinerant service delivery models in education of students who are visually impaired, has become one of the major challenges facing the teachers of today. Some feel that the concept of an "expanded core curriculum" is simply a repackaging of what was formerly referred to as the disability-specific curriculum that has been in place for many years; others feel that additional requirements are being placed on an already-too-large agenda for classroom teachers. The unique approach of *ECC Essentials: Teaching the Expanded Core Curriculum to Students with Visual Impairments* addresses this and related issues head on.

It is the purpose of this book not only to articulate clearly the contents of each of the nine components of the EEC but to suggest as well methods and instructional strategies for integrating instruction of the skills in the nine areas of the EEC. In so doing, the editors and chapter authors have provided a road map to show how teachers can most effectively provide instruction, maximize their own effectiveness, and make the best use of their time. In addition, chapters in this book show how to approach educational goals and skill building in the context of the learning standards in effect in any given state or locality.

ECC Essentials discusses the nine ECC content areas along with relevant assessments, the important roles of teachers of students with visual impairments as well as their students' parents, and learning activities and resources. It also includes additional suggestions on integrating the ECC into the core curriculum, aligning the ECC to state standards, and working with administrators. But overlying this material is the recognition that the acquisition of skills is a developmental and organic process and that the interdependence of the areas of the ECC requires teachers not to address nine separate areas in isolation but to work on several skill areas in a combined way that supports natural skill development. It is truly a different approach and method of teaching that allows for specific and strengthened skill development as well as documentation of success.

The primary audience for this book is the trained teacher of students with visual impairments working in inclusive settings with students of all ages who may be blind or visually impaired as well as those with multiple disabilities, although anyone who works with visually impaired students in any setting, as well as parents and family members, will benefit from the extensive and in-depth information contained in this book. The presentation of the nine components of the expanded core curriculum and their related learning activities allows the teacher to have in one volume virtually all the information necessary to teach the ECC.

Because each student with a visual impairment is unique, it is virtually impossible to list all the potential skills that students may need to learn. However, *ECC Essentials* is the only book to provide a detailed presentation of the range of each area in the ECC and its components in a targeted way supportive of teaching efforts. Finally, here is one book that attempts to cover all the issues that teachers need to deal with as they address the expanded core curriculum!

Although the application of this material can be used in a variety of settings such as teacher training programs, the teacher of students with visual impairments, and especially the itinerant teacher, remains at the heart of the book. It provides information and ideas that can be immediately put into practice and encourages and assists the teacher to extrapolate and expand from the material presented, and in that sense serves as a how-to methods book. In helping teachers address both curricula—the core curriculum and the expanded core curriculum—the editors ultimately aim to ensure that students who are blind or visually impaired develop to their full potential as they grow into adulthood.

It has been encouraging to see the enthusiastic way educators and parents have embraced the ECC as critical to meeting their students' and children's needs. The ECC applies to all students who are blind or visually impaired regardless of their educational placement, intellectual abilities, age, or degree of visual impairment. Commitment to the ECC requires that teachers and parents become aware of all aspects of this instruction, even though they might not be necessary for all children at the same time. Professionals and parents also need to become familiar with this book and all the knowledge it contains regarding the application of the ECC. We can only hope that more children will benefit and be better prepared for adult life through the addition of *ECC Essentials* to the literature of the field.

—Philip Hatlen
retired Superintendent
Texas School for the Blind and Visually Impaired

—Susan Jay Spungin
retired Vice President of International Programs and Special Projects
American Foundation for the Blind

References

American Printing House for the Blind. (2012). *Annual report 2012: Administration of the federal appropriation.* Louisville, KY: American Printing House for the Blind. Retrieved from http://www.aph.org/annual-reports/2012/federal.html

Curry, S. A., & Hatlen, P. (1988). Meeting the unique educational needs of visually impaired pupils through appropriate placement. *Journal of Visual Impairment & Blindness, 82*(10), 417–424.

Mackie, R. P., & Cahoe, E. (1956). *Teachers of children who are partially seeing.* A report based on findings from the study, "Qualification and preparation of teachers of exceptional children." Washington, DC:

Office of Education, U.S. Department of Health, Education, and Welfare.

Mackie, R. P., & Dunn, L. M. (1955). *Teachers of children who are blind.* A report based on findings from the study, "Qualification and preparation of teachers of exceptional children." Washington, DC: Office of Education, U.S. Department of Health, Education, and Welfare.

Spungin, S. J. (1977). *Competency based curriculum for teachers of the visually handicapped: A national study.* New York: American Foundation for the Blind.

Acknowledgments

The preparation for editing *ECC Essentials* really started when we were teachers in the late 1970s, working with our own students with visual impairments. Although we were on opposite coasts, it didn't take us long to realize that our students needed more than academic support from us. Of course, in those days, orientation and mobility was considered necessary only for students in high school, assistive technology (even CCTVs) was just an emerging concept, and Natalie Barraga's work on visual efficiency was just being disseminated. Still, we spent hours talking with students (and often their parents) about issues related to social adjustment and what has come to be known as self-determination. We watched with dismay as our students were excluded from physical education and prevented from joining community recreation activities. Our greatest disappointments, however, concerned those of our students who had seemed to do well in school, but struggled with adult responsibilities because of limited independent living and career skills. More than any one person or group, we want to acknowledge these students and families for all that they taught us about the unique needs of students with visual impairments.

We were not alone in concluding that, based on our experiences, our students needed more from us. Fortunately, Dr. Phil Hatlen, a far more careful observer of the needs of students with visual impairments, was active in the field and was beginning to share his concerns about the unintended consequences of the lack of specialized instruction for this population of students. More than just observing, though, Phil, listened. He worked closely with two private agencies in Northern California, one that served the parents of young children with visual impairments and another with the families of students who were making the transition to adulthood. He listened carefully to what these families were telling him about their needs and, combining what he heard with what he knew about the supports students were receiving in school, asked some troubling questions. Why were preschoolers unprepared to understand concepts used in their reading books? Why were students who could correctly answer complex math problems unfamiliar with a checkbook and how to use it? Why were so many students who had graduated from high school unable to live alone, raise a family, or hold down a job without support?

We want to thank Phil Hatlen for being the kind of person who is always eager to learn more, who is committed to excellence, and who is willing to change his mind when the evidence demonstrates that such a change is needed. As the first to articulate the areas of specialized instruction from which most students with visual impairments benefit, Phil can truly be called the "Father of the Expanded Core Curriculum." He and his work continue to inspire both of us, just as they have inspired most of our colleagues, many of whom are contributors to this volume.

Our work on *ECC Essentials* began nearly a decade ago and, like the ECC itself, this book has evolved since its original inception. It is with great admiration and respect that we acknowledge the many direct contributors to this book. Chapter authors, all experts in the ECC areas on which they were asked to write, were given little initial guidance, frequently asked to make revisions as our conceptions for the book changed, and often went long periods of time without a word from us. We apologize for our inexperience as editors and hope that the final work reflects their understanding of the needs of students with visual impairments and how those needs can be met through careful planning across all ECC areas.

A book of this size and complexity depends on the efforts of a great many people, many of whom are "invisible" to the book's readers. It would be impossible for us to acknowledge them all, but we would be remiss if we didn't mention the three key people who kept us on track. First, we were indeed fortunate to have had as consulting editor a true legend in the field of services to children with visual impairment, Dr. Susan Spungin. Although officially "retired," Susan knows more about what is currently going on in this field (and certainly of its history) than almost anyone else alive. Her ideas and suggestions were invaluable and significantly shaped the final version of *ECC Essentials*. In many ways, *ECC Essentials* is a continuation of her dissertation work on the competencies needed by teachers of students with visual impairments. Thank you, Susan, for all you have done for us and for the field.

Ellen Bilofsky, Managing Editor at AFB Press, was phenomenal, particularly during the last six months, as chapters were reviewed, edited, returned to authors, and reviewed again. Without Ellen, there is no doubt that publication of *ECC Essentials* would have been delayed at least another year. We salute you, Ellen, for all that you have done to make this book a reality.

Finally, we cannot express enough gratitude to Natalie Hilzen, former Director and Editor in Chief at AFB Press, for her guidance and support throughout this long process. Although she'll deny it, Natalie's knowledge of the field is extensive and her appreciation of what is needed by teachers and others working with students with visual impairments is unequaled by anyone else in the publishing business. It was Natalie's vision that encouraged us to begin writing *ECC Essentials* and her belief in our ability that sustained us throughout the process. Her name should be in bold letters on the cover of this book! Since it is not, we will have to be satisfied by recognizing her contributions here. Natalie, we couldn't have done it without you.

Introduction

Students with visual impairments have been included in general educational programs since the early part of the 20th century. However, their teachers have always recognized that many of the skills these children need to learn are not addressed adequately in the general education curriculum and require specialized instruction delivered by professionals who understand the impact of visual impairment on learning. By the early 1990s, dedicated educators began to give these unique skills a name. Hatlen (1996) wrote that teachers of students with visual impairments need to be familiar with a special curriculum known as the expanded core curriculum, accept its importance to the current and future lives of their students, and be committed to making sure that students master the components of this curriculum. One of the primary goals of this book is to help teachers of students with visual impairments become more familiar with strategies for teaching the ECC, renew their commitment to teaching these skills to students, and find effective ways to ensure that students have all the skills they need to enter adulthood prepared for success.

This book, *ECC Essentials: Teaching the Expanded Core Curriculum to Students with Visual Impairments*, focuses on the education of children and adolescents with visual impairments by providing the rationale, suggestions, and strategies for the implementation of instruction in those skills that are typically learned primarily through incidental exposure to them. It has been designed specifically with the teacher of students with visual impairments in mind and seeks to provide these teachers with information, resources, and solutions for addressing the challenges they contend with every day.

There are three parts to this book. Part 1 focuses on the importance of the ECC, as well as the evolutionary, cumulative process through which skills are developed in children. The chapters in Part 1 present the foundations for understanding the unique needs of students with visual impairments and describe how those needs can be met through careful assessment and planned instruction. Part 2 provides specific guidance and strategies for teaching each of the nine areas of the ECC: compensatory access, sensory efficiency, assistive technology, orientation and mobility, independent living, social interaction, recreation and leisure, career education, and self-determination. Although each chapter of Part 2 deals specifically with one ECC area, there is a distinct emphasis on that area's relationship to other areas of the ECC and the importance of teaching skills within meaningful activities that encompass more than one area at once. A major focus of this book is the suggestion to teachers that the myriad of skills that make up the nine areas of the ECC should not be taught in isolation and, indeed, are integral to and complement one another. For this reason, learning activities are provided at the end of each chapter that, while primarily linked to that chapter, provide lessons that combine skills from several areas of the ECC. The intention here is to help reinforce students' skills and maximize teachers' time, planning, and effectiveness. Part 3 of this book is designed to provide teachers with additional resources that support both the ECC and their own effectiveness. It addresses aligning the ECC with state standards, teaching the ECC in general education settings, and maximizing parent involvement.

Although some teachers may view the ECC as an extra set of skills that students need to be taught, it is, in actuality, what teachers do and are supposed to teach. In fact, they must! Without gaining access to the general education curriculum, students cannot learn it. Gaining this access and becoming a competent, independent adult are the goals of education for each student with visual impairments. These goals are embodied in the learning of the ECC. Although there remains much discussion about how many areas of the ECC there are, what they should be called, and how various skills should be grouped, the nine areas as outlined in this book and the table of contents are based on current thinking and our own experiences and the experiences of the teachers we know. The editors of this book fully support ideas that suggest a great deal of overlap in skills within the nine areas, and for that reason, have chosen to provide learning activities that address skills across several areas of the ECC.

Just as there is a great deal of overlap across the areas of the ECC, no area can be considered of more value than the others. An important premise of this book is that mastery in each of the nine ECC areas begins in early childhood and evolves over time. A child whose sensory skills are not established or efficient will not be able to develop the concepts that are in turn central to the formulation of compensatory access skills, engage in leisure activities, or prepare meals. Children who lack self-determination are unlikely to be able to participate meaningfully with friends, make decisions while traveling, or select appropriate assistive technology. The editors considered at length the order in which to present the chapters in this book, but could not identify any skills that are truly prerequisites of any others. All ECC areas are important to the healthy development of the preschooler, just as all are critical to the functioning of the older student. Ignoring the accumulative acquisition of skills in any one area of the ECC has the potential to impose future limitations on the student's functioning. One of the goals in the writing of this book is to prevent these limitations by helping teachers to recognize the evolutionary and prerequisite nature of the mastery of skills.

ECC Essentials: Teaching the Expanded Core Curriculum to Students with Visual Impairments is the first comprehensive book written for teachers that addresses the areas of importance to them as they work to meet the unique needs of all their students with visual impairments. The authors of each chapter in this book are experts in the education of students with visual impairments in general, and specifically within the ECC area that is the focus of their chapters. Their contributions to the important material in this book make *ECC Essentials: Teaching the Expanded Core Curriculum to Students with Visual Impairments* a significant addition to the literature and a powerful tool for both present and future teachers of students with visual impairments.

—Carol B. Allman and Sandra Lewis

About the Contributors

Editors

Carol B. Allman, Ph.D., is a private consultant in special education and assessment issues and was formerly Program Director of Exceptional Student Education Programs at the Florida Department of Education in Tallahassee. She has worked in the field of visual impairment for over 35 years, as a teacher of students with visual impairments, an instructor at Florida State University, and an administrator. Dr. Allman serves as an educational consultant to Florida and other states on issues related to serving students with visual impairments. She is the author of *Test Access: Making Tests Accessible for Students with Visual Impairments: A Guide for Test Publishers, Test Developers, and State Assessment Personnel,* and has authored and co-authored a number of book chapters and articles in several journals.

Sandra Lewis, Ed.D., is Professor, School of Teacher Education, Florida State University in Tallahassee, Florida. She is the Chair of the *Journal of Visual Impairment & Blindness* Editorial Advisory Board and the Treasurer of the Florida chapter of the Association for Education and Rehabilitation of the Blind and Visually Impaired (AER), as well as its past president and secretary and the past president of the Northern California chapter. She is also the recipient of the 2010 Mary K. Bauman Award from AER. Dr. Lewis has worked as an educator of individuals of all ages who are blind or visually impaired and has published widely on the education and assessment of visually impaired students.

Susan J. Spungin, Ph.D., Consulting Editor, is retired as Vice President of International Programs and Special Projects at the American Foundation for the Blind (AFB), where she had served in executive capacities since 1972. She has served as consultant, advisory committee member, and officer of numerous national and international professional organizations, including the World Blind Union, where she served as treasurer from 2004 to 2008, and is currently secretary of the Association for Education and Rehabilitation of the Blind and Visually Impaired (AER). Dr. Spungin has received numerous honors and awards, including the Mary K. Bauman Award from AER and the Wings of Freedom Award from the American Printing House for the Blind. In 2009 she received the AFB Migel Medal, the highest honor in the blindness field.

Chapter Authors

Julie A. Bardin, Ph.D., is a teacher of students with visual impairments North Carolina. She is also an Adjunct Instructor at Florida State University in Tallahassee and West Virginia University in Morgantown. She has published several journal articles and made numerous presentations on the education of children with visual impairments.

Karen E. Blankenship, Ph.D., is Professor of the Practice, Program in Visual Disabilities, Department of Special Education, Peabody College, Vanderbilt University. She is the past chair of the Itinerant Personnel Division of the Association for Education and Rehabilitation of the Blind and Visually Impaired and recipient of its 2010 Judy Cerkovich Award.

Laura C. Brown, M.Ed., is Coordinator of the Visually Impaired Program at the Hillsborough County Public Schools in Tampa, Florida, and Adjunct Professor, Visual Disabilities Program, Florida State University in Tallahassee. She has served as an itinerant teacher, a resource room teacher, and program coordinator, as well as on numerous task forces, advisory committees, and work groups for the Florida State Department of Education. She is a past chair of the Administrative Division and Scholarship Committee of the Association for Education and Rehabilitation of the Blind and Visually Impaired as well as past president of the Florida chapter.

Sue Douglass, M.S., was a teacher of visually impaired students with the Castro Valley School District in California for 29 years and Vision Impairment Specialist with Blind Babies Foundation for five years before her retirement. She was a member of the board of the California Transcribers and Educators for the Blind and

Visually Impaired (CTEBVI) from 2006 to 2012 and chair of the 2009 CTEBVI Conference. She was also a lecturer in the preparation program for teachers of students with visual impairments at San Francisco State University.

Carol Farrenkopf, Ed.D., is Vision Program Coordinator, Toronto District School Board, and Assistant Professor (Limited Duties) at the University of Western Ontario, Ontario, Canada. She is also Associate Editor of the *Journal of Visual Impairment & Blindness.* She has been a teacher of students who are visually impaired, including students with behavioral disorders, for over 20 years. Dr. Farrenkopf is co-editor of *Looking to Learn: Promoting Literacy for Students with Low Vision* and co-author of *Assessment of Braille Literacy Skills.* She has published a number of articles and book chapters on the education of children who are blind or visually impaired and has presented numerous papers at regional, national, and international conferences.

Diane L. Fazzi, Ph.D., a certified orientation and mobility specialist, is Coordinator of the Orientation and Mobility Specialist Training Program, Charter College of Education, California State University, Los Angeles. She is the co-editor of *Early Focus: Working with Young Blind and Visually Impaired Children and Their Families* and the co-author of *Imagining the Possibilities: Creative Approaches to Orientation and Mobility Instruction for Persons Who Are Blind or Visually Impaired,* as well as the author of numerous book chapters, journal articles, and conference presentations on working with young children who are visually impaired.

Missy Garber, Ph.D., is Vision Support Teacher with the Montgomery County Intermediate Unit in Norristown, Pennsylvania. She is also an Adjunct Assistant Professor in the College of Education and Rehabilitation at Salus University in Elkins Park, Pennsylvania, where she was the Director of the Teacher of the Visually Impaired Preparation Program and was the Co-Director of the National Center for Leadership in Visual Impairment. She is the parent of a teenager with a visual impairment.

Susan Glaser, M.S., is Coordinator of the Florida State University Satellite Program in Visual Disabilities at the University Partnership Center/St. Petersburg College in Seminole; Transition Coordinator at the Tampa Lighthouse for the Blind; and teacher of students with visual impairments and orientation and mobility instructor with the Florida Instructional Materials Center for the Visually Impaired, where she coordinates the Florida Regional Braille Challenge and Cane Quest.

Amy R. Guerette, Ed.D., is Associate Dean for Academic Affairs, College of Education at Florida State University in Tallahassee. She serves on national and state committees in the field of visual impairment and deafblindness, as well as various state and university committees regarding teacher preparation and academic integrity. She has published numerous journal articles and has presented widely on the development of literacy skills in students with visual impairments and deafblindness, accommodations and workplace barriers for adults with visual impairments, and teacher preparation.

Deborah Tierney Kreuzer, Ph.D., is Director of Education at the California School for the Blind in Fremont. She has published and presented on language and literacy issues for students with visual, speech, and physical impairments.

Lauren J. Lieberman, Ph.D., is a Distinguished Service Professor in the Department of Kinesiology, Sport Studies and Physical Education, The College at Brockport—State University of New York, where she teaches undergraduate and graduate courses in adapted physical education. Founder of Camp Abilities, a sports camp for children who are visually impaired, blind, or deafblind, Dr. Lieberman is the co-author of *Physical Education and Sports for People with Visual Impairments and Deafblindness,* and has authored numerous books and research articles and presented nationally and internationally on physical activity and individuals with visual impairments. She is the recipient of the 2012 Access Award from the American Foundation for the Blind and the 2012 Professional of the Year Award from the Adapted Physical Activity Council of the American Alliance for Health, Physical Education, Recreation and Dance and is on the board of directors of the U.S. Association for Blind Athletes.

Donna McNear, M.A., is an independent educational consultant focused on services for children and youths with visual impairments. Prior to that she was a teacher of students with visual impairments and orientation and mobility specialist in Minnesota. She currently provides technical assistance to educational agencies and organizations nationally and internationally. Ms. McNear was the recipient of the 2008 Outstanding Leadership Award from the Council for Exceptional Children (CEC) and the 2007 Distinguished Service Award from the CEC Division on Visual Impairments. She was a contributing author of *When You Have a Visually Impaired Student in Your Classroom: A Guide for Teachers;* has written journal articles, book chapters, and reports; and has presented widely, especially on technology and visual impairment.

L. Penny Rosenblum, Ph.D., is a Professor of Practice, Department of Disability and Psychoeducational Studies at The University of Arizona in Tucson. She is the co-author of *Finding Wheels: A Curriculum for Non-drivers with Visual Impairments for Gaining Control of Transportation Needs* and produced the video *Reclaiming Independence: Staying in the Driver's Seat When You No Longer Drive* with the American Printing House for the Blind and wrote the accompanying resource guide. She has published journal articles, has contributed book chapters to *Teaching Social Skills to Students with Visual Impairments* and *Diversity and Visual Impairment: The Influence of Race, Gender, Religion, and Ethnicity on the Individual* and has presented papers at a variety of conferences.

Mary Alice Ross, M.S., is an Adapted Physical Education teacher and a certified orientation and mobility specialist at the California School for the Blind in Fremont. She is the author of *Fitness for the Aging Adult with Visual Impairment: An Exercise and Resource Manual,* has written various journal articles, and contributed a chapter to *Itinerant Teaching: Tricks of the Trade for Teachers of Students with Visual Impairments.*

Sharon Z. Sacks, Ph.D., is Director of Curriculum, Assessment and Professional Development at the California School for the Blind. She was formerly Professor and Coordinator of the Teacher Preparation Program in Visual Impairments at California State University, Los Angeles. She is co-editor of the *Focused On . . . Social Skills* series of videos and study guides, and co-editor of *Teaching Social Skills to Students with Visual Impairments: From Research to Practice* and of *Educating Students Who Have Visual Impairments with Other Disabilities,* and has authored or co-authored numerous book chapters and journal articles. She has presented and published widely throughout the United States and abroad in the areas of social skills instruction for students with visual impairments, transition programming for students with visual impairments and multiple disabilities, psychosocial implications of low vision for students and adults, and issues related to braille literacy. Dr. Sacks is past president of the Association for Education and Rehabilitation of the Blind and Visually Impaired (AER) and the winner of the 2014 Mary K. Bauman Award from AER.

Mildred Smith, M.Ed., is a private consultant for students with visual impairments and for the American Printing House for the Blind (APH) in Louisville, Kentucky. She is the author of *SLK Guidebook and Assessment Forms: Using the Sensory Learning Kit* and *SAM: Symbols and Meaning* and is co-author of *Teaching Students with Visual and Multiple Impairments: A Resource Guide* and the *Barraga Visual Efficiency Program,* forthcoming from the American Printing House for the Blind. She is the recipient of the 2000 C. Warren Bledsoe Award from the Association for Education and Rehabilitation of the Blind and Visually Impaired (AER), the 2001 Virginia Sowell Award from the AER Multiple Disabilities and Deafblind Division, and the 2013 APH Virgil Zickel Award.

Karen E. Wolffe, Ph.D., is the owner of Career Counseling and Consultation in Austin, Texas, and was previously Director of Professional Development and CareerConnect at the American Foundation for the Blind. She is the author of *Career Counseling for People with Disabilities: A Practical Guide to Finding Employment, Transition Tote System,* and *Pre-Employment Programme Trainer's Manual.* She is editor of *Skills for Success: A Career Education Handbook for Children and Youth with Visual Impairments* and co-editor of *Teaching Social Skills to Students with Visual Impairments: From Research to Practice.* She also co-authored *Transition Issues for Students with Visual Disabilities* and *Focused on . . . Social Skills,* a series of instructional videos and study guides. She is the 2002 winner of the John H. McAulay Award from the Association for Education and Rehabilitation of the Blind and Visually Impaired (AER); the 2010 winner of the Robert M. Lambert Award from the AER Psychosocial Division; and the 2014 winner of AER's Ambrose M. Shotwell Award.

Learning Activity Contributors

Nita Crow, M.A., is a certified orientation and mobility specialist at the California School for the Blind. She is a co-author of *Getting to Know You: A Social Skills and Ability Awareness Curriculum*, published by American Printing House for the Blind, and author of several articles in the *Journal of Visual Impairment & Blindness.*

Robyn Herrera, M.A., is a doctoral candidate in the joint doctoral program in special education between California State University, Los Angeles, and the University of California, Los Angeles. She is a recipient of the National Leadership Consortium in Sensory Disabilities Fellowship.

Stephanie Herlich, M.A., is a teacher of visually impaired students, an orientation and mobility specialist, and Low Vision Coordinator at the California School for the Blind in Fremont. She was a researcher on the Alphabetic Braille and Contracted Braille Study (ABC Study), funded by American Printing House for the Blind (APH). She is co-author of *Getting to Know You: A Social Skills and Ability Awareness Curriculum*, contributed a chapter to *Learning to Listen/Listening to Learn: Teaching Listening Skills to Students with Visual Impairments,* and is the author of *Book 3: Learning Braille Contractions for SAL2.* She has also published articles in *Re:view* and the *Journal of Visual Impairment & Blindness.*

Elizabeth Eagan Satter, M.A., a 23-year-veteran in the teaching field, is a teacher of students with visual impairments in Bastrop Independent School District, Bastrop, Texas. She was named the 2006 Texas Council for Exceptional Children (CEC) Teacher of the Year. She has written articles for CEC's *DVI Quarterly* as well as Texas School for the Blind's *SenseAbilities.*

L. Penny Rosenblum

PART I

The Importance of the Expanded Core Curriculum

CHAPTER 1

Learning, Development, and Children with Visual Impairments: The Evolution of Skills

Sandra Lewis and Carol B. Allman

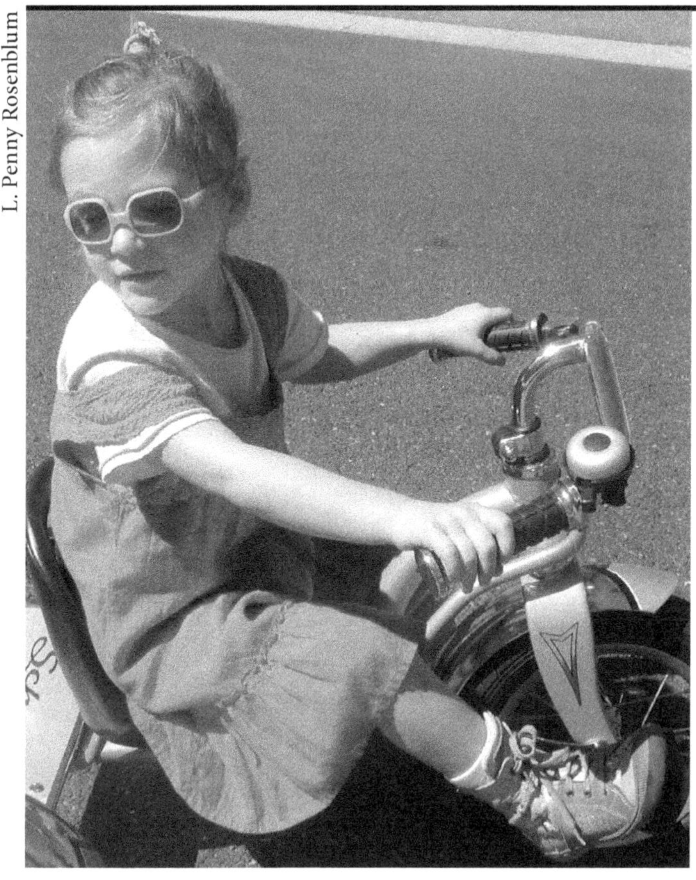
L. Penny Rosenblum

For a child who is visually impaired, learning about the world can be a complicated job. Because vision is the primary sensory system humans use for learning, the very nature of visual impairment means that the process of acquiring new information may be compromised. Because impaired vision affects students' ability to learn by watching other people model behaviors and by observing the operations of the world at large, much of the information available visually to children with typical vision is often not easily accessible to children with impaired sight. Included in this information are both the formal lessons presented in schools and the thousands of pieces of informal information that children, youths, and adolescents gather visually as they construct meaning from their observations and experiences. These informal bits of information include both basic and complex concepts about things, people, space, and the relationships among them.

Since both formally and informally acquired information is critical for successful functioning as an adult and for effective functioning and success in childhood and adolescence for all of us, how, then, can students with visual impairments obtain this information? When a child is not able to access the surrounding environment through his or her vision, the tasks of acquiring information and learning need to be approached and supported deliberately and thoughtfully. Thus, educating children with visual impairments involves unique considerations that must be taken into account in order to provide these students with the tools, skills, and strategies they need to develop alternative ways of obtaining critical information.

Preparing students with visual impairments with the academic, social, and life skills necessary for them to have access to, be integrated within, and participate fully in school, work, and society overall means, then, designing instruction that meets their unique learning styles and their specific needs. Like all children, those who are visually impaired need to learn the general academic curriculum. Unlike other children, visually impaired students also need to be provided instruction in specialized techniques and skills that enable them to have access to the general curriculum and the other formal and informal information they need to navigate the world successfully. These critical skills have come to be known as the expanded core curriculum (ECC), and are encompassed in the nine areas of compensatory access, sensory efficiency, assistive technology, orientation and mobility, independent living, social interaction, recreation and leisure, career education, and self-determination. It is impossible to overstate the importance of these skills in the education of students who are visually impaired.

Why is the ECC so important? As already indicated, this body of skills is necessary for access to and mastery of the core curriculum expected of all students, as well as for successful functioning in life. The knowledge and skills encompassed by the ECC are not acquired naturally through day-to-day life by many children with visual impairments, as they typically are by children with unimpaired vision. Children with limited or no vision often cannot pick up on the visual nuances offered on a daily basis that create the foundation for social and life skills, understanding, and learning. Without these special skills, children with visual impairments may not only be unaware of and uninformed about essential concepts and facts needed for independent functioning by all individuals, but they can also become isolated and overly dependent on others and may lack self-knowledge, self-assurance, and motivation.

The development of skills in the ECC by students with visual impairments requires thoughtful planning not only by their teachers in any one year, but planning and collaboration by and among family members, school administrators, and educators throughout their educational lives. Attention also needs to be directed beyond students' immediate needs to long-term goals. One way to focus attention on these goals is to begin with the end in mind.

BEGINNING WITH THE END IN MIND

Susan and Ed say that they hope their 7-year-old daughter, Kelly, will grow up to have a job, get married, and raise a family. They also would like Kelly to go to college and become employed as a professional of some kind. They dream that Kelly will live near them so that they can be close with their grandchildren and share family holidays. They know that Kelly is smart and believe she will be able to overcome the obstacles presented to her by her congenital visual impairment.

Lisa, Kelly's teacher of students with visual impairments, shares these goals with Kelly's parents and realizes that she must begin early in Kelly's educational programming to focus on skills that will lead to the achievement of these goals. Somehow she must find time to show Kelly how she can overcome the obstacles presented by a world designed for people with vision, while she learns the academic skills necessary for college and employment.

However, when asked when they think they'll allow Kelly to travel by herself on the public bus or in a taxi, Susan and Ed hesitate. "Maybe when she's older," is their indeterminate reply. Their response is similar when asked when they think they might let her go on a date. Of course, dating and riding in a cab alone are not the kind of activities in which most 7-year-olds engage, so many may agree that "when she's older" is an appropriate response.

But Kelly's parents also become defensive when asked when they will allow their daughter to walk by herself to a neighbor's house down the street, offering the following responses: "She can hardly see, you know. It wouldn't be safe." "She might wander into the street." And, "I'd die worrying."

What Susan and Ed may not realize right now is that their dreams for Kelly, although quite realistic, cannot be achieved all at once at some future time unless steps are taken now to prepare the way for them. Kelly's ability to select the right mate for herself will be determined, in large part, on her experiences with dating, which will in turn be influenced by her previous relationships with male and female friends and acquaintances and with her family. Most people do not just decide to get married one day; marriage is the result of a long evolution in the development of relationship skills that begins in infancy.

In a way, relationships are dependent on good travel skills, too. Common sense suggests that Kelly won't be going on a date in her teens unless her parents feel she has the skills to take care of herself in potentially difficult situations, which means being able to take a cab home, if necessary. Usually, the skills required to arrange for and direct a cab driver are built on foundation skills developed over a period of time when one is traveling independently for other purposes and perhaps in a smaller area, such as a neighborhood.

The reality is that by limiting Kelly's travel experiences at age 7, her parents are inadvertently influencing her growth in several areas. Successfully negotiating adult responsibilities—employment, finding a life partner, raising children—requires that children acquire the needed skills in small increments and gradually increase the sophistication of those skills over time. Kelly's parents need help to realize that in order to achieve their dreams for Kelly, they have to keep focused on the long-term goals and create or allow for the opportunities that will facilitate the slow evolution of the skills she will need. In many ways, they have to begin with the end in mind and stay focused on the potential adult they want their child to become.

One of Lisa's key responsibilities in this developmental process of skills building is to help Kelly's parents recognize the particular skills that Kelly will need for adult living. Lisa will also need to provide instruction in these needed skills and work closely with Susan and Ed as Kelly develops toward adulthood. Strong partnerships between parents and teachers increase students' potential for appropriate development. These partnerships can foster coordination of efforts, create supplementary opportunities for practice and repeated exposure to skills, and provide for reinforcement of key concepts and behaviors. Another key responsibility that Lisa will focus on is Kelly's role in developing the critical skills of the ECC; keeping in mind the potential adult Kelly may become will help Lisa sustain this effort as well.

FOCUSING ON THE POTENTIAL ADULT

The first 18 to 21 years of life—the period typically spent by children at home and in school—are but a fraction of the time that most individuals live. In the United States today, the recognition of adult status generally occurs when one's time in high school has been completed or when one begins to assume adult responsibilities, such as living away from a parent's home, working, voting, or raising a family. Even if individuals do not take on these responsibilities until they are older than 18 or 21, they are usually considered "adults" based just on age. They will be expected to manage life as an adult for more than 60 years—nearly three times as long as the period that is complete at the end of high school.

Preparation for adulthood and adult roles occurs throughout the developmental periods of infancy, early and middle childhood, and adolescence. As children mature intellectually, physically, socially, emotionally, and morally, they are developing the knowledge, skills, and attitudes that influence their future behavior and life choices. Growth in these areas generally is shaped by a variety of influences, including biology, personal life experiences, relationships with adults and peers, social institutions, and culture (Shonkoff & Phillips, 2000).

Development, by its very nature, is a process that requires and takes place over time. Mastery of skills *evolves*, knowledge *increases*, and attitudes are *nurtured*. Time is an essential element in each of these processes. Change in children—growth—often is incremental and difficult to recognize immediately; only over time can it be easily measured. Norms have been established that describe the typical development of children, though these quantitative measures usually are accompanied by disclaimers that variations from the norms are common.

In the absence of evidence to the contrary, most adults act in accordance with a subconscious belief that skills will evolve and emerge naturally in children and focus only on what they perceive as a child's immediate needs. That is, parents of toddlers serve meat to their children in bite-size pieces, assuming that the children will develop cutting skills in the future. The mother of an 8-year-old is likely to restrict her son to playing in the local neighborhood. She doesn't plan to maintain this restriction forever, but rather expects that as he matures, she will increase the size of the area where he is allowed to spend time without her.

A key point in these examples is that parents and teachers can more or less assume that the process of development will occur and that skills, attitudes, and knowledge will evolve in children. Although this development will emerge in many areas without much adult direction, it is recognized that growth can and should be influenced by adult intervention. For example, at some point, a child will be taught how to carefully handle a table knife (and then a steak knife). And, as long as students continue to progress in school, they will be taught higher or more advanced skills in the appropriate grades.

Educational systems are designed to assist children with their growth toward adulthood in those areas in which, without intervention, children are less likely to achieve expected development. States in this country have identified the standards of learning for the basic or core curriculum in mathematics, reading, language arts, social studies, and science. Educators at each grade know what knowledge and skills children need to master in order to be prepared for the next level. However, formal standards of learning for social, recreation, or career awareness skills do not exist. Schools place less emphasis on those skills that children are expected to learn without intensive instruction. For example, safe travel in the community and skills related to independent living are not considered part of the standard curriculum. It is expected that students will acquire these skills at the level desired by their families, and it is left to the family to determine how best to provide direction in these skills to the developing child.

Generally, families provide direct instruction in these areas on an as-needed basis. Parents tell toddlers and young children to hold hands and to "look both ways" before crossing the street. Parents demonstrate how to clear the lawn of any rocks or twigs and start the lawn mower; they stay close as the first few strips of grass are mowed, providing advice when necessary. Grandparents make soup with their grandchildren, showing them how to cut the different vegetables and keeping a watchful eye out for unsafe techniques. Parents take their children with them to softball games or track meets, families go hiking, and siblings play board and card games with one another. By watching others, attending to mini-demonstrations ("hold your cards like this"), and getting advice ("it's easier if you shift your weight to the front foot"), children learn most of the everyday skills that will be useful to them as adults.

A common description of parenting, "raising" children, implies that the process takes place in relation to an end point and that the adults are focused on the end product: bringing their child from the dependency of childhood to become a contributing adult who functions competently within an interdependent society. Parents who insist that their children share, help with the housework, and find something to do may be reacting to the needs of the moment, but if asked to think about why they persist with these demands, they recognize that they are preparing their children for their future as adults.

Ed and Susan would argue that they, too, are preparing Kelly for her future as an adult. They encourage her to do well in school and provide a quiet time and space at home for her to do her homework. They attend to her moral education by setting positive examples and making sure that she attends religious services. And, when she is "ready," they will teach her how to cut vegetables, allow her to walk to a neighbor's house, and have her manage her own order at McDonald's.

There are some skills, however, that Susan and Ed haven't yet introduced to Kelly. She isn't assigned household chores because, as Susan explains, "life is so hard for her already." Kelly doesn't help wash the car or weed the garden, "because she's never shown any interest in being outside." They've never really thought of playing board or card games with Kelly. "I guess I just assumed it would be too difficult for her to follow the play of the game," is Ed's explanation. Susan sometimes sums up the situation by saying, "I'd teach her more, but I really don't know how."

Lisa recognizes that Kelly's parents are hesitant and somewhat overprotective of their child. She also understands the reasons for their behavior. Sometimes Lisa wonders if she should "push the issue" with Kelly's parents as she recommends having Kelly take letters to the mailbox and being assigned specific household chores that are appropriate for a 7-year-old. Lisa does not want to alienate these parents, but she sees the need for follow-through at home if Kelly is to develop the skills needed for future mature functioning. She suspects that it would be helpful to spend some time at Kelly's home with her and her parents to help them understand the impact of Kelly's visual impairment and to ease them into the practice of some of the skills that Kelly needs to learn, but Lisa never seems to have enough time to do her job at school, much less add home visits to her schedule.

BARRIERS TO INSTRUCTION PERCEIVED BY PARENTS

Without being aware that they are doing so, Susan and Ed have offered common justifications for delaying or avoiding the introduction of important non-academic skills to children with visual impairments. It isn't that they think Kelly won't be able to play games, prepare meals, travel alone, and manage on her own; they just perceive that she isn't ready *now* to learn how to do them. They think that these skills will gradually emerge, as they do for all children. They haven't taken into account the impact of visual impairment on learning, which is reflected in the explanations they have offered for Kelly's lack of involvement in some areas and activities.

Lack of Interest

"She doesn't show any interest." For children to show interest in performing a task or learning a skill, they first have to be aware that the task exists. In general, children with good distance vision become interested in raking the leaves, making their own breakfast, and playing softball as a result of their visual observations of those activities. Youngsters with visual impairments, who may have poor distance vision, often are not aware of what is going on around them in the same way. They may know that Dad is "making dinner" but may have an incomplete understanding of what "making" means.

In addition, many visually impaired youngsters may not be aware that the tasks occurring around them might be something that others besides a grown-up would do. Children with unimpaired vision often demand to be included. At some point, they typically want to try to vacuum, pour milk, and hold the dog's leash. They may insist on copying what they see on television or in the world around them: they pass footballs, play sandlot baseball, and sleep outside in tents. Many children who are blind or have low vision may not demand that they take on similar tasks. If what is being done around them is done only by grown-ups, then how are they to know that they, too, might be involved?

The Task is Too Difficult

"I assume it will be too difficult for her to do." Of course, adults in the lives of children with visual impairments could propose that the children "help" with whatever task is being performed at the moment. "Come plant flowers with me," or "Fill the glasses with orange juice," or "Let's go toss some hoops," are all phrases that parents of children with visual impairments could utter, but many parents find them difficult to propose. In part, they may avoid asking their children to help because they feel that the task is too difficult or the action too complicated.

That perceived difficulty may have been confirmed to them each time they have tried to teach their child a new skill. Children with significant visual impairments often take more time to learn tasks than children with unimpaired sight. This increased learning time is related to the fact that children with unimpaired vision have the opportunity, through their vision, to observe tasks being performed, often hundreds of times, before they ever begin to try them on their own. They have been learning through observation since infancy, so already understand the concept of what needs to be done, the steps that are required, and the order in which those steps occur. Instruction is primarily necessary to refine techniques and ensure safety. For a child with a visual impairment, however, adults may need to provide instruction on each part of the task, and more than once. Because each of the steps may be unfamiliar to the child, additional practice may be necessary. It is also likely that more frequent messes will be made as the child practices difficult new tasks, such as pouring from a container or washing the car.

It can be challenging for some children with visual impairments to learn new skills. Adults who only have experience teaching children with unimpaired vision can become frustrated or perplexed when working with a child with a visual impairment. Seeing the difficulty that the child has with acquiring a new skill, it may be easy to assume that the skill itself is too difficult for the child, with the result that further instruction is delayed.

The Parents Lack Special Knowledge

"I don't know how to teach her." People who rely on their vision to accomplish everyday living, career, social, and recreation tasks often cannot imagine how a person would manage similar tasks without the benefit of sight. Frequently, this kind of thinking can prevent adults from even trying to teach a child a particular task. Once convinced that a child must learn a skill, adults must then consider how the instruction should occur.

When parents and other adults try to teach new skills to children with visual impairments, they may experience the situation just described, where the "usual" amount of instructional effort and time doesn't seem to be enough; the child needs additional time to understand each step in a task and to master the desired skill. In addition, it may be apparent that the child needs to use different techniques and rely on other senses for key information to learn a skill or complete a task.

People unfamiliar with teaching children with visual impairments may also become discouraged when they realize how traditional teaching typically relies on the learner's ability to observe, imitate, and reproduce actions. "Hold the knife like I'm doing." "Put your foot here and bend your leg just this much." "Well, you almost have it, but you need to stop the bat just a bit sooner, like this." Many skills are taught by having learners watch the task, and then try to replicate it on their own. People working with a student with visual impairments may try to move the child's hands to substitute for the child's limited ability to watch the task. But when adults insert their hands into a task to help a visually impaired child by guiding the child's hands, the "feel" of the task itself changes somewhat for the child, which makes learning it all the more difficult and independent practice of the skill all the more critical to achieve mastery.

Although many of the techniques and strategies used by teachers of students with visual impairments and vision rehabilitation therapists are relatively simple, they are not intuitive to people unfamiliar with living with visual impairment. It is easy to get stuck on the "how" of instruction. Parents frequently need their children's teacher to provide them with suggestions about what can be taught and how to go about teaching it. Usually, once parents learn that the most effective techniques used by teachers of students with visual impairments are common sense and patience, their fears about "teaching the right way" dissipate.

The Child Is Not Ready

"We'll teach her when she's ready." A key idea in this chapter is that skills develop and evolve, and this is equally true for children with and children without visual impairments. Skills, knowledge, and attitudes do not just appear out of nowhere; they develop gradually over time, based on a variety of influences. It is sometimes easy for adults to forget that for children with visual impairments, "readiness" to take on any given task or activity occurs only after hundreds of associated skills are achieved. Kelly won't be "ready" to make and serve breakfast for her family until she knows how to use certain appliances, knows where specific food items and utensils are stored, and knows how to use the needed utensils to perform related tasks like spreading, cutting, and pouring. She will also need to know how to set and clear the table, rinse the dishes, load the dishwasher, and wipe the counters. Long before she is "ready" to make and serve breakfast, she will be (and, at age 7, already is) ready to learn how to perform many of these individual steps. In fact, she probably was ready to learn to put the toast in the toaster, put food in the pantry, empty the silverware basket from the dishwasher, and wipe counters several years ago.

Teachers of students with visual impairments recognize that readiness is an evolving process. They know that the child who can put a play coin in a slot is ready to put the toast in the toaster, that the child who can turn on the water in the sink or bathtub is ready to turn on the water to wash the car, and that the child who can push a toy shopping cart around a play area is ready to help push the lawnmower. They realize that a child doesn't have to "make toast" or "mow the grass"—overwhelming tasks for young children—but that partial participation is enough at first. They expect that over time, the child will do more and more of the task, practicing each of its component steps until the entire task is mastered.

Focusing on the skills that will be needed by the potential adult does not mean that the adults surrounding children with visual impairments need to have them lead a life of all work and no play. Rather, the families and teachers of these children need to keep in mind that there is no "magic moment" at which a skill should be taught. A conscious effort needs to be made to make sure that students with visual impairments are exposed to, assist others with, and gradually become more involved in and responsible for the execution of skills that are expected to be mastered by adulthood. Washing dishes independently is a skill that may be *mastered* by children when they are about 10, for example, but it is *learned* through exposure, partial participation, and practice (both visually and in play) as early as possible. Kelly can help her mother run the water and add dish detergent to the sink if she has a stool to stand on and is allowed to get her hands wet and soapy. Lisa can show Susan which steps Kelly could practice and participate in as they wash the dishes. As Kelly grows older, she will be able to complete this task and many others independently, with instruction and practice, just as her sighted classmates are expected to.

A Teacher's View

Lisa, like many teachers of students with visual impairments, has also identified an important barrier to Kelly's instruction: time. Most of the limited time that teachers do have is available when students are expected to be engaged in learning the core curriculum and other formal requirements.

Detailing all the roles and responsibilities of teachers of students with visual impairments might require several pages in a book such as this (see, for example, Spungin & Ferrell, 2007). Specialized areas in which teachers must regularly participate include:

- assessment and evaluation
- educational and instructional strategies related to adapting the learning environment
- educational and instructional strategies related to adapting the curriculum
- guidance and counseling
- administration and supervision
- school-community relations

There are no easy answers to the problem of not having enough time. Children with visual impairments need to learn the skills of the core curriculum. They also need to learn the ECC, which on its own encompasses hundreds of skills. Teachers of students with visual impairments are often required to make difficult choices about where and how they use their time. Given school systems' demands to ensure that students perform well on statewide accountability assessments and the like, it may seem prudent to forego a planned lesson on the types of balls used in various sporting events to review for an algebra test. Still, too many decisions made in favor of supporting instruction in the core curriculum can result in a student who does not have the skills to be competent outside of school, as a child, adolescent, or adult.

The areas or domains of the ECC—compensatory access, sensory efficiency, assistive technology, orientation and mobility, independent living, social interaction, recreation and leisure, career education, and self-determination (see Chapter 2 for more detailed information)—are closely interrelated. Knowing how to get to the grocery store, for example, may be of little value if one doesn't know how to shop, pay for one's purchases, or interact appropriately with the cashiers or store staff who might provide assistance. It makes sense to leverage these connections and design instruction that takes advantage of these interrelationships. Therefore, teachers of students with visual impairments can make the most of their instructional time by embedding instruction in and practice of as many skills as possible within learning activities. In fact, one activity, if thoughtfully constructed, can help a child develop several skills. The chapters that follow are intended to provide help in implementing this approach to skill development and instruction in the ECC (see Chapters 3 and 13 in particular), and the learning activities presented in Part 2 of this book are offered for use and modification by teachers. Given that skills evolve over time and are interdependent, this way of analyzing and providing instruction supports students' learning in an optimal way.

VISUAL IMPAIRMENT AND LEARNING

The impact that visual impairment may have on a child's ability to acquire information was referred to at the beginning of this chapter. The visual cues provided by sight allow a child with unimpaired vision to acquire new skills and information through casual observation and experience, often without intervention from adults. Learning through casual observation is often referred to as *incidental* learning. Children with visual impairment typically learn differently, since the information that they acquire through their impaired vision and other senses may often be inconsistent and fragmented. In many cases, these children cannot rely on visual information to make sense of the physical and social world around them, and they need to be helped to develop alternate strategies to adapt to its demands.

There are challenges involved in learning with impaired vision. Youngsters with congenital visual impairments start life without the primary sensory system that is typically used to provide contact with the environment, to understand space, to stimulate and inform movement, to understand oneself as separate from others, to reach out to others, to verify information, to receive feedback related to actions, and to provide input for developing a conceptual understanding of objects and their relationships. As a result, areas such as motor, cognitive, social, and language and concept development may need particular attention and support, including early intervention efforts, for children who are visually impaired.

Facilitating optimum growth and development in children with visual impairments is the focus of teachers of students who are visually impaired and has also been the subject of much of the literature (see the end of this chapter for additional readings). Ferrell, for example, has recently (2011) explored ways to support development and learning in young children with visual impairments. As long ago as 1994, Warren concluded that many of the developmental differences observed by researchers between children with visual impairments and those without were not inherently related to blindness. Instead, he theorized that these differences were more likely the result of environmental variables influenced by the presence of visual impairment and of the adaptation of children to those variables. Among these environmental factors were variations in the physical environment, treatment by peers and adults, amount of encouragement to engage with the environment, and expectations of adults for children's success. Notably, these variables were not static, but can be modified to facilitate optimum growth.

Adjusting the variables in the environment to promote the growth and development of children with visual impairments requires care and thought. Opportunities for children to develop and practice important skills need to be offered. In effect, teachers and parents need to create circumstances in which the equivalent of incidental learning—learning from casual and natural (but carefully planned) experiences—can occur for children who cannot easily obtain information through visual observation. In addition to referencing the ECC when undertaking this effort, there are a number of techniques and considerations to keep in mind that will increase effectiveness.

PROMOTING INCIDENTAL LEARNING: THE CAMBOURNE MODEL

As teachers and other adults strive to create the social, psychological, and physical environments that promote opportunities for learning for students with visual impairments, it is helpful to be aware of factors that are thought to facilitate learning in children in general. Although several theories of learning exist, one that is based primarily on the factors that influence and contribute to incidental learning is that proposed by Cambourne (1995). Cambourne's theory may offer some guidance concerning the conditions that teachers of students with visual impairments and other adults might wish to create as they work to facilitate learning among students who are visually impaired.

Essentially, Cambourne proposed that learning takes place when children are interested in and engaged with the material to be learned. He believed that interest in learning develops when children are immersed in an environment or culture in which important skills to be mastered are exercised and when trusted others are demonstrating these skills in their daily activities. Engagement, according to Cambourne, occurs when several conditions are present, among which are high expectations placed upon children, opportunities to improve and practice, and the provision of constructive feedback from trusted others.

Immersion, Demonstration, Engagement

A number of specific conditions for learning were identified by Cambourne. These same conditions have been described as important strategies in the effective instruction of students who are visually impaired (see Chapter 9 on social interaction, Chapter 11 on career education, and Chapter 12 on self-determination). *Immersion* is the first: Cambourne proposed that learners who are "immersed" have opportunities to encounter evidence of what is to be learned. The second of Cambourne's conditions of learning is *demonstration*, which involves exposure to elements or actions in the environment from which people learn. For learners with visual impairments, immersion and demonstration require the adults to be aware that additional efforts to provide suitable experiences, whose purpose is to substitute for visual immersion and experience, may be necessary. Often, these substitutions involve children's participation in experiential learning, as adults ensure that the learner is personally and meaningfully involved in the activity in which the skills to be learned are incorporated. Experiential learning can offer the child who is visually impaired both the conditions of immersion and demonstration, and can provide the means for *engagement* with learning as well.

Cambourne (1988) stressed that learning only occurs when the individual is engaged with the material or task to be mastered and asserted that children become engaged when they perceive themselves as potential "doers" of what the adults around them are demonstrating, when they believe that engaging in the behavior or skill being demonstrated has some purpose in their lives, and when the risks of engaging are not threatening to them. The importance of children with visual impairments being "doers" rather than "done-to-ers," who become accustomed to people doing for (and to) them, has also been emphasized by, for example, Harrell (1992) and Ferrell (1997, 2011).

Additional Conditions for Learning

Cambourne (1988) noted that the probability that children will be engaged in a learning activity increases when five other conditions of learning are present: *expectations, responsibility, approximation, employment,* and *response.*

From Cambourne's perspective, children's engagement in behaviors and skills is often highly dependent on the communication of high expectations. Children's responsibility in the learning process is another important factor and is related to their being given opportunities to practice making choices, which in turn fosters the development of self-directed learning and critical thinking skills. Approximation is a concept recognizing that learners need to be free to make mistakes as they gradually approach a level of proficiency desirable for the performance of the task they are learning (Cambourne, 1988). A related factor is that of employment or use: Learners need frequent opportunities to use and practice their emerging skills within meaningful contexts. Cambourne (1995) recognized that even young children need to see the applicability of the information they are learning and that when they have frequent opportunities to apply new knowledge and skills to real situations, they become more engaged in their learning. He argued against the rote, isolated repetition of parts of tasks and encouraged adults working with learners to involve them across the entire process of the learning activities with which they are presented.

Overall, the need for frequent opportunities for the practice of emerging skills within natural contexts has long been recognized by professionals who work with learners who have visual impairments. As explained in the discussion that follows, in his description of the principles and special methods required in working with children who are blind, Lowenfeld (1973) emphasized the importance of learning by doing, using concrete objects, and being exposed to unifying experiences—the combination of which provides the student with exposure to the conditions of learning outlined by Cambourne (1995).

A final condition of learning emphasized by Cambourne (1988) was response. That is, learners must receive relevant feedback concerning their efforts. To be effective, the response provided needs to be nonthreatening, even when the feedback given is negative, and should assist the student in achieving a closer approximation to mastery of the task. Because students with visual impairments often cannot easily compare their work to the work of others, providing constructive feedback concerning their performance may require more explanation and more focus on what needs to be improved than may sometimes be provided to students with vision. Adults may therefore need to be mindful to emphasize what part of a task was accomplished correctly, to carefully select on which single part of the task to focus immediate feedback, and to gradually shape the desired behavior through positive instruction and frequent opportunities to practice (Wolffe, 1999).

LOWENFELD'S PRINCIPLES OF LEARNING

One of the earliest teachers in the field of services to children with visual impairment was Lowenfeld, who worked first in Europe, then in the United States. Lowenfeld (1973) described three special techniques for use when teaching children who are blind to help them overcome the inherent challenges of blindness: providing concrete experiences, offering opportunities to learn by doing, and ensuring exposure to unifying experiences. These methods continue to be relevant today as the foundation of successful instructional strategies for students with visual impairments.

Concrete Experiences

Much of the information that children with unimpaired vision derive about the objects in their world is known because the objects have been observed. One's understanding and knowledge of such concepts as "in," "bears," "atom bombs," "earth movers," and "the moon" are not usually based on direct personal experience with these objects or concepts, but rather on visual experiences, which may be supplemented by reading about them. However, simply reading about these ideas or objects in the absence of vision is unlikely to produce the same level of understanding, and students who are visually impaired often face the challenge of having to develop understanding without the benefit of clear, accurate visual input. One important way to overcome this challenge is to provide them with real, direct experiences and to encourage their use of all their senses, including tactile contact—that is, having them touch a bear stuffed by a taxidermist, climb on and ride an earth mover, and explore the many ways an object can be "in." Although there are some concepts and objects—such as atoms—that cannot be directly experienced by a person with a visual impairment, providing students with frequent experiences related to a variety of concepts and objects can help overcome barriers to understanding.

Learning by Doing

Just as students with significant visual impairments need to touch or experience real objects to understand them fully, they learn by participating in the real activities that they need to be able to perform. Most children who are blind or who have low vision learn to make toast, to pump gas, to advocate for themselves, or to paddle a kayak not by having the activity explained to them or by being nearby when someone else is engaged in the activity, but by actually being involved in it. Explanations help, but they are not adequate for realized understanding and mastery. It may be said that if a child's hands aren't involved, learning may not be happening.

Unifying Experiences

Many students with visual impairments severe enough to interfere with learning may be analogous to workers on an assembly line. That is, they may learn the parts of activities in which they are regularly engaged, but may have only a vague idea (if any at all) of the other components of the activity down the line. In order for visually impaired students to obtain a full understanding of the activities and tasks in which they need to be engaged and the concepts they need to know, they need to be provided with the "big picture" or overall scope of the activity or concept. When baking cookies, for example, a child cannot just break the eggs to understand how cookies are made. Students who are visually impaired often encounter an object or activity in isolation, without a visual context or accompanying detailed explanations, and for that reason often have only a partial understanding of a concept or task (see Chapter 4 on compensatory access for more on this subject). Mastery requires that students first be exposed to, then gradually practice, and then acquire all the steps and skills involved in an activity or task.

FOCUS ON LEARNING: BUILDING SKILLS

In their work with students with visual impairments, then, teachers can be mindful of Cambourne's conditions of learning and Lowenfeld's principles of special methods to structure opportunities for students to learn "incidentally" in the face of their learning needs. With an understanding of what is different about the way children who are visually impaired learn, teachers can foster experiential learning by:

- providing students with direct experiences with concrete objects
- remembering that learning proceeds from parts to the whole in many cases for students
- promoting immersion by offering multiple instances of explanation and demonstration of concepts and activities
- articulating high expectations for student success
- ensuring repeated opportunities for practice
- allowing students the time they may need for understanding
- providing targeted and realistic feedback

By allowing students to gradually do parts of tasks, as appropriate, and working within activities and contexts that are meaningful to the child, teachers can support students in the direction of making choices, assuming responsibility, and learning by doing.

Using a naturalistic learning approach to present carefully planned opportunities for learning is particularly well-suited to teaching the ECC, which encompasses skills that are rarely mastered in a single lesson or unit, and that typically evolve with use and practice over time. The next chapters focus on the ECC as an essential curriculum for students with visual impairments, describing the individual areas of the ECC, highlighting key skills, and providing strategies for building these skills. By keeping in mind the end that parents and teachers desire for their children and students—that they become adults who lead lives marked by satisfaction and independence to the maximum extent possible—the optimum growth and development of students with visual impairments are more likely to be achieved.

References

Cambourne, B. (1988). *The whole story: Natural learning and the acquisition of literacy in the classroom.* Auckland, New Zealand: Ashton Scholastic.

Cambourne, B. (1995). Toward an educationally relevant theory of literacy learning: Twenty years of inquiry. *The Reading Teacher, 49*(3), 182–190.

Ferrell, K. A. (1997). What is it that is different about a child with blindness or visual impairment? In P. Crane, D. Cuthbertson, K. A. Ferrell, & H. Scherb (Eds.), *Equals in partnership: Basic rights for families of children with blindness or visual impairment* (pp. v–vii). Watertown, MA: Hilton/Perkins Program of Perkins School for the Blind and the National Association for Parents of the Visually Impaired.

Ferrell, K. A. (2011). *Reach out and teach: Helping your child who is visually impaired learn and grow.* New York: AFB Press.

Harrell, L. (1992). *Children's vision concerns: Looks beyond the eyes.* Placerville, CA: Lois Harrell Productions.

Lowenfeld, B. (Ed.). (1973). *The visually handicapped child in school.* New York: John Day.

Shonkoff, J. P., & Phillips, D. A. (2000). Introduction. In Shonkoff & Phillips (Eds.), *From neurons to neighborhoods: The science of early childhood development* (pp. 19–38). Washington, DC: National Academy Press.

Spungin, S., & Ferrell, K. A. (2007). The role and function of teachers of students with visual impairments [Position paper]. Arlington, VA: Division on Visual Impairment, Council for Exceptional Children.

Warren, D. (1994). *Blindness and children: An individual differences approach.* New York: Cambridge University Press.

Wolffe, K. E. (1999). The importance of career. In *Skills for success: A career education handbook for children and adolescents with visual impairments* (pp. 11–28). New York: AFB Press.

For Further Reading

Barraga, N. & Erin, J. N. (2001). *Visual impairments and learning* (4th ed.). Austin, TX: Pro-Ed.

Celeste, M. (2006). Play behaviors and social interactions of a child who is blind: In theory and practice. *Journal of Visual Impairment & Blindness, 100*(2), 75–90.

Coll, C. G., & Szalacha, L. A. (2004). The multiple contexts of middle childhood. *The Future of Children, 14*(2), 81–98.

Fazzi, D. L. (2002). Social focus. In R. L. Pogrund & D. L. Fazzi (Eds.), *Early focus: Working with young children who are blind or visually impaired and their families* (2nd ed., pp. 188–217). New York: AFB Press.

Ferrell, K. A. (1998). *Project PRISM: A longitudinal study of developmental patterns of children who are visually impaired.* Greeley, CO: University of Northern Colorado. Retrieved from http://www.unco.edu/ncssd/research/PRISM/default.html

Ferrell, K. A. (2000). Growth and development of young children. In M. C. Holbrook & A. J. Koenig (Eds.), *Foundations of education: Vol. I. History and theory of teaching children and youths with visual impairments* (2nd ed., pp. 122–126). New York: AFB Press.

Hall, A. (1982). Teaching specific concepts to visually handicapped students. In S. S. Mangold (Ed.), *A teachers' guide to the special educational needs of blind and visually handicapped children* (pp. 10–19). New York: American Foundation for the Blind.

Hatlen, P. (1996). The core curriculum for blind and visually impaired students, including those with additional disabilities. *RE:view, 28*(1), 25–32.

Lieberman, L. J., Byrne, H., Mattern, C., Watt, C., & Fernández-Vivó, M. (2010). Health-related fitness in youth with visual impairments. *Journal of Visual Impairment & Blindness, 104*(6), 349–359.

Lieberman, L. J., & McHugh, E. (2001). Health related fitness of children who are visually impaired. *Journal of Visual Impairment & Blindness, 95*, 272–285.

Sacks, S. Z., & Wolffe, K. E. (1998). Lifestyles of adolescents with visual impairments: An ethnographic analysis. *Journal of Visual Impairment & Blindness, 92*, 7–17.

Sacks, S. Z., Wolffe, K. E., & Tierney, D. (1998). Lifestyles of students with visual impairments: Preliminary studies of social networks. *Exceptional Children, 64*, 463–478.

Strickling, C., & Pogrund, R. L. (2002). Motor focus. In R. L. Pogrund & D. L. Fazzi (Eds.), *Early focus: Working with young children who are blind or visually impaired and their families* (2nd ed., pp. 287–325). New York: AFB Press.

Walker-Andrews, A. S. (1997). Infants' perception of expressive behaviors: Differentiation of multimodal information. *Psychological Bulletin, 121*, 437–456.

Wolffe, K. E. (2000). Growth and development in middle childhood and adolescence. In M. C. Holbrook & A. J. Koenig (Eds.), *Foundations of education: Vol. I. History and theory of teaching children and youths with visual impairments* (2nd ed., pp. 135–160). New York, NY: AFB Press.

Wolffe, K. E. (2006). Theoretical perspectives on the development of social skills in adolescence. In S. Z. Sacks & K. E. Wolffe (Eds.), *Teaching social skills to students with visual impairments: From theory to practice* (pp. 81–121). New York, NY: AFB Press.

Wolffe, K. E. & Sacks, S. Z. (1997). The lifestyles of blind, low vision, and sighted youths: A quantitative comparison. *Journal of Visual Impairment & Blindness, 91,* 245–257.

CHAPTER 2

A Strong Foundation: The Importance of the Expanded Core Curriculum

Carol B. Allman and Sandra Lewis

L. Penny Rosenblum

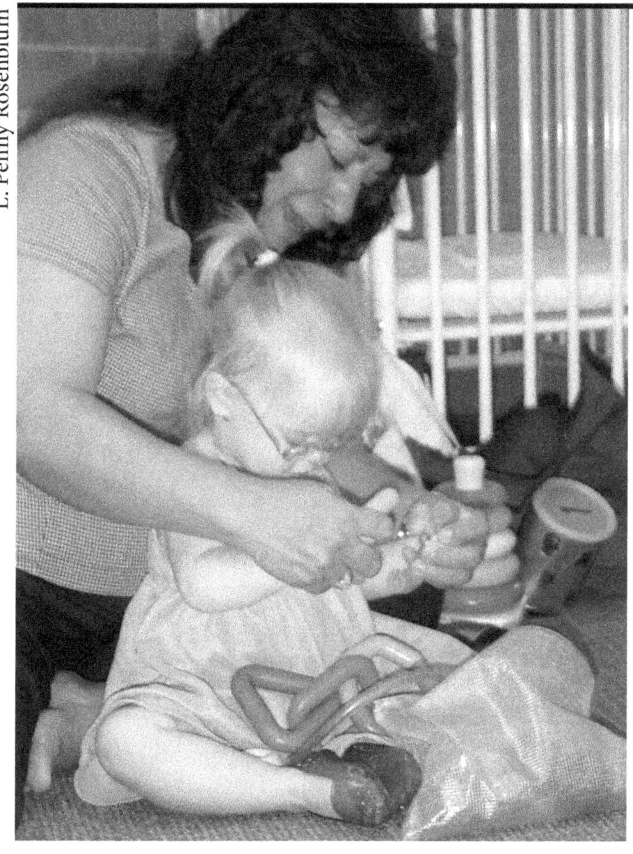

All students who attend school need to learn a common body of knowledge, often referred to as the core curriculum. This core material includes language arts, mathematics, science, and social studies—subjects studied in every school in the United States. Standards of learning for the core curriculum have been developed by states throughout this country, often with reference to concepts outlined by the federal government. These standards are the basis for most academic instruction and the central starting point for initiatives related to assessment, curriculum, and instruction.

Like other students, students who are visually impaired need to master the core curriculum. However, in order to read about, become familiar with, access, and learn this curriculum, they first need to be able to access it. To do so, they need to learn the alternate skills and techniques encompassed by the additional body of knowledge called the expanded core curriculum (ECC) as well (Hatlen, 1996). For many students with visual impairments, the content of subjects like language arts, mathematics, social studies, and science may literally be unavailable unless they can read the material assigned, understand key concepts, and possess the sensory, social, and motor skills necessary to participate in the lessons. The key individual who will help these students learn the skills and techniques necessary, and who may therefore play an essential role in their success in school, is their teacher of students with visual impairments.

THE ECC AS AN ESSENTIAL CURRICULUM

The ECC encompasses skills in areas fundamental to a student's ability to integrate information and to participate with other classmates in school, such as orientation and mobility (O&M), social interaction, independent living, and sensory efficiency. In addition, segments of the ECC, such as social interaction and independent living, enable individuals who are visually impaired to become integrated into their communities more effectively (DeMario, 1990) and participate in life outside school. As students prepare to enter the workforce, they will confront the reality that employers prefer employees who are highly productive and conversant with technology, effective communicators, dependable as well as socially attuned, in possession of good orientation and mobility skills, able to complete tasks independently, and able to use independent living skills effectively (Bina, 1991; DeMario, 1990). Without skills in these areas, students may not only be unable to learn the core curriculum successfully, they may not be able to work and live as independently as they would otherwise be capable of doing. For this reason, the ECC is, in fact, a fundamental curriculum for students with visual impairments. In the example provided in Chapter 1, Kelly's teacher, Lisa, knows that Kelly's success in both school and in life outside school will depend on her acquisition of the behaviors and skills encompassed by the ECC.

The ECC includes the following areas, or domains (Hatlen, 1996; 2003):

- compensatory access (including communication modes that students need to express their ideas and feelings and receive information as well as access the core curriculum)
- sensory efficiency
- assistive technology
- orientation and mobility
- independent living
- social interaction
- recreation and leisure
- career education
- self-determination

Although Hatlen (1996), the earliest of many educators to identify this set of skills as critical for learning by students with visual impairments, enumerated these separate skill areas, discussion concerning the scope of the ECC continues. Areas such as career education and self-determination are in some respects so closely related and aligned that some observers may regard them as encompassing a single area or domain. As indicated throughout this book, ECC areas are interdependent and overlapping, and thus the development of skills in one area will, in fact, support and promote the development of skills in others. Some authors who have studied how the ECC is taught and applied have suggested that there are variations in the emphasis placed on each ECC area. For example, Lohmeier (2005) found that in specialized schools for students who are blind, the areas of the ECC that were most frequently taught were orientation and mobility, career education, and recreation and leisure. Neglected areas included social interaction and sensory efficiency. When Wolffe, Sacks, Corn, Erin, Huebner, and Lewis (2002), observed teachers of students with visual impairments in local schools, they found that the teachers spent the majority of their time focusing on academic skills and tutoring their students. Although 18 percent of the teachers' time was spent addressing communication skills (most closely related to the areas of compensatory access and assistive technology), less than 10 percent of their time was devoted to instruction in the areas of social interaction, sensory efficiency, orientation and mobility, and independent living domains. Teachers were observed addressing skills related to career education only twice.

In all likelihood, the kinds of skills that are addressed by many teachers in various settings and locations may be strongly affected by factors such as school district or state requirements and resources such as time. However, skills in areas like social interaction rarely are included in the academic programs of students with unimpaired vision because such skills are usually learned outside of school or incidentally in interactions with peers. For students with visual impairments, though, skills such as these often need to be specifically addressed in educational programming. Although many factors may determine the variation in emphasis placed on different areas of the ECC, teachers' primary concerns need to be the assessment of the individual ECC areas and the determination of which skills are important to promote for the student (see Chapter 3 for further discussion).

To clarify the terminology used throughout this book, the authors have designated the nine parts of the ECC (compensatory access, social interaction, and so forth) as *areas*, or *domains*. The major segments of content or theme that make up each ECC area, as discussed in current literature, are referred to as *components*. Thus, one of the primary components in the ECC area of compensatory access is communication modes. Likewise, a major component of independent living is personal hygiene and grooming.

THE IMPORTANCE OF EARLY FOCUS ON THE ECC

This book provides strategies and learning activities for teaching the ECC to all students with visual impairments from preschool through high school, but it is important to remember that learning the ECC begins earlier, at ages birth–3, with experiences such as:

- being read to while playing with objects related to a story
- caring for or developing empathy for pets as living creatures
- experiencing family and community events
- using different types of transportation
- being exposed to multiple family members and friends
- eating textured and solid foods as developmentally appropriate
- eating with fingers and then a spoon
- exploring familiar settings around the home and yard or neighborhood
- rolling, crawling, and walking as developmentally appropriate
- experiencing hand and finger play
- discovering different textures to touch and taste
- searching for objects of interest
- being encouraged to be independent
- being praised realistically for accomplishments
- helping with bath time and teeth brushing
- sleeping alone

Young children who are exposed to a variety of early experiences that are accompanied by meaningful verbal explanations of the people, objects, and interactions in the world around them, develop an essential foundation for learning to get along with others, develop a personal point of view, explore, and begin to read and communicate. Experiences such as these lay the groundwork for learning the multiple skills that students who are visually impaired will need to be ready for learning in school, and ultimately, to become successful and happy adults. For this reason, it is important for teachers of students with visual impairments and early interventionists to work with the families of infants and young children to provide and expand experiences and learning opportunities, such as those just described.

THE AREAS OF THE ECC

The nine areas of the ECC are the focus of Part 2 of this book. Each chapter in Part 2 provides specific information about the behaviors, skills, and tasks that are encompassed in each particular area of the ECC. In those chapters, information regarding teaching strategies and priorities, and learning activities for teaching are presented in detail. Although each chapter focuses primarily on one ECC area, there is an emphasis on the integration of skills and instruction among all the ECC domains.

This chapter provides a brief overview of each of the nine areas, with attention paid to why the area is important for students and which components and related skills, based on current literature, are generally included within the given area. As already indicated, many areas overlap with and complement each other. For example, understanding what is meant by personal space may be learned in orientation and mobility, but it is also stressed in regard to social interaction and self-determination. Likewise, learning the organization of school materials as a compensatory access skill is also critical as a student learns to be successful in independent living (when, for example, organizing personal papers becomes necessary), and in orientation and mobility (when a complex trip needs to be planned). It should be noted that the behaviors and skills listed under each component of an ECC area in this chapter are examples provided as a guide to understanding the area and should not be considered a comprehensive list. It should also be noted that, as mentioned earlier in this chapter and in Chapter 1, the interrelationship and overlap among skills in the various ECC areas means that teachers can effectively promote skills in several areas at once through the thoughtful use of activities.

The ordering of the areas in the following discussion was determined by the authors and editors of this book, with consideration given to those that lay a firm foundation of learning (compensatory access, sensory efficiency, assistive technology, orientation and mobility, and independent living), followed by those that help create and support a lifetime of independent functioning (social interaction, recreation and leisure, career education, and self-determination). This order is *not* meant to give any one domain more importance than any other. In fact, it is critical that all domains be thought about, specifically planned for, and taught to students with visual impairments beginning in their early years. For example, although career education and recreation and leisure might seem to be most relevant for older students, very important behaviors and knowledge in those areas need to be taught to young children in order for appropriate growth and learning to occur in those domains and others that are closely related to them.

Readers should also note that not every student will or should learn every skill or behavior that is discussed in this book. In some cases, a skill may only be appropriate if a student has some vision; likewise, a skill may only be applicable if a student has no vision. In addition, some skills may be difficult to perform independently and will need adult or other assistance, especially for some students with multiple disabilities. As with educational efforts in general, the needs, characteristics, and circumstances of the individual student should be the basis of skills targeted for development.

Compensatory Access

Compensatory access (discussed in detail in Chapter 4) is the ECC area often discussed first, not necessarily because it is the most important, but because it is perhaps the most critical for ensuring access to academic learning. Compensatory access refers to skills that must be learned in order for students with visual impairments to have access to information about the world, to be able to communicate, and to be literate and thus to be successful in school.

The ECC area of compensatory access generally includes the following components:

- **concept development**—developing mental ideas about the environment and the objects, people, and processes and interactions taking place in the world
- **spatial understanding**—understanding the physical location of objects in relation to one's self and to other objects
- **communication modes**—developing facility with techniques and tools needed to access information presented in print and to write or communicate thoughts
- **speaking and listening skills**—learning appropriate methods of addressing others in conversation and comprehending what is said
- **study and organization skills**—developing methods that allow a student to maintain order in the use of materials and time and to set priorities for such activities as the completion of school work
- **use of adapted and specialized educational materials**—independently using tools and devices that provide compensatory access

Compensatory access skills are critical to both the long- and short-term success of students. These skills relate to the ability to perform fundamental processes and interactions to learn, form ideas, and develop language. Without knowledge of the components of compensatory access, students with visual impairments will not have the necessary foundation of concepts for human interaction and for learning academic skills. Many of these concepts are ordinarily learned through visual recognition of everyday events, but since children with little or no usable vision frequently miss the nuances of basic concepts (such as characteristics of different animals or how a school is different from the post office) and thus lack the conceptual learning that goes with visual recognition, these concepts and related skills need to be deliberately taught.

For many students with visual impairments, as they get older, the need for compensatory access may become more academic in nature, as they are required to learn how to organize and access increasing amounts of materials for learning. Specific learning activities must therefore be planned by the teacher to ensure that important compensatory skills are learned as appropriate to a student's needs and level of ability and at the appropriate time in the student's educational program.

In addition, it is important for students to have access to multiple modes of communication and opportunities to learn the use of different mediums for learning, both for specific purposes and outcomes and because their visual and other needs may change. For example, although using magnification to read print might be a student's preferred method of accessing most classroom materials, the same student might find the use of recorded materials to access large amounts of material effective.

Given that the skills related to compensatory access provide the foundation for success in school and in many areas of employment and adult integration within the community, the importance of this ECC area cannot be overstated. Deliberate teaching of the behaviors and skills included in this area provides a base for access to academic learning and establishes a framework for future access in a variety of situations.

Sensory Efficiency

Because sensory development is critical to a child's ability to process information and stimuli, sensory efficiency (discussed in detail in Chapter 5) is the ECC area that needs to receive attention earliest in a child's life. This area is most critical for infants and young children and often has particular importance for students with significant disabilities. Because sensory efficiency skills involve the effective use of input derived from the senses, the significance of this ECC area is perhaps the easiest for general educators and the general public to recognize as needing attention for students who are visually impaired. People unfamiliar with the education of students with visual impairments often assume that developing the other senses is a ready answer to meeting the needs of these students, something that is important for teachers of students with visual impairments seeking to enlist resources and support for their instructional efforts to be aware of (see Chapter 13 for more information).

The area of sensory efficiency, previously called visual efficiency (Huebner, Merk-Adam, Stryker, & Wolffe, 2004), is closely related to the area of compensatory access in that it involves the need for students with visual impairments to learn how to use visual, auditory, olfactory, and tactile skills to function efficiently and effectively. When children have impaired vision, they need to learn to develop their sensory functioning abilities to the maximum extent possible so that they can best use any vision they may have, together with their other senses, in order to obtain information about the world around them. For young children just learning about the world and for students who have other disabilities in addition to visual impairment, the development of sensory efficiency skills is critical as they begin to learn how to integrate, interpret, and use the sensory information that they receive. These skills are also important when engaging in other, often more complex activities, such as taking notes from written material on a whiteboard during a lecture, learning to use a stove, and traveling independently.

Skills and behaviors involving the application of sensory efficiency should be incorporated in day-to-day activities and should be highly individualized for each student's particular needs and conditions and the extent of his or her visual and other impairments. Furthermore, lighting, time of day, weather, energy level, and health are just some of the variables that may affect what a student can see, smell, or hear on any given day. The development of tactile discrimination, for example, might be affected by the sensitivity and general health of the student, as well as by the amount of information that he or she can receive through touch and the integration of tactile information with other sensory and developmental learning. In general, the teaching of sensory efficiency is continuous and ongoing, and may need to change based on the variables already mentioned, as well as on the student's age and grade, and the acquisition of skills in other areas of the ECC. The components and skills encompassed in the area of sensory efficiency include:

- **visual function**—fixating, orienting, tracking, and recognizing objects, and using optical devices
- **auditory function**—localization, aural discrimination and presentation, and sound pattern use
- **tactile function**—tactile discrimination, scanning, manipulation, and dexterity

- **gustatory (taste) function**—appreciation for food, discrimination of food types, and recognition of various tastes
- **olfactory (smell) function**—localization of smells, discrimination of odors, and recognition of pleasant and unpleasant odors

In order to learn to develop these skills to attend to and examine objects and events in the environment and to achieve developmental milestones, infants with visual impairments should receive deliberate instruction by a teacher of students with visual impairments. Following, searching for, studying, and identifying objects and persons in the environment are critical skills that fundamentally relate to concept development, but also to the area of social interaction. Practicing sensory-guided motor behaviors (such as reaching for objects, moving toward objects, and searching for objects) is important for orientation and mobility. Other important behaviors and skills in the sensory efficiency area include experimenting and practicing with various low vision or hearing devices; learning to care for, order, and maintain needed low vision or hearing devices; participating in discussions about the best use of the senses in various weather conditions, lighting conditions, and familiar and unfamiliar environments; making environmental adaptations to support one's own learning needs and effective use of visual and other sensory input; and using senses as appropriate and possible to accomplish home and school activities (Corn, DePriest, & Erin, 2000).

Most students will develop a variety of sensory tools and become adept at using multiple sensory input, or input from more than one sense, that is specific to their needs. For example, many students learn that on cloudy days their usable vision may be compromised and that under those conditions, it is necessary to verify what is seen during travel from the classroom by using their senses of smell and hearing to help locate places like the cafeteria.

Assistive Technology

The importance of the ECC area of assistive technology (discussed in detail in Chapter 6) cannot be overstated. Technology has become an integral part of life for all of us, and has enabled people who are visually impaired to have access to printed information, allowing them to obtain a world of information that was previously inaccessible. The term "assistive technology" refers to a wide range of devices and equipment, but in regard to the education of students with visual impairments, the term can be defined as "any item, piece of equipment, or product system, whether acquired commercially off the shelf, modified, or customized, that is used to increase, maintain, or improve functional capabilities of a child with a disability" (Individuals with Disabilities Education Improvement Act of 2004, Sec. 602, 20 USC §1401, 300.5). This definition includes technology needed as an adaptation or accommodation to access the core curriculum (as defined by general standards or modified standards) or technology needed for work, play, and personal care. Assistive technology may consist of high-tech devices, such as screen magnifiers or accessible personal digital assistants (PDAs or electronic notetakers), or low-tech devices, such as magnifiers or canes (Safhi, Zhou, Smith, & Kelley, 2009). Overall, the content taught in the assistive technology area of the ECC includes the use of technological devices that will be most helpful for a student with a visual impairment.

Because technology is a critical tool for gaining access to materials for many students, this domain of the ECC is closely related to the area of compensatory access. The types of devices chosen for students will depend on the age of the student, the expectations of the student's academic program, and the student's future needs. As these needs change, learning media and functional vision assessments (see Chapters 3, 4, and 5 for more information) will help drive the assistive technology assessment required by law, which helps determine the appropriate technology for a student's use (Presley & D'Andrea, 2009). These assessments and their relationship to technology decision-making are discussed in Chapter 6, which addresses specific behaviors and skills related to assistive technology, as well as strategies and learning activities that might be used to achieve assistive technology learning goals.

The components of the ECC area of assistive technology include:

- **access to information**—developing facility with general applications and basic technology skills such as inputting information and producing documents
- **communication**—developing awareness of electronic communication modes and the ability to conduct research and written assignments

- **personal productivity**—practicing the use of basic applications in activities related to learning and daily living

The use of technology will change throughout a child's life (Presley & D'Andrea, 2009). In general, students in preschool and elementary school are expected to be working toward success in reading material, writing information, completing assignments on time, and reviewing what has been read or written. Students in middle and high school are typically expected to use skills learned in early grades to maintain academic learning, manage personal information, and participate in age-appropriate communication. Many students with multiple disabilities may require new communication devices as they develop skills beyond the capabilities of tools previously introduced to them. A child who experiences a change in vision may also need a change in technologies, and the more demanding instructional programs in high school require close evaluation of each student's use of technology. In addition, different assistive technology devices may be needed for different tasks. For example, a student may choose to make a list of needed supplies using a computer or PDA, rather than using a braillewriter. To be able to make such choices, the use of a variety of technology tools needs to be taught to students.

In a national study, Kelly (2009) found that the majority of students with visual impairments were not using assistive technology. Although students who attended residential schools were more likely to use assistive technology than students in local schools, the study found that students overall were more likely to be users of assistive technology if their parents were involved in their education.

It is thus a central concern that consistent attention be devoted to assessing students with visual impairments in regard to their needs for and use of assistive technology and that they receive appropriate training to become effective technology users. Moreover, as they progress through the grades, these students will need to be prepared to access and apply technology that will allow them to meet their states' core standards of learning. Students thus need time to experiment with various technologies and determine the best fit for them for any given purpose at any given time in their lives. In this ongoing effort, teachers of students with visual impairments need to play a vital guiding, supportive, and instructional role.

Orientation and Mobility

Orientation and mobility (O&M) (discussed in detail in Chapter 7) is the area of instruction through which students who are visually impaired learn to be oriented to their surroundings and to move as independently and safely as possible in familiar and unfamiliar settings. Hill and Ponder (1976) stated that the ultimate goal of O&M instruction is to "enable the student to enter any environment, familiar or unfamiliar, and to function safely, efficiently, gracefully, and independently" (p. 1). Orientation and mobility specialists need to provide the majority of instruction for students with visual impairments within this ECC area because such instruction requires special training and certification. Nevertheless, teachers of students with visual impairments need to be involved in the domain of O&M through teaching beginning concepts as well as providing support and reinforcement of behaviors and skills.

O&M is included in the ECC because learning about one's environment and how to move safely and effectively within it is critical to most students.

Specific components and skills in the area of O&M include:

- **body concepts**—understanding body parts and function
- **environmental concepts**—understanding concepts related to the home environment (such as windows and doors), and to buildings, residential and business areas, schools, and streets and intersections
- **spatial concepts**—understanding self-to-object relationships, spatial terminology (such as right, left, and next to), landmarks and cues, and cardinal directions
- **perceptual/sensory skills**—interpreting environmental sounds, applying meaning to tasks, and determining the nature of sensory information
- **mobility skills**—noticing and negotiating unexpected drop-offs, using systematic search techniques, and knowing built elements such as block distances, corners, intersection types, streets, and road structures
- **orientation skills**—knowing routes and understanding layouts
- **interpersonal skills**—requesting directions; arranging for rides; soliciting information from

individuals such as dispatchers, drivers, and store personnel; and using appropriate telephone manners (Emerson & Corn, 2006)

- **decision-making skills**—altering travel in response to inclement weather, choosing appropriate clothing and gear, choosing between routes, knowing the advantages and disadvantages of different modes of travel, and making backup plans

Preschool and elementary level students begin O&M training very early by learning basic body parts and body awareness; practicing movement to develop good gross and fine motor skills; using available vision for orientation and movement at home and in the classroom; and practicing general safety techniques, including sound location, protective arm techniques, and human guide skills. Young children learn, for example, that they can use the odors originating from the school cafeteria to provide information about where they are in their school. Middle school age students need to expand basic O&M learning to include independent travel in the community. Practice with cane travel at school and at home enables students to travel safely and confidently in both familiar and unfamiliar environments.

The connections of O&M training to other areas of the ECC, as well as to the general academic curriculum, provide a good example of how training related to other areas can be integrated into and along with specialized training. That is, success in areas like social interaction, recreation and leisure, sensory efficiency, self-determination, assistive technology and career education rests on the interdependence of skills, including good O&M skills. Skills in math and reading are critical to refining O&M skills and can be practiced within O&M lessons. For example, the ability to understand time, distance, and geometric concepts affects how well a student can travel independently (Smith, 2006) and lessons can be designed to provide practice in these important core curriculum skill areas. Likewise, O&M instruction can reinforce and provide meaning to the skills required for the academic tasks of reading timetables, maps, and graphic information.

Independent Living

Skills within the ECC area of independent living (discussed in detail in Chapter 8) are sometimes referred to as daily living skills. This area incorporates the behaviors and skills involved in managing the daily demands of everyday life and maintaining one's living environments. At first glance, this area may seem to encompass components similar to some courses that are sometimes included in the school curriculum—namely, family life, home economics, and child development. However, the components included in the area of independent living are more targeted to the needs of students with visual impairments than what may typically be taught in these courses. Independent living for visually impaired students includes behaviors and skills that individuals with unimpaired vision usually learn through imitation and incidental learning (Lewis & Iselin, 2002).

More so than perhaps any of the other expanded core curriculum domains, promoting competence in independent living will of necessity require involvement and support from the parents and caregivers of the student with a visual impairment. Lewis and Iselin (2002) interviewed parents to determine their children's mastery of daily living skills and found that as a whole, children who were visually impaired independently performed only half as many daily living tasks as their sighted peers. The learning and the reinforcement of many of the behaviors included in the independent living area are best accomplished in the setting in which the skill would naturally occur—typically at home. Although the teacher of students with visual impairments can plan and provide instruction in many of the behaviors and skills needed in this area, it is important, if not essential, to provide practice for the student in natural environments.

Incorporated into the area of independent living are personal care and management responsibilities needed to function in school and the community, as well as at home. The components, behaviors, and skills included in this area are rarely included in school programs, but are fundamental to successful outcomes, not only in school but in work and community activities.

Components in the ECC area of independent living include:

- **organization**—maintaining school notes and materials where they can be accessed easily, prioritizing daily demands of everyday life and of school and work, and keeping personal objects in a specific location

- **personal hygiene and grooming**— bathing, maintaining feminine and masculine hygiene, and understanding and ensuring privacy

- **dressing**—participating in dressing oneself with independence, and determining appropriate clothing for the weather
- **clothing care**—labeling clothing, selecting appropriate clothing for events, doing laundry, and performing related tasks
- **time management**—establishing a routine of sleeping at appropriate times, recognizing how long it takes to complete a task, using watches and clocks, and maintaining a calendar
- **eating**—eating with utensils, locating food on a plate, using condiments, and using tableware
- **cooking**—preparing and cooking meals, pouring liquids, retrieving utensils, stirring and mixing, spreading and spooning, helping with dishes, using a stove, cleaning up, learning food-related concepts involved in gardening, visiting grocery stores, applying food nutrition, and opening and closing different kinds of packages
- **cleaning and general household tasks**—participating in responsibilities at home and school, retrieving and replacing toys and games, and using cleaning supplies and equipment
- **telephone use**—calling friends, knowing how to make emergency calls, and having a system of phone number retrieval
- **money management**—identifying coins and bills, using ATMs, writing checks, and managing money (Hazekamp & Huebner, 1989; Kelley & Smith, 2000)

Social Interaction

The area of social interaction (discussed in detail in Chapter 9) contains components and behaviors that are needed to participate in social situations appropriately and to prevent social isolation. Some might argue that this ECC domain is, in a sense, the most critical domain overall for individuals with visual impairments because it sets the stage for appropriate and necessary interaction with others, and because so much of social interaction is learned from and based on visual cues. For the most part, students with unimpaired sight learn social interaction by observing how others act and react. For example, parents rarely have to teach their child to smile when receiving a gift or to face a person when having a conversation. Many children with visual impairments, however, are generally not aware of the behaviors involved in being socially appropriate. Despite the obvious importance of social interaction, teachers often seem to find it difficult to include well-developed and creative activities to instruct students in this area during classroom time (Sacks, Kekelis, & Gaylord-Ross, 1997).

The basic components of the ECC area of social interaction include:

- **appropriate body language**—knowing when to lean forward to hear a secret from a friend, maintaining appropriate eye contact, facing a person who is speaking, standing up to greet a new friend, keeping hands to oneself during a group conversation
- **social communication**—engaging in appropriate verbal and nonverbal interaction with others, initiating conversations, expressing needs and wants
- **effective conversation patterns**—asking for help; initiating, maintaining, and ending conversations; extending invitations
- **cooperative skills**—working with another to accomplish a goal, volunteering to help in the classroom, helping with home chores
- **interactions with others**—knowing how to react to humor, identify the person in charge in a given situation, and respond to the presence of a peer; developing dating skills
- **social etiquette**—demonstrating courteous behavior, thanking a friend for a gift, sharing a seat with another on the bus, smiling at others
- **development of relationships and friendships**—taking turns, seeking friendships with others, working effectively in groups
- **knowledge of self**—knowing one's likes and dislikes, taking responsibility for actions, understanding the concept of personal body space, showing pride in accomplished tasks, stating one's own point of view
- **interpretation and monitoring of social behavior**—knowing when to disobey an adult, understanding the appropriate time to ask questions, developing problem solving skills, recognizing sarcasm in a conversation, understanding the difference between reacting to requests from strangers and familiar people (Sacks & Silberman, 2000)

Competence in social interactions provides students with visual impairments with behaviors that are critical for lifelong interdependence, social maturity, and increasing the likelihood of academic and employment success (Wolffe, 1996). The area of social interaction is integrally intertwined with other areas of the ECC. For example, knowing how to react in a social situation may involve understanding key O&M options (such as in instances in which a student may need to leave a situation safely), and may include the need for sensory efficiency skills (as when a student hears unruly behavior that might indicate the need to leave an area).

Recreation and Leisure

The ECC area of recreation and leisure (discussed in detail in Chapter 10) focuses on the development of interests and skills involved in physical and leisure activities. Physical activity is a critical element for good health and a happy lifestyle for all children, including those with visual impairments. Although physical education is one way in which students with unimpaired vision are taught recreation and leisure skills at school, attention to this ECC domain involves more than adapting physical education activities for students with visual impairments. Often participation in recreational and leisure pursuits needs to be deliberately planned for these students because lack of vision may in many cases reduce the opportunity to observe and then choose activities of interest. Most students with visual impairments need to acquire competence in the area of recreation and leisure through thoughtfully planned instruction and demonstration. Planning and instruction in this area are closely related to developing skills related to social interaction, and fostering skills in both areas of the expanded core can often be taught in the same set of lessons. For example, instruction in board or card games can provide an avenue for practicing skills related to interacting with classmates and friends, as well as incorporate reading, language, and mathematical concepts. For some individuals, recreation and leisure pursuits create the foundation for career interests.

The components that are generally encompassed within the recreation and leisure are of the ECC are:

- **play**—interacting through play with peers and siblings, entertaining oneself for various periods of time
- **physical activity**—participating in physical education or other active play activities, taking part in recreation and leisure activities enjoyed by the family
- **health, fitness, and individual sports**—developing a regimen of physical exercise that leads to improvement or maintenance of strength, stamina, and endurance; developing skills for engaging in such activities as track, wrestling, and weight-lifting
- **team and spectator sports**—learning to enjoy competitive and noncompetitive sports activities, such as football, baseball, soccer, golf, baseball or goalball, as a participant or as a spectator
- **leisure activities and hobbies**—being exposed to opportunities for choosing a favorite game or book, experiencing arts and crafts activities, appreciating and enjoying fine arts in such forms as museum visits, theater, dance, opera, and music (McGregor & Farrenkopf, 2000)

Students who are visually impaired need specific instruction in leisure and recreation activities that are of interest to themselves and their families, as well as those that may be available and common in the community. Students, including those who are multiply disabled, need to be exposed to recreation and leisure activities and learn appropriate skills that will enhance their quality of life.

The recreation and leisure area of the ECC is one in which a professional in the field of visual impairment does not necessarily provide instruction in all the behaviors and skills that might be encompassed within this domain. Instead, it is often necessary to collaborate with others, such as physical education teachers, adapted physical education instructors, or community volunteers who are knowledgeable about how a task is taught to interested individuals with unimpaired vision or to those who may have additional disabilities.

Career Education

Although the term "career education" may sometimes be construed to mean education in a specific career of one's choice, career education in general and the ECC area of career education in particular are far broader. In the ECC, career education (discussed in detail in Chapter 11) focuses on components of activities and behaviors and skills needed to prepare students for all the roles they will play throughout their lives, including the maintenance of economic independence in adult life. In general, young people with disabilities continue to fall behind their peers without disabilities on all measures of postschool outcomes (Nagle, 2001), and in the United States, unemployment and underemployment are leading problems facing adults with visual impairments (American Foundation for the Blind, 2013; McDonnall, 2011; Newman, Wagner, Cameto, & Knokey, 2009; Newman, Wagner, Cameto, Knokey, & Shaver, 2010). Lack of preparation in the area of career education has been cited as a major cause of these problems (Wolffe, 1996; Wolffe & Kelly, 2011), and helping students develop skills in this important ECC domain lays the groundwork for full and satisfying lives for students who are visually impaired.

Career education relates directly to other critical ECC areas, such as social interaction, compensatory access, orientation and mobility, and assistive technology (Nagle, 2001), and to self-determination in particular. Career education truly begins at birth and continues throughout the period children are in school. For young children, it involves developing an awareness and understanding of the world around them and the roles they play in it as family members and later as students and members of the community. In addition, it provides opportunities to understand personal interests and abilities and to learn about different workers and professionals and the variety of work that people do. For older students, career education involves making informed choices about future employment and education. Many students with visual impairments may not be aware of the diversity of possible career options because they have not been exposed to—or may not be able to observe—the variety of work people do. For example, students with unimpaired vision whose parents take them shopping are aware that at a grocery store there are people who stock the shelves with products, other people who bag groceries, still different people who perform cashier duties, and still others who oversee activities in the store, assist as needed, or direct workers. Students with visual impairments may need additional guidance to gain awareness of the diversity of work going on around them at the store.

Many secondary schools offer courses in vocational education, and this type of class would be beneficial to students who are visually impaired, but would not be sufficient to teach them a basic understanding of the range of opportunities for work.

Well-planned instruction in career education for students with visual impairments needs to include these components:

- **career awareness**—differentiating between work and play, understanding the value of work
- **career exploration**—developing awareness of careers, researching careers of interest
- **career preparation**—reading and understanding want ads, recognizing typical job adaptations made by workers with visual impairments, developing prevocational skills (such as work habits, attitudes, and motivation), and having vocational interests
- **career placement**—preparing résumés, completing applications, participating in interviews, participating in work

Competence in the area of career education is, in a sense, equivalent to preparation for a satisfying and independent life and as such involves the development of the ability to do the following:

- listen and attend to others
- follow directions
- stay on task
- complete tasks
- play make believe and dress-up activities to imitate adult roles
- have responsibilities at home and school
- recognize different school and community workers
- participate in problem solving (locating lost items independently, for example)
- react appropriately to unexpected changes or events
- learn to work individually and in a group
- learn to be responsible for actions
- recognize that workers get paid
- develop good communication skills
- understand the rewards of work
- organize resources such as time and money
- meet increased responsibilities at home, school and in the community
- show well-developed academic, thinking and work behavior skills
- participate in work activities and jobs and possibly work part-time
- show an understanding of work performed by adults and what is involved in being successful in multiple areas of work
- show interest in particular areas of work
- plan for life beyond high school (Wolffe, 2000)

Because of the wide range of behaviors included in the career education domain, this area overlaps with all areas of the ECC. In a sense, this area encompasses the culminating goal for all individuals, which is to be a self-sufficient adult to the maximum extent possible, so the connection between career education and other areas of the ECC is understandable. Career education is particularly closely related to self-determination, the final area of the ECC.

Self-Determination

Self-determination (discussed in detail in Chapter 12) refers to the ability of a child to advocate for his or her own needs and desires and to make independent choices about personal preferences and goals in life. The inclusion of this area within the ECC is a reflection of the importance of this and related activities for students with visual impairments. Self-determination focuses on teaching children strategies that promote regulation and direction of their own behaviors (Agran, Hong, & Blankenship, 2007). This important domain was added in 2003 to the areas generally agreed to constitute the ECC because of its importance in promoting independence and successful functioning in society, and also because the general skill of self-determination was recognized as a valid predictor of future success (Hatlen, 2003; Sacks, 1996; Tuttle & Tuttle, 2000; Wolffe & Sacks, 1997). Many young children with visual impairments are often encouraged to participate in activities in school and at home with little attention paid to determining their own preferences. In an effort to ensure that children learn essential information and important skills, teachers and parents may sometimes be overly directive and too verbal in their zeal to provide all the information needed by a child to learn an activity, concept, or skill. As a result, students who are visually impaired may not effectively demonstrate self-determination because as with any skill, competence depends in large measure on repeated practice, and many students may not have had opportunities to practice making decisions for themselves.

As part of the ECC, instruction related to self-determination may focus on making sure that young children discover the behaviors and skills that will help them politely tell others what they want to do, where they want to go, or when they are ready for an activity. Students in middle and high school will use these basic behaviors and skills, as well as more advanced methods of negotiation and determination of their own needs, to prepare for becoming independent adults. For students who are visually impaired, self-determination also involves developing an understanding of one's own visual impairment and the adaptations and environmental modifications needed when one has such an impairment, as well as the ability to explain one's impairment to others and to both explain and request specific modifications. The components of self-determination that are considered important for individuals with visual impairments include:

- **self-knowledge**—developing personal preferences, needs, and desires
- **awareness of individual rights and responsibilities**—possessing knowledge of laws protecting people with disabilities
- **capacity to make informed choices**—knowing what to do in an emergency, being able to express one's likes and dislikes
- **problem-solving and goal-setting skills**—making personal and educational goals and interacting with others to obtain assistance
- **ability to engage in self-regulated and self-directed behavior**—developing negotiation skills and skills involved in interacting with others and the public at large
- **self-advocacy and empowerment**—choosing favorite or desired activities and being able to evaluate one's own behavior or progress
- **assertiveness skills**—being able to advocate for one's needs and wants

Self-determination is frequently considered a relatively low-priority area for students with visual impairments, and opportunities for demonstrating self-determined behavior are often limited (Robinson & Lieberman, 2004). However, it is an area that needs to be addressed deliberately because many students without usable vision lack knowledge about themselves and their ability to control what happens to them. Without the impetus provided by vision to explore on their own beyond the bounds of the safety provided by adults or to make choices that aren't explicitly offered, as most children with unimpaired vision do, students who are visually impaired may become accustomed to allowing others to be in control of their lives and their activities, a tendency that may often be reinforced by the adults in their world. It is imperative, therefore, for the long-term benefit and independence of students, that teachers and other adults provide instruction to help them become aware of their needs and appropriate ways to get those needs met.

As already noted, given its focus on self-knowledge and on setting goals and making choices, the area of self-determination has considerable overlap with that of career education. It also has strong connections with the areas of social interaction and independent living.

THE ROLE OF THE TEACHER OF STUDENTS WITH VISUAL IMPAIRMENTS

Based on a comprehensive assessment, members of a student's Individualized Education Program (IEP) team determine the specific instruction in the areas of the ECC that needs to be provided to the student. The members of the IEP team should include:

- the teacher of students with visual impairments
- the O&M specialist
- the student's general classroom teacher
- other special educators, if any
- an administrator
- the student's parents or caregivers
- the student, whenever appropriate

The team may also include other professionals, such as a physical therapist or speech and language pathologist, depending on the student's needs. In general, each team member brings a different kind of expertise to the development of the student's IEP, but the teacher of students with visual impairments and the O&M specialist bring the most extensive knowledge about the needs of children who are blind or have low vision. These two team members therefore have a unique responsibility to help others involved in the education of students with visual impairments understand the tremendous influence that visual impairment has on development and learning, and the importance of focusing on the ECC to improve the student's access to the curriculum and all other aspects of his or her education. Because so many individuals who work with or otherwise come in contact with students who are visually impaired have a limited understanding of the significant impact of visual impairment on development and learning, professionals who specialize in working with students with visual impairments take on a variety of informational, collaborative, and direct service roles to meet their responsibilities to students and to support these students' success in school and throughout their lives.

Providing Information

A challenging role that professionals trained to work with students with visual impairments accept is that of helping others to understand the significant influence of visual learning—or its lack—on all aspects of functioning. Because visual memory has such a profound impact on an individual's perspective, it is extremely difficult for most sighted people to imagine the experiences of individuals who are blind, and whose experiences with the world are based on sensory input different from their own. It is equally difficult to appreciate the challenges and abilities of students who have low vision but are not blind. As a result, those without specialized knowledge often under- or overestimate the abilities of children with visual impairments to learn incidentally.

Teachers of students with visual impairments, therefore, frequently need to consult with others involved in the education of these students in order to facilitate their understanding of the impact of visual impairment on learning and the important role of providing instruction in the ECC in decreasing or eliminating that impact. It is especially important for teachers to spend time talking with school administrators to convince them that without systematic instruction in the ECC, students' access to materials and activities in school, and hence to learning, is further limited, which can result in lower test scores and long-term outcomes. Such discussions are also necessary with many of the providers of services to students with visual impairments to facilitate improved services to students (see Chapter 13 for many strategies and in-depth discussion of this critical topic).

Collaboration

Teachers of students with visual impairments also have a responsibility to talk to parents about how their child typically experiences the world and how ECC instruction can affect their child's long-term functioning. At the same time, teachers also have much to learn from parents and other family members. Developing a close relationship with students' parents is a highly productive way for teachers to spend their time. Ultimately, the child's engagement in activities related to the ECC will in large part depend on the family members' expectations for their child; their facilitation of their child's involvement in personal and household activities, independent travel, and recreation and leisure pursuits; and their encouragement of the child's sensory development, appropriate social interactions, and self-determination skills. (See Chapter 15 for a discussion of families' essential role in supporting the ECC and strategies for working with parents; Part 2 of this book also contains suggestions for working effectively with families in each chapter.)

The engagement of families in providing their own direct instruction in the areas of the ECC will vary. Some families may accept this role with confidence and use their child's teacher of students with visual impairments primarily as a resource for information. Other families may be more tentative, and only become involved after they see progress in the development of new behaviors and skills at home. The partnership between teachers of students with visual impairments and each of the families they serve will be more or less intense depending on many factors, including the family's comfort in involving their children in the kinds of experiences that are key to the acquisition of crucial behaviors and skills over the long term.

Collaboration with other professionals is also usually necessary, especially when the teacher of students with visual impairments must rely on those other professionals to encourage students to use ECC skills and behaviors. Teachers however should always be aware of the extra demands that they may be placing on other professionals to change how or what they have been trained to do. Collaboration with other service providers also may occur when students who are visually impaired are enrolled in courses in which skills associated with the ECC are taught, such as music, art, career education, home economics, and physical education. In these situations, the teacher of students with visual impairments may need to help other educators understand why students' knowledge base may be different from that of their classmates and offer ways to accommodate the students' needs while maintaining high expectations for performance. From these other professionals, teachers of students with visual impairments can learn important information about the subject matter that they can incorporate into their support of other teachers' instruction or in their own extended instruction of that area of the ECC. Additional information about the importance of team collaboration and ideas for making these efforts successful are included in Part 3 of this book.

Assessment and Direct Instruction

Effective assessment always needs to precede instruction and program planning, and this principle pertains to efforts to address the various areas of the ECC with any given student. Teachers of students with visual impairments need to meet the needs of their students by providing instruction in the areas of the ECC that have been identified through a comprehensive assessment (Huebner et al., 2004). By definition, the ECC encompasses those behaviors and skills that students with unimpaired vision typically learn incidentally, without instruction, but for which students who are visually impaired often need direct intervention. In addition to conducting assessments of students in the areas of the ECC, teachers of students with visual impairments also need to ensure that assessments of their students undertaken by other professionals and service providers reflect an understanding of the needs and abilities of visually impaired students and are accessible to students who are being assessed. The chapter that follows and the chapters in Part 2 provide more information on assessment.

CONCLUSION

Knowing the behaviors and skills each student needs to learn and finding time in the school day to teach those behaviors and skills are two very different things! There are challenges to providing instruction in the areas of the ECC, all of which need to be addressed and met by teachers of students with visual impairments. These challenges include:

- identifying what to teach
- coordinating efforts with parents and other school personnel
- having equipment and materials on site for effective instruction
- managing time needed to provide academic support and instruction in all the ECC areas
- convincing school administrators and others of the importance of the ECC
- maintaining students' interest in learning ECC-related skills
- providing practice needed for development and mastery of skills in the areas of the ECC

Throughout this book, tips and suggestions are provided to help teachers of students with visual impairments meet these challenges successfully. In addition, as already mentioned, Chapter 13 specifically discusses supporting instruction in the ECC in general education settings, and Chapter 14 provides a discussion of issues and challenges regarding the ECC and state standards.

Teachers of students with visual impairments are the key coordinators in the important enterprise of making their students' education a valuable experience. They are the professionals with the knowledge and experience to know that failure to assess students in the areas of the ECC and to address instruction when needed can have permanent effects on their students' lifelong functioning. Without this instruction, most visually impaired students are unlikely to reach their full potential as adults. For these reasons, the following chapter presents general principles of assessment and instruction for the ECC. It discusses general assessment of students' needs for instruction in ECC areas, presents principles of instruction for students who are visually impaired, provides useful instructional strategies, and presents key strategies for developing learning activities with accompanying unit plans to help teachers of students with visual impairments.

REFERENCES

Agran, M., Hong, S., & Blankenship, K. (2007). Promoting the self-determination of students with visual impairments: Reducing the gap between knowledge and practice. *Journal of Visual Impairment & Blindness, 101*(8), 453–464.

American Foundation for the Blind. (2013). Interpreting Bureau of Labor Statistics employment data. Retrieved from http://www.afb.org/section.aspx?SectionID=15&SubTopicID=177

Bina, M. J. (1991). Overcoming current obstacles to our hopes for the future: Lessons from our pioneer ancestors. *Journal of Visual Impairment & Blindness, 85,* 410.

Corn, A. L., DePriest, L. B. & Erin, J. N. (2000). Visual efficiency. In A. J. Koenig & M. C. Holbrook (Eds.), *Foundations of education: Vol. II. Instructional strategies for teaching children and youths with visual impairments* (2nd ed., pp. 464–499). New York: AFB Press.

DeMario, N. (1990). *Non-academic competencies for elementary level students with visual impairments.* Toronto: Council for Exceptional Children. (ERIC Document Reproduction Services No. ED321460).

Emerson, R. S. W., & Corn, A. L. (2006). Orientation and mobility content for children and youths: A delphi approach pilot study. *Journal of Visual Impairment & Blindness, 100*(6), 331–242.

Hatlen, P. (1996). The core curriculum for blind and visually impaired students, including those with additional disabilities. *RE:view, 28*(1), 25–32.

Hatlen, P. (2003, December). *Impact of literacy on the expanded core curriculum.* Paper presented at the Getting in Touch with Literacy conference, Vancouver, British Columbia, Canada.

Hazekamp, J., & Huebner, K. M. (Eds.). (1989). *Program planning and evaluation for blind and visually impaired students: National guidelines for educational excellence.* New York: American Foundation for the Blind.

Hill, E. & Ponder, P. (1976). *Orientation and mobility techniques: A guide for the practitioner.* New York: American Foundation for the Blind.

Huebner, K. M., Merk-Adam, B., Stryker, D., & Wolffe, K. (2004). *The National Agenda for the education of children and youths with visual impairments, including those with multiple disabilities* (Revised). New York: AFB Press.

Individuals with Disabilities Education Improvement Act of 2004, Sec. 602, 20 USC § 1401, 300.5.

Kelley, P., & Smith, P. (2000). Independent living skills. In A. J. Koenig & M. C. Holbrook (Eds.), *Foundations of education: Vol. II. Instructional strategies for teaching children and youths with visual impairments* (2nd ed., pp. 569–615). New York: AFB Press.

Kelly, S. M. (2009). Use of assistive technology by students with visual impairments: Findings from a national survey. *Journal of Visual Impairment & Blindness, 103*(8), 470–480.

Lewis, S., & Iselin, S. A. (2002). A comparison of the independent living skills of primary students with visual impairments and their sighted peers: A pilot study. *Journal of Visual Impairment & Blindness, 96*(5), 335–344.

Lohmeier, K. L. (2005). Implementing the expanded core curriculum in specialized schools for the blind. *RE:view, 37*(3), 126–133.

McDonnall, M. C. (2011). Predictors of employment for youths with visual impairments: Findings from the second national longitudinal transition study. *Journal of Visual Impairment & Blindness, 105*(8), 453–466.

McGregor, D., & Farrenkopf, C. (2000). Recreation and leisure skills. In A. J. Koenig & M. C. Holbrook (Eds.), *Foundations of education: Vol. II. Instructional strategies for teaching children and youths with visual impairments* (2nd ed., pp. 653–678). New York: AFB Press.

Nagle, K. M. (2001). Transition to employment and community life for youths with visual impairments: Current status and future directions. *Journal of Visual Impairment & Blindness, 95*(12), 725–738.

Newman, L., Wagner, M., Cameto, R., & Knokey, A.-M. (2009). The post-high school outcomes of youth with disabilities up to 4 years after high school: A report of findings from the National Longitudinal Transition Study-2 (NLTS2) (NCSER 2009-3017). Menlo Park, CA: SRI International. Retrieved from http://www.nlts2.org/reports/2009_04/nlts2_report_2009_04_complete.pdf

Newman, L., Wagner, M., Cameto, R., Knokey, A.-M., & Shaver, D. (2010). Comparisons across time of the outcomes of youth with disabilities up to 4 years after high school: A report of findings from the National Longitudinal Transition Study-2 (NLTS2). Menlo Park, CA: SRI International. Retrieved from http://www.nlts2.org/reports/2010_09/nlts2_report_2010_09_complete.pdf

Presley, I., & D'Andrea, F. M. (2009). *Assistive technology for students who are blind or visually impaired: A guide to assessment.* New York: AFB Press.

Robinson, B. L., & Lieberman, L. J. (2004). Effects of visual impairment, gender, and age on self-determination. *Journal of Visual Impairment & Blindness, 98*(6), 351–366.

Sacks, S. Z. (1996). Psychological and social implications of low vision. In A. L. Corn & A. J. Koenig (Eds.), *Foundations of low vision: Clinical and functional perspectives* (pp. 26–42). New York: AFB Press.

Sacks, S. Z., Kekelis, L. S., & Gaylord-Ross, R. J. (Eds.). (1997). *The development of social skills by blind and visually impaired students.* New York: AFB Press.

Sacks, S. Z., & Silberman, R. K. (2000). Social skills. In A. J. Koenig & M. C. Holbrook (Eds.), *Foundations of education: Vol. II. Instructional strategies for teaching children and youths with visual impairments* (2nd ed., pp. 616–652). New York: AFB Press.

Safhi, M. Y., Zhou, L., Smith, D. W., & Kelley, P. (2009). Assistive technology in teacher-training programs: A national and international perspective. *Journal of Visual Impairment & Blindness, 103,* 562–568.

Smith, D. W. (2006). Developing mathematical concepts through orientation and mobility. *RE:view, 37(4), 161–165.*

Tuttle, K., & Tuttle, N. (2000). Psychosocial needs of children and youth. In M. C. Holbrook & A. J. Koenig (Eds.), *Foundations of education: Vol. I. History and theory of teaching children and youths with visual impairments* (2nd ed., pp. 151–172). New York: AFB Press.

Wolffe, K. (1996). Career education for students with visual impairments. *RE:view, 28,* 89–93.

Wolffe, K. (2000). Career education. In A.J. Koenig & M.C. Holbrook (Eds.), *Foundations of education: Vol. II. Instructional strategies for teaching children and youths with visual impairments* (2nd ed., pp. 679–719). New York: AFB Press.

Wolffe, K., & Kelly, S. (2011). Instruction in areas of the expanded core curriculum linked to transition outcomes for students with visual impairments. *Journal of Visual Impairment & Blindness, 105,* 340–349.

Wolffe, K. E., & Sacks, S. Z. (1997). The lifestyles of blind, low vision, and sighted youths: A quantitative comparison. *Journal of Visual Impairment & Blindness, 91,* 245–257.

Wolffe, K. E., Sacks, S. Z, Corn, A. L., Erin, J. N., Huebner, K. M., & Lewis, S. (2002). Teachers of students with visual impairments: What are they teaching? *Journal of Visual Impairment & Blindness, 96*(5), 293–304.

CHAPTER 3

Instruction and Assessment: General Principles and Strategies

Sandra Lewis and Carol B. Allman

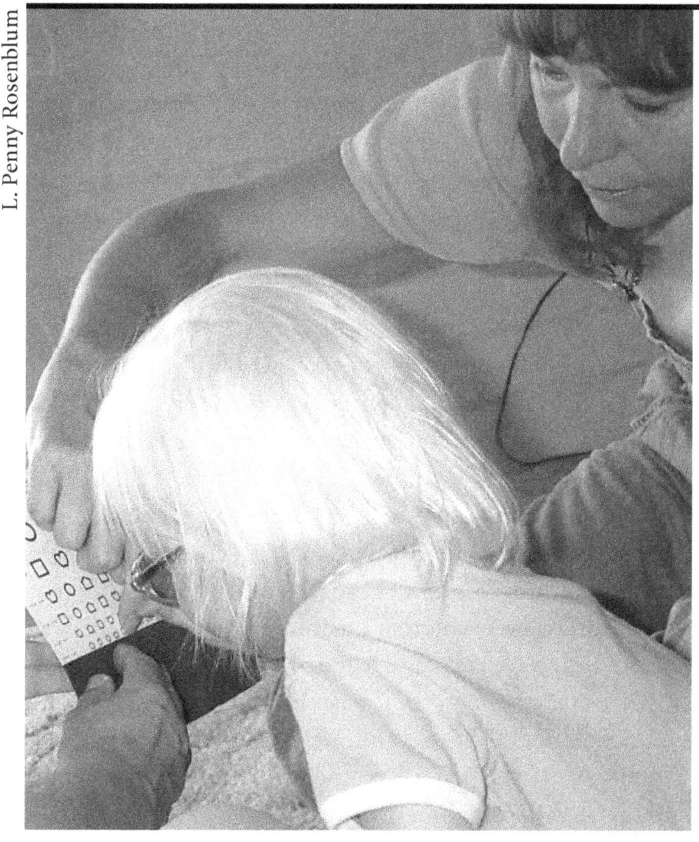
L. Penny Rosenblum

The first two chapters of this book make the case for the importance of the expanded core curriculum. However, anyone who lives or works with a child who is visually impaired and understands the effect of visual impairment on learning knows firsthand the need to help children with visual impairments develop certain essential adaptive techniques and critical skills. As pointed out in Chapter 1, employing the overriding philosophy of beginning with the end in mind helps teachers focus on the adult that each student can potentially become and also can strategically guide instructional efforts. This chapter is intended to provide teachers of students with visual impairments with key suggestions and reminders to support their ECC skills-building efforts with students. Assessment, curriculum, and instruction serve as the foundation of educational planning. The material in this chapter presents general principles and effective strategies in instruction and assessment. Since curriculum is determined at the federal, state, and local levels through adoptions of standards and skills, Chapter 14 provides general strategies for coordinating ECC skills with state standards. Each chapter in Part 2 provides specific information on assessment, instruction, and curriculum pertinent to each ECC area.

INSTRUCTIONAL STRATEGIES

Each student with a visual impairment is different and brings different experiences and abilities to the process of learning. Much has been written about the diversity of students who are visually impaired (see, for example, *When You Have a Visually Impaired Student in Your Classroom*, 2002), and it has even been said that no two children see alike. For this reason, teachers need to adapt their teaching approaches and focus to meet the needs of the individual child and address skills needed by the individual child in each area of the ECC. For example, teaching certain social skills involves providing situations in which students interact with others, while sensory efficiency skills need to be individualized for each student and recreation and leisure skills often depend on students' preferences. There are, however, some general principles of instruction that have proved to be effective when working with learners who are visually impaired. Many of these principles are drawn from solid tenets and models of learning presented in Chapter 1. These principles include the following:

- breaking tasks into their component parts
- making activities meaningful
- working from behind the student
- providing wait time
- giving guidance and support
- creating many opportunities for practice
- allowing learning through improvisation and mistakes

Breaking Tasks into Their Component Parts

It is important to break down the tasks that students with visual impairments need to complete—as well as the skills that need to be learned for the completion of the tasks—into small, manageable steps. This approach allows the teacher to focus on the critical parts of the activity so that each small step can be taught, practiced, and learned as part of the overall process of developing the ability to perform the task. For example, helping to rake leaves at home in the yard requires that a student first learn how to hold the rake and then how to determine the borders of the area being raked as just two of the small parts of the overall task.

Many of the areas of the ECC contain behaviors and skills that are best taught as a series of small steps. Conducting a *task analysis*—a process through which an activity is divided into its smallest component parts—is an effective approach for preparing to teach a task to a student who is visually impaired. As part of the preparation for working with a student who is blind or for whom vision is poor or unreliable, an effective technique for the teacher is to first practice a task blindfolded to determine if all the unique steps have been identified. Steps that are required to complete the task can be recorded, with notes made of each action performed. It is helpful to perform this analysis at the same location where, and in the same way in which, the student will be expected to learn the task. For example, if the skill of loading a dishwasher will be taught to a student in the teacher's lounge, then it may not be accurate or possibly even relevant to conduct the task analysis in a different kitchen or on a different machine. Likewise, if the student is to be expected to load the dishwasher at home, it will be necessary for the teacher to perform a task analysis at the student's home and preferably with the parent's input, since the parent's method of loading a dishwasher may be different than the teacher's.

The teacher will also have to keep the student who is being taught in mind as the task analysis is finalized. Students who have cognitive or motor impairments in addition to their visual impairments may need to have some parts of the task broken into a number of smaller steps. In the example presented in Table 3.1, opening a door requires more steps for some students than it does for others. For a given task, preparing a set of written steps or directions informed by the task analysis is part

TABLE 3.1

Task Analysis of Opening a Door for Three Different Students

Step	Task analysis for student who has low vision	Task analysis for student who is blind	Task analysis for student who is blind and who has limited hand strength
1	Look at door knob	Extend arm	Extend arm
2	Reach for knob with hand	Locate door	Locate door
3	Grasp the knob	Locate door knob	Locate door knob
4	Twist knob to right	Grasp the knob	Grasp the knob with one hand
5	Pull open door	Twist knob to right	Extend other hand to knob
6		Pull open door	Grasp the knob with both hands
7			Twist knob to right with both hands
8			Pull open door

of effective planning for instruction when teaching new processes or solving problems.

Task analysis assists with instruction in two ways. First, it helps the teacher organize instruction. The student eventually will have to combine each of the identified and delineated steps into a fluid whole, which is known as *chaining*. Usually, teachers start with the first step and continue with the next ones in order, so that the child is familiar with the task from start to finish. This approach is known as *forward chaining*. For some tasks, though, the teacher may decide to teach the student by starting with the last step and adding the previous steps in reverse order (known as *backward chaining*). Backward chaining is particularly effective when the task requires many steps to complete and the student is motivated by the end product. For example, a teacher might choose to teach a student how to make a peanut butter and jelly sandwich by teaching the child to cut an already completed sandwich into two pieces first, so that he or she has the immediate reward of eating the completed sandwich. Next the teacher would teach the child to put the two slices of bread containing the peanut butter and jelly together and then cut the bread. Finally, spreading the peanut butter and the jelly would be added to the instruction. It is also sometimes appropriate to start at some other point in a series of steps and add skills in either or both directions. Teachers often save the most difficult part of a task to the end of an instructional unit, as when a student is taught to focus a monocular telescope after the student is already "hooked" on its value for exploring the world.

The second way that a task analysis assists with instruction is by providing a guide for keeping data on the student's acquisition of the steps of the skill being taught. The completed task analysis can be used to create a table that shows the steps in the task, along with a record of the student's performance of each of the steps over time. Table 3.2 provides an example of this type of chart, using the previous task analysis of the steps in opening a door for a student who is blind and has limited hand strength. Each time the student attempts the task, the teacher may record the degree of assistance the student requires for each step. The table thus serves as a monitoring tool for keeping track of the student's progress.

Making Activities Meaningful

Behaviors and skills in some areas of the ECC don't easily lend themselves to a task analysis. Social interaction, sensory efficiency, self-determination, and career education usually don't involve sequential steps per se and often require a different teaching approach that focuses on the recognition of appropriate actions and activities that fit particular occasions.

It is sometimes difficult for students to understand why adults think it is important for them to learn specific skills. For example, it is not uncommon for people to say that budgeting money made more sense to them when they actually had income and expenses to manage. Students with visual impairments are no different from anyone else—it helps them to know why a particular skill is important. Students who have unimpaired vision can often determine why an activity is meaningful through their observations of others performing a task requiring a certain skill. A student who is not visually impaired can see that learning to dribble a ball is

TABLE 3.2

Sample Data Collection Chart for Learning Door Opening

Step	Date							
	10/1	10/2	10/3	10/4	10/5	10/7	10/8	10/9
Extend arm	PP	PA						
Locate door	I	I						
Locate door knob	I	VP						
Grasp door knob with one hand	VP	VP						
Extend other hand to knob	I	I						
Grasp door knob with both hands	PA	PA						
Twist knob to right with both hands	PA	PA						
Pull open door	PA	PA						

Key: PA = Physical assistance; PP = Physical prompt; VP = Verbal prompt; I = Independent

an important component of basketball or that writing one's signature is a task that adults use frequently. A student with a visual impairment may not recognize that these relationships exist between a given task and its usefulness in daily life or a specific activity.

Having students help set up activities is one way to increase the meaningfulness of the activities. For example, if there is a poster to unroll as part of a classroom demonstration, the teacher can let the student take the rubber band off the rolled up poster before starting the demonstration and have him or her roll it back up and replace the rubber band when finished. Similarly, students can be asked to open and close zip-top plastic storage bags; buckle, snap, or zip tote bags or containers; and help clean up after activities. This kind of involvement allows students to practice fine motor skills (opening and closing), independent living skills (cleaning up), and career awareness (understanding what a teacher of students with visual impairment does) within the context of a meaningful activity (K. Mountjoy, personal correspondence, 2006).

Applying the tenets and models of learning presented in Chapter 1, four techniques have been identified that can help students understand important relationships and appreciate the meaningfulness of learning new behaviors and skills.

1. *Teaching in natural environments.* Whenever possible, skills should be taught in the environment in which they will be used. Teaching skills in this way offers students with visual impairments, who may not be able to observe similarities among different environments, the opportunity to focus precisely on how that particular task will need to be performed, thereby increasing their likelihood of success. Performing a skill in the context where it is typically needed also helps student attach meaning to the performance of the skill. In addition, for young children and some students with multiple disabilities, teaching in the environment where the skills will be used is critical to promote *generalization.* Generalization refers to students' ability to use a skill in environments or contexts other than the one in which it was learned, and is often a challenge for some young children with visual impairments and those with multiple disabilities. If, for example, a student is being taught to empty a wastebasket, it is usually more meaningful to take the student to the places where wastebaskets can be found and teach the skill in those locations, rather than bring the wastebaskets to the student.
2. *Teaching within the natural context of the skill.* Learning a skill makes more sense if it is taught in association with the task to which it pertains and is taught at the time when it is usually needed. Brushing one's teeth makes sense immediately after a meal; putting balls and other equipment or toys away makes sense after recess; and emptying wastebaskets seems reasonable at the end of the day when they are full. Students with visual impairments are often at risk of learning isolated skills and tasks that give them only a partial understanding of an activity or concept; it is

important that their teachers help them put the pieces together.

3. *Using routines.* Embedding skills into routines provides students with the opportunity to perform the skills frequently. A routine is any activity or event that occurs in a predictable order, begins with a cue of some sort, frequently takes place at a given time, and results in an observable effect (Browder, 1991). (Teaching within routines is discussed further in Chapter 5.) When routines are used as the framework for instruction, students can begin to memorize the order in which specific steps are to be accomplished. In addition, teachers can assess students' performance more easily within a routine: since routines typically occur often, teachers can recognize even small changes in a student's behavior and can identify *anticipation* and levels of *partial participation* more easily. It is important for the teacher to be alert to instances when a student anticipates the next step in a routine—this behavior indicates that the student is becoming familiar enough with the task to begin performing it without prompting. Similarly, partial participation, which occurs when a student performs some of the component steps in a task or activity, indicates that the student is doing more parts of the task independently. With this information, teachers can increase their expectations of students' involvement or use less intrusive prompts (for example, using a verbal instead of a physical prompt). (Prompts are discussed in greater depth later in this chapter.)
4. *Taking advantage of the teachable moment.* Sometimes when a teacher and student are working together, a situation will occur that is particularly conducive to teaching a skill or behavior, even if that item wasn't intended to be part of the lesson. For example, if during an activity an object drops on the floor, the teacher can use this event to teach or reinforce methods for conducting a tactile search. Similarly, when materials are needed unexpectedly, a student may be taught about where supplies are stored and why that location was selected. These moments spontaneously present the opportunity for learning in a natural environment and at the time when a skill is needed, and it is important to take advantage of them whenever possible.

Working from Behind the Student

When it is necessary to demonstrate a technique to a student who is blind, better results can often be achieved when the teacher stands or sits behind, and places her arms on either side of, the student. In this position, the student can place his arms and hands over or under the teacher's and can imitate the teacher's natural motions as a task is performed. Working from behind the student also feels less intrusive, as the student's hands are not being pulled and pushed. As much as possible, the teacher will want to use the *hand-under-hand* technique, in which the teacher's hands are underneath those of the student. This approach allows the student greater control of the situation, as she can pull away if she feels threatened by unfamiliar or unexpected sensory input. Students are often more willing to try new activities when they have greater control over what happens to them. Because of their size, as well as any cultural prohibitions related to close contact between teachers and older students, working from behind the student is best used with young children and students in elementary school.

Providing Wait Time

Learning through the sense of touch or hearing is less automatic than learning through vision. Unimpaired vision allows the student immediate access to the big picture, which often offers insight into what an activity is supposed to accomplish and how all of its parts fit together. This information is not always immediately available to the student who is blind or has low vision and as a result, it sometimes takes longer for students to process what is being asked of them and how they can accomplish the desired result. Teachers and parents teaching new behaviors and skills to students with visual impairments need to learn to wait . . . and wait . . . and wait. Sitting on one's hands (literally!) is an effective way to prevent helping a visually impaired student too soon, as is counting to oneself. Silently counting the seconds passing provides the added benefit of preventing the offer of a verbal prompt when it isn't necessary. Since it is not uncommon for some students with visual impairments to become dependent on being verbally prompted, these strategies can be particularly important. An appropriate wait time (also known as a *latency* period) depends on each child's circumstances, such as tasks previously done and general learning characteristics. Knowing how long to wait is an example of the "art" of teaching. Waiting involves a teacher's best guess of the child's abilities, frustration level, and familiarity with the task, based on previous experiences with the child.

Giving Guidance and Support

As part of instruction, teachers provide guidance to students in a variety of ways. Frequently, and particularly when students are first learning a skill, teachers offer more support than they expect to have to provide once the student has mastered the targeted task. This support often takes the form of the use of such techniques as *scaffolding, checking for understanding, prompting,* and *praise and reinforcing.*

Scaffolding

Scaffolding refers to the provision by an instructor of a greater number or extent of instructional supports than will be expected to occur after a student has mastered a task. The equivalent of training wheels placed on a bicycle when a child is first learning to balance on a two-wheel bicycle, these supports allow the learner to focus cognitive energy on learning the fundamentals of a skill being introduced or to internalize new information being taught. Scaffolding is usually individualized; that is, its use is dependent on the needs of each learner.

When presenting scaffolded instruction, it is recommended that instructors start with a review of what a student knows or can do, and then gradually increase the level of challenge presented by the task. The challenge should be just beyond the student's current level of mastery and be set at a level that, with instruction, can be achieved relatively quickly. For example, if a student learning braille is going to be asked to read a story in the classroom, the teacher of students with visual impairments might first review the new or more difficult vocabulary words contained in the story by handing the student cards on which the words are brailled and (a) telling the student the word, (b) having the student read the word silently, and (c) asking the student to say the word aloud. Then, when the student reads the story in the classroom, these words will be less likely to present a problem. In this way, the likelihood of failure is reduced and the learner's frustration may be curtailed. The following are some examples of scaffolding strategies:

- pre-teaching, which refers to previewing material that is to be presented in the general education class with the student (for example, if the class will be learning about goods produced in South America, the teacher might pre-teach related map skills so that the student is ready to participate in the class discussion)
- reviewing vocabulary or math facts before initiating instruction
- providing the student with a written or pictorial list of steps required to complete a task
- teaching a mnemonic (such as, the first letters of the names of the Great Lakes spell HOMES)
- modeling the behavior expected of the student

As students master the skill being taught, the teacher gradually reduces the instructional supports and encourages greater independence, always ready to reintroduce support if necessary, or if not, ready to challenge the student to perform at a level just beyond the new level of competence.

Scaffolding strategies reflect the general learning conditions of Cambourne (1988, 1995) and Lowenfeld (1973) described in Chapter 1. They include helping students to understand the purpose of learning, conveying expectations, providing models and concrete experiences, allowing approximations, facilitating engagement and learning by doing, and guiding practice to learn small parts of a larger concept.

Checking for Understanding

During instruction, teachers typically tell students about the steps in the new task to be learned and model for students the behaviors necessary to execute those steps and accomplish the task. It is recommended that throughout instruction, educators also frequently check students' understanding of the instruction that has been provided. Checking for understanding is in fact a method of *formative assessment*—assessment that is ongoing throughout instruction. It provides the teacher with immediate evidence of whether the student is learning the material at hand and allows the teacher to make changes as necessary to meet the student's learning needs. Content area teachers check for understanding when they ask students to reflect on information that has been taught or require students to paraphrase or summarize material. Teachers of students with visual impairments can employ similar strategies, such as when teaching a student about his or her eye condition. A description of the parts of the eye affected by the visual disability might be interrupted by requests to "explain that in your own words for me," or "show me again where the retina is," or "if I said that the lens is filled with aqueous fluid, would I be correct?"

Checking for understanding when teaching a sequence of steps that lead to a finished product or task should be done after each step is taught. After the teacher provides oral instruction and models a particular step, the student should be asked to perform that much of the task, with the teacher using a simple request such as "your turn," or "you try it." If the student can perform that part of the task, then the next step in the sequence of instruction can be introduced. After the teacher has presented the verbal directions and modeling to accomplish this next part of the task, the teacher might ask the student to repeat just that part of the task, or ask the student to "chain" the second step to the first—that is, to perform as much of the task as has been taught thus far.

Formative assessment during instruction not only helps the teacher monitor the student's learning, it also keeps students engaged and helps them monitor their own learning. When undertaken in a non-threatening manner, it encourages students to be aware of misconceptions that may occur, to admit when they are uncertain about something, and to know at what point their understanding of a task breaks down. Armed with this information, they can more easily identify and request the assistance they need to maintain progress.

Prompting

Prompts are cues that teachers offer to students to help them identify what behavior is expected of them. Prompts can be presented in a variety of ways, and are usually classified according to a hierarchy of perceived intrusiveness (from least to most), as shown in Sidebar 3.1.

SIDEBAR 3.1

Hierarchy of Prompts, from Least to Most Intrusive

Natural cue	A natural environmental stimulus that cues the learner, such as the smell of food in cafeteria to suggest that lunch is ready
Gestural prompt	Directing the learner's attention to the task by pointing or nodding one's head toward the task
Indirect verbal prompt	A spoken phrase that indirectly reminds the learner to initiate a behavior, such as, "What do you do next?"
Direct verbal prompt	A spoken phrase that tells the learner what behavior is expected, such as, "You need to get the bowl."
Modeling prompt	A pantomime performed by the teacher that shows the learner what behavior is expected next, such as making a stirring motion over a bowl.
Picture prompt	A picture cue that reminds the learner of the next behavior or step in the sequence
Indirect physical prompt	A nudge or slight tap that directs the learner to the task or expected behavior
Physical prompt	Physical guidance of the learner by the instructor using the hand-under-hand or hand-over-hand technique to demonstrate what is expected of the learner

The selection of the type of prompt appropriate for use during instruction depends on the learner. Prompts such as the use of modeling, pictures, and gestures are only effective with students whose vision allows them to see the prompt. For some students who are blind, verbal prompts are not as desirable as indirect physical prompts, such as gently touching a student's arm when wanting the student to explore a set of objects, because some students can become dependent on receiving verbal input before each step of an activity. This kind of *prompt dependence* maintains the learner's reliance on the assistance of others and is often difficult to reduce.

The lowest level of prompt, if any, that a student requires to perform each step in a task should be noted during assessment. During initial instruction, it is typical to use the level of prompting identified during assessment as a starting point, and then gradually replace that prompt with one that is less intrusive. For example, a teacher who first needs to use a physical prompt (hand-under-hand guidance, for instance) combined with the verbal prompt "open ketchup" to encourage a student to twist the top off a ketchup bottle might only need to prompt the student with the phrase "open ketchup" as the student becomes more familiar with the task. In this instance, the combination of prompts has been replaced with the less intrusive verbal prompt. This practice is referred to as the *fading* of prompts, and it is a desirable technique, given that the use of prompts is associated with greater dependence on others. Particularly when planning instruction for students with more severe cognitive disabilities, but equally applicable when teaching difficult tasks to students whose visual impairment is the only identified disability, it is important for instructors to include these elements in a lesson plan:

- the type of prompt that will be used first
- the period of time that will elapse (referred to as latency or wait time) before additional prompting occurs
- the successive types of prompting that will be provided to the student

Praising, Encouraging, and Providing Feedback

Expressing praise is an important way that teachers signal their satisfaction with the efforts of students, encourage appropriate behavior, and share their enthusiasm over demonstrated progress. Teachers need to use praise carefully, however, because ineffective praise can negatively affect a student's self-motivation and willingness to try more difficult tasks, and ultimately result in learners who are motivated by pleasing others, rather than by the inherent satisfaction in their achievement. In general, praise is considered effective if it is specifically targeted—that is, if it relates to the learner's efforts and achievements and incorporates a description of the characteristics of that achievement. Ineffective praise tends to incorporate a value judgment that encourages learners to strive to please the teacher or adult providing the instruction. Ineffective praise also rewards simply participating instead of the quality of the performance.

Using *descriptive praise*—praise that specifically identifies what a student has done that is worthy of mention—is recommended for all students, but particularly for students with visual impairments, who may have difficulty telling which part of a task they have done well. Specific praise takes the form of recognition, such as "I can see that you worked hard on that assignment," "You almost achieved the goal we set when we started," or "Last week you couldn't make a sandwich, but look at you today—you made one for me and one for you!"

The use of praise with students with visual impairments occasionally substitutes for the nonverbal encouragement that is naturally provided to children with unimpaired vision, such as when an adult smiles at a student to suggest support. As much as possible, teachers will want to find other nonverbal ways of acknowledging and encouraging learners with visual impairments, such as a light touch on a shoulder or pat on the back, or by offering reminders of how good accomplishing the task will feel.

Praise is a form of feedback that adults typically provide to students who are learning new skills and behaviors. Often, though, the feedback that needs to be offered isn't positive. Students with unimpaired vision can easily compare the results of their efforts to produce materials by looking at a model or their performance of a task by observing the performance of classmates. Such comparisons are more difficult to make when students don't have access to models provided or see their classmates' performance with difficulty. Instructors working with students with visual impairments therefore need to find honest ways to offer negative feedback to students without imparting a sense of defeat or impossibility. The use of scaffolding in instruction, as described earlier, is one way to prevent the need to provide too much negative feedback at any one time. Asking students to self-evaluate their performance is another strategy that instructors can use. Teaching students to set goals, monitor and record their own performance, and personally reflect on changes that have taken place is also an effective approach to assuring that students are receiving the kind of constructive feedback that leads to increased learning.

Creating Opportunities for Practice, Practice, Practice

Being engaged in activities is also necessary for students to acquire fluency in performing skills and tasks. All too often, students may be exposed to an activity once or twice but are not given enough opportunities to actually learn the task and the specific skills needed to complete it. Going bowling one time or typing a business letter once provides exposure, but doesn't provide enough of a learning experience, or enough practice, for most students. In general, students need to be given enough practice of a particular skill (called *horizontal development*) so that they can perform the task with ease—with some level of automaticity—and move on to more advanced skills (called *vertical development*). Mastery typically only comes from practice of the skill, first in the environment in which it was taught, then in other more complex or less-familiar environments.

Allowing Learning through Improvisation and Mistakes

As students become skilled at a task or develop a given skill, it is important to encourage them to try techniques or approaches that are different from those they have been taught. Through such improvisation, students can begin to see that problems can be solved in a variety of ways and then select for themselves the approach they prefer.

It is also useful to create a situation in which a mistake is made (these often occur spontaneously!) so students can experience the consequences of the mistake. Having to clean up the mess when the cleanser gets inadvertently knocked over isn't any fun, but it may be the best way to teach a student the value of spatial awareness and carefulness. These opportunities also can be useful for reinforcing problem-solving skills by offering observations such as: "I wonder what you could do now" and "What could you do in the future to avoid this kind of mess?"—phrases that can be used to change an accident into a learning experience.

The principles of instruction just discussed provide a framework of methodology that teachers of students with visual impairments can use to offer instruction via learning activities used to address and develop ECC-related behaviors and skills. The following discussion provides a framework for general assessment of students' skills in the ECC areas.

THE PROCESS OF ASSESSMENT IN THE ECC AREAS

Just as the development of skills in the areas encompassed in the ECC is fundamental to students' success in school, work, and life, the assessment of students' functioning within these areas is fundamental to effective educational planning and is of benefit to the teacher, students, and the students' parents. By identifying what a student needs to learn, targeting critical learning areas, and then devising successful ways of promoting that learning, teachers can make the best use of their talents and time and contribute in an important and satisfying way to each student's educational progress.

Assessment is at the heart of all educational planning and instruction. In order to teach the skills of the expanded core curriculum, the teacher first needs to conduct a functional vision evaluation and learning media assessment to identify the best way to present materials to a given student. For students who are nonverbal or have additional disabilities, gathering the results of assessments conducted by other professionals such as speech-language pathologists or physical therapists will also help in the planning of further assessment. Based on the student's visual impairment, the presence of any other disabilities or health-related conditions, and the student's abilities and needs, the teacher then needs to determine which elements and behaviors within each ECC area to focus on, and identify the tasks and activities conducive to the development of those elements and behaviors. The following steps (adapted from Thomas, Allman & Beech, 2007) provide an overview of how teachers can approach the ongoing process of assessment:

- determine the behaviors and skills the student has mastered within each ECC area by conducting assessments specific to each area (discussed in chapters in Part 2)
- determine the behaviors and skills the student needs to practice in order to maintain mastery
- determine the additional behaviors and skills the student needs to learn
- determine the behaviors and skills the student needs from year to year and in the future
- set priorities for instruction
- develop learning activities and evaluation strategies for each behavior and skill

As already indicated, the ECC-related skills needed by a given student are integrally related to that student's visual impairment and other individual circumstances. To identify these skills, essential assessments for students with visual impairments, namely, a learning media assessment (discussed in Chapters 4 and 5) and a functional vision assessment (discussed in Chapter 5) need to have been conducted for the student. Assessments conducted for each area of the ECC, discussed in each chapter in Part 2 of this book, can then help determine which of the identified skills need development by the student at this time.

Based on the results of these assessments, the teacher of students with visual impairments initially needs to make recommendations about which behaviors and skills in each of the ECC areas are critical for the student's long term success. It is important to remember that all students will not need to learn all behaviors and skills and that the focus of skill-building instruction needs to be individualized. Students with low vision may not need to learn to read braille if they do not have a progressive eye condition and if regular print or print with magnification is sufficient for their needs. Likewise, a student with multiple disabilities and severe physical challenges may not have the physical capability to learn braille and may depend on recordings to access materials. The decisions about which behaviors and skills must be taught should be made at least annually by the teacher of students with visual impairments, with input from other educational personnel who know the student, the student's family, and the student, as appropriate. These decisions must be made with the understanding that it is very likely a student's needs will change over time.

Once the focus for instruction is decided, learning activities can be designed. These activities need to include an evaluation component to determine whether the behaviors and skills taught have been learned. Later in this chapter, some strategies are described for ensuring that assessment is a vital part of learning activities. In addition, sample learning activities included in the chapters in Part 2 contain evaluation sections for the benefit of readers.

Determine Mastery of Skills in Each ECC Area

Teachers who have been working with a student for some time may have a good idea of which behaviors and skills the student has mastered in each area of the ECC. Typically, this kind of information can be acquired through critical observation over time and use of ECC-specific assessments discussed in Part 2. Teachers should mentally assess each student every time they have contact with the student. Although this mental assessment is a first step, it is important to have a way of recording observations when key learning takes place, so that there is a running record of information about each student's mastery of the behaviors and skills within the ECC areas. Teachers may develop their own checklists to record mastery of ECC skills or may use any of the various materials published or otherwise made available to them, such as the example provided in Figure 3.1. The same form, completed for the student Kelly, the 7-year-old who was introduced in Chapter 1, is shown in Figure 3.2 to illustrate how this form might be used. Commercial examples are also available, including the Expanded Core Curriculum Screening Record and Yearly Screening Form (Sanford & Burnett, 2007) from the American Printing House for the Blind. Teachers who don't use some type of record-keeping form run the risk of omitting the assessment of areas that they may not typically teach or have the opportunity to observe in their interactions with familiar students.

Initial Assessment

When a student is new to a teacher's caseload, it is important to do an initial assessment to determine what behaviors and skills she has previously mastered. This assessment might include:

- review of previous IEPs
- review of the most recent functional vision and learning media assessments to determine how to best present materials
- review of any formal or informal assessments, including previous ECC assessments, that have been completed that might indicate behaviors and skills the student has mastered
- review of notes and observations made by other teachers or professionals who have worked with the student
- conducting of interviews with parents, teachers, and other professionals who have had opportunities to observe the student
- execution of planned and structured observations by the teacher that target specific skills within an ECC area to fill in any gaps related to skills development that are not addressed through other methods

If structured observation needs to be planned for this initial assessment of a student, it may be useful to solicit assistance from the orientation and mobility instructor, the parent, or another adult who knows the student well. A structured observation typically involves spending 15–30 minutes recording the targeted behaviors performed by a student in a specific environment. For example, a teacher who wants to assess a student's social interaction or sensory efficiency skills, might observe the student during lunch or in a class that requires social interaction, or in a class such as art or music that requires the use of different senses. It is helpful to start a structured observation with a list of specific behaviors that are expected to be observed. For example, the teacher might want to observe a student's ability to:

- ask questions and talk to the instructor
- explore the environment
- demonstrate interaction with classmates
- understand personal body space
- use visual attending behaviors (maintaining gaze, following)
- move toward objects independently

FIGURE 3.1

Sample ECC Record-keeping Form

This type of chart may be used throughout a student's educational programming to maintain information about progress on all areas of the expanded core curriculum. Specific skills to be listed under each domain or area of the ECC should be identified initially based on observations and evaluation. Additional skills needed would be added with each year of the student's education. Rows and columns can be added as needed. Such a form can serve as an ongoing method of record keeping for each student.

EXPANDED CORE CURRICULUM RECORD-KEEPING FORM

Student's Name: ______________________________

Teacher's Name: ______________________________

ECC Area and Skills	***Date and Grade***			
SENSORY EFFICIENCY				
ASSISTIVE TECHNOLOGY				
COMPENSATORY ACCESS				
ORIENTATION AND MOBILITY				
RECREATION AND LEISURE				
SOCIAL INTERACTION				
CAREER EDUCATION				
INDEPENDENT LIVING				
SELF-DETERMINATION				

Progress Code: I = Independent success; E = Emerging skill; skill needs prompting or assistance to accomplish; — = No opportunity to demonstrate skill or not demonstrated

FIGURE 3.2

Sample Completed ECC Record-keeping Form

The following example has been completed for Kelly, the 7-year-old who was introduced in Chapter 1.

Expanded Core Curriculum Record-keeping Form

Student's Name: *Kelly*

Teacher's Name: *Lisa*

ECC Area and Skills	Date and Grade			
	1/11	1/12	1/13	
	PreK	*K*	*1st*	
Sensory Efficiency				
Differentiates common textures	–	I		
Uses listening to follow three-step directions	–	E	I	
Uses sound and smell clues to identify cafeteria at school	–		E	
Differentiates gradations in size by touch	–	–	E	
Assistive Technology				
Operates Digital Talking Book player from the National Library Service	E	I		
Opens file on notetaking device	–	–	E	
Compensatory Access				
Recognizes 26 braille letters	–	E	I	
Tracks braille letters at 90 lpm	–	–	I	
Functionally uses positional concepts in play and activities	E	I		
Demonstrates understanding of positional concepts on paper	E	E	I	
Writes name with braillewriter	E	I		
Writes signature	E	E	E	
Orientation and Mobility				
Holds cane with proper grip	–	I		
Correctly uses diagonal technique		E	E	
Travels from front of home to backyard	E	I		
Travels from classroom to cafeteria	–	–	E	

FIGURE 3.2 *continued*

ECC Area and Skills	Date and Grade			
	1/11	1/12	1/13	
	PreK	K	1st	
Recreation and Leisure				
Pretend plays with another child	E	E	I	
Can use raised-line coloring book	E	I		
Plays simple card games with peers	—	—	E	
Social Interaction				
Says "please" and "thank you" when requesting/acknowledging assistance	E	I		
Interacts with peers by starting a conversation	E	I		
Asks adults in school office for assistance	E	I		
Career Education				
Can state difference between work and play	E	I		
Can identify three workers who wear uniforms		E	I	
Knows people get paid for working		I		
Independent Living				
Dresses self	E	E	I	
Uses fasteners	—	E	E	
Washes hands independently	E	I		
Sets the table at home	E	I		
Takes letters to mailbox	E	E		
Self-Determination				
Makes choices	E	I		
States preference for preferred toy/friend	E	I		
Can identify one accommodation she uses		E	I	
Identifies name of her visual impairment		E	I	

Progress Code: I = Independent success; E = Emerging skill; skill needs prompting or assistance to accomplish; — = No opportunity to demonstrate or not demonstrated

- make environmental adaptations (move closer to the instructor as needed)
- use hearing to locate other students

These behaviors, possibly along with the skills involved for each, could be listed on a form, along with a place to check them off when each is observed. Many teachers develop lists of behaviors and skills specific to each student to use as a record-keeping form that is updated at grading periods, annually, or at the IEP meeting.

Using observation as a tool to gather accurate information about a student is most effective if done in both familiar and unfamiliar settings. Often students function well in familiar settings, but may have trouble with certain behaviors in unfamiliar ones. Observing a student's ability to adjust to unfamiliar settings is an important part of the assessment process.

Continued Assessment

After the initial assessment, the teacher will have useful information about what the student can do now. However, it is important to carefully record the student's mastery of behaviors, skills, and tasks on an on-going basis. Anecdotal records about mastery and learning within the areas of the ECC should be maintained for each student. A sample form that can be used for observation notes is shown in Figure 3.3.

The information obtained through observation can then be used to complete a record-keeping form, such as the one previously shown in Figure 3.1, which is a valuable tool for planning instruction from grading period to grading period, semester to semester, and year to year, and when writing goals and objectives for the student's IEP. The record-keeping form can also serve as an important information-sharing tool if the student changes teachers or attends another school.

It is important for teachers of students with visual impairments to remember that mastery of a skill or behavior today or in one setting may not necessarily mean that the student has mastered it for life. In addition, as the student matures, more and more complex nuances may need to be taught for each behavior. For example, a student's social interaction at age 5 is expected to be appropriate for 5-year-olds, such as being able to join a group of other children in pretend play. Once the child becomes a teenager, his or her social interactions will require different behaviors, such as joining a peer group by asking appropriate questions, listening to the conversation, and giving appropriate responses. Joining a group of teenagers requires some finesse with body language to physically insert oneself into the group in an appropriate way, whereas 5-year-olds use different skills to enter into a play activity.

Determine Skills that Need Practice

The approach just described for the initial assessment of a student should be repeated on a scheduled basis to keep observations up to date. These regularly scheduled checks, done annually or semi-annually or at the end of each grading period, will give teachers information about behaviors and skills that may need additional practice. This general assessment of the student's performance in the areas of the ECC can be supplemented by more detailed assessments that are used as needed to evaluate specific skills, as described in the chapters in Part 2.

Using the same methods outlined for the initial assessment, teachers of students with visual impairments can maintain a continuous review of behaviors that each student has learned and thereby identify skills and tasks that may need reinforcement from time to time. For example, a student who has mastered one-way street crossing travel through orientation and mobility training may need to have that behavior periodically reinforced if the student's day-to-day travel does not involve those particular kinds of street crossings. In addition, street crossings vary greatly in their characteristics, so the O&M specialist may want to schedule opportunities for frequent reinforcement of the behaviors and skills needed to successfully cross a variety of streets.

Many young children and students with significant cognitive disabilities may not have the ability to generalize a learned behavior to a different setting or task. Requiring them to demonstrate behaviors and skills in different settings can confuse them because the circumstances and the surroundings do not match the setting in which skills were originally learned. It is particularly important for teachers of this group of students, therefore, to teach and reinforce behaviors and skills in different and increasingly complex settings, to use a variety of prompts, and to provide multiple opportunities to practice. For example, if a child learns to locate silverware and set a table in a simulated kitchen at school, locating silverware and setting the table very likely will need to be taught and reinforced at home so that the student can refine these skills in this different location. A child with a severe cognitive disability may learn to exchange money with school lunchroom staff, but may need care-

FIGURE 3.3

Sample Observation Record Form

General Observation Record

Name of Observer: *Margaret White*

Name of Student: *Joshua Martin*

Date	**Observation**	**ECC Areas**
9-20-14	*Josh turned on DAISY player without being reminded.*	*Assistive technology, self-determination*
9-21-14	*Josh greeted peer, Orlando, with "Hi" before science class started.*	*Social interaction*

Source: Adapted from Carol A. Layton, "Comprehensive Assessment," in Alan J. Koenig and M. Cay Holbrook (Eds.), *Foundations of Education* (2nd ed.), *Vol. II: Instructional Strategies for Teaching Children and Youths with Visual Impairments* (New York: AFB Press, 2002), p. 74.

ful instruction and practice in exchanging money at a store in the community. It is thus necessary for teachers to continually be on the alert for behaviors and skills that need reinforcing in different settings or with different adults.

Determine Additional Behaviors and Skills

Keeping an ongoing record of a student's mastery of skills and behaviors within each ECC area allows teachers to identify which additional behaviors and skills a student might need to learn. Input from other school personnel, parents, and the student, as appropriate, can help to identify which skills a student needs at any given time.

As already mentioned, not every student will need to know how to perform every behavior or skill in every ECC domain, as is the situation when considering instruction specific to visual efficiency for a totally blind child. In addition, not every child will have the capability of mastering every behavior. For example, a student with a significant cognitive disability or physical disability may not be able to master cutting with a sharp knife independently and safely. Moreover, some behaviors, skills, and tasks that are not appropriate at the primary level become critical when a student enters middle school. Using a computer at the primary level, for example, is a beginning skill that often results in the ability to play games. At the secondary level, the computer becomes a necessary tool for instructional access that requires a student to know keyboarding skills and to have the ability to use software programs to spell check, edit, and print materials to complete assignments. Thus, the additional skills a student needs to learn changes constantly from year to year because of the student's growth and maturation and the increasing complexity of what is expected of students at school and in the community.

Determine Skills Needed for the Future

For students with visual impairments, who often have difficulty learning new behaviors and skills through observation, it is critical that their teachers and other adults who care about them focus not just on the behaviors needed to be successful in the present, but also on those that they will need in future environments. To determine which behaviors and skills a student will need from year to year, it is imperative that the teacher of students with visual impairments consistently consult with educational personnel, parents, and the student, as appropriate, to consider goals and preferences over a longer period of time than just the year covered by the current IEP. Planning and setting goals for the future should be an integral part of ongoing discussions so that families and the student keep the end in mind and realize that behaviors and skills learned now are laying the groundwork for a successful future.

In general, students with unimpaired vision are constantly developing new behaviors to meet new demands. In order to provide students who are visually impaired with similar opportunities to develop and grow and meet new demands, their teachers need to evaluate the demands that will be presented to them within the environments in which they will be spending time.

Ecological inventories can be useful when trying to determine specific skills that will be needed in the future. Conducting an ecological inventory involves performing assessments in the places where a student will be spending time in the future and determining the behaviors and skills that are needed to function competently in these locations. For example, a teacher of students with visual impairments and an O&M specialist might conduct an ecological inventory at the middle school to which an elementary student will be assigned. A discrepancy analysis, in which a student's behavior is compared to that of his or her peers, might be used by these professionals to determine which of the behaviors and skills required for functioning in the middle school the student has already mastered and which skills are not yet developed. Skills that the student has not yet mastered need to be the focus of present instruction. In this example the student would need to be prepared for functioning with classmates at his or her future middle school, among other things.

Similarly, an ecological inventory of a worksite, grocery store, preschool, or community center can help the teacher of students with visual impairments determine which behaviors and skills need to be taught to a student who will need to function in those various locations. For example, if an ecological inventory of a potential environment shows that the student will have to negotiate stairs and move from one location to another within a certain time limit, a discrepancy analysis would determine whether the student has those capabilities. If the student cannot complete the necessary movement in the time required, then those skills and behaviors would need to be practiced before the student is placed in the new setting.

Figure 3.4 shows a discrepancy analysis from an ecological inventory of a local gym. To begin this assessment, the teacher went to the workout center in the student's neighborhood and identified the skills and behaviors expected of people functioning successfully in that environment, and organized those skills and behaviors according to various sub-environments (at the entrance, in the locker room, within the weights area, and so forth). The teacher then observed the student functioning at the gym and recorded the student's success in performing necessary tasks within the various sub-environments. Based on a discrepancy analysis of the difference between the student's performance and the performance of others, the teacher then targeted specific skills for instruction and identified needed modifications or other measures. For some students with more severe cognitive or physical disabilities, an ecological inventory may be more detailed and result in strategies that involve more instances of partial participation than is shown in Figure 3.4.

Set Priorities for Instruction

Once teachers have used data obtained from assessments to determine the skills and behaviors a student has mastered, the skills and behaviors that the student needs to maintain mastery, and the skills and behaviors that need to be taught for future success, decisions will have

FIGURE 3.4

Sample Discrepancy Analysis

ENVIRONMENT: *LOCAL NEIGHBORHOOD WORKOUT FACILITY*

Sub-Environment	Activity	Rating	Discrepancy Analysis	Modification, Accommodations, or Intervention Necessary
Entrance	*Locates door*	+		
	Locates registration area	+		
	Greets front desk clerk	–	*Voice tone too demanding and loud when saying, "I need help."*	*Needs instruction on social skills of greeting*
	Pays for workout	+		*Note: Uses only bills, no coins*
	Thanks front desk clerk	–	*Just walks away*	*Social skills instruction needed*
Locker Room	*Enters locker room*	+		
	Locates locker	–	*Can't identify locker if it is in center of row*	*Perhaps assign locker at end of first row*
	Uses combination lock	–	*Can't see or remember numbers for combination*	*Use lock that requires a key*
	Stores valuables in locker	+		
	Uses shower	+		
Weights Area	*Locates empty space on floor*	+		
	Selects appropriate weights	+		
	Uses weights correctly	+		
	Returns weights	+		
	Requests assistance, if necessary	+		
Machines	*Uses stationary bike*	–	*Can't adjust controls*	*Area too dark: carry a flashlight to facilitate viewing of controls*
	Uses rowing machine	+		
	Uses treadmill	–	*Can't adjust controls*	*Controls too close together. Use tactile marker.*
Café Area	*Locates café area*	+		
	Orders drink or food item	+	*Note: more demanding than pleasant*	
	Pays for drink or food item	+		*Note: uses only bills, no coins*
	Thanks cashier	–	*Just walks away*	*Social skills instruction*

Key: + = Student completes targeted behavior; – = Student does not complete targeted behavior

to be made about which needs should be given priority and recorded as goals in the student's IEP. It is most important that the teacher determines these priorities with input from the classroom teacher, other educational personnel (the O&M specialist or physical therapist, for instance), the parent, and the student, as appropriate. When setting these priorities, the team needs to take into consideration the student's current needs in relation to academic learning and immediate integration into the learning environment, along with goals related to skills needed in future environments. Priorities must be established at the IEP meeting, but should be given some thought in advance. It is essential to share the results of any assessment with the student's parents in advance of any formal meeting. Doing so will help make sure that the family has input into the behaviors and skills selected as goals for the student.

It is important to note that the student's IEP will most likely contain major categories of skills, not specific details. For example, the IEP might indicate that the student will focus on independent dressing skills, but the small steps—buttoning, snapping, tying, etc.—would most likely not be included, even though these steps may appear on various lists and forms the teacher of students with visual impairments may be using for initial or ongoing assessment.

Setting priorities for learning certain skills will drive the lessons that are developed and used by the teacher with the student. Once those lessons are complete, the performance of the skills that are their focus will need to be assessed.

Develop Learning Activities and Evaluation Strategies

The development of learning activities and lessons is discussed in the following section on instructional planning. Evaluation of the outcomes of those activities—namely, the skills the student may have learned—is part of the teacher's ongoing assessment. Assessment is often overlooked as part of a learning activity, but it is a critical step in determining if a student has mastered the behaviors and skills that were the focus of instruction. Teachers need to decide what they will accept as evidence that a particular behavior or skill has been learned. Some strategies and considerations that help with this decision include the following:

- When beginning to plan instruction, the teacher should write down a description of what the student should be able to do when the behavior or skill is mastered. For example, the teacher might set an objective for the student to maintain a log of homework assignments by making note of daily assignments, estimating the time needed for each assignment, and recording when the assignment is finished. By assessing each component of the homework log, the teacher can determine if the student is successfully maintaining this kind of record and, therefore, if the objective has been achieved.
- For graded performance, it is important to determine what behavior will be considered a passing score. This decision should be made before the activity is taught, and students should be informed in advance of what constitutes a passing score. Using the example of the homework assignment log, the teacher might determine that the student would have to complete all section entries or components of the log for 5 consecutive days to obtain the highest score. Lower scores would be assigned for the completion of only some components on all days or for not recording the required information on some days.
- It is important for teachers to determine if the student understands the content of an activity. It is necessary to be alert for misunderstandings and to have the student demonstrate or explain what he or she has learned. For example, the teacher may need to work with the student to set up the homework log and complete sections of the log with the student for the first week so that the student is clear about the expectations for success. Thereafter, the student can be expected to complete the log independently.

A scoring system is helpful in assigning levels of mastery for skills or tasks. A generic scoring system, or rubric, can be created based on the idea that teachers are always working toward a student's independent mastery of a behavior or skill, with the assumption that different levels of assistance will be provided depending on a student's need. For example:

4 Student demonstrates total mastery of the behavior or skill with no assistance.

3 Student demonstrates mastery of the behavior or skill 3 out of 4 times with no assistance.

2 Student has partial understanding of the behavior or skill but requires some level of assistance.

1 Student needs considerable assistance to complete the behavior or skill or does not demonstrate an understanding of the behavior or skill.

This kind of scoring system can be adjusted by mentioning specific levels of assistance required by the student so that a 5- or 6-point system is used, or by adding additional levels of mastery the student may demonstrate (for example, performing a skill 2 out of 4 times). For example:

6 Student demonstrates total mastery of the behavior or skill with no assistance.

5 Student demonstrates mastery of the behavior or skill 3 out of 4 times with no assistance.

4 Student demonstrates mastery of the behavior or skill 3 out of 4 times with verbal reminders.

3 Student has partial understanding of the behavior or skill but requires simple physical prompt (touch to the arm).

2 Student has partial understanding of the behavior or skill but requires physical assistance.

1 Student needs considerable assistance to complete the behavior or skill or does not demonstrate an understanding of the behavior or skill.

Scoring systems can also be more specific to the task being learned, as demonstrated in the rubric for slate and stylus presented in Sidebar 3.2.

Learning activities need to be adapted to fit the needs of the individual student. For example, a scoring system that requires a student to complete a task independently to obtain a rating of 4 would need to be adapted for a student with multiple disabilities so that completion of the same task with minimal assistance from someone else would score the same rating.

Other types of evaluative assessment include:

- A tally of behaviors on which students are rated on successive days with a plus sign (+) for completing a targeted behavior or a minus sign (–) if they do not complete it, so that the teacher of students with visual impairments can determine if the student is making progress from one day or week to the next.
- A checklist of the key behaviors, skills, or tasks involved in learning an activity, on which the teacher can check off each individual behavior, skill, or task that is part of the activity to signify that the student has performed it.
- A worksheet or test in which the teacher asks direct questions of a student and is answered with a word, a number, or a series of words or numbers, or one that involves matching objects or ideas as appropriate. A test, for example, might be the best way to determine if a student can identify

SIDEBAR 3.2

Rubric for Teaching the Slate and Stylus

SKILLS NECESSARY FOR MASTERY OF THE SLATE AND STYLUS

Score of 1: Demonstrates minimal skills, including:

- Identifies and names a slate
- Identifies and names a stylus
- Scribbles using a stylus on paper that has been inserted into the slate
- Locates first cell on the slate

Score of 2: Demonstrates 50% of all skills, including skills required for a score of 1 and these:

- Holds stylus correctly
- Inserts paper into the slate independently
- Locates first side and second side of the cell
- Identifies top, middle, and bottom of the first side of the cell
- Identifies top, middle, and bottom of the second side of the cell
- Can write the following letters: a, b, l, k, c, and g
- Puts paper into the slate with assistance

Score of 3: Demonstrates 75% of all skills, including skills required for a score of 2 and these:

- Can write the following letters using the stylus: *d, m, n, p, r, u, x, v, w*
- Can write the following letters using the stylus: *e, f, h, l, j, o, q, s, t, z*
- Puts paper into the slate correctly and independently
- Writes three simple words on a line (ball, call, hall)
- Writes names using uncontracted braille

Score of 4: Demonstrates 100% of all skills, including skills required for a score of 3 and these:

- Writes names using contracted braille
- Writes a shopping list using uncontracted braille
- Writes a shopping list using contracted braille

SOURCE: Developed by Sharon Z. Sacks.

the parts of the eye that are relevant to his or her visual impairment.

The type of assessment and scoring criteria used to evaluate a student's level of skill development needs to be determined before an activity is begun. If necessary, adjustments can be made the next time the learning activity is presented to address any problems that occur during initial instruction. It is equally important to keep a record of results. Although many teachers do a mental check of an activity's success or a student's performance without ever writing anything down, it is helpful to note how the student performed and what needs to be changed about an activity or lesson the next time; these notes provide evidence that the skill has been addressed and of the student's progress toward goals.

A critical part of the assessment of a student's performance on an activity is sharing the results with the student. Students benefit from receiving accurate feedback. Often a learning activity lends itself to self-evaluation. In particular, older students can learn to assess their own progress if expectations are shared with them or developed with their input. A scoring rubric, such as the one shown in Sidebar 3.2, is often helpful for communicating expectations to students.

Some teachers have their students assist with recording their own performance of tasks by noting data on charts and graphs, especially when a task requires measurement with numerical data. Students with visual impairments may find large-print graph paper, braille graph paper, and small dot stickers useful for recording this kind of data. The students can then store these data sheets in notebooks so that results can be reviewed and updated frequently. This approach to data management works especially well when noting performance of keyboarding activities, reading and writing speed practice, and listening comprehension practice. Involving the student is not only motivating, but also helps teach the use of charts and graphs, a skill that is part of the ECC area of compensatory access (K. Mountjoy, personal correspondence, 2006).

Each of the learning activities provided in Part 2 of this book includes an evaluation component to emphasize the importance of recording data on students' skills and to demonstrate the many ways it is possible to assess the acquisition of new skills and behaviors. When conducting any assessment, it is paramount to remember that the assessment of students with visual impairments needs to be individualized, based on each student's needs and abilities.

Just as assessment must be individualized for each student, so too must instruction. Given the heterogeneity of the population of students with visual impairments, teachers often create customized instructional activities to meet each student's unique needs. The following discussion provides suggestions for planning such instruction in the skills encompassed by the ECC.

INSTRUCTIONAL PLANNING

Overall, the basis for planning instruction includes the information provided by assessments and the application of general principles of effective instruction. Most teachers are required by school administrators to write lesson plans. Although lesson planning can be time consuming and challenging in a number of ways, it can also be an effective tool for teacher and student success. As many teachers of students with visual impairments are all too often aware, it can be difficult to find the time to address the behaviors and skills of the ECC in addition to supporting students' progress in the core curriculum. Lack of sufficient time to get everything done requires that teachers plan instruction carefully to maximize the value of the learning activities they create. After thinking about instructional objectives and approaches and the evaluation of outcomes appropriate for a given student, a teacher can target related skills in a single lesson or activity, or across a series of lessons.

Learning Activities

Once areas of need have been identified for a student and priorities in these areas have been reflected in the student's IEP, the teacher of students with visual impairments will need to determine how to teach targeted skills and the best ways to integrate the learning of these skills into the tasks and activities the student will be performing throughout the school day. (See Sidebar 3.3 for a checklist that can be used in constructing learning activities.) As already indicated, an effective way of promoting skills is designing instructional learning activities that incorporate the practice of related ECC skills within a single activity or unit and thus address multiple ECC areas at once. Given that the areas of the ECC are closely connected, the thoughtful consideration of an activity and the tasks involved can reveal how a single activity can include behaviors and skills

SIDEBAR 3.3

Activity Planning Checklist

1. Were the goals and objectives identified?
   - What will the student do?
   - How will the student do it?
   - How well is the student expected to perform?
2. Does the teacher describe the activity?
   - How will the student be interested and motivated to engage in learning?
   - How will expectations for the activity be communicated to the student?
   - How will a connection between prior knowledge and skills and this new activity be established?
   - What knowledge and skills need to be taught to achieve the objective of the activity?
   - What parts of the learning activity will require guided practice to support the student's completion of the task?
   - What parts of the activity will the student be able to do without assistance?
   - What parts of the activity will allow the student to practice building speed and proficiency?
   - When might the student's ability to maintain skills learned in this activity be reviewed at a future time?
3. Were ECC behaviors and skills incorporated in the activity?
   - What is the primary behavior of the ECC addressed in this activity?
   - What other ECC behaviors are incorporated in the activity?
4. How will learning be evaluated?
   - How will the student's performance be recorded and reported?
   - How will it be known if the student has learned the intended goal?
   - How will the student's performance be judged?

SOURCE: Adapted from D. Houston and M. Beech, *Designing Lessons for the Diverse Classroom: A Handbook for Teachers* (Tallahassee: Florida Department of Education, 2002).

that extend across several ECC areas. To support teachers in using this approach, the learning activities provided in Part 2 of this book demonstrate that activities and tasks can be designed to incorporate multiple ECC areas, components, and skills. The form used to present those learning activities is provided for readers in Figure 3.5.

For example, the teacher of students with visual impairments who is preparing an activity related to sensory efficiency and plans on having a student listen to a speaker for important information might incorporate an objective related to the social skill of keeping one's face directed to the speaker. An activity focused on learning to play a card game might begin with the opportunity to pop a mini-bag of popcorn in the microwave, bridging the areas of recreation and leisure and independent living. Starting and ending a mobility activity by signing in and out provides the opportunity to practice writing one's name and reading the time on an analog clock to develop O&M, independent living, and compensatory access skills. Teachers of students with visual impairments need to include objectives related to the ECC in their activity plans, if for no other reason than to record that instruction and practice of these important skills is occurring.

Activity plans are not the same as lesson plans, which detail a teaching plan for a single lesson. Typically, lesson plans include information about the activity to be undertaken (benchmarks, objectives, materials needed, time required, and so forth), an introductory section (covering reminders to students about what they've already learned and explanations of how new material applies to previously learned skills and information), the presentation of the activity (what the teacher will say in instruction, how the skill will be modeled, and how the teacher will check for students' understanding), and at what levels of practice the student will be expected to perform the target behaviors (such as with guided practice or independently).

As described here, a learning activity is a more global description of a particular activity, what the teacher desires to accomplish through the activity, and how it will be taught. Several lessons and practice opportunities might typically be required to achieve mastery of the skills being addressed in a single learning activity. An important facet of the activity plan is the method that the

FIGURE 3.5

Form for Planning Learning Activities

Learning Activity: ______________________	
Primary ECC Area: **Grades:**	**Component:**
Other ECC Areas:	
Goal:	
Key Tasks/Concepts to Include:	
Description:	
Instructional Materials and Supplies Needed:	
Settings:	
Duration/Timing:	
Evaluation:	

teacher intends to use to monitor the acquisition of skills over time. The learning activities provided in each chapter of Part 2 of this book are presented using this form. In addition to the typical elements of learning activities, there are places on the form where the teacher of students with visual impairments can list the primary and secondary ECC areas that are the focus of the activity, and ideas for adapting the activity for learners with additional disabilities can be added. (See Figure 3.6 as an example.)

As always, it is important to consult with family members so that the behaviors, skills, and associated tasks to be taught to a student can be identified jointly; instructional strategies discussed together; and agreement reached about activities to teach, reinforce, and monitor within the home. The skills and tasks that are learned most easily through naturally occurring activities at home will be the best place for parents to provide reinforcement, such as in caring for and organizing one's clothes. Many skills in the area of independent living lend themselves to effective instruction in the home and may be the easiest for families to address as well.

Unit Plans

Many teachers find it useful to plan learning activities based on a unit or theme. Typically a unit plan might coincide with other themed activities that are occurring in the student's classroom or school. For example, Thanksgiving is generally a theme around which instructional activities are focused in November. Teachers of students with visual impairments might choose to build on that theme by developing an instructional unit on cooking that, depending on the ages and abilities of the students involved, focuses on instruction in ricing, peeling, or mashing cooked potatoes, stringing green beans, toasting bread for stuffing, opening up cans of olives, or other similar tasks. Although such a unit would focus on instruction in cooking skills, it would also provide students with important conceptual understanding of ideas encountered in class discussions and reading assignments, as well as reinforce other general education skills, such as reading and math.

One approach to unit planning for promoting skills in multiple ECC areas is reflected in the planning guide found in Figure 3.7. This planning tool can be used as follows:

1. In the large box labeled "Skills" in the center of the guide, list some or all of the skills that have been identified as learning needs for the student.
2. A thematic unit that is being addressed in the student's general education classroom as part of the core curriculum or an area of the ECC that needs further attention for the student can then be identified. That topic and a brief description of the unit can be written in the "Title" box.
3. Ways in which each of the areas of the ECC can be incorporated into instruction related to that particular topic can be considered and written in the boxes for the various ECC areas that make up the rest of the form.
4. Activities to support the ideas that have been identified for each of the ECC areas can then be pinpointed.

An example of a completed unit planning guide for Kelly, the student introduced in Chapter 1, is provided in Figure 3.8. Lisa, her teacher of students with visual impairments, created this plan when Kelly's second-grade class was studying community helpers. Lisa wanted to be sure that Kelly understood the concepts of work and community that were key to this social studies unit. She also knew that Kelly had a limited understanding of the concept of "trash" and the various ways that it is handled. She and Kelly's O&M instructor designed a unit plan that would have Kelly travel to the main office daily at 10:00 a.m., where she would be expected to greet the secretary, sign in, remove the trash bag from the can under the secretary's desk and replace it with an empty one, shred a small stack of paper, initiate a conversation with the principal (if he were present), and sign out before returning to her class at 10:30. Each of these tasks reinforced or allowed instruction in IEP goals that had been identified for Kelly. Within the resource room, Lisa planned to spend some time having Kelly explore information on waste and recycling and some of the careers associated with those topics. Two other learning activities that were also incorporated into this unit and that the O&M specialist and Lisa integrated into their work with all of their students included maintenance of an O&M route journal and an "I Can" list—a list of accomplishments that Kelly was expected to maintain. Most of the activities identified in the unit plan example were monitored by a paraeducator, Mr. Daniel, who was assigned to Kelly's general education teacher. He coordinated these activities with Andrew, Kelly's O&M specialist, two days a week.

To perform these activities, Kelly wore a watch that vibrated at 9:55 a.m. to alert her that it was time to put

FIGURE 3.6

Sample Learning Activity

Learning Activity: Find Places for Fun

Primary ECC Area: Recreation and Leisure **Component:** Leisure Activities and Hobbies
Grades: 4–12

Other ECC Areas:

- Compensatory access
- Sensory efficiency
- Orientation and mobility
- Career education
- Self-determination

Goal: The student will become knowledgeable about community resources for recreation and leisure activities. The student will locate places on a map that he or she goes for recreation and leisure activities (such as a neighborhood park or playground, or movie theater).

Key Tasks/Concepts to Include:
The student will:

- Practice map reading
- Practice correct identification of places
- Express preferences of places to go for fun

(Key tasks may need adaptation for appropriate media and mobility capabilities of the student.)

Description:
The student will locate places where recreation and leisure activities occur on a map. The teacher of students with visual impairments will teach, as appropriate, use of a low vision device and tactile graphic techniques, such as systematic searching, scanning, focusing a device, meanings of directional words, tactile discrimination, graphic symbols, and locations of sites in reference to the student's home.

This activity can be conducted over and over again, changing the sites to be located. It can be used for an individual student or several students as a game. Students can use separate maps and practice locating places, depending on their learning medium. The key to this activity is to use it often so that students get a lot of practice in tactile reading of maps or use of low vision devices to locate places on a map. These skills are critical to success in math, science, and social studies as students progress through elementary school. This activity can also be used in higher grades with more and more complex map-reading skills and with the student practicing production of tactile maps and print maps, as appropriate.

Instructional Materials and Supplies Needed:
The teacher will need to prepare maps ahead of time, particularly for younger students. For older students some map construction can be included using tactile graphic kits or other available materials for map building.

Settings:
School (learning of activity), home (practice), or community (visiting locations).

Duration/Timing:
Learning of the tasks needed to do this activity will vary depending on the needs of the students. This activity should be broken into smaller tasks that build on the final goal. Thirty-minute sessions devoted to learning the smaller tasks can be done two or three times a week throughout a six to nine week session with the final goal being the culminating activity that is used to evaluate the student.

Evaluation:
The student can be evaluated using the following rubric:

4 **Student independently finds more than two places of recreation and leisure on a map.**
3 **Student finds two places of recreation and leisure on a map with minimal prompting.**
2 **Student requires step-by-step prompting to find two places of recreation and leisure on a map.**
1 **Student needs hand-over-hand guidance or other physical assistance to find two places of recreation and leisure on a map.**

Note: If a teacher wants to give a grade or evaluate student progress toward the final goal, a similar rubric can be used for each of the skills taught to complete the goal activity. For example, ratings could be given in the following way for a student's ability to correctly identify meanings of directional words: 4, all meanings correct; 3, most meanings correct; 2, at least two meanings correct; 1, no meanings correct.

FIGURE 3.7

Form for Unit Planning

UNIT PLANNING GUIDE

Name of Student ______ Implemented Period ______

Sensory Efficiency	Title	Assistive Technology
	Skills	
Compensatory		Social Interaction
Self-Determination		Recreation and Leisure
Independent Living	Orientation and Mobility	Career

away her materials, get her cane, and meet Mr. Daniel in the hallway. There, they checked the time on Mr. Daniel's braille analog watch to make sure that it was close to 10:00 and started toward the office, with Andrew (when he was present) providing additional instruction related to Kelly's use of the cane in the diagonal position. Once in the office, Kelly was expected to greet the secretary and ask him if any shredding needed to be done. After completing any necessary shredding, Kelly would then say hello to the principal (if present) and initiate a short conversation, which Mr. Daniel would record on a handheld device. After concluding her conversation with the principal, Kelly was expected to empty the wastebasket near the secretary's desk and carry the plastic trash bag to the custodian's cart located on the route back to her classroom. Before entering her classroom, Kelly checked Mr. Daniel's braille analog watch again to see how far the minute hand was from the 10:30 mark.

Even though Lisa wasn't the primary person implementing this routine, she was involved in much of the

FIGURE 3.8

Sample Completed Unit Planning Guide for Kelly

Kelly | **UNIT PLANNING GUIDE** | *First nine weeks of term 9/2–10/31/14*

Sensory Efficiency

N/A

Compensatory

- Organization and planning skills
- Signature practice
- Spelling
- Braille writing

Self-Determination

- Add to braille list of skills that student can do well ("I Can" list)
- Place list in three-ring binder

Independent Living

- Empty wastebaskets in main office of school
- Telling time

Classroom Theme

Community helpers

Skills

- Student will face people talking to her or whom she is addressing.
- Student will initiate and close conversations using a topic of interest to the conversational partner.
- Student will improve braille notetaking ability.
- Student will use a notetaking device for a variety of purposes.
- Student will improve recognition of second-grade word vocabulary in braille.
- Student will use organizational systems.

Orientation and Mobility

- Travel from classroom to office
- Orient to office
- Travel while carrying bag
- Return to class
- Maintain O&M journal

Assistive Technology

- Shred paper
- Explore what happens to trash and recycled materials after leaving school on Internet web page
- Maintain O&M journal

Social Interaction

- Greet secretary appropriately
- Maintain conversation log
- Hold three-minute conversation with principal

Recreation and Leisure

- Discuss weekend sports game with principal
- Learn vocabulary related to sports game

Career

- Discuss careers associated with community workers engaged in recycling, office cleaning, etc. (pay, conditions, hours, etc.)
- Participate in regularly scheduled work task
- Record time of work
- Sign in

instruction related to it. She and Kelly worked on the following skills and behaviors:

- role-playing greetings
- role-playing several conversation starters ("Are you especially busy today?" or "Did you watch any sports on television this weekend?") as well as strategies for ending a conversation ("Well, I've got to get going to my class.")
- reviewing the recorded conversation tape together for feedback purposes

- practicing putting no more than five pieces of paper in the shredder at one time
- gathering the edges of the trash bag together and carrying the bag in this position
- telling time at the hour and half-hour and counting minutes on a braille analog watch

Lisa's work with Kelly incorporated practicing skills in both core curriculum areas (such as writing and telling time), as well as the ECC areas of social interaction, independent living, and orientation and mobility. Similarly, Andrew's role included developing skills from two ECC areas (independent living [telling time], and O&M [movement in a familiar setting]). Mr. Daniel, too, had multiple roles. His primary responsibility was to keep a careful record of Kelly's performance on the targeted tasks, noting how much assistance she required.

Reviewing Unit and Learning Activity Plans

It is important to view learning activities as events that occur over a period of several meetings with the student and not necessarily as individual one-time lessons. Similarly, unit plans typically occur over a longer period of time (several weeks or a grading period). Because learning for students with visual impairments evolves over time and new skills need to be practiced frequently to be mastered, it is essential that instruction in specific skills be repeated while the student is doing the same and different age-appropriate tasks.

Once the teacher of students with visual impairments has developed the unit plan and learning activities, it is helpful to review these plans to make sure that they contain all the important elements that will lead to successful instruction and learning. Using a checklist, such as that provided in Sidebar 3.3, helps teachers make sure that their planning is comprehensive. It is not essential to assess all activities and units using such a checklist, but it can be beneficial for teachers who want to make sure that all critical components have been addressed. It might be helpful for teachers to do this review with another teacher, the parent, or even the student, as appropriate. (Teachers who are experienced in activity planning probably will not need to go through the processes just described every time they plan an activity or a unit.)

CONCLUSION

All the areas of the ECC are important for children of all ages, and teachers of students with visual impairments need to determine the specific skills from each area that should receive attention for each year for each student. A summary of the process looks like this:

- complete assessments of the ECC domains
- set priorities for skills to be taught for the year by determining which skills within each area are critical for the age and grade of the student
- develop activities to teach the skills
- assess the success of teaching the skills

This cyclical process is the basis for ensuring that ECC skill learning is a vital part of the work of teachers of students with visual impairments. Implementing this process will ensure that ECC skills are given the emphasis that is crucial for students' learning throughout their first 21 years of life. Part 2 of this book was designed to support teachers in the processes described in this chapter. The chapters that follow present specific information about each area of the ECC. Each area is described in detail with regard to the components and skills that need to be considered, the assessment of these elements, general considerations for teaching within the particular area, the role of the teacher of students with visual impairments specific to that area, and suggestions for working with parents in developing their children's skills. In addition, learning activities are provided that give examples of how to teach various skills within each ECC area to students of different ages and abilities, and how to incorporate skills from multiple ECC areas. Resources for additional information in each area are also included to help busy teachers promote students' critical skills.

References

Browder, D. M. (1991). *Assessment of individuals with severe handicaps: An applied behavior approach to life skills assessment.* Baltimore, MD: Paul H. Brookes.

Cambourne, B. (1988). *The whole story: Natural learning and the acquisition of literacy in the classroom.* Auckland, New Zealand: Ashton Scholastic.

Cambourne, B. (1995). Toward an educational relevant theory of literacy learning: Twenty years of inquiry. *The Reading Teacher, 49*(3), 182–190.

Houston, D., & Beech, M. (2002). *Designing lessons for the diverse classroom: A handbook for teachers.* Tallahassee: Florida Department of Education.

Lowenfeld, B. (1973). Psychological considerations. In B. Lowenfeld (Ed.), *The visually handicapped child in school.* New York: John Day Co.

Sanford, L., & Burnett, R. (2007). *Functional vision and learning media assessment.* Louisville, KY: American Printing House for the Blind.

Thomas, J., Allman, C., & Beech, M. (2007). *Assessment for the diverse classroom: A handbook for teachers.* Tallahassee: Florida Department of Education.

When you have a visually impaired student in your classroom: A guide for teachers. (2002). New York: AFB Press.

Carol Farrenkopf

PART II

The Skills of the Expanded Core Curriculum: Let's Get Specific

CHAPTER 4

Compensatory Access

Amy R. Guerette

L. Penny Rosenblum

Access to information about the world, the ability to communicate, and literacy are the main themes of the compensatory access area of the expanded core curriculum. Without communication and literacy, it is difficult, if not impossible, for students to derive information from and convey information to the world around them. In the United States today, a heavy emphasis has been placed on literacy in our country's schools. There is increased concentration on the need for all students, including students with visual impairments and those with additional disabilities, to receive high-quality literacy instruction. For students who are visually impaired, this effort entails instruction by qualified teachers of students with visual impairments.

The compensatory access area of the ECC focuses on equipping students who are visually impaired with the capacity to compensate for the unique needs and challenges created by a visual impairment. Compensatory access specifically addresses the ability of students with visual impairments to develop concepts about the world and to obtain and share information with others. Overall, the development of compensatory access skills creates a firm foundation for future growth, learning, and development. The skills encompassed by this area of the ECC are the essential skills needed to access information, including the core curriculum of subjects in school, and they are thus foundational skills without which students cannot participate successfully in school, work, and daily life.

THE CENTRAL ROLE OF COMPENSATORY ACCESS

Ultimately, the skills in the compensatory access area enable students to access the core curriculum. The core curriculum for K–12 students in the United States is guided and shaped by state and national education standards and includes the areas of language arts and reading, mathematics, science, social studies, physical education, world languages, fine arts, and health. Through the passage of the No Child Left Behind Act of 2001 (NCLB), policymakers have demonstrated a renewed focus on the achievement of *all* students, with a strong emphasis on accountability of school districts, school administrators, and teachers. In this environment of increased accountability for learning outcomes for students, all students with visual impairments need to be equipped with the skills necessary to access information and demonstrate mastery of state and national education standards. (For more information on aligning instruction with educational standards, see Chapter 14.)

If students are unable to access information from educational materials used in the classroom, they are not fully engaged in the learning process and, in many instances, may not be able to learn. In addition, if students are not able to produce work that demonstrates what they have learned, their mastery of knowledge and skills cannot be measured. For example, students who are tactile learners cannot fully participate in and master content during lessons on charts and tables if they do not have the ability to read and interpret a tactile graphic. Likewise, a student's knowledge of charts and tables cannot be accurately demonstrated on a statewide assessment at the end of the school year if the student's learning of tactile graphics has been neglected.

The teaching and learning of compensatory access skills does not happen in isolation from the core curriculum or other areas of the ECC. Teachers of students with visual impairments need to be aware of content and scheduling of lessons in all the core curriculum areas to allow for planning and teaching of the skills necessary for students to access information, demonstrate what they have learned, and ultimately be successful and independent in the classroom and in daily life. (For information and suggestions designed to support busy teachers in these efforts, see, in particular, Chapter 13.) In addition, many components of compensatory access lay the foundation for future learning in other ECC areas. There is a great deal of overlap between compensatory access and other areas of the ECC, as will be illustrated throughout this chapter. For example, a student's ability to read and interpret a tactile graphic of a table will have implications for his or her ability to obtain and apply information during activities related to daily life and independent living, recreation and leisure activities, career education efforts, and orientation and mobility (O&M) lessons.

While teachers of students with visual impairments are equipped with the knowledge and skills to teach compensatory access to visually impaired students, they cannot accomplish this goal alone. Collaboration among the members of the full educational team is necessary to prepare students to independently apply the knowledge and skills associated with compensatory access at school, home, and in the community. As is the case with other areas of the expanded core curriculum, families of students are vital partners in teaching compensatory access, as practice and application of the skills are necessary outside of school. Chapter 15 discusses how parents can support their children's development of skills related to the ECC outside of school. Collaboration between the teacher and the student's family is also discussed later in this chapter.

Compensatory access consists of prerequisite skills for accessing the core curriculum and includes six different components, which are discussed in the next section.

COMPONENTS OF COMPENSATORY ACCESS

The compensatory access area encompasses the following components:

- concept development
- spatial understanding
- communication modes
- speaking and listening skills
- study and organization skills
- use of adapted educational materials and specialized equipment

Highly individualized instruction in each of these six components is essential for students with visual impairments to learn about the world, communicate, develop literacy, and access the core curriculum content presented in the classroom. Since the essence of compensatory access is to address the student's particular needs for accessing print and other visually presented information, teaching efforts need to pinpoint and be based on assessment of those needs. In the focus on access to information and communication and the effective use of sensory input, compensatory access is closely related to the ECC areas of sensory efficiency and assistive technology. It should also be noted that because providing compensatory access is so closely tied to the student's unique needs and because students with visual impairments are so diverse in their abilities and needs, this chapter cannot include all possible skills in this area but will discuss more common skills and the strategies to address them.

Each of the six compensatory access components contains unique skills, all of which are necessary to create a firm foundation for learning that occurs at school, home, and in the community. These unique skill areas are discussed in this section, as well as the ways that they overlap with other ECC areas. Strategies for teaching compensatory access skills will be explored later in the chapter.

Concept Development

In essence, *concept development* is the process of (a) understanding the characteristics of an item and (b) understanding the relationship among the item's characteristics and with other objects in the environment (Jacobson, 2013). The importance of concept development for students with visual impairments cannot be overemphasized, largely because most students miss out on many opportunities for learning concepts incidentally, through observation of and participation in the surrounding world.

In general, information gained automatically and effortlessly through incidental learning lays the foundation for concept development for most children. When a young child observes her mother setting the table with plates, napkins, and silverware, she learns over time that this activity indicates that food will be served shortly, thus beginning the process of developing concepts about mealtime. This child may never be formally taught this information; she learns it incidentally through casual visual observation.

For students with visual impairments, however, incidental learning may not take place, or it may be a challenging process, as students with low vision often receive incomplete visual information, and students who are blind typically receive no usable visual information about items and processes in the environment. Students with visual impairments therefore must be exposed formally and deliberately to the kind of information in their environment that is typically accessed visually and incidentally by children without visual impairments. The young child with a visual impairment needs her parent to explain that the table is being set and allow her to visually or tactilely explore the items and their placement on the table. The information the child derives from this and many other similar experiences will enable her to begin to learn about the items used during mealtime and the process of setting the table and thus help her to develop a concept of mealtime as well as other related concepts, such as table manners and the social and familial aspects of eating.

Types of Concepts

Hall (1982) discussed 10 categories of concept development to be understood by students with visual impairments:

- body awareness
- environmental awareness
- awareness of object characteristics
- time awareness
- spatial awareness
- actions
- quantity

- symbol awareness
- emotional and social awareness
- reasoning

Each category is divided into related concepts. For example, the related concept of measurement is listed under the category of quantity. Within measurement, the concepts of inches, feet, and yards are listed. Similarly, the "Concepts Checklist for Visually Impaired Children" from the *Assessment Kit of Informal Tools for Academic Students with Visual Impairments, Part 1* (Sewell, 2001) provides a comprehensive list of 13 categories of concepts and doubles as an informal checklist of skills in concept development. These two resources illustrate two slightly varied ways of dividing the essential concepts for students with visual impairments.

In general, for each concept there are three levels of conceptual understanding that are important to address with students who are visually impaired: *concrete, functional,* and *abstract.* The first level, concrete, encompasses the physical properties of an item. For example, a baseball is white with red stitching, is hard and round, and is made out of smooth leather. The second level involves the functional aspects of the item—what it does. The functional concept of a baseball involves the fact that it can be thrown, hit, rolled, and bounced. Abstract understanding is demonstrated when an individual can generalize from the concrete and functional understanding of an item by reducing the information about it to its most relevant attributes. For example, a student demonstrates an abstract understanding of a baseball when he or she can differentiate a baseball from among a variety of spheres, including baseballs of different colors and materials, yet understands that despite their differences, they are related by their relevant attributes; that is, they are all round and they are all balls.

Abstract understanding is difficult for many students with visual impairments, as they often may not be able to observe objects and frequently do not get enough opportunities to experience the related concepts at the concrete and functional levels that would enable them to create the abstraction. Abstract concepts often involve items that cannot be touched or physically explored. For example, some types of abstract concepts, such as those related to emotions (love, trust, integrity, and so forth), are abstract for people with or without visual impairments. Other concepts are considered to be abstract for students with visual impairments because they are too large, too small, too far, or too dangerous to explore. The sun, moon, and stars can be visually observed in the sky, but cannot be physically touched because of the distances involved. A student cannot have hands-on experiences with an actual, live volcano. However, abstract concepts should be taught and can be understood through well-planned and creative instruction.

Development of Concepts

Children develop an understanding of concepts through a four-step process (Fazzi & Petersmeyer, 2001). It is important to note that children can learn concepts about items only after they are aware that the items exist. The four steps of concept development are:

1. Being aware of the item (for example, a plate)
2. Having a desire to interact with the item (eating off a plate), and being given the opportunity to do so
3. Labeling the item ("The plate is round.") and having multiple experiences interacting with various forms of the item (plastic plates, ceramic plates, dinner plates, salad plates)
4. Classifying other items with similar characteristics that relate to the item (serving platters, soup bowls, pasta bowls, and serving bowls) (Fazzi & Petersmeyer, 2001, p. 97).

Only at the point at which a child develops a sense of "plate-ness," when comparisons to other, related items are made, is the concept of a plate truly formed.

It is essential for teachers and families of students with visual impairments to remember that students with visual impairments may use vocabulary and discuss concepts that they may not fully understand (see Sidebar 4.1 for a real-life illustration). For example, a student may hear a story about an elephant and begin to talk about elephants at dinner that night. The student's teachers and parents then need to begin to ask questions to ensure that the student understands the concepts involved. A parent might say, "Tell me more about elephants. Are they big or small?" Through such conversations a student's understanding of various concepts can be determined.

Spatial Understanding

The understanding of spatial concepts, or *spatial understanding,* has an impact on the development of nearly every area of the ECC, as well as on other com-

SIDEBAR 4.1

When Students Don't Understand the Whole Concept

Teachers of students with visual impairments, general education teachers, and families of students with visual impairments cannot assume that students with visual impairments understand a concept in its entirety just because they can engage in an informed conversation about it. This important point is emphasized by an experience had by the author:

Paul, a 14-year-old student in eighth grade, loved baseball. He lived for the Philadelphia Phillies! He could respond without hesitation to any question about the team, one of its players, or a game or season statistic. Paul was totally blind and listened to the Phillies every night during baseball season and had gone to a few games as well. As we would set up for our daily lessons, Paul would give me the rundown of the prior night's game. One day he said, "I can't believe more people don't hit home runs. It really isn't that far!"

"Not that far?," I thought. Last time I checked, 250-plus feet was pretty darn far! I started to talk to Paul about baseball fields. I asked him to show me how far he thought the pitcher was located from home plate. He stood three feet in front of me. I asked him to show me how far away second base was from home plate. He stood 4 feet in front of me. How far was a home run? He paced off approximately 10 feet in response.

At this point, the elaborate assistive technology lesson I had planned for two hours the night before was scrapped. It was a beautiful day, so we headed out to the baseball diamond at Paul's school and paced off all the bases, the pitcher's mound, the outfield, and the home run fence. This adventure might have been close to a life-changing experience for Paul on that day. For most of his life, he had been a baseball fanatic and had never had an accurate concept of a baseball diamond, the outfield, or the true wonder of a home run. Paul had misunderstood his one true passion in life because for years everyone around him would think, "Listen to that kid—he really knows a lot about baseball!"

pensatory access skills. Fazzi and Petersmeyer (2001) explain that spatial concepts allow students to "understand the placement, arrangement, and spacing of persons or things in relation to one another" (p. 93). Orientation and mobility specialists are key collaborators when teaching spatial concepts to students with visual impairments. For example, the spatial concepts of parallel and perpendicular can apply to both math content and travel on blocks within a neighborhood. For this reason, consultation with a student's O&M instructor on effective ways of teaching and reinforcing spatial concepts may be particularly helpful to the teacher. (It is important, however, that spatial concepts related to mobility be addressed specifically by the O&M specialist, with reinforcement by the teacher of students with visual impairments.)

There are a number of important spatial concepts that children need to understand to further their growth and development. These concepts are addressed by Hall (1982) under the categories of body awareness (left side, right side, above, below, and so on) and spatial awareness (parallel, perpendicular, inside, outside, and so on).

Students first need to be able to understand their own position in space in relation to others and in relation to objects. In general, children develop an understanding of themselves in relation to objects in an egocentric to exocentric manner. In other words, children first understand a concept in relation to themselves before they can understand a concept in relationship to other individuals and items. Physical experiences that help a child develop an understanding of him- or herself in relation to others lay the foundation for development. For example, a child begins to develop the concept of "top" by first experiencing the top of her head and the top of other body parts. Later, after repeated directed experiences, an understanding of what it means to be physically on top of an object becomes clear. Once a student has an understanding of herself in relationship to space, she can begin to apply spatial understanding to objects; for example, she can now begin to comprehend the relationship of one block stacked on top of another, or items on top of the table.

The development of spatial concepts then progresses to the visual and tactile exploration of objects and three-dimensional models. Spatial understanding allows students to visually and tactilely orient themselves for exploration—for example, to apply the concept of "top" to visually or tactilely locate the top of a book, graphic, or globe to explore it further. Only at this point can students begin to effectively use print and tactile two-dimensional materials. However, students with visual impairments do not naturally make the leap from understanding the *top* of a shelf to understanding the *top* of the letter "M" in print or braille, so it is essential that teachers and parents understand this pattern of developing spatial understanding and help children make the necessary connections.

The future development of other components of compensatory access skills relies on a student's spatial understanding, including proficiency in the area of communication modes, the methods used by the student for receiving and conveying information. A student must have strong spatial concepts before being able to be oriented to the formation of letters in print and braille for both reading and writing activities. Students with multiple disabilities need to have a degree of spatial understanding before using a calendar system independently. Study and organization skills such as searching and scanning text or using tactile graphics rely on a solid sense of the spatial orientation of books and diagrams.

In addition, the development of spatial understanding has implications for growth in all areas of the ECC. As already mentioned, there is a strong connection to O&M instruction, in which an understanding of space and the relationship of objects in space is essential for safe and efficient movement within the environment. With regard to developing the social skill of participating in a group conversation, students must first understand the location of individuals around them before they can orient themselves for conversation in a group. The concept of personal space and where one stands during a conversation relies on a student's ability to understand her physical location in relation to a conversational partner. In the area of independent living, spatial understanding is critical to orienting oneself to the rooms in a house before one can engage in activities like cooking, cleaning, or grooming, and then organizing, locating, and using the tools for these activities.

Communication Modes

Communication modes are the methods necessary for receiving and expressing information through visual, tactile, and auditory means and include the methods used to express and receive information from the environment through spoken, signed, and written communication. Print, braille, sign language, choice boards, and calendar systems are among the most common modes of communication utilized by students with visual impairments. The most efficient communication mode for a particular student is determined through careful assessment by the teacher of students with visual impairments, including a functional vision assessment, learning media assessment, and an assistive technology assessment (see the section on assessment later in this chapter as well as Chapters 3, 5, and 6).

Print

For students who are print readers, teachers need to be familiar with and involved in their process of learning to read and write, even though the majority of instruction for most of these students typically is provided in the general classroom by the general education teacher. Students who have low vision often need unique accommodations for print reading and writing. In general, provided modifications should be guided by how the student needs to access materials. One possible approach involves the educational team addressing the accommodations needed by a student in a hierarchical manner, considering the least intrusive accommodations and the smallest degree of adaptation first. When discussing the hierarchy of providing accommodations for students with visual impairments, Stratton (1990) emphasized that "to adapt more than necessary separates the child from the environment" (p. 5). For example, if a student is asked as part of his social studies class to read a map, the use of the map given to all of the students should first be explored. If the student cannot access the details of the map in this format, then use of adaptive devices such as magnification devices should be explored. Only if the student cannot access the needed details of the map with a device should large-print or tactile versions of the map be created. (See also the "least restrictive adaptation" model discussed in Chapter 8.)

If students are unable to read standard print efficiently, the educational team must carefully weigh the advantages and disadvantages of alternate approaches, such as the use of large print or the use of magnifiers or assistive technology (see Chapter 6). Although large-print textbooks are usually available in the K–12 school system, large print is not readily available outside of school. As a result, a student's reliance on large print may lead to limited opportunities for obtaining information elsewhere in life. The team must therefore consider if a student is better served by learning to use low vision devices, which can be used to independently access standard print in any environment. If students continue to struggle with reading print efficiently, the use of braille should be considered.

Braille

Two braille codes are typically taught to school-aged children who are braille readers. The literary braille code involves the various characters and contractions for reading and writing literary materials and is taught as either contracted braille (using short forms) or uncontracted braille (spelled out letter by letter). In 2016, the literary braille code that has been in use since 1959, English Braille–American Edition (EBAE), will be replaced by Unified English Braille (UEB). Although the two codes are very similar, there will be challenges for teachers and students who are accessing materials written in the code with which they are unfamiliar for a period of time. During this transition, it is likely that it will be necessary for readers to be taught key features of both code conventions.

The Nemeth Code for Mathematics and Science Notation is the braille code used for math and science and is made up of numbers and symbols associated with math and science characters and concepts. In the United States, it will continue to be the code used for these purposes, even though UEB has provisions for the preparation of science and mathematics materials. For all braille codes, students must learn both the symbols and the rules associated with the use of each symbol. In addition, students need to be knowledgeable about when to use specific braille codes. For example, when brailling a math problem, a student would use Nemeth code numbers; when brailling dates in a social studies class, the literary braille code would be used.

Sign Language

Students who are deaf-blind have concomitant visual and hearing impairments. Often, but not always, students who are deaf-blind use standard sign language or tactile sign language for receptive and expression communication, that is, for both receiving and expressing information. Sign language is also used with students who have visual and multiple impairments, including language or communication impairments. Teachers of students with visual impairments are not expected to be proficient in sign language, although this knowledge is very helpful when working with students who are deaf-blind or with students for whom verbal communication is not effective. When a teacher is not able to use the student's preferred mode of communication, trained interpreters or interveners—individuals who provide

L. Penny Rosenblum

This student who is deaf-blind is using sign language to communicate with his teacher while exploring rocks and plants.

access to the auditory and visual environment for students who are deaf-blind—should be used when working with the student.

Choice Boards and Calendar Boxes

For students who have visual impairments, establishing predictable routines and encouraging choice making are two essential components of instruction. Making choices helps students develop a sense of cause and effect and also empowers them to feel that they have control over their lives, reducing the risk of developing learned helplessness. *Learned helplessness* is a lack of motivation and effort that can develop "when an individual's efforts have little or no impact on the outcome" (Marks, 1998, p. 200). It is often seen in students with visual and multiple impairments who are not given opportunities for making choices at school or home.

A sense of order is important for these students as well, because routines and predictability can help them develop comprehension of their environment in the face of limited or absent sensory input. *Choice boards* and *calendar boxes* are communication tools that can help students develop a sense of order in and control over the environment. Both tools utilize visual or tactile symbols that are meaningful to the student and are selected based on the student's routines and environment. For example, a seatbelt buckle can be used to communicate that it is time to get on the bus.

Choice boards are used to give students opportunities to make choices throughout their day. On the board, two or more items are presented for the student to choose from in order to communicate his or her preferences about activities (going to the computer or art center, for example) or choices during activities (having pretzels or crackers during snack time, for example).

Calendar boxes are communication systems used to convey a daily schedule to students who struggle with a sense of past, present, and future events. They typically consist of a series of small boxes or containers in which visual or tactile symbols are placed to represent the various activities or classes throughout the student's day at school, home, or in the community. The symbols are objects the student associates with a given activity, such as a spoon to symbolize lunchtime, and they are presented in the sequence in which the student's activities will occur. When first introduced to a student, a calendar box may be quite simple and have two or three bins, among them a Present (what is happening now) bin and a Finished (what is completed) bin. The symbols are placed in the appropriate bin by the teacher before the students arrive for the day. Students usually preview the activities for the entire day in the morning, then select the symbol for the next activity and place it in the Present bin. After each activity is completed, the symbol associated with that activity is placed in the Finished bin to convey that the activity is over and is in the past. Through the use of a calendar box, students can gain a better understanding of future, present, and past events, thus conveying the concept of time or schedule as well as providing a sense of control and empowerment.

Speaking and Listening Skills

It is important that students with visual impairments learn ways to optimize the use of the other senses in order to obtain as much information about the environment as possible. (See Chapter 5 on sensory efficiency for a detailed discussion.) The sense of hearing is typically a critical learning channel for most students, and the development of listening skills needs to be a key focus for instruction (Barclay & Staples, 2012). Effective listening skills are essential in many life, school, and work activities, from being able to follow instructions to being able to distinguish phonemes and begin to read, and eventually interpreting verbal directions or material accessed through recording. In addition, speaking and listening skills relate to many areas of the ECC for students with visual impairments, as they are a prerequisite for development in other areas. One needs to be able to converse and listen actively to others before one is able to form relationships and close friendships (social interaction). Similarly, listening skills are required for such everyday activities as cooking (independent living) or following directions and hearing the approach of oncoming traffic when traveling (orientation and mobility). The ability to listen to and comprehend information is also a prerequisite for the use of screen-reading software or talking devices (assistive technology). Important areas of instruction with students with visual impairments include speaking skills, listening speed, listening comprehension, use of digital talking books and equipment, and the use of readers and personal notetakers.

Listening Skills

The development of strong listening skills is especially important for those students with visual impairments who will use auditory devices and materials in the core curriculum, at home, and in the community. *Active lis-*

tening involves the ability to hear, understand, and interpret information heard from either a person or an enunciating device (Postello & Barclay, 2012). Listening comprehension is an essential component of active listening, as students must not only hear, or perceive, the information aurally, they must comprehend and interpret the information as well. For individuals with visual impairments who use auditory devices and materials, the ability to listen at increased speeds means they can access more information in a given amount of time. However, there is an important relationship between listening speed and comprehension; students cannot increase the speech rate of auditory devices without it affecting their comprehension. Thus, these listening efficiency skills should be formally taught by the teacher as part of compensatory access, as discussed in more detail in the section on instructional strategies.

Speaking Skills

The ability for students to communicate with others is essential to their success in school, in the community, and at home. The verbal language skills of students with visual impairments may sometimes develop in a unique manner, and the educational team must address any differences in development for individual students. For example, a speech-language pathology evaluation may be necessary to diagnose the presence of a speech or language impairment. For many students with visual impairments who do not have additional disabilities, a teacher may assist in ensuring the proper development of speaking skills in academic and social contexts. Challenges for students with visual impairments often include speaking with one's head raised, looking at a conversational partner while speaking, and speaking at a volume that can be comfortably heard. Some students with visual impairments may develop echolalia, speech that is a repetition of what is heard without an understanding of the concepts or content of the speech. The main focus for a student who has an echolalic speech pattern is ensuring comprehensive concept development, a key role of the teacher of students with visual impairments.

Use of Digital Audio Books and Equipment

An audio or talking book is a book whose contents has been recorded so that it can be heard, or "read," by someone who listens to the recording. With the advance of technology, *digital talking books* have been developed. A digital talking book is, "in its fullest implementation, a group of digitally-encoded files containing an audio portion recorded in human speech; the full text of the work in electronic form, marked with the tags of a descriptive markup language; and a linking file that synchronizes the text and audio portion" (Texas School for the Blind and Visually Impaired, 2010). However, digital books or e-books that are not recorded but can be listened to via synthesized speech (or read with a refreshable braille device) are also available for students' use (Postello & Barclay, 2012). Digital talking books (also called digital audio books) may be used by students with visual impairments for whom it has been determined that auditory books are a more efficient option than print or braille for a particular task. Some students will use a combination of braille or print and digital audio textbooks as they become older and reading demands increase in classes, such as in language arts or science. The use of digital talking books should be a decision of the educational team and be based on the results of a learning media assessment (discussed in this chapter in the section on assessment). There are a variety of digital book players designed to play digital audio books for users who are visually impaired. The selection of a specific player for a student should be based on the results of an assistive technology assessment (see Chapter 6), when devices with various characteristics are tried and matched to a student's needs. For some students, for example, the portability of a device may be a key characteristic, while for others, ease of use may be more important.

Use of Readers and Personal Note Takers

While the goal of teaching the ECC is to increase the independence of students with visual impairments, there are situations in which students may need to rely on others to complete specific tasks. Students preparing to go to college or university after high school will need to be knowledgeable about and have practice with using human readers and personal note takers. Personal readers can be used to read materials to students when accessibility cannot be readily provided. For example, a fellow student may read the homework assignments listed on the whiteboard to a student who is a braille reader at the end of the day to ensure all assignments have been recorded properly. Likewise, a human personal note taker can be used in classes when information or diagrams placed on the board are too complex for a student with a visual impairment to interpret at a distance. Additionally, students who make the transition to a work environment may need a reader to give them access to work-related materials that are not available in an accessible format.

Many students do not realize that a teacher of students with visual impairments will not be available beyond high school graduation to braille materials for them, such as those presented on whiteboards or electronic slides. In addition, braille textbooks are often unavailable at colleges or universities. Depending on students' assistive technology skills, they may need to hire readers to access the content of their textbooks and materials by having them read aloud or to hire a personal note taker in classes, such as science and math, in which content is often presented visually. Therefore, skills for locating a reader, managing the use of a reader, and paying a reader are critical for students who intend to attend college or university, as well as for students making the transition to the work environment. (See Trief & Feeney, 2005, for additional discussion.)

Study and Organization Skills

Study and organization skills are often learned incidentally by children with typical sight, but they must be formally taught to students with visual impairments. Organization skills lay the groundwork for success and independence at school, home, and in the community. Study skills are necessary for academic and professional success. Both are essential for equal access to and success in the core curriculum, as visually impaired students often cannot rely on their vision to, for example, quickly scan the contents of their desk, locker, or backpack to locate items. The study and organization component of the compensatory access area includes these behaviors:

- note taking
- searching and scanning written materials
- using reference materials and applying research skills
- interpreting and creating tactile graphics
- using organizational systems

Note Taking

The ability to take notes is an essential skill for success for all students, especially during middle, secondary, and postsecondary education. Students are typically introduced to different note-taking systems and techniques, such as using an outline or other more structured methods, in late elementary school and develop their own methods and systems for taking notes in middle and secondary school. For students who plan to pursue postsecondary education, note-taking skills are an absolute necessity for academic success and organization.

Note taking serves several key purposes. In school, note taking forces a student to participate in active listening and the process of thinking about the information being noted. New content is immediately reinforced by the physical act of notation. The main purpose of note taking, however, is that the notes serve as an important review and study tool a few days, weeks, or months after they were taken. Outside of school, note-taking skills can be useful during a work-related meeting or helpful in creating "to do" or grocery lists. Most important, becoming an effective note taker forces a student to be introspective about his or her personal organization and thought processes, thus engaging in critical thinking skills. By deciding what is important to record and retain, the student exercises judgment, which is itself important as a self-determination skill, but is also helpful in learning how to analyze information.

Searching and Scanning Written Materials

Regardless of whether students use print or braille, it is necessary to be able to efficiently search and scan written materials. *Searching* involves the use of a systematic method to efficiently find a specific piece of information in written materials. *Scanning* involves quickly skimming or glancing over materials and is typically used when searching materials for specific content or when searching graphic materials for information and meaning. Both speed and accuracy should be the focus when teaching these visual or tactile skills. A related skill is highlighting or marking important passages of text for later use through the use of electronic methods, highlighters, bold-line pens, tactile marking stickers, or magnets.

Using Reference Materials and Applying Research Skills

The term *reference skills* refers to the understanding of, and ability to use, reference materials, including but not limited to a dictionary, thesaurus, encyclopedia, atlas and various Internet tools. For example, the ability to use an index, table of contents, or search functions on a digital device to locate a definition of a word or an article on dinosaurs requires the use of reference skills. The term *research skills* refers to the ability to use reference skills to plan the collection of information, then record, organize, interpret, and critically analyze the information found.

Through the use of technology, students, including those with visual impairments, are able to access a nearly unlimited amount of reference material. In the past, braille or large-print dictionaries and encyclopedias were necessary for students with visual impairments, and took up large amounts of storage space in classrooms or media centers. Today, students from a young age are able to access talking dictionaries or thesauruses and software or Internet encyclopedias through much more portable and efficient methods. The Internet itself is a prime source of reference materials and can be searched by various means (see Chapter 6).

It is important to note that although reference materials are more accessible today through the proliferation of many electronic and other types of devices, students with visual impairments need to be taught two key sets of skills in their use: the basic skills to operate electronic devices, and research skills to find information using those devices. Through instruction in the related ECC area of assistive technology (Chapter 6), students can be equipped with the keyboarding skills to input information and specific training on each device, software program, or use of the Internet through the use of accessibility hardware and software.

Students must also be taught the necessary research skills to locate information through the use of technology. Although research skills are often addressed in core curriculum classes, students with visual impairments require instruction in unique techniques, such as how to search for a word in a talking dictionary or how to access the content of visual charts and graphs found as part of a search using the Internet.

Interpreting and Creating Tactile Graphics

Tactile graphics are raised-line representations of print images. They can be used for maps, diagrams, charts, and various pictures used in the classroom. Because tactile graphics are abstract or symbolic two-dimensional representations of concepts, students need both sufficient spatial understanding skills (described earlier in this chapter) and a concrete and functional understanding of the concepts presented in a given graphic before they can begin to interpret the information being presented in tactile charts, graphs, maps, and figures. Students also need to be able to create simple tactile graphics to demonstrate their learning in the classroom.

Using Organizational Systems

Organizational systems can be very simple, such as using folders or binders kept in a backpack, locker, or file box to sort and file materials. However, many students with visual impairments are not familiar with organizational systems, school supplies, and office equipment for three primary reasons. First, they may lack opportunities to develop a general understanding of school and office supplies incidentally, by observing, for example, parents using a stapler at home, classmates using file folders at school, and office supplies on display in stores in the community. Second, for some students, adults may take care of organizing their materials for them, so that a staple seems to "magically" appear to hold their assignments together, or papers become organized through a visit by the "file folder fairy," thus contributing to learned helplessness. Third, some parents and teachers worry that students may injure themselves with items such as scissors, staplers, staple removers, or letter openers, so they don't give them the chance to use these tools.

As a result, the independent use of organizational systems, school supplies, and office equipment for organization and studying purposes needs to be formally taught by the teacher of students with visual impairments in collaboration with parents and others. It is important to teach specific skills based on a student's age or grade. For example, elementary school students should be aware of ways to organize a desk and traditional backpack. Junior high and high school students need the skills to keep a locker and their messenger bag or backpack organized. Parents need to reinforce the independent use of these skills at home and in the community. Additionally, students need to be aware of and learn the use of school and office supplies, such as various types of scissors, staplers, staple removers, paperclips, binder clips, pens, pencils, highlighters, pencil/pen pouches, cups, and boxes, binders (both regular and larger braille binders), folders (both file folders and larger braille folders), dividers (both regular and larger braille dividers), and correction tape or fluid. Students with visual impairments should be aware of various electronic storage devices such as CDs, DVDs, USB drives, digital music players, and external hard drives. Organization of electronic files and folders using these devices is an important skill for both data portability and sharing.

The study and organization component of compensatory access overlaps with the ECC areas of independent living and assistive technology. Office supplies and organizational skills are used in activities of daily living, such as using file folders to organize bills or bank statements. Individuals often use electronic reference and research skills at home to find recipes or home fix-it solutions. Similarly, organization of electronic media enhances students' recreational skills. For example, maintaining a game score on an electronic device will demonstrate a student's ability to participate in a chosen game as the scorekeeper.

Use of Adapted Educational Materials and Specialized Equipment

One of the key components necessary for students with visual impairments to independently access information presented in the classroom is the ability to use adapted educational materials and specialized equipment. The selection and use of these materials is highly individualized and is based on assessment data on students' functional vision, appropriate learning media, and the demands of the classroom environment. Teachers of students with visual impairments need to be familiar with the most current adapted materials and specialized equipment available for their students.

To be successful in the core curriculum, students with visual impairments may need to be taught to use a variety of adapted educational items, as appropriate. The term *adapted educational materials* refers to educational items that are used in the general and special education classroom and that have been adapted specifically for students with visual impairments. Students in the classroom may be using rulers, thermometers, scales, protractors, scientific calculators, and graph paper. Each of these items exists in an adapted form, including large-print and braille rulers; large-display and talking thermometers; talking scales or tactilely-adapted balances; large-print and braille protractors; large-display and talking scientific calculators; and bold-line and embossed graph paper.

In addition to such adapted materials, specialized equipment has been developed to allow students with visual impairments to demonstrate abilities and skills that students with vision demonstrate in slightly different ways. *Specialized equipment* includes both electronic and nonelectronic devices developed specifically for use by individuals with visual impairments. The most common specialized nonelectronic educational materials used by students with visual impairments for academic purposes are the braillewriter, handheld and other magnification devices, the abacus, the slate and stylus, and signature writing guides. Keeping in mind the principles of the least restrictive adaptation model described earlier, these devices should be introduced to the student as appropriate to the student's need. Mastery of these devices requires time and practice and should include an exploration of the times when use of the device is most helpful. Some students may not be comfortable using a particular tool and should be allowed to stop using a device if it does not improve their functioning. The introduction of any specialized material or equipment is intended to provide the student with additional access tools, but it is the student's decision, with the teacher's guidance, to continue use of any particular device.

Electronic educational materials include adapted computer hardware and software and their applications, electric braillewriters, electronic magnification devices, electronic notetakers (or personal digital assistants), and the multitude of other assistive technology that exists for students with visual impairments. These electronic devices are discussed in detail in Chapter 6. Again, an individual student will choose to use devices that are most helpful, but should have the advantage of experimenting with a variety of devices with the help of the teacher of students with visual impairments.

The ability to use these adapted materials and specialized equipment independently is essential for the completion of many life activities at school, home, and in the community. For example, learning to sign one's name is a critical skill and may require the use of a signature guide for some students. In school, students need to sign up for activities or are asked to sign rules and regulations contracts. At home, writing a check or sending a birthday card requires the use of a signature. In the community, one must be prepared to sign credit card receipts and legal documents, such as an apartment lease or banking agreement. The demands for using a legal signature increase with age. Instruction for students needs to begin in elementary school, well before the use of a legal signature is required for life activities at home and in the community. Likewise, learning to use an abacus may be important for some students when use of a calculator is not allowed. The use of the abacus can mirror the use of paper and pencil when calculations are completed on a worksheet without a calculator. The slate and stylus, while not used as much since the development of handheld notetakers and other methods of jotting down information for personal use, can be a useful tool for some students in labeling items, making lists, or writing notes that they might want to be read tactilely.

Students also need to become familiar with the resources and processes for ordering adapted educational materials and specialized equipment and, over time, should become responsible for ordering their own materials and equipment. The ability to obtain or make arrangements for one's own necessary adapted materials is an important skill for successful transition to post-secondary education or work.

ASSESSMENT OF COMPENSATORY ACCESS

Assessment in each of the components of compensatory access is vital for informing instruction in this ECC area. The basic tenets of assessment are discussed in Chapter 3. There are six assessment procedures that can be used to evaluate the current knowledge and skills of students with visual impairments in the area of compensatory access (Salvia, Ysseldyke, & Bolt, 2010):

- observations
- interviews
- informal assessment tools
- criterion-based assessments
- skills inventories
- professional judgment

There are three types of assessments critical to determining the needs of students with visual impairments in the area of compensatory access. The first two are the functional vision assessment and learning media assessment; in addition, a comprehensive assessment of each of the components of compensatory access must be conducted.

The *functional vision assessment* evaluates the student's use of vision in the natural environment (home, school, and community) instead of in the clinical environment of a doctor's office (see Chapter 5 for more information). The functional vision assessment is required by most state education rules or regulations as part of the evaluation and reevaluation process for all students who are visually impaired.

A structured assessment tool, the *learning media assessment* (also discussed in Chapter 5) supports an evaluative process that is required to be completed for all students with visual impairments by many state departments of education and by the Individuals with Disabilities Education Act (IDEA), which mandates that students with visual impairments be evaluated with regard to their need for instruction in braille. A learning media assessment is "an objective process of systematically selecting learning media and literacy media . . . [that] guides the educational team in making deliberate and informed decisions on the total range of instructional media needed to facilitate learning" (Koenig & Holbrook, 1995, p. 2). This essential assessment is a determination of the primary and secondary sensory channels that students use to obtain information, which then indicates the medium or media, such as print or braille, that they will use most effectively for reading and learning. *Learning Media Assessment of Students with Visual Impairments* (Koenig & Holbrook, 1995) was the first resource for conducting structured learning media assessments for students with visual impairments. McKenzie (2009b) provided guidelines for conducting learning media assessments for students who are deaf-blind, including the role of key personnel, accommodations for hearing impairments, and assessment of communication skills when necessary. An additional resource for learning media assessment tools and checklists is the *FVLMA Kit: Functional Vision and Learning Media Assessment Kit* (Sanford & Burnett, 2008). (See the Resources section of this chapter.)

The learning media assessment is critical for identifying a student's efficiency and needs related to reading and writing. Assessment in this area must be ongoing, as a student's effective use of and need for adaptations to instructional materials can vary as vision changes and educational demands increase. Literacy tools (visual, tactile, and auditory) that need to be taught, expanded, or improved are assessed continually so that changes can be made to the student's instruction in accessing media (Koenig et al., 2000). Sidebar 4.2 provides suggestions that can be helpful for conducting a learning media assessment.

Although a comprehensive evaluation of all areas of the ECC will be conducted, for purposes of this chapter, a comprehensive evaluation of compensatory access must be conducted by the teacher of students with visual impairments, using the six assessment procedures identified previously, to determine a student's present level of performance and future instructional needs for educational access. An assistive technology assessment, discussed in Chapter 6, will also be important to use in tandem with the learning media assessment to

SIDEBAR 4.2

Tips for Conducting Learning Media Assessments

The following suggestions are important to keep in mind when conducting a learning media assessment:

1. Use available tools. For example, *Learning Media Assessment of Students with Visual Impairments* (Koenig & Holbrook, 1995) and the *FVLMA Kit* (Sanford & Burnett, 2008).
2. Focus on the sensory channel or channels—visual, tactile, or auditory—used by the student in a variety of activities and tasks.
3. Record observations of the student's use of sensory channels in a variety of settings.
4. Make notes regarding observed sensory channel use on a regular basis.
5. Determine reading efficiency by recording comprehension and words read per minute.
6. Determine the student's ability to read his or her own handwriting.
7. Monitor the student's academic progress and ability to keep up with classroom progress.
8. Consider the student's long-range academic needs and which literacy tools he or she will need to maintain progress.
9. Link the learning media assessment to the assistive technology assessment.

identify literacy tools a student will need for different purposes.

Observations

Observations are critical to determining if a student is able to generalize the use of compensatory access skills to the core curriculum classroom or the community. Observations do not need to involve the use of specific observation tools for data collection. For example, a teacher can conduct an observation of the student's overall use of compensatory access skills in math class or during an O&M lesson at the mall. Such observations are helpful for understanding a student's performance in the area of compensatory access as a whole across different environments. Observations of students should be both announced and unannounced. Unannounced observations allow the teacher of students with visual impairments to truly see the student's performance in natural environments. For example, a teacher can observe a student during math class to make sure that he is able to keep up with the pace of the class through his ability to read the Nemeth code in his textbooks and use specialized educational materials, including the abacus, as needed. If the student is not able to keep up with his peers, intensive instruction can be provided in specific skill areas, as needed, such as Nemeth code, abacus, or organization skills. Observation allows the teacher not only to evaluate how well the student performs a skill, but also to set priorities for direct instruction in compensatory access skills.

Observation of students with visual impairments in the classroom is essential for the functional vision assessment, learning media assessment, overall ECC assessment, on-going assessment of instruction, and determination of the need for accommodations. Classroom observations should focus on the environment, the student's behaviors, and the general education teacher's teaching methods (Loftin, 2005). Items to observe in the environment include the physical layout of the room, the learning materials utilized, use of adapted equipment and materials specifically for students with visual impairments, and the use of paraprofessionals or aides. Student behaviors include organization, participation, social skills, speaking and listening skills, O&M, and the ability to use specialized educational materials. Observation of the teaching methods utilized in the classroom provides the teacher of students with visual impairments with information to suggest targeted accommodations that allow equal participation of a student with a visual impairment. For example, if he or she determines that the general education teacher typically puts a large amount of information on the whiteboard that is essential to understanding the lecture, uses multimedia presentations that are projected onto a screen, or maintains a list of homework assignments on the board throughout the day, special accommodations may be needed to make sure that a student who is visually impaired is able to access that information. The teacher of students with visual impairments will also want to make sure that the general education teacher checks to make sure that all students understand the material before moving onto a new topic.

General classroom observation checklists can be created by teachers of students with visual impairments to meet specific needs (see Chapter 3 for more information about creating and using checklists). Also see the

Resources section at the end of this chapter for information on established classroom observation protocols, including *EVALS: Evaluating Visually Impaired Students* (Texas School for the Blind and Visually Impaired, 2007) and the *FVLMA Kit* (Sanford & Burnett, 2008) mentioned earlier.

Observations can be conducted specifically to observe the utilization of a particular component of compensatory access at school or in the community. Often, teachers of students with visual impairments use predetermined observation tools or checklists to collect information during focused observations. For example, a teacher might use a teacher-created tool for observing the specific skills taught regarding the use of a talking calculator or an abacus in the classroom. Such checklists would include a task analysis of the skills to be used. For example, to evaluate a student's use of the braillewriter in the classroom, the teacher would want to focus on whether the student can successfully perform a variety of related tasks, including:

- determining when the braillewriter was needed
- using the braillewriter in a manner that is not distracting to others
- placing the braillewriter properly on the desk
- removing and storing the dust cover
- locating the correct braille paper
- loading the paper correctly
- using the line advance key to lock in the paper
- using the proper hand and finger placement on the keys
- using correct and consistent pressure when brailling
- estimating correctly the number of cells to braille after the bell
- advancing to a new line when needed
- removing the paper when finished
- covering the braillewriter and placing it in the storage location

A detailed listing of these individual tasks allows the teacher of students with visual impairments to determine which skills need teaching or reinforcing and how to prioritize the teaching of specific skills.

Interviews

Interviews with others can provide important assessment information about a student's performance in the area of compensatory access. It is best to conduct interviews with a variety of individuals, including parents, paraeducators, classroom teachers, or, when appropriate, the students themselves. Parents can provide important information about their child's use of specific compensatory access skills at home and in the community. Classroom teachers and paraeducators can provide similar information regarding the use of skills in the classroom and upcoming needs for instruction in new compensatory access skills. An interview does not need to involve a formal list of questions; consultation and collaboration are imperatives and can take place naturally through regular educational team meetings. For example, when consulting with a classroom teacher, the teacher of students with visual impairments can ask about the student's ability to keep up with classroom instruction or whether the student is arriving with class materials organized.

Collecting information from students is just as important. Asking students to rate their comfort with using new compensatory access skills in the classroom, at home, or in the community encourages open communication with the teacher of students with visual impairments. It can be motivating for both the student and the teacher to see a student's ability and comfort with the use of new skills increase over time as a result of effective assessment and consequent targeted instruction.

Checklists

The majority of tools for assessing and keeping track of a student's ability in the compensatory access area involve checklists of skills for the various components. For example, the *Assessment Kit of Informal Tools for Academic Students with Visual Impairments, Part 1* (Sewell, 2001) contains a checklist for nearly every component of compensatory skills, as does *EVALS* (Texas School for the Blind and Visually Impaired, 2007), a comprehensive assessment kit for all areas of the ECC. The *Assessment of Braille Literacy Skills* (Koenig & Farrenkopf, 1995) is an assessment tool for teachers of students with visual impairments to document development of emergent, academic, and functional braille literacy skills. (See the Resources section at the end of this chapter for more information on assessment tools.)

Criterion-Referenced Assessments

There are a variety of *criterion-referenced assessments* (ones that measure the student's performance against a defined standard or criterion) that have not been designed for students with visual impairments, but are often used by educational teams to assess achievement. Criterion-referenced assessments are used to evaluate a student's learning of specific knowledge and skills and can also be used to assess the compensatory access skills of students with visual impairments. For example, the *KeyMath 3* (Connolly, 2007), is a criterion-referenced math assessment for students in kindergarten through ninth grade. The 1988 version is available in braille from the American Printing House for the Blind (APH) (see the Resources section at the end of this chapter). Skill areas include basic math concepts, operations, and applications, including measurement, time, money, and problem solving. Other popular criterion-referenced tests that are available in braille are the *Basic Reading Inventory* (Johns, 2010), and the *Kaufman Test of Educational Achievement, Second Edition* (Kaufman & Kaufman, 2005), which assesses general reading and math skills. The use of these tests in their alternate formats can provide the teacher with information about student progress in reading and math using particular formats of braille or large print and the use of adapted materials, such as a talking calculator or the abacus.

The *Brigance Diagnostic Comprehensive Inventory of Basic Skills II* (Brigance, 2010) is a criterion-referenced skills inventory that focuses on the more academic skills of reading and math. For students with visual impairments, APH publishes the 1999 version of this inventory in both large print and braille (see the Resources section at the end of this chapter). Portions of the assessment can be used for documenting a student's strengths and weaknesses in reading and writing in print or braille, as well as the use of print or Nemeth code for completion of math-related activities, including measurement, money, time, and other general concepts.

As with all such instruments that are dated or not normed on students with visual impairments, extreme caution must be exercised when interpreting test results. Results are comparable only to those of the population used to develop the standardized scoring, which more than likely did not include students with visual impairments. The team must keep in mind the effects of a visual impairment on the unique development of a child and understand that using criterion- or norm-referenced information may not give an accurate evaluation of a student's performance of the task. For example, test items should be analyzed for the inclusion of concepts that are not completely understood by the student or for the use of visual information that could not be adapted for a student with a visual impairment. In addition, the format of the test and any modifications of items that were made for accessibility purposes, such as creating a braille version of a print test or using real objects in place of pictures, must be considered when interpreting the assessment results, and specifically stated when communicating these results to others. With these caveats in mind, the educational team can use the results of these tests to make some general recommendations for a student with visual impairment.

Skills Inventories

The use of *skills inventories* is important when assessing the knowledge and abilities of students with visual impairments in the area of compensatory skills. Most skills inventories are criterion-referenced assessment tools used to determine a student's present level of performance in various skill areas. Skills inventories allow the assessor to provide information to the educational team regarding the student's overall development in relation to his or her age or grade level. When reporting results, it is important to note whether the skills inventory being used was produced specifically for students with visual impairments, as general skills inventories do not take into account the unique developmental patterns of students with visual impairments. For example, a general motor skills inventory might not consider the unique effects of a visual impairment on the development of motor skills.

Several skills inventories have been used for assessing students with visual impairments in compensatory access skills, some of which were designed specifically for this population. The *Oregon Project for Preschool Children Who are Blind or Visually Impaired* (Anderson, Boigon, Davis & deWaard, 2007) is a complete skills inventory for young children both with and without additional disabilities that includes compensatory and communication sections. *Independent Living: A Curriculum with Adaptations for Students with Visual Impairments* (Loumiet & Levack, 1991) includes a skills inventory assessment tool. While the majority of the curriculum addresses other ECC areas, it also includes components within compensatory access, such as reading, writing, and speaking, science and technology, money management, time concepts, and scholastic success. The inventory provides suggested skill-specific age ranges for students with visual impairments.

For students who are deaf-blind or students who are visually impaired and have severe or profound additional disabilities, the *Callier-Azusa Scale* (Stillman, 1978; Stillman & Battle, 1985) provides a scale for overall development (Scale G) and for development of communication (Scale H). Scale G is further divided into five areas and 18 subscales, including Perceptual Abilities (visual, auditory, and tactile) and Cognitive, Communication, and Language Development (receptive and expressive communication).

Professional Judgment

Because visual impairment is a low-incidence disability, standardized assessments of students with visual impairments that render objective scores are rare. Therefore, the majority of assessment findings made by teachers of students with visual impairments regarding the strengths and weaknesses of students will rely on use of their professional judgment and the knowledge of the development of students with visual impairments.

Teachers of students with visual impairments should ensure that, if possible, all six assessment methods are used to collect data. Through a systematic data collection process using a variety of available tools, a teacher can gather high-quality information on students' compensatory access skills for instructional planning as well as for progress monitoring as skills are taught to students. Assessment results and recommendations should be presented to the educational team in narrative reports, focusing on the student's knowledge and skills, followed by recommendations for accommodations and future instruction.

GENERAL CONSIDERATIONS FOR TEACHING COMPENSATORY ACCESS

As indicated at the beginning of this chapter, when planning instruction in the compensatory access area, it is important to base teaching efforts on the student's individual characteristics and circumstances. Teachers need to be mindful that each student's needs for knowledge and skill are highly individualized, depending on the presence of additional disabilities, level of visual functioning, age, curricular demands, and classroom environment. The reading and writing media of students must also be taken into account during the instructional planning process, especially for students who are dual media (using both print and braille) readers. The teacher of students with visual impairments must consider when and where the student will use each medium. For example, will braille be used for most text-based tasks and print mainly for activities that rely heavily on visual information? Or will both media be used equally for all school activities? (For additional discussion, see the section titled Teaching Print and Braille in Tandem later in this chapter.)

The knowledge and skills associated with the various components of compensatory access need to be taught before students encounter the concepts, codes, symbols, graphics, or equipment used in core curriculum instruction and subsequent learning that require these skills. For example, a student must first learn to interpret a tactile bar graph before being presented with one in math class. In order for students to be successful in the classroom, they must be equipped with the necessary compensatory skills to access the content presented. The method of pre-teaching (teaching in advance) is used by teachers of students with visual impairments to provide compensatory instruction to students *prior* to encountering various concepts in the core curriculum or needing to use a specialized piece of equipment in the classroom. Teachers of students with visual impairments therefore need to carefully and sequentially plan instruction in compensatory access based on state educational standards, school curricular guidelines, and collaboration with the general education classroom teacher. (Collaboration is discussed further later in this chapter and is specifically addressed in Chapter 13.)

To carefully plan pre-teaching, the teacher of students with visual impairments must complete a series of steps to ensure that all compensatory access needs are identified and addressed before they are required in the general education classroom. The process begins during the previous school year and is implemented during the current school year. The following example of an instructional planning sequence is based on a fourth-grade mathematics curriculum for a student who is a braille reader. The teacher of students with visual impairments:

1. Reviews the state mathematics fourth-grade curricular standards and grade level expectations during the summer before the student enters fourth grade.
2. Obtains a copy of the textbook to be used by the classroom teacher and reviews for content.

3. Based on the content of the curriculum and textbook, determines the unique needs for the student in the skill areas of:
   a. concept development and spatial understanding
   b. tactile graphics
   c. Nemeth code symbols and rules
   d. abacus
   e. other specialized and adapted educational materials.
4. Orders specialized educational materials necessary.
5. Consults with the mathematics classroom teacher as school starts regarding the instructional sequence for the upcoming school year, because this may vary from the textbook.
6. Sequentially plans pre-teaching in the skill areas previously listed.
7. Implements the pre-teaching instructional plan, always staying ahead of the content being taught in the math classroom by staying in periodic touch with the classroom teacher.
8. Conducts ongoing assessment and observation of the skills that were pre-taught.
9. Monitors progress of the student in the math class to ensure the student possesses sufficient compensatory access skills for success.

For young students in preschool and early elementary grades, teachers of students with visual impairments generally need to provide frequent and intense instruction in all components of compensatory access, especially concept development, spatial understanding, communication modes, and use of specialized educational materials. For many students, this instruction will take place on a daily basis. As students grow older, their instructional needs change; they generally require less frequent instruction but in more complex concepts, advanced communication modes, and more intense study and organizational skills. If students receive a high-quality and well-organized instructional foundation in compensatory access, the frequency of instruction in this area will usually decrease over time.

TEACHING STRATEGIES FOR COMPENSATORY ACCESS

The following sections suggest strategies for teaching the various components of the compensatory access area of the ECC.

Concept Development

To ensure success in all areas of learning and development for students with visual impairments, concepts need to be formally and deliberately taught, taking into account the sequence of concept development discussed earlier in this chapter. Pre-teaching the concepts that will be encountered in the core curriculum is an essential job role of teachers of students with visual impairments. As noted previously, well-planned, structured, and sequential instruction is necessary and requires extensive collaboration and coordination with the general education teacher. Because pre-teaching must take place *before* a student encounters a concept in the classroom in order for a student to participate in classroom instruction, the teacher of students with visual impairments needs to discuss ahead of time with the general education teacher the types and sequence of concepts that the student will be encountering. If, for some reason, pre-teaching of a concept has not taken place, the teacher can work with the student to clarify confusing content. Careful monitoring of each student's work is necessary to identify such situations.

For example, if a classroom theme relating to apples will be used in the general education classroom, the goal of pre-teaching would be for the student to become familiar with and understand all aspects of the concept of "apple-ness." The student will need not only to have a concept of an apple, but also to know about how apples grow, various types of apples, and the variety of ways in which an apple can be prepared and eaten. Students are more likely to comprehend a book about helping to bake an apple pie with apples gathered from an apple orchard if they are familiar with "apple-ness." It is important that teachers of students with visual impairments incorporate activities relating to other areas of the ECC—such as independent living skill activities like peeling an apple or making applesauce—during pre-teaching to ensure the full understanding of a concept.

Instruction regarding new concepts should involve the use of real objects whenever possible. (See Chapters 1 and 3 for further discussion of effective teaching techniques with students who are visually impaired.) Students with learn concepts best through actual, direct, hands-on experiences with items. Using the example of an apple, the basic concrete concepts of an apple (including a description of skin color, flesh color, seeds, stem, and core) can be discussed while exploring various types of apples and noting differences in appear-

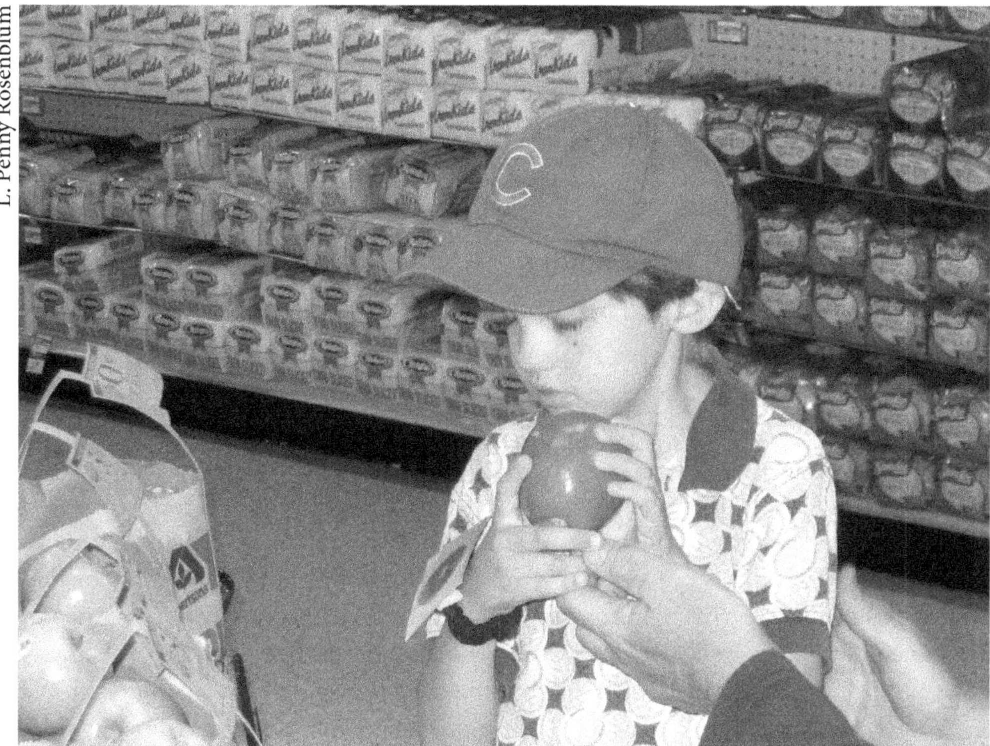
L. Penny Rosenblum

Exploring the characteristics of an apple in a grocery store, using a variety of sensory efficiency skills, is part of learning the concept of "apple-ness."

ance, tactile qualities, and taste. The growth of apples should be investigated, including the exploration of an apple tree and the picking of an apple, as well as the functional nature of apples, including ways for using them (sauce, pie, juice, and so forth). All these experiences can involve hands-on activities with real objects. Students with visual impairments need to be actively involved in learning about their environment and the objects within it so that they can receive direct sensory impressions and repeated contact with items in the environment, which reinforces their learning and helps them integrate information into the concepts they are developing. (See Chapter 5 for additional discussion of learning through senses other than vision.)

Many abstract concepts will be more difficult to teach using real objects. Sayings such as "You're the apple of my eye" can be explained once concrete and functional concepts of an apple are developed, but in these cases there are no related objects to touch. However, the development of some abstract concepts can often still involve hands-on, active learning through the use of three-dimensional models or replicas of items that are too big, too small, or too dangerous to touch. If a student is studying the concept of a cell in science class, the teacher can create a three-dimensional model of a cell and pre-teach associated concepts prior to the student's encountering them in the classroom or textbook. While a student cannot tactilely explore a skyscraper, he or she can experience riding to the top of a skyscraper or climbing many flights of stairs, and the concept can be reinforced with the use of a three-dimensional replica.

As already indicated, hands-on learning activities and learning concepts through "doing" are essential for students with visual impairments to fully grasp all three levels of a concept. For preschoolers and others for whom concrete learning is especially important, teachers of students with visual impairments can take a thematic approach to teaching concepts. For example, an instructional unit on the concept of fruits could be planned before students encounter the concepts in the general or special educational classroom. The teacher of students with visual impairments can plan hands-on learning experiences, such as trips to an orchard and grocery store produce department, to illustrate the farm-to-table cycle of various fruits. Then independent living activities, such as buying fruit, washing fruit, cooking with fruit, and eating fruit, can be practiced. In this instance, the student would have an opportunity to develop an understanding of and ability to compare the difference among several fruits, such as the difference between apples and oranges. While this instructional planning is highly individualized, curricular resources for teaching concepts do exist (see the Resources section at the end of this chapter).

For young students who are visually impaired, instruction and experiences with concepts need to be intense and frequent. Pre-teaching concepts requires not only time for initial instruction, but continued instruction and repeated hands-on experiences with the concept being addressed. For example, after an initial lesson introducing the concept of apple, multiple lessons and experiences with apples in a variety of settings involving other ECC areas will be necessary for full understanding and mastery of the concepts involved.

Spatial Understanding

Through well-planned instruction, students can learn to apply spatial understanding to themselves, objects, and, eventually, to print or tactile materials. Teachers of students with visual impairments need to collaborate with O&M specialists when providing instruction in the area of spatial understanding in the environment. This team approach is important to ensure consistency in instruction, such as the consistent use of terminology or explanations.

Students need to develop spatial concepts first in relation to themselves before they can apply this understanding to real objects, then three-dimensional models, and finally two-dimensional representations. "Where Do I Belong?," an activity in the Learning Activities section at the end of this chapter, provides an enjoyable lesson idea for teaching and reinforcing spatial understanding of oneself in relation to the environment. This activity is a good example of the incorporation of other ECC areas as spatial concepts are learned; it also involves independent living, career education, self-determination, and O&M skills. Because comprehension of the concept of space involves awareness of how objects exist in space in relationship to each other, spatial understanding is more difficult to develop in isolation from other ECC areas. Generalizing the concepts across areas is important for understanding and mastery.

When teaching spatial understanding of two-dimensional representations (such as tactile graphs), skills instruction should begin with the exploration of simple two-dimensional materials and progress to more advanced materials that incorporate greater amounts of information. For example, students must first be exposed to simple tactile graphics, such as large embossed shapes. Then, the tactile detail of the graphics can be increased, with the ultimate goal of reading charts, graphs, and maps. (See the section on teaching tactile graphics later in this chapter for more information.) *Teaching Touch* (Harrell, 2002) is an example of a curriculum that uses beginning tactile graphics teaching materials (see the Resources section at the end of this chapter).

Communication Modes

Print Reading and Writing

For students with low vision, the development of skills related to print literacy is typically considered the work of the general education teacher or reading specialist, who will be primarily responsible for teaching literacy skills to students who read print. Nevertheless, the teacher of students with visual impairments needs to serve as a close collaborator in addressing literacy and vision-related issues and advocating for access to print materials for these students. The teacher of students with visual impairments ensures that a comprehensive learning media assessment is conducted and implements the recommendations of that assessment for print readers. Although conducting learning media assessments is essential to determine appropriate media for all students with visual impairments, particular attention needs to be paid to the needs of students with progressive eye conditions, who may need to be instructed in reading braille as well as print (see the section titled Teaching Print and Braille in Tandem later in this chapter). For the development of literacy, print-rich environments are just as important for students with low vision as they are for all students, so teachers must ensure that students with low vision can easily access these environments and the literacy materials in them. If recommended, students may need to be taught to use low vision devices or be given access to large-print books. A framework of literacy skill areas to be addressed for students with low vision was created by Corn and Koenig (2002; see Sidebar 4.3).

For students for whom low vision devices have been prescribed, the use of these devices to access print in classroom and home environments needs to be formally taught by teachers of students with visual impairments. Instruction and practice in using low vision devices in the community and during travel requires collaboration between the teacher and the O&M specialist. *Looking to Learn* (D'Andrea & Farrenkopf, 2000) provides in-depth information about teaching the use of low vision devices, as well as ideas for learning activities. (More information about low vision devices can be found in Chapters 5 and 6.)

SIDEBAR 4.3

Areas of Literacy Development for Students with Low Vision

The following are descriptions of skill areas in literacy in which teachers of students with visual impairments need to provide instruction for students with low vision, as identified by Corn and Koenig (2002).

EMERGENT LITERACY SKILLS

- supporting the development of literacy in early childhood settings, such as the home, day care, and preschool
- teaching early literacy skills and modeling techniques based on children obtaining knowledge through active experiences for fostering the development of those skills in the home and preschool, such as reading aloud to children, developing book concepts, encouraging early reading and writing skills (pretend reading and scribbling, for example)
- working with parents and others to expand students' experiential base and general concepts
- helping parents and others acquire and create books, labels, and other materials in accessible media
- drawing attention to signs and other forms of environmental print
- assuring models of proficient readers
- bridging emergent literacy to beginning print literacy

INTEGRATED USE OF VISUAL SKILLS

- teaching and reinforcing the development of visual skills in functional contexts, such as visually searching at a distance and visually directed reach
- teaching the integrated use of visual skills in authentic environments and contexts, such as interpreting pictures and graphic displays
- searching and scanning for information on a page in a systematic manner, reading, writing, daily living skills, social skills, and travel skills
- teaching the use of environmental adaptations and nonoptical low vision devices and strategies (for example, light-controlling devices, felt-tip pens, filters, and the angle and position of materials)

USE OF OPTICAL DEVICES IN NEAR ENVIRONMENTS

- teaching the use of prescribed optical low vision devices, such as hand and stand magnifiers and spectacle-mounted devices, for reading in near textual environments (books, newspapers, magazines, and other material involving narrative reading)
- building stamina in students for sustaining textual reading for sufficient periods to complete given tasks
- teaching the integrated use of near low vision optical devices in authentic environments for functional tasks, such as reading menus, time tables, and price tags
- coordinating training with the O&M instructor (map-reading skills)

USE OF OPTICAL DEVICES IN DISTANT ENVIRONMENTS

- teaching students to use prescribed distance optical devices, such as handheld monoculars and binoculars and spectacle-mounted devices, to complete short-term distance tasks (for example, viewing directories in office buildings, menus on walls, signs in grocery store aisles, chalkboards, overhead projectors, charts in classrooms, and demonstrations in classrooms)
- coordinating training with the O&M instructor on tasks such as reading house numbers and street signs
- integrating the use of distance devices in authentic tasks and throughout the day
- teaching the care and importance of the use of the devices to gain independence
- teaching older students how to obtain devices if they need them in the future when their visual demands increase

BEGINNING PRINT LITERACY SKILLS

- teaching formal reading skills in print, including handwriting, decoding, and word-analysis skills, vocabulary development, comprehension skills, and reading for specific purposes
- teaching formal writing skills (manuscript and cursive)
- providing ongoing assessments of literacy skills and literacy media needs
- building reading fluency and stamina; arranging the reading environment
- building motivation for, and the enjoyment of, reading

(continued on next page)

- encouraging leisure reading
- applying literacy skills throughout the day and in authentic contexts
- bridging beginning print literacy skills with intermediate/advanced print literacy skills

INTERMEDIATE AND ADVANCED PRINT LITERACY SKILLS

- building stamina and fluency in reading with or without optical devices
- teaching strategies for gaining access to print information in the environment
- providing ongoing assessments of literacy skills and literacy media needs
- fostering responsibility for accessing visual information
- teaching strategies for determining when to augment visual information with other sources, such as recorded texts and braille
- fostering the enjoyment of reading and leisure reading
- using print literacy skills to complete functional tasks in authentic environments
- applying literacy skills in learning subject matter, such as when studying science
- teaching strategies for transitioning to work environments

BEGINNING LITERACY SKILLS IN DUAL MEDIA (PRINT AND BRAILLE)

For students for whom the educational team has decided that instruction in both print and braille is appropriate, skills include:

- teaching formal reading skills concurrently in both print and braille, including decoding and word-analysis skills, vocabulary development, comprehension skills, and reading for specific purposes
- teaching writing and formal writing skills in both print and braille
- providing ongoing assessments of literacy skills and literacy media needs
- continuing to develop mechanical skills in braille reading
- building reading fluency in both media
- building motivation for, and the enjoyment of, reading
- encouraging leisure reading
- applying literacy skills in print and braille throughout the day and in authentic contexts
- bridging beginning literacy skills and intermediate/advanced literacy skills

BRAILLE LITERACY SKILLS FOR STUDENTS WITH PRINT LITERACY SKILLS

For students for whom the educational team has decided that instruction in braille is appropriate as a supplement to or substitute for print, skills include:

- teaching tactile perception, hand movements, and letter/symbol recognition skills in braille
- introducing braille contractions and rules in meaningful contexts
- teaching braille-writing skills
- integrating the use of braille in practical activities
- providing instruction in contracted and uncontracted braille to address the present and future needs of the individual student
- providing ongoing assessments
- applying literacy skills throughout the day and in authentic contexts

LISTENING, AURAL READING, AND LIVE-READER SKILLS

- fostering the development of auditory skills such as auditory awareness and attention, sound localization, auditory memory, and auditory closure
- teaching and reinforcing the use of listening to gather information
- teaching the mechanics of using recorded textbooks
- teaching strategies for gathering information from recorded textbooks
- teaching strategies for obtaining and purposefully directing the activities of, and gathering information from, live readers
- applying listening, aural-reader, and live-reader skills in authentic contexts

KEYBOARDING AND WORD-PROCESSING SKILLS

- teaching touch-typing techniques via a computer with accessible print and/or speech synthesis
- teaching strategies for using word processing, including creating, editing, saving, and printing text files

SIDEBAR 4.3 *continued*

- building fluency and accuracy in keyboarding skills
- helping students choose a comfortable font, display color contrast, and text size for efficient word processing
- applying keyboarding and word-processing skills in daily activities

TECHNOLOGY SKILLS

- teaching technology skills to facilitate literacy tasks and to gain access to print information, such as the use of closed-circuit television, computers with accessible print, synthesized speech, voice recognition systems, enlarging software, and scanners (to convert print to an accessible medium)
- gaining access to, and information from, the Internet
- applying technology skills throughout the day and in authentic contexts
- teaching the care and maintenance of the equipment
- setting up new equipment

SOURCE: Reprinted with permission from A. L. Corn and A. J. Koenig, "Literacy for Students with Low Vision: A Framework for Delivering Instruction," *Journal of Visual Impairment & Blindness, 96*(5) (2002), pp. 305–321.

Because reading and writing are visual tasks, it is important for the teacher of students with visual impairments to stay in close contact with the reading specialist or general education teacher about a student's successes and struggles with skills needed to access print. Accommodations, such as reading stands, frequent breaks, and preferential seating, may need to be provided to address such issues as limited visual fields, lack of central or color vision, and visual fatigue. The teacher of students with visual impairments is best equipped to suggest such accommodations and monitor their successful implementation. Chapter 5 discusses visual skills that may need to be emphasized with students who have low vision, as well as environmental considerations that need to be taken into account for reading print.

Reading efficiently is sometimes a challenge for many students with low vision, and reading rates and fluency often vary greatly in this population (Koenig, Layton, & Ross, 1992; Kamei-Hannan & Ricci, in press). Strategies for increasing reading speed and fluency that are typically used by the general literacy field can be effective with readers who are visually impaired as well. One such strategy that has been found to be successful with students who have low vision is known as *repeated readings* (Layton & Koenig, 1998). Repeated readings involve having a student read the same passage for one minute multiple times during daily sessions. During each reading, the teacher records the number of words read correctly per minute and tracks the increase in reading fluency and speed until a pre-established goal is achieved. Repeated readings can be motivating to students because achieving the reading speed goal gives struggling readers a sense of accomplishment. If reading speed and fluency continue to be an issue, a comprehensive learning media assessment should be conducted to help the educational team determine if print is actually the most efficient learning media for the student. If a student continues to struggle after the learning media assessment has confirmed that the appropriate reading medium is being used, then a referral to a reading specialist should be considered.

Many students with low vision may have difficulty developing handwriting skills if they are not provided appropriate instruction and accommodations. Because general education teachers often provide handwriting instruction at the front of the classroom on a whiteboard or chalkboard, the teacher of students with visual impairments may need to teach this skill directly. A variety of adapted devices and materials can be explored. For example, the student may require the use of a slant board, video magnifier (closed-circuit television system or CCTV), bold-lined paper, raised-line paper, or a bold pen. A systematic plan formulated by the teacher of students with visual impairments for introducing appropriate accommodations is vital, based on the results of the student's learning media assessment and functional vision assessment, as well as observations in the classroom, taking into consideration the teaching methods and materials used by the general education teacher. An evaluation by an occupational therapist may be needed if handwriting problems persist, to rule out the possibility of fine motor issues. As noted earlier, learning to sign one's name is an important skill, but if the student has a difficult time mastering handwriting and the instruction is time-consuming, the teacher may decide that it is preferable to develop a unique signature that is easy for the student to write. Even initials or a shortened form of a student's name, if written consistently, can satisfy the requirements for a legal signature. Many students may eventually find that taking notes or jotting lists is more time efficient on a computer or handheld electronic device.

Literary Braille

If the educational team has determined, based on the results of the learning media assessment, that a student requires braille instruction, the teacher of students with visual impairments must begin to plan carefully sequenced instruction. Koenig and Holbrook (2000) presented a list of areas of braille literacy development for students with visual impairments (see Sidebar 4.4). Students develop traditional braille literacy skills by progressing through a number of phases:

- emergent braille literacy skills
- early formal braille literacy skills
- beginning braille literacy skills
- intermediate braille literacy skills
- advanced braille literacy skills

Koenig and Farrenkopf (1995) provide an overview of the specific skills to be addressed during the various phases of braille literacy development, including functional application of advanced literacy skills.

Using these areas of braille literacy development as a guiding framework, teachers of students with visual impairments need first to determine a customized approach to braille literacy based on the needs of the individual student; the braille literacy program will be different for every student with a visual impairment.

SIDEBAR 4.4

Areas of Literacy Development for Students Who Read Braille

The following are descriptions of skill areas in braille literacy in which teachers of students with visual impairments need to provide instruction for students who have been identified as having a braille learning medium, as identified by Corn and Koenig (2000).

EMERGENT BRAILLE LITERACY SKILLS

- supporting early literacy development in early childhood settings, including the home, day care, and preschool
- teaching early literacy skills and modeling techniques for fostering the development of those skills in the home and preschool, such as reading aloud to the child, developing book concepts, encouraging early reading and writing skills, such as pretend reading and scribbling
- working with parents and others to expand the child's experiential base and general concepts
- developing skills
- helping parents and others acquire books, labels, and other materials in accessible media
- helping parents acquire a knowledge of braille and resources for learning the braille code
- ensuring models of proficient braille readers
- bridging emergent literacy to early formal braille literacy

EARLY FORMAL LITERACY SKILLS ("PREBRAILLE")

- teaching hand-finger skills, tactile discrimination and perception skills, and hand movements
- fostering early letter- and simple word-recognition skills
- increasing the student's conceptual knowledge and vocabulary skills
- increasing listening skills
- expanding the student's experiential base
- fostering early reading and writing skills
- fostering the motivation for, and enjoyment of, reading
- applying braille in authentic contexts
- bridging early literacy and beginning braille literacy

BEGINNING BRAILLE LITERACY SKILLS

- teaching formal reading skills in braille, including decoding and word-analysis skills, vocabulary development, comprehension skills, and reading for specific purposes
- teaching formal writing skills with the braillewriter
- providing an ongoing assessment of braille literacy skills and literacy media needs
- continuing to develop mechanical skills in braille reading

(continued on next page)

- building reading fluency
- building the motivation for, and enjoyment of, reading
- encouraging leisure reading
- applying literacy skills throughout the day and in authentic contexts
- bridging beginning braille literacy skills and intermediate braille literacy skills

BEGINNING BRAILLE LITERACY SKILLS IN DUAL MEDIA (PRINT AND BRAILLE)

- teaching formal reading skills concurrently in both print and braille, including decoding and word-analysis skills, vocabulary development, comprehension skills, and reading for specific purposes
- teaching formal writing skills in both print and braille
- providing an ongoing assessment of literacy skills and literacy media needs
- continuing to develop mechanical skills in braille reading
- building reading fluency in both media
- building a motivation for, and enjoyment of, reading
- encouraging leisure reading
- applying literacy skills in print and braille throughout the day and in authentic contexts
- bridging beginning literacy skills and intermediate literacy skills

INTERMEDIATE BRAILLE LITERACY SKILLS

- teaching the use of reading as a tool for learning
- teaching flexibility skills (such as studying and skimming)
- teaching and applying reading skills in content areas
- teaching the use of reference books (like dictionaries and encyclopedias)
- continued teaching of editing marks in refining writing drafts
- continued work on fluency and, as needed, on accurate recognition of contractions in the braille code
- continued work on interpreting and reading various formats
- teaching strategies for using a variety of literacy tools
- incorporating technology into literacy tasks
- applying literacy tasks in authentic contexts
- bridging intermediate literacy skills and advanced literacy skills

ADVANCED BRAILLE LITERACY SKILLS

- teaching specialized codes, such as computer braille and foreign-language braille
- continuing the use of Nemeth code in more advanced science and mathematical contexts
- continuing to expand experience with textbook formats
- offering Grade 3 braille as an option for college-bound students
- teaching strategies for balancing emphases among literacy tools (such as braille and recorded material)
- continuing to incorporate the use of technology into literacy tasks
- continuing to apply literacy tasks in authentic contexts

BRAILLE LITERACY SKILLS FOR STUDENTS WITH PRINT LITERACY SKILLS

- teaching tactile perception, hand movements, and letter/symbol-recognition skills in braille
- introducing braille contractions and rules in meaningful contexts
- teaching braille-writing skills
- integrating the use of braille in practical activities
- providing instruction in contracted and uncontracted braille to address an individual student's present and future needs
- providing an ongoing assessment
- applying literacy skills throughout the day and in authentic contexts
- bridging beginning literacy skills and intermediate literacy skills

LISTENING, AURAL-READING, AND LIVE-READER SKILLS

- fostering the development of auditory skills (such as auditory awareness and attention, sound localization, auditory memory, and auditory closure)
- teaching and reinforcing the use of listening to gather information

(continued on next page)

SIDEBAR 4.4 *continued*

- teaching the mechanics of using recorded textbooks
- teaching strategies for gathering information from recorded textbooks
- teaching strategies for obtaining and purposefully directing the activities of, and gathering information from, live readers
- applying listening, aural-reader, and live-reader skills in authentic contexts

TECHNOLOGY SKILLS

- Teaching technology skills to facilitate literacy tasks and to gain access to print information, including the use of braille note-taking devices, refreshable braille displays, synthesized speech, accessible software (such as database and telecommunications programs), scanners (to convert print to an accessible medium), and braille and inkprint printers
- gaining access to, and information from, the Internet
- applying technology skills throughout the day and in authentic contexts

KEYBOARDING AND WORD-PROCESSING SKILLS

- teaching touch-typing techniques via a computer with speech synthesis or a typewriter with verbal feedback from the teacher
- teaching strategies for using word processing, including creating, editing, saving, and printing text files
- building fluency and accuracy in keyboarding skills
- applying keyboarding and word-processing skills in daily activities

SLATE-AND-STYLUS SKILLS

- modeling the appropriate and effective use of the slate and stylus
- teaching the use of the slate and stylus
- exposing students to the various types of slates and styli and the purposes for which each may be used
- building fluency in the use of the slate and stylus
- applying the use of slate-and-stylus skills in practical literacy activities

SIGNATURE-WRITING SKILLS

- teaching skills in signature writing for legal purposes
- exposing students to a variety of writing implements and writing guides
- developing fluency and consistency in signature writing
- teaching strategies for knowing when and why one's signature is required
- assessing a student's need for further instruction in handwriting (beyond a signature)
- applying the use of signature writing skills in authentic contexts

SOURCE: Reprinted with permission from A. J. Koenig and M. C. Holbrook, "Ensuring High-Quality Instruction for Students in Braille Literacy Programs," *Journal of Visual Impairment & Blindness, 94*(11) (2000), pp. 677–694.

The age of onset of vision loss, tactile abilities, chronological age, developmental level, and additional disabilities are all factors that affect a teacher's approach to braille instruction for an individual student. Moreover, some students may have traditional literacy needs, meaning they will be taught literacy skills in the general education classroom through traditional curricular materials, whereas others, such as those with multiple disabilities, may instead need to learn functional literacy skills and vocabulary for basic tasks in daily life (as discussed later in this section).

EMERGENT LITERACY. Students who are not yet reading and writing are considered to be in the emergent literacy phase. Teachers first need to support the development of concepts and meaningful language and address other literacy needs by creating braille-rich environments for these students. Just as students with unimpaired vision are surrounded by print in their environment prior to beginning to read, students who will be braille readers should be exposed to and become familiar with braille. Teachers and family members can model the use of braille and bring the student's attention to its use. Students should be allowed to scribble on braillewriters, play with slates and styli, and encounter braille naturally in the environment, such as by finding braille recipes available for them in a kitchen play area, going to a restaurant where braille menus are provided, or being made aware of braille signage on elevator buttons or ATM machines. In addition, books that include both print and braille should be readily available in the classroom and at home for reading aloud and exploration. Similar efforts need to be made to enhance the environment in an appropriate way for students with visual and multiple impairments who are tactile learners (McKenzie, 2009a; McKenzie & Davidson, 2007). The *Assessment of Braille Literacy Skills* (*ABLS;* Koenig & Farrenkopf, 1995) provides an overview of the skills to be addressed for braille literacy, starting with the emergent literacy phase through advanced literacy skills (see the Resources section at the end of this chapter).

Early Formal Literacy Skills. In the early braille literacy stage of skill development, the focus is on more formal development of students' tactile abilities, such as use of hands and fingers, as well as tactile discrimination and beginning letter recognition. Early braille skills instruction must begin before students are learning their letters in the classroom, so the braille reader is able to participate in instructional activities. Activities and exercises that provide students with opportunities to strengthen their hands and fingers, develop a greater ability to distinguish tactile shapes and textures, and, overall, refine their use of touch are often needed. (See the Resources section at the end of this chapter for commercially available curricula and publications for developing early braille skills, such as tactile discrimination and perception, appropriate hand movements, and knowledge of braille letters.)

Beginning Braille Literacy. During the stage of beginning braille literacy instruction, students with traditional literacy needs continue to learn braille letters (that is, uncontracted braille) and are then taught braille contractions (contracted braille) associated with the literary braille code. Teachers of students with visual impairments need to determine the appropriate method for teaching braille contractions to a particular student, taking into consideration the literacy instruction occurring in the classroom. Contracted braille can be taught in a systematic, prescribed manner, referred to as the basal approach (because of the basal, or basic, readers used), by using various commercially available curricula (see the Resources section at the end of this chapter). However, this specialized basal approach usually does not mirror the reading approach used in the classroom, and words requiring contractions may not be encountered at the same time in the braille readers and in the classroom materials. Teachers of students with visual impairments may therefore decide to teach contracted braille through teacher-made materials as contractions are encountered in the classroom reading curriculum. A variety of resources exist for supporting the use of reading programs being used in today's classroom (see for example, Wormsley & D'Andrea, 1997; Swenson, 1999).

Intermediate and Advanced Braille Literacy Skills. Students progress to the intermediate and advanced phases of the development of braille literacy skills as they begin to apply these skills to use reference materials, learn specialized codes, such as the music braille code, and increase the number of literacy tools (braillewriter, slate and stylus, electronic notetakers, and laptop) used for reading and writing braille. Daily functional use of braille, such as for reading labels on music CDs or flash drives or utilizing braille menus, is the focus during these phases of literacy development. Note that during all phases of braille literacy instruction, the teacher of students with visual impairments must ensure that the student understands the rules of braille contractions. Repeated discussion about the rules of braille will provide the student with a solid foundation of braille reading, writing, and appropriate use.

Functional Braille Literacy

For many students who have visual and multiple impairments, a more functional braille literacy program may be appropriate. This decision should be based on the most recent results of the student's learning media assessment and the input of the educational team. A functional approach typically is appropriate for students for whom learning literary braille in a traditional manner will be difficult due to their intellectual disabilities. In a functional approach, the educational team determines the vocabulary to teach based on the student's needs and current Individualized Education Program (IEP) goals and objectives. For example, it might be important for the student to read a lunch menu or follow the order in which work tasks should be performed. *Braille Literacy: A Functional Approach* (Wormsley, 2004) details a functional braille literacy program starting with high-interest and useful everyday vocabulary.

Teaching Print and Braille in Tandem

For some young students, the learning media assessment may result in a recommendation to teach both print and braille at the same time. These students often have a visual condition that is unstable or has a poor prognosis;

or they may have low vision and function efficiently in both learning media. The teacher of students with visual impairments and the educational team (which may include the student) must decide how literacy instruction will be provided in both media. Often, the student learns the use of print (with accommodations) in the classroom from the general education teacher and learns braille from the teacher of students with visual impairments in a manner that mirrors the classroom print curriculum. The key is for the student to receive equal, consistent, and daily instruction in each literacy medium.

For this student population, the teacher of students with visual impairments and educational team must also decide when the student will use print or braille in school, at home, and in the community. Again, equal use of both is the key to enable the student to generalize literacy skills to both media. The decision about when to use print or braille should be based on the student's unique needs. There may be times in the day where a student needs to use braille due to visual fatigue, or chooses to use print in subjects that are highly visual, such as social studies or science.

Teaching Braille to Students Who Are Print Users

Students with visual impairments who are already established print readers may require instruction in braille for a variety of reasons. For some students, the diagnosis of a progressive visual impairment, such as retinitis pigmentosa, in their late teens would cause the teacher of students with visual impairments and educational team to discuss the need to provide braille instruction as a secondary literacy media. There are also students who may suddenly lose their vision as the result of other medical conditions or accidents. In either case, creating motivation for learning braille is crucial. The use of motivating tasks to practice using braille, such as labeling favorite DVDs with braille or reading passages about favorite bands or actors, can be effective in helping students adapt to the use of braille.

Braille instruction for this population is different from that already discussed because the students are already established readers. These readers don't need to be taught that the symbols on the page represent the sounds in spoken words, but concepts such as braille indicators or contractions will need focused instruction. An emphasis needs to be placed on both reading and writing skills, as well as the rules of braille. There are curricular materials available to teach braille to individuals who are established print readers (see the Resources section at the end of this chapter).

Nemeth Code

For students who are braille readers, instruction in the Nemeth code, the specialized code used in mathematics and science, is necessary for meaningful participation in math and science courses. Generally, the teaching of Nemeth code begins in the early grades as young students are introduced to math and science. The curriculum used in the classroom will be the primary indicator to the teacher of students with visual impairments of what to teach, keeping in mind that the goal is to stay one step ahead of the student's class. Since the curriculum and sequence for teaching math and science varies by state and school district, teachers need to plan a sequence of Nemeth code instruction that is unique to the student and the curricular expectations for his or her grade level. At the end of each school year, the teacher should review the state education standards and discuss the sequence of the curriculum with the math and science educators for the student's next grade level, and obtain a copy of the math and science textbooks to be used to identify challenging concepts that are presented in a visual way. The knowledge and skills needed for participation in math class at the beginning of the next year should be taught prior to the end of the current school year, and materials should be provided for the student to practice with over the summer months.

In Nemeth code, symbols sometimes represent print characters, such as the equals sign. However, students also have to learn the use of indicators that alert the reader to unique items in the material that follow the indicators and that do not always have a print equivalent (such as the number sign, which indicates that a numeral follows, or the superscript indicator), as well as the rules associated with the use of these symbols. Experiences with both reading and writing Nemeth code are vital for students. Although few curricular materials are available for teaching Nemeth code, Kapperman, Heinze, and Sticken (1997) provide some suggestions. Teachers may also find the *Basic Nemeth—Mangold Math #1: Read and Write Braille Numerals* (n.d.) kit a useful tool for introducing reading and writing numbers in the Nemeth code to early learners.

Students who use braille also need to understand the visual aspects of certain mathematic and scientific concepts, in order to fully participate in classrooms where students and teachers may refer to these concepts in visual terms. They need to understand, for example, that visually, a superscript is a number or letter written one level above and to the left or right of the item it is modifying. Tactile graphics that can help in conveying these visual concepts are available from the Project Math Access website (see the Resources section at the end of this chapter).

Braille Writing

Braillewriters. While learning to read the various braille codes, students also need to learn and practice writing braille through a variety of methods using both low-tech and high-tech equipment. Before starting formal instruction in beginning braille-writing skills, students who are tactile learners should be exposed to a braillewriter for the purposes of awareness and exploration. Just as children without visual impairments explore and practice using writing implements long before they formally write letters, students with visual impairments need the opportunity to interact informally with braillewriters and other equipment for writing braille (Wormsley, 1997).

Braillewriters are typically also the first writing device to which students are introduced during the early phases of their formal literacy development. Students need to be systematically shown the parts of the braillewriter, the use of all the keys, and their operation. In addition, students should be taught to use the braillewriter as they learn the Nemeth code and how to spatially arrange math problems.

In addition to the classic mechanical Perkins Brailler, there are several alternatives that are lighter and quieter (including the Perkins Next Generation), some of which offer additional features such as a visual display and voicing of letters and contractions as they are brailled (see Sources of Products in the Resources section at the end of this chapter). The Mountbatten electric braillewriter provides a "high-tech" alternative that is a braillewriter, electronic notetaker, and embosser all in one and that provides both tactile and auditory output. The device also allows teachers to view the student's work on a computer monitor using additional equipment and provides an easier mechanism for students to practice early editing skills.

For students who struggle with the physical ability to push down the keys on a traditional braillewriter, extension keys are available that reduce the strength needed to depress keys or for one-hand use. One innovative teacher secured math manipulative cubes to the keys of the braillewriter with packing tape to create "cubies," to help young students who have difficulty isolating their fingers to keep them on the correct keys.

Slate and Stylus. Although braillewriters are primarily the first piece of equipment taught for writing braille, other devices need to be introduced as students develop mastery of the various braille codes. The slate and stylus provides individuals with a portable, low-tech method for writing braille. It can be used to take a telephone message, create a grocery list, or jot down a new acquaintance's phone number. It is important to expose students who read and write braille to the slate and stylus as one of a number of methods for making notes from which they can choose.

In today's technological world, it can be difficult for students to understand why learning the slate and stylus is important. Motivating activities and modeling by the teacher of students with visual impairments of appropriate uses for the slate and stylus are therefore a must. A game of racing a blindfolded teacher on the slate and stylus is fun for teachers and for students, who may enjoy the idea of beating their teacher at something. Other ideas include having students keep a journal of situations encountered where braille needed to be created on the run or when the slate and stylus was a noticeably convenient tool, such as for creating braille labels for favorite belongings. (See the Resources section at the end of this chapter for a curriculum to teach the slate and stylus.)

High-Tech Braille-Writing Devices. Students also need to learn and practice braille-writing skills using high-tech devices, such as electronic braille notetakers (also known as personal digital assistants or PDAs) and computers, from an early age. Keyboarding skills using standard (QWERTY) keyboards are also essential in today's world. (Instruction regarding assistive technology devices is addressed in Chapter 6.) As students become proficient with all of the available devices, they will have a range of options from which to choose in given situations.

Signature Writing

For students who are blind, the production of a legal signature is often the only writing skill requiring a pen or pencil that is taught. For young children, decisions about the extent of handwriting skills they need to learn may need to be made in conjunction with the child's parents. Early instruction may involve teaching students to make straight horizontal and vertical lines and circles, and combining these strokes to create initials. The teacher of students with visual impairments should begin to teach a student to write his or her signature during the elementary school years. Before beginning this initial signature practice, teachers will need to determine the requirements for a legal signature in the student's state of residence. For older students, this research can be incorporated with lessons in other ECC areas; for example, traveling to or calling a bank to inquire about requirements for a legal signature (O&M and independent living). Typically, a legal signature is one that is consistent in appearance and that fits in the space provided on the front and back of a check. Students should be taught to write their signatures in the actual size they would use in real-life activities, instead of first being taught to write large signatures that eventually are reduced in size.

Koenig and Holbrook (2000) describe several methods for teaching signature writing. The most popular method is typically the forward chaining method, in which the individual strokes that make up each letter of the signature are analyzed and taught in a sequential manner (see Mangold & Pesavento, 1997, for more information). Another approach includes the use of a custom signature-writing template with which the student traces his or her signature to establish muscle memory. (See also the discussion of signature writing guides in the section on Use of Specialized and Adapted Educational Materials later in this chapter.) Ultimately, the memorization of stroke patterns is the key to mastering this skill. Because most students who are visually impaired will not get visual feedback on their performance of signature writing, the teacher is essentially teaching and reinforcing muscle memory of the pattern of strokes that make up the letters and the transitions between the letters that comprise a signature.

Since the exact formation of letters in one's name is not the purpose of a signature, students should be given considerable latitude to form a unique signature that at least resembles his or her name. Given the extensive use of electronic media for writing today, dwelling on exact formation of all the letters of the alphabet requires valuable teaching time that could be spent on more useful skills. "Signature Required," a fun and motivating activity for students for practicing signature writing, can be found in the Learning Activities section of this chapter.

Choice Boards and Calendar Systems

As noted earlier, choice boards and calendar boxes are communication systems often used with students who have multiple disabilities that make use of visual or tactile symbols that have meaning to the individual student. Thus, before teaching the use of choice boards or calendar boxes, the educational team needs to decide on the objects or symbols that will be used with these systems, as well as their physical structure. It is important to carefully consider the continuum from concrete to abstract symbols for students, and whether they are tactile or visual learners, in addition to their individual needs, level of understanding and language development, and preferred communication method.

Blaha (2001) explained the instructional progression of teaching students to use daily, weekly, monthly, and eventually, annual calendars, and provided a summary sheet for educational teams to use when designing calendars for students. For choice boards, it is important to consider how best to present the symbols, taking into account the student's functional vision or physical abilities to explore the objects. It is important for team members to be consistent in instruction and vocabulary as well as the methods of using choice boards and calendar boxes. The teacher of students with visual impairments should be responsible for ensuring consistency among team members when communicating with the student using a choice board or calendar box.

For students to learn and to be able to generalize that learning to other situations, it is important that the symbols used as part of the student's choice board or calendar box also be encountered and used by the student in the environment. For example, the symbols used to represent activities during the school day can also be used to label the places where those activities take place, such as the cafeteria, the gymnasium, or the bathroom. In classrooms that include students who are using various symbols, the labels used for centers or areas can include all the symbols used by students in the class, whether braille, pictures, object symbols, or real objects (McKenzie & Davidson, 2007).

Speaking and Listening Skills

Speaking and listening skills should be taught from a very young age to students in an age-appropriate manner. This includes having normal conversations with children and practicing listening skills by deliberately calling attention to and naming sounds heard in the environment. Speaking and listening skills can be taught and reinforced in such natural contexts as the home and community, by helping children become aware of different sounds and their sources. As students get older, role-play situations can be used for practicing socially appropriate speaking and listening skills, such as interacting with teachers when requesting accommodations in the classrooms.

Teachers of students with visual impairments need to work with parents and other educational team members to reinforce the use of socially appropriate speaking and listening skills. Speaking skills include having informal conversations with peers, presenting a formal point of view in the form of a speech in school, or conversing by telephone or electronic devices. Instruction in formal speaking skills is often addressed in conjunction with social skills instruction by practicing holding conversations while looking at the other participants and using appropriate eye contact (see Chapter 9 for additional discussion). Formal listening skills, such as listening for meaning, listening to localize sounds in independent travel, and listening to distinguish discrete sounds in reading instruction, along with auditory comprehension and interpretation, are typically taught and reinforced through the use of learning activities devised by teachers. (See Chapter 5 for more about listening, and the learning activities "What Is It?" and "Sounds of My World" in that chapter. See also *Learning to Listen/Listening to Learn* [Barclay, 2012] for specific teaching strategies and the Resources section at the end of this chapter for *Listen and Think*, a formal listening curriculum.)

As older students prepare for working or studying independently after high school, they need to be formally taught the speaking, listening, and social skills used with human readers and personal note takers. For using readers, skills include where to find candidates, interviewing, scheduling, methods for working with readers, and even how to fire them, if necessary. When working with personal note takers, secondary students must be taught how to approach and work with them, as well as how to access the notes taken by others in academic classes (see the section titled Study and Organization Skills in this chapter). *College Bound: A Guide for Students with Visual Impairments* (Trief & Feeney, 2005) provides detailed information directed toward students on these topics as well as study, organization, and research skills. See also *Navigating the Rapids of Life: The Transition Tote System* (Wolffe & Terlau, 2011).

Study and Organization Skills

As already indicated, study and organizational skills need to be formally taught to students with visual impairments before the skills are needed for success in the core curriculum classroom. These skills include the use of office supplies, organization of classroom and study materials, note taking during instruction, and scanning and searching resources and references for important information. Learning these skills is critical to success in other areas of the ECC, such as independent living (see Chapter 8) and orientation and mobility (see Chapter 7). Although a curriculum is not available for teaching sequential study and organization skills specifically to students with visual impairments, a list of organization skills for elementary and secondary students with visual impairments is included in Sewell (2001).

Note Taking

Teaching note-taking skills to students with visual impairments is another area that must be individualized to the student, as everyone, regardless of visual ability, has different note-taking styles, strengths, and weaknesses. The first step in introducing note-taking skills is to help students understand the benefit or value of note taking. For example, it can be pointed out that individuals are more actively engaged with the content that is being presented to them when they are taking notes and that they will be able to consult those notes to review and study at future dates. Second, students need to be taught how to select key concepts from material presented orally or in a text. Sometimes, it is helpful to use an audiotaped version of a passage in conjunction with the text and review with the student how authors use bold or highlighted text to guide the reader to important points. Helping students listen for phrases used by presenters to indicate transitions and critical concepts is important. The teacher can also help students develop ways to write information quickly.

Note-taking style is a personal preference that depends on individual cognition and learning styles. Students should be exposed to a variety of note-taking methods so that they can find the ones that work best for them in different circumstances, such as the outline method, visual organization (in which items are listed under headings), and use of the Cornell method, which involves using two columns for taking notes (one column for keywords or concepts and one for notes pertaining to them). Finally, students need many opportunities to practice emerging note-taking skills in order to improve their ability to select key ideas and to increase the speed at which they are able to record them.

An essential area of instruction in note taking for students with visual impairments is how to select the most efficient literacy tools for taking notes in different situations. Teachers of students with visual impairments need to demonstrate and provide opportunities for note taking by students with visual impairments using a variety of tools, such as a traditional braillewriter, slate and stylus, or assistive technology devices (see Chapter 6); all of the options in the writing "toolbox" ought to be explored (Presley & D'Andrea, 2009). Methods of organizing and accessing notes, depending on the literacy tools utilized, are also important to learn. (See Trief & Feeney, 2005, for information on note taking and the use of various techniques and tools for students with visual impairments, and Herlich, 2012, for suggestions for teaching note taking.)

Searching and Scanning Written Materials

The ability to search and scan print or braille materials for pertinent information is required for successful participation in both educational and work settings. Visual and tactile scanning techniques can be taught; specific strategies depend on a student's reading efficiency skills and the media being used. The ability to scan and read graphs, charts, and maps is critical for success in all academic areas as well as other areas of the ECC (including orientation and mobility and assistive technology).

In general, students need to be introduced to the various search tools in computer software programs and on electronic devices and how best to use them to find specific information in electronic materials. In addition, the ability to highlight or mark text of particular interest is essential. For students who are print readers, highlighters or bold-line markers can be used. For students who read braille, such items as raised-dot stickers from craft stores or sticky note flags can be used to mark a place in text for later reference. (APH and assistive technology and independent living vendors also sell products such as tactile stickers or magnetic markers that can be used for this purpose; see the Resources section at the end of this book for more information.) For electronic materials, the highlight, bold, or underline function tools can be used in word-processing programs by both visual and tactile learners.

Reference and Research Skills

Students need to learn what an encyclopedia is and what type of material it contains before they learn about high-tech reference materials and research techniques. Exposing students to print and braille encyclopedias, dictionaries, and other reference materials, such as cookbooks, teaches the initial concept of locating information in such resources. Although many consider the braille versions of these items to be inconvenient, important concepts are developed through exposure to the concrete item before using reference materials with technology. Introduction to many reference materials can begin at an early age with simple instruction manuals, cookbooks, and game instructions.

Although the use of technology for accessing reference and research materials is taught as part of the assistive technology area (see Chapter 6), it is important that teachers of students with visual impairments also introduce students to the concepts involved in researching and obtaining information on a topic, as well as to a variety of reference and research resources. These include the use of:

- electronic library databases for locating books and journals
- the Internet for locating reliable information
- print materials to find research content
- electronic journals and e-books to find research content (Trief & Feeney, 2005)

Students need to be taught to perform basic and advanced searches in library databases and on the Internet. Free, online resources can be used to teach students the tenets of a sound and effective online search. In addition, in today's world, all students need to learn how to identify reliable sources of information on the Internet, a skill that will most likely be covered in the core curriculum classroom. Through the use of assistive technology, students with visual impairments can access reference and research materials in an efficient way, similar to their sighted classmates.

Interpretation and Creation of Tactile Graphics

Instruction in the use of tactile graphics for students who are braille readers often begins with methods for exploring a tactile graphic or gaining an overall understanding of a tactile graphic through the use of both hands in a systematic scanning system. The most common method of scanning begins in the upper left hand corner and proceeds down and up the page in an overlapping, organized fashion until the student reaches the bottom right corner, and in this way comes into contact with all the information displayed (Barth, n.d.).

When teaching interpretation of tactile graphics, the graphics should be introduced in a sequential manner, from simple to more complex. *Teaching Touch* (Harrell, 2002) provides a sequential introduction of simple tactile graphics. The Picture Maker Wheatley Tactile Diagramming Kit (see the Resources section at the end of this chapter) allows teachers of students with visual impairments to create graphics, such as simple room diagrams, spatial organizers, or pictographs used in the classroom, using familiar shapes, thus serving as a transition to more complex graphics. (Presley and D'Andrea [2009], describe a variety of methods for creating tactile graphics.)

Maps, charts, and graphs are more complex tactile graphics that are often used in social studies, math, and science as students move through the core curriculum. The use of maps involves unique concepts, such as borders, compass directions, mileage legends, and symbolic keys, which must be taught formally for students to be able to interpret them appropriately. Tactile maps and globes are available commercially from APH, but are often made by teachers of students with visual impairments to meet the needs of the core curriculum. Pre-teaching of maps should be a focus during elementary school, with the use of more complex maps pre-taught in early secondary grades.

When teaching tactile charts and graphs, a continuum from simple (pictographs, or graphs composed of pictures instead of data points) to more complex (line graphs) should be used. When teaching the use of maps, charts, and graphs, teachers of students with visual impairments should become familiar with the format of tactile graphics used on statewide assessments so that students are exposed to these formats before encountering them in that high-stakes context. Students should be exposed to a wide variety of charts and graphs made from a variety of tactile materials, including embossed braille paper, arts and crafts materials, microcapsule paper, and thermoform paper. (See the Resources section at the end of this chapter for sources of instructional materials.)

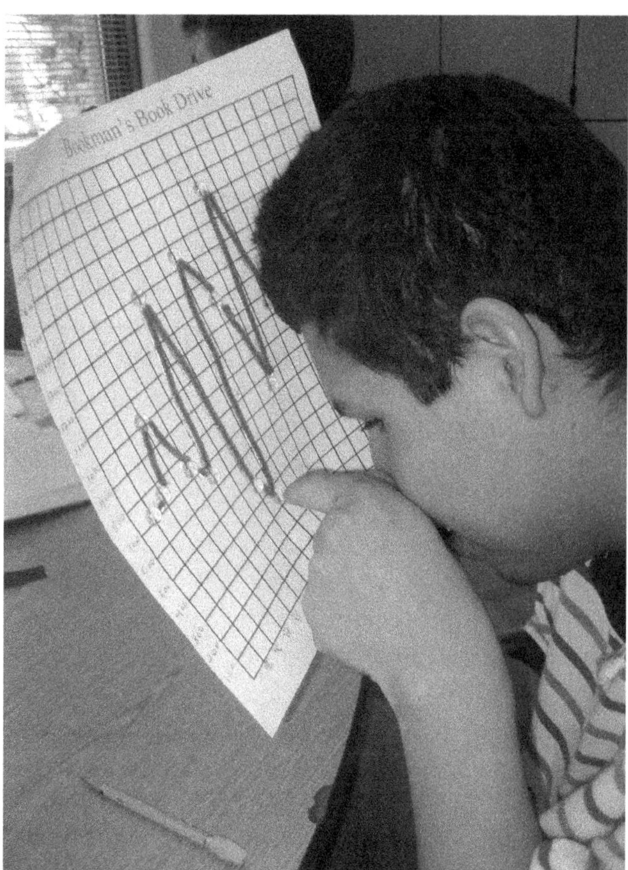

L. Penny Rosenblum

This student uses a tactile line graph to track collections in a book drive, an activity combining compensatory access, sensory efficiency, and social interaction skills with core curriculum math skills.

When learning how to create their own tactile graphics, students need to be taught to determine if a tactile graphic needs to be permanent and portable (such as one that needs to be submitted for an assignment and perhaps saved for an end-of-the-year portfolio), or temporary (such as a tactile graphic created in the classroom to demonstrate understanding of a concept, assessed immediately by the classroom teacher, and then discarded). Or perhaps a graphic might need to be somewhere between those extremes and be sturdy enough to be used over several days. Durability must be considered when selecting creation methods and materials. More durable materials are those that would be fixed to a surface using glue or tape versus using pushpins that can easily be moved. Teachers should also teach their students the use of bold-line and embossed graph paper for creating tactile charts and graphs required in the classroom. The use of tactile drawing boards and tactile drawing paper can also be taught, as well as the use of the Wheatley Picture Maker. Wikki Stix, string, rubber bands, pushpins, and other tactile markers can be used for creating graphics that do not need to be permanent or transported.

Use of Organizational Systems

Although there is no specific curriculum or instructional sequence for teaching how to use a personal organizational system for school materials, such as filing information in folders or binders, teachers of students with visual impairments should introduce the use of supplies before they are necessary for organization or use in the classroom. The use of school and office supplies should be modeled for students and formally taught through real, hands-on experiences and frequent opportunities to practice emerging skills. Ultimately, students should leave school equipped with a "toolbox" of skills for using school and office supplies, which will require that they have both exposure to a variety of materials and the ability to figure out appropriate uses for supplies and equipment in various situations. (See Chapter 8 for additional discussion of organizational skills.)

Use of Specialized and Adapted Educational Materials

The need for specialized educational materials is based on a student's present levels of performance, as determined by a comprehensive assessment, and the curricular demands of the classroom in the various core curriculum areas. The materials used will depend on the student's visual functioning, age, and literacy media needs. Therefore, instruction in the area of specialized educational materials will be highly individualized for each student. As discussed earlier in the section on General Considerations for Teaching Compensatory Access, a sequential approach to identifying curricular needs and planning instruction for specialized educational materials is suggested.

As noted earlier, the abacus and signature guide are among the most common specialized materials that need to be taught. In addition, a variety of adapted devices and materials are available for assisting students with school-related tasks, and students need to be taught the use of these materials as well.

Abacus

Beginning abacus skills can be introduced at a young age to assist students in learning early math skills, such as one-to-one correspondence and place value. The age of introduction should be driven by the classroom curriculum used in the student's locality and state. Through the use of a simplified abacus (such as the Beginner's Abacus available from APH), students can be introduced to the concepts and components of the abacus; this device can also be used for classroom instruction in early math concepts.

After a student learns the basic concepts involved in addition, subtraction, multiplication, and division, instruction in abacus skills corresponding to each of these areas can begin. The abacus enables students to solve more advanced calculation problems that cannot be accomplished using mental math. Teachers should carefully follow state education standards for what needs to be taught and when, and schedule abacus instruction after the student has demonstrated mastery of each basic arithmetic process in the classroom. Collaboration with the general education teacher is essential for determining when these skills are mastered, but it is important to teach the abacus before more complex addition, subtraction, multiplication, and division calculations are used in the classroom. Learning the abacus can be motivating and fun when games are incorporated, such as "Abacus Counts," found in the Learning Activities section of this chapter. For students who have difficulty with the motor skills involved in using an abacus, a large-format abacus with larger beads and columns is available from APH.

The approach selected for teaching the abacus should be based on the unique characteristics of the student, including mathematical knowledge and presence of any additional disabilities. Kapperman, Heinze, and Sticken (1997) describe various approaches for teaching the use of the abacus. Livingston (1997) provides teachers with two approaches for teaching the use of the abacus (logics and counting methods) and offers practice problems for teachers to use during instructional lessons. The DVD *Hands-on Experience with the Cranmer Abacus*, provides lesson ideas for functional uses of the abacus. (See the Resources section at the end of this chapter.)

In many states, the abacus is an allowable accommodation for students with visual impairments for all grade levels and items on statewide assessments in mathematics. In contrast, the use of talking calculators is limited to tests and items for which calculators are used by all the students completing the test. The abacus also has many functional applications outside the classroom, such as keeping track of a grocery bill while shopping or quickly calculating and adding a tip to a restaurant bill. Although there are higher-tech substitutions for an abacus, there is no substitute for having a discreet alternative to performing paper and pencil calculations that does not require power or voice output. For this reason, knowing how to use an abacus, like knowing how to use a slate and stylus, can provide students with an option that can be helpful in meeting specific and spontaneous needs.

Signature Writing Guides

Instruction in signature writing was discussed earlier in the section on communication modes. Signature writing guides are available in various forms, including guides that permit the user to make letters that fall below the writing line. Standard signature writing guides are not required for writing a legible signature and some individuals prefer not to use a signature guide. Some people prefer to use the side of a sticky note or other straight edge to guide their signature writing. While more complex guides for check writing exist, these are typically used by people who once had unimpaired vision. Signature writing guides are available through various companies that specialize in adapted equipment for individuals who are blind (see the Resources section at the end of this book). Raised or bold-lined paper and embossed or high-contrast graph paper are often used while teaching signature writing skills, along with the use of bold-line pens for individuals with low vision.

Adapted Educational Materials

It is important for teachers of students with visual impairments to be thoroughly familiar with and up-to-date in their knowledge of adapted versions of educational equipment that is used in the classroom, such as talking calculators or dictionaries, braille rulers, and the like, that are commercially available from the APH or companies that specialize in adapted equipment for people who are visually impaired (see the Resources section at the end of this book). Teachers of students with visual impairments need to work closely with general education teachers to become aware of the educational equipment used by a student's classmates and to determine if adapted versions are available. This collaboration needs to occur *before* the equipment will be needed in the classroom, so that the teacher of students with visual impairments can plan to teach the use of the adapted equipment well in advance, based on classroom curriculum and state education standards to be covered in the classroom in the near future. Sidebar 4.5 provides an example of planning related to the use of a talking calculator.

Students cannot be expected to be adept in the use of adapted equipment without being formally taught how

SIDEBAR 4.5

Teaching the Use of a Talking Calculator

This sample plan for teaching the use of adapted equipment was developed for Joe, a second-grade student who is blind, by Suzannah, his teacher of students with visual impairments.

PLANNING PROCESS

During the prior school year, Suzannah learns through a review of the state educational standards and Joe's second-grade math curriculum that the use of calculators will be introduced in the math classroom at the end of the first semester of second grade. At the beginning of second grade, Suzannah discusses with the math teacher the specific classroom uses of the calculator that will be necessary beginning in November. Suzannah decides to begin instruction in the use of a talking calculator for Joe in late September and orders an appropriate model of a talking calculator based on the functions needed in the classroom and on the statewide assessment.

INSTRUCTIONAL PLANNING

Suzannah must now determine what knowledge and skills are important for the use of a talking calculator for Joe. She determines that the following skills should be taught:

- Location and function of keys
- Finger placement
  - using number 5 key (typically marked with a tactile bump) as the orientation key for all other keys
  - using the 4, 5, and 6 keys as a home row for their pointer, middle, and ring fingers
  - using the thumb and pinky for keys on the outside columns
- Settings
  - adjusting volume
  - using answer mode, including reading all input or answer only

(continued on next page)

SIDEBAR 4.5 *continued*

- adjusting voice settings, including speed and voice options
- Discreet use in the classroom
  - locating the headset jack
  - using a headset that can be worn in only one ear (such as earbuds) to facilitate class participation while using the calculator

Using this list, Suzannah plans instruction for Joe involving modeling, hands-on experiences, guided practice, and independent practice in the use of the talking calculator over a three week period.

ONGOING ASSESSMENT

Suzannah intends to continue to assess Joe's ability to use the talking calculator through several methods once its use has been introduced in the classroom.

- Observing Joe using the calculator in the natural environment: Is Joe able to generalize the skills from instruction with Suzannah to use in the math classroom?
- Discussing Joe's use of the talking calculator in the classroom with his math teacher and at home with his parents: Is he able to use the device easily or is he experiencing frustration? Can he efficiently keep up with his peers in class or on homework?
- Asking Joe to report his degree of comfort with the use of the talking calculator through informal conversations, more formal questions and interviews, and the use of a journal to note his feelings and reactions to using the talking calculator in the classroom and at home. (Journal use is typically more appropriate with older students.)

to use it. In addition, since students who are visually impaired typically are not able to learn the use of devices in the classroom through observing their classmates or teacher, the use of these items needs to be pre-taught before the equipment is needed in the classroom to ensure the student's successful participation in class, as demonstrated in Sidebar 4.5. For example, formal instruction in the use of a braille ruler should be planned and implemented well before a student is expected to use a ruler in the classroom for activities, homework, or assessments. Finally, classroom teachers and parents should also be introduced to the student's adapted equipment. As part of the planning process, the environments in which the student will be using the equipment should be carefully considered to ensure that individuals who support the student's school efforts are knowledgeable about the items to be used.

ROLE OF THE TEACHER OF STUDENTS WITH VISUAL IMPAIRMENTS

The teacher of students with visual impairments has multiple roles in regard to their students' development of compensatory access skills. Depending on the needs of an individual student, teachers may undertake any or all of the following in an ongoing way:

- planning for potential instructional areas
- assessing the student's skills in those areas
- providing direct instruction
- ordering specialized instructional and educational materials
- creating adapted educational materials
- teaching and modeling the use of specialized and adapted educational materials for others

Collaboration with other educational team members is critical both to make certain that students receive effective instruction and to ensure that the efforts of the teacher of students with visual impairments are supported and reinforced. Access to the general education curriculum and core educational standards depend in part on the student's ability to recognize the need for specialized tools, implement the use of these tools, and continually adjust to both the curriculum being learned and the availability of adaptive tools and materials. It is the role of the teacher of students with visual impairments to ensure effective access for each individual student.

Ensuring Access

As already indicated, pre-teaching of certain concepts and skills is essential for students to participate effectively in the core curriculum, and in order for pre-teaching to occur in a timely way that helps support a student's success, teachers of students with visual impairments need to plan and sequence instruction to teach the knowledge and skills necessary for accessing the curriculum. Planning for instruction can be accomplished through review of state educational standards, individual school and/or classroom curricula, and course textbooks or supplemental materials. Because students need to be prepared to participate in the core curriculum at the beginning of any given school year, instruction in critical concepts, equipment, and skills must occur before the end of the prior school year.

Instruction must be based on and supported by good assessment. Once collaborative planning with the general education teacher and other educational team members has occurred, the teacher of students with visual impairments can better assess a student's knowledge and skills in the components of the compensatory area that are deemed necessary for success in the core curriculum classroom. After assessment has taken place, it is the responsibility of the teacher of students with visual impairments to ensure that the necessary knowledge and skills related to compensatory access appear in the form of goals and objectives on the student's IEP. Then instruction can be planned to address assessment-supported IEP goals and objectives.

Teachers of students with visual impairments are also responsible for direct instruction in compensatory access skills. Because teachers of students with visual impairments have the specialized knowledge of the unique needs and developmental patterns of students with visual impairments necessary for this instruction, they are in fact the student's primary service provider in this regard. Direct instruction can take place with one student or with groups of students who are visually impaired, but should take into account the unique needs of students and use effective teaching strategies, as outlined in Chapter 3. All instruction should be geared toward facilitating students' increasingly independent use of all materials and accommodations.

Ordering the specialized instructional and educational materials needed by students with visual impairments is a key role of the teacher of students with visual impairments. Since the resources and ordering procedures for this equipment vary from state to state, teachers will find it important to become familiar with the way in which this critical activity can be accomplished by checking with their local school districts. Instructional and educational materials are typically purchased either through the use of federal quota funds associated with APH, as described earlier in this chapter, or through direct payment by school districts. Some states have an instructional materials center or instructional resource center for students with visual impairments that is funded through the state education office.

It is essential that teachers of students with visual impairments act as advocates for their students and make clear to district and school administrators the critical need for specialized materials for students with visual impairments. A student's success in accessing the core curriculum is often dependent on the availability of such materials, including textbooks, unique instructional curricula, state and local assessment materials, and equipment.

The specialized instructional and educational materials used by students to participate in the core curriculum classroom may not always be commercially available, and when this is the case, they need to be created by the teacher of students with visual impairments using a variety of adaptation methods. Books, worksheets, tests, maps, charts, graphs, and diagrams that are used in the core curriculum are prepared by teachers of students with visual impairments in advance of students learning to use the materials and their actual use in the classroom. Pre-teaching of these materials is essential when new formats or types of materials are used in a student's classroom. In addition, teachers of students with visual impairments will often need to create adapted materials for providing actual instruction to students with visual impairments in the various components of the compensatory and other ECC areas. For example, a teacher of students with visual impairments may need to create charts and graphs while teaching a student both the interpretation of and the creation of tactile graphics. Similarly, a graphic demonstrating how drop-down and page-up windows are displayed on a computer screen may need to be made before a lesson on technology skills.

It is not enough for teachers of students with visual impairments to order and provide direct instruction in the use of specialized and adapted educational materials. The teacher may also need to help general education teachers, paraeducators, and parents become familiar with the equipment used by students, to provide them with support in the classroom, at home, and in the community. It is important to recognize that classroom teachers and parents spend most of the day with a student and oversee the majority of learning that takes place, either in school or at home while homework is being completed. Their understanding of the specialized and adapted educational equipment used can reinforce and support the student's performance of assignments and help ensure successful learning. Adults who are familiar with these adaptations are also more likely to encourage their use when students are engaged in activities related to other ECC areas.

Collaboration with Educational Team Members

The educational team consists of various individuals involved in the education of a student with a visual impairment and can vary based on the student's needs. At a minimum, this team will include the student's parents, the teacher of students with visual impairments, classroom teacher, administrator, and when feasible, the student. Related service providers, such as O&M instructors, occupational therapists, physical therapists, speech and language pathologists, clinical low vision therapists, audiologists, and paraeducators may also be team members, depending on any additional disabilities and needs of the student. The teacher of students with visual impairments plays a critical role on the educational team in sharing information about the student's visual skills and abilities and his or her learning needs due to the visual impairment, including the student's visual functioning, learning media, strengths, and need for accommodations or adapted materials.

General Education Teacher

Regardless of whether a student is placed in a general or special education classroom, collaboration with the general education teacher is another key to success in the area of compensatory access. Compensatory access allows students with visual impairments to participate fully in the core curriculum, so consulting with the general classroom teacher in a timely fashion regarding the curricular demands that will be placed on students is vital, as is coordinating the pre-teaching of concepts and provision of adapted materials necessary for access to the classroom instruction being scheduled. As already noted, planning for instruction, assessment, and direct instruction in the form of pre-teaching requires knowledge of the student's grade level core curriculum sequence and timeline, including both the concepts included in the curriculum, as well as the need for specialized educational materials. The teacher of students with visual impairments also needs to share with the classroom teacher critical information about the student's visual functioning, learning media, and need for environmental modifications, accommodations, and adapted learning materials.

Parents

Collaboration with parents is vital to ensure that students are utilizing and generalizing compensatory skills to situations outside of the school walls. Students need to apply their knowledge and skills within the components of compensatory skills while completing homework and school projects, as well as while participating in all aspects of daily life. For example, the parents of a student who needs to create a line graph as part of a typical social studies homework assignment can require their child to create and use a similar graph to track the child's progress toward some goal, such as reading for 60 minutes each day. Rapport needs to be built between teachers and families in order to achieve the kind of open communication that is essential for the reinforcement and practice of skills. Teachers of students with visual impairments must ensure that parents are familiar with the knowledge and skills being taught, practiced, and applied at school, in order to promote use and generalization at home and in the community. Teachers of students with visual impairments can review a student's IEP with parents, explaining educational terms or jargon, and discuss with parents ways the child can use compensatory access skills at home. Students benefit when parents and teachers of students with visual impairments are comfortable with providing feedback or asking for assistance from one another, particularly in cases in which a student may be having difficulty mastering skills or may be experiencing frustration with the application or use of various skills.

Orientation and Mobility Instructors

Collaboration and consistency in instruction between the teacher of students with visual impairments and O&M instructor are crucial for a student's success in the area of compensatory access. With regard to concept development and spatial understanding in particular, collaboration in instructional planning, assessment, and direct instruction is necessary. Consistent instructional sequence, methods, and vocabulary used during lessons are important and require discussion in advance. For example, the teacher of students with visual impairments may find that the concepts of parallel and perpendicular will be covered in math class soon. The teacher and O&M instructor can collaborate to plan, assess, and provide pre-teaching of these concepts to the student using real objects, three-dimensional representations, tactile graphics, and physical movement in the school and community before classroom instruction begins, thus repeatedly exposing the student to reinforcing direct experiences and explanations.

Collaboration with the O&M specialist is also necessary when planning to teach many other components of compensatory access. For example, reinforcing the use of appropriate communication modes during O&M lessons is important for helping the student practice communication techniques in real-life situations. Instruction in the use of low vision devices will be shared between the teacher of students with visual impairments and O&M specialist; use of devices in the classroom will be addressed by the teacher of students with visual impairments, and use in the community is usually addressed by the O&M specialist. The use of speaking and listening skills as they apply to social skills and the use of specialized educational materials, such as the abacus and signature-writing guides, can be incorporated into O&M lessons in the community. Study and organizational skills can be practiced when planning routes or researching public transportation options and schedules.

Other Related Service Providers

Collaboration with other professionals, such as occupational therapists, physical therapists, speech and language pathologists, certified low vision therapists, and audiologists, may be necessary to undertake assessment and instruction in many components of the compensatory access area. Occupational therapists and physical therapists should be consulted regarding the use of the student's fine and gross motor skills in relation to such activities as writing print, reading and writing braille, and executing sign language. All service providers should use consistent instruction and vocabulary to promote the student's concept development and spatial understanding, as these elements are applicable across all areas of instruction. When speech and language pathologists use real objects for instruction in concept development and vocabulary, they are valuable partners in instruction of students with visual impairments. Certified low vision therapists and eye care specialists play a critical role in evaluating students' vision and prescribing clinical low vision devices, when appropriate; teachers of students with visual impairments should not provide these devices for students without a prescription. Audiologists are key team members for students who are deaf-blind and can provide the teacher with significant information about a student's hearing and use of auditory information. For students who are deaf-blind, collaboration needs to take place among teachers of students with visual impairments, audiologists, and teachers of students who are deaf and hard of hearing, to determine effective modes of communication and development of speaking and listening skills, due to the significant role that hearing plays in both of these skill areas.

Paraeducators

Paraeducators provide instructional support to students with visual impairments in many components of the compensatory access area, including braille, concept development, listening skills, note-taking skills, and study skills (McKenzie & Lewis, 2008). According to NCLB, paraeducators may provide instructional support under the supervision of a certified teacher; in working with students with visual impairments, "the para[educator's] role is primarily to provide reinforcement and practice of . . . skills" taught by the teacher (McKenzie & Lewis, 2008, p. 463). Given their role, it is important that educational teams provide the training, supervision, and evaluation for paraeducators to successfully support student achievement in the compensatory access area, though direct instruction of new compensatory access skills needs to be provided only by the teacher of students with visual impairments.

SUGGESTIONS FOR WORKING WITH PARENTS

As indicated throughout this chapter, parents are key members of the educational team and need to be included to the greatest extent possible in their child's compensatory access instruction. Many parents believe that they need to have specialized training or knowledge to encourage the development of compensatory access skills, such as concept development, in their children. However, simply having an awareness of a child's developmental needs in this area is usually sufficient to encourage parents to assist in promoting the critical skills of concept development, spatial understanding, and language and literacy skills. The "Learning About the World: Can Do!" video series listed in the Resources section at the end of this chapter is a good source of developmental information for parents.

According to the International Reading Association and the National Association for the Education of Young Children (1998), the single most effective strategy for increasing the likelihood of the development of literacy skills is reading aloud to young children. There is no reason to believe that this advice does not apply to young children with visual impairments. Parents can ask for books in braille and print that are appropriate for their children (see the Resources section at the end of this chapter for some sources). If it is anticipated that the child will be a braille reader, parents can encourage the child to follow the braille while the story is being read. Selecting books that have themes that relate to the child's experiences helps to increase their meaning and relevance. Parents can work with teachers of students with visual impairments to make simple object or experience books that focus on their child's activities and that can reinforce early book skills, like page turning and book orientation, when reading.

Parents can provide natural opportunities in the course of daily life for their child's development, use, and practice of compensatory skills at home and in the community. These opportunities do not need to involve formal instruction. Rather, allowing children with visual impairments to be involved in naturally occurring events at home will create opportunities for the development and use of compensatory access skills. The most common way parents can support compensatory access skill development is to provide natural instruction in concept development in the home and community. Taking children to the grocery store, post office, and restaurants and engaging them in the activities that occur there, can expose children to critical concepts about the world. Behind-the-scenes tours of local businesses, such as a grocery store that allows hands-on experiences, offers the opportunity to expose children to hundreds of concepts that provide a deeper understanding of the world around them. Sidebar 4.6 provides a list of ideas for parents to incorporate the practice of compensatory

SIDEBAR 4.6

Practicing Compensatory Skills in the Community and at Home

The following suggestions and fun activities for practicing and reinforcing a student's compensatory skills can be shared with families when working with them:

AT THE GROCERY STORE

The grocery store is a great place to practice a variety of compensatory skills. Taking a child with a visual impairment to the store regularly will provide multiple opportunities to reinforce these skills.

Keeping Track of Total Cost

Have the child bring an abacus or talking calculator to the grocery store to round up the prices and keep track of how much all the items cost. If the child's total comes within $5 of the final total, he gets to choose what the family will have for dinner.

Selecting Produce

As the child helps pick out and picks up the fruits and vegetables on the shopping list, parents can describe each one: which are big/small, smooth/rough/bumpy, heavy/light, round/long, fat/skinny, and so on. Even if the child cannot see colors, parents should name the colors associated with each item. Everyone should know that bananas are yellow and that apples come in yellow, green, and red varieties. Some adults who are visually impaired do not know that it's okay to separate two or three bananas from a bunch if that's all they want to buy. Teachers and families can help students avoid such misconceptions.

Comparing Like Items in the Dairy Section

In the dairy section, have the child take an item from the shopping list off the shelf, and then compare it to other similar items.

- Compare a container of milk to the other sizes and types of containers in which milk is commonly sold (plastic, paper carton, gallon, half-gallon, pint, etc.). Compare a carton of milk to a carton of orange juice. Parents can talk about what other types of milk are in the store: rice milk, soy milk, almond milk, powdered milk, chocolate milk.
- Explore how eggs are packaged (by the dozen or half dozen, in plastic cartons and paper cartons). Parents can talk about why we can't buy just one or two eggs. At home, parents can "accidentally" drop an egg so the child can find out what happens.
- Cheeses come in plastic wrap, plastic containers, individually wrapped slices, solid blocks, bags that contain crumbled cheese, bags that contain shredded cheese, and so on. Have the child investigate a variety of cheese while the parents describe the differences. Parents can also talk

(continued on next page)

about how shoppers can have cheese sliced at the deli counter.

Paying for an Item (Pre-Elementary)

For children who are not yet in elementary school, parents can bring a wallet with a properly folded $5 bill inside. (Teachers can first explain the folding system used to identify denominations of bills to parents who are not familiar with it.) The child can independently pick out one item that costs less than $5 and pay for it before or after the parent checks out with the rest of the groceries. The child will likely receive $1 bills, or coins, or both, as change. This activity provides practice talking to the cashier, listening for how much to pay, receiving change, and answering the question of "Paper or plastic?" as the clerk bags the item. A young child can more easily put singles or coins back in the wallet because the bills do not have to be folded.

Independent Shopping (Elementary and Older)

Have the child call the grocery store ahead of time to find out when a customer service representative can assist him or her with an independent shopping activity. At the store, the parents can give the child $8 (3 singles and a $5 folded in half), and then drop the child off at the customer service counter to get assistance. The child will then put together a meal for $8 or less, while the parents shop separately. Have the child meet back at the registers in 20 minutes.

Reading Aisle Signage

For students with low vision, that monocular isn't just for school. As parents do their shopping, their child can read the signs that list the items that are found in each aisle. Parents can make it fun by asking the child to identify where the peanut butter and jelly supplies are found, or have the child figure out which aisle to go to next based on the shopping list.

AT HOME

Signing Cards

For signing birthday and holiday cards, the child can use a slate and stylus to braille his or her name and then use a signature guide to sign his or her name above the braille.

Thank-You Cards

The child can braille thank-you cards to friends or family members who have sent gifts. Parents will need to show the child how to address an envelope, where to put the stamp, and how to put the cards in the mailbox so the mail carrier can deliver them. Young children can "scribble" using the brailler, use a stylus or tracing tools to make tactile designs, or attach puffy, tactile stickers for decorations.

Vacation Research

Have the child research fun activities the family would enjoy at an upcoming vacation destination. The child can use the Internet with a speech synthesis program, screen magnification program, or braille notetaker, or call a visitor center in the area. Notes can be typed on a computer or on a braillewriter.

Reading on Vacation

When traveling, parents can bring along plenty of Talking Books or digital books that their child can listen to for entertainment.

Chore List

Parents can create a list of five chores (in print or braille) for their child to do on the same day every week, and attach it securely to the same place (for example, the front of the refrigerator). Every week, the child can choose three out of the five chores on the list to do. The child can indicate when a task is completed by using a dark, bold marker, tactile sticker, or a braille eraser to cross it off, mark it, or erase it from the list.

Ordering Takeout

Have the child order takeout by first recording (in braille, on a braille notetaker, in high-contrast print, or other preferred writing mode) what the family wants to order and the telephone number of the restaurant, dialing the number correctly, answering the questions that the restaurant employee asks (name, phone number, address, and the order), and recording the total price.

SOURCE: WRITTEN BY SUSAN GLASER

skills during regularly occurring events. Additional suggestions to help parents to promote language and literacy skills and concept development in their visually impaired children can be found in *Reach Out and Teach* (Ferrell, 2011).

SUMMARY

Compensatory access skills allow students with visual impairments to obtain information about the world around them. At school, compensatory skills permit access to the core curriculum; at home and in the community, compensatory access is necessary for the performance of a range of functional, everyday tasks, such as writing a letter or ordering from a menu. Through systematic planning, assessment, and sequential instruction by teachers of students with visual impairments, students can be equipped with the skills to develop concepts about the world and to obtain and share information with others. Collaboration with parents and educational team members allows practice of the various components of compensatory skills to continue at school, at home, and in the community. Ultimately, well-developed compensatory access skills allow students with visual impairments to be independent, successful individuals and to form the foundation for active participation in school, work, and life.

References

Anderson, S., Boigon, S., Davis, K., & deWaard, C. (2007). Oregon project for preschool children who are blind or visually impaired (6th ed.). Medford: Southern Oregon Education Service District.

Barclay, L. A. (Ed.). (2012). *Learning to listen, listening to learn: Teaching listening skills to students with visual impairments.* New York: AFB Press.

Barclay, L. A., & Staples, S. (2012). The importance of listening instruction. In L.A. Barclay (Ed.), *Learning to listen, listening to learn: Teaching listening skills to students with visual impairments* (pp. 3–23). New York: AFB Press.

Barth, J. L. (n.d.). *Tactile graphics guidebook.* Louisville, KY: American Printing House for the Blind.

Basic Nemeth—Mangold math #1: Read and write braille numerals. (n.d.). Livermore, CA: Exceptional Teaching Aids.

Blaha, R. (2001). *Calendars for students with multiple impairments including deafblindness.* Austin: Texas School for the Blind and Visually Impaired.

Brigance, A. H. (2010). *Brigance comprehensive inventory of basic skills II* (CIBS II). North Billerica, MA: Curriculum Associates.

Connolly, A. J. (2007). *Keymath 3: Diagnostic assessment.* San Antonio, TX: Pearson Clinical Assessment.

Corn, A. L., & Koenig, A. J. (2002). Literacy for students with low vision: A framework for delivering instruction. *Journal of Visual Impairment & Blindness, 96*(5), 305–321.

D'Andrea, F. M., & Farrenkopf, C. (Eds.). (2000). *Looking to learn: Promoting literacy for students with low vision.* New York: AFB Press.

Fazzi, D. L., & Petersmeyer, B. A. (2001). *Imagining the possibilities: Creative approaches to orientation and mobility instruction for persons who are visually impaired.* New York: AFB Press.

Ferrell, K. A. (2011). *Reach out and teach: Helping your child who is visually impaired learn and grow.* New York: AFB Press.

Hall, A. (1982). Teaching specific concepts to visually handicapped students. In S. S. Mangold (Ed.), *A Teacher's guide to the special educational needs of blind and visually handicapped children* (pp. 10–19). New York: American Foundation for the Blind.

Harrell, L. (2002). *Teaching touch: Helping children become active explorers of tactual materials: A guide for teachers and parents of young visually impaired children.* Louisville, KY: American Printing House for the Blind.

Herlich, S. (2012). Middle school and high school: Advanced skill development. In L.A. Barclay (Ed.), *Learning to listen, listening to learn: Teaching listening skills to students with visual impairments* (pp. 153–195). New York: AFB Press.

International Reading Association and National Association for the Education of Young Children. (1998). Learning to read and write: Developmentally appropriate practices in young children. *Young Children, 53*(4), 30–46.

Jacobson, W. H. (2013). *The art and science of teaching orientation and mobility to persons with visual impairments* (2nd ed.). New York: AFB Press.

Johns, J. (2010). *Basic reading inventory* (10th ed.). Dubuque, IA: Kendall Hunt Publishing.

Kamei-Hannan, C., & Ricci, L. (in press). *Strategies for teaching reading to students with visual impairments.* New York: AFB Press.

Kapperman, G., Heinze, T., & Sticken, J. (1997). *Strategies for developing mathematics skills in students who use braille.* Alexandria, VA: Association for the Education and Rehabilitation of the Blind and Visually Impaired.

Kaufman, A. S., & Kaufman, N. L. (2005). *Kaufman test of educational achievement* (2nd ed.), San Antonio, TX: Pearson Educational.

Koenig, A. J., & Farrenkopf, C. (1995). *Assessment of braille literacy skills.* Houston, TX: Region 4 Education Service Center.

Koenig, A. J., & Holbrook, M. C. (1995). *Learning media assessment of students with visual impairments* (2nd ed.). Austin: Texas School for the Blind and Visually Impaired.

Koenig, A. J., & Holbrook, M. C. (2000). Ensuring high-quality instruction for students in braille literacy programs. *Journal of Visual Impairment & Blindness, 94*(11), 677–694.

Koenig, A. J., Holbrook, M. C., Corn, A. L., DePriest, L. B., Erin, J. N., & Presley, I. (2000). Specialized assessments for students with visual impairments. In A. J. Koenig and M. C. Holbrook (Eds.), *Foundations of education: Vol. II. Instructional strategies for teaching children and youths with visual impairments* (2nd ed., pp. 103–153). New York: AFB Press.

Koenig, A. J., Layton, C. A., & Ross, D. B. (1992). The relative effectiveness of reading in large print and reading with low vision devices for students with low vision. *Journal of Visual Impairment & Blindness, 86*, 48–53.

Layton, C. A., & Koenig, A. J. (1998). Increased reading fluency in elementary students with low vision through repeated readings. *Journal of Visual Impairment & Blindness, 92*(5), 276–292.

Listen and think auditory readiness (AR). Adapted by E. Pester. Louisville, KY: American Printing House for the Blind.

Livingston, R. (1997). *Use of the Cranmer abacus* (2nd ed.). Austin: Texas School for the Blind and Visually Impaired.

Loftin, M. (2005). *Making evaluation meaningful.* Austin: Texas School for the Blind and Visually Impaired.

Loumiet, R., & Levack, N. (1991). *Independent living: A curriculum with adaptations for students with visual impairments* (Vols. 1–3). Austin: Texas School for the Blind and Visually Impaired.

Mangold, S. S. (1994). *Mangold Developmental Program of Tactile Perception and Braille Letter Recognition* (Rev.). Livermore, CA: Exceptional Teaching Aids.

Mangold, S., & Pesavento, M. E. (1997). *Teaching signature writing to those who are visually impaired: A training program for teachers and parents.* DVD. Livermore, CA: Exceptional Teaching Aids.

Marks, S. B. (1998). Understanding and preventing learned helplessness in children who are congenitally deaf-blind. *Journal of Visual Impairment & Blindness, 92*(3), 200–211.

McKenzie, A. R. (2009a). Emergent literacy supports for students who are deaf-blind or have visual and multiple impairments: A multiple-case study. *Journal of Visual Impairment & Blindness, 103*(5), 291–302.

McKenzie, A. R. (2009b). Unique considerations for assessing the learning media of students who are deaf-blind. *Journal of Visual Impairment & Blindness, 103*(4), 241–245.

McKenzie, A. R., & Davidson, R. (2007). The emergent literacy of preschool students who are deaf-blind: A case study. *Journal of Visual Impairment & Blindness, 101*(11), 720–725.

McKenzie, A. R., & Lewis, S. (2008). The role and training of paraeducators who work with students who are visually impaired. *Journal of Visual Impairment & Blindness, 102*(8), 459–471.

No Child Left Behind Act (NLCB) of 2001. Title 20 U.S.C. 6301 et seq.

Postello, T., & Barclay, L. A. (2012). Elementary school: developing and refining listening skills. In L. A. Barclay (Ed.), *Learning to listen, listening to learn: Teaching listening skills to students with visual impairments* (pp. 104–152). New York: AFB Press.

Presley, I., & D'Andrea, F. M. (2009). *Assistive technology for students who are blind or visually impaired: A guide to assessment.* New York: AFB Press.

Salvia, J., Ysseldyke, J., & Bolt, S. (2010). *Assessment: In special and inclusive education.* Florence, KY: Wadsworth Publishing.

Sanford, L., & Burnett, R. (2008). *FVLMA Kit: Functional vision and learning media assessment for students who are pre-academic and academic and visually impaired in grades K-12.* Louisville, KY: American Printing House for the Blind.

Sewell, D. (2001). *Assessment kit: Kit of informal tools for academic students with visual impairments, Part 1–3.* Austin: Texas School for the Blind and Visually Impaired.

Stillman, R. (1978). *The Callier-Azusa scale "G."* Dallas: Callier Center, University of Texas at Dallas.

Stillman, R., & Battle, C. (1985). *Callier-Azusa scale "H."* Dallas: Callier Center, University of Texas at Dallas.

Stratton, J. (1990). The principle of least restrictive materials. *Journal of Visual Impairment & Blindness, 84*, 3–5.

Swenson, A. M. (1999). *Beginning with braille: Firsthand experiences with a balanced approach to literacy.* New York: AFB Press.

Texas School for the Blind and Visually Impaired. (2007). *EVALS: Evaluating Visually Impaired Students.* Austin: Texas School for the Blind and Visually Impaired.

Texas School for the Blind and Visually Impaired. (2010). *Common acronyms used when speaking about accessible textbooks.* Retrieved from www.tsbvi.edu/component/content/article/157-technology/1856-common-acronyms-used-when-speaking-about-accessible-textbooks

Trief, E., & Feeney, R. (2005). *College bound: A Guide for students with visual impairments.* New York: AFB Press.

Wolffe, K. E., & Terlau, M. T. (2011). *Navigating the rapids of life: The transition tote system* (2nd ed.). Louisville, KY: American Printing House for the Blind.

Wormsley, D. P. (1997). Learning to read, reading to learn: Teaching braille reading and writing. In D. P. Wormsley & F. M. D'Andrea (Eds.), *Instructional strategies for braille literacy* (pp. 57–110). New York: AFB Press.

Wormsley, D. P. (2004). *Braille literacy: A functional approach.* New York: AFB Press.

Wormsley, D. P., & D'Andrea, F. M. (Eds.). (1997). *Instructional strategies for braille literacy.* New York: AFB Press.

Compensatory Access Resources

This section provides resources such as assessment tools, publications, and instructional materials that may be used for teaching compensatory access components. For additional resources that relate to the expanded core curriculum in general, see the Resources section at the end of this book.

ASSESSMENT TOOLS

Assessment of Braille Literacy Skills (ABLS)

Population/Age level: Preschool, elementary and secondary students

Component: Communication modes

Source: Koenig, A. J., & Farrenkopf, C. (1995). *Assessment of braille literacy skills.* Houston, TX: Region 4 Education Service Center.

Assessment Kit: Kit of Informal Tools for Academic Students with Visual Impairments

Population/Age level: Elementary and secondary students

Component: All skills

Source: Sewell, D. (2001). *Assessment kit: Kit of informal tools for academic students with visual impairments, Part 1–3.* Austin: Texas School for the Blind and Visually Impaired.

Basic Reading Inventory

Population/Age level: Preschool, elementary, and secondary students

Component: Communication modes

Source: Johns, J. (2010). *Basic reading inventory* (10th ed.). Dubuque, IA: Kendall Hunt Publishing.

Brigance Diagnostic Comprehensive Inventory of Basic Skills

Population/Age level: Preschool through ninth grade

Component: Speaking and listening skills, study and organization skills

Sources: Brigance, A. H. (2010). *Brigance comprehensive inventory of basic skills II (CIBS II).* North Billerica, MA: Curriculum Associates.

Brigance, A. H. (1999). *Brigance diagnostic comprehensive inventory of basic skills (green), Revised: Student Braille Edition.* Louisville, KY: American Printing House for the Blind.

Brigance, A. H. (1999). *Brigance diagnostic comprehensive inventory of basic skills (green), Revised, 1999: Student Large Print Edition.* Louisville, KY: American Printing House for the Blind.

The Callier-Azusa Scale "G"

Population/Age level: Multiply disabled and deafblind students, birth to 108 months

Component: Concept development, spatial understanding, communication modes, speaking and listening skills, use of specialized education materials

Source: Stillman, R. (1978). *Callier-Azusa scale "G."* Dallas: Callier Center, University of Texas at Dallas.

Callier-Azusa Scale "H"

Population/Age level: Multiply disabled and deafblind students

Component: Communication modes, speaking and listening skills

Source: Stillman, R., & Battle, C. (1985). *Callier-Azusa scale "H."* Dallas: Callier Center, University of Texas at Dallas.

EVALS: Evaluating Visually Impaired Students

Population/Age level: All

Component: All skills

Source: Texas School for the Blind and Visually Impaired. (2007). *EVALS: Evaluating Visually Impaired Students.* Austin: Texas School for the Blind and Visually Impaired.

FVLMA (Functional Vision and Learning Media Assessment)

Population/Age level: Pre-academic and academic students in grades K–12

Component: Communication modes

Source: Sanford, L., & Burnett, R. (2008). *FVLMA: Functional vision and learning media assessment for students who are pre-academic and academic and visually impaired in grades K–12.* Louisville, KY: American Printing House for the Blind.

Independent Living: A Curriculum with Adaptations for Students with Visual Impairments

Population/Age level: All

Components: Concept development, spatial understanding, speaking and listening skills, study and organizational skills, use of specialized education materials

Source: Loumiet, R., & Levack, N. (1991). *Independent living: A curriculum with adaptations for students with visual impairments* (Vols. 1–3). Austin: Texas School for the Blind and Visually Impaired.

Kaufman Test of Educational Achievement

Population/Age level: Preschool to grade 3+

Components: Communication modes, speaking and listening skills

Source: Kaufman, A. S., & Kaufman, N. L. (2005). *Kaufman test of educational achievement* (2nd ed.). San Antonio, TX: Pearson Educational.

KeyMath Revised: A Diagnostic Inventory of Essential Mathematics

Population/Age level: Kindergarten through ninth grade

Component: Communication modes, use of specialized education materials

Sources: Connolly, A. (1988). *KeyMath revised: A diagnostic inventory of essential mathematics.* Circle Pines, MN: American Guidance Service.

Connolly, A. J. (2007). *KeyMath 3: Diagnostic assessment.* San Antonio, TX: Pearson Clinical Assessment.

Learning Media Assessment for Students with Visual Impairments

Population/Age level: All

Components: Communication modes

Source: Koenig, A. J., & Holbrook, M. C. (1995). *Learning media assessment of students with visual impairments: A resource guide for teachers* (2nd ed.). Austin: Texas School for the Blind and Visually Impaired.

Oregon Project for Preschool Children Who Are Blind or Visually Impaired

Population/Age level: Birth to 5 years

Components: All

Source: Anderson, S., Boigon, S., Davis, K., & deWaard, C. (2007). *Oregon project for preschool children who are blind or visually impaired* (6th ed). Medford: Southern Oregon Education Service District.

Tactile Test of Basic Concepts

Population/Age level: Kindergarten and grades 1 and 2

Components: Spatial understanding

Source: Caton, H. (1980). *The tactile test of basic concepts: A tactile analog to the Boehm Test of Basic Concepts, Form A.* Louisville, KY: American Printing House for the Blind.

CURRICULA AND INSTRUCTIONAL MATERIALS

Concepts

Drezek, W. (1995). *Move, touch, do!* Louisville, KY: American Printing House for the Blind.

Curriculum for young students with visual impairments, emphasizing use of hands-on learning activities for teaching critical concepts.

O'Sail, B., Levack, N., Donovan, L., & Sewell, D. (2001). *Elementary concepts for students with visual impairments.* Austin: Texas School for the Blind and Visually Impaired.

Thematic curriculum for teaching basic concepts that includes reading, writing, math, social, and independent living skill activities to students with visual impairments who are 12 years of age or younger and are not yet at the first-grade level in the core curriculum.

Spatial Understanding

Harrell, L. (2002). *Teaching touch: Helping children become active explorers of tactual materials: A guide for teachers and parents of young visually impaired children.* Louisville, KY: American Printing House for the Blind.

A set of tactile materials for young children ages 4 to 7 years for developing tactile exploration skills with an emphasis on spatial understanding and tactile awareness.

Communication Modes

Braillewriting Dot by Dot Kit. (1995). Louisville, KY: American Printing House for the Blind.

A kit for teaching beginning writing skills with braillewriters and the slate and stylus.

Building on Patterns: Primary Braille Literacy Program. (multiple dates). Louisville, KY: American Printing House for the Blind.

A complete primary literacy program to teach beginning braille users to read, write, and spell in braille. Addresses basic literacy skills as well as skill areas needed by children who are blind, such as language development, sound discrimination, tactile discrimination, and concept development, and braille contractions.

Freund, E. D. (1995). *Freund Longhand Writing Kit.* Louisville, KY: American Printing House for the Blind.

Kit for teaching cursive writing, with an embossed workbook, a Tactile Marking Mat, embossed-line paper, and a manual.

Harrell, L. (2002). *Teaching touch: Helping children become active explorers of tactual materials: A guide for teachers and parents of young visually impaired children.* Louisville, KY: American Printing House for the Blind.

Curriculum for developing tactile discrimination skills.

Mangold, P. (1994). *Teaching the braille slate and stylus.* Livermore, CA: Exceptional Teaching Aids.

Manual and DVD modeling methods for teaching the slate and stylus to individuals who read braille.

Mangold, S. S. (1994). *Mangold developmental program of tactile perception and braille letter recognition* (Rev. ed.). Livermore, CA: Exceptional Teaching Aids.

Addresses tactile discrimination and perception skills, develops appropriate hand movements, and introduces braille letters in a systematic order.

Mangold, S., & Pesavento, M. E. (1997). *Teaching signature writing to those who are visually impaired: A training program for teachers and parents.* Livermore, CA: Exceptional Teaching Aids.

DVD and manual for teaching signature writing.

On the way to literacy. Louisville, KY: American Printing House for the Blind.

Storybooks for children 2½–5 years of age in large print and braille with tactile illustrations, with handbook, and CD available.

Patterns: Primary Braille Reading Program. Louisville, KY: American Printing House for the Blind.

A basal reading program for teaching braille literacy.

Pester, E. *The braille connection: A braille reading and writing program for former print users.* Louisville, KY: American Printing House for the Blind.

A braille curriculum for former print users.

Speaking and Listening

Listen and think auditory readiness (AR). Adapted by E. Pester. Louisville, KY: American Printing House for the Blind.

Study and Organization

Barth, J. L., & Berla, E. P. (1982). *Tangible graphs.* Louisville, KY: American Printing House for the Blind.

Math builders, unit 8: Data collection, graphing, and probability-statistics kit. Louisville, KY: American Printing House for the Blind.

Kit for teaching tactile graphing to students K–3.

Picture maker Wheatley tactile diagramming kit. Louisville, KY: American Printing House for the Blind.

Kit for making tactile diagrams on a felt-covered board using Velcro-backed pieces in a variety of shapes, sizes, textures, and colors. Includes guidebook.

PUBLICATIONS

Assessment

McKenzie, A. R. (2009). Unique considerations for assessing the learning media of students who are deafblind. *Journal of Visual Impairment & Blindness, 103*(4), 241–245.

Concepts

Fazzi, D. L., & Petersmeyer, B. A. (2001). *Imagining the possibilities: Creative approaches to orientation and mobility instruction for persons who are visually impaired.* New York: AFB Press.

Shafer, S. (1995, June). An introduction to Dr. Lilli Nielsen's active learning. *VISIONS, 3*(2).

Communication Modes

Blaha, R. (2001). *Calendars for students with multiple impairments including deafblindness.* Austin: Texas School for the Blind and Visually Impaired.

D'Andrea, F. M., & Farrenkopf, C. (Eds.). (2000). *Looking to learn: Promoting literacy for students with low vision.* New York: AFB Press.

In-depth information about teaching the use of low vision devices, with ideas for learning activities.

Kapperman, G., Heinze, T., & Sticken, J. (1997). *Strategies for developing mathematics skills in students who use braille.* Alexandria, VA: Association for the Education and Rehabilitation of the Blind and Visually Impaired.

Olson, M. R. (1981). *Guidelines and games for teaching efficient braille reading.* New York: American Foundation for the Blind.

Rex, E. J., Koenig, A. J., Wormsley, D., & Baker, R. (1994). *Foundations of braille literacy.* New York: AFB Press.

Swenson, A. M. (1999). *Beginning with braille: First-hand experiences with a balanced approach to literacy.* New York: AFB Press.

Wormsley, D. P. (2004). *Braille literacy: A functional approach.* New York: AFB Press.

Wormsley, D. P., & D'Andrea, F. M., Eds. (1997). *Instructional strategies for braille literacy.* New York: AFB Press.

Speaking and Listening

Barclay, L. A. (Ed.). (2012). *Learning to listen, listening to learn: Teaching listening skills to students with visual impairments.* New York: AFB Press.

Study and Organization Skills

Trief, E., & Feeney, R. (2005). *College bound: A guide for students with visual impairments.* New York: AFB Press.

Wolffe, K. E., & Terlau, M. T. (2011). *Navigating the rapids of life: The transition tote system* (2nd ed.). Louisville, KY: American Printing House for the Blind.

Specialized and Adapted Educational Materials

Basic Nemeth—Mangold math #1: Read and write braille numerals. (n.d.). Livermore, CA: Exceptional Teaching Aids.

Braille Authority of North America. (2010). *Guidelines and standards for tactile graphics, 2010.* Louisville, KY: American Printing House for the Blind. Available at http://brailleauthority.org/tg/index.html.

Kapperman, G., Heinze, T. , & Sticken, J. (1997). *Strategies for developing mathematics skills in students who use braille.* Alexandria, VA: Association for the Education and Rehabilitation of the Blind and Visually Impaired.

Livingston, R. (1997). *Use of the Cranmer abacus* (2nd ed.). Austin: Texas School for the Blind and Visually Impaired

VIDEOS AND DVDS

Hands-on experience: Tactile learning and skills. Can Do! Series. DVD/VHS. Louisville, KY: Visually Impaired Preschool Services.

COMPONENT: Communication skills

Hands-on experience with the Cranmer abacus. DVD. Louisville, KY: American Printing House for the Blind.

COMPONENT: Use of specialized educational materials

Learning about the world: Concept development. Can Do! Series. DVD. Louisville, KY: Visually Impaired Preschool Services.

COMPONENT: Concept development

Power at your fingertips: An introduction to learning braille. Can Do! Series. DVD. Louisville, KY: Visually Impaired Preschool Services.

COMPONENT: Concept development

WEBSITES

Paths to Literacy
www.pathstoliteracy.org

An online hub for information related to literacy for students who are blind or visually impaired, including those with additional disabilities or deaf-blindness.

Project Math Access
Texas School for the Blind and Visually Impaired
http://s22318.tsbvi.edu/mathproject

Contains information about and suggestions for teaching mathematics, including Nemeth code, to students with visual impairments. The "Spoken Mathematics" section contains an extensive section of tactile graphics for many mathematical symbols and concepts that can be downloaded at no cost and embossed using a braille embosser.

SOURCES OF PRODUCTS

American Printing House for the Blind
1839 Frankfort Avenue
Louisville, KY 40206
(800) 223-1839
info@aph.org
www.aph.org

Sells the "On the Way to Literacy" books, with print and braille and tactile illustrations. Also source for many other braille children's books and early learning materials; tactile maps and globes; abaci; Picture Maker Wheatley Tactile Diagramming Kit; and other educational materials.

Humanware Canada
1800 Michaud Street
Drummondville (Quebec)
Canada J2C 7G7
(888) 723-7273 (Canada and US) or (819) 471-4818
Fax: (819) 471-4828
ca.info@humanware.com
www.humanware.com

Humanware United States
1 UPS Way
PO Box 800
Champlain, NY 12919
(800) 722-3393
Fax: (888) 871-4828
info@humanware.com
www.humanware.com

Distributes the Mountbatten Brailler, along with a variety of assistive technology products.

Kenneth Jernigan Library for Blind Children
American Action Fund for Blind Children and Adults
18440 Oxnard Street
Tarzana, CA 91356
(818) 343-2022
www.actionfund.org

Maintains a lending library of print/braille books as well as braille books for K to 12th grade reading and interest levels.

National Braille Press
88 St. Stephen Street
Boston, MA 02115
(617) 266-6160 or (800) 548-7323
orders@nbp.org
www.nbp.org

Offers a Children's Braille Book Club aimed especially for preschool and primary grade children, featuring popular picture books with clear plastic sheets that contain the braille translation. There is no fee to join the club, and members can buy as few or as many books as they wish.

National Library Service for the Blind and Physically Handicapped (NLS)
Library of Congress
Washington, DC 20542
(800) 424-8567
nls@loc.gov
www.loc.gov/nls

Offers a wide variety of braille books on loan.

Perkins Products
37 Fifield Street
Watertown, MA 02472
(617) 972-7308
Fax: (617) 926-2027
PerkinsProducts@Perkins.org
www.perkins.org/store

Sells the classic Perkins Brailler, Next Generation Perkins Brailler, Perkins Smart Brailler, extension keys and other braillewriter accessories, slates and styli, in addition to a variety of learning, daily living, and assistive technology products.

Seedlings Braille Books for Children
PO Box 51924
Livonia, MI 48151-5924
(734) 427-8552 or (800) 777-8552
seedlink@aol.com
www.seedlings.org

Sells popular, high-quality books for children of all ages, including print/braille picture books and print/braille books for older readers.

Compensatory Access Learning Activities

Contributed by Carol B. Allman, Susan Glaser, and Sandra Lewis

These sample learning activities are presented as examples of activities that teachers can create to work on several ECC skills at once with their students. Activities that help teach compensatory access skills can also be found in other chapters. The activities presented, like all instruction, need to be considered and modified to address the needs of individual students—such as those who are braille readers, have low vision, or have additional disabilities—with adaptations for appropriate media and the physical and other capabilities of the student.

Learning Activity: Where Do I Belong?
Primary ECC Area: Compensatory access **Components:** Concept development, spatial understanding **Grades:** Pre-K–5, students with multiple disabilities
Other ECC Areas ■ Career education ■ Independent living ■ Self-determination ■ Orientation and mobility
Goal: Given a random collection of everyday items, the student will identify the use of each one and return it to where it belongs.
Key Tasks/Concepts The student will: ■ Use problem-solving and critical thinking skills to identify an object out of context and figure out where it belongs. ■ Increase knowledge of everyday objects used for common tasks and activities. ■ Increase spatial awareness by searching for storage locations and putting items away.
Description It is not uncommon for a child who is blind or has low vision to be able to name and describe the function of common objects, but not know how to use them. This reverse scavenger hunt activity will teach and reinforce students' knowledge of typical, everyday items and their functions. In a kitchen, teachers' lounge, resource room, or school classroom, the teacher collects a variety of objects that have a definite place. For example, in a teachers' lounge, the teacher can collect items such as a mug, a pot holder, utensils, a plate, plastic sandwich bags, a napkin, salt and pepper shakers, and place them in a storage container. The students then name each object and explain what it is used for, then put each item back in its correct location within the room. An eating utensil has to be put away in the proper place in the silverware divider inside the proper drawer; placing it on the counter or leaving it on the table doesn't meet the criteria for completing the task. Students may be able to name an item, but not know where it belongs, especially if they are used to the "fairy godmother" (an adult completing the task without involving the student) magically placing items back in their proper locations. With this activity, students will need to decide what each item is used for and determine a logical place where a given item would be kept or stored. If an item of food is used, students need to determine if it should be stored in a cupboard, refrigerator, or freezer.

(continued on next page)

To increase the difficulty of the activity, the teacher can identify a reference point such as the refrigerator, before beginning and have students explain where the item is stored based on its relation to the refrigerator. Example: "I put the spoon in the second drawer to the right of the refrigerator."

This activity can be done in a variety of settings, such as the housekeeping area of a pre-kindergarten or kindergarten class, where the reference point can be "From my chair . . ." or "From the circle area . . ." The activity can be repeated in different settings to focus on office supplies, toys, classroom supplies, and so forth.

To expand this activity to community-based instruction in a grocery store, the teacher can collect items such as peanut butter, jelly, bread, plastic utensils, paper plates, napkins, milk, and orange juice in a shopping cart or basket and have students find the correct aisles to return them to their place in the store. Some students may not realize that like items are found together or that the ends of aisles are labeled. Students can use critical thinking skills to make educated guesses as to where certain items are displayed, as well as practice previously learned skills related to orientation within the store. Students with low vision can use a monocular telescope to read the aisle numbers and signage. As appropriate to each student, the teacher may limit the supplies to be returned to shelves to one small (but expanding) area or an area to which the student has previously been oriented.

Instructional Materials and Supplies Needed

- A storage container
- 5–10 everyday objects, depending on age and ability of student

Settings

School, general or special education classroom, teachers' lounge, media center, home, community

Duration/Timing

- 5–10 minutes to collect items
- 20–30 minutes to complete activity if on school campus (allow more time if in the community)

Evaluation

Student progress can be monitored with a chart to track how many items were identified and put away properly, as in the following example:

Task	Date	Date	Date
1a. Identify ice cream scoop			
b. Describe purpose and uses			
c. Store in drawer and silverware tray			
2a. Identify pot holder			
b. Describe purpose and uses			
c. Store in drawer under microwave			

Key:
I = Independent
V = Verbal direction
P = Physical support

Learning Activity: Abacus Counts

Primary ECC Area: Compensatory access **Component:** Use of specialized educational materials
Grades: 2–6

Other ECC Areas

- Social interaction
- Self-determination
- Recreation and leisure

Goal: The student will increase proficiency in adding and subtracting on the abacus.

Key Tasks/Concepts

The student will:

- Practice correct terminology associated with the abacus.
- Improve basic computation on the abacus using addition and subtraction.
- Practice listening for auditory clues and turn-taking.
- Identify alternate decisions and analyze consequences.

Description

Students with visual impairments are often told what to do, when to do it, and how to do it. Consequently, they do not have a lot of opportunities to think on their own. This activity requires that students identify possible decisions, analyze the consequences of those decisions, and make independent decisions. Through playing the game, basic addition and subtraction computation skills will be improved.

At least two players are needed; there is no limit to the number of students who can play. The teacher or other students who are visually impaired can use abacuses to play, or a student with unimpaired vision can use pencil and paper to play.

1. Before play begins, the players select a number (1–6) to be the "clear" number, and choose a total that will be considered the winning number. The winning number can be as high as 100, 250, or 1,000, or as low as 15 or 20, depending on the time available and the players' abilities. The higher the winning number, the longer the game will take to complete.
2. Players take turns rolling one accessible six-sided die.
3. As each player rolls a number, he or she sets that number on his or her abacus.
4. If a player rolls the "clear" number, then that player's abacus must be cleared and the die passed to the next player to roll.
5. When a player rolls a number that is not the "clear" number, that number is set on that player's abacus. Now a decision must be made. The player can keep the number and pass the die to the next player, or roll again and add the new number to the abacus.
6. Whoever reaches the winning number first, wins.

When students are first learning the game, it is best to select a low winning number, such as 20, to maintain the players' attention span and allow the game to come to a definite end. As the students' understanding of the game increases, less instruction will be needed throughout and a higher winning number can be selected.

This activity can be extended to work on subtraction skills. In this case, a starting number of 20, 50 or 100 should be selected. Each time a player rolls, the number on the die will be subtracted from the starting number. The "clear" number now becomes a "set" number, and the player who rolls it must reset the abacus to the number shown at the start of his or her turn.

Players are required to pay attention to the announcement of each number on the die, as well as their opponents' running totals. Knowing how far ahead or behind opponents are can be a factor in whether a player should roll again or pass the die. If more than two people are playing, each also needs to pay attention to whose turn it is.

(continued on next page)

This game can be used as a reward at the end of a lesson or class. As a student learns the game, classmates can be invited to play for longer durations. Eventually, the student can teach classmates how to play, and the game can be used during game time in the general education classroom.

Instructional Materials and Supplies Needed

- Cranmer abacus
- Accessible dice

Settings

School, home, after school program

Duration/Timing

- 10–60 minutes. This activity can be introduced with just the teacher and a single student spending as little as 10 minutes at a time, with the duration and number of players increasing as the student masters the skills involved.

Evaluation

The teacher can observe a student's participation in the game and evaluate both understanding of the game and use of the abacus. Charts such as those following can be used to monitor a student's progress.

Understanding of Game

Skill	1st Turn	2nd Turn	3rd Turn	4th Turn
1. Rolls die				
2. Sets first number or passes die				
3. Makes decision to roll again or pass die				
4. Adds new number to existing number on abacus				
5. Makes decision to roll again or pass die				
6. Adds new number to existing number on abacus				

Key:
I = Independent
V = Verbal support
P = Physical support

Use of Abacus

Skill	Date	Date	Date	Date
1. Places abacus on flat surface				
2. Uses left index finger as the "helper finger" to find the correct place value column (one column to the left of the number to be set)				
3. Sets correct beads in corresponding place value column				
4. Adds (sets) new numbers accurately to existing number in corresponding place value column				
5. Clears all beads on abacus to bring score back to 0				
6. Verbalizes steps using correct terminology (set, clear, units column, tens column, hundreds column, 1-bead, 5-bead)				

Record how many times during each game the student performs each skill correctly. For example, if a student performs a skill correctly 6 times out of 10 rounds of the game, the progress would be noted as 6/10.

Learning Activity: Creating an "I Can" Book

Primary ECC Area: Compensatory access **Component:** Organizational skills
Grades: 3–12

Other ECC Areas
- Self-determination
- Career education

Goal: The student will increase self-awareness of his or her abilities and use this information to set personal goals.

Key Tasks/Concepts
The student will:
- Create a list of tasks or skills that he or she is able to do.
- Evaluate how frequently and how well he or she does those skills.
- Review these skills over time and add new ones.
- Set goals for improvement.

Description
Students with visual impairments often are told what they cannot do, but do not always have a good sense of what skills they have learned to accomplish. Maintaining a list of accomplishments provides students with a framework for knowing their abilities, soliciting realistic feedback, and setting goals.

The activity starts with students making a list of accomplished tasks or skills. (Depending on the age of the students, the teacher may need to help with list generation, writing, and spelling.) The teacher has the students rate those activities with regard to (a) how frequently they engage in the task and (b) how well they accomplish it.

The list should be reviewed regularly, at least monthly, but preferably more often. Students can identify how performance has changed over the time period and note any relationships among those changes and the frequency with which they perform the task. As new skills and tasks are mastered, they can be added to the list.

This activity can be extended by soliciting the feedback of others to determine if the students' perceptions of their skills are accurate.

Further, this activity can be used to help students identify areas in which they might want to improve. The teachers can assist students with setting goals and developing strategies for making these desired improvements.

Instructional Materials and Supplies Needed
- Writing tools (braillewriter, pen, pencil, slate, stylus, or notetaker)
- Paper
- Notebook

Settings
School, extending to home as appropriate

Duration/Timing
- 8–20 minutes. This activity can be introduced over a period of several days. Discussions can be accomplished during shorter periods of perhaps 8–10 minutes.
- Once the "I Can" book has been created, the review of accomplishments, personal evaluation, and goal setting can be scheduled regularly and will usually require no more than 15–20 minutes.

Evaluation
Evaluation can be through written or oral testing and by observing and recording student's behavior each time the "I Can" book is reviewed.
- Did the student identify a minimum of five areas of accomplishment?
- Did the student solicit realistic feedback on performance from others?
- Did the student identify one area in which improvement is desired?
- Did the student develop a strategy for improving?

Learning Activity: Surveying Favorites

Primary ECC Area: Compensatory skills
Grades: 5–9

Components: Communication modes, speaking and listening skills

Other ECC Areas

- Social skills
- Recreation and leisure
- Assistive technology
- Self-determination

Goal: The student will conduct surveys of classmates about their likes and dislikes on a variety of topics and create a graph that depicts the results.

Key Tasks/Concepts

The student will:

- Choose a topic on which to conduct a survey.
- Determine a method to tally responses.
- Conduct the survey with classmates and keep a tally of the results.
- Add up the tallies and graph the results.
- Use a computer or notetaker to record and produce results.
- Express personal preferences.

Description

For conducting a survey of classmates on their likes and dislikes, the teacher has students choose a topic (such as types of food, pets, or sports), list appropriate choices within that topic, determine a method to tally the responses, figure out a good time to approach classmates, and utilize social skills in talking to the other students. Students can practice each of these key tasks by picking a topic to ask two or three people (classmates or others) about. After practicing the key tasks with two or three people, students can then conduct a survey of their choosing, by questioning at least 15 other classmates or others in the school community.

After tallying the responses, the teacher has the students produce a graph of the results on graph paper. To encompass additional skills, students can produce brief reports composed using a computer or notetaker, which can then be presented to the class. The teacher can take the opportunity to have a discussion with the students about the varied likes and dislikes people have, and to question students about their personal favorites. The discussion can lead to an ongoing conversation that encourages students to make good choices and advocate for their preferences.

Instructional Materials and Supplies Needed

- Graphing paper or other tallying method
- Computer or notetaking device

Settings

Classrooms and other school areas

Duration/Timing

- One week. After practicing the tasks, students should be given a week to complete the survey and prepare their results. Different surveys can be conducted at different times of the year.

Evaluation

To evaluate a student's performance on the stated goal, the accuracy of the final product (graph) in depicting the preferences of peers on a variety of topics would have to be measured. If this activity is repeated with a variety of topics, the work over time could be evaluated as suggested below:

(continued on next page)

Task	Date Sports	Date Foods	Date Pets	Date Fruits
Labels X axis				
Labels Y axis				
Tallies accurately represented on graph				
Highlights personal preference				
Constructs neat and legible graph				

A more socially oriented evaluation of the results of this activity might involve the teacher (or parent) maintaining a record of the number of times that the student expresses in conversation:

1. His or her own likes and dislikes
2. The likes and dislikes of peers
3. A recognition that not everyone has the same favorites
4. Information about other students in the class

The teacher might also assess the level of proficiency with each task, in order to determine if further instruction is needed in any of the areas for a given student. Students can be evaluated on the process (the teacher would have to observe the students doing the questioning and preparing the results) or the end product (just looking at the results and how they were presented).

Learning Activity: Signature Required

Primary ECC Area: Compensatory access
Grades: 3–8

Components: Use of specialized educational materials, communication modes

Other ECC Areas

- Career education
- Independent living
- Self-determination

Goal: The student will use a signature-writing guide to practice signing legal documents or important papers.

Key Tasks/Concepts

The student will:

- Request assistance to line up a signature guide when needed.
- Line up a signature guide on the back of a check on his own.
- Create a signature small enough to fit in a signature guide.

Description

Learning to write a signature can be much more motivating to students when money is involved! So that students do not become fatigued or disinterested in writing a signature over and over again during rote practice, once they have learned the basic skill, a simulated bank can be used as part of an activity that may hold more interest and meaning.

The teacher starts the activity by developing a contract with the students. The contract can be for displaying appropriate behavior, being prepared, completing "chores" at school, or any other behavior or skill the teacher would like the students to improve. Each student will be "paid" with a check on a bi-monthly basis to simulate earning a paycheck from a job. Each student needs to sign in at the start of every lesson and keep

(continued on next page)

track of hours "worked" when with the teacher. Each student will also need to sign and submit a timesheet at the end of every week. On payday, each student receives a practice check, either regular or with raised lines, and needs to sign the back in order to deposit it to the "First Bank of Vision." Older students can keep track of the checks using a check register on a computer, in print, or in large print.

Requesting assistance to write a signature is an important self-advocacy skill. This activity allows the student to practice writing his or her signature while soliciting assistance, when needed, to use a signature guide with regular paper.

Hint: A sticky note or other straight edge can be used as a guide instead of a formal signature guide.

Instructional Materials and Supplies Needed

- Signature writing guide, sticky notes, or other straight edge to use as a guide
- Time card or timesheet
- Sign-in sheet
- Practice checks or raised-line checks
- Practice check register on computer, in print, or in large print

Settings

School or community

Duration/Timing

- 30–45 minutes initially to set up the contract, job duties, and practice signature writing
- 1 minute daily to sign in
- 5 minutes weekly to endorse a check or sign a timesheet

Evaluation

A student's progress can be monitored by keeping a notebook of signed timesheets, endorsed checks, and the sign-in sheet. The teacher can review these materials for accuracy of the signature. Errors or issues with a student's signature should be addressed as soon as possible to avoid the forming of incorrect muscle memory.

CHAPTER 5

Sensory Efficiency

Mildred Smith

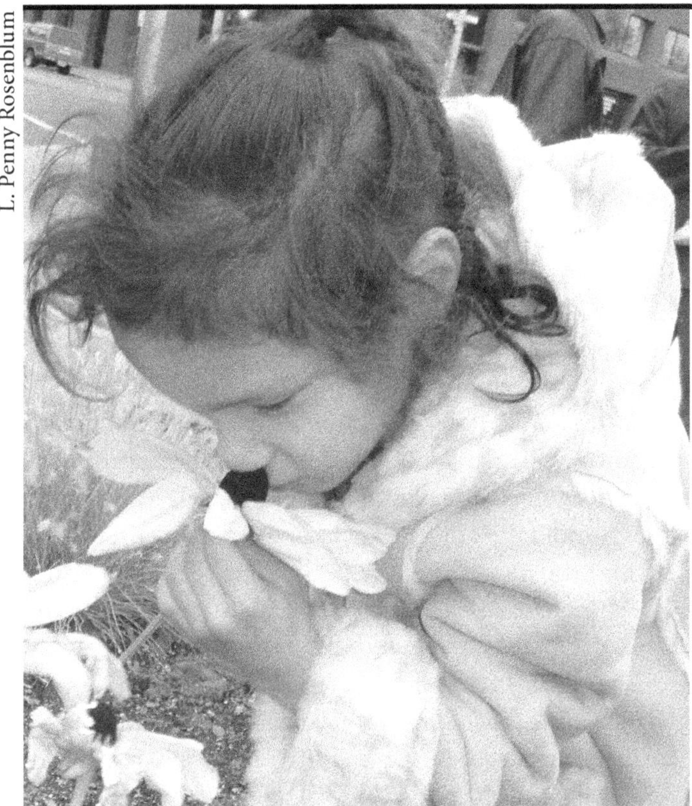
L. Penny Rosenblum

Efficient use of all sensory systems, not just the sense of sight, is essential to the development of students with visual impairments. For this reason, in 2009, sensory efficiency became the new name of the expanded core curriculum (ECC) area previously called visual efficiency (Lohmeier, Blankenship, & Hatlen, 2009). Thus, the consideration of sensory efficiency now refers to how well an individual receives, transmits, and interprets information about people, objects, and events in the environment, using all sensory systems.

Sensory efficiency involves acquiring and mastering skills that contribute to the most effective use of sensory systems for obtaining information. The ability to understand and make sense of what is seen, heard, touched, smelled, and tasted and to react appropriately to that information, is the foundation for development and learning (Langley, 2004). Development of skills in all other areas of the ECC is dependent on the efficient use of sensory information. For these reasons, working with students to help them use their senses to gather information efficiently is a critical focus for teachers of students with visual impairments. Any one of a student's sensory systems can be impaired in a way that causes the system to function less efficiently, thus compromising the quality of the information gathered. When one sensory system is impaired, the efficiency of other systems becomes even more important.

The complexity of the topic of sensory efficiency—especially given the extent of the additional disabilities experienced by many children with visual impairments—calls for a broad understanding of sensory skill development, and a significant portion of this chapter is therefore devoted to this topic. Information is presented here on sensory efficiency for students of all ages and abilities. Describing the critical components of the early development of sensory skills is also a major focus in this chapter because most sensory skills are mastered in the first two years of life, and teachers of students with visual impairments can play a major supporting role in this process. Much of the discussion of early development relates to the needs of infants and toddlers with visual impairments and to the continuing needs of students who have visual impairments and significant multiple disabilities. Subsequent sections of this chapter include discussions of the sensory efficiency needs of students at preschool and academic levels of development, to provide readers with information and resources to foster their knowledge of this critical area. Because of the many varied aspects of sensory efficiency in relation to a diverse student population, the structure of this chapter differs from that of other chapters in Part 2 of the book.

SENSORY SYSTEMS AND DEVELOPMENT

Human beings are equipped with seven sensory systems. The five systems that provide information about the world outside the body are vision, hearing (the auditory system), touch (the tactile system), taste (the gustatory system), and smell (the olfactory system). In addition, there are two internal senses that provide information about the movement, position, and stabilization of the body. These are the proprioceptive and vestibular systems (Bundy, Lane, & Murray, 2002). The proprioceptive sense conveys information about position and movement of parts of the body. The vestibular sense detects changes in the direction of gravitational pull and influences balance, movement, and posture.

Each sensory system is unique and is designed to react to features outside the body (the environment) or inside the body. For example, vision reacts to light rays, touch to pressure and temperature, and proprioception to the expansion and contraction of muscles. If the information received by the senses is perceived to be meaningful and important, it is stored and becomes part of the knowledge that creates understanding (Kolb & Whishaw, 2009).

Importance of Sensory Efficiency

During the first year of life, the weight of the brain doubles in size in typically developing children as a result of the proliferation of neural networks established as sensory information is processed during interactions with people and objects in the environment. Billions of sensory experiences like these are required for this growth (Smith Roley, Blanche, & Schaaf, 2001). As brains grow, cognitive skills develop. Without appropriate interventions, the cognitive development of young children with visual impairments, and especially those with additional impairments, is highly at risk because sources of stimulation that would be available to children without disabilities are less available to them (Barraga & Erin, 2001). As a result, children with sensory disabilities could have far fewer sensory experiences than the billions required for typical cognitive development. Therefore, creating access to sensory information during the early development of children who have visual impairments is essential. Cognition is a process consisting of four stages (Matlin, 2008):

- acquisition of sensory information
- storage, organization, and integration of new and previous sensory experiences
- retrieval of information in response to a specific need
- use of what is retrieved according to a clear intention

Learning begins with the acquisition of sensory information. The other three steps in the cognitive process are impossible without this acquisition. For young children with typical sensory abilities, immersion in sensory-rich environments may provide access to the quantity and quality of sensory experiences sufficient for normal cognitive development. Immersion alone is not sufficient when sensory disabilities are present.

Teachers of students with visual impairments must ensure that sensory efficiency is a major consideration for students so that their developmental potentials can be fully achieved. To do that, teachers need to know how to provide students with materials and experiences that enhance their access to the world around them, while avoiding such common barriers to the use of the senses as specific sensory aversions, superfluous or overwhelming sensory complexity, or pacing of instruction that does not allow enough time for a learner with sensory processing delays to gather information efficiently (Smith, 2005). Enhancing access to the world requires that teachers understand how interest in people, objects, and actions develops in young children. All children, including those with visual impairments, progress through a hierarchy of interactions with their environments. How successful they are at understanding their worlds at each level depends on the experiences provided for them. Teachers of students with visual impairments need to carefully select learning media (materials for learning) at each level so that sensory experiences can be highly effective.

Hierarchy of Learning Media

In general, the learning media used by children develops in the following hierarchy, or levels, starting from birth (Smith, 2012):

1. Own body (passive sensory input)
2. Objects, people, and actions touching the body (early exploration of one primary object of interest at a time)
3. Objects, people, actions, and places beyond the body (exploration of things at distance)
4. Clusters of objects, people, actions, and places that are part of events beyond the body (using integrated multisensory information for understanding relationships between multiple elements)
5. Symbols for objects, people, actions, places, and events
   a. Static forms that remain present over time: objects, part objects, pictures, print, braille
   b. Dynamic forms that go away after presentation: spoken language, signed language

Infants begin life with level 1 media—their own bodies—when they learn that crying and stiffening their limbs is sometimes associated with changes that produce comfort. Later they begin to add level 2 media—objects, people, and actions touching their bodies—for example, when a baby becomes interested in a blanket associated with the warmth that produces comfort and begins to rub his fingers against its surface to explore its texture. A baby begins to anticipate that her dad is going to kiss her tummy when her shirt is lifted and that her mom is going to show her an interesting toy and let her put it in her mouth to explore orally.

Understanding the hierarchy of learning media is important because interventions for young children and students with severe multiple impairments often inappropriately start with objects beyond their bodies (level 3) before they have had sufficient experiences at levels 1 and 2. Teachers of students with visual impairments can determine the appropriate level for beginning an intervention by observing their students' interactions with objects. If a student is passive, not interacting with objects touching his or her body, intervention at the own body level should be the focus of instruction for a period of time. When objects beyond the body are ignored or rejected, either visually or manually, by a student, more work at the level of objects, people, and actions touching the body may be the key to progress.

Using Sensory Information

The use of the senses and movement for exploration are primary activities of learning at the stage of cognitive development that psychologist Jean Piaget (1950, 1954 /2013) called *sensorimotor.* This stage, from birth to approximately two years, is a time when typically developing children are intensely curious about the attributes of people and objects in the environment (Fazzi & Klein, 2002). Three questions are constantly being asked and answered by young children during this stage (Gibson, 1988): "What is it like?" "What does it do?" and "How does it relate to other things?" (These questions are also referred to as *recognition, function,* and *relativity.*) As they use sensory exploration to answer these questions, children develop the cognitive concepts and skills that lay the foundation for understanding: object permanence, imitation, causality, use of tools (means and ends), and spatial relationships (Matlin, 2008).

The use of sensory information continues to be primary as more advanced skills are learned during later stages of cognitive development described by Piaget (the *preoperational* stage, from about 2 to 7 years old, and the *operational* stage, approximately age 7 and older). In these later stages, children use language and other symbols to organize and expand knowledge, build schemas (units of information organized into patterns) that include abstract concepts, and learn rules that structure thought processes, like grammar, mathematics, and logic.

Throughout these three stages (sensorimotor, preoperational, and operational), the content of what is learned changes, but the process of learning does not. Infants who are blind learn to recognize their parents by taking in auditory, tactile, and olfactory information. A 3-year-old with a visual impairment takes in visual, vestibular, tactile, and proprioceptive information as he learns to take a drink from a brightly colored cup placed on a contrasting background. A 4-year-old with functional blindness takes in the tactile properties of a line of braille as she moves her fingers from character to character while her mother reads her a familiar story. A high school student learning to negotiate a street crossing listens carefully to the traffic flow. All learning, including that related to all the areas of the ECC, depends on efficient use of sensory systems throughout the lifetime of an individual and includes the four stages of cognition described by Matlin (2008).

COMPONENTS OF SENSORY EFFICIENCY

The behaviors, skills, and tasks to be taught in the sensory efficiency area of the ECC can be organized in terms of the five external and two internal senses:

- visual function
- auditory function
- tactile function
- gustatory (taste) function
- olfactory (smell) function
- proprioceptive function
- vestibular function

In the following sections, the visual, auditory, tactile, gustatory, and olfactory senses are discussed in terms of the skills that are critical to each of them. The internal senses of proprioceptive and vestibular function are briefly defined, but are discussed in more detail in the section on developmental progression of sensory systems at the sensorimotor stage. These two internal senses are most critical at this early stage of development and are a foundation for movement and balance that becomes important in many ECC areas.

Although the sensory systems are discussed separately, it is important to understand that perception, the result of efficient sensory function, is always multisensory (Mesulam, 2000). Information from sensory systems is integrated as it is processed. Information related to each sensory system is primarily processed and stored in a specific area in the cortex of the brain, but activity in one area stimulates activity in other areas associated with the source of the original stimulus (Mesulam, 2000). Active exploration on the part of the learner is the key factor in the development of the neurological activity that results in sensory integration. Passive sensory stimulation (input provided for the learner by someone else) tends to be primarily subcortical and unimodal (involving one sensory system only).

Visual Function

The efficiency of the function of the visual sense is always a concern when students have visual impairments, specifically behaviors relating to near and distance vision, preferred viewing areas, perceptual abilities, and processing efficiency. For students at the sensorimotor stage—very young children and students with significant cognitive disabilities—critical behaviors include ocular motor skills (fixating, tracking, shifting gaze, and scanning), discrimination skills (recognizing features such as size, shape, and color), and recognition skills (remembering an object or person previously experienced). As students develop into the preoperational and operational stages, the skills of using visual features for matching, sorting, sequencing, and categorizing; using language for identification of visual features such as color and shape; and obtaining information from pictures and text become critical to learning.

Auditory Function

The efficiency of auditory functioning can be a concern for any student with a visual impairment. Certainly, students with deaf-blindness have visual and auditory challenges, but many students who may not meet the criteria for deaf-blindness may have needs related to auditory functioning. Behaviors and skills for both near and distant hearing include:

- localization
- motion perception
- pattern discrimination (loud/soft intensity, high/low pitch, and continuous/intermittent tempo)
- speech discrimination

As a result of the ability to discriminate speech sounds, language develops and is used for abstract thinking and for building concepts and vocabulary. The discrimination of speech inflections is used for understanding emphases, sarcasm, anger, joking, boredom, and detection of truth or falsehood. Academically, auditory learning media become a major source of information for some students with severe vision loss.

Tactile Function

The importance of tactile functioning, especially for students with little usable vision, cannot be overemphasized. The behaviors and skills related to the use of the sense of touch allow students to discriminate characteristics of objects, including temperature, texture, density, weight, volume, and shape. The critical information provided by the sense of touch encourages students to explore their environments and learn important skills, such as recognizing objects based on tactile characteristics and generalizing characteristics of objects for comparison and categorization. Using the sense of touch for exploration serves to encourage the development of fine motor skills used for manipulation and operation of objects. Eventually, the refinement of tactile function allows for the learning of braille.

Virtually all students with visual impairments depend on some aspect of tactile functioning to understand their environments. For example, students with some usable vision are taught to verify characteristics of objects by supplementing visual function with touch. Tactile functioning lays an important foundation for the learning of many other skills in the other ECC areas. For example, children will use tactile functioning in the compensatory access area, particularly if they have little usable vision. Appropriate touch becomes important in social skill development and is also demonstrated in the orientation and mobility (O&M) area when recognition of changes of surface from carpet to tile, for example, is needed for direction.

Gustatory and Olfactory Functions

The gustatory and olfactory functions, or taste and smell, are closely related and include behaviors and skills that provide important information about environments. For example, the recognition of common smells, such as freshly laid asphalt, car exhaust, food at a street fair, and freshly cut grass, can greatly assist a student learning mobility skills in an unfamiliar environment. In school, a student can locate the cafeteria using the sense of smell and good mobility skills. At home, a child can detect where people are and what they are doing when he smells furniture polish, washing detergent, or food cooking.

The sense of taste, likewise, provides important information about foods and liquids. Distinguishing sweet, sour, salty, and bitter are skills that children use from birth to form food preferences. The tactile sense also contributes to food preferences. Children often develop either an aversion or an attraction to a certain foods based on taste and/or texture. Teaching children that tasting some things, such as cleaning products, is dangerous is important. The use of taste for exploring objects should be monitored carefully in young children and students with severe multiple disabilities because of choking hazards.

Proprioceptive and Vestibular Functions

Proprioception is the sense that conveys information to the brain related to the perception of static position and movement of parts of the body. Historically, researchers referred to two senses related to position and movement. They were proprioception, or unconscious awareness, and kinesthesia, or conscious awareness. Later research indicated that this distinction is not functionally accurate (Matthews, 1988). Literature now suggests that both conscious and unconscious perceptions of position and movement should be considered under one sense: proprioception (Smith Roley et al., 2001).

The vestibular sense, like proprioception, is an internal sensory system. It detects changes in the direction of gravitational pull caused by motion and works with vision and proprioception to influence balance, movement, and posture.

The example of Matt, a student with low vision, (see Sidebar 5.1) illustrates how the components of sensory efficiency are utilized in the skills he is developing in his daily activities. The skills that Matt uses in this example are linked to O&M (learning a route),

Components of Sensory Efficiency in Action: Matt's School-Day Activities

The following example of the tasks in Matt's school-day activities illustrates how each of the components of sensory efficiency is involved.

Matt is a 4-year-old prekindergarten student with low vision due to retinopathy of prematurity. His distance vision is corrected to about 20/50 in his better eye, but his near vision is still uncorrected. He will begin to wear bifocals soon. In the meantime, his close-up viewing distance for detail is about 4 inches. He also has restricted peripheral fields. When he gets off the school bus, a classmate guides him to the door of his classroom using the human guide technique taught to her by Matt's orientation and mobility instructor. This method will be used until Matt learns to travel the route independently.

Matt's teacher greets him at the classroom door and tells him to get ready for class, which means he needs to do four things:

1. Get his snack bag out of his backpack and hand it to his teacher.
2. Get his folder out of his backpack and put it in the basket on the floor near the entrance to the classroom.
3. Hang his coat on the hook in his locker.
4. Put away his backpack in his locker.

VISUAL FUNCTION

Matt's primary sensory channel is vision, but efficient use of that channel is compromised by difficulty with seeing detail close up and by difficulty with locating objects outside his central field of vision. Matt's teacher of students with visual impairments needs to make sure that he can use his available vision efficiently on each step of his arrival routine. The critical visual skills to be taught to perform these tasks are localization and scanning. Matt needs to learn to:

1. Visually scan his teacher's body to find her hand.
2. Visually locate the basket.
3. Visually locate his locker and scan his jacket to find the collar before hanging it on the hook.
4. Visually locate his backpack on the hallway floor and re-locate his locker.

AUDITORY AND TACTILE FUNCTION

Matt's secondary sensory channels are hearing and touch. He knows the sources of familiar environmental sounds and his receptive language abilities are typical for his age. He appropriately combines visual and auditory information while performing tasks:

- Matt uses his teacher's voice to guide his visual search for her hand.
- Matt uses the sound of other students' folders dropping into the basket to narrow his search.

Matt's teacher of students with visual impairments has decided that he could become more efficient by using some tactile skills on certain steps, for example:

- Because it is dark inside Matt's locker, he cannot see the hook. He needs to learn to find the hook tactilely and to tactilely align his jacket collar with the hook.

Matt needs to learn that he can advocate for himself by choosing efficient sensory strategies as he performs the tasks in his arrival routine. For example, once his teacher of students with visual impairments has helped him learn to use vision to find the collar of his jacket, he can evaluate whether this is a better strategy than locating the collar tactilely. He needs to have some experience with both strategies before he can make an informed decision about which one he prefers. Matt selects which strategy to use depending on the visual characteristics of the jacket he is wearing. His rain jacket is one color inside and out and the collar does not have any visual characteristics that make it stand out. He prefers a tactile strategy when he wears this garment. Matt's denim jacket has a white fleece collar. Vision is the better strategy when he wears this jacket.

OLFACTORY AND GUSTATORY FUNCTION

Later in the morning, Matt will go to the cafeteria for lunch with his class. Matt's O&M instructor has been working with Matt to plan a route to the cafeteria using the odors from the cafeteria to help guide him. Once seated with his class, Matt will use his senses of taste and smell to identify foods served for lunch that day.

PROPRIOCEPTIVE AND VESTIBULAR FUNCTION

Matt's intentional movements during his performance of these tasks further develop the integrated use of his external senses and his internal proprioceptive and vestibular senses. Balance, posture, and agility improve as subconscious neurological processes in the internal senses combine with consciously directed interactions with the environment using the external senses.

self-determination (advocacy), independent living (dressing), and compensatory access (concept development).

DEVELOPMENTAL PROGRESSION OF SENSORY SYSTEMS

Sensorimotor Stage

In the sensorimotor stage, the first two years of life, taking in sensory information about the environment is an end in itself for a child. The primary learning behavior engaged in by infants and toddlers is sensorimotor exploration, using actions to probe the potential sensory attributes of objects (Gibson, 1988). As noted earlier, sensory exploration is the activity that fuels the development of sensorimotor cognitive skills and concepts: object permanence, imitation, causality, tool use, and spatial relationships. For example, during sensorimotor exploration, an infant might put an object in his mouth to probe attributes related to taste, such as sweetness or sourness. As he holds the object for transfer to his mouth, he might get information about tactile potentials such as density, temperature, texture, and shape. He might get information about the object's color, size, and shape as he looks at it while taking it out of his mouth. Later, he might recall this sensory information to, for example, choose one of two snack items offered by a parent.

Older students with severe cognitive disabilities are also sensorimotor learners, so they may need to begin instruction with oral exploration of objects if they are not engaging in any exploratory behaviors. This does not mean, however, that they do not have the potential to progress to higher levels of sensorimotor performance, including using object recognition for communication skills, such as choice making.

Like all other skills, sensory skills are learned behaviors, different from reflexive behaviors in that they are performed intentionally (Smith Roley et al., 2001). For example, when newborns grasp a finger placed on their palm, this is a reflex, not an intentional behavior. Infants need about four to five months of motor skill practice to develop the ability to intentionally grasp an object. Several more months will be needed to refine this skill (McLinden & McCall, 2002). This is learning. (Suggestions for working with students at the sensorimotor stage are found in the section on General Considerations for Teaching Sensory Efficiency in this chapter.)

All viable sensory systems become more efficient during the sensorimotor stage due to physiological changes in the central nervous system, but these are not learned skills. For example, the shortening of the time required to process information as the nervous system matures is an improvement in efficiency that is unrelated to learning (Eliot, 1999). Sensory skills are learned when three conditions are met. First, the learner must have an intention—a conscious desire to do something. Second, the learner must be able to access sensory information related to the task. Third, the learner must refine skills by practicing them in a variety of contexts.

Teachers of students with visual impairments sometimes think of primary and secondary sensory systems in terms of functionality. A sensory system is considered primary if it works better than others for an important task, like reading. A sensory system is considered secondary if it provides supporting information in a task, but is not the most significant source of information. However, dependence on the use of one primary sense does not work well for students at the sensorimotor stage. Exploration is the important learning behavior of this stage, and exploration is always multisensory (Bundy et al., 2002). Nevertheless, some sensory systems contribute more than others to understanding.

Primary Sensory Systems: Touch and Vision

During the sensorimotor stage, two primary sensory systems provide the quantity and quality of information necessary for building the concepts that establish a child's understanding of the world: touch and vision (Eliot, 1999). These systems are used in combination by children with and without visual impairments as information from these two primary sensory sources is integrated to assign meaning to experiences (Mesulam, 2000). For example, vision alone, even when it is unimpaired, is not sufficient for the development of perceptual skills, such as those required to perceive depth and three-dimensionality. Tactile information must be combined with vision for a period of time before these qualities can be perceived using vision alone. Instruction at this stage needs to provide experiences in which both primary systems—vision and touch—are used in combination to the maximum extent possible when objects are explored. A favorite toy presented to a child within his visual field will be noticed, but then needs to be examined tactilely to help address the questions of recognition, function, and relativity.

During the sensorimotor stage of development, the auditory channel cannot be primary because sensorimotor learners are not yet sophisticated users of language, and environmental sounds have no meaning unless their sources are seen and touched. Teachers need to remember that a sound made by a person or object provides no information about the source of the sound, and using words to describe events that are heard does not help provide meaning if the language used is not comprehended (Dunlea, 1989). Though not primary, auditory efficiency *is* important at this stage, however, because the foundation for understanding environmental sounds and language is being built.

Tactile and visual systems remain primary even when impairments to vision and touch are present. Teachers face a formidable challenge when their students at this stage have impairments in both systems, and this situation occurs with a high degree of frequency. Teachers need to provide accommodations, modifications, and supports for both systems that allow students to use them as efficiently as possible to make sense of their worlds.

Three issues in particular may adversely affect visual and tactile efficiency for children with visual impairments during the sensorimotor stage:

- inadequate time for combined visual and tactile exploration
- pervasive manipulation of the hands by others
- limited access to objects

Inadequate Time for Exploration. More time may be required for exploration by children who coordinate visual and tactile information differently, such as some children with cortical visual impairment (CVI) who may tend to look away while moving their hands toward objects. This behavior does not mean that they are not looking and touching, but that they are doing so sequentially rather than simultaneously because they cannot easily process information from two sensory systems at once. They need more time for sequential exploration and for processing the information from both senses.

Pervasive Manipulation of the Hands by Others. Some children may cry or withdraw when their hands are touched. Sometimes the term "tactilely defensive" is used to describe this condition. However, many such children are not truly tactilely defensive—which is a global tactile dysfunction (not just of the hands) that needs to be evaluated by an occupational therapist (Royeen & Lane, 1991). Rather, they are *manually avoidant*—they do not want their hands to be manipulated by another person. Manual avoidance can be well established in infancy or it may develop later. (See the section on Tactile Modeling and Hand-Under-Hand Guidance later in this chapter for a discussion of how children who are manually avoidant can be encouraged to use their hands to engage in tactile exploration.)

Lack of Access to Objects. Lack of access to objects tends to occur with children who have severe motor impairments. In children who have cerebral palsy, impaired ocular motor abilities and limited hand use may restrict visual and tactile exploratory behaviors. Some of these children also may be unable to move their bodies to access objects. As a result, without intervention, the quantity and quality of visual and tactile experiences may be severely compromised for them. (Strategies to overcome barriers to sensory efficiency like these are discussed later in this chapter.).

Key Points for Use of Primary Sensory Systems

The following section lists key points for early interventionists and teachers of students with visual impairments to consider when working to develop tactile and visual skills with infants and toddlers throughout the sensorimotor stage of development. To provide a summary of typical sensory development at this stage (birth to 2 years old), Table 5.1 outlines the hierarchical development of skills in the primary senses, touch and vision, and the most significant secondary system, hearing.

Birth to 4 Months.

- At this age, comfort levels must be monitored. An infant who feels hungry, tired, anxious, or uncomfortable cannot pay attention to characteristics of objects or use the senses to obtain information.
- The most significant sensory system for all infants from birth through 4 months, whether they have visual impairments or not, is touch. At birth, the neurological development of touch, taste, and smell—the senses related to feeding—is more advanced than that of the other senses (Eliot, 1999). For the next four months, touch gives more detailed information about objects than any other sensory system.

TABLE 5.1

Hierarchical Development of Touch, Vision, and Hearing Skills, from Birth to 2 Years

Touch	*Vision*	*Hearing*
Birth to 4 months	**Birth to 4 months**	**Birth to 4 months**
Uses tongue for information about texture and density	Blinks to light	Differentiates and prefers mother's voice
Detects temperatures and shapes orally	Fixates and briefly follows horizontally	Startles to loud sounds
Clutches objects reflexively, possibly transferring to mouth	Orients to single target	Pays growing attention to soft sounds
Opens and closes fingers in kneading pattern	Sees patterns of light and dark Attends to forms of things explored orally Attends to faces and objects at 2.5 feet Has weak color discrimination Shows interest in complicated patterns in surroundings Smiles when smiled at Tracks horizontally to midline and vertically Recognizes familiar faces based on hairline contours Attends to actions of others Perceives three-dimensional shapes Discriminates red-green Prefers novelty Improved acuities and fields allow exploration of immediate environment Shifts gaze from target to target Tracks past midline Recognizes faces based on internal feature detail	Makes sounds to communicate needs Ignores sounds that are not meaningful Detects absence of expected sounds Prefers human voices Recognizes voices of primary caregivers Stops crying to listen Plays with noise-making toys
4 to 9 months	**4 to 9 months**	**4 to 9 months**
Displays repetitive finger and hand movements: scratching, rubbing, waving, banging, squeezing, poking	Recognizes familiar objects	Begins searching for some sound sources
Transfers objects from hand to hand	Discriminates color at adult levels	Has differentiated responses to different tones
Uses one hand for exploration, the other for stabilization	Looks at objects held in hand during mouthing	Cries if voice heard doesn't match face seen
Perceives texture, density, weight, temperature, size	Observes toys falling and rolling away Tracks diagonally across midline Watches own hands Recognizes distant objects Recognizes partially hidden objects Responds to variety of facial expressions Exhibits interest in pictures	Attends to and responds to vocal affect Enjoys being sung to Likes reciprocal vocal play
9 to 10 months	**9 to 12 months**	**9 to 13 months**
Uses two hands	Avoids obstacles in path	Labels sounds
Explores two objects in coordinated fashion	Imitates actions of others	Sings

(continued on next page)

TABLE 5.1 *continued*

Touch	***Vision***	***Hearing***
9 TO 10 MONTHS	**9 TO 12 MONTHS**	**9 TO 13 MONTHS**
Perceives shape manually	Follows pointing finger Locates object against cluttered background Recognizes self in mirror	Responds to requests Produces first words Localizes sounds in any plane Recalls critical elements of utterances
	12 TO 24 MONTHS	
	Identifies elements in pictured scenes	

SOURCES: E. W. Bushnell & P. Boudreau, "Motor Development and the Mind: The Potential Role of Motor Abilities as a Determinant of Aspect of Perceptual Development," *Child Development,* 64 (1993), pp. 1005–1021; K. A. Ferrell, "Visual Development," in A. L. Corn & J. N. Erin, Eds., *Foundations of Low Vision: Clinical and Functional Perspectives*, 2nd ed. (New York: AFB Press, 2010), pp. 299–338; J. Northern and M. Downs, *Hearing in Children* (Baltimore, MD: Williams & Wilkins, 2002).

- Vision is generally used to find and follow moving objects. Visual alerting—detecting a change in the visual field—arouses curiosity and a desire to get more detailed information by touching (Gibson, 1988).
- Faces are a favorite visual target, and speaking faces are preferred over silent faces, perhaps because they move more, but also because vision and hearing seem to be neurologically connected in a way that coordinates information from the two systems (Kuhl, Williams, & Meltzoff, 1991).
- Sensorimotor exploration is primarily oral. The mouth remains the preferred organ for tactile exploration throughout the first year of life and is still used significantly throughout the second year. Oral exploration, movements of the tongue and lips, may be used intentionally for the purpose of gathering tactile information about an object (Rochat, 1989).
- Stimulation imposed on a child without careful attention to the child's state of arousal (level of alertness, discussed later in this chapter) and emotional tone (positive or negative reactions to stimulation), as evidenced by muscle tone, facial expressions, vocalizations, and movements, can result in sensory avoidance (Bundy et al., 2002; Langley, 1998).
- Exploration should be facilitated during social routines, not in isolation. A smiling face saying playfully, "I'm gonna get you!" just before a kiss; objects used during feeding, dressing, and bathing; and toys that are part of a look-and-touch peek-a-boo game are recommended media for learning.
- Children's self-initiated exploration of their own feet and hands starts very early, but objects are not very interesting in the first three months of life unless they are related to food or soothing touch. Starting at about three months, toys become more interesting. At this time, teachers can begin using visual presentation of brightly colored and light-reflecting objects with different textures and shapes to arouse a child's curiosity.
- Basic visual skills of localization, fixation, tracking, shifting gaze, and scanning begin to be developed during this time and need reinforcement and intervention for infants with visual impairments (Lueck, 2004b). For example, an infant may need a screen that reduces background complexity to be able to fixate on her mother's face. Another infant may be able to shift his gaze from the toy held by his father in one hand to the toy held in the other hand only after the toy is moved slightly in his peripheral visual field. Trief and Shaw (2009) provide activities for developing these skills.

INFANTS AGES 4 TO 9 MONTHS.

- The primary sensory systems for children in this age range are touch and vision used in coordination (Gibson, 1988).
- The quantity and quality of information gathered by infants improves dramatically during this time, as exploratory procedures carried out with the hands get more refined and visual skills improve so that close visual inspection of objects held in the hand is possible. Perceptual skills emerge as coordinated exploratory patterns

SIDEBAR 5.2

Steps in the Exploratory Pattern of Infants

Infants approximately 5 to 8 months old will explore unfamiliar objects in the environment using a combination of vision and touch following a specific pattern of steps:

1. Visually scan environment
2. Fixate on attractive target
3. Reach for and grasp target
4. Move hand to face
5. Look at object held in hand
6. Put object in mouth
7. Explore object with tongue and lips
8. Remove object from mouth and look again
9. Look while rotating object
10. Put object back in mouth
11. Repeat several times

SIDEBAR 5.3

Procedures for Tactile Exploration

The following six procedures are used by people throughout their lives to explore objects and gather tactile information. These procedures may need to be explicitly taught to some students with visual impairments.

- *lateral motion:* movement of the fingers over a surface to obtain information about texture
- *pressure*: pressing a surface to obtain information about density
- *static contact*: touching a surface without movement to obtain information about temperature
- *unsupported holding*: lifting and holding an object to obtain information about weight
- *enclosure*: grasping an object between the hands to obtain information about global shape
- *contour following*: moving a finger or fingers around the edges of an object to obtain information about exact shape.

SOURCE: R. Klatzky and S. Lederman, "Object Recognition by Touch," in J. J. Riser, D. H. Ashmead, F. F. Ebner, and A. L. Corn (Eds.), *Blindness and Brain Plasticity in Navigation and Object Perception* (New York: Lawrence Erlbaum Associates, 2008), pp. 185–207.

integrate information from visual and tactile systems (Mesulam, 2000).

- When an object is unfamiliar, infants combine vision and touch in an exploratory pattern consisting of the specific steps detailed in Sidebar 5.2.
- The hands gradually become more important tools for gathering information about objects. If use of the hands does not increase, or if infants cry or withdraw when their hands are touched, teachers of students with visual impairments must make sure that strategies to facilitate touch (discussed later in this chapter) are put in place immediately (Chen & Downing, 2006; McLinden & McCall, 2002; Smith, 2012). (For information about referral for evaluation of tactile defensiveness, see the discussion of the learning media assessment in the Assessment section of this chapter.)
- Infants at this stage use different kinds of tactile exploration based on the kind of information they are seeking (Ruff, Saltarelli, Capozzoli, & Dubiner, 1992). Descriptions of the tactile exploration strategies used by children at this stage of development can be found in Sidebar 5.3. When a familiar object changes in only one respect, children use more specific exploration strategies. For example, when texture changes, they do more rubbing with their fingers (lateral motion).
- When touch is not paired with an infant's visual response, the visual responses lose their intensity as a component of the infant's effort to interact with and learn about his or her world. Passivity may result. Once the infant fixes on and tracks an object, the infant should also touch it (see the exploratory steps described in Sidebar 5.2; for more information and illustrations of the procedure in Sidebar 5.2, see McLinden & McCall, 2002; Chen & Downing, 2006; Smith, 2012).

Infants and Toddlers Ages 9 to 24 Months.

- Coordinated touch and vision remain primary during these months, but vision and touch develop unique, separate functions. The hands are still used for exploring the tactile characteristics of objects, like temperature, weight, density, texture, shape, and contour, but they are much more important now as tools for making things happen. Vision takes on new functions as well: watching and imitating what other people do with objects and identifying two-dimensional representations of familiar people and objects (simple single-object pictures). (See Kitchel, 2008; Roman-Lantzy, 2010, for adapted materials for learning to use pictures.)

- The hands and eyes become more efficient tools for gathering information as visual acuities and motor skills improve.
- Mobility expands the sphere of exploration from items found in close proximity to the body to objects found anywhere the body can go (Gibson, 1988).
- Places become important as children discover that the location of objects tells them something about how the objects are used and how they relate to other things in the same place: pots and pans are kitchen things, toothbrushes and toothpaste tubes are bathroom things, and so on. Objects need to be explored where they are typically located or used, rather than in artificial or adapted environments.

Modeling teaches the appropriate use of objects. When vision cannot be used for imitation, tactile modeling (demonstrating an activity by having the student feel the modeler's hands and the objects involved) and hand-under-hand guidance (in which the adult's hands are underneath those of the student) become important instructional strategies (see McLinden & McCall, 2002; Chen & Downing, 2006; and the section Tactile Modeling and Hand-Under-Hand Guidance later in this chapter).

Secondary Sensory Systems

The information acquired by the two primary senses, vision and touch, is supported and expanded by use of five secondary systems. Three of these are external senses—hearing, smell, and taste—that provide information about objects and people. Two are internal senses—vestibular and proprioceptive—that provide information about the position and alignment of the body.

Given the multisensory nature of exploration, it is important for teachers of students with visual impairments to understand the unique contributions of additional sensory systems to exploration and acquisition of information, as well as some of the challenges presented by the use of each.

Contributions of Hearing. Hearing is the most important secondary sensory system at the sensorimotor stage. During early infancy, because viewing at a distance is limited by the baby's poor visual acuity, awareness of things beyond the body is primarily olfactory and auditory (Eliot, 1999).

At birth, infants are generally unresponsive to quiet sounds, but they already differentiate their mothers' voices from other voices. From birth to 4 months, the auditory system improves rapidly. At 1 month, infants respond to loud noise by crying or startling. Discrimination of sounds at low frequencies is better than that for sounds at high frequencies. By 2 months, infants respond to approaching sounds and human voices by quieting. By 4 months, they pay attention to voice tone and begin to combine visual and auditory information by turning their eyes toward some sound sources. The process of learning to visually locate the sources of sounds is not fully developed until the age of about 13 months, when sound sources can be located in all positions relative to the head. At the end of the first year, the child can associate a sequence of sounds with specific events (Northern & Downs, 2002). Sounds can then be used as a bridge to gather information at a distance. For example, after many experiences in which the two events are paired, an infant hearing a parent's activities with the microwave in the kitchen can anticipate that he will soon be fed (Smith, 2012).

One of the characteristics that distinguishes human babies from animals of other species is that, from birth, they seem to be neurologically predisposed to pay special attention to speech sounds. Children in the sensorimotor stage work hard to derive meaning from speech sounds. Hearing these sounds is vitally important; it helps them identify people, predict their social availability, encode the rhythms and structure of language, develop phonemic discrimination, and, eventually, understand the meaning of words (Northern & Downs, 2002).

When vision and hearing are impaired (deaf-blindness), children in the sensorimotor stage of development have limited access to sensory information beyond their bodies. Their knowledge of their world is essentially based on what they can touch, smell, and taste. Children who cannot hear environmental sounds do not alert to sounds made by objects, people, or other creatures in their vicinity, which, in turn, affects the visual channel because hearing and looking are neurologically coordinated in infants (Mesulam, 2000). Children who are deaf-blind also cannot anticipate familiar events if they do not hear the sounds associated with them at a distance. If they can hear environmental sounds but not speech sounds, they cannot build the linguistic foundation for thinking and communicating that become the keys to progress at the preoperational and operational stages of cognitive development.

Contributions of Smell. The sense of smell is well developed at birth. It can help create understanding of the world or it can impede that understanding. In infants, certain smells support nutrition by stimulating appetite. Smells associated with people are an important element in early bonding. Smell has a very strong, and sometimes overwhelming, effect on the central nervous system. Certain behaviors related to appetite, sexuality, and aggression are affected by smells (Mesulam, 2000).

Teachers of students with visual impairments at this stage need to be very aware of the influence of smells in the environment and in association with specific people and objects. Smells can capture a child's attention, and when they do, access to sensory information from other sensory systems capable of providing more useful information can be compromised. Ambient odors in the environment should be avoided or suppressed as much as possible so that more discrete odors associated with people and objects can be used for information. Strong smells, such as perfume, aftershave, or scented lotions, are aversive for some children. People, foods, and objects may be rejected quickly and emphatically if their smells are perceived to be unpleasant.

Smell also powerfully triggers memory. Letting a child smell an object associated with an activity is a highly effective way to let her know that a familiar activity is about to start. For example, the odor of toothpaste can be an effective way of communicating to a child that a tooth brushing activity is about to take place.

Random, repeated exposures to strong smells should be avoided, however. This technique can sometimes be seen in activities in which students who have minimal responses to sensory input are exposed to a random array of smells, like vanilla and cinnamon, one after the other in an effort to elicit a response. The use of smells as a tool to alert a child should always lead to engagement in an exploratory activity with the object associated with the smell that brought the child to alertness. For example, if the scent of vanilla is perceived to be pleasant, vanilla scented lotion should be used to alert the child and to communicate to him that his lotion routine is about to start.

Children who have breathing tubes do not inhale through their noses. As a result, they have an absent, or at least much diminished, sense of smell. With these children, smells cannot be used for cueing or for facilitating alertness.

Contributions of Taste. The sense of taste is also well developed at birth. Infants detect four flavors: sweet, sour, bitter, and salty. They prefer sweet tastes and are relatively indifferent to salty ones. Taste strongly affects the entire central nervous system and produces strong feelings of pleasure and displeasure.

Teachers can take advantage of the pleasure produced during taste experiences by using food to motivate participation in instructional activities. When oral exploration is the primary activity of the infant, preferred tastes can be used to facilitate oral exploration. In one study, 3-month-old infants were shown to engage in increased oral exploratory behavior when an object was dipped in fruit juice (Gibson, 1988). When children do not eat by mouth, taste should not be used to encourage oral exploration without medical and parental approval.

During the finger-feeding phase of development, the time during which children pick up bits of food with their fingers and put them into their mouths, motivation to obtain desired foods can be used by teachers to expand exploration to containers, like boxes, jars, bowls, and bags, that hold favorite foods. Later, objects like spoons and dishes that are part of eating routines can be targeted for exploration. Eventually, eating and food preparation can provide an effective context for practicing imitation of actions with objects. For example, a child who is curious about the sound made as his mother uses a whisk to stir ingredients in a metal bowl might reach out to feel her hands to find out what she is doing and then participate in stirring as his mother provides hand-under-hand guidance.

Food should be used for instruction when eating would occur naturally for nutritional purposes. Young children eat frequently. Food should not be used as an external reward for desired behavior in activities that have nothing to do with eating.

Contributions of Proprioception. Proprioception is the basis for the physical sense of self and its interactions with the external world. The interaction of the proprioceptive and tactile senses, along with vision, is integral in the development of the coordinated movements that support the child's ability to plan and execute exploratory patterns of behavior. Proprioception has another important function—regulation. The skillful provision of proprioceptive input can effectively modulate a child's arousal states and emotional tone when drowsiness, fussiness, or agitation are barriers to learning (Smith Roley et al., 2001; for more information, see the section on Teaching Sensory Efficiency later in this chapter).

Self-initiated movement is an essential part of sensory efficiency because it is related to intention. Sensory efficiency cannot improve unless a child intends to interact with something in his environment in order to get information about it. Movement is required for that interaction.

The tactile, visual, and vestibular systems work with proprioception to allow children to develop motor abilities. For example, head control develops as newborns use olfactory, tactile, and proprioceptive information to guide intentional movement of the head in an effort to find sources of food.

Contributions of the Vestibular Sense. The functions of the vestibular sense are well developed at birth and are largely unconscious. Many of a child's early reflexes related to head, neck, and eye movement are a result of vestibular activity (Smith Roley et al., 2001). Activity of the vestibular sense sets in motion the stabilization of retinal images by allowing the eyes to automatically move to compensate for changes in the position of the head. Vestibular input has a profound effect on postural stability, spatial orientation, ocular control, visual alertness, and the regulation of arousal states (Langley, 1998). Infants exhibit a strong need for vestibular input, like bouncing and rocking, that typically peaks at about 6 to 8 months of age (Eliot, 1999).

Abnormal tone and posture, particularly of the head and neck, adversely affect the visual system (Langley, 1998). Teachers of students with visual impairments need to know how to use vestibular input to create visual alertness. For example, holding a child in the lap and rocking back and forth before presenting a visual task can dramatically improve visual responsiveness. They must know how to position and move a child's body so that basic organizational and regulatory processes involving the vestibular and proprioceptive senses can be integrated with vision for optimal ocular motor function. (For detailed information about making postural changes to align the head and neck, using vestibular input to alert and organize the visual system, and facilitating visual-motor responses, see Langley, 1998, Component 5.) Implementation of these procedures should be done in collaboration with physical and occupational therapists. (Suggestions for working with students at the sensorimotor stage are found in the section on General Considerations for Teaching Sensory Efficiency in this chapter.)

The Preoperational Stage

When typically developing children are approximately 2 years old, they enter the preoperational stage where imitation, not exploration, becomes the compelling dynamic in learning. Instead of concentrating on discovering the sensory properties of objects, as they did in the sensorimotor stage of development, children at the preoperational stage, from 2 years old to about 7 years old, use integrated sensory information to accomplish tasks (Lightfoot, Cole, & Cole, 2005). Learners at this stage also include older students with moderate cognitive disabilities, who are learning some of the same skills with a more functional emphasis or academic skills aligned with age-equivalent standards.

At this stage, children are still curious about the sensory attributes of objects and they continue to use sensorimotor strategies to explore new objects, but the primary behavior related to learning becomes a socially motivated desire to imitate the actions of adults and other children (Matlin, 2008). They are usually fascinated by what other people are doing and they want to do it too; they do things over and over in order to improve their motor performance, and they use language for thinking and communicating. They may already know that the word label for the little white circles they eat for breakfast is *banana,* but now they learn that the crescent-shaped yellow object is also banana, that it comes in bunches, and is one of a group of like things called fruit (Dunlea, 1989). These preoperational learners are using sensory experiences to build concepts and schemas that organize and expand their knowledge of their worlds.

It is therefore appropriate that children at the preoperational stage use sensory skills as tools for developing cognitive, communication, motor, social, self-help, and emergent academic skills. Among many other activities, children match and sort; cut and paste; label colors, shapes, letters, and numbers; and use pictures to learn about their communities.

Very few new sensory skills remain to be learned for children developing typically at this stage; instead, established skills are applied in increasingly complex contexts (Gibson, 1988). For example, at this level, the perception of color is not what is being learned when children match and sort colors. They are using color perception that developed to nearly adult levels when they were 4 months old to now learn the cognitive skill of putting like things together. Similarly, when a preoperational stage child cuts along a line with scissors, he is practicing a motor coordination skill. The visual part of the task, looking at high contrast borders and lines, began to be learned in infancy when he observed the hairline on his mother's face and watched her hand as it positioned an object for insertion into his mouth.

In the same way, a child at this stage matching textured blocks or using touch to identify shapes is not learning tactile discrimination skills. He is using tactile discrimination skills learned during earlier sensorimotor exploration to master the cognitive skill of matching and the vocabulary skill of using abstract words to describe shape. Abstract words and comparison words, like curved/straight, rough/smooth, wet/dry, soft/hard, and warm/cold, are cognitively challenging. Young children should be very good at using simple nouns and verbs with concrete referents before they are expected to understand or use words for abstract and comparative concepts (Dunlea, 1989). Inability to sort and match textures and to use abstract and comparative words is more likely related to cognitive and language skills than to sensory skills.

At this stage, then, children are beginning to apply sensory skills that they mastered as infants and toddlers in a wide variety of new contexts related to other areas of the ECC. For example, the strategies learned to visually locate objects in familiar environments are expanded to visually locate objects in unfamiliar environments in early O&M activities (e.g., traffic signals) and to use compensatory skills to read pictographs or signage.

Primary Sensory Systems

The Visual Sense. Learning media assessments and functional vision evaluations (discussed later in this chapter and also in Chapter 3) determine when vision can be used as a primary or secondary source of information for different kinds of tasks and the conditions under which vision can be used most efficiently. Some students with visual impairments who are in the preoperational stage may use the visual skills they developed earlier in life very efficiently as they encounter new environments, deal with more complex learning media, such as books and puzzles, and expand their social experiences through play with peers. Some may not be able to use established skills in new contexts without help and some will need to continue to work on the basic visual skills typically developed by infants and toddlers.

A student's visual learning at this stage greatly depends on the ability of the teacher of students with visual impairments to create access to visual information by providing accommodations based on the student's needs. Teachers must, therefore, evaluate each student's *visual efficiency*—the ability to use visual abilities to the maximum extent possible in regularly occurring activities throughout the day, such as dressing, playing on a swing set, or reading picture books. This evaluation must be ongoing because recommendations based on the observation of one or two activities at one point in time may not contribute information regarding the quality of a child's visual efficiency in other activities. Therefore, whenever the teacher of students with visual impairments works with a student in a variety of different activities and locations, observations of the student's use of functional vision is part of an ongoing evaluation. (Tools for ongoing analysis of specific activities can be found in Smith, in press; Lueck, 2004a; and Corn & Erin, 2010; see the Resources section at the end of this chapter.)

Because learning at the preoperational stage is still dependent upon the efficient acquisition of sensory information, teachers of students with visual impairments need to make sure that visual learning is maximized to the fullest extent possible, given a student's individual physical capacities and preferences. At this stage of development, activities that take place on the playground, in the gym, in the cafeteria, and on shopping trips with family members are just as important as those that take place in the classroom. Since these locations are important learning environments, the activities that take place in them need to be observed during functional vision evaluations.

Creating visual access to learning media for a student at this stage is challenging because of the variety of contexts involved. Without visual access to the calendar being pointed to by the teacher, students with low vision who are primary visual learners cannot learn about the days of the week as effectively as their classmates. The teacher of students with visual impairments must, therefore, provide accommodations that create the access needed. She will start by analyzing the activity to determine the optimum viewing distance for her

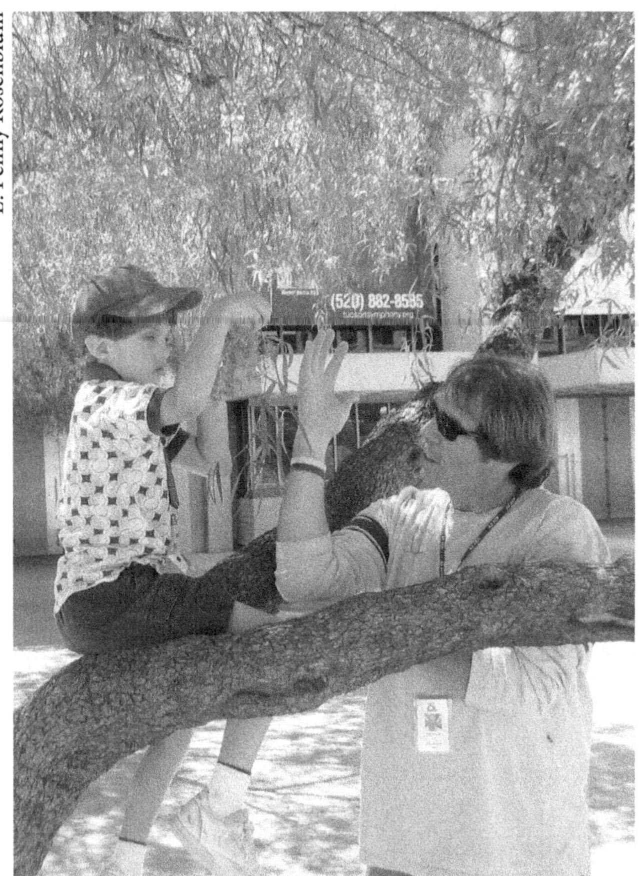

L. Penny Rosenblum

Students need to practice integrating multisensory information in variety of natural environments.

student. If access cannot be created with closer seating for the student, she will need to talk to the classroom teacher about providing additional accommodations such as changes to the calendar related to its size, complexity, and contrast. If these changes fail to provide sufficient access for the student, the teacher may have to provide the student with a personal calendar similar to the one used by the rest of class, so that the student can sit with the group and use near vision to do the same tasks classmates are doing at distance. Some students with low vision begin to use optical devices at this stage; clinical low vision evaluations are essential for all students with visual impairments in order to make this determination.

A student whose assessment indicates that vision is a primary learning system may still be at risk of missing many important learning opportunities when learning media is more than about 16 inches away from the eyes. This risk is particularly acute if the student can be successful using near vision, but has difficulty using distance vision. The teacher of students with visual impairments will, therefore, need to assess the use of near and distance vision for accessing learning media in activities taking place at a variety of distances from the student, so that she can ensure that appropriate accommodations are used. For the student who has difficulty acquiring visual information at a distance, a teacher's demonstrations in front of a group of students during physical education class may not provide any instruction, and the student's motor, social, and recreation/leisure skills will be affected accordingly. Pictures of community helpers and animals held up by the classroom teacher in front of a group are also of little or no use to the student who is dependent on his use of near vision and, without accommodation, his development of concepts will be adversely affected because he hears words about things with which he has little direct experience. In situations like these, teachers of students with visual impairments need to include specific accommodations for acquisition of distance information and make sure that these accommodations are part of the individualized education program (IEP). Accommodations might include close seating, permission to get up and move next to distance media, provision of copies or replicas, or use of optical devices.

The Tactile Sense. The preoperational stage can be a challenging time for the child who uses touch primarily for learning. At this stage, children begin to spend increasing amounts of time developing social skills in play activities with peers and in structured group learning activities. Participation in these groups brings associated challenges related to keeping up with peers and the pacing of instruction. Pacing is a critical factor for primary tactile learners at this age because acquiring information tactilely rather than visually takes more time (Chen & Downing, 2006). Whereas vision provides a comprehensive and broad array of information almost instantaneously with one glance, there is no equivalent when touch is used. Tactile information is gathered one piece at a time in sequential touches. Tactile learning needs adequate time for independent, active execution of important exploratory procedures (Klatsky & Lederman, 2008), as indicated earlier in this chapter.

Another potential challenge for the learner at this stage who uses touch primarily is that the people asking him to participate in structured activities may use inappropriate strategies as they attempt to facilitate participation. Well-meaning adults who want tactile learners to use their hands to stick the straw in a juice box, pull their pants up and down when they go to the restroom, put together a puzzle, and ride a tricycle may think that they are teaching when they use their own hands to manipulate tactile learners using hand-over-hand guidance. Tactile information received passively—when someone else moves the student's hands and fingers—does not provide high-quality, meaningful information because it limits the use of the six procedures that are important for gathering tactile information (see Sidebar 5.3 earlier in this chapter). Passive touch relies almost exclusively on the use of one procedure, static touch, whereas independent movement of the hands and fingers during active or haptic touch makes possible the use of all six procedures (McLinden & McCall, 2002). A better strategy is using hand-under-hand guidance so that the child is planning and initiating her movements and maintaining control over her own hands.

The Auditory Sense. In general, as already noted, the auditory channel cannot be a student's primary system for learning and obtaining information unless the student's language skills are highly developed. Students at the preoperational stage are on their way to being sophisticated users of language, but primary dependence on auditory information for learning at this stage is not a reliable strategy unless auditory information is paired with visual and tactile information. Pairing is essential because the usefulness of language as a source of information depends on the student's ability to comprehend the meaning of words spoken and heard. Children's vocabularies are expanding rapidly at this time, but are still limited. Typically developing children often enjoy listening to language and saying words long before they understand the meaning of the words they hear and speak. As mentioned previously, an understanding of the meaning of words develops when a child has been able to associate words with the concrete objects to which they refer. Children start building their mental dictionaries by asking for labels for their favorite people and objects. They often ask by pointing. They don't really want the thing—they want to hear its name (Dunlea, 1989). They pair the thing they see—the concrete referent—with the word they hear—the symbol for the thing. When a child is blind or severely visually impaired and cannot see an object, she will not point to it to ask its name. Instead, family members and teachers must offer the object manually. A child who is a tactile learner points by touching an object held in the hand of her parent or teacher. This is called *tactile mutual regard*, and it is an essential element of communication development for tactile learners.

Some students with visual impairments have trouble developing an understanding of the meaning of words because they do not have adequate visual or tactile access to the relevant concrete referents (Dunlea, 1989). If they hear words without seeing or touching the things to which they refer, they may speak those words without really knowing what they mean. Adults and peers often have a tendency to assume that some students with visual impairments understand the language they hear based on the fact that the students may say lots of words. That assumption can be a mistake; verbal instruction cannot be a primary learning tool if the language used is not meaningful to the student.

Secondary Sensory Systems

Neurological maturation allows typically developing children at the preoperational stage to acquire and integrate information from different sensory systems quickly and efficiently. A child with a visual impairment at this stage integrates information from primary and secondary systems as well, but the process may be more deliberate and effortful for him. As he walks down a hallway trying to find his classroom, he may use all at once information from the colors of door decorations, the sounds of his classmates' voices, the feel of the things his hand touches as it trails the hallway wall, the smells coming from various sources, and the vestibular sense of how fast he is moving. However, teachers need to keep in mind that young children pay attention to what they find interesting. The parts of their brains that use reason and logic to solve problems and direct activity are not well developed at this age. The focuses of their attention are primarily driven by need and pleasure (Matlin, 2008). Teachers may want them to pay attention to the multisensory cues that may help them find their classrooms, but if something they find more interesting distracts them, their attention will be absorbed by the new object of interest.

Since the use of complex sensory information is typical at this level, an inability to integrate multisensory information may be an indication of difficulties in sensory processing. Some students may have significant delays in response times when they receive simultaneous input from more than one sensory system. Or, they may intentionally limit attention to one system in order to shut out input from competing systems that produce too much complexity. Teachers of students with visual impairments do not generally evaluate sensory processing disorders, but they do evaluate the functional viability of all sensory systems as a means of providing information about the use of appropriate accommodations and other learning considerations. When sensory processing disorders are suspected, students should be referred for additional evaluation by appropriate team members. (Suggestions for working with students at the preoperational stage are found in the section on General Considerations for Teaching Sensory Efficiency.)

The Operational Stage

When typically developing children are approximately 7 years old, they become operational learners and begin to use logic, reasoning, and analysis to achieve skills in reading, writing, mathematics, science, and social studies: the primary focus of learning in schools from kindergarten through high school. Sensory efficiency continues to be critical during the operational stage. Now, however, students' sensory skills are used in even more rapidly expanding contexts, as more complex and demanding tasks and activities become part of students' lives at home and at school. The selection of effective sensory strategies becomes the key to performing tasks efficiently, and the accommodations provided within a student's environments become more specific and more sophisticated. For example, a middle school student may choose to access written text using tactile strategies (such as braille) and maps and graphs using visual strategies (such as a video magnifier). Likewise, he may find that listening to a recording of a novel may expedite the reading of the material.

Primary Sensory Systems

Visual and Tactile Senses. From the elementary grades onward, students' visual efficiency in academic contexts needs to be examined regularly through learning media and functional vision assessments (discussed in more detail in the section on Assessment, later in this chapter, and in Chapter 4). There is no mandated evaluation of factors related to tactile efficiency. Since a student's learning media assessment is typically the only record of tactile performance in regard to academic tasks, specific information about tactile performance in all areas, not just literacy, should be addressed in this report. (Specific tools and detailed instructions for assessing the efficiency of visual and tactile strategies for different kinds of academic tasks can be found in Koenig and Holbrook, 2010).

For some students, learning media and functional vision assessments may indicate the need for instruction using the types of sensory efficiency strategies recommended for young children. For example, an elementary student may need instruction on exploration skills so that he can develop concrete, sensory-based referents for words.

Auditory Sense. Auditory efficiency, listening skills, and language proficiency become a complex and interdependent set of skills by the time students enter elementary school. Phonemic awareness—the ability to identify the small units of sound that combine to make words—is an essential focus of reading instruction, and auditory skills play a key role in the acquisition of skills in this area. Efficient auditory skills are needed for the use of recorded material, for the use of speech output technology like screen readers, for the development of O&M skills, and for use in social skills, such as engaging in conversations.

Secondary Sensory Systems

From infancy, each piece of information from a single sensory system combines with pieces from other systems as they are stored in long-term memory. These associated bits of information form a whole perception upon which concepts are built. By the time typically developing students enter elementary school, their use of multisensory strategies is, in general, highly efficient. Students with visual impairments at this stage generally use integrated primary and secondary sensory systems efficiently with two exceptions. They may need additional time for processing and integrating information in unfamiliar environments and they may encounter some of the same difficulties with sensory processing that can create learning challenges for students without visual impairments. When difficulties occur with sensory integration—the combining of sensory information from multiple systems—they may be related to a number of factors:

- *Multiple demands on the student's attention.* Students in elementary and higher grades deal with a high degree of complexity in their environments, with the learning media used in their instruction, and in their interpersonal relationships with adults and other students. They are constantly deciding what to pay attention to and what to ignore. How they distribute their attention is based on their perception of what is important. A student's inability to ignore extraneous sensory input can create serious problems in the area of sensory efficiency.

- *Specific learning disabilities.* Some students who do not progress as expected in academic areas during elementary school may have difficulties related to their ability to use perceptual skills in certain sensory systems. After careful assessment and diagnosis, interventions need to be designed to respond to these students' unique needs. Students with visual impairments who have these types of perceptual difficulties also need evaluation. A visual impairment makes the need for combining information from multisensory systems more acute, but it does not eliminate the possibility that other problems, such as learning disabilities, may also exist.
- *Stress and anxiety.* Combining information from multisensory systems requires a lot of cognitive energy (Matlin, 2008). Students need to be able to shift focus from one sensory element to another, make conscious decisions about the best sensory strategy for gaining information related to each element, and evaluate the importance of the information received to the goal at hand. Stress and anxiety make sustaining attention very difficult and reduce conscious sensory strategy selection to a subconscious reactive level. Hormones secreted when students are stressed decrease sensory efficiency by shifting the primary activity of sensory processing from the thinking part of the brain, the cortex, to the emotional part of the brain, the limbic area, which does not support efficient cross-modal integration (Mesulam, 2000).

Students at the operational stage in academic settings need time to practice combining information from multiple sensory systems by participating repeatedly in regularly occurring activities. For example, a student who is working on integrating the complex sensory information (visual, tactile, and auditory input) related to ordering a meal at a fast food restaurant cannot achieve success in one visit. Several visits to the same restaurant will be needed and the teacher of students with visual impairments may need to focus on one sense at a time before integrating information from all senses. Practice of this kind will increase the student's ability to make decisions about the most efficient way to negotiate ever-expanding and more complicated environments that are experienced as the student matures. Practice with instruction provided by teachers of students with visual impairments and O&M instructors in complex environments, such as fast food restaurants, will help the student use and generalize efficient sensory strategies that will last a lifetime. (Suggestions for working with students at the operational stage are found in the section on General Considerations for Teaching Sensory Efficiency.)

ASSESSMENT OF SENSORY EFFICIENCY

Teachers of students with visual impairments conduct two primary assessments mandated by the Individuals with Disabilities Education Act (IDEA): the functional vision assessment and the learning media assessment. Through these important processes, they evaluate a student's ability to use vision to perform tasks in a variety of activities and assess the relative strengths of the student's different sensory systems for the use of learning media in a variety of different kinds of tasks. IEP teams decide during annual reviews when assessment information should be revised. Typically, assessments of functional vision and learning media are conducted every three years unless IEP teams indicate otherwise.

Functional assessments of touch and hearing are not mandated by IDEA and are not commonly conducted by teachers of students with visual impairments, except in regard to pre-braille skills and language listening skills. Skills such as tactile exploratory procedures and localization and identification of sound sources may not be addressed. If a student's functional use of tactile or auditory senses has not been assessed, the teacher of students with visual impairments will need to assess these systems as part of her learning media assessment and make appropriate referrals to other team members when needed. Teachers of students with visual impairments work collaboratively with educational team members, such as occupational therapists, physical therapists, speech-language therapists, teachers of students with hearing impairments, and deaf-blind specialists, to assess the functionality of students' use of tactile and auditory senses when impairments in these systems have been identified or referrals have been made because impairments are suspected. The Individual Sensory Learning Profile (see Appendix 5A) can be used to help determine the need for additional assessments. This tool contains important questions about the function of specific sensory systems. If these questions cannot be answered based on existing information, more in-depth assessment is needed.

In general, teachers of students with visual impairments must be prepared to conduct assessments with students who have a range of abilities and ages. Depending on a student's characteristics, including the presence of additional disabilities, different assessment tools may be used and different procedures may be required. For example, when assessing students with multiple disabilities, particular attention may need to be paid to the positioning of the student and to her methods of communicating, including the need to interpret nonverbal responses. Likewise, careful assessment of older students will need to take into consideration needs that may emerge as new, more complex activities place additional demands on sensory systems that previous assessments may have found to be operating efficiently.

Visual Functioning

Functional Vision Assessment

The functional vision assessment provides information about students' ability to use vision to perform tasks. The evaluation procedures involved typically call for observations of students in two or more settings, both indoors and outdoors. For example, a teacher might observe students finding their lockers in a school hallway and for moving around on an outdoor playground. Although observation of two settings may be sufficient for some students, it is not usually adequate for determining the specific accommodations needed by infants and toddlers, preschool students, and students with multiple impairments. These students require observation of important activities at different times of the day, on different days, and over time. The visual behaviors of these kinds of students fluctuate significantly based on health, ambient characteristics of the environment, the quality of social bonding between the student and the teacher, the student's levels of alertness, the attractiveness or unattractiveness of learning media, and the pacing of instruction.

A variety of functional vision assessment protocols are available for use by teachers of students with visual impairments (see Table 5.2; for details about these assessments, see the Resources section at the end of this chapter). They typically include some components from three broad categories of visual function: developmental components, like perceptual skills; ocular components, like visual fields and acuities; and neurological components, such as responses related to movement, familiarity, and complexity. Very few protocols cover components in all three categories. Teachers of students with visual impairments who are assessing young children, students with severe multiple impairments, and students with CVI may have to use more than one protocol to make sure that all the important components are assessed. (See Anthony, 2000, for a detailed treatment of how to perform a functional vision assessment.)

Developmental Components of Functional Vision Assessments

It is essential to use a functional vision assessment protocol with components in the developmental category for the evaluation of infants, toddlers, some preschool children, and students with severe multiple disabilities. These components include:

- ocular motor behaviors, such as localizing, fixating, tracking, shifting gaze, and scanning
- visual motor behaviors, such as visually directed reach and the visual alignment of objects to the body and to each other
- color perception
- depth perception
- visual perceptual skills, such as:
  - figure-ground perception
  - constancy, the ability to recognize an object regardless of its spatial orientation
  - closure, the ability to recognize an object when only a part of it can be seen
  - visual memory

Developmental components are often part of scales and checklists that provide lists of visual behaviors in the order in which they typically develop in infants and toddlers. They can be used to make sure that interventions are effective. Without knowledge of typical visual skill development, teachers or parents might work on skills at inappropriate ages or without sufficient attention to more basic skills (Ferrell, 2010). For example, the ability to fixate must be established before a child can track, and the fourth month would be the appropri-

TABLE 5.2

Tools for Functional Vision Assessments

For more information about the functional vision assessment tools listed in this table, see the Resources section of this chapter.

Tool	Source	Categories of Visual Functioning Addressed: Developmental Components	Ocular Components	Neurological Components
Barraga Visual Efficiency Program	Smith (in press)	x	x	
CVI Range and Resolution Chart	Roman-Lantzy (2007)			x
Functional Vision Evaluation Report: Young Children and Students with Additional Disabilities	Haegerstrom-Portnoy (2004)		x	x
Functional Vision Evaluation Report: Children and Adults	Greer (2004)		x	x
FVLMA: Functional vision and learning media assessment for students who are pre-academic and academic and visually impaired in grades K-12	Sanford and Burnett (2008)		x	
ISAVE: Individualized Systematic Assessment of Visual Efficiency	Langley (1998)	x	x	x
ToAD: Tools for Assessment and Development of Visual Skills	Kitchel (2008)	x	x	

ate time to expect that a child would begin to reach for a visual stimulus (Ferrell, 2010). Developmental scales and checklists can also help teachers identify skill gaps in older children with multiple disabilities that might be improved with better accommodations, different strategies, and additional devices (Langley, 1998).

Neurological Components of Functional Vision Assessments

The use of a functional vision assessment protocol with components in the neurological category is essential for students who have CVI and for students with multiple disabilities. Neurological components help teachers evaluate a student's color preference, responses to movement, preferred visual distances, ability to deal with visual complexity, response delays, stereotypical behaviors, field preferences, difficulty with novelty, and uncoordinated use of vision and reach (Roman-Lantzy, 2007). Information about these components is essential for determining appropriate instructional strategies and accommodations so that environments and learning media contribute to the improvement of visual efficiency over time. For example, visual avoidance of unfamiliar and complex situations can be diminished if teachers provide sufficient experiences in which a student enjoys using vision to look at familiar, simple objects.

Ocular Components of Functional Vision Assessments

Clinical low vision specialists, ophthalmologists, and optometrists have the expertise necessary for the reliable evaluation of ocular components, including ocular reflexes, pupillary responses, contrast sensitivity, color perception, accommodative ability, ocular motor function, visual fields, and near and distance acuities. Teachers of students with visual impairments should read the eye reports available for their students before performing an assessment. Results obtained from the eye report can be informative for the teacher in performing subsequent functional vision evaluations. If an ophthalmologist or optometrist has not evaluated all ocular components for a student, such as visual fields, visual acuities, and ocular motor function, or is unable to evaluate these components, referral of the student for a clinical low vision evaluation is essential.

Reporting Results of Functional Vision Assessments

When reporting results of a functional vision assessment, it is important for the teacher to include detailed information about what was observed, including all activities. Later, the teacher can organize this information into an observation and accommodation guide chart, like the examples shown in Figure 5.1. Information from the chart can serve as the observational data that are the basis of the functional vision assessment report. Data can be summarized in sections of the functional vision assessment report describing areas such as near and distance performance. Specific recommendations for accommodations and modifications can also be included

FIGURE 5.1

Observation and Accommodation Guide from Functional Vision Assessment Results

INSTRUCTIONS

Step 1: Interview

Talk to parents and general education teacher about daily activities. Prioritize activities for observation. Enter priority activities in the left column of the Observation and Accommodation Guide chart.

Criteria for priority activities are the following:

- activity occurs frequently
- activity contains important instructional objectives
- activity is important socially

Step 2: Observe Activities

List the media used in the activity. Include objects and people. Note the following in the observations column:

- size of media and the viewing distance
- preferred viewing area
- areas in which the student reacts to a visual change in the environment (field)
- ability to maintain fixation as object moves from a distance to close up
- use of visually guided reach
- perceptual responses: color, constancy, figure-ground, closure, memory

Step 3: Describe the Accommodation

Describe the accommodation for each learning media item whose use was adversely affected by vision loss. Include information from direct assessment.

EXAMPLES

STUDENT WITH OCULAR IMPAIRMENT: MATT

Activity	***Media***	***Observations (includes size of object and viewing distance)***	***Accommodation***
Arrival	*Teacher*	*Fixation at 4′*	
	Name tag on locker	*3″ at 12″, central fixation, used touch of wrinkled corner to confirm*	
	Zipper on backpack	*1″ at 14″, central fixation, direct visually guided reach*	
	Hook in locker	*Too dark, used tactile strategy*	
	Clear plastic folder	*12″ at 12″, central fixation, poor contrast no problem*	
	Folder basket	*20″ at 3′, central fixation, walked right by it twice, found when heard peer drop folder in basket*	*Teach scanning pattern: last locker to doorframe to basket*

FIGURE 5.1 *continued*

Student with Ocular Impairment: Matt

Activity	Media	Observations (includes size of object and viewing distance)	Accommodation
Reading	Phonics worksheet	1" outline pictures with internal detail at 4"	Reading stand and dome magnifier
	Pencil	Visually guided marking good	

Student with Cortical Visual Impairment: Ashley

Activity	Media	Observations	Accommodation/ Modification/ Support
Music routine	Teacher's face	At 8", glance with upper left peripheral vision, followed by big head turn for central vision	
	CD in "now" container	5" at 14", presented at lower central level (student's lap), head drop for central fixation, .5-second fixation, silver CD in black container, movement, 12-second delay, no reaching (student looks only)	Present at face level centrally at 2', wait 30 seconds for independent reach
	CD player	6" at 2', presentation central, 1-second fixation, red tape on lid of silver player, no object movement, no delay, looks away when reaching for object	
	Switch	12" at 3', central fixation (alerts to sound, no head drop at distance), .5-second fixation, yellow object, movement, no delay, sequential look and reach for switch	Present at face level centrally at 2', wait 30 seconds for independent reach
	CD in "finished" container	Same as "now" container, except container is orange color	

in the report. If approved by the IEP committee, recommended accommodations and modifications should be listed on the student's IEP.

Learning Media Assessment

Learning media are the materials or objects used during instruction. Print might be the medium used during the instruction of reading; a piano, the object used during the instruction of music; a shoe, one of the objects used during the instruction of dressing. Media change in relation to the targeted task and when they change, the sensory strategy used by a student may change, as well. The same student might use vision, with the assistance of an optical device, to read print, hearing alone to play the piano, and touch to put on and tie his shoes.

Nonacademic Learning Media

A learning media assessment for academic students determines the efficiency of touch, vision, and hearing for accessing information with a variety of learning media, such as books, computers, and maps (see Chapter 4 and Koenig & Holbrook, 1995). Learning media assessments that only address literacy needs, however, often fail to address important learning media accommodations needed by the student for instruction in specific content areas, such as science, mathematics, physical education, and art. Language arts, math, and social studies teachers may be able to provide highly effective instruction to a student who is visually impaired when they know that the student needs brailled text and a portable video magnifier for charts, graphs, maps, and pictures. But that student's science and physical education teachers need to know about other kinds of accommodations and supports that have nothing to do with literacy in order to make instruction in their subjects effective. Similarly, learners at the sensorimotor and preoperational stages need accommodations and supports that may not be covered by academic learning media assessments.

Sensorimotor Learners. Infants, toddlers, and older students at the sensorimotor stage of development need a different kind of learning media assessment. Assessment in this case needs to determine which sensory systems work best for exploration of the learning media appropriate at this stage: people, objects, actions, and places. Responses to media using all of a student's sensory systems should be assessed in order to determine how each activity may affect the child's arousal states and the efficiency of the child's other sensory systems.

Preoperational Learners. Teachers of students with visual impairments at the preschool level or older students at the preoperational stage must conduct assessments that allow them to share with others the learning media needs of their students who are unable to use pictures for emergent literacy instruction, for concept development in areas such as weather and community helpers, or in alternative communication instruction, such as picture exchange programs.

See Sidebar 5.4 and the Resources section at the end of this chapter for a list of learning media assessment tools that may be helpful for use with learners at the sensorimotor, preoperational, and operational stages of development.

Results of the Learning Media Assessment

When learning media assessments result in the observation of abnormal sensory responses, referrals for additional assessment by other team members may be necessary. For example, observation of abnormal responses to environmental noises or voices might result in a referral for an audiological evaluation. Observation of touch avoidance or feeding difficulties might result in a referral to an occupational therapist to evaluate the possibility of tactile defensiveness, a sensory processing impairment (see Sidebar 5.5). Intervention needs to be provided as early as possible when auditory and tactile impairments are identified. Failure to respond to these conditions with appropriate accommodations and therapeutic interventions can result in significant difficulties in auditory and tactile learning and social development.

If the teacher of students with visual impairments observes noticeable gaps in a student's use of tactile and auditory skills while conducting the functional vision assessment or learning media assessment, he or she needs to initiate and participate in functional assessments of touch and hearing, even though these evaluations are not required by law. When students do not use their tactile and auditory senses efficiently, functional

SIDEBAR 5.4

Tools for Learning Media Assessment

For more information about the learning media assessment tools listed here, see the chapter references and the Resources section at the end of this chapter.

SENSORIMOTOR STAGE

For students in the sensorimotor stage (infants and toddlers, and older students with severe and profound disabilities):

- *Sensory Learning Kit* (Smith, 2005)
- *Every Move Counts* (Korsten, Foss, & Berry, 2007)
- *Infant/Toddler Sensory Profile* (Dunn, 2002)
- *The Sensory Profile* (Dunn, 1999)
- *The Sensory Profile*—School Companion (Dunn, 2006)

PREOPERATIONAL STAGE

For students in the preoperational stage (preschool students and older students with moderate disabilities):

- *FVLMA: Functional Vision and Learning Media Assessment for Students Who Are Pre-Academic or Academic in Grades K–12* (Sanford & Burnett, 2008)
- Use of Sensory Channels (in Koenig & Holbrook, 1995)

OPERATIONAL STAGE

For students at the operational or academic level:

- *FVLMA: Functional Vision and Learning Media Assessment for Students Who Are Pre-Academic or Academic in Grades K–12* (Sanford & Burnett, 2008)
- A Procedure for Documenting Reading Efficiency (in Koenig & Holbrook, 1995)
- Inventory of Functional Literacy Tasks (in Holbrook, Koenig, & Rex, 2010)

SIDEBAR 5.5

Assessing Tactile Defensiveness

Certain behavioral characteristics are often associated with tactile defensiveness (Royeen & Lane, 1991); the observation of any of the following behaviors over a period of time indicates the need for an occupational therapy referral:

- tensing, crying, or aggression in response to touching of the body by another person, clothing, or objects
- oral refusal of objects associated with eating and drinking like cups and spoons
- rejection of different textures in food
- avoidance of foods that require sucking or licking (popsicles, suckers)
- removal of face, hands, or feet in response to touch
- stereotypical touching of familiar objects such as tapping an object against the teeth or lips
- avoidance of proximity (maintaining distance from other bodies)

assessments of these areas are necessary to make sure that instruction and accommodations related to each are included in the student's IEP. These assessments are not the same as the evaluations conducted by audiologists and occupational therapists to identify sensory system impairments. Functional assessments of auditory and tactile efficiency should include other team members, but need to be initiated by the teacher of students with visual impairments.

Functional Tactile Assessment

While teachers of students with visual impairments may informally observe some aspects of tactile function, they rarely assess the broad spectrum of tactile skills except as part of pre-braille instruction. As a result, tactile efficiency—the efficient use of the sense of touch in a variety of tasks—is sometimes regarded in the field of visual impairments as almost synonymous with the ability to match textures and recognize shapes. However, the effective use of the sense of touch to gather information goes beyond these two abilities. Occupational therapists evaluate functions like tactile discrimination and the ability to recognize objects based on touch alone (Bundy et al., 2002), but they do not assess exploratory procedures used to gather information about objects in the environment, an important skill area for students who are visually impaired. Tactile inefficiency is a common difficulty for children with visual impairments because they often are not provided with guided practice in learning how to explore an object. Sometimes even accomplished braille readers have limited knowledge of the tactile features of objects. In order to plan interventions to increase tactile efficiency, teachers of students with visual impairments should collaborate whenever possible with an occupational therapist to assess their students' functional tactile skills. These assessments should take place when learning media assessments indicate that there are difficulties in this area. (See the Resources section at the end of this chapter for information about tools that may be useful for evaluating tactile function.)

Functional Auditory Assessment

Families and teachers of children with hearing impairments may often be uncertain or confused about what children hear and don't hear. As in any other area, technical information needs to be made practical so that teachers and family members can help a child maximize his or her use of auditory information. A functional hearing evaluation is the tool that translates audiological information describing decibels and frequencies into instructional information about appropriate learning media, like environmental sounds and voices, to be used with a child.

Teachers of students with visual impairments without special auditory training cannot conduct a functional hearing assessment. (Teachers with both vision and auditory expertise are usually deaf-blind specialists.) Nevertheless, they still have an important role related to hearing. They must make appropriate referrals to hearing specialists, participate in assessments, and make sure that accommodations are provided accordingly. Undetected hearing loss, when present, is a serious problem for a child with a visual impairment, and teachers of students with visual impairments can help ensure the early identification of such a loss. Even mild hearing loss is significant, not only because it affects language development, but also because, when combined with vision loss, a child's access to distance information may be limited. Behaviors related to abnormal hearing ability are frequently overlooked or misinterpreted. For example, teachers may assume that a child who responds to environmental sounds and music hears normally and that failure to respond to verbal directions is due to noncompliance or inattention, rather than the inability to hear certain speech frequencies.

Families and teachers generally tend to assume that children can hear. As a result, teachers of students with visual impairments should routinely screen their students for abnormal responses to voices and environmental sounds. This screening may be part of the learning media assessment, but hearing abnormalities are likely to be missed during an observation of an activity when visual and tactile responses are being evaluated at the same time. A separate observation using structured hearing screening tools designed to detect abnormal responses can help ensure accuracy and thoroughness. If screening results in the observation of abnormal responses, appropriate referrals to auditory specialists should follow and audiological and functional hearing assessments should be conducted. Hearing and deaf-blind specialists may not routinely conduct a functional hearing assessment for a student who is visually impaired, unless teachers of students with visual impairments specifically request information about functioning in typical environments and participate in its administration. (See the Resources section at the end of this chapter for a list of tools that may be useful for conducting hearing screenings and functional hearing assessments.)

GENERAL CONSIDERATIONS FOR TEACHING SENSORY EFFICIENCY

Given how important it is for students who are visually impaired to use all available sensory information as efficiently as possible, providing instruction and support to students in this key area of the ECC needs to be a primary concern for the teacher of students with visual impairments, particularly when working with young children and students who have multiple disabilities. The range and diversity of characteristics, conditions, abilities, and needs found among students who are visually impaired requires the consideration of many variables and factors in planning teaching activities.

Enhancing Use of Sensory Systems in the Sensorimotor Stage

In the sensorimotor stage of development, children move from general reactions to targeted reactions (Gibson, 1988). For example, a child may enjoy watching the movement of people around his crib. Later, he may pay careful attention to the differences in the shapes of these people in order to predict which one of them might be his mother. When working with students at the sensorimotor stage of cognitive development, the teacher of students with visual impairments is responsible for designing interventions that result in efficient sensory exploration of people, objects, actions, and places. Some considerations for enhancing the use of sensory systems in young children and older individuals who are at the sensorimotor stage of development are listed in the following paragraphs.

In order to be efficient, sensory exploration must be active. Teachers of students with visual impairments may use passive stimulation to help their students fixate on and track objects, but this should be only the first step in creating an experience in which students interact with the things they see. Instruction needs to be designed to offer sensing and acting experiences that provide answers to the three essential questions of "What is it?" (recognition), "What does it do?" (function), and "How does it relate to other things?" (relativity) (Gibson, 1988). For example, a child who is taught to passively look at and follow the movement of a lighted toy practices and refines the visual skills of fixation and tracking. That is important, but in order to develop those skills, the child must form the intention of wanting to use them to answer the three essential questions about the toy. She needs to help turn it on, hold it, and bang with it, put it in her mouth and explore the parts of it with her tongue and lips, and place it in her toy box with her other toys when she loses interest in it. Many young children who have visual impairments will be unable to do any of those things without the support of specialists who can address their sensory needs by guiding such exploration.

Environmental complexity and sensory aversions influence sensory learning. Careful observation is needed to identify environmental features that contribute to states of arousal—drowsiness, fussiness, and agitation—that prevent targeted attention. Under-stimulation contributes to drowsiness. Sensory complexity and the presence of specific sources with aversive sensory attributes are the two most common environmental features related to fussiness and agitation. Once identified, these environmental features should be eliminated or minimized.

For many children at the sensorimotor stage, and especially those with CVI, sensory complexity prevents them from paying targeted attention to specific people, objects, actions, and places. A complex environment is one in which multiple sources of sensory stimulation activate several of a child's sensory systems randomly and simultaneously. Typical homes are complex. A TV is on. Someone nearby is talking on the phone. Music can be heard from yet another area. The clothes dryer is running. Light is coming from the ceiling, lamps, and windows. Rugs, drapes, clothing worn by people, and furniture coverings are patterned with intricate designs. Objects are crowded together on shelves and in containers. People and animals randomly and unexpectedly touch a child as they move by, and strong smells related to cleaning, cooking, personal hygiene, and decorations are pervasive.

Even when environments are not complex, aversive characteristics of a single feature in the environment related to temperature, odor, lighting, or noise can prevent targeted attention. Sensory responses are very individualized. What is considered pleasant by one person may be a strong source of aversion to another.

Stress caused by sensory complexity and aversion may result in a child's shutting down, which is sometimes called *sensory withdrawal* (Smith Roley et al., 2001). Stress hormones stimulate a flight-or-fight reaction in the subcortical region of the brain. Withdrawal may be thought of as flight, and fussiness and agitation as fight. Until the sources of these unconscious reactions are removed or eased, a child's targeted attention to specific sensory information will tend to be absent or intermittent at best (Smith, 2005).

Self-stimulation prevents exploration. Self-stimulation is a behavior engaged in because of a neurological, subcortical need for more or less sensory stimulation. It is unrelated to learning. For that reason, exploration is to be encouraged, and self-stimulation avoided. Individuals of all ages and abilities engage in self-stimulatory behavior periodically, but when these behaviors occur with significant frequency and intensity in young children, sensory efficiency is compromised and development can be delayed. Self-stimulation can be avoided only by providing environments and experiences with the sensory attributes needed by a child to support alertness. Once established, self-stimulatory behaviors are very persistent, so preventive intervention needs to begin in infancy.

Many factors contribute to a child's need to engage in self-stimulatory behaviors. Sometimes these behaviors calm a child experiencing discomfort resulting from exposure to aversive or overly complex sensory input. Sometimes they excite a child experiencing discomfort due to boredom. Boredom, at the sensorimotor stage, is caused by lack of access to novel objects. A child with no other option resorts to using his mouth to engage in repetitive interactions with his own body or something touching his body, like clothing. This is called oral self-stimulation. Oral exploration, in contrast, provides excellent information about novel objects and is the launching pad for emerging visual and tactile skills. It should be encouraged, not prevented, especially when it is used as a substitution strategy to interrupt oral self-stimulation. As long as exploration is taking place, any sensory strategy is a good one.

Environments that support learning need to be simple, comfortable, safe, and predictable. Infants in simple, comfortable, safe, and predictable environments will start exploring when their familiar caregivers hold them during feeding. They will tend to explore things touching their bodies as they sit or lie in their cribs, on blankets on the floor, and in playpens. They will often reach out to find things around them and confidently move to new areas as soon as they can. Similarly, some older students at the sensorimotor stage of development who have difficulty with complexity and aversion may learn best in simple, comfortable, safe, predictable environments.

As indicated earlier, careful observation is needed to determine appropriate environmental accommodations that increase sensory efficiency for an individual child. Some general principles can be followed, such as controlling the amount of simultaneous sensory stimulation to which a child is exposed and removing sources of aversive stimulation. (The Arousal State Profile in *The Sensory Learning Kit* [Smith, 2005] can be used to identify environmental conditions contributing to children's withdrawal, fussiness, and agitation.)

Lighting conditions influence sensory learning. Since many conditions that cause visual impairment are affected by lighting, the amount and kind of lighting to which a child is exposed need special consideration. Teachers of students with visual impairments should know the lighting needs of their students. They can start by getting general information about lighting needs related to a student's eye condition and then get more specific information during observations of the child in different environments conducted as part of the child's functional vision assessment, discussed earlier in this chapter. (A chart indicating the lighting needs of people with specific eye conditions can be found in Flom, 2004.)

Contraindicated levels of lighting and glare, and positioning a child so he or she is looking directly into light sources need to be carefully avoided. Sometimes room lighting is dimmed when direct lighting is deliberately used to call a child's attention to an object, but this should be a temporary adjustment in cases in which a child's distance vision functions best with normal lighting. Unless a condition necessitates dim lighting, ceiling lights generally work better than area lamps for use of distance vision because the light is more evenly diffused and produces less glare. However, it should be kept in mind that young children and students with severe motor impairments may spend significant amounts of time on their backs, in a supine position. When this is the case, parents and teachers need to make sure that ceiling lights are not directly overhead when children are facing upward, toward the light.

Selecting appropriate learning media is critical. For children and older students at the sensorimotor stage, learning media are the people, objects, actions, and places that they explore. Therefore, the most important consideration at this stage is the careful selection of items with interesting and pleasing sensory characteristics that create curiosity. No one questions this approach with infants and toddlers. Manufacturers of toys for young children strive to make their products highly attractive by appealing to touch, as well as to vision and hearing. The general predominance of brightly colored hard plastic toys with sounds has given way to brightly colored, multi-textured toys with sounds. When older students are at the sensorimotor stage of development, choices about their learning materials can sometimes be difficult. Infant and toddler toys are not appropriate for use after early childhood. Yet, teachers need to continue to facilitate exploration by providing objects that have interesting and pleasing sensory characteristics. A cloth book with brightly colored pictures of toddler toys might need to be replaced for an older student with a cloth book containing brightly colored pictures of objects used during mealtime or pictures of the faces of classmates. The exploratory pattern of looking while holding followed by mouthing has to be facilitated at any age before it can be surpassed. Learning media must be individualized so that they dignify the students who use them and, at the same time, motivate them to explore using more manual rather than oral procedures over time.

The provision of accommodations for learning media is an important consideration for students who have CVI and are at the sensorimotor stage of development. Crucial variables need to be assessed in the child's functional vision assessment and specific considerations in regard to each of these variables need to be included in the child's IEP. Some considerations will relate to characteristics of objects: color, pattern complexity, and luminosity. Others will have to do with the presentation of objects: movement, preferred viewing areas, and distance. Delays in response times are common among children with CVI and children with multiple sensory issues. Teachers need to consider these delays in the pacing of instruction.

Expanding the array of learning media items to include novel items that stimulate exploration may be more difficult with students at this stage because they may tend to avoid unfamiliar objects. In such cases, characteristics of new objects may need to be similar to the characteristics of familiar objects. For example, after a textured ball is familiar, a different toy with a similar texture might be introduced. Another way to address this problem is to introduce novelty by gradually changing small features of a familiar object one at a time. For example, a piece of yellow duct tape might be placed on a familiar red plastic ball. Later, glue might be added to make ridges. (The CVI Range and the CVI Resolution Chart [Roman-Lantzy, 2007], can be used to assess these and related variables.)

Using prescribed optical devices facilitates visual function. Optical devices include eyeglasses and contact lenses that compensate for refractive errors in the eye as well as more specialized lenses, such as magnifiers and telescopes. Children with visual impairments at the sensorimotor stage of development frequently receive prescriptions for corrective lenses if they are examined by eye specialists who understand the importance of maximizing visual efficiency for purposes of promoting cognitive, motor, and social growth. There are, however, some eye specialists who believe that correction of refractive errors is not important until children begin to use symbols and look at pictures. One of the more important roles of the teacher of students with visual impairments, therefore, is to help families make sure that their children see eye specialists who appreciate the significance of optical intervention in early development and who know how to evaluate low vision clients using alternative measures that do not depend on verbal responses or the ability to interpret pictures, symbols, or letters.

Corrective lenses can be prescribed for children of any age. Contact lenses are frequently prescribed for infants after cataract surgery (Zimmerman, Zebehazy, & Moon, 2010). Eyeglasses for correction of near vision are less common in very young children, since many eye specialists believe that eyeglasses for correcting a child's near vision are unnecessary because young children typically have good accommodative ability and can maintain close working distances for long periods of time without fatigue (Wilkinson, 2010). Nevertheless, special attention to the accommodative ability of the eyes of young children is important. A child who looks away when objects and faces come closer may be experiencing confusion as images blur and become unfamiliar (Hyvarinen, 1998). Children at the sensorimotor stage of development rarely use magnifiers and telescopes, but, if they become interested in objects and pictures with small internal detail, a simple magnifier can be made available.

Some children and older students at the sensorimotor stage refuse to wear eyeglasses. Teachers of students with visual impairments should discuss the importance of eyeglasses with parents and teachers to help them appreciate the role eyeglasses can play in promoting exploration and the growth of learning.

Using assistive listening devices facilitates auditory function. Assistive listening devices increase the intensity of sound and manipulate the quality of sound related to ambient noise and reverberation. Audiologists are the professionals who evaluate hearing function and recommend devices. The most common assistive listening devices are hearing aids, which may be worn behind the ear, inside the ear, or inside the ear canal, and frequency modulation (FM) systems, which function somewhat like a personal radio that receives voice signals from a person wearing a transmitter.

Cochlear implants are another type of assistive listening device. They consist of external parts worn behind the ear—microphone, speech processor, and transmitter—and internal parts surgically implanted in the bone behind the ear and in the cochlea—receiver, stimulator, and electrodes. Speech/language therapists work with children who receive implants to help them learn to identify and interpret the new sounds they hear (NIDCD Information Clearinghouse, 2011). Teachers of students with visual impairments and O&M instructors add unique perspectives on the development of these skills by children who have deaf-blindness. They should be part of a team approach to providing instruction that pairs new access to environmental sounds with the tactile exploration that identifies the sound sources so that sounds alone can provide meaningful distance information. The following vignette is an example of how this kind of team approach can work:

A few weeks after Sonny's cochlear implant surgery, he had several programming sessions with the audiologist to adjust and set his device. The speech therapist helped his parents learn to recognize Sonny's reactions to sounds at home. After he began to hear sounds at distance, Sonny's motor development advanced rapidly as, with the help of his teacher of students with visual impairments and O&M instructor, he was motivated to move in order to discover the sources of the sounds he heard. One day, when his mother turned on the radio, Sonny abruptly stopped playing with his blocks and crawled to the radio, demonstrating this association.

Early detection of hearing loss is vitally important. Studies indicate that when children with hearing loss receive intervention before 6 months of age, they develop language, spoken or signed, on par with peers with typical hearing (Northern & Downs, 2002). Infants as young as 4 weeks old wear hearing aids. Behind-the-ear aids are commonly used with young children, partly because ear molds are easy to replace on a frequent basis as these children grow. In general, children at the sensorimotor stage of development cannot maintain their own devices, and their caregivers and teachers need to check them frequently to make sure that they are operating properly. The amount of sound coming out of the ear pieces of hearing aids is set by audiologists using very specialized measurement techniques. If teachers and parents notice that a child begins pulling aids off or resists putting aids on, the audiologist should be alerted, as an adjustment may be needed.

Enhancing Use of Sensory Systems at the Preoperational Stage

Preoperational stage learners with typical vision are involved in many activities designed to foster early literacy skills and compensatory access skills. These children practice visual and visual motor skills related to reading and writing (by the time they start elementary school, for example, they have spent hundreds of hours visually following lines of text as adults read to them). Learners at the preoperational stage who use touch primarily need access to the same experiences with the same frequency. As a result of enjoying stories and understanding that the words read are represented by brailled text, students are often highly motivated to explore the written words on their pages. Reading along by following the reader's hands as they move across lines of brailled text when stories are read aloud helps refine tactile skills in the same way visual skills are refined in a similar reading-along process, during which readers point to print words as they are read.

For children at the preoperational stage, teachers of students with visual impairments need to work with speech-language therapists and other educational team members to evaluate the language skills of their students. The determination of how auditory strategies should be used must be based not only on the viability of the student's visual and tactile systems, but also on the student's language comprehension skills. Some students may prefer using auditory strategies because they find using visual and tactile information too difficult. If listening does not contribute to a student's understanding more efficiently than vision and touch do, it should not be designated the student's primary learning system, even when it is preferred by a child. In such cases, the teacher of students with visual impairments should provide instruction for the student in visual and tactile strategies with appropriate environmental and learning media accommodations so that the sensory systems of vision and touch can be primary for learning if they provide better information to the student. It is important for teachers working with students at this age to keep in mind that their vocabularies cannot expand without efficient use of visual and tactile information to help them establish concrete referents for words. The Symbol and Referent Analysis (SARA) in Smith (2012) can be used for assessment and instruction of common and academic vocabulary.

Teachers of students with visual impairments and O&M instructors who teach students at the preoperational stage need to be effective motivators. The key to supporting a student's sensory efficiency in a given task is getting the student to want something enough that his attention is focused on the materials that are part of the lesson. Frequently, lessons presented in a game format using media with attractive sensory qualities tend to increase a student's motivation to pay careful attention to sensory information. For example, a preoperational stage student might pay more attention to the names of the days of the week if they are sung rather than spoken. Attention to pictures might be better if they are brightly colored rather than black and white. Plastic objects used for counting in math activities might be replaced with objects that have interesting textures.

When students are not able to combine multisensory information, teachers of students with visual impairments should work with other educational team members to provide accommodations in the student's environments and to design instruction so that sensory information is used as efficiently as possible (Bundy et al., 2002). For example, a teacher might stop speaking while her student tactilely explores an unfamiliar object that is part of his instruction so that he does not have to try to process auditory and tactile information at the same time.

Efficient listening skills are also important for students (Barclay, 2012). Listening is a major component of compensatory access (see Chapter 4). The need for instruction in this area is sometimes identified when students do not respond to requests or follow instructions. This behavior may indeed be a problem related to listening, but at this stage, teachers of students with visual impairments should also consider the possibility that a student's lack of response might be related to problems with comprehension or to hearing loss. Teachers of students with visual impairments need to be aware that auditory impairments are sometimes identified when children are at the preoperational stage because the child exhibits significant delays in speech development. A child with a visual impairment and a previously undetected hearing impairment is likely to have significant developmental delays that may be unrelated to cognitive capacity (Nelson, van Dijk, Oster, & McDonnell, 2009). As a result, teachers of students with visual impairments need to carefully observe auditory responses as part of learning media assessments and ensure that additional assessments are conducted when responses are abnormal (Chen, 2014).

Sensory strategies are the decisions children make about how they will use their senses to get the information they desire. According to Klatzky and Lederman (2008), children make these decisions based on the concept of "cost." Cost refers to the amount of effort required by a child to use a particular sense to gather information in a specific situation. A strategy that "costs" less is one that requires less effort and will be chosen over a strategy that costs the child more. By the time they are 2 years old, children have established habits in their use of sensory strategies. For instance, a child who cannot see features in faces may decide that a visual strategy costs too much when he is trying to identify a person approaching him. He may therefore stop looking when people approach him and rely on an auditory strategy. He may also generalize this tendency to the point that he begins habitually to rely on auditory skills to obtain information at a distance.

A teacher of students with visual impairments needs to use a learning media assessment to evaluate sensory costs for her students in a variety of different tasks and to determine whether instruction of new skills with the provision of accommodations might encourage use of more efficient strategies. If the teacher can reduce the amount of effort needed by a student to use a visual strategy by making accommodations in the student's environment and learning media or by helping the student obtain optical devices, she must then also make sure that the student receives instruction that allows him to reevaluate the cost of using his vision. If the student learns that a visual strategy can be easy and more efficient, he may choose this strategy more often and his visual skills may improve. Sometimes, however, the student decides otherwise. At a certain point, after accommodations have been provided and practiced to make strategies familiar, a child's choice of sensory strategies related to a specific task needs to be respected (Corn & Lusk, 2010). Children use different sensory strategies for different tasks and even for the same task in different environments. A child who uses vision to identify people in his classroom may use auditory skills to identify the same people in the cafeteria, where the sensory complexity of the environment may increase the effort—and thus the cost—it takes to use his vision. Another child may prefer tactile strategies for finding his cup at mealtime until his teacher or parent helps him practice finding a brightly colored cup on a contrasting placemat. For some children, visual accommodations can sometimes be gradually eliminated as looking becomes a habit, as a memory bank of meaningful visual experiences speeds up their perceptual processes, and as cortical issues resolve.

Teachers of students with visual impairments teach students to select efficient sensory strategies by expanding the array of options available to them so that they can make informed choices. Each option needs to provide meaningful and important information. Sometimes auditory substitutions are used when vision is not a viable strategy in a given situation. Teachers can encourage parents and teachers to use language, an auditory strategy, to give children information about things they cannot see. Sometimes verbal descriptions of things happening around a child with a visual impairment may be helpful even when the language used is not comprehended. Hearing someone talk about what she is doing lets a young child know where that person is. It may contribute to bonding because the child learns that the other person is socially connected to him even when not physically touching him. This kind of awareness is vitally important.

However, as indicated earlier, hearing someone talk about what she is doing does not provide a child with information about people, objects, actions, and places unless the child comprehends the language being used. When a child has good receptive language skills, including a vocabulary grounded in concrete experiences, he can use these descriptions to increase his understanding of what is happening in his world (Dunlea, 1989). If a child does not have these language skills, talking may only add to the sensory complexity of his environment. He may have to choose one of the several sensory strategies available to him: touching, looking, listening to sounds made by objects, or listening to speech. Because they are neurologically predisposed to do so, young children are likely to choose speech and to listen, even when they do not understand the words being used. As a result, they may not attend tactilely and visually when speech is present and may therefore miss opportunities to learn in a given instance. Teachers may need to be quiet when they want to increase the efficient use of visual and tactile strategies and then use appropriate language to comment on what the child did afterwards.

Because young children are neurologically predisposed to listen to speech, many young children with visual impairments have an overdependence on auditory strategies and, as a result, may have diminished active engagement with things in their environments. Talking to these children remains important: they need time when people describe things and chat with them. However, they also need time when people use very specific instructional language. Instructional language includes clear directions like "Find your sock," repetition of the single word "sock" periodically while the child is touching and looking at the sock, and clear comments about things that have just occurred like "Mary found her sock." This language helps children build experience-based vocabularies. Children also need time when people suspend talk while joining them in the use of sensory strategies involving touch and vision. For these reasons, it is important that teachers of students with visual impairments help parents and other teachers understand the importance of being quiet while they help a child use his vision or his hands, using strategies such as tactile mutual attention and hand-under-hand guidance. (For more information on this topic, see Chen & Downing, 2006, and Smith, 2012).

Reducing sensory complexity in classrooms may be difficult because accommodations needed by one student may deprive other students of access to sights and sounds that are appropriate and desirable for them. As part of the development of IEPs, students' educational teams are responsible for determining appropriate educational settings. Since learning is dependent on students' effective use of sensory information, and sensory efficiency is strongly influenced by ambient environmental characteristics like complexity, settings should be chosen carefully. No setting should be ruled out or included for a student without evaluation of factors related to the support of that student's efficient use of available sensory information.

Environmental Considerations

Schools are complex sensory environments. Gyms and cafeterias tend to be among the most complex, but even individual classrooms are noisy, busy places. Children who have difficulty with sensory complexity may withdraw or become fussy or agitated in these environments. Children with CVI, in particular, may in many cases be unable to use their vision efficiently in complex environments. They may try to reduce complexity for themselves by paying intense attention to single objects held close to the eyes so that they are less aware of activity around them. They may be unable to watch the actions of others because opening up their visual fields for observation of things at a distance lets in too much sensation (Roman-Lantzy, 2007). As a result, they may avoid social situations. They may also miss instruction provided at distance, such as teachers pointing to pictures in books during group reading activities.

The amount and rate of change taking place in active environments affects children's sensory efficiency. As mentioned earlier, students relying on touch for learning in general require more processing time because pieces of information obtained through the sense of touch are gathered sequentially rather than simultaneously (Chen & Downing, 2006). Children with cortical impairments often have response delays caused by neurological difficulties that interfere with the processing of sensory information, and, as a result, require more processing time. If elements in the environment change frequently, these children may spend much more of their energy responding to those changes than children with typical sensory abilities would. While students with cortical impairments are figuring out what is going on, they are paying less sensory attention to information related to the specific task at hand.

As with children at the sensorimotor stage, lighting in the environment must be considered in relation to the visual impairment and the child's lighting preferences. Attention to glare, ambient light, fluorescent lighting, natural light (day and night/cloudy and sunny) are important so that a child can use vision effectively in the classroom, at home, and in the environment.

Learning Media Considerations

Teachers need to provide their students with learning media that offer them access to information using their preferred sensory strategies—those perceived by the student to be of lower cost. It is also important to add experiences requiring the use of other strategies, including those that students have avoided, so that they can learn to make choices about which strategies to use in a variety of situations. In educational settings for preoperational stage learners, such as preschools, typical learning media are predominantly visual and motor in nature. For example, children spend a great deal of time looking at pictures and words in books and practicing gross and fine motor skills, like climbing ladders on playground equipment and coloring between lines. Teachers of students with low vision should try to create access for their students to the same visual materials that are being used by their classmates. To do so, they need to adjust size, reduce complexity, enhance contrast, adjust viewing distances, ensure placement in the student's preferred visual fields, and use direct lighting as needed.

When students need tactile access, the accommodations required may involve the provision of alternate media. For example, when a classroom teacher passes out a worksheet and asks the class to circle pictured objects that begin with the letter B, the teacher of a student with low vision may need to color the pictures if her student cannot recognize outline drawings. But, if the student cannot use vision for this task even with such accommodations, the teacher may need to use auditory and tactile substitutions (Lueck, 2004b). If the pictured object is unfamiliar, she might provide an object corresponding as closely as possible to the item depicted. If the pictured object is something the child has touched many times while learning the word that labels it, the teacher may be able to say the word without presenting the concrete object to which it refers.

Auditory substitutions should be used carefully with students at the preoperational level. In order to be meaningful, words must be paired with the objects to which they refer. Use of words without meaning at this developmental level can adversely affect the student's social, intellectual, and academic performance in an ongoing way. Children at the preoperational stage who cannot use pictures are often given tactile substitutes, like stuffed animals and plastic replicas. These objects, like pictures, look like the things they represent. Their use is appropriate for students who can see them. However, they are not appropriate learning media for students who need tactile access. They do not feel like the things they represent, and often they are not the same size as the real object; for example, a plastic toy airplane does not resemble a real one to a student who can feel it but can't see it. Therefore, such substitutes do not provide information about the object to which a word refers for a tactile learner.

Tactile pictures can be created to represent some items using parts of objects glued on cards (Chen & Downing, 2006). However, some things pictured cannot be tactilely represented. A book or a worksheet might contain a picture of a cloud or a house. The first cannot be touched and the second consists of a whole that is not defined by any of its touched parts. Teachers of students with visual impairments need to appreciate the challenges involved in supporting students' concept development that such sensory limitations create. (See Chapter 4 for a discussion of concept development with students who are visually impaired.) A child who cannot see a variety of different kinds of houses on streets and in pictures can develop a concept of house based only on what he has felt and heard. He may have some idea of the different materials used in construction and know about the function of different rooms. However, rooftops and ceilings may be as mysterious to him as clouds.

Overall, then, teachers of students with absent or very limited vision need to make sure that words and pictures are matched whenever possible with tactile experiences of the things they represent. After a child has touched a real object and been taught the word for the thing while touching it, the word can be used alone meaningfully. If, during a lesson on farm animals, a child is given a stuffed horse toy and told it is a horse, he may have a very distorted concept of what that word represents. He may think a horse is a small, soft, inanimate thing that smells like cloth. Learning about a horse, like everything else, begins with gathering sensory information. Inaccurate and misleading information gathered through the sense of touch is not helpful. A trip to a farm might be optional for a child with typical vision who knows a lot about animals from drives in the country and watching TV, but it is not optional for a child with visual impairment who needs to touch the animal's body, hear it breathe, and feel the ground vibrate as it moves in order to understand that it is alive and big. (Strategies for creating tactile access to people, objects, actions, and places can be found in Smith, 2012).

Concepts can be built by pairing direct sensory experiences with learning media—people, objects, actions, and places—with the words and tactile symbols used to represent them in a developmental hierarchy. Learning of concepts takes place in the following order:

- learning about one's own body in infancy
- learning about media touching the body
- learning about specific media beyond the body
- learning about clusters of related media that are a part of events beyond the body

The strategy of *sensory bridging*, the pairing of near and distance sensory information, is used to develop concepts about media and events beyond the body. For example, a young child who hears barking, but due to visual impairment does not see the source of the barking, cannot develop the concept of "dog" or the real meaning of the word "dog," unless she has help touching the animal as it barks and hears the word used to label the animal while she is touching it. Then, in the future, when she hears a different dog barking, her teacher can use the word "dog" to label that sound so that distance information is meaningful. (Sensory bridging is

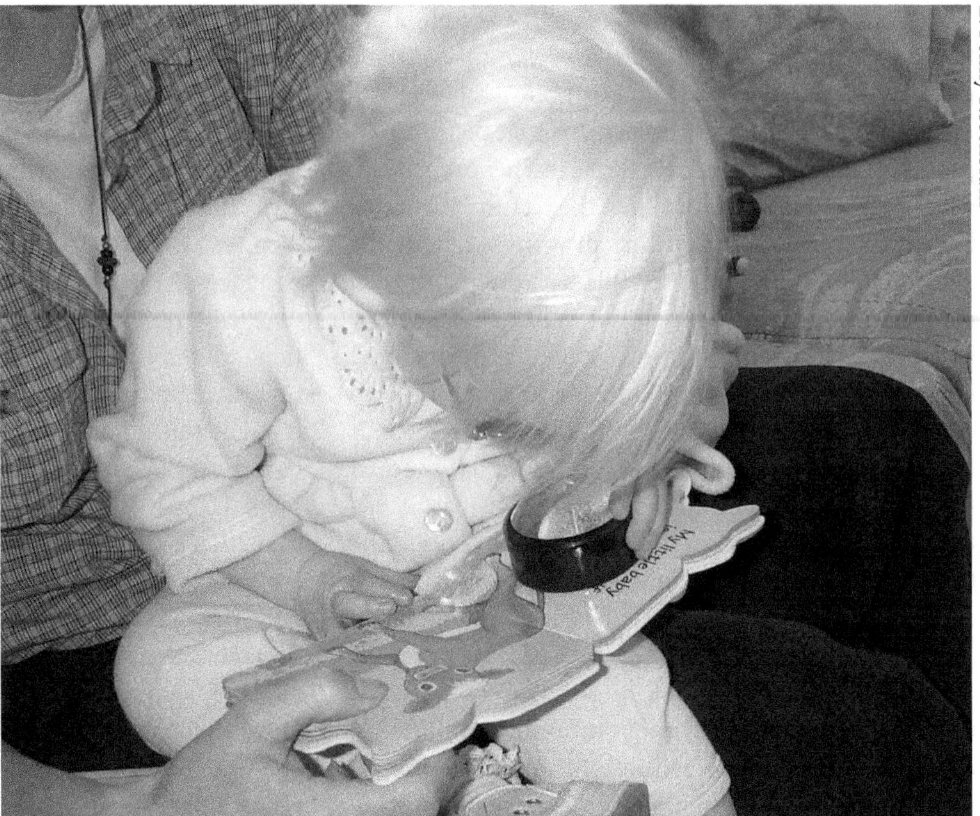

Preschool children may be introduced to optical devices, such as this dome magnifier.

L. Penny Rosenblum

discussed in more detail in the section on Teaching Sensory Efficiency in this chapter.)

Considerations for Introducing Optical Devices

In addition to corrective lenses worn in eyeglasses, preschool children may start to use magnifiers and telescopes for simple discrete tasks. Although the ability to store and maintain devices is sometimes considered a prerequisite for their introduction, teachers may find that earlier exposure to such devices contributes to their later acceptance by a child. For example, teachers can provide magnifiers at appropriate times during activities without asking students to be responsible for their storage and maintenance. The best way to ensure that students do not think that using a device is a high-cost strategy is to make sure that its use is easy and fun. At the end of an activity, a child might be given a dome magnifier to help him choose which sticker he wants. Or, a child might play pirate during recess by using a paper tube to find large targets at a distance. When a child likes using a device for one thing, another application that is enjoyable can be added. For example, the child who enjoyed playing pirate with the paper tube on the playground might be invited to use it to find favorite classmates in the lunchroom or to find specific artwork in an array displayed in a hallway.

Clinical environments are generally less complex than are homes and schools. As a result, low vision specialists may prescribe devices for a student based on the child's performance under very controlled circumstances. Teachers are sometimes disappointed when a student then rejects a device in more normal, uncontrolled settings. Gradual and careful introduction of devices in natural settings is vitally important for young children. (Strategies for the introduction and use of optical devices can be found in Lueck, 2004a; Corn & Erin, 2010; Hotta & Kitchel, 2002; Kitchel & Scott, 2002; and D'Andrea & Farrenkopf, 2000.)

Considerations for Introducing Assistive Listening Devices

A great deal of the learning that takes place at the preoperational stage is language based, and students with hearing impairments, therefore, need IEPs that ensure that they have access to language. Audiologists, speech and language therapists, teachers of students with hearing impairments, and deaf-blind specialists need to work with other educational team members to conduct communication assessments. Assistive listening devices may be one of the accommodations specified. When devices are recommended, all team members need to be trained to support a student's learning using this accommodation. Teachers of students with visual impairments need to work with hearing specialists to make sure that they develop the skills necessary to assist any student they serve whose program includes assistive listening devices.

Some assistive listening devices are designed to emphasize attention to speech sounds. When these types of devices are used, some students with visual impairments may lose access to information provided by particular environmental sounds. Students with low vision who use devices to hear speech may not see things that happen around them because their visual attention is not attracted by the environmental sounds relating to those events, and they may not anticipate events based on auditory and visual cues. As a result, their sensory efficiency is compromised.

Enhancing Use of Sensory Systems at the Operational Stage

Learning to select strategies for the most efficient way to obtain sensory information is part of the development of self-determination and sensory efficiency for students with visual impairments. For development to occur, selection of sensory strategies must be controlled by the student, not the teacher. The role of the teacher of students with visual impairments is to make sure that students try different strategies and evaluate the results accurately so that they can learn to make informed choices.

Teachers can empower students primarily in two ways: They need to make sure students have a menu of strategies from which to choose and that they know how to ask for what they need. Again, the selection of a strategy is based on the cost of the effort involved and comfort with use of a particular strategy. A kindergarten student may be able to see his teacher point to the crossed out days on the group calendar when seated with his classmates, but he may need to get up and stand next to his teacher to read the names of the days of the week and the current date. An older student who selects braille for reading most texts because it is faster for him may select magnification for reading a math text containing charts and graphs. In science class, he may dissect his frog on the tray of a video magnifier. A student who is aware that his reading rate is significantly slower than that of other students may choose to supplement his reading by using an audio book for certain chapters in order to complete an assigned novel in time to turn in his report. (Chapter 4 and Chapter 6 provide more information on strategies for performing specific tasks.)

Teachers of students with visual impairments may find that some students need instruction and accommodations to increase their literacy-related visual and tactile efficiency. For example, a student entering the third grade who has efficient visual tracking and scanning skills when reading the print typically used in books read in primary grades may have to slow down and reestablish those skills starting at a much lower level when he begins reading the smaller font used in upper elementary grades. Likewise, the same student will need to learn new skills when using a computerized text enlargement program or a portable video magnifier. A student who loses visual capacity suddenly due to head trauma or another medical issue may need to begin the transition to the use of braille media.

Often, visual and tactile efficiency needs are related to areas of the general education curriculum other than reading, writing, and math. A proficient braille reader may need help dealing with the sensory complexity of an art activity or a science lesson. A student who uses a video magnifier efficiently for reading may not realize that it is possible to use the same device to identify parts of a plant during a science lesson. Teachers of students with visual impairments need to evaluate students' sensory efficiency in a wide variety of activities in order to help students develop the skills they need to be as independent as possible in all areas of the general education curriculum, as well as all the ECC areas. When students with visual impairments have language and reading difficulties, teachers of students with visual impairments need to work with other members of the educational team to evaluate the contributing factors.

Students may not focus their attention on the targets that their teachers would choose. In recognition of the fact that attention is driven by preference, teachers need to use a variety of strategies to motivate their students to pay attention to an instructional activity. They may use external rewards in the form of prizes or social rewards in the form of praise. They can also use aesthetically pleasing materials to motivate their students to pay attention. Some students with visual impairments may miss the qualities of learning media, such as colors and pictures, that make them attractive to classmates with typical vision. Directing their attention to learning media may be more challenging as a result. Students in early elementary grades need materials with accommodations that provide the same content as that provided to classmates, but also that provide some of the same aesthetic qualities that create sensory attractiveness.

Teachers also need to be aware that having to deal with sensory complexity and unfamiliarity creates stress for students. Students who deal with sensory complexity with a high degree of efficiency in familiar situations may not function as well in equally complex but unfamiliar situations. The child who successfully combines multisensory information efficiently in the school cafeteria where he eats lunch five days a week may need much more help to integrate multisensory information on a field trip to a restaurant.

Many students are expanding their use of assistive technology at this time. The use of listening devices needs to be evaluated in relation to creating access to and increasing efficient use of items, such as tape and digital recorders and players, e-text readers, talking calculators, electronic notetakers or personal digital assistants (PDAs), scanning systems with speech, talking compasses, and talking GPS devices (Presley, 2010; Presley & D'Andrea, 2009).

Environmental Considerations

Students naturally experience more complexity in a greater variety of situations in their schools, regardless of grade level. Environmental characteristics, such as glare, illumination levels, sensory complexity, and the number and rate of environmental changes they encounter, should be carefully observed. Children who have difficulties with transition from one environment to another may be reacting to conditions they find aversive. Situations such as hallways with skylights on bright sunny days, large open areas where sounds bounce off of hard surfaces, floor surfaces with complex patterns, and playgrounds on days when moving clouds cause sudden changes in lighting can cause difficulties for some students.

Unfamiliar or unexplained noises may cause anxiety. Students who cannot see the sources of sounds may be upset by noise created by electrical appliances, such as vacuum cleaners, buffing machines, and ice dispensers, that are immediately understandable to children with typical vision. Teachers of students with visual impairments need to make sure that students continue to have the opportunity to associate unusual sounds and their sources through high school. For example, interpreting the various sounds, including ring tones and sound effects, that are heard on electronic devices like smart phones and tablets could be an interesting lesson. Some students may be too frightened to touch something like a floor buffing machine while it is operating. The teacher may need to let the student listen to the machine a few times until the noise is not threatening. Moving the machine far away from the student or listening to a recording of the sound made by the machine and then progressively moving it closer could help the student who is particularly sensitive to the noise. When the student is more comfortable with the noise, the teacher can then take her to the machine and let her touch it while it is turned off. Eventually, the teacher can turn the machine on in close proximity and the student might volunteer to touch it, or the teacher can show the student how to turn the machine off and on and let the child be in control of when the machine does or does not make noise.

Learning Media Considerations

Students with visual impairments use an array of accommodations and supports as they participate in academic instruction. Magnifiers, enlarged print, braille, audio books, reading stands, tactile rulers, talking calculators, electronic notetakers (PDAs), audio-adapted computers, tactile maps, tactile graphics, and many other assistive technologies provide access to information. In non-academic areas, items like beep balls, templates for microwave and oven controls, and color tags for clothing, provide access to activities engaged in by other students. Other chapters in this book, such as the ones on compensatory access (Chapter 4), assistive technology (Chapter 6), independent living (Chapter 8), and recreation and leisure (Chapter 10) address the specific needs of students in regard to the use of these kinds of learning media. At this level, all accommodations for academic learning media are based on the carefully assessed sensory needs of students. The learning media and functional vision assessments conducted by teachers of students with visual impairments are an essential part of determining what kinds of accommodations and supports work best to increase students' sensory efficiency in various academic contexts. In order to provide the best learning media accommodations for students at this level, teachers of students with visual impairments will need to support their students' use of the ever-expanding array of materials and technologies available.

Considerations for Optical Device Instruction

Around the third grade, some students with low vision begin to depend on the use of optical devices for access to print materials because textbooks no longer have the larger print and expanded spacing typically provided in books for younger students. Magnified print might be a student's primary literacy mode, or it might be supplemental. Telescopes often become a more important part of the menu of sensory strategies available for students to obtain visual information at a distance. As students get older, more sophisticated devices will contribute to sensory efficiency for some. These devices may include items like spectacle-mounted telescopes and prism lenses. Optical devices should always be prescribed for a student by a qualified, knowledgeable low vision specialist, who works with the teacher to ensure that the student knows how to use the device.

The use of optical devices can dramatically improve a student's sensory efficiency. Each time a new device is prescribed for one of their students, teachers of students with visual impairments and O&M specialists will need to provide extensive instruction. Without this instruction, students cannot accurately evaluate the cost in terms of energy necessary to use different strategies and make informed selections. Many devices are rejected because they cost too much (not in dollars, but in the effort to use them), and cost is always too high without guided practice. Teachers must also know how to use the device and provide time and activities for the student to become proficient in use of the device. (For information about teaching students to use magnifiers and telescopes, see Lueck, 2004b; Corn & Erin, 2010; Hotta & Kitchel, 2002; Kitchel & Scott, 2002; D'Andrea & Farrenkopf, 2000; and the Resources section of this chapter.)

Considerations for Assistive Listening Device Instruction

Teachers of students with visual impairments need to instruct students who use assistive listening devices to make sensory strategy decisions for using those devices based on their efficiency in different situations. For example, hearing aids and FM systems increase efficiency for listening to speech, but they may decrease efficiency for listening to environmental sounds for some students. The need to hear environmental sounds to the maximum extent possible expands as students at the operational level participate in activities in a wide variety of settings beyond home and school. Becoming familiar with these sounds is part of the development of concepts about objects and events at distance, such as understanding the traffic noises made by vehicles. Making use of sounds like these is an important part of the development of O&M skills in more complex environments that involve tasks such as street crossings. When speech is not the primary focus of instruction, a listening device used primarily for speech access may need to be removed, readjusted, or replaced with other technology.

Acceptance and efficient use of listening devices at the operational level requires that students learn to independently maintain and manage their devices so that they can make adjustments as they move from setting to setting and as different sensory strategies are selected.

TEACHING SENSORY EFFICIENCY: STRATEGIES IN ACTION

Specific strategies for teaching sensory efficiency and overcoming barriers to efficient use of the senses are discussed in the following section, along with examples of their application by teachers of students with visual impairments. Table 5.3 provides a guide for choosing strategies to address specific barriers to sensory efficiency, referred to frequently in the literature on the special needs of children with visual impairments and described previously in this chapter.

Collaboration with appropriate educational team members is essential in working with the strategies listed in Table 5.3. The strategies are not specifically geared to particular ages or ability levels, but they are especially important for young children, students with multiple disabilities, and students at the preoperational stage. For example, the strategy of sensory bridging, discussed earlier in this section, may be used to help a child with severe cognitive disabilities at the sensorimotor stage learn to identify the source of a sound or to help an academic high school student travel independently from class to class in his school. Adaptive play environments containing age-appropriate objects might be provided for an older student with severe multiple disabilities as part of his recreation and leisure activities or for a prekindergarten student as one of her classroom centers. In the following section, a short vignette is provided to illustrate each strategy described. Each vignette provides only one example of how a given strategy might be used; the same strategy might be appropriate for additional types of students.

TABLE 5.3

Strategies for Addressing Barriers to Sensory Efficiency

A variety of conditions and factors can compromise children's visual and tactile efficiency. Some of the common barriers encountered by teachers in their efforts to help students develop sensory efficiency skills are listed here, along with helpful strategies, which are described in the text. Collaboration with appropriate educational team members is desirable in working with these strategies, and especially necessary in regard to infant massage and techniques for dealing with children's arousal states.

Category	***Barrier***	***Strategy***	***Resources***
Alertness	Unresponsiveness	Infant massage	Newton, 2000
	Extended arousal states (drowsy, fussy, agitated)	Appetite/aversion lists	Smith, 2005; Blaha, 1996
	Self-stimulation	Arousal state management	Smith, 2005
	Passivity	Offering technique	Nielsen, 1993
Tactile efficiency	Not enough time for tactile procedures (pacing of instruction too fast)	Attract-invite-wait-assist procedure	Smith, 2012
	Manual avoidance resulting from pervasive manipulation of hands by others	Tactile modeling and hand-under-hand guidance	Chen & Downing, 2006
	Limited access to objects	Adapted play environments	Nielsen, 1992
		Exploration in natural environments	Smith, 2012
	Limited hand use due to motor impairments	Oral exploration	Smith, 2012
		Tactile exploratory procedures instruction	Chen & Downing, 2006; McLinden & McCall, 2002; Smith, 2012
	Limited use of tactile media for alternative communication	Tactile symbols	Chen & Downing, 2006
	Tactile strategies not implemented in daily instruction	Routine-based learning	Chen & Downing, 2006; Dote-Kwan & Chen, 1999; Corn & Erin, 2010; Lueck, 2004b; Roman-Lantzy, 2007; Trief & Shaw, 2009; Smith, 2005
Visual efficiency	Positioning that precludes or makes difficult visual regard of hands during interactions with objects	Positioning for hand regard	Smith, 2012
	Eyeglasses not worn	Making friends with eyeglasses	Hyvarinen, 1998
	Optical aides not used	Easing into optical device instruction	Bell Coy & Anderson, 2010; Lueck & Heinz, 2004; Hotta & Kitchel, 2002; Kitchel & Scott, 2002
	Limited access to distance information	Sensory bridging	Smith, 2012
	Visual accommodations not used in daily instruction and visual skills not practiced in daily instruction	Routine-based learning	Chen & Downing, 2006; Dote-Kwan & Chen, 1999; Corn & Erin, 2010; Lueck, 2004a; Roman-Lantzy, 2007; Trief & Shaw, 2009; Smith, 2005

Strategies for Teaching Alertness

Infant Massage

Certain kinds of touch promote not only appetite and growth in newborns, but bonding and sensory receptiveness, as well. Infant massage—a structured, neurologically based procedure for using touch to stimulate appetite, reduce fussiness and agitation, improve sensory receptivity, and increase or decrease abnormal levels of muscle tone—may be helpful for many infants, as it was for Manuel:

Manuel was born prematurely. While he was in the neonatal intensive care unit, his parents were taught how to do infant massage. At scheduled times, the parents held Manuel and touched him in the precise ways they were taught. Later, when the parents took Manuel home, if he began showing signs of stress like stiffening and crying, they used the massage techniques to help him relax and get used to the sensory complexity of his new environment.

A program called BART: Bonding and Relaxation Techniques (McClure, 2000) teaches parents to use infant massage techniques to achieve these benefits. (See also Newton, 2000, for information about this program.)

Appetite/Aversion Lists

Van Dijk uses the terms *appetites* and *aversions* to describe strong, neurologically based reactions to specific types of sensory experiences (Blaha, 1996). An appetite is a strong desire for a certain kind of input. For example, at a certain stage of development, children may have a strong need for vestibular stimulation (movement). Left to her own devices, a child may twirl around or rock back and forth in response to this appetite. An aversion is a strong dislike for a certain kind of input. For example, the same child may react to strong smells by biting her hand or screaming.

Appetites can be a part of highly effective instruction when teachers pair sensory appetites with learning media that have similar sensory characteristics. Aversions are often the basis of behavior difficulties in children, ranging in severity from withdrawal to extreme aggression directed at the self or others. It is essential that teachers know their students' sensory aversions and appetites so that they can be avoided or used effectively in instruction. Forcing a student to engage in a sensory experience he finds aversive is a counterproductive and potentially damaging strategy. Accordingly, increasing a student's sensory tolerance requires carefully applied therapeutic techniques and should be carried out under the direction of an occupational therapist (Bundy et al., 2002), as in the following example:

Farna's teacher of students with visual impairments, George, can't get her to look at or touch objects. He knows that Farna, a 14-year-old student with visual, motor, and cognitive disabilities, has the capacity to do both because she spends a lot of time looking at her hands as she moves them back and forth in front of light sources. George decides to create an appetite/aversion list for Farna as part of her learning media assessment (Smith, 2005). He begins by listing items based on the information on Farna's likes and dislikes that he has previously gathered by interviewing Farna's parents and teachers. Farna's first appetite/aversion list can be found in Table 5.4.

George then consults the occupational therapist, who suspects that Farna may be avoiding vestibular sensation, since she enjoys moving her torso and limbs in a small enclosure filled with plastic balls, but does not seem to like actions that include movement of her head. She also suspects that Farna's problem with bathing may be the light touch of the washcloth on her body. George and Farna's special education teacher decide to conduct the Sensory Response Record assessment (Smith, 2005). The teachers present Farna with at least five items in all sensory systems to determine which she likes or dislikes, and to obtain additional information about her response delays and response levels. Farna's appetite/aversion list after assessment can also be found in Table 5.4.

George helps Farna's other teachers understand that the items on her appetite list should be used as learning media in her instructional activities because Farna is motivated to use sensory strategies to explore them. George will also help Farna's teachers use these items to prepare Farna for instruction. They will use appetites with calming attributes to move her from a fussy to an alert state, and they will use appetites with alerting attributes to move her from drowsy to alert.

TABLE 5.4

Farna's Appetite/Aversion Lists

Likes	*Dislikes*
Farna's Initial Appetite/Aversion List	
Hand movement before light source (vision)	Anything unfamiliar
Warm oatmeal (taste, temperature, texture)	Rocking
Limb movement in ball pit (proprioceptive system)	Movement during transitions
Listening to voices (hearing)	Bathing
Farna's Appetite/Aversion List After Assessment	
Vision Hand movement before light source Disco ball Moving objects on lightbox Moving fan blades illuminated by penlight LED candle Optic fiber wand	Anything unfamiliar encountered without proper preparation Anything that combines vision and sounds (toys with lights and music)
Touch Warm oatmeal Warm water on feet and hands Anything heavy on her body (bean bags, weighted blankets) Massage Pressing lips and cheek against bubble wrap under head while prone if covered by something heavy Vibration on shoulders, back, and thighs if vibrator isn't too loud	Light touch Manipulation of hands Unfamiliar textures in mouth Cold, hard surfaces Bubbling water
Proprioception Movement of limbs in ball pit especially with heavier balls Pressing feet against springboard Movement of hands through water Chewing ring dipped in fruit juice Wriggling around in a small sleeping bag especially if there is bubble wrap in it	Manipulation of body during transitions if fast-paced and unexpected
Hearing Talking Tuning forks Simple song (voice only)	Unexpected sounds Loud sounds Complex sounds (two people speaking simultaneously, songs with instruments and voices)
Smell	Strong dislike resulting in withdrawal: use unscented lotions, soaps, etc.
Vestibular System Swinging on platform swing if prone, supine, or side-lying and if swinging is slow	Head movement okay, except when sitting or in stander, or when too fast

Arousal State Management

All people move through a continuum of levels of alertness, or *arousal states*, throughout the day. These arousal states include *asleep, drowsy, quiet alert, active alert, fussy*, and *agitated*. Occupational therapists have traditionally been trained to use sensory input to modulate arousal states. Researchers in the field of severe disabilities have begun to address the use of educational strategies to create and maintain alert states in response to neurological evidence that alert states are required for learning (Guess et al., 1988). Using these strategies, teachers of students with visual impairments who work with students who become fussy when they are asked to participate in instructional activities or who are unavailable for instruction because they are drowsy, can provide sensory input that either alerts or calms the student so that effective instruction can proceed. In order to manage a child's arousal state, teachers learn what kinds of sensory input are typically alerting and what kinds are typically calming for an individual student. They watch their students' reactions to see which kinds of input work best for management of arousal states and use them to create and maintain alertness so that sensory information can be used efficiently, as Farna's teacher of students with visual impairments did:

When Farna is stressed by environmental complexity, unexpected events, or aversive sensations, she gets fussy and starts to chew on her hand. George has a list of different kinds of sensory experiences that Farna enjoys. When Farna is fussy, he chooses one of the items that provides calming sensations. Before each transition or change of activity, he uses a large beanbag to gently compress Farna's shoulders and hips while she lies on her tummy on a floor mat (Bundy et al., 2002). He does these compressions for about three minutes, sits quietly next to Farna for about another minute, and then gives her a touch cue—firm pressure on her upper arms applied with both hands—to alert her that she is about to be moved.

George also wants to help extend the duration of Farna's alert periods. For example, after Farna explores a rubber ball with bumps on it for about a minute, she loses interest and starts to gaze at her hands, so George uses a different kind of sensory input—such as a similar rubber ball that lights up—to regain her attention and alertness for as long as possible. Movement of a novel object with light excites Farna and stimulates her to begin exploration. George knows that strobe lights can cause seizures in some children, so he consulted with Farna's parents before using this item.

Strategies for managing arousal states designed for use by teachers of students with visual impairments can be found in Smith (2005).

Offering Technique

The offering technique is one of several strategies designed by Nielsen (1993) to encourage tactile exploration in children who are reluctant to use their hands to touch objects. (See the Offering Technique activity in the Learning Activities section at the end of this chapter.) In this activity, an adult offers objects by interacting with them in close proximity to the child's hands. Objects that make interesting sounds attract the child's attention and interesting tactile qualities encourage exploration. When the child's exploration of one object subsides, another object is offered. The adult does not touch the child's hands and is silent while the object is offered and during the child's exploration (reducing sensory complexity so that the child can give full attention to the object), as in the following example:

Rashita's mother wants to play with her daughter. The mother sits on a resonance board behind Rashita, supporting her daughter's back against her torso. The mother picks up a plastic bottle about half full of water and holds it in front of Rashita, next to, but not touching, her hands. She then shakes the bottle so that the sloshing water makes an interesting sound. She keeps shaking the bottle until Rashita moves her hands to the object. The mother does not put the object in Rashita's hands or move Rashita's hands to the object. If Rashita doesn't move her hands toward the sound, the mother puts that object away and tries another one. So far, Rashita's favorites are a toy accordion and a whisk in a metal mixing bowl.

Strategies for Teaching Tactile Efficiency

Attract-Invite-Wait-Assist Procedure

The Attract-Invite-Wait-Assist (AIWA) procedure, outlined in Sidebar 5.6, is used to facilitate the active exploration needed for efficient tactile learning. This procedure is based on research indicating that there are four phases in a motor event—preparation, initiation, execution, and termination—and that activity in the cortex of the brain is very high during the preparation and initiation phases (Deecke, 1978; Smith, 2005). Execution of motor actions is strongly related to the development of motor skills, but it is not the most important phase with regard to learning. Designing instruction with an emphasis on preparation and initiation of actions gives students with severe motor impairments the

SIDEBAR 5.6

The Attract-Invite-Wait-Assist Procedure

The Attract-Invite-Wait-Assist (AIWA) procedure is used to facilitate the active exploration needed for efficient tactile learning. The steps in the procedure are the following:

ATTRACT
Choose learning media with characteristics that the student finds highly attractive. The learning media assessment should provide information about attractive media in each viable sensory channel (Smith, 2005).

INVITE
Let the student know that you expect action. Invite action by using verbal prompts, mimicking actions, tactile modeling, pointing, tapping, supporting wrist and elbow, and so forth.

WAIT
After inviting action, wait for the student to prepare and initiate a response. The learning media assessment should provide information about response delays (Smith, 2005). Remember that the response may be subtle. Increases in muscle tone; leaning forward; extending the head, chin, tongue, or the fingers of a fisted hand are all forms of initiating action involving the student's action system.

ASSIST
After the student has responded and executed as much independent movement as he or she can, assist. Use tactile modeling and hand-under-hand-guidance. Provide the least amount of assistance required to allow the student to understand what full execution is like. Pauses that allow the student to prepare and initiate very small actions will keep his or her cerebral activity at a high level.

opportunity to use coordinated sensing and acting for maximum cognitive benefit. The AIWA procedure makes tactile learning more efficient for all students, but it is essential for those who have severe motor impairments. The following is an example of when it would be important to use the AIWA procedure:

Paul's teacher of students with visual impairments, Eric, is concerned that Paul's visually directed reach is very delayed. The teacher has discussed this issue with Paul's other teachers and they decide to use a strategy called *partial participation*, which allows Paul to do everything he can in an activity before a teacher assists with the parts he cannot do. During observations in the classroom, Eric sees the general education teacher conducting fast-paced instruction and completely manipulating Paul's hands. The general education teacher explains that she is concerned that the pacing appropriate for Paul is not appropriate for the other children in her classroom.

Eric shows the IEP team his data showing that Paul's responses during fast-paced instruction are limited to startle reflexes occurring when his hands are touched. The IEP team members agree to use the AIWA procedure in carefully selected activities. When the AIWA procedure is used, pacing will be individualized to meet Paul's needs and he will have time to prepare and initiate his motor responses.

Tactile Modeling and Hand-Under-Hand Guidance

Children who are manually avoidant can be encouraged to use their hands to engage in tactile exploration by combining the AIWA procedure just described with tactile modeling and hand-under-hand guidance, as in the example that follows. (See Chen & Downing, 2006, for information about and illustrations of these strategies; and the Washington Sensory Disabilities Services website [see the Resources section at the end of this chapter] for helpful video examples of hand-under-hand guidance.)

Cruz will not let anyone touch his hands and he does not use his hands for exploration, even though touch is his primary learning system. He spends his time in his pre-K classroom listening, and he especially enjoys language. He can repeat his story tapes verbatim, including beeps and instructions to turn the page. His teacher of students with visual impairments, Clare, knows that, in order to make language meaningful, she will have to get Cruz to touch objects as he learns the words that label them.

Clare begins by consulting with an occupational therapist in order to determine whether Cruz is tactilely defensive. The occupational therapist screens Cruz and tells Clare that Cruz does not exhibit the characteristics of tactile defensiveness, but is manually avoidant. Clare asks Cruz's other teachers to use tactile modeling and hand-under-hand strategies. She models these strategies for the teachers and they practice them with each other. Clare tells them to be patient, since it will take time for Cruz to trust that his teachers are not going to grab his hands or put objects into them.

Now a teacher can hold an object, press the back of her hand against the back of Cruz's hand, and say, "May I show you?" Cruz will turn his hand over and place it over the back of his teacher's hands to signal his assent. When the teacher turns her hand over, he will take the object from her hand and explore it. The teacher labels the object by saying what it is while he explores it.

Adapted Play Environments

A child's sensory exploration may be limited for a variety of reasons. Children with visual impairments may not know that objects exist beyond their bodies because they cannot see them. They may have motor impairments that prevent movement to objects that they can see. Or, they may reject novel objects because too many experiences with unfamiliar things have been unpleasant to them. Adapted play environments are spaces that create access to new objects with attractive sensory characteristics and encourage a child's use of exploration for learning. Lueck and Heinze (2004) called these environments "small worlds," and they provide information about a variety of possible play settings, as well as considerations for setting up these environments. Nielsen (1992) has described a more formal approach, known as the Little Room:

Rashita enjoys playing with objects in her Little Room. Lakshmi, her teacher of students with visual impairments, set it up in the family room, as Rashita's mother requested. When the Little Room was ready, Rashita's mother was skeptical. The objects in the hanging array seemed strange. Rashita's favorite object, her pacifier, was there, but so was a piece of heavy plastic coated chain, a metal cooking pot, and a leather glove. The space seemed small and cluttered. Lakshmi explained that objects with strong sensory characteristics had been chosen: the chain for weight, the pot for coolness, and the glove for softness.

The first time Rashita went into her Little Room, she was very quiet for several minutes. Eventually, she lifted her hand to put her fingers in her mouth. When she did this, her hand brushed past the leather glove and came in contact with her pacifier. She turned her head to the side and grasped her pacifier with her mouth. While sucking, she lifted her hand again. This time she rubbed her hand against the glove. She did this several times. Finally, she spit out her pacifier, used her hand to push the glove toward her face, and rubbed it with her lips. Soon after, Rashita traced the seams of the glove with the tip of her tongue and, eventually, searched the array around her face to find additional objects. After watching her daughter use the Little Room, Rashita's mother understands the significance of these behaviors: learning about gloves isn't important; learning to actively explore her environment is essential.

Exploration in Natural Environments

Teachers need to be sure that young children with visual impairments, including those who have motor impairments, have the same opportunities to learn object and place relationships that children without visual and motor impairments have. Children with visual impairments need to brush their teeth in the bathroom where they can see, touch, and hear things related to this activity (like a sink and water running) and understand that this is the place where their toothbrush is located. They cannot learn these concepts and relationships among objects if their bodies do not move to different places and if objects are taken out of their natural contexts and brought to them, as was the case with Kenny:

Kenny loves reading books with his classmates in the library. When he goes to the library, a teaching assistant wheels him to a table and places several books on it so that he can choose the one he wants to read. Kenny has no idea that there are rows of shelves containing books surrounding him in this environment. After observing this, Kenny's teacher of students with visual impairments works with the teaching assistant to make sure that Kenny is allowed to pull several books from the shelves to take to his table in the future.

Oral Exploration

Children should be encouraged to use their hands for exploration to the maximum extent possible. Some children with very limited vision and severe motor impairments will need to continue to use oral exploration as a primary means of obtaining tactile information well past the developmental stage that is typical for that behavior in children. As noted earlier, for many children who have cerebral palsy, spasticity limits their ability to reach for and grasp objects with their hands, and peripheral nerve damage may reduce the childrens' ability to discriminate the characteristics of objects placed in their hands (Blanche & Nakasuji, 2001). If a child with these characteristics has good head control, the continued use of oral exploration can allow him to use his mouth to obtain information about objects that would be unavailable to him otherwise, as in the following example:

Ben is 3 years old and enrolled in an early intervention program at his neighborhood school. In spite of the fact that his only access to high-quality information about objects—information that is accurate and meaningful to him—is through oral exploration, his teachers feel that what they call "mouthing" is inappropriate. Ben's teacher of students with visual impairments, Mark, knows that he needs to explore objects orally to establish concrete referents for new vocabulary. For example, he hears the word "bell" during music circle, but he never sees or touches the bell. His teacher thinks he knows what the word means because he uses the word "bell" to label the sound he hears, but being able to label the sound of a bell ringing is not the same thing as knowing what a bell is.

Understanding Ben's limited understanding of the objects around him, Mark makes oral object exploration one of Ben's IEP goals. However, the assistive technology team has to be convinced that Ben's "mouthing" should be encouraged. They want Ben to touch adaptive switches. Mark has to explain that Ben needs to understand what those switches are attached to. Ben needs to know what the words "CD player" and "fan" mean. If he only touches a switch to turn these things on and never touches the things themselves, then the words that label the objects that are turned on have no meaning for him. Mark refers to the appendix titled "Limited Hand Use Due to Motor Impairment" in *SAM: Symbols and Meaning* (Smith, 2012) as a guide for incorporating manual and oral exploration of objects into Ben's lessons.

Tactile Exploratory Procedures Instruction

When a young child uses touch primarily for learning, teachers of students with visual impairments may need to teach tactile exploratory procedures (see Sidebar 5.3) as a compensatory skill, just as they might teach braille to an older student. Refusal to explore objects with the hands is a barrier to sensory efficiency for many students with visual impairments, regardless of age or ability level, as it is for Joey in this example:

Joey is a kindergarten student who has resisted touching objects all her life due to tactile defensiveness. She has excellent language skills, but she has many gaps in her understanding of concepts. Her occupational therapist has trained her teachers to use deep pressure techniques (firm, deep, consistent pressure, such as bear hugs and joint compressions, that calm and organize the central nervous system) to prepare her for touching objects during activities. Her teacher of students with visual impairments is using the same techniques to prepare her for instruction in using specific exploratory procedures, such as contour following (see Sidebar 5.3) to explore the exact shape of objects, such as puzzle pieces.

Tactile Symbols

Alternative communication skills are those that compensate for the inability to use speech, by providing instruction in the use of tactile cues, gestures, and sign language, and the inability to see pictures and written words by providing instruction in the use of tactile symbols, such as whole objects, parts of objects, and braille (Chen & Downing, 2006). In the following example, Demarcus uses signed speech and tactile symbols:

Demarcus is a 3-year-old boy with a visual impairment and a profound hearing loss. He is enrolled in a preschool program where he uses signed speech to label people and objects. Since he has very limited peripheral visual fields and needs high contrast for visual discrimination, his teacher of students with visual impairments has worked with team members to make sure that they wear a dark colored vest to increase contrast, and define a specific space for central fixation during presentation of their hands for signing. Demarcus cannot use the pictures used by his peers in choice-making tasks, so his teacher of students with visual impairments has created tactile pictures for him (for example, his picture for "juice" is a juice box straw glued on a card).

Routine-Based Learning

As the term is used in this chapter, a *routine* is an activity with a series of steps performed in the same way and in the same order each time the activity occurs. Routines provide a high degree of consistency, which increases children's participation levels and lowers stress. Activities designed this way can be highly effective. Students with multiple disabilities and young children who are engaged in routine-based instruction can anticipate the steps in an activity because the steps occur in the same order each time the activity is done.

Cruz, who was introduced earlier, now has several routines that are part of his daily schedule. His music routine begins by moving him from a mat to a floor chair. He then closes the lid of the CD player, which is his participation in loading the CD, and finally, he uses a switch to turn on the music. Cruz shows that he knows the steps of his routine when he begins to reach for the switch after he has closed the lid—evidence of anticipation.

Teachers embed IEP skills into activities designed as routines. One of Cruz's IEP objectives is to learn to use a switch to activate a device. The teacher embeds the switch skill in his music routine and over time will embed additional skills, such as tactilely exploring the CD player, within the routine. She also uses a tactile label on the switch so that Cruz will associate it with the device to which it is attached. (See Dote-Kwan & Chen, 1999, and Smith, 2005, for additional information about routines.)

Strategies for Teaching Visual Efficiency

Positioning for Hand Regard

Students at any stage of development who have impaired motor abilities need to be positioned so that they can see their hands. These students cannot use vision and touch in coordination if they are, for example, positioned in travel chairs and wheelchairs that are tipped backward. Good head control is needed to move the head down sufficiently to see hands and objects on lap trays. Some supports provided for head stabilization prevent downward movement of the head. Various supine, prone, and side-lying positions provide efficient visual access to objects and hands. A student with severe motor impairments might lie on his stomach on a mat, head turned to the side, with an attractive object or a touch screen placed so that he can watch his hands interact with it or move his mouth to it for oral exploration or operation of a puff switch. Another student might lie on his back with a hanging array of objects positioned so that he can see them and touch them easily. (For information about positioning to facilitate exploration, see the appendix titled "Tactual Learning with Limited Hand Use Due to Motor Impairment," in Smith, 2012.)

Raffi is a student with a visual impairment and a severe motor impairment. He has lower visual field loss and poor head control. He cannot move his head down far enough to inspect objects on the table surface used by his classmates in a cooperative learning science activity on classification of objects into categories of mineral or vegetable. A swing arm attached to his wheelchair is used to present a hanging array containing the same objects so that Raffi can inspect them using his upper visual field.

Making Friends with Eyeglasses

Many children who need eyeglasses refuse to wear them. Use of eyeglasses needs to be encouraged, while keeping in mind that each child is different and that what works for one does not necessarily work for another. Some strategies that are generally helpful include the following:

- Be sure a child's eyeglasses fit. Some parents prefer eyeglasses that look good, but they may not be the glasses that feel comfortable to the child. Soft frames may help in this regard.
- Allow the child to help select eyeglasses frames.
- Smile while helping a child put eyeglasses on.
- Let the child help put on the eyeglasses.
- Have the child use the eyeglasses for a short time for designated activities, gradually increasing use over time. For example, a child might wear his glasses when he chooses the music CD he wants to play and then take them off.
- Engage the child in an interesting visual activity before putting on eyeglasses. For example, playing an "I Spy" game in which the child uses

his vision to find several CD cases can create a positive feeling about using vision for something easy before the eyeglasses are put on to do something harder, like identifying the contents of the cases by looking closely at their labels.

- If the child takes the eyeglasses off, wait a while before putting them back on and be sure to smile when doing so.
- A change in vision, even for the better, may be disturbing to a child. Gradual increases in corrective power may help a child adjust to the change. Also, wearing frames without lenses for a while may help a child who needs to get used to one thing at a time.
- Suggest to families that putting on and wearing eyeglasses become part of a child's "getting dressed" routine.
- Get a second opinion about the prescription if a child continues to refuse to wear eyeglasses. Sometimes eyeglasses are refused because the correction isn't helpful.

The following example shows how some of these strategies might work:

When he was 3 years old, after a series of surgeries, Matt received his first eyeglasses prescription for correcting his distance vision. At first, he refused to wear his glasses. Matt's mother decided to start by having him wear his eyeglasses while choosing his cereal. She put three single-serving cereal boxes on the counter, about 3 feet away from Matt, and asked him to put his glasses on and choose the one he wanted. She put the boxes at a distance so that Matt couldn't use his preferred strategy of picking them up and holding them close to his eyes. Matt knew he could take his eyeglasses off after choosing his cereal. One morning he looked at the boxes without his eyeglasses, put the eyeglasses on, looked again, and said, "Better."

Easing Into Optical Device Instruction

Optical devices are often rejected or used inefficiently because they are prescribed and supplied without supportive instruction. In general, teachers of students with visual impairments need to make sure that optical devices are used for the specific purposes for which they were prescribed. Teachers may need to help students understand and accept the fact that higher levels of magnification make the area viewable through a device smaller and that, as a result, they may have more difficulty locating objects within a wider field. When motivation is high, teachers can begin to teach information about the device and its care, provide directed practice in the use of the device for a variety of tasks, and help the student identify situations in which he or she should initiate use of the device, as in the following example:

When Jenny was in second grade, a clinical low vision specialist recommended that she start to learn to use a telescope. Jenny's teacher of visual impairments, John, included an objective for the use of the device in Jenny's IEP and provided direct instruction. Jenny enjoyed using her telescope in a "treasure map" activity (see the learning activity "Treasure Map" at the end of this chapter), where she followed lines drawn on a whiteboard in order to find a picture of an object. After she found the picture, she went to the treasure chest to get the corresponding object. When Jenny advanced to the point that she could scan lines of print easily, John and Jenny's general education teacher decided it was time to ask Jenny to use her telescope to read material projected on the screen, rather than giving her desk copies. With help from John and her O&M instructor, Jenny also learned to use her telescope to find her friends on the playground and for many other distance activities.

For information about teaching the use of optical devices, see the Resources section at the end of this chapter.

Sensory Bridging

Children with visual impairments that severely limit their ability to see people and objects at a distance need help getting sensory information about events that take place beyond their visual range. Because they cannot use vision for distance information, they need to depend on auditory information, yet the sounds they hear may or may not be helpful. As noted earlier, sound can serve as a sensory bridge to distance information, but only when the child is able to identify a given sound's source. Sounds cannot be bridges unless hearing and touching are first paired so the child has the opportunity to develop an understanding of the connection between a sound and its source. For example, a child at a birthday party might be able to see the candles on the birthday cake in front of him, but have no idea where the horn noises are coming from because he cannot see the noisemakers used by the other children at the table.

Teachers of students with visual impairments need to ensure that their students who depend on sound for distance information have experiences during which they touch what they hear (Smith, 2012). Once these experiences are well established, the sound alone can convey meaningful information, as in the following example:

Annie spends a lot of her time playing with a toy piano keyboard in her kindergarten class. She becomes very upset when she needs to make a transition from one activity to another, frequently falling to the floor and biting people who try to get her up. Her teacher thinks Annie does not want to leave her piano because it is familiar to her. Several of Annie's educational team members believe she needs a behavior plan consisting of time outs for aggression and rewards for compliance. Her teacher of visual impairments, Martha, suspects that Annie is experiencing high levels of stress because her CVI makes the complex events in her environment confusing and scary. She holds her toy piano against her ear while she manipulates it because it makes her feel safe. More than a behavior plan, she needs sensory efficiency instruction that helps her make sense of the unfamiliar activities and the sounds associated with them.

Martha decides to use sensory bridging materials (Smith, 2012) to help Annie understand the sounds she hears. She starts with an event that occurs several times each day: transition to the restroom in Annie's classroom. Annie finds the sound of the air dryer in the restroom interesting, but she doesn't know what makes the sound. The teacher waits until Annie has finished toileting and washing her hands and then takes her to the air dryer. She provides Annie with several experiences of touching the object before activating it. One day Annie showed that the sound was meaningful to her by getting up by herself and moving to the dryer when she heard its sound. Her teacher now uses the sound of the dryer to let Annie know the destination of her upcoming transition to the restroom, and Annie no longer resists.

Routine-Based Learning

The best way to ensure that visual accommodations will be used and that visual skills will be practiced in daily instruction is to design routines in which accommodations are specified and skills are embedded. This strategy is equally effective for ensuring the use of tactile accommodations and the teaching of tactile skills. Refer to the discussion of this strategy and the examples of tools used to implement it in the previous section on Strategies for Teaching Tactile Efficiency.

Tools for Designing Sensory Efficiency Instruction

A variety of tools are available to help teachers plan sensory efficiency instruction. Figure 5.2 illustrates the use of five such tools as they might be used to plan instruction for some of the students described in this section. The Ecological Inventory is designed to help teachers provide instruction that increases tactile efficiency. The other four tools—Analysis of Daily Routines Form, Observations of Visual Behaviors, Form for Designing an Intervention, and Functional Literacy Tasks—address visual efficiency. The Resources section also lists specific tools for designing integrated sensory efficiency instruction (see D'Andrea & Farrenkopf, 2000; Lueck, 2004a; Corn & Erin, 2010; Roman-Lantzy, 2007; Trief & Shaw, 2009; Smith et al., in press), strategies for teaching integrated tactile skills (see McLinden & McCall, 2002; Chen & Downing, 2006), and tools for the assessment of all sensory systems and the integration of multisensory strategies in routine-based instruction (see Smith, 2005).

ROLE OF THE TEACHER OF STUDENTS WITH VISUAL IMPAIRMENTS

Teachers of students with visual impairments address the sensory efficiency needs of their students by assessing those needs, by working directly with students when that is the most effective way to develop skills, by participating in the selection and design of activities that occur regularly throughout the day, by teaching others who provide instruction on a daily basis to use effective sensory accommodations and strategies, and by helping to revise activities when difficulties are encountered or when embedded skills are achieved and new skills need to be added. Teaching others to provide instruction includes sharing information, modeling effective instruction, and coaching others during observations.

Teachers of students with visual impairments conduct evaluations of new students' functional vision,

FIGURE 5.2

Examples of Tools for Designing Sensory Efficiency Instruction

The following are examples of tools that can be used to design activities for the instruction of sensory efficiency:

ECOLOGICAL INVENTORY: CRUZ'S MUSIC ROUTINE

Steps in Routine	***Instructional Cues***	***Skills Required***	***Tactile Strategies***
Transition from mat to floor chair	*Anticipation calendar* *"Time for music"*	*Recognize new container and object symbol (CD)*	*Wait at least 30 seconds after verbal prompt for independent touch* *Allow at least 30 seconds for tactile exploration of container and object*
Close lid of CD player	*Provide sound cue (closing of lid)* *"Close lid"*	*Differentiate lid from rest of player* *Imitate demonstrated action*	*Tactilely scan player* *Use hand under hand to follow tactile modeling*
Start music with switch	*Provide sound cue (clicking of switch)* *"Start music"*	*Associate switch with music player* *Read label on switch*	*Attach tactile label to top of switch (CD)* *Attach switch to front of player*

SOURCE: Adapted from D. Chen and J. Downing, "Ecological Inventory: Circle Time," in *Tactile Strategies for Children Who Have Visual Impairments and Multiple Disabilities: Promoting Communication and Learning Skills* (New York: AFB Press, 2006), Table 2.2; pp. 37–38.

ANALYSIS OF DAILY ROUTINES FORM: MATT'S ARRIVAL ROUTINE

Daily schedule	***Visual Components***	***Visual Skill Instruction***	***Related Skills***
Arrival routine	*Locate locker*	*Scan row of lockers*	*Left-right progression* *Sequential order*
	Locate folder in backpack		
	Locate folder basket	*Localize position*	*Combine visual and auditory information to narrow search area*
	Put folder in basket		
Restroom			
Journal time			
Morning circle			
Centers			
Snack			
Playground			

SOURCE: Adapted from A. H. Lueck and T. Heinze, "Interventions for Young Children with Visual Impairments and Students with Visual and Multiple Disabilities," in A. H. Lueck (Ed.), *Functional Vision: A Practitioner's Guide to Evaluation and Intervention* (New York: AFB Press, 2004), Figure 8.2; pp. 282–285.

OBSERVATIONS OF VISUAL BEHAVIORS: MANUEL

Visual Behavior	***Specific Skill***	***When***	***Conditions***
Fixating	*Maintain gaze on mother's face*	*Feeding, diapering, and playing peek-a-boo*	*Move face to 2 feet and speak*
Shifting gaze	*Alternately look from mother to bottle*	*Feeding*	*Use red, shiny bottle* *Move bottle slowly in upper left field at 2 feet* *Sit in front of blank wall space*

FIGURE 5.2 *continued*

Visual Behavior	*Specific Skill*	*When*	*Conditions*
Scanning	*Look around to find teddy bear*	*Crib play*	*Yellow bear with black button eyes and red mouth* *Solid, dark color blanket*

SOURCE: Adapted from A. H. Lueck and T. Heinze, "Interventions for Young Children with Visual Impairments and Students with Visual and Multiple Disabilities," in A. H. Lueck (Ed.), *Functional Vision: A Practitioner's Guide to Evaluation and Intervention* (New York: AFB Press, 2004), Figure 8.4; pp. 292–293.

FORM FOR DESIGNING AN INTERVENTION: MATT'S—JOURNAL TIME

Goal	*Scan table area to find materials* *Use magnifier for close-up details*
Activity components	*Share markers with peer partner* *Choose sticker from sheet of small stickers*
Ambient accommodations	*Provide reading stand*
Learning media accommodations	*None*
Optical devices	*Dome magnifier*
Sensory strategy selection	*Allow Matt to use any marker he wants in order to give him a chance to discover which colors he can see best*
Specific visual skill instruction	*Teach up/down/side/side scan pattern* *Teach vertical scanning from row to row with magnifier on sticker page*

SOURCE: Adapted from A. H. Lueck and T. Heinze, "Interventions for Young Children with Visual Impairments and Students with Visual and Multiple Disabilities," in A. H. Lueck (Ed.), *Functional Vision: A Practitioner's Guide to Evaluation and Intervention* (New York: AFB Press, 2004), Figure 8.5; p. 336.

INVENTORY OF FUNCTIONAL LITERACY TASKS: JENNY

Environment	*Task*	*Strategies*
School	*Read textbooks* *Read computer screens* *Read projected material* *Handwriting* *Keyboarding*	*Video magnifier* *Enhanced contrast* *Telescope* *Stand magnifier or black fine-tip felt marker* *Touch typing*
Home	*Texting* *Reading e-mail* *Reading magazines* *Reading the TV channel guide*	*Stand magnifier* *Enhanced contrast* *Video magnifier if necessary* *Telescope*
Community	*Reading menus* *Reading labels* *Reading signs*	*Pocket magnifier* *Pocket magnifier* *Telescope*

SOURCE: Adapted from M. C. Holbrook, A. J. Koenig, and E. J. Rex, "Instruction of Literacy Skills to Children and Youths with Low Vision," in A. L. Corn and J. N. Erin (Eds.), *Foundations of Low Vision: Clinical and Functional Perspectives,* 2nd ed. (New York: AFB Press, 2010), Appendix 13A; pp. 523–526.

learning media, and the ECC as part of the special education referral process and for established students as part of the IEP review process. At IEP meetings, they recommend the type and amount of service they will provide for the coming year. These decisions are based on the needs of the student, as determined by their assessments.

In general, teachers of students with visual impairments need to use a combination of direct and consultative services to address students' ECC needs, including sensory efficiency. Short-term direct pull-out instruction can be highly effective with some students for teaching sensory efficiency skills, such as those related to the use of a new optical device. This type of service works effectively with students who can practice on their own after a skill is taught. When children are young or when they have multiple impairments, direct pull-out instruction may be difficult because these students need frequent practice in order to establish a new skill. These students are not likely to practice a skill without the support of a teacher. Therefore, teachers of students with visual impairments need to work with general and special education teachers to ensure that students have opportunities to practice and master sensory skills. Sensory efficiency skills taught in this way require that teachers of students with visual impairments do the following:

- provide accommodations in environments where instruction will take place
- make sure that learning media used in activities are attractive and accessible to the student
- use modeling and coaching to train teachers and parents to use effective visual and tactile strategies
- conduct ongoing assessment through observation in order to revise instruction and expand on skills to be taught

Promoting a Team Approach

IEPs for students with visual impairments are designed and implemented by teams. Classroom teachers and teaching assistants provide daily instruction. Teachers of students with visual impairments and other specialists work directly with students when appropriate, but the skills they teach must also be part of a student's regular activities throughout the day. In many cases, other members of the educational team may teach the skills related to the needs identified by the teacher of students with visual impairments. To ensure that these sensory efficiency goals are taught and practiced during daily instruction, the teacher of students with visual impairments needs to communicate regularly with other team members, offer them support and consultation, advocate on behalf of the student's visual and other sensory needs, and work collaboratively on an ongoing basis. Sidebar 5.7 offers some suggestions for working with other professionals to integrate sensory skills into daily instruction.

Effective collaboration with parents, family members, and other significant care providers requires teachers to have a unique set of skills. Members of the educational team must consider a family's cultural values, linguistic backgrounds, responsibility and energy loads of individual family members, and interpersonal and psychological factors. To the extent possible, the healthiest collaboration occurs when parents and families are involved in school programs and when professional team members are involved in home programs. Teachers who do not welcome parents in their classrooms cannot expect that they will be welcome in their homes. The trust that makes collaboration possible means that all parties must openly share perspectives and value the significance of understanding each other's points of view (Trief & Shaw, 2009).

Changes and Clarifications to the IEP: Accommodations, Modifications, and Supports

Use of accommodations listed for students in their IEPs is legally mandated, whereas adaptations that may be recommended by teachers of students with visual impairments in their assessment reports are optional. To ensure that needed accommodations are implemented in daily instruction, it is therefore important that teachers of students with visual impairments include a section on "accommodations, modifications, and supports" in their reports of functional vision assessments and learning media assessments, and make sure that items required by students are made part of the accommodations, modifications, and supports section of students' IEPs. The individualized needs of a student in all three areas are established by assessment. Accommodations are changes to the materials or strategies used for the delivery of content or to the methods used by a student to respond to content. Teachers of students with visual impairments should list accommodations such as complexity reduction, enlarged text, and heightened contrast, if assessment

SIDEBAR 5.7

Suggestions for Working with Educational Team Members to Integrate Sensory Skills into Instruction

Teachers of students with visual impairments working with team members to integrate sensory skills into daily instruction may find some of these suggestions helpful.

- Perform evaluations collaboratively when possible.
- Share responsibility for the student's daily schedule by helping to design instruction with embedded sensory skills across times and settings.
- Model strategies.
- Observe frequently to make sure that strategies are being used as modeled.
- Coach team members when changes are needed.
- Use video, e-mail, and text messages to share information and to ask for help from other team members.
- Review progress frequently in order to revise strategies that may not be working well and to add new strategies to teach additional skills.
- ***Allow for environmental differences.*** For many children, sensory responses and the use of sensory systems are quite different at home. Some children might be more efficient in using their senses to gather information at home because environments and objects are more familiar, and strong social bonds reduce stress. Other children might use their senses more efficiently in a school environment if they find it less complex and more predictable.
- ***Involve parents when appropriate.*** Parental help may be needed for some evaluations. For some children who cannot speak and may have a limited range of responses, parents need to be involved to teach other educational team members how to interpret behaviors, like changes in breathing rates, increased movement of the extremities, and other responses that a person less familiar with the student's longstanding patterns of behavior might find ambiguous.
- ***Strive for consistency.*** Strategies like tactile modeling and hand-under-hand guidance are much more likely to increase manual cooperation if they are used consistently by everyone, including family members, and if their use begins as early as possible.
- ***Identify ways to lower stress.*** Avoiding exposure to sensory aversions and providing accommodations to reduce environmental complexity can have a significant impact on a child's behavior. Parents and families may find that these interventions make events like mealtimes, dressing, bathing, and bedtime much less stressful and should therefore be informed about them.

indicates these changes are needed by the student. Modifications are changes to curriculum content. Teachers might list such modifications as shortened assignments and alternative text. Supports may include equipment such as voice recognition programs for computers, staff training on unique needs such as optical device support, or special transportation for mobility lessons. When listing accommodations, teachers need to appreciate that specific information is more helpful than general information to team members providing daily instruction. Short written guides for important instructional activities provided by the teacher of students with visual impairments can be helpful, as in the following example:

At the beginning of the school year, Ashley's teacher of students with visual impairments, Aiko, explained Ashley's accommodations to the teachers in Ashley's self-contained special education classroom and her general education teachers. During scheduled observations, however, Aiko noticed that many of the accommodations were not being used. When Aiko discussed this concern with the teachers, it appeared that the accommodation statements were too vague. Aiko restated the accommodations with more specificity: "Present media centrally" became "Present media centrally at face level at a distance of 2 feet"; "Allow extra time" became "Wait 30 seconds after Ashley looks at an object to allow her enough time to reach for the object independently." Aiko gave Ashley's teachers a reference page showing the application of these strategies in certain activities. She found that after she provided this detailed information for a few important activities, teachers were able to generalize the strategies to new activities without additional help.

SUGGESTIONS FOR WORKING WITH PARENTS

Involvement of parents and families is important in all areas of the ECC (see Chapter 15), but has unique significance in the area of sensory efficiency. Every child is different; instructional strategies and interventions that work for one will not necessarily work for another. Parents and their children's educational teams need to try to make the best decisions about what ideas to try and how to make those efforts effective.

The following suggestions can be shared with families as a menu from which to pick and choose.

- Turn off TVs and music players when you want your child to pay attention to his bottle, your face, a toy, or items used while dressing, eating, or grooming.
- Make sure you know what kind of lighting helps your child see. Windows, area lamps, skylights, ceiling fans, and dim lighting can cause problems.
- Start asking your eye specialist about eyeglasses as soon as you know your child has a visual impairment. If your eye specialist says your child doesn't need eyeglasses because he is too young or because he isn't interested in pictures and written words, get a second opinion. Try to find a clinical low vision specialist who knows about young children and children with multiple impairments. Not all clinical low vision specialists have the skills to work with young children, especially those with special needs. Ask your child's teacher of students with visual impairments to find one qualified to evaluate your child.
- Be a good consumer of the help provided by the team serving your child. Expect them to give you information that allows you to be more successful with the things you want to do at home. Ask for information that demonstrates success with achieving the goals you have agreed on for school.
- Identify a special area for certain types of activities. You are probably going to have to do some things your child hates. Teeth need to be brushed, medications given, and nails clipped. You might try doing these activities in a special place where only these events happen, such as a mat with a special covering, or a chair different from other chairs. It may sound counterintuitive, but it can really help. Your child may learn that if she isn't in the "unpleasant things happen here" place, she can relax. Use a routine so that the "unpleasant things" always happen the same way. When your child knows what to expect, even if it isn't pleasant, she will be less stressed.
- Remove things your child does not like. If your child shows you that he doesn't like something, take it away. If it is something you can't take away, like a toothbrush, give your child frequent breaks from interaction with the object. Make sure you have a touch cue or some other way of letting him know that you are going to start again. Don't try to just force your way through the activity to get it over with. Go slow. Let your child deal with something difficult for a very short time and then rest a bit before you go again. Stay calm. Use a soft reassuring voice.
- Don't make your child touch anything he doesn't like to touch. His hands are his. Your job is to invite, not force.
- Expect your child to participate in activities with you even if she has very limited motor ability. Give her a turn. "Your turn to take a bite" might mean that she opens her mouth. "Your turn to put on your shoe" might be lifting a foot.
- Encourage independent exploration and use of senses. You may need to slow down during feeding, bathing, and other activities to give your child time to take in information and respond to it.
- Children with deaf-blindness may need to establish bonds with parents and other significant people without the benefit of eye gaze and voice recognition. Teachers of students with visual impairments, with the help of deaf-blind specialists, must help parents use touch as a basis for bonding and for building the tactile mutuality that is the foundation of tactile communication (Chen & Downing, 2006).

SUMMARY

Efficient acquisition of sensory information is required for all learning throughout life. Children use five external sensory systems—touch, vision, hearing, taste, and smell—to learn about their worlds. They use two internal systems—proprioceptive and vestibular—to position and stabilize their bodies. Without active exploration, sensory skills do not develop. Without active exploration using sensory skills, understanding of the world does not develop.

Teachers of students with visual impairments provide instruction and accommodations to address the sensory efficiency needs of their students. They design instruction that develops visual and tactile skills and that uses other sensory systems to supply additional information. They teach students to use optical devices and to select appropriate sensory strategies for a variety of different kinds of tasks. They help parents and teachers adapt the student's environments so that the student can use sensory skills efficiently. They also specify accommodations for learning media to make sure materials have the sensory characteristics needed to make them accessible to the student.

In order to determine what skills to teach and which accommodations are needed, teachers of students with visual impairments assess students' functional vision and the efficiency of all sensory systems for accessing learning media. The teacher of students with visual impairments needs to use effective strategies to overcome sensory barriers associated with factors such as unresponsiveness, limited hand use, self-stimulation, and manual avoidance. Effective interventions ensure that students can use sensory skills efficiently for exploration; for learning cognitive, communication, and motor skills; for academic achievement, and for mastery of other ECC skills. These efforts are critical for the growth and development of students, and for their participation in school, work, and life.

References

Anthony, T. L. (2000). Performing a functional low vision assessment. In F.M. D'Andrea and C. Farrenkopf (Eds.), *Looking to learn: Promoting literacy for students with low vision* (pp. 32–83). New York: AFB Press.

Bayley scales of infant and toddler development (3rd ed.; Bayley III). Oxford, England: Pearson Assessment.

Barclay, L. A. (2012). *Learning to listen, listening to learn: Teaching listening skills to students with visual impairments.* New York: AFB Press.

Barraga, N., & Erin, J. (2001). *Visual impairments and learning* (4th ed.). Austin, TX: Pro-Ed.

Bell Coy, J., & Anderson, E. (2010). Instruction in the use of optical devices for children and youths. In A. L. Corn and J. N. Erin (Eds.), *Foundations of low vision: Clinical and functional perspectives* (2nd ed., pp. 527–588). New York, NY: AFB Press.

Blaha, R. (Fall, 1996). Thoughts on the assessment of the student with the most profound disabilities. *SEE/HEAR Newsletter, 1*(4), 13–21.

Blanche, E. I., & Nakasuji, B. (2001). Sensory integration and the child with cerebral palsy. In S. Smith Roley, E. Blanche, and R. Schaaf (Eds.), *Understanding the nature of sensory integration with diverse populations* (pp. 345–364). Tucson, AZ: Therapy Skill Builders.

Bundy, A., Lane, S., & Murray, E. (2002). *Sensory integration: Theory and practice.* Philadelphia, PA: F. A. Davis Company.

Bushnell, E. W., & Boudreau, P. (1993). Motor development and the mind: The potential role of motor abilities as a determinant of aspect of perceptual development. *Child Development, 64*, 1005–1021.

Chen, D. (2014). Understanding hearing loss: Implications for early intervention. In D. Chen (Ed.), *Essential elements in early intervention: Visual impairment and multiple disabilities* (2nd ed., pp. 294–340). New York: AFB Press.

Chen, D., & Downing, J. (2006). *Tactile strategies for children who have visual impairments and multiple disabilities: Promoting communication and learning skills.* New York: AFB Press.

Corn, A. L., & Erin, J. N. (Eds.). (2010). *Foundations of low vision: Clinical and functional perspectives* (2nd ed.). New York: AFB Press.

Corn, A. L., & Lusk, K. (2010). Perspectives on low vision. In A. L. Corn and J. N. Erin (Eds.), *Foundations of low vision: Clinical and functional perspectives* (2nd ed., pp. 3–34). New York: AFB Press.

D'Andrea, F. M., & Farrenkopf, C. (Eds.). (2000). *Looking to learn: Promoting literacy for students with low vision.* New York: AFB Press.

Deecke, L. (1978). Functional significance of cerebral potentials preceding voluntary movement. In D. A. Otto (Ed.), *Multidisciplinary perspectives in event-related potential research: Proceedings of the fourth international congress on event-related slow potentials of the brain* (pp. 343–356). Washington, D.C.: U.S. Government Printing Office.

Dote-Kwan, J., & Chen, D. (1999). Developing meaningful intervention. In D. Chen (Ed.), *Essential elements in early intervention: Visual impairment and multiple disabilities* (pp. 287–336). New York: AFB Press.

Dunlea, A. (1989). *Vision and the emergence of meaning: Blind and sighted children's early language.* New York, NY: Cambridge University Press.

Dunn, W. (1999). *The sensory profile.* San Antonio, TX: Psychological Corporation.

Dunn, W. (2002). *The infant/toddler sensory profile.* San Antonio, TX: Psychological Corporation.

Dunn, W. (2006). *The sensory profile—school companion.* San Antonio, TX: Psychological Corporation.

Eliot, L. (1999). *What's going on in there: How the brain and mind develop in the first five years of life.* New York: Bantam Books.

Fazzi, D. L., & Klein, M. D. (2002). Cognitive focus: Developing cognition, concepts, and language. In R. Pogrund and D. L. Fazzi (Eds.), *Early focus: Working with young children who are blind or visually impaired and their families* (pp. 107–153). New York: AFB Press.

Ferrell, K. A. (2010). Visual development. In A. L. Corn and J. N. Erin (Eds.), *Foundations of low vision: Clinical and functional perspectives* (2nd ed., pp. 299–338). New York: AFB Press.

Flom, R. (2004). Visual consequences of most common eye conditions associated with visual impairment. In A. H. Lueck (Ed.), *Functional vision: A practitioner's guide to evaluation and intervention* (p. 477). New York: AFB Press.

Gibson, E. (1988). Exploratory behavior in the development of perceiving, acting, and the acquiring of knowledge. *Annual Review of Psychology, 39*, 1–47.

Greer, R. (2004). Evaluation methods and functional implications: Children and adults with visual impairments. In A. H. Lueck (Ed.), *Functional vision: A practitioner's guide to evaluation and intervention* (pp. 177–253). New York: AFB Press.

Guess, D., Mulligan-Ault, M., Roberts, S., Struth, J., Siegal-Causey, E., Thompson, B., Bronicki, G., & Guy, G. (1988). Implications of biobehavioral states for the education and treatment of students with the most handicapping conditions. *Journal of the Association of Severe Handicaps, 13*(3), 163–174.

Haegerstrom-Portnoy, G. (2004). Evaluation methods and functional implications: Young children with visual impairments and students with visual and multiple disabilities. In A. H. Lueck (Ed.), *Functional vision: A practitioner's guide to evaluation and intervention* (pp. 115–176). New York: AFB Press.

Holbrook, M. C., Koenig, A. J., & Rex, E. J. (2010). Instruction of literacy skills to children and youths with low vision. In A. L. Corn and J. N. Erin (Eds.), *Foundations of low vision: Clinical and functional perspectives* (pp. 484–526). New York: AFB Press.

Hotta, C., & Kitchel, E. (2002). *Envision I: Vision enhancement program using distance devices.* Louisville, KY: American Printing House for the Blind.

Hyvarinen, L. (1998). *Vision in early development.* Retrieved from: http://www.lea-test.fi

Kitchel, E. (2008). *ToAD: Tools for assessment and development of visual skills.* Louisville, KY: American Printing House for the Blind.

Kitchel, E., & Scott, K. (2002). *Envision II: Vision enhancement program using near magnification devices.* Louisville, KY: American Printing House for the Blind.

Klatzky, R., & Lederman, S. (2008). Object recognition by touch. In J. J. Rieser, D. H. Ashmead, F. F. Ebner, and A. L. Corn (Eds.), *Blindness and brain plasticity in navigation and object perception* (pp. 185–207). New York: Lawrence Erlbaum Associates.

Koenig, A. J., & Holbrook, M. C. (1995). *Learning media assessments of students with visual impairments: A resource guide for teachers* (2nd ed.). Austin: Texas School for the Blind and Visually Impaired.

Koenig, A. J., & Holbrook, M. C. (2010). Selection and assessment of learning and literacy media. In A. L. Corn and J. N. Erin (Eds.), *Foundations of low vision: Clinical and functional perspectives* (pp. 442–483). New York: AFB Press.

Kolb, B., & Whishaw, I. Q. (2009). *Fundamentals of human neuropsychology* (6th ed.). New York: Freeman-Worth.

Korsten, J. E., Foss, T. V., & Berry, L. M. (2007). *Every move counts—Clicks and chats: Sensory-based approach: Communication and assistive technology.* Kansas City, MO: EMC Communications.

Kuhl, P. K., Williams, K. A., & Meltzoff, A. N. (1991). Cross-modal speech perception in adults and infants using nonspeech auditory stimuli. *Journal of Experimental Psychology-Human Perception and Performance, 17*, 829–840.

Langley, M. (1998). *ISAVE: Individualized systematic assessment of visual efficiency.* Louisville, KY: American Printing House for the Blind.

Langley, M. (2004). Screening and assessment of sensory functions. In M. McLean, M. Wolery, & D. Bailey (Eds.), *Assessing infants and preschoolers with special needs* (3rd ed., pp. 123–171). Upper Saddle River, NJ: Pearson/Merrill Prentice Hall.

Lightfoot, C., Cole, M., & Cole, S. (2005). *The development of children.* New York, NY: Worth Publishers.

Lohmeier, K., Blankenship, K. E., & Hatlen, P. (2009). Expanded core curriculum: Twelve years later. *Journal of Visual Impairment & Blindness, 103*, 103–112.

Lueck, A. H. (Ed.). (2004a). *Functional vision: A practitioner's guide to evaluation and intervention.* New York: AFB Press.

Lueck, A. H. (2004b). Overview of intervention methods. In A. H. Lueck (Ed.), *Functional vision: A practitioner's guide to evaluation and intervention* (pp. 89–114). New York: AFB Press.

Lueck, A. H., & Heinze, T. (2004). Interventions for young children with visual impairments and students with visual and multiple disabilities. In A. H. Lueck (Ed.), *Functional vision: A practitioner's guide to evaluation and intervention* (pp. 277–352). New York: AFB Press.

Matlin, M. (2008). *Cognition.* New York: Harcourt Brace Publishers.

Matthews, P. (1988). Proprioceptors and their contribution to somatosensory mapping: Complex messages require complex processing. *Canadian Journal of Physiological Pharmacology, 66*, 430–438.

McClure, V. (2000). *Infant massage: A handbook for loving parents.* New York: Bantam Books.

McLinden, M., & McCall, S. (2002). *Learning through touch: Supporting children with visual impairments and additional difficulties.* London: David Fulton Publishers.

Mesulam, M. (2000). *Principles of behavioral and cognitive neurology.* New York: Oxford University Press.

Nelson, C., van Dijk, J., Oster, T., & McDonnell, A. (2009). *Child-guided strategies: The van Dijk approach to assessment for understanding children and youth with sensory impairments and multiple disabilities.* Louisville, KY: American Printing House for the Blind.

Newton, G. (Fall, 2000). The importance of touch in parent-infant bonding. *See/Hear Newsletter, 5*(4). Available at http://www.tsbvi.edu/seehear/fall00/infantbonding.htm

NIDCD Information Clearinghouse. (2011). Cochlear Implants. National Institute on Deafness and Other Communication Disorders. Retrieved from: www.nidcd.nih.gov/health/hearing/coch.asp

Nielsen, L. (1992). *Space and self.* Copenhagen: Sikon.

Nielsen, L. (1993). *Early learning step by step.* Copenhagen: Sikon.

Northern, J., & Downs, M. (2002). *Hearing in children.* Baltimore, MD: Williams and Wilkins.

Piaget, J. (1950). *The psychology of intelligence.* Oxford, England: Routledge.

Piaget, J. (2013). *The construction of reality in the child.* Oxford, England: Routledge. (Original work published in 1954.)

Presley, I. (2010). The impact of assistive technology: Assessment and instruction for children and youths with low vision. In A. L. Corn and J. N. Erin (Eds.), *Foundations of low vision: Clinical and functional perspectives* (2nd ed., pp. 589–654). New York: AFB Press.

Presley, I., & D'Andrea, F. M. (2009). *Assistive technology for students who are blind or visually impaired: A guide to assessment.* New York: AFB Press.

Rochat, P. (1989). Object manipulation and exploration in 2 to 5 month old infants. *Developmental Psychology, 25,* 871–4.

Roman-Lantzy, C. (2007). *Cortical visual impairment: An approach to assessment and intervention.* New York: AFB Press.

Roman-Lantzy, C. (2010). *CVI complexity sequences.* Louisville, KY: American Printing House for the Blind.

Royeen, C., & Lane, S. (1991). Tactile processing and sensory defensiveness. In A. G. Fisher, E. A. Murray, & A. C. Bundy (Eds.), *Sensory integration: Theory and practice.* Philadelphia, PA: F. A. Davis.

Ruff, H., Saltarelli, L., Capozzoli, M., & Dubiner, K. (1992). The differentiation of activity in infants' exploration of objects. *Developmental Psychology, 28,* 851–861.

Sanford, L., & Burnett, R. (2008). *FVLMA: Functional vision and learning media assessment for students who are pre-academic or academic in grades K-12.* Louisville, KY: American Printing House for the Blind.

Smith, M. (Summer, 1998). Feelin' Groovy: Functional tactual skills. *See/Hear, 3*(3).

Smith, M. (2005). *SLK guidebook and assessment forms: Using the sensory learning kit.* Louisville, KY: American Printing House for the Blind.

Smith, M. (2012). *SAM: Symbols and meaning.* Louisville, KY: American Printing House for the Blind.

Smith, M., with Topor, I., Erin, J., Ferrell, K. A., Orel-Bixler, D., Pogrund, R., Roman-Lantzy, C., & Rosenblum, L. P. (in press). *Barraga visual efficiency program.* Louisville, KY: American Printing House for the Blind.

Smith Roley, S., Blanche, E., & Schaaf, R. (2001). *Understanding the nature of sensory integration with diverse populations.* Tucson, AZ: Therapy Skill Builders.

Topor, I. (2014). Functional vision assessment and early intervention. In D. Chen (Ed.), *Essential elements in early intervention: Visual impairment and multiple disabilities* (2nd ed., pp. 262–266). New York: AFB Press.

Trief, E., & Shaw, R. (2009). *Everyday activities to promote visual efficiency.* New York: AFB Press.

Wilkinson, M. (2010). Clinical low vision services. In A. L. Corn and J. N. Erin (Eds.), *Foundations of low vision: Clinical and functional perspectives* (2nd ed., pp. 238–298). New York: AFB Press.

Zimmerman, G., Zebehazy, K., & Moon, M. (2010). Optics and low vision devices. In A. L. Corn and J. N. Erin (Eds.), *Foundations of low vision: Clinical and functional perspectives* (2nd ed., pp. 192–237). New York: AFB Press.

Sample Completed Individual Sensory Learning Profile

INDIVIDUAL SENSORY LEARNING PROFILE

Child's name: *Rachel Sanduski*

DOB: *3/02/11* **Current age:** *17 months*

Date: *8/02/13* **Completed by:** *Irene Topor, Teacher of Students with Visual Impairments, and Mrs. Sanduski, mother*

Background Information:

Medical diagnoses: *Rachel was diagnosed with Peter's anomaly.*

Current medications and reason for prescription: *None*

Sensory Profile Questions

Vision

Is the child diagnosed as being blind or visually impaired? Yes ☒ No ☐

If so, what is the medical diagnosis? *Peter's anomaly, opacities of the cornea*

Does the child wear glasses or use other optical devices? Yes ☐ No ☒

If so, please give the prescription and/or details about the devices for:

Right eye (OD): ☐ Left eye (OS): ☐

Both eyes (OU): ☐

Does the child visually respond to a human face? Yes ☒ No ☐

Does the child respond to other visual stimuli: Yes ☒ No ☐

If so, what are the characteristics of the visual stimuli?

☒ Illuminating ☒ Shiny/light reflective ☒ High contrast

☐ Pastel colored ☒ Brightly colored ☒ Familiar

Other characteristics or details about visual stimuli: *Rachel prefers toy jewelry that is brightly colored or toys that have brightly colored lights or other similar characteristics.*

Is there an immediate or delayed response to a visual stimulus? Please describe:

Rachel can see her toy jewelry from up to 3 feet away because she moves toward or reaches for these desired items. Rachel notices and crawls to the jewelry after her mom places the objects on the floor when previously there was nothing there. When seated, Rachel will reach for unfamiliar objects if they are presented slightly left of her midline and not more than 4–6 inches away.

What type of environment seems to best support visual responsiveness? Mark all that apply:

Presentation to midline ☐ Left side ☒ Right side ☐ Above eye level ☒

Below eye level ☐

Visual attention distance (describe in inches or feet): *4 to 6 inches*

Illumination preference: *Reduce glare because Rachel is sensitive to light.*

Describe characteristics of familiar setting including items, noise level, visual clutter:

Toys are in box that stays in the same place in the living room. Noise level is kept at a minimum except for background television noise. Visual clutter needs to be minimized to increase visual functioning.

Accompaniment of other sensory stimuli: *light, sound, light box*

Other environmental preferences including positioning needs for visual attending:
Currently using a light box to determine Rachel's color preferences. Rachel sits next to the light box and brings individual pieces of colored Plexiglass to her left eye.

Items that the child shows a visual response/preference for:
Rachel prefers shiny necklaces, objects that produce light (e.g., a musical toy that lights up), high contrast materials (a white and black soccer ball) and familiar objects.

Hearing

Is the child diagnosed as: ☐ deaf, ☐ hard of hearing, or having a ☐ central processing disorder? (check all that apply)

Does the child wear hearing aids or use other sound amplification devices? Yes ☐ No ☒

If yes, please list the listening devices used: ______

Is there a history of ear infections? Yes ☐ No ☒

Does the child attend to auditory stimuli? Yes ☒ No ☐

If yes, what are the characteristics of the auditory stimuli?

Human voice: Yes ☒ No ☐

Environmental Sounds: Yes ☒ No ☐

Sound Volume: Low ☐ Moderate ☒ High ☐

Other characteristics or details about auditory stimuli:
Rachel responds to and participates in familiar songs and sound games with significant caregivers.

Is there an immediate or delayed response to auditory information: Please describe:
Immediate—Rachel turns toward a familiar person who calls her name. She moves toward sound producing toys from up to 5 feet away.

What type of environment seems to best support auditory responsiveness?

Sound presentation distance (describe in inches or feet): ______

quiet ☐ low noise clutter ☒ echolocation boundaries ☐

Accompaniment of other sensory stimuli:
Rachel enjoys familiar sounds such as from toys and people that she knows.

Other environmental preferences for auditory responsiveness: ______

Items that the child shows an auditory response/preference to: ______

Touch / Kinesthetic/ Vestibular

Does the child have a diagnosis of cerebral palsy or other disorder affecting movement?

Yes ☐ No ☒

Does the child benefit from any orthopedic or special positioning, ambulation, or mobility devices?

Yes ☐ No ☒ If yes, please list these devices: ______

Does the child respond positively or adversely to being touched?

Positively ☒ Adversely ☐

Please explain preferences or aversions for being touched (e.g., soft, firm, predictable):
Firm touch is preferred.

Does the child respond positively or adversely to touching people/objects?

Positively ☒ Adversely ☐

Please explain preferences or aversions for touching people/objects:

Rachel prefers hard to soft toys.

Does the child respond positively or adversely to movement:

Positively ☒ Adversely ☐

Please explain preferences or aversions to movement (e.g., slow, rhythmic, predictable, etc.):

Rachel will spin herself around while sitting on the floor when not engaged with people or objects.

Positions that seem to best support overall sensory responsiveness:

Prone (on stomach) ☒ Supine (on back) ☐ Sidelying ☐ Sitting ☒ Sitting with support

☐ Other__________

Olfactory / Taste

Does the child positively or adversely respond to specific smells and/or tastes? Please describe:

Positive responses: *If Rachel smells something sweet such as chocolate, she will work to locate it and try to taste it. She liked the smell of candles and has tried to eat some!*

Negative responses: __________

Summary of Sensory Preferences / Recommendations for Motivating Objects

Visual: *Rachel enjoys brightly colored objects, those that have a light component, and those that are of high contrast. When selecting materials for Rachel, consider offering materials that motivate her to look.*

Auditory: *Rachel uses her hearing to localize sounds in her environment. She is beginning to understand spoken words within familiar activities and responds to her mother's questions such as "Do you want more water? More crackers?"*

Touch/Movement: *Rachel uses both hearing and vision to move within her environment. She may benefit from learning some protective techniques and some search techniques to help her explore.*

Smell/Taste: *Rachel enjoys tasting things that smell good to her. As she does not yet understand which things are safe and which are not safe things to put in her mouth, care should be taken to keep objects that could be dangerous out of her reach.*

Other Recommendations: *Rachel learns best when provided with objects/toys that have multiple sensory characteristics. Light and reflective objects are attractive to Rachel and can be used to enhance and encourage her use of vision. Rachel's hearing is within normal limits and she is beginning to understand spoken words within familiar activities. Caregivers might provide some gentle movement, e.g., put Rachel in a swing or small rocking chair, to prepare Rachel to use other senses.*

Source: Reprinted with permission from Irene Topor, "Functional Vision Assessment and Early Intervention," in Deborah Chen, Ed., *Essential Elements in Early Intervention: Visual Impairment and Multiple Disabilities,* 2nd ed. (New York: AFB Press, 2014), pp. 262–266. Adapted by Irene Topor with permission from T. L. Anthony, "Individual Sensory Learning Profile Interview," in I. Topor, L. P. Rosenblum, & D. D. Hatton, *Visual Conditions and Functional Vision: Early Intervention Issues.* Session 4: Functional Vision Assessment and Developmentally Appropriate Learning Media Assessment, Handout K (Chapel Hill: Early Intervention Training Center for Infants and Toddlers with Visual Impairments, FPG Child Development Institute, University of North Carolina at Chapel Hill, 2004).

Sensory Efficiency Resources

This section provides resources such as assessment tools, publications, and instructional materials for teaching sensory efficiency skills. For additional resources that relate to the expanded core curriculum in general, see the Resources section at the end of this book.

ASSESSMENT TOOLS

Acquiring Information through Primary and Secondary Channels

Vision

Barraga Visual Efficiency Evaluation

Population/Age level: Students at or above the 3-year developmental level

Source: Smith, M., with Topor, I., Erin, J., Ferrell, K. A., Orel-Bixler, D., Pogrund, R., Roman-Lantzy, C., & Rosenblum, L. P. (in press). *Barraga visual efficiency program.* Louisville, KY: American Printing House for the Blind.

CVI Range and Resolution Chart

Population/Age level: Young children and students with cortical visual impairment

Source: Roman-Lantzy, C. (2007). *Cortical visual impairment: An approach to assessment and intervention.* New York: AFB Press.

Functional Vision Evaluation Report: Children and Adults

Population/Age level: Children and adults

Source: Greer, R. (2004). Evaluation methods and functional implications: Children and adults with visual impairments. In A. H. Lueck (Ed.), *Functional vision: A practitioner's guide to evaluation and intervention* (pp. 177–253). New York: AFB Press.

Functional Vision Evaluation Report: Young Children and Students with Additional Disabilities

Population/Age level: Young children under 3 years old and older children with multiple disabilities

Source: Haegerstrom-Portnoy, G. (2004). Evaluation methods and functional implications: Young children with visual impairments and students with visual and multiple disabilities. In A. H. Lueck (Ed.), *Functional vision: A practitioner's guide to evaluation and intervention* (pp. 115–176). New York: AFB Press.

FVLMA (Functional Vision and Learning Media Assessment)

Population/Age level: Pre-academic and academic students in grades K–12

Source: Sanford, L., & Burnett, R. (2008). *FVLMA: Functional vision and learning media assessment for students who are pre-academic and academic and visually impaired in grades K–12.* Louisville, KY: American Printing House for the Blind.

Inventory of Functional Literacy Tasks

Population/Age level: School-age children

Source: Holbrook, M. C., Koenig, A. J., & Rex, E. J. (2010). Instruction of literacy skills to children and youths with low vision. In A. L. Corn and J. N. Erin (Eds.), *Foundations of low vision: Clinical and functional perspectives* (2nd ed.). New York: AFB Press.

ISAVE (Individualized Systematic Assessment of Visual Efficiency)

Population/Age level: Young children and students with multiple impairments

Source: Langley, M. (1998). *ISAVE: Individualized systematic assessment of visual efficiency.* Louisville, KY: American Printing House for the Blind.

Procedure for Documenting Reading Efficiency

Source: Koenig, A. J., & Holbrook, M. C. (1995). *Learning media assessment of students with visual impairments: A resource guide for teachers* (2nd ed.). Austin: Texas School for the Blind and Visually Impaired.

ToAD (Tools for Assessment and Development of Visual Skills)

Population/Age level: 2.5 to 5 years of age

Source: Kitchel, E. (2008). *ToAD: Tools for assessment and development of visual skills.* Louisville, KY: American Printing House for the Blind.

Use of Sensory Channels

Population/Age level: Learning media assessment for preschool and life skills students

SOURCE: Koenig, A. J., & Holbrook, M. C. (1995). Use of sensory channels. In *Learning media assessment of students with visual impairments: A resource guide for teachers.* Austin: Texas School for the Blind and Visually Impaired.

Touch

Feelin' Groovy: Functional Tactile Skills

POPULATION/AGE LEVEL: Children with visual and multiple impairments

SOURCE: Smith, M. (Summer, 1998). Feelin' groovy: Functional tactual skills. *See/Hear, 3*(3). Available at http://www.tsbvi.edu/component/content/article/100/1300-feelin-groovy-functional-tactual-skills

Haptic-Tactile Perception

POPULATION/AGE LEVEL: Infants and toddlers with visual impairments only and older children with visual impairments and additional disabilities; 0–48 months

SOURCE: Nielsen, L. (2005). *Functional scheme.* Kolding, Denmark: Lilli Books.

Object-Related Scheme Assessment Procedure (ORSAP)

POPULATION/AGE LEVEL: Developmentally young children who may have additional physical or sensory handicaps; 0–48 months

SOURCE: Coupe, J., & Levy, D. (1985). The object related scheme assessment procedure: A cognitive assessment for developmentally young children who may have additional physical or sensory handicaps. *Mental Handicap, 13,* 22–4.

Procedure for Documenting Reading Efficiency

Koenig, A. J., & Holbrook, M. C. (1995). *Learning media assessment of students with visual impairments: A resource guide for teachers* (2nd ed.). Austin: Texas School for the Blind and Visually Impaired.

Schemes for Relating to Objects

POPULATION/AGE LEVEL: Infants

SOURCE: Uzgaris, I., & Hunt, J. (1975). Schemes for relating to objects. In *Assessment in infancy.* Urbana, IL: University of Illinois Press.

Hearing

Auditory Perception in Functional Schemes

POPULATION/AGE LEVEL: Infants and toddlers with visual impairments only and older children with visual impairments and additional disabilities; 0–48 months

SOURCE: Nielsen, L. (2005). *Functional scheme.* Kolding, Denmark: Lilli Books.

Early Listening Function

POPULATION/AGE LEVEL: 5 to 24 months

SOURCE: Anderson, K. (2002). *Early listening function (ELF).* Available at https://successforkidswithhearingloss.com/uploads/ELF_Questionnaire.pdf

Functional Auditory Performance Indicators

POPULATION/AGE LEVEL: Children with hearing loss

SOURCE: Stredler-Brown, A., & Johnson, C. (2004). *Functional auditory performance indicators: An integrated approach to auditory development (FAPI).* Available at http://arlenestredlerbrown.org/docs/FAPI-old.pdf

Functional Hearing Assessment

POPULATION/AGE LEVEL: Children with hearing loss

SOURCE: *Functional hearing assessment* (1991). Alabama State Department of Education. Available at http://www.alsde.edu/home/Sections/SectionDocuments.aspx?SectionID=65&Subsection=4

Combining Information from Multisensory Channels

Arousal State Profile

POPULATION/AGE LEVEL: Children with multiple disabilities

SOURCE: Smith, M. (2005). Appetite item menu. In *SLK guidebook and assessment forms: Using the sensory learning kit.* Louisville, KY: American Printing House for the Blind

Individual Sensory Learning Profile Interview

POPULATION/AGE LEVEL: Birth to 3

SOURCE: Anthony, T. L. (2004). Individual sensory learning profile interview. In I. Topor, L. P. Rosenblum, & D. D. Hatton, *Visual conditions and functional vision: Early intervention issues* (Session 4: Functional vision assessment and developmentally appropriate learning media assessment, handout K). Chapel Hill: Early Intervention Training Center for Infants and Toddlers with Visual Impairments, FPG Child Development Institute, University of North Carolina at Chapel Hill.

Infant and Toddler Sensory Profile

POPULATION/AGE LEVEL: Birth to 36 months

SOURCE: Dunn, W. (2002). *The infant/toddler sensory profile.* San Antonio, TX: Psychological Corporation.

Sensory Response Assessment

Population/Age level: Children with severe and profound sensorimotor differences, developmental differences, and autism

Source: Korsten, J. E., Foss, T. V., & Berry, L. M. (2007). *Every move counts—Clicks and chats: Sensory-based approach: Communication and assistive technology.* Kansas City, MO: EMC Communications.

Sensory Response Record

Population/Age level: Infants, toddlers, and older learners who have visual and severe multiple impairments; 0–24 months

Source: Smith, M. (2005). Sensory response record. In *SLK guidebook and assessment forms: Using the sensory learning kit.* Louisville, KY: American Printing House for the Blind.

Symbol and Referent Analysis (SARA)

Population/Age level: Learners with visual impairments of any age who are developing concepts and receptive vocabulary at the late sensorimotor and early preoperational stages of cognitive development; 1–4 years

Source: Smith, M. (2012). Symbol and referent analysis (SARA). In *SAM: Symbols and Meaning.* Louisville, KY: American Printing House for the Blind.

The Sensory Profile

Population/Age level: Individuals with sensory processing issues affecting performance in home, school, and work environments; infants through adults

Source: Dunn, W. (1999). *The sensory profile.* San Antonio, TX: Psychological Corporation.

The Sensory Profile—School Companion

Population/Age level: Children with sensory processing issues in academic settings; 5–18 years of age

Source: Dunn, W. (2006). *The sensory profile—school companion.* San Antonio, TX: Psychological Corporation.

PUBLICATIONS

Acquiring Information through Primary and Secondary Channels

Vision

Analysis of Daily Routines

Sources: Lueck, A. H., & Heinze, T. (2004). Interventions for young children with visual impairments and students with visual and multiple disabilities. In A. H. Lueck (Ed.), *Functional Vision: A practitioner's guide to evaluation and intervention* (Appendix 8.1). New York: AFB Press.

Trief, E., & Shaw, R. (2009). *Everyday activities to promote visual efficiency.* New York: AFB Press.

Characteristics of Instructional Programs to Encourage the Use of Vision

Source: Lueck, A. H. (2004). Overview of intervention methods. In A. H. Lueck (Ed.), *Functional Vision: A practitioner's guide to evaluation and intervention* (Table 7.2). New York: AFB Press.

Design for Instruction

Source: Smith, M., with Topor, I., Erin, J., Ferrell, K. A., Orel-Bixler, D., Pogrund, R., Roman-Lantzy, C., & Rosenblum, L. P. (in press). *Barraga visual efficiency program.* Louisville, KY: American Printing House for the Blind.

IFSP/IEP Intervention Planning Worksheet

Source: Roman-Lantzy, C. (2007). *Cortical visual impairment: An approach to assessment and intervention* (Essential Forms). New York, NY: AFB Press.

Looking to learn: Promoting literacy for students with low vision.

Source: D'Andrea, F. M., & Farrenkopf, C. (Eds.). (2000). *Looking to learn: Promoting literacy for students with low vision.* New York: AFB Press.

Small Worlds for Young Children with Visual Impairments

Source: Lueck, A. H., & Heinze, T. (2004). Interventions for young children with visual impairments and students with visual and multiple disabilities. In A. H. Lueck (Ed.), *Functional Vision: A practitioner's guide to evaluation and intervention* (Sidebar 8.7). New York: AFB Press.

Visual Consequences of Most Common Eye Conditions Associated with Visual Impairment

Source: Flom, R. (2004). Visual consequences of most common eye conditions associated with visual impairment. In A. H. Lueck (Ed.), *Functional Vision: A practitioner's guide to evaluation and intervention* (Appendix). New York: AFB Press.

Visual Goals Integrated into Classroom Activities

Source: Corn, A. L., & Erin, J. N. (Eds.). (2010). Instruction in visual techniques for students with low vision, including those with multiple disabilities. In A. Corn and J. N. Erin (Eds.), *Foundations of low vision:*

Clinical and functional perspectives (2nd ed., Sidebar 11.4). New York: AFB Press.

Touch

Discrepancy Analysis with Tactile Intervention Strategies to Support Participation

Source: Chen, D., & Downing, J. (2006). Assessing tactile skills and planning interventions. In *Tactile strategies for children who have visual impairments and multiple disabilities: Promoting communication and learning skills* (Table 3.4). New York: AFB Press.

Ecological Inventory: Circle Time

Source: Chen, D., & Downing, J. (2006). Supporting interactions through touch. In *Tactile strategies for children who have visual impairments and multiple disabilities: Promoting communication and learning skills* (Table 2.2). New York: AFB Press.

Illustrations of Exploratory Procedures Used for Acquiring Sensory Information

Source: McLinden, M., & McCall, S. (2002). Functions of touch. In *Learning through touch: Supporting children with visual impairment and additional difficulties* (Figure 3.7). London: David Fulton Publishers.

Tactile Learning with Limited Hand Use Due to Motor Impairment

Source: Smith, M. (2012). Tactual learning with limited hand use due to motor impairment. In *SAM: Symbols and meaning* (Appendix C). Louisville, KY: American Printing House for the Blind.

Hearing

Jim Durkel's Advice on Sensory Efficiency Listening Skills

Source: FamilyConnect website. Available at http://www.familyconnect.org/parentsite.asp?SectionID=72&TopicID=382&SubTopicID=183&DocumentID=4680

Combining Information from Multisensory Sources

Arousal State Management (Modulating Sensory Complexity)

Source: Smith, M. (2005). *SLK guidebook and assessment forms: Using the sensory learning kit.* Louisville, KY: American Printing House for the Blind.

Bridging Near and Distance Sensory Information

Source: Smith, M. (2012). Bridging near and distance sensory information. In *SAM: Symbols and meaning.* Louisville, KY: American Printing House for the Blind.

Selecting Sensory Strategies

Sensory Substitutions and Modifications for Students with Low Vision

Source: Topor, I., Lueck, A. H., & Smith, J. (2004). Compensatory instruction for academically oriented students with visual impairment. In A. H. Lueck (Ed.), *Functional vision: A practitioner's guide to evaluation and intervention* (Sidebar 9.4). New York: AFB Press.

Environmental Accommodations

Optimizing the Visual Environment

Source: Topor, I., Lueck, A. H., & Smith, J. (2004). Compensatory instruction for academically oriented students with visual impairment. In A. H. Lueck (Ed.), *Functional vision: A practitioner's guide to evaluation and intervention* (Sidebar 9.3). New York: AFB Press.

Learning Media Accommodations

Attributes of Visual Stimuli to Be Considered in Arranging the Visual Environment of Young Children with Visual Impairments

Source: Lueck, A. H., & Heinze, T. (2004). Interventions for young children with visual impairments and students with visual and multiple disabilities. In A. H. Lueck (Ed.), *Functional vision: A practitioner's guide to evaluation and intervention* (Sidebar 8.5). New York: AFB Press.

Tactile Communication Options

Source: Chen, D., & Downing, J. (2006). Considering multiple communication options. In *Tactile strategies for children who have visual impairments and multiple disabilities: Promoting communication and learning skills* (Table 5.1). New York: AFB Press.

Optical Device Instruction

Activities for Using a Magnifier

Source: Bell Coy, J., & Andersen, E. A. (2010). Instruction in the use of optical devices for children and youths. In A. L. Corn and J. N. Erin (Eds.), *Foundations of low vision: Clinical and functional perspectives* (2nd ed., Sidebar 14.4). New York: AFB Press.

Activities for Using a Monocular

Source: Bell Coy, J., & Andersen, E. A. (2010). Instruction in the use of optical devices for children and youths. In A. L. Corn and J. N. Erin (Eds.), *Foundations of low vision: Clinical and functional perspectives* (2nd ed., Sidebar 14.5). New York: AFB Press.

Considerations for Optical Device Instruction

SOURCE: D'Andrea, F. M., & Farrenkopf, C. (Eds.). (2000). *Looking to learn: Promoting literacy for students with low vision.* New York: AFB Press.

Teaching Telescope Use for School-Age Students

SOURCE: Topor, I., Lueck, A. H., & Smith, J. (2004). *Compensatory instruction for academically oriented students with visual impairment.* In A. H. Lueck (Ed.), *Functional Vision: A practitioner's guide to evaluation and intervention* (Appendix 9.2). New York: AFB Press.

Teaching Video Magnifier Use for School-Age Students

SOURCE: Topor, I., Lueck, A. H., & Smith, J. (2004). *Compensatory instruction for academically oriented students with visual impairment.* In A. H. Lueck (Ed.), *Functional vision: A practitioner's guide to evaluation and intervention* (Appendix 9.3). New York: AFB Press.

Vision Enhancement Using Near Magnification Devices

SOURCE: Kitchel, E., & Scott, K. (2002). *Envision II: Vision enhancement program using near magnification devices.* Louisville, KY: American Printing House for the Blind.

Visual Enhancement Program Using Distance Devices

SOURCE: Hotta, C., & Kitchel, E. (2002). *Envision I: Vision enhancement program using distance devices.* Louisville, KY: American Printing House for the Blind.

WEBSITE

Washington Sensory Disabilities Services

http://wsdsonline.org

Organization that supports the developmental and learning needs of children from birth to age 21 who are deaf or hard of hearing, blind or visually impaired, or have a combined hearing loss and visual impairment. Provides resources for working with these groups, including a video library with examples of hand-under-hand guidance and other strategies for promoting communication and learning for young children and teens with dual sensory loss or deaf-blindness.

Sensory Efficiency Learning Activities

Contributed by Mildred Smith, Carol B. Allman, and Sandra Lewis

These sample learning activities are presented as examples of activities that teachers can create to work on several ECC skills at once with their students. Activities that help teach sensory efficiency skills can also be found in other chapters. The activities presented, like all instruction, need to be considered and modified to address the needs of individual students—such as those who are braille readers, have low vision, or have additional disabilities—with adaptations for appropriate media and the physical and other capabilities of the student.

Learning Activity: <u>Offering Technique</u>
Primary ECC Area: Sensory efficiency **Component:** Tactile functioning **Grades:** Pre-K; students with multiple disabilities
Other ECC Area ■ Compensatory skills
Goal: The student will use different methods of exploring objects.
Key Tasks/Concepts The student will: ■ Follow the movements of a teacher's hands as she demonstrates different ways of interacting with objects. ■ Explore different objects by banging, shaking, and dropping them.
Description The teacher shows the student the symbol for her "Explore Time" activity and sits with the student on the floor mat. The student sits between the teacher's legs with her back supported by the teacher's torso. The student is supported so that her hands are comfortably positioned where she can see them. The teacher presents the first of a set of objects to be explored, holding it near the student's hands. The teacher performs an action with the object, such as banging, shaking, or dropping, that produces an interesting sound, and waits for the student to move her hands to the teacher's hands. If the student does not move her hands to the teacher's hands, the teacher repeats the action closer to student's hands so that some movements touch the student's arms and wrists and waits again for the student to initiate the demonstrated action. When the student's interest in the first action subsides, the teacher models the second action with the same object. When interest in the second action subsides, the teacher models the third action. This procedure is repeated for the other objects in the set. If the student doesn't reach for an object that is presented, even when it has been moved close to her arms or wrists, the teacher should select a different object to present to the student. If the student reaches for an object and has difficulty reproducing the modeled action, the teacher can gently use the hand-under-hand approach to show the student how to reproduce the behavior, carefully attending to the child's response and honoring any response that might indicate that performing a specific action is not desired. The teacher needs to refrain from talking too much during this activity, especially if the student has difficulty processing information from more than one sensory modality at a time. It is important to allow for the response time that the student typically displays with new objects.

(continued on next page)

Instructional Materials and Supplies Needed

- floor mat
- variety of interesting objects

Settings

Classroom, home. If teacher sends home a chart listing the activities, parents can be encouraged to replicate lesson done at school once per day at home.

Duration/Timing

- 30 minutes, including time for transition and positioning, twice a day

Evaluation

Record the name of each object and a plus for each exploratory activity imitated by the student.

Learning Activity: What Is It?

Primary ECC Area: Sensory efficiency **Components:** Auditory, olfactory, and tactile functioning

Grades: Pre-K–5

Other ECC Areas

- Compensatory access
- Orientation and mobility

Goal: Student will demonstrate understanding of concepts using auditory, olfactory, and tactile functioning.

Key Tasks/Concepts

The student will:

- Match objects or concepts to their sound after hearing the sound made by the object.
- Match objects to their tactile characteristics.
- Match objects or concepts to their olfactory characteristics.

Description

1. When a student alerts to a sound, the teacher takes the student to the sound source in its natural context (for example, a door opening and shutting).
2. The teacher helps the student touch the object as it makes the sound that was heard at a distance.
3. The teacher says the name of the object two or three times while the student touches it.
4. The teacher presents the sound of the object and two familiar object sounds (for example, a ball bouncing and a bell ringing).
5. The teacher helps the student go to the source of each of the sounds.
6. The teacher asks the student to find the object associated with one of the sounds.
7. The procedure is repeated for two other objects.

Note: This procedure could be repeated for objects identified through tactile characteristics (carpet/tile floors, bumpy balls or tennis balls), olfactory objects (fruit) or concepts (the cafeteria). Many sounds cannot be presented tactilely to the student and will need to be talked about for the student to understand the concept and its associated sound (for example, rain dripping off the roof, children laughing on the playground, traffic zooming by, footsteps in the hallway). Talking about these sounds can prompt guessing games ("Who is coming to our room?") and encourage social interaction understanding ("Why do you think the children are laughing?")

Instructional Materials and Supplies Needed

Selected objects. (Concepts and objects used should be examined and studied in their natural environments as much as possible and should be appropriate to the cognitive level and age level of the student.)

(continued on next page)

Setting
Home or classroom. Additional environments as indicated by O&M specialist.
Duration/Timing The procedure should be implemented as often as possible whenever the child alerts to sounds, smells, or something encountered tactilely.
Evaluation Record correct matches of sound to object; smell to object or concept; and touch to object. In evaluating this activity, the teacher will need to make notes about the demonstrated capabilities of the student to use auditory, olfactory, and tactile functioning to help identify objects and concepts.

Learning Activity: Sounds of My World

Primary ECC Area: Sensory efficiency **Components:** Auditory and visual functioning
Grades: K–8

Other ECC Areas

- Recreation and leisure
- Orientation and mobility
- Compensatory access

Goal: The student will distinguish the direction of sounds in the environment and their likely sources.

Key Tasks/Concepts

The student will:

- Determine the direction a sound has come from.
- Identify sounds in a general category (for younger students).
- Identify the specific sources of sounds (for older students).

Description

This activity involves the teacher spending some time with a student sitting quietly in a particular area (such as outside the classroom, in the front office of the school, on a park bench in the city, in a rural area, at a mall). When the student hears a particular sound, he or she should point to the direction from which it is coming and identify the sound. This activity will need to occur over and over in multiple settings so that the student is able to learn and practice sound identification.

For students with low vision, practice spotting sound sources with a prescribed monocular could further expand this activity.

If a student can't identify a sound, it might be appropriate for the teacher to guide the student to make predictions about its source, then guide the student to the source of the sound and encourage the student to spend some time exploring it. If that is not possible, the teacher can discuss with the student what the sound represents.

Typical sounds to incorporate include the following:

Outside the Classroom

- wind blowing
- birds singing (as a general category for younger students and specific birds—cardinal, blue jay—for older students)
- children walking
- children running

(continued on next page)

- an adult speaking to another adult or child (specific names of known persons or children for older students)
- door slamming
- door shutting
- children on a playground

Front Office of School

- adults talking (familiar adults by name for older students)
- office equipment (printer, telephone, intercom, fax machine, stapler, file cabinet opening and closing)
- door shutting

In the City

- traffic (cars, buses, trucks)
- a street crossing indicator
- people passing by
- horns honking
- a truck backing up
- sirens
- pigeons

In a Rural Area

- wind blowing
- birds singing
- tractors
- lawn mowers
- animals (cow, goat, horse, dog, cat)

At the Mall

- people passing by
- carts being pushed
- escalators
- elevators
- store clerks' voices
- music
- food court sounds

This activity could also become a game between two students, in which they take turns pointing to and identifying sounds. A student would "win" when the other student could no longer draw attention to a new sound or when the other student erred in determining a sound's location or source.

This is a good game to share with parents, who can play this game with their child from time to time. This activity can be simple or complicated depending upon how often it is done, how many sounds are identified, and the discussion about the sounds and what they mean.

A trained classmate might play this game with a student who is waiting for a bus, thereby also providing an opportunity for social interaction.

Instructional Materials and Supplies Needed

Access to different areas

Settings

The classroom, the school, the community

Duration/Timing

5–40 minutes. The teacher can spend 5–10 minutes with the student doing this activity in small chunks—identify one or two sounds wherever the teacher and student happen to be for practice and gradually increase

(continued on next page)

the duration to sitting in an area for 20–30 minutes, spending some time on sound identification and allowing 5–10 minutes to talk about what caused the sounds.

Evaluation

The evaluation for this activity should focus on the student's ability to locate and identify sounds. The teacher might develop a chart such as the following. A plus (+) or minus (–) sign can be used to indicate whether the student was able to identify the direction of each sound and its source, as in the following example:

Date	Sounds	Student identifies sound direction	Student identifies sound source
9/10	*Crow*	+	–
9/10	*Cell phone vibrating*	+	+
9/10	*Leaf blowing across ground*	–	–
9/10	*Children on playground*	+	+
9/10	*Wasp*	–	+
9/11			
9/11			
9/11			
9/11			
9/11			

Learning Activity: Treasure Map

Primary ECC Area: Sensory efficiency **Component:** Visual functioning
Grades: Students with low vision, grades 2–6

Other ECC Areas

- Orientation and mobility
- Recreation and leisure
- Compensatory access

Goal: The student will locate specified targets at a distance using a telescope.

Key Tasks/Concepts

Using a telescope, the student will:

- Locate a named target.
- Track dotted lines in vertical, horizontal, diagonal, and circular patterns.
- Scan lines of print.

Description

The teacher projects a treasure map on a screen about 12 feet away from the students. The students scan the outside edges to locate the starting place. Students track along vertical and horizontal dotted lines, past landmarks like trees and pools. When students arrive at the treasure chest on the map, an item from a box or container decorated as a treasure chest can be chosen by each student as a reward.

After the students master tracking horizontal and vertical lines, diagonal and circular lines can be added. The distance at which the map is projected can be increased after the students master the activity at a distance of 12 feet.

(continued on next page)

Instructional Materials and Supplies Needed

- Computer
- Projector
- Maps
- Treasure chest
- Rewards (favorites of the students)

Duration/Timing

20–25 minutes, three times weekly

Evaluation

The teacher can use a chart such as the following to record the student's performance each time the activity is done, using plus (+) or minus (–) signs to indicate whether the task was performed or not.

Task	Date	Date	Date	Date
Finds starting point				
Accurately tracks horizontal and vertical lines				
Accurately tracks diagonal and circular lines				
Number of lines of print scanned successfully				

Learning Activity: A Trip to the Grocery Store

Primary ECC Area: Sensory efficiency **Components:** Visual, auditory, tactile, and olfactory functioning
Grades: 7–12

Other ECC Areas

- Compensatory access
- Orientation and mobility
- Assistive technology
- Self-determination

Goal: The student will use a combination of sensory functions to identify appropriate and healthy foods for three meals for one day (breakfast, lunch, dinner).

Key Tasks/Concepts

The student will:

- Make a grocery list.
- Use assistive technology along with sensory skills to identify areas of the grocery store.
- Locate specific foods in the grocery store and read their labels.

Description of Learning Activity

In this activity, the students make a grocery list of desired foods for each meal in a day. Using preferred low vision devices or technology together with auditory, olfactory, and gustatory sensory information, the students scan the grocery store layout and determine what foods are in which sections. Students then use preferred low vision aids to locate items from their grocery lists on the shelves, read the labels for dietary information, and select the best brand based on cost.

This learning activity is the culminating activity of a series of lessons that would also include the following:

1. Determining menus for each meal while discussing healthy food issues and practicing with food labels provided by the teacher or accessed on the Internet.

(continued on next page)

2. Constructing a grocery list of foods needed using chosen technology.
3. Taking a field trip to the grocery store.
   - Using scanning techniques together with other senses to identify the deli section, fresh food section (tactile identification of foods), meat and dairy sections (visual, tactile, and olfactory identification of foods), canned and other food sections (visual and tactile identification of foods). The teacher can point out to the student that aisles are identified with signs above each aisle and that the sections of the store are labeled. In addition, the teacher can note that the sense of smell can detect the fresh food section and the deli section of the store. The teacher can discuss standard layout: most grocery stores have the deli and fresh food sections on either side of the store, meat and dairy are usually in the back of the store, and the canned and other packaged foods are in the middle of the store.
   - Locating desired food and checking dietary labels, costs, and brands for selection. (A good math lesson involving this information would be to determine the calories consumed in each meal.)
   - Checking off foods on list as they are located. (Another good math lesson would be to determine how much was spent on each meal and on the entire list.)

Students will not actually purchase the food during this activity. However, the family of the student could be included in the activity so that the student plans the families' meals for one day, purchases the needed products, and assists in meal preparation.

This activity would be a good one to use several times during a school year so that the student's understanding can be charted for an entire year. Including the O&M specialist in planning and undertaking the trip to the grocery store would also be helpful.

Instructional Materials and Supplies Needed

- Assistive technology of choice
- Food labels
- Calculator
- Internet access (if using for research)
- Lists of healthy food suggestions

Setting

Most of the mini-lessons would occur in the school setting, with the grocery store visit taking place in the community. To extend this activity to include the family, the home setting could be added.

Duration/Timing

- 30 minutes: selecting menus
- 10 minutes: constructing grocery list
- 60 minutes: field trip to grocery store

The entire learning activity would occur over a three- to six-week period, with the culminating grocery store visit occurring at the end of that time.

Evaluation

Each key task should be evaluated using the following rubric:

1. Student completes key task with physical and verbal assistance.
2. Student completes key task with prompting only.
3. Student completes key task with some elements of task missing.
4. Student completes entire key task independently.

Evaluations could also be broken out by meal or by each element of each key task, instead of the entire key task. The results of the evaluation will let the teacher know which parts of the activity are difficult for the student and require further instruction and assistance.

CHAPTER 6

Assistive Technology

Donna McNear and Carol Farrenkopf

Carol Farrenkopf

The area of assistive technology within the expanded core curriculum (ECC) focuses on the knowledge and skills that are essential to learning how to use technology to access all aspects of daily living, whether at school, at work, at play, or at rest. Technology has become a fundamental part of every-day living for most people in the world. It is part of the environment, from touch screens on automatic banking machines to barcode scanners in grocery stores to global positioning systems in our automobiles that direct us through traffic—although today's innovations will be quickly replaced by others. Technological advancements occur rapidly; it seems that new devices come on the market each week and new versions of software and hardware are available within months of their original release. In many ways, technology has made life easier and faster, but the accelerating rate of change has also made it difficult to keep up with the pace. This chapter focuses on what students with visual impairments need to know about technology and how their teachers can keep up with changing technology in order to meet their needs.

TECHNOLOGY AND STUDENTS WITH VISUAL IMPAIRMENTS

Students with visual impairments need to have the same knowledge about technology as typically sighted children their age. For example, they need to know how to create, save, and print documents; to scan a page of print; to send e-mails and text messages to friends; and to communicate through the use of social media. However, the technological devices needed to accomplish many of these tasks often have not been designed for use by individuals who are visually impaired—they are often inaccessible to them—and therefore students with visual impairments must also learn how to use the specialized hardware, software, and devices that give them access to that general technology. Collectively, this specialized equipment and software is referred to as *assistive technology.*

The role of assistive technology is of central importance in the lives of students who are visually impaired. Assistive technology makes information displayed visually and in print available and readable for students, and provides information about the world that might not ordinarily be possible for them to know. Through this access, assistive technology also enables students to participate in the school curriculum. (As such, the ECC area of assistive technology is closely aligned with that of compensatory access.) Assistive technology promotes increased independence for students who are visually impaired, regardless of their ability level, by enabling them to perform tasks that would otherwise have been difficult or impossible for them using the same or similar devices as those used by their classmates. By enhancing or adapting a device, or by adding specialized features such as a special software program, enlarged or tactile labels, or modified hardware, everyday tasks can be accomplished with greater speed, ease, and independence by students with visual impairments.

Assistive technology empowers the student to take personal control of his or her learning environment. Rather than relying on the teacher of students with visual impairments to transcribe into print an assignment that was produced in braille, for example, a student who is blind can prepare the assignment on a computer using either a braille display or speech output software to proofread the assignment, then emboss a copy in braille for his or her future reference, and produce a print copy for the teacher. In such a situation, the teacher wouldn't have to be involved at all—the student can complete the writing assignment completely independently. In fact, the transformative and empowering aspects of assistive technology for students who are visually impaired cannot be overestimated.

The concept of *universal design* (a term originally coined by Mace [1985]) promotes the creation of products and environments that have been designed in such a way that they are accessible to all individuals with and without disabilities. Various technology manufacturers have embraced the idea of creating products that are inherently accessible and that can be used by people with disabilities without being modified—products that don't require any special attachments or software to be added to the basic device. Current examples of such inherently accessible devices include smart phones and computer tablets that have built-in speech output and screen enlargement capabilities from which everyone benefits. Given the rapid pace of technological development, in the future all technological devices may be accessible to people with visual impairments. Until such equal access is realized, however, teachers and students need to learn the technology that is currently available. Therefore, students with visual impairments need to develop skills in the use of *both* mainstream, or everyday, technology and assistive technology. Each student's instruction in this area needs to be customized, however. Students need to learn the use of technological devices that are appropriate for the ways in which they most efficiently access the environment and make effective use of sensory input. Given the diversity of students who require individualized solutions as well as the constantly evolving nature of technology, this chapter can only give a broad overview of how technology is being used at this moment in time.

With age- and developmentally appropriate instruction and time to practice using technology in meaningful ways (such as completing classroom assignments, keeping a personal digital diary, or making choices between two food item pictures displayed on a tablet), students with visual impairments typically can acquire the necessary skills to integrate technology into their daily lives. Teachers of students with visual impairments therefore need to be prepared to teach their students both the general technology-related skills they need and the use of various devices best suited to meet their access needs in order to ensure their full participation in school, work, and life. This chapter is intended to provide support and resources for instruction in this critical area of the ECC and to reassure teachers that they can develop comfort with new technology and knowledge of particular devices needed by their students. As students begin to learn, so too can their teachers. (See The Role of the Teacher of Students with Visual Impairments later in this chapter for a discussion of how teachers can learn more about assistive technology.)

COMPONENTS OF ASSISTIVE TECHNOLOGY

Assistive technology practices in educational settings are shaped by the federal Individuals with Disabilities Education Act (IDEA). Under IDEA, it is the education agency's responsibility to make available both assistive technology and services if required as part of the education of a student with disabilities (Sec. 300.105). An assistive technology device is defined as "any item, piece of equipment, or product system, whether acquired commercially off the shelf, modified, or customized, that is used to increase, maintain, or improve functional capabilities of a child with a disability" (Sec. 602 (20), USC 1401, Sec. 300.5). Thus, devices need not be "high-tech" to fall into IDEA's category of assistive technology.

In addition, assistive technology services encompass a variety of activities, including evaluating a student's needs; acquiring needed assistive technology devices; selecting or designing, adapting, and maintaining devices; coordinating other services with assistive technology devices; training of or providing technical assistance to the student (or the student's family, if appropriate); and training of or providing technical assistance to professionals involved with the student (Sec. 300.6). Thus, the ECC area of assistive technology includes much more than instruction in the use of devices; it encompasses a broad spectrum of educational services and strategies to provide access for students to participate equally in learning and daily living activities.

In general, the area of assistive technology includes the following components:

- access to information, including knowledge of basic general technology skills necessary to use multiple tools, operating systems, and applications (such as inputting information into a spreadsheet or producing documents with a word processor)
- communication, including knowledge of basic skills students with or without visual impairments need to perform school-related tasks, such as reading electronic books, completing written assignments, researching information using the Internet and tasks that require unique access (science, mathematics, images, graphics, distance learning, and the like)
- personal productivity, including the use of basic applications that enhance personal efficiency, productivity, and independence in learning and daily living activities, such as choosing an appropriate method and tool to efficiently complete a classroom assignment and customizing presentation of content on a device, based on personal preferences

The many skills to be learned within these components will be discussed in detail later in this chapter. It should be noted that these components focus on the *functions* of the technology in accessing or communicating information or accomplishing a task, rather than on whether or not the technology might be categorized as assistive or specialized.

Knowledge of Technology in General

The skills required to master technology in general are not unique to students who are visually impaired; they are based on what all students need to learn to effectively integrate technology into their lives. The difference lies primarily in the fact that students without visual impairments may learn many of these general technology functions through incidental learning, that is, through observation of others using technology. Students with visual impairments need to be taught these general skills in deliberate, systematic ways, since their awareness of technology may be limited.

As already noted, however, these students may need certain unique applications, devices, and compensatory skills to access general technology in all areas of the school curriculum and general activities of independent living, which requires that they develop skills in assistive technology. Therefore, before going into detail about the components of the assistive technology area, it is important to review the types of assistive technology available for different populations of students and how they are selected.

Knowledge of Specialized Technology

The particular assistive technology devices selected for each student depend on several factors, including:

- the specific needs of the individual child and the type of access needed, based on the extent of the visual impairment
- the presence of additional disabilities
- the degree to which the child relies on visual, tactile, or auditory input for learning

A wide range of specialized technology, both high-tech and low-tech, is used by students who are blind or visually impaired. Table 6.1 provides an extensive list of assistive technology and other methods used by students to access information. The table classifies the various technologies according to both the student's primary method of accessing information and the purpose of the technology: accessing print, accessing electronic information, producing written communication, or

TABLE 6.1

Types of Assistive Technology and Information Access for Students Who Are Blind or Visually Impaired

	Access Method		
Types of Technology	**Visual Access**	**Tactile Access**	**Auditory Access**
Technology for accessing print	Nonoptical devices • Large print • Reading stands • Acetate overlays • Lighting Optical devices • Handheld and stand magnifiers • Telescopes Video magnification systems Scanning and OCR systems Electronic whiteboards	Braille reading Tactile graphics Tactile math tools	Readers Audio recording • Digital talking books • Other audio formats Specialized scanning systems • Stand-alone electronic reading machines • Computer-based reading machines E-book readers Talking calculators Talking dictionaries
Technology for accessing electronic information	Computers • Screen-enlarging hardware • Large monitors • Adjustable monitor arms • Software options o Operating system display property adjustments o Computer accessibility features o Cursor-enlarging software • Screen magnification software Specialized scanning systems Accessible portable word processors Accessible PDAs E-book readers Large-print and online calculators Online dictionaries and thesauri	Refreshable braille displays Computers Accessible PDAs Touch tablets	Talking word-processing programs Text readers Self-voicing applications Screen-reading software Accessible PDAs Specialized scanning systems E-book readers Talking dictionaries Talking calculators Digital voice recorders

TABLE 6.1 *continued*

Types of Technology	***Access Method***		
	Visual Access	**Tactile Access**	**Auditory Access**
Technology for producing written communications	Manual tools • Bold- or raised-line paper • Felt-tip pens and bold markers • Bold-lined graph paper for math Electronic tools • Dedicated word processors • Accessible PDAs • Imaging software • Drawing software • Talking word processor • Computer with word-processing and screen magnification software • Math software and spreadsheets • Laptop or notebook computers	Manual and mechanical braille-writing devices • Slate and stylus • Braillewriters Electronic braille-writing devices • Electric and electronic braillewriters • Computers with word-processing software • Accessible PDAs • Braille translation software • Braille embosser	Accessible computers with word-processing software Accessible PDAs
Technology for producing materials in alternate formats	Scanning and OCR system Computer with word-processing software Laser printer	Scanning and OCR system Computer with word-processing software Braille translation software Graphics software Braille embosser Equipment and materials for producing tactile graphics Materials for collage Manual devices for tooling graphics Fusers and capsule paper	Digital and analog audio recording devices Scanning and OCR System

Source: Reprinted with permission from I. Presley and F. M. D'Andrea, *Assistive Technology for Students Who are Blind or Visually Impaired: A Guide to Assessment* (New York: AFB Press, 2009), pp. 9–10.

producing materials in alternate formats. Most of the technology in Table 6.1 addresses the first two assistive technology components of access to information and communication.

Specialized Technology for Students with Low Vision

In general, students who have low vision may need to use technology devices that help them maximize the use of their vision. Computers are typically made accessible through the use of screen enlargement or magnification programs that display information in sizes that can be determined by the individual. Speech-output or screen-reading software, which uses synthetic speech to announce what is displayed on the computer screen, makes the computer more easily accessible to many students who need or benefit from auditory information and reinforcement. Print materials can also be scanned and the text manipulated—for example, enlarged or contrast enhanced to make it readable by the student or able to be voiced aloud by the computer. Many devices using touch screen technology have built-in accessibility features that enlarge text and pictures on the computer's monitor, use speech output, and enhance the fore- and backgrounds of documents. Devices for near and distance viewing and stand-alone and portable electronic magnification devices also provide access to concrete materials—such as books, worksheets, objects, teachers' notes on the chalkboard, and pictures on the walls—for students with low vision. A stand-alone video magnifier

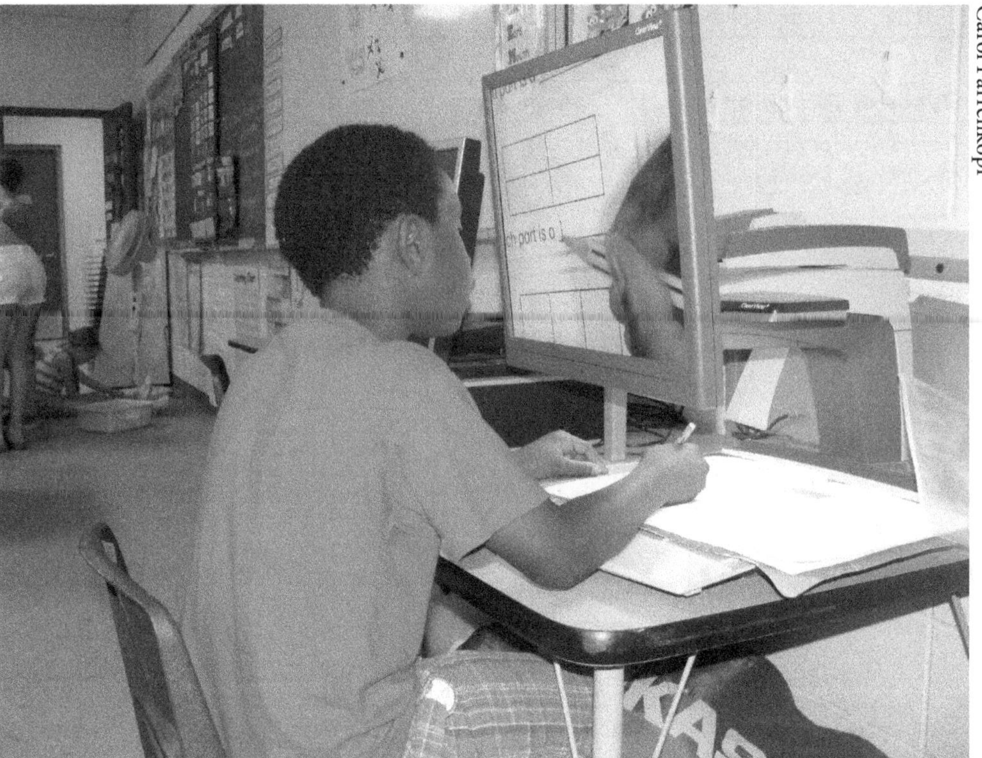

A student with very low vision uses a video magnifier to enlarge and complete a math worksheet.

Carol Farrenkopf

enables students to access their visual surroundings (both up close and far away), with or without being connected to a computer.

Specialized Technology for Students Who are Blind

In general, students who are blind may need to use technology devices that help them maximize the use of tactile information and obtain auditory information or reinforcement. For students who are blind and use braille for reading and writing, it is critical to provide technology with braille input and output. Students need daily opportunities to read and write with braille technology as they develop braille skills to maintain proficiency in braille literacy. Braille tools allow students to develop and demonstrate competencies that auditory input and output does not permit. For example, without braille access, spelling can be misrepresented or misunderstood; proper formatting of text may not be represented clearly; and graphical information without tactile representation may be confusing. With braille and tactile technology (and hard-copy braille when appropriate) students are more likely to spell accurately, develop appropriate and accurate spatial concepts, and understand illustrations and graphics.

Computers are typically made accessible for users who are blind through braille input, which makes use of six-key entry, and braille output using such devices as braille embossers or refreshable braille displays. Specialized technology that supports student access, knowledge, and use of braille literacy skills includes a variety of mechanical braille-writing tools, electronic braillewriters, portable braille notetakers (also called personal digital assistants), book readers with six-key entry and refreshable braille, and braille embossers. Depending on the student, the technology for producing materials in tactile formats, such as braille translation software and tactile image makers and capsule paper, or other tools for creating tactile graphics, needs to be made available for use. It is helpful for teachers to understand the braille tasks that students need to accomplish, in order to make decisions about and to apply the appropriate braille technology tools. To help teachers plan, manage, and instruct students in braille technology, Sidebar 6.1 provides an outline of the braille literacy knowledge and skills that students need to develop at different stages in their education.

Use of speech technology may supplement tactile information through auditory access for some devices. Stand-alone auditory devices, such as book readers, electronic reading machines, and talking calculators, may also support students' access to information. Speech recognition software can replace traditional forms of inputting information into the computer, such as those

SIDEBAR 6.1

Integrating Braille Literacy Tasks and Technology: What Students Should Know and Do

To help teachers integrate technology and literacy to improve students' results, below are braille reading and writing tasks and activities that are important for overall braille literacy and for developing skills in the use of assistive technology tools. The lists do not include all braille skills, but focus on the use of technology to promote students' knowledge and skills. The age ranges are aligned with and influenced by the International Society for Technology in Education Standards (2007a) and Student Profiles (2007b).

EARLY CHILDHOOD: EMERGENT LITERACY

Learning Tasks

1. Displays an interest in tactile graphics.
2. Understands and gains meaning from information represented in a tactile two-dimensional format (tactile graphics).
3. Displays an interest in three-dimensional tactile images.
4. Develops shape discrimination skills (matching, sorting, naming) with tactile graphics.
5. Develops size discrimination skills (matching, sorting, naming) with tactile graphics.
6. Understands spatial concepts (such as top, bottom, left, right) in a two-dimensional format.
7. Displays an interest in braille.
8. Discriminates likenesses and differences in isolated braille cells (match, sort, name).
9. Discriminates likenesses and differences in isolated braille words (match, sort, name).
10. Develops tactile tracking skills (left to right, top to bottom).
11. Gains meaning through tactile books.
12. Experiments with braille writing by making dots, scribbling, and writing on a variety of braille tools.
13. Experiments with drawing and tactile graphics.
14. Writes random letters in braille on a variety of braille tools.
15. Interprets simple tactile pictures.

Daily Living Activities

1. Uses braille and braille tools during play activities.
2. Uses tactile graphics in a variety of play activities.
3. Engages in pretend play with braille, braille tools, and tactile graphics.
4. Imitates adult reading and writing activities using braille and braille tools.
5. Plays simple games with braille and tactile graphics.

Tasks and Activities Providing Access to Content

1. Plays on a QWERTY keyboard and emphasizes commonly used keys such as Enter, Backspace, and Arrows.
2. Plays on a touch screen and emphasizes commonly used motions, such as swiping and tapping.
3. Explores approved early childhood websites.
4. "Reads" and listens to electronic books.

STEM Tasks and Activities

1. Displays an interest in:
   a. Braille numbers and signs of operation in pretend play activities.
   b. Braille and tactile counting books.
   c. Books with maps and tactile graphics.
2. Plays with an abacus.

GRADES PRE-K–2

Learning Tasks

1. Reads and writes letters of the alphabet.
2. Reads and writes literary numbers.
3. Develops mechanics of braille writing using a variety of tools.
4. Reads and writes all braille symbols and contractions.
5. Spells in uncontracted and contracted braille.
6. Expands tactile tracking patterns.
7. Develops tactile scanning techniques.
8. Interprets tactile graphics.
9. Creates simple tactile graphics.
10. Gains meaning from three-dimensional tactile images.
11. Creates braille documents.
12. Creates print documents from braille tools.
13. Drafts, proofreads, and revises written assignments in braille.
14. Continues braille keyboarding.

(continued on next page)

15. Begins using electronic tools with refreshable braille displays.

Daily Living Activities

1. Pretends to read and write in play activities using braille.
2. Writes messages for personal use.
3. Makes lists in braille.
4. Writes messages to others.
5. Creates tactile and braille materials for play.
6. Uses tablet technology with a braille interface to play games and access information for leisure activities.

Tasks and Activities Providing Access to Content

1. Locates and uses commonly used QWERTY keys, such as enter, backspace, and arrows.
2. Uses QWERTY keyboard to access electronic information for braille reading and writing with a braille interface.
3. Uses Apps for reading electronic books with refreshable braille access to device.
4. Shows an interest in QWERTY keyboarding skills with refreshable braille displays.
5. Begins to use multimedia tools to share content, such as presentation tools.
6. Is interested in image descriptions.

STEM Tasks and Activities

1. Reads and writes Nemeth numbers.
2. Reads and writes symbols of operation.
3. Uses braille measurement tools.
4. Understands spoken mathematics notation and concepts in the grade-level curriculum.
5. Understands a variety of tactile images, such as graphs and charts.
6. Explores and plays with a variety of talking calculators.
7. Explores and plays with tools with sonification.

GRADES 3–5

Learning Tasks

1. Reads and writes contracted braille in content areas.
2. Understands and uses a variety of unique braille formats for reading and writing.
3. Interprets tactile graphics in content areas.
4. Creates braille documents with appropriate formatting.
5. Creates print documents with appropriate formatting.
6. Drafts, proofreads, and revises written assignments independently.
7. Completes tests and exams in a variety of formats and media.
8. Develops note-taking skills.
9. Uses electronic tools with refreshable braille efficiently and effectively.
10. Accesses and shares information electronically.
11. Organizes electronic information using a variety of tools.
12. Conducts research activities.
13. Converts text into braille.
14. Converts braille into text.
15. Participates in solving access problems with technology.

Daily Living Activities

1. Completes homework assignments in braille.
2. Builds a personal library of hard copy and electronic braille books.
3. Uses braille in extracurricular activities.
4. Uses braille tools for personal correspondence.
5. Writes notes to family members.
6. Sends special occasion cards.
7. Uses electronic tools with a braille interface to participate in leisure activities, such as games and leisure reading and writing.

Tasks and Activities Providing Access to Content

1. Develops formal keyboarding skills on a QWERTY keyboard and a refreshable braille device to access information efficiently.
2. Locates and downloads books and documents for learning tasks.
3. Locates and uses web-based content for learning tasks.
4. Understands a variety of image descriptions.
5. Uses a variety of electronic tools with braille interface.

STEM Tasks and Activities

1. Understands and uses Nemeth code materials for STEM tasks.
2. Uses speech-adapted tools for laboratory tasks and calculating.
3. Increases skills in using spoken mathematics.

SIDEBAR 6.1 *continued*

GRADES 6–8

Learning Tasks

1. Understands and uses a variety of braille formats for reading and writing.
2. Expands note-taking skills in the content areas.
3. Accesses and shares information electronically.
4. Selects and uses appropriate braille tools for a variety of tasks.
5. Solves problems related to access and technology independently.

Daily Living Activities

1. Creates and follows a schedule.
2. Creates a personal address book.
3. Keeps a personal journal.
4. Accesses materials for community activities.
5. Conducts personal correspondence.

Tasks and Activities Providing Access to Content

1. Is proficient in QWERTY keyboarding skills and refreshable braille displays.
2. Understands and uses a variety of print formats for sharing information using braille access tools.
3. Understands and uses a variety of web-based documents and information.

STEM Tasks and Activities

1. Understands and uses higher level Nemeth code symbols for STEM tasks.
2. Uses electronic tools for laboratory tasks, such as microscopes and speech-adapted data collection tools.
3. Understands spoken mathematics equations, expressions, and notations.
4. Interprets and understands sonification in STEM content.

GRADES 9–12

Learning Tasks

1. Understands and applies special braille symbols and codes.
2. Understands and uses a variety of braille and print formats routinely and efficiently.
3. Creates quality print and braille documents routinely and efficiently.

Daily Living Activities

1. Takes notes on a job interview.
2. Accesses and shares information professionally.
3. Schedules personal commitments and appointments.
4. Uses braille tools for managing and communicating personal and professional information.

Tasks and Activities Providing Access to Content

1. Selects and uses electronic information and tools for research activities.
2. Accesses and shares information electronically routinely and efficiently.

STEM Tasks and Activities

1. Uses electronic resources to research Nemeth code symbols for use in higher level mathematics and scientific notation coursework.
2. Accurately interprets, uses, and creates a variety of images and graphics, such as charts, graphs, illustrations, diagrams, and symbols.

SOURCE: Developed by Donna McNear.

using a standard, or QWERTY, keyboard. Speech recognition software refers to the capability of devices to recognize and use speech to control input into the device, for example, by dictating e-mails and documents, voice dialing, and speaking commands to control operations and functions of devices. Some stand-alone devices, such as digital recorders, support voice input. Some touch screen devices have built-in accessibility features that enable students who are blind to use the device without any special attachments. In addition, smartphone apps can be downloaded that enhance the basic accessibility features and usability of a device for students who are blind—for example, an app that scans barcodes and reads aloud product information that has been printed on a label enhances the everyday usability of the device. Print can also be scanned and translated by specialized software so that it may be embossed into braille, presented on a refreshable braille display, or read aloud by a screen-reading program. Depending on their needs, it will be important for students to develop skills in the use of these devices and equipment.

Specialized Technology for Students with Additional Disabilities

In addition to the equipment and devices already described, some students with additional disabilities will benefit from specialized technology devices that help them perform a variety of functions, such as to communicate or to compensate for the effects of their disabilities on their capacity for engaging in learning and everyday tasks. Specialized technology is frequently used when a student benefits from a communication system. These systems generally employ alternative methods for communicating, commonly referred to as *augmentative and alternative communication*, and include all forms of communication other than oral language used to express thoughts and needs and to participate in literacy learning ("Augmentative and Alternative Communication," n.d.). Computers and communication devices are made accessible to students who have visual and additional disabilities through the use of specialized hardware—such as switches, the use of a roller ball instead of a mouse, or a modified keyboard—and software—such as simplified choice-making programs, speech output, and word prediction programs that automatically complete words after the initial letters are supplied. Although some students are able to independently use simple devices, such as digital recorders with large start/stop switch plates, many students require assistance from someone to operate or set up a device. For example, the teacher of students with visual impairments may create a series of pictures on the computer that change when the student hits the space bar or switch. Visual, tactile, and auditory enhancements may be added to a device to enable better access to the device for the student with visual and additional disabilities. These students will need to be supported in their development of skills to use such equipment and devices, and, as appropriate, to develop more advanced technology skills.

OVERVIEW OF ASSISTIVE TECHNOLOGY INSTRUCTION FOR STUDENTS WITH VISUAL IMPAIRMENTS

A framework with which to view and understand the often complex ECC area of assistive technology, based on the three components outlined earlier, is found in Table 6.2. This overview of assistive technology instruction illustrates the primary tasks, skills, and knowledge that students with visual impairments need in order to use technology effectively at school and in all other areas of their lives. The overview includes skills and knowledge related to technology in general as well as specialized, disability-related knowledge. Teachers of students with visual impairments can use this overview to develop goals and lesson plans for specific learning activities for individual students. In addition, a sampling of learning activities at the end of this chapter is provided for teachers of students with visual impairments to use or adapt in teaching assistive technology. (Note that each learning activity also includes components of other ECC areas so that teaching is not isolated or restricted to only one area of the ECC.) Strategies for teaching the components of the assistive technology area are discussed later in this chapter.

Table 6.2 was developed with awareness of the diversity in the learning characteristics of students with visual impairments and the extensive range of applications required to meet the needs of individual students. The overview does not explicitly refer to students as being blind, having low vision, or having additional disabilities, nor does it refer to their methods of obtaining access to information (learning media)—the needs of *all* students with visual impairments are considered in the overview. It should also be noted that the framework is not exhaustive—it represents the most common and current technology and knowledge students need to use for active participation in the school curriculum and daily life activities. The table focuses on high-tech items and does not include low-tech (or non-technological) devices, handheld optical devices such as monoculars or magnifiers (discussed in Chapter 5), or nontechnical devices such as slant boards and reading stands. The discussion that follows elaborates on the components outlined in the overview.

Access to Information

Certain operational knowledge and general access skills are needed by *all* students so they can use multiple tools and applications throughout their education and be active participants in today's fast-changing world. Five broad skills or tasks are encompassed in the component of access to information:

- input
- output
- program operation

TABLE 6.2

Assistive Technology Instruction: An Overview

General Technology Applications or Components	Skill or Task	Knowledge	Instructional Focuses, Including Specialized Devices
Access to Information	Input	Keyboarding	Standard or QWERTY keyboard Six-key input and braille External keyboards Specialty keyboards (ergonomic)
		Keyboard shortcuts	Computer platforms (computer operating system) Frequently used key combinations Function keys
		Touch screen	Gestures (tapping, swiping, pinching, spreading) Onscreen typing and use of access features (voice, magnification, landscape mode)
		Pointing device (mouse)	Physical features Icons, speed, size Adaptation options
		Keypad	Numeric Specific tools (telephone, combination lock)
		Speech and voice	Voice-activated input, speech recognition Voice recording functions Recording voice notes Digital voice recorders Environmental controls
		Electronic	Scanning Electronic conversion of print to digital (OCR software) Camera technology
	Output	Visual display and format	Printed (paper) Monitor, screen, LCD Visual presentation (size, speed, contrast, letter thickness, background clutter, animation, zoom) Magnification options
		Tactile display and format	Embossed (hardcopy) braille Refreshable braille
		Auditory format	Text-to-speech (TTS) Image description Speech (human narration, digitized) Audio description Video description Speakers, head- and earphones, earbuds
		Customization	Built-in accessibility features Specialized tools

(continued on next page)

TABLE 6.2 *continued*

General Technology Applications or Components	Skill or Task	Knowledge	Instructional Focuses, Including Specialized Devices
	Program operation	Application software	Computer-based • Word processing • Presentation tools • Spreadsheet • Database Web-based (browser) applications Mobile apps
		Software management	Finding, downloading, activating, managing, updating, removing
		File and data management	Navigation Security Storage
		Problem solving	Use of Help option Tech support User groups
	Internet use	World Wide Web	Finding content, searching • Websites • Webpages Accessing text, digital media (pictures, music, media), hyperlinks Web browsers • Navigating functions and features
		E-mail and communication	Sending and receiving Attachments Electronic discussion groups, newsgroups, social media, blogs Social networking and virtual communities
	Ethical and social use of information	Safe Internet and social media use	Safety: risks and benefits Responsible use Electronic etiquette Security, spam, viruses
		Copyright responsibility	Law, fair use, public domain Access under the Chafee Amendment
Communication	Reading	Electronic books and documents • Functions and features of reading devices • File formats • Web-based content • Sources of electronic content	Access formats • Visual • Tactile • Auditory • Multisensory Access contexts • Core curriculum • State standards, assessment • Expanded core curriculum • Multimedia Settings • School • Home • Community • Work
		Navigation • Units • Headings • Controls (e.g. bookmarking) • Scanning, finding text • Address boxes, buttons, scrolling, menus, tabs	
		Interactive study skills • Bookmarking	

TABLE 6.2 *continued*

General Technology Applications or Components	Skill or Task	Knowledge	Instructional Focuses, Including Specialized Devices
		• Highlighting • Word supports • Outlining • Annotating • Inserting text	
	Writing	Creating electronic text • Mechanics (tools, techniques) • Conventions (spelling, grammar) • Organizing • Outlining • Note taking • Writing content	
		Reviewing electronic text • Editing • Spelling • Grammar	
	Science, technology, engineering, and mathematics (STEM)	Calculation	Talking, scientific, and graphing calculators Sonification
		Math equations, expressions, and notation	Spoken mathematics • Terminology, choice in presentation Nemeth code
		Diagrams and accessible images	Reading and interpreting • Understanding described STEM images (e.g. data formats, priority data, organization, processes) • Navigating Writing and producing • MathML, translating into speech
		Laboratories	Electronic microscopes Speech-adapted data collection tools Real-time interactive access to displayed content
	Images, graphics	Interpretation • Elements • Key concepts	Types • Maps • Charts • Graphs • Illustrations • Diagrams • Symbols Presentation • Multimedia tablets • Braille embossers • Tactile images • 3-D tactile images • Image description, alternative text, audio
		Creation	

(continued on next page)

TABLE 6.2 *continued*

General Technology Applications or Components	Skill or Task	Knowledge	Instructional Focuses, Including Specialized Devices
			Methods • Computer drawing tools • Drawing tablets • Tactile picture makers • Image description tools
	Research	Finding content • Online searching • Device-based tools	Search engines Search techniques Browser skills Reference sources (dictionaries, encyclopedias, newspapers, periodicals, indexes, abstracts, documents)
	Distance learning and virtual classrooms	Computer-based communication Web-based homework supports	Internet browser E-mail Electronic forums Videoconferencing Chatrooms Bulletin boards Instant messaging Managing files
	Augmentative communication	Aided communication • Device type and style • Input and selection methods • Symbol and language representation Output methods Literacy learning	Access formats • Visual • Tactile • Auditory • Multisensory Symbol and language representation
Personal Productivity Applications	Accessing instruction	Presentation of information • Distance • Near • Real-time interactive access to displayed content	Lecture text • Manually created • Electronically created Demonstrations Multimedia Models, objects Experiential learning Strategies • Advance preparation • Real-time interaction • Post presentation review
	Accessing materials	Locating Downloading (content) Scanning File formats • Conversions • Transferring Translating	Textbooks Workbooks Worksheets Teacher-generated materials Web content
	Completing assignments and tests	Alternate responses Alternate production Sharing	Hard-copy Electronic file File conversion

TABLE 6.2 *continued*

General Technology Applications or Components	Skill or Task	Knowledge	Instructional Focuses, Including Specialized Devices
	Applying personal management applications	Independence Organization Efficiency	Management • Creating notes and checklists • Calendars • Schedules • Contacts • Financial records • Checkbooks
		Mobile technology	Consuming information • Entertainment • Games • Music • Shopping • Travel • News
	Selecting tools	Purpose and task Advantages and disadvantages	Portability (size, weight, battery life) Ergonomics File types Connectivity with other devices
	Customizing tools for personal use	Accessibility "wizards" Device-based Connectivity with other devices Functions and features Information management Multiple formats	Personal preferences Level of difficulty and complexity Physical dynamics (one-handed use)
	Maintaining devices	Safe use • Planning • Organizing	Battery Back-up storage • Web-based • External devices (thumb drives)
	Solving problems	Locating, searching, asking • Online • Device-based	Help features Manuals User groups Tech support Trial and error
	Applying travel applications (orientation and mobility)	Orientation	Wayfinding Navigation Points of interest Destination travel Routes GPS
		Mobility	Electronic travel aids Obstacles

- Internet use
- ethical and social use

These five tasks relate broadly to most technology operations and are activities in which students who use technology typically participate. Providing students with visual impairments with a strong foundation related to each of these five tasks will enable students to participate in all areas of the core curriculum and ECC that use technology. The knowledge and instructional focuses outlined here have been included because of their importance to students' overall performance in the area of technology and in the application of assistive technology.

Input

Input refers to methods of entering information and data into a computer or electronic tool, and is a major activity for all technology users, including students with visual impairments. Table 6.2 lists the relevant knowledge, skills, and instructional focuses for students who are visually impaired, in regard to the inputting of information using different tools and applications.

Keyboarding. Keyboarding, the process of inputting text into a device through a keyboard, is a fundamental skill for most students. A keyboard is the primary input device used with computers and other electronic tools. Students need to know and use a variety of keyboarding techniques, including the QWERTY keyboard. (QWERTY refers to the standard design for keyboards and gets its name from the first six letters in the upper left area of the keyboard.) Proficiency in QWERTY keyboarding provides students with the ability to use computers in most school and work settings. For students who are visually impaired and who use an auditory learning channel, common tools for teaching keyboarding, as of this writing, are Talking Typer for Windows and Learn Keys: Verbal Keyboard Feedback (both available from the American Printing House for the Blind; see the Resources section at the end of this book). Students using the visual learning channel may be able to access and learn from the keyboarding programs used in their local school districts, with or without accessibility adaptations. There is also a variety of free online keyboarding programs for children of all ages that may be appropriate with or without adaptations for some students. Detailed suggestions for teaching keyboarding skills are found in Presley & D'Andrea (2009).

Students who are learning braille generally learn six-key braille input when they begin writing on manual braillewriters, and it is critical that students using braille master six-key input to develop proficient braille literacy skills (discussed in Chapter 4). This skill can be transferred to electronic tools, such as electric braillewriters and portable braille notetakers, when students begin using braille-related assistive technology devices. Without proficiency in braille writing, the student will not be able to input information quickly and efficiently into a braille-related device.

A variety of external and specialty keyboards, such as ergonomic keyboards, provide options for students who may benefit from uniquely designed physical adaptations to standard keyboards. Some people with visual impairments prefer a traditional external keyboard when using tablet technology.

Keyboard shortcuts. Students can increase their efficiency when inputting by using keyboard shortcuts, which are keys or combination of keys that give the computer or other device a command to perform a certain function, such as Control + S for saving an open document. These shortcuts can substitute for the "point and click" function performed by the navigation device known as the computer mouse (discussed later in this section), for students whose visual impairment or other disability interferes with the use of this device. However, all students with visual impairments, not just students who are unable to use a mouse effectively, benefit from skills in using keyboard shortcuts because these shortcuts typically provide a quicker way to navigate and use a variety of software programs. Thus, common keyboard shortcuts can increase most students' productivity. There are shortcut keys for a variety of computer platforms and software programs, both everyday and specialized technology, as well as methods to create individualized shortcut combinations. (See Sidebar 6.2 for more information about keyboard shortcuts.)

Touch Screen input. Another common input method is direct touch with a finger or stylus on a touch screen. A touch screen is a display on an electronic device that accepts information input directly through the screen; they are standard features on many portable electronic tools, such as smartphones and tablet computers, and are commonly used in activities in which students are playing and learning. Tablet technology uses the touch screen as its primary input method, although external keyboards can also be used for input with these devices. Students need to know the basics of touch screen formats and how people with visual impairments can use this input method accurately and efficiently. As manufacturers redesign electronic tools, such as computers, they are incorporating touch screen input with traditional keyboards. Today's tablet technology requires a variety of human touch input methods, often referred to as "gestures." Students with low vision may need to learn gestures such as tapping on icons, pinching an image with the fingers to make it smaller,

SIDEBAR 6.2

Keyboard Shortcuts

Keyboard shortcuts use individual keys or combination of keys that give a computer or other device a command to perform a certain function. Often they involve alphanumeric keys in various combinations with the Alt, Shift, and Control keys or the use of function keys (such as those numbered F1 to F12). The commands associated with various key combinations change with different operating systems or applications. Use of keyboard shortcuts increases the efficiency of most technology users, especially those who rely on the keyboard for inputting information or data. Keyboard shortcut commands vary, depending on the tool, platform, and software. For example, each of the following might have its own shortcut commands:

- operating systems
- software programs
- applications
- general keyboard shortcuts
- dialog boxes
- accessibility shortcuts

In addition to these, there are special accessibility shortcuts, and it is also possible to create custom shortcuts.

The following are some suggestions for teachers for helping students become more proficient in using keyboard shortcuts.

- Begin teaching the most common keyboard shortcuts related to the students' technology devices and encourage them to become efficient with those before teaching additional shortcuts.
- Research the Internet for information on shortcuts for your students' particular devices. There are many resources, but they change periodically.
- Create helpful references for students, such as a list in print or braille of the shortcuts students prefer to use, that they can keep by their desks or work stations. Create a more detailed electronic file of shortcuts that students can refer to when needed.
- Periodically monitor and evaluate each student's use of shortcuts.

spreading an image apart to make it larger, and swiping the screen to scroll through content.

Students also need to know how to use pop-up graphical keyboards that are programmed to appear suddenly on the touch screen to facilitate the inputting of text information in a variety of contexts. For students who are braille readers and writers, there are six-key braille external keyboards that can be used for input instead. Common access features in many devices, such as voice output and magnification, make onscreen typing easier. Students can learn other strategies, such as using the screen in landscape mode (horizontally oriented), to assist in efficient onscreen typing.

Pointing device (mouse). A pointing device, most often the device referred to as a mouse, is a popular input tool for computer users. Mice can have a variety of physical features and they come in a variety of sizes and shapes, with various button configurations that can be assigned commands, and scroll wheels that can navigate around a document or screen with the movements of one finger (such as when scrolling up or down through a document or website). A variety of mouse adaptations can be made to address the needs of students who also have physical challenges, such as interfacing with switches or joysticks, or a hands-free mode in which the mouse is activated by, for example, the user's voice, chin, or foot. Students who are visually impaired and use a mouse for input need to know features of the mouse and options for adaptations to increase their technological efficiency.

Keypads. A keypad is an arrangement of keys in a specific pattern, such as the numeric keypad on some computer keyboards. In addition to those used on computers and other electronic devices, keypads are features in other common tools, such as phones, calculators, and combination locks. Some specialized tools, such as braille devices, have additional keypads unique to each device that students need to understand and know how to use.

Speech and voice input. Many students increase their productivity through the use of speech and voice functions to input information into devices that have multimedia capabilities. Speech input can be used with devices that are programmed to respond to the human voice. As more technology devices integrate speech recognition and voice-related functions, the use of voice access by many users of technology is increasing. Many specialized devices for students with visual impairments and additional disabilities that focus on visual and tactile learning channels also include speech input capabilities. Through speech input, some students are able to increase their interactions with text through faster navigation, search-and-find functions, and note taking.

Electronic input. *Scanning,* the conversion of print or visual information into an electronic file by means of specialized software, is an essential way for students to access print information independently. Through the use of specialized tools, students can convert print into an electronic format and manipulate the information (Presley & D'Andrea, 2009), providing themselves with immediate access to the print environment. Students need to know how to capture print material through scanning and use optical character recognition (OCR) software to convert the captured digital images into digital text. Students with visual impairments can access the resulting files in a variety of ways appropriate for their needs, including through synthetic speech or devices that produce tactile access in the form of braille. Scanning technology thus provides students who are visually impaired with greater independence, access in real time to instructional materials, and privacy in regard to accessing print-based content. The digital camera technology incorporated into many devices gives users the ability to view content immediately after an image has been taken. Knowledge of camera-based and scanning technologies for classroom and other learning activities, as well as application in daily living tasks, is therefore a valuable skill for students with visual impairments.

Output

Output refers to methods that are used to generate information and data from a computer or electronic device. Students who are visually impaired should be able to use a variety of output methods, using various devices and applications.

Output can be considered in terms of visual, tactile, and auditory formats, referring to the methods and learning channels that students with visual impairments use to create and interact with text. As teachers consider the skills students need to generate output, it is important to think about when it is best for a student to use printed materials or hard-copy braille and when it may make more sense to use electronic presentation of materials using monitors, screens, or refreshable braille. Eventually, students need to be taught to make these judgments independently.

Visual display/format. When students use a visual learning channel and choose to use a hard-copy print paper format, they need to understand and know how to use tools to produce visually accessible content in print documents. For example, students may need to be proficient in the use of a video magnifier (also referred to as a closed-circuit television system or CCTV), which magnifies print material and can be used for either near and distance viewing, or both, depending on the features and functions of the device. When using digital content, they need to know the variety of methods to display information on monitors and screens. Students need to understand the features of tools that manipulate the visual presentation of information, such as size, speed, contrast, letter thickness, background clutter, animation, and zoom capabilities. Understanding the range of magnification options is important to efficiently access visual information.

Tactile display/format. Students who use the tactile learning channel need to know how to use electronic tools to produce hard-copy embossed braille. Creating hard-copy embossed braille is essential for understanding many literacy activities. Students need to know how to use a refreshable braille display (an electronic braille device that produces braille through the raising and lowering of round-tipped pins positioned in the configuration of a braille cell) to read and manipulate text. Using electronic tools with braille output is critical for accurate and efficient learning skills.

Donna McNear

Print can be accessed tactilely through the use of a refreshable braille display.

Auditory format. For many users, an auditory format can supplement information presented as visual or tactile output and can assist in providing access to multimedia materials. When speech is used for output, students need to understand how the speech is generated. The phrase *text-to-speech* (often abbreviated as TTS) refers to the artificial production of speech by an electronic device through use of a speech synthesizer. Human narration is provided through the recording of a human voice. Students need to know how to use the auditory format to access audio descriptions provided for images and videos in electronic learning materials. Students also need to know how to manage the tools to optimize auditory access, such as speakers, head- and earphones, and earbuds.

Customization. A critical skill for students to learn is how to customize output for their needs using built-in accessibility features, now common in many technology devices. When students who are visually impaired use specialized assistive technology tools, they also need to know how to customize the features of the output produced to increase their reading efficiency or ease of access.

Program Operation

Program operation refers to the essential knowledge and skills *all* students need to become proficient in operating programs that enable a computer or other device to perform basic applications essential to using technology. *Program* in this sense refers to software or applications that enable computers and electronic devices to perform their functions, such as word processing or Internet browsing. This proficiency includes knowledge and skills in the following areas:

- application software
- software management
- file and data management
- problem-solving skills

Application software. Students need to have knowledge of and skills in the commonly used applications that enable electronic tools to perform useful functions. Students need to know how to use common computer applications, such as those used for word processing and for creating presentations, spreadsheets, and databases. Navigating the World Wide Web with web browser applications is an essential skill, and students need to understand the features and functions of web browsing. The use of apps (applications for mobile devices) enables students to access and participate in many aspects of daily life.

Software management. Software programs like those just discussed are necessary for performing literacy, numeracy, and learning tasks required in the core curriculum and the ECC. To operate software programs for a variety of electronic devices, students need to know a range of basic functions, such as how to launch programs, create documents and files, enter information and data, format documents, edit and save information, manipulate files, and locate saved documents and files. Students also need to know how to manage apps on mobile devices. They need to know how to find appropriate apps and to download, activate, update, and remove them.

File and data management. Similarly, students with visual impairments need to understand and manage the basic functions involved in use of electronic information, such as those relating to navigation, security, and storage. The basic skills of file and data management that are needed to operate a computer effectively include:

- navigating through menus, dialog boxes, and other elements
- selecting items
- using commands like Find, Cut, Copy, and Paste
- manipulating documents
- navigating by paragraphs, sentences, and lines
- organizing file folders and files
- navigating between applications
- being informed about security issues including knowledge of antivirus programs, firewalls, passwords, and strategies for identifying suspicious requests to download content appearing in e-mails and dialog boxes
- understanding how to maintain privacy through file protection and securing a computer desktop with a password
- knowing how to back up and store information on devices and on the Internet

Problem solving. Problem solving is a critical life skill. It is important to provide opportunities for students with visual impairments to engage in their own problem solving early and frequently throughout their school years, beginning in early childhood. When it comes to assistive technology, it is especially important that students know how to approach problems and troubleshoot issues related to the technology they use. Students who know how to use the Help feature available on most devices, and who understand how to access a variety of technical supports—such as searching for solutions on the Internet, using web-based support, and obtaining telephone support—are generally more independent and productive than students who do not know how to solve problems in this way. As students get older, knowing how to participate in electronic discussion groups and user groups related to preferred and frequently used technology devices is another important set of skills.

Internet Use

The Internet provides a vast array of resources and services, and using it is a basic skill for all students. The processes that students with visual impairments need to learn in using the Internet are similar to what all students need to know and include how to browse the World Wide Web and use e-mail.

World Wide Web (WWW). The World Wide Web (now commonly known as "the web") refers to the information and documents typically presented in the form of pages on a computer or other screen that can be accessed on the Internet using an application called a web browser. Students with visual impairments must know which browsers interact best with assistive technology programs that involve visual, tactile, and auditory formats and functions. If students are using access software, such as speech output or screen magnification, they also need to learn effective strategies for searching, browsing, and navigating. Knowing how to input information and operate programs effectively are important aspects of independent Internet use. The effective use of the Internet is dependent on a student's understanding of key concepts, such as search engines, web addresses or URLs (uniform resource locators), and conventions such as bookmarking. Students should also be able to locate content, read within a website, determine reliable information, and recognize and manage advertisements. It is essential that students know how to retrieve and download content in a variety of accessible file formats to engage in diverse learning activities. The learning activity "Checking Out Movie Listings" at the end of this chapter suggests a way of practicing these types of skills in the context of an activity that also involves skills from a variety of ECC areas.

E-mail and communication. E-mail is one of the most widely used activities related to the Internet and has become a standard way to communicate. It is therefore fundamental that students who are visually impaired understand how to send and receive e-mail messages. They should know how to log on to a server, create new messages, and to send, receive, view, and reply to messages. Similarly, they must be able to create, access, and send attachments with e-mail messages.

In addition to using e-mail, students will want to access the wide variety of communication options that are available on the Internet. They need a familiarity with, and skills in, the use of basic Internet elements, such as electronic discussion groups, newsgroups, social media, and blogs. This knowledge will enable them to make choices about the ways in which they may want to stay in touch with others.

Ethical and Social Use of Information

Instruction in the ethical and social use of electronic devices and electronic forms of communication is essential for all students, but is particularly important for students with visual impairments because of their additional need to use the Internet and electronic devices to access information, participate in learning, and communicate with others.

Safe Internet use. Forms of communication over the Internet such as social networking, social media, and virtual communities are widespread in the lives of all students, and it is important that students who are visually impaired understand how to safely use, negotiate, and learn from informal and virtual environments. Students need to understand the vastness of the information that resides on the World Wide Web and how to use that information responsibly. They also must be taught how to practice safe web browsing, avoid contact with offensive websites and material, recognize spam, and be cautious about opening e-mail from unknown sources. Other essential areas of learning include:

- understanding the elements of creating a positive web presence, such as keeping a clean "e-image"
- developing personal branding
- knowing online dos and don'ts
- managing an online reputation
- protecting privacy

Teachers need to explain how quickly personal information and pictures can be shared with the rest of the world when shared electronically or posted somewhere on the web without a student's knowledge. Students should be taught that if they respond to a blog with a negative comment, or post a compromising photograph of themselves to a social networking site, they may find that these items have an infinitely long virtual life, viewable to all, including prospective employers. Teachers of students with visual impairments can also teach students who are visually impaired to develop skills related to electronic etiquette, such as avoiding the use of all capital letters (as it appears to the reader as overly commanding or loud), appropriate ways to communicate with others electronically, and use of antivirus software to keep a computer running properly and as safely as possible.

COPYRIGHT RESPONSIBILITY. Students with visual impairments need to develop an understanding of the concept of copyright and their responsibilities as users of information. Familiarity with the appropriate and legal use of information and with such practices as fair use of material in the public domain is important, as is knowledge of what is permissible regarding the sharing and duplication of electronic material. It is critical that students (and their teachers) in the United States understand accessibility rights under the Chafee Amendment (P.L. 104–197) to the U.S. Copyright Law. Teachers need to be deliberate about teaching students who use specialized formats that they cannot share these materials with others. Information about which materials can be distributed freely (non-copyrighted) and which cannot (copyrighted) and how states or local governments manage and distribute specialized materials for eligible students can be found on the websites of most states' departments of education.

Communication

The technology component of communication includes a variety of tasks and skills related to the use of technology to perform literacy skills and the application of those skills to learning in the core curriculum and in the ECC, including:

- reading
- writing
- science, technology, engineering, and mathematics (STEM)
- images and graphics
- research
- distance learning and virtual classrooms
- augmentative communication

These seven areas represent the body of essential knowledge and skills in the area of assistive technology that are needed by students with visual impairments to engage effectively in the educational curriculum. This section focuses on elements of literacy and learning in which access and participation can be particularly challenging for students with visual impairments. Students need to read, write, conduct research, and learn using electronic content in a variety of formats (visual, tactile, auditory, or a combination of formats) based on their individual needs. They need to be able to access, read, and write content in a variety of learning contexts, such as when participating in core curriculum subject matter, state standard assessments, ECC learning activities, and increasingly prevalent multimedia educational content. Students need to be able to access, read, and write content in all the settings where they live, work, and learn. For students who benefit from adapted communication strategies and formats, educators need to consider a variety of methods and devices for augmentative communication. Table 6.2 provides a framework of knowledge, skills, and instructional focuses in this area.

Reading

ELECTRONIC BOOKS AND DOCUMENTS. Students with visual impairments, like all students, need to be proficient in all aspects of using electronic materials. As common core educational content moves from hard-copy print textbooks to electronic textbooks (accessed on the web or via devices), content created by teachers, and content accessed on the Internet, students are increasing their use of a variety of electronic devices to participate in the common core curriculum. They are increasing their use of personal devices and the places where they use those devices. Many schools are also integrating distance learning options into their site-based school programs to supplement core content.

As a result, the skills involved in reading books, documents and web-based content electronically are a primary focus of assessment and instruction. The knowledge, skills, and instructional focuses relating to the universal and general application of access to information already described in this chapter—skills related to input, output, file management, navigation, and using the web—set the stage for students to read the full range of electronic materials and thereby participate in literacy and learning activities. As traditional electronic devices for people who are visually impaired increase their capacities for managing the use of electronic books and content, these devices are evolving into electronic reading systems that provide many avenues for reading, writing, and studying. Students need to know the functions and features of a variety of devices that support the reading of electronic books and content, and understand the methods for visual, tactile, and auditory access available on the devices.

Teachers can teach their students with visual impairments to explore the functions and features of different kinds of reading devices and determine whether they support text-to-speech conversion or other output. Students need to recognize and make use of different file formats and determine which are most accessible for their reading purposes and use web-based content for learning. In addition, students need to understand the sources of electronic books and documents and protocols relating to their use, so they do not unintentionally violate copyright laws.

Navigation. Developing the skills for navigating within electronic books and documents so that they can be read by designated units such as characters, words, lines, and paragraphs is important for users who are visually impaired. Students can be taught how to use special controls to efficiently read electronic text. Methods of searching for and locating text in a document or book are critical skills to be learned that, once acquired, can save students a great deal of time. The learning activity "Listening for Nonsense Words" at the end of this chapter offers a fun activity that allows students to practice navigation as well as listening skills that are important for aural reading. Students also need to be able to navigate content on the web for reading, writing, and learning activities, including how to use address boxes, menus, tabs, buttons, and scrolling techniques.

Interactive study skills. An important aspect of reading to participate in the curriculum is using study skills that allow the student to actively interact with text in multiple ways. Many electronic tools have capabilities that increase the student's ability to engage with learning material for study purposes. These include the capability to bookmark and highlight text, access word pronunciation support, create annotations, group ideas, and share editorial remarks in a document that several individuals are working on concurrently. Students with visual impairments need to develop the ability to use these options as support to their own study efforts.

Writing

Creating electronic text. Producing written communication is an essential literacy skill for all students. Students with visual impairments should be able to produce written communication that meets the same expectations and standards that apply to all students. They need to master the mechanics of using and operating devices for written communication, and it is essential that they have the skills needed to produce content in an accessible format for all learning tasks and in all settings. Students need to be able to use portable electronic tools to have the flexibility to create text in any classroom or location.

In addition to learning methods of inputting described earlier in this section, students with visual impairments should know how to organize written documents and have skills for studying efficiently, such as outlining and note taking. In general, students should be taught to use devices that foster the development of effective written communication skills, including using writing conventions, such as punctuation and spelling, in all formats for themselves and other readers. Students need devices that easily integrate reading and writing to efficiently express ideas, so they are able to keep up with the volume of assignments that are required at school.

Reviewing electronic text. Essential to producing written communication is the ability to review what has been written and to modify content. Students who are visually impaired need skills and devices that foster efficiency in editing, spelling, and checking grammar. They should know how to use the features and functions related to reviewing text on all of their devices. If students are using auditory formats, learning how to proofread by *listening* to the spelling of the spoken word can be challenging and is another area of instruction to be addressed.

Science, Technology, Engineering and Mathematics (STEM)

The participation of students with visual impairments in science, technology, engineering, and mathematics—known as STEM—is an area of instruction that requires ongoing attention as accessibility options emerge to improve access. Electronic information in mathematics and related scientific and technical areas is becoming more accessible, and accessible devices for work in these areas are becoming more sophisticated. Teachers of students with visual impairments must help students interpret mathematical, scientific, and technical content and teach them how to write and produce this content appropriately and accurately. Electronic devices such as computers and notetakers that students frequently use for learning applications often need to be used with additional access solutions to be efficient in accessing STEM material. For example, people who are blind sometimes use "alternative" braille codes, such as the computer code, to support mathematical calculations because tools to comprehensively support the Nemeth Braille Code for Mathematics and Science Notation are still emerging at this time. Their teachers need to be prepared to teach all necessary braille codes to their students who may use a variety of codes—old and new. As the Unified English Braille Code (UEB) is integrated into educational learning content in the United States (it is already used in Canada and other English-speaking countries), educators and students need to be prepared to quickly teach and learn new mathematics and computer codes when UEB content is available. Although no research currently exists in the field regarding the usability or ease of UEB and STEM materials, it is anticipated that students will find using a single braille code for literary, math, and science materials to be more convenient than using two codes.

Calculation. Skills in operating accessible electronic devices to perform mathematical calculations are fundamental for students with visual impairments. Accessible calculators are essential electronic equipment for students with visual impairments and have been in use for some time. Talking scientific calculators are also considered fundamental tools and are available as standalone devices or as embedded functions in other electronic devices. Graphing calculators typically offer an audible avenue for understanding graphs (sonification), but some students find it difficult to understand the meaning of the different sounds and pitches of the audible output. In such cases, the student may prefer a tactile representation of a graph. In either case, intense instruction by teachers of students with visual impairments may be necessary for students to achieve proficiency with these tools. Development of skills in the use of these devices is especially important for students taking or planning to take advanced mathematics and science courses.

Math equations, expressions, and notation. Electronic devices are beginning to use emerging image description application tools to create spoken mathematics, enabling the user to access math equations, expressions, and notation. Students need to learn the terminology used to represent mathematical elements in order to access and participate in electronic mathematical content. They need to understand the various methods used to "speak" math elements like fractions and equations.

Students who use braille need to continue to learn the Nemeth code, especially if they are participating in advanced math and science subject matter. Spoken mathematics in electronic tools will need to be supplemented with representation in braille to facilitate accurate comprehension of content. With the advent of UEB, electronic tools will also increase the capacity to provide access in UEB and improve the accessibility of mathematical content.

Diagrams, accessible images. Diagrams are also referred to in the discussion on graphics in the next section but are important to mention in relationship to mathematics and science, because they are frequently used in these areas and are key to understanding this content. Students with visual impairments need experience with understanding and interpreting diagrams and using devices to create and produce diagrams for classroom learning activities, and it is important for teachers of students with visual impairments to provide access to diagrams for students based on their primary and secondary learning media and preferences (discussed in Chapters 4 and 5).

All students need experience in using electronic devices to access content containing image descriptions because this is a primary adaptation for accessing diagrams and other graphic material. For example, electronic books may contain additional text that describes images, which can be accessed through speech or braille. Students need to understand how data in diagrams and tables are organized and described, how to navigate through the descriptions, and how to focus on priority data. Those who use vision as a primary learning channel may need to develop skills in using low vision devices to visually interpret content in diagrams to ensure accuracy, especially when reading numbers. Immediate access to tactile graphics for those who need them is critical in order for those students to keep up with their classmates in mathematics and science. Teachers of students with visual impairments also need to teach students to use technology to create their own diagrams and to use verbal descriptions to communicate content. Multimedia access methods (tools that use both speech and tactile materials), such as talking tablets for tactile representations, are often valuable for this purpose. As MathML (an application to describe mathematical notation) becomes common to tools, students may benefit from greater knowledge in this area to access and participate in STEM activities. (See the section on images and graphics below for more information.)

Laboratories. Technology is improving student access and participation in activities that are undertaken in learning laboratories, but laboratory work remains an area that needs deliberate attention by the teacher of students with visual impairments. Laboratory work is typically challenging for teachers when it comes to devising ways to include students with visual impairments in class activities, but doing so ensures that all relevant information is shared, and also facilitates development and practice of self-determination skills. It is important to plan ahead and decide what will be the most effective teaching strategies and access devices used. Electronic microscopes can improve access for students who are visual learners by enlarging microscopic organisms to a degree that can be seen by students with low vision. However, no such equivalent device exists for students who are blind, so these students must be taught strategies to use when relying on in-depth verbal descriptions and tactile representations of organisms.

Emerging speech technology and speech-adapted data collection tools improve the real-time access and participation of students in science laboratory settings. These tools provide real-time audio output and specialized software provides immediate recording of data so students can navigate, analyze, and output content in a variety of ways. Students need to understand these tools and use them in laboratory studies to increase their independence. (See the Resources section at the end of this chapter for sources of such products.)

Images and Graphics

As already indicated, access to images and graphics is another technology-related area where accessible formats remain challenging. When teachers assess and teach students skills in using images and graphics, they need to consider the variety of images that students are required to access and understand, including maps, charts, graphs, illustrations, diagrams, and symbols. All access methods, whether visual, tactile, or auditory in nature, involve unique challenges in representing content that incorporates graphics. In a visual format, graphics are often complex and not easily viewed, even with magnification devices. Tactile graphics are labor intensive to produce, not always readily available, and usually provide far less information than is found in the original printed items. Auditory access to graphics is also labor intensive, but new tools are emerging, such as talking graphics calculators and electronic applications that describe images. Despite the challenges, skills related to access and to engagement with graphic content are critical for students with visual impairments. (See Chapter 5 for additional discussion of tactile graphics.)

Interpretation. Teachers of students with visual impairments need to teach their students to interpret the images students can access. Teachers especially need to ensure that students learn efficient methods of scanning—that is, using a systematic pattern to examine an image to find its key features—when using visual or tactile media. Students must master use of keys, legends, and other features of graphics important to their use. Teaching students with visual impairments to efficiently interpret maps, charts, graphs, illustrations, diagrams, and symbols can help them understand the larger concepts being taught in a particular subject area and can increase immediate access to instructional materials presented in general education classes. For example, if a student cannot systematically and efficiently scan a tactile map to locate large bodies of water, valuable class time may be spent by the student exploring irrelevant lines and bumps. Students need to be able to identify the elements used in a graphic to communicate an idea and understand key concepts.

Creation. It is not unusual for today's students to be asked to create graphics for class assignments and on standardized tests. Students with visual impairments also need the knowledge and skills to understand the variety of methods used to present graphics and to use tools to create graphics. They may need to be taught how to use computer-based drawing tools, web-based libraries for graphics, multimedia tablets, braille embossers, 3-D tactile image printers, tactile picture makers, and image description tools for this purpose.

Research

Students with visual impairments need focused instruction in order to effectively use research tools in all areas of learning.

Finding content. Students need to become proficient in finding research content using electronic sources, such as the Internet, and references housed in stand-alone devices. They need to know proper research methods for online searching, such as how to use search engines and employ effective browsing and search techniques.

Teachers of students with visual impairments need to teach students to use the features of web-based and device-based dictionaries, as well as how to find information in web-based encyclopedias, newspapers, periodicals, indexes, abstracts, and documents. In addition, it is necessary to provide instruction on how to determine the reliability of Internet sources. Strategies for creating accessible files from sources that provide file formats that are not easily accessible, even with access devices, should also be explored. Possible strategies include the following: downloading the article onto a different device to determine if different functionality will allow access; converting the file to a different format, such as rich text format (rtf); copying and pasting the content into a different program that has a different file format; and printing the file and rescanning it into a device that will permit access.

Distance Learning and Virtual Classrooms

Formal teaching and learning activities are no longer restricted to the classroom, but may occur in many distance learning contexts and in virtual classrooms. Many school districts supplement site-based teaching and learning with supplementary content on the Internet and many students participate in extension courses on the Internet. Students need proficiency in computer-based communication methods—such as e-mail; web browsing; participation in electronic forums, chatrooms, online bulletin boards, instant messaging, and video conferencing; and file management for submitting assignments—to effectively participate in these teaching and learning contexts.

Augmentative Communication

Many students who are visually impaired and have additional disabilities benefit from augmentative communication devices that help them participate in literacy, learning, and daily living activities. When working with a student who is visually impaired and has additional disabilities, it is important to understand the functions and features of any specialized communication devices, including:

- input methods
- selection methods
- symbols
- methods of representing language
- output methods

Teachers of students with visual impairments need to collaborate with other team members to consider what forms of assisted communication will best meet the student's needs and may need to consult with communication specialists and professionals knowledgeable about augmentative communication and appropriate devices. In general, it is the role of the teacher of students with visual impairments to contribute information to the educational team on assistive communication methods and appropriate visual, tactile, or auditory adaptations, based on information from the functional vision assessment and learning media assessment. It may also be necessary to help other team members understand that the association between symbols and the objects they represent can be particularly challenging for students with visual impairments for whom these devices are recommended (see Chapters 4 and 5 for more information).

Personal Productivity Applications

The personal productivity component of the assistive technology area encompasses a variety of skills related to increasing students' independence, efficiency, and productivity. The skills in this area pertain to how students who are visually impaired use assistive technology devices, as well as the technology skills that relate to the first two components, to efficiently and independently meet their personal needs. In general, use of technology needs to be supported consistently and on a daily basis in all learning settings and environments. To do so, teachers can incorporate technology use in the instruction of skills and behaviors of other ECC areas. The broad groups of skills encompassed in the personal productivity component include:

- accessing instruction
- accessing materials
- completing assignments and testing
- applying personal management applications
- selecting tools
- customizing tools for personal use
- maintaining devices
- solving problems
- applying travel applications (orientation and mobility)

Accessing Instruction

Students should be comfortable and competent using their knowledge of assistive technology to access the school curriculum, adapt to the variety of instructional methods used by teachers, and participate in typical learning activities at home, at school, at work, and at play. They should be prepared to use technology for access to and participation in large and small groups and be able to access information for individual use.

Students need strategies and devices that enable them to access content provided by teachers, who deliver instruction using a range of approaches, including through lectures, directly from textbooks, through multimedia presentations and equipment (such as computer projection systems), and by writing information on a variety of boards displayed at a distance. When instruction and information are presented at a distance, students need to be taught to determine the best approach to use so that they can access information in the classroom at the same time as their classmates, using not only their assistive technology devices, but also through commonly used instructional accommodations (see Chapter 4 on compensatory access for more information about accommodations). Students need to participate in real-time interactive learning in their primary learning medium through using tablets, computers, and specialized personal devices integrated with classroom technology to access instructional content presented by the teacher. Students with low vision should be able to use devices or other means, such as wireless connections from the teacher's digital presentation to their own device to access instructional content. With such technology, a student might for example, use a distance magnification device connected to a laptop computer that displays the information in an enlarged format using specialized software to see the steps of a mathematics problem as the teacher records them on a board for the entire class. Students who are blind should be able to use electronic devices that provide braille and/or speech access to the content.

Electronic access methods to participate in classroom instruction may need to be supplemented with other instructional supports, such as manually and electronically created content (especially for images and mathematical content), real items used in demonstrations (models and objects), and experiential learning. Teachers need to be attentive to planning strategies for accessing instructional content and need to use advance planning, arrange real-time interactive access, and provide post-presentation review activities. Providing access to instruction is fundamental in order for students who are visually impaired to participate in the curriculum, but students need to have the necessary skills to take advantage of that access.

Accessing Materials

Accessing instructional materials and, in particular, print materials, is an essential activity for students who are visually impaired. Students must be taught efficient strategies and proficient skills to be able to access such materials independently throughout the school day and under a variety of circumstances. Access includes locating, downloading, scanning, converting, transferring, and translating needed material in or into appropriate file formats. Teachers need to assist students (especially as they get older) in planning, managing, and accessing all learning materials used in instruction, including textbooks, workbooks, worksheets, teacher-generated materials, and web content. Over time, students' options for accessing printed materials should increase, as should their role in selecting which device to use for a specific purpose. As students become more independent in making these choices, their selections should be honored—even if they are not the ones their teachers would have selected—and the natural consequences of those options reviewed with students. These lessons can prove invaluable for increasing students' personal productivity over the course of a lifetime and reinforce self-determination skills as well.

Completing Assignments and Tests

Teachers of students with visual impairments need to help their students develop skills for completing assignments and taking tests and instruct them in how to use assistive technology devices that produce responses in alternate formats for completing assignments and tests. For example, students may answer questions on a test produced in braille using an electronic device that outputs the answers in print or in an electronic word-processed document, so the general classroom teacher can read them. Students need to learn to determine when an assignment or test needs to be completed in print, braille, or in an electronic format and be proficient in performing file conversions to make assignments and tests accessible to a variety of audiences.

Students need to complete computerized standardized tests in their primary learning medium, using the electronic tools they use for everyday learning. It is essential that they have the opportunity to participate in practice tests using the same access and tools that are used in the final test. Teachers need to be diligent in working with district and state assessment personnel to ensure that students with visual impairments who need specialized access and tools are provided with appropriate accommodations.

Applying Personal Management Applications

Students need independence and efficiency in using technology to manage their time and for recordkeeping, and teachers must include lessons in using tools for personal use. Knowing about and using options for planning and creating notes and checklists for personal use that can increase organization are important. Many software programs for both general and specialized devices include operations for calendars, maintaining contacts, managing tasks, and creating and maintaining notes. Teaching students to use electronic calendars for appointments, schedules, and other commitments is important for both personal and school use. Financial recordkeeping tools, such as electronic checkbooks, provide independent access to a task that is otherwise difficult for many people who are visually impaired. Data management tools, such as spreadsheets, assist students with personally managing more complex information. The learning activity titled "Checking out Movie Listings" gives students an opportunity to apply personal management skills along with use of the Internet.

Students need to know how to use mobile technology for accessing and managing information and increasing their independence and personal productivity. Everyday access and information consumption through apps is increasing for all mobile device users, including individuals with visual impairments. Students need to understand how to use mobile technology and mobile apps for entertainment, games, music, shopping, travel, news, and banking. They need to learn which apps work best with accessibility options, such as speech and braille devices. They need to know where to find information to learn about the solutions preferred by many people with visual impairments and understand that these solutions are changing daily.

Selecting tools

In general, the effective use of assistive technology devices depends on the tasks the student needs to accomplish and how appropriate a given device is for a student's needs and circumstances. Given the broad range of assistive technology available for performing various tasks using visual, tactile, or auditory means, students need to have the widest possible experience with the largest variety of devices possible (including mobile technology), in order to be able to make an informed decision about which will provide the greatest efficiency and independence for specific tasks.

When portable devices are considered, the teacher should examine such factors as the device's battery life and the ergonomics involved in using the device, to determine whether the device will meet the student's actual needs and if it can be positioned comfortably in a designated space for the efficient performance of tasks. The difficulty and complexity involved in using different devices is another important consideration in selecting appropriate tools, especially when determining appropriate equipment for younger students and students with additional disabilities. In addition, a tool's physical requirements, such as whether it has an option for one-handed functionality, may also need to be considered for students with a physical disability. Connectivity with other devices and applications also needs to be considered. Students need to be able to efficiently connect with classroom technology, exchange data, and connect to the Internet.

Customizing Tools for Personal Use

Most tools used by students who are visually impaired can be customized to accommodate their personal preferences and accessibility needs. Some technology devices contain their own built-in accessibility "wizards," or helpful pop-up interfaces that help users systematically adjust settings for such features as print size, color selection, and speech input or output. By learning how to customize the settings on their devices, students expand the number and type of devices they can use without having to rely on purchasing additional specialized hardware or software. Teachers can assist students with testing the suitability of various assistive technology devices by collecting information on the student's fluency and accuracy with each device and review this data together with the student. Feedback from the student is critical because ultimately it is the student who will be using the devices every day.

Students' personal productivity can be increased through efficient use of the various functions and features of assistive technology devices, understanding how information is organized and managed by those devices, and knowing which formats a particular device uses. Being able to connect devices with other equipment and to troubleshoot problems will further maximize the student's options in regard to communication and accessibility.

Maintaining Devices

Students need to become responsible supporters of technology by learning how to take care of their assistive technology devices and practice safe use and storage. They can be taught planning and organizational strategies to keep their equipment working well, along with specific maintenance tasks, such as monitoring the battery life of a device and having a plan for recharging devices regularly. Knowing how to pack a device to return it to its manufacturer for repair or cleaning is another skill within this category. Additionally, students need to become personally responsible for backing up and storing their data on external drives or disks, in secure web-based folders, and through other arrangements.

Solving Problems

Problem solving is an essential skill for all students and a critical one for students with visual impairments because of the uniqueness of many of their devices. Often, special devices require specialized maintenance or repair that involves sending equipment back to the manufacturer or vendor, thereby resulting in periods of time during which the student does not have access to the device. Learning how to solve problems and troubleshoot means students may be able to prevent costly and time-consuming periods without their equipment. Becoming adept in the use of support functions, like Help, that are built in to devices and programs; using electronic manuals to search for information; making use of web- or telephone-based support; and accessing user groups are all skills that will promote a student's independence and productivity. Encouraging trial and error when the risks of error are low will allow the student to develop new skills that will prove useful in more important situations.

Applying Travel Applications

Assistive technology devices for orientation and mobility (O&M), including global positioning systems (GPS), are commonly referred to as electronic travel aids or electronic orientation aids (Smith & Penrod, 2010; see Chapter 7 for more information on O&M). This technology is important for students who are independent travelers and should be addressed in planning assessment and instruction. Electronic travel and orientation aids can enhance a student's independence; the development of skills in this area should not be overlooked. It is essential to include certified O&M specialists in assistive technology assessments to determine and address student needs in this regard.

ORIENTATION. Accessible way-finding devices make use of GPS technology to provide travelers ways of maintaining orientation and locating information in outdoor environments via access to commercially available maps and points of interest or to user-generated locations that are stored in databases by category (Smith & Penrod, 2010). Teaching students with visual impairments how this technology can be applied to their daily travel needs, including the functions and features of GPS, such as navigation, destination travel, points of interest, and development of routes for independent travel, is one of the responsibilities of O&M specialists.

MOBILITY. Electronic travel aids are devices that support safe and independent travel for individuals who are visually impaired by identifying obstacles in the user's path via reflected sound (usually sonar) or light (usually laser or infrared) (Smith & Penrod, 2010). The presence of an obstacle is indicated to the user by vibration or audible sound. Currently, there are limited assistive technology solutions for mobility, and these devices typically need to be used in conjunction with a long cane, dog guide, or human guide. Nevertheless, many students need to be made aware of these options and students using these devices need to receive appropriate instruction for them.

ASSESSMENT OF ASSISTIVE TECHNOLOGY

As it is in all other ECC areas, assessment is the foundation for determining the needs of students with visual impairments in the area of technology, and, as noted at the beginning of this chapter, evaluation of a student's assistive technology needs is required under IDEA. A comprehensive assessment in technology may require the knowledge and skills of a variety of professionals and team members. The teacher of students with visual impairments should lead and coordinate the assessment process with support from others, such as parents, an assistive technology specialist, occupational therapist, speech and language therapist, and O&M specialist, as needed. According to Presley and D'Andrea (2009), "the assistive technology assessment should investigate the student's potential to use tools with his or her primary and secondary learning media" (p. 200) in order to determine the devices and equipment that will enable the student to perform important tasks most efficiently.

Presley and D'Andrea (2009) have provided a comprehensive and logical approach for assessing the assistive technology needs of students with visual impairments, based on the educational tasks that students who are visually impaired need to undertake, which include:

- accessing print and electronic text
- producing written communication
- producing materials in accessible formats

An integral part of this framework is assessment of the way in which a student makes use of visual, tactile, and auditory input in accessing information and performing various tasks. Based on an examination of the primary and secondary sensory channels on which a student relies for the performance of an activity (see Chapter 5 for more about sensory efficiency), decisions can be made about the technology that is most appropriate for the performance of a given activity. (Table 6.1, earlier in this chapter, illustrates this framework.) Presley and D'Andrea (2009) describe in detail the process for conducting an assistive technology assessment and provide an extensive checklist for teachers of students with visual impairments and technology specialists to use.

Key Considerations for Assessment

When performing an assessment, the teacher or other technology assessor needs to consider the student's strengths and needs when using visual, tactile, and auditory sensory channels to access the visual environment, communicate with others, and participate in the school curriculum. A student's primary and secondary learning channels should be identified and considered when determining which tools are best for the variety of educational and independent living tasks in which a student participates throughout the day. Therefore, a functional vision assessment (if the student has vision) and a learning media assessment (see Chapters 3, 4, and 5) are essential parts of the assistive technology assessment as well.

A functional vision assessment is critical because it provides essential information about how a student uses vision in natural settings to do everyday living and learning tasks, such as reading, writing, and understanding pictures, and determines preferred viewing distances for near and far tasks in a variety of environments. This information guides teachers in understanding the student's visual strengths and needs in the area of accommodations and specialized technology. The learning media assessment is a systematic process for gathering information about how a student uses visual, tactile, and auditory learning channels; what are the most efficient and appropriate ways for a student to use these learning channels for reading and writing; and what media and tools are necessary for the student to participate in the educational curriculum. This process provides essential information about a student's primary and secondary learning channels that is critical when making decisions about technology use and instruction.

The teacher of students with visual impairments or the technology assessor must also consider the student's personal productivity and how the student can be most efficient and independent. Different devices may be needed to perform different tasks. Maximizing efficiency and independence may require that the student learn to use several devices, depending on the specific teaching and learning task and the student's use of visual, tactile, or auditory input in performing the task. For example, a student with low vision may listen to a lengthy novel as spoken through screen-reading software because it is faster than reading it visually, but will read questions on a history test using a near magnification device, such as a desktop video magnifier, because the student needs to see how the words are spelled. A comprehensive assistive technology assessment includes a broad look at the access and production needs of the student and specific tasks in which the student engages in daily. Students who are comfortable with using many forms of technology and with learning how to use new devices will be prepared to work independently and efficiently through their school and work lives. Table 6.1, which appears earlier in this chapter, can serve as a reference for considering the range of devices that can potentially be included in an assistive technology assessment using visual, tactile, and auditory access methods.

Assessing students in authentic environments—that is, real-world locations, such as in the classroom—is critical. Conducting an assessment of a student's assistive technology needs solely in a sterile technology lab or clinic, for example, will inevitably fall short because observations in such surroundings will not reflect the student's real-life school environment, where near and distance tasks change frequently, the student moves from class to class, and environmental conditions are highly changeable. A portable notetaker may be more appropriate for a student when changing classes throughout the day, while a desktop computer located in a workroom may be best for the purpose of writing an essay. A single device typically cannot meet all of a student's assistive technology needs; additional devices must be assessed for their suitability in the student's real-world daily environment.

FIGURE 6.1

Sample Observations of Task Performance Form

TECHNOLOGY ASSESSMENT: OBSERVATIONS OF TASK PERFORMANCE

Student: *Timothy Chuan, ninth-grade student with low vision* | **Observer:** *Jan Kovarski, Teacher of Students with Visual Impairments*

Setting: *Ninth-grade geography class; students sit at tables*

Date/Time	Environment	Task	Performance	Comments	Appropriate Performance for Task: Effective	Somewhat Effective	Not Effective
1/5/14 *1:00 pm*	*Geography test* *Handout of test questions, 12-point print*	*Read test questions*	*Student held paper with test questions and brought close to eyes, approx. 4–5″ viewing distance*	*Student scanned and read first test question and put paper down on lap.*	X		
1:05 pm–1:15 pm	*Handout of U.S. map on 11″ × 14″ paper, no enlargement*	*Find coordinates on the map to identify a specific location to complete a test item*	*Student used laptop with camera to magnify view of map*	*Student set up equipment prior to beginning the test. Placed map under camera and adjusted enlargement and focus. Moved map in random fashion under camera and rescanned previous sections of map multiple times. Used finger as marker on map.* *Other students appeared to complete the first test item in 2–4 min.*		X	
1:15 pm	*Answer sheet handout, 12-point print*	*Record test items on answer sheet*	*Student used answer sheet provided by teacher*	*Student moved map to position answer sheet under camera. Readjusted focus of camera. Wrote answers in pen.*		X	

Follow up: *Evaluate strategies for using systematic scanning patterns when using magnification devices. Brainstorm solutions for marking locations on map. Evaluate other strategies for writing answers, such as using the laptop computer.*

A sample observation tool for gathering information about how a student participates in the curriculum is included in Figure 6.1 (completed for a sample student). Intended to supplement other ways of gathering information, the tool illustrates how a teacher or other team member might document a student's effectiveness in using solutions to access and participate in teaching and learning tasks in authentic environments, evaluate the student's performance, and consider his or her needs.

Gathering information about the strategies a student uses to participate in multiple activities and settings can shed light on which devices—or how additional instruction in the use of a device—might address the student's access needs. Making sure to have a dialogue with the student about his or her needs and the possible devices he or she might learn to use will encourage the student to take responsibility for decisions about technology.

The Assessment Process

Students' needs change from year to year, semester to semester, and class to class. Sometimes the auditory, visual, or tactile abilities of students also change. Consequently, it is important to conduct assistive technology assessments when functional vision assessments and learning media assessments are completed or when educational team members' concerns about student performance indicate additional information is needed. For example, a technology assessment may have been completed before the end of a school year, but, when the new school year begins, the student's schedule may change, new classroom materials may be used, or the student's visual functioning may have changed. Therefore, new information needs to be gathered to ensure that the current technology solutions meet the ongoing needs of the student. Technology assessments need to be conducted annually, or more frequently if there are changes in the student or in the environmental conditions.

A collaborative approach to assessment is always important, but may be particularly appropriate should the teacher of students with visual impairments have limited knowledge and experience in the area of assistive technology. Rather than trying to meet an unrealistic expectation that the teacher of students with visual impairments must know everything about assistive technology, a teacher can seek the assistance of other experts or school personnel. The teacher of students with visual impairments should lead the collaborative team and the assessment process for students with visual impairments. Depending on each student's characteristics and needs, additional team members should participate, such as parents, assistive technology specialists, general and special education teachers, occupational therapists, speech and language therapists, O&M specialists, and physical therapists. Interagency personnel should also be considered as team members because they may have access to technology solutions that are currently unavailable in the local school. Team members each provide information in their areas of expertise to create a complete picture of the student's technology needs and contribute to determining the most appropriate and effective technology solutions. For example, the teacher of students with visual impairments provides the functional vision assessment and learning media assessment results, so members of the team understand the student's sensory and learning needs and what combination of visual, tactile, or auditory modes the student uses to approach various tasks. If the school district or local educational agency has an assistive technology specialist, this person may be able to assess the student's ability to use a particular computer platform, for example, one that has built-in accessibility features. The teacher of students with visual impairments might also consult an assistive technology specialist from an organization or agency that provides services to people with visual impairments to assess the student's need for and ability to use more advanced functions and features of more specialized access tools, like screen readers. This type of specialist may also have access to a wide range of tools for visual, tactile, and auditory access to information that is often less available at local education agencies. In this manner, the collaborative team may work together to determine the assistive technology needs of the student, even in cases in which the teacher of students with visual impairments may initially be unfamiliar with the assistive technology options available.

Once the student's assistive technology needs have been determined, teachers have two additional tasks to complete. The first is ensuring that appropriate documentation of the student's needs is included in the student's individualized education program (IEP). This documentation includes observable, measurable goals for instruction in the area of assistive technology, as well as the inclusion of appropriate accommodations, materials, and devices. For example, a third-grade student with low vision whose primary learning medium is print and who needs to use specialized technology for reading text presented from a distance in math class might have the following goal:

> The student will increase access to text presented at a distance in her third-grade math class on an interactive whiteboard by independently using a portable video magnification system daily, as observed, charted, and rated on a list of skills by team members.

The specific objectives to achieve this goal might include:

- learning to set up the device
- learning the features and functions of the device
- learning to use the device in a separate setting
- using the device in the math class with support
- using the device independently

The technology and assistive devices that a student needs to use to facilitate participation in the educational curriculum must be identified in the accommodations area of the IEP. For example, a third grade student who is blind and reads and writes in braille may have the following assistive technology accommodations listed on the IEP:

- braillewriters, including both manual and electronic braillers, slate and stylus, and braille notetaker with refreshable braille display
- scanner
- braille translation software
- braille embosser
- fuser and capsule paper (for creating tactile graphics)
- abacus and talking calculator
- laptop with speech and refreshable braille access

The second task involves monitoring the student's progress through the ongoing collection of data on the student's use of assistive technology, according to the goals listed on the IEP. Monitoring how students apply assistive technology in their daily tasks is especially critical. Data collection based on noting a student's performance at frequent intervals helps the teacher of students with visual impairments document and analyze the student's progress toward achieving assistive technology goals, and instruction can be adjusted accordingly when goals are met. Data collection tools such as the Observation of Task Performance Form (Figure 6.1) and individualized skill checklists can be used. For example, after a student is taught how to use a personal digital assistant (PDA) or electronic notetaker for sending and receiving e-mail, the teacher of students with visual impairments can observe the student performing this task weekly for one month and note the student's skills. Similarly, for a student who is learning how to use a new device for reading print, the teacher of students with visual impairments can check and note fluency and reading rates weekly for a specific period of time to make sure that the new device actually increases the student's reading efficiency. With a goal of efficiency in independent reading, consideration should also be given to whether the student can use a device independently or needs verbal or physical assistance. Older students can be involved in analyzing their own efficiency on devices by taking notes in a daily or weekly journal or chart, which also provides practice in compensatory and self-determination skills.

The following questions may be helpful in assisting the teacher of students with visual impairments and other educational team members in assessing a student's use of assistive technology and determining the appropriateness of particular devices in supporting the student's performance in the classroom.

- Is the student reading, writing, and learning under the same expectations as sighted classmates?
- Does the student have the same immediate access to learning materials as sighted classmates?
- Is the student reading, writing, and learning with the same level of participation as sighted classmates?
- Is the student being held accountable for the same level of reading, writing, and learning as sighted classmates?
- Is the student progressing at the same rate in reading, writing, and learning as sighted classmates?

If the answers to these questions are negative, it may be an appropriate time to evaluate whether the student's needs are being met effectively by the devices and equipment the student is currently using, whether additional training and support are needed by the student, or if some other factor is affecting the student's performance.

GENERAL CONSIDERATIONS FOR TEACHING ASSISTIVE TECHNOLOGY

The general teaching strategies that are effective in many areas of the ECC are also applicable to assistive technology; some of these are discussed in the following section. Since assistive technology is tied closely to the development of literacy and independence for students, it is important to be thoughtful, systematic, and deliberate in providing effective assistive technology instruction, based on the results of comprehensive assessment, to students with visual impairments. In addition, the individual student's type and degree of visual impairment, the presence of additional disabilities, and the student's age all affect how assistive technology skills are best taught.

When to Introduce Students to Assistive Technology

The introduction of assistive technology should occur early in the lives of children with visual impairments, just as the introduction of technology occurs early in the lives of their sighted classmates. The variety of new technology tools, their increasing availability, and their increasing affordability are changing how families are using technology in their daily lives. These factors are also changing ideas about the age when sighted children can be introduced to and begin using technology. For example, it is not unusual for 2-year-old children to use the arrow keys on computers to follow along with electronic books, use the apps on cell phones to learn letter recognition skills, and use push button remote control devices to play with toys that move across the room.

Similarly, teachers are changing their ideas about what ages children with visual impairments should be introduced to technology, both general and specialized. It is important to consider that young children who are blind may not be aware that computers are commonly found in libraries, on a desk in the family's den, on the kitchen counter, or in a sibling's backpack, because they cannot see them. Similarly, young children with low vision, with and without additional disabilities, may not understand or recognize what they're seeing. Deliberate exposure to and hands-on use of computers and other electronic devices to perform meaningful tasks, paired with rich verbal descriptions about what the device does and how it is connected or operated, will help young children who are visually impaired understand what these devices are.

Young children are similarly typically unaware of the specialized devices people who are visually impaired use in their daily lives. They need intentional and hands-on experiences with the diversity of specialized access tools, such as magnification software and tools, distance magnification tools, a variety of braillewriters, and speech access tools, to develop an awareness of the value of using such tools, beginning as early as 2 years old.

There are many different attitudes and philosophies that influence the decision about when to introduce assistive technology skills to students with visual impairments. However, there is no "magical" age or grade level that a parent or teacher of students with visual impairments needs to wait for before introducing a child to technology. Keeping in mind that early exposure to assistive technology is critical, there should be little or no difference in the age or grade-level exposure to technology for children with visual impairments as compared to children without disabilities. Table 6.3 presents examples of tasks and skills related to technology, excerpted from the overview offered earlier in Table 6.2, and offers recommendations for the grade levels at which these skills might be introduced to typically developing students with visual impairments. The list in Table 6.3 is not intended to encompass all the skills and tasks students need to know and do, but provides examples to give teachers guidance on when to consider instruction in these areas.

Instruction in assistive technology typically begins slowly for young children, increases significantly through age 16, and then decreases into the early adult years. Teaching preschool students through direct instruction how to use a keyboard to operate a computer and follow the story line of an electronic book is not only an age-appropriate skill, but an essential skill for a young child with a visual impairment. A student with low vision in the first grade can learn to customize the visual appearance of text on a computer screen for his or her personal viewing needs by enlarging the size of print and changing the text and background colors, while a student who is blind in the third grade can use a portable braille notetaking device to read an electronic book in braille.

Another resource to guide teachers in deciding when different technology skills might be introduced is the standards and goals for technology learning provided by the International Society for Technology in Education (2007a, b); see the Resources section at the end of this chapter. This organization also offers recommended learning activities for students at different grade levels.

Presley and D'Andrea (2009) have suggested that assistive technology skills be taught in response to an assessment of a student's current and immediate needs. In considering and planning when to introduce new skills, however, it is important for teachers of students with visual impairments to keep in mind not only the student's immediate needs for certain skills, which may

TABLE 6.3

When to Introduce Technology

This chart suggests grade levels at which a teacher may introduce technology to children with visual impairments. A variety of activities are indicated, based on the technology applications and skills in Table 6.2.

Technology Skills or Tasks	***Preschool***	***Grades K–2***	***Grades 3–5***	***Grades 6–8***	***Grades 9–12***
Input	Keyboarding • Arrow keys on a standard keyboard • Six-key input and braille • Specialty keyboards Pointing device (mouse) Touch screens on computers and portable devices • Gestures Speech and voice input	Keyboarding • Continue keyboarding awareness skills Keyboard shortcuts Keypads Touch screens • Onscreen typing	Keyboarding • Formal keyboarding instruction Electronic • Scanning • Electronic conversions of print to digital		
Output	Visual displays • Magnification • Variety of visual presentation of text Tactile displays • Embossed • Refreshable Auditory format • Text-to-speech (TTS) • Image description	Auditory format • Ear- and headphones, earbuds, speakers Customized output • Built-in accessibility features • Specialized tools			
Program operation	Application software • Computer-based word processing • Web-based applications • Mobile apps	Application software • Presentation tools File/data management • Navigation	Software management • Finding, downloading, removing Application software • Spreadsheet • Database File/data management • Security • Storage	Problem solving • Tech support	Problem solving • User groups

Internet use		World Wide Web • Finding content, searching • Web browsers • Accessing text E-mail and communication • Sending and receiving	World Wide Web • Web browsers • Navigation functions E-mail and communication • E-mail attachments		E-mail and communication • Electronic discussion groups • Newsgroups Social networking and virtual communities
Ethical and social use of information			Safe Internet and social media use • Responsible use • Electronic etiquette • Security, spam, viruses Copyright responsibility		
Reading	Electronic books Web-based content Navigation Access contexts • Multimedia	Documents Functions/features Sources Interactive study skills • Highlighting	File formats Interactive study skills • Bookmarking • Word supports		
Writing	Creating electronic text • Mechanics	Creating electronic text • Conventions (spelling, grammar) • Writing content • Reviewing electronic text • Editing	Creating electronic text • Outlining • Note taking		
Science, technology, engineering, and mathematics (STEM)	Diagrams	Calculation Math notation • Spoken mathematics Diagrams • Reading and interpreting • Writing and producing	Laboratories • Speech-adapted electronic tools • Real-time interactive access		
Images and graphics	Interpretation • Methods: Drawing tablets • Methods: Tactile picture makers • Presentation: Braille embossers Creation	Interpretation • Elements • Key concepts • Methods: Computer drawing tools • Methods: Image description tools			

(continued on next page)

TABLE 6.3 *continued*

Technology Skills or Tasks	**Preschool**	**Grades K–2**	**Grades 3–5**	**Grades 6–8**	**Grades 9–12**
Research		Finding content • Online searching • Device-based tools • Reference resources: dictionaries, encyclopedias	Finding content • Search engines • Search techniques • Browser skills • Reference resources: newspapers, periodicals, indexes, documents		
Distance learning and virtual classrooms		Web-based homework supports	Computer-based communication • Internet browser • Videoconferencing • Managing files	Computer-based communication • Chatrooms • Bulletin boards • Instant messaging	
Augmentative Communication	Aided communication				
Accessing instruction	Presentation of information • Near • Distance • Real-time interactive access • Multimedia • Demonstrations • Experiential	Lecture text			
Accessing materials			Locating Downloading content Scanning File formats • Conversions • Transferring Translating		

Completing assignments and tests		Alternate responses Alternate production	Sharing		
Applying personal management applications	Use mobile technology Consuming Information: games, music	Creating notes Using schedules	Management • Calendars • Contacts	Management • Financial records • Checkbooks	Consuming information: shopping, travel, news
Selecting tools			Function and features • Connectivity with other devices	Advantages and disadvantages	
Customizing for personal use		Accessibility "wizards" Personal preferences			
Maintaining devices		Battery		Back-up storage • Web-based • External devices	
Solving problems	Trial and error		Help features Manuals	Tech support	User groups
Applying travel applications (orientation & mobility)	Orientation • Wayfinding • Points of interest	Orientation • Wayfinding • Navigation • Routes	Mobility • Electronic travel aids		

present themselves before the skills are typically taught to the student's sighted peers, but also the curriculum for the student's current and future grade levels. For example, many sighted students may be introduced to keyboarding instruction in the second or third grade, while some are not formally taught keyboarding in school at all. Since these students are able to see the keyboard, they can begin inputting information as soon as they are introduced to computer use in kindergarten, if not earlier, regardless of whether or not they receive formal instruction in keyboard skills at any point in their education. For the child who uses braille as a literacy medium, grade three may be too late to start learning how to input text on a computer using the regular keyboard. Without deliberate instruction, it is unlikely that the child will pick this skill up incidentally. The teacher of students with visual impairments, therefore, needs to keep pace with the student and teach keyboarding shortly after he or she has learned the basics of computer use, such as turning the machine on and off, exploring the desktop, and opening and closing programs.

General Instructional Considerations

Whenever possible, assistive technology instruction should take place in the actual environments where students learn, live, play, and work. If technology instruction only occurs in isolated settings, the student may not independently generalize the skill to real-life situations. For example, if a student only experiences keyboarding instruction and practice in a resource room when the teacher of students with visual impairments is present, the student may never use keyboarding skills for written assignments in English, science, or other classes. If keyboarding instruction is also presented collaboratively in the student's general education classroom, then a student is more likely to understand the connection, receive the support, and apply keyboarding skills to complete required classroom assignments. Similarly, a student who uses a handheld electronic magnification device should be taught how to use the device to read a note from a classmate as well as a menu in a local restaurant.

Assistive technology instruction should be incorporated into all areas of the ECC to promote students' skills. For example, the teacher can teach a student who will be attending a sibling's tennis match to download information regarding scoring procedures for tennis, and to record scores throughout the game on a laptop computer or other mobile device. This instructional activity covers two areas of the ECC: assistive technology and recreation and leisure skills. Virtually every area of the ECC has skills that either relate directly to assistive technology (for example, those that may be used in a potential career or in O&M), or depend on assistive technology as a method to accomplish tasks (for example, for personal organization, which is an independent living and compensatory access skill).

Expanded opportunities to reinforce and supplement instruction in assistive technology may be provided through several means. For example, students can take technology classes, enroll in special assistive technology summer camps or weekend sessions, take noncredit short courses, or engage in online courses.

Instructional Considerations for Introducing Assistive Technology

The best way to start teaching a new technology is as variable as there are individual learning styles and learning preferences. When choosing a teaching approach, the teacher needs to consider a variety of factors, including:

- age of the student
- individual needs of the student
- previous knowledge and skills of the student
- complexity of the device
- tasks to be accomplished with the device

For example, when considering the environment for learning, the age of the student may be a factor; young children can be taught in a play setting, mid-level students might learn best with a peer, and older students may prefer a more private learning context. The individual needs of the students influence the level of supports that may be needed, such as individualized support through a paraprofessional, use of specific routines and procedures to create a highly structured learning environment, or additional equipment to facilitate independent use of tools. A student's previous knowledge and skills may influence the frequency and variety of learning tasks needed to master new concepts. If a student is transferring from using a notetaker to using a computer, his or her knowledge and skills in using electronic files will facilitate use of the new technology. How complex a device is to use can be influenced by the design of the software—whether it was designed for users with visual impairments or users who are sighted—which can influence a student's speed in acquiring new skills and the intensity of instruction that may be required. The specific tasks the student needs to perform using a device influences how, when, and where instruction is delivered. It may be most appropriate to teach in an authentic context when the student needs to accomplish a task, such as at a restaurant if a student is using a mobile device and app for accessing a menu.

These factors also influence the level of familiarity the teacher should have with the device, the rate of learning anticipated by the student, and teaching style. Depending on all of these factors, the teacher should also consider the variety of teaching roles that are appropriate for teaching technology, such as role model, co-learner, guide, facilitator, and provider of instructional content.

Sidebar 6.3 provides some general suggestions for how the teacher of students with visual impairments can prepare to introduce a new device to a student. The following sections provide additional recommendations for working with students with different conditions and in different age groups.

SIDEBAR 6.3

Getting Started Teaching a Device

The following steps provide an overall guide for getting started with an unfamiliar device. The teacher can begin by becoming familiar with the new device and then introducing it to the student or can work through the initial steps together with the student.

BEFORE USING THE DEVICE

1. Explore the device manual and the options for accessing content from the device manual. For example, many technology tools and devices provide options for downloading manuals from a website. Electronic manuals provide easy access to searching for specific information.
2. Research additional teaching tools that may be available for the device from the manufacturer, other agencies, and colleagues, such as curricula, tips for using the device, "getting started" guides, and FAQs (frequently asked questions).
3. Prepare the manual and other informational tools in the student's preferred learning formats—print, tactile, auditory, or digital.
4. Charge the device or make sure that batteries are available.
5. Gather additional accessories, such as visual displays for tactile devices, flash memory devices for content storage, and headphones.
6. Make sure that appropriate access to the Internet is available in the learning environment, if needed.
7. Prepare teaching files or content for using the device.

WITH THE STUDENT

1. Become familiar with the device's hardware and accessories. This includes all sides of the device and the input and output connections.
2. Connect the device to power and learn about the battery's capabilities.
3. Turn the device on and off.
4. Adjust basic features such as sound and visual display capabilities.
5. Learn basic functions of the device from a "need to know" perspective: What does the student need to know to begin using a device for a priority task?
6. Learn to input information.
7. Learn how to review and output information.
8. Learn basic navigation functions, including exiting from the current activity.
9. Learn menu structure.
10. Learn major programs.
11. Learn Options menus and elements, such as settings for time, speech, braille, keyboard, battery status, and the like.
12. Learn to switch between tasks.
13. Learn to integrate the device with other devices, such as printers and embossers.

IN REAL-LIFE SETTINGS

1. Arrange appropriate security for the device when it is not in use.
2. Provide access to power if the device needs to be charged.
3. Provide appropriate furniture and physical space for using the device.
4. Provide appropriate storage cases for portable devices.
5. Have the student practice using the device in a real-life setting before having to use it for an actual educational task.
6. Make sure the student can set up, turn on, and dismantle the device with ease, efficiency, and safely.

General Considerations for Teaching Students Who Are Blind

There are a number of elements to consider that will promote optimal learning of how to use assistive technology for students who are blind. Depending on the needs of the individual student, the following suggestions may be helpful:

- Work in a quiet workspace to ensure that the student can focus on the task, especially when initially introducing a device.
- Work in an area or a room with ample space for the equipment so the student can easily reach it.
- Whenever possible, use hands-on activities with real devices that students can manipulate, such as pairing a talking calculator with the calculator feature available on a computer.
- Provide opportunities for thorough hands-on examination of devices by the student, combined with rich verbal descriptions by the teacher so the student understands each part of the device, what function it performs, and how it relates to other components on the device.
- Provide a variety of devices with which the student can experiment on a variety of tasks.
- During instruction, pair speech (auditory channel) and braille output (tactile channel) to address the needs of students who prefer and may benefit from a multisensory approach to learning.
- Provide instruction and assistive technology experiences by employing a range of options, such as using braille input with six-key entry, a standard QWERTY keyboard, and a touch screen, to ensure students are able to input information in different ways on different devices.
- Provide opportunities for students to apply assistive technology skills within the classroom and to class assignments, thereby generalizing assistive technology skills.
- Reinforce braille-reading skills using a refreshable braille display (pins that form braille letters and words and that "refresh" themselves as the characters change) in addition to reading hard-copy braille to ensure students are comfortable feeling and reading different types of braille.
- When using a screen reader, adjust its speed to one that the student is able to understand and, as the student attains skills at one speed, increase it gradually to improve fluency.
- As students become proficient with devices, teach them how to independently adjust the devices for maximum efficiency.

Teachers may find it valuable to review with the student each device's user manual and any support materials, such as "quick start" guides, charts of frequently used commands, FAQs, tutorials, and webinars. Working with the student to create personalized "help sheets" that list frequently used procedures, processes, and commands is also helpful.

General Considerations for Teaching Students Who Have Low Vision

Students with low vision may have highly variable needs since their individual visual abilities may change, depending on such factors as their eye condition, their level of fatigue on a given day, and environmental factors. In general, they will need to perform a variety of near and distance tasks in their learning and living environments and thus need to learn how to access information that is up close and far away. Depending on the needs of the individual student, the following suggestions may be helpful when first beginning instruction with a new device:

- Consider the student's need for, or sensitivity to, light. Adjust lighting to reduce glare or to provide more (or less) light, based on the student's need. Position the device to ensure comfort and ease of viewing and use.
- On the basis of the student's assessment, adjust print to the most efficient size for the student to see.
- Adjust the magnification level of the device to the level that is most efficient for the student.
- Adjust the contrast to that which works best for the student.
- Select a font style and type size that is easiest for the student to see, based on the assistive technology assessment ("APH Guidelines," n.d.).
- Personalize the display on the computer screen for the student, paying attention to such elements as colors for the text and background on the monitor that suit the student's visual needs. For example, students who are sensitive to light may prefer yellow letters on a black background.
- Determine keyboard accessibility needs, such as a regular QWERTY keyboard or a large-

print QWERTY keyboard, to address student preferences.

- After the student has learned to use a device independently, teach the student to make adjustments to position it and adjust magnification, contrast, lighting, and color.

General Considerations for Teaching Students with Additional Disabilities

In general, when teaching students who are visually impaired who are diagnosed with other disabilities, teachers of students with visual impairments should begin with the same general considerations for teaching students who do not face additional challenges to learning. However, more individualized approaches need to be developed for many students with additional disabilities. Specific strategies are needed to address physical, developmental, and other sensory conditions that have an impact on a student's functioning. Greater intensity may be required in the initial instruction phase for this population, as in the following example:

> Maurice, a 12-year-old student with low vision, developmental delay, and physical restrictions is making the transition to using an assistive technology device for communication. Maurice is able to make a choice between two concrete objects by reaching for the desired object. Therefore, when considering how to introduce assistive technology to this student, rather than using typical technology like a computer, Diane, his teacher of students with visual impairments, chose to use a tablet on which she can present pictures of two objects side by side in order to offer a choice. After repeatedly pairing the physical objects with their pictorial representations on the tablet, Diane began to teach Maurice to touch the tablet to select his desired object. When Maurice accurately touches the appropriate item, Diane reinforces his behavior by giving him the desired object.

Depending on the visual, sensory, developmental, or physical needs of an individual student, the following suggestions may be helpful:

- Consult, as appropriate, with professionals knowledgeable about the student's other disabilities and specialized technology often used by individuals with additional disabilities, such as an occupational therapist, physical therapist, speech and language pathologist, teacher of students who are deaf or hard of hearing, augmentative communication specialist, or O&M specialist.

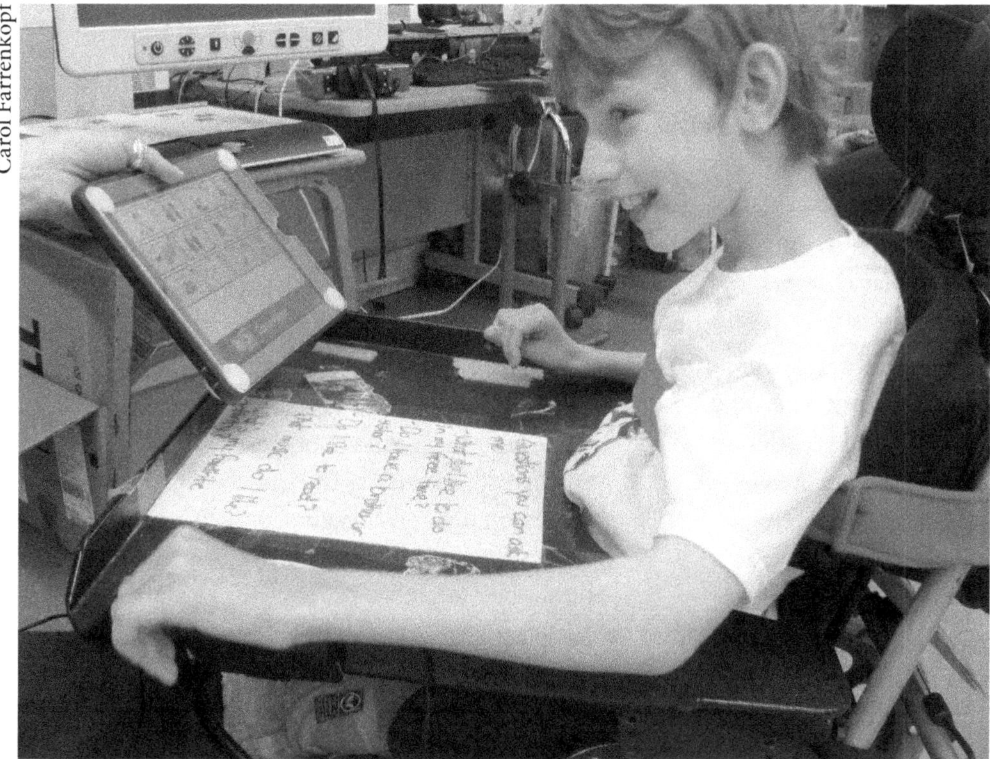

Carol Farrenkopf

A student with low vision and multiple disabilities uses a specialized switch connected to a tablet with speech output to make a choice about what he wants to do next.

- Identify the effects of physical limitations that may warrant the use of modified hardware, such as a modified keyboard, a roller ball instead of a mouse, an adjustable arm mounted to a monitor, and the like.
- Determine comfortable and effective positioning of the student, especially if the student is in a wheelchair.
- Determine the best positioning of the equipment to enhance the student's independence and ease of use. Use explicit procedures, verbal directions, and physical support and guidance to ensure students understand what is being asked of them.
- Use music and auditory feedback to maintain the student's interest in and attention to the activity. For example, since many students are motivated by songs and music, creating a song based on a familiar tune that incorporates directions for using a device for a specific task may be helpful.
- Use physical or verbal prompts to encourage the student to respond.
- Ensure that technology is used for meaningful tasks, such as making choices or activating a favorite toy. Avoid devices that allow students to engage in unproductive repetitive actions.
- Pair hands-on instruction and modeling with verbal descriptions to facilitate better understanding of the concept being taught.
- Provide instruction that is activity based and appropriate for the individual needs of the child, based on age and development. For example, a computer game selected for an older student to use during free time should not be one that is designed for preschoolers. It is better to find a game that the student is able to play that employs images and music preferred by peers.
- Avoid overstimulating or prolonged activities so the student does not tire too quickly and become unable to process information and instruction.
- Avoid rushing instruction—some students are not able to understand fast-paced, multi-level instruction.
- Expect to wait a little longer for students to respond to requests, to give them sufficient time to engage in the often complex process of understanding what was asked of them and then coordinating a response.
- Move beyond the use of technology to teach basic concepts, such as cause and effect, to focus on more complex communication and interaction skills whenever possible. For example, a student who has learned to use a push button switch to turn on and off a fan, a light, and music can expand switch use to communicate a preference for an activity.
- Encourage independent and functional use of devices by students, as appropriate. For example, a student who uses a speech-generating device for augmentative communication can learn to carry the device and use it to respond to yes-and-no questions from the servers in the cafeteria line.

General Considerations for Teaching Preschool Children

Preschool children with visual impairments, like preschool children with unimpaired vision, spend a great deal of time learning through play and hands-on activities. In general, such young learners should also be introduced to assistive technology skills in play-based settings, rather than at a desk in a classroom. Depending on the age and the child's degree of visual and other impairments, the following suggestions may be helpful:

- Provide play-based, concrete activities that lend themselves to the introduction of assistive technology. For example, during pretend play as a doctor, the child can use an electronic device in their primary learning medium to "write" during an examination. When playing simple board games, a child can use an electronic dice app on a mobile device when it is his or her turn.
- Use materials and programs that stimulate the visual, tactile, and auditory senses to maintain the child's interest in the activities.
- Use music, games, and pretend play to maintain the child's attention to the task at hand. For example, when teaching a child to operate a CD player, use familiar songs, such as the alphabet song, to make the lesson fun and engaging, or incorporate scribbling on the slate and stylus by pretending to be a waiter taking an order in a restaurant.
- Keep activities brief to match the length of the child's attention span.
- Encourage a child with low vision to pretend to write using crayons under a video magnification

device to prepare him for formal writing instruction in kindergarten.

- Encourage a child who is blind to pretend to write using a manual or electronic braillewriter to prepare him for formal writing (brailling) instruction in kindergarten.
- Engage parents in the instructional process. When working with the family in their home, include the parents and their child in play activities involving technology, such as taking turns using magnification tools to play a game of I Spy. Parents often need suggestions so that they can include devices in independent living, communication, and recreation and leisure activities when the teacher is not present. (See the section on Suggestions for Working with Parents later in this chapter for additional suggestions.)

General Considerations for Teaching Transition-Age Students

Students with visual impairments who are approaching the end of their high school years and moving into the world beyond school may have already acquired most of the assistive technology skills they need to be successful in college or employment. At this critical stage of development, students are learning how to become more independent in all aspects of their lives. The teacher of students with visual impairments should also be working toward helping the student achieve as much independence as possible through the use of assistive technology. At this stage of students' education, when they may already be making considerable use of technology for compensatory access to classroom instruction and other schoolwork, assistive technology instruction is liable to overlap to a large degree with instruction in career education and self-determination.

The following suggestions may be helpful when working with transition-age students:

- Assess the student's current abilities and future needs for technology-related skills and intensify instruction in those areas in which the student's skills would benefit from improvement.
- Consider the student's self-advocacy skills in terms of expressing his or her needs for assistive technology in the types of situations he or she is likely to encounter in future educational or employment situations. For example, the student could meet with a counselor at a prospective post-secondary institution and describe the accommodations and technology that will facilitate his or her success. The student can also ask about additional skills that may be needed in that setting, such as use of courseware for remote learning.
- Help the student refine his or her assistive technology skills to reinforce the competency and efficiency of assistive technology use.
- Promote independent use of assistive technology to produce classroom assignments and communicate with teachers and classmates electronically with minimal intervention from the teacher.
- Create relevant assignments to solidify assistive technology skills, such as résumé writing, researching careers, or finding out movie times at the local theater (see the learning activity "Checking Out Movie Listings" at the end of this chapter).
- Teach the importance of attending to safety and protection of privacy when using social networking sites, communicating through e-mail, and exploring the Internet.
- Encourage the student to pick the most efficient device for a specific task so the student can maximize personal productivity.
- Ensure that the student is able to troubleshoot independently by seeking solutions from a technician—for instance, by calling a technology company's help desk—reading user manuals, contacting the manufacturer or vendor of a specific device, or asking a friend for help.
- Make sure that the student knows how to investigate and learn about new technologies.

TEACHING STRATEGIES FOR ASSISTIVE TECHNOLOGY

Proficiency in the area of technology depends on repeated use of skills and devices, which often requires increased instructional time. Therefore, as noted throughout this chapter, to ensure that students are receiving the frequency and variety of instruction necessary, teachers need to be systematic and deliberate about planning, organizing, delivering, and evaluating assistive technology instruction (Abner & Lahm, 2002). In addition, it is not unusual for students to be reluctant to use new accommodations and devices that are unfamiliar to them, and teachers may need to focus on overcoming these attitudinal barriers as much as on the procedures necessary to use the device.

When a student is getting started with a new device and learning new assistive technology skills, the frequency and intensity of support from the teacher of students with visual impairments generally needs to be increased, even to as much as daily instruction in some instances, so the student has the opportunity for more practice. As the student begins to apply the new skills to classroom tasks, continued instruction may require increased collaboration and shared responsibility for instruction with classroom teachers, as well as greater flexibility with schedules, as illustrated by this vignette:

After Kirsty mastered basic keyboarding skills through daily direct instruction from her teacher of students with visual impairments, her keyboarding proficiency increased as she used those skills in the classroom to complete assignments. She then required additional short-term specialized instruction, such as strategies to remember and locate keys seldom used and the integration of shortcut keys from the teacher of students with visual impairments, with support from the classroom teachers. This collaboration required more communication and flexibility among teaching colleagues.

The daily practice required to develop proficiency in keyboarding and other technology-related skills may initially need to be monitored by the teacher of students with visual impairments. After this initial period, the student can maintain his or her own keyboarding log and then graphically illustrate personal progress on a frequency chart developed together with the teacher.

Strategies that are useful when teaching assistive technology to students with visual impairments include the following, which are described in the sections that follow:

- task analysis
- pre-teaching and re-teaching
- scaffolding (providing extra supports)
- independent practice
- differentiated, individualized instruction

The use of incentives can also be considered.

The teacher of students with visual impairments must be explicit about establishing teaching routines and procedures that promote independence in the use of assistive technology. Instruction must be individualized to meet the needs of the student and promote independence in the use of assistive technology.

Task Analysis

Task analysis (discussed in Chapter 3) involves listing all the steps needed to learn a task so that they can be taught in the manner and sequence that is most appropriate for a particular student. There are a variety of methods and sequencing strategies used in task analysis. For example, when a student needs to learn to read electronic books, the lesson can begin by showing the student how to read a book that is "student-ready" (that is, one that has already been prepared for the student to be read on an appropriate device) so that the student only needs to enter one command to begin reading and experience success. Then the teacher of students with visual impairments can sequentially teach all of the skills and steps the student needs to independently read the book, including navigating through a book, customizing the device's features, locating a book in the device's storage area, transferring the book to a different device, downloading the book from a website, and locating it within the device. Depending on the student's learning needs and preferences, the teacher can vary the steps to learn a task. They can be expanded, collapsed, taught in a forward sequence, or in a backward sequence. It is important for the student to experience success and for the teacher to deliver the instruction in a manner that allows the student to manage learning the task.

Pre-teaching Skills

As in many other areas of the ECC, *pre-teaching* technology skills—that is, teaching them before students will need them in the classroom—helps to ensure that students will be ready to participate in core curriculum lessons with their classmates. For example, if the mathematics teacher is using a new presentation tool and a student needs to connect his or her device to the teacher's device, it will be necessary for the teacher of students with visual impairments to find a convenient time to work in the mathematics teacher's classroom when other students are not present, to teach the student with visual impairments to connect, activate, and use the assistive technology, so the student is prepared for instruction during mathematics class.

Re-Teaching Content

Re-teaching content that was taught and used in a classroom is an effective strategy to ensure understanding and use of technology knowledge and skills. For example, after a student has been taught some problem-solving strategies for downloading content from the Internet to a device, such as how to access an inaccessible file from the Internet by changing the format of the file to one that is accessible, the teacher of students with visual impairments might create another scenario for which the student needs to use the same problem-solving techniques to resolve a different situation in which inaccessible files need to be used. If necessary, the teacher of students with visual impairments can re-teach the options and steps the student can use to change the file into an accessible format.

Scaffolding

Using *scaffolding* (discussed in Chapter 3) or providing temporary support, such as extra modeling or coaching during the learning process, is often helpful in teaching assistive technology skills. When a student is learning, support strategies may be needed to ensure that the student is able to use a device appropriately. For example, a student who has learned to use a portable device for taking notes in a one-on-one setting with a teacher of students with visual impairments may need to have a checklist of procedures and an accessible chart of basic commands to increase efficiency and help the student transfer use of the device from one setting to another.

Independent Practice

Providing *independent practice* is a critical element in teaching assistive technology skills. It is important for the teacher of students with visual impairments to step aside and allow the student to practice skills independently, asking questions when needed. For example, when a student has received initial instruction in creating, editing, and saving a document, the student should be given the opportunity to independently practice the procedures on new assignments that require these same steps.

Differentiated Instruction

Differentiated instruction, in which multiple ways are provided for students to learn and participate in instruction and instruction is tailored to meet students' individual learning needs, can be particularly important when teaching students with visual impairments. For example, although a teacher of students with visual impairments may have a preference for using the touch typing method (when the fingers are trained to locate keys by position without looking at the letters on the keyboard or having additional tactile markers placed on the keys) for initial instruction in keyboarding skills, this approach may not be the best method for a particular student. In such a case, the instruction needs to be differentiated for the student, who may respond best when the keyboard has enlarged print letters on the keys or tactile markers on certain keys.

Incentives

Using *incentives,* such as positive reinforcement, to motivate learning can increase the rate at which students learn. Teaching with incentives can be as simple as letting progress serve as its own reinforcer by setting an explicit goal with a student and having the student chart his or her own progress. For example, a student who has a goal to increase her braille-writing speed on an electronic braillewriter and who charts her progress weekly toward meeting that goal, is motivated by her own progress and works to beat her last time.

For students who are not as intrinsically motivated, more concrete incentives can be used, such as allowing extra time for a favorite computer game, listening to a favorite song, or the opportunity to attend a special event. Collaboration with parents on appropriate incentives can be effective and is essential if food incentives are being considered.

Routines and Procedures

Teaching through the use of *routines* and *procedures* provides students with structure that can be reinforcing for students and helps them to be organized, because they know what to expect and can focus on the content being presented, rather than the instructional format. (See Chapter 5 for a discussion of teaching through routines.) Repeating systematic and clearly stated steps in an activity can also help in the development of good work habits. For example, when teaching lessons on using a graphing calculator, the teacher of students with visual impairments can use the following consistent procedure:

1. Explicitly review what was taught in the previous lesson
2. Use the same materials as in the previous lesson
3. Ask the student to explain the key concept that was previously taught
4. Introduce a new concept
5. Provide an overview of the materials to be used
6. Teach the new concept

7. Provide independent practice and application of skills
8. Summarize the lesson

As in every area of instruction, the choice of instructional strategies must be based on the student's individual needs and reevaluated as instruction proceeds over time.

ROLE OF THE TEACHER OF STUDENTS WITH VISUAL IMPAIRMENTS

Primary responsibilities for teachers of students with visual impairments in the area of assistive technology include providing direct instruction in use of assistive technology and skills for accessing mainstream technology; ensuring that their students receive an appropriate assistive technology assessment that takes into account the results of functional vision assessments and learning media assessments; and ensuring that measurable assistive technology goals for the student are developed, instruction is provided, and student progress is evaluated. The teacher of students with visual impairments needs to plan, manage, deliver, and evaluate instruction to ensure that the student is accessing and participating in the curriculum and making appropriate progress on all IEP goals, including technology. The teacher may need to consider how to set priorities for the length and intensity of instruction in order to include both one-on-one lessons with a student and collaborative activities that take place in the classroom.

In the course of these responsibilities, teachers must collaborate frequently with other educational team members. For example, the teacher of students with visual impairments who teaches a student to use an e-book reader with refreshable braille in order to read a novel for language arts class, will then need to collaborate with the language arts teacher in teaching the student to use the technology in the classroom to review the text and participate in small group discussions. Ongoing monitoring of students' progress in using assistive technology also entails the teacher of students with visual impairments working closely with general education teachers and other school-based team members who assist with assistive technology instruction or the application of assistive technology in their classrooms to make sure that students have adequate opportunities to practice using devices and technology in class and are able to generalize what they have learned to real-world situations. To provide this support to their students, it is critical for the teacher of students with visual impairments to be present in the settings and environments in which students are actually using their assistive technology devices. The teacher of students with visual impairments needs to arrange a flexible schedule so that he or she can observe, monitor, and adjust instructional strategies without significant delays.

Obtaining Training in Technology

In today's technology-driven environment, it is difficult for most people who are not technology specialists to be experts in the use of every device and emerging technology trend used in education. For teachers of students who are visually impaired who need to help students with visual impairments acquire the essential assistive technology skills to access the school curriculum as independently as possible, there are several strategies that can be helpful. First, teachers can do their best to make sure that experts who *do* possess necessary training and experience, such as an assistive technology specialist in the school district, are part of a student's collaborative educational team. When the teacher of students with visual impairments is the only teacher specializing in working with students with visual impairments in a school district or agency, it is important for that teacher to reach out for the support of other team members in promoting all the skills described in this chapter and other areas of the ECC as well (Edwards & Lewis, 1998).

Second, it is important that the teacher learn as much as possible about assistive technology by taking courses, attending conferences, participating in electronic mailing lists and user groups, accessing information and training on the Internet, and embracing a collaborative approach with other professionals (Zhou, Parker, Smith, & Griffin-Shirley, 2011). Frequent upgrading of assistive technology knowledge and skills through participation in specialized training opportunities, staying current with the professional literature, networking through electronic communication, on-the-job training, and professional development—such as participating in webinars and courses—are also important and supportive to teaching efforts. Teachers need to incorporate ongoing professional development in assistive technology into their professional development plan on a yearly basis whenever possible.

Whenever possible, teachers of students with visual impairments should participate in assistive technology training sessions offered to their students by assistive technology experts. By learning with the student, the teacher of students with visual impairments can increase his or her knowledge, while at the same time making sure that the trainer understands the educational demands the student experiences at school and at home. Often, the manufacturers or distributors of devices and equipment will include a specific number of free training sessions, or training time can be purchased at the same time as the device is ordered. If this is the case, the teacher of students with visual impairments should make sure that the training actually takes place and be present with the student. School districts may also pay for specialized training if no other training sources are readily available.

Typically, training often occurs in one- or two-hour blocks of time, which is generally enough time to learn the basic operations of a device. After this initial introductory training, the student and the teacher of students with visual impairments should practice what they were taught and work together to learn more. When the student and the teacher of students with visual impairments have reached a point where they can go no further on their own, additional training should be arranged to learn how to use more advanced features of the device. Eventually, both the student and the teacher should be able to operate the equipment independently. Though the teacher of students with visual impairments may have started the training process with little or no experience with a new device or technology, by the end of a session, the teacher, like the student, should have acquired valuable skills, knowledge, and experience. Educational agencies are responsible for providing the assistive technology that the educational team determines is necessary for a student who is visually impaired in all settings and environments. However, it is sometimes necessary for the teacher of students with visual impairments to take a leadership role in seeking assistance from other organizations, such as rehabilitation agencies and community organizations, to ensure that appropriate technology is available for a student. (Some suggestions for partnerships between teachers and outside agencies are provided in Chapter 13.)

In addition, it may in fact be helpful for the teacher, if possible, to modify his or her role in the area of assistive technology beyond the traditional teaching role of "director" and "expert." The area of technology is so vast and rapidly changing that teachers may need to move away from "telling" and "directing" learning, to serving as a role model, supporter, guide, facilitator, and co-learner, who provides learning activities and opportunities for students (McNear, 2001). By adjusting their traditional roles, teachers of students with visual impairments may implement assistive technology instruction with greater confidence, knowing that they do not need to know "everything" before they begin instruction with a student who is visually impaired.

SUGGESTIONS FOR WORKING WITH PARENTS

Teachers of students with visual impairments can encourage parents to actively consider and support the needs of their child with regard to assistive technology in all settings and environments, especially at home. In order for children who are visually impaired to acquire and maintain skills at the same rate as sighted classmates, they need access to educational tools in their home environment. When parents participate in educational team meetings, they can ask specific questions about how their child will maintain assistive technology skills at home and in the community. Parents will need specific information about which devices their child should use to complete homework and assignments. If their child reads and writes using braille, parents need to know how their child will read and write braille at home, using the same tools that are used in school. If their child reads and writes in print using assistive technology, they need to know how their child will use assistive technology at home for homework completion. If the child's family has a computer at home that is not accessible to their child who is visually impaired, parents should be provided with information about how their home computer can be made accessible to their child. Often, use of a portable thumb drive on which the access program—screen reader or screen magnification—is loaded is all that is needed.

To ensure that their child is making appropriate progress, parents can expect periodic progress reports from teachers about their child's knowledge and skills in using assistive technology. Teachers can encourage parents to ask questions so they clearly understand how their child is learning to access the visual environment, how their child is making progress in literacy skills, and how their child communicates with others. If there is a specific assistive technology goal in the child's IEP, teachers can provide parents with an assessment result or report on the child's progress toward achieving that goal.

Parents, like teachers and the students themselves, need training and support to learn how to use the assistive technology devices used by their child and to support and encourage the child's use of them. In some cases, it is the teacher of students with visual impairments who provides this training. It may also be possible that a local manufacturer or distributor of equipment will provide the training for the child's parents, especially if the training is part of the original purchase conditions for the device. It is important that parents know how to use the equipment so they can assist their child (especially in the case of younger children) with difficulties, should they arise at home, and so they can help their child be responsible in all settings for independently accessing information, reading, writing, and producing materials in alternate formats.

When parents understand the technology being used by their children, they are better able to set expectations for their children. Parents can work together with the teacher of students with visual impairments and other members of the educational team to determine incentives that will promote efficient and appropriate assistive technology use at home and at school. They can embrace the integration of technology into the student's daily life by ensuring its use in community environments, such as the local library, at the mall, and during club or scouting events, thereby encouraging habits that promote success.

Parents can also encourage a student's siblings and extended family members to learn more about their child's assistive technology and how it is used, fostering a supportive and understanding environment for increased independence and practice in the use of tools for a variety of purposes and tasks. A child with a visual impairment can communicate with grandparents and other family members using e-mail and sending photographs as attachments, thereby practicing personal productivity and the ability to use assistive technology in settings outside of school. Siblings can be engaged with the child's assistive technology by creating home videos together or preparing electronic slideshows and photo albums.

As mentioned earlier in this chapter, students with visual impairments need to learn to use technology in a manner that is ethically and socially responsible. Likewise, parents also need to understand and promote the ethical and social use of technology by their children. If their child is a minor and using electronic books, parents will need to sign forms indicating they understand the use of electronic materials and that those materials will not be sold or distributed once downloaded. Teachers can provide additional information to ensure parents are informed about issues related to copyright. If a child is using technology and copyrighted materials in multiple environments, parents need to follow-up with their child to make sure copyrighted content is not inappropriately being shared with others.

Finally, parents of children who are visually impaired, like parents of children without disabilities, must be vigilant about monitoring their children's safe use of technology, especially when it comes to downloading content from inappropriate sources, using social media, and sharing personal information on social networking sites. Parents need to protect their children from potential dangers that exist in the digital or virtual world by frequently checking their child's computer for its search history and by controlling the privacy and parental settings that are integrated into all computers.

SUMMARY

Observing what students with visual impairments can accomplish through using technology is well worth all the dedicated effort that teachers and other educational team members put forth in regard to this area of the ECC. Engaging students at an early age by using assistive technology in playful ways promotes the development of literacy and communication skills, as well as independence. When technology is integrated into a young child's life, it seamlessly becomes a part of the child's everyday experiences. Encouraging all members of the student's educational team to increase their knowledge and skills with respect to assistive technology, supports the notion that everyone has a role to play in ensuring that the student who is visually impaired is able to live, work, and play with greater independent access to the surrounding world.

References

Abner, G. H., & Lahm, E. A. (2002). Implementation of assistive technology with students who are visually impaired: Teacher readiness. *Journal of Visual Impairment & Blindness, 96*, 98–105.

APH guidelines for print document design. (n.d.). Louisville, KY: American Printing House for the Blind. Retrieved January 31, 2014, from http://www.aph.org/edresearch/lpguide.htm

Augmentative and alternative communication (ACC). (n.d.). Rockville, MD: American Speech-Language-Hearing Association. Retrieved December 28, 2011, from http://www.asha.org/public/speech/disorders/AAC/

Edwards, B. J., & Lewis, S. (1998). The use of technology in programs for students with visual impairments in Florida. *Journal of Visual Impairment & Blindness, 92,* 302–312.

International Society for Technology in Education. (2007a). Standards for Students. Retrieved September 3, 2011, from http://www.iste.org/standards/standards-for-students

International Society for Technology in Education. (2007b). Profiles for technology literate students. Retrieved September 3, 2011, from http://www.iste.org/docs/pdfs/nets-s-2007-student-profiles-en.pdf?sfvrsn=4

Mace, R. (1985). Universal design: Barrier-free environments for everyone. *Designers West, 33* (1).

McNear, D. L. (2001). *A framework for braille literacy: Integrating assistive technology tools in the literacy curriculum.* Loomis, CA: HumanWare, Inc.

Presley, I., & D'Andrea, F. M. (2009). *Assistive technology for students who are blind or visually impaired: A guide to assessment.* New York: AFB Press.

Smith, D. L., & Penrod, W. M. (2010). Adaptive technology for orientation and mobility. In W. R. Wiener, R. L. Welsh, and B. B. Blasch (Eds.), *Foundations of orientation and mobility: Volume I. History and theory* (3rd ed., pp. 241–276). New York: AFB Press.

Zhou, L., Parker, A. T., Smith, D. W., & Griffin-Shirley, N. (2011). Assistive technology for students with visual impairments: Challenges and needs in teachers' preparation programs and practice. *Journal of Visual Impairment & Blindness, 105,* 197–210.

Assistive Technology Resources

This section provides resources such as assessment tools, publications, and instructional materials for teaching assistive technology skills. For additional resources that relate to the expanded core curriculum in general, see the Resources section at the end of this book.

ASSESSMENT TOOLS

Assistive Technology Assessment Checklist for Students with Visual Impairments

POPULATION/AGE LEVEL: All

SOURCE: Presley, I., & D'Andrea, F. M. (2009). *Assistive technology for students who are blind or visually impaired: A guide to assessment.* New York: AFB Press.

EVALS: Evaluating Visually Impaired Students

POPULATION/AGE LEVEL: All

SOURCE: *EVALS: Evaluating Visually Impaired Students.* (2007). Austin: Texas School for the Blind and Visually Impaired.

PUBLICATIONS

Goodman, S. A., & Wittenstein, S. H. (2003). *Collaborative assessment: Working with students who are blind or visually impaired, including those with additional disabilities.* New York: AFB Press.

Lueck, A. H., Dote-Kwan, J., Senge, J. C., & Clarke, L. (2001). Selecting assistive technology for greater independence. In *RE:view,* 33(1), pp. 21–33.

Presley, I., & D'Andrea, F. M. (2009). *Assistive technology for students who are blind or visually impaired: A guide to assessment.* New York: AFB Press.

Smith, D. L., & Penrod, W. M. (2010). Adaptive technology for orientation and mobility. In W. R. Wiener, R. L. Welsh, and B. B. Blasch (Eds.), *Foundations of orientation and mobility: Volume I. History and theory* (3rd ed., pp. 241–276). New York: AFB Press.

WEBSITES

This section offers a sample of websites that provide information on technology for individuals with visual impairments.

AccessWorld

www.afb.org/aw/main.asp

Offers comprehensive product evaluations, user-friendly explanations of current technology, practical tips on using popular technologies, news and reports from the field, and interviews with industry leaders.

AIM Navigator: National Center on Accessible Instructional Materials

http://aim.cast.org/experience/decision-making_tools/aim_navigator

Offers an interactive tool that facilitates the process of decision-making around accessible instructional materials for individual students.

American Foundation for the Blind Product Database

www.afb.org/prodMain.asp

Provides a comprehensive listing of assistive technology products used by people who are blind or visually impaired.

Apple Accessibility

www.apple.com/accessibility

Offers information on the accessibility features built into Apple products.

Apps for Blind and Visually Impaired

http://appadvice.com/applists/show/apps-for-the-visually-impaired

Lists apps available on iOS devices to people with visual impairments.

DAISY Consortium

www.daisy.org

Pools and coordinates resources to ensure that people have equal access to information and knowledge regardless of disability.

DIAGRAM Center

http://diagramcenter.org/webinars.html

http://diagramcenter.org/research/product-matrices-complete.html

Offers free quarterly webinars for content creators on image description, accessible math, and many other topics. Offers a comparison of the features of DAISY Talking Books and a variety of e-book hardware and software.

Microsoft Accessibility

www.microsoft.com/enable/guides/vision.aspx

Offers a guide describing accessibility features built into Windows 7 and 8 and Office 2010 or Office 2013 that are available to address vision impairments and preferences. It also offers information on available assistive technology products.

MOLinsight

www.molinsight.net

Offers free software that allows a screen reader user to access an electronic version of the periodic table and a free program that reads aloud the visual configurations of atoms and molecules.

National Center on Accessible Instructional Materials

http://aim.cast.org

Offers information for students with sensory, physical, cognitive, or learning differences and their teachers about accessible instructional materials.

NASA MathTrax

http://prime.jsc.nasa.gov/mathtrax

Offers MathTrax, a free downloadable accessible graphing tool for middle school and high school students to graph equations.

SciTrain

www.catea.gatech.edu/scitrain

Offers free online courses for high school math and science teachers to train them to be more effective instructors for students with disabilities.

Sharing the SETT Framework

www.joyzabala.com

Provides information and supports related to the SETT (Student, Environments, Tasks, and Tools) Framework, a four-part model intended to promote collaborative decision-making in all phases of assistive technology service design and delivery, from consideration through implementation and evaluation of effectiveness. Also includes links to other areas of interest, particularly Quality Indicators for Assistive Technology Services (QIAT), Universal Design for Learning (UDL), and Accessible Instructional Material (AIM).

SmartBrief on EdTech

www.smartbrief.com/news/edtech

Offers STEM-specific news for career and technical education professionals.

Special Education Technology British Columbia

www.setbc.org/setinfo/projects_archived.html

Assists school districts in educating students whose access to the curriculum is restricted primarily due to the following disabilities: physical disabilities or chronic health impairments, visual impairments, dependent handicaps, deaf-blindness, autism spectrum disorders, and moderate to profound intellectual disabilities.

ORGANIZATIONS

American Chemical Society

1155 Sixteenth Street NW
Washington, DC 20036
(800) 227-5558 or (202) 872-4600
www.acs.org

Independent membership organization for chemistry professionals. Distributes free training materials about classroom modifications for students with vision loss and other disabilities.

Closing the Gap

526 Main Street
PO Box 68
Henderson, MN 56044
(507) 248-3294
Fax: (507) 248-3810
info@closingthegap.com
www.closingthegap.com

Organization focusing on computer technology to enhance the lives of people with special needs through its bi-monthly newspaper, website, and annual international conference.

International Society for Technology in Education

1710 Rhode Island Avenue NW, Suite 900
Washington, DC 20036
(866) 654-4777 or (202) 861-7777
Fax: (202) 861-0888
www.iste.org
iste@iste.org

Membership association for educators and education leaders engaged in improving learning and teaching by advancing the effective use of technology in pre-K–12 and teacher education.

SOURCES OF PRODUCTS

This section offers a sample of companies offering products that make science, technology, and mathematics education more accessible to students with visual impairments.

Anatomical Chart Company

Wolters Kluwer Health
351 West Camden Street
Baltimore, MD 21201
(410) 528-4000
www.lww.com/webapp/wcs/stores/servlet/category_Charts_11851_-1_9012053_50011157_50011157_Y__Y

Sells tactile two-dimensional diagrams of parts of the human body, such as the heart, lungs, nervous system, and digestive system.

Design Science

140 Pine Avenue, 4th Floor
Long Beach, CA 90802
(562) 432-2920
info@dessci.com
www.dessci.com

Offers the MathPlayer software for accessing MathML and MathDaisy software for sighted teachers to create accessible electronic and braille math materials.

eTouchSciences, LLC

309 Highland Meadows Drive
Grafton, WV 26354
mdarrah@etouchsciences.com
www.etouchsciences.com/ets/contactus

Sells educational apps providing math and science lessons with tactile feedback, audio and high-contrast graphics as well as the Novint Falcon haptic device, a 3-D controller that replaces the mouse and offers tactile feedback from computer applications.

Henter Math

PO Box 40430
St. Petersburg, FL 33743-0430
(727) 347-1313 or (888) 533-6284
info@hentermath.com
www.hentermath.com

Sells the Virtual Pencil software for basic math and algebra.

Independence Science

3000 Kent Avenue
West Lafayette, IN 47906
(866) 862-9665
Fax: (765) 807-8665
www.independencescience.com

Sells the Talking Vernier LabQuest adapted data-collection device and offers techniques for creating an accessible laboratory for students who are blind or visually impaired.

Tedco Toys

498 South Washington Street
Hagerstown, IN 47346
(800) 654-6357
Fax: 765-489-5752
www.tedcotoys.com
support@shopatron.com

Sells scientifically accurate three-dimensional models of animal and plant cells, and many other science models that are used by students in elementary school through college.

Texas Instruments

12500 TI Boulevard
Dallas, TX 75243
(972) 995-2011 or (512) 434-1560
www.ti.com

Sells TI interactive software, the TI-84 talking graphing calculator, and the talking TI-34 desktop calculator.

Wolf Products

106 Purvis Road
Butler, PA 16001
(724) 285-5428
Fax: (413) 208-9042
www.mathwindow.com/index.html
wolfproducts@mathwindow.com

Manufactures Math Window, a math teaching tool utilizing magnetic tiles on a conveniently sized work surface.

Assistive Technology Learning Activities

Contributed by Carol Farrenkopf and Susan Glaser

These sample learning activities are presented as examples of activities that teachers can create to work on several ECC skills at once with their students. Activities that help teach assistive technology skills can also be found in other chapters. The activities presented, like all instruction, need to be considered and modified to address the needs of individual students—such as those who are braille readers, have low vision, or have additional disabilities—with adaptations for appropriate media and the physical and other capabilities of the student.

Learning Activity: Cooking with an Audio Recipe

Primary ECC Area: Assistive technology **Component:** Personal productivity
Grades: Pre-K–K, older students with multiple disabilities

Other ECC Areas

- Recreation and leisure
- Social interaction
- Compensatory access
- Sensory efficiency
- Independent living

Goal: The student will follow one- or two-step instructions on a digital voice recorder to make a simple snack.

Key Tasks/Concept

The student will:

- Use the controls on a digital voice recorder to play instructions.
- Follow one direction at a time on the recorder to make a snack.
- After finishing the snack, record a summary of the steps taken to make the snack.
- Offer the finished snack to other students or teachers in the school.

Description

For this activity, the student must have the following prerequisite skills:

- Basic awareness of a recipe
- Dexterity and strength to push a dime-sized button on a recorder
- Auditory discrimination

Making simple snacks such as instant pudding, cheese or peanut butter crackers, or trail mix gives young children experience in the kitchen and teaches them at a young age that they are expected to participate in cooking activities. For preschool-age children with visual impairments, reading a recipe or following the pictures that are often used to help young children follow recipes are not typically an option. Using a very simple digital voice recorder that has only a few buttons is an easy alternative to reading a recipe and also teaches young children that there are many ways to access information and get tasks done without reading print. This lesson can be done over two sessions, and it can be repeated any number of times with the same or different snacks.

The first session will involve collecting the ingredients, and the second will be making the snack. The first step in this activity is for the teacher to choose, ideally with the student, a simple snack. In a school setting, instant pudding is a great option because the student can purchase the required milk for the recipe from the

(continued on next page)

cafeteria, reinforcing even more ECC skills. A refrigerator in a teachers' lounge or pre-kindergarten classroom can be used to chill the milk and the finished pudding.

The teacher will need to create a task analysis of the activity so that each step can be listed separately. The list of ingredients should be pre-recorded by the teacher with each "step" or "file" of the recorder listing just one ingredient or supply needed (pudding mix, milk, bowl, whisk, and so forth). The student listens to one ingredient at a time, collecting each item after hearing it. For the next session, the teacher will pre-record the recipe, including only one simple step at a time for each "step" or "file" of the recorder, so that when the student pushes the Play button, only one direction is heard. Steps should be very simple, such as the following:

1. Open the box.
2. Take out the package.
3. Open the package.
4. Pour the mix into a bowl.
5. Pour the milk into the bowl.
6. [continue]

The complexity or number of steps can be varied depending on the ability of the individual student. Some students will be capable of learning to use the Play, Forward, and Rewind buttons in order to review a direction. For a student with multiple disabilities, pushing a pre-labeled Play button may be an appropriate level of independent participation. The student can then add the ingredients with more assistance.

When the pudding (or other chosen snack) is in the refrigerator and clean-up is finished, the student can record a summary of what was required to make the snack and then listen to it. This can act as a review and/or evaluation of the lesson and will also give the student more practice using the device.

To complete the activity and extend it further to encompass other ECC areas, the student can offer to share the snack with a small group of students, the classroom teacher, or office staff.

Instructional Materials and Supplies Needed

- A basic digital voice recorder
- Ingredients for the simple snack

Settings

Preschool or kindergarten classroom, home

Duration/Timing

- 15–20 minutes for the first session of collecting ingredients.
- 20–30 minutes for the second session of following directions to make a simple snack.

Time will vary depending on the snack selected.

Evaluation

The student's performance can be evaluated by using the following checklist.

Skill	Date	Date	Date	Date
Pushes the Play button to hear ingredients one at a time.				
Collects ingredients.				
Pushes the Play button to hear directions one at a time.				
Follows one direction before pushing the Play button to advance to the next one.				

(continued on next page)

Skill	Date	Date	Date	Date
Repeats a direction to listen to it again.				
Records own voice summarizing activity after snack is finished.				

Key:
I = Independently
MiA = Minimal Assistance
MoA = Moderate Assistance
MA = Maximum Assistance

Learning Activity: Shape Bingo

Primary ECC Area: Assistive technology **Component:** Access to information
Grades: K–5

Other ECC Areas
- Recreation and leisure
- Social interaction
- Compensatory access
- Sensory efficiency

Goal: The student will move the X-Y table on a video magnifier (desktop closed-circuit television system or CCTV) to locate specific shapes while playing a game of Shape Bingo.

Key Tasks/Concepts
The student will:
- Learn the rules of the game Shape Bingo.
- Use previous knowledge of shapes and letters to play a BINGO game.
- Use the Shape Bingo game to practice the use of the X-Y table on a video magnifier.
- Practice scanning horizontal and vertical lines.

Description
For this activity, the student must have the following prerequisite skills:
- Knowledge of the letters B, I, N, G, and O
- Knowledge of the shapes used in the game—circle, square, triangle, heart, and diamond
- Ability to use the basic functions of a desktop video magnifier—on/off, magnification, color, contrast, focus
- Understanding of the difference between vertical and horizontal
- Good visual discrimination skills.

One of the earliest games young children learn to play is Bingo. This learning activity is a variation of that game, except it uses shapes instead of numbers. At least initially, five consecutive squares in columns or rows only, not diagonal lines, are considered a win in Shape Bingo.

After some initial instruction by the teacher regarding systematic scanning (such as top-to-bottom and left-to-right) and practice scanning horizontal and vertical lines, the teacher can introduce the Shape Bingo card to the students so they are are familiar with it before the game begins.

(continued on next page)

Before playing the game, the teacher should review the rules of the game with the students who will be playing the game and make sure that all the children who will be playing the game either are able to play independently or have assistance from another adult in the classroom. Whenever possible, the teacher should include all children in the game.

After all the Bingo cards and playing chips have been handed out to the students, the teacher can give them a moment to look at the shapes on the card. When drawing a shape, the teacher or another adult in the classroom can pull a shape card from a box, bag, or hat and then bring it close to students with low vision so they can see the shape clearly. Frequent breaks may be needed to keep young children on task. As the shapes are called out, students with low vision use the video magnifier to scan their Bingo cards first horizontally to find the appropriate letter and then vertically to find the appropriate shape. When any student finds a called shape on their card, they place a Bingo chip on the shape. This process continues until someone calls "BINGO!"

This activity can be extended to include diagonal lines after the student has mastered vertical and horizontal X-Y table movement. Also, elements such as color or size can be added to the shapes to make the task more visually challenging. For older children, the game can be extended to numbers and number, letter, and word combinations.

Instructional Materials and Supplies Needed

- Specially created Shape Bingo playing cards made on a computer (black, solid shapes on white paper)
- Large single shape cards (black, solid shapes on white paper) to be used by the "caller"
- Bingo playing chips (coins, stickers, cut-out circles) to be used as markers
- Recording sheet so the caller knows which shapes and letters have been called
- Recording sheet so the teacher of students with visual impairments can document proper X-Y table movement

Settings

Preschool or kindergarten classroom, home

Duration/Timing

5–10 minutes per game, depending on the attention spans of the players.

Evaluation

Student performance can be evaluated by using the following checklist, which includes the behaviors involved in vertical and horizontal scanning with Shape Bingo. Anecdotal notes can be included so the teacher is able to target instruction in areas of particular difficulty at a later date.

Skill	With Assistance	Without Assistance	Further Instruction Needed
Locates "B" at top left of Bingo card (the starting point for each new shape scan)			
Slides X-Y table to the **left** to scan the Bingo line to the **right**			
When correct letter is found, stops horizontal scanning			
Moves X-Y table **up** to scan **down** the column for the correct shape			
If shape is located, stops scanning and places chip on shape			
Maintains visual focus on the monitor rather than on the X-Y table			

Learning Activity: Listening for Nonsense Words

Primary ECC Area: Assistive technology **Component:** Communication
Grades: K–12

Other ECC Areas
- Social interaction
- Compensatory access
- Sensory efficiency

Goal: To improve proofreading skills, the student will listen to a story using a screen-reading program and pause the speech whenever he/she hears a nonsense word.

Key Tasks/Concepts
The student will:
- Listen carefully while the story is read aloud by the computer.
- Distinguish between "real" words that have meaning within the context of the story and "nonsense" words that are not "real" words and do not have meaning within the context of the story.
- Make the connection between this activity and proofreading written material.

Description
For this activity, some of the prerequisite skills that the student must have include:
- Ability to use a computer and screen-reading program independently, including how to pause the speech output
- Ability to understand age-appropriate stories
- Ability to hear and understand speech produced through a computer.

Before playing this game, the teacher will need to create or find a number of one- to two-page age-appropriate short stories and insert a particular number of nonsense words in each (10 nonsense words per story is recommended). When playing this game, the computer monitor should be turned off so players with low vision do not have the advantage of reading a nonsense word visually, rather than hearing it. The teacher sets up the game by activating the screen-reading software (if the computer doesn't automatically run the program on start-up) and opening the first story. When the Start Reading function is activated by the teacher, the game begins.

Players listen intently, without making any sounds, until they detect that a nonsense word has been inserted into the story. When they detect a nonsense word, the players press the Pause function key and the teacher records whether or not the response was accurate. Play resumes by pressing the Start function key and continues as the software continues to read through the story.

This game can be played in several different ways:
- The student who is visually impaired can play against herself and try to beat previous scores.
- The student who is visually impaired can play against another student (sighted or visually impaired) and take turns playing with different stories.
- The student who is visually impaired can play with another student (sighted or visually impaired) at the same time—the game becomes a speed challenge to see who will recognize the nonsense word and pause the speech function first.
- The teacher can use an unedited document produced by the student and play the game to "proofread" the document together.

This activity can be extended in a number of ways including:
- Increasing or decreasing the speed of the computer's voice (this may sound so silly that the players will find it funny, but at the same time, it will be more challenging to detect the nonsense words because real words will also sound different)
- Changing the computer's speech-generated voice (e.g., from male to female, from American accent to Australian accent

(continued on next page)

- Making the nonsense words less obviously nonsensical
- Inserting meaningful, but misspelled, words into the passage and asking the student to identify them.

Instructional Materials and Supplies Needed

- Computer with screen-reading software and speakers, if not built into the computer
- A number of one- to two-page age-appropriate short stories
- Word-processing program on the computer in which electronic versions of short stories can be saved
- List of nonsense words within each story so the teacher knows the correct responses
- Checklist to record students' responses

Settings

Classroom, resource room, home (quiet area works best)

Duration/Timing

3–5 minutes to listen to each story, depending on how many times the players interrupt play with false pauses or giggles. Play can continue until the players are ready to stop playing.

Evaluation

Record the total number of nonsense words inserted in the story along with the number of correctly identified nonsense words. A frequency chart can be created to demonstrate achievement over several stories or days. It is recommended that the total number of nonsense words remains the same each time the game is played. Ten nonsense words are recommended.

Date	Story 1	Story 2	Story 3	Story 4	Story 5	Story 6	Story 7	Story 8	Story 9	Story 10

Learning Activity: Checking Out Movie Listings

Primary ECC Area: Assistive technology
Component: Personal productivity
Grades: 4–12

Other ECC Areas

- Recreation and leisure
- Social interaction
- Independent living
- Orientation and mobility

Goal: The student will search the Internet to find the date, time, and location of a specific movie at a local theater.

Key Tasks/Concepts

The student will:

- Learn how to refine Internet search patterns for a specific website.
- Demonstrate the ability to navigate within the website using appropriate menus.
- Determine which local theater (if more than one) is the most easily accessible for orientation and mobility purposes.

(continued on next page)

Description

For this activity, some of the prerequisite skills that the student must have include:

- Independent use of a computer to search the Internet with a screen enlargement or screen-reading/speech-output program
- Previous experience using a computer to explore other websites.

Prior to beginning this activity with the student, the teacher of students with visual impairments should discuss movies of interest to the student. Also, the teacher should explore websites for various nearby theaters so she is aware of what is available on each of the sites (in case the student accesses more than one site).

The student and teacher should find a quiet space to work so the student is not distracted. The teacher will monitor and observe the student as he navigates a website to locate the date, time, and location of a movie they have discussed. When appropriate, the teacher can make suggestions to the student to assist him with the search (for instance, saving a website as a favorite, or bookmarking the site). As the student encounters difficulties, the teacher makes note of the issues that will require targeted teaching after the task at hand is completed.

The task is considered complete when the student has located the desired movie and recorded its time, date, and location.

This activity can be extended by having the student locate other information on the Internet, such as bus, train, and airplane arrivals and departures, or by having the student enter the information into an electronic calendar.

Instructional Materials and Supplies Needed

- Computer with screen enlargement or screen-reading and speech-output software and Internet access
- Notebook or braillewriter to record movie information

Settings

Classroom, library, home

Duration/Timing

30–60 minutes to complete the task, depending on the number of difficulties encountered by the student. This activity can be introduced over a period of several days, including time to discuss various movies currently showing.

Evaluation

Evaluation of this activity can be accomplished by completing a checklist like the one below. Anecdotal notes can be included so the teacher is able to target instruction in areas of particular difficulty at a later date.

Task	With Assistance	Without Assistance	Further Instruction Needed
Locates the most appropriate website.			
Locates the movie on the website.			
Locates the time and date for the movie.			
Finds the theater's address.			
Finds the admission charge.			
Did the student encounter any problems while conducting the search for this activity? If yes, provide details here:			

Learning Activity: Creative Editing

Primary ECC Area: Assistive Technology **Component:** Access to information
Grades: 6–12

Other ECC Areas

- Recreation and leisure
- Social interaction
- Compensatory access

Goal: The student will use a refreshable braille display to search for keywords and replace existing words to create a "Mad Libs" story.

Key Tasks/Concepts

The student will:

- Read a short story or excerpt, two to three paragraphs long, on a refreshable braille display.
- Search for and identify various parts of speech (verbs, nouns, adjectives, pronouns, adverbs, etc.) as directed by the teacher.
- Replace each word with the name of its category (noun, verb, adjective, etc.).
- Start at the beginning of the document and ask a friend, peer, or teacher to replace each type of word.
- Read the new finished story out loud.

Description

For this activity, the student must have the following prerequisite skills:

- Ability to read braille at a fifth-grade or higher level
- Basic use of a refreshable braille display
- Knowledge of nouns, verbs, adjectives, pronouns, adverbs, etc.

The game "Mad Libs" can easily be re-created for a braille reader and friends to enjoy. Students will reinforce their English language skills and have a fun experience using the refreshable braille display through this activity.

The teacher or student can find an excerpt from a required reading book for class, such as a novel, a passage from the English textbook, or an article found online. It can be a serious passage, travel, informational, sports-related, or anything the student is interested in. (A humorous passage should be avoided since the distortion of a serious work will add to the comic relief.) The student or teacher can download the passage from the Internet or open an existing file. It should only be a few paragraphs long, or the listener may lose interest.

Once the short passage is chosen and downloaded to the student's device, it should be read in its entirety on the refreshable braille display. The teacher may have to review the passage to determine what types of words (such as proper nouns, pronouns, verbs, places, animals, or sports) would be best to replace and how many. The student will then go on a "scavenger hunt" through the document to find the types of words the teacher names, replacing the words with their descriptions or parts of speech.

When the document has been edited with targeted words removed, it is time to invite a friend to the activity. The braille reader asks the friend to "name a place," "name a sport," "name a noun, verb, proper noun, etc.," as the document now calls for and inserts the new words into the document in the proper spaces. When all words have been replaced, the student reads back the passage—usually to great comical effect.

Instructional Materials and Supplies Needed

- Electronic notetaker or computer
- Refreshable braille display
- Selection of short passages

(continued on next page)

Settings

School resource room or media center

Duration/Timing

20–30 minutes if the teacher pre-selects a passage or selection of passages.

Evaluation

In addition to the skills in the following data collection chart, the finished passage with replaced words can be embossed or e-mailed to the teacher and used as a sample of the student's work.

Skill	Date	Date	Date	Date
Opens correct file containing passage on device.				
Locates designated keywords using refreshable braille display.				
Replaces keyword with a descriptor.				
Uses navigational keys to locate each replacement word.				
Asks a friend to replace each descriptor.				
Inserts new word into document.				
Reads new passage with replacement words.				

Key:

I = Independently

MiA = Minimal assistance

MoA = Moderate assistance

MA = Maximum assistance

CHAPTER 7

Orientation and Mobility

Diane L. Fazzi

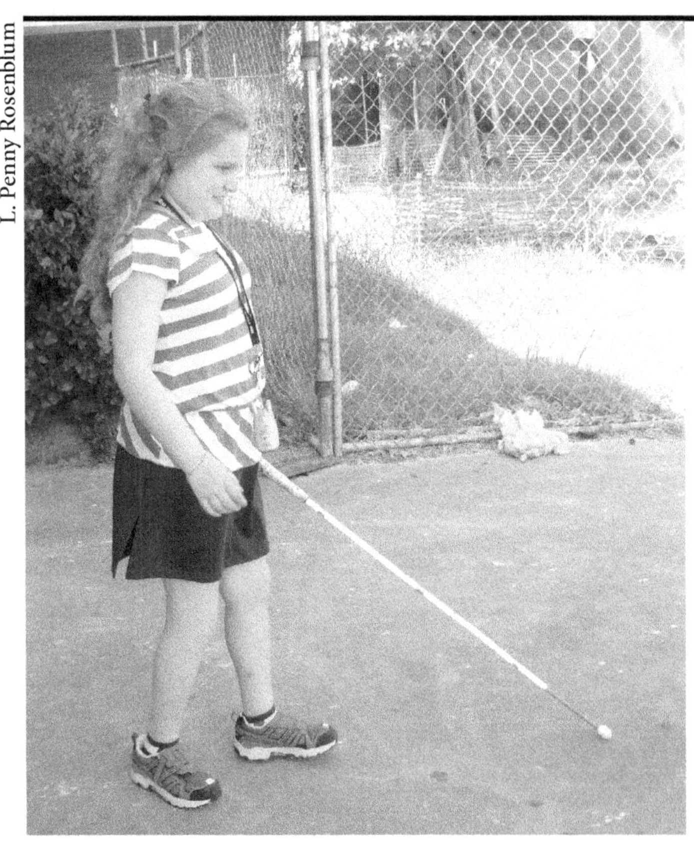
L. Penny Rosenblum

Orientation and mobility (O&M) is the area of the expanded core curriculum (ECC) in which students learn the concepts and skills necessary to get from one place to another safely and efficiently. O&M specialists are the professionals who are specifically trained to work with children with visual impairments, including those students with additional disabilities, to provide this training. It is critical for teachers of students with visual impairments to become familiar with the concepts and skills of O&M in order to effectively support O&M specialists in their efforts to teach students to travel as independently as possible in home, school, and community environments. Therefore, consultation and collaboration between these two professionals are essential to help students who are visually impaired develop not just O&M skills in particular, but all ECC skills.

This area of the ECC encompasses the learning and practice of a body of specific techniques that enable individuals who are blind or have low vision to travel safely on their own. O&M instruction focuses on conceptual understanding of the physical environment, and purposeful movement in home, school, and community environments that is both safe and independent (or interdependent) to the fullest extent of each child's individual ability. (The term "interdependent travel" refers to the fact that, while "independent" travel is a goal to strive for, travel often requires seeking assistance or information from others. Stressing interdependent travel highlights that students who may not have the full potential for "independent" travel also benefit from O&M instruction.)

The O&M area of the expanded core curriculum focuses on two broad interrelated components:

- *orientation:* knowing one's position in relation to other objects, people, and places in one's surroundings and keeping track of how these positions and relationships change as one moves through the environment
- *mobility:* the physical act of moving from one place to another

The development of conceptual understanding of the environment, including physical layout and spatial relationships among people, places, and things, is the foundation for orientation. The development of motor skills, physical coordination, and stamina, and the use of appropriate mobility tools (such as the long cane) are the basis for independent mobility.

The 1997 reauthorization of the Individuals with Disabilities Education Act (IDEA) identified O&M instruction as a related service for students with visual impairments, defined as "transportation and such developmental, corrective, and other support services as are required to assist a child with a disability to benefit from special education" (Section 300.24. 300.24 Related services), and further noted the importance of instruction provided in home, school, and community environments.

LEARNING TO NAVIGATE THE ENVIRONMENT AS A DEVELOPMENTAL PROCESS

Learning about the world and how to navigate through it is a developmental process, in which each new piece of understanding builds on others previously acquired, and strengthens an overall knowledge and broader sense of increasingly larger environments. The knowledge and skills needed for children to get where they want to go increase as their choices, opportunities, and environments expand and as direct supervision provided by parents for movement from one place to another decreases accordingly. Children with visual impairments, like all other children, build their knowledge of how to navigate the world in this developmental and cumulative way, but they do not have the benefit of full visual input while doing so. O&M instruction addresses this circumstance by providing them with techniques that enable safe and independent travel without the use of the sense of sight or with varying degrees of visual impairment.

Development of Mobility in Typical Children

In the toddler period, children want to get to people, family pets, toys, and other objects of interest to them and they do so under the supervision of caring adults. Young children are given opportunities to move independently, but parents also provide physical support for complex movements, such as offering a hand during first steps or placing a hand lightly on the child's back to support climbing onto a slide. Caretakers may use verbal guidance or physical barriers, such as baby gates, to restrict childrens' movements as they feel appropriate for safety in any given situation.

Depending on the neighborhood environment, cultural norms, and general comfort level, parents allow older children more freedom of movement within the neighborhood to play with other children, participate in family outings, and travel with others on school field trips. With good motor skills in place, concern from parents is now focused on the child's judgment and safety when the environmental demands are increased, as in navigating neighborhood street crossings, communicating safety with strangers, and adhering to rules given for increased levels of independence.

Adolescents are often given opportunities to spend time with friends at locations at greater distances from home, such as the community mall, shopping center, or movie theater. Increased understanding of the world is necessary for safely navigating these areas independently. It is likely that children initially became familiar with these travel destinations at younger ages while on outings with the family or under adult supervision in small groups of friends at earlier ages. Hence, the developmental process of learning how to navigate the environment safely takes place somewhat naturally for families and children as they grow and mature.

In the later teenage years, parents teach their children how to drive, use public transportation, or both. In many instances, schools and private companies are available to conduct driver's training lessons—both the conceptual understanding of rules of traffic and pedestrians on the road and the behind-the-wheel mobility skills of operating a vehicle. Teenagers have been learning these skills since childhood through observation of adult driving and simulated experiences with video games and the like. Thus, achieving the ability to travel independently with safety is a developmental learning process for all children and families.

Impact of Visual Impairment on the Ability to Move Safely

Little on the specific subject of O&M is typically covered in the general education curriculum. There are aspects of concepts about neighborhood and community that are addressed in the primary curriculum, and driver's training is addressed in high school at some level. The rest of what needs to be learned about independent travel is mostly acquired through incidental learning (derived from everyday observation of others) and first-hand experiences along the way.

For students with visual impairments, including students with additional disabilities, the knowledge and skills necessary for freedom of movement in home, school, and community settings may not develop as readily as they may for other students. A team approach involving O&M specialists, families, teachers of students with visual impairments, and the various professionals working with a student is necessary for developing high expectations for the student's performance and providing direct exploration and travel opportunities that match the student's individual developmental needs. Children who are visually impaired may learn some aspects of O&M in the home incidentally, through observation and awareness of others and through daily interactions with family members and objects in the home. However, these children may also miss crucial concepts, develop physical skills differently, or be afforded fewer opportunities or less encouragement to explore and move.

Supporting the Development of Orientation and Mobility Skills

Young children who are visually impaired will benefit tremendously from working with an O&M specialist, who can provide structured opportunities for exploration and instruction, suggestions for family activities that will support O&M, recommendations and guidance for the educational team, and introduction to mobility devices and any safety considerations, as needed. Teachers of students with visual impairments can further support the development of O&M skills and concepts in a number of ways, including:

- reinforcing the use of techniques taught by the O&M specialist throughout the school day, such as expecting the student to use the long cane during travel on specified routes
- relating lessons in the core curriculum and ECC to travel experiences in the home, school, and community, such as applying concepts of the perimeter of a rectangle to a residential block in the area
- building on body, spatial, and environmental concepts in the classroom setting, such as labeling and referring to classroom walls according to cardinal directions

Early Motor Development

Attention to the development of O&M skills needs to begin early. Encouragement from the entire early intervention team, including the family, can help promote motor development and skills. At this stage, the teacher of students with visual impairments needs to work closely with the student's family and O&M specialist to encourage the child's use of sensory information for learning and the motivation to move and to provide deliberate and repeated opportunities for the child to explore the world with as much tactile and physical participation as possible. (Families and professionals will find resources, adaptations, and activities and routines to teach skills to and support growth in young children in Ferrell, 2011.) Ways in which teachers of students with visual impairments can reinforce purposeful reaching and movement in young children with visual impairments and young children with additional disabilities include:

- Using defined spaces for learning activities and orienting children to the space by touch and verbal description. For example, if intervention activities are to be completed on a blanket, the teacher can help children explore the perimeter and feel the difference between the soft blanket and the scratchy carpet surface.
- Moving coactively with young children to pull toys and objects from the teacher's basket or bag to support concepts related to object permanence. For example, the teacher needs to make sure that children do not assume that objects magically appear and disappear from reach during intervention sessions by helping them remove and return objects to and from the same container each time.
- Encouraging the use of senses for guided and purposeful reaching. For example, the teacher can give prompts to encourage young children to attend to specific sensory information for determining where to reach for people, pets, or toys.

(For information, resources, and strategies for supporting motor, cognitive, and sensory development in young children, see Pogrund & Fazzi, 2002.)

Conceptual Development

As children with visual impairments grow from infancy into toddlerhood, the type of direct instruction they receive from an O&M specialist typically changes depending on their individual needs. School-age students, including those with additional disabilities, need direct O&M instruction in order to acquire conceptual knowledge, such as:

- how a school building is laid out, including the shape of the perimeter and the arrangement of stories within
- that items or symbols can be representations of other things or activities, like a circle shape on a map representing a drinking fountain in a building or a toilet paper roll in a calendar box representing restroom breaks in the schedule
- how streets and residential blocks are aligned with one another
- how the positions of people and things can relate to one another in the immediate surroundings—for example, the gate to the campus is *in front of* the main office

Teachers of students with visual impairments reinforce such concepts through their work in related academic and ECC areas. For example, understanding the symbolic representation of a calendar box for daily routines can generalize to an understanding of maps for O&M. School-age students, including those with additional disabilities, need direct instruction in mobility skills, such as negotiating a crowded hallway while using a wheelchair, using the long cane effectively on the playground, walking with peers as guides on campus as appropriate, or negotiating specific stairways, large open spaces, or heavy doors throughout the school day. Teachers of students with visual impairments can reinforce these practices during the school day, monitoring their use or follow-through and updating O&M specialists on areas of success and challenge.

Traveling in the Community

Together, O&M concepts and skills will enable students to move comfortably within the school environment and to build the skills necessary for traveling in the community. While a general education kindergarten class may spend one or two days exploring the elementary school campus and making a class map of the area, students with visual impairments will need additional time to learn about, for example, the tactile, olfactory, auditory, and visual landmarks and cues that will help them become oriented. Teachers of students with visual impairments and O&M specialists can work together to ensure that students learn the campus. In addition, further time will be required for the O&M specialist to provide these students with opportunities to learn, for example, what route segments are and how to put them together to travel a route, first with supervision, and then independently.

Elementary school-age students generally learn concepts about neighborhoods and beginning notions about cardinal directions and related geographic content in school, but students with visual impairments, in addition to learning these same concepts in their general education classes, will benefit from O&M instruction that provides in-depth understanding of cardinal directions and how to apply them to maintain orientation during travel in surrounding residential areas, possibly making initial use of a compass and global positioning system (GPS) technology. Teachers of students with visual impairments may teach the use of the braille and assistive technology skills that are needed to use some GPS systems. While high school-age students will learn the rules of the road in driver's education, students who are visually impaired will be traveling in increasingly complex environments, learning to use public transportation independently, and building skills necessary for becoming independent adults. Teachers can collaborate with O&M specialists working on these skills by, for example, selecting career development sites with easy access to public transportation for their students who are also working on career transition goals.

Overlap with Other ECC Areas

Instruction in O&M provides students with the ability to move on their own and to live their lives as independently as possible. Time spent developing and reinforcing O&M knowledge and skills has a beneficial impact on all areas of life and supports learning in other ECC areas. These skills enhance a wide range of experiences, including:

- Increased participation in family routines within the home; for example, being able to move confidently from one place to another in the house becomes an essential part of completing chores, such as bringing groceries in from the car and putting them away in cabinets or dusting the furniture.
- Greater freedom of movement in the neighborhood with peers; for example, being able to go next door to play a game of tetherball with a neighborhood friend or walk together to a corner store or park—which in turn supports the development of friendships and other relationships.
- Enriched social interactions with classmates in school environments; for example, being able to move freely from the swings to the slide to keep up with a small group of friends on the playground, or to manage a cafeteria tray while finding a seat near friends at lunch—which in turn allows the student to be integrated socially and be a full and accepted participant in social interactions.
- Increased opportunities for learning the general education core curriculum; for example, being able to get from one class to another during class-changing periods; using O&M time to solve real-life math word problems, such as calculating distances between three destinations that form a triangle; or having meaningful hands-on experiences to help develop conceptual understanding of abstract concepts, such as the changing position of the sun throughout the day in relation to earth's rotation.
- Increased success in mastery of other areas of the ECC; for example, practicing self-determination by making choices about the most efficient route to travel to a location, using GPS to aid orientation to a local community college as part of career exploration, or applying sensory efficiency skills in real-life situations by using auditory skills to analyze the complexity of an intersection.
- Increased travel opportunities that support leisure, recreation, and activities of daily living in the community; for example, being able to travel alone or in groups by city bus or paratransit to the local YMCA for a yoga class or to the market to shop for personal management items for use in independent living.
- Expanded possibilities for future employment that will be satisfying and promote long-term independence or interdependence; for example, being able to travel to and from a volunteer work experience placement or exploring a variety of transportation options available within the community and in line with a personal budget.

Each element of access promoted by O&M builds confidence and skills, increases opportunities, and becomes a stepping stone to future possibilities.

COMPONENTS OF ORIENTATION AND MOBILITY

The O&M area of the ECC can be broken down into the following components (Wall Emerson & Corn, 2006; Fazzi & Naimy, 2010; Fazzi & Petersmeyer, 2001; Hill & Ponder, 1976; Pogrund et al., 1995):

- body concepts
- environmental concepts
- spatial concepts
- perceptual and sensory skills
- mobility skills
- orientation skills
- interpersonal skills
- decision-making skills

Each of these O&M components is important to students with visual impairments along a continuum of conceptual and skill development that leads to increasing independence as a traveler. O&M incorporates a lifetime of environmental understanding and travel skills that change according to the age of the traveler, the familiarity and complexity of the environment, and the availability of relevant technologies. The list of behaviors and skills encompassed within each component can thus be limitless. Prioritizing the most essential skills and concepts for each student, based on the results of assessment, instructional monitoring, and planning for the future, is a key responsibility for the O&M specialist in conjunction with families, the teacher of students with visual impairments, and the rest of the educational team. Following is a wide sampling of the types of concepts, behaviors, and skills related to each O&M component that will benefit students with visual impairments as they develop skills related to travel in home, school, and community environments. The role of the teacher of students with visual impairments in these processes is also discussed. Although teachers of students with visual impairments do not typically teach specific travel skills, they will be involved in teaching many of the concepts that underlie those skills and will need to coordinate this instruction with the O&M specialist.

Body Concepts

From infancy, families and service providers need to work to strengthen the understanding of and use of body concepts by children with visual impairments. Body concepts include the location, identification, and relationship of various parts and planes of the body, as well as an understanding of the range of movements and functions of those same body parts. Body concepts include, but are not limited to, the following behaviors, skills and understanding:

- location and identification of the body part
- function of the body part
- range of movements of the body part
- body planes

As a part of natural interactions, such as tickle games; family routines, such as bathing and dressing; and literature and interactive media, such as appropriate, child-friendly videos, families support childrens' growing understanding of their bodies. In games of tickle, a parent may gently call out the name of the body part ("tickle on the tummy") before commencing. During bath time, a parent may place the soapy washcloth on the child's arm, call out "Where's the washcloth?", and then wait for the child to locate it and pull it off. Teachers of students with visual impairments can facilitate the development of body concepts by helping parents understand the importance of these kinds of activities and ensuring that young children have access to and participate in movement songs in pre-kindergarten and kindergarten classrooms. Songs, such as "Head, Shoulders, Knees, and Toes," or those that require students to hop, jump, walk, run, or slide, may not be meaningful to a child with a visual impairment who cannot mimic the movements just from watching. The teacher can pre-teach the movements or work with the child while the song plays in class so that the child is not left out of the activity.

Understanding of body concepts, refined proprioceptive skills (a sense of one's body position and relation of body parts to one another, such as recognizing that an elbow is bent), and the ability to make use of a full range of body movements, all assist children with both orientation and mobility skills. The more accurate the body concepts developed by children who are blind (for instance, understanding that the arm reaches in front, to the side, and to the back), the easier it will be for them to use their bodies as a frame of reference in relation to people, places, and things in the environment. Children who can feel that their shoulders are turned are more likely to understand why they made contact with an unexpected obstacle in the hallway and reorient and reestablish their line of direction to maintain better orientation. Children who recognize that their toes are pointed outward, causing them to veer from a straight line when crossing a street, are likely to be able to practice pointing their toes straight forward during O&M lessons, to refine their line of travel and improve mobility skills for street crossings.

Collaborative efforts among teachers of students with visual impairments, O&M specialists, families, and other professionals directed at strengthening body concepts lead to improved O&M outcomes for a lifetime. See Sidebar 7.1 for suggestions for teaching body concepts to students.

Environmental Concepts

Environmental concepts relate to an understanding of the structural and physical properties of elements in the world around us and the way in which they are organized. Sidebar 7.2 lists some typical environments and their related concepts.

All children begin to learn a variety of environmental concepts as they interact with people and things early in life. Children who are visually impaired may become

SIDEBAR 7.1

Supporting the Development of Body Concepts

Teachers of students with visual impairments can support the development of body concepts in the following ways:

- Help families find easy ways to reinforce body concepts within the home and during natural family routines such as diapering, bath time, and play.
- Use body-specific language when working with very young children. For example, "Grab the toy with your fingers," or "Feel the warm grass with your toes."
- Plan activities that involve purposeful use of various body parts within other core or expanded core lessons. For example, have students use measuring tape to measure the length of their hands, feet, arms, and legs, and width of their shoulders, knees, and hips.
- Provide appropriate adaptations of instructional materials for general education teachers to ensure access to curriculum that addresses aspects of body concepts, progressing from the simple to the complex (for example, age-appropriate dolls for learning names of body parts in preschool; tactile diagrams or anatomically correct dolls [approved by the school and the parents] for learning about aspects of body changes that occur with onset of puberty in fifth grade; and tactile diagrams or scientific models that are labeled for learning anatomy as part of more advanced biological sciences in high school).
- Coordinate units on body concepts with the O&M specialist. For example, coordinate the brailling of body part labels to correspond with lessons on learning to use the cane that involve body parts such as wrist, forearm, index finger, and shoulders.

SIDEBAR 7.2

Typical Environmental Concepts

Some typical environments and their related concepts include, but are not limited to, the following:

HOME ENVIRONMENTS

- doors
- windows
- hallways
- rooms
- wall surfaces (wallpaper, paneling, textured drywall, and the like)
- flooring materials (linoleum, carpet, hardwood, and the like)

NONRESIDENTIAL BUILDINGS

Including typical locations, sizes and shapes, and various construction materials of buildings, and standard placement of features such as handrails and doorknobs.

- walls
- doors
- floors
- windows
- rooms
- hallways
- stairs

RESIDENTIAL NEIGHBORHOODS

Including typical locations within neighborhoods, relationships to other neighborhood features, textures, colors, and slopes, and appropriate corresponding cane skills to use when these features are encountered.

- houses
- streets
- sidewalks
- curbs
- driveways
- blocks
- parkways or grass lines
- fences
- mailboxes
- traffic
- street name signage

SIDEBAR 7.2 *continued*

SCHOOLS AND THEIR CAMPUSES
Including features, typical locations, and relations to other key school destinations.

- office
- classroom
- restroom
- library
- cafeteria
- playground

BUSINESS AREAS
Including features, typical locations and relations to other business areas, and appropriate mobility techniques for use in each situation.

- stores
- parking lots
- gas stations
- street furniture
- shopping centers
- escalators and elevators
- automatic and revolving doors

STREETS AND INTERSECTIONS

- intersection shape and type
- traffic and pedestrian controls
- crosswalks
- traffic flow
- phasing of the signals
- medians
- traffic islands

aware of different floor surfaces by crawling across them and feeling the textures of rough or smooth, soft or hard, and the relative temperature of warm or cool. They learn the reflective sound properties of floor surfaces when listening to people wearing hard-soled shoes walk across them or by banging a wooden spoon or bouncing a ball upon them. In the home, young children learn about the typical locations of environmental features, such as windows and doors, and the functions of these features. As they get older, they are exposed to a wide variety of doors and how to locate and perhaps manage a long cane while negotiating them in preparation for more challenging travel in school and community environments. Once again, the environmental concepts first learned at home become the building blocks for future concept and skill development in O&M.

Older students learn a host of more complex and advanced environmental concepts (such as streets, alleys, driveways, and curbs) through direct instruction time in O&M and practice opportunities with their families. An understanding of the environment outside the home is essential, not just for progress toward independence in the activities of daily life, but also for the maintenance of students' safety and well-being. The complexity and importance of intersection analysis is a key area for O&M specialists to address. Students must learn how to determine the safe time to cross a given intersection, depending on their visual and auditory abilities. Students who have low vision may use a monocular telescope to see the pedestrian control signal (WALK/DON'T WALK sign) to decide when to cross a traffic light-controlled intersection, but also need to know the safe time to cross at a complex phasing intersection when pedestrian controls are not functioning properly. Students who are blind need to learn to access this same information through auditory means, and understanding of the environment is key to applying meaning to what is heard at each individual intersection. While teachers of students with visual impairments are not involved in intersection analysis, it is helpful for them to be aware of the complexity of the content that will be covered and to see if there are ways to support this learning. For example, teachers might collaborate with the O&M specialists to develop worksheets for intersection analysis that can be used in the classroom to reinforce important concepts.

In general, students with visual impairments learn environmental concepts through a variety of means. Some initial learning of concepts takes place in the home or indirectly when reading books or watching television or movies. In-depth understanding follows repeated, structured opportunities for hands-on experiences that occur during O&M lessons in appropriate travel environments. For example, a young child who is blind and being pushed in a stroller on a family walk may first hear the word "sidewalk" when Dad says to an older sibling, "Stay on the sidewalk. Don't walk in the street." Other indirect experiences with sidewalks may arise during story time when a teacher reads about a fictional dog character that carries a young child piggyback along the sidewalk in front of a house. Each experience contributes to an initial understanding of the concept of *sidewalk*—an outdoor phenomenon associated with walking either in front of houses or next to streets. When a child lacks vision to help connect and compare the location, color, and length of sidewalks with other neighborhood features, O&M specialists need to use hands-on activities to further develop the concept of *sidewalk*, such as the following:

- feeling the sidewalk with hands, feet, and cane tip
- finding the sidewalk from the grassy yard, cement driveway, and even from the street
- exploring the length of the sidewalk by traveling until the cane tip falls off the edge of the sidewalk
- discovering unfamiliar sidewalks in other neighborhoods and areas for comparison
- building a model of a neighborhood with sidewalks placed next to streets and in between houses and yards

Each experience contributes to the student's ability to put together pieces of sensory and cognitive information to create an understanding of an integrated whole (*part-to-whole learning*). Teachers of students with visual impairments can help reinforce understanding of the concepts involved through reading, writing, math, and science activities.

The structured approach to exploring and learning about environmental concepts through O&M lessons is essential to building strong foundations for both orientation and mobility in ever-expanding travel environments. Collaborative efforts among O&M specialists, teachers of students with visual impairments, families, and other members of the educational team directed at environmental concepts can help provide incentives and greater meaning for exploration, purposeful movement, and travel in a wide variety of environments for students with visual impairments. See Sidebar 7.3 for some ideas teachers can use to support the development of environmental concepts.

SIDEBAR 7.3

Supporting the Development of Environmental Concepts

Teachers of students with visual impairments can support the development of environmental concepts in the following ways:

- Use descriptive language for environmental features present in the learning environment. For example, "The retaining wall between the classroom and the garden is made of brick and is 2 feet high. It keeps the dirt from the garden from moving toward our door when there is a lot of rain."
- Plan activities that involve the use of real objects so that students have multiple opportunities for hands-on learning of environmental concepts. For example, to prepare students for O&M travel on rainy days, develop an outdoor lesson on umbrellas. Teach the shape and range of sizes of umbrellas, and the varied means there are for opening and closing them. Explore the sound made by water bouncing off the top of an umbrella and dripping down the edges, and examine the water-repellent properties of the materials used for umbrella construction.
- Provide appropriate adaptations of instructional materials for general education teachers to ensure access to curriculum that addresses aspects of environmental concepts, from simple through complex. For example, help the general education teacher develop an activity in which students create a model of a Native American mud dwelling for tactile exploration prior to the class field trip to an Indian reservation.
- Coordinate units on environmental concepts with the O&M specialist. For example, if a literature unit on autumn is coming up, work with the O&M specialist to create an "autumn travels" collage or book from leaves gathered at special spots found while on O&M lessons. Students of all different ability levels and mobility challenges can create books and stories from their travel experiences.

Spatial Concepts

Spatial concepts relate to the location or position of stationary and moving elements in the environment. Some important concepts, with examples, include the following:

- self-to-object relationships (*Where am I in relationship to the table?*)
- object-to-object relationships (*Is my chair next to the table?*)
- right and left for self, others, and objects (*Who is sitting to my left?*)

- spatial terminology, such as next to, behind and in front, top and bottom (*The plate is on top of the table.*)
- cardinal directions (*If I am facing north, which direction is south?*)
- parallel and perpendicular (*The aisles in the supermarket are parallel to one another.*)
- landmarks—unique and persistent features of the environment that help travelers determine their location (*The brick retaining wall tells me that I am close to the start of the driveway.*)
- Cues—unique features of the environment that are intermittent or not always present (*The sound of the clothes dryer tells me I am close to the garage.*)
- typical spatial layouts of buildings (*Supermarkets have aisles; office buildings have floors.*)
- typical characteristics of types of areas (*My classroom has a perimeter and the chairs are arranged in a grid; the blocks in my neighborhood are arranged in a grid; addresses in my town get bigger as I walk north.*)
- symbolic representation of locations and destinations on a map (*The small triangle on this map represents the actual location of the men's restroom at the mall.*)

Knowing where one is in relationship to other people, places, and important things is essential to purposeful movement. Keeping track of those relationships while moving is a dynamic cognitive process. Infants with visual impairments, like other children, begin early mental mapping by developing an understanding of the location of their own body parts and their relation to one another, and extend those maps beyond arms' reach to understand where other people and items are located in relation to one another as they explore predictable home environments. They use sensory information, body concepts, and environmental understanding to put together the pieces of the puzzle to recognize the location or placement of people and objects around them and to know the spatial layout of rooms, places, and areas in their surrounding environment and beyond. This component of O&M is crucial for independent and interdependent travel.

Some spatial concepts are more challenging to understand with limited or no vision than others. Vision is a distance sense that gives an immediate "whole picture" of how things are arranged in the environment. These whole pictures are then used to make assumptions about spatial concepts in other unfamiliar areas and in larger areas that cannot be seen. Some children with visual impairments struggle with spatial concepts, partly because relying on auditory, tactile, proprioceptive, vestibular, and olfactory sensory information provides a less complete picture than visual information does for developing understanding (see Chapter 5 for more information on sensory efficiency and development), and partly because spatial understanding is so closely intertwined with comprehension of body and environmental concepts, described earlier. Missing elements in an individual's early understanding of body and environmental concepts will present challenges later on to the development of related spatial concepts. For example, if a teenage student who is blind is trying to understand the spatial layout of an intersection, but has difficulty recognizing the misalignment of her head, shoulders, and toes (body concepts), and does not have a full grasp of traffic and pedestrian control signals (environmental concepts), then she may have difficulty understanding how many audible pedestrian signals are mounted at the corners for pedestrians to see and hear, and the relative location of the pedestrian signal apparatus to the corner, the crosswalk, and her alignment (spatial concepts). As with teaching environmental concept development, teaching spatial concept development requires a structured approach to make sure that students with visual impairments are learning these essential concepts.

Understanding and managing the many spatial concepts inherent in general learning and specific to travel require a coordinated approach to assuring the greatest level of mastery possible. Teachers of students with visual impairments have many opportunities at school, in the classroom, and during lessons—and many unplanned opportunities—to help teach and reinforce these useful concepts. (See Sidebar 7.4 for suggestions teachers can use to support the development of spatial concepts.)

Perceptual and Sensory Skills

The ability to move through the environment with purpose requires the acquisition of a number of important concepts and skills, among them the ability to interpret and understand, and then integrate, information received through all the senses. The perception of sensory information for O&M follows a sequence that happens quickly in the processing centers of the brain.

SIDEBAR 7.4

Supporting the Development of Spatial Concepts

Teachers of students with visual impairments can support the development of spatial concepts in the following ways:

- Use descriptive language when talking about home, school, classroom or field trip environments, as in these examples:
  - rather than handing the student scissors for a craft project, describe the location as "near your left hand next to the paintbrush"
  - describe the position of other students who are lined up to a student with a visual impairment who uses a wheelchair for mobility, so that he understands who is in front and who is behind in the line
  - describe the height of the fence enclosure at the zebra exhibit at the zoo by encouraging the student to raise his cane vertically to see that the fence is taller than both he and his extended cane
- Plan activities that promote the understanding of spatial concepts. For example, have students help create the classroom bulletin board. During the activity, encourage the use of terms such as *bottom, top left corner, next to* or *underneath,* to help students locate items and to add new ones on the board.
- Provide appropriate adaptations of instructional materials for general education teachers to ensure access to curriculum that addresses aspects of spatial concepts, ranging from simple through complex. For example, loan to the general education teacher a small drawer set containing craft supplies, beads, and other small items to substitute for worksheets that are used to teach placement and position concepts to young children. Allow the O&M specialist to use the same drawer set for positional concepts assessment. Or, bring three-dimensional objects to support geometrical concepts in general education math.
- Coordinate with the O&M specialist to plan units on spatial concepts. For example, a map unit planned with the O&M specialist could coincide with a basic geography unit in general education. Plan together a few simple maps to start with. While the teacher of students with visual impairments teaches map-reading skills in the classroom, the O&M specialist can work with the student to gather materials and identify landmarks in a familiar residential area in order to construct his or her own map. Students with dual sensory impairments will also benefit from creating maps or landmark cards that can be used for orientation during routes or for calendar boxes.

1. Receiving the sensory information (hearing a humming noise).
2. Perceiving the sensory information to have meaning (the noise is created by the fan of a drinking fountain).
3. Determining the source of the sensory information (the fan sound is in front of me and slightly to the right).
4. Applying the meaning of the information to a task for use in purposeful movement (I am coming closer to the sound cue and I would like to get a drink).

Perceptual and sensory skills include, but are not limited to, the ability to:

- interpret environmental cues, such as visual, auditory, tactile, olfactory, and proprioceptive cues. *(For example, if I feel that I am walking on a slope, I might be crossing a driveway.)*
- use sensory information systematically to maintain orientation in dynamic environments. *(If I scan systematically, I will find my landmarks along the route.)*
- use low vision devices and electronic travel devices to enhance sensory information for orientation and mobility purposes. *(If I use an electronic mobility aid, I get additional information about how close I am to the end of the hallway.)*

Although all people use their senses while moving through the environment, ready access to an abundance of quick visual details in the distance enables many people to pay less attention to alternative sensory information—that is, to information received from the senses other than sight. However, children who are blind need to learn to use other senses artfully to gather the information they need to get around in home, school, and community environments. Children who have low vision need to make use of their usable or functional vision, along with alternative sensory input (e.g., auditory, tactile, proprioceptive, vestibular, and olfactory) as needed, to enhance their orientation and overall travel skills.

Teachers of students with visual impairments can also reinforce and teach sensory integration skills, as described in detail in Chapter 5. While traveling from one location to another on a school campus, for example, the teacher and student might engage in a sound scavenger hunt, in which each listens for a sound in the environment, identifies where it is coming from, names the sound, and explains what it means. Or, they can use a set of brailled vocabulary cards with words such as "playground," "parking lot," and "water fountain." The student can identify sound cues that indicate they are approaching any of these and guess where the sound is coming from. Or, the teacher and student can listen for interesting sounds along a route, such as a flag flapping in the wind, water dripping from a faucet, loud chatter from a cafeteria that gets louder when a door is opened, vehicles passing by on a nearby road, a lawnmower, and so on. The teacher can lead a discussion of what these sounds mean, how they can be useful to someone traveling, and how they can help that traveler locate a destination. The sound of a dripping faucet can help a student who is blind quickly find the sink for hand washing. The sounds of the flag blowing and flapping in the wind and the rope and metal clips clanking on the flagpole can tell a student where the front of the school is. These types of sounds are not landmarks and cannot be relied on all the time for orientation purposes, but they will help students pay more attention to the environment and what is happening. The teacher can also teach the student that as a sound gets louder, the student is getting closer to the sound's source. For example, the loud hum of children in the cafeteria will become louder as the student approaches. A sound scavenger hunt can be expanded to a sensory scavenger hunt to include smells and textures as well. (See also the learning activities in Chapter 5 on sensory efficiency.)

Teachers of students with visual impairments can play an important role in developing perceptual and sensory skills in the classroom, by focusing on ways in which these skills can be used and applied to their full extent for accessing and understanding sensory information for the benefit of learning, socializing, enjoying recreation and leisure, and developing career, travel, and independent living skills. Several ideas for supporting the development of perceptual and sensory skills are detailed in Sidebar 7.5.

SIDEBAR 7.5

Supporting the Development of Perceptual and Sensory Skills

Teachers of students with visual impairments can support the development of perceptual and sensory skills in the following ways:

- Use descriptive language to talk about changes in sensory information in the classroom or at school. For example, talk about the loud sounds of the lawnmower outside the classroom. Ask students to guess why the mower makes a clattering sound every so often. Point out the smell of cut grass. Explore the small piles of cut grass the mower leaves behind, look for small rocks that may have gotten caught in the mower blades, and relate the rocks back to the clattering noise.
- Provide appropriate adaptations of instructional materials for general education teachers to ensure access to curriculum that addresses simple through complex aspects of sensory perception. For example, provide the general education teacher with a model of the eye that can be used during the academic unit on visual perception and provide support to the student in understanding the principles presented. Work with the O&M specialist to explain the principle of how a moving cane is perceived as more visible to a driver than a stationary cane, prior to street crossings. A similar approach can be used when learning about auditory perception and the application of echolocation.
- Coordinate a sensory skills unit with the O&M specialist. For example, plan in advance for a visual skills unit in which a coordinated set of learning activities are planned to teach and reinforce systematic visual scanning. Activities can be set up along the hallway, classroom bulletin board, and during O&M routes, to scan for puzzle pieces that will eventually fit together at the end of the unit. The puzzle can be made from an actual photograph of a mystery location that the student gets to travel to after completing the scanning unit.

Mobility Skills

Mobility skills include, but are not limited to, the ability to:

- walk with good posture and maintain a straight line of travel
- use systematic search patterns
- ascend and descend stairs with alternating footsteps
- negotiate a variety of types of doors, escalators, and elevators
- make accurate 90-, 180- and 360-degree turns
- use time-distance estimation (using a combination of sensory information and perception of time and distance passing to approximate how far one has traveled)
- use appropriate mobility tools (such as the long cane, monocular telescope, or adapted mobility device) with efficiency

Foundational mobility skills begin with purposeful reaching in infancy and blossom into movement skills such as crawling, walking, and climbing—which require increased strength, coordination, and balance—to get from one place to another. Families encourage purposeful movement in the home through their daily routines—play time, household chores, meal preparation, and bed time routines, to name a few. O&M specialists, in collaboration with teachers of students with visual impairments and other early intervention service providers, support families in this venture by encouraging high expectations for exploration and movement, and by providing concrete suggestions for encouraging, reinforcing, and ensuring safe movement in the home. The mobility arena widens as children go off to school and need to learn to travel from one place to another within increasingly larger school sites. Teachers of students with visual impairments play an important role in communicating with O&M specialists about such issues as:

- travel needs on given school campuses
- concerns voiced by families, teachers, or other school-site staff about a student's mobility
- mobility-related challenges or incidents that may occur
- anticipating future needs

Teachers of students with visual impairments, when working closely with O&M specialists, can be an important monitor of the effectiveness of routes selected on campus or techniques that are being improperly used or not used at all. They can alert the O&M specialist to specific concerns raised by family or other team members, such as the safety of navigating certain activities or locations, and can work collaboratively on ways to address these concerns. O&M specialists and teachers together can address specific incidents that might occur, such as a tripping incident or an instance of disorientation that led to a student being late for class. For older students who may be engaged in advanced O&M lessons requiring bus transfers or travel to and from greater distances, the teacher of students with visual impairments can enable a level of flexibility in scheduling lessons to meet these increasing O&M demands without hampering the student's success in core academic subjects and other ECC areas.

For most students with visual impairments, success in O&M cannot readily be achieved in one or two lessons per week. Rather, there is a need for in-depth preparation for the travel demands of home, school, and community living and a need for consistent practice of skills during and far beyond planned O&M lessons. Students will have much greater success in mastering these skills if other professionals at the school know what to look for and how to reinforce the skills. A simple chart can be developed using teacher-friendly language to describe what cane skills a student should be using and how a teacher at the school can respond to the student, such as the chart in Figure 7.1, created for a student named Leah. This chart can be shared with both classroom teachers and teachers of students with visual impairments.

Delivering the message of the need for constant practice of O&M skills to families and individualized education program (IEP) teams becomes a cooperative responsibility of the O&M specialist and teacher of students with visual impairments. Sidebar 7.6 provides suggestions for teachers to use to support the mobility development of their students. Creative scheduling, teamwork, and a focused vision for O&M skills development are essential for long-term success.

Orientation Skills

While physical mobility skills are an important component of O&M, the purpose behind that movement is rooted in the traveler's orientation skills and understanding. As mentioned earlier, cognitive mapping of physical space and one's surroundings first emerges in early childhood and continues to expand along with exposure to larger, more complex environments.

FIGURE 7.1

Sample Handout for Teachers on a Young Student's O&M Skills

LEAH'S CANE SKILLS (AGE 5)

Skill	*Language Used*	*Leah's Actions*
1. Identify parts of the cane	"Grip is at the top and made of rubber; shaft comes below the grip and is long and smooth and made of aluminum or graphite; tip comes at the very bottom and is round and made of nylon or metal."	■ She should be able to touch each part of the cane and name it on her own. ■ When asked to find any part of the cane ("show me the grip"), she should be able to touch the part named.
2. Position hand/finger on grip *Left or right hand is based on child's abilities.*	"Thumb on top of grip, index finger pointing down the flat side of grip."	■ She should grasp the cane making sure her thumb is extended and on the top of the grip and her pointer (index) finger should be pointing down along the flat side of the grip.
3. Maintain proper cane position	"Center that cane in front of your belly button!"	■ Her cane-holding hand should be positioned in front of her belly button so that she has adequate coverage to the left and right side of her body.
4. Move the cane in an arc	■ "Sweep the cane left and right." ■ "Move your wrist, not your arm." ■ "Keep it moving so it won't get stuck." ■ "Swing the tip of the cane from just outside your left shoulder to just outside your right shoulder."	■ Leah should be able to swing the cane from side to side by moving her wrist, not her entire arm. ■ While moving the cane in an arc, she should be able to extend the cane tip from just outside her right shoulder to just outside her left shoulder. ■ She should be able to keep the cane moving to lessen the likelihood of the tip of the cane getting stuck in a crack in the sidewalk.
5. Using the constant-contact technique	"Keep that cane tip on the ground."	■ In this technique, Leah should keep the cane tip on the floor or ground while sweeping from side to side. ■ Leah should not pick up the cane from the ground; she slides it along the ground.
6. Using the two-point-touch technique *Good to use when traveling on uneven surfaces like grass, dirt, woodchips, sand, or stones. It will prevent the cane from getting stuck in these surfaces.*	"Tap that cane to the left and right."	■ Leah moves the cane in a low arc from side to side, tapping just beyond the width of her shoulders on each side. ■ Her foot and her cane tip touch down at the same time.
7. Carrying the cane when not walking independently	"Hold that cane straight up and down next to your body."	■ When waiting in line, standing still, holding an adult's hand, or walking with a guide, Leah should hold the cane in a vertical position, parallel to her body, so that it does not accidentally trip anyone.

(continued on next page)

FIGURE 7.1 *continued*

Skills for The Teacher and Family		
8. Specific praise *Children very often hear about all the things they are doing wrong, but they need to hear about all the things they are doing right!*	■ "I like the way you are holding that cane right in front of your belly button!" ■ "You are sweeping that cane left and right so well!" ■ "You've got that index finger pointing straight down just like you are supposed to." ■ "You are so responsible with your cane when you hold it still, straight up and down, right next to your body. That way, no one will trip on your cane."	■ Provide positive, specific praise when Leah is demonstrating good cane skills. ■ Don't just say "good job." Tell Leah exactly what she did that was good and why it was good.

Source: Adapted from handout developed by Susan Glaser.

SIDEBAR 7.6

Supporting the Development of Mobility Skills

Teachers of students with visual impairments can support the development of mobility skills in the following ways:

- Encourage the appropriate use and storage of mobility tools, such as the long cane or monocular telescope, at school.
- Plan activities that will incorporate the use of the student's mobility skills. For example, plan for a gardening and plant study unit that will require students to carry small plants from the classroom to the garden area using safe mobility skills, so as not to spill any of the plant packages.
- Reinforce mobility skills with high expectations and positive comments for a job well done. For example, set up a self-check system for remembering to bring the long cane to school each day and compliment students for increased success. Or, encourage social acceptance of monocular use by rewarding other well-behaved classmates with an opportunity to use a spare monocular for a whiteboard task.
- Coordinate mobility units with the O&M specialist. For example, as part of a career awareness unit, co-plan a trip to the local community college to find out about the support services available to students with disabilities, including those specific to visual impairments, as well as other disability-related services as they pertain to individual students. Have the student plan the bus route with the O&M specialist and travel there together.

Orientation skills include, but are not limited to, the ability to:

- relate one's own position to people and objects in the environment. *(Are the swings in front of me, and are there children already using them?)*
- understand that a route is a planned path to get from one place to another that incorporates a sequence of directions (such as, turns and/or cardinal directions), landmarks, and cues (key objects or points of information that help the traveler know where he or she is).
- memorize route landmarks, route segments (steps or sections of a route), full routes (the complete course from point A to B), and return routes (the return route from the desired destination).
- plan, execute, and reverse routes in familiar and unfamiliar areas.
- develop a mental or cognitive map of an area to maintain orientation. *(The block is shaped like a rectangle with two short sides and two long sides, and since I just traveled along a short side, I must be at the corner of X and Y.)*

- reestablish one's location after brief or prolonged disorientation (for example, find the sidewalk after veering into a gas station).
- relate one's own position or other objects to positions on a map.
- use a map to plan, review, or problem-solve along a route.
- update one's location while traveling in relation to other landmarks along a route (spatial updating).
- use orientation aids, such as a map, compass, visual and talking signs, and GPS devices for orientation for travel.
- direct a driver or other pedestrian to a destination.

When children who are visually impaired travel primarily with others using human guide techniques (holding a guide's elbow), they typically become passive about their surroundings and how the surroundings change as they move. Within reason and with the exception of specific social circumstances that may warrant traveling with peers (such as supporting attempts to make new friends or keeping pace with others to get good seats at an assembly), students should be encouraged to travel as independently as possible.

Teachers of students with visual impairments can support good use of orientation skills on school campuses by doing the following:

- helping the student understand the campus layout, numbering system for classrooms and offices, and cardinal directions associated with important locations
- learning the routes that the O&M specialist has taught the student to get to and from specific locations and becoming familiar with the terminology used to describe those routes (making note cards as necessary) in case questions arise or a student needs a reminder
- discussing with the O&M specialist the expectations for independent orientation on campus for given students, in order to reinforce at a consistent level

The entire education team must work together to ensure that students with visual impairments travel at their optimum level of independence, making use of orientation skills on a daily basis to build competence and confidence that will extend beyond the school years. Ideas for supporting the development of orientation skills can be found in Sidebar 7.7.

L. Penny Rosenblum

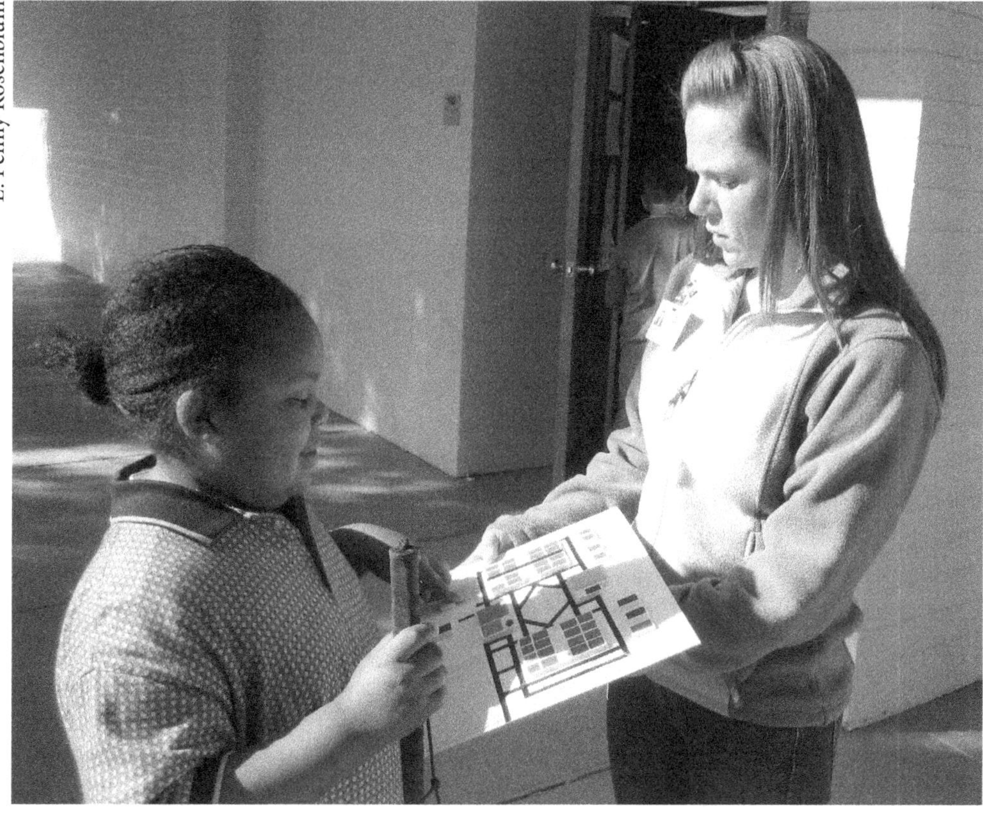

Relating a tactile map to the school campus helps this student learn both spatial and orientation concepts.

SIDEBAR 7.7

Supporting the Development of Orientation Skills

Teachers of students with visual impairments can support the development of orientation skills in the following ways:

- Use descriptive language for the location of important landmarks or safety features in the environment. For example, quickly describe the location of cabinets left open at head-level or ask the student to be your tour guide on campus, pointing out the landmarks that she uses to get from one class to another. Make a note for the O&M specialist to see if those are the same landmarks that have been taught.
- Encourage the use of orientation skills by sending the student on errands to familiar parts of campus for independent practice.
- Provide appropriate adaptations of instructional materials for general education teachers to ensure access to curriculum that addresses simple through complex aspects of orientation. For example, provide the general education teacher with a tactile compass and an accessible GPS system she can show the class to enhance the students' understanding of navigation systems used by early explorers and, today, by everyone from parents to astronauts.
- Coordinate an orientation unit with the O&M specialist to prepare in advance for disaster drills on campus. Despite the fact that classes evacuate together, there will be instances when students are separated—because they are returning from another location or are using the restroom, for example—and they need to be aware of evacuation routes from appropriate places.

Interpersonal Skills

Interpersonal skills cut across all areas of the academic core curriculum and ECC areas, including orientation and mobility (as discussed in detail in Chapter 9). O&M lessons can provide an opportunity to practice communication and other interpersonal skills in real-world situations (for example, asking a store clerk for assistance to find an appropriate greeting card and remembering the social graces that should accompany that request, such as "please" and "thank you"). O&M also presents its own set of demands on interpersonal skills, such as asking for directions when lost, communicating with drivers for bus and paratransit systems, and obtaining information in a mall, to name just a few. The entire educational team, families included, has to address these skills when the need arises. Teachers of students with visual impairments can work with O&M specialists on strategies to promote improved interpersonal skills in their students that can be applied in daily and weekly situations—both fabricated (sending the student to the office to ask for an absence log or other task) and natural (asking for directions when disoriented along a route).

Interpersonal skills include, but are not limited to, the ability to:

- request directions and assistance during a route
- use the telephone or other means, such as the Internet, to obtain information for transportation schedules and routes, destination locations, or emergency situations
- arrange for rides or other travel arrangements
- interact with the public, such as bus drivers or store clerks, to solicit information or to provide information about one's visual impairment or destination
- deal with unwanted or improperly given assistance from familiar and unfamiliar people, as when using the Hines Break technique to politely but assertively remove the unwanted grasp of a stranger who has decided to escort the student across the street

As students build competence in using interpersonal communication skills in controlled environments, such as a small school campus, they will hopefully gain confidence in using similar skills in less familiar environments. Teachers of students with visual impairments play an essential role in promoting interpersonal skill development in their students through both direct instruction and daily reinforcement. For example, a young child learning how to rest her cane against a wall in the cafeteria could become frustrated by well-intentioned adults who grab the cane when it begins to fall. The teacher can teach the student how to graciously decline assistance, advocate for the student to practice independently, and communicate with the O&M specialist to make sure everyone on the team is informed of the issue. Grown-ups and other children love to be helpful and can often be found opening doors, carrying chairs, pushing the water fountain button, and doing many other tasks that reinforce learned helplessness (see Chapter 9) in the student who is visually impaired. The teacher of students with visual impairments can help the student develop the necessary communication skills by role-playing similar situations until the student gains the confidence to advocate more independently. Other ideas for supporting the development of interpersonal skills related to O&M can be found in Sidebar 7.8.

Decision-Making Skills

As children mature, they are faced with increasing opportunities to make decisions in their lives, such as what to play with, what to eat for a snack, which path to take to get to math class, what friends to sit with at lunchtime, whether or not to complete homework, whether or not to follow school or house rules, what college to apply to, and so on. As children make decisions, they are then faced with the consequences of each choice—a good grade for completing homework or a poorer grade for not completing it, for example.

O&M presents numerous opportunities for students who are visually impaired to make decisions. Route plans, technique selections, whether or not to cross a given intersection, whom to ask for assistance, from whom to accept assistance, whether or not to identify oneself as having a visual impairment, which bus to take, and what time to leave the house are just a few of the types of decisions that may need to be made as part of the process of getting from one place to another. Some decisions have high stakes in that they involve factors of safety, whereas others are just a matter of personal choice. Teachers of students with visual impairments also provide students with opportunities for making choices within their school, classroom, and learning environments. Each choice a student makes presents a further opportunity for reflection on the correctness and consequences of the student's selection and, hopefully, informs future choices.

Decision-making skills in O&M include the ability to:

- choose appropriate clothing and gear for various travel situations
- choose among route travel options
- estimate the amount of time needed to travel between locations, including allowances for the early or late arrival of public transportation
- select an appropriate mode of travel based on perceived advantages and disadvantages
- choose to solicit or not solicit information from others
- decide whether or not to accept unsolicited assistance from another person
- alter travel plans due to inclement weather, construction, unexpected circumstances, or another reason
- create and use emergency back-up plans (for example, keeping important phone numbers in a cell phone contact list in case one is separated from the O&M specialist during a bus lesson) (Wall Emerson & Corn, 2006)

Teachers of students with visual impairments can help students with the decision-making process by providing

SIDEBAR 7.8

Supporting the Development of Interpersonal Skills

Teachers of students with visual impairments can support the development of interpersonal skills in the following ways:

- Encourage use of interpersonal skills in the classroom and on the school campus with both classmates and adults. For example:
    - for younger students, establish a routine for greeting the O&M specialist and for letting the classroom teacher know that they will be leaving class for a lesson
    - for older students, arrange for some group study sessions during the free period
    - have older students make telephone inquiries for a community resource of interest such as the YMCA programs or schedule
- Plan activities that require communication skills with peers and other adults at school. For example, for a student who has additional disabilities and uses an augmentative communication system, have the student use it to inform classmates about which area of the playground he or she would like to go to.
- With the O&M specialist, coordinate interpersonal skills units that will promote communication in the community. For example, plan a culminating shopping trip that will bring together basic math skills for budgeting expenditures and the need for asking for assistance in locating some specific items in the store, such as a greeting card, with both orientation and mobility skills.

them with a model that is age-appropriate and can readily be used across a variety of life situations. For example, prior to making an important decision, a simple list of pros and cons can be made (brailled, written, or recorded) and saved as a record. After the results of the decision have been realized—whether they were positive, negative, or a combination of the two—the teacher and student can review the list, identify any areas that were not considered in the decision making process, and perhaps do a self-rating of the decision and changes that might occur in the future as a result.

Ideas that can be used by teachers to support the development of decision-making skills can be found in Sidebar 7.9. Much like the development of interpersonal skills, which is clearly embedded across all core academic areas, decision-making skills also need to be addressed by the educational team to ensure that opportunities to learn, practice, and assess decision-making abilities are offered on a daily and weekly basis throughout the school year.

SIDEBAR 7.9

Supporting the Development of Decision-Making Skills

Teachers of students with visual impairments can support the development of decision-making skills in the following ways:

- Encourage students to participate in decisions about their own needs and goals in advance of IEP and transition planning meetings. For example, together with the O&M specialist, present the student with a menu of choices for IEP goals and transition planning goals; together, rank order those goals in terms of which are considered most important; compare and discuss the results together, finding commonalities and differences.
- Coordinate units on decision-making skills with the O&M specialist. For example:
  - after establishing several important transition goals with the educational team, provide the student with the steps that need to be done to complete one of the goals and ask the student to place those steps in the most logical order possible
  - identify which steps can be done at home, which can be done in class, and which can be done during O&M lessons
  - work with the O&M specialist to complete the steps identified for O&M lessons
  - meet together after all of the steps are completed to reflect on the process, what was learned, and how it might affect future planning

ASSESSMENT OF ORIENTATION AND MOBILITY

General assessment strategies are outlined in Chapter 3 and can be helpful in assisting teachers to assess students' strengths and identify areas for targeted instruction. Because of the specialized knowledge required to evaluate a student's needs for O&M training and subsequently to make appropriate recommendations concerning the student's educational programming and goals in this area, a good starting principle for O&M assessment is to ensure that a certified O&M specialist conducts the assessment. If the responsibility for screening and making referrals of students who are visually impaired is given to other professionals—such as teachers of students with visual impairments or general special education teachers—the assessors may lack awareness of the full scope of O&M instruction and the specific skills from which students may benefit, particularly when students have low vision or additional disabilities. Without the involvement of an O&M specialist in the assessment process, these students may not receive the O&M services they need (Fazzi & Naimy, 2010).

All students with visual impairments should receive an initial O&M assessment from an O&M specialist, at minimum upon referral for special education services, that addresses each of the O&M component areas identified earlier in this chapter. O&M specialists use a combination of the following approaches to assess a student's O&M abilities (for more details, see Bina, Naimy, Fazzi & Crouse, 2010; Jacobson, 2013):

- review of records
- interviews with student and key members of the educational team, including parents and general educators, to determine the student's level of O&M engagement in the home and priorities for and concerns about navigating in school
- interview with the teacher of students with visual impairments to determine any areas of concern and to share other assessment results
- natural observations in the school environment (such as the classroom, playground, and cafeteria)

to assess the student's confidence with O&M skills and to see how and if O&M tools are being used

- route travel assessment to determine the student's confidence and accuracy in traveling routes to familiar (or, for a more advanced traveler, unfamiliar) locations
- other assessment activities, such as playing a game of Simon Says to see how well the child can identify body parts, execute movements, and follow multiple-step directions; or asking the student to move toy cars on a tactile diagram of an intersection to assess the student's understanding of concepts such as intersection and traffic flow

It is important for the teacher of students with visual impairments to collaborate in the assessment with the O&M specialist by sharing information based on observing and working with the student, as well as from the student's functional vision assessment, learning media assessment, and other related activities. In addition, the teacher can make the importance of O&M known to other members of the educational team and work closely with the O&M specialist to make sure that the student is screened or assessed, as needed. While it is ideal for O&M specialists to assess all students with visual impairments to ascertain their individualized need, teachers of students with visual impairments also play a crucial role in alerting O&M specialists when there are significant changes in students' functional performance or travel demands so that O&M specialists can reassess their instructional needs.

Opinion varies about the appropriate frequency of O&M assessments for school-age students with visual impairments (Wall Emerson & Corn, 2006), but at a minimum, a comprehensive assessment should be completed every three years. It is recommended that assessments of progress on IEP goals and consideration of the need for future goals in the area of O&M take place annually or more frequently, depending on the scheduling of the student's annual IEP meeting. Additionally, formal assessments should be conducted whenever a student experiences a significant change in vision, hearing, or other physical or sensory ability, or moves to a different travel environment—transferring from elementary to middle school, for instance—since new skills may be required. Less formal assessments for progress monitoring should be made frequently and are also important to determine instructional effectiveness.

GENERAL CONSIDERATIONS FOR REINFORCING O&M SKILLS

Instruction in the components of the O&M area is typically provided directly by the O&M specialist. The O&M specialist provides instruction in the most appropriate learning environment for the child and for the skills being taught. For example, the specialist may work directly in the home of a young child to support the child's early exploration and purposeful movement. The school campus provides a rich environment for learning beginning O&M concepts, skills, and routes. However, for most students, it is imperative that O&M specialists spend a majority of the time teaching O&M lessons in community environments, where students can learn and apply foundational and advanced skills and concepts in real-life situations. While some initial concepts and skills can conceivably be introduced on a school campus, street-crossing lessons, for example, cannot be simulated and must be taught at actual intersections. Nevertheless, certain O&M skills are commonly reinforced by families at home and in the community and by teachers of students with visual impairments in the school environment, as the examples provided throughout this chapter show.

Although the O&M area of the ECC has a clearly defined curriculum and a specialized service provider (for sample O&M skill and curriculum guides, see Pogrund et al., 1995; Hill & Ponder, 1976; Jacobson, 2013; LaGrow & Weesies, 1994), it is not taught in isolation from the other areas of the ECC or in isolation from the total school experience. In fact, O&M practice and learning happen throughout each and every day, whenever students move from place to place or register awareness of their surroundings, at home, at school, and beyond. O&M specialists work closely with teachers of students with visual impairments, families, and other professionals to ensure that students are supported in their efforts to develop independent travel skills that will serve them throughout their lifetimes.

ROLE OF THE TEACHER OF STUDENTS WITH VISUAL IMPAIRMENTS

The role of teachers of students with visual impairments in orientation and mobility may vary depending on whether or not they are also trained as O&M specialists.

Those professionals with greater training and expertise may be more likely to assume an active role in supporting the development of O&M skills than the teacher who has only a basic awareness of the skills and techniques of the profession. The main difference in role is typically based on how the teaching assignments for dually-trained professionals are made. Some dually-trained professionals, either by choice or by personnel assignment by the school or district, may be assigned to serve one or the other role—teacher of students with visual impairments or O&M specialist—with all or some of the students on their caseload. In such instances, the role of the teacher of students with visual impairments is to play a supporting role to the O&M specialist. Other dually-trained professionals are assigned to provide both services—teacher and O&M specialist—to the same students on their caseloads. This combined role requires a different set of skills to ensure that students are getting what they need in all areas of the core and ECC.

The Teacher's Role in Promoting the Development of Concepts and Skills

As noted earlier, there are many ways that the teacher of students with visual impairments can support the development of concepts and skills related to orientation and mobility. For teachers who are not dually trained or certified as O&M specialists, it is important that they include the following in their support of O&M skills development:

- develop an awareness of the curriculum that their students will be learning
- collaborate with O&M specialists to provide a cohesive assessment and set of interrelated curricula
- communicate and coordinate with O&M specialists to monitor and reinforce important O&M skills and concepts in their students

Awareness of O&M Curriculum

IEP meetings provide an important opportunity to examine the yearly O&M goals that will be addressed for each student, but since O&M is so highly individualized, perhaps the best approach to understanding the curriculum for a given group of students is to discuss the goals and approaches with the O&M specialist on a regular basis, staying informed about the specific instructional units that are being addressed throughout the school year.

Developing a general awareness of the curriculum or units of instruction allows the teacher of students with visual impairments to take a focused interest in students' progress in O&M, by asking specific questions or listening intently to descriptions of routes traveled or community experiences. It is helpful for students to know that others take a genuine interest in their O&M successes in much the same way that they would receive recognition for participating in a school spelling bee. Such awareness also encourages teachers to think of ways of relating O&M activities to the academic core and ECC. (See the Learning Activities section at the end of this chapter for examples of such activities.) Relating learning in one subject or area with another serves to strengthen "big picture" learning—how one skill supports another or how one concept can serve as a bridge to learning a new one.

Collaboration with the O&M Specialist

Although virtually all teachers' daily and weekly schedules are hectic, whether they are teaching in a resource room, special school, or in an itinerant setting, time planned for collaboration between the teacher of students with visual impairments and the O&M specialist is time well spent. Together, these professionals can plan a coordinated approach and optimum sequence for introducing and reinforcing complementary skills and concepts to maximize the efficiency and effectiveness of both assessment and instruction. For example, after reviewing the sequence of several key O&M instructional units, the teacher of students with visual impairments might choose to switch two planned lessons in self-determination to coincide with O&M lessons that will take place at a park near the community library. Similarly, through collaborative planning the two professionals can decide the best time and sequence for training in the use of the monocular telescope, determine who will introduce the skills, and plan how the skills will be reinforced throughout the upcoming weeks. (See Sidebar 7.10 for ideas for finding time for collaborative planning between the teacher and the O&M specialist.)

Another skill that O&M specialists teach their students is room familiarization. Ideally, an O&M specialist would familiarize students to their classrooms and other areas to be used on the school campus. Collaborating with the O&M specialist will allow the teacher of students with visual impairments to reinforce these skills if, for example, the student has difficulty remembering certain locations or requires more repetition. Some teachers may need to familiarize their students to a

SIDEBAR 7.10

Ensuring Collaborative Planning Time

Teachers of students with visual impairments can take several steps to ensure that there is adequate time for collaborative planning with the O&M specialist, including the following:

- Work together at the beginning of the year, if both professionals are itinerant, to develop schedules for working with students, to find time to coordinate combined lessons and to ensure that there is a shared time for meeting with one another on at least a monthly basis.
- For those who have a resource room or self-contained classroom, make sure that the O&M specialist has the daily schedule for their shared students.
- Familiarize the O&M specialist with an overview of the academic content that will be covered during the upcoming grade level, to provide a context for collaborative planning during the year.
- Ensure that the O&M specialist has a list of ECC goals for each student he or she will be working with.
- Obtain a list of similar goals for O&M and ask which concepts and skills can be reinforced within the classroom or school day and how that can be done most effectively.

Each of these steps, if undertaken at the beginning of the school year, can promote better planning, encourage collaborative brainstorming of ideas, and promote reinforcement of knowledge and skills that will ultimately enhance the student's learning.

basic classroom or other area when the O&M specialist is not available. Teachers who have previously worked with the O&M specialist on these skills will be more effective in these situations.

Collaborative decisions can also be made about the most effective instructional approaches, behavior supports, or reinforcement strategies. This coordination will foster more consistency in instruction, which is one of the keys to positive behavior change.

Communication and Coordination

A system for communication can be put in place to make sure that student progress in areas of O&M is monitored in home, school, and community environments by families, teachers, and O&M specialists. When expectations for a student's performance are established—for example, how often a student should be expected to travel independently to and from a class—professionals can clearly communicate with and support one another and the student in achieving those goals. The teacher of students with visual impairments can support good cane skills by maintaining a tactile progress chart in her classroom. The O&M specialist can work with the student to log that progress and the teacher can review weekly progress on the chart, reinforcing not only development of O&M skills, but also math and graphing skills and concepts.

The Role of the Teacher with Dual Certification

Many teachers of students with visual impairments may also be trained as O&M specialists and have attained dual certification. When these teachers are assigned dual roles for the same students, their role is markedly different from that just described. Professionals who are dually certified as teachers and specialists assume complete primary responsibility for both roles with each student they serve, including all assessments, instructional planning, delivery, and monitoring as an O&M specialist and as a teacher of students with visual impairments. For example, a dually-trained professional might be responsible for the following areas of instruction and support for one student:

- literary braille and support of literacy instruction
- Nemeth code and support of math instruction
- adaptation of instructional materials for the general education science class
- preparation of testing materials for the general education social studies class
- cane skills, campus orientation, and residential travel
- all other areas of the expanded core curriculum

Frequently, these professionals also serve as case managers and are responsible for organizing and managing the IEP process and other associated paperwork for the student.

It is imperative that these professionals work to ensure that their students receive the full complement of O&M instruction, in addition to everything else they need to provide as a teacher of students with visual impairments, as determined by individualized assessment and designated in the IEP. It can be challenging to juggle so many sets of goals. It is crucial that dually-certified professionals advocate for a manageable caseload in order to provide both services to the extent required and to have the time to effectively implement the IEP goals.

Dually-certified professionals need to be creative in designing programs that are complimentary to one another. For example, lessons conducted on school campuses to support academics can incorporate a review of route travel. O&M lessons in the community can incorporate braille reading skills for maps, written instructions, or a treasure hunt code. While separate instructional time must be dedicated to each area to ensure adequate coverage and student progress, dually-certified professionals serving in both roles are encouraged to work to ensure that there is maximum reinforcement for all areas of the academic and expanded core.

Activities for Reinforcing O&M and Other Curriculum Areas

The following list provides sample activities for dually-certified service providers or for teachers of students with visual impairments and O&M specialists working together to simultaneously reinforce core academic areas and O&M and other ECC areas across disciplines. (Additional sample activities that can be used to address O&M and other ECC areas appear at the end of this chapter.)

- Work on writing skills (academic core skill) by having students outline a route in the neighborhood and develop details to add, such as sensory information found along the way and other descriptive details (O&M); nouns, verbs, adjectives, and adverbs can be identified within the completed writing sample (academic core); and the writing sample proofread for braille errors (compensatory access).
- Plan a reception for parents at a school open house in which families are invited to see samples of student work and meet with teachers. Activities can include:
  - develop a menu (independent living)
  - list the menu items, ingredients needed, and estimated prices using the market advertisement page viewed with a video magnifier (academic core, independent living, and sensory efficiency)
  - plan a trip to the nearby market (O&M)
  - travel to the market and use a monocular to locate menu items based on aisle signage (sensory efficiency and O&M)
  - purchase items and use math skills to verify the correct change (academic core and independent living)
  - prepare the items for the open house (independent living)
- Have a student create a term paper and presentation on the history of the neighboring community (compensatory skills and academic core), and incorporate the following tasks:
  - travel to the community library to obtain materials and photographs of the community 50 years ago (O&M, academic core, compensatory access, and social interaction)
  - travel to the same locations that were photographed 50 years ago and determine the differences in architecture and location of key businesses (O&M)
  - gather business cards and brochures for presentation and take new photos of the same areas (O&M and social interaction)
  - write narrative for report (academic core, assistive technology)
  - prepare presentation (academic core, assistive technology, social interaction, and compensatory skills)

Ideas such as these can be embedded and reinforced in instruction across disciplines by a dually-certified professional or when a teacher of students with visual impairments is working collaboratively with an O&M specialist. The added advantage when two separate professionals provide instruction in their distinct service areas is greater flexibility and time for lessons. However, additional time is required for collaborative planning to develop rich instructional units to reinforce content knowledge and skills across disciplines.

SUGGESTIONS FOR WORKING WITH PARENTS

Parents and other family members are the first teachers of O&M. As children gain in both motor and cognitive skills, parents' expectations for independent movement are very important for students who are beginning O&M. High expectations for movement and exploration lead to increased opportunities for practicing movement and encouragement for exploring in the home. Each opportunity then can become a step to another level of engagement with people and things in the environment.

Teachers of students with visual impairments can encourage families to support the development of O&M skills and concepts in the following ways:

- Provide young children with a consistent and secure base of support from which to explore the surroundings and check back for encouragement, as in the following example:

A young child who has low vision keeps one hand on his mother's knee and reaches forward with the free hand to explore the furry dog nearby, but only reaches part way before looking at his mother for approval. Seeing no apprehension, the child continues on to pat the dog.

- Bring attention to interesting sensory information by talking about it. For example, parents can talk about the feeling of the breeze on the child's face and touch the child's cheek in the same location.
- Practice naming and locating major body parts during natural routine activities, such as diapering, bathing, dressing, and feeding.
- Practice moving the child's body parts during play routines, such as helping young children move their hands to cover their eyes during peek-a-boo.
- Play with dolls and stuffed animals together with the child to identify body parts, and, later, to work on simple dressing and figuring out which dolls have moving body parts, such as noticing that a particular doll is not able to bend her elbow.
- Practice naming and locating more detailed body parts with slightly older children as part of a game like Simon Says.
- Encourage movement activities and adapt games. For example, the game Twister can be adapted by placing tactile markings around the circles and replacing colors with textures that are easily recognized to make bending, twisting, and playing with others highly motivating.
- Expect that children will participate in household chores (and assist them in doing so), such as sorting laundry, picking up clothes, and dusting clear areas to help with orientation in the home, use of more refined motor skills, and increased spatial and environmental concepts.
- Spend time teaching children to use playground equipment, such as swings, climbing bars, and see-saws, to encourage development of balance, strength, and coordination that will be useful in later motor and O&M tasks and skills.
- Encourage children who are cane users to use their cane in the neighborhood and community.
- Plan family outings using various forms of public transportation to increase their child's environmental awareness and community travel experiences.
- Be receptive to communication with the O&M specialist and teacher of students with visual impairments to ensure that all are aware of successes and challenges in the area of O&M at home, at school, and in the community.

Parents and other family members are a vital part of the educational team and can play an active role in

L. Penny Rosenblum

This child pushing the stop request signal on a bus is learning about public transportation early on.

reinforcing O&M skills and concepts. With increased communication, achieved through a weekly or monthly telephone call, e-mail, or other written communication, families can participate in the individualized O&M program for their child, as in the following examples:

- encouraging the use of the long cane, adapted mobility device, low vision device, or orientation tool at home or while in the community
- reinforcing spatial and environmental concepts, such as those found at the market or community park
- accessing community programs for young children, such as "mommy and me" classes, gymnastics, yoga, martial arts, dance, swimming, and so on
- planning for family outings that will include the use of orientation and mobility skills, such as a drive to a relative's house while using a navigation system (GPS) in the car and talking about what the instructions mean, or to a museum that allows for cane use and/or hands-on exploration

SUMMARY

Orientation and mobility is a key area of the ECC for students with visual impairments, but it takes an "O&M village" to realize greater success and improve students' achievement. In collaboration with each other and the rest of the educational team, the teacher of students with visual impairments and the O&M specialist need to coordinate assessments and plan for instruction that not only meets O&M goals for the IEP, but also supports other areas of the academic core and ECC. They can also emphasize to families and other educational team members that if students are to develop the highest possible level of independence, high expectations need to be reinforced and opportunities to apply these skills need to be provided at home and in the community beyond formal weekly O&M lessons. In this way, teachers and O&M specialists can ensure that students with visual impairments receive the essential O&M instruction they require, practice O&M skills in a variety of environments on an ongoing basis, and apply these skills not only in school, but also in the greater community—and far into the future in their college, work, and living environments.

REFERENCES

Bina, M. J., Naimy, B. J., Fazzi, D. L., & Crouse, R. J. (2010). Administration, assessment, and program planning for orientation and mobility services. In W. R. Wiener, R. L. Welsh, and B. B. Blasch (Eds.), *Foundations of orientation and mobility: Vol. I. History and theory* (3rd ed., pp. 389–434). New York: AFB Press.

Fazzi, D. L., & Naimy, B. J. (2010). Orientation and mobility services for children and youths with low vision. In A. L. Corn and J. N. Erin (Eds.), *Foundations of low vision: Clinical and functional perspectives* (2nd ed., pp. 655–726). New York: AFB Press.

Fazzi, D. L., & Naimy, B. J. (2010). Teaching orientation and mobility to school-age children. In W. R. Wiener, R. L. Welsh, and B. B. Blasch (Eds.), *Foundations of orientation and mobility: Vol. II. Instructional strategies and practical applications* (3rd ed., pp. 208–263). New York: AFB Press.

Fazzi, D. L., & Petersmeyer, B. A. (2001). *Imagining the possibilities: Creative approaches to orientation and mobility instruction for persons who are visually impaired.* New York: AFB Press.

Ferrell, K. A. (2011). *Reach out and teach: Helping your young child who is visually impaired learn and grow.* New York: AFB Press.

Hill, E. W., & Ponder, P. (1976). *Orientation and mobility techniques: A guide for the practitioner.* New York: American Foundation for the Blind.

Jacobson, W. H. (2013). *The art and science of teaching orientation and mobility to persons with visual impairments* (2nd ed.). New York: AFB Press.

LaGrow, S. & Weesies, M. (1994). *Orientation and mobility: Techniques for independence.* Palmerston North, New Zealand: The Dunmore Press.

Pogrund, R. L., & Fazzi, D. L. (Eds.). (2002). *Early focus: Working with young children who are blind or visually impaired and their families* (2nd ed.). New York: AFB Press.

Pogrund, R. L., Healy, G., Jones, K., Levack, N., Martin-Curry, S., Martinex, C., et al. (1995). *Teaching age-appropriate purposeful skills: An orientation and mobility curriculum for students with visual impairments.* Austin: Texas School for the Blind and Visually Impaired.

Wall Emerson, R. S., & Corn, A. L. (2006). Orientation and mobility content for children and youths: A Delphi approach pilot study. *Journal of Visual Impairment & Blindness, 100*(6), 331–342.

Orientation and Mobility Resources

This section provides resources such as assessment tools, publications, and instructional materials for teaching orientation and mobility skills. For additional resources that relate to the expanded core curriculum in general, see the Resources section at the end of this book.

ASSESSMENT TOOLS

Hill Performance Test of Selected Positional Concepts

POPULATION/AGE LEVEL: 6–10 years

SOURCE: Hill, E. (1981). *The Hill performance test of selected positional concepts.* Wood Dale, IL: Stoelting Co.

TAPS—Comprehensive Initial and Ongoing Evaluation

POPULATION/AGE LEVEL: 3–21 years

SOURCE: Pogrund, R. L., Sewell, D., Anderson, H., Calaci, L., Cowart, M. F., Gonzalez, C., Marsh, R. A. & Roberson-Smith, R. (2012). TAPS—*Teaching age-appropriate purposeful skills: An orientation & mobility curriculum for students with visual impairments* (3rd ed.). Austin: Texas School for the Blind and Visually Impaired.

PUBLICATIONS

Brody, J., & Webber, L. (1994). *Let's eat: Feeding a child with a visual impairment.* Los Angeles: Blind Childrens Center.

Chen, D., & Dote-Kwan, J. (1995). *Starting points: Instructional practices for young children whose multiple disabilities include visual impairment.* Los Angeles: Blind Childrens Center.

Chen, D., & McCann, M. (1993). *Selecting a program: A guide for parents of infants and preschoolers with visual impairments.* Los Angeles: Blind Childrens Center.

Chernus-Mansfield, N., Hayashi, D., Horn, M., & Kekelis, L. (1986). *Heart to heart: Parents of children who are blind and partially sighted talk about their feelings.* Los Angeles: Blind Childrens Center.

Chernus-Mansfield, N., Hayashi, D., & Kekelis, L. (1985). *Talk to me II: A sequel to talk to me.* Los Angeles: Blind Childrens Center.

Chernus-Mansfield, N., & Kekelis, L. (1984). *Talk to me: A language guide for parents of children who are visually impaired.* Los Angeles: Blind Childrens Center.

Ferrell, K. A. (2011). *Reach out and teach: Helping your child who is visually impaired learn and grow.* New York: AFB Press.

Hill, E. W., & Ponder, P. (1976). *Orientation and mobility techniques: A guide for the practitioners.* New York: AFB Press.

Hug, D., Chernus-Mansfield, N., & Hayashi, D. (1987). *Move with me: A parents' guide to movement development for visually impaired babies.* Los Angeles: Blind Childrens Center.

Jacobson, W. H. (2013). *The art and science of teaching orientation and mobility to persons with visual impairments* (2nd ed.). New York: AFB Press.

LaPrelle, L. L. (1996). *Standing on my own two feet: A step-by-step guide to designing and constructing simple, individually tailored adaptive mobility devices for preschool-age children who are visually impaired.* Los Angeles: Blind Childrens Center.

Pediatric visual diagnostic fact sheet. (2003). San Francisco: Blind Babies Foundation.

Pogrund, R. L., & Fazzi, D. L. (Eds.). (2002). *Early focus: Working with young children who are blind or visually impaired and their families* (2nd ed.). New York: AFB Press.

Pogrund, R. L., Sewell, D., Anderson, H., Calaci, L., Cowart, M. F., Gonzalez, C., Marsh, R. A. & Roberson-Smith, R. (2012). TAPS—*Teaching age-appropriate purposeful skills; An orientation & mobility curriculum for students with visual impairments* (3rd ed.). Austin: Texas School for the Blind and Visually Impaired.

Recchia, S. L. (1987). *Learning to play: Common concerns for the visually impaired preschool child.* Los Angeles: Blind Childrens Center.

Simmons, S. S., & O'Mara Maida, S. (1992). *Reaching, crawling, walking . . . let's get moving.* Los Angeles: Blind Childrens Center.

Wiener, W. R., Welsh, R. L., & Blasch, B. B. (Eds.). (2010). *Foundations of orientation and mobility* (3rd ed.). New York: AFB Press.

SOURCES OF PRODUCTS

The following companies distribute canes, tips, accessories, independent living aids, and a variety of O&M

products for people who are visually impaired and instructional tools for orientation and mobility teachers.

Advantage Canes
Revolution Enterprises, Inc.
12170 Dearborn Place
Poway, CA 92064
(800) 382-5132 or (858) 679-5785
Fax: (858) 679-5788
www.advantage-canes.com

AmbuTech
34 DeBaets Street
Winnipeg, MB R2J 3S9
Canada
(800) 561-3340
Fax: (800) 267-5059
orders@ambutech.com
www.ambutech.com

American Printing House for the Blind
1839 Frankfort Avenue
PO Box 6085
Louisville, KY 40206-0085
(502) 895-2405 or (800) 223-1839
Fax: (502) 899-2274
www.aph.org
info@aph.org

Independent Living Aids
200 Robbins Lane
Jericho, NY 11753
(800) 537-2118 or (855) 746-7452
Fax: (516) 937-3906
www.independentliving.com

LS&S, LLC
145 River Rock Drive
Buffalo, NY 14207
(800) 468-4789 or (716) 348-3500
Fax: (877) 498-1482
www.lssproducts.com/contact

Maxi-Aids
42 Executive Boulevard
Farmingdale, NY 11735
(800) 522-6294 or (631) 752-0521
Fax: (631) 752-0689
TTY: (631) 752-0738
www.maxiaids.com/store/default.asp

Orientation and Mobility Learning Activities

Contributed by Robyn Herrera, Susan Glaser, and Diane L. Fazzi

These sample learning activities are presented as examples of activities that teachers can create to work on several ECC skills at once with their students. Activities that help teach O&M skills can also be found in other chapters. The activities presented, like all instruction, need to be considered and modified to address the needs of individual students—such as those who are braille readers, have low vision, or have additional disabilities—with adaptations for appropriate media and the physical and other capabilities of the student.

Learning Activity: Think Inside the Box

Primary ECC Area: Orientation & Mobility **Components:** Spatial concepts, mobility skills, orientation skills
Grades: Pre-K, kindergarten

Other ECC Areas

- Social interaction
- Compensatory access
- Recreation and leisure

Goal: The student will participate in play and pretend play activities involving a cardboard box.

Key Tasks/Concepts

The student will interact with the box in various ways, such as:

- Open and close the flaps of the box
- Climb in and out of the box
- Identify the top, bottom, and sides of the box
- Hide inside the box with the flaps closed
- Turn the box on its side
- Turn the box upside down
- Pretend to drive the box like a car
- Pretend to open and close the "doors" of the box as if it were a house

Description

Carefully selected, age-appropriate, and often educational toys are sometimes not the most treasured items after a young child's birthday party is over. A child's imagination applied to a box can easily outperform the bells and whistles of a manufactured toy's design. Children with typical vision often pretend that empty boxes are something else—a car, house, boat, wagon, or fort, for example—but a child who is visually impaired who has not been exposed to many of these other things may not do the same. With this activity, the teacher of students with visual impairments can teach pretend play with a simple cardboard box while reinforcing numerous O&M concepts.

Find a box that is big enough for the student to completely fit inside of, but not so big that the student cannot touch all the sides with her arms outstretched. Show the student the closed box and how to open the flaps. Explore the outside of the box, walk around it, pick it up (is it heavy or light?), and open and close the flaps several times. As the student is exploring, use descriptive language to explain what each part is and how it works. For example, "The flaps of the box open and close. There are four flaps on the top of the box. Let's count them." Start with all the flaps open and, as each is counted, close it.

(continued on next page)

After the box is explored from the outside, use positional concepts to describe the student's position in relation to the box and start changing that position; for example: "You are next to the box. Now it's time to climb inside the box." Assist the student, if necessary at first, to put each hand on opposite sides of the box while climbing in. Have the student stand up, turn around, sit down. If the student has light perception, ask what will happen if the flaps are closed. Show the student how to close the flaps while inside (so as not to take away the student's control), and then pop out of the box. Turn the box around, have the student get out of the box, and help re-orient the student or explain how the direction changed.

Suggest games with the box, such as pretending it is a car. If the student is not familiar with a car other than a car seat, explore a real car first. Using the car/box, suggest the student create a steering wheel and horn. Tactile materials can be added to make wheels, doors, a windshield, radio, etc. Ask the student to call out directions (left, right, reverse) and push the car box to make it "go." Visit various sections of the classroom pushing the car/box and allowing the student to get in and out of it. Run some pretend errands in the car/box.

When the fun of the car/box wears off, the bottom of the box can be opened to create a tunnel. The concept of *tunnel* may need to be introduced, but can lead to more games and fun with the box. Additional boxes can be added to the tunnel, which will require crawling or squatting down and waddling to get to the other side.

The box or a description of the types of activities to do with a similar box can be sent home. Parents of young children who are blind or have low vision often look for special toys or ideas for games to play at home, but some toys do not have to be specialized at all.

Instructional Materials and Supplies Needed

- A box big enough to fit a young child
- Tactile arts and crafts supplies to decorate the car/box, such as paper or plastic plates, cups, textured paper, felt, and glue

Settings

Home, preschool, or daycare environment

Duration/Timing

15–20 minutes

Evaluation

This type of chart can be used to monitor the student's acquisition of skills.

Skill	Date	Date	Date	Date
Opens flaps				
Closes flaps				
Climbs in box				
Climbs out of box				
Uses box for pretend play				
Crawls or creeps through tunnel				
Turns box upside down				
Turns box on its side				

Key:

R = Receptive (student performs skill when asked)

E = Expressive (student names skill/concept as it is being done)

Learning Activity: O&M Story Time

Primary ECC Area: Orientation & Mobility
Grades: K–2, students with multiple disabilities

Components: Orientation skills, environmental concepts, spatial concepts

Other ECC Areas

- Compensatory skills

Goal: Using object cues, the student will sequence the landmarks from the story *Knuffle Bunny: A Cautionary Tale.**

Key Tasks/Concepts

The student will:

- Listen to a story entitled *Knuffle Bunny* about a young child who walks with her dad to a neighborhood Laundromat.
- Explore object cues used to represent the landmarks along the route from the story. (Depending on the student's literacy level, cards with print or braille words can be substituted for object cues.)
- Arrange the object cues in the order in which they are presented in the story.
- Tell the story back using the object cues as prompts.

Description

This literary activity can be done at home with family or at school with the teacher of students with visual impairments.

The adult reads *Knuffle Bunny*, which tells the tale of a father and young daughter who walk together to the Laundromat. They pass a series of landmarks, including a park and a school. They reverse the route to return home and the young girl realizes she has lost her favorite stuffed animal. The family returns past each of the landmarks and finds the bunny at the Laundromat.

In advance, the adult prepares object cues to represent each of the landmarks, such as: a flower for the park; a book, pencil or backpack for the school; and an empty detergent package for the Laundromat. Each item should be individually selected to help the child think of the location. The items should be prepared with a Velcro backing so they can be easily adhered to a long Velcro strip attached to the wall.

After reading through the story once or twice, present the object cues to the child and ask which place the object goes with. After introducing all of the object cues, read the story again and help the child find the correct object cue at the appropriate time in the story. Next, ask the child to remember the story and find the object that comes first, second, and so on and help her attach them to the Velcro strip in order. Help the child tell the story by moving her hand from one object cue to another, in order.

Together, remove all of the object cues and place in a bag with the story book for future readings.

(Note: The object cues represent route segments of the story, and once the child is able to place them in order consistently, she has demonstrated the cognitive ability to remember four steps of a whole route. She can try the reverse route once she is confident with the route to the Laundromat.)

Settings

Home or classroom

Instructional Materials and Supplies Needed

- Velcro to attach to the wall and to each object cue
- Object cues
- Story book
- Bag for contents

* *Knuffle Bunny: A Cautionary Tale*, by Mo Willems (New York: Hyperion Books, 2004).

(continued on next page)

Duration/Timing
20–30 minutes, depending on the attention span and interest of the child. The book takes no longer than 5 minutes to read.

Evaluation
The student can be evaluated on this activity using a rubric, such as the following, for each individual task:

Example 1
1. The child identifies all object cues.
2. The child identifies 3 of 4 object cues.
3. The child identifies 2 of 4 object cues.
4. The child identifies 1 or no object cues.

Example 2
1. The child places the object cues in the correct order (route).
2. The child places the object cues in a partially correct order.
3. The child places the object cues in random order.

Learning Activity: Mail Call

Primary ECC Area: Orientation & Mobility
Grades: K–5
Components: Environmental concepts, spatial concepts, interpersonal skills

Other ECC Areas
- Independent living
- Compensatory access
- Sensory efficiency
- Self-determination

Goal: The student will address an envelope and mail a letter at a nearby mailbox.

Key Tasks/Concepts to Include
The student will:
- Describe the function of the US Postal Service (USPS), including hours of operation and regular and specialty services available
- Identify his or her home mailing address
- Address an envelope
- Mail a letter
- Receive a letter

Description
Prior to this lesson, the teacher should have the student write a letter to his or her family.

Begin the activity by visiting the USPS website for post offices (http://www.uspspostoffices.com), and, with the student, locate the closest mailbox. Review the hours of operation and then talk about the various services provided by the USPS.

Ask the student to identify his or her home mailing address. Review the required information needed for mailing an item and how this information is laid out on the front of an envelope. Model addressing an envelope using the school's address. Have the student address two envelopes: one to the family at home and a return envelope to the student using the school and classroom in the address, so that the family can send a note back. The student can write directly on the envelopes or use an appropriate word-processing program

(continued on next page)

and printer. The student will place the previously written letter or note, along with the return envelope, into the envelope addressed to the family.

The student will travel with the O&M specialist to the closest mailbox to mail the letter. If more than one student has taken part in this activity, they can then take turns checking in the school's main office each day to see if any letters have been received at school and delivering those letters to classmates. (Teachers may also want to mail individual notes to students to make sure that each student receives a return letter, in the event that a given family is unable to follow through with the activity.)

Follow-up lessons can include sending invitations to school events such as an Open House, a Back-to-School Night, and various school plays or performances.

Settings: Classroom and home

Instructional Materials and Supplies Needed

- Computer and Internet access
- Word-processing software and printer for printing on envelopes
- Envelopes
- Stamps

Duration and Timing

- One session of 45–60 minutes for the main components of the lesson.
- The letters and notes to be sent home will need to be completed previously.
- The actual mailing of the letters will likely be completed at a subsequent time, unless the mailbox is in close proximity to the school campus.

Evaluation

The student can be evaluated on this activity using a rubric, such as the following, for each individual task:

Example 1

1. The student identifies three services provided by the USPS.
2. The student identifies two services provided by the USPS.
3. The student identifies one service provided by the USPS.

Example 2

1. The student addresses two envelopes with 100% accuracy.
2. The student addresses two envelopes with 75% accuracy.
3. The student addresses two envelopes with 50% accuracy.

Learning Activity: How Does Your Garden Grow?

Primary ECC Area: Orientation & Mobility

Components: motor skills, spatial concepts

Grades: 6–8, students with multiple disabilities

Other ECC Areas

- Independent living
- Compensatory access
- Sensory efficiency
- Recreation and leisure

Goal: The student will prepare and tend to a small garden, using spatial concepts in the layout.

(continued on next page)

Key Tasks/Concepts

The student will:

- Use a trowel for preparing soil
- Open seed or plant containers
- Plant seeds or small starter plants in well-defined rows
- Using cardinal direction points, identify locations of various plants

Description

This activity can be done in individual or small group rectangular planting boxes, or in a plot of ground on the school or home property. All students can participate with differentiated levels of support.

The teacher will need to identify a few plants (flowers, herbs, or vegetables) that grow quickly in the climate in which the student resides. If several options are available, students should be given the opportunity to select which plants they prefer to grow. Older students may be guided to search online to determine what plants are hardiest or match some other desired characteristic.

Give each student a rectangular box for planting. Ask the students to measure the length and width of the box and to apply math skills in determining the perimeter and area of the box. Have the students identify which side of their boxes will serve as the north side and place labels on the box for north, south, east, and west. Ask the student to identify the cardinal point corners, such as northwest. After reading the planting instructions, have the students predict how many rows of plants can be planted in their boxes and determine what the spacing between each plant should be.

The teacher and students can work the soil in preparation for planting the seeds or starter plants. The students will likely need assistance in learning to use the trowel to dig and turn over the soil. If working outside, the teacher will want to make sure that the ground can be worked fairly easily. When ready to plant the seeds, the teacher and students should read the directions on the seed package together, using optical devices or braille as appropriate, and follow the directions. A tactile ruler can be used to determine the correct depth to plant the seeds. The seeds should be carefully watered.

The date the seeds or starter plants were planted should be noted on a calendar or chart. At least once each week, the garden area should be checked for growth and observations noted on the chart. The students should be taught how to use tactile information to determine if the plant needs watering. Watering should be noted on the calendar or chart.

The products of the garden—herbs, flowers, or vegetables—can be harvested and shared with someone special to each student.

Expansion activities might include visiting a nursery, public garden, or farmers' market. In addition, this activity provides an opportunity to learn and use new vocabulary.

Settings

Classroom, school grounds, or home indoor or outdoor garden.

Instructional Materials and Supplies Needed

- Rectangular planter box or plot of ground
- Trowel
- Small watering can for indoor planting or larger can or hose for outdoor planting
- Seeds or starter plants—directions should be provided in braille, if needed
- Weekly chart for recording measurements
- Tactile or large-print ruler

Duration/Timing

- Up to 60 minutes for the introductory lesson. (Will vary based on student skill and size of plot.)
- 5–15 minutes weekly to check on watering needs and the weekly recording of plant growth.

(continued on next page)

Evaluation

This type of chart can be individualized in order to evaluate most relevant skills related to the introductory lesson and follow-up activities:

Task	Introductory Lesson Week 1	Follow-up Activities Week 2	Follow-up Activities Week 3	Follow-up Activities Week 4
Measures the length and width of the planter box				
Calculates the area of the planter box				
Plants seeds or starter plants in organized rows				
Identifies location of plants by cardinal direction points				
Checks soil for dampness weekly; waters as needed				
Accurately measures plant growth with ruler				
Accurately records plant growth findings on chart				

Key:

M = Mastered skill
D = Developing skill
U = Unable to perform skill

Learning Activity: Career/College Research

Primary ECC Area: Orientation & Mobility
Grades: High school

Components: Environmental concepts, orientation, decision-making

Other ECC Areas

- Assistive technology
- Social interaction
- Career skills
- Self-determination

Goal: The student will research transportation options for two local colleges and two summer employment possibilities.

Key Tasks/Concepts

The student will:

- Identify transportation available to travel to selected local college and employment options
- Compare and contrast cost, travel time, and preferences associated with transportation options
- Describe the college, employment, and transportation options explored through an oral presentation

(continued on next page)

Description

Have students do the research for a paper on transportation options for college and career possibilities using the Internet. First, each student will identify two local community or four-year colleges and two potential sites for summer employment. The students will then explore and report on transportation options for each location. The papers must compare and contrast the available transportation options with regard to cost, travel time, convenience, and personal preference.

The lesson can be introduced by asking students to brainstorm a list of any colleges that they are familiar with in the area and also summer employment options. The students can be given the details of the assignment, along with a scoring rubric. Time will be given during the initial lesson to begin some Internet searches.

Students will be asked to complete the first draft of the research paper for homework and bring the draft to class the following week for peer review and editing. By reviewing and editing each other's papers, students will learn about each other's research and have an opportunity to improve on their writing skills.

Final papers will be due the following week and students will each do a five-minute oral presentation on their findings. They should be expected to prepare note cards for the presentation.

Instructional Materials and Supplies Needed

- Access to the Internet
- Word processor and printer

Settings

School and home

Duration/Timing

- 45–60 minutes for the introductory lesson and to begin work.
- Students can work on completing the first draft at home.
- A second 45–60–minute lesson will be dedicated to time spent with peers reviewing and editing drafts.
- A third 45–60–minute lesson will include oral presentations of each student's findings.

Evaluation

The student can be evaluated using the following type of rubric:

Research Paper	Maximum Points	Score
Research and Writing		
Content		
Paper covers all of the required components	25	
Transportation comparisons are clear and logical	20	
Summary and conclusion are clearly written	10	
Grammar		
Paper is free of grammatical errors	5	
Paper is free of spelling errors	5	
Presentation		
Content		
Identifies two colleges and summer employment options	10	
Identifies and compares transportation options	10	
Oral Skills		
Presents information clearly	5	
Makes eye contact with audience	5	
Projects voice	5	
TOTAL	**100**	

CHAPTER 8

Independent Living

Julie A. Bardin

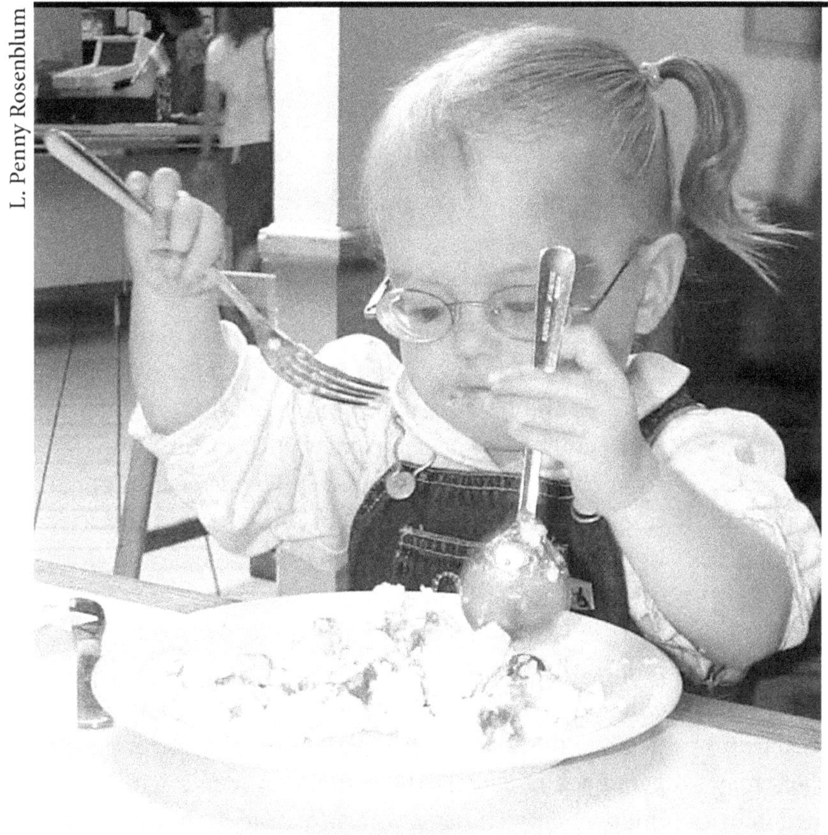

L. Penny Rosenblum

The independent living area of the expanded core curriculum (ECC) addresses activities necessary to take care of one's self, family, and home and to live as independently as possible. In essence, independent living skills enable people, whether sighted or visually impaired, to take care of themselves and others as they meet the demands of everyday life. For students to manage their lives and function in the community, both in the present and later as adults, behaviors and skills related to personal hygiene, eating, dressing, clothing care, time management, cooking, cleaning and household tasks, using the telephone, and money management are essential. Overall, mastering these skills leads to greater independence for students with visual impairments (Pogrund & Fazzi, 2002) and increases the potential for a more satisfying life. In addition, development of these skills is necessary for a student to be successful in other areas of the ECC, especially in the areas of social interaction, career education, and self determination.

In general, typically developing children learn many independent living skills through observation, pretend play, and partial participation in tasks. Through this process of incidental learning, children observe activities occurring around them and learn how they are performed without deliberate instruction. A hungry child with unimpaired vision may arrive home from school and know how to make a peanut butter and jelly sandwich because he has watched his mother take out the materials and make sandwiches many times before. Toddlers mimic self-care tasks when they find a hairbrush and try to brush their own hair. As part of this natural process of learning, adults typically reinforce children's attempts to perform these skills by praising the child and drawing attention to the child's participation or initiation of independent activities.

Many children with visual impairments frequently miss these incidental learning opportunities and as a result may not know how to initiate activities that lead to independence. As described in Chapter 1 of this book, when the child does not attempt such daily living tasks, parents often think the child isn't ready to learn the skill and so they wait to provide direct instruction, in effect lowering their expectations of their child's ability to perform activities independently. In some cases, the wait can lead to a teenager who does not wash her own hair and expects others to continue doing it for her. Such passivity or lack of initiative is referred to as "learned helplessness" (Marks, 1998). Caregivers and teachers may unintentionally promote dependency or learned helplessness in a child by waiting for the child to show interest or develop an "I can do it myself" attitude rather than deliberately helping the child to develop important skills.

Overall, independent living is key to student achievement, independence, and life success. There are many behaviors and skills in the independent living area that need to be intentionally taught to students with visual impairments. Like other ECC areas, the specific behaviors and skills targeted for development for a student will depend on the individual characteristics of each student, including physical and cognitive abilities, needs, age, health condition, and family culture and priorities. Suggested activities for teaching independent living skills, along with other aspects of the ECC, are provided throughout this chapter, as well as in the learning activities provided at the end.

COMPONENTS OF INDEPENDENT LIVING

The independent living area of the ECC can be divided into the following components:

- organization
- personal hygiene and grooming
- dressing
- clothing care
- time management
- eating
- cooking
- cleaning and general household tasks
- telephone use
- money management

Each of these components encompasses many behaviors and skills. For example, the component of cooking requires and involves obtaining, preparing, and storing food, and applying one's knowledge of nutrition. The component of personal hygiene includes bathing, hair care, dental care, gender-specific hygiene, and any activity that influences one's personal appearance and cleanliness.

The ECC area of independent living contains a diverse group of skills that students with visual impairments will need to master to achieve a level of independence, as detailed in the following sections. Although total independence is usually the goal for students with visual impairments, students who have disabilities in addition to visual impairment may need to have independent living tasks modified so that they can participate as much as possible. Such modification requires that teachers of students with visual impairments work with other team members to carefully assess a student's abilities, compare those abilities to the demands of their current and future environments, and provide instruction to increase the student's participation in those environments.

Organization

Behaviors and skills related to the component of organization include:

- storing and retrieving toys and supplies
- organizing closets, cabinets, drawers, and pantries
- developing a labeling system
- handling mail
- creating a filing system
- maintaining records, calendars, and contact lists

In order to develop success in academics and other areas of the ECC, students with visual impairments must have proficient organizational skills. These behaviors and skills transfer to efficiency at home and in the world at large. Erica can't play goal ball if she can't find her equipment; José can't use his low vision devices to do his homework if they are not where he thinks he left them; Betsy can't cook dinner if she can't locate the ingredients in her pantry; and Connor can't manage his household if he doesn't have a system for paying and filing bills. Although these examples all relate to skills and behaviors of teenagers or adults, instruction in organizational skills needs to begin at a young age. Children with vision learn incidentally that the blocks go together on the shelf, dolls and their accessories are stored together, silverware is sorted by type and kept in a drawer, and the spices are kept in a specific cabinet. Many young children with visual impairments miss this incidental information because of lack of opportunities to observe. Caregivers and teachers need to talk about where items are stored and how and why they are sorted, as well as help the child to explore organizational systems and to assist in putting items away.

Organizing Items and Objects

In order to be independent, people with visual impairments need to know where to find their possessions and other items in the environment and where to put them when they are finished with them. Relying on a parent, spouse, teacher, friend, or sibling to store, locate, and retrieve supplies fosters dependency and, in the case of a child or young person, will slow the development of these very important organizational skills. It is not difficult to begin teaching organizational skills to young children. For example, they can help retrieve and put away toys, bath supplies, eating utensils, and clothing items during daily routines. In addition, they can be expected to put items in their appropriate places when they are replaced or replenished after a shopping trip to a store.

When children begin school, they can select their clothing for the next day and lay selected items in a predetermined place. They can pack their materials in their backpacks and assist in making and packing lunches. Once children arrive at school, they can be taught how to unpack materials and where to place completed homework, signed forms, lunchboxes, and jackets. Being taught how to organize a workspace and maintain materials independently at school is also important (see Chapter 4 for more information about these organizing skills).

In order to be successful in all components of independent living, students need certain additional organizational skills, such as how to organize closets, drawers, cabinets, and pantries. Using common sense and everyday items, establishing skills in this area is not difficult. For example, upon returning from the grocery store, young children can take items out of the bags and pass them to the parent to put away while the parent describes where items are being stored. Later, allowing children to put away items themselves helps them to develop physical strength and dexterity, in addition to reinforcing organizational patterns. Several ideas for teaching organizational skills can be found in Sidebar 8.1.

People with visual impairments often have personal preferences about where to store personal items and household objects. Sometimes these preferences may be informed by physical limitations or established based on personal perceptions of efficiency. As systems of organization are established, such preferences need to be considered and honored whenever possible.

Organizing Information, Documents, and Records

In addition to organizing personal items, all individuals need to learn how to organize information in the form of both paper and electronic materials in some kind of systematic way. Doing so is an activity that relates to many areas of life. For example, on any given day a student may need to access the term paper she wrote to submit it to her teacher; a parent may need to access her child's birth certificate in order to register her for school; and a couple may need to find their financial records for a tax audit.

SIDEBAR 8.1

Developing Organizational Skills

The following are some easy activities for teachers and parents to do with a child to develop organizational skills beginning at a young age.

- Establish and maintain consistency early on. Store toys, personal items, and clothing in designated places and always return them to the same location once they are no longer needed.
- Provide verbal description of what is being done when retrieving and putting items away.
- Practice sorting items and storing similar items together.
- Use labels or symbols on multiple containers, notebooks, and folders so that students can distinguish one from the other.
- Use household items to label similarly shaped containers. For example, wrap a rubber band around the conditioner bottle to distinguish it from an identically shaped shampoo bottle.
- Expect students to participate in putting items away or filing papers into notebooks and folders.
- Show students a tidy, well-organized area such as a desk or bookshelf to explore so he or she knows what is expected.
- Have the students develop their own labeling systems and label their own items.

In order to maintain adequate records, students need to be taught how to develop systems to label, sort, and store them. In general, any system needs to have these characteristics:

- be devised by the individual who will use it
- be simple
- be expandable

In addition to creating a filing system, procedures for using the system should be established. Students also need to create plans for such tasks as regularly opening their mail and determining how to access print materials and complete paperwork tasks. Students must also learn how to decide what documents to keep, when they should be filed, and what to purge and when.

Personal Hygiene and Grooming

Personal hygiene and grooming are two of the most fundamental independent living skills a child needs to develop. Good hygiene skills are necessary for a person to stay healthy, feel confident, and be accepted socially. A person with poor hygiene and grooming may be avoided by others, may be unable to obtain a job, and may develop health problems.

Behaviors and skills related to the component of personal hygiene and grooming include:

- washing and bathing
- toileting
- caring for teeth and mouth
- caring for hair
- caring for skin
- shaving
- using deodorant
- applying makeup
- attending to general hygiene needs
- attending to gender-specific hygiene
- choosing appropriate hygiene supplies
- purchasing hygiene items

Students with visual impairments need to be taught hygiene and grooming skills in a deliberate and explicit way, and, just like students without disabilities, they need frequent opportunities to practice the skills themselves. To adhere to best practices, this instruction and practice should take place with the actual items used by the student and in the natural environment where the task typically occurs. Most of the activities related to personal hygiene and grooming require caregivers and teachers to respect the child's privacy and to show sensitivity as well as respect.

For children without disabilities, knowledge of personal hygiene skills typically begins to develop at a young age before actual instruction occurs. The child learns to expect that the phrase "bath time" is related to water, shampoo, soap, and washing, simply through the repetition of being bathed. A child with a visual impairment can benefit the same way if the caregiver provides explicit verbal descriptions and engages the child in the activities associated with bathing. For example, "It's time to wash your hair; help me open the shampoo bottle and squeeze some shampoo into your hand—the shampoo smells so good." The child can develop body concepts and better anticipate what is going to happen next when the caregiver explains what is about to occur, as in "Help me wash your legs; the washcloth feels so fuzzy on them."

As children mature, they have opportunities to manipulate the materials needed for grooming. They may get their toothbrush and try to brush their own teeth or open the toothpaste tube and try to apply paste to the brush. Sometimes these attempts are successful, other times they are not and may result in a mess. Children learn from these failed attempts and messes. They learn that what they did that time did not work, and, with encouragement, can try something different in future attempts. Many children with visual impairments, however, may not initiate such attempts, and may need to be guided to explore grooming supplies. Guidance typically begins with physical prompting through hand-under-hand practice (discussed later in this chapter), during which the child and adult complete a task together. This kind of joint manipulation of personal hygiene tools may be particularly important for students who have low muscle tone or who have had limited opportunities to experience activities that require stabilization of the wrist, as for example, might be necessary when using a hairbrush. Ideas for facilitating the development of personal hygiene skills can be found in Sidebar 8.2.

As the child becomes more proficient in performing a task, prompting should become less intrusive (for example, fading from physical to verbal prompts), and ultimately, the child should be expected and able to complete the task independently. A student learning to wash her hands may first need hand-under-hand assistance to locate the soap container on the wall. After a period of time, the child may just need the physical prompt of a tap on the left shoulder while being told to "get the soap." After the student masters the skill in this manner, she may only need to be tapped on the shoulder, with no verbal guidance. Depending on the student and the presence of additional disabilities, the amount of time to progress through the level of prompting will vary. Some students may always need some level of prompting.

It is valuable for adolescents with visual impairments to have someone they can talk to honestly about their own grooming, as well as about current trends and new products. Family members, peers, teachers, hair stylists, physicians, dentists, or store clerks are examples of individuals who can offer guidance. These discussions should be positive and conducted with the intent of helping the student; they should never be punitive or demeaning. Instruction in grooming and hygiene skills should reflect cultural and current societal norms for the student, as well. For example, some families may have a specific age at which they believe it is acceptable for their daughters to wear nail polish or makeup. For some students, religious beliefs may dictate whether or not they can cut their hair. A same-aged peer, such as a classmate, cousin, or friend, who demonstrates hygiene values similar to those of the student or the student's family can be particularly helpful in identifying fashionable styles and helpful products.

Instruction in hygiene and grooming skills typically needs to continue from early childhood through early adulthood. This may seem like a long time, but hygiene needs change as people grow, and certain skills are only appropriate to teach toward the end of this age range. For example, using deodorant or shaving are personal hygiene skills not needed by young children; they are taught only to older students. Likewise, developing and maintaining gender-specific hygiene skills, such as meeting menstrual needs, are appropriate to teach preteen and teenage girls.

SIDEBAR 8.2

Developing Personal Hygiene Skills

In addition to daily practice, additional activities to assist in the development of grooming and hygiene skills may be needed. Possible strategies and activities include:

- Involve students in organizing, labeling, and storing grooming products.
- Help students make schedules for grooming tasks, including determining if grooming tasks are best performed on a daily, weekly, or other frequency.
- Include students when shopping for and storing hygiene and grooming products.
- Allow students to use their low vision devices to observe someone else doing grooming tasks and to look at product labels.
- Explore grooming product options by visiting the health and beauty aids section of a store.
- Register with health and beauty aid companies to receive free samples of products.
- Work with a local dentist to have students learn about and practice oral care and to have the opportunity to explore models of teeth.
- Schedule an appointment at a cosmetics counter to learn about skin care and makeup needs.
- Meet with a hairstylist to learn about hair care, current trends, and individual needs.
- Interview adults with visual impairments to learn about their strategies for grooming.

For teenagers, part of personal hygiene and grooming may be learning to apply makeup independently, just as their friends do.

L. Penny Rosenblum

Dressing

Like personal hygiene and grooming, clothing can influence self-esteem and others' perceptions of a person. Dressing also has an effect on personal safety. In their daily lives, people select clothing that is appropriate for the settings and the weather they will encounter during their days, as well as for the activities they will perform. As with hygiene and grooming methods, styles in dress are influenced by cultural and societal norms, personal preferences, and functionality. Just like students with unimpaired vision, students who are visually impaired need to learn the many aspects of dressing themselves and maintaining their appearance and comfort.

Typically developing children often start the process of developing dressing skills by engaging in opportunities to undress. Very young children remove their shoes and socks and as they mature, they may remove their pants, shirts, and undergarments. Much to a parent's dismay, sometimes this undressing occurs right after they have been dressed! Although actions like these can be frustrating to caregivers, the process allows a child to learn the easier arm, hand, and body movements for managing clothing. These undressing activities provide the foundation for more complicated tasks associated with dressing.

At a young age, most children have also usually observed their parents getting clothes out of dresser drawers or closets and have seen dirty clothing items placed in hampers. When these children become mobile and can understand directions, in most cases they will be able to get pajamas out of a drawer and put their messy shirts in the hamper with very little instruction. Children with visual impairments who miss these incidental learning opportunities will likely need to be shown where to find their clean clothes and what is expected for them to do with dirty clothing.

Dressing involves much more than just putting clothes on one's body. Behaviors and skills related to the component of dressing include:

- removing clothes
- opening and closing fasteners
- lacing and tying
- identifying articles of clothing
- identifying the parts and sides of clothing (front, back, inside, outside, left, right, top, bottom)
- positioning clothes in order to put them on correctly
- putting on a variety of items (instruction can start simply with elastic waistbands and pull-over shirts, then move on to increasingly difficult fasteners)

- coordinating clothing
- choosing clothes for weather and occasion
- choosing clothes that fit
- choosing stylish, age-appropriate clothing
- ensuring privacy
- organizing and selecting accessories
- shopping for clothes

Sidebar 8.3 presents some strategies and ideas for teaching dressing skills to students with visual impairments.

Putting on Clothes

Instruction in dressing skills for children with visual impairments is frequently most successful when a *backward chaining* approach (discussed later in this chapter) is used. For example, when teaching a child to put on pants with an elastic waistband, the adult can help the child put her feet in the pant legs and partially pull up the pants to, for example, the child's knees. The child then can be expected to complete the task by pulling her pants to her waist. Once she has mastered this procedure, the adult helps the child put her feet in the pant legs and the child pulls the pants all the way up to her waist. The process continues until the child can put her feet in the pants and pull them all the way up on her own. A helpful tip for teaching children to put on their pants and skirts is to start with the child sitting down and then have her stand to pull up the pants or skirt. Adults working with a child in this way should make sure the surrounding space is clear of objects on which the child could hit her head while reaching for her feet.

As when teaching all skills, adults need to make judgments about how much feedback to provide and when to provide it. For the child who is struggling to pull up his pants, it may be more appropriate to praise his success at getting them up, even if the pants are twisted at the waist. Later, after the child has experienced many successful attempts at getting the pants up, the adult working with him can begin to provide feedback on getting them better aligned.

Operating Fasteners

In addition to learning how to put on articles of clothing, children need to learn how to open and close a variety of fasteners, including buttons, snaps, zippers, buckles, laces, and hook-and-loop fasteners. It is important for children to open and close fasteners on articles of clothing while they are wearing them, which allows children

SIDEBAR 8.3

Developing Dressing Skills

Dressing skills can be easily taught using the student's regular routines. Some specific strategies and activities that teachers can do to teach dressing skills include:

- Introduce shoe tying by having seated students tie bows using ribbons around their thighs. This method simulates the necessary movements in the correct direction and can be done without bending over, which can cause students to lose balance.
- Have students try on clothing items that are too large and too small so they can develop the concept of clothes that fit correctly.
- Keep a container of weather-related clothing items, such as raincoats, gloves, shorts, sandals, swimsuits, and boots at school. When elementary classes talk about the weather and types of clothing needed for the day, allow students to select the clothing being discussed.
- Celebrate successes—offer praise, a victory dance, or a small reward whenever a task is successfully and independently done for the first time.
- Encourage parents to include students when choosing clothes for the day. Advise parents to provide the information needed to make an informed decision—"Today is chilly out and we're going to the grocery store. What should you wear?"
- Explain to parents that it's important for the student to be made aware of important information about her clothes, such as its color or any pictures or words that might be visible. It can be embarrassing when someone comments about the color, texture, or graphic shown on an article of clothing and the student is unaware of these features.
- Be sure that students also know which types of clothing are age appropriate and which are not. It may not be appropriate, for example, for a fifth grader to wear a shirt with a preschool-level cartoon character on it.
- Allow the student to express preferences when shopping for clothes and to help select them.
- Collaborate with an occupational therapist on strategies for opening and closing fasteners on clothes and other dressing needs that require fine or gross motor skills.

to perform movements in the correct direction for dressing and not in the opposite direction, as can occur when children are working on simulated zipper and button tasks placed on a table in front of them. Zippers can be adapted, if necessary, by attaching a larger object (a ring or tab, for example) on the zipper pull. An efficient way to teach fastening skills is to modify a vest or pair of pants with larger buttons, zippers, and snaps than those that are on the child's clothes. Because of the fine motor skills involved in manipulating closings like buttons, bigger buttons are often easier to use than smaller ones, so they might be used when providing initial instruction. A vest adapted with a variety of fasteners can be particularly helpful for continuing instruction on these skills even when the child is wearing clothing without fasteners. If two vests are available, a blindfolded peer can be invited to "race" the student with visual impairment to get all the fasteners opened or closed.

Clothing Care

Clothing care is another important life skill that often is ignored when children with visual impairments are growing up. Clothing care isn't typically taught explicitly to children with unimpaired vision, and when instruction does occur, they learn what they need to know pretty quickly. A visual impairment may mean that students learn clothing care skills differently than their sighted peers and siblings do.

Behaviors and skills related to the component of clothing care include:

- determining whether clothes are clean or dirty
- sorting clothes for laundry
- learning about supplies for clothing care (detergent, bleach, fabric softener, stain treatments)
- determining care instructions
- treating stains
- washing (by hand, by machine, and using a Laundromat)
- drying (by machine, on a line, on a drying rack)
- folding
- ironing
- organizing closet and drawers
- labeling items
- hanging items on hangers and on hooks
- polishing shoes
- mending items
- determining when to replace and dispose of items
- using a dry cleaner

It can be easy for teachers and parents to assume that youngsters with visual impairments are no different in the way they learn these skills, but that assumption can be very wrong, as evidenced by this story of Abigail, a high school senior with congenital blindness who was getting ready to go to college.

Abigail was interviewing a college freshman to learn about life on campus as part of a career-education assignment. The freshman mentioned the hassle of doing laundry on campus. Abigail responded, "What are you talking about?" The college student proceeded to explain washing and drying dirty clothes in the dorm's laundry room. Abigail was amazed. She had never encountered washers and dryers or folded laundry. Additionally, she had no idea about laundry soap, fabric softener, or stain treatments.

After the interview, Abigail asked her teacher about laundry. The teacher was equally amazed—how could an honors student not know about laundry? After a discussion with Abigail and her parents, the teacher found out why. In Abigail's house, the washer and dryer were in the garage. The family never parked their car in the garage and because they perceived they were protecting her safety, Abigail was not permitted in that area. During this discussion, the teacher learned that when Abigail took her clothes off to shower, she put them on the bathroom floor and her mother would pick them up while Abigail was in the shower and put them in the hamper. At night, Abigail's mom would wash the dirty clothes. Once they were clean, mom put the clothes back in Abigail's dresser. Abigail admitted that she knew her mother took care of her clothes, but had no idea of the process involved in getting clothes clean.

Helpful ideas and activities for teaching clothing care skills can be found in Sidebar 8.4. The "Hang 10" learning activity at the end of this chapter shows how instruction in some of these skills can be included in an activity that incorporates several areas of the ECC.

SIDEBAR 8.4

Developing Clothing Care Skills

Teaching the following skills for clothing care may require field trips into the community or collaboration with the student's family:

- Explore a variety of washers and dryers in appliance stores.
- Visit the laundry care aisle at the grocery store to explore the variety of products.
- Have students (with the parents' permission) help mark the settings on their home washers and dryers, either tactilely with tape, glue, puffy paint, or Hi Marks or with large print.
- Visit a Laundromat and dry cleaner to explore the machines and become familiar with staff and the processes of washing clothes, and dropping off and picking up dry cleaning.
- Teach students to fold laundry, beginning with simple and symmetrical items like washcloths and hand towels, increasing the level of complexity as skills develop.
  - Teach how to match the corners of a washcloth and fold the cloth first one way, then another.
  - Socks and underwear (panties folded in half lengthwise, then across) are also fairly easy garments to fold.
- Practice ironing with a cold iron.
- Compare clothes that are in good repair to damaged ones.
- Make up riddles or poems about clothing care and supplies—"I should only be used with white laundry. What am I?" "Bleach."
- Have students attach sock mates with safety pins or sock fasteners when they take them off so the socks are still matched after being cleaned.
- Empty the lint trap of a clothes dryer.
- Teach students to hang clothes. A good garment to start with when teaching is a golf or polo shirt.
  1. Lay the shirt on a table or floor, aligned as if it were being worn, with the sleeves spread out, the front pieces neatly placed on top of the inside back of the shirt and the button at the neck of the shirt fastened.
  2. Show students how to slide the hanger through the bottom of the shirt so that the hook of the hanger comes out the neck hole and the hanger is situated appropriately in the arms of the shirt.
  3. Hang the hanger on a closet rod.

Doing Laundry

Children who are visually impaired need to be introduced to laundry-related activities at an early age. Young children should be allowed to explore the washer and dryer used by the family. When adults and older siblings are doing laundry, they should explain what they are doing and, as much as possible, involve the child so that the association of clothing care vocabulary with the appropriate equipment, products, and tasks can begin to develop. Teachers need to remind parents and other caregivers that it is a good idea for adults to allow the young student with a visual impairment to help collect dirty laundry; transfer wet clothes from the washer to the dryer; fold washcloths, towels, and eventually more complicated items; and to put away clean laundry.

Maintaining Clothing

In addition to doing laundry, students need to learn how to maintain their clothing. Occasionally, buttons need to be replaced, seams mended, and shoes polished. Adults can have students explore items that need repair and compare them with items that don't, so that they can develop a sense of when items need attention or need to be replaced. The skills needed to sew a button can be introduced at a preschool age by having the child use lacing cards or thread beads onto a shoelace. As the child's fine motor skills develop, instruction in the use of needles, thread, needle threaders, and buttons can take place.

Time Management

There are a finite number of hours in a day and an infinite number of tasks and responsibilities that one can choose to do in that time. Time management encompasses the behaviors and skills a student needs in order to manage and set priorities for obligations and free time. The following time management skills are among those that form the basis of the ability to manage and set priorities for activities, and will help students to become successful employees and heads of households:

- knowing what comes next or happened before
- following a simple routine or schedule
- estimating the amount of time needed for an activity, including preparation and cleanup
- creating schedules, using day planners and agendas
- using a watch and a clock (digital and analog)

SIDEBAR 8.5

Developing Time Management Skills

Teachers and caregivers can facilitate the instruction of time management skills by exposing children to some of the following activities:

- Estimate the amount of time needed for a task, time it, and compare the estimate to the actual time necessary for completion.
- Explore types of watches (large-face, braille, talking, digital, analog).
- Explore types of agendas (young students can start with simple versions).
- Present scenarios to students to increase time-related skills. For example, "We'll go to art class in 5 minutes. What time will we go to art?" Or, "We'll go to art at 11:00 am and we will be there for 50 minutes, so what time will we leave art?"
- Teach students how to set a watch and how to change it for time changes like moving to Daylight Saving Time.
- Set aside time during the day when students can stop and write assignments, appointments, and other items into an agenda. Students can record due dates for projects, times for orientation and mobility lessons, and homework assignments.
- Have students keep time-tracking journals in which they note how long various tasks took and if more or less time is needed.
- Have students interview a person with a visual impairment to find out how he or she handles time management.

- using a calendar or agenda (paper and electronic)
- weighing the pros and cons of decisions
- setting priorities

The ability to manage time is all the more challenging in today's fast-paced world. To be successful, employable, and independent adults, students need to develop very strong time management skills. Students without visual impairments learn these skills at a very early age through incidental learning and participation. Students with visual impairments need specific and targeted instruction to develop skills in time management, as well as instruction on how to access assistive technology and accessible calendars, clocks, alarms, and agendas. Helpful ideas and activities for teaching time management skills can be found in Sidebar 8.5.

The foundation for time management begins at a young age when children are taught what comes first, next, and last. Most preschool-aged children begin to understand time-related concepts, through conversations, such as that a minute is a small amount of time. Or, perhaps the family uses a timer for cooking or when a child is given a time out, and the child becomes aware that time can be measured in this way.

Using and Reading Timepieces

Students typically are expected to tell time to the hour and half hour in kindergarten, to the quarter-hour and five minutes in first grade, and to the minute in second grade. Students with visual impairments will be exposed to instruction on reading a clock with their sighted peers during math instruction, and students in these grades should be utilizing clocks and watches in a medium appropriate for their vision. There are large-type, high-contrast, tactile, and talking timepieces available.

Many students with visual impairments, however, will not bring the same level of knowledge and experience with watches and clocks to learning activities presented in the general education classroom as their classmates, because they have not shared similar opportunities for incidental learning. Adults working with preschool children with visual impairments will want to provide experiences with clocks and activities that help the children understand time and the vocabulary associated with describing it. Among these experiences are likely to be daily opportunities to review an accessible calendar and frequent opportunities throughout the day to check the time on an accessible timepiece.

Creating Schedules

Children with visual impairments may need to start with an object calendar for early scheduling practice. (An object calendar is one in which objects represent an activity, like a fork for lunch or a book for reading.) Once students are able to use the object calendar to communicate about past or future events, they are likely to be ready to use a more abstract braille or print schedule.

Students usually begin to understand the concept of appointment times and using an agenda or personal calendar in elementary school. At this stage, students need prompting to use their agendas, calendars, or notebooks to record important dates such as appointments, due dates for assignments and homework, and field trips.

For a student with a visual impairment, the agenda can be in print, braille, or an audio or electronic format. Regardless of the format, whatever is used should be simple, easy to access, and allow the child to be independent in recording and reading scheduled tasks. During the school year, the teacher can provide numerous opportunities for the child to record and discuss appointments, due dates, and the length of time needed to complete tasks. An ongoing activity that combines time management with compensatory access skills is using a simple chart or calendar in the student's preferred medium—a braille calendar or object calendar can be used for students with multiple disabilities—to list the times that activities happen for each day of the week. Routine events can be put on the chart or calendar in advance; non-routine events can be inserted as they come up. The teacher of students with visual impairments and the student can discuss how the student might use the times that have no events, incorporating self-determination and possibly recreation or social skills into the activity. This activity can start as a simple day-to-day schedule for young students and, as the student gets older, expand into a method of organizing activities and tasks. The calendar or chart can go home and back to school with the student, making it a good activity in which to involve parents and a good communication tool between the teacher of students with visual impairments and the student's family.

Allocating and Prioritizing Time

As children mature, their time management skills must also evolve. Simply recording events doesn't meet the requirements of older students, who need to allocate time for specific tasks and set priorities among their responsibilities. For example, orientation and mobility (O&M) students working on bus travel skills are taught the importance of allowing extra time to catch buses that may be running early or late, and they experience the consequences of errors in planning when the bus leaves without them.

Similarly, older students with visual impairments may need guidance in prioritizing the use of their time. This is another area in which it is important to know when to step back and let students act independently, even if they may make a mistake. Parents, teachers, and paraeducators often want to help students or save them from consequences by making choices for them or assisting them in completing certain tasks. It is important to remember, however, that people learn from their mistakes. When a student doesn't perform an activity, he or she does not only miss an opportunity to learn how to do the activity, but even more important, he or she misses an opportunity to fail. Failure provides the opportunity to solve problems, learn from mistakes, and make different choices, as this student was able to do in the following example:

When Andrew's history project was first assigned, Ms. Cohen, his teacher of students with visual impairments, worked with him to identify what needed to be done to complete it on time. They reviewed the assignment, discussed what research would be required, and planned how Andrew would be able to complete that research before and after school, since he did not have access to the Internet at home. Together, they established a schedule for Andrew to complete the work and agreed that Ms. Cohen would monitor its completion.

When Ms. Cohen noticed that Andrew had not made much progress on his history report, she expressed her concerns with him. He admitted that he was having trouble getting up early, so he wasn't getting to school early enough to work on his research, as they had planned. They talked about how, if Andrew continued to make the choice to sleep late, he probably would not get his history project finished and would earn a low grade. Unfortunately, Andrew did not change his behavior and not only earned a poor grade on the history assignment, but was not permitted to participate in an overnight field trip with the rest of his class. This consequence gave Ms. Cohen the opportunity to encourage him to learn from his mistake and to further discuss self-determination, goal setting, and time management with Andrew.

Working Pace

An important but often overlooked area of instruction related to time management is the value of helping students with visual impairments increase the pace at which they work. Students who work slowly often do not have a good understanding of how quickly their peers complete the same task. While there may be some very legitimate reasons why some students might work more slowly than their classmates (for example, challenges related to finding information in braille or with a low vision device), to the extent it is possible, teachers should help students identify when the pace at which they are working is unacceptable and what can be done to eliminate these discrepancies. Alternative methods of access might be appropriate in many situations, but students often benefit, too, from self-monitoring and personal goal setting to work more efficiently. Teachers can play an important role in helping students to establish monitoring systems and working with them to identify alternate, more efficient ways to complete tasks.

Eating and Table Skills

Eating is a social activity that has implications for recreation and leisure. People meet to eat for fun, for business, and as part of dating and family life. A person with poor table manners and eating skills may be excluded from social occasions involving meals, lose a big account for work, or make a poor impression with a potential mate. Proper eating habits are also essential for good health and nutrition, which influence the ability to participate in physical work and recreation activities. Students with visual impairments, especially those with additional health conditions, may need to be mindful of any special dietary needs and food allergies they may have and to be taught early about making choices that promote their health. Among the skills associated with eating in which instruction may be necessary are:

- self-feeding
- drinking using cups, glasses, bottles, straws, and cans
- using utensils and napkins
- demonstrating table manners, including chewing with mouth closed
- eating finger foods, such as tacos, sandwiches, pizza, ice cream cones, and the like
- using condiments (including those in standard packaging, single-serving condiment packs, and jumbo-size containers with hand pumps)
- opening containers, such as boxes, plastic bags, milk cartons, jars, cans, plastic ware
- setting a table
- passing food
- eating in a variety of styles and venues such as cafeterias, family restaurants, formal restaurants, and fast food establishments
- accessing a menu
- ordering food
- tipping

SIDEBAR 8.6

Developing Eating and Table Skills

The independent living component of eating has many associated skills. To teach eating skills, teachers might work with students on some of these activities:

- Set the table.
- Teach a child experiencing difficulty with using a straw to “kiss” the end of a short straw
- Practice scooping thicker foods, such as oatmeal, mashed potatoes, or grits, before lighter foods, such as applesauce or cold cereal.
- Practice stabbing food with a fork while holding a roll or piece of bread against the food to stabilize it.
- Practice cutting simple foods such as French toast, pancakes, or waffles before working on meats. When learning to cut meats, start first with items without bones, such as hamburgers.
- Hold food tasting events where students can try new or seasonal foods that require different eating techniques, such as tacos or edamame, and practice using condiments.
- Explore online menus for local restaurants.
- Have O&M lessons that end with a meal at a variety of eating environments.
- Use low vision devices and flashlights, as necessary, to read menus and food labels.

Sidebar 8.6 summarizes some ideas for teaching eating and table skills.

Young children typically begin to learn eating skills when they are less than a year old. Skill development begins through incidental learning and watching others eat, and then may evolve to grabbing the spoon as it approaches when being fed or trying to pick up cereal from a high chair tray. A child with a visual impairment may take longer to initiate the process of self-feeding if she cannot see the spoonful of baby food getting closer to her face or if the color of the cereal doesn't contrast strongly enough with the color of the high chair tray to be seen. With young children with a visual impairment, using hand-under-hand experiences (as discussed later in this chapter) and working from behind during feeding often helps them begin to learn about an approaching spoon and the movements necessary to get food from plate to mouth. Using high-contrast utensils, plates, bowls, and trays may also help children better see the food they are trying to eat.

When children are just starting to learn to eat and for students with fine motor difficulties, it may be helpful to use a bowl or a plate with a raised edge. This adaptation allows children to work on scooping food and decreases the amount of food that gets pushed off the plate. Once children are able to coordinate both hands, they can use a piece of bread or a butter knife to help guide the food onto a spoon.

Knife Skills

In addition to learning the appropriate use of forks and spoons, diners with visual impairments need to develop appropriate and safe knife skills. Typically developing children observe the use of knives during meals and often practice cutting clay with safe plastic knives. The child with a visual impairment can also practice cutting during play, but will need direct instruction on using a knife during a meal. The ability to control the hand at midline is a developmental prerequisite for using a knife. As with using hairbrushes and toothbrushes, the ability to stabilize one's wrist or arm is important when using a knife and may need to be practiced separately before it feels comfortable.

Knives are used for both cutting food items and spreading toppings such as butter, jelly, and peanut butter. Spreading is usually taught before cutting, since a knife with a blunt edge can be used for the task. Part of the struggle with this task, however, is getting the material to be spread out of its container. Some teachers start instruction in spreading skills only after the child has mastered scooping; others use backward chaining (discussed later in this chapter) and complete this part of the task for their students at first. When teaching spreading skills, it can be easier to start with a softer spread, like room temperature butter or whipped cream cheese, and use either toast or frozen bread. When using frozen bread, it is typically thawed by the time the spreading is complete, and like toast, it stays flat better than bread at room temperature. It is not unusual for students to require many practice opportunities before mastering the ability to spread, as the movement of the wrist and arm is so unfamiliar.

Learning to cut with a knife is a skill that is often denied to students with visual impairment based on the perceived safety risks involved. Table knives, however, are not usually so sharp as to create a hazard and can be used to teach the basics of cutting skills. Ideal materials on which to practice emerging cutting skills are pancakes, soft bread (as that used in a sandwich), toast, or a fruit or vegetable that has already been prepared for eating, such as a pineapple slice, half a canned pear, or piece of cooked zucchini. As the child achieves competence and confidence with soft foods and dull knives, instruction should proceed with foods that are more difficult to cut and sharper knives.

Independent Dining Skills

As children mature, expectations placed on them in regard to independent feeding and appropriate manners increase. In order to participate independently at mealtime, especially at school, children must know how to open milk cartons, lunchboxes, food and condiment packages, and also know how to choose the correct utensil and make choices in a cafeteria line. School staff play an integral role in providing opportunities for students to be independent. Once students can complete a task like opening a milk carton at lunch, they should be required to do it from that point forward. This practice allows children to refine their skills and become more efficient at completing expected tasks. Students will also need opportunities to apply the skills they have acquired when eating at home or school to other environments, such as formal and casual meals, delicatessens, cafeterias, buffets, other peoples' homes, and potluck dinners. This kind of generalization occurs through repeated practice in a variety of settings, although new skills may need to be introduced on various occasions, such as determining what is in containers, reading menus, and using utensils with specific purposes like salad forks, soup spoons, and crab forks.

In addition to eating, drinking skills are included in this component of the independent living area. When young children move on from nursing or drinking from a bottle, they frequently begin with covered, non-spill cups, progress to open, non-breakable glasses, and eventually begin using glasses and mugs made of breakable materials. Children who are visually impaired can make this transition as well. Non-spill or sippy cups usually require a child to suck in order to drink, which is similar in many respects to drinking from a breast or bottle. What is different and sometimes challenging is that the child needs to tip the cup in order for the liquid to flow. A child who has been unable to see others tip a cup while drinking may need to be taught with physical guidance how to do it himself. Some young children with visual impairments have difficulty with the motor skills of holding cups or with the oral motor skills associated with drinking; a consultation with an occupational therapist or speech language pathologist may be needed for these children.

While eating skills are being taught, it may be helpful, especially at first, for the table to be set in the same manner at each meal. The child can be encouraged to return utensils and cups to the same place after use. This consistency promotes independence for the child since she can locate items and can decrease spills because she will know where the cup, fork, knife and spoon are usually placed. After the child replaces an item on the table, it is important for adults to leave the item where the child has placed it. If something is moved, the child will not know where the item is located and may spill or make a mess because it was not where she expected it to be. If a cup is not placed in the usual location, the child should be instructed to move the cup and be told why: "Patrick, your cup is too close to the edge of the table and it might get knocked over, so move it to the top right of your placemat, please." This kind of explanation will let a child know where to locate the cup the next time and why the first placement needed to be changed. Alternatively, allowing a spill to happen occasionally teaches an important consequence related to organization and awareness of one's surroundings, and provides an opportunity for the child to practice another independent living behavior: cleaning up spills.

One of the abilities people with sight take for granted is the ease with which they can quickly locate food on a plate. However, people with visual impairments may not be able to see or identify the food on a plate, align the fork, and spear the food onto the fork with success. Diners with low vision may prefer a patternless, solid-colored plate that provides high contrast with most foods. A simple strategy for describing the location of food on a plate is to use a clock-face method, in which the hours on a clock represent the food's location on the plate, for example, "The green beans are at 9:00, and the meat is at 3:00." Teachers and caregivers need to be aware, however, that this method is not useful for children who are unfamiliar with the face of a clock. For these students, one can describe where the food is located on the plate by saying top, bottom, left, and right while guiding the child's hand to each item.

Table Manners

As previously mentioned, the purpose of eating is not just for obtaining sustenance for one's body; eating is often also a social and professional activity. Table manners reflect an individual's social skills. As with other eating tasks, manners typically need to be taught and reinforced at an early age.

Food Preparation Skills

Food preparation is another component of the independent living area that children master through increasingly complex involvement in cooking activities. Typically, most children learn to cook by observing others in the kitchen and demanding to be a part of the action. Adults comply with these demands by selecting the easiest part of the task at hand and allowing the child to help—by dumping dry ingredients into a bowl, using a rolling pin, grating cheese, washing strawberries, retrieving ingredients, and so forth. Based on their observations of the adults in the kitchen and their own limited involvement in such activities, it is not unusual for children to then incorporate further practice of skills in their pretend play.

Children with visual impairments can complete these tasks too, but due to limited incidental learning opportunities, many children may not ask to help their parents or may not imitate cooking skills during pretend play. A parent or caregiver may need to prompt or encourage a child to assist with cooking tasks and provide deliberate instruction when necessary. Such instruction might involve a simple demonstration to show the child how to hold his hands to tear the lettuce or use a potato peeler, but could also involve more complex and carefully designed teaching, such as might take place before using an oven for the first time.

Cooking behaviors and skills for which instruction may be necessary for students with visual impairments include:

- stirring
- pouring
- measuring
- cutting
- using kitchen appliances and utensils
- using hygienic methods
- labeling food
- preparing simple snacks
- preparing meals
- following recipes
- storing food
- making a grocery list
- planning meals and buying food

Brief cooking activities can be easily incorporated into weekly lessons with students, starting with simple tasks like those that follow and working up to more complex food preparation tasks:

- scooping ice cream
- peeling carrots
- rinsing fruits and vegetables
- opening cans of fruit
- slicing bananas
- spreading room-temperature butter on toast
- tearing lettuce for a salad
- toasting bread and waffles; warm toaster pastries
- pouring juice or milk from a small pitcher
- using a blender to make a smoothie or milkshake
- preparing hot cocoa using a microwave oven
- making a melted cheese sandwich in a sandwich maker
- slicing cheese with a cheese slicer; put cheese on crackers
- spreading cheese spread or dip on crackers
- using a melon baller
- preparing a sandwich using cheese and meat slices
- peeling fruit

Additional ideas for providing instruction in food preparation skills can be found in Sidebar 8.7.

In order to help young children with visual impairments be aware of cooking activities in which others are engaged, caregivers and teachers need to "think out loud" while doing food preparation tasks and menu planning—that is, provide full descriptions of what they are doing during these activities. These verbal descriptions can help draw attention to the steps and materials necessary to complete the tasks performed and can help children with visual impairments begin to understand the sequence of an activity and which steps come first, next, and last. As early as possible, though, having the child help with some part of the tasks involved in meal preparation will be critical to the student's long-term successful mastery of this area.

One good place to start is with involving the student in placing newly purchased foods on shelves in cabinets, pantries, refrigerators, and freezers. Combined with helping to retrieve items needed during meal preparation, these activities provide opportunities for the student to learn important information about food storage, to practice spatial awareness and motor planning, to carry objects, and to be involved as a meaningful contributor to the family unit. The importance of

SIDEBAR 8.7

Developing Food Preparation Skills

As with the other components of the independent living area, the best way to promote growth in cooking skills is to provide opportunities for the child to practice.

Before beginning, prepare the environment by making modifications appropriate for the student, such as placing task lighting and other appropriate lighting strategically in the kitchen space and pantry; providing a large-print or talking timer or other adapted kitchen devices; and providing long oven mitts to cover most of the arm when cooking or working near an oven.

The following are some suggestions for working on beginning food preparation skills:

- Practice cutting Play-Doh and soft foods before tackling harder ones.
- Have students help make a simple snack such as carrots and ranch dressing or buttered toast to start.
- Mark the microwave and oven controls for tactile identification or high contrast using puffy paint or Hi-Marks or other tactile marking substances.
- Teach students how to label canned goods with magnet tags, and, when an item is used up, to place the tag in an envelope to indicate which items need to be replaced on shopping day.
- Have students plan, shop for, and prepare a meal for their families.
- Explore large kitchen appliances like the stove, dishwasher, freezer, and refrigerator, and unplugged small ones, like the toaster, blender, coffeemaker, and mixer.
- Pour and measure materials, both dry and liquid.
- Allow students to help with a recipe based on their functional level, gradually allowing students to complete more of the recipe independently as their skills develop.

organization is also emphasized in these activities. As with the other components of the independent living area, organization is crucial to independence in the kitchen. Students benefit from knowing where materials are stored so they can safely locate and replace them, and function most efficiently in a clearly defined and consistently used workspace (at a table, for example, or on a counter). Eventually, they will also need a system for identifying food products in the kitchen pantry or shelves and for putting these items on the family shopping list when replacements are needed.

Spatial organization will also be important when students begin to use appliances. In order for a student with a visual impairment to understand the inside of the oven or the layout of the burners on the stove, she should be guided in a careful examination of cold stoves and ovens. This exploration, which should involve feeling the walls, sides, interior ceiling, and heating elements, and moving racks back and forth, provides an opportunity for the student to understand the spatial arrangement of these cooking units and where to put baking sheets and pans. Similar explorations of other kitchen appliances will assist the student to form mental images of the shelves in refrigerator doors or the layout of the racks in the dishwasher.

Students with visual impairments can be helped to select ingredients and cooking utensils before a cooking activity and to place these items in a specified area within easy reach of the food preparation area. A tray or cookie sheet with raised sides can be used to further define the work area. This strategy keeps the new cook organized and makes messes easier to contain and clean.

Using Specialized Tools

There are many specialized kitchen gadgets for cooks with visual impairments, including liquid level indicators that beep when a container is full of liquid, talking and large-print timers, adapted knives, extra long hot mitts, and so forth. (See the Resources section at the end of this chapter for sources.) Some cooks like specialized tools and others prefer to use common items with little or no adaptation. When deciding whether to use an adapted utensil or a standard one, the following points should be considered: the cost of the device and the student's age, level of motor skills development, amount of vision, comfort level with cooking, and personal preferences. It should be noted, however, that the use of specialized tools may limit the student's ability to generalize skills to other settings. So, the teen who only knows how to pour milk using a liquid level indicator may be at a disadvantage when helping to get ready for dinner in a friend's kitchen.

Cooking is an activity that some people enjoy and pursue as a leisure activity. Some cook elaborate meals, while others dread the task and cook as simply and as infrequently as possible. In order for students with visual impairments to know whether they enjoy cooking or not, they need to be taught basic cooking skills. Regardless of whether or not they will eventually cook five-course meals or prepare frozen dinners in the microwave, basic kitchen competence is critical to independent living.

Cleaning and General Household Skills

It does not matter if people rent or own the place where they live or have roommates or live alone. Nearly everyone needs to know how to clean their living space and complete general household tasks. Failure to learn and apply skills in this component of the independent living area can result in an unsafe and unhealthy living situation. Typically developing youngsters acquire knowledge of cleaning and household tasks through observation and pretend play, and, as they mature, they practice these skills in the form of chores. Doing dishes, sweeping floors, cleaning bathrooms, making beds, and taking out the garbage are all chores completed by children with unimpaired vision. Similarly, students with visual impairments need to be expected to do chores. Not only do they need to learn how to clean their living environment, they can develop a sense of social responsibility and feel proud of their contributions through chores. In addition, as a student's first work experiences, chores are an initial part of career education (see Chapter 11 and the "Home Helper" learning activity in that chapter).

Among the household tasks for which instruction may be necessary for students with visual impairments are:

- putting items in their correct location
- using household cleaning products
- changing linens
- cleaning floors
- cleaning bathrooms
- cleaning kitchens
- emptying trash and taking out the garbage; moving trash cans to the street
- caring for plants

- hanging pictures
- replacing toilet paper rolls
- changing light bulbs
- arranging furniture
- completing simple household repairs
- scheduling maintenance of air conditioning units, septic tanks and other household systems
- caring for lawns and flower beds
- caring for pets

Ideas for providing instruction in household cleaning can be found in Sidebar 8.8.

Just as at home, there are opportunities in the classroom or school for students to contribute through regular chores or jobs. Elementary classes usually have helpers to pass out papers and lead lines of other students, and teachers assign jobs and appoint monitors to certain duties after messy projects, such as the student in charge of sweeping the floor or wiping the tables. In school, students are expected to keep their desk or work area, cubby, or locker tidy and to throw away garbage. In classrooms with a kitchen, students take turns with various aspects of cleanup duty after cooking projects.

Cleaning Skills

The strategies necessary to teach a child with a visual impairment how to clean are relatively simple and can be generalized to multiple cleaning chores. The most basic strategy for cleaning is the use of an *overlapping grid pattern*. This pattern decreases the chance of missing a dirty area while cleaning. When using an overlapping grid pattern, students are taught to start at the top left hand corner of a surface, then to clean to the right, and when the end of the surface is reached, to slide down slightly and clean to the left. Students should be encouraged to overlap the area previously cleaned when moving to clean the next area. When using a *double grid pattern,* when the bottom of the surface is reached, the surface is cleaned again, this time moving in a vertical pattern from top to bottom and then moving to the right and continuing until the entire surface has been cleaned again. The learning activity "I'm Stuck!" at the end of this chapter illustrates a lesson that uses a game to teach students how to clean a table.

Physical or verbal prompting may need to be provided to help the student develop the muscle memory needed to clean and track straight lines. Many tasks, like cleaning countertops and showers, dusting, vacuuming, and mopping, require the ability to use an overlapping

SIDEBAR 8.8

Developing Household Cleaning Skills

Home maintenance and care skills can be a little more difficult to teach at school than some other independent living skills, since the environment and tools for those activities may not be available in the classroom. It may be helpful to send a newsletter home to families that includes a list of strategies for including a student with visual impairments with home maintenance activities.

However, there can also be many opportunities throughout a school day to eat meals or snacks, wash dishes, and clean up afterwards in a natural context. Students who come to school early for breakfast, have snack in the classroom (typically primary grades), or bring/purchase lunch in the cafeteria can participate in a club a few times a week with the teacher of students with visual impairments. It can be the Breakfast Club, Snack Club, or Lunch Bunch. By eating in an area with a sink and cabinets, such as the faculty lounge or cafeteria, the teacher of students with visual impairments can allow students to use real dishes and require all students to rinse, wash, dry, and return dishes to the cupboards.

Some other activities include the following:

- Take a field trip to the cleaning aisle at a local store. Compare brooms, mops, dusters, and cleaning products.
- Interview a plumber, air conditioner repairman, landscaper, and others with careers related to home care and maintenance. Find out about related costs, basic care, and why it is important to maintain home systems.
- Plant seeds and care for plants to learn about plant care.
- Brainstorm to create a list of chores and maintenance tasks students can do at home.
- Assign a chore journal for the students to document chores they are doing at home.
- Practice using basic tools, such as hammers, screwdrivers, and pliers.

L. Penny Rosenblum

Learning cleaning and general household skills, such as doing the dishes, is an important part of learning to live independently.

grid pattern to clean. While wiping counters, students can be taught to use their nondominant hand to check the just-covered surface for cleanliness.

It is recommended that instruction start with smaller spaces or objects to be cleaned, moving to larger items or surfaces as the student develops skills. For example, learning to make a twin-sized bed is easier than learning to make one that is king sized, and thoroughly cleaning a small table or mirror is easier than a large countertop. Learning how to complete the easier, smaller task builds competence, increases confidence, and decreases frustration as the student becomes better equipped to tackle larger tasks.

Telephone Skills

Telephones are an integral tool for communication and, thanks to today's rapidly changing technology and accompanying changes in our society, cell phones, particularly smartphones, perform many other functions as well. It is not uncommon to see children in elementary school and even kindergarten with mobile phones of their own. Previously, the main telephone skills included making and receiving calls, obtaining telephone numbers, and taking messages. As of this writing, telephones are used not just for calls, but for text messaging, connecting to social media, surfing the Internet, sending photographs, checking e-mail, getting and following directions to a location, playing games, and much more. Phones have and will continue to change. Some have push button keypads, touch screens, or voice recognition. Many homes have opted to forego traditional landlines and handsets entirely in favor of mobile phones. Regardless of the type of phone used in the home, young children need to know, at a minimum, where to locate the phone, how to answer it, and how to make an emergency call.

When students first begin to use a phone, their calls tend to be to family members and friends. As they mature, they will be required to make social and business calls. Adults may need to model professional and informal phone calls and have the student describe the differences and the characteristics of each type of call.

In order for students to be independent and employable in the future, it is important that teachers and caregivers allow students to practice the appropriate use of a variety of telephone skills, including:

- Making calls (personal, business, emergency, local, long distance)
- Dialing phone numbers with letters in the numbers, such as 1-407-W-DISNEY
- Having a variety of conversations (casual, formal, professional)
- Taking messages
- Using voicemail and answering machines
- Choosing and arranging phone service (for traditional landline phones and mobile phones)
- Organizing telephone contact information either on paper or electronically

SIDEBAR 8.9

Developing Telephone Skills

In addition to role playing and providing opportunities for children to use the phone, the following suggestions can be used for teaching telephone skills:

- Teach the student how and when to make emergency calls.
- Request a tour of a 911 dispatch facility where students can talk with 911 operators about their jobs and why it is important to call 911 only in a true emergency.
- Encourage the family to have telephones in the home that are accessible to people with visual impairments, and to keep phones in consistent locations so that the student can find them.
- Explore a variety of phones and practice making and receiving calls on different types.
- Teach students safety guidelines for texting.
- Interview a person with a visual impairment to learn about the necessary and desirable features to look for when buying a cell phone.

- Becoming aware of different types of phones (including pay phones) and their features
- Choosing a phone that is accessible
- Telephone safety

Ideas for providing instruction in telephone skills can be found in Sidebar 8.9.

Making Calls

An effective strategy to teach the skills to make phone calls is through role play. It is important to make sure the student understands the controls of the phone being used and how to dial or otherwise initiate a phone call. The teacher can begin by discussing the skill being addressed (such as calling and asking for directions to a business). The teacher can first have the student practice without actually making a phone call, and then practice with a real connection. Once the student is comfortable with role playing more complex telephone skills, the student can be asked to make actual calls. Some meaningful calls to start with include:

- ordering pizza
- calling Grandma to thank her for the birthday gift
- asking a business about their hours of operation
- contacting the public transit company to ask about schedules
- calling a cab company to arrange transportation after school
- contacting a mobility instructor to set up the next lesson

In addition to the mechanics of making a phone call, students may need instruction on telephone etiquette such as how to properly answer a phone, how to politely ask for information, the proper volume and tone of voice to use, taking turns talking, and how to end a conversation. Once students are able to make phone calls, they will need to practice how to take messages or note important information. Some students use electronic tools to take notes and record information, others braille or write their notes, and some students prefer to use an abacus to jot down a phone number. Regardless of the system used, all students need a way to take messages and organize contact information.

Money Management

Money management includes knowing how to make purchases with cash, checks, gift cards, or debit cards; understanding the use of credit and electronic payment systems; identifying money and counting change; preparing a budget; and identifying sources of income and expenses. Skills in the management of money also require the individual to make choices, interact with sales and banking staff, and understand that money has value and can be used to obtain goods and services.

As with the other components of independent living, sighted children tend to learn about money through observation at a very young age. They see siblings put a coin in a machine to get a gumball, they sit in the supermarket shopping cart when dad pays for groceries with his debit card, or they observe mom writing checks to pay the household bills or paying them online. They may have played games, such as Monopoly or Life, that use paper play money. In addition, they may have learned lessons related to spending and saving associated with managing the allowance they receive from their parents.

The money management skills that frequently need to be addressed by teachers of students with visual impairments include:

- Using currency (identifying bills and coins, counting, exchanging money, and making change)

SIDEBAR 8.10

Teaching Money Management Skills

Activities to encourage money management skills can be fun and often involve taking students to locations in the community to learn about finances and complete financial transactions, as in the following examples:

- Play games that use play money (such as Monopoly or Life).
- Pretend play a store or bank.
- Identify, count, and sort money.
- Make a list of items on which people spend money.
- Take a trip to the grocery store. Have the student select the correct bills to pay with and count the change.
- Purchase a snack from a vending machine.
- Develop a list of ways to earn money.
- Take a trip to a bank—find out about the jobs and careers available there, what services are offered, and how to open an account.
- Use an automated teller machine and a credit/debit point of sale device.
- Purchase a bus or train pass at the terminal.

- Organizing financial documents, such as bank statements, credit card statements, and loan documents
- Knowing the differences between credit and debit cards
- Making purchases with and managing credit and debit cards
- Writing and recording checks
- Filling in information on deposit slips
- Using bank accounts, including reconciling accounts
- Developing a personal budget
- Identifying sources of income and expenses
- Maintaining financial records
- Protecting personal and financial information

Suggestions for facilitating instruction in money management can be found in Sidebar 8.10.

Students with visual impairments need to be taught about methods of payment in a direct and deliberate way. This instruction can begin simply with a comment such as, "Daddy is getting his money out of his wallet to pay for the carton of milk." In addition to being provided verbal descriptions of transactions involving finances or money, it is necessary for students to handle currency, checks, and credit cards. Adults will want to provide students with frequent opportunities to use currency and coins to purchase items. Practice with credit cards and checks may have to be limited to exercises provided in class, but still are important for understanding the concepts and activities involved.

Identifying and Counting Currency

When learning to identify and count currency, students with visual impairments need access to real coins and bills. Coin identification is typically taught by having the student learn the sizes of coins and which ones have ridges. For example, dimes are the small coins with ridges on the edge. If a child has some usable vision, he may use his low vision devices to look at the coins and bills while he is handling them, but eventually, it will be important for the child to be fluid in his handling of coins and bills, which may require the use of tactile identification methods or alternate methods of marking bills. Identifying denominations of paper money and learning to mark bills can be included in lessons on using low vision devices or electronic bill readers. For example, one method of storing money is to fold (in half, in quarters, or lengthwise) bills of specified denominations, or turn their corners in a certain way for ease in identification. Students can also be taught to ask a trusted person with vision (cashier, bank teller, or friend) to identify denominations of paper money so that the person with a visual impairment can mark the bills using a preferred system. Some phones now include bill identification applications, increasing the independence of individuals with visual impairments. Practice in using these devices and other approaches may increase their effectiveness.

Lessons in currency denominations and identification and activities such as making change can be supported in the general education mathematics curriculum in elementary school, though the amount of practice provided in this environment may not be sufficient to meet students' needs. (See the learning activity "It Costs How Much?" at the end of this chapter for an example of an activity that reinforces a variety of money management skills.) Many life skills curricula for students with disabilities also include lessons for students to learn about personal finances, computing sale prices, and paying taxes (income, property, and sales). If a student is not enrolled in a class in which these skills are addressed, the teacher of students with visual impairments may want to use these materials as resources when providing this instruction. Money management is much more than identifying currency and making change. Students finishing high school need to be informed about financial options related to saving, investing, and borrowing money.

ASSESSMENT OF INDEPENDENT LIVING SKILLS

When determining the need for instruction in the area of independent living, it can be helpful to use a comprehensive tool that identifies the typical age ranges at which children demonstrate independent livings skills, such as the Oregon Project (Anderson et al., 2007) or the assessment components of the Independent Living Skills Curriculum (Levack & Loumiet, 1993). Less structured, but equally valuable, assessment methods include parent interviews, observation of the child in natural environments, and skill checklists (see Chapter 3 for more information on assessments).

Given the vast number of skills included in the independent living area, assessment can seem like a daunting task. Teachers can begin by interviewing a student's parents and, if applicable, the student's other teachers. It is important to determine what skills the adults who are living and working with the child want to have the child achieve first, as these are the skills for which parents and teachers will encourage students' success. It is also helpful to observe what tasks and activities other children the same age are expected to do and consider any limitations the student may have that affect the way in which a behavior needs to be taught to or completed by the student. By observing students in their routines and discussing family priorities, teachers can help focus instruction on the skills that students and families are likely to actually use, and, as the student masters skills, new ones can be added. The teacher can then begin to set priorities for the skills that the student needs to learn. Once specific skills have been selected for instruction, the next step in determining how instruction of an independent living skill can proceed is using *task analysis* (which is discussed in more detail later in the chapter), and *discrepancy analysis* techniques (see Chapter 3) to determine which steps the child can do independently and which ones require assistance and instruction.

Task Analysis in Assessment

Assessing a student's self-feeding behavior, for example, might start by presenting the student with finger foods to determine whether she can locate the foods, pick them up, get them to her mouth, chew, and then swallow. If she is successful with finger foods, foods and materials for spoon feeding can be provided. The teacher will need to consider all the individual steps in self-feeding with a spoon (task analysis) and then see if the child can locate the spoon, grasp it correctly, dip it into food, scoop food and keep it on the spoon, get it into her mouth with food still on it, close her lips around the spoon and swallow the food. During the observation, a teacher may notice the child can complete the steps up to scooping food onto the spoon. As the child makes a few more attempts at feeding herself, it may become apparent that the bowl is sliding on the table. At that point, the teacher can try to secure the bowl with a nonslip mat or a damp dish towel. After it is secured, the child can be asked to try again. If securing the bowl eliminated the scooping problem, the teacher can continue the observation. If not, it may be necessary to re-evaluate the child's movements while scooping to determine if physical assistance with the spoon is necessary. Further assessment will involve moving forward through the steps of the task analysis to determine where instruction may need to occur.

The input of parents is valuable, but it is still necessary to observe the child during the task to determine whether the child has mastered it completely or to identify at what point the child's ability to do the task fluently breaks down. Occasionally, family members may be embarrassed to admit that their son or daughter does not perform an independent living skill expected of most children at that age. Or, more likely, a parent's perception of completing a task may be different than the teacher's. The parent of a child who holds the toothbrush in his mouth and chews on it, but who does not apply the toothpaste or scrub each tooth, for example, may say the child is able to brush his teeth not to be misleading but because the parent is uncertain about the expectations for a child who is blind. In any event, it is always good to have independent corroboration of the child's abilities. If there are challenges to the child's performance of the task, the teacher can offer family members constructive feedback about instructional strategies and methods with which they may be unfamiliar.

Discrepancy Analysis

Once the task analysis is complete, a discrepancy analysis should be done to determine if there are barriers within the environment that prevent the child from performing the task the way others would do it, and those barriers need to be addressed to facilitate growth and independent functioning. For example, when teaching hand washing, the teacher should determine if the child can manipulate the pump on the soap to dispense the proper amount of soap into her hand. If not, a child who is physically capable of that manipulation may need instruction on using this type of soap dispenser before hand washing instruction can proceed. If the child is not capable of using the dispenser, another solution might need to be found, such as providing a soap bar at that location.

Developing Goals and Evaluating Success

Information received from assessments using task analysis and discrepancy analyses will be valuable in developing instructional goals and objectives.

Once goals are developed and instruction in specific independent living skills have occurred, teachers can use the task analyses that were created for assessment and instruction to evaluate the student's success in learning to complete each step of the skill. This process will give specific information related to the points in the task where the student has achieved mastery and those where remedial instruction may need to occur. For example, if the goal is "Elena will self-feed 100% of the time," supporting objectives would address her specific difficulties during the self-feeding process. One such objective might be, "When scooping pureed food from a bowl with a spoon, Elena will keep the spoon level 5 out of 5 bites."

GENERAL CONSIDERATIONS FOR TEACHING INDEPENDENT LIVING SKILLS

Pogrund and Fazzi (2002) encourage the following practices for teaching independent living skills to children with visual impairments of all ages and abilities:

- consider the future environment
- teach at natural times and in natural environments
- encourage partial participation

Consider the Future Environment

Sometimes, the immediate instructional needs of a student with visual impairment appear to have been met, and no new instruction in independent living skills seems necessary. It is important to not only think about the immediate situation, but also to consider transitions to new environments where independent living skills will be needed. Transitions happen at all ages, as when a child makes a transition from organizing a toy shelf at home to a cubby at preschool, to a desk in elementary school, to a locker in middle school and high school, and a dorm room in college. The ultimate instructional goal is for students to become as independent in life as possible. To achieve this, it is important to teach strategies that can apply to multiple situations as well as situations in the future.

Teach at Natural Times and in Natural Environments

As discussed in Chapter 3, instruction in independent living tends to be more effective when it occurs as part of the actual routines and within the natural environments in which a given task is typically performed. By learning the task during a familiar routine, the student is able to complete the skill at an appropriate time, using authentic materials. It is easier for the student to understand the meaning of the task during a naturally occurring activity than in an arbitrary situation. Simulated classroom instruction of independent living skills can help teach the motor demands of a task, but simulations can make initiating and generalizing the task difficult because the student may not fully understand its purpose and applicability. It is better when teaching a student how to use soap pumps, for example, to have the student use the pump every time she washes her hands. This method allows for numerous opportunities to practice each day with the particular soap pumps the child needs to use. Similarly, practicing food scooping skills naturally occurs at snack and meal time. By teaching scooping skills during these times, the child can develop a framework for understanding when spoons are used. In addition, practicing scooping food when the child is hungry and motivated to eat can be naturally reinforcing.

Encourage Partial Participation

Students with visual impairments should ultimately be expected to complete all the steps of independent living tasks, but for developmental or other reasons, *partial participation,* in which a student who cannot complete an entire activity performs the part he or she can (see Chapter 3 for more information) may be appropriate. An example of partial participation by a student who only has the use of one hand may occur when zipping a jacket. The student may need someone to engage the two parts of the zipper together, but is expected to pull up the zipper. The instructional methods of *forward chaining* or *backward chaining* (discussed earlier in this chapter; see also Chapter 3 for more information) provide opportunities for partial participation by having the child complete portions of the task. By completing part of a task, children build self-confidence, develop necessary cognitive and motor skills, and build their ability to assist in independent living skills as well.

Finally, it is important to provide numerous opportunities for repetition and to expect the child to participate in independent living skills as independently as possible. These opportunities and expectations will make performing independent living skills seem natural to the student.

TEACHING STRATEGIES FOR INDEPENDENT LIVING

Basic Instructional Strategies

Frequently, parents and teachers focus on teaching a child how to complete a specific behavior and miss teaching critical supporting skills. For example, they teach the child how to move the toothbrush over his teeth, but forget to teach him where to reach for the toothbrush, where to find the toothpaste, how to remove and replace the toothpaste cap, and how to squeeze the paste onto the toothbrush. These skills, however, are just the start of learning all there is to know about brushing teeth. As students grow older, they'll need even more information related to this topic, such as types of toothbrushes, toothpaste brands, toothpaste delivery systems (tubes, pumps, or powders), where to purchase these items, how much they cost, and so forth. Instruction in independent livings skills should be comprehensive and include all related tasks and behaviors related to a particular skill.

Task Analysis in Instruction

Before beginning instruction in any independent living behavior, it is important for the teacher to develop a comprehensive *task analysis,* a step-by-step guide that breaks any task into detailed parts (also discussed in Chapter 3). In order to do a task analysis, the teacher should perform each part of the behavior to better identify the steps involved in undertaking the task, with special consideration for completing each step with impaired vision. Blindfolding oneself or using a low vision simulator can be invaluable when completing a task analysis. The task analysis provides an excellent framework for developing a plan of instruction and a tool for recording skill mastery. The teacher can use the task analysis to evaluate the student's ability to complete each step of a task independently or with verbal or physical support, and determine where strengths and potential areas of difficulty occur.

For example, the task of hand washing can be divided into multiple steps. General instruction in this task includes orienting the student to the sink and how to turn on the faucet, using the soap dispenser, and drying the hands. A task analysis of hand washing includes the following steps:

1. Approach sink
2. Stand facing sink
3. Reach for knobs of faucet
4. Turn on water to desired temperature
5. Wet hands
6. Locate soap
7. Apply soap to hands
8. Rub hands together under water
9. Scrub hands for 20 seconds
10. Rinse all soap off
11. Reach for knobs of faucet
12. Turn off faucet
13. Find towel, paper towel, or hand dryer
14. Dry hands
15. Dispose of paper towel or hang up towel

Of course, each of these steps can be further divided into several additional parts through a similar process. An important consideration of how to define each step is the condition under which the task is to be performed. For instance, turning on the water using a water faucet with separate knobs for the cold and hot water is different than turning on the water when using a faucet with a single handle. The determination of how finely to describe the steps of a task also depends on the physical and cognitive abilities of the learner. The task analysis for a learner with the use of only one hand would look somewhat different than that for a two-handed student. Similarly, the step "dispose of paper towel" may involve the following steps for a student who is blind and has a developmental disability:

1. Place towel in left hand
2. Reach for cane with right hand
3. Turn so that sink is on right side
4. Place cane in position for traveling
5. Walk to wall
6. Locate trash can with cane
7. With left hand, locate top of trash can
8. Place paper towel in trash can by releasing paper

Forward and Backward Chaining

Once a task has been divided into individual sequential steps through task analysis, the teacher can teach the skill through *chaining*. Chaining is the process of presenting instruction in a specific order so that the student masters each step of the task before moving on to the next one. Frequently, instruction occurs with the student learning each step sequentially from start to finish, which is referred to as *forward chaining*. For example, a teacher might use forward chaining when teaching a child to make toast by first teaching the student to get out the materials, then teaching how to use the toaster, then showing the student how to spread the butter, then providing instruction on how to cut the toast.

Depending on the activity, however, students with visual impairments may benefit most from learning and mastering the last part of a skill, then adding the previous steps until they are doing the entire task independently. This process of instruction is referred to as *backward chaining*. Backward chaining is particularly effective when a task requires numerous steps and the student is motivated by finishing the task. If a teacher were using backward chaining to teach students to make toast, she would complete all the steps up through spreading the butter and first teach how to cut the toast in half. After the students had mastered cutting, they would then work on spreading the butter, then on slicing a piece of butter from the stick or scooping from a tub of butter, then on using the toaster, with the last lesson relating to locating the materials. Backward chaining, in this example, allows the student to feel proud and successful because he has completed the task and been rewarded each time with toast to eat. Forward chaining relies on the teacher finishing the task from the point at which the student stops, and the student may feel frustrated because he "got stuck" and didn't finish the task.

When teaching independent living skills, teachers and caregivers will want to work from behind students when possible. This positioning enables the teacher and student to be in the same directional plane and move their arms and hands in the same way. Having the direction and patterns the same is important when the student is learning by following the physical movements of the instructor. When the child and teacher are facing each other, the movements and directions are opposite to each other and may be confusing to the student.

Hand-Under-Hand Guidance

Another effective approach when teaching independent living skills is to have the student place his hands on top of the instructor's, a technique referred to as *hand-under-hand guidance*. This arrangement allows the student to have control over his own participation (he can remove his hands when he wants) and to experience the correct motor skills necessary to complete the task. Rarely, it is necessary for the teacher to place her hands over the child's and manipulate them (*hand-over-hand guidance*). This technique takes control of participation and learning away from the child and should be used only when necessary. (See comments about hand-over-hand guidance in Chapter 5.)

Fading Prompts

As soon as a student shows she can complete a behavior somewhat on her own, assistance should be reduced or replaced with less intrusive forms of help. Continuing with physical or verbal assistance when it is no longer necessary does not allow the child to increase her confidence or independence. Providing a physical prompt, such as touching the student's hand or helping to support her elbow, may be the next least intrusive method of encouraging a child to complete a step in a task. Likewise, a verbal prompt such as "keep going" may help a student to complete a step. Gradually replacing intrusive prompts with reminders that are less intrusive or specific is referred to as *fading*. Ideally, all physical and verbal prompts would be faded as completely as possible so that the child develops greater levels of independence.

Wait Time and Stepping Back

Once instructions or prompts have been provided during instruction, adults need to allow plenty of *wait time* for a child to respond. Teachers may sometimes interpret a pause in response as the student's not knowing the answer or correct way to respond, when in reality

SIDEBAR 8.11

19 Ways to Step Back

It often feels right to give help to students with visual impairments, but this may not be in their best interest. Use this list to help yourself to step back.

1. You're stepping back so your students can step forward and become independent. Keep this in mind.
2. Clock how long it actually takes for students to start zippers, pick up dropped papers, or find page numbers. What's a few more seconds in the grander scheme?
3. Sit on your hands for a whole task while you practice giving verbal instead of touch cues. Hands off the hands!
4. If you need touch cues, try hand-under-hand instead of hand-over-hand. This gives students much more choice.
5. Let your students make mistakes and get into trouble. It's part of the human experience!
6. Acknowledge your own needs. There's a reason you chose the helping profession.
7. Sit further away. If you've been within arm's reach, sit just within earshot. If you've been sitting just within earshot, sit across the room.
8. Pat yourself on the back every time you help with seeing, not thinking. Your job is to give information.
9. Even though helping can feel right, be aware that too much assistance is short-sighted. Sometimes less is more, less is better.
10. Catch yourself before you correct your students' work. Don't cover for them. This is about their skills . . . not yours.
11. Commit to no intervention for a whole activity. Take data instead. Things might not fall apart as much as you had expected.
12. "What page are we on?" "What's for lunch?" Have students ask their classmates instead of you, both during school and on the telephone.
13. Assign student learning partners and sighted guides.
14. Teach students to decline assistance, "Thanks, but please let me try it by myself."
15. Whenever you add prompts, include a plan to phase them out.
16. Let the boss know that you need to step back so that your students can be more independent. You're not shirking your responsibilities.
17. Collaborate with other adults to break your habits of helping too much. Agree to remind each other to step back.
18. Try helping only when classroom teachers give you a signal. They may prefer to respond directly or to give students longer to work it out alone.
19. Post a sign, "Are there any other ways I could step back?"

SOURCE: Adapted with permission from Laurel J. Hudson, *Classroom Collaboration* (Watertown, MA: Perkins School for the Blind, 1997).

the student may be processing the request and thinking of how to react. The amount of wait time will vary from student to student. One student may require 10 seconds, while others may require a minute or more. Students who are processing information may need the teacher to wait quietly and not repeat the instruction. Repeating requests and instructions may make the student start processing all over again. "Nineteen Ways to Step Back" (Hudson, 1997), a compilation of useful hints for teachers and parents about allowing students sufficient time and space to act independently, appears in Sidebar 8.11 as a helpful reminder.

Teachers need to know their students well when determining how much wait time is appropriate, as both repeating directions too quickly and waiting too long to rephrase them can interfere with student learning. It may be necessary to keep careful data on students' response times to help in making this determination.

Using Routines

Various techniques can be used to incorporate instruction of independent living skills into school activities. The first step is to determine the school day routines in which the student is involved. These routines typically include arrival at school, transitioning to learning activities, obtaining educational materials, eating lunch, toileting, and departing school. Teaching during routines allows for authentic experiences with real objects that are meaningful to the child. Using a student's own jacket to learn to use a zipper, opening the milk cartons that the student drinks from every day, and washing hands using the faucets, soap dispensers, and paper towels that are in the school are examples of using frequently occurring events for instruction. Using established routines and consistent materials is especially valuable for students who have cognitive disabilities in addition to a visual impairment.

Adapting Activities

When determining which materials should be used in instruction, the "least restrictive adaptation" model (Jones, 2004) is important to consider to reduce the use of specialty or expensive materials or equipment. The model describes four approaches, ranked from least to most restrictive, for adapting activities for individuals with visual impairments:

- modifying behavior
- adapting the environment
- using familiar tools and devices
- using specialty products

(A similar hierarchy for providing accommodations is discussed in Chapter 4.)

Modifying behavior occurs when students change the way they perform a task. For example, instead of asking a parent to hand her the shampoo and conditioner bottles during bathtime, the youngster might be taught to determine independently which bottle is which by always placing the shampoo in a particular location or by learning to distinguish them by the shape or size of the bottle. If this youngster has some usable vision in bright light, a dark shower curtain could be replaced with one that allows enough light in the shower to read the labels on the bottles—an example of *adapting the environment.* To identify the shampoo bottle *using familiar items*, a rubber band could be placed around the bottle of shampoo so it is tactilely distinguishable from the similarly shaped bottle of conditioner, which has no rubber band. These simple approaches eliminate the need to purchase an expensive *specialty product*, such as a special dispenser for the shampoo and conditioner, to accomplish this task. It also results in solutions that can be used in other environments and with other tasks.

The least restrictive adaptation is the one that most closely resembles the strategies used by others and is most easily reproduced in other situations. It often is the approach that is most efficient and least expensive. It also tends to be the solution that is least likely to highlight the differences among people with and without visual impairments. Teachers who teach students to distinguish coins tactilely instead of using a specialized coin counting machine are using this approach (modifying behavior), as are the parents who install a brighter bulb in the clothes closet of their teen with low vision (adapting the environment) so that he can choose his own clothes. Students with visual impairments should be encouraged to be involved in the selection of adaptations that they use. When students are young, adults should share the reasoning behind the selection of a particular adaption. As students mature, it is important that a range of acceptable options be provided to them, their opinions solicited, and their preferences increasingly honored. Long before students finish with school, they should be responsible for making these kinds of decisions as independently as possible.

ROLE OF THE TEACHER OF STUDENTS WITH VISUAL IMPAIRMENTS

While there are numerous ways to teach independent living skills, it is important for the teacher of students with visual impairments to plan to use the home and community in addition to the school setting for instruction, because these settings are the natural environments in which the activities of daily living are performed. When possible, the teacher may need to schedule a home lesson. During this type of lesson, the student is in his or her natural environment with familiar and meaningful materials. Additionally, home lessons allow the student's caregivers the opportunity to observe the instructional strategies used by the teacher and perhaps incorporate them when they help the student with the same skills at other times.

In addition to providing direct instruction to students, the teacher can hold sessions at the school for parents and students where family members can learn skills related to the instruction of independent living skills and their child's abilities. One idea is to offer a group meal that the students make and share with their families. Students can be assigned tasks based on their abilities and needs; there are plenty of activities to do, including buying groceries (collaborate with O&M staff), setting the table, preparing food, serving guests, and cleaning up afterward. Another strategy is to bring family members together and provide instruction. Teachers can offer activities in which sighted family members are blindfolded or wear low vision simulators to experience performing tasks under these conditions, share strategies, and encourage family members to come up with their own ideas of what will work with their child. If the teacher is unable to meet with parents, information about independent living tasks can be provided in a weekly or monthly newsletter.

Finally, the teacher needs to support and encourage the student. Students who are blind or visually impaired have often repeatedly been told they are unable to accomplish many ordinary tasks or activities, and they need someone to believe in them and empower them to succeed.

The suggestions and learning activities presented in this chapter are but a few examples of possible lessons that address independent living. They are intended to be suggestions that can be modified as needed to adjust to the needs of individual students.

SUGGESTIONS FOR WORKING WITH PARENTS

Children spend a majority of their time with family. Just as children with vision learn independent living skills at home, so can children with visual impairments. Parents and caregivers are the ones who are bathing their child, brushing his or her teeth, preparing meals, and helping the child to complete numerous other daily living tasks. As previously discussed, children learn best with consistent routines and using authentic materials, which makes home the perfect place to develop and practice independent living.

Teachers can support a student's development of independent living skills by providing family members with resources and materials and by inviting parents to observe the child learning these skills at school. Suggestions for encouraging independent skill development at home include the following:

- Begin intentional instruction early, when the child is young; don't wait for the child to initiate interest in learning the task.
- Talk to the child about the tasks you are doing, the materials needed, where they are stored and any sensory information (smells, sounds, temperature, texture, and so on) pertinent to the task.
- Allow the child to explore and play with items needed for independent living tasks.
- Teach "in the moment" by having your child participate in some part of what you are doing for him or her. By using this technique, routines are reinforced and success often comes more quickly when the child is engaged in a task.
- When there is time, follow your child's lead. If, for example, he opens his dresser drawer, encourage him to explore its contents and investigate how the drawer opens and closes.
- Have high expectations by encouraging your child to explore her world and participate in independent living tasks.
- Remember the "Nineteen Ways to Step Back" (Hudson, 1997), discussed earlier in this chapter, and incorporate those strategies in your interactions with your child to promote independence.
- Avoid promoting learned helplessness by trying not to help your child complete activities and by expecting him or her to perform them independent of your or other assistance.
- Have fun and enjoy being with your child!

These strategies usually can be easily incorporated into the child's daily routines. When the child wakes in the morning, he can help pull up the covers and make his bed. During dressing time, young children can retrieve their clothes from the dresser or closet. Meal preparation is the perfect time to include a child in learning skills for independence by having her start by tearing lettuce and, as her skills develop, cutting other vegetables for the salad. In addition, many of the suggestions for activities provided throughout this chapter will be useful for parents. Parents and teachers can work together to determine how to include a child with visual impairments in independent living skills.

SUMMARY

Instruction in independent living skills is an integral part of education for students with visual impairments. The ultimate goal for students is to achieve the highest level of independence possible and to feel confident and happy with themselves. It could be argued that independent living skills are more valuable than academic skills or, at least, are more fundamental. Students who struggle academically still need to maintain their appearance, nourish their bodies, and keep their living space safe and clean. In addition, success in the performance of independent living skills has an impact on students' success in the other areas of the ECC. For teachers, independent living skills can be some of the most rewarding skills to teach and are ones that students of all abilities can develop.

References

Anderson, S., Boigon, S., Davis, K., & deWaard, C. (2007). *Oregon project for preschool children who are blind or visually impaired* (6th ed.). Medford: Southern Oregon Educational Service District.

Hudson, L. (1997). *Classroom collaboration.* Watertown, MA: Perkins School for the Blind.

Jones, L. (2004). Least restrictive adaptation model: Anything you need, you can find in the kitchen drawer. *RE:view, 36*(2).

Levack, N., & Loumiet, R. (1993). *Independent living: A curriculum with adaptations for students with visual impairments: Volume II. Self-care and maintenance of personal environment* (2nd ed.). Austin: Texas School for the Blind and Visually Impaired.

Marks, S. (1998). Understanding and preventing learned helplessness in children who are congenitally deaf-blind. *Journal of Visual Impairment & Blindness, 92*(3), 200–211.

Pogrund, R. L., & Fazzi, D. L. (2002). *Early focus: Working with young children who are blind or visually impaired and their families* (2nd ed.). New York: AFB Press.

Independent Living Skills Resources

This section provides resources such as assessment tools, publications, and instructional materials for teaching independent living skills. For additional resources that relate to the expanded core curriculum in general, see the Resources section at the end of this book.

ASSESSMENT TOOLS

Assessment Kit: Kit of Informal Tools for Academic Students with Visual Impairments

Population/Age level: Ages vary

Source: Sewell, D. (1997). *Assessment kit: Kit of informal tools for academic students with visual impairments.* Austin: Texas School for the Blind and Visually Impaired.

Independent Living—A Curriculum with Adaptations for Students with Visual Impairments: Assessment and Ongoing Evaluation Booklet

Population/Age level: School-age to adulthood

Source: Loumiet, R., & Levack, N. (1993). *Independent living: Assessment and ongoing evaluation booklet.* Austin: Texas School for the Blind and Visually Impaired.

Oregon Project for Preschool Children Who Are Blind or Visually Impaired

Population/Age level: Birth to 5 years

Source: Anderson, S. Boigon, S., Davis, K., & deWaard, C. (2007). *Oregon project for preschool children who are blind or visually impaired* (6th ed.). Medford: Southern Oregon Education Service District.

PUBLICATIONS

Chen, D., & Dote-Kwan, J. (1995). *Starting points: Instructional practices for young children whose multiple disabilities include visual impairment.* Los Angeles: Blind Children's Center.

Corn, A. L., Bina, M. J., & Sacks, S. Z. (2009). *Looking good: A curriculum on physical appearance and personal presentation for adolescents and young adults with visual impairments.* Austin: Pro-Ed.

Huebner, K. M., & Swallow, R. (1987). *How to thrive, not just survive: A guide to developing independent life skills for blind and visually impaired children and youths.* New York: American Foundation for the Blind.

Kelley, P., & Smith, P. (2000). Independent living skills. In A. J. Koenig and M. C. Holbrook (Eds.), *Foundations of Education: Vol. II. Instructional strategies for teaching children and youths with visual impairments* (2nd ed., pp. 569–615). New York: AFB Press.

Levack, N., Hauser, S., Newton, L., & Stephenson, P. (1996). *Basic skills for community living: A curriculum for students with visual impairments and multiple disabilities.* Austin: Texas School for the Blind and Visually Impaired.

Lewis, S., Slay, S., & Bischof, E. (2008). *PATTER: Preschool attainment through typical everyday routines.* Louisville, KY: American Printing House for the Blind.

Loumiet, R., & Levack, N. (1993). *Independent living: A curriculum with adaptations for students with visual impairments.* Austin: Texas School for the Blind and Visually Impaired.

Loumiet, R., & Levack, N. (2009). *Independent living: Activity routines.* Austin: Texas School for the Blind and Visually Impaired.

Perwein, V., & Levack, N. (1996). *Independent living: From IEP to teaching strategies . . . how do we get there?* Austin: Texas School for the Blind and Visually Impaired.

Smith, N. (2001). *Calendar: Everyday exposure to experiences for enjoyment.* Louisville, KY: American Printing House for the Blind.

SOURCES OF ADAPTED PRODUCTS AND MATERIALS

The following companies carry a variety of products for independent living. For additional sources of products, see the Resources sections in the chapters on other areas of the ECC; for sources of products for instruction and low vision, see the Resources section at the end of this book.

Independent Living Aids
200 Robbins Lane
Jericho, NY 11753
(800) 537-2118 or (855) 746-7452
Fax: (516) 937-3906
www.independentliving.com

LS&S
145 River Rock Drive
Buffalo, NY 14207
(800) 468-4789 or (716) 348-3500
Fax: (877) 498-1482
www.lssproducts.com/contact

Maxi-Aids
42 Executive Boulevard
Farmingdale, NY 11735
(800) 522-6294 or (631) 752-0521
Fax: (631) 752-0689
TTY: (631) 752-0738
www.maxiaids.com/store/default.asp

ShopLowVision.com
3030 Enterprise Court, Suite C
Vista, CA 92081-8358
(800) 826-4200
Fax: (800) 368-4111
info@shoplowvision.com
www.shoplowvision.com

Independent Living Learning Activities

Contributed by Carol B. Allman and Sandra Lewis

These sample learning activities are presented as examples of activities that teachers can create to work on several ECC skills at once with their students. Activities that help teach independent living skills can also be found in other chapters. The activities presented, like all instruction, need to be considered and modified to address the needs of individual students—such as those who are braille readers, have low vision, or have additional disabilities—with adaptations for appropriate media and the physical and other capabilities of the student.

Learning Activity: Bag of Gold	
Primary ECC Area: Independent living **Grades:** Pre-K–4	**Component:** Money management
Other ECC Areas ■ Compensatory access ■ Sensory efficiency	
Goal: Student will identify coins using tactile sense.	
Key Tasks/Concepts The student will: ■ Use the tactile sense to differentiate each type of coin. ■ Correctly name all the coins.	
Description For students who are blind or who have low vision, being able to identify coins tactilely with ease is an important lifelong skill. This game provides young children with visual impairments an opportunity to develop fluency in the tactile identification of US coins. For some students, it may also provide a first exposure to all of the coins, their names, and distinguishing characteristics. Assuming that a student has had no previous exposure to coins, the teacher of students with visual impairments can start by placing five of one type of coin and one of another type in a gold bag. At first, the teacher will want to choose two very different coins, such as the penny and the half dollar. If the goal were to teach the identification of the penny, one penny would be placed in the bag with the half dollars and the student asked to find the "smallest coin with the smooth edge." After tactilely confirming that the correct coin had been found, the teacher would explain that the smaller coin with the smooth edge was called a penny. The penny would be returned to the bag and the student asked either to find the penny or the smallest coin with the smooth edge. It would not be necessary or advisable to provide the name of the other coin at this point. Once the student could reliably locate the penny by name or descriptor, then the pirate game can be played. More pennies are added to the bag and the teacher puts on a pirate's hat. The teacher draws a card from a pile on which she has brailled or typed directions, such as "Find two pennies, matey," or "Captain Bligh says, 'Find four of the smallest coins with smooth edges.'" If the student finds the correct number and type of coin, the roles reverse and the student gets to wear the pirate's hat and draw the card; the teacher follows the written directions. If an incorrect identification is made, then the hat stays with the current pirate and the player who made the error takes another turn.	

(continued on next page)

As the student becomes proficient at finding the pennies among the half dollars, other coins can be added (quarters, then dimes, then nickels). When dimes are added to the mix, the student's attention will need to be focused on the reeded edges (the edges with ridges) and it may be necessary to play the game with just these two coins (with only the penny actually identified) for a while. When nickels are added to the mix, the focus will need to be on differentiating the coins by weight and size; the penny will still be the "smallest coin with the smooth edge." As with the dime, it may be necessary to work with just these two coins in the bag before others are added.

After the student can find the penny with ease among the coins in the bag, the teacher can ask the student to draw a coin from the bag (either randomly or by direction—"Get me the smallest coin with the rough edge."), which then becomes the target of the next round of instruction. The coin should be named and its tactile characteristics explored by the teacher and student together. The teacher can add additional direction cards to the draw pile and, as with the penny, add additional coins to the bag as the child demonstrates the ability to select the targeted coins with ease.

For students who know the names of the coins and their general characteristics, but who need additional practice to develop tactile fluency, the teacher might introduce the use of a timer into the game. In this variation, the child would try to beat his or her previous time in locating the targeted coins and would be permitted to wear the pirate's hat as long as each turn was completed more quickly than the last.

The timed version of the game could be played with two players, each with a bag filled with identical coin sets. The player fastest at finding the targeted coins wins the round (and the right to wear the pirate's hat).

Because this game is played entirely with the tactile sense, a sighted peer could join without having an advantage.

Instructional Materials and Supplies Needed

- Pennies, dimes, nickels, quarters, half dollars, and dollar coins—at least five of each coin
- Gold bag with drawstring
- Pirate's hat
- Index cards with print and/or braille directions, such as "Find the biggest coin with a rough edge;" "Find two little coins with smooth edges;" "Find the biggest coin."
- Timing device

Settings

Recess area, teacher's meeting area, resource room

Duration/Timing

5–15 minutes. If started when a student is 3 or 4 years old, frequent shorter sessions might be preferred. For older students (7–8 years old) whose peers can identify coins, sessions may have to be longer.

Evaluation

Progress monitoring probes can be conducted biweekly to confirm that the student is acquiring the targeted skills.

Task	Date	Date	Date	Date
Tactilely locates penny within 5 seconds				
Tactilely locates nickel within 5 seconds				
Tactilely locates dime within 5 seconds				
Tactilely locates quarter within 5 seconds				
Tactilely locates half dollar within 5 seconds				
Tactilely locates dollar coin within 5 seconds				

Learning Activity: Dress for the Weather

Primary ECC Area: Independent living **Component:** Dressing
Grades: K–3, students with multiple disabilities

Other ECC Areas
- Self-determination
- O&M
- Compensatory access
- Social interaction

Goal: The student will determine which clothes to wear in different kinds of weather (hot, cold, warm, rain, snow, variable temperatures) and for different functions.

Key Tasks/Concepts
The student will:
- Identify different kinds of weather.
- Determine what clothes to wear for certain kinds of weather and certain kinds of places—school, church, outside, inside, movies, and the like.
- Practice zipping, buttoning, snapping, tying, pulling clothes on, taking clothes off, getting shoes on and off, recognizing the order of items when dressing.
- Identify popular logos on clothing, discuss current clothing styles, and where to shop for clothes.

Description
This activity can occur throughout the year as the weather changes. Students should be taught to be aware of the weather and the seasons, to determine appropriate clothing to wear for different kinds of weather, and to select appropriate clothes to wear to certain events while keeping the weather in mind. The teacher can bring out various types of clothing and, after instruction, ask the student to sort items by what would be worn when it is hot, rainy, cold, windy, and so forth.

Other questions to ask include what to wear if it is:
- raining and you are going to school
- hot and you are going to an outside fair
- hot outside and you are going to a movie
- cold outside and you are going to school
- cold in the morning, turning warm in the afternoon, and you will be outside all day

The activity can be made more fun by having students pull from a pile of cards containing the names of items of clothing and then put on the item selected (preferably in a large size), so that they might end with a rain slicker on over a swimsuit, while wearing snow boots.

Children who are young, nonverbal, or have additional physical disabilities may need to be presented with fewer items at a time and asked to provide responses using the means of communication that has been established for them. For example, a student with limited hand functioning and cognitive impairment might be allowed to examine a jacket and told that it is worn when it is cold outside. Then, presented with a jacket and a flip-flop, the child would be asked which item is worn when it is cold. As students develop mastery with limited numbers of items, additional ones could be presented.

This kind of activity can be adjusted for older students, including teens, to focus less on the weather and more on making dressing decisions based on current fashions.

This is a good activity to share with parents, who can work with children on the key tasks and help their children develop independent dressing skills while expressing preferences for clothing styles and color and picking out the appropriate clothing to wear.

(continued on next page)

Instructional Materials and Supplies Needed

- Cards with names of clothing items on them
- Various items of clothing and shoes, suitable for a variety of different conditions, that can be used to practice zipping, buttoning, snapping, and tying and for matching to the items on the cards
- Clothing catalogs for ideas

Settings

The classroom and home

Duration/Timing

- 5–10 minute discussion—"What is the weather today? What do you have on? Is it appropriate for today's weather?"

or

- 30–45 minute lesson that includes all the key tasks listed in the description

Evaluation

The evaluation for this activity should focus on the student's ability to do each of the key tasks listed. Scoring rubrics, such as the one below, can be developed that evaluate the student's ability to do these tasks.

1 Needs physical and verbal assistance.
2 Needs a prompt.
3 Identifies the weather accurately.
4 Identifies the weather and appropriate clothing.

The evaluation can be altered for students with multiple disabilities by addressing the various levels of prompting needed.

Learning Activity: Who Washes Dishes By Hand Anymore?

Primary ECC Area: Independent living **Component:** Cleaning and general household tasks
Grades: K–8

Other ECC Areas

- Compensatory access
- Career education

Goal: The student will hand wash, rinse, and dry dishes.

Key Tasks/Concepts

The student will:

- Prepare dishes to be washed.
- Determine the order in which dishes will be washed.
- Adjust temperature of water.
- Fill sink with water.
- Squeeze appropriate amount of liquid detergent into sink.
- Wash dishes completely.
- Rinse dishes.
- Dry dishes.
- Put dishes in cupboard.

Description

This activity should start on a limited scale and be increased in scope as the student's proficiency improves. Washing dishes makes good sense after a meal or snack has been eaten. For young students, it may be enough

(continued on next page)

for the teacher to ask them to help bring the dishes from the table to the counter and to hand the dishes to the teacher to be washed. At some point, though, the teacher will want to encourage students to help in other ways—to turn the water on and off, to let the teacher know when the water temperature is just right, to practice squeezing the detergent into the water, and to use a sponge or cloth to clean the dishes. For students who have tactile sensitivity issues, it may be best to start by having the child assist with rinsing and drying, and then as the child's comfort level increases, expand to other tasks.

The complexity of this task can be expanded in the following ways:

- increasing the number and variety of dishware items
- increasing the fragility of the dishware
- introducing different types of dishes (such as pots and pans)
- introducing items with foods that are baked on or otherwise hard to remove

As the student becomes familiar with the skills involved in this activity, the teacher of students with visual impairments can look for other opportunities to practice the skills so that they become more automatic. Arrangements might be made to wash the cups and dishes left in the sink in the teachers' lounge on a specific day of the week. (Crafty teachers might even offer to have this work done for a small sum. Earnings can be used to purchase cleaning supplies or food for cooking lessons.)

Students in elementary classrooms often like to assist their teacher with classroom chores. Including another child in this activity would provide an opportunity for the two children to socialize while working together.

The teacher can discuss the brand of dishwashing soap that has been used, where it was purchased, where else it could be purchased, what it cost, why that brand was selected, and other options that might have been available.

This activity can be extended in the area of career education by visiting a restaurant and talking with the dishwasher. Students could ask the worker basic information about the job, including hours worked, the rate of pay, and the advantages and disadvantages to being a dishwasher.

Settings

Ideally, instruction related to this activity will occur in the student's home. If not, then it may be possible that instruction occurs in the preschool classroom, resource room, or in the teacher's lounge.

Instructional Materials and Supplies Needed

- Dirty dishware
- Liquid dishwashing detergent
- Drying cloths
- Dishrag or sponge
- Dish rack

Duration/Timing

- 30–45 minutes or longer, depending on the skill level of the students and the number of dishes to be washed

Evaluation

The student's progress in the development of mastery of dishwashing skills can be measured using a tool based on a task analysis* of the activity, such as the one below. Performance can be measured during every session or probes taken less frequently, such as once each month.

Task	Date	Date	Date	Date
Prepares dishes for washing				
Prioritizes dishes for washing				
Adjusts temperature of water				

(continued on next page)

Fills sink				
Squeezes dishwashing liquid				
Washes drinking glasses				
Washes silverware				
Washes plates				
Washes serving dishes				
Washes pots/pans				
Rinses items thoroughly				
Dries items thoroughly				
Stores items				

* The task analysis for students who are very young or have additional disabilities who are being taught this task or taught to engage in parts of this task would be more detailed and recognize the specific learning needs of each student.

Key:
I = Independent
VD = Verbal direction
P = Physical support

Learning Activity: Hang 10

Primary ECC Area: Independent living **Component:** Clothing care
Grades: 2–10

Other ECC Areas

- Compensatory access
- Career education
- Sensory efficiency

Goal: The student will fold and hang articles of clothing.

Key Tasks/Concepts

The student will:

- Fold washcloths.
- Fold towels.
- Fold tee-shirts.
- Fold underwear (briefs, boxers, bras, panties).
- Match socks.
- Hang button-front shirt on hanger.
- Fold pants.
- Hang pants on hanger.
- Hang a dress on a hanger.
- Hang a skirt on a skirt hanger.

Description

The teacher of students with visual impairments will need to consult with the student's family to determine the techniques that are used in the home to handle clean clothes. Not every family folds clothes the

(continued on next page)

same way; not every family even folds clothes after they are washed. Still, it is important for the student to know about these skills, as clothing organization is a valuable tool for maximizing efficiency as an adult. Whenever possible, the family's preferences should be honored in the instruction, especially for younger students. (It might be appropriate for older students to be shown other options.)

Parents may choose to send a bag containing clean clothes for the teacher to use when teaching the student folding skills at school. Alternatively, the teacher may elect to bring some of her own clothes for this purpose or to keep a bag of discarded items at school for this purpose.

This activity is useful for teaching children with limited experiences that different people wear different sizes and types of clothing, which may help students to develop knowledge of themselves and others. The teacher can use the folding activities to discuss concepts of size ("Whose underwear is smallest?") and gender-specific garments ("Who wears a bra?").

When working with hangers, the teacher can discuss with the student where one purchases hangers, how much the different types of hangers cost, fabrics, fabric care, and laundry options. The teacher can also provide information to the student about the people whose work involves these same skills.

Speed and fluency in getting clothes folded and hung is important. These skills will need to be practiced frequently, so that automaticity can be achieved. Timing the student who has acquired the skills, yet whose pace is still slow, may be of value in the development of mastery.

Students who are not motivated to learn hanger skills may need more incentive. Job readiness can be further incorporated by having students earn coins or tokens depending on how productive they are (paid in tokens for hanging clothes). The tokens can later be exchanged to "buy" free time activities that the student prefers, such as computer time, listening to music, or cooking a meal.

Partial participation of students with severe intellectual or physical disabilities might involve identifying the way certain types of clothing are to be stored (such as folded or hung), making initial folds on items, or handing the item to be folded or hung to the peer or adult who is performing the task.

Settings

Ideally, instruction related to this activity will occur in the student's home. If not, then instruction might occur in the resource room or space assigned to the itinerant teacher. Since this skill is one that other children learn incidentally, it may not be appropriate to provide instruction on this skill in the presence of peers.

Instructional Materials and Supplies Needed

- Plastic and metal hangers
- Specialized hangers for skirts or pants
- Clean clothes
- Sock sorters (if necessary)

Duration/Timing

The time required for this activity will depend on a number of factors that can be controlled by the teacher. A lesson on folding one garment (with opportunities for guided and independent practice) may take 25–30 minutes. A lesson focused on developing speed when folding several similar garments may require less time.

Evaluation

The student's progress in the development of these clothing care skills can be measured through a tool based on articles of clothing or skills involved. Performance can be measured during every session (as in the example below) or probes taken less frequently, such as every two weeks. For some children, it may be necessary to prepare a detailed task analysis of every step of folding or hanging each type of garment and use that task analysis as a basis for measuring progress.

(continued on next page)

Task	Date	Date	Date	Date
Folds washcloths				
Folds towels				
Folds tee-shirts				
Folds underwear (briefs, boxers, bras, panties)				
Matches/folds socks				
Hangs button-front shirt on hanger				
Folds pants				
Hangs pants on hanger				
Hangs a girl's dress on a hanger				
Hangs a skirt on a skirt hanger				

Key:
I = Independent
VD = Verbal direction
P = Physical support

Learning Activity: I'm Stuck!

Primary ECC Area: Independent living **Component:** Cleaning and general household tasks
Grades: 2–5

Other ECC Areas

- Compensatory access
- Career education
- Orientation and mobility
- Recreation and leisure

Goal: Student will use a grid pattern to clean a table top

Key Tasks/Concepts

The student will:

- Evaluate the cleanliness of table.
- Use an organized pattern to find the food on table.

Description

This activity takes the form of a game the object of which is to be the first to wipe the assigned area of a table thoroughly using the double grid pattern. Before playing the game, the teacher will need to have demonstrated to the student how to use a double grid pattern to wipe a table clean. The student will also need to be shown how to wring the water from the sponge or paper towel.

When first instructing the student in the use of the grid pattern, the teacher can speak aloud the steps that she is using on her side of the table and have the student follow along. "My right hand is leading the way as I move from the left side of the table to the right side. Oops! I'm stuck! I found something messy! I'll just wipe it up with my sponge until I can't feel it any more. Now I'm at the side of the table. Guess I'll have to go back to the left and start again."

For the game, the teacher will need to divide a small table top into two sections using Wikki Stix or some other semi-permanent item (two tables could also be used). The student would be asked to smear some sticky

(continued on next page)

food (such as honey, jam, peanut better, or mayonnaise) on several places on one side of the table while the teacher does the same on the other side of the table. (The number of smears and the substance used could be agreed upon in advance by the student and teacher.) One of the players starts the timer, and each player does the following:

1. Dips a sponge or paper towel in warm water
2. Wrings out the water
3. Wipes clean the assigned side of the table
4. Dries assigned side of the table

When the timer rings, the two players switch sides to check the other's work, again following a grid pattern to identify if the work was done well. If there is a doubt about whether the mess has been cleaned or if the table is dry enough, the students can place a tissue on the surface to see if it sticks.

For each area that isn't thoroughly cleaned or that is left too damp, a point is assessed. The player with the fewest points wins.

This game could also be played with a blindfolded peer or another student with visual impairment.

A variation of this game is to use dry or crumbly food on the table and to spread a towel or table cloth on the floor to catch food that the students push off the table instead of catching. The player with the cleanest table and the cleanest floor cloth would be the winner.

Instructional Materials and Supplies Needed

- One or two small tables
- Wikki Stix to divide table
- Sticky or messy food item
- Paper towels, dishcloths, or sponges
- Timer
- Blindfold for teacher or peer
- Bowl or pail filled with warm sudsy water
- Tissues

Settings

The teacher's meeting area, a resource room, or the student's home

Duration/Timing

The length of time required to play this game can be managed by adjusting the number of food smears on each side of the table, the time set on the timer, and the number of rounds that are played. More time should be allowed if two children are playing.

Evaluation

If the evaluation is done during every lesson, the data sheet might look like the following:

Task	Date	Date	Date	Date
Uses organized technique to identify food on table				
Locates sticky messes				
Wrings water thoroughly from dishrag				
Thoroughly cleans mess from table				
Wipes table dry				

Key:
M = Mastery level
D = Developing
U = Unacceptable

Learning Activity: It Costs How Much?

Primary ECC Area: Independent living **Component:** Money management
Grades: 4–10

Other ECC Areas

- Compensatory access (counting, ordering)
- Assistive technology (cost of equipment)

Goal: Student will place a series of items in order, based on their relative costs.

Key Tasks/Concepts

The student will understand that:

- Objects that people use cost money.
- Not all objects cost the same amount.
- The size of the object isn't necessarily related to its cost.

Description

The teacher can collect a variety of items familiar to the student, like a pack of gum, a compact disc, a can of soda, a cane, a candy bar, a brailler, a television, a cell phone, a package of socks, and a toy.

Selecting two of the items with different costs, but still within the student's numeracy understanding (the gum and the CD, for example), the teacher would explain that the gum costs about $2 and the CD costs around $15. Students who are concrete learners, such as those who are younger or who have additional disabilities, could be asked to count out the number of dollar bills needed to purchase each item. A third item—the socks, for instance—could then be introduced and the student told their cost and asked to count out the number of dollar bills necessary to pay for them. The student could then be asked to put the items in order from most to least expensive. Additional items could be similarly introduced, with discussions centering on why some items cost more than others. As the student becomes more familiar with items that have prices within easy counting range, more expensive items could be included, such as the brailler or television.

It would be valuable for the teacher to find out from the family a list of items that they purchase regularly, such as types and brands of groceries, items of clothing, and places they go for meals out and for entertainment. Whenever possible, the teacher should include the same or similar items in the lesson.

Families can be involved further by discussing with the student the prices of the items that they purchase when shopping, explaining how they get the money to pay for them, and describing how they make shopping decisions.

For students who are older and who don't have an intellectual disability, it isn't necessary to use real items or to count out bills. Instead, the cost of a broader range of objects, including adaptive technology, can be discussed. It is still important to focus on objects familiar to the student. It may be of value to include in discussions the fact that some items that look similar can cost very different amounts.

Instructional Materials and Supplies Needed

- Dollar bills
- Items whose prices are being discussed

Settings

Meeting area or resource room

Duration/Timing:

- Segments of 5–7 minutes, or longer.

This lesson could be presented in short segments of approximately 5–7 minutes each, for example: "Let's take a break from reading for a few minutes. Remember last week when we talked about how much your cane cost? What did we say it cost? That's right, about $20. You asked me then to bring something today that costs

(continued on next page)

less than a cane, but more than that $6 package of socks. Look what I found. It's a desk fan, and it cost $13. I got it at Sears. So, we have a package of socks, a desk fan, and a cane. Put them in order for me, with the most expensive on the right and the least expensive on the left."

This lesson also could be presented over a longer period of time, with more objects introduced and a longer discussion of their relative values.

Evaluation

If the evaluation is done during every lesson, the data sheet might be set up as follows:

Task	Date	Date	Date	Date
Organizes 3 items from least expensive to most expensive, with no errors				
Organizes 5 items from least expensive to most expensive, with no errors				
Organizes 10 items from least expensive to most expensive, with no errors				
Organizes 20 items from least expensive to most expensive, with no errors				

A more summative evaluation of the student's knowledge of the relative cost of items might be determined through a unit test, as follows:

1. Which costs more, a desk fan or a pair of socks?
2. Which costs more, a candy bar or a cane?
3. Which costs less, a package of gum or a package of cereal?
4. Which costs less, a brailler or a CD player?

CHAPTER 9

Social Interaction

Sharon Z. Sacks

L. Penny Rosenblum

Social interaction is an essential area of the expanded core curriculum (ECC) for students with visual impairments. Social skills permeate all aspects of a student's life and are in addition an integral part of other areas of the ECC, such as compensatory access, recreation and leisure, independent living, and self-determination. For children and adolescents who are sighted, the acquisition of social skills occurs naturally by imitating visually observed events. Sighted babies, for example, will react to the smiles of their parents and other family members by one month of age. In contrast, babies who are blind or visually impaired may not respond to social cues such as smiling unless they also receive verbal or tactile cues.

It has been estimated that almost 80 percent of what is learned socially is taken in through the visual sense (Hill & Blasch, 1980). Many students with visual impairments may therefore have difficulty acquiring information about their social environment, engaging in social activities, and understanding and interpreting the social nuances involved in everyday interactions. Students who have congenital visual impairments—who have been visually impaired since birth—are more dependent on others, such as family members and friends, to obtain valuable information about the social worlds in which they live and the intricacies involved in developing and maintaining social relationships. Also, students who have disabilities in addition to visual impairments may not understand the abstract concepts involved in acquiring a repertoire of social skills. These students may need to learn social skills in a more concrete and structured manner.

Of all the developmental processes, social development for students with visual impairments, including students with additional disabilities, is perhaps the most highly dependent on the support of teachers, family, friends, and others to bring the social world to the child. How others react to and interact with students who are blind or visually impaired can play a significant role in students' self-perception. Also, when students are not given opportunities to engage with others, make choices and decisions, and learn the social rules of their environment, they can become socially isolated and experience poor self-esteem, which may negatively affect their success in the academic arena.

Acquiring social interaction skills can often be an ongoing process for students with visual impairments. Students who have congenital visual impairments, as well as students who acquire a visual impairment at a later age, require instruction that is consistent, regularly monitored by teachers and family members, and that provides opportunities to practice a repertoire of social skills in a variety of natural settings. In order for students with visual impairments, including students who have additional disabilities, to be successful in social environments, they need to be motivated to engage with others and experience the world around them. Providing students with numerous hands-on experiences and facilitating opportunities to engage with others are essential elements in establishing a strong social foundation. Because of the prevailing emphasis on academic subjects for all students, including those with disabilities, instruction in social interaction may often be minimized or overlooked. This chapter provides suggestions and strategies designed to help effectively promote the social interaction skills that are so important to students' well-being and life success.

DEVELOPMENT OF SOCIAL SKILLS

Social skills include knowing the social rules—typically based on social beliefs and mores—at work in a culture or society. Often, these rules involve comprehending nonverbal cues, which requires sophisticated problem solving and analysis. The acquisition of social skills allows students to communicate effectively with others, engage in positive interactions, and establish and maintain relationships with other students, friends, classmates, and adults.

It is important to recognize that social skills are influenced by additional factors, such as family values and beliefs, socioeconomic status, culture, and, for people with visual impairments, beliefs about the competence of people who are blind or visually impaired. In addition, teachers of students with visual impairments, orientation and mobility (O&M) specialists, and other professionals may have their own biases regarding social propriety. Nevertheless, beliefs and values held by members of a student's educational team should not influence what they teach. Rather, their instruction should be based on thoughtful assessment and knowledge of how students with and without visual impairments develop socially.

When considering how children with visual impairments learn social skills, it is important for professionals and families to recognize that their social development process may be different than that of children who are sighted. The social development process for students with visual impairments, including students with additional disabilities, can be conceptualized as progressing through three levels, which might be termed awareness, interaction, and evaluation (Sacks, 2006; Sacks & Silberman, 2000). While children who are sighted may, as noted earlier, move through these levels with little adult support and for the most part acquire a repertoire of social skills through visual imitation, children with visual impairments require that the social world be brought to them.

Initially, students with visual impairments develop an *awareness* of others and a sense of self-identity. For example, a young child who is deaf-blind and exhibits cognitive challenges may not respond to family members or siblings in a positive manner unless he is helped to understand the existence of others outside of himself and is provided with a tactile cue, such as a light touch to the arm or shoulder coupled with a greeting, to alert him to others entering his world.

At the next level, students with visual impairments develop skills and strategies to *interact* with other students and adults. For example, a student who is congenitally blind needs to learn to turn her head toward the person speaking when conversing with a friend or teacher.

The third level requires a student to be able to interpret social situations, *evaluate* each social encounter, and use a range of social strategies to engage with others. For example, an adolescent with low vision may not be able to see the nonverbal cues of friends hanging out in a group. He may need to listen to the conversation of others, obtain clarifying information from a trusted friend, or physically get closer in order to determine the tenor of the group.

COMPONENTS OF SOCIAL INTERACTION

The area of social interaction includes at least nine components. While the following list of components is not exhaustive, it is based on research completed by experts in the field of blindness and visual impairment (Sacks, Kekelis, & Gaylord-Ross, 1992; Sacks & Wolffe, 2006b; Sacks, Wolffe, & Tierney, 1998; Wolffe & Sacks, 1997).

- appropriate body language
- social communication
- effective conversation patterns
- cooperative skills
- interactions with others
- social etiquette
- development of relationships and friendships
- knowledge of self
- interpretation and monitoring of social behavior

Within each of these components, there are numerous behaviors and skills to be learned by students with visual impairments. Some of the skills discussed in this chapter overlap with those that fall under other ECC components. For example, in the ECC area of recreation and leisure, children also learn to engage and greet one another through pretend play. While taking responsibility for one's actions may be an important skill in the area of career development, teaching students to understand how their social behavior affects others is an important component of developing relationships and friendships. The following sections address each component and its related skills. It is important to remember that social skills instruction for many of these behaviors is an ongoing process that requires consistent practice over time, throughout a student's educational career.

Appropriate Body Language

Body language is the way in which people move or position themselves physically and in so doing, communicate their thoughts and feelings. To demonstrate appropriate body language, students need to learn the following skills:

- maintaining appropriate eye contact
  - turning head toward the direction of the speaker's voice
  - keeping head up
  - looking at a person
- demonstrating appropriate body posture
  - standing and sitting in an erect and relaxed manner
  - placing arms and hands close to body
- maintaining personal body space
  - engaging with others without getting too close (remaining 12 to 18 inches away)
  - using appropriate touching when engaging with others
- utilizing and responding to gestures and facial expressions
  - using facial expressions that are representative of mood or emotional state (smile, frown, angry, sad, frightened)
  - nodding or shaking head appropriately to indicate affirmative or negative responses
  - waving hello and good-bye
  - pointing
  - performing hand motions to communicate "stop" or "come closer"
  - performing thumbs-up and thumbs-down gestures
  - interpreting facial expressions or gestures from other students or adults by using vision or verbal feedback

- refraining from socially unacceptable mannerisms
  - recognizing behaviors that are socially inappropriate in public (such as nose picking, licking or smelling arms or hands, masturbation)
  - understanding the concepts of public and private
  - refraining from inappropriate touching
  - replacing rocking as an expression of happiness or stress
  - replacing eye poking or light gazing as an expression of boredom or an attempt to obtain stimulation

At the most basic level, developing an awareness of oneself in relation to others is an essential component of acquiring skills to use body language in ways that are considered socially acceptable by others. Many of the behaviors students need to learn in this area typically are acquired through the use of vision. Therefore, alternative strategies should be employed to help youngsters develop these skills. For example, teaching students to turn their heads in the direction of the speaker or keeping one's head up during a conversation may not occur naturally without physical or verbal reminders. Teachers and family members may need to reinforce these behaviors by demonstrating them to the student in a variety of environments beginning at an early age.

Teaching social behaviors, like maintaining body posture and body space, may be influenced by the student's culture and beliefs. In some families, it is acceptable for children and adults to have close physical proximity when engaging with others. Yet in Western society, there are unwritten social rules that require individuals to engage with one another from a distance of about 12 to 18 inches. In some cultures, slouching connotes laziness or disinterest. Students with visual impairments may be unaware of such societal rules unless they are provided with the information or training to follow them. Sighted children can observe other people's body stance and the distance they maintain from others. They learn relatively early, through imitation and visual observation, that people stand in an erect position, for example. Students with visual impairments need to learn the difference between standing in a stiff, erect position and standing or sitting in a more relaxed manner. The nuances of these behaviors and how to teach them are important for professionals to consider.

Again, learning nonverbal behaviors, such as gestures and facial expressions, requires deliberate instruction and structured support from professionals and family members. It is common for young children who are sighted, for example, to nod their heads to say "yes" or shake their heads for "no" and wave good-bye when disengaging with others. Imitation allows them to learn more complex gestures. In school settings, teachers may ask students to use "thumbs up" or "thumbs down" gestures to indicate whether students have completed their work or require more time. In play, children learn that a palm held up and facing outward means that they should stop moving. Unless provided with this information, students with visual impairments may miss these essential social cues. The same is true for learning facial expressions. For example, a child who is blind may smile when she is scared or angry. Conversely, a student with a severe visual impairment may frown or grimace when having his picture taken if he has not been taught to smile.

Many students who are blind or have low vision exhibit behaviors that may be considered socially inappropriate. Students exhibit these behaviors for many reasons. For example, for some students, rocking back and forth, twirling, or hand flapping provides sensory stimulation. Some children may exhibit these behaviors because they are overly stressed. Others may do so because they are happy, excited, or bored. For some students, these behaviors may be habitual. Eye poking or light gazing may also be indicative of specific visual impairments. For example, children with glaucoma may poke their eyes in an effort to relieve pain. Students with cataracts, and sometimes students with cortical visual impairments, may enjoy gazing at sunlight or colored lights while moving their hands or fingers in front of their eyes.

While these behaviors may be considered socially unacceptable by many, several things need to be determined by professionals and families before pursuing a change in the behavior:

1. Why the behavior occurs.
2. If the behavior serves a purpose.
3. Whether the behavior should be extinguished, changed, or redirected.
4. If there are contexts where it might be considered socially appropriate for the behavior to occur.

For example, allowing students to rock in a rocking chair is considered more age-appropriate and socially acceptable than self-stimulatory rocking while seated in a desk chair during class. Many students with visual impairments do not realize that others can observe their behavior. It is important to help students understand that when they exhibit behaviors that are considered undesirable by others, it is likely that they will be excluded or ignored from social interactions and opportunities. Students with additional disabilities may require more structured intervention to reduce or change socially distancing behaviors. Such intervention may involve redirection of the behavior by changing the behavior to a more acceptable behavior.

Learning of appropriate body language begins when children are very young and develops as experiences occur that allow for natural teaching opportunities. For example, if a student sits quietly at the lunch table in a slouched position with his head down, his teacher should encourage appropriate posture at the table for all students and remind the group that having a conversation with the other students at their table is appropriate. An additional reminder to the student with a visual impairment might include a cue to look up so others at the table will know he is listening to the conversation.

Social Communication

Social communication is the ability to interact with another person or group of people using verbal or nonverbal forms of communication. Behaviors and skills in the area of social communication require engagement and interaction with family members, teachers, and classmates. For social interaction to occur, students typically need to exhibit a communicative intent, whether through speaking or through other expressive means, such as a squeal, crying, or laughter. To demonstrate social communication, students need to learn the following skills:

- initiating contact with and greeting others
  - approaching a person
  - looking at a person
  - using an appropriate greeting for a given situation
- engaging with others
  - showing interest in people
  - being willing to be touched
  - reacting positively to cuddling, tickling, or hugs
- expressing wants and needs
  - using expressive language to communicate wants and needs
  - using signs, gestures, tactile symbols, or augmentative devices to communicate wants and needs
- making choices
  - using expressive language to communicate choices
  - using signs, gestures, tactile symbols, pictures, or augmentative devices to communicate choices
- responding appropriately to positive and negative feedback
  - saying, signing, or using an augmentative device to say "thank you" or other pleasantries
  - refraining from having tantrums, crying, or inappropriate verbal or signed responses

Young children who are sighted develop social communication behaviors almost from birth. Newborns, for example, will respond to their caregivers by looking at them when they are spoken to. Likewise, babies who are sighted make their wants and needs known through social engagement with caregivers and family members. Young children who are blind or who have low vision do not learn these behaviors incidentally. Parents and family members may need to develop alternate strategies, such as verbal reinforcement, physical contact, or moving the child in position to look at another person when creating reciprocal interactions. Also, families need to interpret their child's communicative intent to determine basic wants and needs (Chen, 2014). Creating a communicative rhythm and exchange between parent and child may sometimes be difficult, particularly when a young child is resistant to touch or cuddling. Many young children with visual impairments require and react positively to a verbal anticipatory cue like, "It's Mommy! I'm going to pick you up."

As children with visual impairments grow older, it is important to find ways for them to make choices. Preschoolers need to be given opportunities to make choices about what they might like for a snack or what clothing they would like to wear to school. Providing these opportunities establishes the foundation for autonomy and for students to become socially assertive later in life. Many students with visual impairments and additional disabilities may not be able to express themselves verbally, but can engage with others through gestures, sign language, or communication devices that speak for them. It is extremely important for families and professionals to find ways to ensure that these students have opportunities to make choices and decisions when interacting with others.

Learning to greet and initiate interaction with others usually involves the use of vision. Students with visual impairments need to learn to use their auditory skills to recognize when classmates and adults in their lives are approaching them. When greeting others, youngsters should incorporate body language skills, such as looking at the other person, and use gestures and facial expressions correctly to match the verbal greeting. Students who have additional disabilities and visual impairments may learn to use augmentative communication devices that are programmed to state a greeting when activated by the student. In order to promote positive interaction with other children, it is important for the device to have an age-appropriate voice recording the greeting. (See the learning activity "Greetings" at the end of this chapter for ideas on how to teach greeting skills.)

Social communication at a higher level involves understanding how one's behavior influences others. Complimenting friends and classmates and showing empathy toward others are critical behaviors for developing positive social relationships. Because many students with visual impairments cannot always visually interpret nonverbal behavior from peers or adults accurately, it can be difficult for them to understand the information others are communicating without the support of a trusted friend or caring adult.

Effective Conversation Patterns

Understanding effective conversation patterns allows students to engage in topics of interest with friends, classmates, and adults. Conversations involve two or more people exchanging ideas in a reciprocal manner. The behaviors and skills needed for students to engage in conversation are multi-faceted. To demonstrate effective conversation patterns, students need to learn the following skills:

- initiating a conversation with peers or adults.
    - using "icebreakers" (such as, "What did you do this weekend?") to start a conversation
    - having a repertoire of experiences to draw on to start a conversation
- sharing appropriate information with peers and adults
- maintaining and expanding a conversation
    - listening attentively to others
    - staying on topic
    - knowing when to insert a comment
- knowing how to end a conversation
    - listening for a lull in the conversation
    - realizing when another person is ending a thought
    - saying or signing "good-bye" or some other indicator that the conversation has ended
- knowing how to take turns when in a conversation
    - understanding the give and take involved in a conversation
    - waiting for the speaker to stop talking
    - using body language or gestures to indicate that it is another person's turn to speak
    - being aware of the length of his or her comments when conversing with others
    - demonstrating awareness that a speaker's comments have concluded
- knowing how to ask for help or assistance
    - making requests in a pleasant manner
    - not demanding assistance from others
- inviting friends for special activities
    - asking friends to participate in a special activity
    - using the telephone to ask a friend to a special event
    - giving a friend a written invitation for a special event
    - using e-mail or a social networking site to invite a friend for a special event

In order for students with visual impairments to engage in conversations with peers or adults, they need to understand that a conversation is an exchange of thoughts and not simply a one-way outlet for their own expression. Having a conversation also requires that students have a variety of experiences to draw on and share in order to initiate, maintain, and expand conversational topics. For example, when children with visual impairments have had hands-on experiences with recreational activities, like playing on the play equipment at the park, riding on amusement park rides, or navigating a climbing wall, they can share their personal views with others. Also, students need to learn the give and take that occurs when engaging with another person. Students need to learn to listen for a lull in the conversation, wait a couple of seconds to respond, get the attention of the other person involved in the conversation, and hold the interest of others while speaking by staying on topic. Students also need to be flexible enough to change topics as the conversation progresses.

Many students with visual impairments and additional disabilities use alternative means to engage in conversations with peers and adults. Some students may use a combination of sign language and augmentative and alternative communication devices (discussed in Chapter 6), which will speak for the student when activated by a button or switch. Simple types of these devices use basic phrases to ask for assistance or to make wants and needs known to others. More complex devices allow the student to engage in a typical conversation. Just like other students with visual impairments, these students should learn to initiate a conversation, wait their turn to speak, and find ways to end a conversation.

As students with visual impairments become more skilled at conversing with others, they will recognize that conversations can be brief and that topics can change rapidly. Students need to learn to be flexible and willing to shift the conversational flow quickly. Not only do students need to learn how to converse face-to-face with peers and adults, they need to develop similar behaviors for conversing on the telephone, such as greeting, initiating a conversation, maintaining the conversation, shifting topics, and ending the conversation. In addition, students need to become skilled at conversing with others on social network sites, including developing an understanding of what information is appropriate to post on public sites. Teaching students to distinguish between sharing public and private information is critical to ensure their safety and well-being.

Cooperative Skills

Of all social skills that are taught to students with visual impairments, becoming skilled at cooperating with others is one of the most essential for life. Whether a young child with a visual impairment is in a play group, or an older student is engaged in competitive work, they will need to learn how to work with others in a cooperative and collaborative manner. Students who dominate group activities or try to change the focus of the activity are at risk for social isolation or group rejection (Corsaro, 1985). By contrast, students who take an equal but active role in social activities, such as choosing a game, are more likely to be included with their peers.

In order for students to be able to demonstrate positive cooperation, they need to learn the following behaviors and skills:

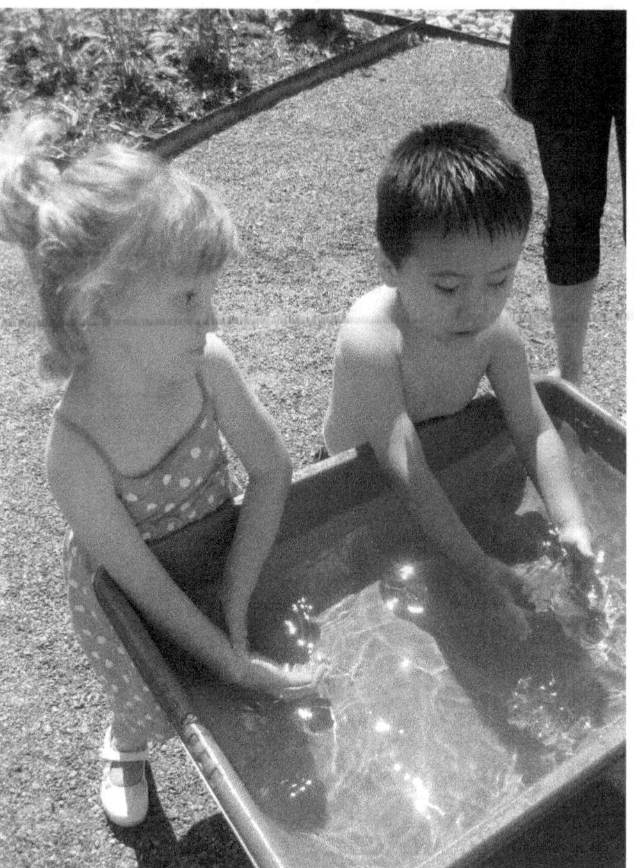

Anchor Center for Blind Children, Denver, CO

Learning to play side by side with other children and share toys is the beginning of learning cooperative skills.

- Understanding of group dynamics
  - Developing awareness of other members of a group
  - Understanding that one individual leads a group or activity
  - Understanding rules or expected behavior for specific group activities
- Sharing in group activities
  - Knowing how to initiate group interactions
  - Knowing how to enter a group in a positive manner
  - Knowing how to contribute to group choices and decisions
  - Demonstrating active participation in group activities
- Understanding roles and responsibilities of group members
  - Understanding the concept of a group leader
  - Understanding the role of a group member
  - Understanding the concept of cooperative learning groups and their function

  - Identifying roles and responsibilities in cooperative learning groups
- Understanding reciprosity and shared responsibilities in a group
  - Understanding the concept of give and take in making group decisions
  - Demonstrating flexibility in making choices or decisions
  - Complimenting and reciprocating when another group member helps or assists the student with a visual impairment

Helping students with visual impairments to develop cooperative skills begins at an early age. Families, with the support of the teacher of students with visual impairments or early intervention specialist, need to provide opportunities for young children to learn to share toys or take turns on play equipment. Structured group lessons led by a teacher of students with visual impairments provide students with a basic understanding of group dynamics: that they are part of a group, that the group is led by a teacher, and that there are specific activities to be accomplished during the lesson. Families can follow up with these concepts by using mealtime or family outings to reinforce sharing, waiting to take a turn, or initiating a desire to engage in a group activity.

School-age students with visual impairments engage in cooperative activities on a daily basis. For example, students in many general education classrooms engage in group projects and activities. Students with visual impairments need to know how to share and interact with their peers. They need to be aware of the roles and responsibilities within groups. Most important, they need to be taught how to take an active role in cooperative lessons or group projects. Too often, students with visual impairments are not given a leadership role in cooperative activities because they may not be assertive enough or feel that they have the skills or abilities to assume a leadership role.

Teachers of students with visual impairments and family members need to support students by providing opportunities to practice a variety of group roles in stress-free environments with familiar peers or adults so that they can learn how to

- contribute to choices and decisions as part of a group by providing a perspective or opinion, but realizing that the final decision or outcome may be different
- take an active role in completing group projects by having the necessary materials and adaptations to contribute to the finished product
- share in group activities without dominating the group by asking for assistance or support

As students with visual impairments in adolescence encounter greater independence and the potential for work, greater emphasis is placed on the ability to collaborate and cooperate in community and work settings. Adolescents and young adults with visual impairments need to know how to work effectively within a team model. They need to understand their role within a group, including how to work effectively with a team leader, know how to disagree with team decisions in a positive and proactive manner, how to take responsibility for completing tasks determined by the group, and effective ways of assisting the group to complete a project or work activity.

Interactions with Others

Students with visual impairments need to develop a repertoire of behaviors and skills in order to interact effectively with peers and adults. Interaction with others is based on an awareness of the fact that other people are human beings with needs that are to be respected and that courtesy, consideration, and respect are basic ingredients of interaction. Skills in this area are essential to the development of friendships and other relationships, and critical if a student is to successfully engage in a variety of activities in school, at home, and in the community. To demonstrate effective interactions with others, students need to learn the following skills:

- greeting others and saying "hello" or "good-bye" when appropriate
  - approaching friends, classmates, or adults to greet them
  - using a variety of greetings depending on the person being greeted and the occasion (see the learning activity "Greetings" at the end of this chapter for ideas on how to teach this skill)
  - using appropriate gestures and facial expressions when greeting someone
- maintaining interactions with peers and adults
  - understanding that an interaction has a beginning, middle, and end
  - understanding that an interaction involves turn taking
  - using age-appropriate topics to maintain an interaction

- knowing how to respond to teasing
- recognizing and knowing how to report bullying

■ compromising
- sharing toys, games, and possessions
- understanding that others may have likes and dislikes
- engaging in an activity that may not be favored or liked
- being willing to allow others to make choices or decisions

■ showing empathy and sympathy for others
- recognizing a variety of feelings and emotions
- demonstrating awareness of others and their feelings
- supporting classmates and friends in games, sports activities, and in the classroom
- supporting a friend or classmate when she is ill or hurts herself or otherwise needs help
- supporting a friend or classmate when he shows feelings such as sadness, fear, or disappointment

■ complimenting and encouraging the efforts of others
- using positive statements when someone else does something special
- demonstrating unselfish behavior when engaging with others
- showing good sportsmanship in play activities and games in school or in the community

■ demonstrating gratitude toward others
- saying "thank you" when peers or adults have assisted or done something special for the student (see the learning activity "Showing Gratitude" at the end of this chapter for ideas on teaching this skill)
- understanding and using the concept of reciprocation

Developing positive interaction skills allows students with visual impairments to engage effectively with others. Families of young children with visual impairments set the tone for social interactions by encouraging and fostering reciprocal interactions. Through play and cuddling, families teach their child the give and take of interactions. As children grow older and develop a means to communicate, whether via verbal language, signs, gestures, or augmentative communication devices, they learn to engage by approaching others and gaining attention. It is not uncommon for toddlers to wave hello or good-bye, and to say, "hi" or "hello." Young students with visual impairments need to be encouraged to approach classmates to initiate greetings or conversations. It is important for families and teachers to model positive social interactions, as well.

When students are in elementary and middle school, their social groups widen. Expectations increase for students to engage with classmates in sports, recreation activities, group work in class, and social activities. Students should be able to expand their greetings into conversations that peers will find interesting. They should learn to share their ideas and belongings, as well as share in making decisions about games or activities others might want to enjoy. Learning to compromise and understand that others have feelings and preferred activities is critical in order to develop friendships and lasting relationships.

Students need to learn to strike a balance between complimenting too much and ignoring the accomplishments of others. Sometimes it is useful for teachers and other caring adults to provide feedback about students' behavior. For example, a teacher might inform her student that a friend scored a home run during recess so that he can provide a compliment to his friend.

Students who are blind or who have low vision need to reach beyond themselves and learn the importance of letting peers and adults know that their assistance is appreciated. Expressing gratitude when others have done something special for the student is an essential part of positive social interactions. As students grow older, teaching them to reciprocate when peers or adults provide assistance on a regular basis is another key skill to emphasize when teaching positive social interactions. (See the learning activity "Showing Gratitude" at the end of this chapter for ideas on reinforcing appreciation skills.)

Much of what makes social interactions positive involves nonverbal behavior. Students with visual impairments often miss subtle cues and are unaware that peers may be exhibiting emotions or feelings unless they receive feedback from others. Helping students interpret emotions and feelings by using their auditory and cognitive skills requires a more sophisticated level of social thinking. Complex social thinking is particularly important for helping students understand the difference between teasing in a positive manner (for instance, saying, "You're so ugly," in a light tone of voice and with a smile), teasing to hurt another person's feelings (for instance, hiding a student's cane), and bullying (such as threatening the student with isolation from the group at recess). Often, students with visual impairments have difficulty distinguishing these behaviors, and may overreact because they are unable to read the nonverbal cues from others or figure out how to interpret the social situation.

Social Etiquette

Just like their sighted peers, students with visual impairments need to exhibit good manners when interacting with others in the home, at school, and in the community. To demonstrate social etiquette, students need to learn the following skills:

- saying or signing "please" and "thank you" given the situation
  - saying or signing "please" when requesting assistance
  - using "thank you" in an appropriate manner, such as after someone has provided assistance
  - saying or signing social amenities spontaneously without prompting
- using manners when eating
  - eating with mouth closed
  - saying or signing "excuse me" after burping
  - eating with utensils (fork, spoon, knife)
  - wiping mouth with a napkin after eating
  - passing food when eating family style
- sharing toys, games, and activities with others
  - inviting friends, classmates, or adults to play
  - demonstrating willingness to share a toy with a classmate or friend
  - allowing others to select a chosen activity
- waiting for his or her turn
  - waiting patiently while others engage in an activity
  - not insisting on going first when playing a game or engaging in an activity
- reciprocating when others provide assistance
  - understanding the concept of reciprocation
  - willingly exhibiting a desire to give to others

Demonstrating good manners in a variety of social situations is a skill that all children are expected to acquire. Children with visual impairments should be given the feedback and cues to learn when these behaviors and skills are expected in their daily lives. One of the first behaviors sighted children learn is to say "please" and "thank you." Toddlers imitate this behavior by responding to the cues from their family members in a variety of social situations. Students with visual impairments should be given a variety of opportunities to practice these skills. As with sighted children, children with visual impairments may need to receive verbal prompts from their teachers or family members to help them know when to use these pleasantries.

In the same vein, students with visual impairments need to learn and demonstrate appropriate eating skills. Not only should students learn techniques for using eating utensils, as discussed in Chapter 8, they need to learn the social rules surrounding eating. Students should learn which foods are acceptable to eat with their fingers or hands—such as chunks of cheese, crackers, raw vegetables, sandwiches, tacos, fried chicken—and which foods require utensils. Also, students need to be given experiences to learn how to determine how much food should be placed in one's mouth, the importance of closing one's mouth while eating, and appropriate posture when bringing food to one's mouth while seated at a table. Finally, students need to learn the social graces surrounding eating. Because eating can be a social event, students need to learn to refrain from speaking with a full mouth, say or sign "excuse me" if they burp or belch, and use a napkin to wipe food off face and hands.

In school settings, students with visual impairments need to learn the social rules of waiting their turn, raising their hands to be acknowledged, and sharing toys, games, and materials with classmates. Often, students with visual impairments miss nonverbal cues, such as a nod of the head or a wave of the hand, that indicate it is time to answer a question or join a group. Teachers and family members can assist students by remembering to provide a verbal cue paired with a physical cue. For example, having the classroom teacher say the student's name while standing close to him or providing a physical prompt, such as a gentle tap on the shoulder, may help reinforce a student's sense of turn taking and prevent him from calling out responses to a teacher's question instead of waiting to be called on. Having peers place a hand on the student's shoulder, paired with "wait a second," may encourage greater success for the student who is attempting to join a group engaged in a play activity in knowing when it is appropriate to speak.

The importance of reciprocation is a key concept for students with visual impairments to acquire, especially in secondary and post-secondary settings. Students with visual impairments need to understand that positive social relationships are built upon mutual caring and concern and that they cannot simply expect to receive assistance and support from others without reciprocating in some way. Also, students need to learn the social rules involved in demonstrating genuine appreciation for the assistance and support given by others. If students are perceived by their sighted peers as always needing help, without some sort of social reinforcement from the student who is visually impaired, it is likely that the student will eventually experience isolation. Providing opportunities from an early age for students with visual impairments to learn to reciprocate is critical. For example, having students write thank-you notes, bake a batch of cookies, create a special piece of art, or buy a favorite food item helps others to know that students recognize and appreciate the assistance that has been provided. (See the learning activity "Showing Gratitude" at the end of this chapter for more ideas on teaching these skills.) Also, teaching students to reach beyond themselves provides students with a sense of altruism. Developing community service projects, such as sponsoring a canned food drive during the holiday season or collecting food for an animal shelter, teaches students with visual impairments that reciprocation is a two-way street. By giving to others in addition to having others give to them, students are observing social amenities in a positive manner.

Development of Relationships and Friendships

Many of the skills described in previous sections are prerequisites to developing and maintaining relationships and friendships. To demonstrate the ability to develop relationships and friendships, students need to learn the following skills:

- knowing the differences between family, friends, acquaintances, and strangers
  - naming family members
  - identifying friends
  - naming and identifying acquaintances
  - knowing what information can be shared with a stranger and what can be shared with an acquaintance or friend
- seeking other children as friends
  - selecting friends with similar interests
  - showing mutual care and respect for friends
  - spending extended time engaged in play and social activities with friends
- sharing in group activities
  - engaging in age-appropriate sports
  - engaging in age-appropriate art and recreational activities
  - showing interest in activity choices of other peers
  - engaging in structured group activities, such as scouts, youth group, drama group
- demonstrating concern for friends
  - being aware of friends' feelings
  - showing empathy toward friends
  - showing genuine appreciation for friends
- interacting with peers outside of school
  - having play dates
  - engaging in after-school activities (swimming, gymnastics, dance, athletic teams, and the like)
  - having sleepovers
  - attending events with friends (such as movies, plays, and sports events)
  - knowing how to hang out
- demonstrating age-appropriate knowledge of human sexuality
  - knowing body parts on self
  - knowing body parts on opposite sex
  - understanding the concepts of public and private
  - understanding the difference between a platonic friendship and a close relationship
  - understanding concepts of sexual intercourse
  - knowing about birth control
- understanding dating
  - knowing how to flirt to get the attention of a person of interest
  - knowing how to ask a person for a date
  - understanding that dating involves a special social relationship
- using appropriate social behavior in a work setting
  - knowing how to respond to a supervisor
  - knowing how to interact with colleagues
  - knowing how to take a break
  - knowing how to work with a team
  - taking criticism and feedback in a positive manner

The skills children need to exhibit in relationships change and develop as they get older and find themselves in different settings.

Home Environment

The home environment and family milieu set the stage for children with visual impairments to develop and maintain positive peer relationships and friendships. Parents create trust and familiarity for their children by encouraging them to engage with others. Family gatherings and playgroup activities allow young children with visual impairments to experience a wide range of people and children. Through these experiences, children may show interest in other children and demonstrate greater independence.

Preschool

Developmentally, as children move into preschool settings, they demonstrate a willingness to share toys and engage in interactive play with children their same age. Young children with visual impairments may need support from adults to gain entry into groups or to maintain group involvement in a game or activity. It is critical that these young students and their families recognize early on that these relationships are based on mutual respect and interests. Therefore, it is important for the student who is visually impaired to have exposure to a variety of play activities, social environments, and experiences with children who are and are not visually impaired. Also, encouraging these children to explore and physically interact with the world around them promotes greater autonomy and interdependence. Providing opportunities that facilitate meaningful social exchanges with peers is the first step toward developing lasting friendships.

Elementary and Middle School

School settings allow children to expand their relationships with peers. In fact, researchers believe that the school environment provides the structure and establishes the social rules for developing and maintaining friendships. MacCuspie (1996) asserted that in order for families and teachers of students with visual impairments to truly understand how children develop friendships, they need to be knowledgeable about the children's culture. The social culture in school teaches students the social rules in the classroom, as well as how to play age-appropriate games and maintain social exchanges with classmates on the playground or at lunch. It also establishes norms for appropriate dress and physical appearance. Often, students with visual impairments feel isolated from their peers because they may lack the skills or experiences to easily engage with them in unstructured settings. Also, students may not have the level of sophistication necessary to analyze social situations, interpret the feelings of others, or to determine the best way to respond. Structured social skills interventions (described in greater detail later in the chapter), provide students with visual impairments the tools to develop and maintain friendships.

As students engage in positive experiences with classmates in school, they should be encouraged to maintain relationships outside of school, in environments that are less structured. Giving students opportunities to join after-school groups, such as the Boy and Girl Scouts, or to participate in service groups or youth group activities allows students to make friends in their neighborhoods or local communities. Participation in athletic activities provides students with opportunities to work on a team and meet students who have similar interests. Teaching students to become computer literate in elementary school allows them to engage with peers through e-mail or social networking sites, although close monitoring by teachers and families is critical to ensure personal safety.

Students' understanding of friendship is heightened when students become interested in close social relationships with the same or opposite sex. To ensure that students are safe and have a positive sense of self, issues around human sexuality should be addressed by teachers and families. At the most basic level, students with visual impairments need to know the concept of public and private, and the social behaviors that are appropriate in these situations. Also, students need to be familiar with their own bodies, and able to distinguish between male and female body parts and their functions. Understanding the difference between a platonic relationship and a love relationship may be difficult for some students with visual impairments because of the nonverbal communications involved in these relationships. Teachers, counselors, and families need to provide students with hands-on information (by using anatomically correct dolls, for instance) about sexual intercourse, protected sex, and homosexuality so that students with visual impairments have the understanding necessary to make appropriate and safe decisions.

High School and Transition

Social relationships in adolescence require that students have knowledge about dating, hanging out with friends, and using appropriate social behavior at work. Knowing how to flirt and gain the attention of a person of interest requires that students combine gestures, emotions, and social communication. Often, students with visual impairments, particularly those who have additional disabilities, may have difficulty "reading" the social cues of others. They may misinterpret kind deeds exhibited by their sighted classmates as an indication of friendship or a close social relationship, when in fact these classmates may merely be acquaintances. In addition, if their views are based on what is presented in the media or what occurs in their home environment, rather than experiences with their contemporaries, many adolescents with visual impairments may have a skewed perspective about dating or marriage. Providing students with accurate information about how teens engage with one another, initially in groups, and then in more intimate situations, allows them the opportunity for greater social success.

Work, whether it is volunteer or paid, provides an outlet for teens to demonstrate their abilities and skills. In order for students with visual impairments to be successful at work, they need to be able to complete job tasks in a timely and efficient manner. Also, they need to demonstrate a repertoire of social skills that can greatly influence their success on the job, such as being punctual, interacting effectively with someone in authority, knowing how to ask for assistance, getting along with colleagues, dressing appropriately for the work setting, knowing how to engage with colleagues at break or at lunch, and knowing how to join and interact with colleagues in after-work settings.

Knowledge of Self

The development of social skills by students with visual impairments is contingent upon those students having a positive sense of self. In other words, students need to have a clear and realistic view of who they are as individuals. To demonstrate knowledge of self, students need to learn the following skills:

- taking responsibility for personal actions
  - understanding when a mistake is made
  - apologizing for an inappropriate action
  - understanding consequences
- understanding and explaining visual impairment
  - naming visual impairment
  - explaining the causes of the visual impairment
  - explaining what accommodations or modifications need to be made
- demonstrating awareness of competencies and limitations
  - stating competencies in a realistic manner
  - recognizing limitations and can communicate them
  - developing alternative solutions for limitations
- advocating for self at home, in school, and in the community
  - communicating needs to others
  - asking for assistance in a positive manner
  - distinguishing when assistance is necessary and when it is not needed
- demonstrating assertiveness in an appropriate manner
  - identifying the difference between passive, aggressive, and assertive behavior
  - using assertive statements when communicating with others

One of the goals of teaching students with visual impairments is for the student to develop and maintain a positive sense of self. For many years, educators who provided services to students with visual impairments believed that these youngsters reached developmental milestones in the same manner and at the same age as sighted children their same age. There was no recognition that students with visual impairments acquired skills and concepts in a different manner (see, for example, Ferrell, 1998; Warren, 1994). As a result, students were not exposed to a disability-specific curriculum like the ECC, and were not given opportunities to view themselves as individuals with visual impairments.

When students know about their visual impairments, they have valuable knowledge about themselves. Being able to provide information about their needs and the accommodations that allow them to function independently gives students an opportunity to view themselves as capable and proactive. Also, when caring adults provide realistic feedback about students' skills and abilities, it helps them understand their strengths and limitations and allows them to make choices about their level of independence. Professionals and families can help students analyze the skills needed to accomplish tasks, provide alternative solutions, and give honest feedback when appropriate.

Achieving autonomy and independence has long been considered the goal of adolescence (Wolffe, 2006). Students with visual impairments grapple with the lack of control they may have in their lives and the skills they need to be independent. It is not unusual for students with visual impairments to be dependent on adult support to provide assistance with schoolwork, independent living skills tasks in the home, or independent travel in the community. Finding the balance between too much and too little support can be difficult for adults who provide support to students with visual impairments. If too much support is provided, students may demonstrate learned helplessness (Seligman, 1990), a situation in which they stop trying to accomplish daily routines or expectations independently. In some cases, students are not expected to make choices or decisions or to act in a socially appropriate manner. When students are not expected to behave in an age-appropriate manner and are given special considerations for completing class assignments or job duties, they are not being held accountable for their actions. Learning early that there are consequences for one's behavior and actions helps students become responsible for how they engage with their classmates, friends, and adults.

Understanding how to communicate needs or requests to others is another important component of social skills instruction. Teaching students the difference between passive, aggressive, and assertive behavior helps them to recognize how their communication style affects the behavior of others. For example, if a student demands, in an aggressive manner, that his teaching assistant get his braille books, the aide may be less willing to support the student. On the other hand, the assistant would be more likely to help the student if the student uses appropriate social etiquette and an assertive communication style, such as, "I'm having trouble finding my books, can you help me please?"

Interpretation and Monitoring of Social Behavior

Social perspective taking is the ability to analyze or interpret social situations and take the perspective of others. To demonstrate appropriate interpretation and monitoring of social behavior, students need to learn the following skills:

- asking questions at the appropriate time
  - listening to the conversation
  - finding a lull in the conversation to ask a question
  - making sure the question is on topic or appropriate to ask
- interpreting nonverbal cues from others
  - demonstrating knowledge of gestures, facial expressions, and body posture when they are verbally described
  - enlisting the assistance of a trusted friend or colleague to provide verbal interpretation
  - using auditory cues to assist with interpreting nonverbal cues
  - asking for clarification about nonverbal behaviors or cues
- understanding risk taking
  - understanding that adults can see and observe behavior
  - knowing where and when to use certain behavior
  - determining situational limits and understanding consequences if those limits are exceeded
  - knowing how to inform others of inappropriate advances
- understanding and interpreting sarcasm
  - interpreting a variety of voice qualities, such as humor, anger, and sarcasm
  - identifying sarcasm
  - knowing how to react when a person makes a sarcastic remark
- monitoring behavior in a variety of situations
  - analyzing social situations and using appropriate social behavior accordingly
  - demonstrating an ability to correct a behavior in a specific social situation
  - seeing humor in own social mistakes
- interpreting others' behavior in social situations
  - interpreting feelings and emotions of others correctly
  - recognizing when another's feelings have been hurt
  - taking the role of others and understanding their view
  - soliciting feedback from others to clarify the interpretation of behavior

The ability of students with visual impairments to analyze and monitor their social interaction skills requires that they use auditory, visual, and cognitive abilities to scope out and analyze a social situation. To be effective, students need to have a range of social experiences to draw on as opportunities to practice and receive feedback from trusted friends and adults occur.

Often, students with visual impairments ask many questions to gain access to information or to mediate a social situation. When engaged in a social interaction, students need to learn to listen to the conversation, identify a lull, and determine if the question they want to ask is relevant to the social exchange. In a similar manner, students are more likely to be successful in gaining entry into a group or maintaining social contacts with peers if they can analyze the context of a social gathering or group activity, determine their role, engage in an appropriate manner, and quickly evaluate if the exchange was positive.

Some professionals who work with students with visual impairments remark that students with visual impairments do not take risks or get into trouble like their sighted classmates do. Students who can see are able to determine when an adult is monitoring their behavior. Students who are blind or who have low vision are at a disadvantage because they cannot visually monitor the situation or change their behavior in a matter of seconds to adhere to adult expectations. Again, teaching students to listen carefully to determine who might be in their immediate environment and to develop an understanding of the accepted social rules for a given situation can help students to demonstrate more typical social behavior.

Interpreting others' emotions and feelings and putting oneself in another's place are difficult skills for some students with visual impairments. These sophisticated skills require that students are able to interpret nonverbal cues. Without auditory feedback, students may misinterpret overtures made by classmates or adults. It is important for students who are blind or who have low vision to learn alternate ways to gather this information. For example, teaching students to use facial expressions and gestures in a variety of social environments or providing activities where students listen carefully to various voice intonations to determine their meaning assists students in developing these skills. It is particularly important for middle school students and adolescents with visual impairments to be able to understand and interpret sarcasm. If students have little exposure to the peer culture or have limited experiences using the language of their classmates, they may misinterpret these exchanges as negative or disrespectful rather than recognizing the playful intent of the interaction.

ASSESSMENT OF SOCIAL INTERACTION

Assessment of social skills is the first step in determining what needs to be taught. There are numerous ways to assess social interaction skills, including:

- observation
- interviews
- social skills checklists
- role-playing situations
- audio and video assessment
- problem-solving scenarios
- student self-evaluation

Observation

Observation is the first step in the social skills assessment process. This form of assessment allows teachers, family members, and other professionals to gain insight into the social lives of their students with visual impairments. Observation is a valuable tool for evaluating students' social performance on an ongoing basis in a variety of natural environments. By observing students in their daily activities, the teacher can obtain a snapshot into their social worlds: their behavior with classmates, interactions with classmates and adults, the quality and quantity of social activities, and the way in which friendships are developed and maintained. Observation allows teachers and other professionals with opportunities to document a student's social behavior over time by providing anecdotal information.

When considering observation as a tool for social skills assessment, it is important to observe students in many different environments to obtain a clear picture of the student's social competence. Often teachers use checklists as a framework to observe the social behavior of students with visual impairments. Checklists and social skills rating scales (discussed later in this chapter) provide guidelines for the evaluator to monitor a student's social behavior on an on-going basis.

According to Sacks and Barclay (2006), when observing students with visual impairments, the following behaviors may be considered:

- number of social contacts during an observation period
- behaviors that work for a student during a social interaction
- behaviors that create obstacles for the student in the social interaction process
- ability to sustain conversations that are age-appropriate
- diversity of conversation topics that are meaningful and engaging
- turn taking during conversations and social interactions with peers and adults
- length of social interactions
- interest in peers and peer topics
- knowledge of peer culture: games, dress, language, and communication styles
- awareness of nonverbal communication: gestures, facial expressions, body language

- social balance: is the student regarded by classmates or peers as someone who is desirable as a friend or is the student perceived by peers as needing care and support within social contexts (p. 288)

Thorough observation of social performance by students with visual impairments should occur in the home, the school, and in the community. Observing how the student engages with his parents, siblings, and extended family provides the evaluator with valuable information about the level of expectations family members have for the student's acquisition and maintenance of social skills. Careful observation of students in their general education classes, on the playground during recess, and in the cafeteria during lunch helps the evaluator to know more about how students engage with peers in structured and unstructured settings. Also, the information gained during school observations provides information about the type of activities students may engage in with and without adult support.

Observing students who are visually impaired in community settings provides information about how the students interact with individuals outside of the home and with the public. Observations of young children in child care settings or in playgroup activities allow the evaluator to see how the child interacts with caregivers who are less familiar to the child. Also, viewing the young child as part of a group allows the observer opportunities to determine how interactive the child might be with other children and with an array of adults. Observing elementary-age students with visual impairments on field trips or middle school students on trips to the mall provides the evaluator with rich information about how the student with a visual impairment interacts and maintains social exchanges with his or her peers over an extended period of time. Observations of adolescents and young adults in community settings examine the strategies students use to engage with store personnel, passengers on public transit, restaurant and fast food personnel, and pedestrians when soliciting assistance or making a purchase.

Another form of assessment often used to evaluate students' social interaction skills involves audio or video taping of students engaged in a range of activities with peers. Teachers of students with visual impairments, O&M specialists, and families can listen to or view these recordings to obtain an authentic perspective of how students engage with others. For example, voice quality, length of conversation, and dominance in a conversation topic can be measured by listening to audio recordings of student interactions. In a similar manner, videotaping students engaged in social activities provides the evaluator with information about the quality and quantity of social interactions and the ways in which students use a variety of social behaviors to engage with classmates and adults.

Social Skills Interviews

Interviews with families, students, and teachers are another effective tool in the social skills assessment process. Structured interviews with families provide a formal way for professionals to gather information about the priorities and needs the family may have for teaching social interaction skills. The teacher can also use these interviews to gather more information about the social dynamics and family culture in the home. For example, the teacher may find that for cultural reasons family members do not establish eye contact with unfamiliar people. This information would be helpful to obtain, so that the teacher could modify instruction or work with the family to help them understand the expectations of Western culture. Examples of interview questions for families may include:

- How do you view your child's social skills?
- What are some social behaviors that you think your child might need support to acquire or to improve?
- What does your child do for fun during free time or in structured activities?
- Who are your child's friends and how did he or she develop those friendships?
- How does your child feel about being visually impaired? (Sacks & Barclay, 2006, p. 303)

Interviews with students with visual impairments provide a vehicle for the students to express their thoughts and perceptions about their level of social competence. By using this assessment tool, teachers can ask students to evaluate their social abilities and determine if their perceptions about themselves are accurate. Student interviews can also assist teachers in determining what needs to be taught. Having students prioritize the social skill areas that are important to them allows teachers to make instruction more motivating and meaningful. Interview questions for students with visual impairments may include:

- Tell me what you do with friends on the playground.
- How do you know when friends want to play with you?
- How do you find your friends on the playground?
- What do you do for free time at home and at school?
- What do you tell your teachers and your classmates about your visual impairment?
- What does it mean to be popular? Can you describe a person in your class who is popular?
- What characteristics do you have that make you likable by others? (Sacks & Barclay, 2006, p. 304)

Interviews with classroom teachers, counselors, and other program personnel provide information about how the student with a visual impairment engages in group learning activities in the classroom, as well as in other school settings, like the playground during recess, gym class, or in the cafeteria during lunch. These professionals can provide valuable information about how students interact with classmates, which activities facilitate social exchanges with classmates, the effectiveness of a given communication style with classmates and adults, and the people students interact with during free time. The following interview questions may be considered:

- During group lessons, does the student engage with his or her classmates? How often, and for what reasons?
- Where is the student seated in the classroom? How do you facilitate social contacts with peers for all of your students?
- What does the student do for free time in the classroom?

Social Skills Assessment Checklists

Social skills checklists and social rating scales provide a structured way for teachers and other professionals to evaluate a student's level of social competence. Checklists provide a streamlined way to examine a variety of behaviors and skills, rate them, and rank what needs to be taught in a systematic fashion. Many social skills assessment checklists and rating scales are available to professionals and families. Few, however, have been designed to address the specific social skills needs of students with visual impairments. While it is possible for teachers and other professionals to create checklists that meet their individual needs, some assessment tools have been used consistently with a wide variety of students who are blind or visually impaired. The Social Skills Assessment Tool for Children with Visual Impairments–Revised (SSAT-VI:R; Sacks & Wolffe, 2006) evaluates social behavior in three areas: basic social behavior, interpersonal relationships, and cognitive social behaviors. This tool provides a framework for teachers and others to observe specific social behaviors in a sequential manner, from very basic (uses eye contact) to quite advanced (interpreting nonverbal behavior). The evaluator is asked to rank each behavior on a scale from 1 (absent) to 6 (excellent). Figure 9.1 provides an excerpt from the SSAT-VI:R. The SSAT-VI:R can be used as a tool for ongoing assessment.

Another social skills checklist that is designed for students with visual impairments is the Social Competence Assessment from the *Independent Living* curriculum (Loumiet & Levack, 1991). This social skills assessment tool allows the evaluator to use a scale to examine interactions with family, peers, and others. Areas included in the evaluation include self-concept, recognition and expression of emotions, nonverbal communication, values clarification, personal and social aspects of sexual behavior, courteous behavior, problem solving and decision making, scholastic success, and personal and civic responsibility. This checklist allows the evaluator to tie the assessment directly to the student's individualized education program (IEP) or individualized transition program (ITP). An excerpt from the checklist can be found in Figure 9.2.

When using this checklist, the assessor indicates the school year at the time of the assessment for each behavior. If the assessor observes the student using the behavior in an appropriate manner in at least one environment, the box labeled "Competence" is checked. If the behavior is observed in several different environments, the box labeled "Generalized Use" is checked. The checklist items with an asterisk indicate that they are essential skills. Like the SSAT-VI:R, the Social Competence Assessment checklist can be used on an ongoing basis.

Additional social skills checklists are commercially available, and many are used widely by school psychologists and teachers in general education settings, but have not been designed for students with visual impairments. The *Social Skills Rating System* (*SSRS*; Gresham & Elliot, 1990) is one of the most comprehensive tools

FIGURE 9.1

Social Skills Assessment Tool for Children with Visual Impairments: Revised (SSAT-VI:R)

Student:____________________ Assessor: ____________________ Date: ____________

Rate each item as:
1 Absent
2 Poor
3 Fair
4 Adequate
5 Good
6 Excellent

BASIC SOCIAL BEHAVIORS

A. Body Language

1. _____ Maintains appropriate eye contact.
2. _____ Demonstrates appropriate body posture.
3. _____ Maintains appropriate personal body space.
4. _____ Utilizes and respond to gestures and facial expressions.
5. _____ Refrains from engaging in socially unacceptable mannerisms.

B. Communication Skills

1. _____ Positively initiates interactions with others.
2. _____ Exhibits age-appropriate interactions and conversations.
3. _____ Expands conversations.
4. _____ Listens well.
5. _____ Compliments.
6. _____ Interrupts appropriately.
7. _____ Demonstrates empathy and sympathy.
8. _____ Responds appropriately to positive and negative feedback from peers and adults.

C. Cooperative Skills

1. _____ Demonstrates cooperation and understanding of group dynamics.
2. _____ Demonstrates respect for group leader.
3. _____ Sustains group involvement.
4. _____ Shares in group activity.
5. _____ Initiates joining a group.
6. _____ Leads group activity.

INTERPERSONAL RELATIONSHIPS

A. Social Interaction

1. _____ Greets others and says "good-bye," as appropriate
2. _____ Interacts with others: ____ adult ____ disabled peer
   ____ nondisabled peer ____ younger children ____ older children.
   Comment on type and style of interaction:
3. _____ Is able to compromise.

(continued on next page)

FIGURE 9.1 *continued*

4. _____ Encourages the efforts of others.
5. _____ Demonstrates gratitude towards others.

B. Play Skills/Recreation and Leisure

1. _____ Takes turns and shares.
2. _____ Plays with others: ____ one ____ small group ____ larger group.
   Comment on quality of play:
3. _____ Demonstrates ability to engage in a variety of play activities.
4. _____ Shows awareness of common activities and interests.

C. Developing Friendships and Relationships

1. _____ Demonstrates an understanding of differences between family, friends, acquaintances, and strangers.
2. _____ Develops friends and is liked by peers.
3. _____ Demonstrates appropriate behaviors for attending social events.
4. _____ Interacts with peers outside of school.
5. _____ Understands the needs of others.
6. _____ Demonstrates an age-appropriate awareness of human sexuality including concepts of public vs. private, and societal values and attitudes.
7. _____ Demonstrates an age-appropriate awareness of job-related concepts including assuming responsibility and relating to others in work situations.

SELF-IDENTITY AND SELF-MONITORING

A. Self-Identity

1. _____ Demonstrates understanding of visual impairment.
2. _____ Demonstrates awareness of personal competencies and limitations.
3. _____ Demonstrates awareness of possible adaptations.
4. _____ Advocates for self in school, home, and community environments.
5. _____ Demonstrates assertiveness in appropriate manner.

B. Self-Monitoring

1. _____ Observes and identifies opportunities for social interactions.
2. _____ Interprets social cues and generates strategies for interaction.
3. _____ Anticipates consequences of strategies and selects most desired.
4. _____ Initiates and performs appropriate behaviors.
5. _____ Takes responsibility for own actions and behavior.
6. _____ Generalizes social skills to a variety of situations.
7. _____ Sustains social competency over time.
8. _____ Demonstrates ability to evaluate and monitor own social performance realistically.
9. _____ Demonstrates ability to adjust own behavior accordingly.

SOURCE: Revised by Sharon Z. Sacks and Karen E. Wolffe, California School for the Blind, Fremont, CA, 2006.

FIGURE 9.2

Social Competence Assessment

Interaction with Family, Peers, and Others

Age (Years)	Skills	IEP School Year	Competence	Generalized Use
0–1	1 Respond to an adult's attempt to interact.*			
	2 Initiate interactions with an adult.*			
	3 Demonstrate the ability to differentiate between familiar people and strangers.*			
	4 Respond to the presence of a peer.*			
	5 Accept a substitute activity that replaces a socially unacceptable mannerism.			
2–3	6 Demonstrate understanding of approval and disapproval of adults.*			
	7 Address parents or other familiar adults by name.*			
	8 Associate particular adults with routine activities.*			
	9 Engage in same activity as a peer.*			
	10 Comply with simple directions and limits from adults.*			
	11 Interact with peers or siblings.*			
	12 Address siblings by name.*			
4–7	13 Interact with blind, low vision, and sighted peers in common situations.*			
	14 Identify the person in charge in various situations.*			
	15 Identify situations in which an adult should not be obeyed.*			
	16 Initiate interactions with peers.*			
	17 Share toys or other items with a peer.*			
	18 Use a peer as a resource.*			
	19 Indicate preferences in playmates.*			
	20 Discuss the concept of friendship.			
	21 Describe other people.			
	22 Take turns.*			
	23 Determine when it is not appropriate to share something, and communicate it in an assertive manner.*			
	24 Identify the consequences of behaviors in social interactions.*			
	25 Name family members, and discuss the relationship to each of them.			
	26 Maintain contact with parents, guardians, and family members when separated for a long period of time.*			
	27 Respond to humor, and use it in social situations.			
	28 Recognize sarcasm, and respond in an effective manner.			
	29 Interact with blind and low vision adults in a variety of situations.*			

(continued on next page)

	30 Initiate, continue, develop, and conclude conversations.*			
	31 Discuss the personal likes and dislikes of other people.			
	32 Recognize behaviors that can cause social isolation and demonstrate alternative behaviors that promote social integration.*			
8–11	33 Demonstrate affection in socially acceptable ways, considering the person, place, and situation.			
	34 Demonstrate the ability to resist peer pressure when resistance is necessary or desirable.*			
	35 Demonstrate skills for resolving conflicts with siblings and peers.*			
	36 Deal with personal insults, ostracism, ridicule, or other mistreatment.			
	37 Tolerate some unusual or unexpected behaviors from others.*			
	38 Seek interactions with blind, low vision, and sighted peers and adults in a variety of situations.*			
12–15	39 Interact positively with friends.*			
	40 Discuss some problems that might arise with family members or with friends, and suggest strategies that could be used to resolve them.*			
	41 Identify how different friends can meet different needs.			
	42 Demonstrate various aspects of planning and carrying out social activities with friends.*			
	43 Use assertive techniques in appropriate social situations.*			
	44 Discuss the rights and responsibilities of an individual in a relationship.*			
16–21	45 Establish and maintain a variety of friendships.			
	46 Work effectively in various groups that have a defined purpose or structure.			
	47 Discuss the concepts of role model(s) and/or mentor(s) for self.			
	48 Discuss the concept of networking, and demonstrate an understanding of its value.			

Self-Concept

Age (Years)	Skills	IEP School Year	Competence	Generalized Use
0–1	1 Recognize and respond to name.			
	2 Demonstrate interest in a mirror image.*			
	3 State own first name.*			
	4 Demonstrate a strong desire to perform tasks independently.*			
	5 Demonstrate awareness that his behavior has an effect on others.*			

(continued on next page)

FIGURE 9.2 *continued*

Age	Skill			
2–3	6 Indicate a preference.*			
	7 Demonstrate recognition of own image in a picture or on a videotape, and/or demonstrate recognition of own voice on an audiotape.*			
	8 Use personal pronouns *I*, *you*, and *me*.*			
	9 Use a variety of methods to get own way.*			
	10 Demonstrate an awareness of himself as a separate person.			
	11 Show pride in accomplishing tasks.*			
	12 State own first name, last name, and age.*			
4–7	13 Separate own possessions from those of others.*			
	14 Name things that she can do now that she was unable to do at an earlier age, and name things that she will learn to do in the future.*			
	15 State basic information about self.*			
	16 State basic information about family members.*			
	17 Indicate awareness of own visual and other physical abilities, and differences between his abilities and those of others.*			
8–11	18 Discuss personal likes and dislikes.*			
	19 Provide basic information as to own ethnic origin, religious preference, and family background.*			
12–15	20 Evaluate own personality traits, and attempt to modify those that are not functional.*			
	21 State own point of view on various specific topics.			
16–21	22 State own social security number.*			
	23 Obtain and use an identification card.*			
	24 Show pride in personal achievements.			
	25 Express realistic views of own capabilities and limitations.*			
	26 Demonstrate confidence in own decisions, values, and beliefs.*			

*Skills considered essential

SOURCE: Excerpted with permission from R. Loumiet & N. Levack, *Independent Living: A Curriculum with Adaptations for Students with Visual Impairments, Vol. I: Social Competence* (Austin: Texas School for the Blind and Visually Impaired, 1992), pp. 210–214.

to measure the social competence and academic performance of students without disabilities. Teachers of students with visual impairments can use this checklist as a baseline for measuring social expectations for their students based on sighted student norms.

Role-Play

Role-playing scenarios allow teachers and other professionals who teach social skills to evaluate a student's social competence by using typical situations that students encounter during the school day or in after-school activities with friends and classmates. This form of assessment allows professionals to evaluate acquisition of specific skills, such as the use of eye contact when greeting peers at recess or the quality of how the student interrupts a group involved in a game. When role-playing for the assessment, a student with visual impairments can be paired with an adult (teacher) or a classmate to perform. Examples of role-plays for assessment purposes may include:

- You are working on an art project with a group of students. You touch the art supplies to determine their location on the table. Another student in the group pushes your hand away and says, "Don't touch that." What do you say and do to handle this situation?

- You have won an award for your science project. You will be honored at an all-school assembly, and given the award by the school principal. What will you do when you are on the stage receiving the award?
- One of your classmates is playing with a favorite toy during free time. You want to play with it, too. What do you do and say?

Problem-Solving Scenarios

Like role-playing scenarios, problem-solving scenarios create a situation where students with visual impairments need to evaluate and analyze a social situation. This form of social skills assessment allows the evaluator to examine how students with visual impairments perceive social encounters with others. Using analytical skills, students should be able to evaluate a situation, determine what social behaviors need to be used, initiate the encounter, and evaluate the choices made during the exchange. In addition, problem-solving scenarios provide the teacher with valuable insight into how students interpret the social interaction skills used by others and whether they have the skills to take another's role. Because so much of what is involved in social communication relies on nonverbal cues, students with visual impairments often miss or misinterpret overtures made by others. A student who is blind may think that another student is her friend because she says "hello" each morning. Or, the student who is visually impaired may not realize that her sighted classmates engage with many students in the same manner, but choose to "hang out" with only a few friends.

The ability to understand and perceive what others are thinking or feeling can be assessed through problem-solving scenarios and social stories. Social stories usually present a moral dilemma or issue that students need to resolve. These stories allow the evaluator to examine how the student views himself in relation to his classmates, thinks about how to solve the social situation, and evaluates how others may feel or react to a given outcome. This form of assessment requires the student who is visually impaired to have had numerous experiences to draw upon and the cognitive skills to interpret a range of social situations. Examples of problem-solving scenarios that can be used to assess these skills include:

- You learn that one of your classmates has taken your long cane and put it in another student's backpack. How do you handle this situation? What do you say to the peer who has taken your cane? How do you think the other students feel about this?
- You are on a mobility lesson with another student. You are given $10 to purchase some groceries. Your O&M teacher waits outside while you and your friend purchase the items after obtaining assistance from customer service. While in the checkout line, you realize that your friend has pocketed the change. Your friend tells you not to say anything to your O&M teacher. What do you do? What do you tell your friend? How do you handle the situation with your O&M teacher when she realizes some of the change is missing?

Like role-plays, problem-solving scenarios can be used for both instructional and assessment purposes.

Student Self-Evaluation

Another form of social skills assessment asks students to evaluate themselves on a variety of established criteria. Students with visual impairments can be asked to rank themselves in relation to their peers on qualities such as personal appearance, ability to interact with others, ability to share belongings and toys, and level of friendliness.

Another self-evaluation technique allows students to listen to an audio recording of themselves engaged in a social exchange with peers. Students are asked to rate themselves using a scale of 1 (low) to 5 (high) on criteria such as voice quality and tone, quality and length of the interaction, and range of conversation topics used during the interaction. Videotaped social interactions provide another way for students with visual impairments to self-evaluate their social behavior. Students with low vision can examine how they engage with their peers, and evaluate the ways in which they join groups, maintain social contacts, and use social behaviors, such as eye contact, gestures, or mannerisms. By using this form of assessment, students become more aware of their strengths and limitations when interacting with peers.

Self-evaluation of social interaction skills can also be examined by having students write or tape a description of their feelings about themselves and their classmates. Teachers and other professionals can use this information to determine the students' social strengths and weaknesses. Younger children with low vision can draw pictures of themselves, their families, and their friends. For students who are functionally blind, using clay or other materials to create a representation of themselves and others in their lives can be an effective assessment technique. Consultation with an art therapist is recommended to assist with the interpretation of these products.

GENERAL CONSIDERATIONS FOR TEACHING SOCIAL INTERACTION

Teaching social interaction skills to students with visual impairments is a process that requires ongoing assessment and consistent instruction by professionals and families alike. Because so much of what is learned socially is typically interpreted through the visual sense, it cannot be assumed that students with visual impairments will learn social skills incidentally. Rather, these skills need to be deliberately taught and reinforced throughout these students' educational careers. Opportunities in real-world settings need to be created to encourage students who are visually impaired to engage with others, participate in social activities, and learn the social rules in various social situations, such as playing games at recess or hanging out with friends at the mall. Students with visual impairments and additional disabilities in particular need opportunities to learn social skills in realistic situations. Teaching social skills within the context of daily routines—for example, greeting classmates and the teacher when entering the classroom, choosing a play activity with a classmate during recess, and sharing snacks during lunch—helps students with visual impairments generalize social interaction skills and use them in different environments. In addition, students should be expected to act in a manner that is considered socially acceptable by others. Consistent feedback from caring professionals and family members is essential for developing social competence.

Nurturing Social Competence

In order for students to be socially successful, they need to develop a social presence. Having a social presence means showing interest in others, experiencing a variety of activities that involve risk taking and decision making, demonstrating a repertoire of social behaviors that promote positive interactions with others, and developing a personal style that is age-appropriate. Socially competent students with visual impairments understand that learning these skills helps to facilitate friendships and establish positive relationships with peers and adults. Youngsters who have a strong social presence take responsibility for their actions. They learn that both verbal and nonverbal

L. Penny Rosenblum

Everyday settings and daily routines, such as eating lunch in the school cafeteria, provide excellent opportunities to observe students' social skills and provide instruction.

behavior communicates a message to others. These students feel confident and comfortable with themselves. They have a sense of humor and can laugh at themselves when social mistakes are made.

Because social skills instruction requires time, practice, and support, professionals need to be as creative as possible in the way they deliver this instruction. Infusing social skills into existing lessons provides students with many opportunities to practice a specific behavior or skill. For example, students can practice social greetings each time they work with the teacher of students with visual impairments. During this time the teacher can focus on specific social behaviors, such as teaching eye contact, body posture, social initiations, and formal and informal greetings. It is also important for teachers of students with visual impairments and O&M specialists to observe their students in a variety of school environments in order to monitor how students use skills learned during instruction.

Creating Opportunities to Promote Social Skills

Likewise, it is important for teachers to create opportunities for students with visual impairments to practice their social interaction skills with their visually impaired and sighted peers. Forming lunch buddy groups and using ability awareness curricula, like *Getting to Know You: A Social Skills and Ability Awareness Curriculum* (Crow & Herlich, 2012), helps to promote friendships and establish positive social relationships among classmates. For students with visual impairments who are served in resource rooms or special day class settings, more formal social skills instruction can occur. Working collaboratively with general education teachers who promote affective or character education in their classrooms can help to facilitate positive social interaction skills for all students.

Social interaction skills cannot be taught in a vacuum. The responsibility for teaching social skills creates a partnership between families and professionals. It is essential that families be involved in the social skills assessment process and help to determine what skills need to be taught. While the school setting may seem like the natural place for teaching social skills, it is essential that learning and use of these skills carries over to the home and the community. Teachers of students with visual impairments and O&M specialists need to share teaching strategies with families, and together design effective interventions that can occur easily and consistently. Suggestions to support parents in teaching social skills are provided later in this chapter.

Finally, opportunities for students with visual impairments to meet and interact with students who have similar disabilities allow them to develop a strong sense of identity as a person with a visual impairment. Providing opportunities for students to meet socially competent adolescent or adult role models provides a natural way for students to learn strategies that foster social competence and interdependence. Teachers and other professionals can facilitate these relationships by providing opportunities for younger students to meet older students during recreational activities, events at organizations for individuals who are blind or visually impaired, or during weekend and summer camp experiences for visually impaired youngsters.

TEACHING STRATEGIES FOR SOCIAL INTERACTION

Sacks and Wolffe (2006b) provide numerous strategies for teaching social interaction skills to students with visual impairments. Many of them are presented in this section and the learning activities included at the end of the chapter. Instructional techniques that can be used by teachers, O&M specialists, and families to teach a range of social skills include the following:

- structured behavioral interventions
- peer-mediated interventions
- classmate support models
- role-playing scenarios
- cognitive-behavioral strategies
- mentors and role models
- five-minute lessons

Structured Behavioral Interventions

This form of instruction is based on behavior modification strategies and follows this type of sequence:

1. The teacher introduces a skill.
2. The teacher models the skill for the student, such as making a social greeting, or introducing himself.
3. The student practices the skill.
4. The teacher provides verbal feedback and, when appropriate, physically models or positions the student to assist in learning the skill.
5. The student practices the skill again.

SIDEBAR 9.1

Sample Structured Behavioral Intervention: Joining a Group

Jenny is a third-grade student who is included in her general education class. She works with her teacher of students with visual impairments for three 1-hour sessions per week. Jenny has been functionally blind since birth.

Teacher: Good morning, Jenny. Today we are going to talk about joining groups of friends on the playground. I've noticed that sometimes you have a hard time knowing when to join in. Can you tell me the kinds of activities kids play or do at recess?

Jenny: Well, sometimes the girls just talk to each other. Sometimes they play jump rope, wall ball, or tether ball.

Teacher: Those are great activities. Do you know how to play these games? Do we need to spend some time working on learning how to play these games?

Jenny: I know how to play jump rope and wall ball, but I need to learn how to play tether ball.

Teacher: Okay, I will work with you on that, but let's talk about the steps for joining a group. First, you have to find the group. You may need to ask for assistance to find a specific group of friends. Then, you sort of hang out. Remember, we talked about body space, and listening for a lull in the conversation. When there is a pause, you would face the group of students (physically demonstrate facing the group), casually greet them, and ask "what's happening" or "what's going on." Wait for a response from someone in the group. If there is no response, try the process again with someone whose voice is familiar to you. Then, if the activity is something you want to do, ask if you can join in. You might need to be a bit assertive. Do you remember what that word means?

Jenny: Yes, assertive means that I just don't jump in or get too pushy. I use words like, "I'd really like to play the game. I know I can do it."

Teacher: That's great. Now tell me the steps you would use for joining a group. [Has the student retell the steps filling in where needed.] You did a good job describing the steps, but you forgot about facing the students and using eye contact. Remember, that's an important way to get your friends' attention. Remember, it's important to keep an "imaginary fence" of 12 to 18 inches of space between yourself and the person you're talking to. Let's practice that.

Jenny: [Jenny stands, and turns her head toward her teacher, looking at her and making sure she is a reasonable distance from the teacher.]

Teacher: Yes, that is very good. You've got the idea. Now, I'm going to give you a typical situation you might encounter with your friends on the playground. I'll be your friend Jane, and you'll be yourself. Here's the situation. It's snack recess, and a group of girls from your class are standing around. They are sharing their snacks with each other, and talking about a movie they saw over the weekend. What do you do?

Jenny: I walk up to the group with my snack (a bag of chips). I listen for a few seconds, and wait for a break in the conversation. Then, I turn to my friends Jane and Alison, and ask if they want some chips. If they want chips I give them some, and get involved in the conversation. If not, I try to get involved in the conversation, waiting my turn.

Teacher: Good, you've got the idea. Now let's role-play.

6. Eventually the student uses the skill in a real setting.
7. After the student uses the social skill in a natural context, such as the cafeteria or the playground, the teacher provides feedback.

Sidebar 9.1 provides an example of how this technique might be used to teach the social interaction skill of joining a group.

This strategy is even more effective when sighted classmates are used to model appropriate social behavior. Classmates can provide natural feedback when engaged in teaching a specific social skill.

Peer-Mediated Interventions

Teachers of students with visual impairments need to work collaboratively with general education teachers to implement the peer-mediated intervention strategy. After specific social interaction skills are targeted for intervention, the teacher of students with visual impairments and the general education teacher need to recruit same-aged classmates who exhibit age-appropriate social skills. It is most effective if the students selected show a genuine interest in working with and being a friend to the student who is visually impaired. Initially, the classmate receives instruction from the teacher of students with visual impairments about the student's visual impairment and his or her visual functioning. The teacher and the classmate brainstorm about the kind of activities the two students can do together. However, final decisions regarding activities are made mutually between the students. Within the context of the activity, the sighted classmate provides modeling, cues, and feedback to help the student who is blind or has low vision learn a specific social skill. Throughout the intervention, the sighted peer meets with the teacher of students with visual impairments to receive support and guidance regarding specific teaching strategies, but the student with a visual impairment is unaware of the adult support.

Peer Support Models

Another model that is used with students who are blind or visually impaired in general education classrooms uses sighted peers as support for the student. Sighted peers have three functions in this model:

- They can help the student with a visual impairment interpret social behaviors and cues in the classroom. For example, the sighted peer might assist a student who is blind in knowing when to raise his hand during a class discussion rather than interrupting the conversation.
- They can provide assistance with materials and equipment. For example, if a student has a visual impairment and a physical disability, a sighted peer might provide support in retrieving equipment or helping the student position him- or herself at a computer station.
- They can assist the student with a visual impairment outside the classroom, such as by guiding him on the playground or acting as a buddy at lunch.

The overall goal with this method is to help the student who is blind or visually impaired feel included in the classroom milieu. It is always important to include the student who is visually impaired in the selection of his or her support team. Sighted students who are selected as peer supports need to be closely monitored by the general education teacher and the teacher of students with visual impairments. These professionals ensure that the sighted peers are providing socialization opportunities while striking a balance between nurturing independence and providing too much support. Teachers meet weekly with the peer support team and the student with a visual impairment to provide feedback and to discuss strategies to promote positive social relationships.

This model encourages students with visual impairment to develop positive social relationships and friendships with their classmates. With this technique, not only are students encouraged to be supported by their classmates, they can also be taught how to reciprocate and demonstrate appreciation for that assistance. Also, students can be taught the difference between a friend and an acquaintance, including that friends have similar interests, they show mutual respect for one another, and they enjoy being together. Friends share personal information, while acquaintances interact on a more superficial level.

Role-Playing Scenarios

Earlier in this chapter, role-plays were mentioned as a vehicle for social skills assessment. Role-playing scenarios can also be used as a teaching tool. Role-playing scenarios allow students with a visual impairment to experience in a safe setting typical situations they may encounter with classmates at school, with family members at home, and with adults in the community. Usually role-playing scenarios are acted out by the student who is visually impaired and classmates who may be either sighted or visually impaired.

Role-plays allow students with visual impairments to take on the role of a sighted classmate, a sibling, a teacher, or a stranger in the community. The teacher or O&M specialist sets the stage for the role-play by targeting specific social interaction skills, describing the role-play, assigning roles, and providing feedback after the students have completed the scenario. After the students complete the role-play, they can also share their unique perspectives. For example, a sighted student might point out that the student who is blind always whines when he doesn't get to play his favorite board game. In a similar manner, a student with low vision can point out that his classmates move game pieces too quickly when playing Monopoly, which causes him great frustration.

Teachers of students with visual impairments can create role-playing scenarios to suit specific situations that their students already face or need to be able to handle. Sample role-playing scenarios are provided in Sidebar 9.2 for students in elementary, middle, and high school to assist in implementing this teaching strategy. Role-playing scenarios are also an effective instructional tool for other areas of the ECC, such as when teaching job interviewing skills in the career development area, or when modeling self-advocacy skills in the self-determination area.

SIDEBAR 9.2

Sample Social Interaction Role-Playing Scenarios

ELEMENTARY SCHOOL

1. You are in your general education class, and your teacher has just written some math problems on the smart board. Your teacher of students with visual impairments has not put the problems into braille or large print. How will you let your general education teacher know you need assistance? How will you ask for assistance?
2. During recess a group of kids in your class does not want you to play four-square with them. They tell you that you don't know how to play the game. What would you tell the kids?
3. You are working in class using your Braille-Note. One of the students comes up to you to ask if he can try it out. What would you say and do?
4. Your classroom teacher never asks you to take the attendance to the school office even though you know the route very well. What could you say to your teacher?
5. Every time you use your special eyeglasses in class, the kids whisper and make fun of you. What could you say to make them stop teasing you?
6. Yesterday students in your table group wouldn't let you be the leader of the science experiment. They said you were not paying attention to the teacher's directions because your head was down on the table. What can you say and do to make them want you to be the group leader?
7. At lunch you are at a table with a couple of students you know from class. They are talking about what they have for lunch. What will you do to get involved in the conversation?
8. Whenever you go to the computer lab or the library with your class, one of the students takes your hand, and drags you along. You want to stay with the class, but you don't want to be dragged. What can you do?
9. During morning meeting you want to share special news from home. What do you do?
10. You are in the lunch line waiting to buy your lunch. You are rocking and talking to yourself. You bump into the student in front of you. The student pushes you and says, "Stop it." What can you do?
11. Your family is having a big reunion. You are expected to greet all of the relatives. What will you say and do?
12. Many of your classmates have chores at home and get an allowance. You want to be paid for your work at home as well. What can you say to your parents?

MIDDLE SCHOOL

1. Girls in your sixth-grade class are teasing you about your eyeglasses. They call you weird and ugly. What do you say?
2. You are friendly with a couple of students in your English class. They invite you to have lunch with them. Every time you try to find them in the cafeteria, they are nowhere to be found. What do you do?
3. Your social studies teacher never calls on you even though you raise your hand. It's like you don't exist. How do you let her know you want to contribute to the class discussion?
4. None of the students in your science group will let you work on the experiment. They continually say that you can't see the equipment. What do you say or do?
5. You want to join the swim team, and the coach tells you that you can't because you are blind. How do you handle this situation?
6. You want to go to the mall with a friend from school. Your parents are reluctant to let you go. How can you convince them that you have the ability and skills to go to the mall?
7. You are at the school dance. It's loud and very difficult to see anyone. How are you going to find someone you know?
8. It's the beginning of the school year, and you want to get to know some of the people in your class. What can you do to get their attention in a positive way?
9. Your teacher asks everyone in class to introduce themselves. When it is your turn, you introduce yourself. One student asks about your cane and your braille notetaker. What do you say or do?

(continued on next page)

SIDEBAR 9.2 *continued*

HIGH SCHOOL

1. During passing period you notice that a student always waves to you and says, "Hi," but you can't quite figure out who the student is. What do you do to make contact with this person?
2. Every time your English teacher shows PowerPoint slides, you ask her for a copy in braille [or large print], but she ignores you and continues to forget. What can you do to solve this problem? What can you say to your teacher? What other strategies could you use with classmates?
3. You are a new student at your high school. One of your classmates notices that you use a long cane to travel from one class to another, but you read both print and braille. He approaches you and asks, "Hey, are you blind or what?" How do you respond?
4. You are on a job interview for a summer job at a local business. The employer has never met you. You walk in with your braille notetaker in hand. When you take it out to take notes, his demeanor changes from interested to ending the interview immediately. What can you do to make the interview continue and end successfully?
5. You are out in the community at a fast food restaurant. You cannot read the menu. What can you say to and do with the service person behind the counter to place your order?
6. You are traveling to your local bank to deposit your check from work. You need cash back, and cannot complete the deposit slip on your own. What do you do and what do you communicate to the bank teller?
7. It's prom time and you want to ask a sighted classmate to the prom. You haven't figured out transportation yet. Your friend doesn't realize you have a visual impairment, and thinks you can drive. What do you say and do when your friend asks about how you two are going to get to prom?
8. You have been given a shopping list for the grocery store. You have to purchase several items, and you don't like to ask for assistance. How do you handle the situation and find all of the items at the grocery store?
9. You want to travel on the city bus to get to the mall. You have accomplished this route with your O&M teacher. Even though your teacher has said that you are very confident traveling on the bus, your parents refuse to let you do this independently. What do you say and do to convince your parents you can do this on your own?
10. You will be graduating from high school at the end of the school year, and will be attending a four-year college. You have been assigned a roommate in the dorm for the fall semester. You have been e-mailing back and forth. You have similar interests, but you have not mentioned that you are visually impaired. How would you handle this situation? What would you say to your new roommate?

Because role-play allows students with visual impairments to take the role of others, it provides opportunities for them to discover behaviors that they weren't aware of exhibiting, and the unintentional impact of their behavior on other students. For example, if the student who is blind tends to whine when waiting in the cafeteria line, the teacher can set up a role-playing scenario in which a sighted peer takes the role of the student who is visually impaired, and the student who is blind assumes the role of the sighted peer. After the role-play, the teacher can turn the evaluation of the scenario into a discussion about the behaviors that were exhibited. The students can discuss their feelings about students who whine or complain.

Cognitive-Behavioral Strategies

Cognitive-behavioral teaching strategies emphasize the use of student self-evaluation and analytical thinking. Students with visual impairments need to be able to examine a social situation they have encountered and determine the aspects of the interaction that were positive and the aspects of the interaction that need improvement. This strategy is particularly useful for adolescents and young adults in learning how to analyze nonverbal communication, understand how others perceive them, and appreciate how their behavior impacts and influences other people in their lives. Teachers of students with visual impairments can facilitate this strategy by observing the student in a variety of social situations, discussing with the student who is visually impaired the events of the social interaction, the aspects that went well, and how the student might change his or her behavior in a subsequent situation. The teacher can provide feedback regarding the observation and offer strategies to enhance the social exchange. Teachers can also use situation role-plays to assist students with developing these skills.

The following examples of role-plays for evaluation and analysis can be used with individuals or in a group.

- You are at a dance with a group of friends. It's very dark, and you ask the wrong person to dance. What do you do? How do you think the person feels? What could you have done differently?
- You are in the cafeteria line at lunch. Two students bump into you while waiting in line. What do you think they were doing? Were they intending to tease you or cut in line? How would you handle the situation?
- Your math teacher writes problems on the whiteboard, and does not verbalize any of the information even after you have asked him to do so. What can you do to resolve this situation? What can you say to your teacher?

Mentors and Role Models

One of the most powerful tools in teaching social interaction skills to students with visual impairments is recruiting older students or adults with visual impairments who are socially successful. These individuals can share their personal experiences about how they use social interaction skills in their daily lives. Also, they can demonstrate and discuss how they enter groups, develop friendships, interpret nonverbal communication, use gestures and facial expressions, and more. Role models and mentors can talk to students openly and honestly about their visual impairments. They can demonstrate and model how they let others know they have a visual impairment. (For information on using role models and mentors for career education, see Chapter 11.)

Five-Minute Lessons

All the strategies described thus far require that a designated time commitment be allotted for teaching social interaction skills to students with visual impairments. While it is important for teachers to include this area of the ECC in what they teach and provide structured interventions based on ongoing assessment, academic priorities and large caseloads often make it difficult to consistently implement these strategies. Therefore, providing shorter lessons on a more consistent basis may provide more positive outcomes. Sidebar 9.3 provides a

SIDEBAR 9.3

Five-Minute Social Skills Lessons

The following lessons are examples of short activities that teach social skills for different age groups. These can be done either as parts of other lessons or individually during a short break.

PRESCHOOL

- Introduce students to games that require a partner or a small group of students—London Bridge, A-Tisket, A-Tasket, and the like—and practice the game.
- Teach students to play on playground equipment such as swings, slides, and climbing structures.
- Demonstrate the use of favorite toys in the classroom; have students practice using the toy.
- Teach simple ball games like Hot Potato.
- Role-play asking a friend to play or join an activity.
- Create opportunities for students to engage in pretend play by bringing in toys, objects, and clothing that encourage make-believe play.

ELEMENTARY SCHOOL

- When working directly with students, create opportunities to practice greetings, introductions, social niceties, and turn-taking.
- Engage students in reciprocal conversations about topics of interest.
- Create opportunities for students to practice facial expressions and gestures through role-playing or drama experiences.
- Discuss mannerisms that are acceptable and those that are not. Have students create a list of each. Discuss situations or environments in which certain mannerisms are okay.

(continued on next page)

- Work with students to create lists of activities they can do or want to learn to do with classmates and friends during recess. Spend time teaching new activities to the students.
- Provide opportunities for students to learn board games, hand-clapping games, and other interactive games.
- Help students compile lists of games, activities, movies, videos, and toys that are popular with classmates to assist with age-appropriate conversations and gaining entry into groups.
- With classmates, give each student "emotion cards" to act out. Each card needs to have an emotion or feeling printed on it in braille, large print, or standard print. The printed word can be paired with a picture depicting the emotion.

MIDDLE SCHOOL

- Help students learn phrases (ice breakers) that will promote interactive relationships and entry into social groups.
- Have students create lists of the things they do well or excel in at school, at home, and in the community in order to improve self-esteem and an increased awareness of their abilities.
- Have students make a list of sayings middle school students use in greetings and conversations.
- Have students practice making positive statements about themselves and others.
- Have students examine teen magazines to discuss styles and dress.
- Discuss ways for students to disclose their visual impairments and practice them.
- Bring in a variety of skin care products and makeup or shaving lotions to try out.
- Practice effective ways to enter and leave a group in social situations.

HIGH SCHOOL

- Have students demonstrate the differences between passive, aggressive, and assertive behavior when communicating.
- Create situations for students where they have to problem-solve and analyze a social situation. Encourage students to describe how they would handle each situation.
- Provide opportunities for students to make a list of "text-message talk," and practice it on their cell phones or on e-mail.
- Teach students to use social networking sites and to develop an understanding of the safety issues surrounding them.
- Teach students to flirt and demonstrate other means of nonverbal communication.
- Hold mock job interviews where students practice greetings, shaking hands, making eye contact, disclosing visual impairments, and listening to questions and answering them in a succinct manner.
- Help students practice asking a classmate or friend on a date.

WORKING WITH STUDENTS WHO HAVE ADDITIONAL DISABILITIES

- Practice greetings using sign language, picture cards, or augmentative communication devices.
- Engage students in group conversations and reinforce taking turns by using a rain stick (a tube filled with beads that move slowly from the top to the bottom when turned upside down) or timer to help students know when to talk.
- Provide opportunities for students to choose activities, food items, or classmates and friends to play with during activities in class or in the community.
- Reinforce head-up behavior, eye contact, and body space when students talk to other people in the classroom or in the community.
- Teach students to play outdoor games or activities with classmates through co-acting and physical imitation.
- Expect students to use social amenities like saying "please" and "thank you" when interacting with others.
- Encourage the use of gestures like nodding the head for "yes," shaking the head for "no," palm flat and facing out for "stop," thumbs-up for approval, and thumbs-down for disapproval.
- Encourage students to communicate emotions or feelings by using picture cards or word cards with simple phrases, like: "I'm happy," "I'm sad," "I'm angry," and "I need help."

list of "five-minute lessons," categorized by age groupings, that teachers and O&M specialists can try with their students.

ROLE OF THE TEACHER OF STUDENTS WITH VISUAL IMPAIRMENTS

The teacher of students with visual impairments and the O&M specialist play a significant role in teaching social interaction skills to students with visual impairments. These professionals understand and can articulate to others the impact of a student's visual impairment on his or her social development. In addition, the teacher and O&M specialist should be able to understand and communicate how additional disabilities, like autism, intellectual challenges, neurological disabilities, and hearing impairments, in conjunction with a visual impairment, influence the acquisition of social interaction skills. The teacher and O&M specialist can share with general education teachers and special education colleagues from other disciplines valuable insights into how students with visual impairments, and especially those students with additional disabilities, develop and maintain positive social interactions with others, including the following:

- Students with visual impairments learn best about their social environment through real, hands-on experiences.
- Students learn appropriate social behavior by being provided with consistent verbal and physical feedback.
- Teaching of social interaction skills should take place in daily routines within naturally occurring activities.
- Verbally interpreting students' own social behavior and that of others helps them understand emotions and feelings in a variety of settings.

The teacher and O&M specialist should view themselves as the primary assessor of social interaction skills. Partnering with parents, siblings, and other family members to prioritize what social interaction skills need to be taught is critical. Teachers and O&M specialists should be able to communicate the importance of teaching social interaction skills to families, while being sensitive to the cultural values and beliefs those families practice. When working with families, teachers and O&M specialists need to strike a balance between recognizing that families may have low expectations or negative beliefs about blindness, visual impairments, or disabilities in general, and helping families understand that using appropriate social interaction skills is critical if students hope to gain acceptance by classmates, be included in group activities, live independently, attract a mate, or find and secure a job. (Other suggestions for working with family members appear in the next section.)

The teacher and O&M specialist can also facilitate and promote social skills instruction in general education and community contexts. Teachers and O&M specialists should view social skills instruction as an essential part of a student's IEP or ITP. Working with the general education classroom teacher or other professionals to create a classroom environment that nurtures and values affective education is critical. (Affective education, sometimes referred to as "character education," refers to the development of skills in social values and ethical practices.) Finding and recommending for their students classrooms that are organized, structured, and provide students with visual impairments the opportunity to work in small groups, take leadership roles, make decisions and choices, assume responsibility for their actions and belongings, and have clear expectations regarding social performance is essential.

Teachers should work collaboratively and take the lead in ensuring that students have opportunities to practice and use the social interaction skills learned in school or community settings. These professionals are responsible for making available the tools and resources that enable families, general and special education teachers, and other professionals to reinforce appropriate social behavior for students with visual impairments. For example, sharing an abilities awareness curriculum in which students learn about the capabilities of people with disabilities or role-playing scenarios designed especially for students with visual impairments can facilitate positive social experiences for all students in a particular classroom (see, for example, Crow & Herlich, 2012). Also, teachers and O&M specialists can provide valuable information about specialized courses or training for families related to social interaction skills at schools for the blind and rehabilitation agencies.

SUGGESTIONS FOR WORKING WITH PARENTS

Families play an integral role in helping students with visual impairments learn social interaction skills. Parents and other family members are the first teachers of social skills, and with the support of caring professionals, the home environment provides opportunities for children with visual impairments to learn to engage with others, develop close and trusting relationships, and become a valued member of the family unit. However, in order for students to be viewed as socially competent, there needs to be a strong partnership between the home and the school. Teachers and O&M specialists must work with families to implement social skills instruction.

As has been stressed throughout this chapter, learning social interaction skills is not spontaneous for children with visual impairments, nor is it instinctive for the adults around these children to demonstrate skills and to bring the social world to and interpret it for the child. Teaching social interaction skills is an ongoing process that requires consistent messages from parents, siblings, other family members, teachers of students with visual impairments, general education teachers, and other professionals. It is important that everyone who works with a student provides the same information. The following suggestions can be offered as guidelines for families to follow in nurturing and supporting social interaction skills in the home.

- Create realistic expectations for the child to develop an array of social interaction skills.
- Include the child in all family activities. Try to verbalize what is happening, and provide hands-on experiences for as many parts of the activity as possible. Try to vary spectator activities, such as attending games or shows, with active ones, such as hiking or bowling.
- Encourage rough-and-tumble play and allow early exploration of the environment.
- Provide opportunities for the child to make choices and decisions—such as choosing food items, selecting clothing, and selecting a favorite game—to help him or her develop a sense of independence and autonomy.
- Provide opportunities for the child to take responsibility for his or her belongings, chores around the house, and completing homework.
- Provide opportunities for the child to be involved in group activities, like scouts, sports, music groups, and church groups.
- Encourage the child to invite classmates and friends for birthday parties, sleepovers, and play dates. The parents can work on making the home a place where the child's friends want to congregate. As the child grows older, the parents can make the home available for larger group events in which the child is involved, like cast parties, club gatherings, team get-togethers, and the like.
- Encourage participation in summer camps and recreational activities for students who are blind or visually impaired.
- Assist the child in learning about age-appropriate dress styles, and make sure that the child's personal appearance is socially acceptable.
- Encourage taking turns and model appropriate conversations during mealtime or other social activities.
- Encourage the child to use proper social etiquette in the home and in the community.

SUMMARY

Teaching social interaction to students with visual impairments is an essential part of the ECC. It is clear that teachers of students with visual impairments, O&M specialists, families, and other professionals must work together to ensure that students with visual impairments receive training and support to develop a sense of social competence. By using the strategies for assessment and instruction detailed in this chapter, teachers can implement ongoing evaluation, as well as create lessons that meet the individual needs of the student. Direct instruction in social interaction skills can be integrated into other ECC content areas or into instructional activities in the classroom, and can also take place within structured lessons.

No matter what approach is taken, it is essential for teachers and O&M specialists to recognize that they are an essential piece of the social skills puzzle. Their role is pivotal in educating families and other professionals and in helping students understand and use socially appropriate behavior in every aspect of their lives. Without such advocacy efforts and specialized knowledge and skills in teaching social interaction skills, students with visual impairments may be subject to social isolation from classmates and friends and have difficulty maintaining employment or living independently as adults. When students receive consistent messages about their social performance, use the skills and strategies they have learned, and experience clear and realistic expectations from caring adults, they demonstrate a strong social presence and develop a sense of self-worth—the ultimate goals of social skills education.

References

Chen, D. (2014). *Essential elements in early intervention: Visual impairment and multiple disabilities* (2nd ed.). New York: AFB Press.

Corsaro, W. A. (1985). *Friendship and peer culture in the early years.* Norwood, NJ: Ablex.

Crow, N., & Herlich, S. (2012). *Getting to know you: A social skills/ability awareness curriculum.* Louisville, KY: American Printing House for the Blind.

Ferrell, K. A. (1998). Project PRISM: A longitudinal study of developmental patterns of children who are visually impaired. Greeley: University of Northern Colorado. Retrieved from www.unco.edu/ncssd/research/PRISM/default.html

Gresham, F. M., & Elliott, S. N. (1990). *Social skills rating system.* Circle Pines, MN: American Guidance Service.

Hill, E., & Blasch, B. B. (1980). Concept development. In R. L. Welsh and B. B. Blasch (Eds.), *Foundations of orientation and mobility* (pp. 265–290). New York: AFB Press.

Loumiet, R., & Levack, N. (1991). *Independent living: A curriculum with adaptations for students with visual impairments.* Austin: Texas School for the Blind and Visually Impaired.

MacCuspie, P. A. (1996). Promoting acceptance of children with disabilities: From tolerance to inclusion. Halifax, Nova Scotia: Atlantic Provinces Special Education Authority.

Sacks, S. Z. (2006). Theoretical perspectives on the early years of social development. In S. Z. Sacks and K. E. Wolffe (Eds.), *Teaching social skills to students with visual impairments: From theory to practice* (pp. 51–80). New York: AFB Press.

Sacks, S. Z., & Barclay, L. A. (2006). Social skills assessment. In S. Z. Sacks and K. E. Wolffe (Eds.), *Teaching social skills to students with visual impairments: From theory to practice* (pp. 279–331). New York: AFB Press.

Sacks, S. Z., Kekelis, L. S., & Gaylord-Ross, R. J. (1992). *The development of social skills by blind and visually impaired students: Exploratory studies and strategies.* New York: AFB Press.

Sacks, S. Z., & Silberman, R. K. (2000). Social skills. In A. J. Koenig & M .C. Holbrook (Eds.), *Foundations of education: Vol. II. Instructional strategies for teaching children and youths with visual impairments* (2nd ed., pp. 616–642). New York: AFB Press.

Sacks, S. Z., & Wolffe, K. E. (2006a). *Social skills assessment tool for children with visual impairments: Revised.* Fremont: California School for the Blind.

Sacks, S. Z., & Wolffe, K. E. (2006b). *Teaching social skills to students with visual impairments: From research to practice.* New York: AFB Press.

Sacks, S. Z., Wolffe, K. E., & Tierney, D. (1998). Lifestyles of students with visual impairments: Preliminary studies of social networks. *Exceptional Children, 64,* 463–478.

Seligman, M. E. P. (1990). *Learned optimism.* New York: Alfred A. Knopf.

Warren, D. (1994). *Blindness and children: An individual differences approach.* New York: Cambridge University Press.

Wolffe, K. (2006). Teaching social skills to adolescents and young adults with visual impairments. In S. Z. Sacks & K. E. Wolffe (Eds.), *Teaching social skills to students with visual impairments: From theory to practice* (pp. 405–440). New York: AFB Press.

Wolffe, K. E., & Sacks, S. Z. (1997). The social network pilot project: A quantitative comparison of the lifestyles of blind and sighted young adults. *Journal of Visual Impairment & Blindness, 91*(3), 245–257.

Social Interaction Resources

This section provides resources such as assessment tools, publications, and instructional materials for teaching social skills. For additional resources that relate to the expanded core curriculum in general, see the Resources section at the end of this book.

ASSESSMENT TOOLS

Social Skills Assessment Tool for Children with Visual Impairments–Revised (SSAT-VI: R)

POPULATION/AGE LEVEL: Pre-K–12

SOURCE: Sacks, S. Z., & Wolffe, K. E. (2006). *Social skills assessment tool for children with visual impairments: Revised.* Fremont: California School for the Blind.

Social Competence Assessment

SOURCE: Loumiet, R., & Levack, N. (1991). *Independent living: A curriculum with adaptations for students with visual impairments, Vol. I: Social competence* (pp. 210–214). Austin: Texas School for the Blind and Visually Impaired.

PUBLICATIONS

Books

Fazzi, D. L. (2002). Social focus: Developing social skills and promoting social interactions. In R. L. Pogrund & D. L. Fazzi (Eds.), *Early Focus: Working with young children who are blind or visually impaired and their families* (2nd ed.). New York: AFB Press.

Garcia Winner, M. (2007). *Inside out: What makes a person with social cognition deficits tick?* Los Gatos, CA: Social Thinking.

Garcia Winner, M. (2008). *Think social.* Los Gatos, CA: Social Thinking.

MacCuspie, P. A. (1996). *Promoting acceptance of children with disabilities: From tolerance to inclusion.* Halifax, Nova Scotia: Atlantic Provinces Special Education Authority.

McCallum, B. J., & Sacks, S. Z. (Eds.). (1993). *Social skills curriculum for children with visual impairments.* Santa Clara, CA: Score Regionalization Project.

Sacks, S. Z. & Wolffe, K. E. (2006). *Teaching social skills to students with visual impairments: From research to practice.* New York: AFB Press.

Sacks, S. Z., Kekelis, L. S., & Gaylord-Ross, R. (Eds.) (1992). *The development of social skills by blind and visually impaired students.* New York: American Foundation for the Blind.

Sacks, S. Z., & Silberman, R. K. (2000). Social skills. In A. J. Koenig and M. C. Holbrook (Eds.), *Foundations of Education: Vol. II. Instructional strategies for teaching children and youths with visual impairments* (2nd ed., pp. 616–652). New York: AFB Press.

Seligman, M. E. P. (1990). *Learned optimism.* New York: Alfred Knopf.

Seligman, M. E. P. (1996). *The optimistic child.* New York: Harper Collins.

Tuttle, D. W., & Tuttle, N. (2004). *Self-esteem and adjusting with blindness* (3rd ed.). Springfield, IL: Charles C Thomas.

Wolf, A. E. (1991). *Get out of my life but first could you drive me and Cheryl to the mall?: A parent's guide to the new teenager.* New York: The Noonday Press.

Wolf, A. E. (1995). *It's not fair, Jeremy Spencer's parents let him stay up all night!* New York: Farrar, Straus and Giroux.

Wolffe, K. E. (Ed.). (1999). *Skills for success: A career education handbook for children and adolescents with visual impairments.* New York: AFB Press.

Curricula

Cleveland, J. R., Clinkscales, M., Hefner, N., Houghtling, D., Kubacak, C., & Sewell, D. (2007). *Empowered: An activity based self-determination curriculum for students with visual impairments.* Austin: Texas School for the Blind and Visually Impaired.

Corn, A. L., Bina, M., & Sacks, S. Z. (2009). *Looking good: A curriculum on physical appearance and personal presentation for students with visual impairments.* Austin, TX: Pro-Ed.

Corn, A. L., & Rosenblum, L. P. (2000). *Finding wheels: A curriculum for non-drivers with visual impairments for gaining control of transportation needs.* Austin, TX: Pro-Ed.

Loumiet, R., & Levack, N. (1993). *Independent living: A curriculum with adaptations for students with visual impairments* (2nd ed.). Austin, TX: Texas School for the Blind and Visually Impaired.

Wolffe, K. E., & Sacks, S. Z. (2000). *Focused on: Social skills.* New York: AFB Press.

Journal Articles

D'Allura, T. (2002). Enhancing the social interaction skills of preschoolers with visual impairments. *Journal of Visual Impairment & Blindness, 96*(8), 576–584.

Griffin-Shirley, N., & Nes, S. L. (2005). Self-esteem and empathy in sighted and visually impaired preadolescents. *Journal of Visual Impairment & Blindness, 99*(5), 276–285.

Huurre, T., Komulainen, E. J., & Aro, H. M. (1999). Social support and self-esteem among adolescents with visual impairments. *Journal of Visual Impairment & Blindness, 93*(1), 26–37.

Jindal-Snape, D. (2005). Use of feedback from sighted peers in promoting social interaction skills. *Journal of Visual Impairment & Blindness, 99*(7), 403–412.

Kef, S. (1997). The personal networks and social supports of blind and visually impaired adolescents. *Journal of Visual Impairment & Blindness, 91*(3), 236–244.

Peavy, K. O., & Leff, D. (2002). Social acceptance of adolescent mainstreamed students with visual impairments. *Journal of Visual Impairment & Blindness, 96*(11), 808–811.

Pogrund, R. L., & Fazzi, D. L. (Eds.). (2002). *Early focus: Working with young children who are blind or visually impaired and their families* (2nd ed.). New York: AFB Press.

Rosenblum, L. P. (1997). Adolescents with visual impairments who have best friends: A pilot study. *Journal of Visual Impairment & Blindness, 91*, 224–235.

Rosenblum, L. P. (1998). Best friendships of adolescents with visual impairments: A descriptive study. *Journal of Visual Impairment & Blindness, 92*, 593–608.

Sacks, S. Z., & Gaylord-Ross, R. J. (1989). Peer-mediated and teacher-directed social skills training for visually impaired students. *Behavior Therapy, 20*, 619–638.

Sacks, S. Z., & Wolffe, K. (1992). The importance of social skills in the transition process for students with visual impairments. *Journal of Vocational Rehabilitation, 2*(1), 46–55.

Sacks, S. Z., & Wolffe, K. E. (1998). Lifestyles of adolescents with visual impairments: An ethnographic analysis. *Journal of Visual Impairment & Blindness, 92*(1), 7–17.

Sacks, S. Z., Wolffe, K. E., & Tierney, D. (1998). Lifestyles of students with visual impairments: Preliminary studies of social networks. *Exceptional Child, 64*(4), 463–478.

Wolffe, K. E., & Sacks, S. Z. (1997). The lifestyles of blind, low vision, and sighted youths: A quantitative comparison. *Journal of Visual Impairment & Blindness, 91*(3), 245–257.

Social Interaction Learning Activities

Contributed by Nita Crow and Stephanie Herlich

These sample learning activities are presented as examples of activities that teachers can create to work on several ECC skills at once with their students. Activities that help teach social interaction skills can also be found in other chapters. The activities presented, like all instruction, need to be considered and modified to address the needs of individual students—such as those who are braille readers, have low vision, or have additional disabilities—with adaptations for appropriate media and the physical and other capabilities of the student.

Learning Activity: Showing Gratitude

Primary ECC Area: Social interaction **Component:** Interactions with others
Grade: Pre-K–12, students with multiple disabilities

Other ECC Areas

- Assistive technology
- Orientation and mobility
- Career education
- Self-determination

Goal: The student will be able to show appreciation and gratitude toward others.

Key Tasks/Concepts

The student will:

- Make choices
- Organize materials
- Write a note using an appropriate device
- Deliver note

Description

The expression of gratitude is one of the foundations for developing and maintaining positive social relationships. This thank-you note activity will teach and reinforce students' knowledge of common ways we express gratitude, and develop an awareness of others' actions for which gratitude is an appropriate response.

The teacher can discuss with students the importance of showing appreciation and gratitude, asking students if someone has ever shown or demonstrated appreciation or gratitude to them for something they did.

- How did that feel?
- Was it important? Why?

The teacher can ask students if they have done something for someone else that shows appreciation or gratitude. The teacher may want to begin the discussion with a personal example, as necessary.

For younger students: The teacher will explain that a mailbox will be placed in the classroom and that all students will write at least two notes each week telling another student or a staff member that they did something that was appreciated. The teacher may need to keep a list of classmates' names in a braille or large-print list near mailbox. The teacher can encourage students to write to different people each week.

(continued on next page)

A template such as the following can be provided to students for a thank-you note:

Dear ________________,

I liked it when you ________________________.

It made me feel __________________________.

Sincerely,

____

The teacher can have older students write an e-mail, note, or text to at least one person each week expressing gratitude for something the recipient did. Some students may need instruction in composing an appropriate note.

Instructional Materials and Supplies Needed

- Braille notetaker, brailler, paper, bold-line markers or pens, magnifier, computer with appropriate software
- For older students, personal equipment such as students' cell phones for texting
- For younger students, mailbox
- List of students' names
- Template, if using

Settings

The resource or itinerant teacher's regular meeting room. The activity can also be a project for the whole class within the general education classroom. Participants can be students with visual impairments and sighted peers.

Duration/Timing

10–15 minutes of "gratitude time" once or twice each week.

Evaluation

An evaluation tool such as the following can be used to record students' progress in completing the elements of the activity over the course of several weeks.

Task	Date	Date	Date	Date
Chooses person				
Uses template				
Composes letter without template				

Key:

I = Independent

WA = With Assistance

Learning Activity: Hold It!

Primary ECC Area: Social interaction

Components: Development of relationships and friendships

Grades: K–5

Other ECC Areas

- Recreation and leisure
- Compensatory access
- Sensory efficiency
- Independent living

Goal: The student will interact appropriately when playing a tactile game with a classmate.

(continued on next page)

Key Tasks/Concepts

The student will:

- Play a game with a classmate using appropriate turn-taking and social interaction skills.
- Identify objects tactilely.
- Describe objects using specific descriptors.

Description

The teacher prepares two bags or boxes with an identical variety of common items in each (the more unfamiliar the items are to the students, the better), and closes the containers so that the participating players can access the objects only by reaching into them. The game is played in pairs, with each player receiving one of the containers. Each round will last one minute. The first player, the describer, reaches into the box, selects an item, and, without using the name of the object, describes the item to the other player. The second player, the matcher, then has to locate the same item in his or her container. Once a match is selected, the second player says, "Got it!" If the correct item is selected, the describer moves on to describe another object. Play continues until the timer rings. At the end of the round, the describer gets 2 points for every item the matcher guessed correctly. The matcher gets 1 point for every item guessed correctly. Students reverse rolls after tallying their points. The game continues until each child has had a specified number of turns or the time available has expired. At the end of the game, the children add their points, and the player with the highest number of points is declared the winner.

The players can be encouraged to determine some of the rules, such as how to decide who plays first and what to do with the items that have already been described—whether they are put back into the container and possibly be described multiple times or are put aside, out of the game.

Depending on the skills of the students, the teacher may want to have the student with a visual impairment practice this game before involving classmates. Collaboration with the speech and language pathologist to identify classmates who need practice with these same skills may ensure that the vocabulary skills of the two players are similar.

Instructional Materials and Supplies Needed

- Accessible timer that measures seconds
- Chart for recording times in the student's preferred medium
- Two boxes (or bags) with holes cut into the lids or sides
- Pairs of items to describe and locate, such as:
  - slates
  - braille erasers
  - pencils
  - individual hole punchers
  - staple removers
  - buttons
  - coins
  - toothpicks
  - marbles
  - socks
  - silverware
  - hair clips
  - household tools
- Tactile clock with movable hands

Settings

Classrooms and other school areas, including playground

(continued on next page)

Duration/Timing

- Approximately 5 minutes per round (each player taking one turn), expandable depending on how much time is available.
- Inclusion of additional skills (time tracking, clock skills, and the like) will increase the time required to complete the activity.

Evaluation

The evaluation for this activity focuses on game skills, such as turn taking, following rules, putting away the game, and tallying the scores, as well as social interaction with the other player. The evaluation tool might appear as follows, using plus or minus signs to indicate whether the task was performed or not:

Task	Date	Date	Date	Date
Retrieves game materials from activity shelf				
Accurately reviews game rules before start of game				
Cooperates with fellow player in determining turn order				
Follows rules of game				
Records players' scores				
Displays players' scores on tactile clock				
Assists with returning game materials to shelf				
Interacts politely with other player				

Learning Activity: Greetings

Primary ECC Area: Social interaction **Component:** Interactions with others
Grades: K–12, students with multiple disabilities

Other ECC Areas

- Compensatory access
- Career education
- Sensory efficiency

Goal: The student will be able to appropriately greet people of all ages within a variety of settings.

Key Tasks/Concepts

The student will:

- Make choices
- Work in a team
- Take turns

Description

The teacher creates the scenario cards described below, using an appropriate medium for the students, and additional cards based on students participating in the group. It is recommended to have a minimum of eight cards available for the 30-minute session. Each card lists a setting, a person being greeted, and three choices of a greeting for the students to choose from. For example:

(continued on next page)

After you wake up in the morning, you go to greet Mom in the kitchen. You:
(a) shake hands with her
(b) give her a hug
(c) give her a high five

Participants can be students with visual impairments and classmates with sight. The cards should allow the students to imagine themselves in these scenarios as well as to imagine different age groups. Students need to learn appropriate behaviors based on their own ages and interactions with people of other ages.

To begin the activity, the teacher discusses different forms of greetings based on the person being greeted and the setting, such as the following:

Informal greetings:
- waving
- saying "hi"
- high fives
- special handshakes
- head nods
- hugs
- kisses on the cheek

Formal greetings:
- shaking hands
- saying "hello"
- bowing

The teacher needs to make sure each student can physically demonstrate each type of greeting.

Participants can discuss which type of greeting would be used in a variety of settings, such as school, home, work, store, a friend's house, out in the community.

After the discussion, the teacher passes out the scenario cards and explains that more than one greeting may be appropriate for a given situation.

For younger students or students with multiple disabilities: The students are divided into pairs. One pair can act out the scenario and the other students can decide if an appropriate greeting was used. If students cannot read, the teacher can read the card.

For older students: The students can choose to act out scenarios or to discuss what greetings are appropriate and why.

Instructional Materials and Supplies Needed

- Scenario cards in appropriate medium (large print, braille, or both). Examples:
  - Child wakes up in the morning and goes to greet mom in the kitchen: (a) shakes hands, (b) gives a hug (c) gives a high five
  - Student sees friend at the mall: (a) gives special handshake (b) waves (c) ignores
  - 15-year-old student sees favorite teacher in the hallway: (a) hugs (b) waves (c) high-fives
  - Preschooler sees favorite teacher in mall: (a) hugs (b) waves (c) ignores
  - Familiar clerk at grocery store greets student at checkout stand and student: (a) hugs (b) shakes hands (c) says "hello"

Settings

The resource or itinerant teacher's regular meeting room.

Duration/Timing

- About 30 minutes. Can take place in the regular meeting room or in the general classroom.

(continued on next page)

Evaluation

An evaluation tool such as the following can be used to record how students greet classmates, other students, and other school staff. At least one evaluation should take place before lesson is taught.

Task	Date	Date	Date	Date
Morning greeting of friend				
Morning greeting of teacher				
Midday greeting of familiar school staff				
Afternoon greeting of bus driver (if appropriate)				

Key:

A = Appropriate
NA = Not appropriate

Learning Activity: Say "Excuse Me!"

(Contributed by Lisa LaDue, Sarasota, Florida)

Primary ECC Area: Social interaction **Component:** Social etiquette
Grades: 2–6

Other ECC Areas

- Recreation and leisure
- Sensory efficiency
- Compensatory access
- Self-determination

Goal: Students will identify polite behaviors they are expected to use in various social situations.

Key Tasks/Concepts

The student will

- Distinguish between polite and impolite behaviors
- Learn about behaviors that are socially unacceptable
- Play a game
- Use magnification

Description

This game reinforces classroom rules and behavior that are typically addressed in the classroom during the first week of school. It would be appropriate to play this game in the general education classroom and include classmates with sight. It can also be played just with the teacher of students with visual impairments or at home.

Preparation: The teacher has the students generate a list of the types of polite behaviors that are expected of them at home, school, and with classmates, and their "opposites"—impolite behaviors that are discouraged in these environments. One student writes or brailles each behavior on an index card (or the teacher can do this, depending on the students' ages and abilities). For example, one card might say: "I say 'excuse me' when I burp," and the opposite card might say, "I like to burp as loud as I can in class." Generating ideas of impolite behaviors is especially fun for students. The teacher can guide students to identify rude behaviors that they might be likely to exhibit, such as holding one's head down when talking to someone else, eye pressing, or bumping into people without offering an apology.

(continued on next page)

Dice, a number of game pieces equal to the number of players, and a game board with spaces need to be prepared for the game. (Each player can have an individual game board or all of the players can use the same one.) Depending on the age and physical and cognitive functioning of students involved, the game board can be very simple or more complex. The rules of the game should also be prepared in each student's preferred medium for students to read.

The teacher has each student roll one die to see who goes first (whoever rolls the highest number). The first player then rolls the die, draws a card, and reads it aloud. If it is a polite behavior, the player moves his or her game piece forward the number of squares indicated by the die. If the behavior described on the card is an impolite one, the player moves the game piece backward the specified number of squares. When a rude behavior is read, the other player or players can exclaim, "I will not tolerate that behavior from you!" The player who gets to the finish first wins the game.

The game is more fun if several players are involved and they act out the polite behaviors before moving their game pieces.

Instructional Materials and Supplies Needed

- Accessible dice
- Game board (the configuration of squares can be a simple line or more elaborate, depending on the age and skills of the students; the board can be created on fabric that has a nap, so game pieces can be attached with Velcro)
- Game pieces—any object that fits within the game board's playing area and is not likely to move far if inadvertently bumped
- Cards with polite and impolite behaviors written on them
- Game rules written in print and braille

Settings

Initially at school. Can also be played at lunch or recess, or taken home.

Duration/Timing

- 10–20 minutes to make the cards.
- 30 minutes or more for a complete game in the general education classroom.
- A game can also be completed in 5-minute segments each day that the student is seen by the teacher of students with visual impairments. (In this event, it would be wise to use game pieces that adhere to the game board so their positions remain undisturbed between rounds.)

Evaluation

The student's performance on the game itself or the student's actual behaviors with others can form the basis for evaluation. For example:

- Did the student identify polite and impolite behaviors with 90% accuracy each time the game was played?
- Are the student's spontaneous positive behaviors increasing while waiting in lunch line?

The following is a sample rubric to measure observed generalization of skills, using plus or minus signs to indicate whether the task was performed or not:

Task	Date	Date	Date	Date	Date
Does not touch other children in line	+				
Says "sorry" when cane hits another person	–				
Says "thank you" to cafeteria worker when paying for meal	–				
Politely asks for assistance with carrying tray	+				

Learning Activity: What Are You Feeling?

Primary ECC Area: Social interaction **Component:** Interactions with others
Grades: 7–12

Other ECC Areas

- Compensatory access
- Assistive technology
- Sensory efficiency
- Orientation and mobility

Goal: The student will identify the feelings that are being expressed by others by replicating their body language and facial expressions.

Key Tasks/Concepts

The student will:

- Identify emotions expressed by others
- Practice facial expressions associated with certain emotions
- Practice body language associated with certain emotions
- Practice voice tones associated with certain emotions

Description

The teacher asks students to name common feelings—such as mad, sad, happy, excited—and talk about other feelings that one might experience—such as proud, disappointed, pity, envy, appreciation, worry, loneliness, contentment, and belligerent.

The students each make a list of these feelings using preferred media (braille, print, technology device, or other).

The teacher and students choose two or three emotions at a time to discuss for each session. Talk can be about facial expressions, body language, and voice tones used with each emotion; the teacher should practice these with the students.

The teacher can walk around the school environment with the students with the purpose of identifying the feelings of people encountered based on visual and auditory cues. The teacher may need to quietly describe facial expressions or body stance and movement of people of interest. A greater variety of emotions can probably be observed in other environments, such as on buses, or in stores and parks.

The teacher has students practice facial expressions, voice tones, and body language associated with various emotions. The teacher may need to model expressions and gestures and assist the student by manipulating body positions. The teacher might also take this opportunity to discuss with the student the appropriateness of showing various emotions in public, with friends, and at home. Role-playing with other students can be incorporated if desired.

Students can maintain journals that record the emotions they recognize in others and in themselves.

Instructional Materials and Supplies Needed

- Journaling materials in the appropriate media—braille, print, or technology device.

Setting

School, home, or community

Duration/Timing

- 15–20 minutes for the introductory discussion, depending on the age and awareness of the child.
- 5–10 minutes scheduled as a weekly activity so that a variety of emotions and settings can be explored.

Evaluation

This activity can be evaluated using the following rubric:

(continued on next page)

Mark plus sign (+) if an emotion is properly demonstrated, based on the teacher's judgment, through voice (V), body language (B), or facial expression (F). Mark minus sign (–) if the emotion is not demonstrated or is demonstrated incorrectly.

	Date			Date			Date			Date		
Skill	V	B	F	V	B	F	V	B	F	V	B	F
Demonstrates fear												
Demonstrates anxiety												
Demonstrates loneliness												
Demonstrates pity												
Demonstrates pride												
Demonstrates anger												
Demonstrates joy												

CHAPTER 10

Recreation and Leisure

Carol B. Allman and Sandra Lewis,
with Lauren J. Lieberman and Mary Alice Ross

L. Penny Rosenblum

The recreation and leisure area of the expanded core curriculum (ECC) focuses on the knowledge, behaviors, and skills that allow individuals to participate in a healthy level of physical activity and enjoy fun and relaxing activities in their free time. It includes the general aspects of being physically and mentally active that lay the groundwork for healthy leisure and recreation choices that last a lifetime. Being engaged in recreation and leisure offers opportunities for social interactions and is critical for the physical and mental health and well-being of individuals throughout their lives (Edginton, Jordan, DeGraaf, & Edginton, 2002).

BENEFITS OF RECREATION AND LEISURE

Leisure activities provide opportunities to rest, release tension, slow down mentally, share experiences with friends, meet new people, practice autonomy, and increase self-reliance (Edginton et al., 2002). Recent national attention on the importance of physical activity focuses on its significance in maintaining normal weight and avoiding chronic diseases and other health problems (Physical Activity and Health, 2011). Physical activity has been shown to reduce certain diseases, help maintain appropriate weight, provide for mental and emotional well-being, and generally allow individuals to be self-confident and live healthy, happy lives (Lieberman, Schedlin & Pierce, 2009). Physical activity improves respiratory, muscular, and cardiovascular system health, which in turn has an impact on one's attitude, posture, and sense of well-being (Physical Activity and Health, 2011).

Students who are involved in recreation and leisure activities are more likely to be included in school and family recreation activities, which increases their opportunities to practice other important ECC skills, including social interaction, orientation and mobility (O&M), and self-determination. Students who participate in activities typically enjoyed by others in their age group also have more opportunities to share interests and conversations with peers, which is the foundation of true friendships.

Typically sighted children are aware of a wide variety of recreation and leisure activities because they observe individuals involved in these activities on a daily basis. Since children with visual impairments have limited opportunities to incidentally observe others engaged in recreation and leisure activities, their chances for becoming interested and involved in these activities are lowered. There is evidence that children with visual impairments engage in more passive, and fewer, leisure activities than their age-mates with unimpaired vision (Kroksmark & Nordell, 2001; Wolffe & Sacks, 1997). These children also have fewer opportunities to participate in activities that enhance physical development, a limitation that results in delays in motor skill development (Celeste, 2002) and physical activity (Lieberman, Byrne, Mattern, Watt, & Fernandez-Vivo, 2010; Lieberman & McHugh, 2001).

Students with a visual impairment need to be exposed directly to the skills needed for incorporating recreation and leisure activities into their lives and offered safe, non-threatening opportunities to try those activities. When given an equal opportunity to participate, children with visual impairments exhibit comparable levels of fitness to their peers (Blessing, McCrimmon, Stovall, & Williford, 1993; Ponchillia, Powell, Felski, & Nicklawski, 1992; Williams, Armstrong, Eves, & Faulkner, 1996). The barriers to engagement in recreation and leisure opportunities listed by parents include fear of possible injury, lack of available activities for children, and the inability of physical education teachers to help children with visual impairments (Conroy, 2012; Lieberman, Stuart, Hand, & Robinson, 2006). Other barriers include lack of opportunities to be active, absence of other children to participate with, and negative attitudes on the part of other people about the participation of visually impaired individuals in sports and recreation activities (Lieberman, Ponchillia, & Ponchillia, 2013).

Involvement in recreation and leisure activities helps students practice skills from other areas of the ECC. Social interaction and self-determination are enhanced for children engaged in recreation and leisure (Shapiro, Lieberman, & Moffett, 2003), and they need to practice appropriate O&M skills and sensory efficiency skills to participate effectively. In addition, some recreation and leisure activities develop technology and compensatory access skills, such as when walking with talking pedometers (Lieberman, Stuart et al., 2006), monitoring health with talking heart-rate devices, participating in electronic exercise games (discussed later in this chapter), or using the Internet to research activities and events, as in the learning activity "Finding Places for Fun" at the end of this chapter.

Recreation and leisure activities also provide opportunities for students to demonstrate career, independent living, and self-determination skills. For example, a student is more likely to actively participate in a craft activity of building a birdhouse in art class at school if she is self-assured and can gracefully join a group while volunteering to help with the project, move about the art class independently to help gather materials, effectively use hearing to understand directions and the purpose of the activity, and demonstrate independence and self-determination in explaining to the group what she can do to help with the project. Having had experiences with similar building activities prior to instruction in class will further facilitate the student's success.

In general, people have varied interests and develop their own opinions about what areas of recreation and leisure are best suited to them. For students with visual impairments to develop these interests and establish opinions about the areas of recreation and leisure they prefer, a variety of options need to be introduced and students need to be provided with opportunities to learn enough about each option to determine which they would like to explore further. Teaching recreation and leisure skills can be fun and exciting for the student, the parents, and the teacher of students with visual impairments, but, like other areas of the ECC, recreation and leisure skills need to be taught in a systematic way beginning at an early age, with the provision of many opportunities to practice.

A study by Stuart, Lieberman, and Hand (2006) listed parents' solutions to addressing recreation and leisure skill development, among which included:

- encouraging practice
- providing positive encouragement
- instilling confidence
- offering a variety of activities in safe areas
- using sighted peers as helpers
- increasing parent involvement

As they learn and practice recreation and leisure skills, students are more likely to spend free time appropriately and establish a foundation for adding new pursuits as additional opportunities of recreation and leisure arise.

COMPONENTS OF RECREATION AND LEISURE

The recreation and leisure area includes the following components:

- play
- physical activity
- health, fitness, and individual sports
- team and spectator sports
- leisure activities and hobbies

Within each of these components are a great many possible behaviors and skills. For example, the component of hobbies might include board games, computer games, gardening, arts and crafts, reading, fine arts (music, singing, and acting), joke telling, and generally any activity that a student can enjoy during leisure time. Likewise, the component of health, fitness, and individual sports includes a vast variety of exercise routines and individual sport activities in which a student can participate. Each of the components is outlined in the following sections, with specific considerations for students with visual impairments.

Play

The component of play includes the following skills and behaviors:

- entertaining oneself (finding an activity to do on one's own)
- engaging in parallel play (playing side-by-side with others)
- engaging in pretend play (dress up, playing store or school)
- engaging in give-and-take with others (taking turns in a game, social exchanges)
- sharing with others (allowing others to play with one's toys or games, using toys or games together)

Play is perhaps the most important component of recreation and leisure for young children, as the behaviors that provide a foundation for positive engagement with others throughout life are developed through play. If basic play skills are not developed at an early age, the probability of being successful in other areas of recreation and leisure is diminished (Anthony, 2013). Children with visual impairments need to be taught how to play, and each aspect of play may have to be taught, demonstrated, practiced, talked about, and allowed to develop over the course of the early years (Anthony, 2013). The teacher of students with visual impairments needs to give verbal feedback about what other students are doing and demonstrate what type of activity is happening for many students with visual impairments to be successful in all areas of play. Sidebar 10.1 provides suggestions for teachers and family members about helping young children learn how to play.

The interactive play of children with typical sight is often based on visual reconstructions of the world around them. For example, parallel play often is demonstrated by reproducing the actions of another child, as when a child observes a peer push a toy truck across the room and imitates this activity. A teacher or parent might need to describe what the other child is doing, show the child with a visual impairment where the toy trucks are kept, and demonstrate how to push one of them to encourage him or her to participate in this activity. Participating as a competent actor in pretend play (dress up, playing store or school) is facilitated by having

Learning How to Play

The roots of play form in a child's early development, when infants first learn to interact with people and objects. This learning process can be more difficult for infants whose visual impairments prevent them from seeing where people or objects are in their environment or what effects their own actions have on their caretakers or on the objects they touch. Children with visual impairments may need deliberate instruction in play throughout their childhood. Following are some guidelines and suggestions that professionals and families can follow when helping visually impaired children to be ready for play:

EARLY PLAY INTERACTION

Early on, face-to-face interactions during everyday routines such as diaper changing and feeding are important to start teaching social interaction and communication. The parents may imitate the infant's babbling, movements, or facial expressions (if the baby has some vision), and then prompt the baby to respond in kind; or they may develop routines involving tickling or touching and labeling the infant's body parts. These early routines can evolve into social games, such as peek-a-boo or patty cake. During this play, it is important to include opportunities for touch and physical contact and lots of verbal feedback.

IMITATION AND TURN TAKING

As these early play interactions with other people become more complex, the baby learns skills of imitation and turn taking. When a baby is reinforced for touching her daddy's hand to continue a fun activity, such as a tickling or bouncing game, she is expanding her understanding of cause and effect in physical activity—that is, "I do something and something happens."

SENSORY EXPERIENCES

Young children also need to be deliberately exposed to a variety of sensory experiences and to objects in the environment that they can act on to produce a result such as a sound or movement. They can lie on their back under "activity gyms" from which shiny objects or toys containing bells can be safely suspended within reach, or placed on their stomachs on a blanket within reach of toys that have auditory and tactile properties, as well as bright colors.

TOYS AND OBJECTS

As children's physical skills develop, they need to be exposed to toys and objects they can manipulate. Toddlers may need to be shown how to stack blocks or put objects into containers and dump them out again, for example, or be guided to explore the parts of toys that have various buttons and knobs to find out that they produce sound or motion.

PRETEND PLAY

Children of preschool age enjoy dramatic or pretend play, in which they may dress up and imitate the activities of people they have seen around them in their everyday lives. The more hands-on experiences children who are blind or have low vision have had with everyday events and environments in their homes, schools, and community, the more they will be able to engage in pretend play with other children. They need to know what police officers, firefighters, office workers, and mommies and daddies do, what tools are used in a variety of jobs, and what people wear when they are at work if they are going to be able to join in these games.

GAME RULES

Children preschool age and older begin to recognize that some games have rules that have to be followed in order to play with others, including early motor games such as hide-and-seek or easy board games. Children with visual impairments may need extra instruction (see the section on teaching strategies later in this chapter). It may be helpful to provide a human guide in the beginning for games that involve circling around a group of children such as duck, duck, goose. Tactile adaptations may be needed in board games.

PHYSICAL SKILLS

Children do not automatically know how to perform basic physical skills that are important in children's games, such as running, jumping, or throwing and kicking a ball. Young children with typical sight absorb these skills largely through incidental learning, visual observation, and a lot of practice. Children who are blind or visually impaired do not have the advantage of seeing others running or throwing, and may need to be taught such skills deliberately. If a child has little or no vision, the best approach may be allowing the child to tactilely examine someone performing the skill to get an overview of how it works

(continued on next page)

SIDEBAR 10.1 *continued*

and then breaking the skill down into its component pieces to teach it (see the section on teaching strategies later in this chapter).

SPATIAL CONCEPTS

Concepts of space that are important for physical activities also are not learned automatically by children with visual impairments. Orientation and mobility professionals can help their students to be ready for active games by making sure they understand body concepts, their relationship to the space around them, and concepts such as:

- in front and behind
- high and low
- forward and backward
- near and far
- straight and curved
- fast and slow
- hard and soft

PLAY AS SOCIALIZATION

The older children get, the more socializing with other children becomes a part of their play. Joining the play of others can be difficult for children who can't see their classmates or exactly what they are doing. Younger children need to have play dates arranged to begin learning how to play with others. Older children may need to practice how to find other children in the school yard or playground and to use their hearing to find out what they are doing. Role-playing ways of approaching others and asking to join in can be helpful.

SOURCES: Adapted from T. Anthony (2013), "Early Childhood Development: Movement and Play in Early Childhood," in L. J. Lieberman, P. E. Ponchillia, and S. V. Ponchillia, *Physical Education and Sports for People with Visual Impairments and Deafblindness: Foundations of Instruction* (New York: AFB Press); and K. A. Ferrell (2011), *Reach Out and Teach: Helping Your Child Who Is Visually Impaired Learn and Grow* (New York: AFB Press).

experienced the "real" activity, but the relationship between the pretend play and reality can be challenging for some young students to understand. Thus, some children with visual impairments may need to be taught to engage in typical pretend and imagination-based activities. (See the learning activity "Dress Up and Pretend" at the end of this chapter for an example of such instruction.)

It is important to remember that students with visual impairments also need to learn how to use free time appropriately when they are not engaged with others. For example, when a student has free or down time at home in the afternoon, that time should be used as the student desires by practicing a favorite game, reading a book of interest, or dabbling in a fun hobby. Often, teachers and parents need to help direct the child to an appropriate activity. Teachers and parents can encourage children to entertain themselves by keeping a "fun box" that is easily accessed by the child and that contains activities that he or she can do independently. After practice with the activities in the box, the adult can suggest that the student select a favorite while the adult is "busy" with another task. During this free time, the teacher should make note of the child's behaviors and identify the length of time that the child is appropriately engaged. Over time, this period should be increased. This same strategy is a good one to share with parents.

Learning how to give, take, and share during play are skills that need reinforcing even for children with unimpaired vision. One often hears parents or teachers say "share your doll with your friend," or "let Debby have a turn at swinging." Teaching, expecting, and reinforcing these appropriate play behaviors in young children with visual impairments lays a foundation of social interaction that will benefit the child in future social situations and when participating in recreation and leisure activities.

Physical Activity

Physical activity includes development of:

- strength
- dexterity
- coordination
- safety
- fine and gross motor movement

Although "children with visual impairments are born with the same potential to develop both motor skills and a healthy level of fitness as their sighted peers" (Lieberman et al., 2009, p. 173), they face a number of barriers that can interfere with their ability to learn the skills or find the opportunities necessary to participate in physical activities. Factors such as lack of opportunities, limited expectations, and absence of familiar adults who are knowledgeable about physical activity appear to be influential in the relative inactivity of children with visual impairments (Lieberman et al., 2013).

Very young children with early-onset visual impairments often have delays in reaching milestones related to developing muscle tone and gross motor skills such as sitting, rolling, crawling, and walking—or even lifting their heads (Strickling & Pogrund, 2002). Families and early interventionists who work with these children need to understand the importance of actively and deliberately working with children on these skills and motor development in general, in collaboration with other team members such as O&M specialists and occupational and physical therapists. (Many suggestions for activities and interventions can be found in Anthony, 2013; Ferrell, 2011, Strickling & Pogrund, 2002.)

Some parents may worry about being too rough with their young children who are visually impaired, but (unless a child has a medical condition that requires special treatment) providing opportunities for active and rough-and-tumble play can facilitate motor development, improve coordination, and prepare children for games and activities they will encounter with their playmates and in preschool and elementary school (see Sidebar 10.2 for some suggestions). As children get older, they can be encouraged to take part in active play and games involving movement such as:

- ring-around-the-rosy or Simon says
- using the slides, swings, and climbing equipment in the playground
- riding tricycles or scooters
- skating
- running, climbing, crawling, and jumping activities

The learning activity "Hula-Hoop Fun" at the end of this chapter is an example of an activity that can help

SIDEBAR 10.2

Early Rough-and-Tumble Play Activities

The following activities can help young children with visual impairments become used to rough-and-tumble play, starting when they are infants and continuing in more active ways throughout toddlerhood, and prepare them for interacting with other children.

Body-on-body play: A young baby is placed on her tummy on top of an adult's reclining body, as the adult rocks gently so the baby can feel the to-and-fro movements. As the infant's motor control becomes more established, the adult can exaggerate the body movements so that the child experiences more of a need to respond to the pull of gravity. Once the baby is able to stay upright, they can play games such as "horsey" with the child positioned on the adult's knee, so that the child feels the up and down of the adult's leg against her body.

Mad tickle games: When the child has the benefit of the floor supporting the length of her body, the adult can play a tickle game where the adult's hands move from one limb to another in a fun tickling fashion. As the child squirms from the tickling hands, she will experience the feel of movement of her body on the ground surface.

Hammock play: In a swaddled position in a blanket, the child can feel the rhythmic movements of being rocked back and forth by an adult at each end of the blanket.

Airplane: With proper support, the child can feel the "whoosh" of air as she is lifted up in the air in safe hands.

Moving or dancing to rhythms or music: With the steady tap of a drum, favorite song, or an activity song, the child is given free rein to move to the beat or follow a specified routine of body movements such as raising hands in the air, clapping, stamping feet, spinning, etc.

Throwing and chasing balls: The child catches or chases a rolled or thrown ball. As the child becomes more proficient, the distance can be increased. Balls with bells can be used for children who are blind or have a severe visual impairment.

Obstacle course: Navigating through tunnels, over gym mats, up and down stairs, and the like will build balance, physical strength, and motor planning skills.

Physical play can involve learning how to sequence one action or body movement after another, such as how to get on and off a rocking horse, go up and down a slide, or follow a sounding ball and throw it back to a friend.

(continued on next page)

SIDEBAR 10.1 *continued*

The game Simon Says is a great way for children to practice listening and following specific and varied directions, such as: walk slow; walk fast; turn in a circle; put your hand on the floor; put your hand in the air, and so on. The preschool child is often especially interested in rough-and-tumble play where children run and chase one another or engage repeatedly and happily at self-initiated action. Later, children will rock back and forth on their hands and knees to feel the movement of their bodies in this new weight-bearing position.

Very young children will enjoy bouncing on an adult's knee, being tickled, or being swung in a blanket. Parts of the child's body can be specifically targeted in games of "I'm going to get your [insert the name of a body part]," as the adult names the body part to be touched and watches for the child's reaction when the right or the wrong body part is tickled.

SOURCE: Reprinted from T. Anthony (2013). "Early Childhood Development: Movement and Play in Early Childhood," in L. J. Lieberman, P. E. Ponchillia, & S. V. Ponchillia, *Physical Education and Sports for People with Visual Impairments and Deafblindness: Foundations of Instruction* (New York: AFB Press), p. 179.

students increase motor coordination and endurance while having fun.

It is also important for teachers to facilitate the development of fine motor skills through engagement in activities that require children to use the small muscles of their hands. Even when eye-hand coordination is challenging or not possible because of limited vision, children need to learn to use their hands as efficient tools. The kinds of play activities in which young children are often asked to engage are designed specifically for the purposes of improving finger isolation, finger and hand strength, and coordination of the hands. So, for example, young children can be asked to stack blocks, manipulate puppets, handle writing implements, operate clothing fasteners as they play dress-up, use scissors, paste artwork, string beads, finger paint, and work with clay during play times. Older children can manipulate game pieces, pick up bowling balls, strum ukuleles, make jewelry, and so forth to continue to refine these hand skills.

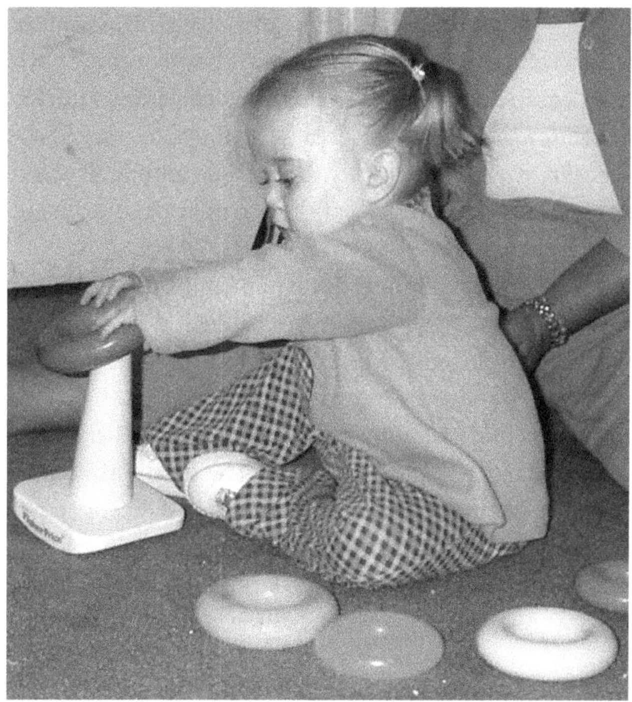

L. Penny Rosenblum

Play activities for young children, such as stacking rings, serve to develop their fine motor skills and improve strength and coordination of the fingers and hands.

Teachers of students with visual impairments need to be aware of the importance of developing strength, dexterity, coordination, and fine and gross movements of young children and encourage the practice and refinement of these skills through physical education, art, and music classes, in O&M training, during manipulation of materials in the classroom, and through activities at home and in the community. Teachers need to allow students to reach for and lift materials and equipment used in the classroom and encourage parents to allow their child to lift, carry, and adjust household items during daily activities in the home. Physical involvement in ordinary, everyday activities can help develop strength, dexterity, and coordination, as can deliberate conditioning exercises. Too often, adults and classmates assume that they are helping the child by doing things for the child with a visual impairment. It is important that visually impaired children learn from an early age that they can and should actively participate in day-to-day routines that involve physical strength, dexterity, and coordination.

At all times the teacher of students with visual impairments should be alert to safety issues, help children understand the importance of safe practices, and remind them of strategies that will keep them safe. For example, when cutting paper with scissors, the teacher can demonstrate (perhaps using hand-over-hand or hand-under-hand techniques) the movement of the scissors so that the hand holding the paper is not in the path of cutting. This type of demonstration should include conversation about safety with scissors and how to avoid getting cut. As the teacher works with students on how to be safe when participating in recreation and leisure activities, she can remind other adults that teaching students to be alert and utilize safe behaviors allows students to feel comfortable doing an activity and less likely to be fearful and anxious about participating in activities that are intended to be fun and interesting for them. Teachers can also address safety issues with parents or caregivers and explain how children can be allowed to explore in a safe environment. For example, parents can create a safe area to ride a push scooter in the driveway with tactile boundaries and describe the importance of the boundaries in terms of safety.

While physical motor development is typically associated with younger children, middle and high school students may also need specific time set aside for instruction and practice in improving motor skills. Coaches can assist in developing physical activity routines specific to particular students and provide the time and space for them to practice skills. Music, dance, and art teachers and therapists can also offer activities that facilitate increased control of large and small muscle groups. As students grow and refine strength, dexterity, and coordination, they can develop skills that are likely to lead to a lifetime of healthy habits that are centered on the enjoyment of physical activity.

Health, Fitness, and Individual Sports

Generally, any physical activity that a student chooses to do individually for fun or health maintenance falls in the health, fitness, and individual sports component of the recreation and leisure area. While these activities can be enjoyed with others, they usually do not require many adaptations for people with visual impairments, and in fact, it is possible for many individuals who are blind or who have low vision to participate in them without additional assistance. Among the types of activities that fall within the health, fitness, and individual sports component are:

- swimming
- boating
- skiing
- skating and roller blading
- running, walking, and hiking
- weight lifting
- exercising
- aerobics
- using jump ropes, hula hoops, and pogo sticks
- biking
- canoeing and kayaking
- track and field events
- wrestling
- dancing
- martial arts (judo, tae kwan do, karate)

Participating in these activities requires skills from other components of the recreation and leisure area, such as play and physical activity. For example, fine and gross motor skills, strength, and dexterity are needed to accomplish most health and fitness routines.

The inclusion of students with visual impairments in health and fitness routines and individual sports is most easily accomplished if particular modifications are implemented as needed. Some modifications that might be appropriate for students when learning to engage in these activities include the following (Lieberman, 2002; Lieberman et al., 2013):

- working with a sighted partner, with or without a tether, for skating, skiing, swimming, track, and canoeing
- using a tandem bicycle
- using equipment with audible capability, such as a jump rope with bells on it or beeping targets
- modifying boundaries for swimming, track, wrestling events or martial arts
    - tactile: guide wire system, rope taped to the floor, large cones
    - auditory: using a human caller or audible device
    - visual: using contrasting or bright tape, cones, or ribbons

Some activities, such as running on a treadmill, using a stationary bicycle or a bicycle stand, floating in a pool, treading water, jumping rope, or doing yoga, require no modification. While these activities may not need to be modified, it is likely that students will require instruction

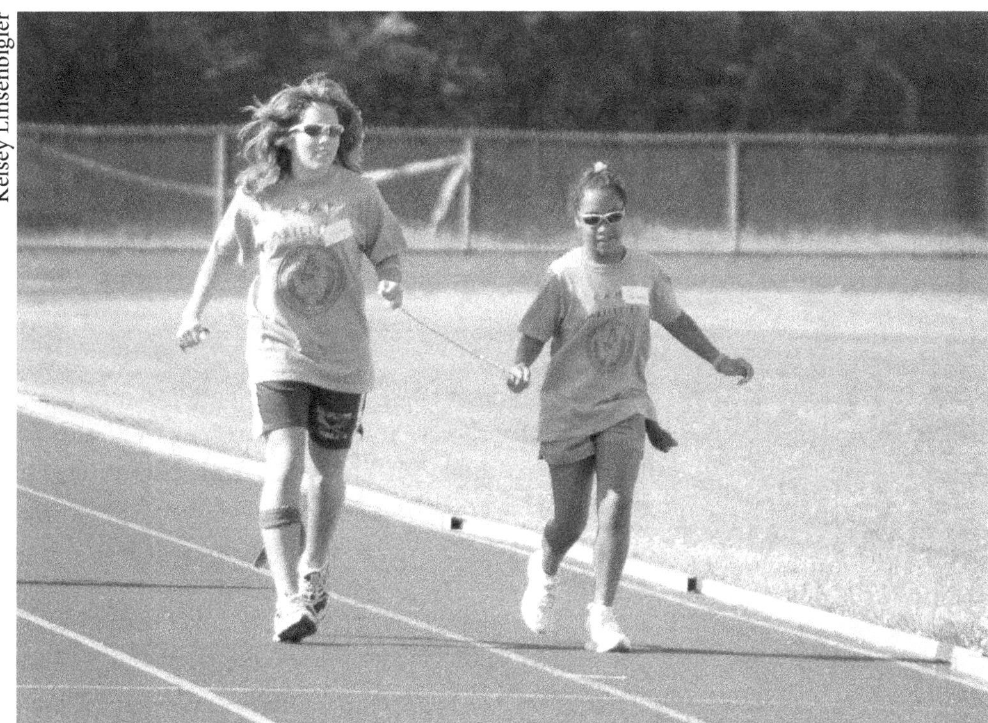
Kelsey Linsenbigler

Students with visual impairments can often participate in individual sports and physical fitness activities with only simple modifications, such as running with a guide using a tether.

and practice with adult supervision for safety purposes, at least initially.

Instruction in an activity may need to be modified by breaking down the steps of the activity for students to understand and practice first. For example, using a stationary bike or a bike in a special stand, the activity of bicycle riding can be divided into several small steps, such as:

- rotation of the pedals
- operation of the brakes
- changing of the gears
- forward movement of the bicycle

When engaged in bicycling students will incorporate other ECC skills, like directionality and safety (O&M) and communicating with a partner on a tandem bicycle (social interaction). (See the sections on general considerations and teaching strategies later in this chapter for additional discussion of adaptations and teaching methods.)

Fitness activities such as aerobic exercises, weight lifting, and general stretching and strengthening conditioning exercises require little adaptation, but may entail modifications in teaching the activities (as described later in this chapter). For older students, the controls of exercise machines can be modified to make them more accessible and easier to use (Burton & Huffman, 2007). Participating in electronic exercise games can be a fun and motivating way to encourage students to get exercise. For example, active sports and game formats for the Wii home video game console (in which players imitate the movements of activities such as tennis or bowling) and Dance Dance Revolution (a video game in which players stand on a marked-up mat or stage and step on colored arrows laid out in a cross, following musical and visual cues from a music video) have been studied and adapted for individuals with visual impairments (Morelli, Folmer, Foley & Lieberman, 2011; Gasperetti, Milford, Blanchard, Yang, Lieberman, & Foley, 2010; see also www.vifit.org).

Students with multiple disabilities also need to participate in health and fitness activities and learn the necessary skills. Like other students, in addition to enjoying the activities themselves, students with visual impairments will derive important health benefits and experience increased social interaction as consequences of their participation. Modifications to the way these activities are taught and performed and to the equipment that is used may be necessary for students with multiple disabilities, such as using a side-by-side bike or a tricycle with Velcro on the pedals. Partial participation may be an appropriate goal for some students.

As with most recreation and leisure activities, repeated practice in health, fitness, and individual sports activities is necessary for mastery. It is a good idea to

L. Penny Rosenblum

Partial participation, along with modifications such as this batting tee, allows students with multiple disabilities to enjoy and benefit from health and fitness activities.

have "experts" and people with visual impairments who participate in the areas of the student's interest available for instruction and practice in activities.

Preference for, and whether to participate in, specific health and fitness activities and individual sports is up to the individual student. The teacher of students with visual impairments needs to approach this component of the recreation and leisure area with the understanding that students' physical capabilities, interests, and preferences will influence their individual choices, as will the availability of facilities and experts in the health and fitness areas each student is interested in. Often a discussion of the various options in health and fitness will help students determine if they are interested in trying a proposed activity. For many students, it will be necessary to demonstrate the skills and behaviors involved in an activity and have the student try it over a period of time in order to make an informed decision. Prioritizing the areas that are of interest to the student will facilitate learning and save the teacher valuable instruction time. Learning each of the activities listed takes considerable time; choosing the activities that are most likely to interest the student is a wise instructional strategy (Lieberman, Modell, & Jackson, 2006).

Team and Spectator Sports

Team and spectator sports involve the playing and observing of various sporting activities, including:

- basketball
- football
- baseball
- softball
- tennis
- goalball
- soccer
- bowling

Children often begin to develop an interest in team and spectator sports in the early years as games such as kick ball or soccer are introduced and played during physical education classes. Interest in other sports develops through exposure to local sporting events when local high school, college, or professional teams are reported on the news, shown on television, or talked about in the community and at home. The young child's interest in these areas will be enhanced if the teacher of students with visual impairments takes time to talk about the sports and uses the interests of the school and community as a basis for determining which sports to highlight. The interests of parents and other family members influence children's awareness of certain team and spectator sports; family members can be important partners in talking about the team and spectator sports they enjoy and in practicing the skills involved with the student. For example, learning to throw and catch a ball, exploring equipment, and participating with the school or family when engaged in an activity are ways to facilitate a student's interest and knowledge in an activity. If the family goes bowling, for instance, they can make sure that their child participates at whatever level he or she is able.

Students can learn about team and spectator sports through after-school and recreation department programs, although consultation with instructors may be necessary for students to gain full benefit. Using the summer for special sports activities or accessing a residential school or specialized sports camp for students with visual impairments can enhance students' recreation and leisure skills and offer them the opportunity to learn basic skills they may have missed, as well as develop increased confidence. Students who attend a residential school for the blind or summer sports camps may become more active in sports played at that school or in the community and develop a particular interest in sports such as goalball (a fast-paced goal sport played with a ball containing bells that was developed specifically to be played by people with blindness) or wrestling.

Adapting Team Sports

The types of adaptations and modifications that may be needed for team sports include the following:

- use of audible balls, goals, or boundaries
- tactile or visual modifications to balls, goals, or boundaries
- use of buddies as sighted guides for running or to give verbal guidance about the location of a ball, for example
- revision to the rules of the game while learning is taking place; for example, allowing two bounces of the ball instead of one in tennis or three chances for a strike in bowling instead of two

Sidebar 10.3 provides additional information about adapting sports for students with visual impairments; sources for modified games and equipment can be found in the Resources section at the end of this chapter. Lieberman et al. (2013) provide detailed information about modifying specific sports to include students with visual impairments.

As with health, fitness, and individual sports activities, it is important for teachers to be selective in the sports that are taught, keeping in mind students' interests and abilities and the availability of the sport in the school and community. There are many choices, as the list at the beginning of this section indicates, although inclusion on this list does not mean that each and every sport must be taught to every student.

Developing Confidence and Competence

Developing a sense of their own competence enables children with visual impairments to feel comfortable when participating in physical activities. One strategy to help students develop a belief in their own competence in sports is the use of role models (Aillaud & Lieberman, 2013). Teachers can talk about people with visual impairments who have been successful in sports, such as James Mastro (wrestling, track and field, goalball, judo), Erik Weihenmeyer and Bill Irwin (mountain climbing), Marla Runyan and Tim Willis (distance running), and Trischa Zorn (swimming) (Shapiro et al., 2003). Students can research such individuals and even write reports about them (practicing compensatory access skills). They can also be encouraged to follow athletes in the Paralympic Games who are blind or visually impaired. The teacher may also invite any local sportspeople with visual impairments to the classroom. The United States Association for Blind Athletes (USABA), an organization that promotes participation in sports for individuals with visual impairments, can be a source of information for locating athletes with visual impairments living in

SIDEBAR 10.3

Adapting Physical Activities and Sports for Students with Visual Impairments

With appropriate instruction and adaptation, students who are visually impaired can participate in virtually any physical activity, game, or sport. The AccesSports model, developed by Paul Ponchillia (1995; Lieberman, Ponchillia, & Ponchillia, 2013) is a method of analyzing activities to determine what adaptations might best accommodate a student's needs. The basic principles of this model are:

1. The instructor considers the abilities and current skills of the student, any disabilities in addition to visual impairment, and the effects of the activity's environment (such as glare or noise) on the student.
2. Based on these factors, the instructor then examines three main aspects of the activity to see which are likely to serve as a barrier to the student's participation: targets and goals (including equipment), boundaries, and rules of activity.
3. Adaptations are then selected to address the barriers that have been identified. Adaptations can involve auditory or tactile adaptations, assistance from sighted guides, or modifications to rules of play.
4. The adaptations are put into practice, evaluated, and modified as needed.

Generally, it is best to use the fewest adaptations necessary to enable the student who is visually impaired to participate. These principles can also be used to analyze recreational activities such as skiing or snowshoeing,

The following chart gives examples of potential barriers to participation in physical activities and how they can be addressed.

(continued on next page)

SIDEBAR 10.3 *continued*

Aspect of Activity	***Examples of Barriers to Participation***	***Methods of Adapting***	***Examples of Adaptations***
Targets and goals (including equipment)	Perceiving the location of the basketball net, soccer goal net, baseball/softball bases, volleyball net, archery target. Perceiving the location of the balls in any sport.	Increase visibility of target or goal by making it larger or by increasing contrast. Use auditory or tactile cues.	A sound beacon for the basket in basketball Bells in a volleyball or soccer ball
Boundaries—the sides of a playing field or court	Perceiving boundaries that delineate the outline of a playing area, such as a tennis court, or that mark off particular zones or locations within a game such as the free-throw line in basketball. In swimming, the swimmer may have trouble staying in the lane and knowing when the wall is coming up.	Increase visibility of boundaries. Add auditory or tactile cues.	Identify boundaries with tactile indicators, such as rope covered with gym tape Identify boundaries with audible indicators, using a sound beacon
Rules of activity		Provide special assistance to the student with a visual impairment or deafblindness, such as verbal description of the play. Simplify the activity or decrease the complexity of the playing environment by decreasing the number of players, decreasing the difficulty of locating the goal or target, increasing the ease of scoring, or decreasing the possibility of injury.	Allow a sighted guide for running a race Allow a bounce before returning the ball in volleyball

Source: Based on L. J. Lieberman, P. E. Ponchillia, and S. V. Ponchillia, *Physical Education and Sports for People with Visual Impairments and Deafblindness: Foundations of Instruction* (New York: AFB Press, 2013).

specific regions of the country (see the Resources section at the end of this chapter).

Another strategy for helping students achieve physical competence and confidence in their skills uses assessments of motor behavior (Shapiro et al., 2003). Determining competence in specific skills needed in a particular sport gives students reinforcement for what they do well and helps them focus on areas that need improvement. As students develop specific skills needed for sports activities, they become more confident and motivated to participate in the activities.

The section on assessment later in this chapter discusses some tools for evaluating physical fitness (see also the Resources section at the end of the chapter). In addition, teachers can develop individual rubrics or a checklist of specific skills that breaks down a specific sport into skills areas and addresses the skills needed by the individual student. The Camp Abilities Activity Assessment (Lieberman et al., 2013) is a checklist that provides a kind of breakdown that could be used by teachers to pinpoint specific skills needed by individual students. This checklist includes areas of track and field, beep baseball, goalball, tandem bike, gymnastics, judo, and orientation and mobility. (Excerpts from this checklist appear in Appendix 10A at the end of this chapter.)

Older students who develop an interest and competence in a particular sport or sports may be motivated to join school or community teams. Although not always necessary, competitions specifically for people who are blind or visually impaired, such as those sponsored by the USABA or the Canadian Blind Sports Association, are attractive to some students. Students can aspire to competition on an international level through the Paralympic Games or the International Blind Sports Federation World Championships (see the Resources section at the end of this chapter for contact information). Information on sports adaptations and rules of competition can be obtained from the websites of these organizations.

Even if students do not have the physical skills or interest necessary to actually play sports, it is important that they have personal experiences with various sports so that interest as a spectator can be developed. (See the learning activity "Whose Ball is This?" at the end of this chapter for an example of an activity to help students develop beginning familiarity with different sports.) Given the general interest in sports in the United States, having a basic knowledge of and direct experience with specific sports (including types of equipment, rules, teams, and famous players) can add to a student's ability to have mutually satisfying conversations with others—an important social and career skill. (See, for example, the vignette in Sidebar 4.1 about a totally blind 14-year-old who was an expert on baseball.) If conversation about team and spectator sports becomes common practice with the teacher of visually impaired students, parents, and other school personnel, the student's interest and understanding of this component of recreation and leisure will be refined. Students who have the opportunity to develop an understanding of and engage in team sports as a participant or a spectator can converse with others appropriately and use their understanding to be active in recreation and leisure activities for a lifetime.

Leisure Activities and Hobbies

The preferences that people develop for participating in leisure activities and hobbies are often guided by observation of peers and family members taking part in such activities or through television, video, or motion pictures. As discussed throughout this book, incidental observation is often difficult for students with visual impairments. For that reason, it is imperative that teachers devote specific time to investigating various leisure activities and hobbies with their students so that informed choices can be made about how to spend this time. Common leisure activities and hobbies include:

- gardening
- arts and crafts
- knitting/crocheting/needlepoint
- reading
- cooking
- acting and enjoying theater productions
- visiting museums
- music (listening to music and playing instruments)
- singing alone or in a group
- telling jokes
- playing board games
- collecting (stamps, sport cards, coins)
- taking photographs
- playing computer and video games
- attending movies and theater performances (with audio description, as needed)

Groundwork for the establishment of leisure activities and hobbies can be laid when young children develop an interest in reading, arts and crafts, music, and collecting. These early years are the time to explore some of the games that children play, such as dominoes, Lotto, and simple card games. Games played by other children at school or in the child's neighborhood are a good place to focus instruction at first. Young children begin to explore leisure activities and hobbies as they practice scribbling, coloring, cutting, finger painting, using modeling clay, growing plants from seeds, putting puzzles together, reading jingles, making ceramics, using various art media to construct projects, playing simple board games, telling knock-knock jokes, playing games on the computer, collecting items of interest (shells, stuffed animals, books), putting on plays or music demonstrations, singing, and showing an interest in music. Some games are available in commercial versions with tactile or large-print modifications or braille overlays, including Monopoly, Scrabble, checkers, chess, and cribbage, and teachers can create their own adaptations in many cases. (The Resources section at the end of this chapter includes sources for adapted games and computer software for students with visual impairments.)

As students take part in such activities using appropriate accommodations provided by teachers, they will begin to devise their own methods of participating. Engaging in activities that are enjoyable and that others consider sources of leisure will encourage students to develop opinions about leisure activities and hobbies, thus laying the groundwork for making their own choices, a key component of another ECC skill, self-determination.

Students in middle childhood typically enjoy a wide variety of leisure activities and hobbies. This period is the critical time for them to make decisions about what is fun and interesting to do so that activities and hobbies can be refined for lifelong participation. Focusing on board games and computer games is often convenient, because they are most readily available at school, can be easily modified, and frequently reinforce development of academic skills, but as part of preparing students for a lifetime of recreation and leisure activities, options need to be much broader. Helping students understand what is available to them is one important role that the teacher plays. Incorporating conversations and activities that include information about gardening, needlework, reading, cooking, and starting collections of interest will allow students to become aware of the wide variety of hobbies that one can have. Teachers can use school time already allotted for instruction in music, drama, art, and crafts to expand students' interests and understanding in these areas, although scheduling constraints may present challenges. Teachers should not forget to teach students how to tell jokes, listen to jokes told by others, and react appropriately by telling a joke of their own or by simply laughing and saying that they can never remember good jokes.

Whereas students with unimpaired vision typically are influenced to try new activities by their families and peers, family members may be reluctant to include a child with visual impairment in preferred leisure pursuits for many reasons, including fear of injury, reluctance to put the child in a situation where initial failure seems likely, and not knowing how to make the appropriate accommodations. As a result, the evolution of knowledge, skills, and competence in recreation and leisure that is common among students with unimpaired vision does not occur as easily for students who are blind or who have low vision.

The families of many youngsters may need encouragement to include their child in their typical leisure time pursuits or to develop new interests in which their child can participate more easily. (See the section titled Suggestions for Working with Parents later in this chapter.) They may need assistance to learn how they can increase the child's understanding of the activity and facilitate his or her meaningful participation. To accomplish these objectives and expand the knowledge base of students, teachers will likely need to develop specific lessons focused on the skills and behaviors in this ECC area.

ASSESSMENT OF RECREATION AND LEISURE

Assessment in the recreation and leisure area of the ECC follows the general strategies discussed in Chapter 3, including determining which skills the child has mastered, which skills need practice to maintain mastery, and which additional skills the student needs to learn. If particular skills are not assessed through a formal instrument, the teacher can use questioning and observation strategies to identify a student's interest, knowledge, and skill level in the various components of the recreation and leisure area. In addition to these general strategies, the impacts of the following considerations on a student's ability to participate in recreation and leisure activities need to be considered:

- recreation and leisure activities available at school and in the community
- favorite activities of the student and his or her family
- availability of knowledgeable individuals to assist with instruction in specific areas
- preferences for certain types of activities, such as outside or inside, individual or group, competitive or noncompetitive, or strenuous or nonstrenuous

Recreation and leisure activities lend themselves to assessment by observation. It will often be clear to a teacher what skills a student has by observing a child participating in or attempting various activities. Since the behaviors and skills taught in this ECC area are so individual, depending on each student's ability and interest and the availability of different activities, it is important for teachers to get a general sense of how these variables relate to each student. It may be necessary to investigate the availability of facilities and experts in a particular component to assist with this assessment. A simple assessment form for recreation and leisure activities that is used at the California School for the Blind appears in Figure 10.1.

Some formal tools for recording and further assessing the recreation and leisure area of the ECC are listed in the Resources section at the end of this chapter, including the Camp Abilities Activity Checklist discussed earlier and excerpted in Appendix 10A. The resources listing is by no means a complete catalog of evaluative instruments that may be considered for the recreation

FIGURE 10.1

Sample Recreation and Leisure Checklist

RECREATION AND LEISURE

Rating Scale:
1 not achieved
2 emerging with prompts
3 partially achieved (50 percent without prompts)
4 achieved (performs skill independently)

Recreation and Leisure	***Fall 2014***	***Spring 2015***	***Fall 2015***	***Spring 2016***	***Fall 2016***	***Spring 2017***
Demonstrates solitary play						
Demonstrates interactive/pretend play						
Plays card games						
Plays board games						
Plays computer games						
Walks for fun						
Runs for fun						
Understands turn taking						
Uses a treadmill						
Uses an exercycle						
Uses weights						
Can swim						
Can bowl						
Can roller skate						
Can ice skate						
Can hike						
Uses play equipment in an age-appropriate manner						
Rides a bike independently						
Rides a tandem bike as a passenger						
Plays kickball						
Plays goalball						
Plays beep baseball						

SOURCE: Adapted with permission from Expanded Core Curriculum Minimum Standards (Fresno: California School for the Blind, n.d.).

and leisure area, but it provides a sense of the wide range of specific skills and assessment options available.

It is important that teachers make use of the expertise of other school personnel, such as physical education teachers, coaches, O&M specialists, physical therapists, art, music, and dance teachers, preschool teachers, and librarians, as well as individuals in the community, such as coaches, artisans, and musicians who can help to identify skills needed for various activities. Local community or recreation centers are good resources for individuals involved in various recreation and leisure activities.

GENERAL CONSIDERATIONS WHEN TEACHING RECREATION AND LEISURE

As noted throughout this chapter, students with visual impairments need deliberate and repeated exposure to a variety of recreation and leisure activities in order to develop skills and individual interests within this area of the ECC. When considering instruction in recreation and leisure, the overall goal of the teacher of students with visual impairments is providing an environment where children can:

- experience a range of recreation and leisure activities
- practice and succeed in activities of interest to them
- choose and practice an activity
- use recreation and leisure time appropriately
- make use of constructive feedback to refine their skills

For students to have a solid knowledge base of specific recreation and leisure activities, teachers of students with visual impairments will need to ensure that certain general information about each activity is included in their instruction, including:

- purpose and outcome or objective of the activity
- specific skills needed to do the activity
- rules for scoring or means of measuring success
- time requirements to complete
- expectations of sportsmanship
- rules of the game
- location where the activity typically takes place
- supplies, materials, or equipment used and purpose of each
- impact of weather
- physical fitness requirements (upper body strength, abdominal strength, body mass index, cardiovascular endurance, flexibility, coordination, dexterity)
- modifications that can be made to the activity
- expert guidance, as needed

Accommodations and modifications are often necessary for students with visual impairments to participate in targeted recreation and leisure activities, as described in the earlier sections of this chapter. Teachers should use the principles of adaptation of materials that are utilized for other instructional areas when adapting recreation and leisure materials, focusing on identifying the least restrictive adaptation that facilitates learning and participation (discussed in Chapters 4 and 8). In general, a greater number of modifications may be necessary for students with visual impairments who are first learning an activity or for students who have additional disabilities. These adaptations should be faded as the student becomes more competent in the activity to facilitate greater inclusion, as appropriate.

Although it is sometimes necessary to adapt materials, it is more common to have to modify the instruction that is provided to students with visual impairments, as described in the next section, Teaching Strategies for Recreation and Leisure. Students who are blind or who have low vision often require targeted instruction to ensure that they understand details about an activity that are usually available visually or that are most easily taught through demonstration ("hold your cards like this"; "watch as I use my finger to poke a hole in the ground where we'll put the seed") and are often not described verbally by an instructor. Instruction for students with visual impairments will likely involve careful examination of materials before teaching the actual activity, as well as exploration of how those materials change during the activity ("Let's go see what happened to the bowling pins—I didn't hear any fall, but let's check it out."). These modifications to instruction generally necessitate that more time be allotted for the development of fluency.

Discovering and sampling different activities with other people who enjoy and understand the activities can be fun for students. The ideas provided in this chapter and in the Learning Activities section at the end are intended to be suggestions for teachers of students with visual impairments to use, and to modify, expand, or adjust as needed to make them meaningful and fun for their students.

TEACHING STRATEGIES FOR RECREATION AND LEISURE

Teachers of students with visual impairments will need to use a variety of methods for teaching skills in the recreation and leisure area of the ECC. The following sections summarize several of the most useful strategies. (For more comprehensive resources for teaching recreation and leisure skills, see Lieberman et al., 2006; and Lieberman et al., 2013.) Note that any of these teaching methods requires substantial practice and ongoing feedback for students to be able to appreciate and choose the recreation and leisure areas that are most interesting to them.

Whole-Part-Whole Instruction

Whole-part-whole instruction involves familiarizing a student with the entirety of an activity before teaching the parts that comprise it. Then the activity is learned through practice of each part, until the entire activity is mastered. When working on an arts and crafts activity, for example, it might be helpful to have a copy of the finished product for students to examine before beginning and while completing the project. This approach is particularly effective when teaching sports and fitness activities and games (Lieberman et al., 2009). As students become adept at the parts of the game, they can play practice games and then competitive games, helping them put the individual skills together.

Task Analysis

Task analysis is similar to whole-part-whole instruction in that parts or steps of the activity are identified and taught individually until the entire task is mastered. (See Chapters 3 and 8 for more detailed discussion of task analysis.) Breaking down a recreation or leisure activity into steps can facilitate a student's thorough understanding of the activity. For example, learning the game of goalball involves mastering throwing the ball, catching the ball, positioning the body to block a ball, sound identification, body positioning, and communication with teammates. In turn, each of these skills can be broken down into their individual steps in order to teach them. Once these skills are mastered individually, the student can be more successful in participating in and practicing the sport of goalball.

Demonstration and Modeling

Demonstration and modeling is perhaps the least intrusive method of teaching activities. Students with enough vision to be able to copy movements and skills can benefit from demonstration and modeling. For example, learning to jump rope may best be taught through demonstration, with opportunities for the student to practice what is being shown. Demonstration or modeling teamed with practice is a useful strategy for learning many activities. Use of monoculars for distance viewing and other optical devices may be beneficial during these sessions, providing an opportunity to practice a sensory efficiency skill.

Tactile Modeling

Tactile modeling is useful when the skill can be demonstrated by having the student feel the instructor or a classmate performing the desired motion or activity. Similar to hand-under-hand instruction (see Chapter 5), this strategy requires more active body and limb contact. Verbal explanation is helpful when using tactile modeling (O'Connell, Lieberman, & Petersen, 2006). Tactile modeling is especially useful for small motor activities, such as folding, cutting, moving game pieces, and exploring and holding game and sports apparatus.

Physical Guidance

Physical guidance is most useful when a skill cannot easily be demonstrated visually or through tactile modeling. With this method, the instructor physically moves the student through the necessary motions for a skill, such as moving a student's arm in the motion used to throw a ball or to make a lanyard. It is important to ask students' permission before touching or manipulating parts of their bodies. Again, physical guidance should be paired with verbal explanation. Having the student practice a skill with physical guidance and then fading guidance is helpful for students who need assistance to perfect skills needed for particular activities.

Peer Tutoring

Peer tutoring involves the use of a trained classmate to assist a student with particular skills. For example, a peer can demonstrate skills for a student, provide feedback and guidance on skills, describe environmental cues, facilitate socialization, and ensure the use of adaptations and modifications identified by the teacher of students with visual impairments. It is important for the peer to be trained and supervised by the teacher and other professionals so that the peer understands what he or she is expected to do and how to work with a student who is visually impaired (Wiskochil, Lieberman, Houston-Wilson, & Peterson, 2007).

Peer tutoring should only be used when the student with a visual impairment is willing to have a peer tutor and is comfortable with feedback and guidance from a classmate. The teacher should first demonstrate alone with the student strategies such as methods of demonstrating skills, providing feedback and guidance, and describing the environment; then practice them with the peer present; then allow the peer tutoring to occur with the teacher observing; and finally permit the peer tutoring to occur without the teacher's presence. It will be important for the teacher to get feedback from both the student with a visual impairment and the peer about the progression of the student's skills using this method.

Mentor Guidance

Mentor guidance refers to obtaining assistance from an individual with a visual impairment who is successful in a particular activity. It is a good strategy to use when students need to understand and recognize that other people with similar disabilities can and do enjoy recreation and leisure activities. Working with a mentor with similar visual functioning provides the student with the opportunity to ask questions, seek guidance, and observe demonstration of skills with someone who has been through a similar learning process.

Guided Discovery

Guided discovery encourages students, especially those with low vision, to discover movements that will accomplish a given task. For example, if students with low vision are asked to "kick the ball as far as you can" or "throw the ball," they will often demonstrate the correct motion and, with minimal feedback, discover from their own experiences the movements that are most effective and practice them to improve their skill (Shapiro et al., 2003). This type of guidance allows students to learn at their own pace with only occasional direction, which can increase their engagement in the activity and their sense of competence (Shapiro et al., 2003). While probably not appropriate for use in a large class, it may be an effective strategy for teaching some skills one-on-one or in small groups.

Pre-Teaching

Pre-teaching refers to giving a student instruction in skills and concepts that will be taught in physical education, art, music, or other classes and familiarizing the student with any equipment involved to help the student understand the activity before it is presented to an entire class. Because instruction often requires more time for students with visual impairments (if they need additional modeling of an activity or to explore equipment, for instance), pre-teaching provides students with enough preparation to be able to participate in the activity along with classmates.

The teacher of students with visual impairments will want to share these methods with other educators teaching similar skills. For example, physical education teachers may not be aware of the special techniques that may need to be employed with students who have not had the opportunity to carefully observe others doing physical activities or have only rarely actively participated in such activities with peers. Even in home economics, art, and music classes, the general educator may be unaware of strategies that will ensure that students with visual impairments can grasp the purpose of or benefit from demonstrations. The teacher of students with visual impairments will likely need to share information with these other school personnel about the specific accommodations and modifications that may be appropriate so that students can learn skills that are the current focus of instruction. Likewise, with adequate communication, the teacher of students with visual impairments can reinforce skills being taught by other members of a student's educational team. The teacher of students with visual impairments can also use a student's time in physical education, art, home economics, and music class to work closely with the student to discover a variety of recreation and leisure activities that are first introduced as "schoolwork" in these courses. The techniques just described can be used in those classes by the teacher of students with visual impairments or in other settings where one-on-one or small groups of students are receiving instruction.

THE ROLE OF THE TEACHER OF STUDENTS WITH VISUAL IMPAIRMENTS

As already noted, which recreation and leisure activities should be the focus of instruction for a student is often dependent on local availability, individual preferences of the family and the student, the student's physical abilities, and availability of experts and coaches. Some general tips for selecting activities include:

- asking parents which recreation and leisure activities they participate in and value
- identifying the activities in which the student's friends and classmates are engaged

- determining the availability of the activity of interest in the community
- determining the availability of experts or coaches to teach or demonstrate the areas of interest

Although it is also important to solicit the opinions of students, it is important to remember that students may have limited information on which to base their opinions. Wise teachers will choose to first introduce activities that they believe match students' current abilities and preferences, then gradually broaden their instruction to include novel activities that challenge students' comfort levels.

When selecting recreation and leisure activities, consideration should be given to students' perspectives and their ability to engage in the activity at the same level of independence as peers. Some art activities, such as painting or drawing, may not be of interest to students who are totally blind, since their ability to appreciate their own work is limited. However, other students who are blind may enjoy the feeling of the brush or pencil on paper and be unconcerned with being able to examine their finished product. Some students will find great pleasure at attending movies, sports events, and theater productions with friends and family, while others may find that these events result in boredom.

Teachers will want to be sure the student has experienced a particular recreation and leisure activity in a safe and comprehensive way before the student is encouraged to decide if it is one he or she would like to discontinue. If an activity is not presented in an accessible way, the student may believe he doesn't like it. For example, a student thrown into a soccer game with no modifications and no explanation of what is happening may be hit by the ball a few times, which may result in the student believing that she is not skilled and will not enjoy soccer. Before actually playing in a soccer game, a student with a visual impairment must be taught the format, rules, and general intent of the game using a brightly colored ball of good contrast or a beeping soccer ball. Playing on a small field with fewer players and using a companion player would give the student a sense of the game, allow for some level of participation, and provide more information on which to base a decision to continue to engage in the activity or not.

Once an activity has been introduced appropriately and students have had a chance to learn about it, it is never a good idea to force the activity on students who have no interest in it. Having a frank discussion with students about what they find exciting, relaxing, and fun to do is important, as is honoring those preferences. Even if a student doesn't like an activity that has been appropriately presented, it may be worthwhile to present it again when she is older and has developed other skills and interests.

Teachers of students with visual impairments need to rely on a variety of people to assist with the introduction and teaching of recreation and leisure activities. Coaches; sports enthusiasts; physical education, art, home economics, and music teachers; physical therapists; role models who are visually impaired; and other young people with hobbies of interest to the student are just a few of the people who can be recruited to assist with instruction in recreation and leisure activities. In these situations, often the primary role of teachers of students with visual impairments is to focus on making adaptations and modifications that are important and necessary for the student to be successful, as well as to communicate appropriate teaching methods to other personnel, as already noted.

There are recreation and leisure skills that can be taught directly by the teacher of students with visual impairments. For example, while it is unlikely (and probably inappropriate) that the teacher instruct a student in how to play the clarinet, it is appropriate for the teacher to take the student to the band room and explore differences between the clarinet and other musical instruments. Introducing and teaching students to use less complicated instruments, such as recorders, marimbas, bongo drums, and harmonicas, can be done in short instructional segments that may result in the development of a lifelong leisure pursuit. Similarly, instructional units that focus on stamp and coin collecting (great activities for developing visual efficiency skills and reinforcing math or geography skills) can introduce students to activities enjoyed by many adults.

Other general categories of activities in which teachers can provide instruction include board and card games, simple exercises (such as stretches, sit-ups, and squat thrusts), use of hand weights, arts and crafts, joke telling, computer or video games, needlework, and appreciation of spectator sports. Of course, teachers of students with visual impairments who are unfamiliar with specific techniques related to the activities they are teaching will need to consult with others for guidance.

Students also benefit when teachers include instruction in some of the prerequisite knowledge and skills that are required for success in other classes, such as art and physical education, that other students may be absorbing through vision-based incidental learning. The teacher of students with visual impairments might choose to spend some instructional time exploring the differences between roller skates and roller blades before a physical education skating unit. This instructional exploring, or pre-teaching (discussed earlier in this chapter and in Chapter 4), should take place before any unit that is new to the student so the student has a clear understanding of the equipment, concepts, rules, and strategies that will be taught (Lieberman et al., 2013). Instructional time with the teacher might be spent teaching the student to put on different skates, helmets, wrist guards, and elbow and knee pads. Encouraging the student to practice skating while wearing just one skate in a quiet hallway might result in increased confidence for skating with a larger, noisier group and, eventually, on two skates.

The teacher of students with visual impairments can enhance students' appreciation for recreation and leisure activities by maintaining a positive focus on the activities and helping students understand and share in the enjoyment that others experience while involved in them. It is important to keep in mind that learning new recreation and leisure skills without the use of vision can be extremely challenging. Especially at first, when basic skills are being learned, students may question the potential for enjoyment in what probably feels like hard work. Teachers of students with visual impairments may need to encourage perseverance, incorporate goal setting, and celebrate small victories until fundamental skills are developed. While the immediate goals are to expose students to opportunities and teach basic skills, ultimately the goal is for recreation and leisure choices to be defined by the individual, with activities selected because the individual finds them intrinsically valuable and enjoyable.

Finding time to address these skills can also be a challenge. Teachers of students with visual impairments can use instruction in recreation and leisure skills as a way to facilitate the practice of skills in other areas of the ECC, in particular social, self-determination, and O&M skills. For example, using a student's interest in board games, the teacher can teach social skills of sharing and turn-taking and the compensatory skill of reading. Choosing and participating in a favorite sport reinforces self-determination, sensory efficiency, and O&M skills. Some teachers plan special activities for groups of students with visual impairments where the students meet once a month at a specified location to participate in a thematic activity—for example, to participate in favorite board games or a special arts and crafts project (K. Mountjoy, personal correspondence, 2003).

Other methods of providing opportunities to participate in recreation and leisure activities may include involving students in a special summer camp session or extended school year program where students who are visually impaired meet together to experience various recreation and leisure activities. Special schools for students with visual impairments typically provide these types of summer experiences as well. As much as possible, it is important to make sure that the selection of activities that are the focus of these camps provides opportunities for students to be engaged as participants, and not just as passive observers of others.

The teacher of students with visual impairments will need to check with family and school personnel to make sure that older students are using free time wisely and are able to entertain themselves in appropriate leisure activities. Opportunities to share games, books, and sports talk are important for students in high school, and the teacher should use other school personnel and the family to help provide these opportunities. Teachers can encourage parents to talk about their own hobbies and the interests of the student, question if the student might want to learn about a particular hobby, or use the summer to focus on a special set of recreation and leisure skills. Likewise, the teacher and other school personnel can involve the student in conversation about recreation and leisure interests.

The teacher of students with visual impairments will recognize that many of the skills taught by O&M specialists are skills that will be important to achieve success in recreation and leisure activities. Working closely with the O&M specialist is often critical in this important ECC area.

The involvement of the teacher of students with visual impairments in teaching of recreation and leisure skills is generally fairly constant throughout the school years, but the focus of instruction changes over time as new skills are introduced. It is important for the teacher to address age-appropriate recreation and leisure skills throughout a student's schooling, keeping in mind that the end goal is an adult who has developed preferences for activities based on previous direct experiences with a variety of recreation and leisure activities.

SUGGESTIONS FOR WORKING WITH PARENTS

For most students with visual impairments, their earliest exposure to recreation and leisure skills will more than likely occur at home. Similarly, the recreation and leisure pursuits of students will be influenced by the ways that their family members spend their free time. To encourage the development of recreation and leisure skills, parents should involve their children in these kinds of activities as early as possible; teachers can provide important guidance with this process.

The family's involvement is key to encouraging the child's participation. Parents who ride and care for horses can involve their young children in this activity by allowing them to sit with them on the horse and to hold equipment when grooming and preparing a horse for riding. Older children can help with grooming, retrieving and storing equipment, feeding, and cleaning up the stables. Families who enjoy boating can have their child help with equipment, learn to buckle life vests, and handle the bumper as the boat leaves or approaches the dock. Families who enjoy camping as a leisure activity can involve children of all ages in various aspects of preparing the equipment, packing and preparing food, setting up sleeping areas, and storing equipment to keep it safe from wildlife.

When first having their children participate in these activities, parents should start with the simplest of actions (holding equipment, handing parents items when requested), and allow the child to watch from as close as necessary or to feel the parent's hands as the parent demonstrates what needs to be done. Parents should allow as much time and repetition as the child needs to understand and practice performing appropriate tasks. Of course, careful attention should be paid to ensure safety and to teach the child to be responsible for safe behaviors in the environments in which recreation and leisure activities occur.

Teachers of students with visual impairments and O&M specialists can remind parents that they are available for assistance with ideas about how to adapt materials and instruction for specific activities in which the families typically engage. Sometimes the best advice is to keep in mind the perspective of the student and the impact that the student's visual impairment has on understanding the activity and its component parts. For example, parents who enjoy model car shows may want to explore ways for their child to get close enough to examine (either visually or tactilely) the distinguishing features (headlights, tail fins, bumpers, emblems) of the automobiles on display. Students who have low vision and who have been prescribed a telescope can use this tool to help identify these features and share the telescope with family members (or family members can use binoculars and share with the student). With young children, it might be best to target just one feature at first, then gradually increase the range of exploration.

Keeping in mind that children with visual impairments often do not have the ability to resolve details at a distance, it is advisable to encourage exploration of the area in which an activity will occur before starting it. Time at the neighborhood basketball court might include walking around the court to get an idea of how big it is, walking from the center court to each basket (maybe counting steps to discover that the distances are equal), walking around the key (it's not really like a house key!), and being held up to explore the height of the basket. Similarly, allowing a child to work her way around the edge of a pool while being held by the parent in the water can give her a better idea of the size of the pool and the location of important features, such as the diving board, the shallow end, and the stairs. While not always possible, the time taken to explore new environments can help the child feel more secure, can increase vocabulary, and encourage independence.

Parents can help their children learn motor skills associated with some sports by making simple changes to the equipment or area of play. Lowering the net for volleyball and the backboard and net for basketball can make it easier for the child to get the ball over or through the net. As appropriate, the adaptation should be faded as the child becomes proficient with the skill.

Parents can also help children learn about the recreation and leisure activities of interest to others in the community and beyond. Discussing the status of national, university, and high school sports teams can provide youngsters with information that they can share in conversations with peers (and in the future, with work colleagues). Parents can describe the kinds of weekend activities that are listed in the local newspaper or community website (such as garden shows or bridge competitions) and respond to their child's questions and comments about those activities. Parents will want to be alert to gaps in the child's knowledge that are expressed in these conversations and, whenever possible, provide opportunities for the child to have related experiences, such as comparing pitcher's and catcher's mitts, examining a stock car, walking the length of a football field, visiting an ice skating facility, examining coin collections in antique stores, or copying tai chi movements. A local sporting goods store (especially one that allows customers to explore unpackaged equipment) can provide the venue for some of these casual hands-on learning opportunities.

Families that have the financial means to enroll their children in commercially available classes can be encouraged to do so. Children with visual impairments often can participate in music, crafts, art, dance, photography, needlework, yoga, and other classes with other students their age, with minimal adaptations. Of course, selection of these classes should be made with care and with the needs of the child in mind. Instructors should believe that successful involvement of a child with visual impairment is possible and welcome the child to the class. Parents can be reminded that teachers of students with visual impairments and O&M specialists frequently are willing to help the instructors of these classes make appropriate modifications to materials and instruction. In general, it is probably best if these classes are relatively small in size, so that the individual needs of the child can be addressed and the child can get the attention needed to learn the skill being presented.

Enrolling students in summer day and overnight camps also provides a way for students to be exposed to and learn important recreation and leisure skills. Camps for individuals with visual impairments, including specialized sports camps, often offer opportunities for children and youths to learn new and challenging skills taught by counselors familiar with visual impairment in environments that have been designed to accommodate the needs of these students, including those with multiple disabilities. However, many students, especially those who have well-developed social and self-determination skills, do well at camps that accept children with and without disabilities. When selecting the best camp for a particular child, parents will want to investigate the level of support provided as students learn new skills, the willingness of counselors to accommodate students with special needs, and the degree to which students are protected (or overprotected) within these environments.

Parents will discover that it becomes second nature to include their child with visual impairment in the activities that they enjoy, first through partial participation, then with higher expectations for involvement. The most difficult step in the process is letting go of any preconceived notions of what children with visual impairments are able to do. Expectation, experimentation, patience, and repetition, along with an appreciation of the activity from the perspective of the child, are most of what is required for parents and other family members to facilitate the evolution of recreation and leisure skills in their child with visual impairment.

SUMMARY

The learning activities provided at the end of this chapter are designed to address the components of play; physical activities; health, fitness, and individual sports; team and spectator sports; and leisure activities and hobbies. Recreation and leisure is a critical area of the ECC that needs to be deliberately introduced to children with visual impairments to allow them to explore the various and multiple options that exist for having fun, high-quality, and interesting leisure time, by themselves and with others. The activities and suggestions provided in this chapter offer a variety of options to consider, but they are by no means the only ones. It is important to remember that many kinds of recreation and leisure activities are seasonal and available only in certain areas, so teachers need to check local media for availability and scheduling.

Teaching students with visual impairments how to participate in recreation and leisure is critical to their long-term healthy development and inclusion in society. In addition, incorporating skills from other areas of the ECC into recreation and leisure can add fun to instruction in those areas.

References

Aillaud, C. L., & Lieberman, L. J. (2013). *Everybody plays: How kids with visual impairments play sports.* Louisville, KY: American Printing House for the Blind.

Anthony, T. (2013). Early childhood development: Movement and play in early childhood. In L. J. Lieberman, P. E. Ponchillia, & S. V. Ponchillia (Eds.), *Physical education and sports for people with visual impairments and deafblindness: Foundations of instruction* (pp. 159–186). New York: AFB Press.

Blessing, D. L, McCrimmon, D., Stovall, J., & Williford, H. N. (1993). The effects of regular exercise programs for visually impaired and sighted schoolchildren. *Journal of Visual Impairment & Blindness, 87,* 50–52.

Burton, D., & Huffman, L. (2007). Exercising your right to fitness: An overview of the accessibility of exercise equipment. *AccessWorld, 8*(5). Retrieved from http://www.afb.org/afbpress/pub.asp?DocID=aw080603

Celeste, M. (2002). A survey of motor development for infants and young children with visual impairments. *Journal of Visual Impairment & Blindness, 96,* 169–174.

Conroy, P. (2012). Supporting students with visual impairments in physical education: Needs of physical educators. *Insight, 5*(1), 3–10.

Edginton, C. R., Jordan, D. J., DeGraaf, D. G., & Edginton, S. R. (2002). *Leisure and life satisfaction: Foundational perspectives* (3rd ed.). Boston: McGraw Hill.

Ferrell, K. A. (2011). *Reach out and teach: Helping your child who is visually impaired learn and grow.* New York: AFB Press.

Gasperetti, B., Milford, M., Blanchard, D., Yang, S., Lieberman, L., & Foley, J. (2010). Dance Dance Revolution and Eyetoy kinetic modifications for youth with visual impairments. *Journal of Physical Education, Recreation, & Dance, 81,* 15–17, 55.

Kroksmark, U., & Nordell, K. (2001). Adolescence: The age of opportunities and obstacles for students with low vision in Sweden. *Journal of Visual Impairment & Blindness, 95*(4), 213–225.

Lieberman, L. (2002). Fitness for individuals who are visually impaired and deafblind, *RE:view, 34*(1), 13–23.

Lieberman, L. J., Byrne, H., Mattern, C., Watt, C., & Fernandez-Vivo, M. (2010). Health-related fitness in youth with visual impairments. *Journal of Visual Impairments & Blindness, 104*(6), 349–359.

Lieberman, L. J., & McHugh, B. E. (2001). Health-related fitness of children with visual impairments and blindness. *Journal of Visual Impairment & Blindness, 95,* 272–286.

Lieberman, L. J., Modell, S., & Jackson, I. (2006). *Going PLACES: A transition guide to physical activity for youth with visual impairments.* Louisville, KY: American Printing House for the Blind.

Lieberman, L. J., Ponchillia, P. E., & Ponchillia, S. V. (2013). *Physical education and sports for people with visual impairments and deafblindness: Foundations of instruction.* New York: AFB Press.

Lieberman, L., Schedlin, H., & Pierce, T. (2009). Teaching jump rope to children with visual impairments. *Journal of Visual Impairment & Blindness, 103*(3), 173–178.

Lieberman, L. J., Stuart, M. E., Hand, K., & Robinson, B. (2006). An investigation of the motivational effects of talking pedometers among youth with visual impairments and deaf-blindness. *Journal of Visual Impairment & Blindness, 100*(12), 726–736.

Morelli, T., Folmer, E., Foley, T., & Lieberman, L. J. (2011). Improving the lives of youth with visual impairments through exergames. *Insight Journal, 4,* 160–170.

O'Connell, M., Lieberman, L., & Petersen, S. (2006). The use of tactile modeling and physical guidance as instructional strategies in physical activity for children who are blind. *Journal of Visual Impairment & Blindness, 100*(8), 471–477.

Physical activity and health: The benefits of physical activity (2011). Atlanta, GA: Centers for Disease Control and Prevention. Retrieved from http:www.cdc.gov/physicalactivity/everyone/health/index.html

Ponchillia, P. (1995). AccesSports: A model for adapting mainstream sports activities for individuals with visual impairments. *RE:view, 27,* 5–14.

Ponchillia, S. V., Powell, L. L., Felski, K. A., & Nicklawski, M. T. (1992). The effectiveness of aerobic exercise instruction for totally blind women. *Journal of Visual Impairment & Blindness, 86,* 174–177.

Shapiro, D. R., Lieberman, L. J., & Moffett, A. (2003). Strategies to improve perceived competence in children with visual impairments. *RE:view, 35*(2), 69–80.

Strickling, C. A., & Pogrund, R. L. (2002). Motor focus: Promoting movement experiences and motor development. In R. L. Pogrund & D. L. Fazzi (Eds.), *Early focus: Working with young children who are blind or visually impaired and their families* (2nd ed., pp. 287–325). New York: AFB Press.

Stuart, M. E., Lieberman, L. J., & Hand, K. (2006). Parent-child beliefs about physical activity: And examination of families of children with visual impairments. *Journal of Visual Impairment & Blindness, 100*(4), 223–234.

Williams, C. A., Armstrong, N., Eves, N., & Faulkner, A. (1996). Peak aerobic fitness of visually impaired and sighted adolescent girls. *Journal of Visual Impairment & Blindness, 90,* 495–500.

Wiskochil, B., Lieberman, L. J., Houston-Wilson, C., & Petersen, S. (2007). The effects of trained peer tutors on the physical education of children who are visually impaired. *Journal of Visual Impairment & Blindness, 101*(6), 339–350.

Wolffe, K., & Sacks, S. (1997). The lifestyles of blind, low vision, and sighted youths: A quantitative comparison. *Journal of Visual Impairment & Blindness, 91*(3), 245–257.

APPENDIX 10A

Excerpts from Camp Abilities Activity Assessment

CAMP ABILITIES ACTIVITY ASSESSMENT

Camper ______________________________

Counselor ______________________________ Date ______________

Track and Field Assessment Checklist

	Criteria			
Skill	***Verbal Cue***	***Partial Physical Assistance***	***Total Physical Assistance***	***Other***
Long Jump	Personal Best: ______________			
Start with take-off foot				
12–18 strides				
Accelerate to maximum speed				
Knees up and tall in last strides				
Jump up and out				
Drive up knee and opposite arm vigorously				
Curve body like half moon				
Arms above head and behind shoulders				
Close jackknife				
Collapse buttocks to heels upon landing				
Arms thrust forward				
Feet together				
Shot Put	Personal Best: ______________			
Wrap four fingers firmly around shot				
Keep shot firm against neck				
Push shot past head				
Punch out				
Think position facing back toward direction of throw				
Hips rotate				
Kick backward with nonsupport leg				
Left leg straightens hard, right leg pushes up and out, causing a shooting motion				
Slap and pull				
Discus	Personal Best: ______________			
Hold the discus open-handed with an eagle claw grip				
Release discus, palm down, off index finger				

Keep body in wound-up position until thrown, then shout				
Rotate hips				
End throw with a long pull, head and chest up, facing sector				
Block-push-shoot				
Running				
Body erect, relax face, neck, shoulders, and arms				
Rest thumb on index finger				
Swing arms forward and back				
Open stride				
Strike heel and roll to toe				
Toes straight ahead or slightly out				
Head facing straight ahead				

Beep Baseball Assessment Checklist

	Criteria			
Skill	***Verbal Cue***	***Partial Physical Assistance***	***Total Physical Assistance***	***Other***
Running Bases				
Standing at home, turn toward and point to beeping base				
Walk to beeping base with guide				
Walk to beeping base without guide				
Jog to beeping base with guide				
Jog to beeping base without guide				
Fielding the Ball				
Assume a ready stance (feet apart, knees bent, hands ready)				
Go to ground slowly—lie on one side, body bent slightly at the waist, arms and legs outstretched				
Go to ground into fielding position rapidly				
Field a ball rolled gently				
Field a ball rolled with force				
Field a batted ball				
Hitting				
Hold a bat properly				
Swing a bat with smooth, level swing				
Swing bat and hit ball off a tee				
Swing bat and hit pitched ball				

Goalball Assessment Checklist

	Criteria			
Skill	***Verbal Cue***	***Partial Physical Assistance***	***Total Physical Assistance***	***Other***
Ready Position				
Face the other team				
Knees bent				
Hands on knees				
Underhand Roll				
Shift weight back and bring ball back with dominant hand				
Step forward with opposite foot				
Shift weight forward				
Release ball in front (ball should drop within 8′ of release)				
Follow through in front				
Falling to a Lying Position				
Ready position				
Determine if ball is to left or right				
Lie on ground with legs together and arms above and in front of head				
Passing				
Realize when to pass ball to teammate (player already passed twice in a row)				
Say teammate's name				
Bend down				
Roll ball toward team member				

Tandem Biking Checklist

Skill	***Day 1***	***Day 2***	***Day 3***	***Day 4***
Preparation Skills				
Wear appropriate footwear				
Closed-toe shoes				
Sneakers				
Put on helmet				
Make sure helmet is secure on head				
Straddle seat in ready position				
Push off				
Put feet on pedals				
Dismount Skills				
Put foot on ground				

Maintain balance				
Bring leg around, dismount bike				
Take helmet off				
Distance				
1/8 mile				
1/4 mile				
1/2 mile				
1 mile				
2 miles				
3 miles				
4 miles				
5 miles				
5+ miles				

Gymnastics Assessment Checklist

Skill	***Criteria***			
Single Bar				
Grip bar				
Jump to front support				
Forward roll over bar				
Pull over				
Front support, cast				
Cast, back hip circle				
Single leg around				
Single knee swing up to support				
Straight body hang from high bar				
Straight body swing from high bar				
Balance Beam				
Step onto beam				
Step into squat position				
Front support mount				
Front support to straddle sit				
Jump to one-foot squat support				
Stand from a squat position				
Stationary stand				
Stationary stand on one foot				
Squat stance				
Balance on hands and knees				
Sit on beam				
Beam walk on hands and knees				
Slide steps sideward				
Walk sideways				
Walk forward				

Dip steps forward				
Dip steps backward				
¼ turn (straight stand or squat position)				
½ turn (straight stand or squat position)				
One whole turn (straight stand or squat position)				
Walk forward, ½ turn				
Walk backward, ½ turn				
Step off end of beam to straight stand				
Straight jump dismount				
Tuck jump dismount				
Straddle jump dismount				
Rings				
Straight body support				
Tuck support				
Inverted straight body support				
Inverted tuck support				
Straight arm support				
Pike support (L position)				
Dismount (swinging with straight body, land on two feet)				
Side Horse				
Jump to front support				
Jump to single leg straddle support				
Front support, single leg straddle				
Straight body travel, to opposite end of horse				
Single leg circle				
Double leg circle				
Floor Exercise				
V sit				
Knee scale				
One leg scale				
Jump ½ turn				
Jump one whole turn				
Tuck jump				
Pike jump				
Straddle jump				
Log roll				
Tuck forward roll				
Straddle forward roll				
Tuck backward roll				
Straddle backward roll				
Mule kicks				
Handstand				
Cartwheel				

Combination of Floor Skills				
Jump ½ turn, jump one whole turn				
Tuck jump, straddle jump				
Tuck jump, pike jump				
Forward roll, jump ½ turn, backward roll				
Forward roll, straddle forward roll				
Backward roll, jump ½ turn, forward roll				
Backward roll, backward straddle roll				
Handstand forward roll				
Handstand forward roll to a cartwheel				
Handstand forward roll, jump ½ turn or one whole turn				

SOURCE: Excerpted from L. J. Lieberman, P. E. Ponchillia, and S. V. Ponchillia, *Physical Education and Sports for People with Visual Impairments and Deafblindness: Foundations of Instruction* (New York: AFB Press, 2013), pp. 363–374.

Recreation and Leisure Resources

This section provides resources such as assessment tools, publications, and instructional materials for teaching recreational and leisure skills. For additional resources that relate to the expanded core curriculum in general, see the Resources section at the end of this book.

ASSESSMENT TOOLS

Brigance Diagnostic Inventory of Early Development: APH Tactile Supplement.

POPULATION/AGE LEVEL: Birth–7 years

SOURCE: *Brigance diagnostic inventory of early development: APH tactile supplement* (1991 & 1992). Louisville, KY: American Printing House for the Blind.

Criterion-referenced assessment designed to identify the level of mastery achieved by a young child has on selected skills, including preambulatory motor skills and behaviors, gross motor skills and behaviors, and fine motor skills and behaviors.

The Brockport Physical Fitness Test (BFFT)

POPULATION/AGE LEVEL: 10–17 years

SOURCE: Winnick, J. P., & Short, F. X. (1999). *The Brockport physical fitness test manual.* Champaign, IL: Human Kinetics.

Measure of health-related physical fitness for children with a variety of disabilities, including visual impairments, rated on several fitness tasks against age- and disability-based standards for what is considered healthy.

Camp Abilities Activity Checklist.

POPULATION/AGE LEVEL: 9–18

SOURCE: Lieberman, L. J., Ponchillia, P. E., & Ponchillia, S. V. (2013). *Physical education and sports for people with visual impairments and deafblindness: Foundations of instruction.* New York: AFB Press.

Checklist of performance of sports-specific skills for beep baseball, bocce, goalball, gymnastics, judo, swimming, tandem biking, track and field, and orientation and mobility.

The Hill Performance Test of Selected Positional Concepts

POPULATION/AGE LEVEL: 6–10 years

SOURCE: Hill, E. (1981). *The Hill performance test of selected positional concepts.* Wood Dale, IL: Stoelting Co.

Measure of the development of basic spatial concepts in children who are visually impaired.

Oregon Project for Visually Impaired and Blind Preschool Children

POPULATION/AGE LEVEL: Birth-6 years

SOURCE: Anderson, S., Boigon, S., & Davis, K. (1991). *Oregon project for visually impaired and blind preschool children.* Medford, OR: Jackson County Education Services.

Includes assessments of fine motor and gross motor skills.

Peabody Mobility Kit for Infants & Toddlers

POPULATION/AGE LEVEL: Birth–24 months

SOURCE: Harley, R. K., Long, R. G., Merbler, J. B., & Wood, T. A. (1988). *Peabody mobility kit for infants & toddlers.* Wood Dale, IL: Stoelting.

Provides assessment of and training in functional movement for children who are visually impaired with multiple disabilities.

Test of Gross Motor Development-2 (TGMD-2)

POPULATION/AGE LEVEL: 3–11 years

SOURCE: Ulrich, D. A. (2000). *Test of gross motor development-2* (2nd ed.). Austin, TX: Pro-Ed.

Assesses locomotor and object control skills; can also be effective for measuring skills in older children with developmental lags in physical skills. Has been validated for use with children with visual impairments from 6–12 years of age

PUBLICATIONS

Blakely, B., Hart, R., & Lang, M. (1991). *Getting in touch with play: Creating play environments for children with visual impairments.* New York: Lighthouse National Center for Vision and Child Development.

Kelley, J. D., & Frieden, L. (Eds.). (1989). *Go for it: A book on sport and recreation for persons with disabilities.* Orlando, FL: Harcourt Brace Jovanovich.

Lieberman, L. J., Modell, S., Jackson, I. (2006). *Going PLACES: A transition guide to physical activity for youth with visual impairments.* Louisville, KY: American Printing House for the Blind.

Lieberman, L. J., Ponchillia, P. E., & Ponchillia, S. V. (2012). *Physical education and sports for people with visual impairments and deafblindness: Foundations of instruction.* New York: AFB Press.

Loumiet, R., & Levack, N. (1993). *Independent Living: A Curriculum with Adaptations for Students with Visual Impairments. Vol. 3: Play and Leisure.* Austin: Texas School for the Blind and Visually Impaired.

WEBSITES

Parent/Teacher Resource for Children with Sensory Impairments: Promoting Physical Education and Recreation

American Printing House for the Blind
www.aph.org/pe

Contains a wide range of information on health, fitness, and physical education for children with visual and other impairments as well as extensive resources for equipment, products, camps, organizations, and additional information.

Products for People Who Are Blind or Visually Impaired

American Foundation for the Blind
www.afb.org/prodmain.asp

Product database includes listings of games and activities, including accessible computer games.

Texas School for the Blind and Visually Impaired
www.tsbvi.edu

Contains ideas for games to develop and adapt for students with visual impairments.

VI Fit
www.vifit.org

Contains information about using electronic exercise games for fitness and provides downloads of games that can be played without visual feedback using the Wii remote motion sensing controller, which provides vibrotactile and audio cues.

VIP Conduit
https://www.vipconduit.com/index.php

Includes listing of computer games for users who are blind or have low vision.

WonderBaby
Perkins School for the Blind
www.wonderbaby.org/articles/best-accessible-computer-games-blind-kids

A listing of the best accessible computer games for kids who are blind.

ORGANIZATIONS

Camp Abilities
The College at Brockport
State University of New York
350 New Campus Drive
Brockport, NY 14420
(585) 395-5361
Fax: (585) 395-2771
www.campabilitiesbrockport.org

Developmental sports camps with sports and recreation activities adapted and modified for deafblindness. Website also provides links to instructional materials about how to teach sports and recreation to children with visual impairments or deafblindness as well as links to other Camp Abilities around the country.

Canadian Blind Sports Association
325-5055 Joyce Street
Vancouver, BC V5R 6B2
Local: (604) 419-0480
Fax: (604) 419-0481
Toll free: (877) 604-0480
info@canadianblindsports.ca
www.canadianblindsports.ca

Organization serving individuals with visual and other impairments. Serves as the national governing body for goalball in Canada. Provincial and territorial member associations provide support for Canadians with visual impairments who are involved in a range of sports.

Challenge Aspen
PO Box 6639
Aspen, CO 81615
(970) 923-0578
(800) 530-3901

Fax: (970) 923-7338
possibilities@challengeaspen.com
www.challengeaspen.com

Organization offering skiing, snowmobiling, ice skating, and many summer activities such as hiking and rock climbing for people with disabilities. Hosts daily adaptive ski and snowboard programs and camps in Snowmass Village, Colorado, making winter sports accessible to people with any physical or cognitive disability.

International Blind Sports Federation
www.ibsa.es

International organization developing and promoting sports for people who are blind or visually impaired. Organizes competitive events, develops and finalizes rules and conditions for individual sports, and raises awareness of the participation of people with visual impairments in sports. Holds World Championship Games every four years. Provides descriptions of adapted sports, including rules and regulations, and a calendar of upcoming competitions.

United States Association of Blind Athletes
1 Olympic Plaza
Colorado Springs, CO 80909
(719) 866-3224
Fax: (719) 866-3400
www.usaba.org

National organization providing sports opportunities to children, youths, adults, and veterans with visual impairments or deaf-blindness in sports including, but not limited to, track and field, Nordic and Alpine skiing, biathlon, judo, wrestling, swimming, tandem cycling, powerlifting, and goalball. Offers detailed information about individual sports and adaptations; maintains a calendar of upcoming events and competitions. Sells goalballs and instructional goalball videos.

United States Paralympics Committee
1 Olympic Plaza
Colorado Springs, CO 80909
(719) 866-2032
Fax: (719) 866-2029
www2.teamusa.org/US-Paralympics.aspx

Division of the U.S. Olympic Committee responsible for selecting and managing the U.S. teams that compete in the Paralympic Games. Offers information such as game rules and schedules, and general resources for competitors.

VSA
John F. Kennedy Center for the Performing Arts
Department of VSA and Accessibility
2700 F Street, NW
Washington, DC 20566
(800) 444-1324
(202) 467-4600
www.kennedy-center.org/education/vsa

International organization on arts and disability that offers opportunities in both the performing and visual arts for artists with disabilities nationally and through the VSA State Affiliate network. Also provides resources about accessibility, arts, and education for teachers, students, parents, artists and arts administrators.

SOURCES OF GAMES AND ARTS AND CRAFTS MATERIALS

American Printing House for the Blind
1839 Frankfort Avenue
PO Box 6085
Louisville, KY 40206
(502) 895-2405
(800) 223-1839
www.aph.org
info@aph.org

Future Aids: The Braille Superstore
33222 Lynn Ave.
Abbotsford, BC V2S 1C9
Canada
(800) 987-1231
(604) 852-6341
Fax: (800) 985-1231
www.braillebookstore.com

Independent Living Aids
200 Robbins Lane
Jericho, NY 11753
(800) 537-2118
(855) 746-7452
Fax: (516) 937-3906
www.independentliving.com

LS&S Group
145 River Rock Drive
Buffalo, NY 14207
(800) 468-4789

Fax: (877) 498-1482
TDD/TTY: (866) 317-8533
www.lssgroup.com

SightConnection
9709 Third Avenue NE, #100
Seattle, WA 98115-2027
(206) 525-5556
(800) 458-4888
Fax: 206-525-0422
www.sightconnection.org
info@sightconnection.org

Recreation and Leisure Learning Activities

Contributed by Carol B. Allman and Sandra Lewis

These sample learning activities are presented as examples of activities that teachers can create to work on several ECC skills at once with their students. Activities that help teach recreation and leisure skills can also be found in other chapters. The activities presented, like all instruction, need to be considered and modified to address the needs of individual students—such as those who are braille readers, have low vision, or have additional disabilities—with adaptations for appropriate media and the physical and other capabilities of the student.

Learning Activity: Dress Up and Pretend
Primary ECC Area: Recreation and leisure **Component:** Play **Grades:** Pre-K–5; students with multiple disabilities
Other ECC Areas ■ Social interaction ■ Independent living ■ Self-determination ■ Career education
Goal: The student will dress up for a specified pretend activity.
Key Tasks/Concepts The student will: ■ Determine appropriate clothes for a specified activity. ■ Learn independent dressing skills. ■ Distinguish between real and pretend activities.
Description The student is given a pretend activity (shoveling snow, going to the gym, walking the dog, cooking dinner, going to work, etc.) and selects what clothes to wear for the activity. The student practices putting on different types of clothes, using appropriate conversation for the activity chosen, and performing the activity. This activity is best completed with two or more students who can interact about a pretend activity and actually pretend play together. The teacher may have to serve in the role of a participant. The teacher may need to spend some time discussing the "right" clothes to wear for various activities and pretend play with the student so that the student develops an understanding of what is expected. This is an excellent activity to share with parents so that dress up and pretend play can occur at home with siblings and peers. Career skills could be infused as students pretend to take on the roles of workers with whom they are familiar. The teacher can use this learning activity as an opportunity to discuss the concepts of real and pretend.
Instructional Materials and Supplies Needed An assortment of dress-up outfits should be available in a location of the classroom so that the student can easily access the clothes. For students who have motor impairments, clothing with Velcro closures might facilitate the ease with which clothes are put on and removed.
Settings Classroom or home

(continued on next page)

Duration/Timing

Depending on the abilities of the child, 5–10 minutes to select and dress in appropriate clothing and 15 minutes for the pretend play session.

Evaluation

The teacher might want to evaluate the student's engagement in this activity by noting the level of assistance that it was necessary to provide, using the following rubric:

1. Needs considerable assistance to participate in all components of this activity.
2. Requires step-by-step instructional assistance to participate in this activity.
3. Participates in this activity with minimal assistance (limited verbal prompting).
4. Participates in this activity independently.

This is the type of activity that the teacher might not want to evaluate formally but rather provide as a free-time option because pretend and dress up are typical activities for children ages 3 to 8. Informal evaluation would consist of noting the student's ability to independently put on clothes properly, select appropriate clothing, and carry on appropriate conversation that fits the pretend activity.

Learning Activity: Hula-Hoop Fun

(Contributed by Kimberly Mountjoy, Nashville, TN)

Primary ECC Area: Recreation and leisure **Component:** Physical activity
Grades: 3–8

Other ECC Areas

- Social interaction
- Sensory efficiency
- Compensatory access
- O&M (motor skills)

Goal: Students will increase motor coordination and physical endurance by timing one another to see how long each participant can keep a Hula-Hoop going.

Key Tasks/Concepts

The student will:

- Use a Hula-Hoop
- Use low vision or tactile strategies to read a clock or use a stopwatch or other method of timing.
- Chart minutes on a graph or other paper.
- Interpret another student's chart.
- Take turns and compare results with fellow student.

Key tasks may need adaptation for appropriate media and physical capabilities of the students.

Description

This activity is best done with two or more students who are 6 to 8 years old. Students work in pairs and take turns timing each other using a Hula-Hoop. The duration of successfully keeping the Hula-Hoop in motion is charted in minutes on graph paper. Students compare times and read each others' charts.

Prior to participating in this activity, each student will need to know how to do the following:

- use a Hula-Hoop
- use a graph for charting time
- use a clock or other timing device

(continued on next page)

This activity provides exercise, socialization with peers, and practice with timing and charting progress. Students may be paired with classmates who are not visually impaired.

Depending on the proficiency of the students involved, it may be appropriate to blindfold students with sight while they are using the Hula-Hoop.

Instructional Materials and Supplies Needed

- Hula-Hoops
- Graph paper in the medium used by the student with visual impairment
- Marking devices
- Timing devices accessible by all students involved

Settings

A large room that has enough space to do the activity and where there are tables for the students to use when filling out the charts. Adequate lighting for students to read the timing devices is necessary. Depending on the lighting needs of the students with visual impairments, this activity may not work as well when undertaken outside.

Duration/Timing

- 15–20 minutes minimum
- This activity can be repeated once a week over an indefinite period of time

Evaluation

The goal of this activity is to improve motor coordination and physical endurance. The teacher might choose to evaluate progress in these areas indirectly by keeping track of the longest period of time that the student with visual impairment was able to keep the Hula-Hoop in motion during each session. If desired, data on students' progress on reading a clock or timer correctly, reading another's graph, correctly charting time on a graph, and demonstration of appropriate play skills could also be collected.

Skill	Date	Date	Date	Date
Longest period of time keeping Hula-Hoop in motion (record time)				
X-axis is labeled				
Y-axis is labeled				
Represents score accurately on graph				
Reads stopwatch accurately				
Checks classmate's graph and confirms accuracy				
Plays well with classmates (takes turns, uses appropriate language, acknowledges classmate's comments, refrains from being bossy)				

Key:

I = Independent
VD = Verbal directions
PS = Physical support

Learning Activity: Whose Ball Is This?

Primary ECC Area: Recreation and leisure **Component:** Sports
Grades: 3–10

Other ECC Areas
- Compensatory access
- Social interaction
- Sensory efficiency

Goal: The student will match ten balls with the sports or games in which they are used.

Key Tasks/Concepts
The student will:
- Recognize that different sports use different balls.
- Learn that balls are not always the same, can be of made of different materials, and differ in size and shape.
- Learn that some sports don't use a ball.

Description
In this activity, the student will match ten different balls with the appropriate sports or games.

One way to approach this activity is to introduce one ball at a time to the student. The teacher can tell the student in what sport the ball is used and what the ball is called, and then encourage the student to describe the ball and its characteristics. When the student has explored one ball sufficiently and can name it when shown (or select it from a group of other balls), then a new ball can be introduced.

Another approach is to introduce several or all of the balls at one time. The teacher can ask the student to categorize or sort the balls using whatever method appeals to the student. The teacher can then assist the student in sorting the balls using alternative criteria (weight, size, outside material, texture, and the like.). As the student is engaged in these activities, the teacher can name each ball and the sport in which it is used.

Instructional Materials and Supplies Needed
- Golf ball
- Soccer ball
- Bowling ball
- Tennis ball
- Ping-pong ball
- Baseball
- Basketball
- Softball
- Hockey puck
- Football

Setting
This activity can occur in a resource room or other area where the teacher provides services to the student. Smaller settings are recommended, as balls have a way of traveling long distances if not controlled.

Unless peers are to be included in some meaningful way, it is probably best not to conduct this lesson where peers can observe, since it may prompt teasing (if peers don't understand why a student who is visually impaired is being provided this instruction) or disrupt other planned classroom activities.

Duration/Timing
- 10 minutes per ball for the one-ball-at-a-time approach, followed by longer sessions for comparing and contrasting multiple balls
- up to 1 hour to introduce all balls at once, followed by additional opportunities for exploring

(continued on next page)

Evaluation

The evaluation tool below reflects the student's ability to name the correct sport when the associated ball is presented.

Task	Date	Date	Date	Date	Date	Date
Names baseball						
Names basketball						
Names softball						
Names football						
Names ping-pong ball						
Names tennis ball						
Names bowling ball						
Names soccer ball						
Names golf ball						
Names hockey puck						

It would also be possible to have the student find the ball when a particular sport is named. In that case, then, the chart would appear as below:

Task	Date	Date	Date	Date	Date
Locates baseball					
Locates basketball					
Locates softball					
Locates football					
Locates ping-pong ball					
Locates tennis ball					
Locates bowling ball					
Locates soccer ball					
Locates golf ball					
Locates hockey puck					

Key

I = Independent
VD = Verbal directions
PS = Physical support

Learning Activity: Finding Places for Fun

Primary ECC Area: Recreation and leisure **Component:** Leisure activities and hobbies
Grades: 4–12

Other ECC Areas

- Compensatory access
- Sensory efficiency
- Orientation and mobility
- Career education
- Self-determination

Goal: The student will become knowledgeable about community resources for recreation and leisure activities. The student will locate places on a map that he frequents for recreation and leisure activities (such as a neighborhood park or playground or a movie theater).

Key Tasks/Concepts

The student will:

- Practice map reading.
- Practice correct identification of places.
- Express preferences of places to go for fun.

Key tasks may need adaptation for appropriate media and the mobility capabilities of the student.

Description

The student will locate on a map places in the community where recreation and leisure activities occur. The teacher will teach low vision device use and tactile graphic techniques such as systematic searching, scanning, focusing of device, directional word meanings, tactile discrimination, graphic symbols, and locations of sites in reference to the student's home. This activity can be conducted repeatedly, changing the sites to be located, and can involve one or more students. With multiple students, each can use a separate map to practice locating places. The key to this activity is to use it often so that students get lots of practice with reading of tactile maps or using low vision aids to locate places on a map. These skills are critical to success in math, science, and social studies as students progress through the grades. This activity can also be used in higher grades with more and more complex map reading skills and with the student practicing production of tactile maps and print maps as appropriate.

Instructional Materials and Supplies Needed

The teacher will need to prepare maps ahead of time, particularly for younger students. For older students some map construction can be included using tactile graphic kits or other available materials for map building.

Settings

School (learning of activity), home (practice), or community (visiting locations)

Duration/Timing

- Learning of the tasks needed to do this activity will vary depending on the needs of the students.
- This activity should be broken into smaller tasks that build toward the final goal.
- 30-minute sessions devoted to learning the smaller tasks can be done two or three times a week over a six- to nine-week period, with the final goal being the culminating activity that is used to evaluate the student.

Evaluation

The student can be evaluated using the following rubric:

1. Needs hand-over-hand or other physical assistance to find two places of recreation and leisure on a map.
2. Requires step-by-step prompting to find two places of recreation and leisure on a map.

(continued on next page)

3. Finds two places of recreation and leisure on a map with minimal prompting.
4. Finds more than two places of recreation and leisure on a map independently.

If a teacher wants to give a grade or evaluate student progress toward the final goal, a similar rubric can be used for each of the skills taught to complete the goal activity. For example, ratings could be given for student ability to correctly identify meanings of directional words with 1 for no meanings correct, 2 for at least two meanings, 3 for most meanings correct, and 4 for all meanings correct.

Learning Activity: Fun in the Workshop

Primary ECC Area: Recreation and leisure **Component:** Leisure activities and hobbies
Grades: 5–12; students with multiple disabilities

Other ECC Areas

- Sensory efficiency
- Compensatory access
- Independent living
- Social interaction
- Self-determination

Goal: Student will use woodworking skills to create a gift.

Key Tasks/Concepts

The student will:

- Follow written directions.
- Use low vision devices, as appropriate, to monitor own work and read directions.
- Use sandpaper of different grades to smooth edges of wood.
- Use a screwdriver.
- Make choices.
- Organize materials.

Key tasks might need adaptation for appropriate media and the physical capabilities of the student.

Description

The teacher will need to create samples of several easy-to-create woodworking projects that are appropriate for the level of the students involved. Ideas include:

- Key hook—a storage place for keys to be hung in the garage or by the entry door of the house or classroom.
- Wind chime—a wind chime from which small metal items are hung
- Planter box—a box to raise flowers or herbs
- Napkin or mail holder—a box to keep napkins or mail upright

The teacher may start by informing the student that many people make gifts for others in their free time and that in their free time after lessons, they will be working on a gift project. The teacher can encourage the student to choose a recipient for the gift, facilitating this decision through a discussion of why gifts are given—for birthdays, for holidays, to say thank you, because the recipient isn't feeling well, and just to express love. Using a calendar in this discussion to check upcoming special events would add a chance to practice another ECC skill.

Once the recipient of the gift is identified, the teacher can show the student the options for projects and discuss the new skills involved and how much time will be required to make each item. Students should be encouraged to use this information, along with what they feel the gift recipients would like, to select what item each will make.

(continued on next page)

The teacher would then prepare the directions for the selected project in either braille or print. If the student has low vision, reading the directions with a prescribed magnification device will add another ECC skill to this lesson.

After the student has completed one project, it is recommended that a second project be started so that the newly learned skills can be practiced.

Students with additional cognitive or motor impairments can also be involved in gift-making activities that use workshop tools, though it may be necessary to select an activity that requires less detailed fine motor skills. Partial participation may also be appropriate. For all students engaging in this type of activity for the first time, having a finished version of the final project will enable them to understand what they are creating.

Instructional Materials and Supplies Needed

For key hook:

- 8″–10″ piece of 1 × 2 lumber
- Sand paper
- 4–5 cup hooks
- Picture frame hanging wire
- Screws
- Screwdriver
- Measuring device

For wind chime:

- 8″–10″ piece of 1 × 2 lumber
- Sandpaper
- Piano wire
- Screws
- Screwdriver
- Discarded metal toys, silverware, electronics parts
- Measuring device

For planter box:

- 3 pieces of 1 × 6 lumber, 12″–15″ long (for long sides)
- 2 pieces of 1 × 6 lumber, 6″ long (for short sides)
- Wood clamps
- Glue
- Screwdriver
- Screws
- 8 braces
- Measuring device

For napkin or mail holder:

- 1 piece of 1 × 6 lumber, 4″ long
- Sandpaper
- Glue
- Screwdriver
- Screws
- 4 tongue depressors, 6 popsicle sticks or other narrow wood pieces
- Measuring device

Settings

The resource or regular meeting room.

(continued on next page)

Duration/Timing

Sanding of wood pieces can be completed in free time in the general education classroom or in short sessions at the end of lessons with the teacher. Longer sessions of approximately 30–45 minutes will be required to teach the skills of screwing, measuring, gluing, etc. Ideally, once these skills have been introduced, the student can practice them in shorter sessions. That is, once the student has attached one brace with screws, other braces could be completed in opportunities for free time in the general education classroom and during time with the teacher.

Evaluation

The evaluation tool will depend to some extent on the project selected by the student and how frequently the teacher probes the skills being practiced by the student, but can look something like the following:

Task	Date	Date	Date	Date
Refers to directions				
Keeps materials organized				
Uses sandpaper				
Recognizes when wood is smooth				
Uses measuring device				
Screws with screwdriver				
Uses wood glue				

Key:

I = Independent
VD = Verbal directions
PS = Physical support

CHAPTER 11

Career Education

Karen E. Wolffe

L. Penny Rosenblum

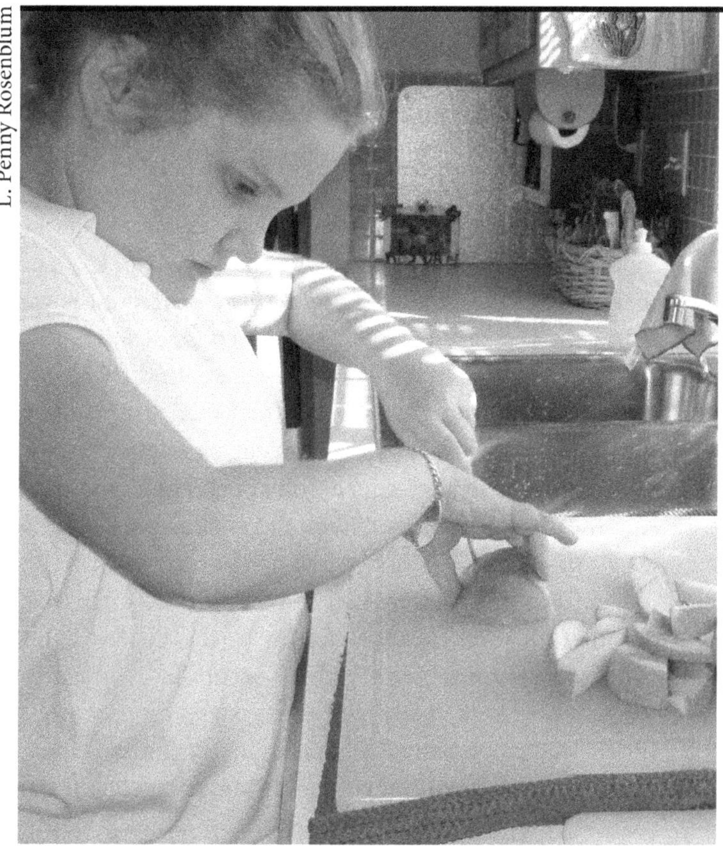

Career education focuses on the development of knowledge, the refinement of innate talents, and the promotion of skills, including the work habits or behaviors needed for success in employment and other life roles. Although there is a particular emphasis on obtaining and maintaining employment in the area of career education within the expanded core curriculum (ECC), career education also is about preparing for the student's "next environment." That is, career education helps parents prepare their children to move from home to school, helps teachers prepare their students to move through grades in school, and helps young people prepare not just for work, but for all the roles they will play over the course of their lives. In this sense, career education encompasses a broad understanding of the world and how it works. As a result of instruction in career education, students develop greater understanding of the many activities of life and the various occupations that people pursue, as well as how they may fit into this great continuum. Career education, then, involves promoting awareness and knowledge, as well as the development of specific skills.

THE IMPORTANCE OF CAREER EDUCATION

Although most students can benefit from career education, it is of critical importance for children and adolescents with visual impairments because they, perhaps more than their sighted classmates, may rely on the skills and knowledge gained from this area of instruction to determine their life and career paths: what life roles they may play; what occupational areas are of greatest interest to them; what jobs they might be able to perform; and how to go about finding, obtaining, and maintaining employment. Most people in Western society need and seek employment to support themselves and their families; in fact the majority of households in the United States have two working adults (Haupt & Kane, 2004). Adults are generally expected to work in some capacity, whether in the form of maintaining the household, taking care of family members like children or elderly relatives, or holding down a job. Effective career awareness, exploration, and preparation can be determining factors in the trajectory of an individual's life and in his or her life satisfaction.

Current evidence indicates that young people who are visually impaired are, after graduating from high school, almost as likely to enter college as students without disabilities, but they are far less likely to be working, living independently, or engaging in marriages or relationships when compared to most other students with or without disabilities (Kef & Tielen, 2008; Newman, Wagner, Cameto, & Knokey, 2009; Newman, Wagner, Cameto, Knokey, & Shaver, 2010). It is likely that there are many reasons for these discrepancies, though a lack of instruction geared to skill development and the way students with visual impairments learn about career education appears to be a contributing factor (Wolffe, 1996; Wolffe, Roessler, & Schriner, 1992; Wolffe, Sacks, Corn, Erin, Huebner, & Lewis, 2002; Wolffe & Kelly, 2011). This chapter defines the needs of children and adolescents in the area of career education and provides practical activities to support the acquisition of skills in this important area of the ECC.

Early Intervention and Incidental Learning

Starting a structured program of career education early in a child's life is crucial for students with visual impairments because they may not be able to learn or obtain information related to the world of work incidentally—by happenstance or casually—using vision. As described in Chapter 1 and elsewhere in this book, children with typical vision learn a great deal about what is going on in their environment through everyday observation—incidentally—and this is particularly significant in regard to the area of career education, where so many aspects of the environment are relevant to the world of work.

For instance, a sighted child who may have stayed home from school with a cold may happen to look out of her bedroom window and notice that a work crew is resurfacing the road outside. Without conscious thought, she will catalog, by visual observation, that there is a foreman directing the crew, and that there are workers breaking up the road surface, preparing a fresh surface with gravel or dirt, mixing asphalt or concrete, and paving the road. The workers will be operating tools such as jackhammers, bulldozers, asphalt or concrete mixers, pavers, backhoes, spreaders, and dump trucks. She will see that they wear construction gear—heavy shirts and slacks, steel-toed boots, gloves, earmuffs or plugs to protect their ears, safety glasses or goggles for their eyes, helmets, and possibly face masks and bright, reflective vests for visibility. If they are working with asphalt, she will see that it is hot, dirty work that requires strength and accuracy. In just a few moments she will have learned about the jobs being performed by the different workers and how this kind of work improves the roadway, because she will see the road before and after the work, and what the tools of the trade are, all through the sense of sight.

In contrast, a child without vision or with impaired vision may well be aware of something going on outside the window, but may not be able to capture the details of what is occurring. She may have to rely on her senses of hearing and smell rather than vision and will be unable to explore the worksite tactilely because of being confined indoors. This child will probably hear the noise made by the equipment and possibly the workers' voices, and will smell the tar or asphalt. But without direct intervention, the child who is visually impaired may miss the number of workers and the roles they play, as well as the variety, size, and color of tools being used; may miss the amount of work and type of tasks being performed; and may not realize the safety features in place to protect the workers. Even if a parent or caregiver describes what is going on outside the window, it is unlikely that the child will comprehend the scope of the project, how each worker's efforts complement the others', or what it takes to do the jobs associated with the work in terms of strength, endurance, and sheer physical size. Each missed opportunity to learn incidentally about work roles, jobs, and careers helps minimize the child's general understanding of the world in which he or she lives and how the work being performed by adults contributes to the overall community. It is also a missed opportunity for the child to learn about what he or she might or might not like to do as an adult.

Children with impaired vision therefore need opportunities to learn about the world and life in general by exploring their environment and what's happening in it—just as children with unimpaired vision do through visual observation—by touching what they cannot see or getting close enough to see. If neither is possible, the people in their lives need to verbally describe what is occurring and what is relevant and then, whenever possible, relate their descriptions to something known by the child. This exposure to the environment and the serendipitous learning that takes place because of that exposure is the essence of incidental learning, and although it happens casually for sighted students, it must be planned and structured for children with severe visual impairments.

For these reasons, instructional staff and caregivers need to enrich the flow of information that children with visual impairments receive. For example, if describing the dump truck used in the earlier example, an observer might relate the truck to the child's family's small pickup truck, explaining that the dump truck is bigger and heavier (almost like two small pickups collapsed into one truck), that its bed is hinged (like a cheese grater or other kitchen tool that can be shown to the child), that the dump truck gate may open from the bottom rather than the top so that the dirt or rocks can be poured out when the bed is tipped, and that while the family's compact truck has four wheels (two under the cab and two under the bed), a dump truck used in road work typically has four double tires under the bed (eight tires) and a pair of wheels under the cab (ten tires in all). If the child has a realistic toy dump truck, the person can use it to show how the real dump truck works and then relate the size to vehicles with which the child is familiar, for instance, the family car compared to a small pickup truck compared to a full-sized pickup truck compared to a bus. At the earliest convenience, it would be ideal for the child to tactilely explore an actual dump truck.

Since children with visual impairments may not be able to learn about what's happening outside of their homes and schools and infer who is doing what kinds of jobs by simply listening to things happening around them, reading books about careers, or hearing about the things that others observe visually, they need to receive the same information deliberately. They need to investigate what they have heard and read about to ensure they've understood; hearing someone mow a lawn or reading about it doesn't give children who are blind information about the equipment being used (a push mower, a riding mower, or a weedeater) nor the safety considerations the worker employs (glove, safety goggles, or a hat). They need to learn about the multiple roles and responsibilities working adults perform through active engagement with others and the environment—by visiting worksites and meeting workers, exploring uniforms, tools, and equipment used on jobs, and doing age-appropriate chores or volunteer work. It is essential, in other words, that students with visual impairments receive a structured career education program.

Because career education encompasses such a broad range of knowledge and skills, it of necessity intersects with all the other ECC areas. Sidebar 11.1 explains how the skills learned in each of the other areas are also important to career education. In particular, the areas of career education and self-determination (discussed in Chapter 12) overlap in many ways, including exploration of one's interests, abilities, values, and learning skills for self-advocacy; therefore, some writers consider them to be one content area (Brolin, 1997; Wolffe, 1996, 2000, 2007, 2013). It is therefore suggested that both chapters be read together and the content considered in tandem for programming.

SIDEBAR 11.1

Career Education and Other Areas of the ECC

In a sense, all areas of the expanded core curriculum are intertwined, and for that reason promoting skills in one area through some thoughtful planning can help develop skills in other areas at the same time. Career education overlaps with and is therefore integrated into the teaching of all the other ECC domains.

COMPENSATORY ACCESS

Compensatory access includes the skills and concepts, including modes of communication, necessary for children with visual impairments to be successful in their education. The disability-specific skills taught in this area are critical to career education. For instance, students apply their skills in reading and writing with braille, optical devices, or assistive technology to explore career opportunities, learn how others with visual impairments are contributing in their communities, and perform tasks in volunteer or paid work.

SENSORY EFFICIENCY

Being able to use one's senses of hearing, vision, taste, smell, or touch alone or in combination with other senses enables students to maximize their knowledge of the world and what's happening around them, which is a critical skill for success in life and work.

ASSISTIVE TECHNOLOGY

Assistive technology has gained importance in the last few decades as technology and assistive devices that enable access for people with visual impairments have provided entry into jobs and life activities formerly closed to them. Thanks to technology, information in print does not have to be read to a person who is blind by a sighted person, and everyday activities, such as depositing one's paycheck, can be handled electronically and privately. Students therefore need to understand how to use technology to their advantage. Most jobs in the 21st century require workers to be able to use technology and workers with impaired vision must know how to use both mainstream and assistive technology to be competitive in today's labor market.

ORIENTATION AND MOBILITY

Being able to travel safely and independently enables students with visual impairments to explore the environment and find out what goes on in their communities. For example, O&M facilities learning about where adults and other children go during the day to play out their roles as workers and students and how to get around in their communities and find locations of interest where they might want to live and work in the future.

INDEPENDENT LIVING SKILLS

Students need to be able to take care of their persons and possessions in order to successfully move into working life. Keeping an organized workspace, being able to reliably retrieve work and work tools, and welcoming coworkers and others into one's home are just a few of the independent living skills that directly affect a student's ability to obtain and maintain employment.

SOCIAL INTERACTION

Being able to communicate and interact effectively with employers and coworkers is important for both obtaining and maintaining work, and is often a required skill for many jobs. In addition, having friends and acquaintances is fundamental to networking, a critical way in which people find jobs and convince prospective employers that they can contribute in the workplace.

RECREATION AND LEISURE

Having recreational and leisure pursuits and interests helps keep students fit and happy. Such interests also help students connect with others by giving them the ability to convey an interest in activities that others may find interesting.

SELF-DETERMINATION

This area of the ECC focuses on a student's ability to make life decisions and everyday choices as independently as possible. It is about establishing an internal locus of control, or a belief that students are able to affect outcomes in life through their own decisions and actions. For students with visual impairments, self-determination encompasses a skill set that will enable them to demonstrate their competence to others and make good decisions for themselves in career planning and implementation. Students also use self-determination to describe their disabilities and explain the accommodations or modifications that would enable them to contribute to or participate in an activity—in other words, self-determination is the basis of the ability to speak up or advocate for students' needs and preferences.

Students with Multiple Disabilities

For students with multiple disabilities, career education is as important as it is for students whose only disability is visual impairment. Students with multiple disabilities may require intervention by a team of professionals who have expertise in the areas of their additional disabilities. For example, students who are deaf-blind will benefit from working with a teacher of students with visual impairments, a teacher of deaf students, and a deaf-blind specialist; students who have physical disabilities and visual impairment may benefit from working with a teacher of students with visual impairments, an occupational therapist, a physical therapist, and a speech/language specialist depending on the severity of their physical impairments. Ideally, students with multiple disabilities receive assistance with their educational programs from interdisciplinary or transdisciplinary teams. The learning activities that are presented at the end of this chapter focus on adaptations for students with visual impairments; for students with multiple disabilities additional individual modifications and techniques may be needed. For example, when picking up toys or tools (see the learning activity "Put That Away!" at the end of this chapter) a student with limited use of his or her limbs may find it helpful to have a mechanical grabber to pick things up. Because the abilities and disabilities of students vary widely, it is particularly important to consider the individual conditions and circumstances of each student and to work closely with the student's family as well as relevant specialists during assessment and planning in regard to career education.

Other factors to consider when students with visual impairments have additional disabilities, particularly cognitive impairments, are that some students may need to work on tasks for longer periods of time to achieve competence or mastery, will benefit from clear and consistent instruction, and may have difficulty transferring skills from one environment to another. In the later stages of the career development model described in this chapter, as students begin to focus on their specific interests and career possibilities, many such students may benefit from:

- Repeated opportunities to explore jobs and parts of jobs to determine the most appropriate career fields.
- Deliberate and planned instruction in the environments where they will be expected to use the skills they are taught, such as learning to wipe tables at a restaurant rather than in a classroom.
- Teacher- or counselor-facilitated placement on jobs in chosen career fields with support from job coaches or trainers.

It is important to remember that not all children will grow up to find jobs on their own, successfully compete for those jobs, or work in full-time competitive employment. Some children with severe multiple disabilities may be too medically fragile to work or they may have mental health issues that inhibit their inclusion in such settings. However, most children grow up wanting to contribute in some way—perhaps through part-time work or volunteer activities—and many will be candidates for competitive employment. Professionals and families need to balance the needs of students with the needs of employers as they consider appropriate work options for students with multiple disabilities because many of these students will require external supports. In such cases, someone other than the student will need to evaluate the student's abilities, limitations, interests, and values; someone else may need to match the student to appropriate work environments and teach the skills needed in the identified area; and someone else may need to persuade or otherwise work with the employer to hire the student. In addition, someone other than the employer may need to support the student to be successful in a work environment, at least initially and possibly for the long term.

An approach known as person-centered planning (Everson & Zhang, 2000; Moss & Wiley, 2003; Mount, Ducharme, & Beeman, 1991; Test, Aspel, & Everson, 2006) can be very helpful in planning for the future with students who have multiple disabilities, including visual impairment, as they approach the end of their time in school. Person-centered planning (discussed in more detail in Chapter 12) involves bringing together people who are involved in every area of a student's life, such as relatives, friends, neighbors, and educational and rehabilitation professionals. Together they compose a picture of who the student is, including strengths and abilities, and who he or she would like to be in adulthood, and develop a plan to achieve that goal. The concept behind this ongoing process is that by viewing the individual as a whole person and listening to his or her preferences and needs, a vision for the student's future can be developed that the members of the group can help support.

COMPONENTS OF CAREER EDUCATION

As already explained, career education entails developing not only specific skills, but also a broad awareness based on exposure to a wide variety of life activities and to the occupations and life roles of family members, friends, and others in the student's environment. It encompasses a wide variety of knowledge and experiences, and teachers and families play a key role at each stage of education in providing the exposure and activities that will enable children to understand the range of life options available and which ones best suit their interests, needs, and abilities. In the area of career education, teachers therefore need to help broaden students' knowledge of human activities and occupations as well as help them develop work-enhancing skills.

Career Education Model

Proponents of career education (Brolin, 1995; Hoyt, 1982; Marland, 1971; Wolffe, 1996, 1999, 2000, 2006a) believe that people develop their life work or careers through the roles they play out over the course of their lives. The roles that children play teach them the skills they need to be successful in school and at home; the roles young adults take on in their first jobs and in early adult life teach them the skills they need to be successful friends and partners, workers, parents, and so forth; and the roles adults play in their working lives prepare them to be successful mentors of another generation of workers and responsible adults.

This lifelong learning model for career education encompasses six levels of activities, the first four of which make up the components of career education that are taught as part of the ECC in school:

- career awareness
- career exploration
- career preparation
- career placement

The knowledge, skills, and abilities that students need to acquire during these four stages are described in the following sections.

The other two levels of activities in this model, maintenance and mentoring, take place in adulthood. Career maintenance involves retaining employment, advancing according to plan, and ultimately achieving career goals. Career mentoring is the stage in which successful adults mentor younger workers and advise them along their career paths. These levels are the focus of service providers who assist working-age people and adults over the age of 21.

In addition to general, age-specific needs, such as learning about job roles and responsibilities, identifying the knowledge, skills, and abilities required to perform in various careers, and working at home or for others in the community, students with visual impairments have unique needs that must be met at each stage of the career education model. A student with visual disabilities may need to start career education activities at an earlier age and continue with them longer than a student who is fully sighted because of a variety of factors, including:

- an inability or restricted ability to learn incidentally through vision about the environment and what people do for work
- others' lowered expectations based on misperceptions of what people who are blind or visually impaired are capable of doing
- lack of realistic feedback that compares the student's performance to that of classmates without disabilities and the student's inability to see what classmates can do
- limited exposure to role models of successful adults with visual impairments

Career Awareness

Young children from birth through elementary school need to learn what work is, what roles they and their classmates play at this time in their lives, and what responsibilities children their age share. Children do this, in part, by coming to understand their places within the family and at school. They affirm their roles as family members through active participation in daily activities, including chores; their roles as students through engagement in academic activities; their roles as friends and acquaintances through interaction with other children and reciprocity in activities, such as active play, birthday parties, and sleepovers. In each of these roles, children with visual impairments need to engage in several activities, including:

- learning the skills being taught to sighted children
- accessing general classroom information by applying nonvisual techniques, such as using tactile or verbal cues to explore materials and environments

- receiving structured input from family members and professionals to help develop their knowledge about what is going on in their communities and neighborhoods

In addition, children with visual impairments need to learn that adults—along with being family members and neighbors—expend energy to produce a product or provide a service, such as building a house (construction worker) or patrolling a neighborhood to protect its residents (police). They also need to learn that adults typically work to support themselves and their families as well as to contribute within the community.

To develop career awareness, young children with visual impairments need to master both the skills other children their age are mastering and the skills needed as a result of their visual impairment to engage with those children in activities appropriate to their age. For instance, all young children benefit from exploring their environment, and sighted students will see things of interest to investigate, such as an older sibling coloring, a parent preparing a meal, or a neighbor's child outside swinging in his backyard. For the visually impaired child, participating in any of these activities and learning what's involved will not necessarily occur without meaningful sighted assistance from parents and professionals and the development of specific strategies to accomplish those tasks (often referred to as *disability-specific skills*). To compensate for lack of visual input, they also need to learn effective listening skills, tactile exploration, and questioning techniques to probe for information from other children and adults, among other skills.

In the career awareness component, children need to master a variety of skills and knowledge, including:

- organizational skills
- following directions
- information about work
- positive work habits
- basic work skills
- incidental information about the world and how it operates

Organizational Skills

To be successful in most career roles, people with impaired vision need organizational skills. The ability to organize physical objects leads and is related to, if appropriately supported, the ability to organize one's activities, time, and thoughts. Learning about organizational principles is therefore critical for children. At the most basic level, students with visual impairments need organizational skills because they may be unable to rely on vision to, for example, find items that are out of place. Without such skills, locating various objects can take so much time that individuals can come to be viewed as inefficient at school or on the job. Organizational skills include:

- knowing how to distinguish between items by touch, smell, taste, or use of functional vision
- being able to identify different kinds of containers and furnishings by size, texture, and color
- being able to identify storage for personal things (clothes, toys, toiletries, books, school materials and supplies) via tactile markings
- being familiar with systems—such as braille, print, pictorial, or tactile markers or labels—for finding and retrieving items

Young children learn about organization by exploring organized areas within their homes, such as pantries and linen closets or silverware drawers and tool boxes and investigating how their parents stack pots, plates, and other dishes; match shoes and socks; and file papers such as important correspondence or other materials such as wrapping paper or decorations. Parents need to encourage such exploration, and teachers can help make students aware of the special importance of doing so.

Following Directions

Following directions includes:

- attending to verbal or signed instructions to initiate and complete activities
- attending to written instructions or instructions in symbolic systems, such as calendar boxes (see Chapter 4 for more about calendar boxes)

Following directions is both an important life skill and one that is fundamental to completing any kind of assigned task or chore. Children who are blind or who have low vision may need hand-under-hand demonstrations or physical guidance (described in Chapter 5 on sensory efficiency) to understand what they are being asked to do, and adults need to use this technique to engage them in the steps of activities.

Games involving songs and nursery rhymes, such as Ring-around-the-Rosie, the Hokey Pokey, or One, Two, Buckle My Shoe, are an effective, fun, and entertaining way to introduce children to following directions. These nursery rhymes and songs also help them with counting, basic concepts, and body imagery. Students who are blind or have very limited functional vision may need to be taught what to do at the appropriate times in these activities. A useful approach is what is referred to as *co-active movement*, in which an adult moves with the child through the movements of an activity. For example, to show children how to make a small circle holding hands, facing the center of the circle, and moving with the other children (left or right) while singing Ring-around-the-Rosie it is best to go through the motions with them (even sitting down at the verbal cue, "We all fall down!"), rather than simply telling them what to do. Once they know the routine, children can usually perform on their own, or they can be asked "What do you need to do?" or, instructed, "You need to hold hands and form a circle with your friends to play Ring-around-the-Rosie."

Information about Work

Information about jobs and work roles is acquired at every stage of career education, with students' knowledge building on what they have learned before. Young children typically start by learning what jobs are being performed by members of their families and other adults they know in the community. Children with visual disabilities need to know more than these adults' job titles. They need to learn about the locations, clothing, tools, and equipment associated with each job, along with which jobs are performed behind-the-scenes at various worksites. One important strategy is to have children visit worksites with their parents and significant other adults in their lives and explore the work environment, meet the workers, and learn what's going on at the workplace. In addition to suggesting this strategy to parents, teachers can plan visits to different community locations to expose children to different kinds of jobs.

Caregivers and professionals need to talk about the work they see occurring in the community and whenever possible take children who are visually impaired up close so that they can inspect and learn what's being done and how. For example, a teacher of students with visual impairments might notice that the school custodian, with whom the visually impaired student will likely have had minimal contact, waxes the floor in the gymnasium once a week. The teacher might ask him for a few minutes of his time to explore the work task being performed and his tools with the student. In this way, the student can tactilely explore the buffer; learn how the polishing pads are put on and taken off, how the wax is applied, how the task is performed—the pattern that the custodian follows to cover the entire floor with wax and then polish it; smell the wax and feel it before it is applied and after it hardens on the floor, and so forth. The teacher and student might also visit the school nurse or the secretary in the office to learn about their jobs and the tools they use.

Positive Work Habits

Positive work habits and behaviors include, for example:

- following instructions
- assuming responsibility for one's self and possessions
- being prompt
- completing tasks in a timely way
- cooperating while at play, in classes, or at work

To develop good work habits, children who are blind or visually impaired need to hear from others when their behaviors are satisfactory and when they fall short. They also need adults surrounding them who will express their expectations and then hold the children to those expectations, rather than people who tend to make special allowances or excuses for them or allow misbehavior.

Basic Work Skills

In addition to basic academic skills, such as reading, writing, speaking, listening, and calculating, young children need to learn basic work skills. These skills include, for example:

- sorting
- assembling things that need to be put together
- using hand tools like scissors and staplers
- matching items by size or shape or texture
- building and dismantling things
- using adapted tools or equipment like audible scales and tactile measuring devices
- organizing possessions

Too often, well-intentioned adults do things for children with visual impairments because they think such tasks cannot be done, or are too dangerous to be done, by the children themselves. Typically, young children learn to cut with scissors that have rounded ends and are fairly blunt and then they progress to using sharper, pointed scissors. Children with visual impairments need to learn how to use scissors in the same fashion. If children with visual impairments do not learn basic work skills at home and in school at the same time as children their age or earlier, they may encounter situations in their later lives in which they are more vulnerable because they don't know how to use hand tools properly or haven't been given opportunities to practice with them. Because many children with visual impairments may not have seen others doing these activities, they will not be able to emulate valuable role modeling and demonstration. For this reason, it is time well spent to expose students with impaired sight to these skills earlier than their fully sighted peers.

In general, children typically learn basic work skills by performing simple tasks or chores at home, as they are learning early independent living skills, and later in school and in the community. Children who are blind or visually impaired need to be encouraged to do the same, as explained in Sidebar 11.2 and in the learning activity "Home Helper" found at the end of this chapter. More information about helping parents to teach their children to perform such everyday chores appears in the section on working with parents, and also in Chapter 8.

Incidental Information

Information about the world and how it operates—for example, such concepts as time of day and year or accepted social conventions—are important for young children to learn in order to become independently functioning individuals in society and also because such basic knowledge is essential within the school community and, ultimately, the workplace social milieu. As already noted, children with visual impairments may not be able to learn such concepts incidentally and therefore need to be taught directly and through hands-on experience what other people are doing and how things happen in their homes and schools. These rules and concepts can then be applied in home, school, community, and work settings.

CONCEPTS RELATED TO TIME

- Understanding morning, noon, evening, dawn, dusk, and so on, and their implications for activities at home, school, and in the community.
- Being on time and what constitutes lateness.
- Learning about time commitments that parents and others make to work—for example, that firefighters and police officers work different schedules from store clerks, and that store clerks may work on holidays because their stores have sales but that office workers will likely have the holiday free.

SOCIAL RULES AND EXPECTATIONS OF THE LARGER SOCIETY

- Using social etiquette such as saying "please" and "thank you."
- Not interrupting others when they are speaking.
- Greeting people and responding to their greetings.

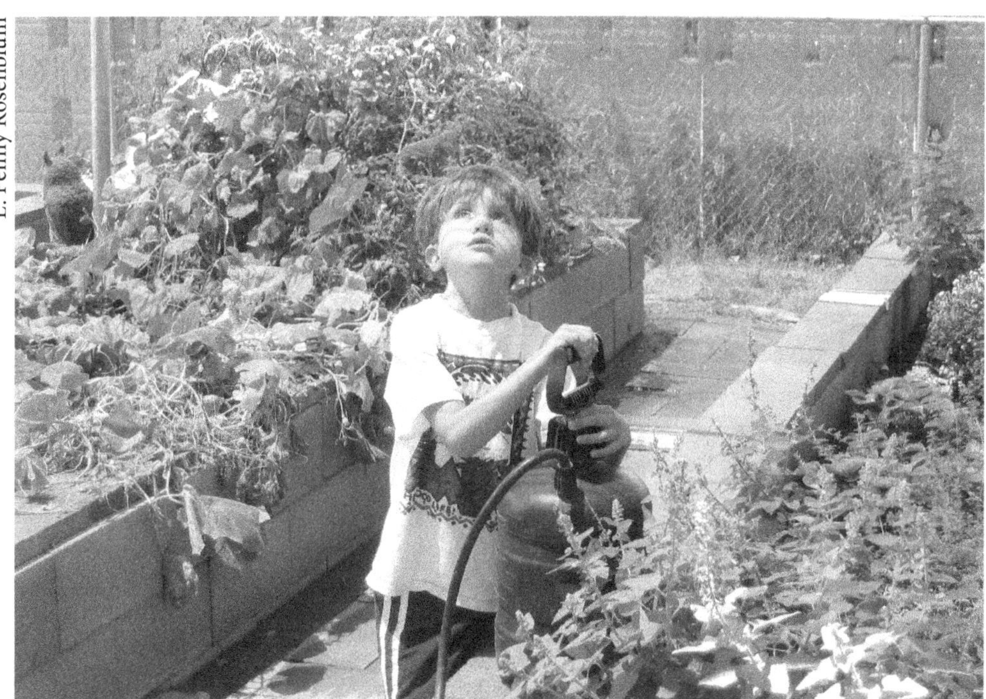
L. Penny Rosenblum

While helping in the garden, this boy is learning early work skills in addition to independent living skills.

SIDEBAR 11.2

Chores at Home and in School: Learning Basic Work Skills and Habits

Chores present teachers and families with opportunities to help children learn about working and develop good work-related skills and behaviors. Students with visual impairments need to do the same tasks that students without visual impairments are expected to do, such as helping around the house and doing assigned jobs in the classroom.

Teachers can suggest to families that children be taught to do chores at home. Chores may consist of any activities the family and child need to attend to for comfortable living. Depending on a child's age and physical abilities, these might include:

- picking up and putting away toys
- folding and hanging up clothing
- putting dirty clothes in a hamper or the washing machine
- sorting or doing laundry
- setting the table or getting out eating utensils for the family
- making beds
- washing and drying dishes
- taking out the trash
- watering plants
- feeding and walking the dog or taking care of other pets
- watching younger children in the family
- sweeping or mopping the floor
- vacuuming and dusting
- working in the yard and garden
- washing and vacuuming family vehicles

In the classroom, teachers can assign children who are visually impaired a variety of tasks including:

- passing out supplies or worksheets
- putting away art supplies or playground equipment
- taking attendance
- conveying messages to the main office
- cleaning up the classroom
- taking care of classroom pets or plants

Eventually, the skills learned in completing such chores can become the basis for student's early paid work experiences—perhaps a job running errands, raking leaves, or pet sitting for extended family members, neighbors, or family friends and acquaintances. Parents or teachers may need to work beside the student initially to be sure she can apply skills she has learned in one setting—home or school—to the other.

THE SEASONS OF THE YEAR AND REPRESENTATIVE ACTIVITIES. Particularly with holidays, children can participate in social and community-based activities and learn work-related skills, such as cooking, planning parties, and decorating their homes and classrooms at school.

- Understanding holidays and holiday traditions for families and community—for example, Thanksgiving occurs in the fall and is when many people provide food to families in need as well as give thanks for what they have, or July 4th is celebrated with fireworks, flags, and barbeques.
- Learning about conditions and activities associated with the seasons—for example, summer is often associated with sunshine, beaches, sand and swimming; winter with snow, ice, shorter days, and sledding.

Career Exploration

For students moving into middle school, career education becomes more focused on investigating various jobs to determine which jobs and careers are of interest to them and are feasible based on their interests, abilities, skills, and values. A related effort is investigating what further skill development or knowledge they will need to pursue to prepare for jobs of interest. Work in the component of career exploration typically begins when students enter middle school and is completed in the first or second year of high school. If students with visual impairments have been encouraged to learn and apply what they have learned during the stage of career awareness, they will in effect also have begun to explore careers. They will have an established awareness of what kinds of jobs are available in their communities and perhaps beyond. In the career exploration phase, they can begin to work on deepening that awareness by exploring options that match their interests, abilities, values, and personalities.

The skills and knowledge that students need to acquire during the career exploration stage include a variety of components, including:

- time management
- advanced content, skills, and techniques
- understanding related positions within a profession
- refinement of work habits
- ability to articulate vocational interests, abilities, skills, values, and liabilities

Time Management

As they grow, students need to participate in a variety of family, secular, school, extracurricular, and religious activities. As children mature, they are expected to do more and more in the way of household chores, schoolwork, and extracurricular responsibilities. By the time students are in the career exploration phase, these responsibilities require so much time and attention that priorities need to be set and some activities culled. This process—balancing what has to be done for home and school with what students want to do—whether performed consciously or unconsciously, encourages students to consider their innate talents, learned skills, and values. The narrowing of commitments and prioritizing of responsibilities is a precursor to deciding what career to pursue.

Advanced Content, Skills, and Techniques

Developing areas of knowledge that are relevant to students' future academic and vocational aspirations prepares students to succeed in both life and work. As students refine and enhance their knowledge, skills, and abilities—including their compensatory, sensory, and assistive technology skills—they apply what they've learned in their everyday experiences and examine how their performance matches up to or surpasses that of their classmates. This evaluation against others helps children determine what areas of work or careers would be most appropriate for them based on their interests and talents.

Understanding Related Positions within a Profession

Understanding how jobs of interest are related and how certain sets of jobs require similar skills and abilities helps students explore the kinds of jobs that they might want to do. For instance, if a student thinks she'd like to be a buyer for a clothing store, it can help her to understand that buyers fall into the broader category of sales and service occupations so that she can also investigate related jobs (such as sales representatives) and fields (like marketing, public relations, or promotions). The Bureau of Labor Statistics (2012) *Occupational Outlook Handbook,* which is also available on an interactive website (www.bls.gov/ooh), provides detailed information about different careers in 25 occupational groups.

Refinement of Work Habits

Specific work habits, skills, and behaviors are critical to maintaining a job and a career, including:

- demonstrating good attendance
- being punctual
- cooperating
- following complex written and oral instructions
- managing time, space, materials, and money properly and reliably
- being trustworthy
- exhibiting self-initiative

Refined work habits such as these are critical extensions of the organizational skills learned in the career awareness component as well as in the compensatory access and independent living skills areas of the ECC. Students with visual impairments need to be responsible for tracking their performance in terms of attendance and punctuality. To develop skills in this area, teachers can encourage students to use an electronic or hardcopy (print or braille) calendar to keep track of school assignments, recreational or school-related events, and other types of obligations, such as doctor's appointments.

Students who are visually impaired also need to receive consistent verbal and written feedback from the teachers, coaches, and other significant adults in their lives about these work habits. Students who cannot see the impact of their behaviors on others need to hear about how their performance and behavior affects others in their lives (both children and adults). For instance, if a visually impaired student trips another student with his or her cane or bumps into someone on the playground or in the cafeteria, whether or not the student apologizes, he is unlikely to see the reaction of the other students or observers. The student may need someone to describe how others' facial expressions and body language indicate how they were affected by what happened. Students also need to know how their performance compares to that of other students their age; for example, what is their ranking in the class with regard to attendance? How many times have they been late in comparison to the other students?

Ability to Articulate Vocational Interests, Abilities, Skills, and Values

Students need to investigate what they might want to do in life based on their innate talents (abilities), what they've learned to do well (skills), what they enjoy doing (interests), and what's important to them (values). During this period, students need to examine themselves closely and determine what they have to offer an employer. There are a vast number of activities that can help students learn more about work in general and their specific vocational interests, abilities, skills, and values. Sidebar 11.3 lists a selection of activities; others are detailed in the learning activities at the end of this chapter.

Students ultimately need to be aware of their own preferences and the challenges they will face as they move into the labor market. Students who are visually impaired may need help with identifying their best abilities—areas in which their performance is as good or better than other students' work. Teachers can, for example, share anonymous examples of other students' work, put into an accessible format, so that visually impaired students can see how their work compares to those other students' efforts. Similarly, teachers can announce how many students in the class received each score on an assignment or test so that students who cannot see others' work can understand how their effort compares.

SIDEBAR 11.3

Investigating Career Interests, Abilities, Skills, and Values

Students in the career exploration phase of career education can investigate their vocational interests, abilities, skills, and values through activities such as those listed below. Students beginning career exploration may start with activities such as reading about careers, going on field trips to workplaces, and listening to guest speakers. Then, students can move on to perform volunteer work or internships and paid work on their own, and may become involved in job shadowing. As students progress into the later stages of career preparation and career placement, they will continue to be involved in these activities, but with greater emphasis on investigating specific interests and careers that they have identified and actual workplace experiences.

READING ABOUT CAREERS

Give students plenty of opportunities to read about work in general, and what jobs of specific interest require in terms of workers' talents, skills, abilities, values, and personality characteristics. Students with visual impairments need to read about work being performed by individuals with disabilities, including those with blindness and low vision, as well as about jobs being performed by individuals without disabilities. Having students read biographies and autobiographies is an excellent assignment to encourage this kind of general exploration of careers.

WORKSITE VISITS

The teacher can take classes to workplaces such as fire stations, police stations, bakeries, museums, nature preserves, pioneer villages, or city halls. These experiential learning opportunities can help students learn firsthand what is involved in performing a variety of jobs. They can find out about details, including:

- typical wages
- work schedules
- tools and equipment used by the workers
- uniform or typical apparel, including any safety features
- where such jobs are located
- popularity of the job
- qualifications, knowledge, skills, and abilities required

Students with visual impairments may need to be given specific assignments to capture information beyond what is obvious. For instance, they may benefit from an assignment to find out how many workers are at the location visited, what their job titles are, what they do on a daily basis, and what tools they use. As an example, a popular field trip for elementary and middle school students is a trip to an aquarium or zoo. Since children with visual impairments may find some of the exhibits uninteresting if they are not allowed to touch or get too close, the experience can be enhanced by making such a visit a cooperative learning experience, in which children work together in groups to learn or accomplish a task. The teacher can give the students assignments to complete together, such as:

- identify a certain number of mammals and reptiles and the attributes of the animals that enable them to camouflage themselves or attract mates
- research a variety of jobs being performed at the zoo before their visit and to choose which types of workers to interview
- interview one of the animal handlers or curators

When the trip is finished, the students can all report back what they've learned.

GUEST SPEAKERS

Invite guest speakers with and without visual impairments to class to talk about their work lives and how they obtained their jobs. Talks can cover a variety of topics, including:

- training
- experiential learning (learning by doing on the job or by doing related activities)
- career progression and path taken to current position
- daily work
- likes and dislikes

Often a teacher will invite people with disabilities to expand students' understanding of diversity; for instance, an adult who is blind may want to share information about reading and writing with braille or using a dog guide as well as talk about his work life. When these opportunities arise, the teacher of students with visual impairments or parent of a student with visual impairment can encourage students who are blind or have low vision to also ask questions about the speaker's career—what roles he plays, what jobs he has held, how he manages his responsibilities, what assistive technology and disability-specific skills he uses on a daily basis, and what his current work entails.

CAREER PORTFOLIO

A career portfolio is a collection of documentation about a student's interests, abilities, skills, and values that is saved for future reference. This documentation can include:

- assessment results
- evidence of input shared formally with students such as grade reports, awards, certificates, and so forth
- information obtained from Internet and library searches, readings, films or videos about careers and positions within those careers
- documentation of any work experiences (volunteer or paid), the tasks accomplished, dates of engagement, and the employers, who may also serve as future references
- photographs of the students at work or accomplishing tasks that demonstrate their abilities or skills. Photographs that show students working with hand tools or equipment that might be used on a job site can be particularly valuable, as they can be used to show prospective employers evidence of ability.

For students with multiple disabilities who may not be able to easily articulate their attributes, a career portfolio is of critical importance because it not only documents for the students and their families what has been accomplished toward achieving career goals, it also helps service providers and ultimately prospective employers understand what interests, abilities, skills, and values the students possess. Career portfolios provide tangible records of the kinds of work-related activities students have participated in and show the skills and work habits they've developed.

INFORMATIONAL INTERVIEWS

To perform an informational interview, students need to develop a series of questions about jobs or careers and then reach out to adults in those work situations to interview them about their work responsibilities and training. Informational interviewing is not about applying for work; rather, it is about seeking information about jobs of interest. For future reference, students should keep a record—either a summary or a full transcript or recording—of every informational interview they accomplish. The career portfolio is an ideal storage place for their informational interviews.

VOLUNTEER WORK

Many community-based organizations rely on unpaid volunteers to help with routine tasks such as fundraising and promotional work, while others use volunteers to help with special projects such as neighborhood clean up after severe weather. Performing volunteer

(continued on next page)

SIDEBAR 11.3 *continued*

work gives students the opportunity to explore a variety of jobs and responsibilities and determine whether they are of sufficient interest to want to prepare for similar paid employment. Employers may be more open to engaging inexperienced workers or students with disabilities as volunteers than as paid employees. For students, volunteering is an opportunity to work and explore a potential career field without the productivity demands of paid employment or making a long-term commitment to an employer.

Teachers can help their students find volunteer opportunities by helping local organizations and agencies understand the importance of opening their doors to students with visual impairments and encouraging the students to help out in their communities. Hospitals, nursing homes, recreation centers, churches, synagogues, schools, day care centers, food banks, and many other organizations welcome volunteers and will make spots available for students with visual impairments if they understand what the students' abilities are and how to make the environment accessible to them.

JOB SHADOWING

Participating in job shadowing, in which a student follows a worker in a profession of interest through some portion of his or her day, can help students learn about the responsibilities of the worker through observation and asking questions. If a student is unable to visually observe working conditions, the teacher may want to send a pair of students—one with sight and one with a visual impairment—into a job shadowing experience to work together to analyze what's going on at the worksite. The sighted student can take the lead for visual observation and the blind student can take the lead in asking questions and recording the worker's responses.

Job shadowing experiences may last for an hour, half a day, a full day, or longer periods of time, depending on the availability of the worker and the student's needs. Teachers, working with rehabilitation counselors or school vocational instructors, can help identify an appropriate work setting and arrange for a student to shadow an employed adult. Occupations that lend themselves to job shadowing typically don't require security clearances or pose serious safety concerns to untrained observers. Office environments, restaurants, retail businesses, and service providers are ideal locations for job shadowing. The notes students collect during their job shadowing experiences can be added to their career portfolios.

Students also need to be encouraged to explore how their interests and talents can lead to new opportunities. For instance, a student who is interested in music or sports needs to explore how that interest might be parlayed into more advanced school-based activities, such as auditioning for the school band or competing for a place on the swim team, or even into some type of work such as playing with a band for pay or collecting tickets at sports events.

During career exploration, students begin to define themselves and determine where their strongest talents, knowledge, skills, and abilities lie. Through this process of self-exploration and analysis of career options, they identify the kinds of courses and activities they will be engaged in during high school and in postsecondary settings. It is important that students with visual impairments receive realistic feedback concerning their performances at home, school, and in the community throughout their elementary and middle school years. This feedback, and having access to work environments through structured exploration (reading, going on field trips, hearing from workers in various jobs, and participating in job shadowing), can help students understand which job options are appealing. Middle school is the time for skill refinement and an initial narrowing of interests in preparation for work and adult responsibilities. It is also the ideal time for visually impaired students to begin volunteering in their communities.

Career Preparation

Career preparation is the career education component that focuses on learning the knowledge and skills needed to enter into a particular career that a student might have identified during the stage of career exploration. It takes place primarily during high school for most students, but students with visual impairments, including those with additional disabilities, are served most effectively when career preparation starts earlier. Students with visual impairments can benefit tremendously from engagement in volunteer work in middle school or junior high school that highlights

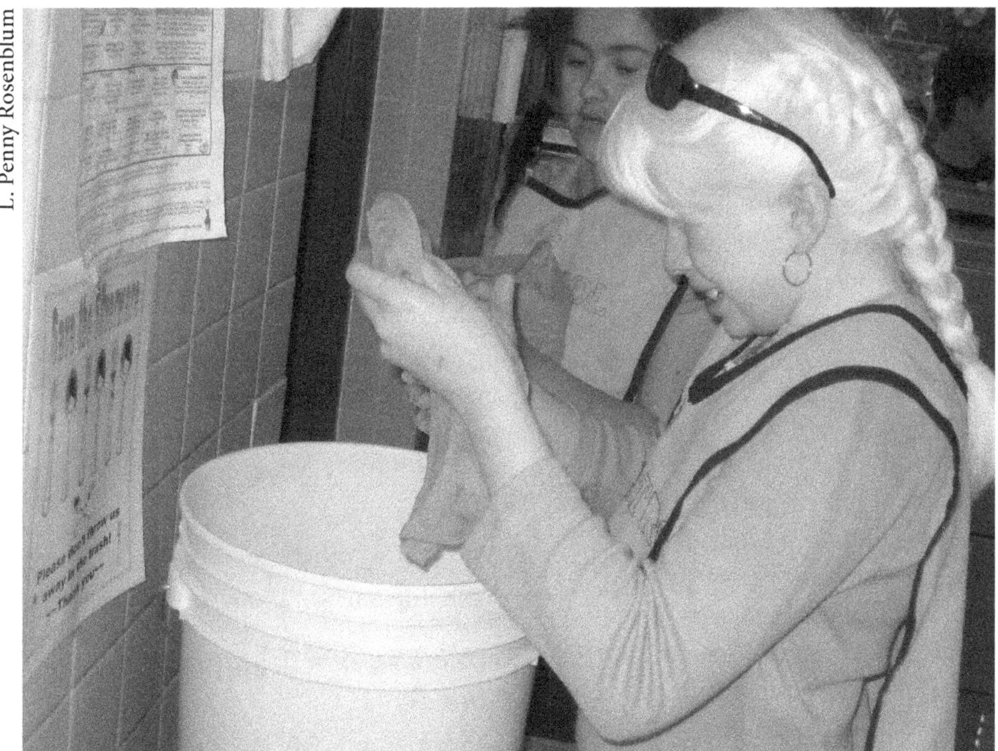
L. Penny Rosenblum

Volunteering as a helper, as here in the school cafeteria, is a good way to learn work-related skills.

what they know and can do, as well as where their deficits are.

Students who are visually impaired generally learn best by doing, and learning about work is no different. At this stage, students can be working at school and in the neighborhood or community at large, doing paid or volunteer tasks, such as babysitting, helping with yard work, washing cars, and caring for pets. As students mature, they are typically encouraged to participate in volunteer experiences, part-time work during and after school, summer jobs, or work-study programs, and it is important that students with visual impairments have the same opportunities as their sighted classmates do. The more opportunities that students have to actively participate in work, the more they will learn about jobs, careers, what they are good at doing, and what they enjoy.

The knowledge, skills, and abilities students need to develop or refine during high school to be prepared to move into work or to participate in career-related postsecondary training include:

- application of learned concepts in daily roles and responsibilities
- clear life and career values
- personal and vocational goals
- an understanding of available work and life resources
- interpersonal skills
- ability to select, use, and maintain equipment and tools
- self-esteem and self-reliance

Application of Learned Concepts in Daily Roles and Responsibilities

Students should be able to do more than simply respond to test items correctly—they need to be able to perform tasks using the knowledge and skills they've been taught in school. Examples include:

- Using math skills to set up and manage a checking account or to apply for a credit card and assume responsibility for paying the balances due.
- Using language arts skills to correspond with prospective mentors about career opportunities.
- Using science skills developed for a science fair project to present accomplishments to a prospective employer or advisor.

Clear Life and Career Values

Most people are likely to feel most comfortable and work most effectively when their careers or jobs align with their values. Teachers can help students with values clarification in a number of ways, primarily through discussion related to class activities and lessons, interpretation of stories and reading assignments, and consideration of community and world events. Through assessment, instruction, and monitoring of behavior, teachers can point out to students what their values seem to be, and give them feedback to that effect. (For further information about instructional activities related to values clarification, see Gevirtz Graduate School of Education, 2012; Raths, Harmin, & Simon, 1978; Simon, Howe, & Kirschenbaum, 1972).

Personal and Vocational Goals

By the time students are in high school, it is important for them to have mastered the ability to solve problems and set goals. If they haven't done so, at this point they need to come to understand that employers will expect them to bring these skills with them to the workplace. Setting goals and devising plans to achieve them requires the ability to think creatively and problem solve. One way to foster these skills is to encourage students to participate in the development and implementation of their Individualized Education Programs (IEPs), by attending IEP meetings, advocating for what they need and want to accomplish while in high school, and documenting their progress toward achieving their goals. Students should come to IEP meetings with an understanding of their challenges (for example, the skills or knowledge they still need to acquire to help them attain a job or placement into postsecondary training programs) and be prepared to set goals to resolve those issues—such as, determine a career objective and figure out what classes they want to take that will help them prepare for that career—and incorporate those goals into their IEP.

An Understanding of Available Work and Life Resources

During career preparation, students need to investigate the financial, emotional, social, and physical assistance their family members and community agencies or service providers may have available to support them in their pursuit of training, education, or career goals. They need to learn how to allocate the time, money, materials, space, and energy necessary to accomplish their career goals. For instance, a student may realize that he needs help to pay his tuition for appropriate training. He would need to research what options were available to him: financial support from his parents, an educational loan from the government, a tuition waiver from a postsecondary institution, financial assistance from vocational rehabilitation, and so forth. Most students at this stage need to be able to determine, based on research and thoughtful consideration, what help they will need beyond graduation, and a sense of how they might obtain the help they need. Students with severe cognitive impairments may need an advocate to do such research for them.

Interpersonal Skills

A variety of interpersonal skills are important in the area of career education, including:

- interacting effectively, such as the ability to meet and greet new people, put people at ease with disability concerns, and initiate and maintain a conversation with peers and strangers
- working in teams
- teaching and leading others
- working with different kinds of people

Ability to Select, Use, and Maintain Equipment and Tools

Students need to know about the high-, medium-, and low-tech tools required to perform competitively in postsecondary and work settings, such as:

- high-tech: desktop or laptop computers, tablets, electronic notetakers
- medium-tech: digital recorders, cell phones, general office equipment
- low-tech: mechanical braillewriters, optical devices, non-mechanized tools

Students also need to develop the ability to use equipment and tools to

- acquire, evaluate, and use information (complete research-driven projects)
- organize and maintain data files (produce and retrieve data gathered for work)
- communicate with and use electronic and social media sites efficiently

Self-Esteem and Self-Reliance

In the area of career preparation, demonstrating self-esteem and self-reliance means students are able to:

- match and coordinate their interests, abilities, and values with career options
- find and obtain jobs with minimal or no external assistance
- maintain their jobs

Engaging in work experiences, whether voluntary or paid, is critical to the career preparation phase for students with visual impairments. Too often an emphasis on the acquisition of academic skills can preempt engagement in work for students. However, without work experiences in middle and high school, students with visual disabilities may be unprepared for the next stage of their lives. Preparation for postsecondary education or training needs to be connected to students' interests or career goals; otherwise, many students may have difficulty understanding its relevance.

Career Placement

Career placement, in which students are expected to find work outside of their home and school, should begin no later than high school and continue through early adulthood. It is the time when experiential learning or on-the-job training is important. During this period, many students find out as much about what they don't want to do for lifelong work as they do about what they do! The more paid and unpaid work-related opportunities that students take advantage of during their secondary and postsecondary experiences the better their understanding of what their choices in entry-level work are likely to be when they graduate from school and move into employment or actively begin to search for jobs on their own.

The career placement component focuses on students' application of what they have learned in the previous stages of career education about the importance of work; their own knowledge, skills, and abilities; and the specific skills for the fields they would like to pursue, and begin to work, if possible, in jobs that are related to their career goals. Up until this point, learning in school and at home has dominated their time, and resources have been almost exclusively devoted to enhancing their repertoire of knowledge and skills. The shift from home and school to the outside world is inherent in career placement—at this time, students are expected to make the transition into adulthood and adult responsibilities. If further study is needed at the postsecondary level, the expectation is that the study will be relevant to a chosen career and focused on developing skills specific to jobs within that field.

Although the knowledge and skills that are critical for students in the career placement stage may overlap and at times seem redundant with those in earlier stages, they will be more sharply focused on the future for young adults in transition from school to work. What is essentially different regarding career placement is that students are expected to find work outside their home and school environments, apply what they have learned there, and ultimately achieve independence through their efforts. At this stage, students need to develop and master the following skills and abilities:

- preparing for and participating in career-related training
- participation in work experiences
- refining work-related skills and habits through volunteering
- pursuing advanced career-related information
- refining interests and experiences based on work trials
- preparing for post-graduation support
- planning for life and career advancement

Preparing for and Participating in Career-Related Training

Many young adults with visual impairments will need or want to attend training after high school in order to reinforce or develop their vocational skills. They may attend a community college or technical school and work toward a certificate indicating they have marketable skills in certain occupational areas, or they may choose to attend a four-year college or university to earn a degree or certificate related to what they want to do for work following graduation. During high school, students who intend to continue their training beyond high school need to research which schools or training programs offer the training they need, determine the entry-level requirements for participation, and make application to those programs.

Participation in Work Experiences

For students in high school, work experiences tend to occur after school, on weekends, or during school holidays. Many youngsters have early experiences with community-based work close to home such as babysitting, pet sitting, camp counseling, tutoring after school, and working at retail stores, grocery stores, or local offices. Young adults with visual impairments need to do these same kinds of activities with support, if necessary, from family and instructional staff, and need to use assistive technology and alternative skills in these environments to perform competitively. In some states or countries, rehabilitation agencies or nonprofit organizations offer assistance to students who are visually impaired as they search for early jobs. Teachers and parents can facilitate contact with such service providers to encourage students to participate in their programs or seek their assistance with finding work. (See the Resources section at the end of this chapter for other sources of information and assistance.)

Young adults with visual impairments who attend university or college programs can, usually as part of their financial aid package, also participate in work-study programs. These programs provide students with part-time on-campus positions such as computer lab assistants, library clerks, administrative assistants in academic departments, and the like. If students are unable to work during the academic year, they may want to find jobs in the summer and during breaks between semesters or academic quarters, if at all possible.

Refining Work-Related Skills and Habits through Volunteering

Teachers and parents can encourage young adults to be actively involved in volunteering their time through secular or religious organizations in local communities (see Sidebar 11.3). While attending school or participating in extracurricular activities, students with visual impairments need to track their attendance and punctuality and gather examples of their other work-related skills and habits for future reference. For example, if a student competes on the debate team or publishes an article in the school newspaper, these accomplishments, which are evidence of work-related skills and habits, can be documented in a career portfolio and used when approaching prospective employers. Teachers and related service providers can assist in this area by helping students with visual impairments perceive how their performances compare to those of other students without vision problems. If a student with visual impairment is not doing as well in these areas as classmates without disabilities, it may be necessary to set goals to improve performance—for example, to decrease the amount of time it takes to complete work-related assignments by five minutes every two weeks until a student can do them as quickly as her classmates—and document efforts to achieve those goals over time.

Pursuing Advanced Career-Related Information

During the earlier stages of the career education process, career-related information will have typically been acquired from reading books, journals, newspapers, and online material. Once students have gathered information through reading and research online, they can reach out to adults working in the fields they like to arrange informational interviews (as described in Sidebar 11.3 and in the "Workers I Know" learning activity at the end of this chapter). They may also want to seek out prospective career mentors—adults working in fields of interest who are amenable to supporting or providing guidance to a young person through the early stages of her or his career. If possible, it can be very helpful to a young adult to make contact with an adult who is working in a field of interest who is also visually impaired. (See the Resources section at the end of this chapter for sources of assistance for locating prospective mentors with visual impairments.) Other ways to gain more advanced career information include participation in long-term job shadowing (see Sidebar 11.3) lasting six weeks to six months, internships, and apprenticeships.

Job shadowing is an appropriate activity for students who are still in secondary school and don't have time in their schedules for actual work experiences. As part of a six-week project, for example, students might sign up to observe and work without pay beside someone in a job similar to one they are interested in doing. Students should be asked to complete a job analysis for each job they observe (an example of a completed job analysis is included in Figure 11.1). Typically part of postsecondary training, apprenticeships and internships, in which a student works under the supervision of a master craftsman or seasoned professional, can be part of standard training requirements for some occupational or professional areas. Students may also independently seek out internship opportunities to gain advanced knowledge about jobs of interest.

Refining Interests and Experiences Based on Work Trials

It may be necessary to provide work trials for students with visual impairments and additional disabilities to see where they perform most effectively and are most comfortable. These experiences can help refine career goals and determine if the work suits the student's personality and skills. In a work trial, a student is placed at a job site, usually with a job coach or trainer who assists with on-the-job training, for a defined period of time (weeks or months). This technique may also be useful with students who are visually impaired and uncertain about the kind of work they want to do. If a work trial is arranged for career exploration purposes, it will often include rotation through a variety of jobs at a particular location. For example, a student may do a work trial at a grocery store and work for a short period of time in the deli section cutting and wrapping meats or cheeses, then

FIGURE 11.1

Sample Completed Job Analysis Form

Name: Clara Cluster **Date:** 8/21/2013

Job Title: Food Service Worker **Sources:** Occupational Outlook Handbook, O*NET

Purpose: *Food service workers serve food and drinks to customers and make sure that they have what they need for a pleasant dining experience (cutlery, napkins, condiments, and so forth).*

Setting and Physical Demands: *Food service workers work in restaurants or cafeterias, typically indoors but may be required to serve in outdoor settings such as patios as well. They are often standing for long periods of time. They often work evenings, weekends, and holidays. They often work part time.*

Major Tasks: *Food service workers typically do the following: Prepare and clean assigned work areas; replenish and stock service stations, cabinets, and tables; serve food and drinks to customers; greet customers, escort them to their seats, and hand them menus; answer customers' questions about menu items and specials; clean tables and dining areas; and set tables for new customers.*

Equipment and Tools Used: *Many restaurants use point-of-sale (POS) software on their computers. Other equipment often found in restaurants and cafeterias may include: carbonated and non-carbonated beverage dispensers, commercial coffee and/or iced tea makers, and garnishing tools.*

Qualifications (Knowledge, Skills, Abilities): *Food service workers are not required to have a high school diploma, though many do have a high school diploma or equivalency and some have college degrees. On-the-job training is required. Bilingual skills are preferred in some communities. Most importantly, employers look for people who are friendly, customer-service oriented, well-groomed, and display maturity and good judgment.*

Wages: Median wages (2010) *$8.72/hour, $18,130/year (40 hrs/week)*

Projected Growth: *Faster than average (14% to 19%)*

Additional Information Sources: *National Restaurant Association (http://www.restaurant.org)*

Related Occupations: *Bartenders, cashiers, cooks, food preparation workers, and waiters/waitresses*

Comments: *I need to find out if the cafeteria in my neighborhood provides on-the-job training or if I could get some training in the school cafeteria.*

shift to work in the back of the store with inventory management, then shift to working in the administrative department, and so forth. If a student is unable to do these jobs, he might be rotated through other jobs, such as wiping the grocery store shelves and dusting products, sweeping or mopping, or stocking shelves. The point is to cycle students through a variety of jobs to determine what they are interested in doing and where their performance is most successful.

Work trials are typically set up by vocational rehabilitation counselors or school-based vocational instructors or coordinators, people who have experience placing young adults with employers and who know the local job market. These individuals or teams find appropriate work opportunities, negotiate with employers for placement sites, and then coach or teach the student how to do the tasks required. Teachers often assist with analyzing the prospective worksites to determine what tools and techniques the student has learned that might assist with the work to be performed. Teachers might also provide direct instruction to the student on the job if a job coach is not available to perform that function.

Preparing for Post-Graduation Support

When young people with visual impairments leave the public school system at graduation from high school or in the academic year they turn 21 years old, they enter an environment with far fewer external supports than they may have received under the Individuals with Disabilities Education Act (IDEA), the federal law that regulates their education up to that point. IDEA mandates that all services, materials, and supports necessary for full access to education be made available to children with disabilities. After graduation, these services may or may not be available. Regardless, after a student leaves the public school system, these services are not mandated by federal legislation, so in order to receive available services to assist with integration into work and adult life, young adults with disabilities must know how to apply for those services. It is therefore important that young people who are visually impaired network with adult service providers while they are still in the public school system and covered under IDEA, so that there is not a gap in services when they need them.

If possible, students should begin the application process while they are still in high school for any services they'll need following completion of their high school education. For instance, if a student knows that she will need orientation and mobility (O&M) skills training or assistance with job training and finding employment, she may want to initiate an application for rehabilitation services in advance of high school graduation. Teachers are responsible for working with transition-aged students to identify post-school goals related to education or training, employment, and independent living (if applicable) and document those goals on their IEPs. Likewise, teachers are charged with identifying the services their students will need to receive during their final years of secondary school, and for noting those services on their IEPs. Teachers can work collaboratively with vocational rehabilitation and other adult service providers to help students find out how to obtain services from these professionals once they are out of high school.

Planning for Life and Career Advancement

At the career placement stage, it is necessary for students with disabilities to think actively and concretely about what they want from life and make plans to achieve the objectives they identify. Students need to understand the importance of setting short-term and long-term goals, both about what they want to achieve or acquire in their lives and about the kind of person they aspire to be. Teachers can encourage goal setting through their assignments—asking students to document what they want to achieve over the course of the term, the semester, the year, or further into the future, and asking students to describe how they plan to achieve their goals. (Activities to facilitate this process are available in the Resources section at the end of this chapter.) For students with multiple disabilities, person-centered planning, discussed earlier in this chapter and in Chapter 12, can be a key part of this process.

Planning is also a large part of what is required for career advancement throughout life. Students need to understand that there is a path to recognition and advancement. They need to learn how to determine what the path is and how to negotiate it by consulting their supervisors or using other strategies to identify how to move forward. Then, they need to develop a plan to make advancement a priority. Students with visual impairments may need to learn—from supportive adults in their lives and mentors on the job—how to approach an employer to obtain this kind of information and what behaviors or attitudes need to be demonstrated on the job to ensure that their worth is recognized.

Postsecondary Life

In an ideal scenario, career placement is well under way by the time students leave the public school system or enter postsecondary education. Career maintenance and mentoring of younger workers, the remaining two stages of the career education model described at the beginning of this chapter, are practiced by adults who have obtained jobs and are progressing toward their career goals or adults who have been placed by others, in the case of individuals with severe multiple disabilities, which may often include intellectual disability. Although it may seem incongruous to some that individuals with multiple disabilities can mentor others, they do so when they work by serving as an example to others. These two areas are not detailed here as they are beyond the scope of instruction in the ECC, although teachers and others working with students who are visually impaired will want to mention these stages to students so that they may anticipate them.

ASSESSMENT OF CAREER EDUCATION

It is vital that caregivers and professionals determine what a student knows and does, with or without assistance, before initiating a career education training plan. Although an all-in-one formal test that assesses the competencies of students with visual impairments in the area of career education does not exist, there are a number of assessment tools and strategies that professionals and family members may want to consider.

The assessment tool may be a simple, teacher-made checklist such as the one in Figure 11.2 (Wolffe, 2000, 2006b, 2012a), which can be used to observe a child

FIGURE 11.2

Sample Career Education Observation Checklist

OBSERVATION CHECKLIST

Student: ____________________

Placement: ____________________

Date of observation: __________ Observer: ____________________

Observation time: __________ Location: ____________________

Task(s) performed and skills utilized: ____________________

Work behaviors observed:	Yes	No	N/A
Is punctual	____	____	____
Initiates work	____	____	____
Follows instructions	____	____	____
Attends to task	____	____	____
Attends to detail	____	____	____
Cooperates	____	____	____
Works consistently	____	____	____
Dresses appropriately	____	____	____
Solicits help, as needed	____	____	____
Solves problems that arise during task	____	____	____
Interacts with coworkers	____	____	____
Follows work rules	____	____	____
Attends to safety concerns	____	____	____
Completes tasks	____	____	____
Puts tools and materials away	____	____	____

Comments: (List overall strengths and weaknesses. Make recommendations. Note level of supervision required to perform tasks assigned. For example, can student perform tasks independently when given verbal, signed, or written instructions? Can student perform with demonstration or tactile cues? How often does the student require prompting to stay on task? Does the student respond to certain people in the work environment more favorably than others? Note the accommodations necessary for the student to perform optimally.)

SOURCE: Adapted from Karen Wolffe, "Career Education," in Alan J. Koenig and M. Cay Holbrook (Eds.), *Foundations of Education (2nd ed.), Vol. 2: Instructional Strategies for Teaching Children and Youths with Visual Impairments* (New York: AFB Press, 2000), pp. 679–719.

working at home, in school, or on a formal worksite. Or, a more formal instrument may be used, such as the two checklists provided in Appendixes 11A and 11B, which were developed to evaluate overall understanding and competence in career education, and specific competencies for older students as they prepare to make the transition from school to work and adult responsibilities.

The Career Education Competencies Checklist (Appendix 11A; Wolffe, 2000) lists the various skills, abilities, and knowledge detailed in this chapter and is completed by simply checking the box beside each competency as the child accomplishes it. The Transition Competencies Checklist (Appendix 11B; Wolffe, 2011a) is a forced-choice instrument that asks the student to answer yes or no for each item on the checklist, with the exceptions of the questions about reading and writing preferences that ask the student to rank order preferences, and an open-ended query about work experiences. It is designed as a self-evaluation for students able to read and write to respond to the items, or for someone to complete for students unable to respond independently. The Transition Competencies Checklist assesses students' skills in the following areas:

- leisure and socialization
- problem-solving
- self-advocacy
- compensatory access (or alternative techniques to using vision)
- work experience

In addition, the Transition Competencies Checklist assesses students' understanding of the following areas:

- work based on real-life experiences (such as chores or engagement in community-based activities)
- career options and sources of information
- levels of ability and their impact on job placement
- career counseling content areas such as self-awareness, career exploration, job-seeking skills, job-maintenance skills, and employment skills
- employers' concerns

In addition to these two instruments designed for students with visual impairments, the *EVALS* package from the Texas School for the Blind and Visually Impaired (2007) also includes a career education checklist for visually impaired students that reflects core curriculum performance standards used in the state of Texas; website links for other states' performance standards are included.

As with other areas of the ECC, assessment resources designed specifically for children with visual impairments in the area of career education are limited. Nevertheless, a number of resources can be used by teachers and other professionals in evaluating students' skills and awareness in career education, and these tools are also listed in the resources for this chapter. Many teachers evaluate students with teacher-made checklists or use checklists or tools designed for other populations of students with and without disabilities. Tools designed for students with learning or intellectual disabilities that are often used with other special education students, including students with visual impairments, include the Council for Exceptional Children's *Life Centered Career Education Curriculum* (Brolin, 2004), which includes assessment instruments; the *Transition Skills Inventory* (Halpern, Herr, Doren, & Wolf, 2000); and the *Transition Planning Inventory* (Clark & Patton, 2009). To use these tools, teachers need to determine whether they can be made accessible for their visually impaired students; that is, whether the print versions can be enlarged or recorded or whether there are braille editions available. If the tool is available in an electronic format, as many now are, the teacher needs to ensure that students can navigate and respond to the instruments using their preferred reading and writing tools.

Many teachers and evaluators also assess students with visual impairments using career exploration and vocational interest, ability, and values tools designed for individuals without disabilities, such as those available through the U.S. Department of Labor Occupational Information Service (O*NET), and others, such as the young adult version of the Self-Directed Search (Holland, 1994). (See the Resources section at the end of this chapter for additional information.) For students with intellectual disabilities and low vision, the *Reading-Free Vocational Interest Inventory* (Becker, 2000) is often used, but it is not appropriate for use with students who are functionally blind because it is entirely pictorial.

The National Secondary Transition Technical Assistance Center (www.nsttac.org) maintains a listing of age-appropriate transition assessment tools, though information specific to individuals with visual impairments is not available on the site. If readers want to use any of these materials, it is essential to first evaluate them for accessibility and validity for individual students before giving them to students with visual impairments. An instrument's administration manual often contains useful information about the populations used to develop the evaluation and its availability in alternate formats. Other information to ascertain about a tool is whether it includes questions, tasks, or activities that are essentially visual or pictorial; if so, how could students with visual impairments access the information or perform the task, and would the task or information be meaningful to someone without vision? If the teacher chooses to use an instrument designed for use with populations other than those with visual impairments, the teacher will have to supplement the assessment with evaluation of the student's skills in other ECC areas, such as reading and writing with braille or optical devices, use of assistive technology, orientation and mobility, and so forth.

Once a student has been evaluated and his or her strengths, needs, and personal interests determined, it is important to incorporate both strengths and needs into the goals and objectives specified on the child's Individualized Family Service Plan (IFSP) or IEP and to evaluate the child's progress toward achieving those goals over time.

GENERAL CONSIDERATIONS FOR TEACHING CAREER EDUCATION

As has been emphasized throughout this chapter, career education needs to start as early as possible and in fact encompasses virtually all of life's activities. Teachers and parents should think about giving students the widest possible direct exposure to experiences and concepts related to work in the broadest sense.

In addition to providing students with information, knowledge, and skills related specifically to career education, it is important for parents, teachers, and other adults in children's lives to pay attention to the following five key factors, which should underlie all instructional efforts and interactions with students. Moreover, these factors are also critical to all other areas of the ECC and demonstrate the interconnection of career education with those areas.

Conveying High Expectations

The messages students with impaired vision will receive from the general public are often that individuals who are visually impaired are to be pitied and helped throughout their lives. Significant others in the lives of students with impaired vision need to counter these inaccurate messages by routinely conveying their high expectations of such students. Children need to hear that the people who know them and care about them believe that they can and will grow up to be successful, establish families, and contribute to the larger society through work and engagement in the community. Statements that convey high expectations include:

- "What do you need to do to prepare for school?"
- "I expect you to help out at home" (or at school, at church or synagogue, in the yard, in the neighborhood, or at Boy or Girl Scout troop meetings).
- "I expect you to actively participate in swimming" (or other sports).
- "I expect you to act your age."
- "What do you want to be when you grow up?"
- "I expect you to have a job and help support your family when you're an adult."

Adults' expectations of students with visual impairments need to be articulated, and when the students meet these expectations, they need to hear that their efforts were recognized and appreciated. If they don't perform or behave in the way that they are asked to, students need to hear that the caring adults in their lives are disappointed and expect them to improve; and adults also need to give students specific ideas for how to improve their performance and then monitor what happens.

Encouraging Socialization

Socialization is an aspect of career education that perhaps relies most heavily on incidental learning, which is learning that takes place by observing how others behave and the impact of those behaviors on other people. Many social nuances (such as flirting, cues to attend to or ignore, conveying subtle feelings to reinforce or reject another's interest, formality or informality of greetings) are conveyed nonverbally through body language, facial expression, and eye movements, and all of these conventions must be learned by children and students who are blind or who have low vision in order for them to be socially integrated into the sighted community. As discussed in Chapter 9 on social interaction, children need to learn how to interpret nonverbal behaviors, body language, and facial expressions and to convey their own messages nonverbally. When children with visual impairments exhibit an appropriate facial expression or indicate with their body language how they are feeling in a way that is understandable and unobjectionable to a sighted audience, they need positive, verbal feedback from those around them—parents, teachers, other service providers, and extended family members.

Although social interaction is covered in Chapter 9 of this book, it is important to recognize that the critical need for social skills in career education is twofold:

- Having positive relationships, such as friendships with schoolmates, helps children develop social networks that may help them find jobs later in life; it is through networking that most people find the best matches for themselves in the labor market.
- Developing good social skills and the ability to get along with others is imperative for keeping jobs and career advancement. If coworkers and supervisors like an individual, they are likely to

help that person retain employment and capture promotions; if they don't like an individual, they will not be supportive and may even sabotage that person's efforts on the job.

Developing Alternative Techniques

Alternative techniques are the competencies, skills, and procedures people with visual impairments learn as substitutes for using vision. Reading and writing with braille; using optical devices and other compensatory skills; using O&M skills to travel; using assistive technology to access computers and other mainstream technology; and using nonvisual approaches to independent living, job seeking, social interaction, and other functional life skills are all examples of alternative techniques. Alternative techniques are of critical importance in the lives of students with visual impairments because they enable them to access the world around them, which has been designed with sighted people in mind.

Students with visual impairments learn many alternative techniques from teachers of students with visual impairments, O&M specialists, and other professionals employed by education and rehabilitation agencies. While these capabilities are covered in the ECC primarily in areas relating to sensory efficiency, compensatory skills, assistive technology skills, and independent living skills, they are also important in the career education area. Students need to learn how to find job openings without being able to read written announcements, explain how they can do a job to someone with sight, describe and demonstrate their knowledge of technology and how to use assistive technology to perform on a job. Skills learned in the area of self-determination are also important in finding job opportunities and asserting the ability to handle job-related tasks. In addition, students must learn to perform other life skills, such as banking, managing time and money, comparing prices, completing forms, and so forth, tasks that most people rely on vision to perform.

Providing Realistic Feedback

Students with impaired vision need to receive realistic feedback from family members and significant others concerning their performance of tasks. Both strengths and weaknesses need to be reviewed with students, and they need to know how their performances compare to those of classmates without disabilities and to understand what's expected of typically developing students their age, as well as younger and older children.

Due to limitations that may be posed by their vision impairment, students who are blind or who have low vision may need additional time and practice to master content and activities in school and in life. They need to work toward this mastery and improvement over time so that as they mature, their performances become more and more similar (rather than different) to the performances of classmates with typical vision.

Children with visual impairments in school are often given time-and-a-half or double the amount of time as children without disabilities to complete work, tests, or classroom projects, regardless of whether or not the additional time is actually needed. Although they may need this extra time initially, students with visual impairments need to understand that classmates without disabilities do not receive the same allowance and that they will want to continuously strive toward accomplishing what other children their age do, and in the amount of time they are allowed, because those students will ultimately be their competitors in life and work environments. If they never receive realistic feedback, many students with visual impairments may leave school thinking that they will always be allowed to do less or perform more slowly than their sighted classmates or coworkers. Likewise, adults who care about these students need to consider how the students are performing in comparison to others their age so that they can provide students with a realistic understanding of and feedback on their performance. This effort requires adults to take the time to observe children and adolescents without visual impairments to see how they behave and how their performance in school, work, home, and the community is like or different from that of students with visual impairments.

Promoting Opportunities for Work Experiences

All children with visual impairments, regardless of the presence of additional disabilities or the extent of their visual impairments, need to experience work as early as possible in their lives. For most children, first work experiences are typically obtained by doing chores at home, as described earlier in this chapter. Chores at home are often followed by helping out at school and in the neighborhood or community at large, on a voluntary or paid basis, depending on the child's interests, abilities, and circumstances. Students with visual impairments may need specific instruction in how to do certain tasks, such as babysitting, car washing, pet care, yard care, or other activities extended family members and neighbors might be willing to pay them to do. Once they've mastered the required skills, they may need to demonstrate how they can perform these jobs before strangers will be willing to hire them. Students with visual impairments can learn these skills and they need to experience the full range of work opportunities available to them—both for work experience and to have something socially appropriate to share with their peers who are also engaged in these early work activities. Parents and professionals need to be available to them to support them in the learning process and then they need to let them get under way!

These five overarching factors—conveying high expectations, encouraging socialization, developing alternative techniques, providing realistic feedback, and promoting opportunities for work experiences—are focuses to be shared by teachers, families, and other adults throughout a student's early childhood and ensuing life. They are addressed in detail with structured learning activities for children and adolescents with visual impairments in *Skills for Success* (Wolffe, 1999).

ROLE OF THE TEACHER OF STUDENTS WITH VISUAL IMPAIRMENTS

As with every other area of the ECC, the role of the teacher of students with visual impairments in the area of career education is multifaceted. It includes providing direct instruction in the specific skills students with visual impairments need to learn to pursue career education, collaborating with families and other service providers, sharing of information and resources, and modifying visual instruction so that it is accessible to students without vision or with severely impaired vision.

Provision of Direct Instruction

Following assessment of students' skills and knowledge in the area of career education, as described in the previous section, teachers of students with visual impairments are often called on to provide direct instruction in areas in which students exhibit a lack of knowledge and skills. During this process, the teacher needs to work in cooperation with the student or the student's parents or caregivers, depending on the student's age and functional abilities, to set goals and objectives in areas that appear to need attention. At a minimum, these goals and objectives need to be reevaluated annually for reporting on the student's IEP. The skills for which the teacher needs to provide instruction to students will flow from the assessed areas of need.

For example, if a young child is assessed using the *Career Education Competencies* checklist (see Appendix 11A) and there is evidence that the child has not learned to follow directions (spoken or signed), the teacher needs to work on developing that skill. The teacher should indicate on the student's IEP that learning to follow directions is a goal for both compensatory or academic access and career education, and is critical to participation in academic settings and employment. Or, the teacher may find that the student has identified a need for instruction in home management skills on the *Transition Competencies Checklist* (see Appendix 11B). In that case, the teacher may generate an action plan with the student, family members, and adult service providers to include on the student's transition plan and to guide direct instruction. The areas of knowledge or skills described in the previous sections of this chapter for each stage of career education offer the teacher guidance as to the kinds of content and activities appropriate for direct instruction of students with visual impairments. In addition, the learning activities at the end of this chapter provide ideas for helping to promote the development of skills.

Collaboration with Families and Other Service Providers

Teachers of students with visual impairments are responsible for the coordination of educational programs of students with visual impairments and often serve as case managers during their students' public school careers. They coordinate the services that students need to receive in order to benefit from the instruction they are receiving in school. They spend a considerable amount of time collaborating with families and other service providers, such as general education teachers, occupational therapists, physical therapists, speech and language specialists, orientation and mobility specialists, rehabilitation practitioners, and paraprofessionals, to ensure that everyone working with these students understands the impact that visual impairment may have on their ability to actively participate in the educational milieu.

Other people in the lives of students with visual impairments need to understand the critical importance of career education; developing this awareness is one of the teacher's critical roles. As described at the beginning of this chapter, it is important that career education instruction be started as early as possible in the life of a child who is visually impaired. Determining what knowledge can and ought to be included in the teaching of skills and building of expertise in this area is vital to a student's future well-being. Teachers may find themselves in the role of explaining career education and the needs children with visual impairment have for structured learning in this area, particularly with young children, because many people, including parents, assume that anything related to careers will occur much later in their children's lives. What others in the lives of these students need to understand is that career awareness will not happen surreptitiously or incidentally for these students because of their difficulties observing what is going on outside of their reach or visual abilities.

To help support a student in this essential area, the teacher will want to relate goals and objectives that are included on the student's IEP to career education-related skills whenever possible to reinforce instructional efforts in all areas and to help ensure coordination among service providers. For example, if the teacher of students with visual impairments, O&M specialist, parents, occupational therapist, and paraprofessional are all working on an aspect of identifying and counting money to make grocery purchases, and the student has an appropriate IEP goal that indicates this effort is a component of daily living skills or independent living skills, the teacher will want to indicate that it is also a career education goal and important in managing personal finances, which will be essential to the student as an adult with a job and family or lifestyle to support. In addition to helping all members of the student's educational team and the student understand the interconnectedness of career education and other areas of instruction (in the example of money management, math, reading, compensatory access, orientation and mobility, independent living, social integration, and sensory efficiency are all relevant), linking goals to career outcomes can help students and their families understand the reason for instruction in the classroom and can also increase the meaningfulness of school-based activities.

Another important element of collaboration is sharing of information and resources, which is discussed in the following section. This effort encourages all individuals working together to achieve a common goal—what is best for the child with a visual impairment—and to work in synch with one another. Often, the teacher of students with visual impairments is the most knowledgeable member of the team concerning the education of children with visual impairments, how to make the learning environment and educational materials accessible, and what resources are available to support team members in their work with students related to the ECC. In addition to helping to identify and define IEP goals and objectives, the teacher can help the other team members understand how to work with the student most effectively and, when the student is old enough, to help the student advocate for the meeting of his or her career education needs.

Information and Resource Sharing

Teachers of students with visual impairments share information and resources with families, related service providers, students, and others in the students' immediate environment, such as general and other special educators, paraprofessionals, school-based staff and administrators, as well as the general public. With families, the teacher shares information about career education in general and specific concerns for children with visual impairments in particular.

If possible, teachers need to share information and resources about career education as a component of early childhood intervention efforts. Although it may seem as though there is plenty of time to discuss career education later, the earlier this information and resource sharing happens, the better off the child will be as he or she moves from environment to environment—home to preschool, preschool to elementary school, elementary school to middle school, and high school to postsecondary training or work.

Early career education resources that the teacher may want to share with parents and other family members include:

- tip sheets on topics ranging from organizational skills to listening efficiency, age-appropriate chores, and checklists of skills for consideration as students mature
- books and journal articles on career education content and the lives of successful adults who are blind or visually impaired
- films and video recordings of activities and careers that adolescents and adults with visual impairments are engaged in across the world
- websites (see the Resources section at the end of this chapter)

Some of these materials are of immediate interest and some are for future reference, to reassure parents and help them recognize that their children can grow up to have successful, productive lives.

Specific career education resources that the teacher may want to introduce include books, such as *Skills for Success: A Career Education Handbook for Children and Adolescents with Visual Impairments* (Wolffe, 1999), and those that profile children and adolescents who are blind or have low vision, such as *Knots on a Counting Rope* (Martin & Archambault, 1987), *Brian's Bird* (Davis, 2000), *Ben and Buzzy's Busy Days* (Scannell, 2007), *All Children have Different Eyes: Learn to Play and Make Friends* (Glaser & Burgio, 2007), as well as the *Jobs that Matter* series from AFB, which profiles adults who are blind or visually impaired who are working as teachers, health care workers, and entrepreneurs (Kendrick, 1993, 1998, 2000, 2001). *The Transition Tote System* (Wolffe, 2012b) is a curriculum designed specifically for adolescents with visual impairments. It covers self-awareness, career exploration, and job-seeking and job-keeping skills, and also comes in a kit with manuals and materials for both student and teacher. Related information appears on the CareerConnect website (www.careerconnect.org) and the Project Aspiro website (www.projectaspiro.com). See the Resources section at the end of this chapter for these and other career resources that can be shared with families and other professionals.

Modification of Instruction and Materials

As in the other areas of the ECC, the teacher of students with visual impairments has traditionally been the professional who makes materials accessible to children with visual impairments in learning environments that are designed for fully sighted students. Based on assessments of the student's needs, including learning media and assistive technology assessments, the teacher produces or oversees the production of texts, worksheets, and other learning materials, as well as tests and related study guides, in braille, large print, electronic files, or other appropriate formats; trains students with low vision in the use of prescribed optical devices for reading and writing tasks at school; and produces or oversees the production of tactile graphics for access to diagrams, charts, maps, and other pictorial information when required.

In addition, teachers advise other educational personnel on how to make instruction accessible to students with visual impairments, for example by reading aloud what they post on the board or around the classroom, voicing when they would typically gesture or demonstrate using nonverbal techniques, asking open-ended questions of students to ensure they've understood concepts shared during lessons, seating the student in the best position for seeing or hearing classroom proceedings, and otherwise modifying the environment for better viewing or listening. Teachers also demonstrate to other professionals and paraprofessionals other aspects of working with students who are blind or who have low vision, such as sighted guide techniques, hand-under-hand or hand-over-hand instruction, tactile marking or labeling, and the like.

In addition to making these traditional modifications to instruction and materials related to career education areas, the teacher needs to make sure that students with visual impairments have opportunities from an early age to explore their environment and what adults and students, both their age and older, are doing in the school and community, as discussed earlier in this chapter. The most important modification to instruction in the area of career education is implementing an emphasis on active engagement with tools, equipment, and materials to promote an understanding of roles that others play. Whether it is the array of equipment a baseball team requires or the tools a painter uses to paint a house, the child with impaired vision needs to touch, get closer to, and otherwise explore those items to know about them and to understand how they fit into the work performed by another human being. Students who are blind or have low vision need hands-on experience whenever possible, and the teacher may be instrumental in paving the way for their active participation outside the classroom in athletics, scouting, or other extracurricular activities that help refine students' talents and help them apply what they are learning in the classroom in real-life settings. By helping coaches and other adult leaders of extracurricular offerings make their environments and meetings accessible, the teacher can help students with visual impairments expand their roles and responsibilities while they are young and may be eager to do so.

SUGGESTIONS FOR WORKING WITH PARENTS

Parents are the first and typically the most consistent teachers of their children. They are the adults who are available day and night in the life of a child. Parents share their values and beliefs, their knowledge of the world, and the social and cultural rules of their communities. Over time, they have a stronger influence over their children than virtually all other individuals in their children's lives. In ideal circumstances, parents of children with visual impairments are actively involved with other important players in their children's lives, including service providers—such as therapists, teachers of students with visual impairments, O&M specialists, assistive technology specialists, and rehabilitation personnel—as well as general and other special education teachers, coaches, troop and youth group leaders, tutors, and paraeducators. Parents need to be encouraged to work with service providers in an ongoing way to plan educational programs for their children and help other individuals, whether students or adults, understand the abilities of their children and how to modify the environment so that they can be included in activities and events of importance.

In the area of career education, parents can play an extremely important role by paying attention to the five overarching factors just described—that is, by exhibiting high expectations for their children, modeling socially appropriate interactions, reinforcing the skills their children learn in school that are specific to their visual impairment (such as use of braille or optical devices to read and write, use of assistive technology with mainstream technology to access information and perform tasks, and O&M skills), providing realistic feedback to their children on how their performance compares to other children their age, and promoting opportunities to work. Of equal importance is that parents convey the expectation that work will be an important part of their child's adult life. In the following sections, suggestions and information are discussed that the teacher of students with visual impairments can share with parents.

Early Childhood Needs

As parents nurture and care for their very young children, they have important roles to play from the perspective of career education. A parent's primary role, from this point of view, is to bond with the infant, which helps the child understand that there are others in the world; and to settle the child into a routine or schedule of activities (eating, sleeping, bathing, playing), which helps the child come to understand sequencing and predictability in preparation for engaging with others (other family members, or other children in day care settings or babysitting co-ops, for example).

Infants who are blind or who have low vision need their parents to "bring the world" to them—literally to put things into their hands or within close proximity (such as mobiles and toys that make pleasant sounds or are brightly colored, depending on whether the child has vision or not) and let them know those objects are there. Babies with visual impairments need to be forewarned when people reach out and touch them or move them from place to place; this warning can be easily done simply by speaking (for example, "Good morning, my love, let's get you something to eat!" "Are you ready for your bath?" "Ready or not, here I come!") or crooning to the child before he or she is touched or lifted. As many children do, a baby without vision may enjoy a lullaby, a story, or a favorite musical toy at bedtime, after which a verbal cue from the parent should be used to let the child know that the adult is leaving the room.

Parents in general do many of the things from which babies who are visually impaired benefit, based on their own exposure to nursery rhymes, games, and the interaction they experienced with their own parents. For instance, a parent may manipulate a baby's little hands and clap them together while singing, "Pat-a-cake, pat-a-cake, baker's man / Bake me a cake as fast as you can." The parent rolls the baby's hands, pats the baby's tummy, and draws the letter B on the child's tummy or chest while singing, "Roll it and pat it and mark it with B," then gestures between baby and self, while finishing the refrain: "Put it in the oven for baby and me." Children with visual impairments need their parents to do things with them, just as in this nursery rhyme game; moving together with the parent helps the child without vision perceive the world and what's going on in it.

Being aware of an external world and others in that world is the first stage of career awareness, and parents need to help their children explore the larger world by doing things with them. When washing dishes, parents may want to place their baby in a front-facing infant carrier or in an infant seat and let the child sit up on the counter. The parent can splash water from the sink or let the child splash. When shopping or walking in the neighborhood, parents can consider putting the child on their back in a child carrier so that he or she feels the parents' movements and can hear what's going on in the environment. Parents can encourage the child to try different flavors and tastes, and expose her to different textures, shapes, and sizes of things.

Whenever possible, parents need to talk about the things that the child is seeing or touching. Parents need to bring their baby who is visually impaired to family gatherings or leisure activities, such as playing games or watching movies. They can hold the baby or make a safe space, using bolsters and pillows as boundaries, in which the baby can roll about without coming to harm and be near family activity, while parents narrate the events. For example, "Amanda, Daddy's throwing the ball to Kevin! Kevin, show Amanda that ball you caught and then you can throw it back to Dad." They can also be engaged in the interactions: "What does Jaime want to do? Do you want to sit with Mommy and dangle your feet in the pool? We can watch Maria swimming, too!" Even though the child may not understand the words, hearing and taking part in the give-and-take of the social interactions is helpful.

Babies and toddlers with impaired vision need their parents to help them explore the world around them. They need to be encouraged to move about in the environment and explore both their physical surroundings and the objects they find in the environment. They may need parents to encourage them to stand and to walk. By the time they are 1 or 2 years old, they need to begin doing simple, age-appropriate chores, such as picking up their toys and putting them away, putting dirty clothes in the hamper rather than dropping them to the floor, and hanging their towel on a hook. Like children with typical sight, children who are visually impaired need adult monitoring when they are very young. A significant difference for children with visual impairments is that a parent or caregiver will need to do more hands-on demonstration of what needs doing. For example, when a typical 1-year-old is being encouraged to put away toys, the parent may ask the child to put a toy away and then point to the toy box. With a child with visual impairment, the parent may ask the child to pick up the toy, then go to the child and be ready to assist in picking up the toy, and, rather than pointing, tap the toy box or place the child's other hand on the box to let the child know where it is.

Encouraging children to "play along" while their parents do routine chores in their homes or the community, such as vacuuming or shopping, helps children learn routines that they are not yet expected to do, but that are an integral part of daily life. If the child startles at loud noises (such as a vacuum cleaner being turned on), the parent can help her anticipate by saying that the vacuum needs to be turned on and letting her flip the switch. Often, a child's startle reflex is due to fear—the child doesn't see what is making the noise and doesn't expect the noise. Allowing the child to control the source of the sound allows her to prepare for and become accustomed to it.

School-Aged Children's Needs

As children move from home to school, they need to be prepared to manage most of their personal care needs, such as toileting and feeding (unless they are children with multiple disabilities who may have been unable to acquire such skills due to cognitive or physical limitations). Parents teach and reinforce these independent living skills on an everyday basis. If the parents have been working with a teacher of students with visual impairments or early childhood specialist, they will have received information and resources to support their efforts. The Resources section at the end of this chapter also includes information about independent living skills instruction, and parents can also consult the websites listed there, such as FamilyConnect (www.familyconnect.org), Project Aspiro (www.projectaspiro.com), or sites maintained by many of the specialized schools for children with visual impairments for further information.

Chores

As noted elsewhere in this chapter, learning to do everyday chores at home helps children with visual impairments learn basic work skills and habits, such as planning, organizing, and following through with tasks. Doing these chores also gives children the satisfaction of contributing to the well-being of their families. In addition, a great deal of the work performed through the different jobs within everyday experiences, such as those outlined earlier in Sidebar 11.2, teaches children the use of basic hand tools, equipment, and materials. This knowledge, coupled with the results of their efforts—clean dishes or clothes, healthy pets, and so forth—helps children learn that work can have positive outcomes. Many children are paid an allowance contingent on completing their chores, and this payment is another way to underscore the importance of producing results that earn a reward, much like working.

Teachers can show parents the techniques for performing and teaching such skills to their children. It may take a little longer for children with visual impairments to learn to perform these chores than their sighted classmates because they will not have the advantage of seeing how others do the task, but there are a variety of methods that can be used, including hand-under-hand or hand-over-hand techniques; task analysis, in which a job is broken down into its individual steps (see Chapters 3 and 8); and allowing the child to explore "before and after" during the various stages of a project to see how the whole was accomplished. For instance, before asking a child to wrap a package, it will be helpful to show the child a wrapped package and the steps completed to wrap it. Likewise, before asking a child to fold a towel or washcloth the child should see (either literally or figuratively through touch) how a folded towel appears. After a particular skill is mastered, the child should be encouraged to find new ways to accomplish the task. Once a child has mastered folding a washcloth, the parent may want to ask him to fold dishcloths, then hand or bath towels; then fold pillowcases, flat sheets, fitted sheets, and so forth. It is important to allow as much independence as possible, even if it means taking longer to accomplish the chore than if the parent did all the steps alone.

Supporting Children in School

Parents can support their child's acquisition of knowledge, skills, and abilities at school by monitoring and reinforcing their efforts at home. For example, parents can begin to learn braille (sighted parents typically read braille visually rather than tactilely) or find out about low vision devices prescribed for their child, and learn how to use the assistive technology that their child needs to access the general education environment. Chapter 15 and the Resources section at the end of this chapter provide resources to help parents obtain information about the skills their children are learning.

Parents need to ask their children about what they are learning in school and review their work whenever possible. Finding out what skills their child has learned and asking the child to demonstrate them helps parents reinforce those skills and conveys to children that the work they do at school is important. Many teachers will send home notes to parents describing what they've been working on at school, and it is important for parents to review those notes and discuss them with their child or the teacher if they have questions or need further detail. Parents' active involvement in their child's education will reinforce the importance of education and encourage the child to be productive in school, which sets the stage for productivity in the workplace.

It is also important for parents to observe whenever possible their child's classroom, playground, and cafeteria to see how their child is performing in comparison to his or her sighted classmates, who are future competitors for the jobs that their child will eventually want. Parents need to understand that after graduation from the public school system, fewer supports and services will be available to their child, so it is important that their child learn how to manage as independently as possible and understand how to negotiate for assistance. Moreover, the more external assistance young adults need as they grow up, the more restricted the choices will be in terms of entering into the world of work. For these reasons, therefore, parents may want to encourage their child to strive to perform in similar fashion in school to classmates with typical sight. If the student is not able to keep up, parents can help set goals to increase productivity over time.

In addition, if the child is working with a paraeducator or receiving other external support from adults to function in the general education environment, parents can help school personnel determine how to reduce the level of support that their child needs over time. While it sometimes seems as if having a dedicated paraeducator, aide, or teacher's assistant with the child ensures that she will be fully integrated, it often works in the opposite way. Paraeducators may do tasks for a child that the child is able to do for herself, reinforcing the idea that she is "unable," rather than "able." Also, many children without disabilities are less likely to approach a child who is always in the company of an adult, so that having a paraeducator with a child who is visually impaired can inhibit his or her interactions with other children. This situation, in turn, risks limiting a child's social networks and, ultimately, his or her opportunities in the workplace.

If a child truly needs external support from an adult because of additional disabilities beyond a visual impairment, parents need to be aware that there may be difficulty in obtaining such assistance beyond age 21 and that they will need to make provisions for that level of assistance either through private (a trust fund, for example) or public funds. Because individuals must be deemed eligible for such limited public support, parents of children with severe or profound multiple disabilities may want to investigate registration for these kinds of services as early as possible in their children's lives. They may also want to investigate options for limited or full guardianship in their state or country through Internet research, in addition to consulting nonprofit disability advocacy and disability rights groups, local attorneys, and estate planners who specialize in making provisions for severely disabled children and adults.

IEP Meetings

By the time children with visual impairments are in middle school or high school, the expectation is that they will be attending and, ideally, leading their IEP meetings. Parents can help in this effort by encouraging their children to consider what they are learning with their teacher of students with visual impairments, O&M specialist, or special education instructors, as well as general educators, and what they feel they need to learn, so that they can discuss those areas at their IEP meetings. These discussions can occur as early as elementary school, but are critical as children move into secondary school. Children often question why they are being asked to perform certain chores or attend classes. Integrating the goal "preparation for self-sufficiency in life" in the IEP process, whenever feasible, can help children and their families understand how what they are studying now is relevant to the future.

As their children's first and most consistent teachers, parents contribute to their children's career education in many and diverse ways throughout their lives. Teachers of students with visual impairments and other related service providers can support parents by sharing information about ways in which they can support career education goals while engaging in the everyday activities of their lives. Through modeling positive work habits and encouraging their children's active participation in chores and work outside the home, parents set the stage for their children to believe that they can work and be successfully integrated into the community.

SUMMARY

The first four components of the career education model described in this chapter—career awareness, career exploration, career preparation, and career placement—typically involve learning and activities taking place from early childhood through the end of secondary or postsecondary school. For children and adolescents with visual impairments, structured learning and deliberate exposure to all aspects of the environment are critical for learning about and preparing for career and life roles. Teachers, related service providers, and families play an essential part in supporting students' awareness of, interest in, and ability to succeed in this critical area of the ECC, which serves as a major foundation to a student's ability to succeed in life beyond school.

References

Anderson, S., Boigon, S., & Davis, K. (1991). *The Oregon project for visually impaired and blind preschool children* (5th ed.). Medford: Jackson Education Service District.

Becker, R. L. (2000). *Reading-free vocational interest inventory* (2nd ed.). Columbus, OH: Elbern Publishing.

Brolin, D. E. (1995). *Career education: A functional life skills approach* (3rd ed.). Englewood Cliffs, NJ: Merrill.

Brolin, D. E. (2004). *Life centered career education curriculum.* Arlington, VA: Council for Exceptional Children.

Bureau of Labor Statistics (2012). *Occupational outlook handbook* (2012–13 ed.). Washington, DC: United States Department of Labor.

Clark, G., & Patton, J. (2013). *Transition planning inventory* (2nd ed.). Austin, TX: Pro-Ed.

Curran, E. (2010). *Just enough to know better: A braille primer.* Boston: National Braille Press.

Davis, P. A. (2000). *Brian's bird.* Walnut Creek, CA: Shen's Books.

Everson, J. M., & Zhang, D. (2000). Person-centered planning: Characteristics, inhibitors, and supports. *Education and Training in Mental Retardation and Developmental Disabilities, 35,* 36–43.

Gevirtz Graduate School of Education. (2012). Values clarification. Santa Barbara: University of California. Retrieved from http://www.education.ucsb.edu/webdata/instruction/hss/Values_Clarification/ValuClarif_Method_Outline.pdf

Glaser, E. A., & Burgio, M. (2007). *All children have different eyes: Learn to play and make friends.* Whittier, CA: Vidi Press.

Halpern, A. S., Herr, C. M., Doren, B., & Wolf, N. K. (2000). *Transition skills inventory.* Austin, TX: Pro-Ed.

Haupt, A., & Kane, T. T. (2004). *Population Reference Bureau's population handbook* (5th ed.). Washington, DC: Population Reference Bureau. Retrieved from http://www.prb.org/pdf/PopHandbook_Eng.pdf

Holland, J. L. (1994). *Self-directed search: Form R* (4th ed.). Odessa, FL: Psychological Assessment Resources.

Holland, J. L. (1996). *Self-directed search: Form E* (4th ed.). Odessa, FL: Psychological Assessment Resources.

Holland, J. L., & Powell, A. B. (1994). *Self-directed search: Career explorer.* Odessa, FL: Psychological Assessment Resources.

Hoyt, K. (1982). Federal and state participation in career education: Past, present, and future. *Journal of Career Education, 9*(1), 5–15.

Kef, S., & Tielen, L. (2008). Touch of love: Research on dating, courtship and sexual experiences of Dutch youth with visual impairments. Proceedings of the 9th International Conference on Low Vision, Vision 2008; Montreal, Canada.

Kendrick, D. (1993). *Jobs to be proud of: Profiles of workers who are blind or visually impaired.* New York: AFB Press.

Layton, T. L. (2004). *Developmental scale for children with Down syndrome.* Durham, NC: Extraordinary Learning Foundation.

Marland, S. (1971). *Career education now.* Speech presented before the annual convention of the National Association of Secondary School Principals, Houston, TX.

Martin, B., & Archambault, J. (1987). *Knots on a counting rope.* New York: Harry Holt.

Moss, K., & Wiley, D. (2003). *A brief guide to personal futures planning.* Austin: Texas School for the Blind and Visually Impaired. Retrieved from http://www.tsbvi.edu/Outreach/deafblind/pcp-workbook.pdf

Mount, B., Ducharme, G., & Beeman, P. (1991). *Person centered development.* Manchester, CT: Communitas, Inc.

Newman, L., Wagner, M., Cameto, R., & Knokey, A. M. (2009). The post-high school outcomes of youth with disabilities up to 4 years after high school: A report of findings from the National Longitudinal Transition Study-2 (NLTS2) (NCSER 2009-3017). Menlo Park, CA: SRI International. Retrieved from www.nlts2.org/reports/2009_04/nlts2_report_2009_04_complete.pdf

Newman, L., Wagner, M., Cameto, R., Knokey, A. M., & Shaver, D. (2010). Comparisons across time of the outcomes of youth with disabilities up to 4 years after high school: A report of findings from the National Longitudinal Transition Study-2 (NLTS2). Menlo Park, CA: SRI International. Retrieved from www.nlts2.org/reports/2010_09/nlts2_report_2010_09_complete.pdf

O'Shea, A. J., & Feller, R. (2000). *Harrington-O'Shea career decision-making system* (rev.). San Antonio, TX: Pearson Education.

Raths, L. E., Harmin, M., & Simon, S. B. (1978). *Values and teaching* (2nd ed.). Columbus, OH: Charles E. Merrill.

Scannell, S. (2007). *Ben and Buzzy's busy days.* Houston, TX: Region IV Education Service Center.

Simon, S. B., Howe, L. W., & Kirschenbaum, H. (1972). *Values clarification: A handbook of practical strategies for teachers and students.* New York: Hart Publishing.

Smith, M., & Levack, N. (1997. *Teaching students with visual and multiple impairments: A resource guide (*2nd ed.). Austin: Texas School for the Blind and Visually Impaired.

Test, D. W., Aspel, N. P., & Everson, J. M. (2006). *Transition methods for youth with disabilities.* Upper Saddle River, NJ: Pearson Education.

Texas School for the Blind and Visually Impaired. (2007). *EVALS: Evaluating visually impaired students.* Austin: Author.

Wolffe, K. E. (1996). Career education for students with visual impairments. *RE:view, 28*(2), 89–93.

Wolffe, K. E. (Ed.). (1999). *Skills for success: A career education handbook for children and adolescents with visual impairments.* New York: AFB Press.

Wolffe, K. E. (2000). Career education. In A. J. Koenig & M. C. Holbrook (Eds.), *Foundations of education: Vol. II. Instructional strategies for teaching children and youths with visual impairments* (2nd ed., pp. 679–719.). New York: AFB Press.

Wolffe, K. E. (2006a). Skills for success: Career education for young people with sight problems. *Insight, 1,* 10–14.

Wolffe, K. E. (2006b, July). *Assessment of students' competencies in the expanded core curriculum: A school-wide approach using observational protocol.* Paper presented at AER Biennial International conference, Snowbird, UT.

Wolffe, K. E. (2011a). *The transition checklist.* Austin, TX: Author.

Wolffe, K. E. (2011b, May). *Working with youth in transition: Overview of transition from evaluation to inception.* Paper presented for Calgary Board of Education in Edmonton and Calgary, Alberta, Canada.

Wolffe, K. E. (2012a). *Career counseling for people with disabilities: A practical guide to finding employment* (2nd ed.). Austin, TX: Pro-Ed.

Wolffe, K. E. (2012b). *The transition tote system* (rev.). Louisville, KY: American Printing House for the Blind.

Wolffe, K. E., & Kelly, S. (2011). Instruction in areas of the expanded core curriculum linked to transition outcomes for students with visual impairments. *Journal of Visual Impairment & Blindness, 105,* 340–349.

Wolffe, K. E., Roessler, R. T., & Schriner, K. F. (1992). Employment concerns of people with blindness or visual impairments. *Journal of Visual Impairment & Blindness, 86,* 185–187.

Wolffe, K. E., Sacks, S. Z., Corn, A. L., Erin, J. N., Huebner, K. M., & Lewis, S. (2002). Teachers of students with visual impairments: What are they teaching? *Journal of Visual Impairment & Blindness, 96,* 293–304.

APPENDIX 11A

Career Education Competencies: A Checklist

PRESCHOOL COMPETENCIES

Learning to listen

- ☐ Orients toward the speaker
- ☐ Attends to the speaker
- ☐ Responds (smiles, laughs, coos) to the speaker

Learning to follow directions

- ☐ Follows the teacher's movements (such as in hand-under-hand or hand-over-hand manipulation of tools)
- ☐ Follows one-word directions ("sit," "stand")
- ☐ Follows more complex directions ("Get your coat," "Get your backpack," "Pick up your toys")

Learning to be responsible

- ☐ Takes turns at games and waits in line at school
- ☐ Puts his or her clothes and supplies where they belong
- ☐ Follows class rules (no running, no hitting, raise your hand to speak)

Learning basic organizational skills

- ☐ Uses a designated cubby to store school supplies and tools
- ☐ Uses tools, such as a backpack, to keep up with personal items
- ☐ Uses appropriate space, like a lipped tray, to store pieces of a project

Fantasizing about adult roles

- ☐ Participates in creative dramatics (classroom or school plays)
- ☐ Engages adults (parents, grandparents, friends, neighbors, community workers) in conversations about their work
- ☐ Participates in make-believe or dress-up activities (playing school, hospital, fire station, grocery store)

Learning to play

- ☐ Engages in play with others (board games, playground games, manipulatives, building toys like LEGOS or Lincoln Logs)
- ☐ Plays alone (reads, puts together puzzles, watches television or videotapes, listens to music)

ELEMENTARY SCHOOL COMPETENCIES

Learning to follow more complex instructions

- ☐ Follows oral or written directions to order materials from a variety of sources, such as the American Printing House for the Blind, BookShare, LearningAlly, and the National Library Service's regional library
- ☐ Follows oral or written directions to complete classroom assignments and homework

- ☐ Follows oral or written directions to complete correspondence (letters, cards, e-mail messages, and so forth)

Learning to work individually and in a group

- ☐ Initiates class work without prompting
- ☐ Works unassisted on classroom assignments, using adaptive tools and materials
- ☐ Actively participates in and contributes to classroom academic projects, such as group reports or group experiences
- ☐ Actively participates in class projects such as bake sales and car washes
- ☐ Successfully engages with peers in projects such as bake sales and car washes

Learning to respond appropriately to adults and peers

- ☐ Successfully engages peers in conversations
- ☐ Actively engages with peers during free time
- ☐ Understands the rules of interacting with adults (raises hand to be called on, does not speak out of turn)
- ☐ Exchanges pleasantries with adults (says "hello" to a cafeteria worker before placing an order, says "thank you" when order is received)

Learning to be responsible for actions

- ☐ Puts materials away in an appropriate location (classroom, cupboard, backpack, closet, locker)
- ☐ Brings assistive devices to class in working order
- ☐ Brings low vision devices (eyeglasses, magnifiers, telescopes) to class
- ☐ Demonstrates socially responsible behavior (covering mouth when sneezing or coughing)
- ☐ Tidies work area at the completion of any project

Learning to organize work and school materials

- ☐ Uses a backpack or similar tool to manage assistive devices and materials
- ☐ Uses three-ring binders or similar tools to organize class assignments and products

Assuming responsibilities at home and at school

- ☐ Uses a calendar to keep up with assignments, projects, or tests
- ☐ Keeps desk tidy and can retrieve materials when asked to do so
- ☐ Helps with simple, age-appropriate, household chores
- ☐ Helps younger children at school with classroom assignments or homework

Identifying different work roles and assuming them in fantasy and play

- ☐ Acts out play roles as physician, lawyer, pilot, teacher, and so forth
- ☐ Talks about vocational dreams and aspirations (fantasizes about being a ballerina, football player, space explorer)
- ☐ Participates in class or school plays that include different work-related roles with appropriate costumes and actions

Recognizing different community workers

- ☐ Identifies common community workers (police officer, firefighter, mail carrier, nurse, emergency medical services worker, librarian) by describing the services they perform

- ☐ Identifies whom to call on in the event of an emergency (hospital worker, doctor, police, firefighter)
- ☐ Demonstrates an understanding of the functions performed, attire worn, and types of experience necessary to engage in community service jobs

Understanding the rewards of work

- ☐ Identifies the sum earned for specific tasks performed
- ☐ Demonstrates an understanding of how payment for work is affected by sloppy or inadequate performance
- ☐ Demonstrates an understanding of the consequences of nonperformance (the concept of no work equals no pay)

Learning to solve problems

- ☐ Attempts to find things before asking for help
- ☐ Asks others how they have resolved problems and tries the ideas to see if they will work
- ☐ Tries different approaches to problem solving if the first attempt at solving a problem does not work

Developing good communication skills

- ☐ Attends to others when they are speaking, as demonstrated by orienting towards the speaker, occasionally nodding his/her head, smiling, or frowning at appropriate comments, doing nothing else when someone is speaking, except taking notes or listening
- ☐ Responds appropriately when addressed by answering questions accurately, sharing topic-related information in a conversation, and waiting until the speaker has finished speaking before commenting
- ☐ Stays on topic in conversations and does not change the focus to him/herself, to some irrelevant detail, or to an unrelated topic

Developing basic academic skills

- ☐ Demonstrates grade-level reading skills using his or her preferred medium (braille, large print, recorded, electronic format)
- ☐ Demonstrates grade-level writing skills
- ☐ Demonstrates grade-level calculation skills

MIDDLE SCHOOL COMPETENCIES

Meeting increased demands for organizing time

- ☐ Demonstrates the ability to organize school activities by arriving to classes on time with completed homework assignments
- ☐ Demonstrates the ability to organize school activities by participating in school clubs or groups
- ☐ Demonstrates the ability to organize school and extracurricular activities by participating in extracurricular activities routinely, and maintaining schoolwork

Meeting increased responsibility at home and in the community

- ☐ Demonstrates responsibility at home by completing assigned chores
- ☐ Demonstrates responsibility at home by performing volunteer and paid work for neighbors and family members

- ☐ Demonstrates responsibility at school through work for clubs, participation in a band, and the like
- ☐ Demonstrates responsibility in the community by volunteering

Meeting increased demands for skill development

- ☐ Performs learned skills in academic areas independently
- ☐ Demonstrates greater speed in using skills at school (in a specific academic or other identified area, such as playing a musical instrument)
- ☐ Demonstrates greater accuracy in using skills

Showing a full understanding of the work performed by adults

- ☐ Can identify the work performed by family members
- ☐ Can provide details (hours worked, major job duties, salaries, qualifications) about the work performed by family members
- ☐ Identifies major community workers and their roles (police, firefighters, physicians, lawyers, social workers, teachers)

Showing a beginning notion of the work he or she wants to do as an adult

- ☐ Reads about the lives and work of famous Americans, including those with disabilities
- ☐ Writes book reports on materials read
- ☐ Reads about careers in general—what is available nationally, regionally, and locally
- ☐ Discusses careers of interest with teachers, parents, and other significant adults
- ☐ Identifies specific jobs related to career interests and abilities

Investigating identified areas of interest

- ☐ Reads about specific careers of interest
- ☐ Conducts informational interviews with adults in the community who perform jobs that are of interest
- ☐ Participates in job-shadowing experiences

HIGH SCHOOL COMPETENCIES

Showing well-developed academic skills

- ☐ Demonstrates well-developed reading, writing, arithmetic, listening, and speaking skills by performing comparably to sighted peers (define the classroom standards without adjusting quantity or quality of work for the student's visual impairment)
- ☐ Demonstrates well-developed reading, writing, arithmetic, listening, and speaking skills by performing at a level commensurate with the demands in the vocational area of interest (define the occupational standard for entry-level workers in this area)
- ☐ Consistently and satisfactorily completes classroom and homework assignments without assistance

Showing well-developed thinking skills

- ☐ When asked to think creatively, the student uses her imagination, connects known ideas in new ways, makes connections between seemingly unrelated ideas, and considers alternatives to known ideas
- ☐ Demonstrates the ability to set goals based on an analysis of the array of choices available to him

- ☐ Demonstrates the ability to recognize that a problem exists, defines the problem, identifies possible solutions, devises an action plan to resolve the problem, initiates the plan, evaluates its success, and revises the plan as needed
- ☐ Recognizes and uses her own learning style (visual, auditory, tactile, kinesthetic), adapts to new situations and tools, and uses formal learning strategies (note taking, repeating new content aloud)
- ☐ Uses logic to draw conclusions from the content presented in the classroom and textbook

Showing well-developed work behaviors

- ☐ Sets and meets self-directed standards for performance
- ☐ Pays attention to details
- ☐ Performs tasks even when the tasks are unpleasant or difficult
- ☐ Describes his/her interests, abilities, values, and liabilities
- ☐ Is aware of the impression he/she makes on others
- ☐ Can describe his/her own needs and how to address them
- ☐ Works well with others
- ☐ Interacts with classmates and adults appropriately
- ☐ Can be trusted with materials and tools

Participation in work activities

- ☐ Volunteers to help others
- ☐ Performs work tasks at home and at school
- ☐ Performs a job for pay in the community

Planning for life beyond high school

- ☐ Investigates postsecondary education or training options
- ☐ Develops a plan for postsecondary education or training related to vocational interests, abilities, and values
- ☐ Develops a plan with short-term, intermediate, and long-term goals for achieving satisfaction in life
- ☐ Identifies the supports he or she will need to move from high school into postsecondary environments (housing, transportation, access to information, child care, personal care, home care, time management or money management, assistance with leisure and recreational activities)

SOURCE: Adapted from Karen Wolffe, "Career Education," in Alan J. Koenig and M. Cay Holbrook (Eds.), *Foundations of Education* (2nd ed.), *Vol. 2: Instructional Strategies for Teaching Children and Youths with Visual Impairments* (New York: AFB Press, 2000), pp. 679–719.

Transition Competencies Checklist

Student Name: ______________________________ Date: ____________________

Address: ____

Telephone Number: ____________________ E-mail: ______________________

School: ______________________________ Grade: ____________________

Address: ____

Telephone Number: ____________________

If someone other than the student completes this checklist, please complete the following section.

Informant: ____

Relationship: ____

Address: ____

Telephone Number: ____________________ E-mail: ______________________

Date(s) of Observation: ____

Student's Placement: ____

DIRECTIONS

The Transition Competencies Checklist is a tool designed for you to complete independently. The Checklist can help you figure out your strengths (competencies) and weaknesses (problems). Once you know, you can decide what you need to work on while you are in high school to prepare for what you want to do after graduation. You can use the Checklist to help you decide what goals to include on your Individualized Education Program (IEP). Or, you can use the Checklist to set personal goals. There are no right or wrong answers—just what is true for you.

Please read each item (indicator) carefully and answer either yes or no. Try to think of examples from your life as you respond. For example, if the item is "I perform chores at home," think of the things you do to help out at home such as washing the dishes or putting away your clothes. Your teacher or counselor may ask you for examples when you share your completed Checklist. Please respond to each item. There is no time limit for completing the Checklist—take as much time as you need to read and respond to the items. You may change an answer, if you have second thoughts and feel you should have answered differently. Remember—there are no right or wrong answers! If you have questions or need help understanding an item, please ask your teacher or counselor.

Transition Competency #1
An understanding of work based on real life experiences.

Indicators	Yes	No
I perform chores at home.		
I perform chores at school.		
I participate in community activities (food drives, litter pick-up, fundraising, etc.).		
I participate in school and community organizations (Girl/Boy Scouts, youth groups, clubs, etc.).		
I volunteer.		
I know about the jobs my family members do.		
I know about the jobs my neighbors do.		

Transition Competency #2
Well-developed leisure and socialization skills.

Indicators	Yes	No
I like people.		
Other people like me.		
I like to watch television.		
I like to listen to the radio.		
I like to read books, magazines, or the newspaper.		
I like to go out with friends.		
I like to go out by myself.		
I participate in athletics.		
I like to watch athletic events.		
I like to go to clubs.		
I like to dance.		
I like to sing.		
I like to go to the movies.		
I like to play video games.		
I like to walk.		
I spend time on my hobbies.		
I get a lot of exercise.		
I often go out at night.		
I feel comfortable eating out.		
It is difficult for me to go out and have a good time.		
I provide favors for others, for example, helping another student with homework.		
I return favors that have been done for me, for example, helping to pay for gas when a friend drives me places.		
I use gestures when I communicate (head nodding or shaking, hand motions, etc.).		
I am a good listener.		
I am a good speaker.		
I am comfortable asking for help.		
I am comfortable speaking with someone I've just met.		

Transition Competency #3
Well-developed problem-solving skills.

Indicators	Yes	No
I recognize when I have a problem.		
I try to solve my problems myself.		
I ask for help with a problem when I need it.		
I consider several solutions to my problems.		
I understand the possible consequences of my choices.		
I take steps to solve a problem.		
I evaluate the outcome of my solutions.		
Other people try to solve my problems for me.		
I feel comfortable asking others not to interfere when I am trying to solve a problem.		

Transition Competency #4
Application of self-advocacy skills

Indicators	Yes	No
I describe my disability to others.		
I describe the accommodations that I need to others.		
I ask for accommodations when needed.		
I handle my own affairs (doctor's appointments, school scheduling, meetings, etc.).		
I know what resources are available to assist me in meeting my future goals.		
I understand my legal rights and responsibilities.		

Transition Competency #5
Application of compensatory skills

Indicators	Yes	No
I read using: (***Rank order your choices —1 = preferred***)		
Regular print without low vision devices.		
Regular print with low vision devices.		
List devices: ____________________		
Large print. Size: ______________		
Braille (Grade 1/uncontracted or Grade 2/contracted).		
Computer with speech output.		
Cassette tapes or CDs.		
Digital books.		
Reader (paid or volunteer).		
Reading machine.		
My reading speed is: ___________		
I can read at that speed for (length of time): _______		
I typically write: (***Rank order your choices—#1 = preferred***)		
I write notes in regular print.		
I write notes in cursive script.		

Indicators	Yes	No
I use a computer (wordprocess/type notes).		
I use a slate and stylus to write notes in braille.		
I use a brailler to write notes in braille.		
I use a notetaking device; list: ____________________		
I use a recorder for notes.		
I can access printed materials.		
I can generate printed materials.		
I use orientation and mobility skills.		
I usually travel in the following ways:		
Family or friends drive me places.		
Someone helps me arrange transportation.		
I use school transportation.		
I use public transportation (bus, train).		
I use paratransit services (special transit).		
I drive my car (motorcycle).		
I have a driver (paid).		
I use private cab companies.		
I walk with a cane.		
I walk without a cane.		
I walk with a dog guide.		
I usually walk with a sighted guide.		
I use a sighted guide in new locations.		
I know how to route plan in my neighborhood.		
I can read a map.		
I know pertinent bus/train schedules.		
I travel outside of my home town (by air, train).		
I do the following:		
Purchase my own clothes.		
Shop for groceries.		
Attend to personal hygiene needs.		
Laundry (wash/dry).		
Store (fold and hang) my clothes.		
Bank (checking or savings).		
Vacuum, dust room(s).		
Wash/dry dishes.		
Take out the trash.		
I receive an allowance contingent upon my performance.		
I receive an allowance which is not contingent.		
I keep a calendar.		
I make and keep appointments.		

Indicators	Yes	No
I have money for incidentals at the end of the month.		
Sometimes I wonder if I can afford the things I want.		
I know the schedule for trash collection at my house.		
I pay my bills on time.		
I know when holidays are upcoming.		
I plan meals in advance.		
I have too many things to do.		
I don't have enough things to do to stay active.		
When I shop, I take a shopping list.		
I budget my money.		
My room/apartment is well organized.		
Other people say my room/apartment is tidy.		
I have trouble keeping my clothes clean.		
Other people say that I look well groomed.		
When I have an emergency, I know what to do.		
I use the following technology devices:		
Computer with speech output; software:		
Computer with magnification; software:		
Computer with braille output; list: ____________________		
Braille embosser		
Electronic notetaking device; list: ____________________		
CCTV or video magnifier; list: ____________________		
Reading machine/scanner		
Voice activated computer		
Talking calculator		
Talking watch		
Electronic dictionary		
Specialized work tools with speech/audio output; list items: ____________________		
I use the Internet.		
I use a GPS system; list: ____________________		
My keyboarding rate is ______ wpm.		
I have participated in a career education program.		
I have participated in vocational education classes.		
If yes, list classes completed: ____________________		

Transition Competency #6
Knowledge of career options and sources of information

Indicators	Yes	No
I know how to find information about jobs.		
I know the most popular fields of work in my community.		

Indicators	Yes	No
I know the most popular fields of work in my state.		
I know the most popular fields of work in my country.		
I know the most popular fields of work being performed by other blind and visually impaired people.		
I have used the following resources to find out about jobs:		
AFB CareerConnect website		
Public/school library		
Telephone		
Internet		
Attending consumer group (American Council of the Blind or National Federation of the Blind) conventions or meetings		
Attending special interest (science fiction, technology, writing, acting, etc.) meetings or conferences		
Community resources (Chamber of Commerce, workforce development centers, Better Business Bureau, etc.)		
Career interest software; list:		
Other resources; list:		

Transition Competency #7
An understanding of levels of ability and impact with regard to job placement

Indicators	Yes	No
I have found my own job(s).		
I can find my own job in the future.		
Others have helped me find a job.		
I know what assistance I will need to work in the future.		
In order to work, I will need help with transportation.		
In order to work, I will need help with housing.		
In order to work, I will need help with managing my home.		
In order to work, I will need help with scheduling my time.		
In order to work, I will need help with managing my money.		
In order to work, I will need help with performing on the job (job coaching).		
In order to work, I will need help with tools, equipment, etc.; List: ______________________________		
I learn best by: (**Pick one only please**)		
Reading a manual or directions		
Listening to someone describe what to do		
Watching someone perform a task		
Doing the task while someone watches me and provides feedback on my performance		
Having someone show me how to perform by doing the task with me; hand-under-hand or hand-over-hand		

Transition Competency #8
Mastery of career counseling content areas

Indicators	Yes	No
Self-Awareness		
I know my interests.		
I know my abilities and strengths.		
I know my values (beliefs).		
I know my weaknesses and barriers to work.		
I know how others view me.		
I know what kind of work best fits my personality traits.		
I have reasons to go to work.		
Career Exploration		
I know what jobs are available.		
For the jobs I know about, I can describe:		
The salary range.		
The work environment.		
The required training.		
The availability of these jobs in my community.		
I have explored jobs in the following ways:		
Reading about jobs.		
Informational interviews with sighted workers.		
Informational interviews with visually impaired workers.		
Job shadowing.		
Job site visits.		
Job analysis.		
Job-Seeking Skills		
I am comfortable calling for information about job openings.		
I can get to a business to apply for a job.		
I have a personal data sheet.		
I use my personal data sheet to complete job applications.		
I have a résumé.		
I know how to use a résumé.		
I know how to find job leads.		
I can follow-up on a job lead.		
I know when it is appropriate to disclose my disability to an employer.		
I know how to prepare for an interview.		
I have interviewed for a job.		
I have followed-up after an interview.		
I keep records of interviews I have had and with whom I've interviewed.		

Indicators	Yes	No
Job Maintenance Skills		
I have good attendance at school.		
I have good attendance at work.		
I am punctual at school.		
I am punctual at work.		
I have worked.		
I have held a job for a year or more.		
I can list my best work habits.		
I know when to ask for help on a job.		
I get along well with my coworkers (peers).		
I make friends easily.		
I can't say "no" to people.		
I can usually speak up for myself.		
I go to the doctor often.		
I miss school/work at least one day a month.		
I often feel lonely.		
I do not like to ask for help.		
I have applied for and received promotions.		
I become upset if someone tells me I'm not working well.		
I have been fired from a job.		
I always try to do a good job.		
I have met some of my present friends at work.		
I have completed a personnel evaluation with an employer.		
Employment Skills		
I am employed.		
I understand my paycheck (net income versus gross income, voluntary versus involuntary deductions).		
I have notified the Social Security Administration that I am working (if necessary).		
I know what work benefits I am eligible for (sick leave, medical/dental insurance, retirement, etc.)		
I understand my current work status (probation period, amount of leave time, disciplinary actions).		
I have records of my work experience.		
I have been oriented to the rules and regulations of my work place (emergency evacuation plan, purchasing, getting supplies, paperwork procedures).		
I understand the chain of command at my work place.		
I know whom to go to if I need assistance on the job (supervisor, O&M instructor, rehabilitation engineer, rehabilitation counselor, job coach).		
I use my compensatory skills on the job (O&M, notetaking skills, etc.).		

Transition Competency #9
Evidence of participation in work experience opportunities

Indicators	Yes	No
I have participated in non-paid work.		
I have participated in paid work.		
List all of the jobs (paid and non-paid) you have had:		

Job Title	Employer	Dates	Paid Yes/No

Transition Competency #10
An understanding of employers' concerns

Indicators	Yes	No
I can address employers' safety concerns.		
I can explain how I access printed materials.		
I can explain how I generate printed materials.		
I can get to and from work.		
I can travel within a work environment without assistance.		
I can produce as much work as my sighted peers.		
I do not make any more mistakes than my sighted peers.		
I understand how employers' expectations change over time.		

SOURCE: Reprinted with permission of the author from Karen Wolffe, *Transition Competencies Checklist,* © 2011.

Career Education Resources

This section provides resources such as assessment tools, publications, and instructional materials for teaching social skills. For additional resources that relate to the expanded core curriculum in general, see the Resources section at the end of this book.

ASSESSMENT TOOLS

Career Decision-Making System (online version)

POPULATION/AGE LEVEL: 12 and older; reading level: 4th grade (level 1), 6th grade (level 2)

SOURCE: O'Shea, A. J., & Feller, R. (2000). *The Harrington-O'Shea career decision-making system* (rev). San Antonio, TX: Pearson.

EVALS: Evaluating Visually Impaired Students

POPULATION/AGE LEVEL: School-age

SOURCE: Texas School for the Blind and Visually Impaired (2007). *EVALS: Evaluating Visually Impaired Students.* Austin: Texas School for the Blind and Visually Impaired.

Life Centered Education: Assessment Protocol

POPULATION/AGE LEVEL: Special education high school students (not specific to students with visual impairments)

SOURCE: Brolin, D. E. (2004). *Life centered education (LCE) transition curriculum.* Arlington, VA: Council for Exceptional Children.

Reading-Free Vocational Interest Inventory

POPULATION/AGE LEVEL: 12 to adult (MR, LD, regular classroom, disadvantaged, sheltered work populations—normative samples); pictorial assessment tool is not appropriate for students without functional vision.

SOURCE: Becker, R. (2000). *Reading-free vocational interest inventory: 2* (2nd ed.) Columbus, OH: Elbern Publications.

Self-Directed Search Career Explorer

POPULATION/AGE LEVEL: 11–17 year olds; 3rd grade reading level (print only)

SOURCE: Holland, J. R., & Powell, A. B. (1994). *Self-directed search: Career explorer.* Lutz, FL: Psychological Assessment Resources.

Self-Directed Search Form E

POPULATION/AGE LEVEL: High school and adult populations with limited reading ability (4th grade); also provides a simplified scoring system (2-letter code rather than 3-letter) and provides job matches that require high school or less in terms of preparation (print only)

SOURCE: Holland, J. R. (1994). *Self-directed search form E* (4th ed.). Lutz, FL: Psychological Assessment Resources.

Self-Directed Search Form R

POPULATION/AGE LEVEL: High school, college, adult

SOURCE: Holland, J. R. (1996). *Self-directed search form R* (4th ed.). Lutz, FL: Psychological Assessment Resources. (Also available in an electronic version online.)

Transition Competencies Checklist

POPULATION/AGE LEVEL: High school students with visual impairments

SOURCE: Wolffe, K. E. (2011). *Transition competencies checklist.* (See Appendix 11B.)

Transition Planning Inventory—Second Edition

POPULATION/AGE LEVEL: High school students with disabilities (not specific to students with visual impairments)

SOURCE: Clark, G. M., & Patton, J. R. (2013). *Transition planning inventory* (2nd ed.). Austin, TX: Pro-Ed.

PUBLICATIONS

Anderson, S., Boigon, S., & Davis, K. (1991). *The Oregon project for visually impaired and blind preschool children* (5th ed.). Medford: Jackson Education Service District.

Capella-McDonnall, M. C., & Crudden, A. (2009). Factors affecting the successful employment of transition-age youths with visual impairments. *Journal of Visual Impairment & Blindness, 103*(6), 329–341.

Christen, C., & Bolles, R. N. (2010). *What color is your parachute? For teens: Discovering yourself, defining your future* (2nd ed.). New York: Ten Speed Press.

Cline, F., & Fay, J. (1990). *Parenting with love and logic.* Colorado Springs, CO: Piñon Press.

Cline, F., & Fay, J. (2006). *Parenting teens with love and logic.* Colorado Springs, CO: Piñon Press.

Crary, E. (1990). *Pick up your socks . . . and other skills growing children need!* Seattle, WA: Parenting Press, Inc.

Davis, P. A. (2000). *Brian's bird.* Walnut Creek, CA: Shen's Books.

DeMario, N. (1992). Skills needed for successful employment: A review of the literature. *RE:view, 24*(3), 115–125.

Freeman, P. (2001). *Deafblind disabled baby: Program of care for parents of the deafblind baby with multiple disabilities.* Retrieved from http://www.nationaldb.org/documents/products/freeman-4.doc

Fryer, J. (2012). *The teen's ultimate guide to making money when you can't get a job: 199 ideas for earning cash on your own terms.* Ocala, FL: Atlantic Publishing Group Inc.

Glaser, E. A., & Burgio, M. (2007). *All children have different eyes: Learn to play and make friends.* Whittier, CA: Vidi Press.

Hanye, R. (1998). The missing link: Real work experiences for people who are visually impaired. *Journal of Visual Impairment & Blindness, 92*(12), 844–847.

Jorgensen-Smith, T., & Lewis, S. (2004). Meeting the challenge: Innovation in one state rehabilitation system's approach to transition. *Journal of Visual Impairment & Blindness, 98*(4), 212–227.

Kendrick, D. (1993). *Jobs to be proud of.* New York: AFB Press.

Kendrick, D. (1998). *Teachers who are blind or visually impaired.* New York: AFB Press.

Kendrick, D. (2000). *Business owners who are blind or visually impaired.* AFB Press.

Kendrick, D. (2001). *Health care professionals who are blind or visually impaired.* New York: AFB Press.

Kerlin, M., & Schneider, S. (2008). *Grow up. Get a job.* Del Mar, CA: Tailwag Studio.

Layton, T. L. (2004). *Developmental scale for children with Down syndrome.* Durham, NC: Extraordinary Learning Foundation.

Lewis, S., Bardin, J., & Jorgensen-Smith, T. (2009). After one year: Self-reported transition skills of teens with visual impairments. *AER Journal: Research & Practice in Visual Impairment, 2*(2), 84–96.

Martin. B., & Archambault, J. (1987). *Knots on a counting rope.* New York: Harry Holt.

Miller, L. S., Glascoe, L. G., & Kokaska, C. J. (1986). *Life centered career education activity books.* Arlington, VA: Council for Exceptional Children.

McBroom, L. W. (1995). *Transition to work following graduation from college: Experiences of employees with visual impairments and their employers* (technical report). Mississippi State, MS. Rehabilitation Research and Training Center on Blindness and Low Vision.

McBroom, L. (1996). *Transition activity calendar for students with visual impairments.* Mississippi State, MS: Rehabilitation Research and Training Center on Blindness and Low Vision.

Nagle, K. M. (2001). Transition to employment and community life for youths with visual impairments: Current status and future directions. *Journal of Visual Impairment & Blindness, 95*(12), 725–738.

Oddo, N. S., & Sitlington, P. L. (2002). What does the future hold? A follow-up study of graduates of a residential school program. *Journal of Visual Impairment & Blindness, 96*(12), 842–851.

Sacks, S. Z., Wolffe, K. E., & Tierney, D. (1998). Lifestyles of students with visual impairments: Preliminary studies of social networks. *Exceptional Child, 64*(4), 463–478.

Sacks, S. Z., & Wolffe, K. E. (2000). *Focused on: Teaching social skills* (videos & booklets). New York: AFB Press.

Sanford, C., Newman, L., Wagner, M., Cameto, R., Knokey, A. M., & Shaver, D. (2011). *The post-high school outcomes of young adults with disabilities up to 6 years after high school. Key findings from the National Longitudinal Transition Study-2 (NLTS2)* (NCSER 2011–3004). Menlo Park, CA: SRI International. Available at www.nlts2.org/reports

Scannell, S. (2007). *Ben and Buzzy's busy days.* Houston, TX: Region IV Education Service Center.

Shaw, A., Gold, D., & Wolffe, K. E. (2007). Employment-related experiences of youths who are visually impaired: How are these youths fairing? *Journal of Visual Impairment & Blindness, 101,* 7–21.

Smith, M., & Levack, N. (1997). *Teaching students with visual and multiple impairments: A resource guide* (2nd ed.). Austin: Texas School for the Blind and Visually Impaired.

Tieger, P. D., & Barron-Tieger, B. (2001). *Do what you are: Discover the perfect career for you through the secrets of personality type* (3rd ed.). New York: Little, Brown and Company.

U.S. Department of Labor Wage and Hour Division. (2010, July). Child labor provisions for nonagricultural occupations under the Fair Labor Standards Act. Retrieved from http://www.dol.gov/whd/regs/compliance/childlabor101.pdf

Wolffe, K. E. (1997). The key to successful school-to-work work programs for blind or visually impaired students, *Journal of Visual Impairment & Blindness, 91*(4), pp. 5–7.

Wolffe, K. E. (1998). Transition planning and employment outcomes for students who have visual impairments with other disabilities. In S. Z. Sacks and R. Silberman (Eds.), *Educating students who have visual impairments with other disabilities.* Baltimore, MD: Paul Brookes.

Wolffe, K. E. (Ed.). (1999). *Skills for success: A career education handbook for children and adolescents with visual impairments.* New York: AFB Press.

Wolffe, K. E. (2000). Career education for children and youths with visual impairments. In A. J. Koenig & M. C. Holbrook (Eds.), *Foundations of education: Vol. II. Instructional strategies for teaching children and youths with visual impairments* (2nd ed.). New York: AFB Press.

Wolffe, K. E. (2000). Making it! Successful transition competencies for youth with visual disabilities. *SEE/HEAR, 5*(2), 19–24.

Wolffe, K. E. (2004). Add a tool to your transition toolbox. *Howe's Now, 8*(2), 20–22.

Wolffe, K. E. (2004). So, what do you want to be when you grow up? *SEE/HEAR, 9*(4), 30–33.

Wolffe, K. E. (2004). Transitioning young adults from school to public transportation. *EnVision: A publication for parents and educators of children with impaired vision, 8*, 7–9.

Wolffe, K. E. (2009). The transition from school to adult roles and responsibilities. *Insight, 23*, 10–13.

Wolffe, K. E. (2011). *Career counseling for people with disabilities: A practical guide to finding employment* (2nd ed.). Austin, TX: Pro-Ed.

Wolffe, K. E., & Erin, J. N. (2012). Transition for students who are blind or have low vision. In M. L. Wehmeyer and K. W. Webb (Eds.), *Handbook of transition for youth with disabilities.* New York: Routledge, Taylor and Francis.

Wolffe, K. E., & Johnson, D. (1997). *Navigating the rapids of life video and booklet.* Louisville, KY: American Printing House for the Blind.

Wolffe, K. E., & Sacks, S. Z. (1997). The social network pilot project: A quantitative comparison of the lifestyles of blind, low vision, and sighted young adults. *Journal of Visual Impairment & Blindness, 91*(3), 245–257.

Wolffe, K. E., & Terlau, M. T. (2012). *The transition tote system* (rev.). Louisville, KY: American Printing House for the Blind.

WEBSITES

CareerConnect

www.careerconnect.org

An employment information resource website developed by the American Foundation for the Blind for job seekers who are blind or visually impaired. It presents employment information, career exploration tools, and job-seeking guidance for students and adults with vision loss and the professionals who work with them.

FamilyConnect

www.familyconnect.org

An online, multimedia community created by the American Foundation for the Blind and the National Association for Parents of Children with Visual Impairments to give parents of children with visual impairments a place to support each other, share stories and concerns, and link to local resources.

National Secondary Transition Technical Assistance Center

www.nsttac.org/content/nsttac-products-and-resources

A national technical assistance and dissemination center funded by the United States Department of Education Office of Special Education Programs and directed and staffed by the Special Education Program at the University of North Carolina at Charlotte, in partnership with the Special Education Program at Western Michigan University. Provides technical assistance and disseminates information to state education agencies, local education authorities, schools, and others to implement evidence-based practices leading to improved academic and functional achievement for students with disabilities, preparing them for college or other postsecondary education and training and the workforce.

O*NET Online
www.onetonline.org

The Department of Labor Occupational Information Service, a tool for career exploration and job analysis. Offers a variety of tools such as the Ability Profiler, Interest Profiler, Computerized Interest Profiler, Work Importance Locator, and Work Importance Profiler.

Project Aspiro
www.projectaspiro.com

A collaborative project between the World Blind Union and the Canadian National Institute for the Blind, this website describes employment resources for youth and adult job seekers; service providers working with people who are visually impaired; friends and family members of children, youth, and adults with visual impairments; and employers.

Washington State School for the Blind
www.wssb.wa.gov/Content/offcampus/Video.asp

Links to instructional video clips on independent living topics, which have an impact on employment readiness.

YouthRules!
www.youthrules.dol.gov

An initiative of the United States Department of Labor to promote positive and safe work experiences for teens by distributing information about young workers to youth, parents, employers and educators.

Career Education Learning Activities

Contributed by Elizabeth Eagan Satter, Karen E. Wolffe, Carol B. Allman, and Sandra Lewis

These sample learning activities are presented as examples of activities that teachers can create to work on several ECC skills at once with their students. Activities that help teach career education skills can also be found in other chapters. The activities presented, like all instruction, need to be considered and modified to address the needs of individual students—such as those who are braille readers, have low vision, or have additional disabilities—with adaptations for appropriate media and the physical and other capabilities of the student.

Learning Activity: Put That Away!
Primary ECC Area: Career education **Component:** Career awareness **Grades:** Pre-K–4; students with multiple disabilities
Other ECC Areas ■ Independent living ■ Sensory efficiency ■ Orientation and mobility ■ Compensatory access
Goal: The student will clean up his or her bedroom or play area (or work area for older students with multiple disabilities) in a timely manner when asked to do so.
Key Tasks/Concepts The student will: ■ Locate items that need to be put away ■ Identify and find appropriate storage spaces ■ Put items away
Description This activity is appropriate for young children to perform with their parents or caregivers at home or with their teachers in preschool and kindergarten classes, and for older children who have multiple disabilities in a classroom or work environment. The techniques are essentially identical for learning to clean up either a play area or work space. First, the teacher of students with visual impairments or other professional needs to make sure that the student is oriented to the setting, whether it is a bedroom, classroom, or work area, and knows where the appropriate storage spaces—such as toy or tool boxes, drawers, closets, storage bins, and cubbies—are located. The storage spaces should be clearly marked with high-contrast print or braille labels, tactile symbols, or different colors for different groupings of items, depending on the student's learning medium and any learned methods of organization. The storage spaces need to remain in place so that the child knows where to find them. Next, the teacher needs to show the student how to locate items that need to be put away. The teacher can demonstrate both visual scanning and nonvisual search techniques to use in the area where the student has been playing or working or across the entire room. With younger children, the teacher or parents might start by designating a smaller space with clear boundaries for them to play in to limit the area that subsequently requires cleaning up.

(continued on next page)

As the child gathers toys, materials, or tools, it can be helpful to collect the items temporarily in a tote bag, paper or plastic bag, box, crate, or a small, clean trashcan lined with a plastic bag. If the student is working at a workstation, a tray with a lip can be used to help keep tools and materials contained and prevent items from rolling off a table. When searching for items to put away, the student can be shown how to move items found to the center of the tray or put them into a temporary container such as a bag or box. Initially, the parent or instructor will want to work side-by-side with the child and help collect the items or hold the bag for the child to place found items in.

After the student has collected the items to put away, the teacher or parent needs to help him or her figure out where to put each item. The teacher can have the student identify each item and then discuss with the student what kind of object it is and where it belongs. For example, a stuffed animal might go in the toy box, a puzzle might belong on the shelf, a book would go in the bookcase, and a shoe belongs in the closet.

If mobility or orientation is difficult for the student, a sound source can be helpful. A sound source provides a constant or consistent noise, such as a clock ticking or a radio playing, and is a technique used to help with orientation. For example, the clock or radio might be on the child's dresser and the toy box located just to the right or left of the dresser. The child would move toward the sound source, find the dresser and then move either left or right to find the toy box.

Once the student knows how to search for objects, where things go, and can consistently put them away, the task can be made more difficult by introducing distractions such as extraneous noise, obstructions in the path to the storage area, or a full toy or tool box.

To give a student additional practice in finding and putting away his or her toys and materials, the teacher can devise a game in which specific items are placed around the room for the child to find. Depending on the student's abilities, he or she can be given a list of items to find, put away, and check off, or the teacher can give a the student one item at a time to find. A point might be awarded for each item found and correctly put away, and the total points accumulated each time the game is played could be compared to assess progress.

Instructional Materials and Supplies Needed

- Designated toy box or container for toys (or tools and materials), which is clearly labeled or marked to be identifiable to the child
- Container for collecting the items to be put away, such as a tote bag or paper/plastic bag, box, or crate
- Tray to contain items at a workstation
- Sound source locator (optional for students with mobility issues)

Settings

The child's bedroom or play area (or workstation with older children) or a preschool classroom. For older students with disabilities, a workstation or work area. Any extraneous sound (radio or television not being used for orientation purposes) needs to be turned off and voices (parents, other adults, siblings, coworkers) need to be minimized, if possible, in the early stages of this activity. This quiet environment will allow the child to listen for environmental cues or a designated sound source as they pick up and put away toys or other materials.

Duration/Timing

30 minutes, minimum

Evaluation

Skill	Date			
	I	SI	AN	U
Locates items that needed putting away				
Picks up items				
Finds where the items belong				

(continued on next page)

Puts the items away in the appropriate storage unit				
Solves problems in tidying up (interfering noise, obstructions in the path to the storage area, a full toy or tool box, and the like)				
Total				

Key:
I = Independent
SI = Semi-independent (student initiates activity and requires minimal assistance)
AN = Assistance needed (task is started for student and then student completes task)
U = Unable to perform

Learning Activity: Workers I Know

Primary ECC Area: Career education **Component:** Career exploration
Grades: 3–8

Other ECC Areas
- Self-determination
- Assistive technology
- Compensatory access
- Social interaction

Goal: The student will gain a more realistic understanding of specific jobs by collecting information about different jobs performed by adults he or she knows and considering whether he or she might have an interest in those jobs.

Key Tasks/Concepts
The student will:
- Develop a list of people who can be asked about their jobs
- Conduct a survey
- Develop a format for recording the job information and use it to record information from the survey
- Discuss and evaluate the jobs in the survey to see if they would be a good match

Description
Students will conduct a "mini-survey" of adults they know, such as parents, other family members, parents of friends, and adults at school to find out what job they do and additional information about their jobs, including job titles, job descriptions, skills needed for each job, and likes and dislikes.

Before the interviews are conducted, the teacher of students with visual impairments will help students prepare in the following ways:
- identify potential interview subjects
- determine what questions to ask
- discuss how to document the information obtained from the interviews
- establish how many interviews need to be completed and recorded to complete the activity (recommendation is three to five interviews)
- practice interview strategies

Students can be involved on any level appropriate for their abilities, and can work independently or with helpers. Interviews should be set up by the students, whenever possible, with the teacher monitoring progress.

(continued on next page)

Students should record the information in a format that is easy for them to consult, such as the following chart for a student with low vision, or a straightforward list for a student who is blind:

Person's Name	Job Title	Job Description	Special Skills Required	Like/Dislike
Dad	*Plumber*	*Repair bath and kitchen pipes and resolve water leaks or other plumbing problems (hot water heater malfunctions, for example)*	*Knowledge of plumbing tools (pipe wrenches, sump pumps, soldering torch, hack saw, etc.) and repair applications, willingness to work in tight places or crawl under homes to access pipes, physical strength (digging, breaking frozen fittings, etc.); computer software for appointment setting and billing*	*Most of the time he likes his job, although sometimes he gets tired and his back hurts*
Mrs. Tucker	*Princi-pal*	*In charge of school – supervises teachers and staff, monitors students' progress*	*Knowledge of teaching, how to work with people, budgeting, hiring and firing of people, and school scheduling; computer skills (word-processing software, Department of Education software)*	*She likes to help children learn.*

This activity can be expanded by having the students further investigate jobs included on the surveys using computer searches to determine what training is required to perform them, what other jobs are related in some way, and so forth. Detailed career investigation of one job a month could be incorporated into the teacher's routine time with each student. Students can also survey classmates about their parents' jobs to determine most common jobs, most unusual jobs, etc.

At completion of the surveys and related job research, students should be asked to evaluate each job to determine whether the job is of interest to them, whether they could do the job—either with or without further training—and what accommodations they would need to perform the job as an individual with a visual impairment. If possible, students should rank the jobs researched from most like what they want to do to least like what they want to do.

Instructional Materials and Supplies Needed

- Charting materials such as paper and pen or braille writer, digital recorder, laptop or electronic notetaker
- Telephone (if interviews need to be done by phone rather than in person)

Settings

Resource room or area where teacher meets with students and the environments where the interviews will take place (home, school, community)

Duration/Timing

15–45 minutes depending on activity phase taking place (setting up the survey or interviewing, etc.)

Evaluation

Skill	Date			
	I	SI	AN	U
Develops a system for collecting information (chart)				
Lists prospective interviewees				
Demonstrates interviewing skills				

(continued on next page)

Performs interviews agreed upon				
Captures pertinent information on chart				
Reviews information with instructor				
Completes additional research on interviewees' jobs				
Compares jobs to self				
Ranks jobs from most to least of interest				
Total				

Key:
I = Independent
SI = Semi-independent (student initiates activity and requires minimal assistance)
AN = Assistance needed (task is started for student and then student completes task)
U = Unable to perform

Learning Activity: Name That Worker!

Primary ECC Area: Career education **Component:** Career exploration
Grades: 2–5

Other ECC Areas
- Social interaction
- Recreation and leisure
- Sensory efficiency
- Compensatory access
- Independent living

Goal: The student will identify workers based on a description of associated job responsibilities.

Key Tasks/Concepts
The student will:
- Identify job responsibilities of community workers
- Increase work-related vocabulary

Description
For this activity, the teacher and students play a game that involves moving a game piece around a game board. At the beginning of each turn, the player draws a card on which is written work-related information, such as:
- This is a worker who spends most of the time putting new soles on shoes, but also repairs broken straps on purses.
- This worker gets to work very early in the morning so that there will be fresh baked goods, like doughnuts, for people to buy for breakfast.
- This worker answers the phone and greets people who come to visit a place of business. Move forward 2 extra days if you can name the person who does this job at your school.

The game board could be prepared with messages in the squares, such as:
- Late to work, go back 2 days
- The boss sees you working hard, advance 3 days
- You've worked at the same job for a year. Take a week's vacation and move forward 5 days.

(continued on next page)

As an alternative to creating an entire game board, an abacus or talking calculator could be used by each player. The messages could all be printed and brailled on cards to be drawn in turn by the players. If a student answers a question correctly, he or she adds 3 points to the abacus/calculator. If the student draws a card that says "late to work," he or she subtracts 2. The teacher would have to keep track separately or watch the student make the calculations.

As a third alternative, a calendar with tactile lines could be used instead of a game board.

Instructional Materials and Supplies Needed

- Game board in the shape of a 30-day calendar or an actual calendar with tactile lines between the boxes; last day is labeled "Pay Day"
- As an alternative to the game board, use an abacus for each player
- Tokens
- Cards on which career information has been typed or brailled

Settings

Resource room or meeting area used by the teacher

Duration/Timing

10–30 minutes, depending on how elaborate the game board is

Evaluation

A chart such as the following could be used to monitor the student's accurate identification of the workers included in the game cards during each time the game is played:

Skill	Date	Date	Date	Date
Identifies secretary				
Identifies police officer				
Identifies baker				
Identifies grocer				
Identifies waitperson				
Identifies truck driver				
Identifies nurse				

Key:

+ = behavior present

– = behavior absent

Learning Activity: Home Helper

Primary ECC Area: Career education **Component:** Career exploration

Grades: K–12

Other ECC Areas

- Independent living
- Self-determination
- Compensatory access

Goal: The student will become aware of and participate in jobs and chores that must be done inside and outside the home.

(continued on next page)

Key Tasks/Concepts

The student will:

- Understand the types of chores that must be done around the home
- Complete simple chores or parts of chores at home
- Complete and maintain a reporting system for chores accomplished

Description

The teacher can begin the activity with a conversation about jobs that are done at home to maintain the home environment, such as:

- Picking up and putting away items (clothes, dishes, food, etc.)
- Vacuuming
- Mopping and sweeping
- Setting the table
- Getting and opening mail
- Paying bills
- Grocery shopping
- Changing linens and towels
- Cleaning bathrooms
- Making beds
- Cleaning kitchen
- Dusting
- Feeding pets
- Washing car
- Mowing grass
- Raking
- Shoveling snow

This list can be expanded or shortened depending on the abilities of the students.

The teacher has students pick out certain jobs or parts of jobs that they can help with. Families should be involved in these discussions and agree to allow the students to participate in jobs at home. Students can keep charts at school of chores they're doing to facilitate discussions about success and completion of jobs and to begin to recognize what additional skills students might need to learn to do the jobs. If possible, it would be preferable for the teacher to work with students in their homes on this activity.

This activity allows students to make choices about chores or jobs they are interested in doing and helps students recognize skills that are needed to do the jobs. It also gives students the expectation that they are contributing members to their households. This activity can begin simply and increase in difficulty as the student becomes competent in skills needed for the jobs.

An expansion of this activity might be a discussion about hiring and paying others to do some of the jobs needed to maintain the home environment.

Instructional Materials and Supplies Needed

Supplies will vary depending on the skills that the student needs to develop.

Settings

Home to demonstrate the skills; charting and discussions can take place at school. If collaboration with the family is not an option, many of these jobs or chores can be performed at school in the child's classroom, teacher's office or workspace, cafeteria, main office, and the like.

Duration/Timing

Discussions and charting can be done in 15–20 minutes. Completion of the actual jobs may take longer. If the teacher of students with visual impairments goes to the home, more time will be required.

(continued on next page)

Evaluation

Evaluation can consist of the student's chart of jobs done at home and skills that the student determines he or she needs to learn, as in the following example. Evaluation can also be done by rating skills that have been learned.

Day or Date	Job or Chore	What I Did	Skills I Need to Learn
Monday 3/23	*Made my bed*	*Put sheets on my bed*	*Putting pillowcases on*
Wednesday 3/25	*Fed the dog*	*Put food in his bowl*	*Putting water in the bowl*

Learning Activity: I'll Work for You!

Primary ECC Area: Career education **Component:** Career preparation

Grades: 3–8

Other ECC Areas

- Independent living
- Self-determination
- Compensatory access
- Orientation and mobility

Goal: The student will learn about characteristics of workers that are valued by employers and demonstrate them by performing a variety of job tasks for others.

Key Tasks/Concepts

The student will:

- Develop a list of desirable work behaviors
- Develop a list of tasks the student can perform independently for others
- Perform tasks, demonstrating the desirable behaviors

Description

The student and teacher of students with visual impairments will discuss behaviors that are desirable when performing work for others, including:

- a positive attitude
- arriving when promised
- asking if there is more work to be done
- being polite
- working efficiently

Then the student and teacher will create another list of tasks the student can do independently and that he or she can perform for another person at the school site. Jobs that might be appropriate for students include:

- cleaning the sink in a classroom
- stapling a set of papers
- collating papers
- watering plants
- dusting plants
- straightening books on a shelf
- making a cup of tea or hot chocolate
- making a snack (popcorn, cheese on crackers)
- getting a drink or snack from the vending machine
- wiping tables
- putting flyers in teachers' boxes

(continued on next page)

For this age group, the teacher will probably need to arrange in advance for the student to work for another adult at the school, though some students might benefit from being present when these arrangements are finalized to hear the discussion.

The teacher should prepare an accessible list of the desirable workplace behaviors discussed earlier and review it with the student before each work event. Acting as a "job coach," the teacher can model for the student these behaviors. Talking out loud can help the student develop awareness of the desired behavior. For example, the teacher might say, "We promised Mr. Marks we'd be there at 3:10. I'd better check the clock to see what time it is. Check the clock with me. Oh, look! It's 3:05 now, so we'd better leave. Good workers show up a few minutes early."

All students will probably need the teacher to demonstrate the actual task that needs to be completed. Because the selected task should be one that the student can perform independently, these sessions should be focused more on orientation to the environment, if it is new to the student, than on instruction.

After the first work experience, the person for whom the student did the work should be asked to provide honest feedback about the student's work behaviors, including the quality of the job done, in a face-to-face session with the student and the teacher. Similar reviews should occur regularly.

After each work session, the list of desired work behaviors should be reviewed again and the student asked to evaluate whether the behavior was demonstrated or not and to rate the quality of the work completed. The teacher should provide honest feedback to the student about the work completed and the behaviors demonstrated.

Instructional Materials and Supplies Needed

- Depends on the job to be performed

Settings

School rooms where work can be performed (classroom, offices, cafeteria, playground, lawn/landscaping beds)

Duration/Timing

Once the work routine has been established, the pre- and post-review of the work behaviors should require about 5 minutes each. Travel time to work location and time to complete the work will increase the period of time set aside for this activity.

The activity should be performed at least weekly.

Evaluation

The teacher should periodically question the student to determine if the student can identify at least five valued workplace behaviors.

The checklist of desired behaviors could serve as the teacher's monitoring of the student's development of the targeted skills, as follows.

Behavior	Date	Date	Date	Date
I had a positive attitude				
I arrived on time				
I asked about more work				
I was polite				
My work was neatly done				
I worked efficiently				
My work was done correctly				

Key:

+ = behavior present

– = behavior absent

CHAPTER 12

Self-Determination

Karen E. Wolffe and L. Penny Rosenblum

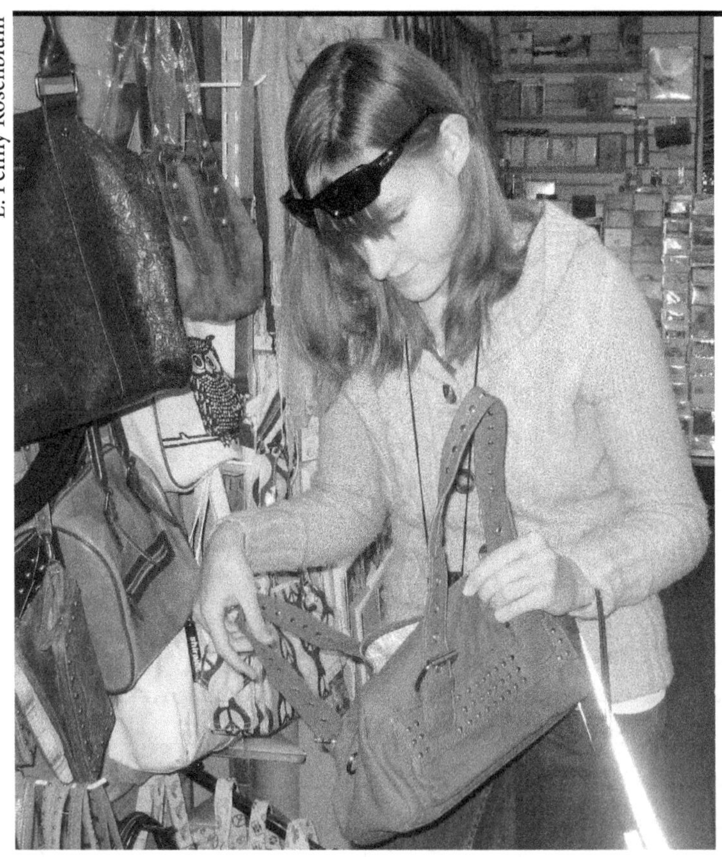
L. Penny Rosenblum

In the expanded core curriculum (ECC), the area of self-determination focuses on skills that enable students to advocate effectively for their own needs and goals. Self-determination refers to an individual's ability to decide what he or she wants and needs, and, by extension, to make decisions about his or her own future. For teachers working with students with visual impairments, helping children develop these skills often becomes a matter of increasing concern as the transition from school to adulthood approaches and the need to be able to make choices, express preferences, and look out for one's own interests and well-being becomes a priority.

As already noted in Chapter 11, the areas of career education and self-determination have considerable overlap and have sometimes been treated as one content area (Brolin, 1997; Wolffe, 1996, 2000, 2007). Both involve self-exploration and an understanding of the impact of one's behavior on other people; both encourage problem solving, goal setting, and self-advocacy. Therefore, readers are encouraged to consider this chapter on self-determination together with the chapter on career education to get the maximum benefit from both.

In addition to career education, the self-determination area overlaps most specifically with skills in the areas of social interaction and independent living. Social interaction and self-determination both encompass assertive communication skills, including the ability to understand differing points of view and relate to people who hold different perspectives; it is through acquiring techniques of assertiveness that individuals learn to speak up or advocate for themselves. Thus, self-advocacy, the ability to express one's needs and desires appropriately, is a fundamental component of self-determination and is also integral to social interaction as well as career education. Finally, many of the opportunities for students to make decisions both at home and at school relate to independent living, particularly when choices need to be made concerning, for example, whether to wash clothing in hot or cold water; whether to organize a drawer of socks by rolling, folding, or pinning them together and stacking or bundling like colors; and whether to take a shower or bath.

The positive outcomes of teaching youngsters self-determination skills and self-directed and self-regulated behavior are well-documented (Abery & Eggebeen, 2001; Agran, Hong, & Blankenship, 2007; Field & Hoffman, 1994; Algozzine, Browder, Karvonen, Test, & Wood, 2001; Hoy, 1986; Mithaug, 1991; Wehmeyer, 1992, 2003; Wehmeyer, Agran, & Hughes, 1998; Wehmeyer, Abery, Mithaug, & Stancliffe, 2003). However, there has not always been a clear understanding of what content should be covered or what theoretical base supports teaching in this area (Wehmeyer, 2003). Self-determination theory, which focuses on whether behavior is internally or externally motivated (referred to as intrinsic versus extrinsic motivation; Deci & Ryan, 2008), has evolved primarily as a result of mounting empirical evidence in the fields of philosophy and psychology that an *internal locus of control*—a belief that one should be guided by one's own values and preferences rather than those of others, and that one can choose how to react to events and control outcomes—tends to lead to greater success in life (Mithaug, 1991; Wehmeyer, 2003). For individuals with disabilities, the concept of self-determination came into vogue with the disability rights movement of the 1970s. Nirje (1972), for example, focused on the right of people with disabilities to self-govern or self-determine, and he advocated for them to have control over their destinies and to be able to make decisions about their education, work, and community activities.

SELF-DETERMINATION AND VISUAL IMPAIRMENT

Self-determination is as important for children and adolescents with visual impairments as for anyone else. However, the way in which students with visual impairments need to be taught the techniques that enable them to apply their knowledge, skills, and abilities in this area differs from the instruction provided to sighted youngsters. Something as fundamental to self-determination as choice making may not be easily learned by students with visual impairments. Sighted students learn a great deal about the choices available to them and the techniques others use to arrive at decisions incidentally, through observation of available choices and the actions of those around them. Children who are blind or severely visually impaired need to be exposed to the same information through hands-on exploration and verbal (or signed, in the case of children who are deaf-blind) explanations.

For example, sighted children typically begin to express their clothing preferences when they are preschoolers because they've seen the choices available to them: the colors, styles, and accessories worn by their siblings and other children in preschool or in pictures. Boys may want to wear blue shorts, tee-shirts with action hero pictures on them, or baseball caps; and girls may want to wear pink dresses, tee-shirts with pictures of fairy princesses on them, and ribbons because they've seen these types of clothes on other children or advertised in magazines or on television. (Although this example may seem gender biased, readers may want to consider how many gender-based clothing decisions children make based on what they've seen other children and adults of their gender wearing.) Many children who are blind, however, may have their clothes chosen for them and may not even know the colors, styles, and accessories they are wearing, much less how their clothes

L. Penny Rosenblum

Expressing preferences and making choices, as in choosing one's own clothes, is an early step toward self-determination.

compare to what other children are wearing. They need caring adults and older children or friends to show them clothing options in stores and closets; they need to receive information about what other children are wearing, why a child might have chosen a particular article of clothing, and what choices meet their families' expectations or values. Children with visual impairments need to be given the opportunity to choose what they'd prefer to wear based on the available options. Initially, it may be most effective and meaningful to give children choices based on general style (such as short versus long sleeves, shorts versus slacks versus a dress, or a dress versus a skirt and blouse) or accessories (such as shoes that tie or have Velcro closures versus slip-ons or sandals) rather than based on color. Children without good vision need to know colors and how to work with various colors to get the effect they might want; however, nuances related to issues like shades of color need to be taught over time.

Without structured intervention to learn self-determination skills, children with visual impairments may be at risk of remaining dependent on others for life. Much has been written about the phenomenon known as "learned helplessness," which is associated with poor psychological well-being, passivity, depression, and low self-esteem (Reed & Curtis, 2012; Seligman, 1990, 1996, 2002). When children always have things done for them or to them, they learn or come to believe that others are more capable than they are, that they cannot control the world in which they live, and that their freedom to take risks and succeed is limited. Self-determination is the polar opposite of learned helplessness—it is the ability of individuals to make choices and exercise control over their lives, to achieve their goals, and to acquire the skills and resources necessary to participate fully and meaningfully as adults in society (Deci, 1992; Deci & Ryan, 1985, 2008; Field, 1996; Morgan, Bixler, & McNamara, 2002).

STUDENTS WITH MULTIPLE DISABILITIES

Like students whose only disability is visual impairment, students who are visually impaired and have additional disabilities need instruction and guidance in self-determination. However, many students with multiple disabilities are likely to require intervention by a team of professionals who have expertise in the areas of their other disability or disabilities in addition to the teacher of students with visual impairments. For example, students who are deaf-blind will benefit from working with both a teacher of students with visual impairments and a teacher of students with hearing impairments who collaborate to plan and implement instruction; depending on the severity of their physical impairments, students who have physical disabilities and visual impairment may benefit from working with a teacher of students with visual impairments, occupational therapist, physical therapist, and speech and language specialist, who all work together to design instruction.

For students with additional disabilities, the strategies and activities presented in this chapter may require additional modifications and techniques. For students with severe or profound multiple disabilities, activities such as goal setting and developing disability statements, discussed later in this chapter, may require extensive input and support from the teacher; in some cases, the teacher may have to complete the activity for the student and then work with the educational team—including the family and the student to the greatest extent possible—on how best to support the student in pursuing goals.

Another factor to consider when students with visual impairments have additional disabilities, particularly cognitive disabilities, is the need to work on tasks for longer periods of time to achieve competence. Students will benefit from clear and consistent instruction, but they may have difficulty transferring skills from one environment to another. Depending on level of ability, the student may need ongoing support for life and may have to rely on assistance from advocates and caregivers. However, most students can achieve some level of self-determination, such as being able to recognize their name and those of significant others and expressing preferences for activities, food, and clothing. In general, teachers need to apply patience in work with students who have multiple disabilities and give them time to make choices, to solve problems, and to achieve goals.

COMPONENTS OF SELF-DETERMINATION

Researchers and practitioners in special education and specifically the education of children with visual impairments have identified important components of self-determination (Agran et al., 2007; Deci & Ryan, 1985; Lewis & Wolffe, 2006; Mithaug, 1991, 2003; Nirje, 1972; Perske, 1972; Wolffe, 2012). Each component supports and contributes to the success of the others; development of all the components results in the achievement of self-determination. These components include:

- self-knowledge
- self-advocacy and empowerment
- assertiveness
- informed decision making
- problem solving and goal setting
- self-directed and self-regulated behavior

Each component and its development are discussed in the following sections, and further, along with strategies for teaching them, in the section titled Role of the Teacher of Students with Visual Impairments.

Self-Knowledge

Self-knowledge entails an understanding of one's own personality and behavior traits, including one's strengths and limitations and awareness of individual rights and responsibilities. For students who are visually impaired, an awareness of the nature and aspects of their visual impairment and any other disabling conditions, as well as the impact of these conditions on one's needs, are part of self-knowledge. Understanding their visual condition allows students to provide information to others, including details about their visual limitations and the accommodations and modifications necessary for accomplishing tasks.

Infants and babies first develop a sense of self-knowledge by exploring their feet and hands and learning to respond to their name. As children grow older, their knowledge of self expands to recognition of feelings, strengths, and weaknesses. Children begin to understand how, as an individual, they affect other people and they recognize ownership of feelings and possessions. This critical development of self-knowledge must be supported and mentored in children with visual impairments by teachers and families so that children can grow into self-assured young people and adults capable of being successful in life.

Also part of self-knowledge is an awareness of individual rights and responsibilities, including knowledge of what to expect and what to contribute as an individual. Young children begin to understand their "rights" when they are provided with the necessities of life (food and shelter), and they explore their responsibilities when they are encouraged by family members and the teacher to take on small household or classroom jobs such as setting the table, dressing, or putting away materials and toys. As students with visual impairments grow older, they need to be taught their rights as outlined in disability legislation and their responsibilities to home, school, and community such as respect for others, participation in class activities and supporting the community through volunteer work and voting.

Self-Advocacy and Empowerment

Self-advocacy means speaking up for oneself. Every individual has the right to speak up for him- or herself by expressing wants and needs. Individuals who feel that they have control over their own life are empowered and tend to grow up to be self-assured adults.

Young children learn self-advocacy and empowerment strategies by expressing what they like or don't like and by feeling safe in expressing their wants and needs. Children often have favorite toys or favorite foods and should be encouraged to talk about what they like about favorites. Developing opinions leads to the ability to advocate for oneself and to the secure feeling of empowerment. Teachers and family members can enhance skills in self-advocacy and empowerment by providing safe environments for children with visual impairments to express themselves and be confident making decisions.

Assertiveness

Assertiveness includes the abilities to communicate effectively and confidently with others, to negotiate with other people to arrive at mutually agreed-on options for action rather than passively or aggressively engaging with them, and to present oneself as a competent, well-adjusted human being. The components of self-knowledge and self-advocacy and empowerment lay the groundwork for developing appropriate assertiveness skills. Young children develop assertiveness skills by communicating their preferences and behaving in a way that brings what they want to them. Sometimes this behavior is not acceptable—for example, having a tantrum to obtain a wanted toy—and teachers and families need to model and mold socially acceptable behavior from the child's earliest years. Assertiveness is critical for successful adults and is closely linked to appropriate social interaction and self-advocacy. Young people hone assertiveness skills by, for example, successfully negotiating with friends to agree on a particular activity, by discussing issues with friends and stating their own opinions, and by presenting themselves as competent and self-assured.

Informed Decision-Making

Self-determined individuals have the capacity to choose from a range of options and make informed decisions based on those options. Young children show preferences for certain foods or toys and express basic likes and dislikes. Older children learn to make choices using strategies that lead to sound decision making. For example, a young child might display his anger at a toy that isn't working by smashing it to the ground. The consequences of such an action might not be evident to the child until the next time he wants that particular toy and then realizes that it is broken beyond repair. Older children can learn to anticipate potential problems and make decisions based on that knowledge. For example, a student can make the decision to use a cane for a street crossing, knowing that it is a safer way to cross the street, and thus avoid a potential problem of unsafe travel. If teachers and families allow children to make informed decisions by discussing potential hazards and talking through the ramifications of choices, children with visual impairments are more likely to grow up to be adults who know how to make decisions based on their range of options and information about those options.

Problem Solving and Goal Setting

Problem solving and goal setting are closely linked to informed decision making in that understanding the ramifications of choices helps to guide one's ability to effectively solve problems and to set reasonable goals. Young children may attempt to solve problems by seeking comfort with a parent or other favorite person. As children grow older they learn to express the need for assistance and to solve simple problems, for example, by using an umbrella to get to a friend's house in the rain. Young people learn to set personal goals for themselves based on recognized need for improvement. As self-knowledge is developed and strengths and weaknesses are discussed with adults or peers in a comfortable setting, a student with a visual impairment can be encouraged to address weaknesses by developing strategies for improvement. For example, if a student feels that she can't contribute to a discussion about the latest trends in clothing, she can address this weakness by asking the teacher of students with visual impairments or a special friend to tell her about clothing choices and what is currently popular. When children and young people are given opportunities to work out the solutions to problems and set goals throughout their school years, they can develop into adults who can solve more critical problems and set important personal goals using strategies that they have learned and practiced.

Self-Directed and Self-Regulated Behavior

Self-directed behavior means choosing what one would like to do. Closely related to making informed decisions, this component of self-determination is important because it allows students with visual impairments to make individual choices and feel that their choices are under their control, not forced by others. Self-regulated behavior involves monitoring the impact of one's behavior on others and controlling that behavior to adjust to social demands. Young children are self-directed when they can choose the toy they want to play with. They demonstrate self-regulated behavior when they learn to politely ask for a drink of water or ask to share a toy. Older children learn self-directed behavior by participating in a favorite sport activity and demonstrate self-regulated behavior when they follow the rules of the game and feel accepted as a participant. Learning self-directed and self-regulated behavior is critical for successful life functioning. Being responsible for one's actions develops self-assurance and recognition that behaviors can impact others negatively or positively.

At the most basic level, *self-directed behavior,* in which individuals choose what they would like to do, is demonstrated when children decide between two or more options or opportunities. As children mature, they demonstrate self-directed behavior when they understand and can apply problem-solving skills to set goals, make plans to achieve their goals, and realistically evaluate whether their plans are working or need to be revised. *Self-regulated behavior,* in which individuals adjust their behavior according to its impact on others or their awareness of its appropriateness in terms of social standards, is demonstrated when people understand and can express their needs (based on self-knowledge), listen to others' feedback, and respond appropriately, and then modify their behavior to meet the demands of society. At its most basic level, self-regulated behavior occurs when children learn appropriate responses to situations in which they either don't get what they want (for example, losing a game and not having a tantrum), or do get what they want (winning at a game and not gloating or making fun of the loser).

Learning the self-determination skills related to the components of self-knowledge, advocacy and empowerment, assertiveness, informed decision making, problem solving and goal setting, and self-directed and self-regulated behavior typically leads to high levels of self-esteem and self-confidence. *Self-esteem* is a feeling of satisfaction with oneself—often referred to as "feeling good about oneself." *Self-confidence* is a belief and expectation that one will typically perform well or be successful in most circumstances in one's life. Self-determination, which is in essence autonomy, or the idea that one has control over one's own destiny and can make one's own choices, contributes to enhanced self-esteem and self-confidence. Table 12.1 lists many of the essential skills related to self-determination and also shows the approximate ages at which children and youngsters with visual impairments typically develop them.

ASSESSMENT OF SELF-DETERMINATION

Although a definitive tool for assessing students with visual impairments on the components of self-determination has yet to be developed, various tests and techniques have been used to assess the self-determination skills of students with other disabilities. Some generic tools have also been used to assess students with visual impairments. Teachers of students with visual impairments can investigate these instruments and consider their use, provided that specific assessment items are appropriately adapted if necessary and the results of the assessment make clear that the instrument was adapted for use with a student with a visual impairment.

Two assessments, in particular, that can be used in this way are the Minnesota Self-Determination Scales, specifically the Importance Scale (Abery, Elkin, Smith, Springborg, & Stancliffe, 2000) and the Self-Determination Exercise Scale: Student Edition (Abery, McGraw, & Smith, 1995) and *The Arc's Self-Determination Scale* (Wehmeyer & Kelchner, 1995). Some sections of the Transition Competencies Checklist (Wolffe, 2011) and the *EVALS (Evaluating Visually Impaired Students)* assessment toolkit from the Texas School for the Blind and Visually Impaired (2007) can also be used for self-determination assessment. In addition, teachers can use informal methods of data collection to monitor a student's strengths and needs in the area of self-determination, such as structured interviews, observations, and informal checklists.

Minnesota Self-Determination Scales

The Importance Scale of the Minnesota Self-Determination Scales (Abery et al., 2000) and a modified version of the Self-Determination Exercise Scale: Student Edition (Abery et al., 1995) have been used in studies with students who are deaf-blind (Abery & Eggebeen, 2001) and have visual impairments (Robinson & Lieberman, 2004). However, the developers of the scale now view it as unreflective of some of the different aspects of self-determination. In 2005, the University of Minnesota Research and Training Center on Community Living team introduced a new scale for elementary and middle school students based on what the team now views as the three aspects of self-determination: (1) degree of control exercised, (2) decision-making preference, or how much control the person desires,

TABLE 12.1

Self-Determination Skills and Typical Ages of Acquisition for Children with Visual Impairments

	Components/Skills				
Age Levels*	**Self-Knowledge**	**Self-Advocacy**	**Assertiveness**	**Decision Making/Problem Solving/Goal Setting**	**Self-Directed/ Self-Regulated Behavior**
0–3 years	■ Responds to name ■ Voices or signs name	■ Chooses a toy or favored object for comfort when stressed or unhappy	■ Communicates favorites ■ Makes known activities that are liked or disliked	■ Shows preferences of toys and food ■ Seeks comfort with mother or favorite person	■ Knows behavior affects others
4–7 years	■ States full name and contact information ■ Provides detailed information about who is in family ■ Provides basic description of disabling conditions	■ Expresses oneself when sad or happy ■ Selects favorite clothing	■ Converses and makes plans with friends	■ States basic likes and dislikes ■ Expresses need for assistance ■ Is aware of making choices ■ Chooses a favorite activity	■ Controls behavior when angry or sad
8–13 years	■ Provides detailed personal information ■ States rights and responsibilities ■ Understands own personality type	■ Speaks up when not happy about an issue ■ Describes preferred foods, music, activities, etc.	■ Negotiates with friends to agree on an activity ■ Demonstrates self-assurance	■ Chooses favorite leisure activities ■ Has a hobby ■ Solves simple problems ■ Sets goals for self-improvement	■ Sets a schedule for getting schoolwork done
14–21 years	■ Knows how to locate specific federal regulations related to disability ■ Articulates own strengths and weaknesses ■ Describes impact of visual impairment on activities such as driving, transportation, movie going	■ Negotiates with others for needed assistance ■ Is confident making decisions and expressing needs ■ Participates in or conducts IEP meeting	■ Uses appropriate behavior to make needs known ■ Presents self as competent ■ Communicates assertively with others	■ Solves complex problems ■ Sets goals for personal development and achievement ■ Chooses part-time work or volunteer job ■ Selects favorite hobby with understanding of limitations ■ Provides input to class schedule selections	■ Uses effective behavior strategies to make friends ■ Routinely engages in self-regulated and self-directed behavior

*Although children acquire skills at varying ages, the ranges here indicate typical ages at which a particular skill may be developed.

Source: Based on information from R. Loumiet and N. Levack, *Independent Living: A Curriculum with Adaptations for Students with Visual Impairments,* 2nd ed., 3 Vols. (Austin: Texas School for the Blind and Visually Impaired, 1993).

and (3) importance, which focuses on how important an aspect of life is in this area (B. Abery, personal communication, June 9, 2011).

With the new scale, rather than asking students to rate themselves in regard to various aspects of their capacity for self-determination, a set of scenarios is presented to which students respond. For example, a teacher might present a scenario in which two students have a choice between chicken and pizza for dinner. The student taking the test is then asked whether he or she is more like the student who can't decide or the one who knows immediately whether he prefers chicken or pizza. The evaluator considers the student's answer, as well as information from teachers and parents, to assess the extent to which the student possesses the skills, knowledge, and attitudes found to be associated with self-determination (B. Abery, personal communication, June 9, 2011).

The Arc's Self-Determination Scale

One of the earliest and arguably one of the more widely used assessment tools for self-determination is *The Arc's Self-Determination Scale* (Wehmeyer & Kelchner, 1995). It is intended as a student-directed assessment, and was originally designed for students with learning and intellectual disabilities. This scale asks students to report on a variety of behaviors, including:

- self-directed behaviors or autonomy in personal care and independent living skills, social and recreational activities, academic and vocational activities
- self-regulated behaviors in problem solving and goal setting
- level of psychological empowerment or ability to self-advocate and feel as if they can achieve desired outcomes
- self-awareness or self-realization in the form of an understanding of abilities, limitations, and feelings

The Arc's Self-Determination Scale includes four subscales (personal autonomy, autonomy in career planning, self-realization, and psychological empowerment). Items are structured in such a way that students select from an array of choices that relate to having opportunities to demonstrate skills, choosing a scenario that would best fit with a social occurrence, and selecting a statement that best describes feelings or wants. When the scale was used to assess the self-determination of students with visual impairments in the second National Longitudinal Transition Study (NLTS2), the results for personal autonomy, career planning, self-realization, and psychological items were largely positive, and they were not substantially different from the results for students with other disabilities (FACTS, 2005), possibly indicating that the test may not be subtle enough to tease out students' strengths and weaknesses in this content area. Therefore, teachers are cautioned to use this test only in conjunction with other evaluative tools such as structured interviews, observations, and behavioral checklists.

Other Assessment Tools

The Transition Competencies Checklist (Wolffe, 2011), a behavioral checklist designed specifically for students with visual impairments, includes many of the components of self-determination proposed by Wehmeyer (1996), such as problem solving, self-advocacy, and self-awareness. This checklist is designed as a self-reporting tool for students with visual impairments and can be used by teachers to assess and focus on specific skills. If the student is unable to complete the checklist, it can be completed by an evaluator during or following observation of the student. In addition, there are parallel versions of the tool that can be completed by parents or caregivers and educational staff for comparisons to the student's self-assessment. (The Transition Competencies Checklist appears in Chapter 11, Appendix 11B.)

The *EVALS (Evaluating Visually Impaired Students)* assessment toolkit (Texas School for the Blind and Visually Impaired, 2007), which has also been used nationally (Wolffe, Blankenship, & Hatlen, 2010), correlates areas of the expanded core curriculum such as self-determination to Texas state educational standards to determine a student's current performance against those standards. Although this series of checklists refers to Texas state standards, it provides information that allows teachers of students with visual impairments to correlate their students' performances to the standards of other states. In addition, Levenson's (1981) Locus of Control Scales and Rosenberg's (1965) Self-Esteem Scale (see the Resources section at the end of this chapter) may provide useful information about a student's abilities in self-regulated and self-directed behaviors and self-esteem.

Structured Interviews

Teachers may want to use structured interviews to assess students' skills regarding specific components of self-determination. In structured interviews, teachers and students talk about identified issues either in small groups or one on one. For a structured interview, the teacher prepares a series of open-ended questions to pose to a student to encourage discussion, such as the following:

- How do you feel when someone tells you what to do and gives you no choice about it? This question would help determine whether students feel they have an internal or external locus of control in the decision-making process.
- What can you do if someone tells you to do something one way and you'd prefer to do it another way? This question might help the teacher discover whether the student can demonstrate negotiation skills that are critical to assertively advocating for a preferred option in informed decision making.
- What can you do if someone offers to do something for you and you'd prefer to do it for yourself? This question can ascertain if the student understands how to graciously refuse assistance from others.
- How would you respond if you're asked to make a choice between two activities or things and you don't like either choice? This question would determine how a student evaluates options to arrive at a decision.

During structured interviews, teachers document the students' responses. Although the list of questions related to decision making in this example is not definitive, the questions would be helpful in initiating a conversation on this topic. Likewise, questions can be developed that determine a student's understanding of self-knowledge, self-advocacy, and assertiveness, as well as a student's ability to self-regulate, self-direct, solve problems, and set goals.

If students struggle with responses, the teacher might suggest two or three ideas and ask the student or group of students to comment. It is preferable for the teacher to suggest more than one thought or response so that the students don't assume that the teacher's idea is the correct approach or correct way to feel. For example, in a discussion about what to do if someone tells you to do something one way when you prefer to do it another, the teacher could suggest that the student could ignore the suggestion, ask for a detailed description of the suggestion, or thank the person for the suggestion and explain that he wants to use his own method. These types of responses could each be brainstormed to examine their potential effect on the outcome of the situation. The overall aim is to encourage students to consider and explore topics and situations.

Observations

Observations entail the teacher setting aside time routinely to watch students in a variety of settings and activities to see whether a desired behavior occurs. Teachers of students with visual impairments are encouraged to keep anecdotal records of their observations. In addition, they may want to note observations shared by family members, teachers, and other team members. Sidebar 12.1 provides an example of this approach.

Reviewing anecdotal notes periodically can help establish students' strengths and needs in the area of self-

SIDEBAR 12.1

A Teacher's Anecdotal Notes on Student Observations

Mr. Bryant, a teacher of students with visual impairments, worked twice a week with Aja, an 8-year-old with a combined vision and hearing loss. Aja attended a self-contained special education classroom with 6 other students, staffed by a teacher, Mrs. Thomas, and a paraprofessional, Sandy. Mr. Bryant noted the following observations of Aja over the course of several weeks.

1/7: I observed Aja going through the lunch line with Mrs. Thomas. Shown 2 meal choices she independently signed her lunch choice (chicken). Shown carton of milk and carton of juice she independently selected milk. Mrs. T. gave Aja 5 minutes when she sat at the table to see if she would sign "help" to get assistance opening her milk carton. Aja did not request help. Mrs. T. said she has been waiting 5 minutes each lunch period before helping and Aja rarely signs "help."

1/28: Came to Mrs. T's class to get Aja for our session. Found her on the floor having a tan-

(continued on next page)

SIDEBAR 12.1 *continued*

trum. Mrs. T. reported that when she had Aja go to the calendar box to see what activity was next (me), Aja took symbol for me and threw it on floor. When Mrs. T. had her pick it up and put it up on the board she got angry and collapsed to the floor having a tantrum. Not sure what is going on, as usually she is all smiles for our sessions. We had a good session 1/26. Once I sat on floor next to Aja and showed her my watch (name sign), she began to quiet after about 5 minutes. We stayed in the classroom and worked on an experience story, as I wasn't comfortable taking her out of the room.

2/12: Spoke to Aja's mother about upcoming IEP meeting. She told me that Aja is making more choices at mealtime at home. She has been having Aja bring dishes to the sink after meals. Asked me if I thought Aja should wash them. Yes! Will bring up independent living goals with Mrs. T. Based on talk with mom, we need to all be consistent in how we handle behavioral outbursts. How can our team help Aja learn to deal with changes to schedule or scheduled activities she doesn't want to do? Right now it seems more often than not she has an outburst and sometimes a full tantrum when there's an unexpected change or she's asked to do something she doesn't want to do.

2/19: Arrived in classroom 5 minutes early so I could see how Mrs. T. is cueing Aja with calendar box to let her know I am coming for our session. It went like clockwork! Mrs. T. signed "finished" to Aja after her snack. Aja trailed to calendar box shelf. She put snack symbol in finished box and got out my symbol and put it on the board. She did the sequence with only two prompts from Mrs. T!

Mr. Bryant's four entries over this period didn't take long to write and aren't detailed; however, there is enough information, given with enough frequency, for him to review and determine whether Aja is doing well with her self-determination skills or needs assistance. Through his observations and communication with Aja's classroom teacher and mother, he gathered additional information he could not have observed. He learned of one instance where Aja did not have success with her calendar box and one where she did. Perhaps when he observed on January 28, Aja wasn't feeling well, she was annoyed that an activity she enjoyed was coming to an end, or she didn't remember that the watch symbolized time with Mr. Bryant.

Perhaps speaking with the communication specialist about Aja's not signing "help" to get assistance with the milk carton would give Mrs. T an idea of how to get Aja to spontaneously ask for help in this situation and others that might be occurring during the school day. Incorporating activities in which Aja needs to ask for help into his own lessons is something he can do immediately to reinforce her self-determination skills. For example, Mr. Bryant might put her story materials into a box Aja can't open and see if she will sign "help" to get him to open the box for her.

Through his discussion with Aja's mother, Mr. Bryant also learned that she was having Aja bring dirty dishes to the sink; and that helped him identify a skill—dishwashing—that could be worked on at school and reinforced at home. Observations such as the ones Mr. Bryant made here could also be shared with other members of Aja's educational team to inform their work with Aja and to make sure all team members had the same understanding of her behavior.

determination. Teachers can use these observations to give students feedback and help them recognize what they are doing successfully and what skills and behaviors could be improved. Teachers can also develop formal lessons based on their observations and be on the lookout for incidental opportunities to have their students practice with self-determination skills such as choice making, self-advocacy, self-directed behavior, and self-regulatory behavior.

Informal Checklists

As in many areas of the ECC, teachers and counselors can develop informal checklists to evaluate students' skills related to self-determination. For example, the faculty members at the Colorado School for the Deaf and Blind have designed a series of checklists to evaluate students, including one focused on self-determination (Wolffe, 2006), which is included in Figure 12.1.

FIGURE 12.1

Example of Teacher-Made Checklist

SELF-DETERMINATION AND SELF-ADVOCACY OBSERVATION CHECKLIST

Student: ______________________________

Placement: ______________________________

Observer: ______________________________

Date of observation: ______________________________

Observation time: ______________________________

Location: ______________________________

Directions: Please rate the student's performance by placing a checkmark in the appropriate column.

Behaviors Observed	***Yes***	***No***	***N/A***
Attends to others			
Recognizes own name			
Communicates needs to others			
Explains desires to others			
Describes disability candidly			
Chooses from 2 options			
Chooses from array of options			
Recognizes when a decision is needed			
Can describe alternatives			
Sets goals			
Recognizes he/she is different from others			
Develops action plan to achieve goals			
Works consistently on action plan			
Evaluates decisions and acts accordingly			
Solicits help, only when needed			
Problem solves challenges			
Accepts consequences of decisions			

Task(s) performed/skill utilization:

Comments:

List overall strengths and weaknesses. Make recommendations. Note level of supervision required to perform tasks assigned. For example, can student perform tasks independently when given verbal, signed or written instructions? Can student perform with demonstration or tactile cues? How often does the student require prompting to stay on task? Does the student respond to certain people in the environment more favorably than others? Note accommodations necessary for the student to perform optimally.

SOURCE: Developed by Karen E. Wolffe and faculty at the Colorado School for the Deaf and the Blind, Colorado Springs, CO.

GENERAL CONSIDERATIONS FOR TEACHING SELF-DETERMINATION

No matter what a student's age, visual abilities, or level of academic or physical functioning, the teacher of students with visual impairments can routinely incorporate instruction in self-determination and opportunities to perform learned skills into the student's educational program as well as in learning activities that focus primarily on other ECC areas, as shown in the learning activities presented in the chapters on each ECC area in this part of this book. It is important to recognize, however, that collaboration among teachers, students, family members, and other professionals is essential to students' successful development of self-determination skills.

Overall, three critical strategies can be used by teachers of students with visual impairments to teach self-determination skills: modeling behaviors, providing practice opportunities, and providing direct instructional time. These same strategies are useful in teaching other ECC area skills, in particular those related to social interaction, recreation and leisure, and independent living.

Modeling Behaviors

Modeling involves exposing students to the use of self-determination skills by significant adults in the child's life (parents, teachers, related services personnel, and others). An activity related to modeling is introducing students to role models: adults with visual impairments who may demonstrate these skills in action. Support for *peer modeling* is another closely related activity. (Additional discussion of role models and peer modeling is presented in the following section of this chapter.) Peer modeling typically involves students coming together with other children and adolescents who have visual impairments to share ideas about how they have spoken up for themselves, solved problems on their own, set and planned to achieve goals, or demonstrated other skills of self-determination. For young children and older students, parents and teachers can, for example, demonstrate and verbalize making choices about favorite foods or activities, express a need for assistance, and describe their own strengths and weaknesses.

Providing Practice Opportunities

Providing opportunities for students to practice self-determination skills and receive realistic feedback from significant adults in their lives is a powerful reinforcing strategy. The value of practice relates to the need for children with visual impairments to learn by doing—not just hearing or reading about skills, but actually performing them—and then receiving input that helps them understand how their efforts compare to those of other children their age with typical vision.

Providing Instructional Time

Setting aside instructional time with students to allow both explicit and incidental opportunities to build self-determination skills is another important strategy. This focus encourages teachers to remember that their students with visual impairments need planned, carefully organized learning opportunities because they may not be able to learn self-determination skills through casual observation. Teachers need to incorporate into their lesson plans instruction that addresses self-determination skills, such as techniques for decision making, problem solving, goal setting, and assertiveness. (The learning activities at the end of this chapter provide some examples, and others are offered in the following section of this chapter.) These efforts can include, for example, coaching students on how they might participate in their own Individualized Education Program (IEP) meetings most effectively, and then encouraging and supporting them in attending and later leading their IEP and transitional IEP meetings.

The section that follows details the key role of the teacher of students with visual impairments in helping students develop self-determination skills, particularly making use of the strategies just described, and an explanation of the activities the teacher can pursue to support this important ECC area.

ROLE OF THE TEACHER OF STUDENTS WITH VISUAL IMPAIRMENTS

General Teaching Strategies

The teacher of students with visual impairments may be the most likely professional—in some cases, the most likely adult—in a child's life to fully understand the importance of supporting the child's development of self-determination skills. However, the role teachers of students with visual impairments play in teaching these skills will vary, depending on the responsibilities they have and environments in which they work. Itinerant teachers may provide less direct instruction, for example, than resource room teachers or teachers in special schools for children with visual impairments, because their students need less instruction in this area or because other educators take a lead role in their instruction, as might occur when a student has multiple disabilities. Regardless of the way in which services are delivered to the student, the teacher of students with visual impairments needs to help all team members recognize the importance of addressing the issue of self-determination. In addition, the teacher can have a powerful impact on a student's development of self-determination skills by modeling such skills, providing access to role models and opportunities for peer modeling, facilitating opportunities to practice self-determination skills, and offering direct instruction in self-determination skills.

Modeling

In their daily lives, sighted children effortlessly and often unconsciously observe the way others move through and interact within their environment. They see how adults and other students make choices in their lives when opportunities present themselves, as when someone who is walking on a sidewalk sees a downed branch and can choose to avoid it by stepping out into the street, walking through a yard, or taking an alternative route along another sidewalk. Students with typical vision see how others arrive at decisions through negotiation and compromise, or exchanges that are more passive or aggressive in nature (and see as well the associated facial expressions and body language of the partners in the interchange to understand what communication worked effectively). For the child with a visual impairment, observational opportunities are frequently limited or may be lacking altogether.

Teachers of students with visual impairments can assist their students by modeling the use of self-determination strategies, such as listing alternatives, problem solving, or requesting assistance, and then discussing what they've done, as in the following example:

Mr. Harkins met his second-grade student, Gabe, who is blind, as Gabe and his classmates came in from recess. Together, Mr. Harkins and Gabe walked to the library, where they usually met for their one-on-one sessions. As they approached the library, Mr. Harkins saw that a book fair was going on and that he and Gabe would not be able to find an available space in which to work. Rather than simply walking to another part of the school to find an unoccupied space, he decided to use the opportunity to model the self-determination skill of problem solving for Gabe. After they looked for an open space in the library without finding one, Mr. Harkins asked Gabe what he thought they should do. Gabe suggested they not meet because there was no space in the library. Mr. Harkins then outlined several possible alternative solutions to their problem, including:

- asking if the book fair organizer could free up space for them
- going to the office to ask if there was another work area they could use
- going back to Gabe's second-grade classroom and working together there.

By modeling how the problem might be solved proactively, involving Gabe in making the choice of how to solve it, and then explaining and reviewing what they had just done, Mr. Harkins helped Gabe recognize that giving up was not the only response to their problem.

Teachers of students with visual impairments can also take advantage of the modeling that others, with and without visual impairments, can provide for their students. When a teacher observes others in the environment using self-determination skills, he or she can describe their actions to the child who cannot see or may miss the nuances of the person's action and the responses of others. Sometimes children with visual impairments simply need to know about the visual subtleties in the environment and how those cues may facilitate or inhibit a person's self-determination.

For instance, a student with low vision may not see how another customer in the grocery store goes to the door of the meat department and rings a bell to call the butcher when the product the customer wants is not on the shelf. Rather than simply providing this information to the student, the teacher might ask the child how she would cope in a situation where she wasn't able to find a particular cut of meat at a grocery store—how would she manage such a challenge? Together the teacher and child might write out a list of options:

- scrutinize each item within reach
- politely ask another customer whether he or she sees the item the child is trying to locate
- go to the customer service area for help
- ask a cashier or another store worker

The teacher might then request that the orientation and mobility (O&M) specialist working with the student accompany the child to the grocery store and let the student try one of the strategies. If her strategy works, the O&M specialist and student should discuss what she learned from the experience (perhaps that there is a door with a buzzer where a customer can call the butcher). If the student's strategy doesn't work, the O&M specialist might choose another idea from the list, such as going to the customer service desk and, when the customer service representative tells them about the door with the buzzer, asking the representative to show them how to find it. At their next meeting, the teacher needs to ask the student how she and the O&M specialist resolved the problem.

By working collaboratively and involving others (the customer service representative or anyone else they encountered in the grocery store to ask for assistance), the teacher and O&M specialist may help the student recognize that when she next visits the grocery store, she can go to the door, ring the bell, and request a specific cut of meat. More importantly, they help the student understand that if there is something that she wants at a store (in this instance, a particular cut of meat), that she may need to ask more than just the obvious question of whether it is available in the store. She may also need to ask someone for assistance (to show her where the item is or how to obtain it) in order to be more independent in the future. By brainstorming solutions and taking turns trying the ideas out, the instructional staff help the student understand that there is often more than one way to solve a problem.

ACCESS TO ROLE MODELS WITH VISUAL IMPAIRMENTS. Teachers can also play a pivotal role in connecting their students with visual impairments to successful adults and competent older students who are blind or have low vision so that they can learn from these prospective role models some of the important skills that enable them to function independently and effectively when conveying their needs and solving problems. Teachers with resource rooms or who are teaching in special schools for children with visual impairments can invite adults or older students with visual impairments to come and make presentations or do volunteer work in the classroom. Itinerant teachers can encourage general education teachers to do the same in classes where there are children with visual impairments.

In the United States there are several organizations, including the American Council of the Blind, the National Federation of the Blind, National Association for Parents of Children with Visual Impairments, the National Organization for Albinism and Hypopigmentation, and the CareerConnect program of the American Foundation for the Blind through which adults with visual impairments may be identified (see the Resources section at the end of this book for more information). Likewise, public and private rehabilitation agencies often have access to successful and productive adults with visual impairments in local communities who are willing to act as role models or mentors.

The teacher of students with visual impairments can orient these speakers or volunteers so that they understand that students are exploring self-determination and provide guidelines for volunteers in the classroom, including:

- allowing students to do things for themselves whenever possible
- offering ideas for problem solving rather than simply telling students the answer to a problem
- describing to students the volunteer's own self-determination behaviors

In this way, teachers can make sure that the adults who volunteer address the ways in which they practice self-advocacy and assertive communication and how they respond to others whose communication styles may differ. Volunteers can share ways they've learned to solicit aid and to determine the array of choices available when confronted by challenges or problems. In addition, volunteers can tell students about their own goals and how they monitor their progress (self-regulation).

OPPORTUNITIES FOR PEER MODELING. Other children, whether they are siblings, classmates, or others in the community of a similar age, often are excellent resources for students with visual impairments. For example,

---

When Hector was born with cortical visual impairment and other disabilities, his parents grieved the loss of the typical son they were expecting. Hector's 4-year-old sister simply saw a baby—one with whom she had waited months to play with. She had no reservations about interacting with Hector and was the one who got him to pick his head up for the first time, roll over, and pass a toy from hand to hand.

Students with visual impairments of varying ages and ability levels can also learn from coming together with others who have visual impairments. Through sharing experiences they can find out, for example, that they are not the only ones who have accidentally walked into the boys' restroom rather than the girls' restroom because the picture on the door was visually confusing or that other students have followed another child wearing a tee-shirt the same color as a friend's, only to discover that the person wasn't the friend at all!

The role that teachers play in the process of engaging students with and learning from their classmates is to facilitate the inclusion of students with visual impairments in the social environment of school: on the playground, in the cafeteria, in the hallways, while waiting for the bus to come or an assembly to begin, and in all the other situations where there are opportunities for social interaction among students. Teachers need to ensure that their students with visual impairments know what's going on—who's playing or sitting with whom, what the other children are doing in addition to talking (passing notes, texting, playing video games, sharing pictures). If teachers pay attention to what the other students are discussing, they can role-play such discussions with their students so that they are comfortable with similar topics. Feedback from the teacher about how the student is being received socially will also be helpful in facilitating self-determination.

Teachers need to let children know what behaviors are working well for them and encourage them to continue to use those skills to establish friendships and to self-regulate behaviors, as in the following example:

Ms. Presley observed that 9-year-old Divya was often reaching out and touching other children as the class waited in line or sat at an assembly. She saw that children were moving away from Divya because they thought she was going to touch them. Ms. Presley shared this observation with Divya when they met in the resource room. They talked about the concept of personal space and how people do not like to have their personal space invaded by a classmate. They also brainstormed ways Divya could find out who was standing or sitting next to her without reaching out to touch them. Together they decided Divya could ask, "Who's sitting to my right?" when she sat down for the weekly assembly or "Who's standing in front of me?" when the class lined up.

Engaging the general education teacher in this process may be equally as important. The teacher of students with visual impairments can encourage the general education teacher to use cooperative learning (in which children work together in groups, with each child having specific responsibilities such as a time keeper, note taker, and materials gatherer), ensuring that the child with the visual impairment is an active participant in class activities, to help the students get to know one another better.

Another important role for the teacher of students with visual impairments is to help children who are blind or have low vision find out where and how to meet other children who are also visually impaired. Many students with visual impairments are the only child in their school or community with impaired vision. To meet other children who are blind or have low vision, students and their families need to know the resources available to them, including summer camps and weekend activities designed for children with visual impairments and membership groups that offer support to families. Information about many such organizations and sources of additional information appears in the Resources section of this chapter. Teachers of students with visual impairments can share these resources with families and encourage their students to participate.

The value of such experiences to children with visual impairments can be seen in the following example, from the second author of this chapter, who has low vision:

I attended a public school where I was the only child with a visual impairment. For two weeks each summer, I went to a camp for children with visual impairments where I was just another camper. I felt no pressure to try to figure out visually what was going on in the environment. Activities at the camp were accessible to all children, and if something was not clear to me, I felt comfortable asking a counselor or another camper with more vision for the information.

Attending camp was a pivotal force in helping me build skills in many areas of the ECC, including self-determination. Camp was the first place I learned about the United States Association for Blind Athletes (USABA), an organization consisting of athletes with visual impairments who reside throughout the United States (see Chapter 10 for more information). While at camp, as a middle school student, I set one of my first long-term goals after hearing about the experiences of other campers who were USABA competitors, deciding that I wanted to swim in a competition for the New Jersey Association for Blind Athletes in order to qualify for the national USABA competition. To reach this goal I had to investigate where I could swim locally during the school year, explain my goal to my parents and get their support (especially with transportation), and develop a training schedule. Coming in fifth in my first race didn't earn me a first-place ribbon or qualify me for the USABA nationals, but it was one of my proudest moments as an eighth grader. I had set a goal and had worked tirelessly to try to achieve it. The lessons of preparing for and participating in that swim meet have lasted well into adulthood.

Providing Opportunities to Practice

Providing opportunities for students to practice self-determination requires the teacher to let students apply or use the skills they've learned when situations present themselves in the course of the instructional day. Many situations lend themselves to practicing different self-determination skills. For example, when students need to select courses they will take or decide whether to join a school club or sports activity, rather than tell them what they need to do, the teacher can ask what their thoughts are and what choice they might make based on the information they have. Students may need encouragement to ask what options are available, for instance, what foods are being offered in the cafeteria or what activities are available during free times. Almost as important as letting students make decisions for themselves is letting them learn firsthand the consequences of their decisions: giving them praise for making good decisions and helping them figure out how to choose differently in the future if a decision goes awry.

ROLE-PLAYING. Role-playing is an excellent way to practice self-determination skills as well as a valuable tool the teacher of students with visual impairments can use in structured instructional time to teach self-determination skills. The teacher can act out specific scenarios with a student who is visually impaired and discuss the different solutions that were evidenced in their role plays, as in the following example:

Nikki, a sixth grader who has low vision and is cognitively and physically impaired, often experiences teasing by other students and becomes upset when this occurs. Rather than telling Nikki that she should go to an adult or walk away from the group if she is teased, Ms. Tannenbaum, Nikki's teacher of students with visual impairments, role-plays the scene with Nikki. Ms. Tannenbaum does this several times with Nikki playing the classmate doing the teasing and the teacher playing Nikki.

Each time the teacher, in the role of Nikki, reacts differently to the teasing. After several rounds of role playing, the teacher guides Nikki in a discussion of what her different reactions were to the teasing. Together they discuss which of the possible solutions Nikki might use if she is teased again. They then reverse roles, with Nikki playing herself and the teacher playing a classmate who is teasing. This way Nikki is able to practice the solution or solutions she thinks she can try the next time she is teased on the playground. By supporting Nikki in exploring options, the teacher is helping her develop her problem-solving and self-advocacy skills. Ms. Tannenbaum can monitor Nikki's progress by asking the classroom assistant to keep a record of what she observes happening when Nikki is on the playground and then meeting with Nikki weekly to talk about how she reacted if any teasing occurred since their last session.

WORKING OR VOLUNTEERING. An important role teachers can play in the development of self-determination is to encourage students to work for pay or as a volunteer while they are in school, providing additional opportunities to practice the skills they have learned. According to one research study (McDonnall & Crudden, 2009), individuals with visual impairments who had taken part in volunteer or paid job experiences by the time they completed high school reported higher levels of self-determination compared to those without such experiences. Volunteer work experiences can begin as early as elementary school, and the teacher of students with visual impairments can play an integral part in setting up these experiences. Volunteer jobs might include filing in the school office, watering plants, setting tables in the lunchroom, sweeping or mopping, or distributing notices to teachers' mailboxes. Having a job to do and receiving realistic feedback about one's performance can be helpful in laying the groundwork for self-determination. As children move into the middle and high school years, the teacher of students with visual impairments can work with the student, family, and other professionals to seek volunteer or paid job opportunities for the student outside of the school setting. These work experiences enhance critical career and social skills needed for a lifetime as well as students' self-determination skills.

Structuring Instructional Time: Lesson Plans and Curricula

The teacher of students with visual impairments can teach most of the components of self-determination directly by structuring learning experiences in the classroom (see the learning activities at the end of this chapter for ideas). For example, the teacher might teach and reinforce choice making by having three or four activities planned for the time she is with a student and allowing the student to determine the order of the activities. To encourage self-regulation, she might allow the student to earn points or tokens for specific behaviors or activities such as completing homework assignments or maintaining proper hand positioning when reading a braille passage. Once the student earns an agreed-on number of points or tokens, she can select an activity she would like to do.

To work on goal setting, the teacher and student may want to develop a *behavioral contract.* Teachers can use behavioral contracts with children of any age. The student can take the lead in deciding what behaviors she wants to strive for and what the consequences will be if she doesn't attain her goals. She can also decide what the reward will be when she does succeed. Use of a behavioral contract gives the student a vehicle with which to monitor her behavior. A well-designed contract helps all involved know what is expected. An example of a student's behavioral contract is presented in Figure 12.2.

Teachers and other professionals can bring students with visual impairments together for structured learning in groups. Several curricula are available that focus on teaching self-determination skills with groups of students (see the Resources section at the end of this chapter for information). An annotated review of many of them is included in *A Practical Guide for Teaching Self-Determination* (Field, Martin, Miller, Ward, & Wehmeyer,

FIGURE 12.2

Sample Behavior Contract

Goal: *For the next two weeks, you will do your best work in your computer skills class and complete all your assignments in a timely manner without arguing.*

To earn an award, you must meet the goal for 10 consecutive days.
Possible rewards for fulfilling your contract (pick one):

1. *Pizza party for the whole class*
2. *Luncheon date with any teacher or administrator of your choice*
3. *Bowling with your technology teacher and a friend of your choice*

Consequences for not fulfilling your contract:

1. *First breach of contract: You will complete your assignment in the dorm as homework and a staff member will have to sign that you completed it in a timely manner.*
2. *Second breach of contract: You will stay after school and complete your assignment with me.*
3. *Third breach of contract: You will write a letter to your parents explaining why you are not completing your work and the school will send it return receipt requested, meaning your parents must sign for the letter to let us know they received it.*

____________________ ____________________
Student's signature Date

____________________ ____________________
Teacher's signature Date

SOURCE: Lisa Foust, technology teacher, Arizona State Schools for the Deaf and the Blind, Tucson.

1998). One curriculum designed specifically for students with visual impairments is *Empowered: An Activity Based Self-Determination Curriculum for Students with Visual Impairments* (Cleveland, Clinkscales, Hefner, Houghtling, Kubacak, & Sewell, 2007). Although students can move through curricula such as these without other students, there can be tremendous benefit to working with a group so that students can share their experiences, bounce ideas off each other, and learn together through the curricular activities. Finally, examples of learning activities for teaching self-determination skills appear at the end of this chapter.

Teaching Self-Determination Components

This section focuses on teaching the components of self-determination students need to learn and provides examples of strategies that can be used, including those described earlier.

Self-Knowledge, Self-Advocacy, and Assertiveness

Self-knowledge is in many ways the foundation of self-advocacy and is critical for students of all ages. Students with visual impairments need to have the self-knowledge to be able to describe their impairment and the accommodations or modifications they will need to fully participate in activities (a process sometimes called *self-disclosure* or *disability disclosure*). Important opportunities for putting these skills into practice occur when students move into classes with new teachers, work with substitute teachers, or engage in activities with children without disabilities whom they don't know. For instance, a kindergarten student with low vision can remind her classmates and teacher that she needs to sit up front to see the pictures in the big book the teacher is sharing or a high school freshman who is blind can let a substitute teacher know that he will be talking with a classmate during a presentation that includes video to learn what is happening visually.

As children mature and develop more formal methods for telling a variety of people—such as classroom teachers, coaches, and, ultimately, employers—about their disabilities, the explanation they provide may be referred to as a *functional disability statement* because it expresses how the student will function, or perform tasks, in the situation or circumstances in question and what accommodations or modifications will be necessary to support or address the student's particular physical or sensory limitations. The teacher may initially use modeling to show the student an appropriate explanation of his or her impairment for others and review the critical components of the disclosure statement with the student. They might role-play together what to do when different people ask about the student's visual impairment. Then, the teacher needs to step back and allow the student to speak for herself. A simple response to questions from classmates and staff members about a student's visual impairment can be practiced and ready for use when a child enters elementary school. For example:

> Amanda, a first grader with albinism, knows what to say when someone says, "Why is your hair so white?" or "You can't wear sunglasses inside." Her teacher and her parents have helped her practice disability disclosure. "I have albinism—that's why my hair is so white. It's why my eyes don't work well, too. Bright light hurts my eyes so I wear sunglasses almost all the time and sometimes I need to get really close to things to see them."

Development of a functional disability statement needs to be started while students are in the elementary grades and routinely practiced with staff and visiting professionals. Students with cognitive impairments or other additional disabilities that might make it difficult for them to explain their disability or understand when it is appropriate to reveal that they are disabled can be expected to have a simple disability disclosure statement prepared and be able to use it by third or fourth grade. Such a statement could be preprinted on a card to be used by the student or the student's advocate.

Children have different needs for self-disclosure as they mature. A kindergartener or first grader simply needs to be able to answer questions from classmates and teachers about his or her disability without going into great detail. By third or fourth grade, a simple statement that includes more detail about the student's visual impairment and how it affects learning and socialization is important. In upper elementary grades and middle school or junior high school, students will be expected to articulate their needs for accommodations and modifications and will need to explain how they manage day-to-day activities and learning responsibilities with their disabilities to different teachers and staff. Sidebar 12.2 provides an example of a disability

SIDEBAR 12.2

Example of a Seventh-Grade Student's Functional Disability Statement

TO: *Ms. Adams*
FROM: *Paula Kissinger*

I'm scheduled to participate in your class this year. My teacher of students with visual impairments and I thought it would be a good idea to inform you about my visual impairment. I am proud to say that I usually do not need extensive help. However, I do need help with seeing things that are far away, reading small print, and seeing anything in bright sunlight. I also have a bit of trouble seeing colors. The following is a list of accommodations that can help me learn:

- It is good if I can sit at the front of the classroom. I prefer to be away from windows to avoid glare. If you're demonstrating something to the class, I may need to get up close to see.
- My best vision is within 10 inches. I will receive large print exams for state-required testing and may need to enlarge reading material that has small print. When I read books or use the computer, I usually get very close to the screen or page.
- I can see the shape of people and objects that are within about 8 feet, but without detail. It is helpful if you verbally describe things that are far away. I won't bump into you in the hallway, but I won't know if you are smiling or frowning and I may not recognize you by sight. My hearing is excellent, however, and I will quickly learn your voice. When you see me in the hallways or in town, please tell me who you are until I learn your voice. Thanks.
- My retinas did not form correctly and I sometimes can't differentiate between colors. I see best with high contrast; for example, black on white or white on black is easier for me to see than blue on grey or green on yellow.
- I have a machine called a Lynx that I can use in class. It is bigger than a laptop, and it helps me to see the board or an image that is projected at the front of the classroom. It has a camera connected to an arm that brings images from pretty far away to a small screen on my desk. I may need a few minutes to set it up at the beginning of class since it's heavy and not easily portable. I may not need this tool in your class; it will depend on how small you write on the board or if you have a projector in your classroom. Occasionally, I may need to be dismissed a couple minutes early from class so I have time to get through the hall with my Lynx machine.
- Other tools: I also have a tiny monocular that I can use to see things far away. Sometimes if I don't have my Lynx, I can use the monocular as a substitute. Electronic or online textbooks are great since I can enlarge the print on my home computer. I also have a device at home called a CCTV or video magnifier that I can use to view printed documents, and an iPad for reading books.

I will let you know if I need anything to help me learn in your class, so you don't need to worry. If you have any questions about my disability or needs, please let me know. I'm a hard-working student who likes a challenge. I'm looking forward to working with you this semester (or year). Thank you

SOURCE: Written by Paula Kissinger, seventh-grade student, Boulder, Colorado. Reprinted with permission.

disclosure statement written by a seventh-grade student for her teachers.

In high school, students will be expected to use and modify their disability statements for different people at school and in the community, depending on the roles they want to play in those different environments. In all instances, disability statements should focus on the skills that enable students to function in situations in which most other students will use vision to perform and the accommodations or modifications that will help them participate in activities or undertake tasks.

Awareness of one's rights and responsibilities can also be incorporated into the development of functional disabilities statements. Older students need to be apprised of individual rights as outlined in federal disability legislation, including the Individuals with Disabilities Education Act (IDEA; P.L. 108–446), the Rehabilitation Act of 1973 (P.L. 93–112), and the Americans with Disabilities Act of 1990 (P.L. 101–336). Participation in the development of an IEP allows students to further develop self-knowledge and self-advocacy skills. Students can be encouraged to search the Internet for the latest information regarding federal disability legislation, thus enhancing their assistive technology skill development along with their self-knowledge.

Assertiveness, too, relates to the components of self-knowledge and self-advocacy and can be learned through activities that promote the student communicating effectively (in development of functional disclosure statements, for example), negotiating with others (by making choices for class scheduling based on preferences, for example), and in presenting herself as competent (such as by participating in or conducting her IEP meeting).

Assertiveness (including communicating effectively) and self-advocacy skills can be fostered by structuring lessons for students to explore their interests, abilities, and work habits (as discussed in Chapter 11). Development of this understanding will help them know and articulate what they have to offer in an employment situation. Being able to articulate their needs for accommodations while in school can help students clearly communicate to prospective employers how they can comfortably fit into an organization or business.

Teachers can also facilitate their students' efforts to be assertive and advocate for themselves effectively in future work or training situations by working with them on how to be effectively included in IEP and transition meetings. Since the focus of the IEP is to make a long-term plan for the next year of a student's life, who better to have input about what the student is going to do for the next year than the student? Beginning in the late elementary years, children need to be prepared to play an integral part in the preparation for their IEP meetings and can be expected to participate during the actual meeting, as in the following example:

Ms. Tsai is a teacher of students with visual impairments working with Lamont, a fifth grader with glaucoma. As the time for Lamont's IEP approaches, Ms. Tsai talks with Lamont about the need to update his functional vision assessment and learning media assessment. She involves Lamont in scheduling their sessions and has him help with recording the data for his reading speed and visual acuity and selecting the sunshades that he feels provide him the greatest reduction in glare. Ms. Tsai talks with Lamont and his father about possible IEP goals for Lamont for the next year, and she practices with Lamont what he will share with the members of the team when they meet. Lamont's participation in the meeting is essential for helping him in the development of self-determination.

Each year as he moves through middle school and then into high school, Lamont's responsibilities in these meetings will increase. In middle school Lamont might assist Ms. Tsai in making a handout about what accommodations he needs, such as being allowed to close window blinds when the sun is causing glare on the board and being allowed to move closer to demonstrations. In high school, Lamont can develop this handout on his own and demonstrate to his teachers the equipment he will use in their classes. By high school, Ms. Tsai can set the stage for Lamont to lead the meetings with his other teachers and for her to provide consultative help only. By having the opportunity to be involved in his IEP meetings from a young age, Lamont is learning how to set long-term goals and the short-term objectives he'll need to meet to achieve those goals, how to solve problems, and how to plan for the future, and he is practicing his self-advocacy skills.

For students with significant additional disabilities, a *person-centered planning process* may be used to complement the IEP or transition meeting process. Person-centered planning (also known as *futures planning* or *MAPS*—making action plans) involves all those who have a stake in the child's life (family members, neighbors and other members of the community, education and rehabilitation personnel, and the student) coming together to plan for the student's future (see, for example, Furney, 1996; O'Brien, O'Brien, & Mount, 1997; Moss & Wiley, 2003; and the resources at the end of this chapter). Together they develop a shared vision of who the individual is now and who he or she would like to be in adulthood (what she would be doing and where she would be living, working, and playing). The team considers the skills the student has now and the skills she needs to develop to achieve her goals, as well as what supports he or she will need in the future and who will provide them. Typically, the team meets together to talk about the individual's current and future goals. The group often draws charts or maps that focus on topics such as communication, likes, dislikes, and wishes to facilitate the discussion of how to achieve the student's wishes. Setting long-term goals in this manner is not only a way for the person with the significant disabilities to have a say in what direction his life is moving but it also allows family, friends, and others to share that vision and what they will do together to make it become a reality.

Decision Making, Problem Solving, and Goal Setting

When developing decision-making and problem-solving skills, the objective is to help students solve problems and make decisions on their own, rather than having problems solved or decisions made for them. There are numerous opportunities for practicing these skills throughout the school day. Simple guidelines can be provided for decision making, such as the following, depending on the situation:

1. Compile (or explore) a list of options.
2. Gather information about each one, if appropriate.
3. Identify advantages and disadvantages for each of the possibilities.
4. Use the information to make a decision.

Students with visual impairments need to experience the natural consequences of their actions and learn to set goals and objectives to alter their behavior when necessary to get the results they desire. When students encounter challenges, teachers need to follow these steps:

1. See if students can solve their problems without assistance.
2. Ask what choices students believe they have in responding to the challenging situation.
3. Provide additional ideas (more than one suggestion) and let the student choose one.
4. Wait to see what happens.

Students who are new to decision making and problem solving on their own may need a bit of extra time to think through situations and consider what options they have. If a chosen strategy works, the teacher should give students positive feedback; if it doesn't work, the teacher can ask the student to rethink the situation and refer back to the list of ideas they generated and to pick another option to try.

Students need to understand that solving a problem sometimes requires some change in the student's behavior, which entails setting a goal to achieve that change. For example, a student who continually interrupts the teacher in the general education classroom to ask a question must be made aware that this behavior creates a situation with the others in the class that is not positive for the student with the visual impairment. The student, now armed with information, needs to decide whether to change this disruptive behavior in an effort to change the reactions of the other students, or to continue doing what he pleases. If he chooses to change his behavior, he needs to consider his teacher's suggestions about how and when to ask questions during class. Setting a goal to control question-asking behavior allows the student to find more appropriate ways to gather information and ultimately allows the student to integrate more fully into the social milieu of the classroom.

Teachers need to help students understand that the decisions and choices they make have consequences. If a student wants to be liked, for example, he needs to treat others as he would wish to be treated; if he ignores the rights of the other students, he is liable to be disliked, ignored, or treated as if he is odd or unacceptable. For students with visual impairments, however, the normal consequences of some decisions may be distorted if well-meaning school personnel do not enforce classroom policies because of their disabilities. For instance, a classroom teacher may refrain from lowering a score for a student with a visual impairment when she does not turn in a homework assignment on time, even though other students' scores are marked down under similar circumstances. This approach does not send the right message to the student, the student's family, or the student's classmates about her ability to perform at the same level as the rest of the class. It also inhibits the student's goal setting: Why try to improve if one's performance is already receiving positive or neutral feedback? How would the student know what behavior requires improvement without receiving realistic feedback?

If, for example, Heather does not do her English homework, she should receive a poor grade in her English class. The teacher of students with visual impairments can work with her if he or she recognizes that there is a problem and set a goal to improve: in this case to get her homework in on time. Helping Heather set a short-term goal for improvement of her English grade, with objectives such as improved organizational skills and time management, gives her an opportunity to practice both goal setting and self-regulation. If Heather wants to complete high school successfully, the teacher can help her understand that to reach that long-term goal she first needs to attend to the short-term goal of improving her English grade. If Heather doesn't meet her short-term goal and continues to perform poorly in her English class, the teacher can continue to coach and support Heather while at the same time making sure the English teacher and other staff members all treat Heather the same way they would a student with typical sight.

A technique that teachers may want to use for teaching goal setting is known by the acronym SMART (Meyer, 2003), which stands for specific, measurable, achievable, relevant, and time-bound. The teacher can explain to students that the best goals are clearly defined and easily understood. The SMART approach can help students develop goals that are clearly defined and easily described by following these guidelines:

- Make the goal specific—clearly define the desired outcome.
- Make the goal measurable—specify action steps the student will undertake, and include a targeted time to complete.
- Make the goal achievable—ensure the goal can be accomplished in the time available.
- Make the goal relevant—determine what makes the student feel it is worth the effort to change.
- Make the goal time-bound—specify when the goal will be achieved.

Teachers can help students brainstorm ways to make a goal "smart."

Self-Directed and Self-Regulated Behavior

Many of the strategies discussed for decision making and goal setting relate directly to teaching self-directed and self-regulated behavior because these components are all so closely linked.

Sometimes children with visual impairments are unaware of problem situations because they do not receive appropriate feedback about their behavior. Others in the school or community may have never encountered a child with impaired vision and may assume that inappropriate behavior or actions that are unexpected for someone of the child's age may simply be "what a person with a visual impairment does." In other words, they may not have high expectations for the child. An important role for the teacher of students with visual impairments, therefore, is to help students understand unspoken or assumed standards for behavior (particularly related to self-directed and self-regulated behavior) and to give students realistic feedback about their actions and interactions. By doing so, the teacher helps the student recognize problem situations and decide whether and how to address them.

For example, the teacher might provide a young student with this type of feedback about his actions on the playground: "You walked in front of Carlee and Samantha, who were both waiting in line for the swing. They looked at each other and shrugged their shoulders as if to say, 'What can you expect—that kid doesn't know the rules!' They both had unhappy looks on their faces when you got on the swing before them, after they had been waiting their turns." Helping the child understand how his actions affect others (including providing descriptions of facial expressions) in such a situation is important for the student to develop an overall awareness of the impact his behavior has on other students. Sometimes students may need to be taught the concept of what it takes to be a team player, for example. This kind of opportunity can also provide the teacher with a chance to talk to the student about playground rules. The teacher and student can discuss how to find out if there is someone in line for the swing, rather than the student just assuming he can go to the swing whenever he wants. Problem solving, in this example, requires input from the individual who saw the social misstep to help the child figure out what the expected behavioral choices are so that he can make an informed decision about what to do.

Teaching a student *internal messaging* or *cuing* is one way to assist a student with self-regulation. For instance, it might be helpful to have a key phrase that the teacher and the student can use as a way to remind the student of what he or she needs to do in order to stay focused and on task, as in the following example:

Lyle, an eighth grader, was reluctant to approach teachers to advocate for himself. He preferred to not do his work rather than to ask for assistance or clarification, and he often felt the work he did wasn't as good as that done by his sighted classmates.

Lyle wanted to join the wrestling team and needed to have a B average to do so. Ms. Garland, Lyle's teacher of students with visual impairments, seized on this opportunity as a way to motivate Lyle. Together they developed a checklist of phrases Lyle needed to say to himself to help him understand and remember the expectations for his behavior with regard to his schoolwork. They created an acronym to help him remember what he needed to do to keep focused and on task. The acronym, **FAST**, stood for **find** out what the task is, **ask** if you don't understand it, **set** a time limit to complete the task, and **take time** to praise yourself for getting things done on time. When Lyle worked with Ms. Garland twice a week they talked about times during the week he was FAST and times he could have been FAST and wasn't. They discussed how Lyle could implement his FAST plan in a similar situation in the future. Helping Lyle to develop self-monitoring skills increased his self-confidence and his ability to regulate his behavior more appropriately.

SUGGESTIONS FOR WORKING WITH PARENTS

The number of small things parents do with their children that set the stage for future independence, and thus self-determination, is vast. From the time their children are infants, parents help them develop self-determination skills. When a child's toy is across the room and he has to figure out that he can roll or creep over to get it or when he has to open a bag in order to get the snack he wants, the child is learning to solve problems and the parent is helping him do so by letting him do these things independently. Helping him learn to calm himself when he is upset, encouraging him to choose which outfit he wants to wear, and allowing his tower of blocks to topple when he chooses to build the base with blocks that are too small or too far from one another are all ways he can learn skills that pave the way for self-determination. Young children need opportunities to make choices, solve problems, set goals, and regulate their behavior.

As they get older, children need to learn how their actions affect others and how to set longer-term goals to achieve what they want in life. The first time they buy a book or video game with money they saved from their allowance or gifts is evidence that they set a goal and worked to achieve it. Staying overnight at a friend's house, joining a club or scout troop, or volunteering to watch the neighbors' pets while they are out of town are ways in which young students begin to demonstrate greater independence and self-reliance. For teens, having a checking account, buying clothes for themselves, and getting a first paycheck are indicators that they are fast approaching adulthood. Each of these behaviors is tied to self-determination because the child needs to make decisions and set goals to achieve an outcome.

Parents and other family members communicate a great deal, often unintentionally, to children. Without realizing it, their actions and comments may communicate to the child that the child is not capable. When a parent tells a child who is visually impaired to let a brother or sister do something because "he can do it faster than you can" or plans an outing to the theater with other siblings and doesn't include the visually impaired child because "you won't be able to see the action on the stage," the message the visually impaired child receives is "you're not worthy or capable of doing this because you don't see well." Parents therefore need to be encouraged to choose their words carefully and, if such situations are inevitable, to balance them with other opportunities for the child who is visually impaired to do something that their siblings don't.

Parents can do many things to foster self-determination as their children grow. In the following sections, ideas are presented for parents by the age range of the child: early childhood (infants, toddlers, and preschoolers), elementary-school students (first through sixth grades), and middle-school and high-school students (seventh through twelfth grades).

Infants, Toddlers, and Preschoolers

During the first few years of a child's life, it is important for her to be as active and involved in all aspects of family life as possible. The more she understands about her environment and the stronger her communication and social skills, the greater the probability that she'll develop a high level of self-esteem and confidence to go out into the world, make her own choices, and live her dreams. Self-esteem and confidence are characteristics that promote self-determination. From infancy, parents can help their children build confidence and self-esteem by taking measures such as the following:

- Orienting them to their homes—showing children what is in each room and how to move from room to room, and establishing where their things are by providing designated spaces with labels.
- Encouraging them to make choices—letting children decide what snacks they would like to have or what toys they would like to play with when they go to the park.
- Putting toys, clothes, and snack food items that children like where they can get to them easily. (Parents will need to supervise children closely when they are very young, but as they mature, they will become more self-reliant.)
- Having children store and retrieve their belongings, such as toys or clothing, rather than having things just appear and disappear as if by magic.

- Encouraging children to share their toys and snacks with siblings and playmates.
- Taking children into the community (for instance, to the grocery store, post office, park; or to the sporting events or performances of older siblings, cousins, or neighbors) to meet and interact with others.
- Making sure when children attend events or go places that they understand who is present, what others are doing, and what they are allowed to do in particular situations. For example, running and jumping are appropriate behaviors at the park where other children are doing these things as well. At the grocery store, running and jumping are not appropriate; the child should be expected to sit in the shopping cart or to walk alongside the cart helping to pick items off the shelf and put them in the cart.

Young children need praise when they truly are doing something well or appropriately, but there is a tendency in some families to overpraise children, which gives them an unrealistic understanding of their behavior, skills, and abilities. Parents need to understand the importance of giving their children realistic feedback. If a child doesn't do something well, the parent can suggest how the child could behave or perform better. For example, if a mother is with her daughter at the playground and the child cuts in front of another child in line, the daughter needs to be told, "You must wait your turn. There is a boy here who wants to go on the slide and he was here first. You may use the slide after him." If she does wait her turn, the mother needs to let her know that she did the right thing. She might say something like, "I like how you waited for that boy to finish on the slide before you took your turn."

Elementary School Years

Parents will see tremendous growth in their children during the elementary school years. This is a stage of rapid development, due in part to children's exposure to so many new and different people in their lives. When children enter elementary school, teachers, other school-based professionals, classmates, community-based group leaders, and children in the neighborhood influence their development, as well as their family members. Children with visual impairments may need to be encouraged to meet others and become involved in activities outside of home and school. Finding opportunities for children to engage in activities that they enjoy during elementary school can help develop lifelong interests and can positively affect many aspects of personal and social development, including fostering self-determination skills. Parents can focus on children's interests and look for clubs, recreational activities, or classes for their child to join. Parents or teachers need to be prepared to help group organizers understand how to accommodate a child's visual impairment.

At home, parents need to give children with visual impairments increasingly challenging responsibilities. During this time in children's lives they are often assigned chores to complete (taking out the trash, loading the dishwasher, sorting laundry, feeding a pet, watering the lawn, and so forth). Although it may take children with visual impairments longer than their sighted brothers or sisters to learn to complete their chores, having this type of responsibility is important for a variety of reasons (including learning independent living skills and developing career-related skills and habits). Children who have chores and perform them well learn that they can effect change through their behaviors (taking out the trash not only pleases their parents, it makes the living environment more pleasant for everyone), which is a critical step in children acquiring an internal locus of control—the belief that they can control their lives ultimately.

Children in elementary school can also begin to exercise self-regulation, another important characteristic of self-determination. They can learn to set alarm clocks so that they can get themselves up and ready for school with minimal parent involvement. Upper elementary students can develop their own schedules for completing homework, participating in athletic or recreational activities, and doing their chores. Parents will need to monitor their children's progress closely, but occasionally need to allow them to make mistakes and face the consequences. For example, if the child has a book report due at school and doesn't schedule time to work on this long-term project, the parent may opt to let the child miss the deadline for turning in the assignment and thus receive a poor or failing grade. No parent wants to see his or her child fail; however, it is sometimes necessary for children in such situations to experience the natural consequences of their behavior so they begin to recognize that they need to plan their time more efficiently. Talking with the child about what happened and problem solving together about how to keep

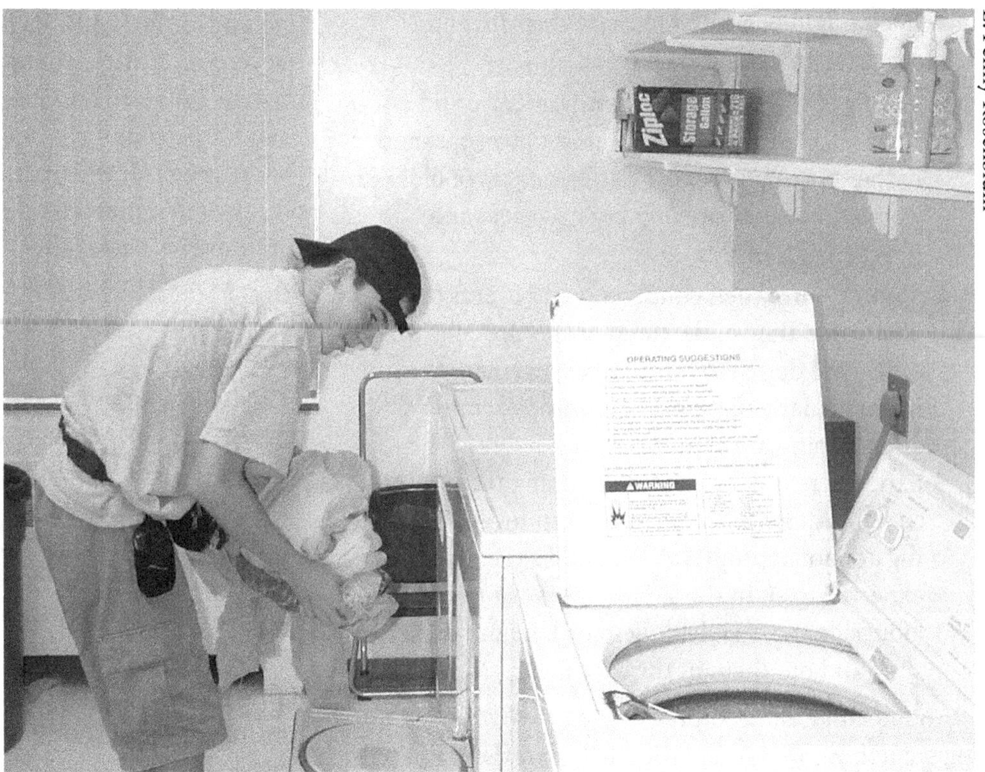

L. Penny Rosenblum

When students take responsibility for chores at home, such as doing the laundry, they are also learning that they can exert control over their lives.

this from happening again in the future helps him or her with both self-direction and self-regulation. Showing him or her how to break the task down into smaller steps can make a large task, such as a book report, more manageable.

By the time children are in elementary school they need to understand, at a basic level, the cause of their visual impairment, its impact on their performance, and what accommodations they need to be successful in given situations. They need to be able to verbalize this information to others, as noted earlier. For example, the parents of 6-year-old Elle have encouraged her to explain to friends' parents, her Scout leader, and the Sunday school teacher: "I was born 3 months early and my eyes don't work well. I don't see things unless I'm really close to them. I have to use my cane to help me find things so I don't trip over them." Even when her parents are standing next to Elle and could easily do this for her, they recognize the value of teaching her to advocate for herself. Elle is able to remind others that she needs to sit up front to see or that she'd like to be able to hold something in her hands to explore it.

If a child is receiving special education services, the parents will want to work with school personnel on the development of the child's IEP. Parents need to talk with other team members about how to involve their child in the IEP process. By late elementary school grades, a child without significant other delays can and needs to be encouraged to attend IEP meetings and share what he views as some of his strengths and needs, as well as what he would like to work on during the coming year. He should have self-determination goals, such as self-advocacy, on his IEP and be expected to help at the beginning of the year in letting teachers and peers know about himself and the accommodations he needs.

Middle School and High School

The teenage years are a time of continued growth toward independence. Many parents find this time in their children's lives to be challenging, yet at the same time rewarding, as they see their children gaining skills and moving into young adulthood. It's important for parents, professionals, and the teens themselves to have a shared vision of what these students want to do following high school. Parents and teens need to meet with the professionals who are supporting their educational programming to discuss post-high school plans. If students want to attend college, get jobs, or live on their own, then short-term and intermediate objectives need to be developed to support them in achieving these goals. Waiting until children are close to graduation is often too late. These discussions need to occur regularly beginning in middle school.

Parents will want to continue to support their children in developing and exploring their interests during the middle and high school years. If a teenager enjoys the arts, then parents can support him or her in joining a local theater group, taking an art class after school, or doing volunteer work for a local advertising company. Volunteer and paid work experience is important for the development of career and social skills, but also facilitates self-determination. Parents can help their children seek work experiences and encourage them to demonstrate appropriate work habits, such as being on time, solving problems with coworkers, or setting short-term goals to achieve at work.

Work at home is equally important. By the teenage years, youngsters need to have responsibility for cleaning their bedrooms and bathrooms, doing their own laundry, helping with cooking and cleaning the house, shopping for groceries, and buying their own clothing. Initially parents may need to monitor teens closely as they do these chores and provide them with feedback on their performance. However, by the time teens are nearing high school graduation they can be expected to do these everyday activities without supervision. Parents need to keep an eye on the future, because before they know it, their children will be out on their own, and may not have a roommate or spouse around to make sure they've separated whites and darks properly or that they've used dishwashing soap to do the dishes. Acquiring independent living skills is an essential part of developing an internal locus of control.

Building self-confidence, self-reliance, and problem-solving skills during the teenage years is important. Learning to manage money and transportation are two ways parents can work with their children to develop these skills. Teens can have a savings or checking account along with a debit card and be given responsibility for managing money for purchases, such as lunch, transportation, and clothing. If a teenager is not going to be a driver, he needs to learn alternative ways (other than taking the school bus or asking for rides from family and friends) to get independently to the places he wants and needs to go. Parents can talk with professionals, such as O&M specialists, and, whenever possible, with visually impaired adults who don't drive about skills and strategies for helping teenagers maximize their ability to travel independently in their present and future communities.

By their teenage years, young people need to be actively involved in their IEP and transition meetings. Ideally, they will be running these meetings by the end of high school. Parents can talk with other team members about how to facilitate their children's involvement and increasing responsibility in conducting these meetings. Teenagers need to have the skills and the confidence to negotiate with teachers and other professionals concerning the accommodations they will need in classes or training. Parents and professionals can ensure that teens meet with their teachers before the school year begins or during the first week of school so that they can share what they need and work out mutually agreed upon systems for communication and sharing of materials. Whether teenagers plan to work or attend college directly after high school graduation, they will need to have the skills to advocate with bosses, coworkers, professors, roommates, and the public. The high school environment is a safe place where these skills can be practiced so that students gain the confidence necessary to be successful as a self-advocate.

Another area where parents can assist young adults is helping them to discover what local groups or summer and weekend programs statewide or nationally may be available for teens with visual impairments. Some groups may focus on sporting activities, others on job or college readiness, and yet others on independent living skills and recreation or leisure activities. Often spending time with others who have visual impairments can be very beneficial to teenagers. In addition, parents may find it valuable to meet other parents of young adults with visual impairments and share their experiences as well. Teens may also find it helpful to join organizations that have a focus on public speaking or leadership skills development. The wider the array of experiences the teen has, the more likely it is that her confidence, understanding of self, and goal setting will expand, leading to greater levels of self-determination.

Parents play many roles in the lives of their children, and these roles change as children age. Along with loving their children unconditionally and accepting their abilities and limitations irrespective of disability, it is important that parents help their children develop the skills to manage without them or other adults. In this way, parents enable their children to achieve the highest level of independence that they are able.

SUMMARY

This chapter discussed the critical skills involved in the area of self-determination for students with visual impairments, along with strategies for assessment. Ideally, the self-determination skills of children and adolescents with visual impairments will be evaluated regularly and often informally so that teachers and parents are aware of these youngsters' strengths and needs in self-determination.

A considerable body of evidence supports the importance of teaching these skills (Algozzine, Browder, Karvonen, Test, & Wood, 2001; Wehmeyer, Agran, & Hughes, 1998), which are particularly critical for young adults with visual impairments, who may be at great risk of being underemployed or unemployed in general (Newman, Wagner, Cameto, & Knokey, 2009; Newman, Wagner, Cameto, Knokey, & Shaver, 2010; Wolffe & Kelly, 2011).

Teachers, parents, and others who care about students who are visually impaired can do a great deal to ensure that they develop the array of skills that will help them succeed in school, work, and the community at large. Teaching students the critical skills that support self-determination is a major contribution to helping them learn how to make good decisions for themselves, solve problems and set goals, speak up for themselves and communicate effectively, and, in general, develop higher levels of self-esteem and self-confidence. Professionals concerned about the welfare of students need to provide opportunities for them to develop and practice these important life skills.

References

Abery, B. H., Elkin, S. V., Smith, J. G., Springborg, H. L., & Stancliffe, R. J. (2000). *Minnesota self-determination scales: Importance scale. Self-report edition*. Minneapolis: University of Minnesota, Research and Training Center on Community Living, Institute on Community Integration.

Abery, B. H., & Eggebeen, A. (2001). *Self-determination and deafblindness: A comparative study of the self-determination levels of young adults with deafblindess* (Technical Report No. 2). Minneapolis: University of Minnesota, Institute on Community Integration.

Abery, B., McGraw, K., & Smith, J. G. (1995). *Self-determination exercise scale: Student edition*. Minneapolis: University of Minnesota, Institute on Community Integration.

Agran, M., Hong, S., & Blankenship, K. (2007). Promoting the self-determination of students with visual impairments: Reducing the gap between knowledge and practice. *Journal of Visual Impairment & Blindness, 101*, 453–464.

Algozzine, B., Browder, D., Karvonen, M., Test, D. W., & Wood, W. M. (2001). Effects of interventions to promote self-determination for individuals with disabilities. *Review of Educational Research, 71*, 219–277.

Brolin, D. E. (1997). *Life-centered career education: A competency-based approach* (5th ed.). Reston, VA: Council for Exceptional Children.

Cleveland, J., Clinkscales, R. M., Hefner, N., Houghtling, D., Kubacak, C., & Sewell, D. (2007). *Empowered: An activity based self-determination curriculum for students with visual impairments*. Austin: Texas School for the Blind and Visually Impaired.

Deci, E. L. (1992). The relation of interest to the motivation of behavior: A self-determination theory perspective. In K.A Renningger, S. Hidi, & A. Krapp (Eds.), *The role of interest in learning and development* (pp. 43–70). Hillsdale, NJ: Lawrence Erlbaum Associates.

Deci, E. L., & Ryan, R. (1985). *Intrinsic motivation and self-determination in human behavior*. New York: Plenum Press.

Deci, E. L., & Ryan, R. M. (2008). Self-determination theory: A macrotheory of human motivation, development, and health. *Canadian Psychology, 49*, 182–185.

FACTS from OSEP's National Longitudinal Studies (2005, June). Washington, DC: Office of Special Education Programs.

Field, S. (1996). Self-determination instructional strategies for youth with learning disabilities. *Journal of Learning Disabilities, 29*, 40–52.

Field, S., & Hoffman, A. (1994). Development of a model for self-determination. *Career Development for Exceptional Individuals, 17*(2), 159–169.

Field, S., Martin, J., Miller, R., Ward, M., & Wehmeyer, M. (1998). *A practical guide for teaching self-determination*. Arlington, VA: Council for Exceptional Children.

Freedman, Judy S. (1999, Spring). Easing the teasing: How parents can help their kids cope. *Early Childhood* (pp. 1, 4). Retrieved from http://ecap.crc.illinois.edu/eecearchive/digests/1999/freed99.html

Furney, K. S. (1996). Making dreams happen: How to facilitate the MAPS process. Burlington: University of Vermont, Center for Transition and Employment.

Hoy, C. (1986). Preventing learned helplessness. *Academic Therapy, 22*(1), 11–18 (ERIC Document Reproduction Service No. EJ 341 266).

Levenson, H. (1981). Differentiating among internality, powerful others, and chance. In H. Lefcourt (Ed.), *Research with the locus of control construct: Vol. I* (pp. 15–63). New York: Academic Press.

Lewis S., & Wolffe, K. E. (2006). Promoting and nurturing self-esteem. In S. Z. Sacks & K. E. Wolffe (Eds.), *Teaching social skills to students with visual impairments: From theory to practice* (pp. 122–162). New York: AFB Press.

McDonnall, M. C., & Crudden, A. (2009). Factors affecting the successful employment of transition-age youngsters with visual impairment. *Journal of Visual Impairment & Blindness, 103*(6) 329–341.

Meyer, P. J. (2003). *Attitude is Everything: If you want to succeed above and beyond*. Waco, TX: Meyer Resource Group.

Mithaug, D. E. (1991). *Self-determined kids*. Lexington, MA: Lexington Books.

Mithaug, D. E. (2003). Adjusting beliefs about self-determination. In M. L. Wehmeyer, B. H. Abery, D. E.

Mithaug, & R. J. Stancliffe (Eds.), *Theory in self-determination* (pp. 5–24). Springfield, IL: Charles C Thomas.

Morgan, S., Bixler, E., & McNamara, J. (2002). *Self-determination for children and young adults who are deaf-blind* (Research paper). Retrieved from National Technical Assistance Consortium for Children and Young Adults Who Are Deaf-Blind website: http://www.nationaldb.org/documents/products/self-determ.pdf

Moss, K., & Wiley, D. (2003). A brief guide to personal futures planning: Organizing your community to envision and build a desirable future with you (booklet). Austin: Texas Deafblind Outreach. Retrieved from http://www.tsbvi.edu/attachments/other/pcp-manual.pdf

Newman, L., Wagner, M., Cameto, R., & Knokey, A. M. (2009). *The post-high school outcomes of youth with disabilities up to 4 years after high school: A report of findings from the National Longitudinal Transition Study-2 (NLTS2)* (NCSER 2009-3017). Menlo Park, CA: SRI International. Available at www.nlts2.org/reports/2009_04/nlts2_report_2009_04_complete.pdf

Newman, L., Wagner, M., Cameto, R., Knokey, A.M., & Shaver, D. (2010). *Comparisons across time of the outcomes of youth with disabilities up to 4 years after high school: A report of findings from the National Longitudinal Transition Study-2 (NLTS2).* Menlo Park, CA: SRI International. Available at www.nlts2.org/reports/2010_09/nlts2_report_2010_09_complete.pdf

Nirje, B. (1972). The right to self-determination. In W. Wolfensberger (Ed.), *Normalization: The principle of normalization* (pp. 176–200). Toronto, Canada: National Institute on Mental Retardation.

O'Brien, C. L., O'Brien, J., & Mount, B. (1997). Person-centered planning has arrived . . . or has it? *Mental Retardation, 35*, 480–484.

Perske, R. (1972). The dignity of risk. In W. Wolfensberger (Ed.), *Normalization: The principle of normalization in human services* (pp. 194–200). Toronto, Canada: National Institute on Mental Retardation.

Reed, M., & Curtis, K. (2012). Experiences of students with visual impairments in Canadian higher education. *Journal of Visual Impairment & Blindness, 106*, 414–425.

Robinson, B. L., & Lieberman, L. J. (2004). Effects of visual impairment, gender, and age on self-determination. *Journal of Visual Impairment & Blindness, 98*, 351–366.

Rosenberg, M. (1965). Society and the adolescent self-image. Princeton, NJ: Princeton University Press

Seligman, M. E. P. (1990). *Learned optimism.* New York: Alfred Knopf.

Seligman, M. E. P. (1996). *The optimistic child.* New York: Harper Collins.

Seligman, M. E. P. (2002). *Authentic happiness.* New York: The Free Press.

Texas School for the Blind and Visually Impaired. (2007). *EVALS (Evaluating Visually Impaired Students).* Austin: Author.

Wehmeyer, M. L. (1992). Self-determination: Critical skills for outcome-oriented transition services. *The Journal for Vocational Special Needs Education, 15*, 3–9.

Wehmeyer, M. L. (1996). Self-determination as an educational outcome: Why is it important to children, youth and adults with disabilities? In D. J. Sands & M. L. Wehmeyer (Eds.), *Self-determination across the life span: Independence and choice for people with disabilities* (pp. 15–34). Baltimore, MD: Brookes.

Wehmeyer, M. L. (2003). Self-determination: A review of the construct. In M. L. Wehmeyer, B. H. Abery, D. E. Mithaug, & R. J. Stancliffe (Eds.), *Theory in self-determination* (pp. 5–24). Springfield, IL: Charles C. Thomas.

Wehmeyer, M. L., Abery, B. H., Mithaug, D. E., & Stancliffe, R. J. (Eds.). (2003). *Theory in self-determination.* Springfield, IL: Charles C. Thomas.

Wehmeyer, M. L., Agran, M., & Hughes, C. (1998). Teaching self-determination to students with disabilities: Basic skills for successful transition. Baltimore, MD: Paul H. Brookes.

Wehmeyer, M. L., & Kelchner, K. (1995). *The Arc's self-determination scale.* Arlington, TX: The Arc National Headquarters. Retrieved from http://www.thearc.org/document.doc?id=3670

Wolffe, K. E. (1996). Career education for students with visual impairments. *Re:view, 28*(2), 89–93.

Wolffe, K. E. (2000). Career education for children and youths with visual impairments. In A. J. Koenig & M. C. Holbrook (Eds.), *Foundations of education: Vol. II.* New York: American Foundation for the Blind.

Wolffe, K. E. (2006, July). *Assessment of students' competencies in the expanded core curriculum: A school-wide approach using observational protocol.* Paper presented at AER Biennial International conference, Snowbird, UT.

Wolffe, K. E. (2007). Transition planning for the world beyond school. In S. LaVenture (Ed.), *A parents' guide to special education for children with visual impairments.* New York: AFB Press.

Wolffe, K. E. (2011). *Transition competencies checklist.* Austin, TX: Author.

Wolffe, K. E. (2012). *Career counseling for people with disabilities: A practical guide to finding employment* (2nd ed.). Austin, TX: PRO-ED.

Wolffe, K. E., Blankenship, K. E., & Hatlen, P. (2010, March). *Just the facts!* Paper presented at the Josephine L. Taylor Leadership Institute, Seattle, WA.

Wolffe, K. E., & Kelly, S. (2011). Instruction in areas of the expanded core curriculum linked to transition outcomes for students with visual impairments. *Journal of Visual Impairment & Blindness, 105*, 340–349.

Self-Determination Resources

This section provides resources such as assessment tools, publications, and instructional materials for teaching self-determination skills. For additional resources that relate to the expanded core curriculum in general, see the Resources section at the end of this book.

ASSESSMENT TOOLS

The Arc's Self-Determination Scale

POPULATION/AGE LEVEL: Adolescents with cognitive impairment

ECC COMPONENT: Self-determination

SOURCE: Wehmeyer, M. L., & Kelchner, K. (1995). *The Arc's Self-determination Scale.* Arlington, TX: The Arc National Headquarters. Retrieved from http://www.thearc.org/document.doc?id=3670

EVALS (Evaluating Visually Impaired Students) toolkit

POPULATION/AGE LEVEL: School-aged children and youth with visual impairments

ECC COMPONENT: All

SOURCES: Texas School for the Blind and Visually Impaired. (2007). *EVALS (Evaluating Visually Impaired Students).* Austin: Texas School for the Blind and Visually Impaired.

Levenson's Locus of Control Scales

POPULATION/AGE LEVEL: Adolescents and adults

ECC COMPONENT: Self-determination, career education

SOURCE: Levenson, H. (1981). Differentiating among internality, powerful others, and chance. In H. Lefcourt (Ed.), *Research with the locus of control construct: Vol. I.* New York: Academic Press. Retrieved from www.hannalevenson.com/ipcscales.pdf or http://cart.rmcdenver.com/instruments/multidimensional_locus.pdf

Rosenberg's Self-Esteem Scale

POPULATION/AGE LEVEL: Adolescents and adults

ECC COMPONENT: Self-determination, social interaction

SOURCE: Rosenberg, M. (1965). *Society and the adolescent self-image.* Princeton, NJ: Princeton University Press. Retrieved from http://www.yorku.ca/rokada/psyctest/rosenbrg.pdf

Self-Determination Exercise Scale: Student Edition

POPULATION/AGE LEVEL: Adolescents with deaf-blindness

ECC COMPONENT: Self-determination

SOURCE: Abery, B. H., & Eggebeen, A. (2001). *Self-determination and deafblindness: A comparative study of the self-determination levels of young adults with deafblindess* (Technical Report No. 2). Minneapolis: University of Minnesota, Institute on Community Integration.

Transition Competencies Checklist

POPULATION/AGE LEVEL: Adolescents with visual impairments

ECC COMPONENT: Self-determination, career education

SOURCE: Wolffe, K. E. (2011). *Transition competencies checklist.* Austin, TX: Author. (See Appendix 11A in this book.)

PUBLICATIONS

Alberti, R., & Emmons, M. (2001). *Your perfect right* (8th ed.). Atascadero, CA: Impact Publishers.

Babcock, J., Daugherty, W., Fusilier, T., Martinez, F., Newton, L., del Rosario, J., & Uriegas, O. (2012). Self-determination daily dozen do's and don'ts. Texas School for the Blind and Visually Impaired. Retrieved from http://www.tsbvi.edu/component/content/article/7-instructional-resources/3717-dosanddonts

Brown, D. (n.d.). Three things parents should know about self-determination skills for deaf-blind students. FamilyConnect. Retrieved from http://www.familyconnect.org/parentsite.asp?SectionID=72&TopicID=382&SubTopicID=186&DocumentID=4712

Cleveland, J., Clinkscales, M. R., Hefner, N., Houghtling, D., Kabacak, C., & Sewell, D. (2007). *Empowered: An activity based self-determination curriculum for students with visual impairments.* Austin: Texas School for the Blind and Visually Impaired.

Corn, A. L., Bina, M. J., & Sacks, S. Z. (2009). *Looking good: A curriculum on physical appearance and personal presentation for adolescents and young adults with visual impairments.* Austin, TX: PRO-ED.

Corn, A. L., & Rosenblum, L. P. (2000). *Finding wheels: A curriculum for non-drivers with visual impairments for gaining control of transportation needs.* Austin, TX: PRO-ED.

Covey, S. R. (1989). *The 7 habits of highly effective people.* New York: Simon & Schuster.

Covey, S. R. (2004). *The 8th habit: From effectiveness to greatness.* New York: Simon & Schuster.

Davies, L. (n.d.). Assertiveness training for children. Retrieved from Kelly Bear website: http://www.kellybear.com/TeacherArticles/TeacherTip74.html

Field, S., Hoffman, A., & Spezia, S. (1998). *Self-determination strategies for adolescents in transition.* Austin, TX: PRO-ED.

Field, S., Martin, J., Miller, R., Ward, M., & Wehmeyer, M. (1998). *A practical guide for teaching self-determination.* Arlington, VA: Council for Exceptional Children.

Feinberg, J. (2011). Becoming commuters: Teaching students traveling to work using public transportation. *Journal of Visual Impairment & Blindness, 105*, 262–265.

Guerette, A. R., Lewis, S., & Mattingly, C. (2011). Students with low vision describe their visual impairments and visual functioning. *Journal of Visual Impairment & Blindness, 105*, 287–298.

Harter, S. & Bukowski, W. M. (2012). *The construction of the self: Development and sociocultural foundations.* New York: Guilford Press.

Jones, M. (2006). Teaching self-determination: Empowering teachers, empowering students. *Teaching Exceptional Children, 39*, 12–17.

Karvonen, M., Test, D. W., Wood, W. M., Browder, D., & Algozzine, B. (2004). Putting self determination into practice. *Exceptional Children, 71*, 23–41.

Lawson, J. (2011). Improving assertive behavior. Retrieved from Live Strong website: http://www.livestrong.com/article/14699-improving-assertive-behavior/

Lewis, S., & Wolffe, K. E. (2006). Promoting and nurturing self-esteem. In S. Z. Sacks & K. E. Wolffe (Eds.), *Teaching social skills to students with visual impairments: From theory to practice* (pp. 122–162). New York: AFB Press.

Mancini, M. (2007). *Time management: 24 techniques to make each minute count at work.* New York: McGraw-Hill.

Morgenstern, J. (1998). *Organizing from the inside out.* New York: Henry Holt.

Morgenstern, J. (2000). *Time management from the inside out.* New York: Henry Holt.

Parker, D. R., Field, S., & Hoffman, A. (2013). *Self-determination strategies: Case studies of adolescents in transition* (2nd ed.). Austin, TX: PRO-ED.

Sanford School of Medicine—Center for Disabilities, & South Dakota Department of Education. (n.d.). Transition guide for students who are deaf-blind. Retrieved from http://www.usd.edu/medical-school/center-for-disabilities/upload/transitionguide.pdf

Seligman, M. E. P. (1990). *Learned optimism.* New York: Alfred A. Knopf.

Seligman, M. E. P. (1995). *The optimistic child.* Boston: Houghton Mifflin.

Seligman, M. E. P. (2002). *Authentic happiness.* New York: The Free Press.

Senge, P. M. (1990). *The fifth discipline: The art and practice of the learning organization.* New York: Doubleday.

Sewell, D. (2008). Becoming empowered through self-determination skills. Retrieved from the Texas School for the Blind and Visually Impaired website: http://www.tsbvi.edu/resources/2680-becoming-empowered-through-self-determination-skills

Smith, M. (1975). *When I say no, I feel guilty.* New York: Bantam.

Wolffe, K. E. (Ed.). (1999). *Skills for success: A career education handbook for children and adolescents with visual impairments.* New York: AFB Press.

Wolffe, K. E. (2012). *Transition tote system: Navigating the rapids of life* (2nd ed.). Louisville, KY: American Printing House for the Blind.

Wolffe, K. E., & Erin, J. N. (2012). Transition for students who are blind or have low vision. In M. L. Wehmeyer & K. W. Webb (Eds.), *Handbook of transition for youth with disabilities.* New York: Routledge, Taylor and Francis.

PERSON-CENTERED PLANNING RESOURCES

Furney, K. S. (1996). *Making dreams happen: How to facilitate the MAPS process.* Burlington: University of Vermont, Center for Transition and Employment.

Moss, K., & Wiley, D. (2003). A brief guide to personal futures planning: Organizing your community to envision and build a desirable future with you (booklet). Austin: Texas Deafblind Outreach. Retrieved from http://www.tsbvi.edu/attachments/other/pcp-manual.pdf

O'Brien, C. L., O'Brien, J., & Mount, B. (1997). Person-centered planning has arrived . . . or has it? *Mental Retardation, 35*, 480–484.

WEBSITES

Office of Disability Employment Policy (ODEP)—Youth

http://www.dol.gov/odep/categories/youth

Identifies and discusses key educational and career development interventions that can help youths, including those with disabilities, to make a successful transition into adulthood.

Person-Centered Planning / Personal Futures Planning for Students with Disabilities
Perkins Scout
Perkins School for the Blind

http://www.perkins.org/resources/scout/transition/person-centered-planning.html

Offers information about and links to numerous resources on person-centered planning.

Project Aspiro

www.projectaspiro.com

A career-planning and employment resource for people who are blind or partially sighted, created in partnership with CNIB and the World Blind Union, that provides information, tools, and resources for people who are blind and partially sighted, their friends and family, service providers, and employers in Ontario and around the globe, with the end goal of improving the overall quality of life of those living with vision loss.

Self-Determination Learning Activities

Contributed by Carol B. Allman, Sandra Lewis, and Karen E. Wolffe

These sample learning activities are presented as examples of activities that teachers can create to work on several ECC skills at once with their students. Activities that help teach self-determination skills can also be found in other chapters. Most of the activities presented can be extended to include all students—such as those who are braille readers, have low vision, or have additional disabilities—with adaptations for appropriate media and physical capabilities of the student.

Learning Activity: Ready or Not, There It Goes!

Primary ECC Area: Self-determination **Component:** Self-advocacy
Grades: Pre-K–1

Other ECC Areas

- Orientation and mobility
- Sensory efficiency
- Social interaction
- Compensatory access

Goal: The student will develop a sense of control and problem-solving skills.

Key Tasks/Concepts

The student will:

- Decide when to surrender a toy/object in possession.
- Learn to problem solve in order to keep the toy/object.
- Anticipate when a toy/object might be removed from possession.

Description

There are many instances when a parent, teacher, or other adult feels it is necessary to take an item away from a young child. Perhaps the activity or snack is over but the child does not understand; or a parent says "no more" and the child does understand but does not want to listen. It is easy for students with typical vision to anticipate when mom, dad or another grown-up is about to pick up an item or take something away. They see the adult coming and then hold onto the desired item a little bit tighter, turn away, or put the item away quickly without the adult's intervention. Students who are blind or who have low vision may feel helpless or lacking control when things are grabbed from them unexpectedly. Developing a sense of control in life can lead to self-determination.

In this activity, the student will learn that it is possible to have control over one's actions, even when it is not possible to control others' actions.

Using age-appropriate language, start with a brief discussion about how sometimes grown-ups pull things away from children unexpectedly. It can leave the student feeling confused, upset, or worried, not knowing when this will happen again. Explain that there are ways to prepare for these situations.

Tell the student, "Let's pretend I'm going to take your ________ (book, candy, toy, napkin, juice, etc.), but you don't want me to. There are some things you can do to be ready for this."

- The student can tell the grown-up, "Can I hand it to you myself, please?" Practice this option with the student. Give her a book or item that she likes, announce, "Give me that book," then hold onto the book and

(continued on next page)

slowly start to pull it away from the student. Prompt or give verbal guidance as necessary so that the student holds on tighter and says, "Can I hand it to you myself, please?"

- The student can ask for more time to finish with the item. Give the student a toy to play with for a few minutes then announce, "Time to clean up." Without giving the student any time to clean up, reach for the toy to pull it away. Prompt or give verbal guidance as necessary so that she holds on tighter and says, "Can I finish playing first?" This may require the teacher to negotiate. Recognize that the student is advocating for herself and make a deal so that the child can play for another 2 or 3 minutes.
- Another option for the student, although likely the least preferred for the teacher or parent, is that the student does not give up the item without a conversation or negotiation. This option yields an opportunity for the student (and the grown-up!) to practice problem solving. Practice by giving the student a desired snack. After she eats a few pieces, announce, "Snack time is over." Prompt or give verbal guidance as necessary so that the student says, "No." Explain the rules of snack time and the consequences of not listening. Be prepared to make a deal, such as allowing the student to have one more bite or piece of the snack this time, but next time there will be less.

Practice each strategy a few times with various items and record the student's responses. Further practice opportunities can be provided by creating a board game where landing on certain squares or pulling a specific card requires the student to demonstrate a specified strategy.

After the student demonstrates an understanding of the options and strategies during practice sessions, the teacher can monitor and record responses in authentic situations throughout the school day.

Instructional Materials and Supplies Needed

Any items that the child likes or is likely to be engaged with in an activity, such as a toy, book, snack, juice box, etc.

Settings

Any setting in which natural interaction takes place with a young child such as a table, floor, couch, indoor play area, playground, bathroom, grocery store, retail store, etc.

Duration/Timing

- Allow 20 minutes for initial instruction.
- 15–20 minutes to practice the strategies at a later date. Time will depend on the age and language level of the child.

Evaluation

Enter the date and the name of the item, and place a check or X in the box corresponding to the student's response or reaction.

Student's Response	Day Item	Day Item	Day Item	Day Item	Day Item
No verbal or physical response. Allows item to be taken.					
Requests to be allowed to hand over the item without it being taken.					
Advocates to have more time with the item.					
Refuses to turn over the item, requiring the grown-up to initiate negotiations.					
Other response:					

Learning Activity: The Eyes Have It

Primary ECC Area: Self-determination **Component:** Self-knowledge
Grades: 1–3

Other ECC Areas

- Social interaction
- Compensatory access

Goal: The student will survey classmates and make a chart comparing physical attributes.

Key Tasks/Concepts

The student will:

- Design a brief survey about eye color and use/non-use of eyeglasses.
- Ask each member of the class, including adults, the survey questions.
- Document participants' responses.
- Create a chart visually/tactually showing the survey results.

Description

To develop a positive self-concept, it is important for students to learn about themselves first, then about others in their world. A student who is visually impaired should also learn about his or her visual impairment and its impact on learning. It can be a difficult subject to learn about, depending on how much the student already knows, family reactions and support, peer reactions and support, and even community reactions and support. Learning about a visual impairment early will likely lead to a healthy self-concept for the student.

The eyes are a good place to start this discussion because everyone has eyes with different characteristics. Bringing attention to eyes is just like bringing attention to other physical attributes, such as gender, hair color, or height. This activity can be used as a beginning step to learning about a student's visual impairment.

Help your student design a simple survey that can be administered in class to find out what color eyes everyone has and who wears eyeglasses or not. The survey can be handwritten by the student, produced together on the computer or brailled. Creating it in the form of a chart, as in the example below, will reinforce additional academic skills. Be sure the student gives the chart a title.

Eyes in Room

Name	Brown	Blue	Green	Wears Glasses
Jamie		*X*		
Lisa			*X*	
Tony	*X*			*X*
Jose	*X*			
Claudia		*X*		
Mrs. Simpson	*X*			*X*
Me	*X*			*X*
TOTAL	*4*	*2*	*1*	*3*

When the survey is ready, the student can go around the room with a clipboard and pencil marking classmates' responses. The adults in the room should also be surveyed (teacher, aides, volunteers). The total for each column should be added along the bottom. To keep track of students and the correct columns, the student can be shown how to use an index card or ruler under each student's name.

(continued on next page)

Once all the members of the class are surveyed, the information can be put into a bar graph or pie chart to show the data, using a crayon that corresponds with each eye color. For braille readers, a tactile chart or graph can be produced. A discussion with the entire class and/or the individual student about the results can help produce the realization that everyone is made up of differences that are not under their control—it is just how people are born.

The activity can be extended with future lessons that focus on why some people wear eyeglasses and some do not. A lesson on the basic anatomy of the eye will help further this understanding. Once the student has an understanding of how the eye works, lessons can move toward how a visual impairment makes vision different.

Instructional Materials and Supplies Needed

- Graph paper, blank paper, or braille paper
- Pencil/marker
- Clipboard
- Brown, blue, green crayon/marker
- Tactile craft supplies

Settings

Elementary classroom, teacher's workroom

Duration/Timing

- 20–25 minutes to create the survey
- 15–20 minutes to survey members of the class and have a brief discussion
- 25–30 minutes to create a chart to depict the data

Evaluation

The completed survey and final chart/graph will be used to show completion of the activity. It is not necessary to document the level of assistance required, as participation in the activity and discussion is the focus. The following questions can be used to document the student's understanding:

1. What color are your eyes?
2. What color eyes do your classmates and teachers have?
3. How many people in your classroom wear glasses?
4. Are everyone's eyes the same?
5. How are people's eyes different?

Learning Activity: <u>I Can Handle It!</u>

Primary ECC Area: Self-determination **Component:** Self-advocacy
Grades: K–12

Other ECC Areas

- Social interaction
- Compensatory access

Goal: The student will demonstrate three effective strategies for dealing with teasing.

Key Tasks/Concepts

The student will:

- Identify why people tease one another.
- Recognize when teasing is good natured or hurtful.

(continued on next page)

- Handle teasing through a variety of methods.
- Recognize when teasing has become harassment or bullying.
- Report bullying and harassment.

Description

This activity begins with the teacher playing recordings of students who are being teased in both good natured and hurtful ways. The teacher asks the students how they think the person being teased felt and how the teasing was handled. The teacher contributes ideas following the students' input. The teacher then asks the students about incidents of teasing that they have experienced and discusses students' reactions and resultant feelings.

The teacher and students can brainstorm reasons why people tease one another, which may include:

- to get attention
- to be accepted by peers
- to feel powerful
- to act like someone else (perhaps a parent, or older sibling)
- because differences are misunderstood or feared and may produce nervous responses to entertain or to make someone laugh

During subsequent meetings, the teacher can introduce various approaches handling teasing such as the following (see Freedman, 1999, for details):

- Positive self-talk such as "I'm okay. I can handle this situation. I am not like the person or thing being described."
- Ignoring and walking away from the teaser.
- Reframing the teasing remark.
- Agreeing with the teaser.
- Using "I" messages such as "I feel uncomfortable when you say such things," or "I feel sad or anxious when others say things like this."
- Responding with, "What are you trying to tell me? Are you serious or are you teasing?"
- Using humor.
- Visualizing a protective shield.

These can be introduced one at a time in very short sessions, with a brief explanation of the strategy, followed by practice using it in a role-playing scenario. The value of these sessions can be enhanced by inviting carefully selected peers to participate.

Students can be asked to be on the alert to times when they hear others being teased and to pay attention to the strategies that their peers use to handle teasing. Sharing these incidents with the teacher will provide opportunities to explore strategies that work or don't.

Students can be asked to maintain a personal chart indicating which strategy they have used when being teased and to share it with their teacher on a weekly or monthly basis, depending on the number of incidents they experience. Successes and failures can be discussed and reviewed.

The teacher will need to emphasize how to determine when teasing has become bullying and teach the student to whom to report bullying incidents.

Instructional Materials and Supplies Needed

- Audio or audio/video recordings of students being teased.
  (Good-natured teasing is often part of family-centered situation comedies, which students usually enjoy watching as part of a school lesson. Recordings of hurtful teasing can be located in curriculum packages focusing on bullying available in many school districts.)
- Audio or video player.

Settings

Classroom

(continued on next page)

Duration/Timing
20–30 minutes for the introductory discussion
5–15 minutes for subsequent lessons

Evaluation
Practicing strategies for dealing with teasing through role playing can be evaluated using the following data-collection tool:

Strategy	Date satisfactorily demonstrated		
Role-plays self-talk			
Role-plays agreeing with facts			
Role-plays saying, "What are you trying to tell me? Are you serious or are you teasing?"			
Role-plays complimenting teaser			

Use of appropriate strategies in real-life situations should be noted when observed, discussed with student, and recorded as an observation.

A more meaningful evaluation tool would be a chart that the students (particularly young students) maintain based on personal experiences, possibly using stickers to indicate how each experience felt to them:

I "handled" the teasing of others by:	Date	Date	Date
Telling myself "I can handle it!"			
Agreed with facts			
Said "So?"			
Complimented teaser			

Key:
Worked for me ☺
I felt sad ☹
I felt angry ☹

Learning Activity: What Do You Do If . . .

Primary ECC Area: Self-determination
Components: Problem solving, informed decision making
Grades: K–12

Other ECC Areas
- Career education
- Independent living
- Social interaction
- Compensatory access
- Orientation and mobility

Goal: The student will propose solutions to a problem presented in hypothetical situations.

(continued on next page)

Key Tasks/Concepts

The student will:

- Develop strategies to deal with unexpected situations at home and school.
- Practice problem-solving strategies.

Description

Being able to solve problems is a critical skill for students to learn.

The teacher can begin with discussions of some possible scenarios that might happen at school, such as the following, and ask how the student might deal with the situation. (Possible solutions that can be part of the discussion are included in parentheses.)

- Finding a seat in the lunchroom. (Approach a table and ask if you can sit; before entering the lunchroom, ask a classmate to sit with you.)
- Needing help opening a door if your hands are full of books. (Knock with your foot or ask if someone nearby can open the door for you.)
- Responding to an alarm. (Listen and follow instructions; follow class rules such as calmly staying with a classmate.)

The teacher can also have discussions about some possible scenarios that might happen at home and how to deal with them:

- Someone in your family is watching something on TV and you would like to change the channel. (Ask politely if you may change the channel or when you may change the channel.)
- A meal includes food that you don't like. (Ask if you may help cook or prepare something that you like and/or ask if you may suggest a menu option once a week.)
- Your sibling is moving things in your room. (Ask your sibling if things could be put back where you can find them or that you be told if things are moved.)

These discussions should always be positive and nonthreatening and should allow the students to brainstorm ways they might want to deal with situations, considering the feelings and needs of others.

Instructional Materials and Supplies Needed

None

Settings

School, community, and home

Duration/Timing

10 minutes maximum at a time and should take place at times when situations occur naturally as much as possible.

Evaluation

This type of activity would not need to be evaluated formally but the teacher should note how the student typically responds to unexpected events and discuss with the student and the parents appropriate ways to deal with such situations.

Learning Activity: Take Action

Primary ECC Area: Self-determination **Component:** Goal setting

Grades: 8–12

Other ECC Areas

- Compensatory access
- Career education
- Assistive technology

(continued on next page)

Goal: The student will set a personally meaningful short-term goal.

Key Tasks/Concepts

The student will:

- Create a short-term goal.
- Create an action plan for accomplishing the goal.
- Keep a record of the steps as they are accomplished and describe any barriers encountered.
- Evaluate level of success in meeting the goal.
- List changes to the goal, action plan, or actions taken that would improve the likelihood of meeting the goal in the future.

Description

Ask students to describe prior experiences they may have had with setting and working toward goals. Have a short discussion to create a working definition of personal goal, including some basic components of a SMART (specific, measurable, achievable, relevant, and time-bound, as described in this chapter) goal.

Give examples of short-term and long-term goals. Discuss goal-setting as an effective way to achieve desired outcomes. Tell the students that it takes practice to become skillful at setting and achieving goals. Remind them that an action plan to achieve a goal requires more than one step.

Introduce the assignment, making it clear that each student has the freedom to choose a goal. A template for goal setting like the one provided at the end of this activity can be provided to assist the students. Offer support as needed, including:

- Help identify possible goal areas while preserving the student's freedom to choose (for example, social engagement, exercise, gaining access to information, getting somewhere, or the like).
- Provide sample written goals and associated action plans and assist with development of a daily log using appropriate assistive technology.
- Brainstorm ideas for making the goal SMART (specific, measurable, achievable, relevant, and time-bound). If needed, provide more support (such as a short list of suggestions) to keep the process moving and to help the students maintain focus on the goal.
- Set time aside once a week (at least) to examine the daily log and discuss progress toward goal(s).

Once the students have written their goals, help them develop and write out action plans. Students frequently need support in breaking a goal into discrete, measurable actions. Encourage the student to begin each step with an action verb (this provides specificity). Ask the student to write a short daily report of his or her efforts and successes in following the action plan.

At the end of the time period identified in the steps of the action plan, review the daily reports with the students, reinforcing their efforts to document the process and follow their action plans. Remind the students that the goal of the activity is to learn an effective way to achieve the things they want or need to do.

Finally, ask the students to evaluate their level of success in meeting the goal. Review the daily reports once again, and guide the students to think of ways to make the process easier and/or more likely to be successful.

Instructional Materials and Supplies Needed

- Materials for writing in student's preferred medium
- Sample goals and action plans in the student's reading medium
- Optional goal-setting template

Settings

Classroom with teacher

(continued on next page)

Duration/Timing

30 to 60 minutes for the initial session to discuss what a goal is, to set a goal, and to develop an action plan. 5–10 minutes for each daily check-in session. If the teacher is itinerant, she will need to allow more time to review the student's daily log when they meet.

Evaluation

The following chart could be used for evaluation of the activity:

Key Tasks	Date	Date	Date	Date	Date
Keeps data showing steps toward achieving goal.					
Reviews goal and adjusts strategies toward goal as appropriate.					
Makes progress toward goal.					
Achieves the set goal in the designated period of time.					

Template for Goal Setting

Name:

Date:

Goal-Writing Steps:	**Your Work**
Specific—define the goal (**what** do you want to achieve?)	
Measurable—describe the action plan with targeted dates for each step (**how** will you do what needs doing and by **when**?)	
Achievable—determine whether you can accomplish this goal (do you have enough time, energy, resources to do this goal?)	
Relevant—explain the reason you want to change (**why** is this goal important to you?)	
Time-bound—state **when** you expect to achieve the goal	

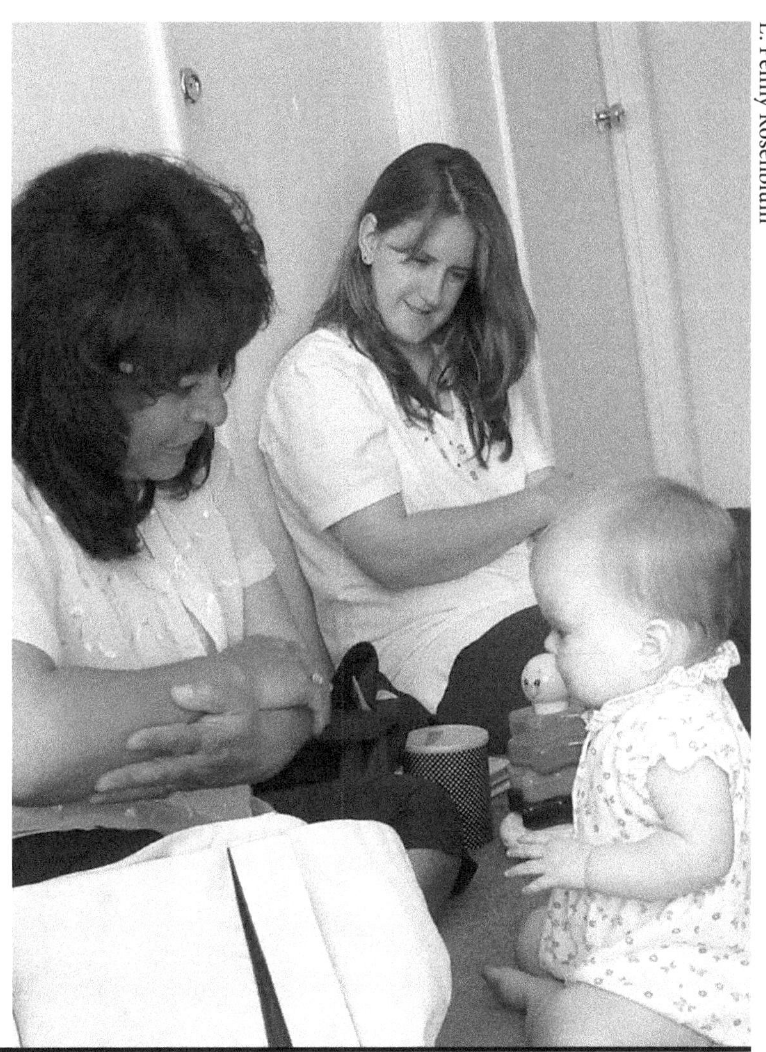

L. Penny Rosenblum

PART III

Supporting the Expanded Core Curriculum

CHAPTER 13

Teaching the Expanded Core Curriculum in General Education Settings

Laura C. Brown and Susan Glaser

American Foundation for the Blind

As the previous chapters of this book have explained, the curriculum for students with visual impairments essentially consists of two parts. The first parallels that provided to sighted students. The second part, known as the expanded core curriculum (ECC), addresses the unique, specialized needs of learners with visual impairments. The ECC is the particular focus of the teacher of students with visual impairments (Huebner, Merk-Adam, Stryker, & Wolffe, 2004, pp. 13–15), who supports students' access to and participation in the overall curriculum by teaching compensatory access skills.

Incorporating the various aspects of the ECC into a student's educational program and typical day can be challenging, but it is crucial to a student's well-being and can feasibly be done. Teachers can work to embed many ECC skills and related activities in the general education curriculum. Most general education studies include the use of skills that overlap with the ECC, such as working in groups (social interaction), learning about different jobs (career education), reading a map (orientation and mobility [O&M]), and working with money (independent living). Teachers of students with visual impairments and O&M specialists can pre-teach, co-teach, and reteach ECC concepts that are partially covered by the general curriculum as one way to incorporate the ECC into a student's education (Sapp & Hatlen, 2010).

There is no question that doing all this is challenging. Teachers of students with visual impairments report that they do not have as much time as they would like to teach ECC lessons because of other responsibilities, including adapting education materials, needing to provide assistance with academic areas that require accommodation, planning and performing in-service activities, and so forth (Blankenship, Hatlen, & Lohmeier, 2009). The purpose of this chapter, therefore, is to provide readers with useful and effective strategies, suggestions, and resources for this essential effort.

THE EXPANDED CORE CURRICULUM: COLLABORATIVE EFFORT

Picture a typical preschool classroom: every color of the rainbow from the floor to ceiling, the alphabet written across the board, a rug with pictures of objects that begin with each letter, enticing toys on shelves, a cozy housekeeping area with appliances that look real, books with exciting covers, and a board filled with materials for learning activities, such as a calendar, cards displaying days of the week, symbols for the weather, a daily attendance chart, a hundreds chart, and charts showing word clusters. What young student would not be immediately captivated by this exciting new world of kindergarten? What parent would not be comforted knowing that this room can provide everything a child needs to learn, grow, and become successful?

Now, consider this same kindergarten classroom from the perspective of a child with a visual impairment. The information on the walls and shelves is inaccessible from a distance, the rug is scratchy, the play kitchen shelves and cabinets are no different from the shelves and cabinets of the free-reading area and so are not delineated from one another, accessible books cannot be found anywhere in the room, and the board does not display a single learning activity that incorporates items to touch and explore. How many parents of children with a visual impairment would want their child to be assigned to this classroom?

This classroom stimulates different responses for parents depending on how they perceive the needs of their child. Parents of children with unimpaired vision who show up for the open house the evening before school begins will be very pleased with the environment in which their children will learn. They will go home with a warm, excited feeling about their child's first encounter with school. Parents of children with a visual impairment may go home feeling nervous and unsettled, wondering how their child is going to experience and learn the same things as the rest of the children in the class.

Creating an accessible learning environment to ensure use by all children is the focus of teachers of students with visual impairments, and they can help general education teachers create a classroom that will be attractive and stimulating for all children. Making such an environment a reality requires the cooperation of school administrators, general education teachers, support staff, community service providers, and parents. To ensure access to the environment and to the curriculum and to promote the development of students' skills, teachers of students with visual impairments need to recruit the help of, collaborate with, and train a variety of school personnel, including classroom teachers, administrators, office staff, cafeteria staff, and others at the school who will be involved in the education of the student or students with visual impairments.

The goal of this chapter is to focus on those issues that frequently impede the implementation of the ECC in educational settings and to offer strategies for addressing those impediments. By addressing some of the key challenges teachers face on a daily basis—role recognition, time management, relationships with administrators, and access to school, school district, and community resources—the chapter is intended to provide readers with a toolbox of solutions in support of teaching the ECC.

ROLE RECOGNITION: EXPLAINING AND DEFINING RESPONSIBILITIES

The prevalence of visual impairment in the general population remains relatively low. Therefore, the presence of students with visual impairments in a given school is uncommon. Few people know any children who are visually impaired and even fewer know that there are teachers who specifically teach these children. With so many misconceptions about blindness in society, it is no wonder that very few people know the crucial role that teachers of students with visual impairments have in the education of their students.

A first and critical step in supporting the ECC for students, therefore, may be educating others about the needs of children with visual impairments. A central part of this process is making sure that everyone involved in the education of a student who is visually impaired understands the role of the teacher of students with visual impairments, including school administrators, other teachers, paraeducators, and school personnel. (For additional suggestions and related information, see the discussion later in this chapter on communicating with administrators.)

It may seem obvious, but it is important to understand clearly what one's role is before trying to explain it to others. Teachers of students with visual impairments know what their jobs entail, and they need to be able to quickly and articulately explain to a variety of audiences what they do. For example, since visual impairment is a low-prevalence disability, when a school enrolls a child who is blind or visually impaired, it may be assumed that the child will have a one-on-one aide or paraeducator to help him or her throughout the school day. If no one at the school has had prior experience working with children who are visually impaired, the school staff may believe that a child who is blind cannot receive the same education as the rest of the students without this one-on-one assistance.

When a teacher of students with visual impairments arrives at this school, she may be ready to adapt a student's classroom, obtain materials that need to be brailled, and meet with classroom teachers to review the student's Individualized Education Program (IEP). However, without an understanding of this teacher's responsibilities and how she is important to a student's successful educational experience, the general education classroom teachers may think this person is there to serve as an independent teacher or as an aide or student assistant. The classroom teacher may be confused about why requests are being made for lesson plans, books, and worksheets, and why discussions about rearranging the layout of the classroom are being held. Although the child with a visual impairment may be physically included in the general education classroom, a lack of clarity about the role and responsibility of his or her specialized teacher can lead to the exclusion of the student from instruction in the curriculum.

Overall, if the general education teacher does not understand that one role of the teacher of students with visual impairments is to make the core curriculum accessible to students who are visually impaired and that this teacher is also responsible for teaching the ECC—and if the general education teacher does not understand what the ECC is—valuable time and effort can be wasted. Without clearly outlined roles and responsibilities, the efforts of both educators can be undermined. In some cases, this situation may lead to the teacher of students with visual impairments slowly taking on the role of an academic teacher or tutor, helping students complete assignments and catch up, instead of focusing on the ECC. Having a discussion about teachers' roles with the general education teacher before students begin the school year is therefore extremely important as well as beneficial.

In-Service Presentations

Organizing an in-service presentation at the beginning of the school year or at the time a child with a visual impairment starts school can be a valuable tool for defining roles, including those of the teacher of students with visual impairments, classroom teachers, school administrators, parents, and students. Not everyone has time to deliver in-service training in every school in which students are served, and the thought of finding a time that fits everyone's schedule can be daunting. However, instead of trying to track down a dozen teachers and staff members to make a meeting happen, teachers of students with visual impairments can work with school staff to identify times when teachers are already available in groups. Many schools hold weekly faculty meetings after school, and it is not unusual for teachers of specific grade levels to hold regular meetings to plan and discuss curriculum. Teachers of students with visual impairments can contact the principal, assistant principal, or program specialist and request to attend these meetings.

These administrators in all likelihood may want to be apprised of what training their teachers receive, and they may be interested in the training themselves.

When planning an in-service training session, it is important to keep it simple and short! General education teachers have much work to do and a limited amount of time in which to do it. They will want to meet the needs of a student who is visually impaired just as much as they will want to meet the needs of all their other students, some of whom may have other types of disabilities. Elaborate, lengthy presentations may not keep the attention of a group of very busy teachers. Sometimes creating and using a handout about a student, similar to Figure 13.1, "Meet Leah," can be more useful than an elaborate slideshow presentation.

This kind of handout provides teachers with something for their further review, at their convenience, and, when printed double-sided on bright, eye-catching paper, can be distributed in mailboxes for teachers who could not attend a presentation. Handouts should be clear, specific and memorable. Because teachers in general enjoy hearing stories about children, whether the stories be funny, sweet, endearing, heartwarming, or even sad, using the real student's story to illustrate each point on a handout can be very effective. Information shared this way will be more meaningful and memorable if the teachers can relate it to the student. In addition, general education teachers will be more likely to view the teacher of students with visual impairments as a teacher, and not as an aide or tutor, after reading or hearing such stories.

A number of topics can be covered in in-service activities. In addition to the needs of students with visual impairments and the role of the teacher specializing in work with them, the appropriate role of paraeducators, importance of assistive technology, and areas included in the ECC are possible subjects to be covered. (See Holbrook, Croft, & Kline, 2000, for additional information on making such presentations.)

An in-service session or informal meeting is also a good time to explain how a classroom can be adapted and why. An example, such as the one at the beginning of this chapter that describes differing perceptions of a visually appealing classroom can be used to illustrate how children with visual impairments depend on appropriate accommodations. A child with a visual impairment in the classroom described would have limited access to many learning materials and consequently might not learn nearly as much as the other children in the class who have visual access to all of the available materials. At an in-service meeting, the teacher of students with visual impairments can provide examples of how a classroom can be made more accessible by using a braille or large print label maker to create labels for different areas or shelves in the room, or providing tactile graphics or real objects to adapt a lesson. A three-ring binder in which information found on the board in a student's classroom is presented in clear, high-contrast print or in braille could also be shown as another example. It is the responsibility of every IEP team member, and every teacher who provides educational services to exceptional students, to ensure that the IEP is fully implemented. The teacher of students with visual impairments can make the oftentimes legal-sounding language of the IEP more understandable and real to classroom teachers by providing concrete examples of accommodations with which classroom teachers may be unfamiliar. Educators participating in such training will find it more meaningful if accommodations and the methods for making them are demonstrated rather than just talked or read about.

Additional Information Sharing

A helpful handout that explains the role of teachers of students with visual impairments can be found in Figure 13.2. Material such as this can be given to teachers or reviewed at an in-service training or other meeting to explain what general education teachers are responsible for teaching and what teachers of students with visual impairments are responsible for teaching. If conducting an in-service presentation is not feasible, similarly visually attractive, simple brochures or handouts can be distributed in teachers' mailboxes or at meetings. At the next staff meeting or other opportunity, teachers can be asked if they have any questions about the information distributed to ensure that they understand the material. *When You Have a Visually Impaired Student in Your Classroom: A Guide for Teachers* (2002) and *When You Have a Visually Impaired Student with Multiple Disabilities in Your Classroom: A Guide for Teachers* (Erin, 2004) are good sources of concise information aimed specifically at general education and special education teachers to include in your handouts or to suggest as recommended reading for teachers who are open to learning more.

It is important to share this same information with the parents or family members of the child who is visually impaired, because they also may not know what the teacher of students with visual impairments is responsible

FIGURE 13.1

Sample Handout about a Student

MEET LEAH

There's a new student in Mrs. Turner's class. Leah loves songs and music, nursery rhymes, movement, and toys. She has a mild hearing loss and should be wearing her hearing aids at all times. She is also totally blind and learns through her other senses. Leah needs a lot of teachers *to teach her about her world. She* does not *need a lot of* helpers *to do things for her!*

Be **FIRM**—Leah is a very self-determined little girl and she knows what she wants. She is also used to getting what she wants. She needs us to teach her appropriate behaviors in school. If other students are not allowed to hug and kiss each other, sit on laps, or throw or slap, then Leah should not be allowed to either—having the same standards for Leah as you do for other children helps her learn independence. It is not the blindness that disables, but people who try to help too much.

Act **NORMAL**—When Leah walks down the sidewalk, enters a room, eats breakfast, or plays on the playground, remember to go about business as usual. Greet her when she comes by, then continue talking or doing whatever you were doing. If you stop talking when she walks by, jump out of her way, make other children clear a path, or stare at her as she walks past, she will not receive any kind of auditory feedback or clues about where she is or what is around her. It's okay if she bumps into something or someone. How else will she learn to say "excuse me" or meet new people?

Promote **INDEPENDENCE**—Many children who are blind are further disabled by other people helping too much. If someone is always there to pick something up, open a door, open a package, or put items in a backpack, how will Leah learn to be independent? Touch her as little as possible and give her plenty of wait time to figure out doors, knobs, latches, containers, packages, faucets, toys, and manipulatives. Remember to "sit on your hands!"

PART-TO-WHOLE learning—Children who are blind learn by taking in one part of an entire object or task at a time. They then put all the parts together to understand the big picture. Sighted children learn incidentally, by watching, and through whole-to-part learning. They see the entire picture, object, or task at one time and then understand how the little parts make it work. If a blind child does not *see* something happen, then she does not know *how* it happened or sometimes even *that* it happened.

Talk, Talk, **TALK**—Say, "Hi Leah, it's ____________," so she will learn your voice and name. The more descriptive your conversations, the better. Use lots of adjectives and verbs to describe what she is doing, touching, walking on, hearing, and smelling. Language is meaningless to a blind child unless she is involved in meaningful experiences at the same time.

Use **DIRECTIONAL WORDS**—*Here, there, this,* and *that* are very ambiguous. Be very specific when giving directions, such as, "the book is on the table," "John is sitting next to you," or "the handle is on your left."

Maintain **HIGH EXPECTATIONS**—Leah just turned 3 and has a lot of pre-K skills to learn. Expect her to perform the same tasks and learn the same skills as other 3-year-old children. She can learn to count, read, write, identify days of the week and months of the year, take turns, interact appropriately, wait patiently, etc. She has a lot of learning to do; *expect* that she will learn successfully.

Encourage exploration of the **CONCRETE** world—To prevent Leah from feeling like she is "lost in space," encourage her to maintain contact with the concrete world. Trailing a wall with her hand, using her cane to find walls and obstacles, and similar methods for maintaining contact with what is around her will help increase her spatial awareness.

All kids **BOUNCE BACK**—Do you know a child who has *never* slammed her finger in a door, scraped his knee, bumped her head because she wasn't paying attention—or had any kind of injury? Leah is no different than any other student. She will fall down and get back up again. She will scrape her knee and get a Band-Aid. She may even bump her head and have to get ice from the nurse. Just like all the other children.

100 TIMES—Remember, for every 1 time a sighted child does something, a blind child should do it 100 times in order to master and perform the task or skill at the same level as sighted peers. If grown-ups are always doing things for her, how will Leah learn to do things on her own?

100-TIMERS CLUB CHALLENGE

Try these activities 100 times *without using your vision*! It might be slow at first, but after 20, 30, or 40 times, you'll get better and faster. Turn in your checklist of completed activities to earn a special braille keychain!

- Insert a key to lock or unlock a door—without looking.
- Tie your shoes—without looking.
- Pour a glass of water—without looking.
- Apply toothpaste on a toothbrush—without looking.
- Dial a phone number—without looking.

FIGURE 13.2

Sample Handout about the Role of TVIs

Teachers of children with visual impairments

TAKE A CLOSER LOOK AT THE ROLE OF A TVI

the Expanded Core Curriculum

What Classroom Teachers Teach

Classroom teachers are responsible for teaching the *core curriculum* to students from kindergarten through twelfth grade. The core curriculum primarily involves academic subjects, such as language arts, mathematics, science, social studies, health, physical education, history, etc. It can be adapted for blind and visually impaired learners; however, the core curriculum does not address the concepts and experiences that most sighted students learn incidentally, by observing others. These skills must be taught to blind and visually impaired students through systematic and sequential instruction.

What TVIs Teach

The additional concepts, experiences, and skills that students who are blind or visually impaired do not obtain incidentally is known as the *expanded core curriculum.* It consists of knowledge and skills that students will need in order to be INDEPENDENT.

Areas of the ECC:

- *Compensatory or functional academic skills, including communication modes:* concept development, spatial understanding, study and organizational skills, speaking and listening skills, adaptations needed to access the core curriculum (braille, large print, regular print with low vision devices, recordings).
- *Sensory efficiency skills:* Utilizing one's remaining senses (vision, auditory, olfactory, and tactile) to function more efficiently and effectively. (use of environmental cues, nonoptical tools, optical low vision devices, etc.)
- *Self-determination:* Teaching students to be in control of their lives. (self-awareness, knowledge of one's visual impairment, self-advocacy, choice making, self-evaluation and adjustment, etc.)
- *Use of assistive technology:* electronic note-takers, screen enlarging software, speech synthesis, digital media, video magnification, etc.

- *Career education:* Basic knowledge of the world of work, transition from school to post-secondary options, etc.
- *Orientation and mobility:* body and spatial awareness, independent travel, use of long cane, protective techniques, cardinal directions, mental mapping, etc.
- *Social interaction skills:* Socially appropriate behavior, such as facial expressions, body language, eye contact, etc. are primarily learned by watching others.
- *Independent living skills:* Everyday activities that allow a person to lead independent lives (personal hygiene, food preparation, money & time management, organization, etc.)
- *Recreation and leisure skills:* Development of life-long skills beyond team sports (play, recreational reading, athletics, hobbies, etc.)

Use these resources to learn more about the Expanded Core Curriculum

- www.tsbvi.edu
- www.afb.org
- National Agenda for the Education of Children and Youths with Visual Impairments, Including Those with Mulitiple Disabilities
- A TVI in your school district

Anywhere School District
Visually Impaired Program

4201 W. 15th Street
Anytown, USA

Mrs. Slate, Teacher of Children with Visual Impairments

Phone: 555.678.0123
Fax: 555.678.3210
E-mail: slate@anytown.k12.us

for. These roles and responsibilities should be briefly reiterated at IEP meetings and, as necessary, at parent conferences. Parents can be reminded of the information in a handout the next time they ask their child's teacher of students with visual impairments to review or teach a core curriculum activity, such as reviewing vocabulary words. Teachers of students with visual impairments do not have time to teach in areas that are not their responsibility. Instead, when services are initiated they can teach parents and others about their role and its critical importance for the student's education and reinforce this message as needed throughout the school year. Eventually, parents can become advocates on behalf of the teacher of students with visual impairments when others suggest that the teacher take on tasks unrelated to this defined role.

Adherence to One's Role: A Key Focus

Many students who are blind or visually impaired require more time and need additional practice to master skills and concepts that their classmates with typical sight may grasp with practically a glance. It is easy for teachers specializing in work with visually impaired students to feel as if the ECC needs to wait until a student has demonstrated required academic concepts. And, when the student's parents, classroom teachers, administrators, or other educators at the school talk about how poorly the student is doing academically, they often expect this teacher to provide academic assistance. However, the role of the teacher of students with visual impairments is to work with the educational team to make sure that appropriate accommodations and considerations are in place. Sometimes it may help to remember that if the student were not visually impaired and were struggling academically, his or her parents, classroom teachers, and administrators would work together to find solutions. After-school tutoring programs, volunteer tutors, intensive math or reading sessions, small-group instruction, or any other instructional programs to support struggling learners are in place to help all students at the school, including students who are blind or visually impaired.

There are plenty of teachers within a school who can help a student with issues like spelling, grammar, paragraph structure, reading, and math skills. It is important to keep in mind that there is only one teacher who can teach a child who is blind how to read and write braille, how to use an electronic notetaker to complete assignments, how to use a screen reader to access a computer and the Internet, and how to use a knife safely to cut vegetables. There is only one teacher who can teach a child who is visually impaired how to use low vision devices efficiently, how to access a computer and the Internet using a screen-enlarging program, or how to use other senses more efficiently. The teacher of students with visual impairments is responsible for a great many skills contained in the domains of the ECC that no other teachers at the school can teach. These teachers are *teachers*, not tutors or academic assistants, to students who are visually impaired. In life, and in school, it is impossible to play every role. Teachers of students with visual impairments need to be a positive role model of self-determination by knowing their role and how to implement it.

TIME MANAGEMENT

One of the more difficult challenges encountered by teachers of students with visual impairments is managing time. For any teacher, it is easy to feel as though there is simply not enough time in a day, or week, to accomplish all the necessary responsibilities of educating students. For a variety of reasons, teachers specializing in working with students who are visually impaired typically face multiple challenges when it comes to the issue of time.

First, and unlike the experience of many other teachers, the majority of the students with whom the teacher of students with visual impairments works are typically in multiple locations. Most teachers of visually impaired students are itinerant, and travel from place to place where their students may be, so a typical class schedule does not define the teacher's day. Not only can students be spread out over several schools and multiple grade levels, but many students may not even be in the same city. In addition, teachers of students with visual impairments may be assigned students with a wide variety of ages and abilities. More often than not, teachers of students with visual impairments work alone; they do not have an entire school network of teachers like them with whom they can share the load, bounce ideas around, or solve problems related to issues specific to serving children with visual impairments. They may only see their professional colleagues on a limited basis or not at all until monthly, quarterly, or yearly district or state program meetings occur. Teachers of students with visual impairments in rural districts may well be one of a kind—the only teacher specializing in work with children who are visually impaired. Although it can be beneficial to be the sole expert in a district and to make program decisions as needed, it is also a great responsibility to be the one expert, without ongoing support from colleagues and peers.

Another unique challenge is that teachers of students with visual impairments are not only preparing and teaching their students compensatory skills to access the general education curriculum, but they are also ensuring that their students have appropriate social, recreation and leisure, orientation and mobility, career development, assistive technology, self-determination, sensory efficiency, and independent living skills for adult living. Students' present and future needs must be considered, and the focus of the teacher must be on achievement of desired outcomes for a student's adult life.

Many teachers of students with visual impairments may find themselves wondering exactly how they are supposed to adapt their students' classrooms, make adaptations for all the core curriculum lessons, produce materials in accessible formats, manage paperwork and stay up-to-date on important documents, provide in-service training at multiple school sites, and teach the ECC. Without effective time management and other strategies, teachers can become overwhelmed. As the earlier chapters in this book have pointed out, developing lessons and activities to address several areas of the ECC at once can be an important way to maximize teacher efficiency and also help students develop strong integrated skills. Suggestions for activities both within and outside of school are shared later in this chapter and in the chapters contained in Part 2 of the book.

Just as students with visual impairments may often feel alone, so may their teachers. It is important to remember that there are many other teachers having the same thoughts and feelings, whether they are in rural, urban, or suburban areas. Two strategies to help students overcome the feeling of "I'm the only one" are to connect them with positive role models and support networks, such as peer groups or local organizations that provide services for people who are visually impaired. These same strategies, along with others described in the following section, can be used by teachers to manage time effectively and ensure that the ECC is integrated into the general education setting for all of their students.

Caseload Issues

The size of a teacher's caseload is a factor that can have perhaps the greatest impact on a teacher's activities and use of time overall. For that reason, addressing the size of one's caseload and the location and specific needs of the students assigned for the year is the basis for much of any teacher's planning.

Caseload management decisions that are based on actual data and current information are more likely to lead to measurable change in students. The results of academic assessments, functional vision assessments, learning media assessments, and ECC assessments should be used to develop IEP goals and objectives that address the learning needs of individual students. These recommended goals and the reasons behind them need to be discussed with the student's IEP team. Using information from these sources, teachers can analyze what needs to be done for a student and can then identify how much time is necessary to serve him or her, and in what way. Services should only be provided to students who qualify for them, based on a state's established criteria. With a clear knowledge of eligibility criteria, teachers of students with visual impairments can identify which students are eligible for services.

Division 16, Itinerant Personnel, of the Association for Education and Rehabilitation of the Blind and Visually Impaired, has studied the issue of caseload management (Association for Education, n.d.) and has issued the position paper presented in Sidebar 13.1 containing information suggested for consideration when conducting a caseload analysis. When teachers have concerns about the size and nature of their caseload, they need to share those concerns with their supervisor.

Caseload issues should be discussed with district personnel after a caseload analysis has been conducted. Much of the information outlined in Sidebar 13.1 is informative for administrators and others who may be unaware of the many responsibilities of the teacher of students with visual impairments and students' learning needs. When teachers are unable to provide needed services to students because of time limitations, data should be used to advocate for these students with school district administrators. A list of identified student needs that cannot be addressed in a teacher's schedule should be provided to the pertinent administrator, who can assist in the identification of resources to meet those needs.

Quality Programs for Students with Visual Impairments (QPVI; www.qpvi.com) is a program improvement process that uses a systematic method of self-study to improve services and outcomes for students with visual impairments. The process is based on student-centered

SIDEBAR 13.1

Position Paper of the Association for Education and Rehabilitation of the Blind and Visually Impaired, Division 16, Itinerant Personnel

CASELOAD ANALYSIS: A CRITICAL COMPONENT OF QUALITY SERVICES FOR STUDENTS WITH VISUAL IMPAIRMENTS

Caseload analysis is a powerful tool for administrators to use in addressing both efficient use of monetary and human resources and quality issues related to student outcomes. The goal of caseload analysis is to provide consistent, quality, cost effective service to all students with visual impairments. Annual caseload analysis, resulting in a manageable number of students, is a critical component of quality services for students with visual impairments. The majority of students with visual impairments are educated in public schools where the itinerant service delivery model predominates. Itinerant teachers' caseloads must be determined analytically based on the needs of the individual students.

It is the position of AER Division 16, Itinerant Personnel, that a valid caseload analysis must encompass the following.

1. Identification of a standard method that assesses the program's needs in relation to individual students.
2. Training of Teachers of Students with Visual Impairments (TVIs) and supervisory staff in the use of the procedure.
3. Annual analysis of caseload accomplished jointly by TVIs and supervisors.
4. Interpretation of results with recommended action.
5. Presentation of results to administration for action.

The extreme low incidence of students with visual impairments, including those with multiple disabilities, requires that general and special education administrators, as well as legislators, receive background information relating to needs specific to this population. An appropriate caseload analysis includes these considerations:

1. Children with visual impairments are an extremely heterogeneous group. They vary in age, degree of vision loss, cognitive ability educational needs and may have additional disabilities.
2. Because of this heterogeneity, TVIs fulfill a variety of roles that differ widely from the typical roles of classroom teachers.
3. Student instruction focuses on the acquisition of skills to allow access to the general curriculum, where appropriate, and to compensate for visual loss.
4. Students require access to an Expanded Core Curriculum of compensatory skills to meet their unique needs. Skills such as: compensatory skills, orientation and mobility, social interaction skills, independent living skills and personal management, recreation and leisure, career and vocational education, assistive technology, visual efficiency skills and self determination must be addressed.
5. Service is time intensive because of the variety of students and the typical "one on one" nature of instruction.
6. Needs of individual students change over time, therefore caseload analysis must be done annually.
7. Students' need for specialized services should be considered annually.
8. Service must be provided in a timely manner; access to instruction and materials must be provided to the student at the same time as sighted peers.
9. Newly blind students or newly diagnosed blind infants and children must receive early and immediate intervention with a high degree of intensity.
10. Service to students provided by TVIs may include instruction, collaborative consultation, material adaptation, ordering and production, instructional planning, assessment, case management, required meetings, and travel.
11. Staff members trained in visual impairment are more effective and efficient in service delivery to this population than generically trained teachers.
12. Equitable allocation of caseloads among itinerant staff can best be addressed through caseload analysis.

(continued on next page)

SIDEBAR 13.1 *continued*

13. The availability or non-availability of support staff to the itinerant teacher (e.g.: resources center, braillists, paraeducators) must be included in the analysis.
14. Planning time varies for novice and experienced teachers depending on the demands of their caseloads (e.g.: new technology, advanced braille instruction, etc.)
15. Sophisticated and constantly changing specialized software and hardware requires ongoing training, instruction and troubleshooting.

Conclusion: The over-arching goal of educating students with visual impairments is to allow each individual to become as independent and self-supporting as possible. A significant percentage of these students graduate from high school, go on to post secondary education, and/or enter the work force. Others may need some level of support throughout their lives, but can achieve a level of independence when given adequate educational programming and intervention. AER Division 16, Itinerant Personnel, supports quality services to students with visual impairments and caseload analysis as a strategy for achieving that goal.

Information and assistance in conducting caseload analyses can be obtained from AER, Division 16 Itinerant Personnel at: http://www.aerbvi.org/Division16

SOURCE: Retrieved from Association for Education and Rehabilitation of the Blind and Visually Impaired, Itinerant Personnel Division website: http://aerbvi.org/modules.php?name=Content&pa=showpage&pid=70

data and best practices in the field of educating students with visual impairments and provides for the practical application of individual state requirements for the provision of services. Results from assessments of individual students and for the caseload as a whole are directly applied to the provision of strong, effective instructional services. (See Toelle and Blankenship, 2008, for more information about the QPVI process.)

Organization, Organization, Organization

The following anecdote may sound familiar to many teachers of students with visual impairments:

Sarah is serving a student in 10th grade who is researching how to find and apply for jobs, and how to prepare for a job interview. Soon after arriving at the student's high school, Sarah realizes that the job applications she printed in preparation are still sitting on the printer at the elementary school she left about 10 minutes ago. Earlier, she had planned to work with a first grader at that school on independent living skills, but had to change those plans when she discovered that the instant pudding mix and carton of milk that she had procured to facilitate the lesson and stored in the teacher's lounge refrigerator the previous afternoon are missing. Later, having had to pull together two impromptu lessons in a row, Sarah was determined to get to her next student's middle school on time and ready to teach. She pulled into the parking lot just in time to see her student's class boarding a bus to go on a field trip for the afternoon.

Some teachers have days like this every now and again, while others have days like this every week. With careful planning and organization, however, the frequency of days like these may be noticeably reduced.

Being organized is an effective way to manage time. Getting organized and staying organized can be easier said than done, but it is a necessity for the successful teacher of students with visual impairments. Having what he needs, when and where it is needed, can save time and help a teacher accomplish what he needs to, thereby increasing that teacher's feelings of accomplishment as well as the benefit to students. Being organized also helps a teacher model proficiency for students, who need to learn organization skills. Teachers new to the field or even veteran educators who find themselves struggling with staying organized can benefit from a positive role model. *Itinerant Teaching: Tricks of the Trade for Teachers of Blind or Visually Impaired Students* (Olmstead, 2005) is an invaluable resource that provides numerous useful tips, forms, and checklists for staying organized.

When preparing a teaching schedule for themselves, teachers of students with visual impairments should do so based on identified student needs. As much as possible, students should be scheduled in a geographically logical order; it doesn't make sense to zigzag back and forth among schools and districts. Teachers should share their schedules with all the schools at which their students are enrolled so that school personnel who provide support in meeting the instructional needs of students stay informed and can coordinate their efforts with those of the teacher. Sharing that schedule with community rehabilitation providers and state agency personnel may increase support from these agencies as well. (See Olmstead, 2005, for more information about scheduling students.) Using a system of data management, such as a list of all assigned students for the year and upcoming dates related to legal requirements, compliance matters (such as medical eye exam reports), IEP meetings, and reevaluations), is a helpful tool for busy teachers. A number of other useful strategies can help as well.

Keep a To-Do List

A to-do list is one of the best places to start. Throughout the day and at the end of every day are good times to jot down reminders, lists of materials to pick up, and notes about anything that may need attention. The hardest part about a to-do list may be remembering to check it, but wise teachers consult their lists before getting out of the car to meet a student or leaving a school.

To-do lists also offer busy teachers a prime way of helping students develop ECC skills. Students can be taught valuable compensatory access skills if they are involved in creating or checking a to-do list. For example, a teacher might ask a student to braille or type the list as it is dictated, or the student can record the list with a digital voice recorder. For younger students, teachers can model use of the braillewriter or slate and stylus and create their lists in braille. In turn, students can be encouraged to create their own to-do lists, both for their schoolwork and for their lives outside of school.

Be Familiar with Each School

Teachers of students with visual impairments will want to remember that it's the little things that count—that is, keeping track of the little things can save a lot of time. When becoming introduced to a new school and its staff, it is a good idea to keep a checklist of important information to learn that will make the job go more smoothly, including:

- identifying where the teacher workroom is located and taking note of what resources are available there: copy machine, paper, computer, printer, Internet access, wireless access, arts and crafts supplies, and so on
- finding out if the school requires codes for using copy machines and other equipment and if you can have your own or need to use another teacher's
- locating all the faculty bathrooms and finding out if a key is required
- meeting the secretarial and custodial staff and briefly explaining to them the role of the teacher of students with visual impairments
- learning if there are volunteers who help at the school who can be used to enlarge materials, input information on a computer to be translated into braille later, create basic tactile graphics, or perform a variety of other tasks

Many teachers will spend the beginning of the school year rearranging their classrooms, obtaining new furniture, and getting rid of old furniture. The week before school starts is the time to go "shopping" and locate any shelving, desks, tables, chairs, or other items that could be helpful in setting up an office or teaching area. Even if the area is a large closet or storage space between two classrooms, furniture of some sort likely will be needed. The custodial staff can assist with moving the furniture or helping to locate needed items for office space.

Keep a Binder or File Box of Important Forms

An easy way to lose time is by having to chase down important forms, such as a medical release, photo release, emergency record, medical eye exam report, field trip permission, important phone number list, or any document that may not be needed on a daily basis but is essential when required. These forms can easily be stored in a student folder at the school's main office or at the home base of the teacher of students with visual impairments, but undoubtedly one or more of these important papers will be needed when the teacher is not at either of those locations. Maintaining a system that works for the individual teacher, such as a three-ring binder with copies of these forms for all the students on one's caseload, can make the retrieval of what is needed quick and easy when it's required. These forms are frequently needed unexpectedly. For example, a teacher may find that on the day of a community-based instruction trip, the school secretary is out and the principal cannot locate a copy of a parent's approval form, which was signed and returned earlier. If the signed form is in the teacher's binder, the trip or lesson can occur as planned. Or, the teacher of students with visual impairments may observe an impromptu meeting between the parent of a student and the classroom teacher, and, because a release form is easily accessible in the teacher's binder, can obtain the parent's permission for a vocational evaluation that will be completed at a summer transition program.

Plan for Paperwork

On occasions when paperwork demands prevail and it feels as though the lesson planned for that day is not going to come to fruition, a teacher may in fact turn the paperwork *into* the lesson. If a student's medical eye report is set to expire in a month and the teacher has not yet found the time to request a current report, the student can be asked to use a screen reading or screen enlarging software program on the computer to locate a business letter template previously used by the teacher to request an updated report from the parent or doctor. The student can also practice keyboarding skills by including a personal note about why this form is so important and when it is due. The form and note will need to be saved, printed, and placed in an envelope addressed to the appropriate party, then dropped off at the school office to go out in the mail. Students can practice these skills, or the teacher can use this opportunity to teach them. The student can even follow up in a week by calling the parent or doctor's office. Instead of the teacher feeling as though the time with the student had to be cancelled or an entire schedule shifted, the student can learn valuable ECC skills in the areas of assistive technology, compensatory access, social interaction, career education, and self-determination.

Plan Ahead

Planning for every day is critical to the success of teachers of students with visual impairments. Very few teachers, if any, can walk into a classroom, regardless of how many students are in attendance, and start teaching effectively. If the lesson is to run smoothly, if learning objectives are to be met, if students are to be motivated, and if time is to be used efficiently, planning and preparation have to happen in advance. Lack of planning can result in the need to reteach skills, or move a lesson to another day or put it off indefinitely, none of which will benefit the student. Planning ahead and developing appropriate lesson plans that incorporate learning activities like the ones found in Part 2 of this book help ensure that the skills involved in the ECC will be mastered by students.

School districts may have different requirements about the types of lesson plans that need to be completed or submitted ahead of time. Many districts will in all likelihood require objectives to be aligned with state standards (see Chapter 14 for information on this important topic) and clearly written for each lesson, with some type of progress monitoring tool used to keep track of a student's achievement of objectives. Most teachers who completed a personnel preparation program learned to write lengthy, detailed, formal lesson plans. Over time, those lesson plans gradually tend to become more concise, more specific, and easier to write.

Not all classroom teachers plan ahead. There are many who plan their lessons with timelines so short that the teacher of students with visual impairments is put in the position of scrambling to meet the needs of her students. Administrators, teachers, and all members of the educational team need to understand the lengthy process of adapting materials and making accessibility accommodations for students and to understand the ramifications of a lack of collaborative planning. Parents are important members of the team, and they can be very helpful in advocacy efforts. Students can also advocate for themselves and talk to their teachers about their needs.

General education teachers who do plan ahead can be a tremendous asset when it comes to providing services to students. Teachers of students with visual impairments can find out when their students' general education teachers devote time to planning and can arrange to work with them if possible. While the general education teacher is planning lessons for the following week, the teacher of students with visual impairments can determine what pre-teaching of concepts or skills needs to be done, what adaptations need to be made, what materials need to be adapted, and which areas of the ECC can be incorporated.

For example, a kindergarten lesson on the fall season may consist of comparing and contrasting apples, including their color, taste, size, and weight. Students with visual impairments can be taught organizational skills by having them separate the different types of apples, placed on high-contrast, non-slip mats, into red, yellow, or green bowls corresponding to the color of the apples. They may also be taught how to use an apple slicer to cut the apples. When the lesson is finished in the classroom, the teacher of students with visual impairments may extend it by teaching the student with a visual impairment to cook the sliced apples in the microwave, crush them, and add cinnamon to make applesauce. With all this sticky apple business going on, an opportunity to teach the student how to clean the table and dishes has been created. If time does not allow for an extended lesson on a given day, the applesauce can perhaps be made the next day by having the student store the apples in an available refrigerator and then retrieve them. Thus, the kindergarten teacher's lesson on apples can result in instruction in three areas of the ECC: compensatory access (in the form of organizational skills), sensory efficiency, and independent living. And, if an extended lesson requires refrigerating and then retrieving the apples, the area of orientation and mobility has been added.

If the teacher of students with visual impairments is unable to meet to plan directly with general education teachers, teacher's editions of textbooks can be reviewed. Supplemental materials from these books can be brailled or adapted ahead of time after checking with the classroom teacher to determine if the lessons are followed as outlined in the teacher's editions. In addition, many teachers maintain a web page (particularly for parents) that can be used by the teacher of students with visual impairments to become familiar with a classroom teacher's curriculum plans. Math and science materials that will be used in upcoming lessons, such as braille or high contrast rulers or thermometers, tactile geometry graphics, and bold lined graph paper, can be collected in advance. These items can be organized and labeled with the names of the lessons with which they will be used in a box in the classroom. Students can practice their self-determination skills by having the responsibility to collect the materials before the class period in order to participate.

A great deal of time can be saved by continuing to plan ahead and come prepared with all the necessary materials for instruction. In being prepared, a teacher of students with visual impairments will also serve as a positive role model to students to show the benefits of being organized and planning ahead. On those days when teachers are not prepared for a lesson, they can take advantage of this opportunity to tell students, "look what happens when we don't prepare," and teach what can be learned from these situations. Everyone makes mistakes, but what matters is what can be learned from those mistakes and how behavior is changed so the same mistake is not repeated. Teachers need to be careful though; this lesson can only be used once with each student!

Take Advantage of Teachable Moments

Teachable moments are opportunities to provide instruction, share information, or practice skills that arise unexpectedly during time with students. Teachers of students with visual impairments can take advantage of such moments and incorporate instruction in the ECC during these opportunities, even if there is no planned lesson involved. For example, if something has been left in the teacher's car that is needed for a lesson, the teacher and student can walk to the parking lot together to retrieve it. This unplanned activity may require the student to travel a route that is unfamiliar (O&M), talk to teachers along the way about where he is going and why (social interaction), and use the teacher's car key or keyless entry remote to open the trunk or car (independent living).

The same types of skills can be practiced if the missing materials are unavailable. If similar items can be obtained from the school office or another classroom, the student can help to get them, practicing making eye contact when requesting the specific item from staff members. Whatever items have to be retrieved, the student can carry them to build hand, arm, and shoulder strength and to practice organizing items so that they can be carried more easily. Students can be encouraged to use problem-solving skills to determine if more than one trip is needed or if using a bag or box will help. Some students will say they cannot carry a box, hold a cane, and open a door at the same time. Maybe they cannot at first, but they can certainly learn how with practice. If ingredients for a cooking lesson have been left at another school, teachers of students with visual impairments can involve their students in critical thinking by brainstorming together about all the items and ingredients that might be available at the current school. A school cafeteria, home economics room, teachers' lounge or prekindergarten classroom may provide a variety of options. Schools typically are filled with resources. Teachers of all subjects forget materials all the time and there often are multiple resources within a school that can be identified so that instruction can move forward. When students are involved in problem solving, they may learn more than the lesson that was originally planned, including the ability to identify strategies that they can use in other similar situations.

Review Caseloads and Collaborate with Peers

It is valuable for teachers of students with visual impairments to step back occasionally and review their caseloads. When doing so, students who are or should be learning the same skills can be identified, and if appropriate, lessons with two or more students can be combined. Younger students can benefit from the modeling provided by older classmates, who often profit from demonstrating their more advanced skills to others. Similarly, teachers can plan to teach the same lesson to several students on their caseload if it is appropriate, and in that way repurpose the content efficiently to save valuable time. Although each student will have individual needs and accommodations that must be considered before instruction takes place, the bulk of the planning and preparation will in all probability overlap.

If more than one teacher of students with visual impairments is in a school district, these teachers can discuss their caseloads and the skills their students are learning. If there is overlap in students' needs to develop skills in particular areas of the ECC, teachers can devise a plan to share lesson ideas and materials. Each teacher can create multiple sets of materials and pass the additional sets on to the others, who, in turn, will share their materials for different lessons with the group.

In other cases—for example, when a teacher is the sole teacher of students with visual impairments in a school district—the teacher may find it helpful to discuss caseloads with other teachers of students who have a low-incidence disability (such as teachers of students with hearing or physical impairments) or with other service providers (such as occupational or physical therapists) to exchange information and advice and provide each other with practical and emotional support.

Manage and Prepare Materials

As already noted, a three-ring binder is a useful tool for keeping materials organized. Instead of carrying around file folders for each student on the year's caseload, teachers can keep one binder for each student, in which they have condensed the most important frequently used information for the student. This binder may take some time to put together at the beginning of the year, but the investment of time will ultimately save valuable hours over the course of the school year. In addition to maintaining sections of important information for each student, a section of the binder can be dedicated to blank forms that are needed on a more frequent basis. (See Sidebar 13.2, "Binder Resources," for a list of documents to keep on hand for easy access.)

SIDEBAR 13.2

Binder Resources

The following items might be stored for easy access in a three-ring binder so that teachers of students with visual impairments always have needed information, forms, and materials at their fingertips.

STUDENT INFORMATION

- emergency contact information
- school bell schedule
- student schedule with names of teachers (including special instructional areas, such as art, music, and physical education)
- school and teacher contact information
- a list of priority ECC skills to be addressed
- medical eye report and/or fact sheet on student's eye condition(s)
- field trip permission forms signed by parents
- media release form in case video or photographs are taken
- notarized medical release in case of accident or injury on field trip so student can be treated by medical personnel
- signed release of records form
- IEP
- progress-monitoring tools and data collection charts

BLANK FORMS

- field trip permission forms
- release of records
- procedural safeguards
- district medical eye form
- medical eye request for upcoming expired medical eye reports

OTHER MATERIALS

- "Role of the TVI" handout to share with teachers or anyone who works with the student (see Figure 13.2)
- business cards

FUNCTIONAL VISION AND LEARNING MEDIA ASSESSMENT KIT. An essential part of the job of the teacher of students with visual impairments is to conduct functional vision and learning media assessments (discussed in Chapters 3 and 5). These assessments can be required as part of an annual review or three-year reevaluation, for transferring a student, or for establishing initial eligibility of a newly referred student. The process of conducting assessments definitely necessitates having critical resources on hand. To save time, teachers of students with visual impairments can create a com-

SIDEBAR 13.3

Functional Vision and Learning Media Assessment Kit

A large storage container or several smaller containers can be used to contain a comprehensive kit of materials for conducting both a functional vision assessment and a learning media assessment for students of any age. The materials in the kit should be able to be used to assess such areas as the following:

- basic visual skills in children of various ages
- near and distance vision
- mode of reading (regular print, large print, with optical devices, etc.)
- color vision
- field of vision
- functional use of vision in daily activities

ITEMS TO INCLUDE

- penlight (with motivating toy)
- occluders
- stopwatch
- tape measure
- eye charts to test near, distance, and intermediate vision
- various styles of paper (college-, high school-, and elementary-ruled; bold-, black-, and blue-lined; plain white; colored construction)
- scissors, glue, tape
- writing tools (markers, crayons, pens, pencils of various thickness, bold-line pen, dry-erase markers, chalk, etc.)
- recipes from cookbooks and packages (oatmeal, macaroni and cheese, microwave popcorn)
- TV listings magazine
- movie listings from newspapers
- classified ads
- telephone book pages
- dictionary pages (various grade levels)
- color filters
- maps (neighborhood, county state, country)
- price tags and receipts from local stores
- restaurant menus
- clothing tags
- medicine boxes and containers
- applications (job, credit card, voter registration, college, Division of Blind Services)
- checkbook (checks, register)
- blank envelopes (for students to address)
- money (coins, bills)
- toys: Slinky, balls, wind-up cars, lights, toys with movable parts, toys that make sounds
- rubber mats (various colors)
- poor photocopies of worksheets, high-contrast photocopies of worksheets
- worksheets with a lot of color (matching, reading, scanning)
- pages from academic books (algebra, geometry, history, science, English, etc.)
- slant board/reading board
- *Learning Media Assessment* book (Holbrook & Koenig, 1995) and copies of forms
- reading inventory and blank assessment forms (regular print, large print, braille)
- parent, teacher, and student interview questions
- *EVALS: Evaluating Visually Impaired Students* (Texas School for the Blind and Visually Impaired, 2007).

SOURCE: Adapted from T. Anthony, "Performing a Functional Low Vision Assessment," in F. M. D'Andrea & C. Farrenkopf (Eds.), *Looking to Learn: Promoting Literacy for Students with Low Vision* (New York: AFB Press, 2000), p. 43.

prehensive functional vision and learning media assessment kit that fits into one large storage container or several smaller containers. Using some type of system on wheels can be very beneficial in moving such a kit from the parking lot to various areas around a school campus with ease. For maximum efficiency, a functional vision and learning media assessment kit should be so complete that it can be used to assess a child of any age or ability across school, home, and community settings. (See Sidebar 13.3 for a list of suggested items to maintain in such a kit; for more details, see Anthony, 2000.)

A functional vision and learning media assessment kit is another resource that will take some time to create, but will save hours in the long run. A teacher can easily spend one or two hours just preparing to assess an individual student by collecting forms, assessment booklets, toys, and a variety of reading materials specific to the student about to be assessed. By devoting six to eight hours at the beginning of the school year to collecting materials that cover the assessment of students of all ages and abilities, teachers can save enormous amounts of time when the assessments are actually required. In addition, a teacher can have a student help compile the kit. There are many ECC skills that can be taught or reinforced by putting together these materials, including:

- organizing papers and various items,
- using office tools (binder, hole puncher, laminator)
- printing documents from a computer
- inserting paper into a printer
- replacing ink cartridges
- hooking up cables
- plugging or unplugging equipment
- cards
- using a copy machine
- collating
- handling a variety of storage containers

TACTILE GRAPHICS AND LABELING KIT. Many teachers of students with visual impairments also spend a good deal of time making adaptations for student assignments that require tactile graphics. A portable tactile graphics and labeling kit that can be used in the classroom, office, or car will be a timesaver and a lifesaver! Assembling items for the kit at the start of the year is both a valuable and a strategic use of time. A smaller storage container that has numerous drawers or compartments can be used to keep small items separated when the materials for the kit have been collected.

A tactile graphics and labeling kit should be kept readily available when working with students at the beginning or emergent literacy level, as the materials in this kit can be used for making experience or concept books. After a field trip, an assembly, a presentation by a guest speaker, a cooking session, or any concept-building experience, it is beneficial to create a tactile experience book so the young student can learn about the symbolic relationship between the experience and the oral and written language that describes it. If the teacher has to track down all the materials necessary for creating a book, however, not only is valuable time taken away from the lesson, but also from involving the student in the bookmaking process on the spot, when the connection between a fresh experience and a description or concept can be made and reinforced. If all of the required materials are on hand, the child can be a more active participant in learning by retrieving the tactile graphics and labeling kit from its storage place, opening the container, and assisting in pulling out the tools to make a book. (See Sidebar 13.4 for suggested items to put in a kit.)

SIDEBAR 13.4

Tactile Graphics and Labeling Kit

The following items would be useful to have on hand for adapting students' educational materials, and particularly when working with students in the beginning stages of literacy:

- scrapbooking stickers and decorations of various shapes, sizes, textures
- brads of various shapes and sizes
- various sewing notions: snaps, Velcro, textured fabrics, strings of very small beads
- foam shapes of various shapes, sizes and colors
- cotton-coated floral wire
- fabric glue
- storage containers and bags
- bendable sticks (wax covered cotton such as Wikki Stix)
- pipe cleaners
- textured shelf liner
- materials with adhesive backing
- three-ring binders
- zippered binder insert or pocket to store supplies
- ruler
- stickers of various shapes and sizes
- permanent markers (variety of colors)
- ball-point pens (variety of colors)
- scissors
- sticky tack
- index cards
- rubber bands

SIDEBAR 13.4 *continued*

- push pins
- paper clips
- key identifiers
- puff paint and glue pen
- tape (including double-sided and packing tape)
- variety of medium and large safety pins
- buttons of distinguishable shapes (square, circle, flower, heart)
- corkboard
- magnetic board with variety of magnetic lines/ shapes
- tactile and high contrast ruler and protractor

The American Printing House for the Blind publishes a wealth of materials for tactile graphics production. At the current time their offering includes the following products (see the Resources section at the end of this book for contact information):

Swail Dot Inverter
Graphic Art Tape
Various Graph Sheets
Picture Maker Storage Panel
Picture Maker: Textured Strips
Wheatley Tactile Diagramming Kit
Chang Tactual Diagram Kit
Draftsman Tactile Drawing Board
Crafty Graphics: Stencil Embossing Kit
Crafty Graphics II
Tactile Graphics Kit
Tactile Graphics Starter Kit
Assorted Feel 'n Peel stickers

SOURCE: Adapted from Lucia Hasty, *Creating Tactile Graphics/ Production Methods.* Presented at the Florida Department of Education/Florida Instructional Materials Center for the Visually Impaired, Weekends with the Experts, Tampa, FL, February 2010.

Students with visual impairments will also need to create tactile graphics at school and home in order to complete the same assignments as the rest of the class. There are many materials readily available that a student can use to produce the "pictures" required for assignments, but he will need to have these materials easily accessible and know how to use them. In addition, students will benefit from learning about a variety of methods for labeling personal belongings, school materials, assignments, lockers, cubbies, and other items or areas within the classroom. Students can help create their own labeling and tactile graphics kits, and in doing so, they will learn how to use each of the tools and materials collected along the way, thereby working on skills that are part of the ECC.

ALPHABET OBJECT BOX. Teachers of students with visual impairments assigned to work with young children might also consider creating an alphabet object box. Such a box, which contains objects beginning with each of the letters of the alphabet, is useful not only for bookmaking projects, but also for use during literacy lessons, circle time, speech therapy sessions, or for completion of assignments that involve pictures. Since preschool or kindergarten teachers use a great many pictures during literacy lessons and circle time activities so that children can see a picture together with the word that represents it and hear the word simultaneously, it is important for the teacher of students with visual impairments to have easy access to real objects that begin with each letter of the alphabet to create alphabet books in print, braille, or both. In this way, the student with a visual impairment has the same experience as her classmates and gets to read in the same way they do. If, for example, the classroom teacher is working on the letter *D* for the week, the teacher of students with visual impairments can go to the alphabet object box and pull out all the *real* objects that begin with the letter *D* such as a dish, dollar, dime, and disc and work with the general education teacher to include these objects in a discussion or lesson. Sidebar 13.5 provides a list of common items that can go in such a box.

Speech-language therapy sessions are also more meaningful for a young child with a visual impairment if real objects are used instead of plastic models. To help establish and reinforce comprehension and connections, the teacher of students with visual impairments can easily pull out all the objects that start with the sounds or vocabulary that the speech-language therapist is working on during a particular session.

Having the names of objects in braille or printed in bold, high-contrast ink on durable index cards is a good

Alphabet Object Box

This alphabetical reference list of objects, actions, and food can be used instead of pictures for language development, alphabet books, and other instructional activities. Most of these objects are readily available and familiar to children.

A
abacus
acorn
alarm clock
album
aluminum foil
anchor
antenna
antler
apple
arrow
avocado

B
bag
ball
balloon
banana
Band-Aid
barrette
basket
battery
beads
beanbag
beans
bell
belt
block
boa
bone
book
bottle
bow
bowl
box
brick
brush
button

C
camera
can
can opener
candle (household)
candle (birthday)
candy
cane
cap
cardboard
cell phone
circle
clay
colander
comb
cookie cutter
cotton ball
crayon
crown
cup

D
diamond (shape)
diaper
dice
doll
dollar
domino
door knob
dress
drill
drum

E
earmuffs
earring
easel
egg
eggshells
electric toothbrush
envelope

F
fan
feather
file
film
filter (coffee)
flag
flashlight
flower
folder
football
fork
frame
fur

G
gift
glasses
globe
glove
glue
grapefruit
gum

H
hair
hair tie
hammer
handkerchief
handle
hanger
harmonica
hat
headband
heart (shape)
helmet
hole
hook
horn
hose

I
ice cream (carton)
ice cube tray
incense
inch
iron
ivy

J
jacket
jacks
jar
jeans
jellybeans
juice box (crushed)
juicer
jump rope

K
kazoo
ketchup
kettle
key
keyboard
kite
kiwi

L
lace
ladle
lamp
leaf
leash
leather
lemon
letter
lid
life jacket
light bulb
lipstick
lock
lollipop
lunch box

M
macaroni
magazine
magnet
mail
marble
marker
marshmallow
mask
mat
match
measuring cup
microphone
milk (carton)
mitten
mouse (computer)
mug
mustard

N
nail
name tag
napkin
necklace
necktie
needle
net
newspaper
noodle
nozzle
nut
nutcracker

O
oatmeal (packet)
oil
ointment
onion
orange
ornament
oval
oven mitt
overalls

P
paintbrush
pajamas
pan
pants
paper
paperclip
peanut
pebbles
pecan
pedal
peg
pen
pencil
penny
pepper
pillow
pin
pipe
pitcher
pizza box
plate
plug
pocket
popcorn
pot
potato
powder
pudding
pumpkin
puppet

SIDEBAR 13.5 *continued*

purse
puzzle

Q
quarter
quill
quilt

R
radio
raincoat
rattle
remote
ribbon
rice
ring
rock
rope
rubber band
rug
ruler

S
salt
sand
saucer
saw
scarf
scissors
screwdriver
shell
shirt
shoe
shower cap
slate
Slinky
soap
sock
spaghetti
spoon
square
star
stick
stockings
straw
string
stylus
sweater
switch

T
tape
tea bag
telephone
thermometer
thread
tie
tile
timer
tissue
toaster
tongs
toothbrush
towel
triangle
trumpet
tweezers

U
ukulele
umbrella
underwear

V
vacuum cleaner
valentine
vanilla
vase
veil
Velcro
velvet
vest
videotape
vine
vinegar
violin
visor

W
wallet
walnut
washcloth
washer
watch
water
watermelon
wax
web
wheel
whistle
wire
wishbone
wood
wool

X
X-ray
Xerox copy
xylophone

Y
yardstick
yarn
yo-yo
yogurt

Z
zigzag
Ziplock bag
zipper
zucchini

SOURCE: Adapted with permission from Texas School for the Blind from Terri Bohling, "Alphabet Objects," *See/Hear, 3*(3), (Summer 2009). Retrieved from http://www.tsbvi.edu/resources/3098-alphabet-objects.

idea, and taking the time at the beginning of the year to create these cards will save time once daily instruction gets under way. The alphabet object box should be organized so that all objects of the same letter are stored together, either in many small boxes or one large box with the same letter objects stored in large, resealable bags. Whatever system is preferred, the objects should be stored in a consistent place for quick retrieval.

COMMUNICATION WITH SCHOOL ADMINISTRATORS

Administrators have the same responsibility to educate students with visual impairments as they do to educate all students. School administrators are generally concerned with students as a whole, and typically tend to think of them as a group. Core curriculum concepts are basic knowledge to them, and implementation of the core curriculum and deployment of resources, including textbooks, supplemental materials, and teachers certified in content areas, are a daily part of their jobs. Often, there are others at additional administrative levels—such as assistant principals, resource teachers, and department heads—who assist in the implementation of the core curriculum for all students.

Overall, administrators—who are typically former teachers themselves—are usually keenly aware of the qualifications and responsibilities of the general education teachers on their staff. They understand the general education environment and the important role of the administration's in it. Most administrators are frequently open-minded and receptive to input about providing services to students at the schools for which they are responsible. As the role of the principal and other administrators continues to change over time, with increasing responsibility and accountability for the learning of all students, so does their need to know more and more about instructional design for all students.

All that being said, very few administrators and general education teachers in the general education environment are knowledgeable about the specific aspects of providing services to students with visual impairments. Their previous experiences probably relate more to general education settings with students who are nondisabled. Although administrators may have had students with a variety of disabilities included in their general education classes, it is not likely that they have ever worked with a student with a visual impairment. In general, then, administrators need to learn about this heterogeneous population of students in order to fulfill their responsibility to educate every student in their school.

By sharing clear and focused information at the start of the school year about students who are visually impaired—including student needs, service and equipment requirements, and the activities in which teachers of students with visual impairments need to engage—a teacher can go a long way toward increasing understanding and support of his or her efforts and the learning needs of the students involved. The beginning of the school year (or several weeks before a student starts at the school) would be an ideal time for the teacher to meet with the school's administration about much of the information described in this section. Oftentimes, the luxury of time is not afforded to teachers or the school, as it is not unheard of for a family to suddenly change schools in the middle of a term or for a student who is visually impaired to move into a district with no records or information from the family or prior school district. A teacher of students with visual impairments has to expect that these types of situations will arise and arrange to collaborate with the school's administration as soon as possible.

In the case of general education students, the population is large and many researched-based curricula are available, providing administrators and schools with numerous options from which to select core curriculum materials, and interventions. This is not the case for students who are visually impaired. This population is very small, and the research base supporting appropriate interventions, although growing, is still limited. In addition, the effective delivery of instruction in the curriculum is impeded by the very variety of service delivery systems found among states and school districts in this country. When asked to provide support for a core curriculum area in which their faculty needs training, administrators in general education settings may have multiple training opportunities from which to choose, many of which include follow-up activities to ensure appropriate implementation. These supports are not naturally in place for the ECC or for the teachers of students with visual impairments who provide instruction in these important skill areas.

Overall, administrators have little knowledge of how the teacher of students with visual impairments fits into their school and into the educational life of students who are visually impaired, and it is therefore important that the teacher informs administrators about his or her critical role in educating and supporting students with visual impairments so that administrators will be more understanding and supportive of the teacher's activities. A valuable tool for educating administrators is the position paper adopted by the Division on Visual Impairments of the Council for Exceptional Children defining the role and function of teachers of students with visual impairments (Spungin & Ferrell, 2007). Another useful tool is *Blind and Visually Impaired Students: Educational Service Guidelines* (Pugh & Erin, 1999). This publication, written by representatives of national consumer and advocacy groups and educational organizations, is designed to provide critical information to state and local agencies on the specific issues involved in providing services to people (including students) with visual impairments.

Administrators who understand the specialized skills of teachers of students with visual impairments and the role they play in the success of their school as a whole are more likely to support instructional efforts to address the ECC. Since these teachers often serve an important role as collaborators with a variety of school staff to address the multiple needs of their students, administrators frequently come to rely on these professionals for their contributions.

Many teachers of students who are visually impaired tend to be comfortable communicating with school personnel who deal directly with students, such as classroom teachers, guidance counselors, social workers, psychologists, and paraprofessionals. Typically, information exchanged with these team members is student-centered, focusing directly on the learning needs and outcomes for the student and on how collaborative efforts in support of the student can be put in place. When speaking with administrators, however, the same language that teachers use when talking to other teachers and direct service personnel may not be as effective. Although administrators may also be focused on students, the information they need to support the efforts of teachers of students with visual impairments and the students they serve is different from that required by direct service personnel, and includes:

- overall programming goals for students with visual impairments

- needs of individual students
- concerns and strengths of the students' families
- issues with funding and compliance
- needs of the teacher of students with visual impairments for space and other resources in the school
- issues related to off-campus instruction

Teachers who can provide this information to the administrators with whom they work are in fact supporting their own efforts, to the benefit of their students.

Program Goals

The National Agenda for the Education of Children and Youths with Visual Impairments, Including Those with Multiple Disabilities (Huebner, Merk-Adam, Stryker, & Wolffe, 2004) formulated a set of overall goals toward which educators should strive in order to provide the type of education to which every student with a visual impairment is entitled. These goals, which are presented in Sidebar 13.6, can also serve as goals for a program for students with visual impairments. Therefore, the National Agenda is a helpful resource for teachers who need to share information with the administrators of their schools; it can serve as a starting point for a conversation with administrators about issues related to providing services to students with visual impairments and reinforce the importance of these services by placing them within a broader national perspective. The National Agenda can also pave the way for grassroots cooperative local efforts to address students' ECC needs. One way to begin such an effort is to develop a local task force made up of members of each local agency that provides services to students with visual impairments and that meets on a regular basis to plan for implementation of instruction in the ECC. A clear understanding of the benefit of such implementation to administrators and others in the school system can lead to effective change.

SIDEBAR 13.6

Goals of the National Agenda

The National Agenda for the Education of Children and Youths with Visual Impairments, Including Those with Multiple Disabilities sets forth in clear and concise terms a vision and plan of action for the future of the education of children who are blind or visually impaired, as well as those who are visually impaired and have other disabilities. The agenda consists of 10 goals:

1. Students and their families will be referred to an appropriate education program within 30 days of identification of a suspected visual impairment. Teachers of students with visual impairments will provide appropriate quality services.
2. Policies and procedures will be implemented to ensure the right of all parents to full participation and equal partnership in the education process.
3. Universities with a minimum of one full-time faculty member in the area of visual impairments will prepare a sufficient number of teachers and O&M specialists for students with visual impairments to meet personnel needs throughout the country.
4. Caseloads will be determined based on the assessed needs of students.
5. Local education programs will ensure that all students have access to a full array of service delivery options.
6. All assessments and evaluations of students will be conducted by and/or in partnership with personnel having expertise in the education of students with visual impairments and their parents.
7. Access to developmental and educational services will include an assurance that instructional materials are available to students in the appropriate media and at the same time as their sighted peers.
8. All educational goals and instruction will address the academic and expanded core curricula based on the assessed needs of each student with visual impairments.
9. Transition services will address developmental and educational needs (birth through high school) to assist students and their families, in setting goals and implementing strategies through the life continuum commensurate with the student's aptitudes, interests, and abilities.
10. To improve student learning, service providers will engage in on-going local, state, and national professional development.

SOURCE: K. M. Huebner, B. Merk-Adam, D. Stryker, & K. Wolffe, *The National Agenda for the Education of Children and Youths with Visual Impairments, Including Those with Multiple Disabilities* (revised) (New York: AFB Press, 2004).

Needs of Students

As mentioned earlier, many administrators and general education teachers are not aware of the generalized, comprehensive impact that a visual impairment may have on a student's overall development, both academically and socially. Once program goals for visually impaired students are discussed from a general perspective, administrators need to understand the specific aspects of the program designed to address a particular student's needs. Important principles of learning that administrators need to know include:

- that touching and hearing are not a substitute for vision
- that students with visual impairments need repeated exposure to direct experiences as well as extensive accompanying explanations of what is occurring around them
- that materials placed in tactile or auditory formats are not equivalent to those presented visually
- that direct experiences also need to be taught in many environments, including off-campus sites

Information about the learning strengths and needs of specific students, including students with multiple disabilities and visual impairments, is available in IEPs that are well written and based on a variety of assessment data, including assessed needs in the ECC. This information should be shared as appropriate with the administrators in a student's school. Another powerful tool is a student-developed portfolio or video résumé that introduces the student and explains his needs to administrators. With parents' assistance, these portfolios can be developed with even the youngest students and those students with additional disabilities. They are a creative way to show administrators and teachers students' successes and capabilities. Depending on the teacher's time, resources, and subject matter, the portfolio can take a variety of different forms, including:

- a three-ring binder that contains pictures of the student engaged in various activities that demonstrate ECC skills, with an explanation of each activity
- a collection of work that the student has produced in braille, such as the student's first sentence in braille from the beginning of the year along with monthly writing samples that show progress
- a collection of sign-in sheets showing the progression of a student's signature over time
- a log that shows a student's progression in learning a multitude of concepts throughout the school year

The possibilities are limited only by a teacher's creativity. Portfolio assembly is also an excellent way to help students develop skills in ECC areas such as career education and self-determination.

Families' Strengths and Concerns

When administrators know that family members will support a student by working with him or her at home and reinforcing the school's efforts to serve the student, administrators will tend to approach the student's learning needs with a more positive attitude and be more responsive to parents' concerns. When all team members work together, the result is a positive, educational experience for the student. Teachers of students with visual impairments can inform administrators of the strengths of individual students' families, and assist in building strong relationships between school personnel and families.

In addition to the wealth of knowledge that families can share about their children, they can also bring individual family resources to bear on the provision of instruction in the core and ECC. For instance, a family member who is employed by a local restaurant may be instrumental in providing an instructional site in the community where students might visit or pursue work opportunities or experience. Similarly, a family member who has a unique hobby may be willing to share information about that hobby and offer a unique learning experience to all students in that school and with other students with visual impairments in the district.

Funding

The typical school administrative framework is built to support large numbers of students. Local, state, and federal funding are predicated on funding for all students. Federal legislation, such as the Individuals with Disabilities Education Act (IDEA), and the No Child Left Behind Act, requires schools, and therefore their leaders, to adopt research-based curriculum. Professional development places heavy emphasis on curricular implementation with fidelity, in the manner in which standard curricula are designed. State and local funding formulas often include provisions for students with disabilities.

This information should be provided to administrators to ensure that appropriated funds are tapped. In some states, there are special sources of funding for low vision services or expensive books and equipment. Topics such as how the teacher of students with visual impairments is paid and who pays for assistive technology and other special materials should be discussed with site-based administrators in order to help them understand their options.

Compliance with State and Federal Laws

Compliance requirements for meeting state and federal laws regarding identification of students who qualify for services and the provision of such services are different for programs for students with visual impairments than they are for other special education programs in that they require the application of certain specialized information. For instance, many administrators may need assistance in understanding the educational implications of eye conditions and the development and implementation of IEPs for students who are visually impaired. Identification and implementation of unique instructional accommodations needed for students to access general education curriculum and statewide testing (such as braille, text-to-speech, electronic digital text) may need to be discussed with administrators. Eligibility requirements vary from state to state, so it is imperative that the teacher of students with visual impairments understand those requirements and their implementation in the provision of high-quality educational services. Many states include requirements for medical eye reports, low vision evaluations, and specialized assessments to address unique skills. These specialized assessments typically include functional vision assessments, learning media assessments, and O&M evaluations.

A federal policy guidance paper titled *Educating Blind and Visually Impaired Students* (U.S. Department of Education, 2000) provides useful information regarding requirements of IDEA1997 related to services for school-aged children (Part B) and can be shared with administrators and others. (It should be noted that documents such as these are updated periodically, as legislation and regulations change, and teachers need to check on their currency.) The 2004 reauthorization of IDEA specifically stated that "IEPs must address students' functional performance and must meet each of the students' other educational needs that result from their disabilities" (CFR 34 § 300.320(a)(1)). Although the ECC is not explicitly mentioned, the reauthorization clearly supports the provision of instruction in all its domains, since these are the "functional and educational needs that result from a visual disability."

Maintaining complete and accurate records of the performance of students with visual impairments is critical to the provision of services and acquisition of educational materials through federal or state programs. For example, a thorough, comprehensive assessment of a student's needs provides the IEP team with information to make decisions regarding special education and related services, including learning media, assistive technology devices, and low vision devices. Compliance documents, such as medical eye reports, low vision examinations, or functional vision and learning media assessments, that are kept up to date and relevant to the needs of students will support the provision of specialized materials for these children, including textbooks and other tangible apparatus available from the American Printing House for the Blind under the Act to Promote the Education of Blind Children (known as the Federal Quota Program). Therefore, keeping records current is an effective investment of time in helping to promote students' skill development; efforts to help administrators understand the importance of these activities in turn supports the teacher's own effort to provide services and implement the ECC.

Needed School Resources

Like other educators, teachers of students with visual impairments need specific resources to provide educational services to and for their students. However, these resources are not always easily identifiable by administrators, who typically are unfamiliar with students with visual impairments and their educational programming needs, and teachers may often need to advocate more than expected for essential resources. As indicated earlier, if administrators understand what the ECC is, why it is so important, and that the role of the teacher of students with visual impairments is to teach the ECC, they are in general more likely to help make needed resources within a school and district readily available.

As stated earlier, administrators have the same responsibility to educate students with visual impairments as they do to educate all students. School resources that are available to all students should thus also be available to students who are visually impaired. Teachers of students with visual impairments can assist administrators in identifying and using the resources that will help make them more effective educators. For example, visually impaired students who need instruction in cooking can use on-campus kitchen facilities designed for family and consumer science classes; instruction in recreation and leisure skills or O&M can be readily provided in areas typically thought to be reserved for physical education classes; and assistive technology skills can be taught and practiced in the school media center.

The teacher of students with visual impairments should inform the administrator of his or her need for space and other facilities as soon as the need is recognized, such as during a meeting before the student begins school. Typically, many administrators' lack of knowledge concerning the program needs of students who are visually impaired will be evident in their willingness to provide only a small area for the teacher to use when at the school. It is therefore important to discuss the space that a teacher of students with visual impairments requires, as well as the space needed by the student, with a school's administration. Storage needs should be explained, as should the need to provide secure areas for using expensive and sometimes loud equipment. Overall, administrators in general education settings have no idea how much space equipment or devices require, or how much space a braille textbook will take on a shelf in a classroom. As more and more texts become available in electronic formats, some of these space needs will be decreased, though it only takes one 96-volume braille math book to make the case for additional storage space for such books.

In general, teachers of students with visual impairments need to inform the administrators of the schools their students attend of the many ways they as teachers support the education of the diverse students on their caseloads. Administrators who have the responsibility to support all teachers need tools to do so effectively; teachers of students who are visually impaired can bring resources to these administrators that may prove helpful in their efforts to create effective learning environments for their students. Among these resources are those used in the education of other professionals through in-service training, as mentioned earlier in this chapter, on topics such as adaptation of materials and provision of specialized equipment.

A number of resources specific to students with visual impairments can be shared with administrators, such as *Administrator's Toolbox,* available online from the Texas School for the Blind (www.tsbvi.edu). This toolbox provides a variety of materials that can be used to support both administrators and teachers. For instance, administrators can find information regarding job descriptions of various professionals serving students with visual impairments and resources to assist them in developing caseloads based on data. Teachers can use the toolbox to assist them when working with administrators to address student needs based on best professional practices. Teachers will also find information to support instruction in important ECC domains. In addition, publications such as *When You Have a Visually Impaired Student in Your Classroom: A Guide for Teachers* (2002) and *Seeing Eye to Eye: An Administrator's Guide to Students with Low Vision* (Lewis, Allman, & D'Andrea, 2000) are materials that may be helpful to share.

Instruction On and Off Campus

Instruction of general education students takes place for the most part inside buildings that house classrooms with four walls, one teacher (occasionally two or more), varying numbers of students (frequently 15–30), and with a district- or state-supported curriculum and materials. The majority of administrators have a keen understanding of the facility needs of their school and are comfortable within the classroom environments under their roofs. They are not usually aware of the fact that instructional settings for students with visual impairments can and should include on- and off-campus locations, especially when addressing the skills encompassed in the ECC.

Teachers of students with visual impairments will want to work closely with school-based administrators before the student starts school to discuss such details as the times that they are scheduled to be at the school and how much of that time will be spent in the classroom with students and how much will involve "pull-out" services. It will be necessary to explain how pull-out services will be scheduled so that students do not miss instruction in the core curriculum. If it is important to students' success, then requesting that periods of common planning time with classroom teachers be set aside so that instructional accommodations and modifications as needed by the student and outlined in the IEP are provided. Once initial arrangements have been made, discussions should be held on an ongoing basis to adjust to the student's acquisition of skills.

As part of this effort and to demonstrate why students may often need to be instructed off site, administrators should be provided information regarding federal guidelines for the implementation of instruction. Discussion may be most effectively scheduled for when the off-campus instruction is approaching. Teachers of students with visual impairments are supported by a wealth of information from professional and federal sources that reiterate the necessity of providing instruction in numerous environments, including instruction in community settings. Among these resources are the previously mentioned policy guidance paper, *Educating Blind and Visually Impaired Students* (U.S. Department of Education, 2000), as well as the contents of IDEA (2004; 34 CFR Sec. 300.34(7)(i)), which deals with related services—including O&M instruction—for children with special needs, which can be shared with a school's administration.

Information on state standards in support of community instruction is also important. For instance, in the state of Florida, a state education system description for a course entitled "Expanded Core Competencies," designed to address unique learning needs of students with visual impairments, notes:

> Instructional activities involving practical applications of course requirements may occur in home, school (including separate setting, small group, and individually), and community settings for the purposes of acquisition, practice, generalization, and maintenance of skills. These applications may require that the student use related technology, tools, and equipment. Activities may be arranged to extend beyond scheduled school hours. To address the full range of special skills, students may also be enrolled in an Orientation and Mobility Skills Course. (Expanded Core Competencies, n.d.)

Administrators who are informed about this kind of specific state curricular information will find it much easier to support the efforts of teachers who provide services to students who are blind or visually impaired. Administrators may need assistance from the teacher to make the connection between the ECC and academic success, especially if instruction in important areas is to take place off campus, as is done in the example presented in Sidebar 13.7 of a proposal for community-based instruction prepared for submission to administrators at district schools.

Conversations with administrators regarding off-campus instruction frequently lead to questions about

SIDEBAR 13.7

Community-Based Instruction Proposal

The Visually Impaired Program proposes taking students on community-based instruction once a month during this school year. This year's trips are designed to address skills outlined in the expanded core curriculum for students with visual impairments. The tentative list of trips includes:

September:	Scavenger hunt in grocery store
October:	Tour of the airport
November:	Cooking at the Lighthouse for the Blind
December:	Holiday gathering with Lions Club at a local restaurant
January:	Tour post office
February:	Bowling
March:	Tour of football stadium
April:	Picnic and recreational day at a local park
May:	Scavenger hunt at mall

There are two main reasons why these community experiences are essential for students with visual impairments. First, there are many skills that most people learn visually, but must be taught directly to a student who is blind or who has low vision. Instruction in unique skills for students with visual impairments can be provided through the expanded core curriculum to address issues such as handling money, asking for assistance from people in the community (such as store clerks), practical application of math skills and literacy skills, and practice of orientation and mobility in unfamiliar environments (just to name a few). For these skills to be transferred into practical application, they must be practiced in real-life situations.

The second and equally important reason is to improve academic skills in core curriculum areas like math and reading. It is estimated that 70 to 80 percent of what we learn is through vision. We look at the world, we look at pictures, and we learn. For students with visual impairments (especially severe visual

(continued on next page)

SIDEBAR 13.7 *continued*

impairments), this is not an option. Therefore they need to learn through other processes. There are concepts commonly taken for granted within basic reading curricula that students who are blind will not understand fully if they have not experienced the concept—they have absolutely no frame of reference for such things. The circus, farms, zoo animals, airplanes, and baseball games are just a few examples of the many things we learn about from pictures when we are young that students with visual impairments only vaguely understand. Without a good grasp of a concept, it is very difficult for a student to comprehend what she is reading or writing about that concept.

This relationship between experience and literacy is supported by research within the field of reading. In *Put Reading First: The Research Building Blocks for Teaching Children to Read Kindergarten Through Grade 3* (National Institute for Literacy, 2001), the authors state that "*Using their experiences and knowledge of the world*, their knowledge of vocabulary and language structure, and their knowledge of reading strategies (or plans), good readers make sense of the text and know how to get the most out of it" (p. 48, emphasis added). Students with visual impairments already have a limited knowledge of the world because of their lack of vicarious, vision-based learning. Only increasing their experiences will increase this general world knowledge, and thereby allowing them to reach their full potential to be good active readers.

An article called "Leadership Letters: Issues and Trends in Reading Best Practices in Vocabulary Instruction" (Blachowicz, n.d.) echoes these same beliefs about how we learn vocabulary. The article states:

> Vocabulary learning takes place when students are active in discovering ways in which words are related to experiences and to one another. In a good learning situation, learners are actively engaged in constructing their own meanings. Many comparisons of instructional methodologies suggest that having learners take an active role in constructing a network of meaning for a word is critical. For example, *learning new words through new experiences is one of the most durable and long lasting ways to develop a rich vocabulary.* We learn new words like thread, needle, selvage, pattern, and dart naturally in the context of learning to sew. We learn the special meaning of hit, run, base and fly as we learn to play baseball (p. 2, emphasis added).
>
> . . . . .
>
> When the goal is to have students gain control of vocabulary to use for their own expression, students need many experiences that allow them to use words in meaningful ways (p. 5).

If we provide our students with visual impairments with direct, active experiences to supplement their academic instruction, they are more likely to become good active readers and learners.

It is respectfully requested that the above community experience trips be approved. Pre- and post-trip instructional activities can be produced and submitted upon request. Parent permission forms will be the responsibility of the teacher of students with visual impairments.

SOURCE: Adapted from a written proposal by Kathryn Kremplewski, teacher of students with visual impairments, Hillsborough County Public Schools, Tampa, FL.

student safety and the liability of the district or teacher. To ensure the safety of all students and staff, districts develop procedures that will protect students and staff both on campus and when in the community. Administrators are aware of these procedures as they apply to the student population as a whole. These same procedures can be used to protect students with visual impairments while they receive instruction in community settings as well. Teachers of students with visual impairments will therefore find it helpful to familiarize themselves with these procedures and the safety resources of their districts. Before proposing off-campus instruction, a teacher of students with visual impairments will find it greatly beneficial to gather and share information and learn about required procedures, such as those described in the following sections.

District Safety Office Contact

Every school district has an office or department that oversees district safety issues. The teacher of students with visual impairments should know the name of that office and the name of the contact person in each district in which they provide services in case a situation arises in which they need to contact the office.

Field Trip Procedures

Districts frequently develop procedures for field trips that apply to all students who are preparing to participate in off-campus activities. These same procedures may apply to situations involving students who are visually impaired. Forms such as medical release forms, media release forms, and parent permission forms are likely to be already in place in most districts. Teachers need to locate these forms in their districts and have them completed when requesting permission to leave campus for instructional purposes. Teachers should also have a thorough and complete understanding of all safety procedures to follow in case of an emergency.

Transportation

Teachers of students with visual impairments should consult the district administrator who oversees the expenditure of IDEA funds to request use of those funds to pay for district school buses for transportation of students to off-campus instruction and field trips. If teachers are considering using a personal vehicle to transport a student, it is important to know the limits of coverage from their personal insurance carrier. Teachers should also consult the school district safety office regarding personal vehicles that are approved for student transportation (many districts and states maintain a list describing approved makes and models of vehicles), and ensure that their vehicle is on this list if they plan on providing transportation in their own car. It is also advisable, whenever possible, to plan to have another adult in the car when transporting students so that additional assistance is available in case of an emergency.

In many instances, using leased vehicles to transport students to community settings is an alternative to teachers transporting students in private automobiles. Athletic teams, driver's education staff, and music departments frequently transport students to various community functions. Districts that provide general education students with transportation to such activities are likely to have a leasing agreement or purchasing bid in place with a vendor to provide vehicles. Teachers of students with visual impairments should check to see if their district provides leased vehicles for these purposes and determine if there is a possibility of using that resource to provide a leased vehicle for their off-campus instructional activities. If such an agreement is not in place, the teacher can check with the school's principal to see how the school funds transportation to sporting events for various athletic teams. It may be possible to use some of those funds for community instruction in the crucial skills of the ECC.

RESOURCES FOR SUPPORTING INSTRUCTION IN THE ECC

When it comes to implementing the ECC, all members of students' educational teams can and should be enlisted as valuable resources. The provision of instruction is a team effort, and teachers of students with visual impairments will want to use the educational team as an extension of themselves. Parents and general education teachers, as well as the student, can offer valuable expertise in developing ECC instructional strategies. Teachers of students with visual impairments will want to provide these other team members with any needed information, guidance, and materials, and accept their information, guidance, and materials in return. Other supports and resources described in the following sections can and should also be enlisted to the maximum extent possible.

School-Based Subject Area Department Experts

Experts in specific subject areas, such as department heads or lead teachers, and other general education teachers, are a valuable source of information on the general education curriculum. Through collaboration and consultation, a teacher of students with visual impairments and these subject experts can create strategies for the provision of instruction to address both the general education arena and the ECC. The core curriculum offers natural opportunities for instruction and practice in ECC areas. For example, the high school computer class is the perfect place to practice the functional application of assistive technology to access computer monitors; and the elementary school cafeteria is a natural environment in which to practice social skills, independent living skills, and orientation and mobility. All students, in fact, whether their vision is impaired or not, are practicing important ECC skills in these environments on a daily basis.

For instance, teachers of students with visual impairments who want their students to learn about musical instruments before a class trip to an orchestral concert can contact the music department within a school district to find a music teacher willing to provide an opportunity for experiential hands-on learning. Since many students who are visually impaired often cannot consolidate conceptual meanings without direct experience, such an experience will help students recognize the instruments in an orchestra, improve their understanding of what an orchestra is, and provide them with the vocabulary to participate meaningfully in class discussions about the trip. In addition, they can practice the social skills needed to request additional information about something they don't understand and self-determination skills as they learn more about and express their personal preferences for the sounds that different instruments make. The student who finds an instrument that piques his or her curiosity and interest may also have been introduced to a future recreation and leisure skill or to an area that leads to competence as a musician in later life.

Similarly, the culinary arts program of a local high school can be used as a resource for teaching cooking. General education teachers who are certified to deliver instruction in culinary arts have a wealth of skills and knowledge in this area. Working together with teachers of students with visual impairments, the culinary arts personnel can help promote independent living skills that can serve visually impaired students for a lifetime. The art teacher is also a good friend to have at a school site for help with tactile graphics supplies, bookmaking materials, and items needed to make lesson adaptations.

Given the nature of the teaching profession, most teachers are caring and giving. Teachers give a lot of their time to students, but many still find time after work to volunteer or participate in community activities. Teachers who volunteer their time to work with children after school are often willing to help students with visual impairments and may have the talents necessary to provide music, art, dance, or swimming lessons, or yoga, martial arts, or technology instruction.

School-Based Administrators

Although school-based administrators are typically knowledgeable in at least one, if not more, content areas, their knowledge of the ECC, like their knowledge of the needs of visually impaired students and the role of the teacher of students with visual impairments, is limited. As already mentioned, these administrators are more likely to support the efforts of the teacher of students with visual impairments and make needed resources within a school and district available if they understand the importance of the ECC, its component areas, and how work in the ECC relates not only to the success of the student, but to the overall success of the school.

The importance of specially designed instruction delivered in appropriate formats and environments therefore must be shared with a school's administrators and general education teachers. They need to know that success on high-stakes tests, such as those linked to graduation and to college entry, is often dependent on the competence of students with visual impairments in the ECC. Sharing the resources and materials mentioned throughout this chapter with administrators is an important way of enlisting their support or help in implementing the ECC.

District-Level Administrators

Although district-level administration varies from district to district, the structures of most districts include school board members, superintendents, assistant superintendents, exceptional student education directors, exceptional student education supervisors, and district content area supervisors. These professionals have an abundance of knowledge regarding district resources, and are usually ready and willing to learn about the needs of students with visual impairments. Along with receiving the same types of information provided to school-level administrators, these individuals should be invited to events involving students who are visually impaired. Invitations to attend instructional activities in the community can be valuable, especially if it is known that an administrator has a particular interest in the community site or the skills being taught there. Administrators can also be invited to provide input about the program to teachers of students with visual impairments. Invitations like these can open up a world of resources and support from important, knowledgeable sources.

Funding Resources

Finding funding for the special needs of a program for students with visual impairments can be challenging since this population requires extensive concrete experiences that often incur costs associated with the purchase of real objects (as opposed to models or pictures), community outings, and transportation. As teachers discuss general funding issues with administrators, they should also provide information on their efforts to supplement the program through the solicitation of sources that typically support efforts to assist students who are visually impaired. Teachers of students with visual impairments have an advantage when they are aware of funding sources in their respective communities that may be available to them. It helps, too, if they are willing to expand their definitions of "funding" and "involvement" broadly to include contributions of time, talent, and location, not just dollars and cents.

IDEA funds are allocated to every school district to educate students with disabilities and are a viable funding source for the provision of ECC instruction. Grants to obtain these funds are generally written annually by school districts and submitted to the state, and then the federal government, for approval. Student needs in assistive technology, community-based instruction, orientation and mobility, and other ECC areas should be made known to the district administrator who is responsible for submitting this grant so that they can be included in the district's proposal. The needs of all students with visual impairments, including students with multiple disabilities, should be considered in any grant proposal. The teacher of students with visual impairments can help to make sure this happens by communicating with the district's administration about the unique needs of children with visual impairments and how, for example, the lack of incidental learning negatively affects their education.

Lions Club International (www.lionsclubs.org) is an organization that promotes community and worldwide involvement in issues affecting people who have visual impairments. Many communities have several chapters, and each chapter has particular interests, but local club members in general are responsive to the needs of students in their local schools when they are made aware of those needs. A presentation to a local club can be as simple as speaking at one of their monthly meetings to provide club members with basic information about students with visual impairments and their needs, including information about ideas for possible community-based instruction. The beginning of the school year is a good time to make a presentation. Some Lions Club members may be in professions that can provide students with experiences that enrich their understanding of the world around them. Offering exposure to work possibilities is the kind of resource that does not require a monetary donation. For example, a Lions Club member who owned an outlet that sold tractors allowed visually impaired students from the local district to spend an afternoon exploring the equipment in his showroom.

Another organization, Civitan International, is a service organization with a focus on individuals with developmental disabilities. Since more than half the population of students with visual impairments have additional disabilities (Lueck, Erin, Corn, & Sacks, 2011), Civitan Clubs in the local community may be interested in supporting efforts on behalf of these students.

There are fraternal organizations, such as the Delta Gamma sorority (www.deltagamma.org), with philanthropic missions dedicated to providing support to people who are visually impaired. Teachers of students with visual impairments can contact local university and alumnae chapters to ask for their assistance. Requests for support should be specific, especially if what is needed is money or the purchase of a special technology device. Organization members can also provide support as volunteers to assist as chaperones or with fundraising or other projects.

Local businesses are another valuable source of possible funding. Many large businesses offer incentives to employees who provide community services. One school district discovered that a trip to a local home supply center provided a treasure chest of opportunities to learn a number of independent living and recreation and leisure skills. Activity centers were set up in locations around the store. Small groups of students rotated among the activity centers and experienced each activity with instruction from employees who had volunteered their time. (The planning document used for this trip can be found in Sidebar 13.8.) Teachers of students with visual impairments located in small communities can work with a local hardware store to set up a similar activity for their students.

A number of companies encourage employees to participate in service activities. Teachers of students with visual impairments can submit a request to sponsor an ECC instructional field trip, which can involve a team of employees assisting in a recreational field day for students. Volunteers can help during various field day activities, such as setting up and cooking food, cleaning up, and assisting with getting students to and from buses. It can be motivating for employees of companies that conduct research or sell products that benefit people who require some level of eye care to get out of their offices and spend time with some of the people who directly benefit from their work.

It can be a productive idea in general to approach businesses that have an interest in what is being taught for assistance in carrying out instruction. For instance, when planning a lesson to expand a student's knowledge of his or her eye condition, contacting a local eye care corporation or provider may result in a donation of funding, time, or other resources. Many local optometrists or ophthalmologists are eager to teach children

SIDEBAR 13.8

Home Supply Center Lesson Plan

The following lesson plan was developed by Elizabeth Underwood, Darcy Stafford-Freer, and Angela Esparza, teachers of students with visual impairments, Hillsborough County Public Schools, Tampa, Florida. Sixty-five students participated in the trip, which included lunch at a pizza restaurant in the shopping plaza.

GOAL

To increase knowledge of the use of basic hand tools to perform basic home-maintenance tasks; job awareness; and concept development. Students will increase social skills by interacting with other trip participants and store employees.

OBJECTIVES OR LESSON PLAN IDEAS

These are suggestions and topics to prepare students for the lesson or to focus on while on the home supply center field trip.

- Can you name five departments in the home supply center?
- When planting a plant what are three other items you would need besides the plant?
- In which section or department of the home supply center would you find plants or flowers?
- If you wanted to move something heavy from the back yard to the front yard such as a big bag of fertilizer, what tool could you use?
- What is fertilizer used for?
- Would you find light bulbs in the plumbing or electrical department of the home supply center?
- What are three different wattages of light bulbs?
- What does the saying "Righty tighty, lefty loosey" mean?
- Name three items or appliances that would require a bulb.
- If you were building a dog house what tools would you need besides a hammer? (Name at least three tools.)
- Is there such a thing as a cordless drill? If so, what does "cordless" mean?
- True or false: I would find a toilet plunger in the plumbing section of the home supply center.
- Is a toilet plunger the only way to unclog a stopped up toilet? If not, what other ways could you unplug the toilet?
- If you had to get a key made what department would you go to at the home supply center?
- True or false: The only kind of battery is a car battery. If false, explain.

ACTIVITY CENTERS

Activity Centers will be prearranged by the home supply center. Students will be grouped into small groups as they arrive. Each group will rotate among the following centers until all centers have been experienced.

Plumbing

- A toilet will be set up (without water)
- A variety of plungers will be available
- Students will learn the various parts of a toilet
- Students will plunge toilets

Lighting

- Several different kinds of light bulbs will be on display
- Several different kinds of switches will be on display
- Students will screw in various types of light bulbs
- Students will activate various types of switches
- Students will identify different uses of different kinds of bulbs

Locks

- Several different kinds of locks and keys will be on display
- Students will use each kind of key and lock
- Students will explore various door handles and activate their respective locks
- Students will identify locks for various purposes

Gardening

- A wheelbarrow will be on display
- A large bag of soil will be on display
- Gardening trowel, small pots, and small plants will be available
- Students will transport the large bag of soil in the wheelbarrow
- Students will plant a small plant in a clay pot
- Students will take plants home with them

SIDEBAR 13.8 *continued*

Tools

- Hammer, screwdriver, cordless drill will be on display
- Boards and various types of nails and screws will be available
- Students will hammer nails into small sections of 2x4 boards
- Students will use screwdrivers to tighten screws into various surfaces
- Students will use a power drill to drive a screw into a wooden board

Batteries

- Various types of flashlights and batteries will be on display
- Students will place appropriate batteries into flashlights

Tour Group

- One group of students will tour the store with a store employee who will introduce them to the various departments, types of shelving, types of displays, forklifts, and different jobs in the store.

about eye conditions or demonstrate low vision devices. For lessons on cooking, a local grocery store, cooking school, or culinary arts class at a nearby high school may be willing to assist with instructional or material support.

Fundraisers involving students offer an effective opportunity for direct instruction in many ECC areas. The value of students' involvement in earning money to support their own learning goals is incalculable, and the connection to vocational skills in these fundraising efforts is another benefit. Perhaps even more powerful than these benefits, however, is the incidental learning of the concepts in which the students engage. For instance, students who participate in a fundraising car wash activity have the opportunity to learn about a variety of vehicles on the road, thus extending their knowledge of "cars" to include minivans, recreational vehicles, smart cars, compact cars, and trucks. They also have a chance to greet customers, interact with other students to achieve a common goal, practice money handling skills, and participate in the obligatory hose fight that will likely occur.

Rehabilitation service delivery agencies in the community, such as private agencies that serve adults who are blind, may have resources that can be available to school district personnel who work with students who are visually impaired. Most community rehabilitation providers have on staff grant writers who may be willing to assist teachers of students with visual impairments in procuring funds from local foundations or charities. These agencies also have a shared interest in helping young children develop into competent, employable adults. They are familiar with the employment issues and needs of people with visual impairments and often have clients who can assist teachers and district school programs in helping students develop career interests and possibly other instructional programs. Clients of these agencies can also benefit from practicing skills while teaching or assisting students. This kind of collaboration can be a step in improving learning outcomes for students and employment outcomes for adults, and in fostering a valuable mentoring program.

Teachers need to step out, be bold, and ask for support and assistance. Even teachers who are not comfortable asking need to do it anyway. Preparing students with visual impairments for adulthood is part of meeting those students' needs. Teachers who ask for what their students need and who expect a positive response may find that they receive those positive responses more often than not!

Instructional Resources

When a teacher of students with visual impairments starts a school year, it is not likely that there will be a room waiting, filled with electronic notetakers, braillewriters, tablet devices, computers with speech synthesis and screen enlarging programs, low vision devices, reading stands, tactile graphics supplies, a kitchen, pots and pans, food supplies, a washer and dryer, laundry baskets, labeling tools, braille books, or any other materials necessary for teaching the ECC. All these materials are not necessary for every teacher at the start of a school year; what is necessary will depend on the individual needs of the students on the teacher's assigned caseload. Nevertheless, teachers of students with visual impairments need to be creative about finding the instructional resources and time required to teach ECC activities and skills.

Teachers providing instruction in the areas of the ECC will benefit from exploring and using the many resources that may be available to them within the school district and community. In particular, members of a student's educational team—the student, parents and family members, school faculty and staff, administrators, and community agencies—can all be potential resources or sources of ideas. The general education teacher, for example, may have a sister-in-law who is a personal trainer and it just so happens that fitness and personal training are career interests of the student. The sister-in-law may be open to a job-shadowing experience or informational interview.

As already suggested, parents and family members represent one of the more powerful resources available within the educational team. The teacher of students with visual impairments will therefore want to, if possible, meet students' family members when students become part of their caseloads and establish effective communication and working relationships with them. By coordinating efforts with the teacher, families can provide students with opportunities to practice skills at home and in the community, thus strongly reinforcing learning in different contexts. Using a collaborative, problem-solving approach to share information with parents and other educational team members and administrators about a child's needs and strategies for meeting those needs may also prompt ideas for family members to arrange events that are fun for the entire family and that provide the student opportunities to learn and practice important skills. (Suggestions for working with families appear in each chapter of Part 2 of this book and are also discussed in Chapter 15.)

Families can actively support students' school careers in many ways, including:

- following through with school assignments (homework, extracurricular activities, social activities)
- becoming involved in school activities, such as the parents' association
- maintaining positive relationships with teachers

In addition to the websites of local school districts, state departments of education, and parent support networks that are useful resources providing guidance on addressing the needs of children, there are many valuable websites for parents of children with visual impairments, including FamilyConnect (www.familyconnect.org) from the American Foundation for the Blind and the Parent Resources page (http://nfb.org/parent-resources) of the National Organization of Parents of Blind Children, part of the National Foundation for the Blind (see the Resources section at the end of this book for more information). These websites provide information that can help parents understand the unique needs of their child and how those needs can best be met within family activities. Guided by this knowledge, parents can be better prepared to suggest needed areas of instruction, advocate for their child with the school district, and support their child's learning when they are not at school.

Agencies that provide adult services and rehabilitation programs in the community can also play an important role in the education of students with visual impairments by providing valuable resources, support, and possible alternate funding options in some situations. More information about the valuable role of these agencies is discussed later in this chapter.

School-based faculty and staff, including administrators; classroom teachers; art, music, and physical education teachers; front office staff; guidance counselors; cafeteria workers; paraeducators; and any other personnel whom students may encounter on a daily basis play a larger role than they (and perhaps, some teachers of students with visual impairments) realize. These educators and related personnel can provide students who are visually impaired with daily opportunities to practice skills in natural contexts. They may not realize the impact they have on a child with a visual impairment in school, but their actions can greatly influence the learning outcomes of students.

School and District Resources

In general, students who are visually impaired benefit greatly from being around other students with visual impairments. Meeting others with visual impairments who are the same age helps students realize they are not the only ones experiencing certain issues and challenges. Younger students can look up to older students, who can act as positive role models. Students of all ages may feel more comfortable being around others who understand what it means to have a visual impairment, and this contact may result in increased self-esteem, forged emotional connections, participation in recreation activities, and enhanced social interaction. With a team of dedicated professionals and careful planning, visually impaired students of all ages and abilities can participate in a field day of activities designed just for them, such as the one outlined in Sidebar 13.9, with a multitude of ECC skills embedded throughout. It may also be helpful for teachers to keep in mind that in addition to making use of the other time-saving and supportive activities suggested throughout this chapter, they may need to consider the use of summer and after-school programming to cover all the skills their students need to develop.

Frequently, rich instructional sites and appropriate materials can be found right in the students' schools

SIDEBAR 13.9

Plan for Field Day Activities

A field day that brings together all the students with visual impairments in a particular district or area can provide substantial benefits for the students, such as the opportunity to encounter role models, make friends who have similar concerns and issues, and practice skills in the ECC areas of social interaction, recreation and leisure, and orientation and mobility, among others. The following plan for one such field day shows how it might be organized.

HILLSBOROUGH COUNTY PUBLIC SCHOOLS
VISUALLY IMPAIRED PROGRAM
TRANSPORTATION-THEMED FIELD DAY

Location: Lettuce Lake Park
Date: March 23, 2012
Time: 10 am–1 pm
Student Population: Sixty-four students in preschool through 12th grade (all blind or visually impaired, including students with multiple disabilities)
Transportation: District school buses
Teachers: Thirteen teachers of students with visual impairments; four teachers with visual impairments /O&M specialists; one administrator; twelve paraprofessionals; five parents
Lunch: Noon–12:30 pm, donated by Lions Eye Institute Foundation from a local fast food restaurant, or bag lunches brought by students from home or school, depending on dietary needs.
Reminder: You know your students and their needs; adapt as needed.

General Instructions

- Determine groups and group sizes.
- Have groups rotate on their own, spending an average of 15–20 minutes per activity. Some activities may take longer or shorter to complete.
- Not all centers have to be completed. Work with your group to decide which activities are most appropriate, depending on student age, ability, and interest, and available time.
- Label centers with a brightly colored sign and their corresponding numbers. Students can use monocular telescopes to scan the park for the signs.
- Suggested accommodations for students with additional disabilities:
  - adult or teammate pushes student in a wheelchair for the suitcase relay
  - adult or another student provides stability for a student with cerebral palsy at the Big Shoes center
  - student may use a bucket to "catch" balloons at the water balloon toss
- Activities with an asterisk (*) are related to transportation (kind of!).

*__Nature walk.__ Walk through the woods with your friends. What kind of animals, birds, leaves, sounds, smells can you find? Climb a tree, skip over logs, have fun. Save your treasures and make an experience book back at school. *Recommended for after lunch.*

Free time on the playground. *Recommended for after lunch.*

Hula-Hoop pass relay. Two teams of students each form a circle. Slide a Hula-Hoop onto the arm of one child on each team and have all the children in each circle hold hands. On "Go," the students have to wiggle and pass the Hula-Hoop over/under each person without letting go of each other's hands until it goes around the whole group and back to the start. Time the groups on each round to see if they can get faster. Lead discussion on teamwork and problem solving (such as, did the students figure out to arrange the students in the group in size order, from tallest to shortest, so the Hula-Hoop is always going down?).

*__Big Shoes.__ Use two long two-by-fours with three pairs of large men's shoes securely attached so that one shoe from each pair is on each board, all facing the same direction. Students insert their feet into each pair of shoes as if wearing the shoes, one foot on each board. Teams walk in the shoes as a group from

(continued on next page)

SIDEBAR 13.9 *continued*

the start to the finish line (Jones, 1998). Classmates stand at start and finish line to act as sound sources to help the walkers stay oriented.

***All Aboard.** Spread a large blanket on the ground. Students get "All Aboard," by stepping on the blanket. When they step onto the blanket and realize how easy it was, chase them off. Fold the blanket so that it is smaller. Have the students get "All Aboard" again. Keep making the blanket smaller until the students have to really squeeze to fit and then problem solve and team build to stay on the blanket. Students may get creative and hold each others' hands from opposite sides of the blanket while leaning back. One may step on another's feet to stay planted. Others may push their way on, causing students on the opposite side to have to step off! Lead a discussion at the end on teamwork, problem solving, personal space, and how is this like riding on a crowded bus or subway? (From http://wilderdom.com/games/descriptions/AllAboard.html)

***Musical foam squares (for younger students).** Place foam squares on the ground in a circle. Each student sits on a square. When the music starts, students walk around the circle while the teacher takes away one square. When the music stops, everyone sits on a square. The student without a square is out. Last one standing can choose the next activity.

Water balloon toss. Two students stand across from each other (start at two feet). One tosses a water balloon to the other. When caught, the student takes a step back and then tosses back to her partner. Students should call or whistle to their partners.

***Suitcase relay.** Divide students into teams. Have two suitcases filled with the same amount of large, silly clothes (skirts, shirts, hats, scarves, mittens) for each team to put on. First teammate runs to base (such as a picnic table across from start line) with the suitcase, opens it, puts on the clothes, runs back to the start line, removes the clothes, places them back into suitcase, closes it, and tags the next teammate who completes the same task. First team with all members to complete the task is the winner. (Make sure any students who have a contagious skin or hair condition such as lice, ringworm do not participate in this game.)

***Transportation freeze tag.** Whoever is "it" runs around chasing friends. When a student is about to be tagged, he should squat down and yell out a form of transportation (bus, car, bike, tugboat, plane, train, canoe, helicopter, walking), which makes the student safe and "it" person have to move on. If a student is tagged before she yells a form of transportation, then she is out.

***I'm going on a trip with the ABCs.** Have students sit in a circle. The first one says, "I'm going on a trip and I'm going to pack [an item beginning with the letter *A*, such as 'my *a*ction figures.']" Next student says, "I'm going on a trip and I'm going to pack my action figures and [an item beginning with the letter *B*, such as 'my *b*low dryer']. Next student says, "I'm going on a trip and I'm going to pack my action figures, my blow dryer, and [an item beginning with the letter *C*, such as 'my *c*omb.']" Continue with each student repeating the previous items and adding a new one that begins with the next letter of the alphabet.

Field trip planning committee: Laura Brown (coordinator), Tiffany Conrad (teacher of students with visual impairments /certified O&M specialist), Jessie Cox (teacher of students with visual impairments), Susan Glaser (teacher of students with visual impairments), Lisa Merwarth (teacher of students with visual impairments).

and within the district. Even the school bus can be used to teach important skills related to the ECC (see Sidebar 13.10).

Knowing where these types of resources are located and how to access them can take some detective work, often requiring a little creativity, organization, and time management.

Common School Resources

Common school resources that can be used for teaching ECC skills include:

- Bathrooms are easy-to-access places that can be used to teach cleaning skills, the use of a plunger, the importance of disinfecting, and the use of different types of cleaning products.
- A teacher's lounge can be used to teach basic cooking skills or food preparation on a weekly basis after obtaining advance permission from the school principal.
- A variety of surfaces such as tables, floors, chairs, and carpets can be used to teach cleaning

SIDEBAR 13.10

Buses Are Classrooms, Too

Many students with visual impairments ride the bus to and from school or on field trips. They may be able to explain what the bus is, where they sit, and the name of their bus driver, but do they *really* know what a bus is? Do they know how big it is, how many tires it has, how many seats it has, what the driver's seat looks like, how the door opens and closes, how the windows open and close, how the back or emergency doors open and close? Probably not! Some schools have buses parked in the parking lot during the day, ready to serve as a valuable "classroom" for a child with a visual impairment.

1. Have the student start with the outside of the bus and feel how big the tires are, how big the lug nuts are, and explore the bumpers, headlights, taillights, reflectors, and the stop sign that swings out from the side of the bus.
2. Have the student try to find all the mirrors, inside and out.
3. Have the student compare the bus to a car: Do cars have stop signs? Does the bus have a trunk? Are the tires the same size?
4. Have the student walk all the way around the bus, keeping track of the starting point so he knows where to stop.
5. After touching all the parts of the outside of the bus and trailing around it, it will be time to find an outside hose or a water spigot (check outside of the cafeteria), to wash hands. This provides additional opportunities for learning concepts: on, off, fast, slow, wet, dry, feet spread apart, "lefty loosey, righty tighty," and eventually, time management (don't be late for class!).

On the next day, explore the inside of the bus.

1. Have the student sit on the springy driver's seat and compare it to the passenger seats.
2. Count how many seats are on the bus going down the long aisle. Some buses may have seats of different lengths on either side, some may have seatbelts, and some may have an opening where a wheelchair can be secured.
3. Have the student find the seats that have a hump on the floor. Then go outside and find the wheel well. Help your student be a detective to figure out why certain seats at the front and back of the bus have humps on the floor.
4. Also, be sure to open and close all the doors and windows. The windows are probably very tricky to open and require a lot of finger and arm strength. If students don't develop strength through everyday activities, they will not be able to open those windows and will have to rely on another student—maybe a younger student. Such feedback on a student's abilities is invaluable.
5. Reinforce positional and spatial concepts, such as front, back, side, open, close, left, right, up, down, near, far, around, and under while exploring the school bus. Other concepts: A bus has very *steep* steps, the driver sits in a seat that is very *bouncy*, and the steering wheel and mirrors are *huge*.

After exploring the bus, teachers can work with younger students to make an experience book. Older students might be asked to braille or type a story about a bus trip, make a comparison chart between a bus and a car, read books about school and other types of buses, or even start a project on transportation.

A field trip to the district's bus garage may be in order if a school bus does not park at your school, but such a trip can also provide an exciting way to extend what is learned in the school's parking lot.

---

skills such as wiping, scrubbing, sweeping, and vacuuming.

- Tables in the cafeteria offer an opportunity to master the use of the overlapping grid pattern (see Chapter 8 for a description) for cleaning (the student may also gain valuable pre-vocational skills, enhanced spatial awareness, a sense of responsibility, and opportunities to practice time management and socialization).
- Trash cans in classrooms and offices can be used to practice taking out the trash and replacing trash bags.
- A housekeeping center in a preschool setting can offer the opportunity for young students to learn to sweep with a small broom and dustpan, to set a tablecloth on a small table, and to store and retrieve items from cabinets.

- Naptime is an opportunity for young students to be responsible for unfolding a sleeping mat and laying a blanket on top of it and for folding the blanket and mat back up when naptime is over.

Home Economics Classroom

An advantage to working in a middle or high school is that often these schools will have a home economics classroom. The home economics teacher most likely does not have a class every single period of the day, and the teacher of students with visual impairments can work with this teacher to create a schedule to use the kitchen once or twice a week while it is not being used for instruction. If the teacher of students with visual impairments has his or her students bake cookies, brownies, or cupcakes to share with other school personnel, using this classroom will not seem so much like an intrusion! Skills that can be learned in the home economics classroom include:

- researching and reading a recipe
- obtaining needed ingredients
- using appliances
- measuring dry and wet ingredients
- learning safety techniques and adaptations for working in a kitchen
- cleaning the dishes
- understanding the importance of hygiene
- applying mathematics (when doubling a recipe, for example)
- using time management to finish a recipe in the allotted time
- using social skills to distribute baked goods to teachers and staff at the school

With additional organization and planning, students can progress to taking weekly orders for particular baked goods from school employees, which can facilitate learning pre-vocational skills, more advanced time management skills, use of spreadsheets to stay organized, additional mathematics skills, written and verbal communication skills, and self-confidence.

Washer and Dryer

Some schools may have a clothes washer and dryer available. Students whose families have these appliances may have different machines at home, but the concept of "doing the laundry" can be taught and reinforced at school. For example, elementary school students can collect art smocks that the art teacher or individual classroom teachers use and wash the smocks once a month, or can do so for one classroom per week. Skills that can be learned with regular laundry practice include:

- distinguishing clean smocks from dirty smocks
- developing strength from carrying smocks from classroom to laundry room
- using a laundry basket or clothes bag
- measuring detergent and learning about various types of detergents (liquid, powder, cubes)
- practicing using labels to set dials and buttons on machines
- pulling heavy, wet clothes from the washer and placing them in the dryer
- using fabric softener
- folding the dry smocks and returning them to the correct classroom

In addition, capabilities in such areas as time management, verbal communication, social interaction, protective techniques, search patterns, and self-confidence can be expanded.

Cooking or Culinary Programs

Schools offering cooking or culinary programs for students offer a wide range of learning opportunities that the teacher of students with visual impairments can leverage as well, as noted previously. Visiting a culinary program at a high school can be a valuable hands-on field trip for elementary or middle school students who are visually impaired. The chef of the program, as well as the high school students who are enrolled in it, can talk about the various jobs in the field, the tools and appliances used in the kitchen, what type of training and education are required, and common working environments and conditions. (Culinary programs can sometimes also be used to provide meals at a discounted rate for activities that a school district's program in visual impairment may be hosting, such as bag lunches for a picnic at a local park or a buffet dinner at an end-of-year award ceremony with students and families.) Teachers seeking to make arrangements with programs like these can point out the mutual advantages, such as the high school students in the program having the opportunity to benefit by improving their public speaking skills and learning more about people with disabilities.

Performing Arts Programs

Visits to middle and high schools with performing arts programs can also provide a variety of opportunities for learning for students with visual impairments. In addition to exploring the various instruments that are available at these sites, students can learn about other types of performing arts at the school. They can stand on a stage, explore the orchestra pit, see where dressing rooms are in a theater, learn how quickly performers must change costumes in between scenes, experience and learn about the acoustics in an auditorium, and learn how the stage curtains open and close. Actors, singers, and dancers are only one part of a stage performance, and students can get a more complete and realistic sense of what is involved through direct experience. For example, they can see or otherwise learn firsthand where the music comes from, how stage lighting is changed, and what other types of work—and careers—are involved behind the scenes of a production. They can learn about choreographers, set designers, costume designers, sound engineers, writers, and directors. A variety of follow-up activities can extend these experiences, such as writing thank-you letters, writing a play, performing a play, designing a costume for a storybook parade at school, or putting together a soundtrack to go with a favorite play. As with so many other activities, direct experiences can generate deeper understanding, increase curiosity, and inspire creativity.

Other District Resources

There are many other resources within a school district that can help teachers of students with visual impairments teach the areas of the ECC. Schools with an auto shop, agricultural or environmental education center, or career/technical center have a variety of experiences to offer. Visits to a high school's auto shop may help students who are visually impaired learn about an essential part of the environment. Though they may not be drivers when they are adults, students with visual impairments do need to know about automobiles and perhaps some basics of how to take care of them. Agricultural programs can teach students with visual impairments about farming, farm equipment, running a business, and animal husbandry, and provide exposure that may spark an interest in a career in one of those areas. Career or technical centers are valuable places to not only learn about different professions, but also to meet professionals in those fields and discover what education and training are needed, what working environments will be like, and what job duties are expected of employees. During such in-district field trips, students have opportunities to use low vision devices, canes, protective techniques (such as the human guide technique), socially appropriate behaviors, verbal communication, and assistive technology to record information or take notes.

Another source of learning within a school district includes visiting administrative offices to learn about how the school district itself is run. Many children think that a school district consists only of teachers and principals. At a district office, they can learn about the hierarchy of school administrators and other school personnel and how many offices and employees it takes to run a school district. They also benefit from learning what happens in an office setting and what tools and equipment are used, including computers, copiers, filing cabinets, and multi-line phones. Back at school, teachers can expand on such a visit by finding the same office tools in the students' school. Students can investigate how a school office (or a teacher's desk) is similar and how it is different from those found at the district office. They can also identify the tools and other items that professionals in general use in an office (stapler, phone, copy machine, computer) and begin to explore what other jobs require employees to use these same tools.

As discussed previously in this chapter, before taking students off the school's campus, it is important to review appropriate policies and procedures and to pursue all necessary notifications, whether to school administrators or other staff or students' families. Moreover, the first and foremost consideration when using resources in the community is the safety of students. Field trip handbooks and district policies should be researched and followed when taking students on field trips or inviting members of the community to work with students. A separate field trip notebook or a binder of important forms and information (described earlier in this chapter) should be carried by teachers on all trips so that permission forms, emergency contact cards, and any other required information is easily available. Teachers should also remember that it is necessary to obtain permission from students' parents or guardians to photograph or videotape students in advance of such trips. When attending special events, there may be news media representatives present who will not be able to photograph or videotape any children unless permission has been granted. Not having required forms available can result in the loss of an important opportunity for free publicity about the district program or the abilities and needs of students who are visually impaired.

Agencies Serving People Who Are Blind

State agencies providing services to people who are blind and private agencies that deliver rehabilitation services are an additional resource that may be helpful to the teacher developing an instructional program focused on the ECC. Community rehabilitation providers will provide services to many students in the future and often are a valuable source of disability-specific information in areas of the ECC that are addressed by agency staff. For example, vision rehabilitation therapists (formerly known as rehabilitation teachers) employed by these agencies can assist teachers with techniques to address independent living skills. These providers may also have facilities that students and teachers may use, such as kitchens adapted for instructional purposes. Assistive technology labs may also be available and can offer students and their families opportunities to explore valuable tools. Clients who have received services through these providers and are now successful adults can be linked with younger students to provide mentoring. If the community rehabilitation provider, the state agency, and the school district are willing to work together and allow their resources to be shared, the possibilities can be endless.

Community Resources

Visits to businesses in the community and places such as the public library or local area recreation center are valuable experiences for students with visual impairments. All field trips or site visits can involve and be followed with additional lessons in the areas of the ECC. With some thought and consideration for a given student's needs, almost any number of activities designed to promote the development of skills can grow out of such visits. For example, teachers can have their students write thank-you letters to businesses and programs they visit, reinforcing writing skills (including the use of braille, or print, or keyboarding), assistive technology skills (such as using an electronic notetaker or a computer with speech synthesis or a screen enlarging program), reading skills, and more. Teachers can also have their students include information they learned from various site visits in their career portfolios (discussed earlier in this chapter). The students can undertake additional research on a career of interest that they were exposed to on a trip, using assistive technology to access the Internet. If necessary, teachers can ask subject area supervisors to provide additional instructional support. For example, an English or writing supervisor may be willing to offer needed lessons in writing skills after a student's field trip.

Many businesses and individuals in a community care about being involved and giving back to the community at large, but they may not do this unless they are asked, and asking the right person is key. Making a phone call to a local business and requesting a donation or permission to set up a field trip may lead to a response like, "I'm sorry, but we're unable to assist with your needs," from the receptionist, cashier on duty, or any other employee who does not have the authority to make such decisions. However, going in person to a location and asking to speak to the owner or manager may yield different results. Teachers pursuing this course of action should be sure to wear a school district identification badge and bring a business card to confirm their position. They can explain how children with typical sight learn incidentally, through observation, and how children who are blind or significantly visually impaired learn by doing. Teachers can also explain how being involved in concrete, hands-on experiences can help students learn about the world at large and develop a variety of skills, including basic skills such as how to read.

One local business donated several boat rides in its water taxi to elementary, middle, and high school students in the community. One of the employees was overheard explaining to someone else how this experience could help students become better readers because the next time they read a story that involved a boat, they could relate to what it felt like to be on a boat, what happens when the boat goes fast, what happens when they stand up, and what would happen if they leaned over too far.

Teachers of students with visual impairments might want to discuss with their supervisors wider possibilities, such as getting school district support to send a visually impaired student to the Space Camp for Interested Visually Impaired Students at the U.S. Space and Rocket Center in Huntsville, Alabama (www.tsbvi.edu/space). In conjunction with families and the school district, fundraising can be planned, with the students' involvement, to raise money to support travel costs for such a program. Students who are involved in raising money to fund a trip will in general find the experience more meaningful and will take more complete ownership of the entire project. Fundraising provides opportunities for the practice of math, social, and compensatory skills, and for the use of assistive technology and written and verbal communication. Teachers of students with visual impairments can as part of this activity invite district science teachers to act as chaperones, thereby helping them increase their understanding of the needs of visually impaired students in their classes. (See the section on funding resources earlier in this chapter for additional suggestions.)

Some school districts may be located in close proximity to their state's residential school for students who are blind. In these circumstances, teachers of students with visual impairments in local districts can team with professionals at residential schools to provide workshops and training for teachers and families. Residential school athletic coaches can put on seminars to teach adaptive physical education techniques specific to students with visual impairments to local physical education teachers, teachers of students with visual impairments, families, and students who are visually impaired. Use of available dormitory space in residential schools can provide additional opportunities for students to practice ECC skills. By taking an overnight trip to the residential school, students can learn and practice a multitude of independent living, social, and O&M skills in a rich but unfamiliar learning environment.

Table 13.1 presents a variety of community resources that can be and have been used to facilitate learning of the core curriculum and the ECC. Resources outlined here are designed to give teachers helpful suggestions about extending learning in both the core and the ECC as interrelated areas that are not taught in isolation but are presented to students with visual impairments as real life experiences.

TABLE 13.1

Using Community Resources to Teach the Expanded Core Curriculum

The following table lists community resources that can serve as sites for activities that teach skills in the ECC and gives examples of such activities. These suggestions are all based on actual ECC lessons provided at each of the community resources listed.

Community Resource	***Purpose/Suggested Activities***
Community rehabilitation provider (no cost)	Visiting the community rehabilitation provider lets students establish a natural connection to the resource and develop an understanding about how they will benefit from this resource when they are adults. • Use as a meeting area for students and/or families to host trainings or guest speakers. • Use kitchen and independent living skills lab, and technology lab for more intensive instruction. • Use facilities to offer a summer program as part of extended school year.
Fast food franchise (no cost)	• Take a tour of the restaurant, including behind the counters and kitchen area. • Have students make their own ice cream cone or call out the number of an order that is ready for pick up.
Hardware store (no cost)	• Take a tour and set up stations to learn how to use the tools in each area including plumbing, gardening, hardware, and lumber.
Theme park (discounted admission)	• Tour the park with a group of students and teachers using a map to find specific rides and areas. • Eat lunch at a park restaurant and browse gift shops. • Explore behind-the-scenes work that takes place to discover more about careers and to use social skills.
Government office (no cost)	• Tour a variety of offices (City Hall, the Mayor's office, disability services, the public defender's office) and listen to guest speakers.
Public transportation (no cost or discounted fares)	• Take a trip on local public transportation, such as bus, trolley, subway, train, or even taxi. • Have a destination with an activity planned once you arrive. • For example, take the bus to the mall to have lunch in the food court.

(continued on next page)

TABLE 13.1 *continued*

Community Resource	Purpose/Suggested Activities
County or state parks (no cost or discounted admission)	• Set up a field day with various stations (a refrigerator box for rolling down hills, three-legged race, beeping egg hunt, water station, etc.). • Have a cook-out with help from community volunteers.
Sports arena (no cost)	• Take a tour of a local sports arena. • Learn about locker rooms, the size of the field or court, stands and seating, concessions, and behind-the-scenes offices.
Bowling alley (no cost or discounted games)	• Find a bowling alley willing to give lessons, a tour of the backside of the lanes, and information about various jobs. • Play a few games and teach students how to keep score (the old fashioned way), exchange their shoes, order snacks, take turns bowling, etc.
YMCA (no cost)	Depending on the community, YMCAs offer a variety of exercise equipment, sports, and classes. • Have students explore the swimming pool, basketball court, racquetball, rock climbing wall, play area, weight equipment, cardiovascular equipment. • Learn about the various types of jobs.
Petting zoo/farm (no cost or discounted admission)	Children cannot begin to understand what a plastic cow, goat or chicken is if they have never been exposed to a real cow, goat, or chicken. • Find a local farm or petting zoo to pet, hold, or ride the animals and learn how they live, what they eat, and what they do.
Post office (no cost)	• Have students write a letter or make a card before the trip. They can put their note in an envelope, address it to the student or teacher, include a return address, and leave off the stamp. • At the post office, have the students buy stamps and put their letters in the mailbox. • Arrange ahead of time a tour of the post office to find out where the letters from the mailbox go. • Try to get the students a peek inside a mail truck. • In a few days, the letter will arrive and the student will know where it came from.
Airport (no cost)	Airlines and airports will have someone assigned to meeting the needs of customers with disabilities. If you find the right person, you could get a very in-depth tour of the airport and quite possibly get your students on an actual airplane. • Show students where to check in, place bags, find the terminal, read the monitors or request assistance to check flight status, go through security lines, etc.
Grocery store (no cost)	A grocery store is an expanded core curriculum heaven! The possibilities are endless. • With one student, teach the layout of the store, benefits of customer service, food groups, budgeting, requesting assistance, paying, bagging, etc. • On a field trip with several students, arrange a behind-the-scenes tour to learn about the freezers, loading, inventory, storage, various jobs, etc.
Mall (no cost or discounted snack)	• Set up a scavenger hunt at a local mall or strip mall. • Students should have the list of items and information to seek (hours of the mall, how many bathrooms are in the mall, what department store is on the east side, etc.) in print, braille, or auditory format and can work in teams or small groups to find the items on the list. • Items should be selected so that students will be required to talk to a variety of individuals, learn about different services in the mall, maintain orientation, etc.
Hotel (no cost)	A local hotel is crawling with skills to teach and careers to explore. There's the bellman, valet service, concierge, front desk staff, managers, accountants, restaurants, housekeeping, pool, fitness center and then some. • Find a time of the year that is not busy and arrange a tour with a manager. • Have kids practice cleaning an entire room from changing the bed sheets to scrubbing the toilet!

Note: The authors wish to acknowledge the work of the teachers, staff, and families of students in the Hillsborough County Public Schools Visually Impaired Program and the assistance of the Florida Division of Blind Services and the Tampa Lighthouse for the Blind, in creating these activities and many others.

CONCLUSION

Integrating the ECC into general education environments can be accomplished. As with any valuable instructional undertaking, some planning and forethought are needed, and teachers of students with visual impairments need administrative support to accomplish this critical goal on their students' behalf. Instruction needs to occur on and off school campuses to perpetuate the development and transfer of skills in natural settings. Effective time and caseload management techniques can be applied to free up time that previously may have been spent on less productive and meaningful tasks. With careful scheduling, thoughtful selection of instructional settings, and, sometimes, creative funding, students' opportunities for learning can be enhanced and their chances for post-school success increased.

Meeting the needs of students may sometimes seem challenging and at times even overwhelming, but teachers of students with visual impairments are the kind of creative people who are up to this task. When teachers feel overwhelmed, the support of other colleagues who share the same experiences and challenges can be invaluable, so reaching out to professional groups, electronic mailing lists, and other teachers is another important investment of time. Administrators and teachers working together to provide appropriate instructional activities in the areas of the ECC are in fact changing the trajectory of educational outcomes for students with visual impairments. Through thoughtful and concerted efforts, students who are visually impaired can be helped to develop the skills they need for ongoing success in school, work, and life.

REFERENCES

Anthony, T. (2000). Performing a functional low vision assessment. In F. M. D'Andrea & C. Farrenkopf (Eds.), *Looking to learn: Promoting literacy for students with low vision.* New York: AFB Press.

Association for Education and Rehabilitation of the Blind and Visually Impaired, Division 16, Itinerant Personnel (n.d.). Caseload analysis: A critical component of quality services for students with visual impairments. Retrieved from http://aerbvi.org/modules.php?name=Content&pa=showpage&pid=70

Blankenship, K., Hatlen, P., & Lohmeier, K. (2009). Expanded core curriculum: 12 years later. *Journal of Visual Impairment & Blindness, 103*(2), 103–112.

Blachowicz, C. L. Z. (n.d.). Leadership letters: Issues and trends in reading best practices in vocabulary instruction. Retrieved from https://perspective.pearsonaccess.com/content/resources/teachingresources/professionaldevelopment/blachowicz.pdf

Erin, J. N. (2004). *When you have a visually impaired student with multiple disabilities in your classroom: A guide for teachers.* New York: AFB Press.

Expanded core competencies: PK–5 (n.d.; course number 7763080). Retrieved from the CPALMS website: http://www.cpalms.org/Public/PreviewCourse/Preview/332

Holbrook, M. C., Croft, J. E., & Kline, C. (2000). Presenting information to the general public. In A. J. Koenig & M. C. Holbrook (Eds.), *Foundations of education: Vol. II. Instructional strategies for teaching children and youths with visual impairments* (2nd ed., pp. 753–768). New York: AFB Press.

Huebner, K. M., Merk-Adam, B., Stryker, D., & Wolffe, K. (2004). *The national agenda for the education of children and youths with visual impairments, including those with multiple disabilities* (revised). New York: AFB Press.

Jones, A. (1998). *104 activities that build: Self-esteem, teamwork, communication, anger management, self-discovery, coping skills* (p. 28). Lusby, MD: Rec Room Publishing.

Lewis, S., Allman, C. B., & D'Andrea, F. M. (2000). *Seeing eye to eye: An administrator's guide to students with low vision.* New York: AFB Press.

Lueck, A., Erin, J. N., Corn, A. L., & Sacks, S. Z. (2011). *Facilitating visual efficiency and access to learning in students with low vision: A position paper of the Division on Visual Impairments, Council of Exceptional Children.* Retrieved from http://www.cecdvi.org/positionpapers.html

National Institute for Literacy (2001). *Put reading first: The research building blocks for teaching children to read.* Retrieved from http://www.nichd.nih.gov/publications/pubs/upload/PRFbooklet.pdf

Olmstead, J. (2005). *Itinerant teaching: Tricks of the trade for students with visual impairments* (2nd ed.). New York: AFB Press.

Pugh, G. S., & Erin, J. N. (Eds.). (1999). *Blind and visually impaired students: Educational service guidelines.* Watertown, MA: Perkins School for the Blind.

Sapp, W. K., & Hatlen, P. (2010). The expanded core curriculum: Where we have been, where we are going, and how we can get there. *Journal of Visual Impairment & Blindness, 104*(6), 338–348.

Spungin, S. J., and Ferrell, K. A. (2007). The role and function of the teacher of students with visual impairments. Retrieved from http://community.cec.sped.org/dvi/resourceportal/positionpapers

Texas School for the Blind and Visually Impaired. (2007). *EVALS: Evaluating Visually Impaired Students.* Austin, TX: Author.

Toelle, N., & Blankenship, K. E. (2008). Practice report: Program accountability for students who are visually impaired. *Journal of Visual Impairment & Blindness, 102*(2), 97–102.

U.S. Department of Education, Office of Special Education and Rehabilitative Services. (2000). *Educating blind and visually impaired students; policy guidance* (Federal Register. June 8, 2000, vol. 65, Num. 111, pp. 36585-36594). Retrieved from http://www2.ed.gov/legislation/FedRegister/other/2000-2/060800a.html

When you have a visually impaired student in your classroom: A guide for teachers. (2002). New York: AFB Press.

Wolffe, K., Sacks, S., Corn, A., Erin, J., Huebner, K., & Lewis, S. (2002) Teachers of students with visual impairments: What are they teaching? *Journal of Visual Impairment & Blindness, 96*(5), 293–303.

CHAPTER 14

Aligning the Expanded Core Curriculum with State Standards

Sharon Z. Sacks, Karen E. Blankenship, Sue Douglass, and Deborah Tierney Kreuzer

L. Penny Rosenblum

In recent years, school districts and state departments of education have been called upon with mounting insistence to increase student achievement by enforcing standards-based education for all students. The 2004 reauthorization of the Individuals with Disabilities Education Act (IDEA) and the enactment of the Elementary and Secondary Education Act of 2001, sometimes known as No Child Left Behind (NCLB), have largely been responsible for this trend. These important legislative landmarks changed the way in which students with disabilities receive educational support throughout the nation and in many ways influenced the focus of educational services overall.

As part of this environmental shift, teachers throughout the country now face a number of pressing new realities: general education and special education teachers are being held accountable *in direct ways* for the academic success of their students. On one hand, curricula designed for reading, language arts, mathematics, science, social studies, and additional core content areas are being based on standards set forth by individual state departments of education. On the other hand, many states have worked in partnership with the National Governor's Association to establish a set of national common core standards (CCS) (found at www.corestandards.org). Although the emphasis on standards is now a matter of widespread attention nationwide, the selection and application of standards varies dramatically from state to state. Some states have aligned their state standards with those of the CCS; others adhere to separate standards determined by the state.

Students with visual impairments are not exempt from these mandates and need to meet the state standards for all students. Furthermore, the mandates of IDEA stipulate that students with disabilities are entitled to the same core academic content as students without disabilities, and the law requires that students with disabilities participate in district-wide and state assessments. However, as has been pointed out previously in this book, students with visual impairments need to learn both the core curriculum and the additional skills encompassed in the expanded core curriculum (ECC), which are essential to their participation in this critical core content. How can their teachers help them successfully address these important demands on their skills?

Some states—such as California, Maryland, and Utah—have created braille reading and mathematics standards, like the Maryland Common Core State Curriculum Frameworks for Braille (Maryland State Department of Education, 2012), that parallel the state's English-language arts and mathematics standards. By creating these standards, these states have provided their teachers of students with visual impairments with a blueprint for adaptations and content specific to the needs of visually impaired students in the areas in which the parallel standards exist. For example, the braille reading standards provide guidelines for when the braillewriter, slate and stylus, or braille notetaking device should be mastered by students and designate at what grade level abacus instruction should begin. Before the establishment of these standards, specific guidelines had not been provided to professionals serving this population of students. Nevertheless, not every state has to date laid out standards that have provided teachers of students with visual impairments with guidelines. In addition, states differ in their perspectives on the ECC itself.

The purpose of this chapter is therefore to familiarize professionals with the issues and activities involved in integrating the ECC into standards-based education and suggest strategies and approaches that can be used. That being said, it is important to note that as of this writing, some states, like Iowa and Texas, have only adopted core content standards and do not incorporate the ECC as essential content at the state level. Other states, like California and Arizona, have matched the ECC to core content standards. In still other states, the ECC may be considered a statement of special education needs or accommodations—both required elements of the Individualized Education Program (IEP)—and in still others, IEP goals are required to only address state standards. It is essential, then, for teachers to learn the prevailing landscape. Professionals who provide services to students with visual impairments need to know how their school districts and state departments of education view the integration of the ECC with academic standards and proceed accordingly.

WHY STANDARDS ARE IMPORTANT

Generally, in the field of education a standard describes what students are expected to accomplish at a particular grade level. Standards are similar to guidelines and help teachers determine what needs to be taught in a sequential manner for each subject area. According to the Association of California School Administrators (ACSA) Special Services *Handbook of Goals & Objectives* (2007), standards have the following characteristics (p. 6):

- are used as a framework for teaching
- provide an educational sequence to learning
- apply to *all* students
- inform *what* to teach, not *how* to teach
- describe what students are expected to perform in each subject area and grade level (as referenced in "present levels of performance" goals or objectives/benchmarks)

- develop a method of assessing the level of student achievement and a way to communicate with the public regarding student performance
- are the criteria used to define accountability

One of the important aspects of standards is that—because they define what needs to be taught—they provide a common language for special educators and their general education counterparts. They allow all professionals to share in the development of ongoing assessment and instruction. State content standards can provide educators with a road map for creating and choosing appropriate curricula for their students and need to be used by teachers of students with visual impairments to help determine what their students need to learn.

A key way in which teachers of students with visual impairments can help their students demonstrate that they do meet the standards required by their state is through designing Individualized Family Service Plans (IFSPs), IEPs, and transition IEPs (sometimes called Individualized Transition Programs or ITPs) that relate to core content standards. Some states in fact require that IEP goals address state standards, and the process through which this effort can be successfully done is described in the following sections of this chapter. A standards-based IEP can serve many functions, including:

- supporting a student in achieving academic goals equivalent to grade-level outcomes
- ensuring participation in district and statewide assessments
- providing an objective measure for a student to advance from grade to grade
- establishing criteria for graduation or exit from formal educational programs

In addition, in states where it is allowed or required, standards-based IFSPs, IEPs, and ITPs can help special educators to link alternative or functional curricula to academic content, which is particularly important in regard to students with visual impairments and additional disabilities. By creating standards-based IFSPs, IEPs, and ITPs, service providers can justify the need for and importance of the development of skills related to the ECC.

The role of the teacher of students with visual impairments and the orientation and mobility (O&M) specialist in implementing standards-based instruction is both important and essential. Not only do these professionals need to demonstrate expertise in the specialized services students with visual impairments require, they need to work closely with their general education colleagues to perform educational assessments and implement high-quality instruction. At a minimum, service providers should be able to assist general educators in adapting and modifying academic curricula. In some instances, the knowledge of teachers of students with visual impairments and O&M specialists needs to cross disciplines. For example, it is the responsibility of the teacher of students with visual impairments to teach students to read and write braille. However, in order to do so effectively, these professionals need to be skilled reading teachers. They need to understand how to teach reading and promote literacy, and to be aware of the expected outcomes for reading achievement for each grade level. Overall, teachers of students with visual impairments need to collaborate closely with the general educator responsible for students' success in the core curriculum presented in the classroom, and that collaboration needs to focus on the ECC.

DESIGNING STANDARDS-BASED IFSPs, IEPs, AND ITPs

Each state has its own requirements for how IFSPs, IEPs, and ITPs are developed and written. Whether students with visual impairments are served in general education contexts or in specialized schools, professionals and family members need to be knowledgeable about writing standards-based documents because these documents provide critical information about student progress both in the core curriculum and the ECC. Integrating the ECC into standards-based documents may not be a viable alternative in some states. However, compiling a framework that integrates the ECC with standards governing core content may help teachers and families include these essential skill areas in IFSPs, IEPs, and ITPs. Table 14.1 provides an example of how such a framework may be constructed: the matrix matches state standards with areas of the ECC and related instructional activities.

As teachers of students with visual impairments approach the need to align their work with students with the standards prevailing in their states or localities, collecting certain information and using the following process may be helpful:

1. Contact a program supervisor or state vision consultant to determine if goals and benchmarks

TABLE 14.1

A Framework for Integrating State Standards with the ECC

Standard	*Primary ECC areas addressed*	*Possible additional ECC content areas*	*Possible ECC instructional activity*
READING			
Grade 3: Read with sufficient accuracy and fluency to support comprehension.	Compensatory access	Self-determination	Student sets word-per-minute goals for improving braille reading fluency and completes weekly timed probes and keeps own data as part of an independent study.
Grade 4: Interpret information presented visually, orally, or quantitatively (e.g., in charts, graphs, diagrams, time lines, animations, or interactive elements on webpages) and explain how the information contributes to an understanding of the text in which it appears.	Compensatory access	All areas	Student learns how to interpret detail in charts used in the textbook (either with a near optical device or a tactile graphic).
Grade 8: Analyze in detail the structure of a specific paragraph in a text, including the role of particular sentences in developing and refining a key concept.	Self-determination	All areas	Student reads about her eye condition and completes an outline of key information on the computer or braille notetaker.
Grade 9: By the end of grade 9, read and comprehend literary nonfiction in the grades 9–10 text complexity band proficiently, with scaffolding as needed at the high end of the range.	Career education	All areas	Student reads both a fiction and non-fiction book on teaching.
WRITING			
Grade 5: Write narratives to develop real or imagined experiences or events using effective technique, descriptive details, and clear event sequences.	Self-determination	Compensatory access	Student researches and writes a report on his eye condition as part of self-determination.
Grade 6: Write informative and explanatory texts to examine a topic and convey ideas, concepts, and information through the selection, organization, and analysis of relevant content.	Social interaction	Compensatory access	Student keeps a journal for the instructional sessions in social skills where students work on two-way peer interaction.
Grade 6: With some guidance and support from peers and adults, develop and strengthen writing as needed by planning, revising, editing, rewriting, or trying a new approach.	Self-determination	Assistive technology Compensatory access Career education	Student edits his research paper on his eye condition prior to turning it in to the teacher of students with visual impairments for review.
Grades 9–10: Use technology, including the Internet, to produce, publish, and update individual or shared writing products, taking advantage of technology's capacity to link to other information and to display information flexibly and dynamically.	Self-determination	Assistive technology	Student develops an outline of his eye condition for his family and a PowerPoint presentation for the classroom.

TABLE 14.1 *continued*

Standard	Primary ECC areas addressed	Possible additional ECC content areas	Possible ECC instructional activity
MATHEMATICS			
Kindergarten: Understand the relationship between numbers and quantities; connect counting to cardinality.	Compensatory access, Nemeth code	Assistive technology	Student learns one-to-one correspondence with counting bears and writes the Nemeth numbers on the braillewriter.
Kindergarten: Solve addition and subtraction word problems, and add and subtract within 10, e.g., by using objects or drawings to represent the problem.	Compensatory access, Nemeth code	Assistive technology	Student learns addition and subtraction on the abacus and writes the problems in Nemeth code on the braillewriter.
Grade 3: Measure and estimate liquid volumes and masses of objects using standard units of grams (g), kilograms (kg), and liters (l). Add, subtract, multiply, or divide to solve one-step word problems involving masses or volumes that are given in the same units, e.g., by using drawings (such as a beaker with a measurement scale) to represent the problem.	Independent living	Compensatory access	Student is baking cupcakes for the FHA bake sale and measuring dry ingredients using an adapted measuring cup.
Grades 6–7: Solve real-world and mathematical problems involving area, volume, and surface area of two- and three-dimensional objects composed of triangles, quadrilaterals, polygons, cubes, and right prisms.	O&M	Compensatory access	Student creates a scale model of an O&M route.
Grade 8: Understand that patterns of association can also be seen in bivariate categorical data by displaying frequencies and relative frequencies in a two-way table. Construct and interpret a two-way table summarizing data on two categorical variables collected from the same subjects. Use relative frequencies calculated for rows or columns to describe possible association between the two variables.	Compensatory access, Nemeth code	Self-determination	Student develops a data sheet and uses it to collect data on her rate of reading (words per minute) in braille.
Grade 8: Understand that patterns of association can also be seen in bivariate categorical data by displaying frequencies and relative frequencies in a two-way table. Construct and interpret a two-way table summarizing data on two categorical variables collected from the same subjects. Use relative frequencies calculated for rows or columns to describe possible association between the two variables.	Self-determination	Compensatory access	Student constructs and interprets charts and bar graph.
PHYSICAL EDUCATION			
Grade 1: Demonstrate competency in motor skills and movement patterns needed to perform a variety of physical activities.	O&M	Independent living Recreation and leisure	Student decreases the amount of time required to travel from his class to the playground.

(continued on next page)

TABLE 14.1 *continued*

Standard	**Primary ECC areas addressed**	**Possible additional ECC content areas**	**Possible ECC instructional activity**
Grade 2: Demonstrate understanding of movement concepts, principles, strategies, and tactics as they apply to the learning and performance of physical activities.	Orientation and mobility	Recreation and leisure Independent living	Student problem solves with the O&M specialist to safely travel from home to school.
Grade 5: Exhibit responsible personal and social behavior that respects self and others in physical activity settings.	Recreation and leisure	Independent living	Student creates a weekly schedule and identifies priorities for a healthy lifestyle that includes physical activity.
Grades 9–12: Lifetime Wellness. Acquire the knowledge and skills necessary to maintain an active life: movement, physical fitness, and nutrition.	Recreation and leisure	Orientation and mobility Social interaction Independent living	Student participates on the goalball team.
SCIENCE			
Grades 11–12: Integrate and evaluate multiple sources of information presented in diverse formats and media (e.g., quantitative data, video, multimedia) in order to address a question or solve a problem.	O&M	Independent living Compensatory access	Student discusses and problem solves around environmental hazards on her route from home to school.
Grades 11–12: Integrate and evaluate multiple sources of information presented in diverse formats and media (e.g., quantitative data, video, multimedia) in order to address a question or solve a problem.	Self-determination	Social interaction Compensatory access Career education	As part of instruction in problem-solving student compares and contrasts three possible solutions to a chosen problem.
Grades 11–12: Integrate and evaluate multiple sources of information presented in diverse formats and media (e.g., quantitative data, video, multimedia) in order to address a question or solve a problem.	Social interaction	Compensatory access Self-determination Social interaction	Student completes the six-step decision-making process to address negative comments with a classmate who is making comments about his optical devices.
SOCIAL SCIENCES			
Grades 6–8: Identify key steps in a text's description of a process related to history/social studies (e.g., how a bill becomes law, how interest rates are raised or lowered).	Self-determination	Independent living	Student studies the components of an IEP and the applicable law in order to begin to lead her IEPs as part of self-determination.
Grades 6–8: Identify key steps in a text's description of a process related to history/social studies (e.g., how a bill becomes law, how interest rates are raised or lowered).	Self-determination	Compensatory access Career education	Student researches ADA law and develops a timeline as part of her portfolio for accommodations.
Grade 7: Solve real-world and mathematical problems involving area, volume, and surface area of two- and three-dimensional objects composed of triangles, quadrilaterals, polygons, cubes, and right prisms.	Orientation and mobility	Independent living Career education	Student creates a model of landmarks for a new route between buildings downtown.

TABLE 14.1 *continued*

Standard	**Primary ECC areas addressed**	**Possible additional ECC content areas**	**Possible ECC instructional activity**
Grade 8: Analyze how a text makes connections among and distinctions between individuals, ideas, or events (e.g., through comparisons, analogies, or categories).	Career education	Compensatory access Orientation and mobility Self-determination	Student researches possible career choices, developing a grid that compares and contrasts each and then develops a presentation based on the research.
Grades 11–12: Follow precisely a complex multistep procedure when carrying out experiments, taking measurements, or performing technical tasks; analyze the specific results based on explanations in the text.	Independent living	Career education Self-determination Compensatory access	Student creates a budget that includes any stipends provided by vocational rehabilitation and SSI for their freshmen year in college.
TECHNOLOGY			
Grades 11–12: Integrate and evaluate multiple sources of information presented in diverse formats and media (e.g., quantitative data, video, multimedia) in order to address a question or solve a problem.	Self-determination	Assistive technology All ECC areas	Student uses technology to research and create an electronic portfolio that includes his disability statement, résumé, sample cover letter, and needed accommodations.
Grades 11–12: Integrate and evaluate multiple sources of information presented in diverse formats and media (e.g., quantitative data, video, multimedia) in order to address a question or solve a problem.	Assistive technology	Self-determination	Student problem solves when braille notetaker won't work.
COMMUNICATION			
Grade 6: Include multimedia components (e.g., graphics, images, music, sound) and visual displays in presentations to clarify information.	Compensatory skills	Sensory efficiency Assistive technology	Student listens to textbook on an audio book player and completes class assignment.
Grade 6: Present claims and findings, sequencing ideas logically and using pertinent descriptions, facts, and details to accentuate main ideas or themes; use appropriate eye contact, adequate volume, and clear pronunciation.	Self-determination	Compensatory access Sensory efficiency Social interaction	Student uses problem-solving steps to address how to complete a group project efficiently.
Grade 8: Integrate multimedia and visual displays into presentations to clarify information, strengthen claims and evidence, and add interest.	Career education	Compensatory access Sensory efficiency Assistive technology Social interaction Self-determination	Student creates a PowerPoint presentation on her chosen career path and presents to class.
Grade 8: Integrate multimedia and visual displays into presentations to clarify information, strengthen claims and evidence, and add interest.	Self-determination	Compensatory access Sensory efficiency Social interaction	Student asks participants for feedback on electronic portfolio and evaluates any needed changes.

SOURCES: Standards taken from Common Core Standards, available at www.corestandards.org/the-standards; and National Association for Sport and Physical Education, "National Standards and Grade-Level Outcomes for K–12 Physical Education," available at www.aahperd.org/naspe/standards/nationalStandards/PEstandards.cfm.

can be written for the ECC, either alone or integrated with the common core standards.

2. Become familiar with each school district's IFSP, IEP, and ITP processes and forms.
3. Determine if ECC goals and benchmarks need to be tied to state core content standards.
4. Determine if the state has braille reading, language arts, and mathematics standards or other standards that may be specific to students with visual impairments.
5. Become familiar with allowable accommodations for assessment and instruction for students who are visually impaired.
6. Write goals and benchmarks so that they are measurable.
7. Use ongoing evaluation to measure students' progress and performance.

It is important that professionals design instructional goals and benchmarks for students that are based on credible assessment, and instructional strategies that are based on research whenever possible and that adhere to best practices. As part of this overall effort, teachers need to be knowledgeable about and able to perform valid and reliable assessments in a collaborative way in the areas of the ECC. Through the use of ecological inventories and other assessment techniques (see Chapter 3 for an in-depth discussion of this topic), professionals can set priorities for what needs to be taught and can then design goals that are unique to their students' needs and incorporate the development of skills related to core content and the ECC. Although in most cases teachers of students with visual impairments provide services on a pull-out basis—often in isolation from general education or special day class settings (although this is changing as a push-in model has become more favored)—in light of the need to work effectively with other members of the student's educational team and the prevailing current emphasis on outcomes-based education, professionals providing services to students with visual impairments need to design instruction and IEP goals in consultation with other professionals and students' families. The following procedure may assist teachers and other service providers in the development and implementation of standards-based IFSPs, IEPs, and ITPs.

Step 1: Examine and Identify Standards

- Review core content standards for the student's specific grade levels. Each state's core content standards are usually available on the Department of Education's website.
- Meet with classroom teachers, family members, and the student to obtain information regarding skills and access to content for determining, along with results from assessments such as the functional vision and learning media assessments, appropriate accommodations.
- Educate families and other professionals about the areas of the ECC, explaining their relevance to the student and how the acquisition of ECC skills helps ensure access to academic learning. (See Chapter 13 for suggestions and strategies for providing information to other professionals and Chapter 15 for suggestions about providing information to families.)

Step 2: Conduct Appropriate Assessment

- Provide specialized assessment to the student in the areas of the ECC as determined by the educational team.

Step 3: Select Goals and Benchmarks

- Once the student's present levels of performance have been determined through assessment, design measurable goals and benchmarks for all identified ECC areas.
- Examine core content standards related to the student's grade and ability level, and match or align relevant content standards with the student's ECC goals. For some goals, this step may be a straightforward match. For example, a state content standard might be to "use word origins to determine the meaning of unknown words." To achieve this standard, a student who is a braille reader will need to access a braille dictionary (a compensatory access ECC skill). For other goals, teachers may need to identify standards that may seem unrelated to goal content. For example, a goal related to teaching a student about his or her visual impairment may most closely be aligned with a health education standard, such as "Students will demonstrate the ability to advocate for personal, family, and community health."
- Often an individual standard has several components. For students with visual impairments and additional disabilities, it may be useful to match a goal with only a part of a standard—this practice

is referred to as *unpacking* the standard. Teachers who unpack a standard teach one part of the standard at a time, allowing a student to work on a grade-level standard, but at a slower pace. For example, a mathematics standard may require students to generate and draw conclusions from graphing data by using line graphs, bar graphs, and pie charts. The teacher of students with visual impairments may assist the classroom teacher by teaching the student to generate and evaluate the data for a bar graph only. Once that part of the standard is achieved, the additional components of the standard can be addressed.

- Many students with visual impairments are unable to perform to the grade-level standards expected of students of the same chronological age. A standard approach is to begin by selecting the content standards that match the student's age and grade level (such as referencing the standards for grade 11 for a 16-year-old). If the student is unable to work on grade level standards, then the teacher of students with visual impairments or O&M specialist can select standards that are below the student's grade level but match the student's ability level. This strategy is referred to as *trellising*.

Step 4: Implement the Standards-Based IFSPs, IEPs, and ITPs

- Design instruction that is based on assessment and evidence-based strategies. Whenever possible, use methodologies that have been researched and tested, and that are considered best practices in the education of students with visual impairments.
- Employ teaching strategies that meet the individual and unique needs of each student: one strategy or technique does not fit all students.
- Use assessments that allow for ongoing evaluation. The teacher of students with visual impairments and O&M specialist should continuously evaluate student performance in targeted areas of the ECC that are aligned or matched with standards.

INDIVIDUALIZED FAMILY SERVICE PLANS

Since 1986, early intervention services for infants and toddlers (birth through 3 years) with disabilities have been a part of IDEA. The IFSP is a family-centered document, analogous to an IEP, that is constructed by the early intervention team for the family of a child under 3 years old. The IFSP differs from an IEP in a number of ways ("IFSP process," 2014):

1. Whenever possible, services are to be provided in a natural environment, such as in the child's home or elsewhere in the community.
2. The IFSP should address the resources, priorities, and concerns of the family and the supports and services necessary to enhance the family's capacity to meet the developmental needs of the infant or toddler with a disability.
3. The IFSP needs to include an evaluation of the child's level of functioning in all five of the following developmental areas:
    a. cognitive development
    b. physical development, including vision and hearing
    c. communication development
    d. social or emotional development
    e. adaptive development
4. In addition to the developmental domains just listed, IFSPs are required to address the three early childhood outcomes (ECOs):
    a. positive social-emotional skills, including social relationships
    b. acquisition and use of knowledge and skills, including early language/communication
    c. use of appropriate behaviors to meet their needs
5. Services are to be provided with the ultimate goal of promoting a child's optimal development in each of the five developmental areas and the three early childhood outcomes.
6. A review of the IFSP must be conducted at least every six months. New goals (called "outcomes" on an IFSP) may be written during these periodic reviews. A meeting must be held annually to evaluate the IFSP for a child and the child's family, and, as appropriate, to revise its provisions.
7. Services are to be provided year round rather than only during the school year.
8. Service coordination may be provided by a school district or a private agency case manager, depending on who has responsibility for ensuring delivery of services.

Increasingly, statewide assessments and standards are being expanded to include states' preschool, toddler, and infant populations. California, for example, uses an instrument called the Desired Results Developmental Profile (DRDP) against which young children need to be evaluated. Most, if not all, of the measures and standards used in the DRDP can be used with or in reference to the ECC. Either the statements in the DRDP themselves can be used to assess progress in regard to the ECC, or the conditions under which the measures are evaluated can include components of the ECC. The following case study of a toddler illustrates how ECC-related content can be integrated into the outcomes selected for a child's IFSP based on California's standards as laid out in the DRDP. (Readers should note that in some instances terminology used in California's DRDP has been changed for clarification purposes for this book.)

Sample Integration of ECC Content and IFSP Outcome: Meet T.J.

Background

T.J. is 2 years, 8 months old and is functionally blind due to cortical visual impairment (CVI). He responds by looking briefly at a red pom-pom and a strand of large red beads against a black background and turns his head toward a light source. T.J. is an only child and lives with his parents. T.J.'s father works full-time. His mother, who is eight months pregnant, works part-time. His maternal grandmother has come to the United States on a special visa from Cambodia to assist in T.J.'s care and looks after him when his parents are at work. She speaks only Cambodian to him. His parents speak to T.J. both in Cambodian and in English. His early intervention specialists speak with his parents and with T.J. in English. In addition to CVI, T.J. has infantile spasms that are not well controlled. The family has tried many seizure medications and a special diet to try to get the seizures under control. His early intervention services include weekly physical and occupational therapy. Currently T.J. is in a center-based program for toddlers with developmental delays. His teacher of visual impairments visits him once every two weeks at the center and provides on-going consultation to T.J.'s family and teachers.

T.J.'s Current Levels of Functioning upon Assessment

Cognitive development: Based on assessment using the Hawaii Early Learning Profile (Parks, 2006), T.J. has cognitive skills averaging in the 3- to 4-month range.

Physical development: At this time, T.J. can roll over in both directions and can prop himself up briefly while on his tummy. He is beginning to prop sit, with weight bearing through his shoulders. He does not reach out for objects on his own, but will interact with objects his hands encounter while lying under a toy frame.

Communication development: T.J.'s mother says he has different cries for discomfort, for hunger, and for boredom. He makes occasional open vowel sounds. When he is excited (as when he sees a red pom-pom), he makes a series of open vowel sounds and moves his arms from the shoulder.

Socio-emotional development: T.J. recognizes his parents' and grandmother's voices and smiles when he hears them. He does not call out for attention. Much of his attention appears to be directed toward his bodily experiences, as he smiles and cries when it is not obvious what is prompting him.

Adaptive development: T.J.'s visual skills in carefully controlled environments are improving. He looks at objects for increasingly longer periods of time and looks at a wider variety of objects with slightly different properties. He can grasp an object with both hands and bring it to his mouth. He can use his thigh to turn on a switch and is beginning to use his hand to find and turn on a yellow switch to play a tape recorder with music he likes or a disco ball. He listens carefully to auditory input.

Family Concerns

T.J.'s mother is most concerned about his seizures, as she believes they are not only upsetting to T.J., but they are delaying his development. T.J. spends a lot of time mouthing and biting his hands and his family would like to find a way to stop this behavior. His family would like to see him learn to sit on his own, crawl, and walk. His mother and grandmother are distressed that they are frequently not able to determine what is upsetting T.J. when he cries.

IFSP Developmental Area: Communication Development

Desired result: Children are personally and socially competent

Measure: Expresses self through language

Developmental level: Child does actions and makes sounds intentionally but does not yet realize he or she can communicate something using his or her behavior

Desired outcome: By six-month review date, T.J. will make sounds or initiate actions that will be interpreted as attempts to attract attention to himself. Examples might be crying when he cannot hear another person, calling out in a loud voice when he cannot hear another person, or pressing a communication switch that calls out, "Mama!"

Relevant ECC areas: Social interaction and self-determination

Teaching focus: To accomplish this result, the teacher of students with visual impairments will focus on the following:

- using a communication matrix to observe and analyze skills introduced and taught to T.J.'s family and other early intervention providers
- using a talking switch, such as a Big Mack

IFSP Developmental Area: Physical and Cognitive Development

Desired results: Children are effective learners.

Measures:

- Shows cognitive competence and problem solving skills through play and daily activities
- Pursues knowledge or understanding of new materials or activities.

Developmental level: Child stores, retrieves, and uses visual information about both familiar and unfamiliar objects and people.

Desired outcomes:

- By the six-month review, T.J. will view for 10 seconds a red pom-pom, a red slinky, and a red hat against a black Invisiboard with a black blanket on the floor. Once achieved, he will work on looking at his teacher when she is sitting in front of the Invisiboard while wearing the red hat.
- By the six-month review, T.J. will recognize and smile at Elmo when Elmo is in front of the Invisiboard on a black blanket.
- By the six-month review, T.J. will simultaneously grasp three different objects (other than a pom-pom and beads) with one hand or both hands or an object in each hand while lying or sitting.

Relevant ECC areas: Sensory efficiency

Teaching focus: To achieve these outcomes, the teacher of students with visual impairments will focus on the following:

- ensuring a controlled environment for T.J.
- using an Invisiboard and black blanket for viewing objects in isolation
- determining the signs that indicate T.J. is looking or not looking at something
- teaching other service providers the hand-under-hand method of presenting objects to T.J.
- teaching other service providers a toy offering technique, as demonstrated by Lilli Nielsen videos (www.lilliworks.com)
- identifying appropriate toys for T.J.
- providing a toy "vest" for T.J., so that whenever he touches his chest, he will encounter objects to feel
- teaching others how to cue T.J. that he is about to be moved from one place to another

The identified IFSP outcomes for T.J. address three of the five areas that the families prioritized—cognitive, sensory, and socio-emotional development—as well as important ECC areas.

INDIVIDUALIZED EDUCATION PROGRAMS

Mandated for all school-age students with disabilities, the IEP is designed to provide a framework for what the student will learn over the course of a calendar year. IEPs begin to be developed for a student when he or she enters a school program at age 3 and end when the student exits a school program (no later than age 22). IEPs for students who are blind or visually impaired need to focus on the areas of the ECC while integrating core curriculum content.

When creating standards-based IEPs, professionals need to include the following:

1. A statement of the student's academic achievement and functional performance
2. A statement of measurable annual goals, including academic and functional goals
3. A description of how the student's progress toward meeting the annual goals will be measured and when periodic reports on progress toward the

annual goal will be provided (such as through the use of quarterly or other periodic reports, concurrent with the issuance of report cards)

4. A statement of the special education and related services and supplementary aides and services that will be provided
5. An explanation of the extent, if any, to which the student will not participate with nondisabled students in the regular class and in activities
6. A statement of any individual appropriate accommodations that are necessary to measure the academic achievement and functional performance of the student on state or district-wide assessments
7. If relevant, a statement detailing why the IEP team has determined that the student shall be evaluated by means of an alternate assessment on a particular state or district-wide assessment of student achievement

The following sections provide some examples of how core content standards and ECC-related goals may be integrated and suggest some activities that might be appropriate to help meet each standard. (The standards relate to the third, fifth, and eighth grades and the material presented is adapted from California's Special Education Administrators of County Offices of Education [Special Education, 2000].)

Integration of Core Content Standards and ECC Goals: Vocabulary and Concept Development

Third Grade

State content standard: Use a dictionary to learn the meaning and other features of unknown words.

Braille standard: Use a braille dictionary to learn the meaning and other features of unknown words.

ECC-related activities:

- Introduce the student to a braille, print, online, or talking dictionary and practice using it to complete general education assignments (assistive technology, sensory efficiency).
- Demonstrate how a dictionary is used by determining the first letter of the word, using guide words, and locating the specific word (compensatory access, assistive technology, sensory efficiency).
- Have the student design his or her own dictionary by listing new words related to cooking terms and food items encountered in ECC-related lessons and finding their definitions, with and without assistance (independent living).
- Have the student design a dictionary of O&M terms (orientation and mobility).

Fifth Grade

State content standard: Use word origins to determine the meaning of unknown words.

Braille standard: Same as state content standard.

Alternative standards:

- Understand that printed materials provide information.
- Identify environmental symbols/signs/cues.
- Match a symbol/cue to an activity or function.
- Follow a list or schedule of activities.

ECC-related activities:

- Determine the origin of a word by using a braille, print, or auditory dictionary (compensatory, assistive technology, sensory efficiency).
- Play a game in which the student has to guess the origin of a word by its sound; students whose guesses are challenged must check them in a braille, print, or auditory dictionary (recreation and leisure, compensatory access, assistive technology, sensory efficiency).
- Have the student create a list of food words that have a foreign origin (pizza, crepe, bologna, taco), but are commonly used in daily life (compensatory access and independent living).
- Have the student create a word list of commonly used sayings that have a foreign origin (top o' the mornin', *capiche?*) (compensatory access and social interaction).
- Have the student read or listen to stories and information about the customs of other countries, in which words are used and explained (compensatory access, social interaction).

Eighth Grade

State content standard: Analyze idioms, analogies, metaphors, and similes to infer the literal and figurative meanings of phrases.

Braille standard: Same as state content standard.

Alternative standards:

- Read one-syllable or high-frequency words.
- Identify high-frequency functional words (those that are important in everyday life, such as "stop" or "exit").
- Share information and ideas, speaking audibly in complete, coherent sentences.
- Communicate information using a complete sentence, gestures, actions, voice output devices, or vocalizations.

ECC-related activities:

- Use idioms in group discussions (social interaction).
- Use problem-solving strategies in O&M lessons to demonstrate the difference between literal and figurative language (compensatory access, O&M, career and self-determination).
- Use real objects (the literal) and objects of representation (the figurative) to support the student's learning of a concept (for example, introducing the student to a stuffed animal dog and a real dog) (compensatory access).

(Reading and language arts standards and mathematics standards with ECC-related activities can be found on the website of the California School for the Blind [www.csb-cde.ca.gov]. As of this writing, Utah has also created braille reading and mathematics standards.)

In addition, the following two student scenarios provide examples of appropriate IEP content for students with different needs.

Sample IEP Content: Meet Jessica

Background

Jessica is 8 years old. She has been blind since birth due to retinopathy of prematurity. Jessica's primary learning medium is braille, and her secondary learning medium is auditory input. Although Jessica is included in a third-grade classroom, her academic skills are estimated to be at the second-grade level as measured by the *Woodcock-Johnson III: Diagnostic Reading Battery* (Woodcock, Mather, &. Schrank, 2011) and the *Johns Basic Reading Inventory* (Johns, 2008). Jessica receives direct support from a teacher of students with visual impairment three times a week for one hour each day. Also, Jessica receives O&M instruction one time per week for one hour. She receives speech and language therapy in a group setting once every week for articulation and pragmatic (social language) issues. She also receives assistance from an instructional aide who supports all the children in Jessica's classroom. Consultation is provided by an adapted physical education teacher.

Focus of Jessica's Program

Jessica's IEP focuses on the following ECC areas:

- compensatory access skills of braille reading and writing, organization, and math concepts (purchasing/money)
- assistive technology
- sensory efficiency including listening skills
- social interaction
- orientation and mobility

Goal 1: Braille Reading

Present level of performance: Jessica is able to read all braille contractions with 100 percent accuracy. She is able to answer simple comprehension questions about factual information using text from first-grade materials. She has not had experience finding information from diagrams, charts, or graphs.

Grade 3 state content standard: Interpret information from diagrams, charts, and graphs.

Braille reading standards:

- Interpret information from diagrams, charts, and graphs by using systematic tactile scanning.
- Use transcriber's notes.
- Use both hands in a coordinated fashion to access information simultaneously on two different pages (such as reading a graph or map with one hand and the accompanying key with the other hand).

Annual goal: By the time of the annual review, the student will read five second-grade–level stories in contracted braille and recall important factual information by using diagrams, charts, and graphs with 80 percent accuracy on 4 out of 5 trials as measured by work samples and pre- and post-test evaluations.

Teaching focus: To accomplish the annual goal, Jessica's teacher of students with visual impairments will focus instruction on the following:

- introducing transcriber's notes that describe a diagram or graph
- teaching systematic tactile scanning of graphs, charts, and diagrams

- teaching systematic tactile scanning of maps and use of a key

Goal 2: Braille Writing

Present level of performance: Jessica uses a Perkins braillewriter to write sentences and short paragraphs. She is familiar with the parts of a braille notetaking device, but has not used one for class assignments.

Grade 3 state content standard: Write a friendly letter complete with the date, salutation, body, closing, and signature.

Braille reading standard: Using a braillewriter, braille notetaking device, or screen reader, write a friendly letter complete with the date, salutation, body, closing, and signature.

Annual goal: By the time of the annual review, the student will write a friendly letter or thank-you note using correct format on the braillewriter and braille notetaker, containing date, salutation, body, closing, and signature with 80 percent accuracy on 4 out of 5 trials. Accuracy to be determined by a rubric or scoring tool developed by the IEP team to score use and correct formatting of all five parts of the letter or note. (For more information on progress monitoring, assessment, and the use of rubrics, see Chapter 3.)

Teaching focus: To accomplish the annual goal, Jessica's teacher of students with visual impairments will focus instruction on the following:

- using the braillewriter to format a friendly letter using margins, line spacing, and indentation
- using the braille notetaker to write a friendly letter: creating a file, opening a file, naming a file, formatting a letter, saving the file, printing the letter
- promoting an understanding of the concepts of paying complements and of reciprocation through the writing of a friendly letter or thank-you note
- writing one's signature

Goal 3: Mathematics

Present level of performance: Jessica is able to add multi-digit numbers. She is familiar with a talking calculator, and is able to add numbers on the abacus without carrying.

Grade 2 state content standard: Add and subtract three-digit whole numbers that require regrouping.

Braille mathematics standard: Using the braillewriter or abacus, set up three-digit addition and subtraction problems with regrouping.

Annual goal: By the time of the annual review, the student will calculate the cost of three items on a shopping trip by using an abacus and a talking calculator to check the total amount with 90 percent accuracy on 4 out of 5 trips using a checklist of skills to measure successful completion of each step in the purchasing process.

Teaching focus: To accomplish the annual goal, Jessica's O&M specialist and teacher of students with visual impairments will coordinate and focus their instruction on the following:

- creating a shopping list on the braillewriter
- traveling to the grocery store to purchase items
- learning the cost of selected items
- teaching simple addition and subtraction calculations with the abacus
- teaching making purchase with the talking calculator

Sample IEP Content: Meet Andrew

Background

Andrew is an extremely bright 13-year-old who is mainstreamed into honors classes at his local middle school. Andrew was diagnosed at age 9 with a brain tumor that caused damage to his optic nerves before it was removed. Andrew's measured visual acuities are 20/800 with best correction in both eyes. Andrew uses a combination of braille, print, and recorded material to complete class assignments. He is functioning above grade level in English, mathematics, science, and social studies. He is also learning to use assistive technology and low vision devices to help with the myriad assignments he must complete. He receives services from a teacher of students with visual impairments three times per week for a total of 120 minutes. Also, he works with an O&M specialist one time per week for 90 minutes. Andrew receives no additional services. Although some of Andrew's goals focus on academic content, they include the areas of the ECC.

Focus of Andrew's Program

Andrew's teacher of students with visual impairments and O&M instructor work together to develop goals and objectives that meet his unique educational needs. The following ECC areas are included on Andrew's IEP:

- assistive technology
- compensatory access
- orientation and mobility
- self-determination
- social interaction
- career education

Goal 1: Research

Present level of performance: Andrew has been introduced to using the Internet by using a screen reader (JAWS). He has completed research reports with the support of a personal reader, but has not located information using assistive technology. Also, Andrew has not made formal presentations using PowerPoint.

Grade 8 state content standards:

Write a research report that satisfies the following criteria:

- defines a thesis
- reports important ideas, concepts, and direct quotations from significant information sources, and paraphrases and summarizes all perspectives on the topic, as appropriate
- uses a variety of primary and secondary sources and distinguishes the nature and value of each
- organizes and displays information on charts, maps, and graphs

Braille reading standard: Use a screen reader, scanner, and other assistive technology to complete assignments including a research report.

Annual goal: By the time of the annual review, the student will complete a research project related to his visual impairment using the Internet and other computer-based resources, and present the information via a PowerPoint presentation. The presentation and project will be evaluated by completion of each component of the grade 8 standard, as defined in a rubric.

Teaching focus: To accomplish the annual goal, Andrew's teacher of students with visual impairments will focus instruction on the following:

- using the Internet with a screen reader or video magnification software
- scanning pertinent information using adaptive scanning devices
- discussing the student's visual impairment with him
- using PowerPoint to present information
- employing appropriate social skills when giving a presentation

To accomplish the annual goal, Andrew's O&M specialist will focus instruction on:

- moving easily around the classroom when making a presentation
- disclosing one's visual impairment or information about specific needs to strangers or acquaintances in the community

Goal 2: Career Development

Present level of performance: Andrew uses a screen reader to complete class assignments. He has written letters to friends, but has not written a formal business letter, nor has he used assistive technology to complete a job application.

Grade 8 state content standard: Write documents related to career development, including simple business letters and job applications.

Braille reading standard: Using screen readers, scanners, or video magnification devices, write documents related to career development, including simple business letters and job applications.

Annual goal: By the time of the annual review, the student will explore three careers of interest and interview and/or visit three employed adults with visual impairments who have jobs related to the student's interest. Andrew will be evaluated based on his accurate completion of information worksheets on each of the three reports.

Teaching focus: To accomplish the annual goal, Andrew's teacher of students with visual impairments will focus instruction on the following:

- completing job applications and information worksheets
- interviewing employers about jobs of interest on the telephone or in person
- demonstrating social skills appropriate for telephone conversation (introducing oneself, taking turns)
- using appropriate social greetings with potential employers

Goal 3: Assistive Technology

Present level of performance: Andrew understands how to calculate rate and percentage problems by using a talking calculator. He uses a braille notetaking device for keeping track of class assignments, schedules, and his address book. He has not been introduced to the scientific calculator function of the notetaker.

Grade 8 standard, algebra: Use algebraic techniques to solve rate problems, work problems, and percent mixture problems.

Braille mathematics standard: Using a braille notetaker with the scientific calculator function, use algebraic techniques to solve rate problems, work problems, and percent mixture problems.

Annual goal: By the time of the annual review, the student will use the scientific calculator function on the BrailleNote to solve problems with 90 percent accuracy on 4 out of 5 trials while using real life examples.

Teaching focus: To accomplish the annual goal, Andrew's teacher of students with visual impairments will focus instruction on the following:

- using the braille notetaker
- using the scientific calculator function of the notetaker
- performing price comparisons for shopping
- using the scientific calculator function of the notetaker when shopping

The two scenarios just described demonstrate how parts of a student's IEP can address the concerns related to the ECC identified by the IEP team and link to standards related to core content. This linkage can be fairly straightforward if the IEP team keeps in mind that students with visual impairments can meet core content standards with the appropriate interventions, accommodations, and special teacher services.

INDIVIDUALIZED TRANSITION PROGRAMS

Most states have developed IEP forms that include transition requirements for students 14 or 16 years of age (depending on state regulations) and that are used statewide. Transition services are a coordinated set of activities focused on improving the academic and functional achievement of the student with an IEP and are intended to prepare the student for the transition to adulthood beyond school. IDEA (2004) notes under the "Definition of Individualized Education Program" (300.320) that transition services should begin no later than the first IEP to be in effect when the child turns 16, or younger if determined appropriate to do so by the IEP team, and updated annually. Thereafter the IEP must include: (1) appropriate measureable postsecondary goals based upon age-appropriate transition assessments related to training, education, employment and, where appropriate, independent living skills; and (2) transition services (including course of study) needed to assist the student in reaching those goals. IDEA 2004 brought with it a new standard for ITPs, moving toward a results-oriented process in the areas of education, living, and working that requires assessments, activities, or instruction, and ongoing evaluation to show progress.

A critical partner in developing an ITP is a disability-specific vocational rehabilitation counselor. The counselor assists in developing collaborative activities to address chosen outcomes. The counselor brings a wealth of information about opportunities within the state and region to assist the student in reaching post-school goals. Some vocational rehabilitation agencies offer weekend or summer opportunities to build or enhance a student's skill set and become a true collaborative partner in teaching ECC areas. If these opportunities are not available, organizations of people who are blind, such as the American Council of the Blind or the National Federation of the Blind (see the Resources section at the back of this book), offer innovative transition programs that may be available locally or online. For example, the Jernigan Center in Baltimore offers programs in science and assistive technology. In addition, some schools for blind students and local agencies such as community rehabilitation providers offer short courses and summer programs that focus on career development, activities of independent living, and assistive technology. Some schools offer fifth-year programs that are for transition-age students who have graduated from high school. Other resources include the American Foundation for the Blind CareerConnect website (www.afb.org/CareerConnect).

ITPs are an essential part of the IEP process for transition-age students with visual impairments. Typically, ITPs include the following areas: career/vocational, education/training, independent living skills, recreation/leisure, and community travel. In addition, the ITP should include the following elements (Bateman, n.d.):

1. Student's (with family's assistance if needed) chosen post-school outcome(s)
2. Identification of ECC-related skills needed for chosen post-school outcome(s)
3. Review of ECC-related screening tool(s) and valid assessments to identify the student's strengths and needs related to skills needed for the chosen outcome(s)
4. Development or review of a program of studies that addresses chosen post-school outcome(s) over the course of the next four years (for example, whether a diploma is required, higher-level coursework that may be needed, vocational classes that may be needed)
5. A list of the student's strengths and needs
6. Measurable goal(s) statement(s) and objectives (if required) for each need listed in item 5
7. A link between the goal(s) and the state standards or alternate expectations

The following student scenarios demonstrate how alignment can be achieved among transition goals, the ECC, and state requirements.

Alignment of ITP, ECC, and State Requirements: Meet Evan

Background

Evan is a 17-year-old student with low vision due to albinism who exhibits an identified learning disability in reading. He goes to the special education classroom for work in reading to improve his literacy skills. He just recently received a low vision exam for the first time and was prescribed optical devices for near and distant tasks, as well as a bioptic driving aid. Evan has been using a magnification device in the classroom for near tasks and physically moves to the whiteboard to access distant tasks in the classroom. Large-print books are ordered every year, but typically remain on the bookshelf and are not accessed for schoolwork. Evan's mom has been reading his schoolwork to him at home since he started school.

Evan has a four-year program of study in place and is on track to graduate with his peers with a basic diploma. Evan does not currently have a rehabilitation counselor from the state's vocational rehabilitation agency, but a representative from this agency has been invited to participate and collaborate on his transition IEP.

Transition Outcomes for Evan

- Employment—work as a plumber at his father's business
- Education and training—complete a technical program to obtain a license as a certified plumber
- Independent living—would like to live in his own apartment

ECC Focus of Evan's IEP

- Sensory efficiency—learn the efficient and effective use of prescribed optical devices (for near and distance work in the classroom or school environment). Instruction will be provided in the classroom during study hall (5 hours per week for 6 weeks, with maintenance provided for 12 weeks at 1 hour a week) and monitored during general education classes by the general education teacher and student. Bioptic training will be conducted by an optometrist who teaches driver education for patients.
- Compensatory access—reading fluency will be practiced with the special education teacher using the student's optical device. Instruction will be provided during literacy instruction in the special education classroom (3.5 hours per week for 18 weeks, fading to 2 hours per week for the remaining 18 weeks) and monitored by the special education teacher and student daily.
- Orientation and mobility—work on efficient travel using a monocular with the O&M specialist.

Goal 1: Reading: Use of Near and Distance Vision

Present level of performance: Evan is not able to describe or demonstrate proper function and use of optical devices as measured by *Evaluating Visually Impaired Students* (Texas School for the Blind and Visually Impaired, 2007). He has difficulty finding specific content in textbooks and locating information on the whiteboard. In the community, Evan cannot read street signs from a distance, nor can he read menus in fast food restaurants.

Common core content reading standards for literacy in history/social studies/science (grades 6–12):

- Integrate information from diverse sources, both primary and secondary, into a coherent understanding of idea or event, noting discrepancies among sources.

- Follow a multi-step procedure when carrying out experiments, taking measurements, or performing technical tasks; analyze the specific results based on explanations in the text.

Integrated transition goals:

- After 6 weeks of instruction, using his magnifier, Evan will locate 5 job titles and 5 facts about each job from the *Dictionary of Occupational Titles* within a 20-minute period with 100 percent accuracy on 4 out of 5 trials (career education and assistive technology).
- After 6 weeks of instruction, Evan will read using his near optical device and copy 35 words per minute with 100 percent accuracy when using his social studies textbook on 4 out of 5 trials (compensatory access and sensory efficiency).
- After 36 weeks of instruction, Evan will fluently read student-selected fiction and non-fiction materials on an eighth-grade reading level at 100 words per minute using his magnifier, and answer comprehension questions about what has been read with 95 percent accuracy (compensatory access and sensory efficiency).
- During an O&M lesson in the community, Evan will read 5 street signs with his monocular with 100 percent proficiency (sensory efficiency and O&M).
- Using his near optical device, Evan will find and read 2 recipes from cooking magazines to be used for a cooking activity within a 20-minute time period on 4 out of 5 trials (sensory efficiency and independent living).

Teaching focus: To accomplish these goals, Evan's teacher of students with visual impairments will focus on the following:

- providing instruction in the function and use of Evan's prescribed near optical device for use in the classroom, in the school environment, and in the community
- teaching Evan to complete a job application using his near optical device
- providing instruction in the function and use of the prescribed monocular for classroom and community use
- developing data sheets with Evan so that he can self-monitor his fluency (grade level of materials, words read per minute, and comprehension rate)

To accomplish these goals, Evan's O&M instructor will focus on teaching Evan the following:

- scanning using the monocular
- scanning for information in textbooks
- locating street signs using the pole of the street sign as a guide
- stopping and using the monocular to locate street signs while walking

Goal 2: Writing: Use of Near and Distance Vision

Present level of performance: Evan has not yet learned to demonstrate the use and function of his newly prescribed monocular or magnifier. Evan copied 8 words per minute with 75 percent accuracy from the whiteboard using his newly prescribed optical device.

Common core content writing standard:

- Produce clear and coherent writing in which the development, organization, and style are appropriate to the task, purpose, and audience.
- Write routinely over extended time periods and shorter time periods for a range of tasks, purposes, and audiences.

Integrated transition goals:

- After 6 weeks of instruction, Evan will copy 15 words per minute with 100 percent accuracy off of a whiteboard during English Literature class using his distant optical device (sensory efficiency and compensatory access).
- After 6 weeks of instruction, Evan will complete a summer job application for his father's plumbing business with 100 percent accuracy using his near optical device (career education and sensory efficiency).
- After 6 weeks of instruction, using his magnifier, Evan will accurately copy the information from two food recipes to construct a shopping list with 100 percent accuracy on 4 out of 5 trials (independent living and sensory efficiency).
- After 15 weeks of instruction, using his monocular, Evan will determine the prices for food items at his favorite fast food restaurant with 100 percent accuracy on 4 out of 5 trials (independent living and sensory efficiency).

To accomplish these goals, Evan's teacher of students with visual impairments will focus on the following:

- providing instruction in the function and use of the prescribed magnification device for copying information in the classroom, in the school environment, and in the community
- teaching Evan to complete a job application using the magnifier
- providing instruction in the function and use of the prescribed monocular for copying information in the classroom and in the community
- developing data sheets with Evan for use in self-monitoring the time spent copying information using the magnifier and the monocular
- teaching Evan to scan for information in textbooks and record information
- teaching Evan to complete a job application using the magnifier
- providing opportunities for Evan to read and copy favorite recipes into a recipe binder

To accomplish these goals, Evan's O&M instructor will focus on the following:

- teaching Evan to read from a menu in a fast food restaurant using the monocular

Goal 3: Career Education

Present level of performance: Although Evan has worked at his father's business during summers, he is unable to identify the job skills needed as a plumber and requirements for licensure in his chosen field as measured by a teacher-developed checklist. In addition, he has not explored possible technical schools in his area that offer apprenticeship training in the area of plumbing.

Common core content writing standards:

- Conduct short as well as more sustained research projects to answer a question or solve a problem.
- Gather relevant information from multiple authoritative print and digital sources, using advanced searches effectively; assess the strengths and limitations of each source in terms of the specific task, purpose, and audience; integrate information into the text selectively to maintain the flow of ideas, avoiding plagiarism and overreliance on any one source and following a standard format for citations.

Integrated transition goals:

- Using multiple resources (in print and online), Evan will explore the needed skill set for an apprentice plumber and create an electronic presentation describing this skill set that incorporates a skills checklist (assistive technology and career education). Accuracy to be determined through use of a rubric.
- Using the Internet, Evan will locate and explore three technical schools in his geographic area using the checklist developed as a guide to identify appropriate programs with 100 percent accuracy (compensatory access and career education).
- Evan will arrange for tours of at least two technical schools and develop a compare-and-contrast essay describing the cost, travel options, accessibility, and coursework available at each with 100 percent accuracy (independent living, O&M, compensatory access, career education, and self-determination).
- After completing his job exploration and tour of potential schools, Evan will develop and implement an action plan delineating needed steps and timelines to complete paperwork for admission to his chosen program with 100 percent accuracy (career education and self-determination).

Teaching focus: To accomplish these goals, Evan's teacher of students with visual impairments will focus on:

- working with Evan to construct career-related checklists and a career-related action plan
- working with Evan on designing and presenting a PowerPoint presentation on his career choices
- teaching Evan to use the Internet to locate technical schools and their requirements
- assisting Evan to evaluate his personal characteristics with those needed for this line of work

To accomplish these goals, Evan's O&M instructor will focus on the following:

- reviewing transportation options with Evan for selected training programs
- assisting Evan in planning routes, and accessing public transportation to get to specific job tours
- teaching Evan to access Internet map sites to obtain directions to the training schools

Alignment of ITP, ECC, and State Requirements: Meet José

Background

José is a 19-year-old student with low vision due to optic nerve hypoplasia (ONH). Ophthalmological reports indicate that José's visual acuity is 20/800 in both eyes. He also exhibits a significant intellectual disability and participates in his school district's alternate assessment. His initial assessment, completed by his teacher of students with visual impairments and O&M specialist, found that he is able to access printed materials that use a 24-inch font and 5-inch pictures with good contrast. He has not had a low vision evaluation and does not have prescribed optical devices. He uses a calendar system effectively for his daily routines and is able to use colored photographs of the activities on his calendar system. He is currently in a community transition program working at a department store, where he sorts and attaches security bars to merchandise; at a local zoo, where he sorts and measures the food for a small group of animals; and at a food distribution center, where he sorts and fills bags with food and other grocery items. José is able to travel independently around each worksite. He walks to school with his sibling or catches a ride with his mother on her way to work when his younger brother is not available.

José is able to complete basic personal hygiene tasks. He is able to shower, shave, and dress himself independently. He requires assistance to prepare simple meals at home. José is quite social and enjoys talking to his coworkers during break time at work.

José has a five-year program of study in place and is not on track to graduate with his peers. He will remain in school for an additional year to complete instruction in specific ECC areas that include independent living, social interaction, and career development. José will receive a certificate of attendance in lieu of a general education diploma. He has a rehabilitation counselor from the state vocational rehabilitation agency and José and his counselor are exploring post-school programs, such as sheltered employment (at, for example, Goodwill) and independent living programs.

José's teacher of students with visual impairments works collaboratively with José's transition team to ensure that all of his materials are in an accessible format. For example, the teacher of students with visual impairments reviews José's routines and activities three weeks in advance to make sure that the calendar system pictures are appropriate to maximize José's visual functioning at each worksite. Also, the teacher of students with visual impairments co-teaches at one of the three worksites each week for two hours per week, to provide input about how to best accommodate José's visual needs and set up work tasks so that José acquires greater independence and autonomy. The O&M specialist consults with the transition team on effective ways to promote independent travel during break times and at lunch. The teacher of students with visual impairments and the O&M specialist meet with the team to collaborate on a monthly basis. Each team member takes turns collecting data on the speed and accuracy of each job task performed at each job site. In addition, the teacher of students with visual impairments works with José on providing personal information for job applications, understanding who should receive personal information (teaching José the concept of a stranger, acquaintance, friend, and family member), and purchasing snacks and lunch to prepare in a microwave at the worksite.

Transition Outcomes

- Employment—Work with the Department of Rehabilitation to place José at the local grocery store as a bagger and customer service assistance with the support of a job coach.
- Education and Training—José will attend a post-secondary independent living program in his community to improve independent living skills and O&M skills.
- Independent Living—José would like to live in a group home with opportunities to cook, clean, and participate in community recreational activities.

ECC Focus of José's IEP

- Career education—learn a sequence of job tasks using a calendar system
- Independent living—learn skills to live in a group home
- Social interaction—know the difference between a stranger, acquaintance, or friend and who can be given personal information

Goal 1: Career Education: Sequencing Job Tasks

Present level of performance: José was able to complete only one step of a four-step picture sequence in one work environment using a calendar system.

José was able to identify individual pictures, but was unable to connect each step in the completed job sequence.

Common core content reading standard: Analyze a complex set of ideas or sequence of events and explain how specific individuals, ideas, or events interact and develop over the course of the text.

Alternate performance indicators (data analysis and probability): Recognize representations of data using concrete objects, pictures, and simple graphs.

Integrated transition goal: After 36 weeks of instruction José will complete a four-step task, using his calendar system with 100 percent accuracy in three different work environments on 5 of 5 trials as measured by a teacher-made rubric for each worksite.

Teaching focus: To accomplish the integrated transition goal, José's teacher of students with visual impairments will focus on:

- visually recognizing information provided in pictures
- following a sequence of tasks using a calendar system
- completing specific jobs using a pictorial calendar system
- performing specific work behaviors (following directions, staying on task, increasing speed and accuracy to complete a job task)

Goal 2: Independent Living Skills

Present level of performance: At each worksite, José has access to a small café where he can purchase snacks and lunch. He enjoys break time, using pictures to find the items he wishes to purchase. In preparation for living in a group home, José is learning to use the microwave. He can locate the on and off buttons, but needs to learn how to use the number pad to cook a snack or simple meal.

Common core content reading standard: Follow precisely a complex multistep procedure when carrying out experiments, taking measurements, or performing technical tasks; analyze the specific results based on explanations in the text.

Alternate reading performance indicators: Develop the reading and listening skills necessary for word recognition, comprehension, interpretation, analysis, and evaluation.

Integrated transition goal: By the end of the academic year, José will follow a pictorial sequence to prepare five different microwavable snacks or lunch items (such as popcorn, burritos, hot pockets, and soup) that he has purchased with assistance with 80 percent accuracy on four out of five trials, as measured by a teacher-made task analysis. (For more discussion of task analysis and other assessment, instructional, and scoring techniques, see Chapter 3.)

Teaching focus: To accomplish this integrated transition goal, José's teacher of students with visual impairments will focus on the following:

- visual sequencing of pictures
- following pictorial directions
- locating numbers on the microwave
- setting the time on the microwave using the number pad
- taking the cooked item out of the microwave

Goal 3: Social Interaction

Present level of performance: José is quite friendly, and enjoys talking to his friends and coworkers. In preparation for completing job applications, José has learned to provide personal information (name, address, cell phone number, home telephone number, and social security number) using a series of printed information cards. During casual conversations during break time, José provides this information to his coworkers. José does not know the difference between a stranger, an acquaintance, and a friend. Also, he does not differentiate to whom personal information can be given.

Common core speaking and listening standard: Present information, findings, and supporting evidence, conveying a clear and distinct perspective, such that alternative or opposing perspectives are addressed, and the organization, development, substance, and style are appropriate to purpose, audience, and a range of formal and informal tasks.

Alternate performance indicators: Develop the structure and creative skills of the writing process necessary to produce written language that can be read, presented to, and interpreted by various audiences.

Integrated transition goal: Within 36 weeks, using role-playing scenarios, José will demonstrate who can receive personal information, on 5 out of 5 trials with 100 percent accuracy as measured by a skills checklist in the *Safe and Sound Curriculum* (Dowling & Greenberg, 2007).

Teaching focus: To accomplish this goal, José's teacher of students with visual impairments will focus on the following:

- developing a method of providing personal information (such as social security number, date of birth) for a job application
- teaching the concepts of public and private
- developing the ability to distinguish between a stranger, acquaintance, friend, and family member
- developing the ability to determine who receives personal information

These transition plan examples provide evidence of how José's and Evan's transition teams developed parts of their ITPs so that common core standards and transition goals would link to the ECC-related goals that are desirable for students with visual impairments who are preparing to function in society as working adults.

ONGOING EVALUATION

In order to create effective standards-based IFSPs, IEPs, and ITPs, the teacher of students with visual impairments needs to have current evaluation data for each student in all areas of the ECC. Ongoing evaluation is essential, as it documents students' progress for the determination of IFSP, IEP, and ITP goals and facilitates the planning of instruction in the areas of the ECC. Chapter 3 of this book offers a comprehensive discussion of assessment and evaluation. The evaluation process discussed there provides for continuous assessment of student outcomes over time.

CONCLUSION

The integration of core content standards with the ECC is a critical goal for professionals and families to achieve for students with visual impairments. This process requires collaboration among general education teachers, teachers of students with visual impairments, O&M specialists, early intervention specialists, and vocational rehabilitation counselors. During a time or in localities when specialized services for students with visual impairments may be questioned because of economic constraints, philosophical perspectives, or other factors, it is important for teachers and families to have the tools needed to document students' progress in a systematic way. Presenting anecdotal information regarding student-related outcomes is not sufficient, and the documentation of these outcomes needs to be based on measurable indicators and lead to goals valued by schools and society. By setting goals for students that enable them to meet state requirements, teachers can help students benefit educationally and ensure that the ECC, so essential to educational progress, is supported and affirmed.

REFERENCES

Association of California School Administrators, Special Services/Special Education Council. (2007). *The ACSA handbook of goals & objectives related to state of California standards.* Sacramento, CA: ACSA Media Relations.

Bateman, B. D. (n.d.). Legal requirements for transition components of the IEP. Retrieved from Wrightslaw, http://www.wrightslaw.com/info/trans.legal.bateman.htm

Dowling, R., & Greenberg, M. D. (Eds.). (2007). *Safe and sound: A safety awareness curriculum for students who are visually impaired and have multiple disabilities.* Fresno: California School for the Blind. Retrieved from http://www.csb-cde.ca.gov/learning_resources.htm

IFSP process: planning and implementing family-centered services in natural environments. (2014). Early Childhood Technical Assistance Center. Retrieved from http://ectacenter.org/topics/ifsp/ifspprocess.asp

Hatlen, P. (1996). The core curriculum for blind and visually impaired students including those with additional disabilities. *RE:view, 28*(1), 25–32.

Johns, J. L. (2008). *Basic reading inventory: Prep-primer through grade twelve and early literacy assessments* (10th ed.). Dubuque, IA: Kendall/Hunt Publishing Co.

Maryland State Department of Education. (2012). Maryland common core state curriculum frameworks for braille. Retrieved from http://mdk12.org/instruction/commoncore/braille/index.html

Parks, S. (2006). *Hawaii early learning profile (HELP).* Palo Alto, CA: Vort Corporation.

Special Education Administrators of County Offices. (2000). *Curriculum guide for students with moderate to severe disabilities: Core content access.* Los Angeles, CA: Lakeshore.

Texas School for the Blind and Visually Impaired. (2007). *Evaluating visually impaired students (EVALS).* Austin, TX: Author.

Woodcock, R., Mather, N., & Schrank, F. A. (2011). *Woodcock-Johnson III: Diagnostic reading battery.* Rolling Meadows, IL: Houghton Mifflin Harcourt–Riverside Publishing.

CHAPTER 15

Integrating the Expanded Core Curriculum at Home and in the Community

Missy Garber

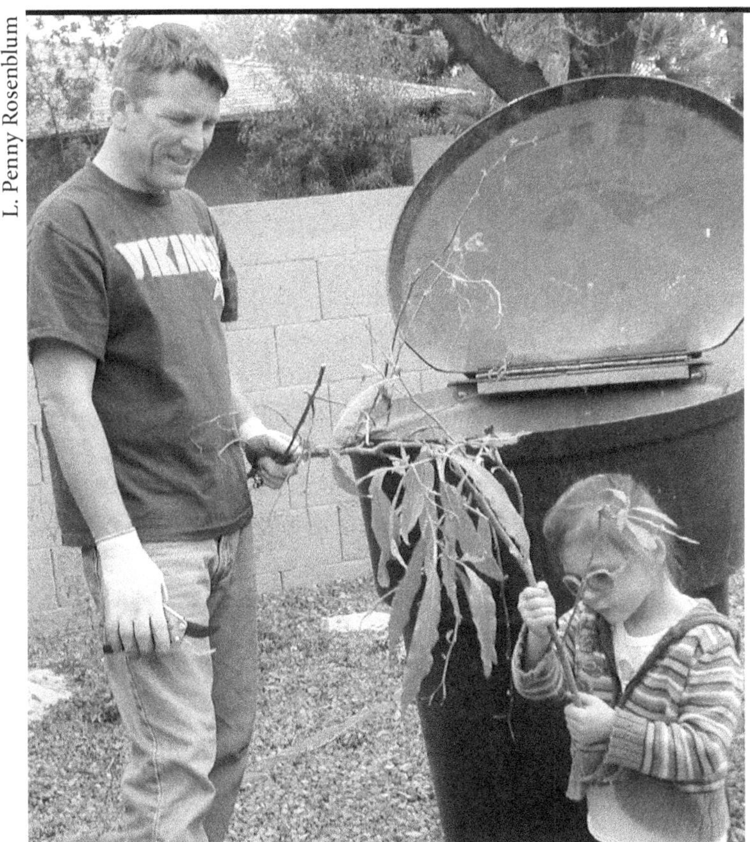

L. Penny Rosenblum

Although school is where much of our learning takes place, most of a student's time is spent outside formal education programs, at home and in the community. This is true whether we look at the hours in any given day a student might spend in school versus at home and in the community, or the number of years a person typically spends in school over the span of an entire lifetime. It is therefore essential that efforts to help students develop skills related to the expanded core curriculum (ECC) include considerable attention to learning opportunities within families and outside of school. Family members need to understand how essential they are to their child's development of skills and learn how to take advantage of *teachable moments*—those times when opportunities occur that especially lend themselves to teaching skills related to the ECC. In turn, teachers need to learn to partner effectively with parents, caregivers, and other family members.

In many ways the development of skills related to the ECC at home and in the community is similar to the development process at school, but it is also different. This chapter discusses how to see the ECC in opportunities at home and in the community and how important learning may be integrated into daily life once that life is viewed through the lens of the ECC. Included are specific ways in which teachers can collaborate with families to incorporate the learning of the ECC outside of school, as well as more general suggestions for how to work effectively with families.

THE ECC OUTSIDE OF SCHOOL

In some respects promoting the development of skills in the ECC during out-of-school time is similar to promoting these skills within a formal education program. In both cases those involved in the care and education of a child with a visual impairment must intentionally address the ECC as a body of knowledge and set of skills that individuals with visual impairments must acquire in order to develop into independent, competent adults. As discussed throughout this book, because of the nature of visual impairment, the skills and knowledge encompassed by the ECC are not acquired informally or casually by students with visual impairments—as they are for most individuals whose vision is intact. Explicit instruction in and deliberate integration of the ECC needs to take place, whether at school or out-of-school, using the same basic effective practices. Families play a central role in the development of skills in out-of-school situations, so it is essential that parents and caregivers become familiar with these effective practices and understand why they are necessary. Table 15.1 presents a summary of some of those practices along with rationales and examples that can be explained to parents.

The development of ECC-related skills at home and in the community also differs from the development of skills at school in several significant ways, and it is important that teachers be aware of and appreciate these differences. The obvious distinction between the two settings and processes is *who* is doing the teaching. Outside of school, teaching—whether deliberate or not—generally is done by parents, caregivers, other family members, and, sometimes, community members; however, these additional "teachers"—family members in particular—do not come to their tasks of teaching and reinforcing the ECC by the same route as school staff do. Teachers and specialists willingly choose their line of work and understand that it has to involve intense attention to skill development in their students. For most families, the presence of a child with a disability is unanticipated. Although a child with a visual impairment may be intentionally adopted into a family or be born into a family with a known genetic cause of visual impairment, it is likely that family members did not choose this new role as an at-home teacher. Families may accept different levels of responsibility in this situation and may be more or less able to cope and undertake different degrees of participation, but all are faced with the challenge of how to integrate providing extra instruction to their child into their existing obligations toward the needs of all household members.

Families' responsibilities differ from those of school personnel in another significant way because they fill a unique role in their child's life. Children certainly benefit from carryover and consistency between school and home as well as strong relationships between their caregivers and teachers, but there are times when children need their caregivers to be just that: caregivers. This means families may very well make choices about how to handle potential learning situations that differ from what teachers might choose. For example, it may be clear to a teacher that expecting a toddler or preschooler (who is able to do so) to walk independently is important, because doing so will encourage independence in the child. A parent may be aware of—and even agree with—this expectation in principle, but may nevertheless decide to pick up and hold the child if he or she feels the child is anxious in a new environment. This parent might believe that the benefits of the child's feeling secure and thus more likely to eventually explore on his or her own outweigh the benefits of independent walking in that specific situation. Families are—and need to be—something other than and *more* than the implementers of a curriculum. Teachers may work with families to help them integrate the development of ECC-related skills outside of school, but they need to remember that families have other needs to fill in the lives of their children besides instruction.

TABLE 15.1

Effective Practices for Teaching Children with Visual Impairments: Suggestions for Families

Effective Practice	*Rationale*	*Examples*
Senses: Provide opportunities for multi-sensory, hands-on exploration.	Without intact vision, other senses, such as hearing, smell, and touch, must be used to take in information and learn about the world.	While riding home from school on the bus, Caroline, who is sighted, notices spring flowers emerging from the ground in some parts of her neighborhood. Her brother Max is visually impaired and doesn't observe this through the school bus window. Later, when walking to a neighbor's, Max's mom draws his attention to the sprouting flowers and encourages him to touch and smell them.
	Some information may need to be communicated to an individual with a visual impairment through explanation. When it is not feasible to use hands-on exploration, verbalize.	From across the room Evan, who has low vision, wonders why his grandmother did not answer his grandfather when his grandfather asked her a question. His grandmother realizes that Evan wasn't aware that she had nodded her head up and down to indicate "yes." She explains to Evan about "yes" and "no" head gestures and makes an effort to point out to him when people are using nonverbal communication, both in real life and on television.
Time: Allow enough time for exploration as well as independent completion of an activity.	Vision allows us to perceive and understand objects and situations quickly; using other senses to perceive and to build up accurate understanding may take longer.	With a glance out the bus window Caroline instantly notices the springtime changes in the neighborhood. It takes Max longer to "see" this change through touch, smell, and explanation by others. It may take several walks and hands-on experiences with the growing plants over time for Max to build up an accurate understanding of change in his neighborhood.
	Intact vision provides countless opportunities for children to observe how activities are completed before others expect them to carry out these activities themselves. Without vision, learning to complete activities independently involves deliberate instruction and a lot of practice. While developing proficiency, it may take an individual with a visual impairment longer to carry out an activity independently.	Grace is learning to get ready for bed herself, with little to no assistance from her parents. When brushing her teeth she needs to find her toothbrush and toothpaste, apply the right amount of toothpaste, and carry out the other steps of this activity. It takes her a long time in the bathroom to carry out all of these steps. Only through numerous opportunities to practice the steps herself, however, will she become faster at it.
Completeness: Provide experiences with all their parts and in all their various forms to develop an understanding of the whole.	Vision allows us to perceive objects, activities, and situations all at once and to quickly understand how individual components are related to form a whole; without vision, complete and accurate understanding needs to be pieced together.	It wouldn't be enough for Max's sister to pick a flower for him from the neighborhood and bring it to him. A more complete understanding of the spring changes in his neighborhood occurs when Max feels the sprout and notices its location in an area of soil next to the sidewalk. On other visits he notices the petals, leaves, and stem. He may smell the bouquets of flowers at the produce stand on his street. While helping his mom plant annuals in their window box, he'll be able to feel the roots of the plants.

(continued on next page)

TABLE 15.1 *continued*

Effective Practice	***Rationale***	***Examples***
Provide a finished product for child to examine before teaching him or her how to carry out the parts of a task.		When Evan was first learning to complete puzzles his grandmother made sure he examined a completed puzzle first, which they then took apart together and finally re-assembled.
		Before Max began learning how to load the dishwasher after dinner, he first learned how to unload it. This meant he had plenty of opportunities to see how a correctly loaded dishwasher was organized, where various utensils and dishware were placed, and how they were best oriented. When it came time for him to begin loading the dishwasher himself he had a solid understanding of what the end product of his efforts should be.
Work toward "start-to-finish" experiences.		Grace's parents want to make sure Grace learns to carry out activities in their entirety—such as preparing a snack, eating it, and cleaning up after herself—or at least understand what the activity in its entirety entails. However, they don't always have enough time to work with Grace to carry out all the steps herself. At such times, they make sure they at least verbalize to her what they are doing for her, so she is aware that there are additional steps. "We're in a rush, so I'll help you by wiping up the crumbs you left on the floor after you ate your muffin. You put your napkin in the trash," her mom tells her.
Environment: Adapt settings, tasks, and behaviors to facilitate nonvisual or reduced visual learning.	Many times a child's environment can be easily adapted to allow them to use their intact senses more effectively.	As a toddler, Max could more easily use his residual vision when provided with additional lighting, so his mom placed a flexible arm desk light over the back of his high chair tray. He was then better able to accurately reach for pieces of cereal on his high chair tray.
		Since he is a preschooler with low vision, Evan's grandmother places children's books on low shelves, magazines and newspapers on the coffee table, and flyers, invitations and a calendar on the refrigerator. These locations are all at his eye level and thus increase his exposure to print in his environment, an important component of literacy development.
		With reduced vision and physical limitations, Grace has a hard time finding and keeping up with the fast-moving kids in the neighborhood who quickly move from place to place while playing outside. Because of this, she misses out on many spontaneous play situations and valuable opportunities for social interaction. Her parents found that by setting up several play areas with boundaries in their yard—such as a play house, sandbox, and a slide—the kids were more likely to stay put and play near, and eventually with, Grace.
		In middle school Max began using a screen reading software program on the computer. Max's mom realizes that when he uses the program to complete homework, check his e-mail, or carry out an Internet search, talking to him interferes with his ability to use the computer. She limits how much she talks to him during these times.

Note: For more extensive discussions of methods for teaching children with visual impairments see Ferrell, 2011 and Koenig & Holbrook, 2000.

It is also important to remember that families and households are different in a range of ways, including:

- attitudes toward disability
- values related to dependence, independence, and interdependence
- approaches to discipline
- household structure and the roles of members
- interaction patterns regarded as acceptable between caregivers and children
- quantity and quality of available resources
- influence of religion on family life
- beliefs about how children learn (Fazzi, Klein, Pogrund, & Salcedo 2002)

This variability makes it difficult to generalize about how to work effectively with families, but anticipating this diversity is a good starting point.

In addition to this immense variability among families of students with visual impairments is the existence at home and in the community of additional people who, although not specially trained as teachers, may offer strengths, talents, and additional attention and other resources that can positively influence the development of skills in a child. Extended and blended family members, neighbors, childcare providers, religious school teachers, camp counselors, coaches, store merchants, and bus drivers are all sources of potential instruction. Families can learn to spot these talents and enlist the help of others in the community. An after-school sitter who loves to knit, or who knows cell phone text messaging language can share her interests with the child, or an elderly relative living in the home might cook with the child.

Just as it is important for teachers to be mindful about aspects of family life that contribute to the development of ECC-related skills, it is important for families to be made aware that some interactions with a child with a visual impairment promote learning and others may impede it. In a large household, for example, there may be so many people around to carry out daily tasks that the contribution of a child with a disability may not be needed and therefore never sought. Siblings ready to lend a hand may automatically "help" a brother or sister who is visually impaired by picking up dropped items and physically guiding the sibling or otherwise anticipating needs. A camp counselor who has not been given basic information about how to include a camper with a visual impairment in camp activities may limit the child's participation and thus opportunities for learning in that setting. An after-school babysitter may feel she is being responsible by meeting a preteen at the door of the bus after school each day, not realizing that her presence could interfere with the student's ability to participate in conversations with friends as they congregate at the bus stop and make social plans.

Another important way that acquiring and practicing ECC-related skills in the home and community differ from learning in an educational program is that learning opportunities outside school are not constrained by the time limits of instructional periods or the boundaries of a teacher's scheduled service. There are certainly different kinds of time constraints at home, such as the need to get dinner on the table or hurry to the theater before a movie starts, but for the most part, complete, start-to-finish, hands-on learning opportunities that are meaningful for a particular family are plentiful outside of school. These opportunities occur spontaneously and constantly. Armed with a little additional planning and a repertoire of strategies for making the most of these teachable moments, families can take advantage of learning opportunities to benefit their child with a visual impairment. The first step in being able to do this is developing an ECC "lens" or prism—that is, raising one's consciousness about the ECC and the importance of practicing skills and learning to view daily life as a rich source of ECC-related learning opportunities.

SEEING THE ECC

Although the term "expanded core curriculum" sounds specialized and complex, in actuality, it can be found all around us. The challenge for those charged with educating and raising children with visual impairments is to pay attention to the numerous areas of life the ECC encompasses and to make sure children are developing proficiency in all of them to the best of their abilities. As earlier chapters have pointed out, for children with visual impairments learning in most ECC areas or domains generally does not take place incidentally or automatically, as it does for children with typical sight. It may seem daunting to both teachers and families that all these areas need to be monitored and addressed throughout the life of a child, but these areas do not have to be approached as specialized bodies of knowledge and collections of skills to be explicitly addressed.

Instead, it is more accurate and reassuring to think of the ECC as something that is all around us, always. Support for developing skills in various areas of the ECC can be as big and deliberate as setting aside time to teach a complex skill such as making a bed, or it can be as small as a teachable moment in which a father tells a child that he is nodding his head as he is speaking to her, and that this gesture means "yes" to those who see it.

Overall, then, "integrating" not only means bringing seemingly disparate parts of the ECC together, but incorporating the ECC into a family's daily life. The ECC need not be viewed as a separate specialized curriculum that a family transposes from school into their home and household and community life, but instead can be regarded as a lens through which daily life, rich in opportunities for learning, may be viewed.

Integrating the ECC at home and in the community involves pulling opportunities for ECC-related learning from daily life. Table 15.2 lists the nine ECC areas or domains and everyday examples of what a skill in that area might look like.

PROMOTING THE ECC OUTSIDE OF SCHOOL

What follows are three illustrations of how multiple ECC areas are integrated into the lives of children and youths with visual impairments. These vignettes show how opportunities for learning are always present and how a family may take advantage of them. Each example emphasizes one primary ECC area, such as independent living, social interaction, or compensatory access, but it can be seen that additional areas are involved. These scenarios also include examples of the role teachers can play in promoting the integration of the ECC at home and in the community.

Independent Living: Helping in the Kitchen

Max is a 14-year-old eighth-grader who attends his neighborhood middle school. Diagnosed with an inherited degenerative retinal condition soon after birth, Max is an auditory and tactile learner who now uses braille as his primary literacy medium. He lives at home with his younger sister, Caroline, and with his mother who works full time outside their home.

On weekdays dinnertime is somewhat rushed in Max's house. His mom might bring home takeout, prepare a quick meal, or defrost a dinner she prepared over the weekend. Although Max loves helping out around the house—especially in the kitchen—he has a lot to learn and needs close supervision and support for many of the cooking activities in which he is interested. For this reason Max's mom is less likely to accept his offers of help in the kitchen during the week—or his sister's either, for that matter. However, she does try to involve him in at least one step of meal preparation—a step he can carry out independently—because she knows how important it is for Max, as a teen with a visual impairment, to learn by doing, and to make real contributions to the work of the household. She asks him to carry out smaller tasks that she has taught him in the past and that he can now do on his own, such as peel vegetables, husk corn, fill water glasses (independent living), or walk to their neighbor's house to ask for an ingredient they ran out of (O&M). One of Max's daily chores is to set the dinner table. In addition to setting the table, each day he is also responsible for emptying the waste baskets, feeding the pets, and taking out the family's recycling (career education).

Max's mom is able to spend extra time in the kitchen on the weekends, preparing the more involved recipes her family loves. Since she has more time, she makes more of an effort to involve her children in the meal, and to work on one recipe each week. On this particular weekend day it is Max's turn to cook with his mom (recreation and leisure). When he arrives in the kitchen in the morning he hears her sitting at the table turning pages as she reads through a book of recipes. As Max pours himself a bowl of cereal, his mom reads to him the names of several dishes she is considering (compensatory access—listening/using a live reader) and asks him to help choose what they will make that day (self-determination). After Max chooses a recipe for baked ziti, his mom reads the recipe out loud and Max uses his braillewriter to make a list of those ingredients they will first need to get at the grocery store before they begin cooking (compensatory access, assistive technology).

For most writing tasks Max uses either his school-provided electronic personal digital assistant (PDA; also called an electronic notetaker) with a refreshable braille display or his laptop equipped with screen-reading software, both of which are charging on his desk in his bed-

TABLE 15.2

Seeing the ECC: Everyday Examples of ECC Skills at Home and in the Community

What is known as the ECC area of . . .	*Looks like . . .*
Compensatory Access	Staying organized by gathering ahead of time all needed ingredients for a recipe and keeping them within reach on a tray Braille reading and writing Understanding concepts related to time and space Using keyboarding skills to write a birthday message to a sighted friend Having an organized work space at home with books, special equipment, and supplies for completing homework
Sensory Efficiency	Using environmental smells and sounds to determine that one is passing the bakery Using vision to systematically track left to right and top to bottom as when using a calendar Knowing when to limit chatting in order to attend to environmental sounds and cues
Assistive Technology	Using a braillewriter to create a grocery list Using a computer with screen magnification software Knowing how and when to use low-tech and high-tech assistive technology, such as a slant board, reading stand, and optical devices
Orientation and Mobility	Using various forms of transportation to run errands with family members Developing an awareness of a community—its features, routes, and distances—through a family's use of a GPS device Attending to and accurately interpreting environmental sounds
Independent Living	Helping prepare meals, filling water glasses, setting the table Making a telephone call Using a system of bill folding to identify money Preparing a snack
Social Interaction	Approximating eye contact with others during conversations Reciprocating favors Responding to a party invitation using the telephone Greeting hosts Showing interest in others
Recreation and Leisure	Spending free time participating in activities one enjoys, such as cooking Learning party games and dances
Career Education	Carrying out daily responsibilities at home, such as setting the table, emptying trash bins, feeding pets, and taking out the recycling Being responsible for one's belongings Communicating with an adult role model with a visual impairment
Self-Determination	Having opportunities to choose what the family will have for dinner Figuring out mistakes and correcting them Choosing what to buy a friend for her birthday Speaking for oneself when others are curious about one's disability and equipment

room this morning. For this grocery list today, however, Max uses his braillewriter. He is still learning how to be careful at home with his advanced technology equipment. His mom and teacher have emphasized to him that is best not to use his electronic devices near food and drinks, so he chooses the braillewriter for this particular writing task in the kitchen.

Max's braillewriter has been in his family's home since he was a baby, brought by the teacher who provided his early intervention services. At that time, the teacher also gave Max's mom information about a distance education course through which she could learn basic information about braille, including the alphabet. After completing the course she was able to label objects around the house in braille and add braille to some of the children's books they owned. When Max began formal braille instruction with his teacher, his mom continued learning braille, moving on to braille contractions and the rules for their use. When Max read at home and encountered a contraction that he had not yet been taught at school, she was able to explain to him what it was. She also helped him form characters as he pressed the keys of the braillewriter. Now Max's mom uses her knowledge of braille to write him letters when he is at camp, label his birthday and holiday gifts, put inspirational quotes in his lunchbox, and help him check his homework when needed. Max is now a competent braille reader and writer and is putting his skills to use as he creates the grocery list for his trip to the store with his mother. (See Sidebar 15.1 for more information about how families can support their children's use of braille.)

For transportation to the store, the family takes the bus, gets a ride with a neighbor or relative, or calls a taxi on those days when they need to do a lot of shopping. Planning for transportation to run weekend errands is done by Max's mom, but taking part in her decisions is especially important for Max, who will not be able to drive a car when he is older and will need to be comfortable with a variety of methods for getting where he needs to go (orientation and mobility). On this particular day, Max and his mom made arrangements to get a ride to the store with their neighbor. Max's mom has decided to make a casserole for her neighbor as a way to thank her for the favor, and

SIDEBAR 15.1

Supporting a Child's Reading Medium Outside of School: Families Learning and Using Braille

One of the key ways families can integrate the ECC into life outside of school for their child who is visually impaired is by sharing their child's primary literacy medium. By law—the Individuals with Disabilities Education Act, or IDEA—all children who are visually impaired must be considered candidates for instruction in braille, unless their IEP team determines that braille would be an inappropriate literacy medium. A learning media assessment, which is carried out by a teacher of students with visual impairments, helps educational teams make this determination.

For children who are or will be print readers, sharing a child's literacy medium is a fairly straightforward process and usually requires no additional learning on the part of families, except perhaps how to best present print materials visually and develop an awareness of contrast, reduced visual clutter, optimal print size, and favorable lighting.

If braille is or will be a child's literacy medium, learning this new code requires more of a commitment on the part of family members. The presence of someone at home who shares the child's literacy medium is important for several reasons, including:

- helping provide a braille-rich (and thus literacy-rich) environment by labeling belongings and objects and by adapting books
- participating in teaching a child to read and write by taking advantage of the many literacy-related teachable moments that occur outside of school—for example, drawing the child's attention to braille in an elevator and on signs, examining a braille menu in a restaurant, and explaining an unfamiliar symbol as they read together
- communicating with the child in a way that is accessible to him, for example by writing braille notes, cards, letters, and overall providing opportunities when the child does not have to rely on a sighted person to read for him
- helping make homework go more smoothly by supporting the child when learning to read and write in the early years and by identifying possible braille errors that will confuse and frustrate her
- reinforcing the use of braille writing for functional activities, such as using a braillewriter or slate and stylus to label belongings, create a "to do list," label print homework documents and memos that need to be handed in to sighted teachers, and to jot down phone numbers
- Assisting the child in her use of braille-based assistive technology, such as electronic PDAs and

(continued on next page)

SIDEBAR 15.1 *continued*

refreshable braille displays, which can require knowledge of six-key entry and braille symbols for writing and for entry of commands.

For various reasons, some families are not able to learn braille or help integrate it into life for the child outside of school. However, for those families who are interested in learning braille and integrating it into their child's life outside of school, a teacher can support them by doing the following:

- emphasizing the importance of understanding and sharing a child's literacy medium
- providing information about resources for learning braille, such as the Hadley School for the Blind (www.hadley.edu), local courses at a rehabilitation agency for individuals who are blind, and DOTS for Families: Ongoing Literacy for Families of Children with Visual Impairments (www.pathstoliteracy.org/dots-families), an online course open to parents anywhere. (See the Resources section at the end of this book for details, as well as the Directory of Services on the website of the American Foundation for the Blind [www.afb.org/directory.aspx].)
- conducting a braille course or workshop for interested families
- spending some service time working directly with family members on braille and answering their questions
- inviting parents to periodically sit in on braille lessons with their child
- linking parents to adult braille readers and consumer organizations that provide braille resources and mentors. (See the Resources section at the back of this book for information about organizations and possible sources of mentors; see also Sidebar 15.2 for online resources.)
- providing resources and equipment such as a braillewriter, braille paper, labeling materials, and braille reference or "cheat" sheets. Some useful learning resources include *Just Enough to Know Better* (Curran, 1988), *The Bridge to Braille* (Castellano & Kosman, 1997), and, for more in-depth learning, *Ashcroft's Programmed Instruction: Unified English Braille* (Holbrook & D'Andrea, in press).

she makes sure Max is aware of her plan (social interaction).

Once they have finished their shopping trip, while cooking Max's mother incorporates several adaptive strategies suggested to her by Max's teacher over the years. For example, after reviewing the recipe they are about to make, they first gather all the needed ingredients and place them on a tray close to the area where they will be working (compensatory access, organization). Although this takes a little more time than if she were to do it herself, Max's mom asks Max to get each ingredient and bring it to the area on the counter where they are working. This assignment helps him learn where items and ingredients are located in their kitchen (orientation and mobility). The tray creates an area with boundaries to contain the various ingredients, which makes it easier for Max to find what he needs more quickly. Another strategy his mom uses is to have Max place a piece of anti-slip material under a bowl containing ingredients for him to stir together. If Max is working with a single ingredient, they place it on a cutting board that provides visual contrast. Max places a finger over the edge of any container into which he pours liquids so he knows when the liquid is nearing the top. Although many of the food items in the house are tactilely distinct and Max knows what a particular item is by the size and shape of its container, for those items that are not so easily identifiable he and his mom have made braille labels.

When working in the kitchen, Max now and then makes mistakes—for example, sometimes he reaches toward the shelf where the cups are stored when he is looking for a bowl. It would certainly be faster if his mom jumped in and corrected him but she knows Max will eventually figure out the problem and solve it himself (self-determination).

The house is quite active and noisy when everyone is home; Max's sister watches television close by, listens to the radio, or plays a video game. Max's mom tries to limit outside noise when Max is learning a new skill and needs to listen to her directions and the sounds that help him when he is cooking. She has noticed that Max seems to pay closer attention to what she says when there is no other source of interesting noise to compete for his attention (sensory efficiency).

When the ziti is finished baking, Max and his mom bring a second casserole to their neighbor who had driven them to the store. Before ringing the doorbell, she quietly reminds Max to look in the direction of their neighbor's face to approximate eye contact (social interaction).

Max's mom plans to talk to his teacher about compiling a binder of brailled recipes he has helped to prepare and can work toward completing independently. She expects him to make dinner when he is a little older to help her out on weeknights and to make his own breakfast and lunch when he is in high school.

Social Interaction Skills: Attending a Birthday Party

Grace is a 9-year-old third-grader with mild cerebral palsy and a visual condition of retinopathy of prematurity. She reads enlarged print but is also learning braille as a secondary reading medium. When Grace arrives home from school one day, her mom tells her there is an envelope addressed to Grace in the day's mail. Grace reaches for the pile of mail on the table near the door in the entranceway and finds the envelope in question. Grace has limited use of her left hand, so she stabilizes the note with her left hand against her chest and opens it with her right. It is an invitation to a classmate's birthday party.

After checking her own calendar, Grace's mom is certain her daughter is free on the day of the party. However, she takes advantage of the opportunity to engage Grace in a discussion of time and planning by suggesting Grace check the large print and braille calendar hanging on the bulletin board in the kitchen. Grace locates today's date on the calendar, and while her mom points to each day—moving left to right, and top to bottom—Grace uses her vision to track across the rows (sensory efficiency: vision) and counts the remaining days until the party—a little over two weeks. She and her mom then figure out how many days they have to make a card for her friend and to buy a present (compensatory access, concept development: time).

Grace is learning to use the telephone, and her mom knows that replying to the invitation will be a good opportunity for her daughter to practice her developing telephone skills. Before making the call, they review what Grace should say when someone on the other end answers the phone, or if instead she gets an answering machine (social interaction). Grace's teacher showed Grace and her mom a technique that individuals with visual impairments use for dialing the phone: placing the middle finger on the 5 button, which usually has a little tactile nib on it to make it easier to find, and using the 4-5-6 row of buttons as a "home row" from which the other numbers can easily be located. Grace will use this dialing technique on the family's landline today when replying to the party invitation (independent living). She also uses this method at school to locate the numbers on the numeric key pad of her computer keyboard and when using a talking calculator (though the placement of the numbers differs on these devices). Grace is also learning to place calls using voice commands on her mom's smart phone.

Several days before her classmate's party, Grace and her dad drive to the store in town that sells toys, games, and crafts to pick out a birthday present. Although Grace's dad knows the way to this particular store, he programs the destination into his GPS device. As they drive, Grace listens to the GPS speak the street names, distances, and directions to their destination (O&M, compensatory access: concept development, listening).

When browsing in the store, Grace's dad reminds her of the price range they can spend on the gift, and they ask the salesperson for her help in suggesting gifts in this price range that might appeal to a girl who is turning 9 years old. The sales clerk suggests several possibilities and Grace's dad allows her to choose among them (self-determination). Knowing that Grace will participate in the purchasing of the gift, her dad has folded the bills in his wallet in such a way as to make each denomination tactilely distinct (independent living). He suggests that Grace hand the $20 bill (folded lengthwise and again widthwise) to the sales clerk and tells her how much change they expect to receive back.

Several days before the party, the mother of the birthday girl gives Grace's parents a call. She indicates that she and her daughter are excited Grace can come to the party. However, she is curious to know if Grace's parents have any suggestions for making sure Grace is included as much as possible in the party activities. They discuss the activities being planned, and agree they will give it some thought and talk again in the next day or two. Some of the activities planned are pass-the-parcel, freeze dance, and a treasure hunt.

Grace's parents subscribe to an e-mail list for parents of children with visual impairments. They learned about this list from Grace's teacher when Grace was first diagnosed with a visual impairment and beginning to receive early intervention services (see Sidebar 15.2 for more information about online support for families). The parents in this online group often discuss toys and games that are especially enjoyable for children with visual impairments, and Grace's dad has saved some of the more helpful postings for future reference. He doesn't recall any recent discussion about strategies for including children who are visually impaired in party games and activities, so he posts a question of his own along these lines to the group. The other parents on the list, as well as adults who are visually impaired who participate in the group, make various suggestions. Perhaps when it comes time for the treasure hunt, Grace can partner with another child at the party. The group agrees there is no real need for a complicated adaptation to pass-the-parcel, in which the children pass around a package that is elaborately wrapped in many layers and contains small gifts in each layer for the person who is holding it when the music stops to unwrap and find; however, the birthday girl's mother will need to verbalize clear instructions about how to play the game and make sure that Grace hears these. Freeze dance involves dancing to music and then freezing in a pose when the music stops at random times during the dancing; the mailing list participants suggest that Grace's parents show her ahead of time some silly poses as well as some ways they've observed kids her age dancing (recreation and leisure). Because of her physical limitations, Grace's parents teach her poses she can assume while leaning on her walker and that only require the use of her right arm.

Grace spends some of her time at school working directly with a teacher of students with visual impairments. Some time with this teacher is spent learning to write using a computer, a screen magnification program with speech, and an adapted keyboard, and she

SIDEBAR 15.2

Online Support for Families

Online communities are vital sources of support and information for families of children with visual impairments. Because visual impairment is a low-incidence disability, a family may very well find that they are one of only a few families or even the only family in a particular town or school raising a child with the specific set of needs associated with visual impairment. Through online communities, however, families from all over the world come together around topics related to visual impairment, and families soon find they are surrounded, virtually, by other families with similar concerns, questions, and needs.

Online communities can assume the form of blogs, forums, message boards, e-mail lists, and social networking sites. Such communities can be formed around topics as general as parenting a child with a visual impairment or as specific as home-schooling a child who is blind. There are also numerous online communities focused on specific eye conditions. Online communities not only offer opportunities for parents to provide support and information to other parents, but they also connect families of children with visual impairments to adults with visual impairments—perhaps even with the same eye conditions—and to professionals working in the field of blindness and visual impairment.

The following list provides a sample of e-mail lists and websites that offer online communities as well as information and resources for parents of children with visual and other disabilities. In addition, parents can investigate the websites of such organizations as the American Council of the Blind (www.acb.org), American Foundation for the Blind (www.afb.org), American Printing House for the Blind (www.aph.org), and National Federation of the Blind (www.nfb.org) and its affiliate, the National Organization of Parents of Blind Children for additional sources of information, resources, and online communities (refer to the Resources section at the end of this book for more information on these and other organizations). Because information on the Internet can be transient, readers should be aware that the following information may be subject to change.

BLINDKID

listserv@nfbnet.org

An e-mail list sponsored by the National Organization of Parents of Blind Children, a division of the National Federation of the Blind, whose purpose is to share information about the welfare and development of blind children.

(continued on next page)

BVI-PARENTS

bvi-parents-subscribe@yahoogroups.com

An e-mail list for parents of children who are blind or visually impaired, whose purpose is to network and share ideas and experiences.

CENTER FOR PARENT INFORMATION AND RESOURCES

www.parentcenterhub.org

A central online resource for information and resources that connects parents of children with disabilities to the Parent Training Information Centers and Community Parent Resource Centers located in every state. These federally funded centers provide parents with information and training about disabilities; parent and children's rights under the IDEA and other relevant laws; and resources in the community, state, and nation.

FAMILYCONNECT

www.familyconnect.org

An online, multimedia community created by the American Foundation for the Blind and the National Association for Parents of Children with Visual Impairments for parents of visually impaired children to find information, support each other through online message boards, share stories and concerns, and link to local resources.

KIDS TOGETHER

www.kidstogether.org

An online forum maintained by a grassroots, all-volunteer organization that advocates for the rights and interests of people with disabilities and provides information, resources, educational materials and trainings on educating children with disabilities in general education settings.

NOAH'S ALBINISM ONLINE COMMUNITY

www.albinism.org/aoc.html

An online community of the National Organization for Albinism and Hypopigmentation in which people and families affected by albinism and others interested in learning more about the condition can ask questions, share experiences, and support each other.

PARENTS HELPING PARENTS

www.php.com

A parent-directed, community-based organization that provides an online source of information and support for parents of children with special needs.

POP-UP IEP FOR PARENTS/ADVOCATES

www.unco.edu/ncssd/bviIEP/index.shtml

A guide for parents from the National Center on Severe and Sensory Disabilities about issues frequently faced by parents in regard to developing Individualized Educational Programs (IEPs) for their children and attending IEP meetings.

PROJECT SALUTE (SUCCESSFUL ADAPTATIONS FOR LEARNING TO USE TOUCH EFFECTIVELY)

www.projectsalute.net

An online resource for families and service providers on tactile learning strategies for working with children who are deaf-blind or who are blind with additional disabilities.

SPARKLE (SUPPORTING PARENT ACCESS TO RESOURCES, KNOWLEDGE, LINKAGES, AND EDUCATION)

www.sparkle.usu.edu

An online resource that provides information and training for parents of children who are deaf-blind through DVDs and the Internet.

WONDERBABY

www.WonderBaby.org

A website sponsored by Perkins School for the Blind with articles and resources for parents of children who are blind, including a list of the best sources of braille books for children.

WRIGHTSLAW

www.wrightslaw.com

An online source of in-depth information about special education law, education law, and advocacy for children with disabilities for parents, educators, advocates, and attorneys.

applies her developing skills to write a birthday message to her friend using the family's desktop computer at home, which also has this technology (compensatory access: communication, assistive technology). With an enlarged pointer, cursor, icons, and font, Grace is able to navigate the computer independently, open a word processing document, and type the message for her card.

On the day of the party, Grace and her family make their way to their door to leave, but Grace realizes she still needs to put on her shoes. She usually takes them off by the front door when she enters the house, but this time her shoes are not there. Instead of finding them for her, her mom asks Grace to think about the other places where the shoes might be. Grace goes to the back door to see if she left them there—still, no shoes. Grace's parents know very well that Grace's shoes are on the floor by the couch where Grace took them off the previous night. However, they did not move them and do not immediately tell her they are there. They want her to find her shoes herself and to make the connection between where she leaves something and where it can be found (compensatory access: organization). Knowing from experience that this process takes a little extra time, her parents have deliberately allowed enough time so they will not be late for the party. After a quick reminder from her mom ("Where did you take off your shoes yesterday?"), Grace remembers taking them off last night by the couch and realizes where they must be.

Grace is still mastering some of the dressing skills that would otherwise be carried out by children her age who do not have the fine motor challenges associated with her cerebral palsy and visual impairment, such as fastening zippers, buttoning, and tying shoe laces. She is learning the steps for putting on her shoes from beginning to end, with an adult carrying out the final steps she has not yet mastered. Today she sits on the floor, orients her shoes by pointing them away in front of her, slides her foot into each one, pulls the laces to tighten, and then crosses over the laces to make an X. Her mom then finishes tying the knot and bow, verbalizing the steps she is carrying out (independent living).

As the family nears the house where the party is taking place, Grace's parents give her a few reminders about how to interact appropriately with other people at the party, such as the need to greet the person who answers the door, wish the birthday girl "happy birthday," and say "please" and "thank you" (social interaction). At school Grace has been practicing with her teacher ways to expand conversations and show interest in the person with whom she is interacting. Grace's conversations tend to be "me" focused; her teachers and parents have noticed that other children, although kind, seem to grow tired of talking to Grace about the topics on which she dwells with little apparent awareness of the interests and needs of other speakers. As a way to make her more aware of what is going on in her social environment so she has more to talk about besides herself, school staff and parents have been describing to Grace what is going on in her social environment. These descriptions give her a better sense of who may be present in certain situations, what they are doing, and how they are doing it. These adults have gently explained and described to Grace how her self-centered conversations sometimes affect others; for example, two children rolling their eyes, or a classmate looking bored.

As the family approaches the house where the party is taking place, Grace is her usual chatty self, talking about something of interest to her and unrelated to the party ahead. Her parents ask her to hold off on talking for now, since listening to the noises from the house will help her to begin to piece together a picture of what might be going on inside (sensory efficiency).

Upon entering the party, a young cousin of the birthday girl, comes up, curious about the new guest. She points to Grace's walker and looks up to ask Grace's dad, "Why does she have that?" He looks at Grace and says with a smile, "You can ask Grace. She'll tell you" (self-determination).

Compensatory Access Skills: Homework

Evan is an 11-year-old fifth-grader with a diagnosis of albinism. He lives with his grandparents in a large city where he attends his neighborhood school. Evan is primarily a visual learner who reads and writes in print with the use of various low-tech low vision devices, such as bold-line paper, a dark art pencil, a slantboard, and a reading stand, as well as a video magnifier when necessary.

Today, after he arrives home from school, prepares himself a snack (independent living), and watches some television (recreation and leisure), Evan begins his homework. His grandmother is home and available to help him, but she tries to let him complete as much as possible on his own. Today, Evan is confused about the directions for his math homework and asks his grandmother to explain. As she looks over the directions and begins her explanation, she notices that Evan's head is oriented downward and that he does not appear to be paying attention to her. She is about to reprimand him, but then hears a fire truck several blocks away and wonders if this has caught his attention. "I bet you're listening to that fire truck down the street," she remarks (orientation and mobility, sensory efficiency). "When we watch the news tonight, let's see if there's a story about a fire," she says. Noticing that Evan is clearly interested in the sirens, she waits until the sound fades before resuming with her explanation of the homework directions. After acknowledging the distraction, she reminds him that it is polite to look in her direction when they are speaking to each other (social interaction).

Evan and his grandmother view the first problem on his math worksheet using the video magnifier, which is set up in the corner of the den where he does his homework and keeps his school supplies, books, and equipment (compensatory access: organization). Evan uses a video magnifier both at school and at home when he needs to access small print and details found in his instructional materials and leisure reading and activities (assistive technology).

This particular video magnifier has been in Evan's home since he was a preschooler. At an early meeting of Evan's Individualized Family Service Program (IFSP) team, his grandmother had mentioned to the other team members that Evan could not identify letters or point to details in pictures found in magazines or books as her own children and other grandchildren had. His teachers agreed it was essential that he, like all children, be exposed to print and other visual information in his environment as part of his literacy and overall concept development. Since then his family has helped him position under the magnifier and scrutinize mail, comics, children's books, photographs, food item labels, objects (such as coins and insects), and, in more recent years, homework (compensatory access: concept development, sensory efficiency). As Evan's teacher of students with visual impairments instructs him in specific techniques for maximizing his use of his vision, including strategies for reading and writing more efficiently with the use of the video magnifier, she has also shown these to his grandmother, so she can help Evan carry over these skills at home.

In addition to working with Evan's grandmother to familiarize her with his equipment and his developing skills, Evan's teacher linked his family to a special resource that has proved invaluable to them over the years: Ed, an adult in the community who also has albinism. Ed is a lawyer with a family of his own who lives and works in the same city as Evan's family. Evan's grandmother sometimes calls Ed when she has questions about growing up with a visual impairment and albinism. Ed is always willing to answer her questions and spend some time with Evan, and in turn, links Evan and his family to an entire community of individuals with visual impairment in general as well as albinism in particular. Evan's grandmother is thankful that as he grows older Evan will have a positive role model who has experienced similar needs and challenges (career education).

PARTNERING EFFECTIVELY WITH FAMILIES

Given that it is so essential to the growth and independence of a child with a visual impairment to integrate all the different aspects of the ECC into his or her life at home and in the community, how can teachers work with families to incorporate the ECC into the child's life outside of school as the families of Max, Grace, and Evan did? On an even broader level, what can teachers do to facilitate an overall effective partnership with the families of the students they serve?

These are not simple questions to answer, because families vary at least as much as students do. In addition to those areas in which differences among the families with whom teachers work may typically be seen—such as values, attitudes toward disability, home language, expectations for individuals with disabilities, demands at home for limited time and resources, to name just a few—there also exists immense variability in the quality and intensity of relationships between families and school personnel. One student's family may not respond to teachers' telephone calls or e-mail messages, or even official letters from administrators. Another student's family may inundate school staff with phone calls, e-mails, and requests for meetings. A student's caregivers may be eager, passive, creative, hostile, curious, disinterested, uninvolved, enmeshed, overwhelmed, unavailable, and any combination of any or all of these! Plus, this is a partial list of variables on the *family* side of the relationship and doesn't take into account differences that the *teacher* will bring.

Because of such variations, the quality of a teacher's relationship with a family and thus how effectively he or she can partner with them to integrate learning of the ECC across the student's environments are not entirely under a teacher's control. Though it may not be possible to arrive at a list of universal generalizations for working effectively with all families, there are nonetheless some areas over which teachers have a greater degree of control and that can potentially lead to effective partnerships with families to help expand ECC-related learning outside of school. These areas include:

- serving as a respected professional resource to families
- providing critical information to them about the ECC and to help reinforce their efforts
- collaborating with them based on their expressed interests, needs, and goals

In addition, Sidebar 15.3 offers some more specific suggestions for effective ways of working with families. Sidebar 15.4 provides an example of a newsletter focusing on topics related to the ECC that teachers could send home to the families of their students.

SIDEBAR 15.3

More Suggestions for Partnering Effectively with Families

In addition to the ideas discussed throughout this chapter for working effectively with families, here are more suggestions for teachers of students with visual impairments to consider implementing:

- Making contact with caregivers within the first few weeks of the school year. New teachers can introduce themselves; returning teachers can inquire about any changes in vision and other updates the family may want to share.
- Implementing communication systems and schedules that are convenient for families. Whereas one family may like e-mail or telephone contact, another may wish to have a communication book that goes between home and school in the student's backpack.
- Ensuring communications with families are equally, if not more often, positive in nature rather than focused on problems or issues.
- Creating ECC "newsletters" or other topic-focused handouts in addition to providing information to families that may be of interest to them (such as information about community events, summer programs, and special workshops). (See Sidebar 15.4 for more information.)
- When leading a meeting, taking steps to ensure that it is productive and runs efficiently, and that team members, including caregivers, are treated respectfully:
    - providing clear communication ahead of time about the time and location of the meeting
    - sending a reminder a day or two before the meeting
    - making sure all the necessary people are present, for example an administrator who might need to approve the purchase of a piece of equipment
    - being on time
    - greeting caregivers when they enter the room
    - being prepared with any necessary paperwork
    - having participants introduce themselves
    - paying attention to your body language and positioning
    - ensuring the student's caregiver is not alone on one side of the table
    - positioning a laptop (if it is absolutely necessary to use one) in such a way that the screen does not create a physical barrier between the teacher and the other team members
    - giving the meeting and the attendees full attention
    - printing out a list of agenda topics to be covered, if there are numerous issues to consider
- Conveying reliability, keeping promises, following through. Maintaining a running list of "action

(continued on next page)

SIDEBAR 15.3 *continued*

items" for yourself as the meeting progresses, so you don't forget.

- Conveying high expectations of students to all team members, including families. At a preschool family service plan meeting for a student who will be a braille reader, for example, "When Melissa takes chemistry in high school, she'll need to know what a 'V' is in print. For example, H_2O is a V-shaped molecule. That's just one reason why it's important she have some understanding of print letters, even though she's developing as a braille reader."
- Conveying enthusiasm for one's work and students.
- Finding a way to maintain empathy when working with a student whose family's interpersonal relationship with you is difficult. The teacher can identify at least one quality to appreciate about the family and keep this quality forefront in her mind as she goes about interacting with them. For example, the teacher might think, "Kevin's behavior is challenging, and his mom really makes my job difficult by 'wordsmithing' the entire IEP, insisting that related services begin on the first day of school, and requesting numerous face-to-face lengthy meetings. But I have to admire how she advocates for him so thoughtfully and persistently. She wants what is best for him, and despite her complaints, I've never heard her make a negative comment or criticism about a teacher or staff member."

Note: For an extensive discussion of many topics related to building effective partnerships with families see A. Turnbull, H. R. Turnbull, E. J. Erwin, L. C. Soodak, and K. A. Shogren, *Families, Professionals, and Exceptionality: Positive Outcomes Through Partnerships and Trust,* 6th ed. (Upper Saddle River, NJ: Pearson Education, 2010).

SIDEBAR 15.4

Sample Newsletter for Parents

HELPING YOUR CHILD DEVELOP GOOD ORGANIZATION SKILLS

It's not unusual for a family to find that one or more of its members can be a "little" or perhaps even "very" disorganized, whether this means having a messy room or a cluttered desk, not being able to find something when it's needed, or misplacing important things such as homework. When a person is organized, the things he needs can be found easily. An organized person also knows what needs to be done and how to do it efficiently.

Children with visual impairments sometimes have more difficulty developing good organization skills than other children. Without good vision to quickly and accurately scan their surroundings, children with a visual impairment may take longer to find something they need. Also, their vision may not be reliable enough to quickly tell the difference between two similar-looking objects, such as the same brand of shampoo and conditioner.

Another way impaired vision might have an impact on the development of organizational skills is that children with vision challenges simply may not observe—and thus not learn—how people organize their homes or classrooms or belongings. Also, when too much help is provided, children with visual impairments may get fewer opportunities to practice being organized, to feel the benefits of being organized, and to experience the negative consequences of being disorganized.

Here are some ways families can help their children develop good organization skills at home.

Provide Experiences with Organized Spaces

There are many activities a child can participate in at home that provide experiences with organized spaces and thus help a child develop an understanding of how to store and arrange objects. At home a child with a visual impairment can help with the following:

- putting away groceries
- emptying the dishwasher or dish-drying rack
- setting the table for a meal
- putting away laundry

Work with Your Child to Create an Organized Environment

Implement simple labeling systems:

SIDEBAR 15.4 *continued*

- If the shampoo and conditioner bottles are practically identical, wrap an elastic band around one so it is easy to distinguish by touch from the other.
- Place a bright ribbon on a child's musical instrument case so it can be easily located among all of the similar cases at school.

Group objects that go together:

- Place all of the items a child may need for a bedtime bathroom routine in his own caddy.
- Use small boxes or drawer dividers to separate kinds of clothing in a drawer, such as socks, underwear, T-shirts, and the like.

Help Your Child Plan Ahead

- Together, look up the weather forecast, think about activities that are going to take place the next day, and lay out clothes before bedtime.
- Make a grocery list together and check each item off as it is found at the store.

More Great Resources on Organization

- Search for websites, blogs, and Pinterest boards related to organization. There are a lot of good ideas out there!
- *Skills for Success: A Career Handbook for Children and Adolescents with Visual Impairments*, by Karen Wolffe.

SOURCE: Missy Garber, Teacher of Students with Visual Impairments

Professional Preparation and Development

Effective partnerships are grounded in mutual respect. Families are more likely to listen to and implement a teacher's suggestions if they respect the teacher as a professional and trust that he or she is competent. The foundation of this respect is the confidence of the family—and the IEP team in general—that the teacher of students with visual impairments is *the* expert on their team on the educational needs of students who are visually impaired. This means the teacher needs to be at the very least proficient in the competencies specified for teachers of students with visual impairments by the Council for Exceptional Children's Division on Visual Impairments and the state in which the teacher practices (Division on Visual Impairments, n.d.).

It is therefore important for teachers to consider whether their own professional knowledge base is what it needs to be to provide accurate and important information to families and other members of students' educational teams. Asking oneself a number of questions such as the following can be an important exercise:

- Do I know basic terminology related to the functioning of the visual system?
- Can I explain the effects of visual impairment on development?
- Can I explain the effects of my students' particular eye conditions to their families?
- What are some strategies for teaching social, daily living, and functional life skills?
- Which of these can I share with families to use at home?
- Am I up-to-date and current in what I need to know to provide essential services effectively, such as how to create high-quality adaptations of instructional materials in braille, teach the use of the abacus, and administer and interpret critical assessments related to visual impairment?
- When I'm not sure of the answers to questions posed by parents or other IEP team members or need to refresh and/or develop skills in a particular area, such as a special braille code or a piece of technology, do I know what to do or where to find answers?

There are many professional competencies expected of teachers of students with visual impairments. Lack of familiarity and proficiency in these areas will undermine the respect and confidence that is the foundation of effective partnerships with families of students.

In addition to preservice preparation as a professional, it is likewise important that teachers remain lifelong learners and continue to stay current with developments in the field of blindness and low vision. In order to share up-to-date information with parents and other team members, teachers need to have up-to-date information themselves. A teacher's professional development activities need to focus at least in part on visual impairment, including developments in promising practices, technology, and changes to the braille code. Some ways a teacher can stay current include the following:

- belonging to professional organizations such as the Association for Education and Rehabilitation of the Blind and Visually Impaired and the Division on Visual Impairments of the Council for Exceptional Children
- subscribing to sources of current information such as professional journals (for example, the *Journal of Visual Impairment & Blindness*) and general and specific (such as those that center around a specific topic, such as braille, O&M, teaching math, and so forth) e-mail lists
- attending local and national conferences
- maintaining skills, including proficiency in braille and technology updates, by participating in workshops and refresher courses
- getting on the mailing lists of vendors of blindness-related products, such as the American Printing House for the Blind, Exceptional Teaching, and others

(See the Resources section at the back of this book for more information on these and other sources of information, and see Sidebar 15.5 for additional sources of information that can be provided to parents.)

Aside from knowledge of current developments in the field of blindness and visual impairment in general, it is also important to maintain current knowledge about

SIDEBAR 15.5

Additional Resources for Parents

A variety of resources are available to help parents learn about the general academic skills and knowledge their children are learning in school and the special skills their children need to master as a result of their visual impairments. Additional information can be found in the Resources sections at the end of this chapter and at the end of this book. The Texas School for the Blind and Visually Impaired also maintains a dynamic listing of resources related to the expanded core curriculum at www.tsbvi.edu/recc, which also includes resources in areas such as art, deaf-blindness, math, science, physical education, and social studies.

LOW VISION DEVICES AND ASSISTIVE TECHNOLOGY

The American Foundation for the Blind website provides a comprehensive online database (www.afb.org/prodmain.asp) of low vision and assistive technology devices used by people with visual impairments. Parents can see and touch many of these devices and tools before buying them by attending a convention of one of the primary membership organizations of people who are blind or visually impaired—the American Council of the Blind (www.acb.org) or the National Federation of the Blind (www.nfb.org; see the Resources section at the back of this book)—where they can get hands-on demonstrations from participating vendors.

INDEPENDENT LIVING

A variety of techniques that people who are blind or visually impaired use to accomplish independent living tasks are demonstrated in a series of video clips posted on the website of the Washington State School for the Blind (www.wssb.wa.gov/Content/offcampus/Video.asp). On the same page there is also an instructional guide, *Parent Education Daily Living Skills Guide*, which can be downloaded or printed out.

The FamilyConnect website (www.familyconnect.org) provides many suggestions for parents about helping children with visual impairments learn age-appropriate everyday skills. The VisionAware Everyday Living (www.visionaware.org/info/everyday-living/1) and the Lighthouse Lifestyle and Independence (www.lighthouse.org/services-and-assistance/lifestyle-independence/living-better-at-home/online-lessons/) websites provide instruction for adults on independent living techniques that can easily be adapted for children as well.

GENERAL ACADEMIC SKILLS

Most school districts adhere to state standards that detail the core curriculum and provide benchmarks for acquisition of knowledge and skills. Some states have parallel documents that describe how the ECC fits within the core curriculum and offer guidelines for knowledge and skill acquisition by students with

SIDEBAR 15.5 *continued*

visual impairments. (To find such documents, parents can search online or contact their child's teacher of students with visual impairments for information.)

SKILLS FOR CHILDREN WITH MULTIPLE DISABILITIES

If their child is in need of greater external assistance due to multiple disabilities or severe cognitive or physical limitations, parents may want to review guidelines appropriate to the child's developmental stage such as the *Oregon Project for Visually Impaired and Blind Preschool Children* (Anderson, Boigon, & Davis, 1991) or the *Developmental Scale for Children with Down Syndrome* (Layton, 2004). In addition, parents may want to review materials designed specifically for instruction of students with multiple disabilities, such as *Teaching Students with Visual and Multiple Impairments: A Resource Guide* (Smith & Levack, 1997).

SOURCE: Written by Karen E. Wolffe

community events and local programming that might be of interest to students and their families and help extend ECC-related learning outside of school. Is there a theater near a student's home that offers audio-described releases for viewers with visual impairments? What kinds of summer programs are offered at a nearby residential school for students who are visually impaired or in the community for students with disabilities? Is there sports programming for students with visual impairments? Has the teacher recently eaten at a restaurant that had menus available in braille and noted the information for families? Or does the teacher know adults with visual impairments who could serve as role models and resources for students and their families? Before they can become involved in activities that promote the learning of skills outside of school, families may need their child's teacher to provide information about what activities and resources are available. Families themselves may be excellent sources of this kind of information, in which case teachers can help share information with other families who may not be aware of such opportunities.

Information Sharing

In addition to the work needed on the part of a teacher in assuming the role of expert on visual impairment, staying up-to-date with developments in the field, and remaining knowledgeable about community activities and resources that may benefit students with visual impairments, there also exists the need for teachers to effectively share this information with families. The most fundamental topic about which teachers may need to educate families—especially families unfamiliar with or not yet knowledgeable about visual impairment—is what the ECC is, why it is necessary, and why their child's competence in the areas of the ECC should be a common goal shared by family, teacher, and student. This includes helping families understand:

- when skills are typically expected for any child (in terms of growth and development)
- why additional effort is needed to make sure a child with a visual impairment acquires these skills and the ways in which these children may learn differently and therefore need to be taught differently
- why an appropriate education for students with visual impairments is not entirely academic and that goals related to the areas of the ECC will need to be incorporated into a student's IEP
- why the ECC cannot be delegated solely to teachers and school personnel and ideally should be integrated into a student's life outside of school
- where learning opportunities to develop skills might exist in a family's daily life
- how a family can help their child acquire needed skills

One particularly helpful starting point for discussions with families about the expanded core curriculum is the FamilyConnect website (www.familyconnect.org) from the American Foundation for the Blind (AFB) and the National Association for Parents of Children with Visual Impairments (NAPVI). In addition to information on eye conditions, medical professionals, legal rights, and growth and development, FamilyConnect includes an extensive area devoted to all areas of the ECC, with experts' explanations and suggestions for enhancing skill development at home, and provides opportunities for parents to interact with members of other families.

Collaboration

Although every child with a visual impairment needs to develop skills in all areas of the ECC, the particular form specific ECC-related skills will assume for any given child is shaped by familial and cultural factors. Because of this, teaching of the ECC and other information is not simply teaching, but enculturation. By taking over some instruction in eating, food preparation, social skills, or recreation and leisure skills, for example, a teacher is adopting a role that for the vast majority of people in society is taught by families incidentally through the process of enculturation, or socialization. What this means is that teachers should not assume that a skill they feel is important will be a priority for the family or that their way of executing a skill is the way a particular family does it, or that they will even accept the teacher's method. For example, if eating skills is an area of need for a student, what is it that the family likes to eat? In which particular skill would instruction be most helpful? How do family members tend to carry out that skill? Max's family butters a roll by cutting it in half and then spreading butter across each half before eating it. In Grace's family bite-size pieces of roll are broken off and buttered individually as they are eaten throughout a meal. When targeting the ECC for instruction and determining what a particular skill might look like in a student's home and community, collaboration between teachers and families is essential.

Collaboration between teachers and families also increases the likelihood that skills being addressed at home may be carried over at school and that skills being learned and mastered in the school setting may be embedded in a student's life outside of school. A child who has learned to identify her coat, orient it correctly, put it on, and zip it at school can be expected to do that at home. A student who has learned to cut food no longer needs someone at home to do it for her at meal times.

There are several basic strategies for working with families to integrate the learning of ECC-related skills outside of school, including the following:

- welcoming family members to observe and participate in some lessons the teacher is carrying out with their child
- teaching family members the specific strategies being taught to their child.
- involving family members in training that may be scheduled at an agency or the school, such as a visit by a representative from a technology company or a braille refresher workshop
- providing information about further learning, such as distance education courses, or offering training by the teacher for families on the teacher's caseload
- providing needed materials and equipment for a student's use at home
- helping families link with services and resources that enhance learning at home, such as sources for accessible books, movies, magazines, and news
- sharing developmental checklists and curricula so families are aware of essential skills and when to expect them to emerge and develop
- connecting families to other families and individuals affected by visual impairment

CONCLUSION

The development of skills in the areas of the ECC is at the heart of educational efforts and programming for students who are visually impaired. Teachers of these students have a pivotal role to play in this process, but so do families, who in fact are among the most powerful resources that teachers have available to them. By working together, as collaborators and partners with the same goals who seek to reinforce each others' efforts, teachers and families can help students achieve success and maximum independence in school, work, and life.

References

Anderson, S., Boigon, S., & Davis, K. (1991). *The Oregon project for visually impaired and blind preschool children* (5th ed.). Medford, OR: Jackson Education Service District.

Castellano, C., & Kosman, D. (1997). *The bridge to braille: Reading and school success for the young blind child.* Baltimore, MD: National Organization of Blind Children.

Curran, E. (1988). *Just enough to know better: A braille primer.* Boston: National Braille Press.

Division on Visual Impairments, Council for Exceptional Children (n.d.). *CEC DVI knowledge and skills for initial special educators serving students with visual impairments.* Retrieved from http://community.cec.sped.org/dvi/professionalstandards

Fazzi, D. L., Klein, M. D., Pogrund, R. L., & Salcedo, P. S. (2002). Family focus: Working effectively with families. In R. L. Pogrund & D. L. Fazzi (Eds.), *Early focus: Working with young children who are blind or visually impaired and their families* (2nd ed., pp. 16–51). New York: AFB Press.

Ferrell, K. A. (2011). *Reach out and teach: Helping your child who is visually impaired learn and grow.* New York: AFB Press.

Holbrook, M. C. (Ed.). (2006). *Children with visual impairments: A parents' guide* (2nd ed.). Bethesda, MD: Woodbine House.

Holbrook, M. C., & D'Andrea, F. M. (in press). *Ashcroft's programmed instruction: Unified English Braille.* Germantown, TN: SCALARS Publishing.

Koenig, A. J., & Holbrook, M. C. (2000). Planning instruction in unique skills. In A. J. Koenig & M. C. Holbrook (Eds.), *Foundations of education: Vol. II. Instructional strategies for teaching children and youths with visual impairments* (2nd ed., pp. 196–221). New York: AFB Press.

Layton, T. L. (2004). *Developmental scale for children with Down syndrome.* Durham, NC: Extraordinary Learning Foundation.

Smith, M., & Levack, N. (1997). *Teaching students with visual and multiple impairments: A resource guide* (2nd ed.). Austin: Texas School for the Blind and Visually Impaired.

Turnbull, A., Turnbull, R., Erwin, E., & Soodak, L. (2006). *Families, professionals, and exceptionality* (5th ed.). Upper Saddle River, NJ: Pearson.

Wolffe, K. (Ed.) (1999). *Skills for success: A career handbook for children and adolescents with visual impairments.* New York: AFB Press.

General Resources

This General Resources section is provided as a central listing of sources of information and referrals on the expanded core curriculum (ECC) for teachers of students with visual impairments, other professionals, and family members. It is intended to complement, not duplicate, the resources provided in Part 2 of this book. Therefore, for more in-depth resources and information on individual areas of the ECC and for related assessment instruments and publications, see the chapter dealing with the specific ECC domain. Additional resources specifically for parents and family members of children who are blind or have low vision are listed in Chapter 15.

The first section contains an extensive list of national organizations that provide information and resources in the field of blindness and low vision and particularly the education of children, many of which are referenced throughout the book. A variety of publications with background information on the ECC are listed in the second section; again, more detailed lists appear in Part 2. The third section lists a number of websites that provide information related to the ECC. The information provided was current at the time it was compiled, but readers should keep in mind that websites are always subject to change. Finally, a representative list of companies and organizations that supply products and services is provided, including books for students who are blind or who have low vision.

For more detailed listings of organizations and sources of products and services, see the American Foundation for the Blind's Directory of Services online at www.afb.org/directory.aspx.

National Organizations

American Association of the Deaf-Blind
8630 Fenton Street, Suite 121
Silver Spring, MD 20910-3803
TDD/TTY: (304) 495-4402
Fax: (301) 495-4404
www.aadb.org

A national consumer organization of, by, and for deaf-blind Americans and their supporters serving as an information clearinghouse to promote better opportunities and services for people who are deaf-blind and ensure that a comprehensive, coordinated system of services is accessible, enabling deaf-blind people to achieve their maximum potential through increased independence, productivity, and integration into the community.

American Council of the Blind (ACB)
2200 Wilson Boulevard, Suite 650
Arlington, VA 22201
(202) 467-5081 or (800) 425-8666
Fax: (703) 467-5085
info@acb.org
www.acb.org

A national consumer membership organization that strives to increase the independence, security, equality of opportunity, and quality of life, for all blind and visually impaired people. Maintains state affiliates and local chapters across the country.

American Council on Rural Special Education (ACRES)
West Virginia University
509 Allen Hall, PO Box 6122
Morgantown, WV 26506-6122
(304) 293-3450
acres-sped@mail.wvu.edu
acres-sped.org

A membership organization of special educators, general educators, related service providers, administrators, teacher trainers, researchers, and parents committed to the enhancement of services to students and individuals living in rural America. Distributes information, publishes a newsletter and a journal, and advocates for the rights of people with disabilities.

American Foundation for the Blind (AFB)
2 Penn Plaza, Suite 1102
New York, NY 10121
(212) 502-7600 or (800) 232-5463
Fax: (212) 502-7777
info@afb.net
www.afb.org

A national organization serving as an information clearinghouse for people who are visually impaired, their families, professionals, schools, organizations, corporations, and the public. Operates a toll-free information hotline; conducts research and mounts program initiatives to promote the inclusion of people with visual impairments, especially in the areas of literacy, technology, aging, and employment; and advocates for services and legislation. Through AFB Press, its publishing arm, publishes books, pamphlets, DVDs, and electronic and online products including the *Directory of Services for Blind and Visually Impaired Persons in the United States and Canada* (www.afb.org/directory.aspx), the *Journal of Visual Impairment & Blindness* (www.jvib.org), and *AccessWorld: Technology and People with Visual Impairments* (www.afb.org/aw). AFB maintains a number of web-based initiatives, including FamilyConnect (www.FamilyConnect.org), an online, multimedia community for parents and families of visually impaired children created with the National Association for Parents of Children with Visual Impairments; CareerConnect (www.CareerConnect.org), a resource for learning about the range and diversity of jobs performed by adults who are blind or visually impaired throughout the United States and Canada; and VisionAware (www.VisionAware.org), an informational website for adults with vision loss, their families, caregivers, health-care providers, and social service professionals maintained with the Reader's Digest Partners for Sight Foundation.

American Printing House for the Blind (APH)
PO Box 6085
Louisville, KY 40206-0085
(502) 895-2405 or (800) 223-1839
Fax: (502) 895-1509
info@aph.org
www.aph.org

A national nonprofit organization that offers educational, workplace, and independent living products and services for persons with visual impairments. Administers the Federal Quota Program to provide funds for purchase of educational materials for students with visual impairments; conducts educational research and development; and maintains the AFB M. C. Migel Library. Maintains an informational website, reference-catalog databases providing information about textbooks and other materials produced in accessible media, and houses the National Instructional Materials Access Center. (See also listing under Sources of Products and Services.)

Association for Education and Rehabilitation of the Blind and Visually Impaired (AER)
1703 N. Beauregard Street, Suite 440
Alexandria, VA 22311
(703) 671-4500 or (877) 492-2708
Fax: (703) 671-6391
aer@aerbvi.org
www.aerbvi.org

The primary professional organization for teachers, counselors, orientation and mobility specialists, and other professionals in the field of blindness and low vision. It is organized into a variety of special divisions. Promotes all phases of education and work for people of all ages who are blind or visually impaired, strives to expand their opportunities to take a contributory place in society, and disseminates information.

Braille Association of North America (BANA)
c/o Frances Mary D'Andrea
5714 Beacon Street
Pittsburgh, PA 15217
literacy2@mindspring.com
www.brailleauthority.org

An organization consisting of representatives of North American organizations in the field of blindness that works to assure literacy for tactile readers through the standardization of braille and/or tactile graphics by promoting and facilitating the uses, teaching, and production of braille.

Canadian National Institute for the Blind (CNIB)
1929 Bayview Avenue
Toronto, ON M4G 3E8
(416) 486-2500 or (800) 563-2742
Fax: (416) 480-7700
info@cnib.ca
www.cnib.ca

The primary national resource for Canadians who are blind or who have low vision, with offices in communities across the country.

Carl and Ruth Shapiro Family National Center for Accessible Media at WGBH (NCAM)
One Guest Street
Boston, MA 02135
(617) 300-3400

TTY: (617) 300-2489
Fax: (617) 300-1035
ncam@wgbh.org
http://ncam.wgbh.org

The research and development arm of WGBH's Media Access Group, involved in technology, policy, and program development to ensure that the nation's media and technologies are fully accessible to people with disabilities.

Closing the Gap
526 Main Street
PO Box 68
Henderson, MN 56044
(507) 248-3294
Fax: (507) 248-3810
info@closingthegap.com
www.closingthegap.com

An organization providing assistive technology resources and training opportunities through its bimonthly magazine, webinars, and annual international conference for people with special needs.

Council for Exceptional Children (CEC) Division on Visual Impairment
2900 Crystal Drive, Suite 1000
Arlington, VA 22202-3557
(888) 232-7733
Fax: (703) 264-9494
service@cec.sped.org
www.cec.sped.org
http://community.cec.sped.org/DVI/home/

A professional organization for educators and other individuals serving children with disabilities and children who are gifted and is organized into a variety of specialized divisions. The Division on Visual Impairment works to advance the education of individuals with visual impairments and to promote related educational, scientific, and charitable purposes and publishes *DVI Quarterly.*

Described and Captioned Media Program (DCMP)
National Association of the Deaf
1447 E. Main Street
Spartanburg, SC 29307
(864) 585-1778 or (800) 237-6213
TTY: (864) 585-2617 or 800-237-6819
Fax: (864) 585-2611
info@dcmp.org
www.dcmp.org

A clearinghouse for information about description and captioning of visual media for people who are blind or have low vision intended for consumers, agencies, corporations, and schools. Offerings include numerous print and online informational resources as well as a gateway to accessibility information from DCMP and its many collaborators.

Early Childhood Technical Assistance Center
CB 8040
Chapel Hill, NC 27599-8040
(919) 962-2001
Fax: (919) 966-7463
ectacenter@unc.edu
http://ectacenter.org

A federally funded national center to support early intervention and preschool special education programs and practitioners and assist states in building effective, efficient systems by scaling up and sustaining effective services and promoting research-based interventions for infants, toddlers, and preschoolers with disabilities and their families.

Hadley School for the Blind
700 Elm Street
Winnetka, IL 60093-0299
(847) 446-8111 or (800) 323-4238
Fax: (847) 446-9916
info@Hadley-School.org
www.hadley-school.org

An accredited distance education program that allows students to study at home with free correspondence course materials. Courses are offered to parents of blind children, professionals working with people who are blind or who have low vision, high school students preparing for college, and adults who have become blind.

Helen Keller National Center for Deaf-Blind Youths and Adults
141 Middle Neck Road
Sands Point, NY 11050-1299
(516) 944-8900
Fax: (516) 944-7302
TDD/TTY: (516) 944-8637
hkncinfo@hknc.org
www.hknc.org

A national rehabilitation program serving youth and adults who are deaf-blind providing short-term rehabilitation services, comprehensive vocational and personal adjustment training, job preparation and placement, and diagnostic services to people who are deaf-blind through its national center and 10 regional offices. Provides technical assistance and training to those who work with deaf-blind people. Publishes *Nat-Cent News.* Sponsors the National Family Association for the Deaf-Blind.

Lighthouse Guild
111 East 59th Street
New York, NY 10022
(212) 821-9200 or (800) 829-0500
info@lighthouse.org
www.lighthouse.org

An organization that provides vision rehabilitation services; conducts research and advocacy; trains professionals; engages in advocacy; and provides educational and professional products and adaptive devices through its catalogs.

National Association for Parents of Children with Visual Impairments (NAPVI)
1 North Lexington Avenue, 8th Floor
White Plains, NY 10601
(212) 769-7819 or (800) 562-6265
TDD/TTY: (800) 562-6265
napvi@guildhealth.org
www.napvi.org

An organization for parents and families of children and young adults with visual impairments that provides leadership, support, and training. Operates a national clearinghouse for information, education, and referral; initiates outreach programs and networking; and advocates for the educational needs and well-being of children who are blind or visually impaired. Publishes the newsletter *Awareness.*

National Association of State Directors of Special Education (NASDSE)
225 Reinekers Lane, Suite 420
Alexandria, VA 22314
Fax: (703) 519-3800
nasdse@nasdse.org
www.nasdse.org

A membership organization of state directors of special education and others employed in state education agencies who direct, coordinate, or supervise programs and services for the education of students with disabilities. Provides assistance to state education agencies in the delivery of quality education to children and youths with disabilities through training, technical assistance, research, and policy development; offers consultative services; publishes newsletters; and sponsors conferences.

National Braille Association
95 Allens Creek Road
Building 1, Suite 202
Rochester, NY 14618
(585) 427-8260
Fax: (585) 427-0263
nbaoffice@nationalbraille.org
www.nationalbraille.org

Organization providing continuing education to those who prepare braille and braille materials to people who are visually impaired. Provides braille transcription and production services and consultation. Also maintains a depository of music materials in braille. Publishes manuals and guidelines for the production of braille and publishes a quarterly bulletin.

National Center on Secondary Education and Transition
Institute on Community Integration
University of Minnesota
6 Pattee Hall, 150 Pillsbury Drive SE
Minneapolis, MN 55455
(612) 624-2097
Fax: (612) 624-9344
ncset@umn.edu
www.ncset.org

Provider of technical assistance and disseminates information, resources, and publications on secondary education and transition services for students with disabilities.

National Consortium on Deaf-Blindness (NCDB)
c/o Teaching Research
Western Oregon University
345 North Monmouth Avenue
Monmouth, OR 97361
(503) 838-8756
Fax: (503) 838-8150
TDD/TTY: (800) 854-7013 or (800) 438-9376
info@nationaldb.org
https://nationaldb.org

A national federally funded technical assistance center working to improve the quality of life for children who are deaf-blind and their families by conducting initiatives and activities to increase the capacity of state and local early intervention and education agencies to improve policies and practices for children and youth who are deaf-blind; promoting the use of evidence-based practices; and enabling families to develop relationships with other families and service providers and expanding their knowledge of deaf-blindness and skills in self-advocacy and self-empowerment. Maintains DB-Link, the largest collection of information related to deaf-blindness.

National Federation of the Blind

200 East Wells Street at Jernigan Place
Baltimore, MD 21230
(410) 659-9314
Fax: (410) 685-5653
www.nfb.org
nfb@nfb.org

A national consumer organization that strives to improve social and economic conditions of people who are blind and to integrate people who are blind or who have low vision as equal members of society. Evaluates and assists in establishing programs and provides public education and scholarships. Interest groups include the National Organization of Parents of Blind Children and the Committee on the Concerns of the Deaf-Blind. Publishes *The Braille Monitor* and *Future Reflections*, a magazine for parents.

National Information Center for Children and Youth with Disabilities

PO Box 1492
Washington, DC 20013-1492
(202) 884-8200
TDD: (800) 695-0285
Fax: (202) 844-8441

A national clearinghouse for information about children and youngsters with disabilities. Provides information and referral to national, state, and local resources. Disseminates numerous free publications.

National Organization for Albinism and Hypopigmentation (NOAH)

PO Box 959
East Hampstead, NH 03826-0959
(603) 887-2310 or (800) 473-2310
Fax: (603) 887-2310
info@albinism.org
www.albinism.org

National organization that provides information on albinism and hypopigmentation, offers peer support, sponsors conferences, and publishes a newsletter.

Office of Special Education Programs (OSEP)

U.S. Department of Education
400 Maryland Avenue, SW
Washington, DC 20202
(202) 205-5507
http://www2.ed.gov/about/offices/list/osers/osep/index.html

The federal agency that administers the Individuals with Disabilities Education Act (IDEA) and related programs for the free appropriate public education of children and youth with disabilities from birth through age 21, including research and demonstration projects, support to states and local school districts for the education of disabled children, and special programs, such as centers and services for children who are deaf-blind.

Perkins School for the Blind

175 North Beacon Street
Watertown, MA 02472
(617) 924-3434
info@Perkins.org
www.Perkins.org

A school for the blind that also publishes books; sells products for students with visual impairments; and offers an informational website that includes teaching resources and instructional strategies, professional development, and parent support. (See also Perkins Products under Sources of Products and Services.)

Prevent Blindness America (PBA)

211 West Wacker Drive, #1700
Chicago, IL 60606
(312) 363-6001 or (800) 331-2020
Fax: (312) 363-6052
info@preventblindness.org
preventblindness.org

A national organization that conducts a program of public and professional education, research, and industrial and community services to prevent blindness, including public education concerning vision conservation, vision screenings in schools, promotion of industrial eye safety, and efforts to improve environmental conditions affecting eye health in schools and colleges. Collects data on the nature and extent of causes of blindness and impaired vision. Maintains the PBA Fight for

Sight research division and the PBA Center for Sight information line.

TASH

1001 Connecticut Ave., NW, Suite 235
Washington, DC 20036
(202) 540-9020,
Fax: (202) 540-9019
E-mail: info@tash.org
www.tash.org
info@tash.org

An advocacy organization for professionals who work with infants, children, and youths with severe disabilities and their families. Promotes full inclusion and participation of people with disabilities in all aspects of life through local chapters. Publishes a monthly newsletter, quarterly journal, and other publications.

Texas School for the Blind and Visually Impaired

1100 West 45th Street
Austin, TX 78756-3494
(512) 454-8631 or (800) 872-5273
Fax: (512) 454-3395
TTY: (512) 206-9451
www.tsbvi.edu

A school for the blind that publishes books and offers online information and resources about visual impairment, instruction, technology, assessment, and a wide range of other topics related to the education of students who have visual and multiple disabilities and publishes professional books, assessments, and curricula, including the Resources for the Expanded Core Curriculum (RECC) section on its website.

Zero to Three

National Center for Infants, Toddlers and Families
1255 23rd Street, NW, Suite 350
Washington, DC 20037
(202) 638-1144
Fax: (202) 638-0851

A national nonprofit, multidisciplinary organization that informs, trains, and supports professionals, policymakers, and parents in their efforts to improve the lives of infants and toddlers. Publishes the *Zero to Three Journal*, a bimonthly publication ideal for early childhood experts, early interventionists, and child care professionals. Also holds the National Training Institute, a comprehensive and multidisciplinary conference that focuses on cutting-edge research, best practices, and policy issues for infants, toddlers, and families, annually.

Publications

Barclay, L. (Ed.). (2014). *Learning to listen/Listening to learn: Teaching listening skills to students with visual impairments.* New York: AFB Press.

Barraga, N., & Erin, J. N. (2001). *Visual impairments and learning* (4th ed.). Austin, TX: Pro-Ed.

Bishop, V. (2004). *Teaching visually impaired children* (3rd ed.). Springfield, IL: Charles C Thomas.

Chen, D. (Ed.). (2014). *Essential elements in early intervention: Visual impairment and multiple disabilities* (2nd ed.). New York: AFB Press.

Corn, A. L., & Erin, J. N. (Eds.). (2010). *Foundations of low vision: Clinical and functional perspective* (2nd ed.). New York: AFB Press.

Curry, S. A., & Hatlen, P. H. (1988). Meeting the unique educational needs of visually impaired pupils through appropriate placement. *Journal of Visual Impairment & Blindness, 82(10)*, 417–424.

Ferrell, K. (2011). *Reach out and teach: Helping your child who is visually impaired learn and grow* (2nd ed.). New York: AFB Press.

Goodman, S. A., & Wittenstein, S. H. (Eds.). (2003). *Collaborative assessment: Working with students who are blind or visually impaired, including those with additional disabilities.* New York: AFB Press.

Hatlen, P. (1996). The core curriculum for blind and visually impaired students, including those with additional disabilities. *RE:view, 28*(1), 25–32.

Hatlen, P. H., & Curry, S. A. (1987). In support of specialized programs for blind and visually impaired children: The impact of vision loss on learning. *Journal of Visual Impairment & Blindness, 81*, 7–13.

Holbrook, M. C. (Ed.). (2006). *Children with visual impairments: A guide for parents* (2nd ed.). Bethesda, MD: Woodbine House.

Holbrook, M. C., & Koenig, A. J. (Eds.) (2000). *Foundations of education: Vol. I. History and theory of teaching children with visual impairments* (2nd ed.). New York: AFB Press.

Koenig, A. J., & Holbrook, M. C. (Eds.) (2000). *Foundations of education: Vol. II. Instructional strategies for teaching children and youths with visual impairments* (2nd ed.). New York: AFB Press.

LaVenture, S. (Ed.). (2007). *A parents' guide to special education for children with visual impairments.* New York: AFB Press.

Lohmeir, K., Blankenship, K. E., & Hatlen, P. (2009). Expanded core curriculum: Twelve years later. *Journal of Visual Impairments & Blindness, 103*, 103–112.

Lueck, A. H., & Dutton, G. N. (in press). *Vision and the brain: Understanding cerebral visual impairment in children.* New York: AFB Press.

Olmstead, J. E. (2005). *Itinerant teaching: Tricks of the trade for teachers of students with visual impairments* (2nd ed.). New York: AFB Press.

Pogrund, P. L., & Fazzi, D. L. (Eds.). (2002). *Early focus: Working with young children who are blind or visually impaired and their families* (2nd ed.). New York: AFB Press.

Roman-Lantzy, C. (2007). *Cortical visual impairment: An approach to assessment and intervention.* New York: AFB Press.

Salvia, J., Ysseldyke, J., & Bolt, S. (2010). *Assessment: In special and inclusive education.* Florence, KY: Wadsworth Publishing.

Sapp, W., & Hatlen, P. (2010). The expanded core curriculum: Where we have been, where we are going, and how we can get there. *Journal of Visual Impairments & Blindness, 104*(6), 338–348.

Sewell, D. (1997). *Assessment KIT: Kit of informal tools for academic students with visual impairments.* Austin: Texas School for the Blind and Visually Impaired.

Smith, M., & Levack, N. (1996). *Teaching students with visual and multiple impairments: A resource guide.* Austin: Texas School for the Blind and Visually Impaired.

Websites

AIM Navigator

National Center on Accessible Instructional Materials
http://aim.cast.org/experience/decision-making_tools/aim_navigator

Serves as a resource for educators, parents, publishers, conversion houses, and accessible media producers by providing an interactive tool to facilitate the process of decision-making around accessible instructional materials for individual students.

Braille Bug

American Foundation for the Blind
www.braillebug.org

Introduces sighted children in grades 3 through 6 to basic braille concepts. Provides teachers with tools to bring braille into the mainstream classroom. Designed for use by children, parents, and teachers, and includes games, secret messages, a reading club, and information about Helen Keller and Louis Braille.

CareerConnect

American Foundation for the Blind
www.CareerConnect.org

Presents employment information, career exploration tools, and extensive job-seeking guidance for students and adults with vision loss, professionals who work with them, and others who want to learn about the range and diversity of jobs performed by adults who are blind or visually impaired throughout the United States and Canada.

FamilyConnect

American Foundation for the Blind and National Association for Parents of Children with Visual Impairments
www.familyconnect.org

Provides parents of visually impaired children with extensive online information about raising a child with visual impairment, message boards for support and sharing stories, and links to local resources. Contains a section on the expanded core curriculum with suggestions for parents from experts.

Paths to Literacy for Students Who Are Blind or Visually Impaired

Perkins School for the Blind and Texas School for the Blind and Visually Impaired
www.pathstoliteracy.org

Provides an online hub for information related to literacy for students who are blind or who have low vision, including those with additional disabilities or deaf-blindness.

Perkins Teaching Resources

Perkins School for the Blind
www.perkins.org/resources

Offers a variety of online resources for educators of students who are visually impaired, including webinars and webcasts; the Samuel P. Hayes Research Library & Archives; curricular resources, including accessible science; and Perkins Scout, an information clearinghouse on blindness and visual impairment.

Resources for the Expanded Core Curriculum (RECC)

Texas School for the Blind and Visually Impaired
www.tsbvi.edu/recc

Offers a searchable database of available tools and materials for teaching the different areas of the expanded core curriculum.

Texas School for the Blind and Visually Impaired

www.tsbvi.edu

See listing under National Organizations.

What Works Clearinghouse (WWC)
Institute of Education Sciences
U.S. Department of Education
(866) 503-6114
ies.ed.gov/ncee/wwc

Reviews studies on education programs, products, practices, and policies; provides accurate information on education research; conducts thorough reviews of the research literature and critically assesses the evidence presented; and delivers information from its reviews through the "Find What Works" tool, a searchable database of research studies and publications.

Sources of Products and Services

Accessible Book Collection
12847 Point Pleasant Drive
Fairfax, VA 22033
(703) 631-1585
Fax: (206) 600-7957
customerservice@accessiblebookcollection.org
www.accessiblebookcollection.org

Offers a large selection of e-books in HTML that are high interest and low reading level for students with print disabilities.

American Printing House for the Blind
1839 Frankfort Avenue
PO Box 6085
Louisville, KY 40206-0085
(502) 895-2405 or (800) 223-1839
Fax: (502) 899-2274
www.aph.org
info@aph.org

Produces a variety of books and learning materials in braille and other media; manufactures computer-access equipment, software, and special education and reading devices for people who are visually impaired; and distributes a variety of educational products and teaching materials designed for people of all ages who are blind and visually impaired. (See also listing under National Organizations.)

Bookshare
480 California Avenue, Suite 201
Palo Alto, CA 94306
(650) 644-3400
Fax: (650) 475-1066
info@bookshare.org
www.bookshare.org

Maintains an accessible digital library for people with print and learning disabilities, with free membership to qualified schools and students.

Enhanced Vision Systems
5882 Machine Drive
Huntington Beach, CA 92649
(714) 374-1829
Fax: (714) 374-1821 (Fax)
TDD/TTY: (888) 811-3161
marketing@enhancedvision.com
www.enhancedvision.com

Manufactures and distributes a variety of low vision devices and video magnifiers.

Exceptional Teaching
3994 Oleander Way
Castro Valley, CA 94546
(510) 889-7282 or (800) 549-6999
Fax: (510) 889-7382
www.exceptionalteaching.com
info@exceptionalteaching.com

Manufactures and distributes educational materials and equipment for visually impaired students, including tutorial and other educational software programs and braille materials for reading readiness, math readiness, and math practice.

Future Aids: The Braille Superstore
33222 Lynn Avenue
Abbotsford, BC V2S 1C9
(604) 852-6341 or (800) 987-1231
Fax: (800) 985-1231
info@braillebookstore.com
www.braillebookstore.com

Distributes braille books and devices, low vision devices, and speech software.

Independent Living Aids
200 Robbins Lane
Jericho, NY 11753
(800) 537-2118 or (855) 746-7452)
Fax: (516) 937-3906
www.independentliving.com

Sells adapted games and other recreational items, adapted household products, braille label makers, and other materials for creating adaptations.

Learning Ally
20 Roszel Road
Princeton, NJ 08540
(609) 452-0606 or (800) 221-4792
Fax: (609) 987-8116
info@learningally.org
www.learningally.org

Provides recorded and computerized textbooks, library services, and other educational resources to people who cannot read standard print because of visual, physical, or specific learning disabilities. Maintains a lending library of recorded books and acts as a recording service for additional titles.

LS&S
145 River Rock Drive
Buffalo, NY 14207
(800) 468-4789 or (716) 348-3500
Fax: (877) 498-1482
www.lssproducts.com

Offers an online catalog of products for people who are visually impaired and hard of hearing, including optical devices, braille labelers, educational products, games, and products for independent living.

Maxi-Aids
42 Executive Boulevard
Farmingdale, NY 11735
(800) 522-6294 or (631) 752-0521
Fax: (631) 752-0689
TTY: (631) 752-0738
www.maxiaids.com

Offers a wide variety of independent living products, low vision devices, and other products for people with vision, hearing, and mobility disabilities.

National Braille Press
88 St. Stephen Street
Boston, MA 02115
(617) 266-6160 or (800) 548-7323
Fax: (617) 437-0456
www.nbp.org

Publishes braille works and promotes literacy for blind children and adults. With Seedlings Braille Books for Children promotes ReadBooks! Program, a national children's braille literacy program encouraging families with blind children to read print/braille books together. Also has a Children's Braille Book Club.

National Library Service for the Blind and Physically Disabled (NLS)
Library of Congress
1291 Taylor Street NW
Washington, DC 20542
(202) 707-5100 or (800) 424-8567 or (888) 657-7323
Fax: (202) 707-0712
TDD/TTY: (202) 707-0744
www.loc.gov/nls
nls@loc.gov

Administers a free library program of braille and digital audio materials circulated to eligible borrowers in the United States by postage-free mail through a national network of cooperating libraries. Also maintains an electronic library for e-text for registered users.

Perkins Products
Perkins School for the Blind
175 North Beacon Street
Watertown, MA 02472
(617) 972-7308
PerkinsProducts@Perkins.org
www.perkins.org

Manufactures and distributes the Perkins Brailler, braille slates, and drawing tools; publishes books for families and professionals; and distributes educational and daily living products, low vision devices, assistive technology, and other products for people who are blind or visually impaired.

Seedlings Braille Books for Children
PO Box 51924
Livonia, MI 48151-5924
(734) 427-8552 or (800) 777-8552
Fax: (734) 427-8552
www.seedlings.org
info@seedlings.org

Publishes braille books for children and distributes Twin Vision print/braille books.

ViewPlus Technologies
1965 SW Airport
Corvallis, OR 97330
(541) 754-4002
Fax: (541) 738-6505
info@viewplus.com
www.viewplus.com

Manufactures braille embossers and a variety of adapted educational products.

Vision Associates
295 N.W. Commons Loop, Suite 115-312
Lake City, FL 32055
(407) 352-1200
Fax: (386) 752-7839
www.visionkits.com

Distributes a variety of vision assessment materials and vision kits.

Index

M

P

Printed in the USA
CPSIA information can be obtained
at www.ICGtesting.com
LVHW061357120724
785287LV00003B/13